Essential LightWave® v9

The Fastest and Easiest Way to Master LightWave 3D

Steve Warner, Kevin Phillips, and Timothy Albee

Technical review by
César Alejandro Montero Orozco

Wordware Publishing, Inc.

Library of Congress Cataloging-in-Publication Data

Warner, Steve, 1970-
    Essential lightwave v9 / by Steve Warner, Kevin Phillips, and Timothy Albee.
        p. cm.
    Includes index.
    ISBN 978-1-59822-024-7 (pbk., companion DVD)
    1. Computer animation.   2. Computer graphics.   3. LightWave 3D.
    I. Phillips, Kevin.   II. Albee, Timothy.   III. Title.
    TR897.7.W375 2007
    006.6'96--dc22   2007015547
                                                            CIP

ISBN-10: 1-59822-024-1
ISBN-13: 978-1-59822-024-7
10 9 8 7 6 5 4 3 2 1
0705

All inquiries for volume purchases of this book should be addressed to Wordware Publishing, Inc.,
at the above address. Telephone inquiries may be made by calling:

(972) 423-0090

Dedication

To all those who have yearned to create great works with LightWave yet found themselves facing a steep and seemingly insurmountable learning curve. We know exactly how you feel. This book was written for you. We hope that it causes you to grow in your skills and inspire others with your wonderful artistic visions.

Steve Warner and Kevin Phillips

Contents

Contents

Contents

Contents

Acknowledgments

This book would not exist were it not for the help of the following people:

Kevin Phillips: You brought your vast expertise to this project and made it possible to create a book of this magnitude. It would not have been possible without you. I am in your debt and am honored to call you my friend. Thank you.

Wes Beckwith: You gave me the opportunity to pursue my vision for this book. Thank you for believing in me. I owe you my deepest thanks.

Tim McEvoy: You provided unwavering support throughout the production of this book, even when the deadlines flew by. You believed in the work we were doing and it allowed us to produce a book that we are proud of. Thank you.

Cesar Montero: You offered invaluable feedback that strengthened the book and ensured it addressed the needs of a broad range of users. I couldn't have asked for a better tech editor. Thank you.

Tim Albee: You started a grand tradition with the *Essential LightWave* series. I am honored to have the opportunity to continue that tradition. Thank you.

Michelle Warner: You stood by me while the months rolled on, the bills went unpaid, the dishes stacked up, and our time together dwindled. This has been an enormous project, and your faith and support sustained me through the difficult times. I love you.

To you, the reader: In purchasing this book, you have shown your support for the work we have done over the past year and a half. Thank you. I hope that you are enriched by the information contained in these pages.

—Steve Warner

I don't think I would have ever gotten through this project if it hadn't been for some key people along the way. It's all been possible because of:

Steve Warner: The captain of the *Essential* ship. You took us sailing through the storms and turbulent sea, and got us safely to the other side. You've been a great driving force and your valuable feedback and consistent communication along the way has helped keep us from ever sinking. Thanks loads for letting me work with you on this fantastic project, and for being such a good friend!

Tim McEvoy and the team at Wordware: Thank you for supporting us all the way and helping us craft something extremely cool for the LightWave-using artistic community! You've been fantastic to deal with, and many thanks for making the journey so comfortable.

Cesar Montero: A man who helped serve up plenty of correction cocktails on our cruise. Your feedback was invaluable in helping mold and polish the work inside the book. Many thanks for your time and efforts!

Wes Beckwith: A man who's always been a driving force behind training for the LightWave community and initially brought me onboard to sail with Steve on the ship. Thanks for your trust in me, and making it possible for me to share what I have to offer with the community!

Marija Phillips: The person who supported me in many more ways than I can ever appreciate, from her patience, feedback, and critique to just those many, many coffees and hours of housework while I sat endlessly behind the computer. Huge hugs and kisses, and loads of love for everything. Thanks for not throwing the dongle overboard!

Max: Our faithful "PC pussycat" for keeping the mouse pad coated in reflective hairs that I'm sure improve the accuracy of the optical mouse, for licking the keys clean on the well-loved keyboard, and wiping the dust from both the screen and my face with his tail as he trampled over my typing fingers. Without you, the process wouldn't have been half as much fun, nor would my computer (and face) be as clean and tidy.

Everybody who uses, loves, or just plays with LightWave: Without you, well, let's face it… there would be no need for this book! I sincerely hope that this book will make your artistic visions easier to achieve, and help drive that creative passion that comes from knowing your tools intimately! This book is for you — Enjoy!

—Kevin Phillips

Introduction

When NewTek announced the upcoming release of LightWave v9, we immediately began planning a new edition of the *Essential* book with hopes of releasing it around the time that LightWave v9 shipped. However, we decided early on that racing through the production was not our highest priority. Rather, our goal was to produce the most complete and thorough LightWave book possible. We wanted to create a book that would grow with you, regardless of your skill level, and bring you years of enjoyment. Nearly a year and a half later we finished what we believe to be the most comprehensive LightWave book on the market. You now hold that book in your hands. Welcome to the all-new *Essential LightWave v9*!

This edition of the *Essential* book is bigger and better than ever! It's more than twice as long as the original and a full third larger than its predecessor, numbering almost 1,000 pages. It's packed with detailed information about LightWave's new features and contains in-depth information on topics that were only touched on before, such as UVs, character modeling, dynamics, and rigging. We've also added new chapters for advanced subjects such as expressions, network rendering, and even a quick look at LScript programming. And if that weren't enough, we've included nearly 14 hours of video training material on the companion DVD to further your understanding of the information presented in the book.

This book is structured according to skill level, making it ideal for use both in a classroom and for self-study. The Basic, Intermediate, and Advanced sections build on one another, allowing you to develop your skills gradually over time. Each chapter is fairly self-contained, however. You don't have to work through the text in a linear fashion if you don't want to. If a particular chapter interests you, jump right in. If it requires a certain set of skills in order to complete it, we'll let you know.

If you're feeling a bit overwhelmed because you're just starting out with LightWave or are new to 3D in general, don't worry! The first seven chapters have been specifically designed to ground you in the basics and will give you all the information you need to become a productive user. (Even if you've been using the software for a while, the first seven chapters contain a wealth of information that can make you more productive, so don't skip over them just because they're in the Basic section!)

We wrote this book for LightWave v9; however, v9.2 was released during production. In order to stay current with the latest version of LightWave, we're including video tutorials about those new features on the DVD that comes with this book. The DVD also contains all the chapter images (useful for seeing all the detail in the images) as well as necessary LightWave files, textures, and plug-ins. There's a lot of great stuff on the DVD, so be sure to check it out.

Thank you for giving us the opportunity to help you develop your skills as a LightWave artist. We had a blast working on this book and hope it comes through on every page. If you have any questions along the way, feel free to drop us a line and let us know.

steve@stevewarner.com
kevman3d@xtra.co.nz

Chapter 1

An Introduction to the World of 3D

The world of 3D holds a special, almost magical appeal. Perhaps like me you found yourself awed by the unlimited potential offered by programs like LightWave and hoped that someday you'd be able to create the types of images you see in print, movies, and on TV. I've got good news for you: You can. And this book is going to show you how. But before we talk about subpatch modeling, particle animation, or character rigging, we've got to ground ourselves in the basics. If you've been using LightWave for a while, you can skip over this chapter. If you're new to the world of 3D and are feeling a tad overwhelmed, then this chapter is for you.

Understanding 3D Space

In my experience, one of the most difficult challenges new users face is becoming comfortable working in a 3D environment. Let's be honest. When you look out at the world, you don't see things simultaneously from four different viewpoints. The whole notion of a top, side, back, and over-the-shoulder perspective view is completely unnatural. But in order to become proficient with 3D software, seeing things from these vantage points must become second nature to you. Therefore, we'll begin with a discussion of 3D space.

When you open LightWave (or any other 3D program for that matter), you're seeing things through one or more "viewports." A viewport is nothing more than a window into the 3D world. Different windows show the 3D world in different ways. The most common viewports are Perspective (which Layout defaults to and Modeler shows in its upper-right quadrant), Top, Back, and Right. The Perspective view is pretty self explanatory. You're seeing the 3D world from a slightly removed vantage point. The Top, Back, and Right viewports are known as "orthographic" viewports. They display the 3D world without any perspective distortion.

The names of the orthographic viewports can be a little misleading. "Back" does not mean that you're looking *toward* the back of your object. Rather, it means you're viewing the 3D world *from* the back, which means you're really looking *toward* the front. This is exactly the type of thing that makes it difficult for new users to orient themselves within the 3D world. As you're starting out, you may find it helpful to insert the words "from the" before the name of any viewport to better remember what you're really seeing.

Objects in the 3D world are positioned via coordinates (really just a fancy word for numbers) along three different axes (or directions). The three axes are X, Y, and Z. In LightWave they represent right/left, up/down, and forward/back, respectively.

Figure 1-1: Viewports are windows into the 3D world. They allow you to see your world simultaneously from different vantage points. This makes it easy to locate and adjust the objects in your scene without constantly changing views.

Since each axis must account for two directions (i.e., X is used to denote both left and right), a simple approach is used to distinguish between the two. Positive numbers are assigned to one direction and negative numbers are assigned to the other. The point where left and right meet is given a value of 0, since 0 is neither positive nor negative. The zero point where all three axes meet is known as the origin.

Items to the left of the origin are said to be on the –X-axis. Objects to the right of the origin are said to be on the +X-axis. If you move something up from the origin, you're said to be moving it on the +Y-axis. If you move it down below the origin, you're moving on the –Y-axis. Likewise, if you move forward, you're moving on the +Z-axis. And backward is the –Z-axis.

The orientation of the axis in relation to the origin is known as a "coordinate

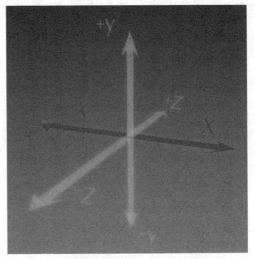

Figure 1-2: Objects are positioned in 3D space along X, Y, and Z coordinates.

system." In Modeler, you are always dealing with a "World" coordinate system. Up will always be oriented in the +Y-axis.

In Layout, you can choose between three different coordinate systems. The default is "Parent," but you can also choose "World" and "Local." Each represents a different way of defining an object's position and rotation in space. It's not important at this stage to worry about the differences between the various coordinate systems; it's simply enough to know that they exist.

All of this technical talk about numbers can be a bit mind-numbing, especially if you're more of an artist than a mathematician. But trust me when I say that they're really only there for technical accuracy. In practice, dealing with objects in the 3D world is a much more fun and intuitive process.

Now that we've examined how objects are *positioned* in the 3D world, let's talk about how they're *rotated*. Many 3D programs use the same axes (X, Y, and Z) to describe position and rotation. But LightWave uses a slightly different approach. Instead of X, Y, and Z, it uses the terms heading (H), pitch (P), and bank (B).

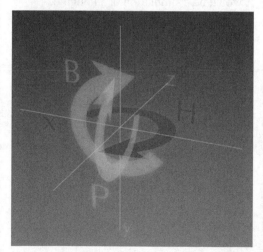

Figure 1-3: Objects are rotated in 3D space along their heading, pitch, and bank.

Stand up for a moment and face straight ahead. Turn your head to look to the left. Now turn your head to look to the right. This is an adjustment to your *heading*. Face forward again. Now look up and down. This is an adjustment to your *pitch*. Finally, cock your head left and right. This is an adjustment to your *bank*.

The 3D world uses the origin to determine an object's position. But the object's *rotation* isn't based on the origin. Instead, it's based on a virtual point known as the "pivot point." Each object in LightWave has its own pivot point. Rotations around the pivot point are described in terms of degrees and, just like X, Y, and Z positions, they can be either positive or negative.

You can create complex rotations very easily by creating a hierarchy of objects in LightWave. For example, you could recreate the workings of our solar system by making the Sun the top level of a hierarchy. By placing the Earth underneath it in the hierarchy and then rotating the Sun 360 degrees along its heading, you would cause the Earth to orbit around it. If you created a moon and placed it on a third tier under the Earth, you could have the moon orbiting the Earth while orbiting the Sun!

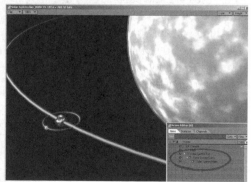

Figure 1-4: By creating a simple hierarchy, complex motions like that of planetary orbits can be created.

Hierarchical motion is the key to complex animation in LightWave, and we'll teach you all about it as we get into later chapters. If you're just getting started and are feeling a bit overwhelmed, don't worry. These can be hard concepts to grasp. But stick with it and you'll soon find yourself not only seeing the world but also thinking of the world in 3D terms.

Before we wrap up this section, we need to address the issue of units. LightWave defaults to using the metric system for measuring things. If you're an American, you're probably much more comfortable with the idea of inches and feet than you are with centimeters and meters. But when you start working in the 3D world, you're going to be multiplying and dividing on a fairly regular basis. The metric system works off of 10's, which makes for easy math. If you're thinking you'd rather stick with the English system because you're more comfortable with it, consider these two questions:

- How many feet are there in a quarter of a mile?

- How many inches are there in a quarter of a mile?

If it took you more than five seconds to answer either question, you should be using the metric system. It may be a struggle to adapt, but you'll thank me for it later.

Understanding the Nature of 3D

As you start down the path toward becoming a 3D artist, I want you to remember one important word. Remembering this one word can save you countless hours of confusion, frustration, and angst. Are you ready? The word is *simulation*.

Go to a window and look outside. Stare at the world around you. The buildings, the trees, the cars, the people; they are all real. Now fix your eyes on something specific. Anything will do. Stare at it and memorize its features. Now close your eyes and picture that thing you just saw. Recall its size, color, and all of the details. What you are seeing in your mind's eye is not real. It is only a *simulation* of reality.

Now pay close attention because this is important. The 3D world is a lot like your mind's eye. It can recreate exacting details, but none of the things you encounter there are real. They are only simulations of things you encounter in the real world.

When you create a 3D model of a car, it's not a real car. It's a simulation of a car. It doesn't run on gas. There's no transmission fluid. It probably doesn't even have an engine unless you specifically make one. And even then, it wouldn't be a real engine. It would be a simulation of an engine.

When you point a light at that car in the 3D world, you're not shining a real light on it. You're only simulating the effect of light. When you adjust the surface properties to make the paint metallic and the leather seats leathery, that's not real paint or leather; it's a simulation of these physical properties. When you animate the car and its wheels rotate according to the speed it's moving, it's a simulation of motion and physics. And when you render the final image, it's not a real car you see. It's a clever combination of all the above, finessed with artistic touches to simulate reality.

Everything you do in the 3D world is a simulation. The tools provided to you in LightWave are there to simulate various real-world properties, and they do a great

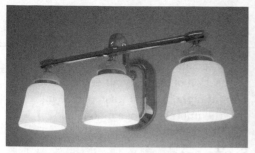

Figure 1-5: These are real lights. Their intensity is limited to the wattage of each bulb.

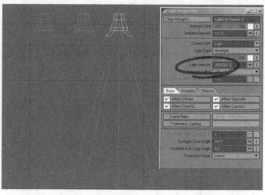

Figure 1-6: These are simulated lights. Their intensity isn't limited. You can set the light to whatever you want. Note that the intensity of the light on the right, which is normally 100%, has been increased to a whopping 25,000%!

job, but they are not and never will be real. *So don't treat them as such*. If a light isn't bright enough and it's already at 100%, bump it up to 200%. If there's too much light in a scene, set the light's intensity to a negative number. There's no such thing as a negative light in reality, but we're not dealing with reality, so it doesn't matter.

Don't expect LightWave's tools to work exactly like their real-world counterparts. Remember, *they are only simulations*.

Understanding the 3D Pipeline

The process of creating a finished 3D animation is fairly straightforward. There are five distinct stages that every project goes through. They are:

1. Modeling
2. Lighting
3. Surfacing
4. Animating
5. Rendering

These stages form what is known as a "pipeline." Over the next few pages, we'll briefly discuss each stage of the pipeline. I'll introduce you to the main concepts and then we'll spend the rest of this book examining each one of them in detail.

Modeling

The first stage of the pipeline involves the creation of 3D models. When you model something, you're simulating its form. Having a good understanding of the object you want to create and how it was originally

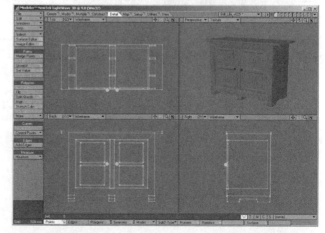

Figure 1-7: Modeling is the process of simulating real-world objects.

constructed will often help you achieve the best results. Modelers typically use reference photos, blueprints, and measurements from real objects to help them recreate their 3D counterparts.

Models are composed of "points" that are connected together to form "polygons." These polygons are what LightWave's virtual camera sees when it draws or "renders" the final image. Typically, models are constructed in the object creation application called Modeler. This is a dedicated environment that provides a focused toolset for building complex 3D objects.

Lighting

Once your objects have been built, they are placed on a virtual soundstage in a program called Layout. It is here that you perform the remaining stages of the pipeline, including the second stage: lighting.

Lighting is often the most overlooked phase of the 3D pipeline, yet it is one of the most important in achieving a good-looking final product. Lighting is much more than making an image look bright. Artistic and creative lighting is used to establish location, time of day, and mood through the use of color and shadow. If your scene takes place at sunset on the edge of a volcano, the use of red and orange lights will help create a sensation of heat. If your scene takes place at night, a broad wash of blue light will give the impression of a moonlit sky.

Surfacing

Once your objects are lit, you can begin giving them specific attributes that will help identify their unique physical properties. Every object in the real world has particular qualities that we associate with it. Apples are red and shiny. Water is transparent and reflective. Leaves are green and translucent. The part of the pipeline that deals with these visual attributes is known as surfacing.

Surfacing also involves the painting of "texture maps," which are applied to your object like decals. Painting maps is one of the most artistic parts of the pipeline, and texture artists spend a good deal of time working in programs like Adobe Photoshop and Corel Painter.

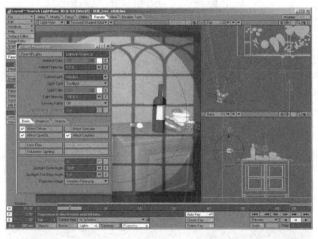

Figure 1-8: Lighting is the process of simulating local and ambient illumination as well as conveying mood and location through the use of color and shadow.

Figure 1-9: Surfacing is the process of simulating an object's appearance by assigning it real-world properties such as color, transparency, and reflection. Surfacing also involves the creation of hand-painted texture maps.

Animating

Animation is the fourth stage of the 3D pipeline. Here, you set up your camera and arrange the objects that will play a part in your scene.

Animation is the process of imbuing life-like qualities to various components in your 3D world. Whether it's twinkling stars or stampeding dinosaurs, any property that changes over time is technically considered animation.

The simplest animation consists of just two frames and the change of a single parameter such as position, rotation, or size. But upon this simple base rests the foundation of all animation.

Rendering

The last stage of the pipeline deals with preparing the computer to generate your 3D images. When the computer looks at your objects, evaluates the lighting, simulates surface properties, accounts for the changing values over time, and then draws the final image, it is said to be "rendering."

The rendering stage of the pipeline involves more than just pressing a button and heading out for lunch. Output settings need to be adjusted to balance computation time with image quality. Pre- and post-processing filters can be used to adjust the look of your final image. And depending on your setup, you may want to distribute the rendering over multiple computers through a network. All of these components are handled during the rendering stage of the pipeline.

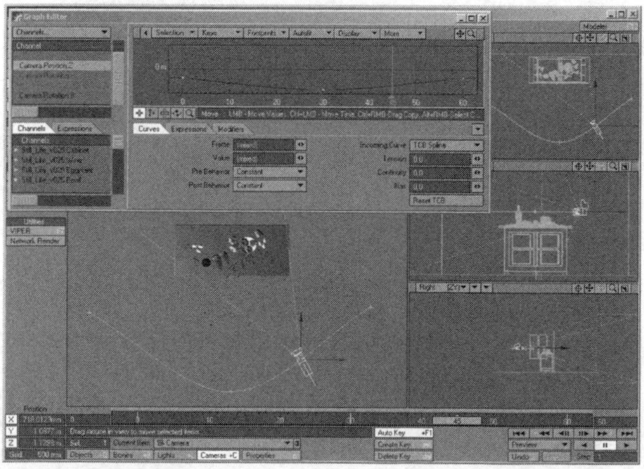

Figure 1-10: Animation is the simulation of lifelike qualities. The simplest animation involves moving an object from one position to another over time.

Figure 1-11: Rendering simulates the process of painting/drawing your final image.

Conclusion

The 3D world is a fantastic place where you can bring your creative visions to life. While points, polygons, axes, and origins may sound highly technical, these are just the mechanics behind a virtual playground that will bring you much enjoyment. Hopefully this brief introduction has taken away some of the mystery surrounding this strange new world.

As you move on to the more detailed chapters of this book, remember that everything you encounter in the 3D world is just a simulation. Experimentation with the tools you're introduced to is encouraged and often rewarded.

The concepts you've learned here about each stage of the production pipeline will form the basis for the rest of our exploration. Now let's move on to a detailed look at the suite of tools we call LightWave 3D!

Chapter 2

The LightWave Suite

When we speak of LightWave, we're really referring to a suite of applications. LightWave utilizes a "division of labor" philosophy. Each component is designed to perform a specific set of tasks. By breaking down the workload, each application's toolset can be streamlined to provide a more responsive and efficient working environment.

There are five main components to the LightWave suite:

- Modeler
- Layout
- Plug-ins
- The Hub
- ScreamerNet

- **Modeler** is the workshop where you build virtual objects to populate your 3D universe.

- **Layout** is the soundstage where all the action in your scene takes place. Here your objects are positioned, textured, lit, animated, and rendered.

- **Plug-ins** are external programs that run inside Modeler or Layout and extend each application's functionality.

- The **Hub** is the server that synchronizes data between Modeler and Layout. If you are working with an object in Layout, you can send it to Modeler with the click of a button and any changes you make will be updated in Layout automatically. The Hub is also responsible for various LightWave preferences. Everything from automated saving options to button color adjustments can be configured through the Hub.

- **ScreamerNet** is a network rendering application. This tool allows you to use every computer at your disposal to assist in the rendering process.

In this chapter, we'll examine each component of the LightWave suite. We'll talk about how the interface is structured (as it's quite a bit different from other graphics applications). We'll also discuss some of the more useful interface tools and look at helpful preferences.

Modeler

Modeler's default interface is comprised of four viewports, a column of tools running down the left side of the screen, a row of tabs running across the top of the screen, and a set of buttons and informational displays along the bottom.

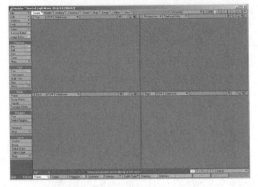

Figure 2-1: LightWave Modeler's interface.

Viewport Settings and Controls

The four windows in the center of Modeler's interface are known as *viewports*. They make up what is often called a "quad display." Each viewport displays your object from a different vantage point. The default configuration provides Top, Back, Right, and Perspective views. Learning how to work with a quad display can be challenging, especially if this is your first experience with 3D software. It takes time to know which viewport you should be working in, and how the changes you make in one viewport will be represented in the others. It also takes time to become comfortable navigating through the displays and working with the various controls.

Viewport Settings

In the upper-left corner of each viewport you'll find the Viewport settings. These pop-up menus let you quickly change a viewport's display angle and type.

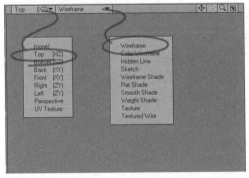

Figure 2-2: The Viewport settings are located in the upper-left corner of each viewport.

> **Note**
>
> A pop-up menu in LightWave is indicated by a small downward-pointing triangle next to a tool or button. These triangles let you know that there are more options than what is shown. Clicking on a pop-up menu presents you with a list of other options to choose from.

The left pop-up menu allows you to adjust the view angle. The view angle determines the orientation of a specific viewport. While there are certainly times when you'll want to change the view angle (for example, to display UV textures), the default configuration of Top, Back, Right, and Perspective typically won't need to be changed.

The right pop-up menu adjusts the view type. The view type (also known as the display type) determines the level of OpenGL rendering that will be applied to a particular viewport. There are 10 view types you can choose from, each of which is illustrated in Figures 2-3 to 2-12.

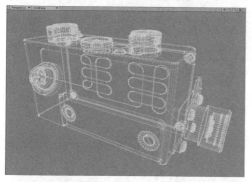

Figure 2-3: The Wireframe display is the default display type for orthographic viewports. It depicts the points and edges of your polygons, but the surfaces of the polygons are not shown.

Figure 2-5: The Hidden Line display type is also similar to the Wireframe display; however, only the polygons that fall within a 90-degree arc of the current viewpoint will be displayed. Polygons that are farther than 90 degrees away will be hidden, making it easier to see and edit the frontmost portions of your object.

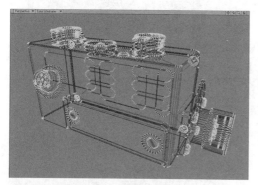

Figure 2-4: The Color Wireframe display is similar to the Wireframe display, but it also takes into consideration the "sketch color" (the wireframe

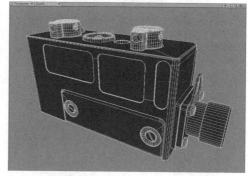

Figure 2-6: The Sketch display type will show a solid object with white wireframes. The polygons in this display type will not show any kind of lighting or surfacing attributes, but they will appear in whatever sketch color you have assigned for them.

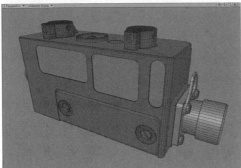

Figure 2-7: The Wireframe Shade display shows surface coloring and the rudimentary lighting that Modeler uses to help you determine the direction each poly is facing. It will also display the wireframes in their respective sketch color.

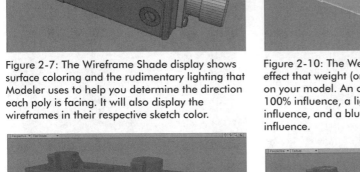

Figure 2-8: The Flat Shade display shows your model as a solid object without any kind of smoothing between polygons; that is, each polygon comes to a sharp edge when it meets its neighbor, regardless of its surface smoothing settings. (For more information on surface smoothing, see Chapter 6.)

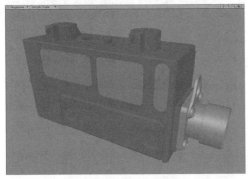

Figure 2-9: The Smooth Shade display shows your model as a solid object with its surface smoothing settings applied.

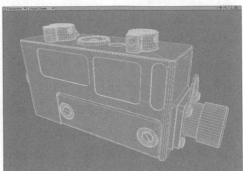

Figure 2-10: The Weight Shade display shows the effect that weight (or "influence") maps will have on your model. An orangish-red color indicates 100% influence, a light-green color indicates 0% influence, and a blue color indicates negative influence.

Figure 2-11: The Texture display shows the effect of image maps applied to the color texture channel of your polygon's surface.

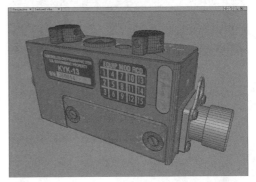

Figure 2-12: The Textured Wire display shows textures and rudimentary lighting along with wireframes rendered according to each polygon's sketch color.

Viewport Presets

I typically leave my Top, Back, and Right viewports set to Wireframe; however, I change my Perspective viewport frequently while I work. To quickly change between viewport settings, you can create viewport presets. Let's do that now.

1. Leave the Top, Back, and Right views set to Wireframe. Now change the Perspective view type to Textured Wire. This is the view type I use most, so in conjunction with the Wireframe display in the other viewports, this constitutes my default configuration — the one I always come back to.

2. Hold down the <Ctrl> key and press the **5** key on your numeric keypad. The Save View Preset window will appear.

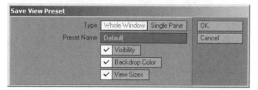

Figure 2-13: Pressing <Ctrl> + a number from 1 to 9 on the numeric keypad allows you to save your viewport settings to that shortcut assignment.

3. Change Type to **Whole Window**. This will save the settings for all viewports. For Preset Name, type the word **Default**. Make sure Visibility, Backdrop Color, and View Sizes are all checked. Then press **OK**.

4. Now place your mouse over the Perspective viewport. Hold down the Ctrl key again and press the **2** key on the numeric keypad. Change Type to **Single Pane**. Enter **Textured Wire** for Preset Name. Leave all the other settings at their default and hit **OK**.

5. Switch the Perspective view type to **Texture** and repeat the process outlined in step 4 (making sure your

mouse is over the Perspective viewport), but this time, press the **1** key and type **Texture** for Preset Name.

6. Finally, change the view type to **Wireframe** and save this preset to the **3** key on your numeric keypad.

You have now created presets to control individual viewports as well as the entire quad display. If you ever tweak your viewport layout (by dragging the edge divider between viewports, for example), you can use these keys to return to your original configuration.

Place your mouse over *any* viewport and press the 1, 2, and 3 keys on the numeric keypad. You'll see that viewport switch to a Perspective view with Texture, Textured Wire, and Wireframe display. Now place your mouse over the column of buttons on the left side of the screen. Press the 1, 2, and 3 keys on the numeric keypad again. All your viewports will change to match your presets. To return to your default configuration, hit the 5 key on the numeric keypad.

Press the 5 key on the numeric keypad to restore your default display configuration before continuing.

Viewport Controls

In addition to the controls that change the viewport's angle and display type, the top of every viewport has four control buttons that let you move, rotate, zoom, and minimize or maximize the view.

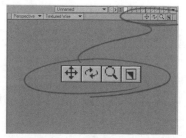

Figure 2-14: These tools control the position, rotation, zoom, and size of the viewports.

Note

The process of clicking your left mouse button, holding it down, and moving the mouse
around is known as "clicking and dragging."
You'll use this process frequently while working in LightWave and we'll refer to it
throughout the course of this book. Unless
otherwise indicated, the term "clicking and
dragging" assumes the action will be performed with the left mouse button.

Note

Hot keys (also called keyboard shortcuts) are
essential for taming the learning curve and
increasing your productivity. This is true for
any software, but it's doubly so with
LightWave. While you don't have to memorize every single hot key that comes along,
there are several that are definitely worth
learning. I'll set these apart in special "Hot
Key Block" sections where applicable.

Figure 2-15:
Pan button.

Figure 2-17:
Zoom button.

Figure 2-16:
Rotate button.

Figure 2-18:
Min/Max button.

Note

LightWave's hot keys are case sensitive! If
you're having trouble with a particular shortcut, make sure that Caps Lock isn't on.

Clicking and dragging on the Pan button
will scroll the viewport around so you can
center the display on different things. (All
viewports that do not have Independent
Center checked under Edit | Display
Options | Viewports will also move when
you pan around your viewport. We'll examine this further in the "Modeler Options"
section.)

Clicking and dragging on the Rotate button will orbit a Perspective viewport around
its center. (This button is inactive in
non-perspective views.)

Clicking and dragging on the Zoom button will zoom in and out of the viewport
(and just as with Pan, all viewports without
Independent Zoom selected will respond).
Drag to the left to zoom out, and drag to the
right to zoom in.

Clicking on the Min/Max button will toggle the viewport in and out of full-screen
mode. You can also tap the 0 key on your
keyboard's numeric keypad to enter and
exit full-screen mode.

Hot Key Block

Viewports

<a> zooms the display to fit your objects
within the visible viewports.

<A> zooms in on just the selected points,
polys, or edges.

<g> centers the view at your mouse
pointer.

<,> (comma key) zooms out by a factor of
1.

<.> (period key) zooms in by a factor of 1.

<<> (less than key) zooms out by a factor
of 2.

<>> (greater than key) zooms in by a factor
of 2.

<Ctrl>+<Alt> and dragging in a viewport
zooms in and out, just like clicking and
dragging on the Zoom button.

<Alt> + dragging in an orthographic
viewport (any view that isn't a Perspective
view) scrolls that viewport in the direction
you drag the mouse.

<Alt> + dragging in a Perspective viewport
orbits the view around its center.

<Shift>+<Alt> and dragging in a Perspec-
tive viewport scrolls (pans) it in the direction
you drag the mouse. (In an orthographic
view, this works just the same as <Alt>
dragging.)

Object and Layer Controls

In the upper right-hand corner of Modeler's screen are the Current Object and Object Layer controls.

Objects

LightWave keeps a running list of all objects open in both Modeler and Layout. The current object's filename is shown in the Current Object pop-up menu.

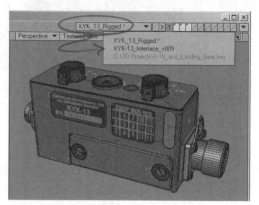

Figure 2-19: The Current Object pop-up menu provides a list of objects open in Modeler and Layout.

Clicking on this pop-up menu shows the list of objects currently open in Modeler and Layout. Objects open in Modeler are shown in black. Objects open in Layout but not currently open in Modeler are shown in gray. Objects that have been modified in Modeler or Layout and have not been saved are shown with an asterisk (*) after their name.

Layers

One of the most powerful and versatile features in LightWave is its layers. In Modeler, layers are like storage bins, but they can be used for much more than organization. Layers allow you to reference another object in the same 3D space where you work without worrying about accidentally altering your reference material. They allow you to create object hierarchies for animation. They even allow you to perform complex modeling functions such as Booleans and Rail Extrusions.

Figure 2-20: The Layer controls are easy to use but have a tremendous amount of power.

Layers can exist in one of four possible "conditions":

- A layer can be empty with nothing in it.

- A layer can have something in it, you can see its contents, and you can directly manipulate what you see. (This is called a "foreground" layer.)

- A layer can have something in it and you can see its contents, but you cannot directly manipulate what you see. (This is called a "background" layer.)

- A layer can have something in it, but its contents are not visible because the layer is not selected or the contents have been hidden.

The content of foreground layers will be shown in the appropriate display type for each viewport. The content of background

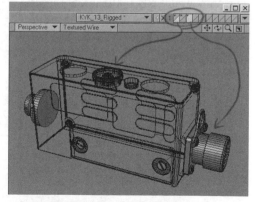

Figure 2-21: You can identify the state of a layer by looking at its icon as well as looking at how the objects are depicted in your viewports.

layers will be displayed as black wireframes. This allows you to visually determine what objects are in the foreground and background without looking at the layer settings.

Layers with content have a little black triangle in the upper-left corner of their icons. Layers in the foreground have their entire Layer icon highlighted. Layers in the background have only the bottom half of their Layer icon highlighted.

In programs like Photoshop, Illustrator, and Flash, you create new layers when you need them, but Modeler doesn't work that way. Instead, layers are immediately available when you create a new object.

There are 990 layers at your disposal, but only 10 of them are shown on the main interface at any given time. These 10 visible layers are known as a "layer bank." There are 99 layer banks available with each object.

Figure 2-22: The "<" and ">" buttons to the right of the Current Object pop-up menu let you move forward and backward through the layer banks. The current bank number is shown to the left of the first layer icon.

The number directly to the left of the first layer shows which bank you are currently viewing. The "<" and ">" buttons shift you up and down through the "banks."

Layers are saved with the object. When you load an object that has content in different layers, each layer will be in exactly the same position it was when you last saved the object — even blank layers!

When you bring a model into Layout, each layer that contains geometry is handled as its own, separate object. This allows you to save a complex model in a single file and still animate its various parts with ease.

The Layers Panel

The layer bank controls make it easy to work with a handful of layers, but what if you want to manage dozens (or even hundreds) of layers at the same time? The Layers panel allows you to do just that. You can access the Layers panel from Windows | Layers Panel.

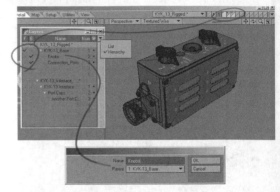

Figure 2-23: The Layers panel allows you to rename layers, establish hierarchies, and control which objects get loaded into Layout.

The Layers panel shows all objects currently open in Modeler, each layer of those objects, and the hierarchy of the layers (if the Hierarchy view is selected from the pop-up menu in the upper right of the Layers panel).

Note

When you have two items and you want one to be linked to the other while at the same time allowing each to be animated independently (like a hat on a character's head), you have to establish a hierarchy for the objects. In 3D terminology, this is considered a "parent" and "child" relationship.

Child items inherit (follow implicitly) the motion applied to their parent items (which can in turn be children of other items). Child items can be adjusted independently, but whatever happens to the parent item will always affect the child.

When you double-click on a layer in the Layers panel, you will be presented with the option to name the layer and assign it a parent.

Foreground layers in the Layers panel have a check under the "F" column. Background layers have a check under the "B" column. If you have Hierarchy view active, you can assign a layer's parent simply by clicking and dragging it under the desired parent layer.

By clicking the check mark at the very top level for an object in the Layers panel, you can quickly select all layers. This makes it easy to select the dozens or even hundreds of layers that can make up a single object so you can see the layers in relation to one another.

Linking to Layout

The pop-up menu without a label in the upper-right corner of Modeler provides options for linking to Layout through the Hub. (When you are running Modeler with the Hub disabled, this pop-up menu isn't visible.) The Hub acts as a server between Modeler and Layout, allowing you to share data between the two programs.

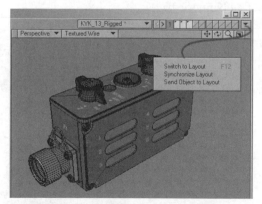

Figure 2-24: The Layout Link pop-up menu allows you to send models directly to Layout.

The Layout Link pop-up menu lets you switch your focus to Layout (Switch to Layout), make doubly sure that Layout has the most recent changes that you've made in Modeler (Synchronize Layout), or send a model that you've just sculpted (or just loaded into Modeler) directly into Layout (Send Object to Layout).

Vertex Maps

Looking at the lower-right corner of Modeler's interface, we find a set of buttons that allow us to create "vertex maps." The "W" button lets you create and select weight maps. The "T" button lets you create and select UV texture maps. The "M" button lets you create and select morph maps. The "C" button lets you create and select color maps. The "S" button lets you create and select selection maps. Vertex maps are simply groupings of points; however, they serve some incredibly powerful purposes.

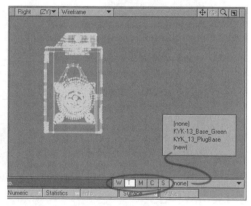

Figure 2-25: The Vertex Map buttons and pop-up menu allow you to create new maps and select existing ones.

Weight Maps

Weight maps define areas of influence. They are frequently used in character animation to limit the influence of bone deformations; however, they can be used for everything from advanced texturing to creating soft selections when modeling.

Texture Maps

Texture maps allow you to "unwrap" your 3D model and place it on a 2D surface so that you can easily paint textures for it in your favorite paint program.

Morph Maps (also known as "Endomorphs")

Endomorphs allow you to store specific deformations with your object. Where programs like Maya require you to store each deformation as a separate object, LightWave allows you to keep them all in a single file. You can use endomorphs for facial animation or to sculpt specific deformations as directed by bone rotations. For example, bending a character's forearm could automatically cause the bicep to bulge into the shape you've sculpted!

Color Maps

Color maps allow you to apply color to individual points. Unlike the colors applied to an object's surface (which are assigned to polygons), color maps are applied to points and can utilize falloff to provide a soft, feathered edge. Color maps are most useful when used in conjunction with surface colors and texture maps to provide localized color "boosts."

Selection Maps

Selection maps (also called selection sets) enable you to store point selections. When modeling, you can use selection sets to quickly select frequently used or hard-to-reach points on your object (such as the points that make up a character's lower jaw). When animating, selection maps allow you to restrict dynamics functions to specific parts of your object.

Adjustment Windows

Running along the bottom of Modeler's interface is a series of buttons that provide access to the most commonly used tools. There are four buttons that open adjustment windows you'll find yourself using on a regular basis. They are the Numeric, Statistics, Info, and Change Surface windows.

Figure 2-26: The most commonly used windows can be opened from these buttons.

Hot Key Block

<n> opens the Numeric panel for the tools in LightWave (creation, modification, or otherwise).

<w> opens the Statistics panel, giving you information about the points and polygons in your object.

<i> opens the Info panel, which gives you detailed information about the selected points or polygons.

<q> opens the Change Surface window, allowing you to assign surfaces to the polygons in your object.

Numeric

The Numeric panel allows you to adjust the properties for many of Modeler's tools. The options displayed in the Numeric panel are context sensitive to the currently selected tool. Many users (myself included) keep this window open all the time and never close it.

Figure 2-27: The Numeric panel allows you to adjust the properties for many tools in Modeler.

Statistics

The Statistics panel gives you *general* information about the points, polygons, and edges in your object. This panel is context sensitive and the information it displays is determined by the current selection mode. You can use this panel to make complex selections and to identify problem areas in your model. Like the Numeric panel, many users keep the Statistics panel open at all times.

Figure 2-28: The Statistics panel gives you general information about the points, polygons, and edges in your object.

Info

The Info panel gives *specific* information about the currently selected points and polygons in your object and allows you to edit many of their properties. (It currently does not work with edges.)

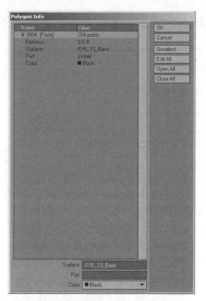

Figure 2-29: The Info panel gives you detailed information about the currently selected points and polygons.

Change Surface

The Change Surface window allows you to assign a new surface to the currently selected polygons. If no polygons are selected, the surface will be assigned to all polys in the currently selected foreground layers.

Figure 2-30: The Change Surface window allows you to assign new and existing surfaces to your polygons.

Selection Modes

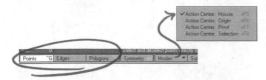

Figure 2-31: The selection and action modes determine what gets selected and how it is modified.

Objects in Modeler are comprised of points that are connected together to form polygons. The link between any two points in a polygon is known as an "edge." As you build your objects, there will be times when it will be best to work with only the points, only the polygons, or only the edges. To determine which of these you're working with, you must choose a "selection mode."

Polygons mode lets you select the geometric shapes that make up your object. Points mode lets you select the individual vertices that make up each polygon. Edges mode allows you to select the portion of a polygon between two points.

Selecting and Deselecting

- To select elements (points, polygons, or edges, depending on your selection mode), simply left-click on them (or right-click to "lasso" around them if you like).

- To deselect individual elements that have already been selected, simply left-click them again (or right-click and "lasso" around them).

- To add elements to an existing selection, hold down <Shift> while left-clicking on them (or right-click, "lassoing" them).

- To completely deselect everything you have selected, press </> (or left-click any blank (unused) portion of the interface).

Note

Modeler and Layout provide more keyboard shortcuts than any other program I've encountered. While this enhances the workflow, it comes at a price. You have to pay close attention to case sensitivity. Capital letters will do drastically different things than their lowercase counterparts. If you're using keyboard shortcuts and are not getting the results you expect, check to make sure Caps Lock is not turned on.

Note

Modeler's interface shows Polygons and Points selection modes as <Ctrl>+<G> and <Ctrl>+<H>. This may give you the impression that you need to use <Ctrl>+ <Shift>+<G> and <Ctrl>+<Shift>+ <H>. But that's not the case. The correct keyboard shortcuts are <Ctrl>+<g> and <Ctrl>+<h>.

Symmetry

The Symmetry mode can assist you in creating symmetrical models such as cars, planes, and even people. With Symmetry active, what you do to the right side of your object is automatically mirrored to its left side.

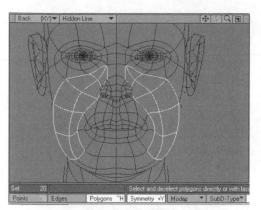

Figure 2-32: With the Symmetry action mode active, selecting the polygons on the right side of a model's face automatically selects their counterparts on the left side. Any tweaking of the points, polygons, or edges on the right will automatically be mirrored on the left.

Note

Symmetry only works when the geometry on the negative side of the X-axis is exactly the same as what is on the positive side of the X-axis. Just being close won't cut it. If you're modeling something symmetrical but Symmetry mode isn't working, delete the left half of your object and use Multiply | Duplicate | MirrorX tool to restore its symmetry.

If you are planning to make something that is symmetrical, start out with your base form perfectly centered along the X-axis (press the F2 key to center your object in Modeler) and always make sure you have Symmetry active when you are sculpting.

Action Centers

The Action Center modes allow you to determine where the action of the modification tool takes place. This has a tremendous impact on how you use two of the most common modification tools: Stretch and Rotate. Let's look at how the various Action Centers affect our use of the Rotate tool.

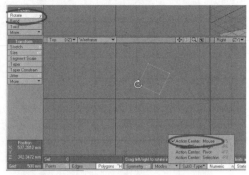

Figure 2-33: Action Center: Mouse — Rotation will occur around the position of the mouse.

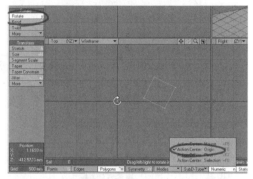

Figure 2-34: Action Center: Origin — Rotation will occur around the origin (the point where X, Y, and Z all equal zero). The position of the mouse has no effect on the action.

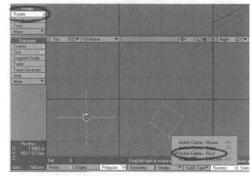

Figure 2-35: Action Center: Pivot — Rotation will occur around the foreground layer's pivot point (each layer in Modeler has one distinct pivot point that can be set via View | Layers | Pivot tool). The position of the mouse has no effect on the action.

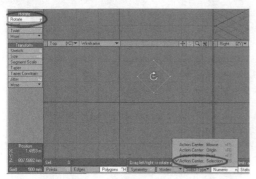

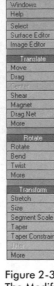

Figure 2-36: Action Center: Selection — Rotation occurs around the center of the selected geometry. If nothing is selected, Modeler will calculate the center based on all visible geometry. The position of the mouse has no effect on the action.

Action Centers are most frequently used with the Stretch and Rotate tools to alter the size and shape of your objects.

Quick Info Display

In the lower-left corner of Modeler is a readout that quickly lets you know the exact position of your mouse, how many elements you have selected, and how much area each grid square represents.

Figure 2-37: Modeler's Quick Info display gives you important feedback on the position of your mouse, the grid size, and the number of points, polygons, or edges selected.

Modeler Toolsets

On the left-hand side of Modeler's interface is a column of tools. The tools you see are directly linked to the tabs at the top of Modeler's window.

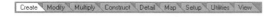

Figure 2-39: The Modify menu tab.

Figure 2-38: The Create menu tab.

Figure 2-40: The Multiply menu tab.

When the Create tab is active at the top of the screen, the primary set of tools used to create geometry are displayed. This includes "primitives" such as boxes, balls, and cones as well as text, points, polygons, and curves.

> **Note**
>
> Any time you see a pop-up menu with "More" on it, that means there are additional tools that aren't being displayed because of the screen size. You can access these tools through the pop-up menu.

The Modify tab contains a collection of tools that modify existing geometry by moving, rotating, and resizing it.

Figure 2-41:
The
Construct
menu tab.

Figure 2-42:
The Detail
menu tab.

Figure 2-43:
The Map
menu tab.

Figure 2-44:
The Setup
menu tab.

Figure 2-45:
The Utilities
menu tab.

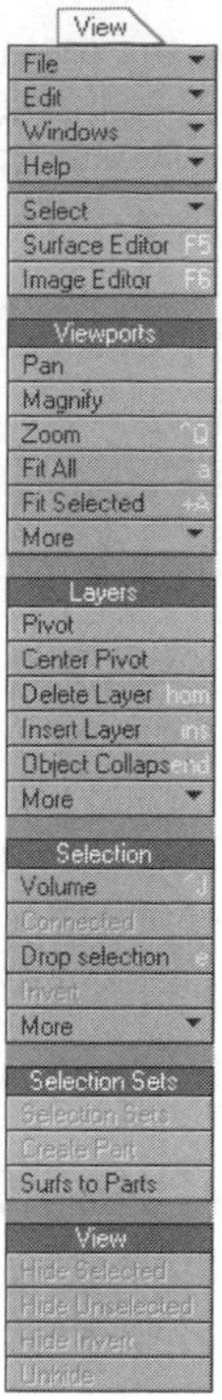

Figure 2-46:
The View
menu tab.

It's a pretty simple way to think about it, but you create objects with the tools under the Create tab and you modify them with the tools under the Modify tab. With these tools, you can move, rotate, drag, bend, twist, size, and stretch your objects.

The Multiply tab contains the tools that take existing geometry and make more of it (for example, extruding, cloning, or slicing it in half).

The Construct tab is home to the tools that affect the construction (makeup) of your geometry (such as Booleans and point/polygon reduction).

The Detail tab holds the tools that focus on the detail-oriented aspects of modeling. You can assign a sketch color, fuse (weld)

two vertices into one, and add edges to your object.

The Map tab houses most of the tools used to modify and refine vertex maps. Using the tools in this section, you can create UV textures, morph targets, and weight (influence) maps, which will give you tremendous control over the appearance of your objects.

The Setup tab contains the tools you'll need to set up and adjust a character's skeleton (used for character animation) as well as add "gons" (polygons that can be converted to various objects such as lights in Layout).

The Utilities tab allows you to add plug-ins and launch custom scripts (known as LScript commands). The Utilities tab also features a "catch-all" pop-up menu called Additional. All of the third-party plug-ins you bring into Modeler will appear in this menu by default.

The View tab controls zooming and panning. It lets you hide and unhide selected elements, make complex selections, and create groups of polygons and points. The View tab also features several layer tools that allow you to add, delete, and merge the layers of your object.

The tabs and buttons in Modeler's interface can be completely customized (as we'll see shortly). The default layout follows a logical flow and suits most people's needs, but you are not stuck with it. You can change the layout to match previous versions of LightWave or even match that of popular studios like Digital Domain. LightWave's interface flexibility allows you to completely customize the program to look and feel the way you're most comfortable with.

Modeler Options

Modeler keeps its program preferences in two separate locations.

General Options

Modeler's basic preferences can be set in the General Options window, which can be found under Edit | General Options.

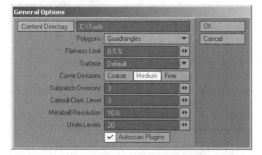

Figure 2-47: The General Options window.

Here's a quick rundown of the settings:

- **Content Directory** — This tells LightWave the default root path where models, textures, and scenes for your current project are kept.

- **Polygons** — This tells LightWave what base shape to use in geometry creation whenever possible. Quadrangles work best when creating subdivision surfaces for high-resolution models, while triangles work best for some game engines.

- **Flatness Limit** — This is a setting you will probably never need to change. (I've never touched it in all my years of using LightWave.) It tells Modeler how much deviation is acceptable among the points that define a flat, planar polygon before it is considered non-planar.

- **Surface** — This determines what surface gets applied to any newly created geometry.

- **Curve Divisions** — This determines how many points will be used when you convert a spline (spatial line) into a polygon. The default of Medium is often more than adequate, and I find that Coarse works well in the majority of situations.

- **Subpatch Divisions** — This tells LightWave how many virtual polygons to use when you convert a low-resolution "cage" object into a subdivision surface object using Modeler's subpatch mode. Higher numbers yield smoother surfaces but are much slower to work with.

- **Catmull-Clark Level** — This tells LightWave how many virtual polygons to use when you convert a low-resolution cage object into a subdivision surface object using Modeler's Catmull-Clark mode. Catmull-Clark sub-ds are similar to subpatches but will work with polygons consisting of more than four points.

- **Metaball Resolution** — This tells Modeler how many polygons to use for displaying and "freezing" metaballs, a kind of digital clay. The default of 10 provides a good balance between quality and performance.

- **Undo Levels** — This tells LightWave how many levels of "undo" to keep in memory. (The default is 20, but I set mine to 100 so I can feel free to experiment.)

- **Autoscan Plugins** — Keeping this option checked will ensure that Modeler scans its install directory for any new plug-ins you drop into it. If you uncheck this, you will have to add new plug-ins manually.

Display Options

Most of the preferences that affect how you interact with Modeler are found in the Display Options window, which is accessible through Edit | Display Options.

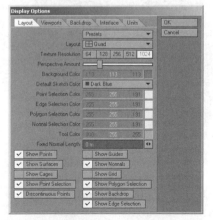

Figure 2-48: The Layout tab of the Display Options window lets you adjust settings that affect all viewports by default.

When the Display Options window is first opened, the Layout tab is shown. Here you can adjust the way that points, polygons, and edges are displayed. You can change the OpenGL texture resolution, alter the amount of perspective distortion shown in the Perspective viewports, and change the default wireframe color for your objects. You can also determine what you see and don't see in your viewports by checking/unchecking the various "show" buttons at the bottom of the Layout tab.

I typically uncheck Show Cages (the polygonal base of subpatches) as I find them distracting. The same is true for their "guides." I also turn off the grid by default and only turn it on when it's necessary. I occasionally turn on and off Show Point Selection and Show Polygon Selection when it suits the type of work I'm doing.

One important thing to make note of is that LightWave Modeler's familiar "quad"-style layout can be changed here by selecting another style from the Layout pop-up menu. Don't feel like you have to stick with the quad layout. The other layouts can be quite helpful.

Note

LightWave's Viewport layout can be further tweaked by clicking and dragging on the bars that separate the viewports, resizing them to your exact needs.

On the Viewports tab, you can make specific changes to the preferences for each viewport.

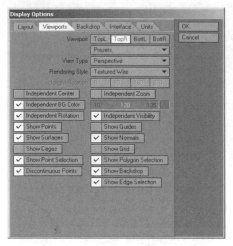

Figure 2-49: The Viewports tab lets you customize the settings for each individual viewport.

- **Independent Center** and **Independent Zoom** let you pan and zoom around a viewport without disturbing the other viewports that might be centered in on some important details.

- **Independent BG Color** lets you change LightWave's hallmark gray background to any color you like. I prefer a grayish-blue.

- **Independent Rotation** lets you unlink the rotation of this viewport from all others. In a typical quad layout with one Perspective viewport, this won't do much. But if you set multiple viewports to Perspective, the rotation of one will affect the rotation of all the rest. If you want to be able to rotate just one while leaving the other views where they are, Independent Rotation will let you do that.

- **Independent Visibility** allows you to alter the same settings found in the Layout tab, but they will only affect the specific viewport you've chosen.

The Backdrop tab lets you put an image into the background of any orthographic viewport. This is helpful when you're

building a model from reference photos or drawings.

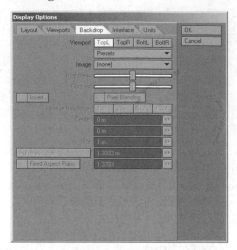

Figure 2-50: The Backdrop tab allows you to place images into your orthographic viewports for use as modeling references.

The Interface tab lets you adjust how you interact with Modeler's interface.

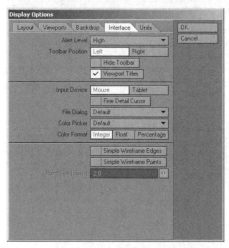

Figure 2-51: The Interface tab affects how you interact with Modeler's interface.

One of the more useful settings on this tab is **Alert Level**. The Alert Level determines whether or not you are presented with a notification window after performing various operations. If you're just starting out, I'd recommend setting this to High. Once you feel comfortable using Modeler, you may want to consider setting this to Medium or Low. The notices will still appear, but rather than popping up in a window, they'll appear in the status bar above the selection modes.

Other useful settings are **Simple Wireframe Points** and **Simple Wireframe Edges**. If you're working on an older graphics card and notice that selecting points and polygons slows down your system, you may find it helpful to select these settings.

The Units tab allows you to determine whether you want to work in metric units or English units. For most projects, **SI** or **Metric** works best as the metric system allows for easy multiplication and division of values. However, if you're working on an architectural project, for example, and know that you need 10-foot ceilings, you can set Unit System to English to make your calculations a bit easier.

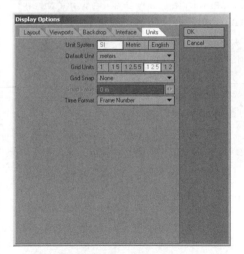

Figure 2-52: The Units tab lets you select the system of measurement.

The **Default Unit** setting determines what value Modeler assumes you're using if one is not specifically stated. For example, if the default unit is set to meters, entering the number 4 into a field would set the value to 4 meters. If your default unit is set to millimeters, entering the number 4 into a field would set the value to 4 millimeters.

> **Note**
>
> You can override the Default Unit setting by simply specifying the exact unit you want to use. For example, if Default Unit is set to meters, entering "6 ft" into a field will result in 1.8288 meters, which is exactly 6 feet.

You can also adjust the Grid Snap setting here. Personally, I find Grid Snap to be annoying, and I make a point of turning it off unless I'm doing something very specific such as working on an architectural model.

The options for Grid Snap are:

- **Standard** — This lets you quickly position elements with respect to decent-sized (one-tenth) segments of Modeler's visible grid.

- **Fine** — This breaks Modeler's Standard snap into even smaller units for precise positioning, still respecting units of its visible grid.

- **Fixed** — This lets you specify exactly what interval to which you wish to adhere your movements, regardless of the visible grid.

- **None** — This lets you move elements with complete freedom.

Menus

The File Menu

In the upper-left corner of Modeler is the File pop-up menu. Here you will find the Load, Save, Import, and Export commands.

The Edit Menu

The Edit pop-up menu, located just below the File pop-up menu, provides traditional edit

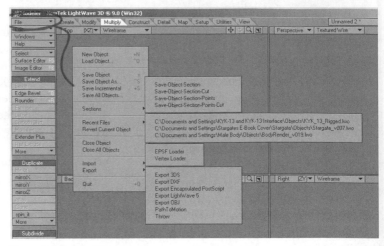

Figure 2-53: The File pop-up menu.

functions (cut, copy, paste, etc.) as well as access to the commands that allow you to customize almost every aspect of Modeler. With the saving and loading of preferences, keyboard shortcuts, and menu layouts, you can take your personal customizations with you wherever you go.

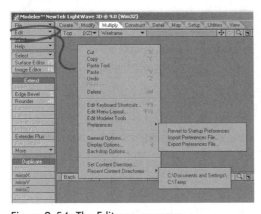

Figure 2-54: The Edit pop-up menu.

The Windows Menu

Just below the Edit pop-up menu is the Windows pop-up menu. Here you'll find access to three additional panels, which let you adjust layers, modify vertex maps, and manage surface presets. You can also use this menu to hide any floating windows and turn on and off the toolbar.

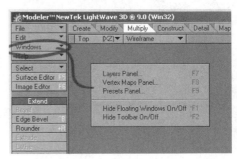

Figure 2-55: The Windows pop-up menu.

The Help Menu

When you run into trouble or have questions about a particular aspect of the software, the Help menu is the first place to turn. The Help pop-up menu provides access to local as well as online web-based documentation. Completely rewritten for LightWave v9, these files contain a wealth of useful information to aid in your understanding of the software.

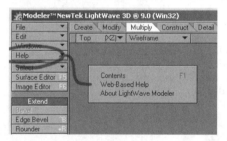

Figure 2-56: The Help pop-up menu.

The Select Menu

The Select pop-up menu provides quick access to some of Modeler's more useful selection tools. For example, you can select loops of points, polygons, and edges with the Select Loop tool. You can select alternating points on an object with the Select Nth tool. Many of these tools (as well as other powerful selection tools) can be found in the View tab under the Selection | More | More pop-up menu.

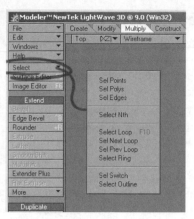

Figure 2-57: The Select pop-up menu.

Modeler Quick Menus

The LightWave manual calls these "contextual pop-ups." I prefer the term "quick menus" because that's really what they are. By placing your mouse over a viewport and holding down <Shift>+<Ctrl> + either the left, right, or middle mouse button, these menus appear. They let you do all sorts of things you would normally have to sift through a few layers of pop-up menus to get at. (These menus are fully customizable, as are all of LightWave's menus.)

Figure 2-58: <Shift>+<Ctrl>+clicking the left, middle, or right mouse button will produce these context-sensitive menus.

Hot Key Customization

If you come to LightWave already accustomed to certain hot keys doing certain things, or if you've been using the software for some time and just want quicker access to your favorite tools, you can assign them a keyboard shortcut.

Modeler's default keyboard shortcuts are pretty good, but I find the process of clicking a blank portion of the interface (or tapping the </> key) to deselect things rather cumbersome. I really like keeping my left hand on the keyboard while I work, so I typically assign the Deselect command to the <e> key. Let's look at how easy it is to do this.

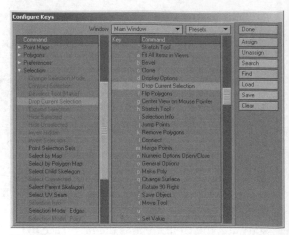

Figure 2-59: You can use the Edit | Edit Keyboard Shortcuts command to assign any Modeler tool to virtually any key or key combination.

1. Choose **Edit | Edit Keyboard Shortcuts** to bring up the Configure Keys window. Expand the selection menu from the Command list on the left by clicking on the small white arrow next to its name. Then click on the **Drop Current Selection** command to highlight it.

2. Scroll through the Key list on the right until you've found the keyboard shortcut you want. For me, this would be the <e> key. Click on it to highlight it.

3. Currently, the <e> key is assigned to the Extender Plus tool. Click on the **Unassign** button to remove the Extender Plus tool from this keyboard shortcut.

4. Click on the **Assign** button to assign the Drop Current Selection tool to the <e> key.

5. Click **Done**.

Now when you select points, polygons, or edges, you can simply tap the <e> key and they will be deselected.

Note

Under the Presets pop-up menu are the default hot key mappings for LightWave v9, as well as presets for versions of LightWave going back to 6.0. You can also switch your settings to match those used in professional studios by choosing Studio Production Style. If you don't like the changes you've made, you can always switch back to the LightWave v9 defaults.

Note

You can click the Save button in the Configure Keys window to back up your hot keys so you can use them on another computer or share them with friends.

Menu Layout Customization

If you want to completely restructure LightWave's menu layout, you can do so. You can add, delete, and rearrange the menu tabs and customize the way each and every menu is displayed. Once you get a taste for how customizable LightWave is, you'll wish all your other programs offered this much control.

One of the first things I do to configure Modeler is add a "Plugins" tab. This allows me to add buttons for my favorite third-party tools. Let's take a look at how easy it is to do this.

1. Open up the Configure Menus window by choosing the **Edit | Edit Menu Layout** command.

At first glance, this long list can be very intimidating. But in most cases, you'll likely only ever change the items found under the main menu. So begin by closing all of the top-level menus by clicking on the white arrow to the left of their names. This makes it a bit easier to see what we're working with.

2. Toggle open the **Main Menu** tree. You'll notice that the subcategories under Main Menu match the tabs at the top of the interface. Click on the **View** group, but don't toggle it open. Now click on the **New Group** button to the right of the window.

A new tab appears in the interface and a new group (appropriately called "New Group") gets added to the tree.

3. Click on **New Group**, click the **Rename** button to rename it, and type **Plugins** for the new name. Then hit **OK**.

4. Now toggle open the **Additional** menu on the left side of the screen. This is where the plug-ins you add can be found. (Even if you haven't added any plug-ins yet, you'll still find a long list of tools in this menu.) Click on one of

them and drag it until it "snaps" into place under the Plugins group. Release the mouse. A button for this tool will now be placed in the Plugins tab on the interface.

5. Repeat this process for any other tools you'd like to have a button for. You can remove tools from the interface by selecting them and clicking on the **Delete** button. This will not remove the tool from your computer; it will only delete the button from the main interface.

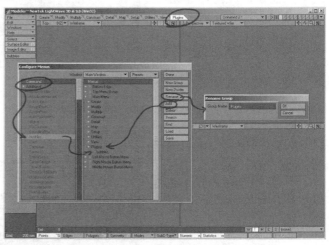

Figure 2-60: You can use the Edit | Edit Menu Layout command to completely customize the interface. Here, a Plugins tab is created and the bubbles tool is assigned to it by dragging and dropping it from the list on the left. You can see that a new tab has been created on the main interface and a button is now available for the bubbles tool.

Note

As is the case with keyboard shortcuts, you can experiment with the various menu presets from the Presets pop-up menu in the Configure Menus window. You can also export your menu layout by clicking on the Save button. This allows you to use your custom menu settings on other computers or to restore them quickly after an update or reinstall.

Layout

Layout is where you position your objects, hang your lights, and make your objects move over time (if you're animating). Layout is also the application where you render your images as either still pictures or animated movie files.

Layout has a lot in common with Modeler. The tabs, menu styles, viewport controls, and Quick Info display readout are all pretty much the same. The differences between Layout and Modeler are so small that you'll likely begin to think of them as one single program.

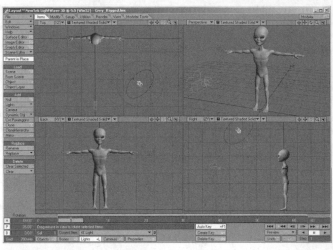

Figure 2-61: The Layout interface with the familiar quad display.

Viewports and Display Modes

Layout's viewports are nearly identical to those found in Modeler. The biggest difference comes from the addition of three extra viewport options. In Modeler, you can only view 3D objects through orthographic and Perspective viewports. Layout builds on this by allowing you to view your objects through a virtual camera, through a light in your scene, or as an organizational chart known as a "schematic."

Layout's real-time OpenGL display modes are also similar to Modeler's, but these too offer a few twists.

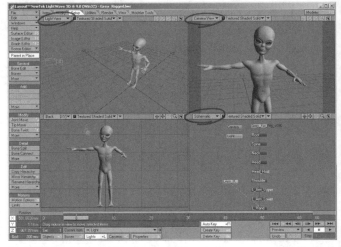

Figure 2-62: Layout adds three additional viewport types: Light, Camera, and Schematic.

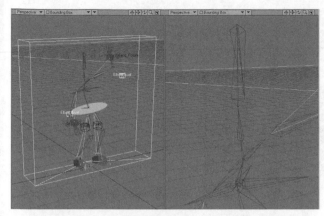

Figure 2-63: Bounding Box does away with all but the simplest geometry. Objects are represented only by a bounding box that encompasses the object's volume. (Bones, lights, cameras, and other "iconic" items are shown normally.)

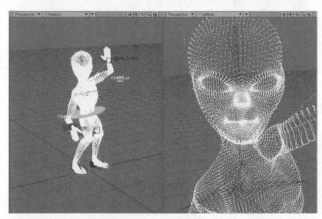

Figure 2-64: Vertices displays only the points in your objects.

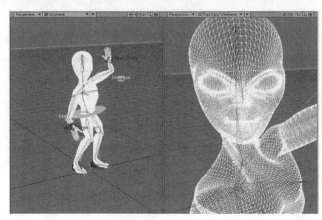

Figure 2-65: Wireframe and Front Face Wireframe are similar to Modeler's Wireframe and Hidden Line display types. These modes speed up refresh rates (how quickly LightWave is able to redraw the screen) and are useful when you start to populate your scene with dozens of objects.

Figure 2-66: Shaded Solid and Textured Shaded Solid are similar to the same display types found in Modeler; however, they are prettier than Modeler's because Layout accounts for up to eight lights in its OpenGL rendering.

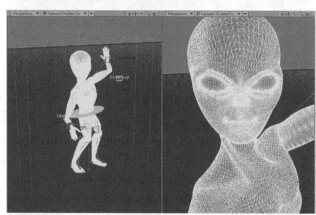

Figure 2-67: Textured Shaded Solid Wireframe is similar to Modeler's Textured Wire view type.

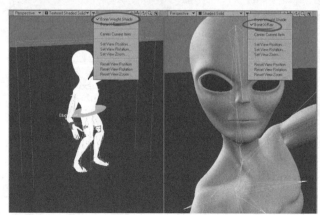

Figure 2-68: Bone Weight Shade shows the effect that bones have on an object. Colors are determined by the bone's color, and the blending shows the effect of the various bone weight maps that limit the bone's influences. Bone X-Ray lets you see the bones that may be hidden inside your object.

Viewport Controls

The viewport controls in Layout are almost exactly the same as Modeler's. Move (Pan), Rotate (Orbit), Zoom, and Min/Max all do exactly the same thing. The one change to the viewport controls is the addition of the little symbol on the left that looks like a gun sight or crosshair. That symbol toggles on and off Center Current Item mode. When active, LightWave will center that viewport in all three dimensions around your current item's pivot point.

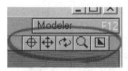

Figure 2-69: Layout's viewport controls.

Note

It's easy to forget you've got Center Current Item active. If Center Current Item is active when you switch to another item, that viewport will "jump" to center that item in the viewport. If you're going to use the Center Current Item feature, I recommend turning it on to center your object, then immediately turning it off again.

Moving and Rotating Objects in Layout's Perspective Views

In Layout, it's not uncommon to move and arrange objects while viewing your scene through a single perspective viewport (such as the Camera View). However, your mouse can only move left, right, up, and down. It can't account for movement in all three dimensions. To overcome this, Layout uses a clever methodology.

To move an object forward, backward, left, or right (this is the X-Z plane), simply activate the Move tool (keyboard shortcut

<t>), then click and drag with your left mouse button.

To move an object up or down (this is the Y plane), simply click and drag with your right mouse button.

The same concept applies to panning a viewport. You can click on the Pan icon and move in the X-Z plane by dragging with your left mouse button. Likewise, you can pan in the Y plane by dragging with your right mouse button.

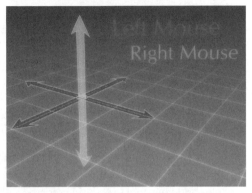

Figure 2-70: Click and drag with your left mouse button to move in the X-Z plane. Click and drag with your right mouse button to move in the Y plane.

Rotating an item (keyboard shortcut <y>) or orbiting a viewport follows a similar convention. While holding down the left mouse button, you can rotate the heading and/or

Figure 2-71: Click and drag with your left mouse button to rotate heading and pitch. Click and drag with your right mouse button to rotate bank.

35

pitch. Holding down the right mouse button rotates in bank only.

In addition to using the viewport controls, you may find it helpful to use the following keyboard shortcuts:

• To pan in a Perspective viewport, just as in Modeler, hold <Shift>+<Alt> while dragging your mouse (still following the above rules for left and right mouse buttoning).

• To orbit about a Perspective viewport's center, hold <Alt> while dragging the mouse (still following the above rules for left and right mouse buttoning).

Linking to Modeler

Layout's link to Modeler is the Modeler button in the upper-right corner of the window. (This button is only visible when running Layout with the Hub active.) When you click on this button, you will be taken to Modeler and your most recently selected object will be opened and ready for you to modify.

Figure 2-72: The Modeler button.

The Timeline

The Timeline is a ruler for measuring the duration of your animation. The length of time (measured in frames) that is currently visible can be adjusted by changing the numbers on either side of the Timeline.

This allows you to zoom in and out of various portions of the Timeline and focus on specific events within your animation.

The default Timeline length is 60 frames, which equals two seconds of animation at the NTSC standard of 30 frames per second. The blue bar with the number at its center is the Current Frame indicator. It is also known as the Frame Slider. You can drag this to any frame in your animation to see what's happening at that particular instance in time.

Note

The Current Frame indicator can be set to show frames (fractional and whole), SMPTE time code, feet and frames (Film Key Code), and the scene's time in seconds. We'll look at which preferences control this in the "Layout Preferences" section of this chapter.

Playback Controls

In the lower right-hand corner of Layout are controls similar to those found on a DVD player. These buttons let you play your scene immediately (without having to render anything), forward or backward, in all viewports, respecting each viewport's maximum render level.

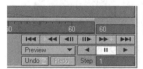

Figure 2-74: The Playback controls.

Figure 2-75: The Previous Key Frame and Next Key Frame buttons.

Figure 2-73: The Timeline and Current Frame indicator are at the bottom of Layout's viewport(s). On either side of the Timeline are input fields for the Start Frame and End Frame. (You can click in these fields and change how long your scene is; negative numbers are okay.)

You may not have seen buttons for Previous Key Frame and Next Key Frame before. We'll take a detailed look at key frames in Chapter 4, but for the moment, you can think of these as the Next/Previous Chapter buttons on a DVD player. They allow you to jump directly to the important events that take place in your scene.

At the bottom of the interface is the Step input field. You can click in this area and tell LightWave to play every frame (1), every other frame (2), every third frame (3), etc. Increasing the Step setting can improve playback performance on complex scenes at the cost of playback accuracy.

Note

You can further improve playback on complex scenes by changing your view mode to Wireframe, switching to a quad view, and disabling three of the four viewports by changing their view angle to (none).

At the left side of the playback controls is the Preview pop-up menu. The options here allow you to build a RAM preview to ensure that your animation plays back at exactly the same frame rate as it would when rendered. The RAM preview uses the upper-left OpenGL viewport to render your animation, and can be a good way to proof your work for clients before committing to a lengthy rendering session. You can even save your RAM preview in the file format and codec of your choice by clicking on the Preview pop-up menu and choosing Preview Options.

Under the Preview pop-up menu, you'll find Layout's Undo/Redo button. The number of undos available can be set in the General Options panel. You can also undo and redo using the keyboard shortcuts of <Ctrl>+<z> and <z> respectively.

Hot Key Block

Playback Controls

<**Left Arrow**> steps to the previous frame of your scene. (Clicking this at the first frame of your scene will cause the Current Frame indicator to "wrap around" to the last visible frame of your scene.)

<**Right Arrow**> advances to the next frame of your scene. (At the end of your scene, the Current Frame indicator "wraps around" to the beginning.)

<**Shift**>+<**Left Arrow**> jumps to the previous key frame of the currently selected item.

<**Shift**>+<**Right Arrow**> jumps to the next key frame of the currently selected item.

<**Page Up**> plays the animation forward.

<**Page Down**> Plays the animation backward.

<**Insert**> Pauses/stops the animation playback.

Key Creation/Deletion

Just to the left of the frame controls are the buttons that let you create and delete key frames for your items.

Figure 2-76: The Create Key and Delete Key buttons.

Clicking on the Create Key button brings up a window where you can tell LightWave to remember the position, rotation, and/or scale along any axis for your choice of items.

Figure 2-77: The Create Motion Key window lets you create a key frame for the currently selected items.

Delete Key works the same as Create Key, only it deletes key frames rather than creating them.

> **Note**
>
> You can put any frame number into the Create Key At field. You aren't limited to creating key frames only on your current frame.

> **Note**
>
> To create a looping animation, simply move the Current Frame indicator to the first frame of your scene, click on the Create Key button, type the number of the last frame of the scene into the Create Key At box, and choose All Items in the For pop-up menu.

The Auto Key button will automatically create key frames for any item you move, rotate, or resize. This is a great thing for newcomers to animation because it frees you from having to remember to create a key frame every time you modify an item in your scene.

The Auto Key function is actually a two-part system. Auto Key will not work unless both parts are active. In addition to having the Auto Key button turned on, you must also tell LightWave on which channels (axes) you'd like to create keys. You can choose to create keys on only the channels you've already modified, or all channels regardless of whether they've been modified before. This information is set in the General tab of the Preferences window under the Auto Key Create pop-up menu.

Item Selection

Just as you must decide whether you want to work with points, edges, or polygons in Modeler, you must choose the type of item you want to work with

in Layout. To the left of the Create Key/ Delete Key buttons are the item selection mode buttons. These tell Layout whether you want to manipulate the objects, bones, lights, or cameras in your scene.

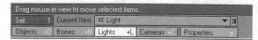

Figure 2-78: The item selection mode buttons.

I'm going to skip over the Properties button right now because there are so many properties for each kind of item. We'll explore these in more detail as we get into later chapters.

Above the item selection mode buttons is the Current Item pop-up menu. Here you will find a list of the items available in your scene. The Current Item pop-up menu filters items based on the current selection mode. For example, if you have the Objects button selected, only objects will appear in the Current Item pop-up menu. If you have the Bones button selected, only the bones of the most recently selected object will appear in the Current Item pop-up menu. The same holds true for lights and cameras.

Just to the right of the Current Item pop-up menu is the List Manager icon. Clicking this icon opens a window with an inventory of the items available in your scene as determined by your current item

Figure 2-79: The List Manager provides an inventory of the items in your scene.

selection mode. For example, if the Lights button is selected, clicking on the List Manager icon will open a window showing all the lights in your scene.

Separate List Manager windows can be opened for each item type and can remain open while you work. You can search for specific items and reorder the list to your liking, making it easy to find just what you're looking for. The List Manager also allows you to create "sets" that display only the items you choose. All of these options work together, giving you a powerful way to organize the content of your scene and making selecting items quick and easy.

Directly above the Current Item pop-up menu is an information bar that Layout uses to keep you on top of what's going on. Information about using the current tool can be found here, such as "Drag mouse in view to move selected items." Error messages also appear here. If something has you stumped, take a peek here — it might give you a clue that will help unravel your mystery.

Quick Info Display

Layout includes a readout of important information such as position, rotation, scale, how many items you have selected, and how much area each grid square represents in the lower left-hand corner of the window.

Figure 2-80: Layout's Quick Info display.

The difference between Layout's Quick Info display and Modeler's is that Layout's is *interactive*. You can enter data into each of these fields to set their properties.

Note

What is currently shown as position information changes to show rotation and scaling, etc., when Layout's active tool is changed.

You can protect an axis from accidental manipulation by clicking on it. For example, clicking on the X will deselect the channel and change the button from white to blue. When a channel is deselected, you will no longer be able to adjust it in Layout's viewports. You can still enter values for it directly into the field, but you won't be able to make changes interactively through the viewports.

The Dope Track

Just above the Timeline but below the viewport window(s) lies a small gray bar. Clicking the small textured area at the center of this bar will pop up the Dope Track. The Dope Track allows you to create and modify your key frames. We'll talk more about the Dope Track and its cousin, the Dope Sheet, in Chapter 4.

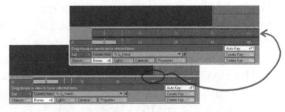

Figure 2-81: The Dope Track.

Layout Menu Tabs

Let's take a look at the menu tabs found in Layout.

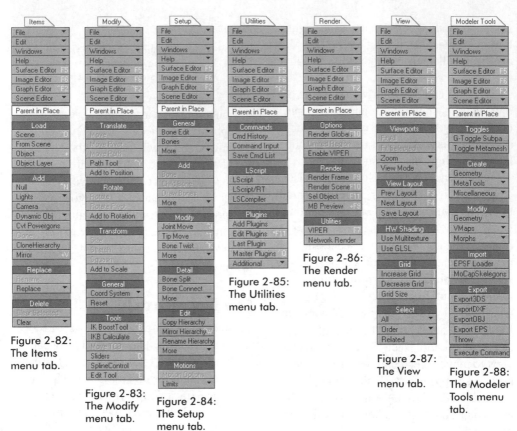

Figure 2-82:
The Items
menu tab.

Figure 2-83:
The Modify
menu tab.

Figure 2-84:
The Setup
menu tab.

Figure 2-85:
The Utilities
menu tab.

Figure 2-86:
The Render
menu tab.

Figure 2-87:
The View
menu tab.

Figure 2-88:
The Modeler
Tools menu
tab.

The Items menu tab provides tools that let you load, add, replace, and delete the different items in your scene. We'll cover these options more in later chapters.

The Modify menu tab contains tools to move, rotate, and resize the objects in your scene. You'll also find tools to adjust key frames and unleash the power of LightWave's IK Booster tool on your characters (more on that in Chapter 24).

The Setup menu tab gives you access to LightWave's powerful character rigging tools. If you've ever rigged a character in another package, you know what a pain it can be. But these tools make it a breeze to create, edit, adjust, and save a character's skeleton. We'll be taking a closer look at character rigging in Chapter 23.

The Utilities menu tab in Layout is virtually identical to the one in Modeler. The Additional pop-up menu here functions just like its counterpart in Modeler and houses the third-party plug-ins you've loaded into Layout.

The Render menu tab lets you change your rendering options (such as turning on ray tracing and choosing an output format for your animation). You'll also find tools to render individual objects, single frames, or full animations, as well as the ability to activate LightWave's Versatile Interactive Preview Renderer (VIPER), which lets you see changes to your surfaces in real time.

The View menu tab gives you the ability to change your viewport setup, activate hardware OpenGL shading, adjust the grid, and make complex selections.

The Modeler Tools menu tab allows you to run a number of Modeler's tools right in Layout. From this tab, you can turn subdivision surfaces on and off, create primitive objects, modify an object's vertex maps, import EPS artwork, and export your models in a variety of formats.

Menus

The File Menu

The File pop-up menu in Layout has many of the same functions that are found in Modeler and a few new options as well.

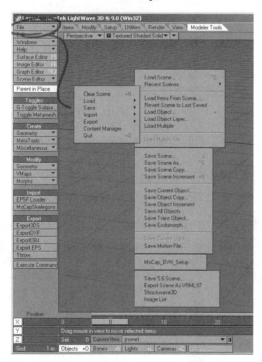

Figure 2-89: The File pop-up menu.

Let's look at some of the more esoteric options.

● **Load Items From Scene** loads the objects (and lights, if you wish) and all their motions into the scene you are currently working on. This is a great way of creating a complex scene from a collection of smaller and simpler scenes.

● **Load Object Layer** lets you load just a single layer from an object rather than loading all its layers at once (which is what Load Object will do).

● **Load Multiple** loads multiple instances of a single object. This eliminates the process of cloning an object once it's already in Layout and is useful for populating a scene with multiple items such as trees, rocks, cars, etc.

● **Save Trans Object** "freezes" an object's deformations, position, orientation, and scale into a single object. This can be handy for saving out models that have been deformed with cloth dynamics, allowing you to further enhance the object's shape in Modeler.

● **Save Motion File** saves all of an item's movement, rotation, and scaling into a single file, which you can then load onto any other item.

● **Content Manager** is a tool used to consolidate the items in your scene and gather all the resources used into one central location. This can be a lifesaver when you need to share your complex scenes with others or simply need to port the scene between work and home.

The Edit Menu

Like its counterpart in Modeler, the Edit pop-up menu houses most of Layout's customization functions.

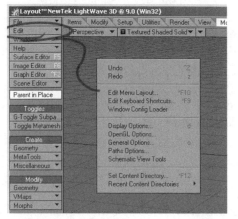

Figure 2-90: The Edit pop-up menu.

The Windows and Help Menus

The Windows pop-up menu provides access to many of Layout's floating palette windows, while the Help pop-up menu offers local and web-based support options.

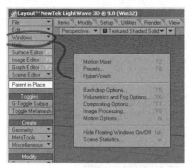

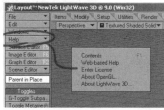

Figure 2-91: The Windows and Help pop-up menus.

Layout Quick Menus

As with Modeler, using the combination of <Shift>+<Ctrl>+ one of the three mouse buttons produces a context-sensitive quick menu.

Figure 2-92: <Shift>+<Ctrl>+clicking the left, middle, or right mouse button will produce these context-sensitive menus.

- <Shift>+<Ctrl>+left-click opens a menu that gives you instant access to many of Layout's most frequently used commands.

- <Shift>+<Ctrl>+right-click brings up a menu that lets you quickly launch different editing windows and select from various rendering options.

- <Shift>+<Ctrl>+middle-click gives you swift access to a plethora of character rigging tools.

Layout Preferences

Layout's Preferences window (which can be opened by pressing the <o> keyboard shortcut) contains several tabs. Let's look at some of the more useful settings found on each tab.

The General Tab

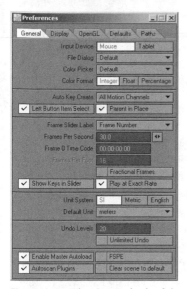

Figure 2-93: The General tab of the Preferences window.

The General tab contains options that affect how you work with Layout's interface.

- **Auto Key Create** works in conjunction with the Auto Key button on the main interface. The options here determine whether keys will be created for all channels, only the modified channels, or none of the channels (essentially turning the feature off).

- **Left Button Item Select** means that you can left-click on an item to select it. (Note that Layout doesn't use the same selection rules that Modeler does. Clicking on an item to select it, then clicking again to deselect it will not work. To deselect an item, you simply select a different item in your scene.)

- **Frame Slider Label** tells Layout what time format you want to see in the Frame Slider (also known as the Current Time indicator). The options available are Frames

(via the Frame Number option), SMPTE, Feet/Frames, or Seconds. Film work is typically done at 24 frames per second. If you need to render to the NTSC television frame rate of 29.97 FPS, you could change this value and your animation would automatically be stretched to fit the new frame rate. If you were to do this, many of your key frames might fall on fractional frames. In order to adjust those frames, you must enable the **Fractional Frames** option.

- **Show Keys in Slider** makes the key frames for the current item appear as yellow "tick-marks" in the ruler-like portion of the Timeline. (I've never found a reason where I've wanted to not show key frames in the Timeline, but I once accidentally deactivated this setting and it took far too long for me to figure out how to get them back.)

- **Play at Exact Rate** is a setting that applies only to the real-time playing of your scene through the playback controls in the lower-right corner of Layout. With this active, Layout will make sure the playback is exactly at whatever FPS you have set in your Frames Per Second option, skipping frames if necessary if your scene is too complex for your video card to handle at real time.

- The **Clear scene to default** option will load any "Default.lws" scene file that it finds in your current content directory whenever you start Layout or clear your scene. This enables you to set up common properties such as light and camera configurations and have them ready to go when you start a new project.

The Display Tab

The Display tab options affect how things are displayed in the main interface.

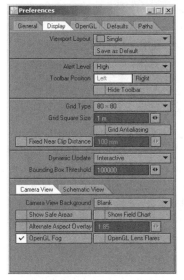

Figure 2-94: The Display tab of the Preferences window.

v9.2 Note

The Display Options window has been updated in LightWave v9.2 to give you control over the new Photo-real Motion Blur and Depth of Field options. For details on the changes, check out the Depth of Field and Motion Blur Preview video in the LightWave 9.2 Videos folder on the companion DVD.

• **Grid Type** is where you can turn off Layout's grid if you need to. You can also specify how large it is (anywhere from 10 x 10 to 100 x 100).

• **Grid Square Size** is where you manually type in how much area you want each grid square to represent.

• **Grid Antialiasing** makes the distant grid squares look nicer (but it also can slow down your video card's display).

• Layout automatically hides geometry that is "too close" (determined by some mysterious referencing of the Grid Square Size setting). Using **Fixed Near Clip Distance**, you can force Layout to draw things it may be leaving out because it thinks they're "too close."

• When LightWave first offered dynamic updating (move a slider and see the results immediately in the viewports), it could be pretty darn sluggish in certain areas. The **Dynamic Update** pop-up menu allowed you to tell Layout to hold off updating the viewports until you're done making adjustments. Now, with LightWave v9, every aspect of dynamic updates (that I've found, at least) is lightning-fast. I've yet to see a reason to change this from Interactive in the recent versions of LightWave.

• **Bounding Box Threshold** tells Light-Wave how many polygons an object has to have before it substitutes a bounding box for it while you're manipulating it. (It shows the object again once you've finished moving/rotating/sizing it.)

• **Camera View Background** shows the background image (still image, image sequence, or movie) you are compositing your LightWave render onto when looking through a Camera View viewport. (You assign the background image using Windows | Compositing Options | Background Image.)

Show Safe Areas turns on a pair of ovals that can be seen through the Camera View viewport. These rings represent the safe zones when working with overscan television frames. Overscan ensures that your picture fills the entire TV screen, but things that move toward the edge of the screen can easily get cut off. Turning on Show Safe Areas lets you determine where the Action Safe and Title Safe areas of your screen are.

The OpenGL Tab

The options in the OpenGL tab affect the degree of detail that will be shown in your viewports.

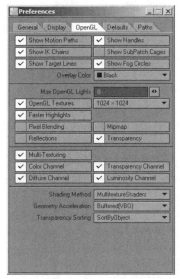

Figure 2-95: The OpenGL tab of the Preferences window.

Show Motion Paths displays the currently selected item's path in the viewports. Key frames are shown with large ticks, while in-between frames are shown with smaller ticks.

Show IK Chains draws a line from an IK chain's root to its goal.

Show Target Lines will draw a dashed line between, for instance, a camera or a light and the item it is targeting.

Show SubPatch Cages shows a ghosting of the polygonal mesh that is the base for your subpatch object.

Show Handles turns on the little arrows and rings that show translation, rotation, and scaling axes for the currently selected items. (You can click directly on a handle and manipulate the item in only that one clicked axis; this overrides the left and right mouse button conventions mentioned earlier.)

Show Fog Circles draws dotted circles (in the overlay color) around the camera (as seen in the orthographic viewports), indicating where objects begin to be affected by LightWave's fog and where they disappear completely into it.

Max OpenGL Lights tells LightWave how many lights you want it to factor in when shading its OpenGL viewports. Eight is the current maximum number of lights; each extra light will slow your system slightly and take away from your ability to see multi-textures on your objects.

Multi-Texturing allows you to preview the effects of procedural textures right in your OpenGL display. Depending on the power of your video card, you may or may not see the benefit from turning on the options found in this section of the OpenGL panel. There's no hard-and-fast rule here, so I'd encourage you to turn them all on and see how responsive your system is. If you find that your display becomes sluggish, try turning off the various channels below the Multi-Texturing setting.

The Defaults Tab

The Defaults tab lets you specify default camera and scene settings.

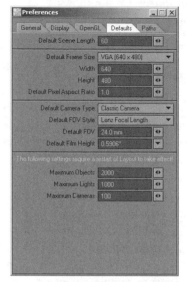

Figure 2-96: The Defaults tab of the Preferences window.

- **Default Scene Length** sets the default length of the Timeline.
- **Default Frame Size** sets the default image size for LightWave's camera.

You can also set camera-specific properties such as the camera type, the field of view (FOV), which is also known as Zoom, and the maximum number of lights, objects, and cameras from this tab.

The Paths Tab

The Paths tab allows you to set the content directory as well as use custom directories for specific types of content.

The content directory is one of LightWave's most overlooked features. It allows you to define a relative path (i.e., "Project/Objects") for all the items used in a given project, including objects, textures, scene files, etc. If you don't specify a

Figure 2-97: The Paths tab of the Preferences window.

content directory, LightWave will look for a fixed path (i.e., "C:/My Files/Current Work/Project/Objects") when loading content. If it does not find that exact path (which is typically the case when loading archived files or scenes originally created on another computer), you'll get an error message because LightWave can't find what it's looking for.

- **Auto-Detect** tells Layout to recognize the folders that typically make up a LightWave content directory. If you load a file in a different content directory, Layout will ask if you'd like to reset the path to this new content directory. This greatly simplifies the process of loading items from many different project folders.

- The **Use custom paths** setting allows you to use different folders for content than those typically required by the content directory. For example, you can place your hand-painted textures in a "Textures" folder and tell Layout to look in it rather than the default "Images" folder.

• The **Create Directories** button will generate folders for the various types of content used by LightWave. Simply click the Content Directory button, specify a root folder, then click the Create Directories button. It will appear as if nothing has happened. However, if you check the content directory, you'll find that over a dozen new folders have been created.

Plug-ins

Plug-ins are external tools that extend LightWave's functionality. Many of these tools are provided free of charge thanks to the generosity of the plug-in authors in the LightWave community.

Plug-ins can do an amazing range of things. For example, the Replace Beep plug-in from Jon Tindall/Binary Arts (which you can find on the DVD that came with this book) allows you to use a custom sound file to alert you when a render has completed. Likewise, the RMan plug-in by Denis Pontonnier (also on the book's DVD) adds 28 amazing procedural textures based on Pixar's Renderman shaders. And the commercial FPrime plug-in from Worley Labs allows you to completely replace LightWave's rendering engine.

Plug-ins have virtually unfettered access to every part of LightWave, and a lot of tools we think of as a standard part of the program (like loading Wavefront .obj files into Modeler) are in actuality plug-ins.

If you have the Autoscan Plugins option enabled in Modeler and Layout, any plug-ins you place in your install/plugins directory will be automatically added and available for you to use. You can also manually add plug-ins through the Utilities | Plugins | Add Plugins menu command in Modeler and Layout.

You can examine plug-ins that you've added with the Edit Plug-ins window. Plug-ins can be grouped either by category or by file. You can also remove plug-ins by selecting them and clicking on the Delete button. (The plug-in isn't deleted from your hard disk — only from being integrated into LightWave.)

LightWave ships with a number of useful plug-ins, but you can also find third-party plug-ins available on the Internet. See Chapter 27 for a list of our favorite third-party plug-ins.

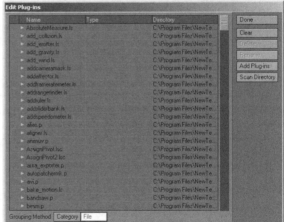

Figure 2-98: Plugins can also be added and removed through the Edit Plug-ins window, launched via the Utilities | Plugins | Edit Plugins menu command.

The Hub

The Hub is a separate application that runs by default whenever Layout or Modeler is started. It acts as a bit of a "client" and a bit of a "server," and in truth, it is quite a bit of both.

Whenever you switch between Layout and Modeler (with the Link button in either program or by using <Alt> + <Tab>), the Hub makes sure both programs are using the most up-to-date versions of objects, surfaces, and other files LightWave uses to get its job done.

Double-clicking on the Hub will bring up the "server" properties and allow you to see the technical details of what the Hub is keeping track of.

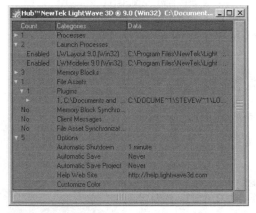

Figure 2-99: The Hub interface.

Would you ever want to run LightWave without the Hub? Yes, sometimes. The Hub, because of all that it does, makes starting up or switching to Layout or Modeler notably slower. If either Layout or Modeler crashes (thankfully, this is rare), the Hub often "gasps" for resources. If you try to restart the crashed program, it can really bring things to a crawl.

Note

Since the Hub acts as both a client and a server, it can cause red flags in certain firewall software. Don't be alarmed if you see this happen. LightWave does not contain spyware! The Hub is simply sending data back and forth between the two principal applications.

PC-Specific Info

To disable the Hub, right-click on the icons for Modeler and/or Layout and click **Properties**. The first field is called "Target." Click in this field and tack on a " –0" (space, minus, zero) after the name of the executable.

Mac-Specific Info

To disable the Hub on a Macintosh, enter the Programs folder in the LightWave folder, and then edit the Modeler cmdLine (or Layout cmdLine) file in your favorite text editor. (This file may or may not already have stuff there.) Enter " –0" as the first line of the document, and then save the file. When you run Modeler with " –0" added to the first line of Modeler cmdLine, you will run without the Hub active. (You can keep a little folder somewhere to hold different versions of your *cmdLine files so you can quickly alternate between using the Hub and not using the Hub.)

You can run multiple instances of LightWave; however, only the first instance will be connected to the Hub (assuming that instance is started from a Hub-enabled icon). All subsequent instances will run without the Hub active until you close the instance that is already connected.

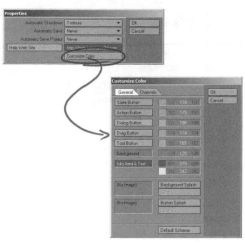

Figure 2-100: The Hub Properties and Customize Color windows.

In addition to ensuring that data is synchronized between Modeler and Layout, the Hub also offers several advanced preferences that affect both Modeler and Layout. Right-clicking on the Hub (Command-clicking on the Mac) while it's running and choosing Properties will bring up a small window. Here you can determine whether the Hub will automatically shut down if Modeler and Layout are closed. You can also enable auto-saving for objects and scenes. And lastly, you can change the interface colors to suit your particular taste.

LightWave ScreamerNet

LightWave ScreamerNet is a stand-alone program that does nothing but render. The programmers at NewTek have managed to condense LightWave's awesome rendering power and fit it into a 528 KB program known as ScreamerNet. This little command-line program is small enough to fit on a floppy disk!

Using LightWave ScreamerNet and a local area network, you can expand your rendering capabilities to include almost any machine on your LAN. (Don't throw out that old 366 MHz laptop! Hook it up and use it as part of your render farm!)

Figure 2-101: As simple as it may look, this little thing has all the power of LightWave's renderer at its command.

Note

Because of the way networks generally handle filenames, never have spaces in the names for your objects or scenes if you plan on rendering over a network. Even if you don't immediately think you'll be rendering across multiple machines, not using spaces in your LightWave names is just a good habit to get into. (That's why you'll frequently see the filenames in this book divided with underscores (_) instead of spaces.)

We'll take a more detailed look at network rendering in Chapter 26.

Conclusion

Modeler, Layout, the Hub, the wide range of plug-ins, and the tiny-but-powerful ScreamerNet all make up the suite of tools we call LightWave. As you're probably beginning to realize, LightWave is an enormous program! But in the coming chapters, we'll break it down and give you the essential information you need to become a productive user.

In the next two chapters we'll start modeling and animating. When you've finished working through these chapters, I'd encourage you to come back and reread this chapter. A lot of the options we've covered here will make more sense once you've had some one-on-one time with the program.

Alright! No more delays. Let's start modeling!

Chapter 3

Basic Skills: Modeling

In this chapter you will learn the foundations of 3D modeling. Modeling, as we've discussed previously, is the art of simulating real-world objects. You begin by creating simple shapes and then, using a powerful set of tools, you develop them into more complex models. One of the most amazing things about modeling is that creating most objects only requires a handful of tools. This chapter will teach you about these tools.

If you're new to modeling, take your time and just play with the tools described in this chapter. Tinker with each of them, one at a time. Don't worry about building something useful or making something pretty. The most important thing at this stage is to get a feel for how the tools work. If you were learning to paint, you'd have to get a feel for the variety of brushes at your disposal. Learning to model is no different. If you spend the time learning each of the tools, you should be able to follow along with the video tutorial (described at the end of the chapter) with relative ease.

Before we start looking at the essential modeling tools, let's back up for a minute and discuss the basics.

3D models are made up of a series of points. These points are connected

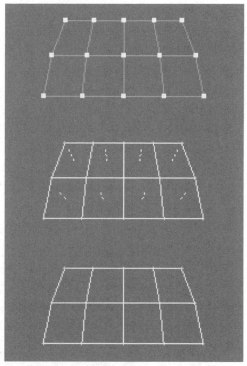

Figure 3-1: Models are made up of points (top), polygons (middle), and edges (bottom).

together to form polygons. The line connecting any two points on a polygon is known as an edge. Let's take a brief look at each of these elements.

Points (Vertices)

point *n.* Math. A dimensionless geometric object having no property but location. (*The American Heritage Dictionary*)

Points exist within three-dimensional space; however, until they are assigned as a part of a polygon they do not render (show up) in Layout's finished drawings or movies.

Points are created using the Create | Points | Points tool. When you left-click in the viewport with the Points tool active, you get a point that you can drag around until it is in the place you want it.

Right-clicking accepts the position of the point you were working with, giving you a new point to position and leaving the other points you have created selected in the order in which they were created.

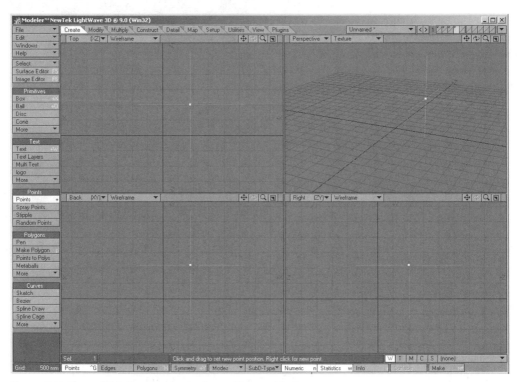

Figure 3-2: The point is the most basic element in an object.

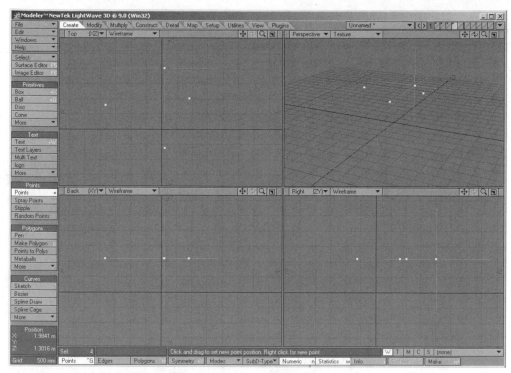

Figure 3-3: Right-click to create and position multiple points.

Polygons

polygon *n*. A closed plane figure bounded by three or more line segments. (*The American Heritage Dictionary*)

Polygons (also called polys) are the elements that show up in LightWave's renderer. The most common polys you'll be working with will have three or four points. These are known as tris (triangles) and quads (quadrangles). But you aren't limited to tris and quads. You can make individual polygons with up to 1,023 points!

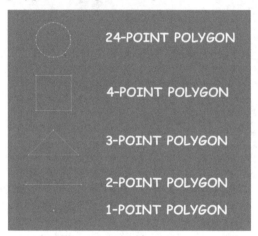

Figure 3-4: Polygons in LightWave can be made up of as many as 1,023 points or as few as a single point.

You can have two-point polygons and even single-point polygons; however, these are typically not used in the creation of "standard" objects. Two-point polygons are often used as "hair guides" for directing the flow of LightWave's hair simulator. Single-point polygons are typically used as stars or other small points of light.

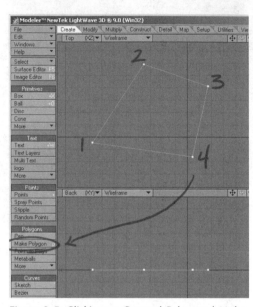

Figure 3-5: Clicking on Create | Polygons | Make Polygon creates a polygon from the points you have selected.

Note

The Pen tool in Modeler (under Create | Polygons | Pen) combines the acts of making points and connecting the dots to make a polygon into one easy tool.

When you're building a polygon (or an entire object for that matter), you should always strive to use the fewest points possible to hold the shape you're after. The more points you have, the more polygons you'll end up with. And large numbers of polygons can bog down the rendering engine, forcing you to wait as the computer crunches all the data. Highly detailed objects are only required when they appear close to the camera. As they move farther away, a high-resolution object and a low-resolution one will begin to look the same. So keep this in mind as you construct your models. Less is often more.

Edges

edge *n.* The line of intersection of two surfaces; a dividing line or border. (*The American Heritage Dictionary*)

The boundaries of each polygon are known as its edges. Unlike points and polygons, edges aren't directly created. Rather, they are a byproduct of the polygon creation process.

Edges serve several useful purposes in 3D modeling. By following an edge as it runs over the surface of a model, you can trace its "flow." This can be particularly useful in character modeling, where the flow of polygons needs to mimic the musculature of the character. Edges also make selections a bit easier. Rather than selecting two points, you can simply select one edge. Additionally, edges can be "weighted" to affect the shape of subdivision surface models and alter how object deformations take place.

Edges can be selected and deselected just like points and polygons. You can add edges to a polygon or an entire object with the Detail | Edges | Add Edges tool. You can also delete them with the Construct | Reduce | Dissolve tool.

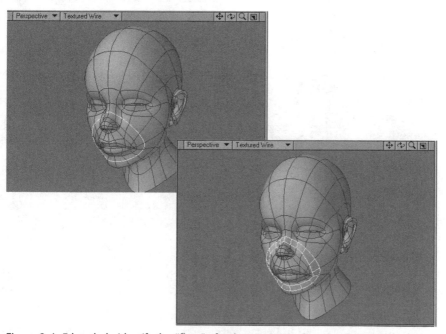

Figure 3-6: Edges help identify the "flow" of polygons. Here, the edge that defines the masseter muscle group has been beveled with the Multiply | Extend | Edge Bevel tool to create additional geometry.

Normals

normal *adj.* Math. Being perpendicular at right angles. (*The American Heritage Dictionary*)

When you make a polygon, LightWave assigns it a surface (initially a light gray color). Once a polygon has a surface, LightWave's camera can "see" it, but only if the *visible* side of the surface is pointing toward the camera. Visible side? Does that mean there's an invisible side? Yes. LightWave only applies the surface to *one* side of each polygon in order to speed up calculations during the rendering process. The side you can see is said to be "facing" you, and its direction is indicated by a "surface normal."

The surface normal appears as a dashed line rising up from the surface of a selected polygon. You can control the length and color of the surface normal in the Display Options window (keyboard shortcut <d>). A Fixed Normal Length setting of 0 m will cause Modeler to automatically adjust the size of the normal based on how close Modeler's virtual camera is to it.

You can force the surface of a polygon to be visible from both sides by setting the Double Sided surface attribute in the Surface Editor (Surface Editor | Double Sided). The reason this attribute isn't active by default is that most objects are only seen from one side,

the outside — like a basketball or a jet fighter. So LightWave culls the back side of its surfaces in order to speed its displays and its rendering.

The direction in which a polygon faces isn't set in stone. If you find that your polygons are facing the wrong direction, you can easily flip them by using the Detail | Polygons | Flip command or by simply pressing the <f> keyboard shortcut.

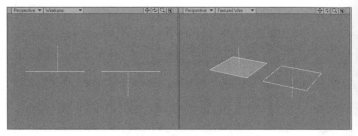

Figure 3-7: The surface normal is a dashed line rising up from the center of each selected polygon. The surface normal indicates which direction the polygon is facing. The front side (from which the normal emanates) will be visible. The back side will appear to be invisible.

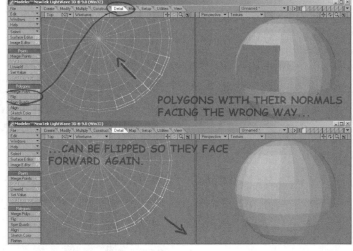

Figure 3-8: The top ball appears to have a rectangular hole in it. But if you look at the polygons selected on the left, you can see that their normals all face inward. This isn't a hole. The polygons are still there; they're just facing the wrong way. To correct this, simply run the Detail | Polygons | Flip command on the selected polygons.

Planar vs. Non-Planar

planar *adj.* 1. Of, pertaining to, or situated in a plane. 2. Flat: a planar surface. (*The American Heritage Dictionary*)

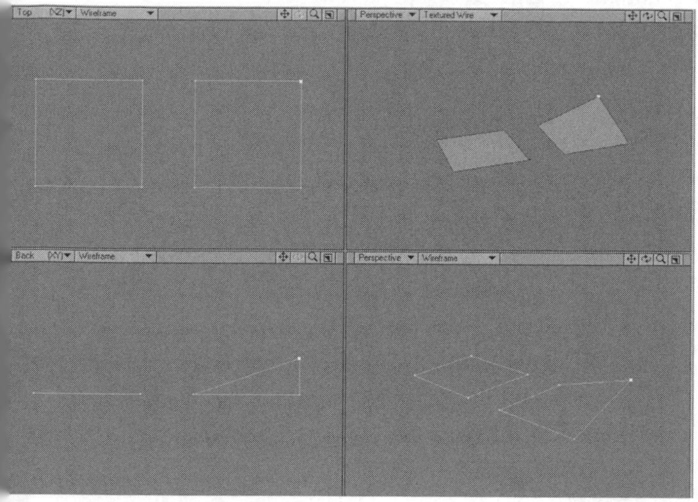

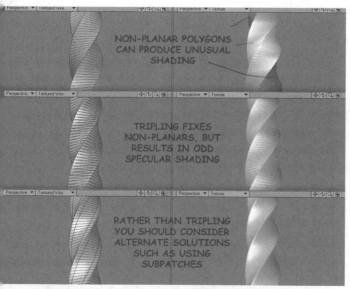

Figure 3-9: A single point on the right polygon has been moved up, making it non-planar.

Figure 3-10: Non-planar polygons can produce shading errors (top). Tripling fixes non-planar polygons by converting them into triangles (which are always flat), but it can create its own weird shading problems (middle). Before tripling non-planar polygons, you should seek out alternate solutions. Here, the polygons have been converted to subpatches (bottom).

As a rule of thumb, the points that make up each polygon should line up to create a perfectly flat plane (and hence a perfectly flat polygon). When they do, the polygon is said to be "planar." When they do not, the polygon is said to be "non-planar."

Non-planar polygons typically result in rendering errors. On still frames, you'll probably notice unusual shading. In animations, you'll typically see strobing or flashing.

Certain modification tools (such as Magnet, Twist, and Jitter) are prone to creating non-planar polygons. Some users try to rectify this by converting the non-planar polygons into triangles, since triangles by their nature are always flat. This process is known as "tripling" and can be accomplished by using the Multiply | Subdivide | Triple tool.

Tripling isn't the best solution for fixing non-planar polygons. It works, but it also increases the number of polygons in your object. In some cases, it can even cause undesirable artifacts on the shading of your surface that require a lot of fiddling in the Surface Editor to correct. Before tripling non-planar polygons, you should consider whether there are other techniques (such as converting your non-planar polygons into

57

Catmull-Clark subpatches) that will achieve the same result without the potentially negative side effects.

Polygons that are *extremely* non-planar will exhibit obvious shading errors. This makes them easy to spot. But the points in a polygon don't have to move much for it to become non-planar. Subtle problems often won't show up until you've finished the model and are trying to render it. So what's the best way to check for non-planar polygons in your object? That's easy. Just use the Statistics panel.

Statistics Panel

The Statistics panel tells you pretty much everything you need to know about the points, polygons, and edges in your object. This panel is context sensitive, and the information it displays will change to match the current selection mode. You can access the Statistics panel through the Statistics button found at the bottom of Modeler's interface.

Hot Key Block

Statistics Panel

<w> opens the Statistics panel.

Let's take a look at what the Polygon Statistics panel tells us about the polygons in this Stargate object:

- **Total** — There are 52,698 polygons in this object.

- **Faces** — Of those 52,698 polygons, 52,698 of them are faces (standard polygons).

- **Curves** — The object has no curves as part of its geometry.

- **SubPatches** — There are no subpatches in this object either.

- **Skelegons** — There are none of Modeler's

bone-placement objects, known as skelegons.

- **Metaballs** — There are no instances of metaballs, a kind of digital clay item.

- **1 Vertex** — There are no polygons made up of a single vertex (point).

- **2 Vertices** — There are no polygons that are made up of only two vertices.

- **3 Vertices** — There are 3,168 triangles in this model.

- **4 Vertices** — There are 49,334 quads in this model.

- **>4 Vertices** — There are 196 polygons with more than four points in this model.

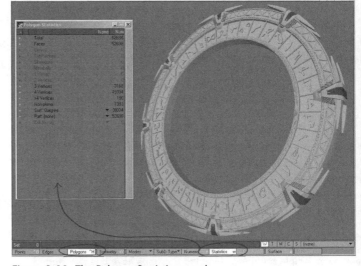

Figure 3-11: The Polygon Statistics panel.

- **Non-planar** — Of all these polys, 1,393 of them are non-planar.

- **Surf: Stargate** — 38,034 of these polys have the "Stargate" surface applied to them. (This and the remaining items in the Polygon Statistics panel are pop-up menus that display lists of the surfaces, parts, or sketch colors you've created for your object.)

- **Part: (none)** — All 52,698 polygons in this object belong to the part None (that is, no polys have been assigned to a part; this is just a way of grouping polys so you can easily sift through them later).

- **Col: (none)** — None of the polygons have been assigned a sketch color (another way of identifying and keeping your polygons separate).

Changing the selection mode to Points updates the Statistics panel with information about the points in our object. Looking at the Point Statistics panel, we can see that:

- **Total** — There are 53,721 total points in this object.

- **0 Polygons** — There are 50 points that don't belong to any polygons. (Usually these are leftovers from common modeling operations and can be deleted, though there are times when you will want to have a point without a poly.)

- **1 Polygons** — There are 0 points that belong to only one polygon each.

- **2 Polygons** — There are 428 points that are shared between two polygons.

- **3 Polygons** — There are 9,534 points that are shared among three polys.

- **4 Polygons** — There are 40,781 points that are shared among four polys.

- **>4 Polygons** — There are 2,928 points that are shared among more than four polys.

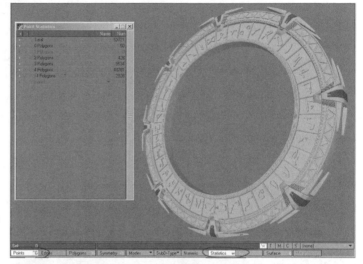

Figure 3-12: The Point Statistics panel.

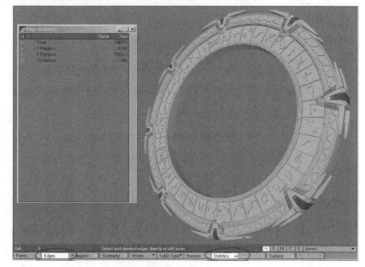

Figure 3-13: The Edge Statistics panel.

• **(none)** — There are no points belonging to a point selection group. (This pop-up menu lists the point selection sets (if any) you've created for the object.)

Changing the selection mode to Edges updates the Statistics panel with information about the edges in our object. Looking at the Edge Statistics panel we can see that:

• **Total** — There are 106,873 edges in this object.

• **1 Polygons** — There are 4,380 open edges that are only connected to a single polygon.

• **2 Polygons** — There are 101,613 edges connected to two adjacent polygons.

• **>2 Vertices** — There are 880 edges connected to multiple polygons that share two vertices. (This is an unusual occurrence and can be an indicator of overlapping polygons.)

The Statistics panel also shows information about the items you currently have selected.

When some of the elements in your object (points, polygons, or edges) are selected, the text and numbers in the Statistics panel will display as light gray. When all of the elements in a category are selected, the text and numbers in the Statistics panel will display as white. When none of the items in a category are selected, the text and numbers will display as black.

The ability to see what's happening with your model at a glance is very powerful. But the Statistics panel does more than just give you information; you can use it to make complex selections. Clicking on the + or – in the columns on the panel's left side

adds or subtracts all the polys from that category, respectively.

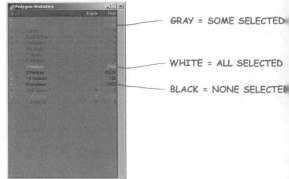

GRAY = SOME SELECTED

WHITE = ALL SELECTED

BLACK = NONE SELECTED

Figure 3-14: The color of the text in the Statistics panel signifies whether some, all, or none of the elements in a category are selected.

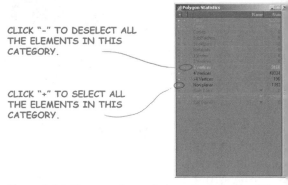

CLICK "-" TO DESELECT ALL THE ELEMENTS IN THIS CATEGORY.

CLICK "+" TO SELECT ALL THE ELEMENTS IN THIS CATEGORY.

Figure 3-15: The + and – symbols on the left side of the Statistics panel let you select and deselect elements in a particular category.

Let's take a look at how I would use the Statistics panel to help me fix the non-planar polygons in my object.

1. The first thing I do is switch to Polygons selection mode by clicking the button at the bottom of the interface or by pressing the <**Ctrl**> + <**h**> keyboard shortcut.

2. Now I make sure that nothing is selected. I glance down at the Quick Info display in the lower-left corner of Modeler. It should say "Sel: 0". If it does not, I press the "/" key (or the "e"

key, which was mapped as the Deselect command in Chapter 2).

3. Next, I open the Statistics panel. Then I click on the "+" to the left of the word "Non-planar." 1,393 polygons are selected.

All the non-planar polygons in the object should now be selected and the text for this category should be white.

4. From the SubD-Type pop-up menu at the bottom of the interface, I select **Catmull-Clark**. This allows me to convert polygons with more than four points into subpatches.

5. Finally, I press **Tab** to convert these polygons to subpatches. Then I deselect everything. Looking at the Statistics panel, I see that I have 1,393 subpatches and 0 non-planar polygons.

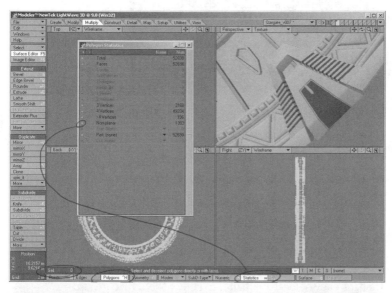

Figure 3-16: To fix the non-planar polygons in this object, I make sure nothing is selected, then open the Statistics panel and click the "+" next to the "Non-planar" category. This ensures that only the non-planar polygons are selected.

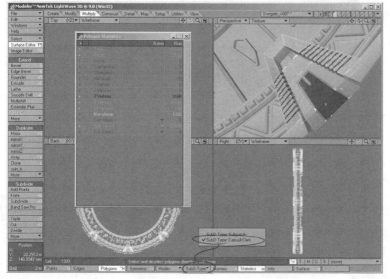

Figure 3-17: Switch the SubD Type to Catmull-Clark.

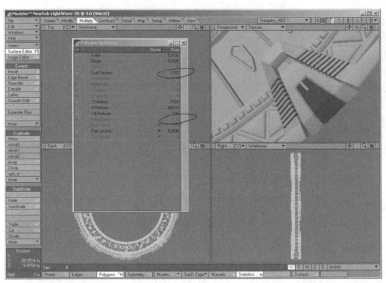

Figure 3-18: By pressing the Tab key, I converted the non-planar polygons into subpatches. Note that the number of non-planar polygons in the Statistics panel is now 0.

> **Note**
>
> Converting non-planar polygons to Catmull-Clark subpatches will work in some cases but not in others. Having a good understanding of how subpatches work (as described in Chapter 15) is essential to getting good results from this trick. If you wind up getting unsatisfactory results, you may opt to triple your non-planar polygons or manually correct each offending polygon one at a time.

Grouping Polygons and Points

In programs like Illustrator and Flash, you can group objects together for easy selection and manipulation. You can do the same basic thing in LightWave. Groups of polygons are known as "parts" and groups of points are called "selection sets." The grouping controls can be found under the View | Selection Sets menu option.

There are two important distinctions that should be made between LightWave's groups (parts and selection sets) and those you find in Illustrator or Flash. The first is that every LightWave group is required to have a name. The second is that selecting elements in a LightWave group will *not* cause the entire group to become selected. Instead, you must choose the name of the part or selection set and use the Statistics panel to select the entire group.

This workflow can take a bit of getting used to, but it has definite advantages. You can quickly recall different groups, and you never have to ungroup to manipulate a single element in the group.

Parts

To group polygons into a part, simply select them and choose the Create Part button. Enter a name for the part and click OK. The Part heading in the Polygon Statistics panel will show stats for the parts you've created as part of its pop-up menu.

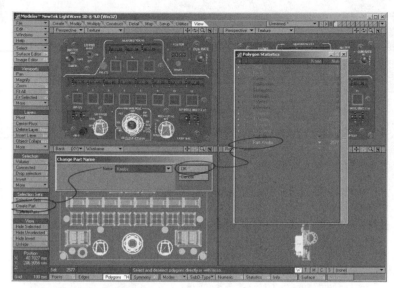

Figure 3-19: The Change Part Name window lets you add, change, and remove groups of polygons known as parts.

To remove a polygon selection from a part, simply leave the Name box blank in the Change Part Name window.

It's important to note that a polygon may only belong to one part at a time. If a polygon belongs to a certain part and you include it in another part, it will no longer be a member of the previous part.

Selection Sets

Assigning points to a selection set is similar to assigning polygons to a part. Simply choose the points you want to group together and click the Selection Sets button. Type in a new selection set name and click Create. The selection set will be available in the Point Statistics panel and will appear in the Vertex Map pop-up menu in the lower-right corner of the interface.

You can remove specific points from a selection set by selecting them, clicking on the Selection Sets button, clicking the Point Set pop-up menu, choosing the name of your selection set, clicking the Remove Points button, and clicking the Create button. It may seem a little counterintuitive to

Note

The very last entry on the Point Statistics panel allows you to work with selection sets. This entry is a pop-up menu. You must click it to see the list of available sets. Its gray color can be confusing, because in other programs this indicates that the item is "ghosted" and unavailable. If you have created a selection set and see the word "(none)" listed here, simply click the word "(none)" and choose your selection set. You can then use the "+" and "−" to select and deselect the points in the set.

click the Create button to remove points from a set, but essentially what you're doing is creating a new version of your set that no longer contains the points you've designated.

You can delete an entire selection set by choosing it from the Point Set pop-up menu and then clicking on the Delete button.

Unlike parts, a point may belong to more than one selection set. You can use this fact to overcome the limits of parts. By selecting a group of polygons and running the Select | Sel Points command, the points that make up those polygons will be

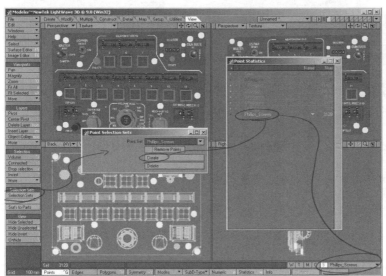

Figure 3-20: The Point Selection Sets window lets you add and remove groups of points.

Note

You can create selection sets by clicking the "S" button in the lower-right corner of the interface, then clicking the Vertex Map pop-up menu to its right (see Figure 3-20) and choosing "(new)." This will bring up the same window that appears when you select View | Selection Sets | Selection Sets. You can also choose selection sets from the Vertex Map pop-up menu, but to actually select the points associated with a set, you must use the Statistics panel.

selected. You can now store these into a selection set. To restore the polygon selection, you would select the point selection set and run the Select | Sel Polys command.

Note

The Select pop-up menu is located in the upper-left corner of Modeler's interface, directly under the Help pop-up menu.

Selection Tools

In Chapter 2 we talked about the basic techniques for selecting points and polygons. Now we're going to look at the tools that allow us to make complex selections. Unless otherwise noted, these tools will work the same for points, polygons, and edges.

Hot Key Block

Selection Tools

<]> Select Connected

<"> Invert Selection

<}> Expand Selection

<{> Contract Selection

<=> Show Only Selection (Hide Unselected)

<\> Show All

<-> Hide Selection

<|> Invert Hidden

Select Connected

Select Connected (View | Selection | Connected) selects every polygon directly "connected" (sharing points with neighboring polygons) to those you currently have selected.

With one or more polygons selected, using Select Connected allows you to instantly select an entire subset of a complex object. You can also use Select Connected with points and edges. The concept is the same, except that points or edges are selected instead of polygons.

Invert Selection

Invert Selection (View | Selection | Invert) swaps what you've currently got selected with what is currently not selected.

Expand/Contract Selection

Expand/Contract Selection (View | Selection | Expand and View | Selection | Contract) can be used to select/deselect the points/polys/edges that are on either side of your current selection.

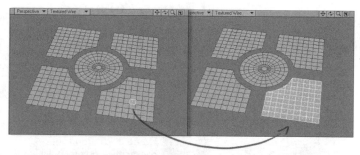

Figure 3-21: Select Connected selects all the points/polygons/edges that are connected to those currently selected.

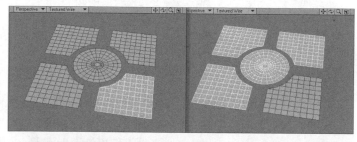

Figure 3-22: After Invert Selection, what was once selected is now unselected and vice versa.

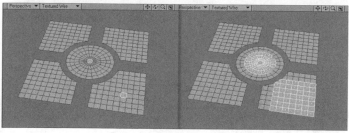

Figure 3-23: Expand Selection causes your selection to grow outward each time it is run. The selection on the left was expanded three times.

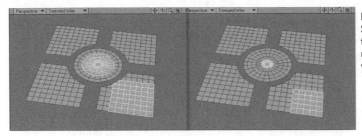

Figure 3-24: Contract Selection causes your selection to shrink inward each time it is run. The selection on the left was contracted two times.

Select Loop

The Select Loop tool (Select | Select Loop) allows you to select bands of points, quad polygons, or edges in your object. You'll probably find yourself using this tool quite a bit (I know I do), so it's worth assigning a keyboard shortcut for it.

Select any two adjacent points/polys/edges and run this tool to quickly select the entire loop. The selection will stop when it reaches a non-quad polygon or it winds its way around and loops back on itself.

Additional bands can be selected by holding down the <Shift> key, selecting two more adjacent points or polys, and running the tool again.

Select Points/Polygons

The Select Points tool (Select | Sel Points) converts your polygon selection into a point selection. Conversely, Select | Sel Polys will convert your point selection back into a polygon selection.

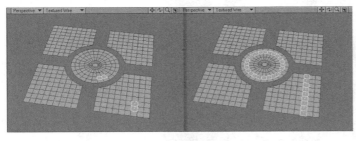

Figure 3-25: Bands of consecutive points, polys, and edges can easily be selected with the Select Loop tool. Here, two polygons on each shape were selected. This defines the loop direction. Running the Select Loop tool causes the entire band of polygons to be selected.

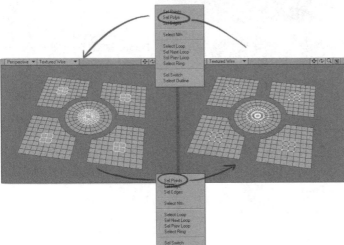

Figure 3-26: The Select Points tool converts your polygon selection into a point selection. Switching points back to polygons can quickly be done with the Select Polygons tool.

Select Nth

The Select Nth tool lets you create staggered selections and is great for alternating point, polygon, and edge selections. You begin by selecting all the elements (points/polygons/edges) on your object that you want affected. Running the tool brings up the Select Nth Poly window.

The n setting determines the spacing between selections. Setting this to 2 will cause every other element to become selected. Setting this to 3 will cause every third element to become selected, and so on.

Offset controls the shift away from your original selection. Leaving this at 0 will start the selection with your first selected element. Setting this to 1 will cause the element next to your original selection to be selected first.

When you click OK, the Select Nth tool will deselect unnecessary polygons from your total selection.

v9.2 Note

LightWave v9.2 features several additional selection tools. For information on these new tools, check out the Select Path and Select Surface videos in the LightWave 9.2 Videos folder on the companion DVD.

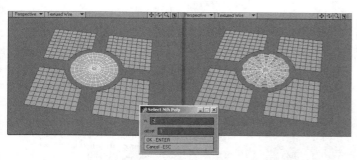

Figure 3-27: The Select Nth tool allows you to create staggered selections.

Hiding and Revealing Selections

In programs like Photoshop, you can mask portions of a layer so that only specific parts are shown. You can do the same thing in Modeler with the various unhide and hide selection commands.

Hide Selected

The Hide Selected command (View | View | Hide Selected) will remove any selected polygons from view. The polygons still exist on that layer; they simply won't be visible.

Hide Invert

The Hide Invert command (View | View | Hide Invert) will swap the visible polygons with those that are hidden.

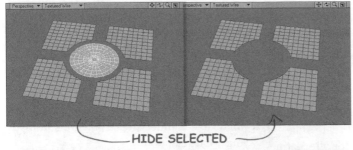

Figure 3-28: The Hide Selected command allows you to mask your polygons, thereby removing them from view.

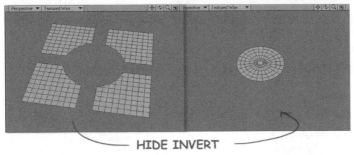

Figure 3-29: The Hide Invert command swaps the visible polygons with those that are hidden.

Hide Unselected

The Hide Unselected command (View | View | Hide Unselected) will remove any unselected polygons from view, leaving only your selected polygons.

Unhide

The Unhide command (View | View | Unhide) will make any hidden polygons visible again.

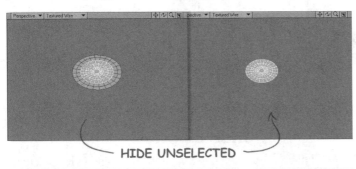

Figure 3-30: The Hide Unselected command masks out any unselected polygons, leaving only the selected polygons visible.

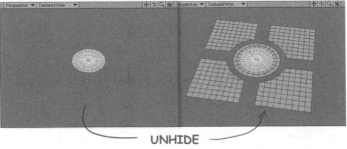

Figure 3-31: The Unhide command makes all hidden polygons visible again.

The various hide and show commands allow you to isolate parts of your object while you're working so that you can focus on them without fear of inadvertently affecting other parts of your model. It's important to note, however, that you cannot use these commands to *permanently* mask out portions of your object. Once you save and close your object, all the hidden geometry will be restored the next time it is loaded.

Primitives

primitive *adj.* 1. a. Of or pertaining to an earliest or original stage or state. b. Archetypal. 2. Math. A form in geometry or algebra from which another form is derived. (*The American Heritage Dictionary*)

Primitives (found in the Create tab) are the building blocks for a wide range of 3D objects. Modeler provides several dozen primitives, including boxes, balls, discs, cones, capsules, gears, and even gemstones. While each of these has a purpose, most objects can be built from either a box or a ball.

Hot Key Block
Primitives
<**X**> Box
<**O**> Ball

Let's look at how to create primitives.

Box

Select the Box tool from the Create | Primitives menu. Then click and drag in one of your orthographic viewports. This will create a basic 2D shape. In the case of the Box tool, it will create a square or rectangle.

Once you've drawn the basic shape, you can click any blank portion of your viewport to size the primitive toward the location of your mouse. The blue handles on the corners and sides allow you to precisely size the primitive to suit your needs.

Clicking in another orthographic viewport turns your 2D shape into a full-fledged 3D object. You can continue to use the blue handles to reshape the object.

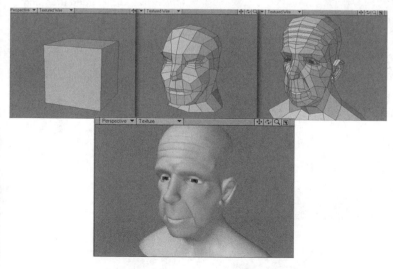

Figure 3-32: This character began his life as a simple box.

If you know the exact size of the shape you need to create, you can enter those figures into the Numeric panel (keyboard shortcut <n>). You can also use the slider buttons

to the right of each data field to interactively adjust these values.

The Numeric panel also allows you to adjust the advanced features for each primitive. For the Box tool, these include segmentation (how many divisions to cut across each axis) as well as smooth edges and round corners (adjusted via the Radius and Radius Segments settings).

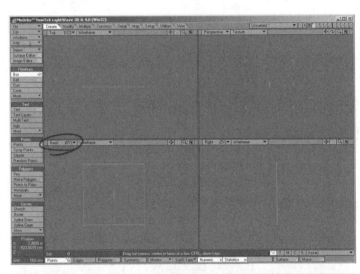

Figure 3-33: With a primitive tool active, clicking and dragging in one viewport creates a 2D shape.

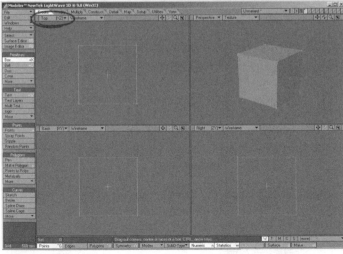

Figure 3-34: With the tool still active, clicking and dragging in a second viewport creates a 3D object.

Some of the Numeric panel's controls can be adjusted via the keyboard. You can adjust the segments for each axis by placing your mouse over each viewport and tapping the up, down, left, and right arrow keys.

When you're happy with the object you've created, simply press the Enter key or the Spacebar to drop the tool.

> **Note**
>
> The standard Enter key works differently than the one on the numeric keypad. The numeric keypad's Enter key will advance through any active data fields. The standard Enter key will accept the value in a data field, but will not advance to the next field.

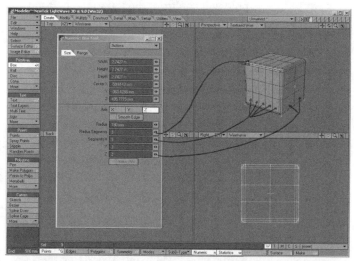

Figure 3-35: The Numeric panel allows you to specify an exact size for your primitives. It also gives you access to the tool's advanced controls.

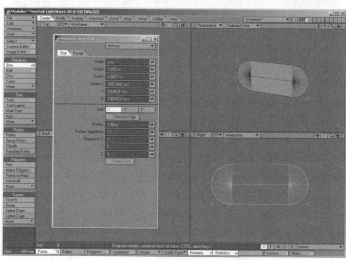

Figure 3-36: Creative use of the advanced controls in the Numeric panel allow you to easily make complex shapes.

Note

If you have made changes in the Numeric panel by entering data directly into one of the fields, you will likely need to press the Enter key twice to drop the tool. The first time you hit it, it will accept the data in the current field. The second time will drop the tool.

Creative use of the settings found in the Numeric panel will allow you to create shapes you never thought possible with these "simple" primitive tools. For example, by dragging out a standard rectangle and increasing the Radius and Radius Segments settings, you can quickly create a rounded rectangle.

Ball

The Ball tool (Create | Primitives | Ball) works similarly to the Box tool. Clicking and dragging in one viewport will create a 2D circle. Clicking and dragging in a second viewport will create a 3D ball. You can hold down the <Ctrl> key while dragging (or simply click-drag with your middle mouse button) to create a perfect circle or sphere. You can also use the handles to

interactively adjust the shape of the circle and/or ball.

One important thing to consider when you use the Ball tool is the orientation of the pole. The pole will be oriented with the viewport in which you draw your 2D shape. Consider Figure 3-37. The 2D circle was drawn in the Top viewport. Therefore, the pole will run from the top to the bottom, regardless of which viewport I click in next.

A circle in Modeler is nothing more than a radial array of points and edges that are connected together to form a polygon. The more points and edges you have, the smoother the circle will appear. Modeler's default for the Ball tool uses 24 edges, which it calls "Sides" in the Numeric panel. This is a good default number; however, if you're going to see this object close-up, you'll likely want to increase the Sides setting to 48 or higher.

Increasing the number of sides can be helpful, but things get really fun and interesting when you begin to *decrease* the number of sides. Many common 2D shapes are just circles with a relatively low number of sides. For example, an octagon is nothing more than an eight-sided circle. A pentagon

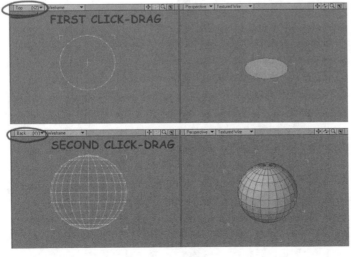

Figure 3-37: The Ball tool works just like the Box tool. Click and drag in one viewport to create a 2D circle. Click and drag in a second viewport to create a 3D sphere.

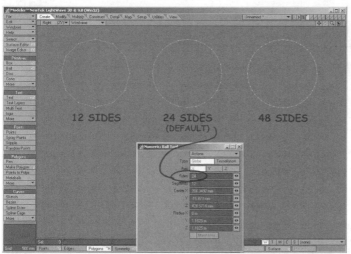

Figure 3-38: A circle is nothing more than a sequence of points and edges. The more points and edges (called sides) you have, the smoother the circle will be.

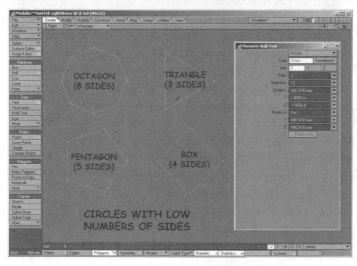

Figure 3-39: The Ball tool allows you to create a variety of useful shapes simply by decreasing the number of sides in the Numeric panel.

is a five-sided circle. A square is a four-sided circle. And a triangle is a three-sided circle!

As I said earlier, creative use of the settings found in the Numeric panel will allow you to create shapes you would never think of as being boxes and balls. Spend time experimenting with the rest of the primitives and the various options found in the Numeric panel. But dedicate yourself to understanding the Box and Ball tools, as you'll be using these on a regular basis.

Text

Modeler has several tools for creating text objects. When you launch Modeler, it will scan your system for any active fonts, including those enabled via a font management tool like Extensis Suitcase. If you have a font that is not currently available to your system, you can manually add it via the Create | Text | Manage Fonts utility.

To create text, select the Create | Text | Text tool, click in any viewport, and begin typing the text you want. You can change the position of the text by clicking and dragging the text block. You can change the kerning (space between letters) by dragging the small tick mark under the first letter of the text. Opening the Numeric panel after typing your text allows you to change the font, size, alignment, and kerning, and lets you specify whether or not sharp corners are beveled.

Figure 3-40: To create text, activate the Text tool, click in any viewport, and begin typing. You can interactively adjust the position and kerning of the text right in the viewport. Advanced options can be set via the Numeric panel.

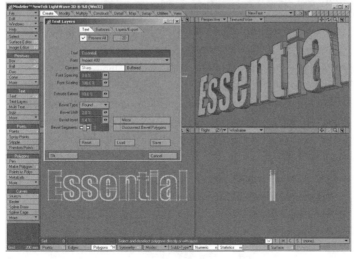

Figure 3-41: The Text Layers tool can create 2D and 3D text with slick beveled edges.

There are several other text tools at your disposal. The Text Layers tool will create 3D text with beveled edges. It has the ability to place each letter or even entire words on separate layers, making it easy to animate the text in Layout. The Multi Text tool can be used for creating longer blocks of text. The Logo tool will create a 3D block of text in a single pass. And the Make Text tool can create extremely long blocks of text from a raw text file.

Modification Tools

Once you've created geometry (either by laying down points to make polygons or by generating 2D/3D shapes with the primitive tools) you can adjust it by using the modification tools found in the Modify tab. Move, Rotate, and Stretch/Size are the primary tools you'll use to get this done.

Hot Key Block

Modification Tools

<t> Move

<y> Rotate

<H> Size

<h> Stretch

Move

Move (found under the Modify | Translate menu) allows you to reposition elements (points, polygons, or edges) freely by clicking and dragging in any viewport. (See Figure 3-42.) When you use the Move tool in the orthographic viewports, the movement will be restricted to the axis of each viewport. For example, if you create a box and place your mouse over the Top (XZ) viewport, you can use the Move tool to move it left and right (along the X-axis) or forward and backward (along the Z-axis).

To move the box up and down, you would need to place your mouse over the Back or Right viewports, as these allow movement along the Y-axis.

You can constrain the motion of the Move tool to a single axis by holding down the <Ctrl> key before you begin your move. If you have a three-button mouse, you can simply click and drag with the middle mouse button to constrain your movement.

Note

Many of the modification tools can be constrained with the <Ctrl> key (or by click-dragging with the middle mouse button), including Move, Rotate, and Stretch.

Rotate

Rotate (found under the Modify | Rotate menu) allows you to swivel your object (or just specific elements) around a specific point. This rotation point is determined by the Action Center mode, which was described in Chapter 2. To rotate an object, place your mouse over one of your viewports, then click and drag. (See Figure 3-43.)

75

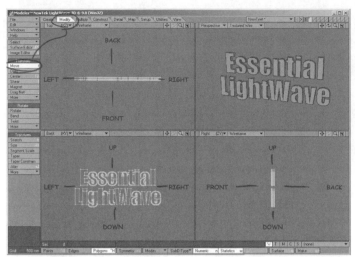

Figure 3-42: Use the Move tool to reposition specific elements (points, polygons, or edges). If nothing is selected, everything in the foreground layer(s) will move.

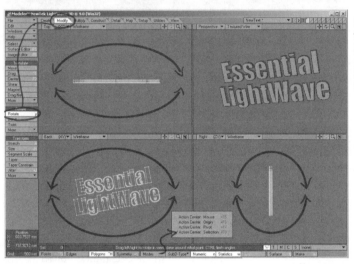

Figure 3-43: Use the Rotate tool to swivel specific elements (points, polygons, or edges). If nothing is selected, everything in the foreground layer(s) will rotate.

Size/Stretch

Size and Stretch (found under the Modify | Transform menu) both change the proportion of your object (or selected elements in the object). Size will scale your object evenly in all three dimensions, regardless of which viewport you place your mouse over. Stretch, on the other hand, takes into account the viewport your mouse is in and will only resize along those two axes. As a rule of thumb, you should only use the Size tool when you want to make an entire object bigger or smaller. The rest of the time, you should use the Stretch tool.

Falloff

The Falloff settings in the Numeric panel allow you to apply the effect of a tool incrementally over a specific region. These settings expand the basic functions of the Move, Rotate, and Size/Stretch tools, allowing you to perform complicated transformations.

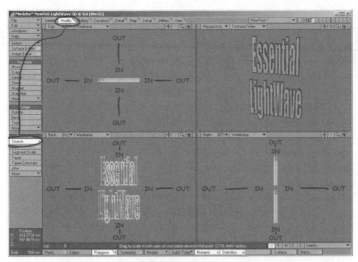

Figure 3-44: Use the Stretch tool to resize specific elements (points, polygons, or edges). If nothing is selected, everything in the foreground layer(s) will be stretched.

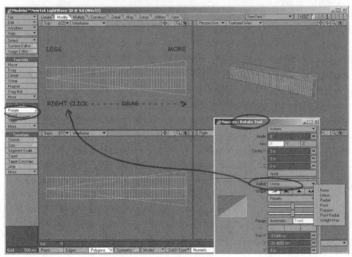

Figure 3-45: The Falloff controls in the Numeric panel let you distribute the effect of a tool over a specific range.

To adjust the Falloff settings for one of the modification tools, click the Falloff pop-up menu in the Numeric panel. Then choose from one of the available Falloff types.

- **None** turns Falloff off.

- **Linear** causes the effect to increase from least to most over a straight region.

- **Radial** causes the effect to increase from the center of a circular 3D region.

- **Point** restricts motion based on the available points in your object.

- **Polygon** restricts motion based on the available polygons in your object.

- **Point Radial** causes the effect to increase from the center of a circular 2D region.

- **Weight Map** allows you to use a weight map to define where the effect is strongest and weakest throughout your entire object.

For Linear, Radial, and Point Radial falloffs, you right-click and drag in one of your viewports to define your falloff region. Then

77

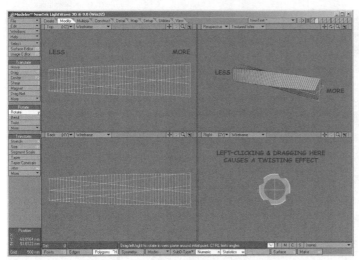

Figure 3-46: Once you've defined a Falloff region, use the tool as normal.

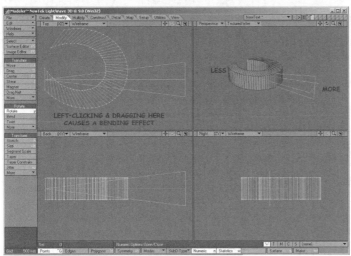

Figure 3-47: Using the tool in different viewports will produce different results.

left-click and drag in any viewport to see the effect of the falloff.

When you combine the Falloff setting with the various Action Center modes discussed in Chapter 2, you will find that these simple tools can do so much more than you ever imagined. If you're just getting started, take some time to make a few primitive objects such as balls and boxes. Then play with the Move, Rotate, and Size/Stretch tools. Get a feel for how each of these tools works. When you're comfortable with their basic usage, change your Action Center

mode to see how that affects their performance. Finally, experiment with the Falloff controls in the Numeric panel. This will give you a real taste of what can be done with a small but powerful set of tools.

> **Note**
>
> The Falloff settings for each tool remain enabled until you turn them off. (Deactivating the tool will not disable the Falloff controls.) If you're using one of the modification tools and get unusual or unpredictable results, check the Falloff settings in the Numeric panel to ensure they are turned off.

Multiplication Tools

The multiplication tools (found under the Multiply tab) serve one common purpose: to increase the amount of geometry available in your object. In this section, we'll briefly touch on the most important tools and how they are used.

Hot Key Block

Multiplication Tools

<E> Extrude

<e> Extender Plus (unless you've remapped this as described in Chapter 2)

<b> Bevel

<Ctrl>+<b> Edge Bevel

<V> Mirror

Extrude

Extrude allows you to take a flat 2D shape and give it 3D volume. It works by adding polygons to every edge and mirroring the shape from one end of the extrusion to the other.

To use the Extrude tool, activate it from the menu (or use the <E> keyboard shortcut) and place your mouse over a viewport that contains the axis you'd like to extrude along. Then click and drag *away* from your polygon's normal. If you'd like to add segments to the extruded geometry, you can tap the left and right arrow keys or increase the Sides setting in the Numeric panel.

Note

If you extrude in the direction of your polygon's normal, the resulting 3D object will appear to be inside out. To correct this, either flip the polygons (keyboard shortcut <f>) or undo and extrude again.

Extender Plus

Extender Plus allows you to extrude individual edges rather than entire polygons. To use the Extender Plus tool, you must first select a group of points or edges on your object. Then click on the tool in the Multiply | Extend menu. It will appear as if nothing has happened. In reality, new geometry has been created. The only thing left for you to do is modify it, typically by moving or resizing.

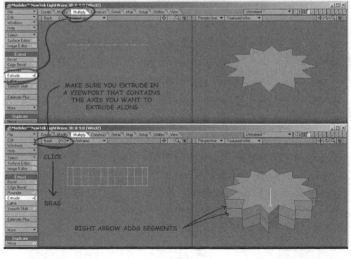

Figure 3-48: The Extrude tool turns 2D shapes into 3D objects.

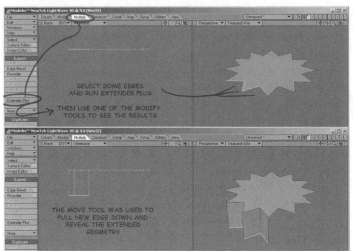

Figure 3-49: The Extender Plus tool extrudes individual edges. You must modify the selection after running this tool in order to see the results.

Bevel

The Bevel tool combines the act of extruding and resizing in one easy step.

To use the Bevel tool, select the polygons you want beveled. If nothing is selected, every polygon in the foreground will be beveled individually. Activate the tool from the Multiply | Extend menu. Click and drag up (or down) to shift your polygons. Drag left (or right) to scale (or *inset*) your bevel.

Note

The edges of every object should have some amount of beveling on them. Without bevels, the edges won't properly catch the light and your object will look unrealistic. There are a variety of tools in Modeler for creating bevels. Some of them will be discussed here; others will be discussed in Chapter 8. You should familiarize yourself with each of these tools in order to improve the appearance of your finished objects.

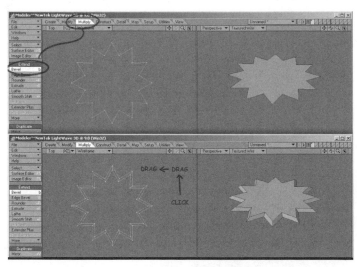

Figure 3-50: The Bevel tool shifts and scales individual polygons.

You can create a sequence of bevels by right-clicking and dragging. It's important to note that the standard Bevel tool does not allow you to edit the bevel sequence. Rather, you must use the modification tools at your disposal after the fact if you want to edit the sequence. You can overcome this limitation by using the Multishift tool.

Multishift

Multishift is an advanced beveling tool with a wide range of options. You can use it to bevel an entire group of polygons as well as perform multi-step bevels that can be edited to your liking.

To use the Multishift tool, begin by selecting one or more polygons. Then activate the tool from the Multiply | Extend menu. Multishift works just like the standard Bevel tool. Click and drag up (or down) to shift your polygons. Drag left and right to adjust the size (inset) of the bevel. You can create multiple bevels by right-clicking and

dragging. Each additional right-click and drag will create a new bevel.

Both the Shift and Inset routines can be adjusted, giving you greater control over the look of complex group bevels. Multishift bevels can also be quick-stored or saved, allowing you to recall them for future use.

You can adjust a bevel sequence while the tool is still active by clicking on the Next Shift or Previous Shift buttons and then adjusting the Shift and Inset controls at the top of the panel. Once you drop the tool, however, the bevels will be "fixed" in place, requiring you to use the modification tools for any further adjustments.

If you're not certain about the look of a particular bevel, it's best to Quick Store it. This allows you to drop the tool and examine the bevel in detail. If you don't like it, you can simply hit Undo, reactivate the Multishift tool, and restore the bevel for further tweaking.

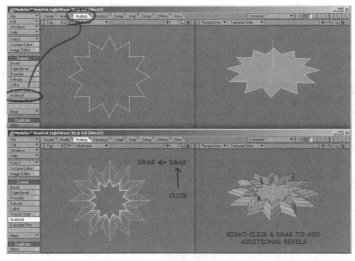

Figure 3-51: Multishift performs multi-step bevels that can be stored and recalled for later use.

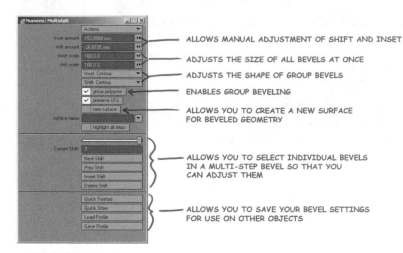

Figure 3-52: Multishift has a wealth of features available in the Numeric panel.

ALLOWS MANUAL ADJUSTMENT OF SHIFT AND INSET

ADJUSTS THE SIZE OF ALL BEVELS AT ONCE

ADJUSTS THE SHAPE OF GROUP BEVELS

ENABLES GROUP BEVELING

ALLOWS YOU TO CREATE A NEW SURFACE FOR BEVELED GEOMETRY

ALLOWS YOU TO SELECT INDIVIDUAL BEVELS IN A MULTI-STEP BEVEL SO THAT YOU CAN ADJUST THEM

ALLOWS YOU TO SAVE YOUR BEVEL SETTINGS FOR USE ON OTHER OBJECTS

Edge Bevel

The Edge Bevel tool allows you to add simple bevels between any two adjacent polygons.

To use the Edge Bevel tool, select one or more edges on your object. Then activate the tool from the Multiply | Extend menu. Click and drag left and right to adjust the size of the bevel.

Mirror

The Mirror tool allows you to duplicate polygons across a specific axis, creating a mirror image of them.

To use the Mirror tool, select the polygons that you'd like mirrored (or select nothing to have all your polygons mirrored), then activate the tool from the Multiply | Duplicate menu. Click and drag in one of your viewports. The *location* you click and drag will define the center of the mirroring action. The *direction* you click and drag will define the axis that the polygons will be

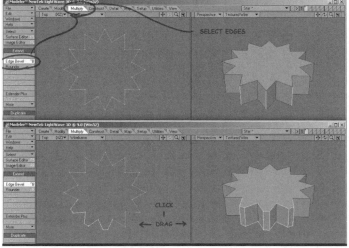

Figure 3-53: Edge Bevel adds simple bevels between adjacent polygons.

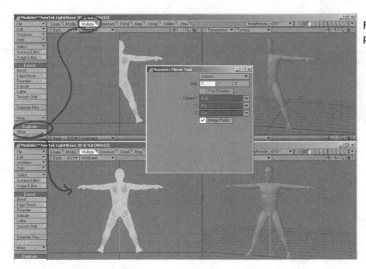

Figure 3-54: Mirror replicates polygons across a specific axis.

mirrored across. You can also open the Numeric panel and enter exact coordinates for the center and axis to mirror along.

In most cases, you'll be mirroring directly across the X-axis at the origin (X=0). This allows you to use the Symmetry mode to affect the points, polygons, and edges on both sides of the X-axis at once.

Note

The Mirror tool typically constrains your mirroring along a straight line. Clicking the Free Rotation button in the Numeric panel allows you to mirror at any angle. You can also mirror in 15-degree increments by <Ctrl> + clicking and dragging (or simply click-dragging with the middle mouse button).

Construction Tools

The construction tools (found under the Construct menu tab) allow you to enhance the structure of your model. In this section, we'll look at two of the most important construction tools: Drill and Boolean.

Hot Key Block

Construction Tools

<B> Boolean

<R> Drill

Drill

The Drill tool allows you to use one object to cut shapes into another. If you're familiar with the Pathfinder tools in Adobe

Illustrator, you'll quickly feel at home with this powerful tool.

To use the Drill tool, you must have an object in the foreground and an object in the background, as shown in Figure 3-56. The background object will be used to alter the shape of the foreground object. The background object does not need to intersect the foreground object; it only needs to line

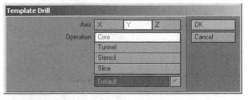

Figure 3-55: The Drill options allow you to determine exactly how the background object affects the foreground object.

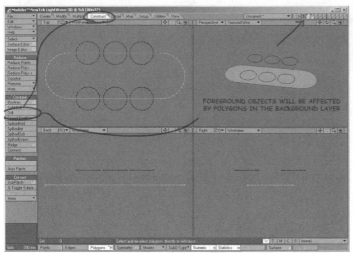

Figure 3-56: Drilling allows a background object to affect the shape of a foreground object. Here, the circles will be used to cut into the rounded rectangle.

up with the foreground object in one of the three axes in order to work.

When you run the Drill tool from the Construct | Combine menu, a window will appear that contains several options.

• **Axis** — This setting determines the direction of the cut. If you're not certain which axis to choose, exit out of the Drill options window, press <'> (single quote) to swap the foreground and background layers, then select the polygons you're using to do the cutting. Look at the direction the

normals face. This is the axis you should use in the Drill options window.

• **Operation** — The buttons under this heading determine the type of cut that will be made.

  • **Core** will cut out everything *except* the area affected by the cutting object.

  • **Tunnel** will cut out just those areas affected by the cutting object.

  • **Stencil** will cut the shape of the background object into your foreground object, giving you the option to assign a

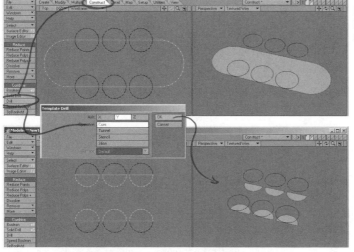

Figure 3-57: The effect of the Drill tool when using the Core setting.

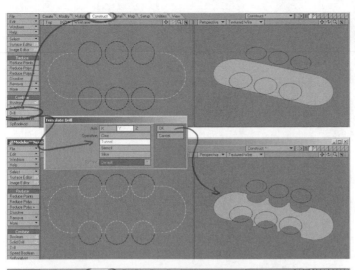

Figure 3-58: The effect of the Drill tool when using the Tunnel setting.

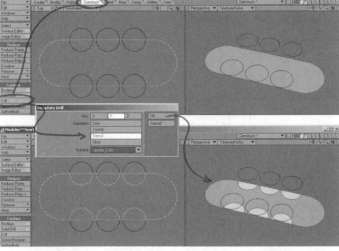

Figure 3-59: The effect of the Drill tool when using the Stencil setting.

surface to the stenciled shape. You can use the new surface name in conjunction with the Statistics panel to easily select the stenciled polygons.

- **Slice** is similar to Stencil; however, you don't have the option to assign a new surface.

The Drill tool will slice through your entire object unless you specifically tell it not to.

You can do this by selecting only the polygons in the foreground layer that you want affected.

Drilling is an essential component in most polygonal modeling, which would include everything from cars and trains to lamp posts and sewer grates. However, drilling lacks the ability to create depth from its cuts. To do this, we need to turn to a different set of tools: Booleans.

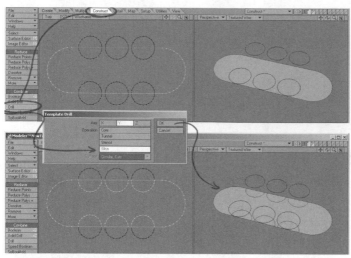

Figure 3-60: The effect of the Drill tool when using the Slice setting.

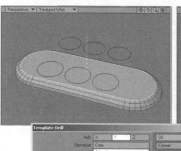

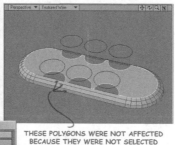

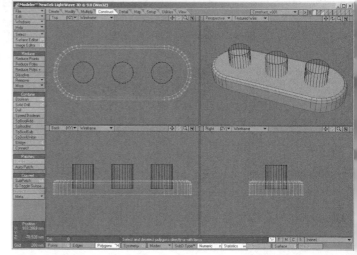

Figure 3-61: Selecting polygons before running the Drill tool limits its effect to the selected polygons.

THESE POLYGONS WERE NOT AFFECTED
BECAUSE THEY WERE NOT SELECTED

Boolean

The Boolean tool works similarly to the Drill tool. A cutting object is placed in the background and is used to affect a foreground object. Unlike the Drill tool, however, the Boolean tool requires the background object to be a 3D shape that intersects with the model in the foreground layer.

Figure 3-62: The Boolean tool requires that you use a 3D object in the background that intersects with the object in the foreground.

When you run the Boolean tool from the Construct | Combine menu, a window appears with the following options:

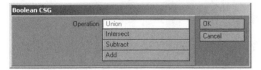

Figure 3-63: The Boolean options allow you to determine exactly how the background object affects the foreground object.

- **Union** combines the background object with the foreground object. The portion where the two objects intersect is removed.

- **Intersect** removes everything except the portion where the two objects intersect.

- **Subtract** removes the intersecting portion of the background object from the foreground object.

- **Add** is similar to Union; however, the portion where the two objects intersect is not removed.

In addition to the standard Boolean tool, Modeler offers "Speed Booleans." These allow you to perform standard Boolean functions without having to use foreground and background layers. You simply intersect your 3D objects, select a single polygon on each cutting object (which would normally be placed in the background), and run one of the Speed Boolean tools.

Note

After running the Boolean tool, you will likely need to run the Detail | Points | Merge Points tool, as the portions of your object that overlap will not be fused together.

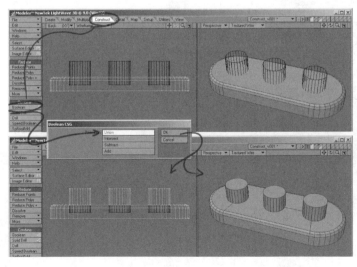

Figure 3-64: The effect of the Boolean tool when using the Union setting.

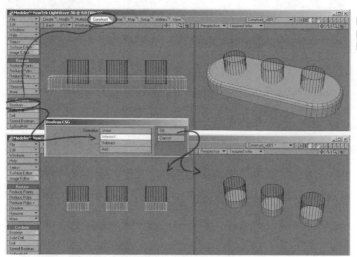

Figure 3-65: The effect of the Boolean tool when using the Intersect setting.

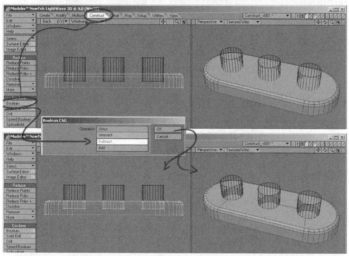

Figure 3-66: The effect of the Boolean tool when using the Subtract setting.

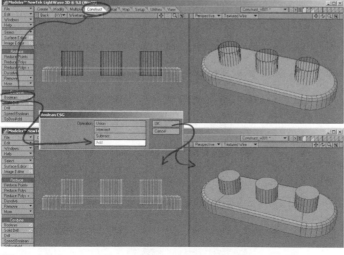

Figure 3-67: The effect of the Boolean tool when using the Add setting.

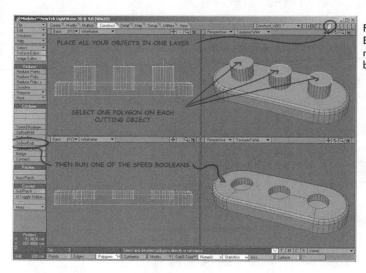

Figure 3-68: The Speed Boolean tools eliminate the need for foreground and background objects.

Detail Tools

The detail tools (found in the Detail tab) allow you to clean up the points and polygons in your object. In this section we'll take a brief look at a few indispensable detail tools.

Hot Key Block
Detail Tools
<m> Merge Points
<Z> Merge Polygons

Merge Points

It's not uncommon for the points on various objects to overlap but not be connected. This will often be the case after using the Boolean tool.

There is nothing wrong with separate objects that have overlapping points; however, some tools require that these points be fused together in order to work properly. When you need to connect overlapping points, you can use the Merge Points tool.

Running the Merge Points tool from the Detail | Points menu (or by pressing the

<m> keyboard shortcut) brings up the Merge Points window.

- **Range** determines how close two points must be before they will be fused together. Automatic requires that each point share exactly the same X, Y, and Z coordinates. Fixed allows you to set a maximum distance. Any points within this distance will be fused together.

- **Keep 1-Point Polygons** ensures that you don't lose any single-point polygons that overlap with regular points when you run the Merge Points tool.

- **Merge UVs** will merge texture map data when fusing points together.

Pressing OK will pop up an information window telling you how many points were merged together.

Note

If you've set your Alert Level to Low in the Interface tab of the Display Options window, this notice will appear in the status bar at the bottom of Modeler's interface.

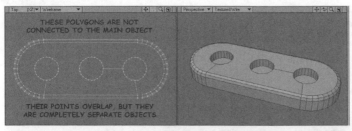

Figure 3-69: Just because objects bump up against one another does not mean they are connected.

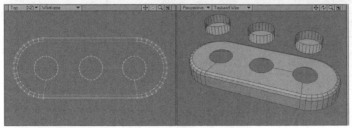

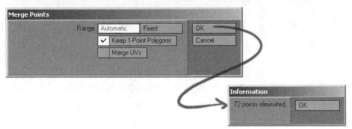

Figure 3-70: The Merge Points window lets you determine how close a point must be to its neighbor before the two will be fused together.

Merge Polygons

The Merge Polygons tool allows you to remove unnecessary polygons from an object while maintaining the object's overall shape.

To use the Merge Polygons tool, you must first select the polys you wish to merge. Then run the tool from the Detail |

Polygons menu or use the <Z> keyboard shortcut.

After running Merge Polygons, you will likely wind up with stray points that are no longer connected to any polygons. These can easily be selected with the Statistics panel and deleted by pressing the Delete key.

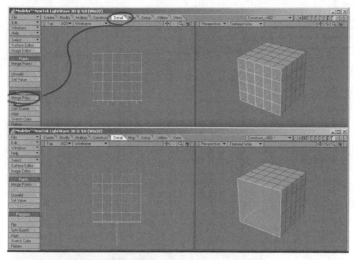

Figure 3-71: The Merge Polygons tool lets you simplify unnecessarily complex objects.

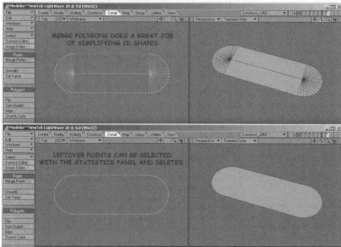

Figure 3-72: You can streamline 2D shapes with the Merge Polygons tool.

Tutorial

We've taken our first look at the tools involved in the modeling process. Knowing *about* the tools, however, will never replace hands-on experience with them. As I mentioned at the beginning of this chapter, it's important to spend time working with each tool to become comfortable with it. Once you've gained that familiarity, you can move on to the video tutorial found in the Video Tutorials\Chapter 03 folder on the DVD that came with this book.

The video tutorial walks you through the process of building a robot using nothing more than the tools covered in this chapter. The video is broken down into nine parts and contains nearly four hours of instruction. You'll learn how to apply the tools you've seen in this chapter to a real-world modeling project.

I highly encourage you to watch each video segment before attempting to follow along. Once you understand *how* and *why* things are done, it will be easier for you to repeat the process on your own.

If you find yourself struggling, stop the video and practice. The point of this tutorial is to hone your skills, not to rush through to the end. Remember, nothing can replace hands-on experience with the software. So take your time and work at your own pace.

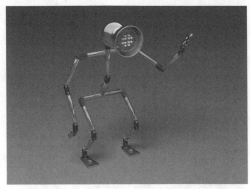

Figure 3-73: This LightBot character was created entirely with the tools mentioned in this chapter. A full-length video tutorial showing how to build it can be found on the book's companion DVD.

Conclusion

We've covered a lot of ground in this chapter. We've seen how points, polygons, and edges are the fundamental components of 3D models. We covered all of the basic tools needed to begin creating your own objects and we've learned how to construct an entire character with them. Not bad for your first foray into modeling! Before moving on, make sure that you're comfortable with the tools covered in this chapter. They are the foundation for the rest of the modeling work we'll be doing in this book.

Now that you've gotten a taste for modeling, let's move on to the next chapter where we'll take our first look at the animation process!

Chapter 4

Basic Skills: CG Filmmaking

One of the best ways to think about the whole process of 3D is to equate it to building scale models and then photographing them. All of the processes are the same. You've got to "sculpt" the pieces that you'll eventually photograph or film, sometimes "kit-bashing" free models found on the Internet or "cannibalizing" old pieces laying around in an attic-like part of your hard drive. If you were working with *practical* ("real") models, you'd paint the models so they looked just the way you wanted, from whatever camera angle you were going to shoot them. You'd find a private stage to set them up. You'd get lights to shine on them and bounce off of diffusing boards and screens. You'd look through your camera's or director's viewfinder and see what needs to be touched up on the models, their placement, or the lighting. You'd possibly add some smoke or wind and, making sure exposure, filters, and camera speed are all correct, you'd let the cameras roll!

The best-looking work I've seen from 3D artists is from people who were thinking as though they were "doing this in real life." 3D is just a tool to give you rent-free, unlimited soundstage space. Once you get beyond the fact that you can't really "hold" what you're working on, becoming good in 3D is mostly a matter of finding out how what you know about your physical, *practical* reality translates into the tools you use to manipulate this *virtual* reality.

> ## Note
>
> Some of the most impressive work to come out of *Babylon 5* was from a guy in his late 40s who, until he was hired, had never worked in 3D CGI before. He was a photographer, and as such, *he understood how light behaved.* After he got the knack of LightWave's controls, his 3D work began to reflect how he would light and shoot an event in "real life." Being a computer whiz has very little to do with being good at 3D. After you know your way around the tools, it's all about what you choose to focus your camera on and how you choose to showcase that environment. *Anyone,* given the time, can learn the tools — possibly one of the most liberating things about working in 3D. There are no limits!

New Camera Technologies — The Low-down

LightWave v9 is unlike any previous version of LightWave, as it has a completely re-engineered camera system that lets you select from a variety of new kinds of cameras that will extend your creativity like never before!

If we want to really understand how to best use the new camera systems in LightWave v9, it's important that we learn a little technobabble and understand how cameras in 3D work to create the images in LightWave. I'll keep this as simple as possible so that it doesn't create mass hysteria for those who are not techno-savvy! After all, it's not often artists need to understand the complex mechanics behind the tools they use. However, in this case, I felt it essential to know a little to help understand a lot later on!

Have you ever created a pinhole camera? It's a fun little camera that you can make by placing a piece of unexposed film at the back of a sealed cardboard box, then poking a tiny hole at the other end to let the light in to take the picture. A standard CG camera system works in a similar way, where the scenery is focused back to a single point, or virtual pinhole.

To create a 3D image in LightWave, the camera fires out a ray from the camera location for each pixel it needs to render in the image. These rays are spread out over an angle both horizontally and vertically. This spread is known as the field of view, as shown in Figure 4-1.

When each ray hits something, it reports back to the camera what it saw, and this information is used to tell LightWave what color to use for the pixel in the image it is creating.

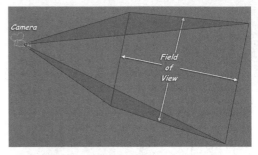

Figure 4-1: The field of view.

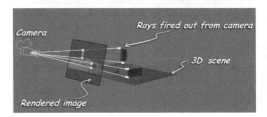

Figure 4-2: How the camera works.

Obviously, there are a lot of these "rays" firing out, looking for things in front of the camera. This spread of rays gives the image we create perspective, providing the illusion of depth in our renders.

Now, that wasn't too painful, was it?! With that snippet of info under our belt, we're ready to move forward.

LightWave's Camera

Like its real-world movie counterpart, computer animation needs a way to be filmed so that you can create that movie reel to show your audience. LightWave includes a virtual camera system to give you the ability to film your masterpiece onto your hard drive's film stock.

Now, if you were to go out and look at a 35mm motion picture camera, or even a professional-level 35mm single-lens reflex camera, you'd see a whole lot of settings that you can play with. LightWave does a lot to pattern its camera's adjustments after its real-world counterpart, so if you come to LightWave knowing how to use a film camera, the transition will be very smooth. Even if the most you've done to study photography is take a night course at a local college, you'll notice things like focal length and F-stop that at the very least should sound familiar.

LightWave's Camera Properties window, accessible by clicking **Properties** (<p>) while the camera is selected, gives you access to many of the settings that control how your filmed footage will look.

- The **Current Camera** pop-up menu lists all the cameras you have in your scene; each camera can have its own, separate settings. Let's run through the rest of the settings, and learn what these are all about.

Note

You can click in the Current Camera text box and edit the name of the camera directly, should you want to rename it. These small, seemingly insignificant details in the LightWave interface are major time-savers and greatly improve the ease and speed of working in LightWave!

What Kind of Camera?

You've just walked into your local camera store, and now you've got to decide what kind of camera gear you want to buy to shoot your masterpiece with. Each camera has its own set of features, complete with various pros and cons. The first section of the Camera Properties window is like our camera store, letting us choose the *virtual hardware* for our camera (however, you don't have to pay extra to get a new camera in LightWave). The NewTek development team has completely re-engineered the camera system for LightWave v9, and we'll be looking at each of these new camera types in much more detail later in this chapter. For now, let's just work our way through the basics of the standard camera type in LightWave v9 — the Classic Camera.

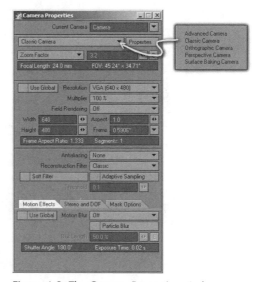

Figure 4-3: The Camera Properties window.

- The **Camera Type** pop-up menu starts out with the default Classic Camera (Light-Wave's original camera system from previous versions of the software) and lets us select what type of camera we want to use. Next to this is a **Properties** button, which opens the more advanced properties for certain types of cameras if they can't be displayed on the Camera Properties window itself. We'll look at the different properties for each camera in more detail later in the chapter.

- The **Zoom Factor** pop-up menu allows you to choose how you want to change the camera's zoom lens. Changing Zoom Factor to Lens Focal Length, Horizontal FOV (Field of View), or Vertical FOV changes the input field to the right to reflect that setting.

Each of these Zoom Factor options may sound different, but they all relate to each other. While we can change the zoom using only one setting at a time from this pop-up, the changes we make are reflected in a readout below this pop-up to show how

they relate to the others (as shown in Figure 4-4.)

The information at the top of the Camera Properties window is related to the specific camera chosen; it changes for other camera types. We'll review the differences later on as we look at each camera type in this chapter. However, the rest of the information in the Camera Properties window is used across the board, no matter which type of camera you plan on using.

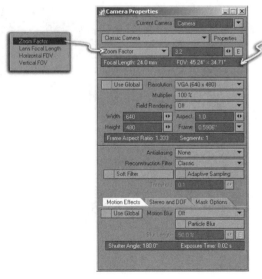

Info line showing the relationship between Focal, Zoom, and FOV

Figure 4-4: We can see how zoom changes the Focal Length and FOV values.

Processing the Virtual Print

Once we've got our basic camera type established, we need to tell it the size of the *output footage* we'll be filming with our camera. In a way, we're telling LightWave the size of the final print from our virtual film work. Is it a high-definition image for printing in a magazine, a logo created at a resolution for TV broadcast, or a small graphic for display on a web page? Well, this is the place where we make that decision.

Figure 4-5: Loading up the virtual print information.

• **Use Global** is an option added in LightWave v9 that lets us tell the camera to use some predefined global details (found in **Render | Render Globals**) for the quality and size of output. This option, along with how it works and relates to rendering (the *virtual processing* of our film), is covered later in Chapter 7, where we discuss what Render Globals is all about.

• The **Resolution** pop-up menu lets you choose from a list of presets that define just how large the "base" size you're rendering will be.

• **Multiplier** is a pop-up menu that lets you *scale* your image (a multiplier of 50% on a resolution of 640 x 480 would yield a rendered image of 320 x 240) while still letting any special post-processing filters that calculate on a per-pixel basis think in terms of the "base" size set under Resolution. (See the following note if this is confusing.)

> **Note**
>
> One of my favorite post-process filters is the Glow Effect, which we cover in Chapter 10. The way its settings work tell it how many pixels out from a "glowing" surface to spread the glow's effect.
>
> With the Multiplier setting, I can do a test render with a multiplier of 25% to save time. If the "base" resolution of my render was 640 x 480, it would then be reduced to 160 x 120, meaning that LightWave would only have to figure out the colors of 19,200 pixels, not 307,200 pixels. Because Multiplier is used (instead of manually setting the image size), the pixel-based setting in Glow Effect is *also* scaled.
>
> Once I get the look I want in my test render, I can return the Multiplier setting to 100%, knowing that the effect I saw in the tiny, quick test will be the same in the full-size render.

• **Field Rendering** lets you render to the scan-line fields that make up an NTSC or PAL image. Think of every row of pixels as being numbered from 0 to 479. (The Even First setting renders the even fields one frame before rendering the odd fields; the Odd First setting does the opposite.)

> **Note**
>
> NTSC may run at 30 frames per second, but each frame is actually made up of two interwoven "sub-frames," the even fields making up one of these sub-frames and the odd fields making up the other. When a TV set plays back a frame, it draws one field first. Then when those phosphors are "dying out," the scan-line goes back to the top of the screen and draws the second field. The result that our eyes perceive is 60 complete images per second, even though the data is only streamed through at 30 frames per second!

You use this setting when you want to get the absolute smoothest possible output on video and the tool you use to get your animation from your computer to video doesn't automatically separate your playback into fields, or when you are compositing to "raw" captured video that hasn't been "de-interlaced."

- **Width** and **Height** change to reflect the combination of the resolution and its multiplier. You can enter values here directly if you need to render to unique-sized formats.

- **Aspect** is an input field that changes automatically when you select a (base) resolution from the pop-up menu. This setting defines the pixel aspect ratio and takes into account the fact that the pixels (picture elements) for PAL and NTSC aren't perfect squares, as they are on a computer monitor. PAL and NTSC, and their regular and wide-screen modes, each have separate aspect ratios. Because this field is automatically updated when you change the resolution to one of these television formats, you'll probably never have to worry about this value. But here it is, just in case.

- The **Frame** pop-up changes the size of the "gate" inside LightWave's virtual camera. It is a measure, in inches, of just how tall the exposed frame of film would be were it a "real-world" camera. You use this when you are matching your rendered imagery to be composited onto film that has been shot with a real camera. It affects how LightWave's camera calculates the depth of field and lens focal length. This value defaults to the height of a frame of 35mm motion picture film. Many other presets are

available through the pop-up to the field's right.

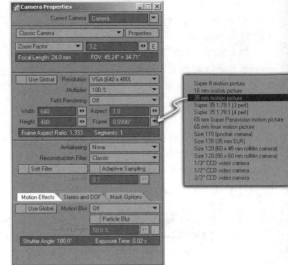

Figure 4-6: The Frame pop-up gives us plenty of options.

- **Frame Aspect Ratio** is a readout that tells you about the ratio of your frame's width to its height. In Figure 4-6, the Frame Aspect Ratio setting reads "1.333" because with a pixel aspect ratio of 1.0 (1 to 1), dividing width by height gives you 1.333. (The industry officially calls this "1 to 1.333" or "1:1.333.")

- **Segments** tells you how many segments LightWave will need to render an image the size you've asked for with the amount of memory allocated under **Render | Render Globals | Segment Memory Limit**. (Render Globals is covered in detail in Chapter 7.)

Print Quality

Once we've established our camera hardware and output size, we'll also want to tell LightWave the quality that we want to see from this footage.

Figure 4-7: Quality controls for our output from the camera.

CG generates images by building them up with single colored dots, or pixels. When we get diagonal lines or details in an image, it can look a little blocky, as seen in Figure 4-8. This effect is referred to as *aliasing*, and it's something we want to try to avoid at all costs wherever possible if we're to get slick and smooth-looking images.

Figure 4-8: Aliased, or jaggy pixels!

> **Note**
>
> Aliasing issues are also commonly known as *jaggies*, obviously because of the jagged appearance!

To alleviate this characteristic of digital art, we luckily have tools that are designed to *antialias* the imagery in LightWave.

- The **Antialiasing** pop-up menu gives you a list of settings ranging from **None** to

Classic, Enhanced Extreme that specify how many passes LightWave makes to take the "jaggies" out of a picture.

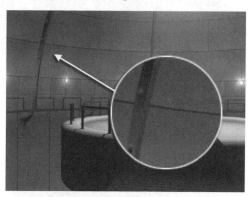

Figure 4-9: Antialiasing the jaggies.

> **v9.2 Note**
>
> LightWave v9.2 features brand-new Antialiasing options as well as revisions to the way Adaptive Sampling works. For information on these new features, check out the Antialiasing video in the LightWave 9.2 Videos folder on the companion DVD.

> **Note**
>
> The difference between all the antialiasing settings in LightWave is the number of passes used to "explore" the detail areas of a piece. The first collection of settings is obvious as they specify the number of passes in their description. For those last few options (these are termed Classic, because they came from earlier versions of LightWave before PLD was introduced in version 8.2), the number of passes is pretty easy to remember. Classic, Low makes five passes, Classic, Medium makes nine passes, Classic, High makes 17 passes, and Classic, Extreme makes 33 passes. With each pass, LightWave is able to figure out more and more details that are smaller than a pixel. (The Enhanced versions of the Classic antialiasing options provide the same number of passes but take more samples into consideration, which yields a higher quality image.)

What Is PLD?

You'll notice in the pop-up that a majority of the antialiasing options start with "PLD." PLD stands for *Pixel Lattice Deformation*, and simply looks at the information about how edges of objects in your scene fall within a rendered image's pixels.

When rendering is finished, the rendered image is *deformed* (the pixels are shifted about) to best fit the shape of the geometry in LightWave in terms of where it lies in relation to the rendered image. This has the advantage that it's a lot faster to warp the image slightly then to re-render the image again. There is a trade-off, though. It doesn't antialias details that do require re-rendering (tiny surfacing details, or intricate texturing with detail smaller than a single pixel).

Note

PLD antialiasing can be a major time-saver when creating renders for quick approval by clients. Often a quick test render may go without antialiasing if there is no time available. With PLD 1-Pass mode, we can smooth our test renders just a small amount, ridding the evilness of having jaggies and obviously looking a little slicker to the client!

- The **Reconstruction Filter** pop-up menu lets us specify the method in which LightWave will reassemble all the antialias passes it creates into the final image. The default of Classic works fine in most cases. The two that have the most visual impact on the output are Gaussian and Lanczos, shown in Figure 4-10. Gaussian tends to create quite soft results and may be useful when rendering scenes needing a filmic quality or containing lots of motion blur or depth of field effects. Lanczos, on the other hand, generates quite defined edges and could be useful when rendering animations with a drawn or illustrative appearance.

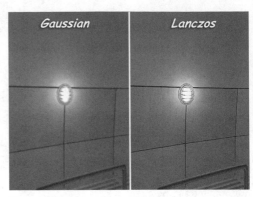

Figure 4-10: Gaussian and Lanczos reconstruction filters at work.

- **Soft Filter** renders the objects in your scene with the "softness" of film (the background isn't affected by Soft Filter). This setting doesn't seem to be a blur of a kind that post processing can mimic; it appears to actually change the way LightWave renders. If you're looking for a more "filmic" render, as opposed to something more "video-like," this, in conjunction with a Film Grain image filter, is your key to getting that look.

- **Adaptive Sampling** is normally used when smoothing an image. This means that after it renders a pass, it goes around and finds all the pixels that differ by a certain amount from their neighbors. (This level of acceptable difference is set in the Threshold input box.) LightWave then re-renders *only* those pixels, letting everything else stay as it is.

Using Adaptive Sampling, you can get a very good-looking image in a fraction of the time it would take to render and antialias on most other rendering engines. Beware, however, that using Adaptive Sampling can cause issues with fine detail in a render, and really isn't a good option for final quality animations. Small details can be partially rendered, as we see in Figure 4-11. If this is then used in an animation, these gaps appear to move between frames, creating a symptom known as pixel crawl.

Without Adaptive Sampling, LightWave re-renders everything in the entire frame for each pass. This is good for when you have tiny surfacing details or intricate texturing with detail smaller than a single pixel of the rendered image. Rendering without Adaptive Sampling helps keep these sub-pixel textures from "crawling" during an animation.

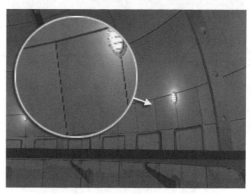

Figure 4-11: Adaptive Sampling misses details.

Note

Adaptive Sampling tends not to do so well when rendering text that is just a set of flat polygons. When rendering text, it is best to deactivate Adaptive Sampling and switch to an enhanced level of antialiasing (one of the Classic modes), which figures in almost twice as many samples per pixel.

Camera Effects

Imperfection is something we're all attuned to in reality. We know when something is out of focus, or if something is traveling too quickly to see clearly by the blurring of our vision (or the vision of the camera). It's these imperfections that CG can also recreate to help add that extra level of reality to our otherwise perfect CG world.

We're now almost done with looking at the basic properties of the camera. We've set up what kind of camera we want, told it how big the output imagery should be, and specified the quality in terms of Antialiasing levels. At the very bottom of the Camera Properties window are three tabs that let us set up some in-camera effects to help further process the look and feel of our art.

Motion Effects

In the real world, film is exposed while the shutter on a camera remains open. Light is let in through the lens, and it gets permanently recorded on the chemical emulsion of the film. Of course, if an object happens to be moving faster than the speed that the shutter opens and closes, then it will appear as a blur or smear on the film. LightWave doesn't use photosensitive film, and its shutter speed has no delay at all. This means that in the virtual world, we can record everything instantly without any blur if we want to; however, this makes for sometimes quite un-dynamic footage if we happen to be creating exciting action sequences. After all, nothing says *fast action* better than animation with a little motion blur!

Figure 4-12: The Motion Effects tab.

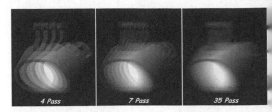

Figure 4-13: Motion Blur at varying levels of antialiasing.

While we've got our virtually perfect shutter, LightWave does give us options to simulate this less-perfect effect so that we can create a dynamic feeling of movement. The Motion Effects tab is where we'll find these options.

• **Use Global**, like we saw previously in the render output properties, tells the camera to use the **Render | Render Globals** settings to determine the motion effects of this camera.

• The **Motion Blur** pop-up becomes an option when you activate Antialiasing. With Motion Blur set to Normal, each anti-aliasing pass is not only rendered in its entirety, but each pass is also rendered from a slightly different point on LightWave's Timeline. (Adaptive Sampling is *not* active when rendering with the Motion Blur or Depth of Field settings, even though the Adaptive Sampling box may remain checked.) The result of this is an image that shows the precise effect of your object's motion that would be too quick for LightWave's "shutter" to "freeze."

Because of the way this motion blur is calculated, factoring in a minutely different point on LightWave's Timeline for each antialiasing pass, the more passes, the smoother and more realistic the render will be. So, the higher the level of antialiasing, the better your rendered image; this is why you'd want to use high levels of antialiasing passes when rendering motion blur (or depth of field).

Alternatively, a Motion Blur option of **Dithered** will split each antialiasing pass in two (as well as split the distance along the Timeline into twice as many steps), each pass only rendering 50% of the pixels at a time in an alternating checkerboard pattern. Dithered can create a smoother result than Normal (but with a slightly longer render time).

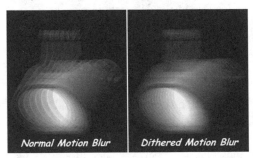

Figure 4-14: Dithering adds a little more softness to motion blur at seven passes.

• The **Particle Blur** check box tells LightWave whether or not you want to blur single-point polys (sometimes also referred to as *partigons* (*parti*-cle poly-*gons*)) as well as regular objects. This option is great when creating star fields for those sci-fi projects!

> **Note**
>
> With the implementation of new camera technology in LightWave v9, we need to use a Classic Camera type when rendering one- or two-point polygons. The other cameras work differently and do not render these at all.

• As seen in Figure 4-12, the **Blur Length** setting is linked to the **Shutter Angle** and **Exposure Time** readouts below it, which tell you about your Blur Length setting in terms a cinematographer is familiar with. The higher the number, the longer the blur. (You can get some neat effects by having Blur Length well over 100% or well under –100%.)

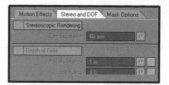

Figure 4-15: The Stereo and DOF tab.

> ## Note
>
> The Motion Blur settings in the Camera Properties window give you the most accurate kind of motion blur, but they aren't the only way to have your objects blur in relation to their change in position over time. A huge factor in creating any art is to "give the illusion of" rather than "exactly recreating."
>
> Clever artists/programmers found out that they could "smudge" the pixels of an object based on its motion data available for that particular frame. And so came about a neat little plug-in called Vector Blur. You can find it under **Windows | Image Processing | Add Image Filter**. You can find out more about this plug-in in the LightWave manual, but in short, it is a way of quickly giving the illusion of motion blur without LightWave having to go through all the steps necessary to create good-looking *exact* motion blur.

> ## v9.2 Note
>
> LightWave v9.2 features brand-new Photoreal Motion Blur and Depth of Field options. For details on these great features, check out the Depth of Field and Motion Blur Preview video in the LightWave 9.2 Videos folder on the companion DVD.

Stereo and DOF

Under the Stereo and DOF tab, we find the options for recreating two very cool effects: Stereoscopic Rendering (the kind you've probably experienced at the movies or your local IMAX theater) and Depth of Field.

The latter of these two — Depth of Field — is most likely going to be of interest. The Depth of Field settings let us create a

camera that behaves more naturally by limiting its focus capability from the unnatural, infinitely perfect focus of the CG world. More attention can be drawn to a subject in a scene by placing everything around the subject *out of focus* (blurring it), and the effect adds some real polish and a level of coolness to our work! However, like motion blur, lots of antialiasing is often required to get the best visuals from this tool.

Let's look at what these settings are all about.

• **Stereoscopic Rendering** will save your renders as *two separate images*, with the camera for each "eye" separated by the distance in the **Eye Separation** input field. (These can be combined into the kind of "red/blue" stereograph shown here using the Anaglyph Stereo: Compose image filter. See the LightWave manual for more information on this filter.)

Figure 4-16: Using Stereoscopic Rendering can give our 3D image a sense of depth when viewed with the right type of special glasses.

• **Depth of Field** becomes an option when you specify any antialiasing option that is set to render nine passes or more.

As with motion blur, the higher the level of antialiasing, the better the final render will look. **Focal Distance** tells LightWave how far in front of the camera you want the "focus" to be. The **Lens F-Stop** setting tells LightWave how much area around your *focal distance* will be "in focus." (Just like a real camera, the higher the F-stop, the larger the area that will be in focus.)

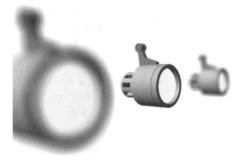

Figure 4-17: Depth of field at work.

While depth of field can be a complex concept to get your head around, it's not that hard to grasp some basics to get it up and running in LightWave. Let's take a look at how we can use the Depth of Field settings to bring a subject into focus in a scene.

1. Start out in Layout by loading the **Scenes\Chapter 04\depth_of_ field.lws** scene file from the companion DVD. This scene contains three

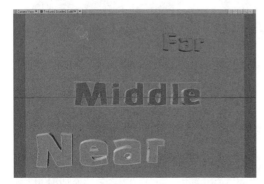

Figure 4-18: Three objects in the scene, all in perfect focus.

simple text objects spread varying distances from the camera. By default, LightWave creates images that are perfectly in focus. However, let's say we wanted to draw the viewer's attention to one of the three objects. If we were to be able to focus the camera lens like a real camera on one of the objects, that would help tremendously — and this is exactly where depth of field comes in.

2. Let's make the **dof_objects:middle** object (easily identified by the fact that it's a 3D model of the word "Middle") in the scene our item of interest by using the Depth of Field setting to focus the camera on it. Select the camera, and then open the Camera Properties window (**<p>**). Set the Antialiasing option to **PLD 9-Pass**. Click on the Stereo and DOF tab and activate the **Depth of Field** option.

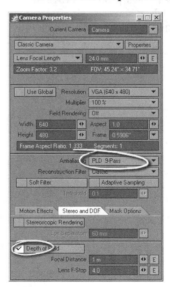

Figure 4-19: Setting up the camera to use depth of field.

Can we see what this looks like? Sure. However, before we do, let's make sure that the viewport is set to **Camera View**, as shown in Figure 4-20. (It should be by default when you loaded the scene, but it doesn't hurt to check.)

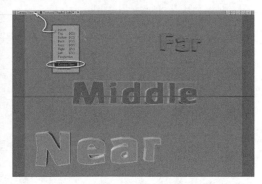

Figure 4-20: Make sure the viewport is set to Camera View first.

3. Click on **Render | Render | MB Preview** (<**Shift**>+<**F9**>). MB Preview will create a quick preview of any motion blur and depth of field effects in Layout (as seen in Figure 4-21). Depth of field is seen through the camera, which is why we need to make sure that the viewport is set to Camera View first.

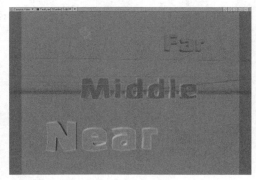

Figure 4-21: MB Preview shows us a quick preview of the depth of field.

Hmmm. That's not quite what we want. The middle object is out of focus; well, to be more accurate, *everything* is out of focus here! The default Focal Distance for the depth of field is set to **1 m** in front of the camera, and the objects in our scene lie *farther away* than 1 meter; hence they all appear slightly blurry and out of focus!

To focus on the dof_objects:middle object, we need to tell the Focal Distance how far away it is, so that it becomes the location where the focus is sharpest in the image. This leads us to ask one simple question: How far away is the middle object?

4. Select the **dof_objects:middle** object and then open the Object Properties window (<**p**>). Under the Geometry tab, select **Range Finder** from the Add Custom Object pop-up. Custom objects are useful visual tools that display information in the viewports of Layout. Range Finder measures the distance of the item it's added to from other items in the scene, then tells us how far it is in meters. This distance can then be used as the Focal Distance for the depth of field.

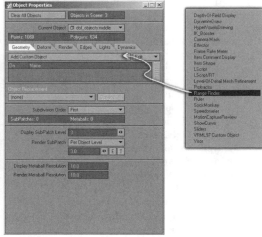

Figure 4-22: Adding Range Finder to the middle object.

5. By default, the Range Finder will measure the distance between the item it's applied to and the camera. When added, the distance is displayed in the Custom

105

Object list as **Range to Camera: 11.1189**, as shown in Figure 4-23.

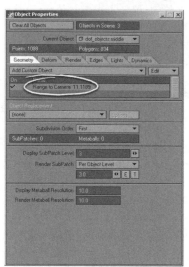

Figure 4-23: The Range Finder displays the distance to the camera after being added.

Note

Range Finder can measure the distance to any other item in the scene, not just the camera. It can be useful when you need to know how far away something is when creating animation or laying out virtual scenery. To change the item to which the Range Finder measures the distance, simply double-click on **Range to Camera: 11.1189** in the custom object list to open the Range Finder window. Select the item you want to measure the distance to from the **Item** pop-up. Check the **Draw Link** option if you want Layout to display a visual line in the viewport to show the link between the two items. When you close the Object Properties window, the **Range to** text in the custom object list will update to show the distance to the new object.

Figure 4-24: The Range Finder properties allow you to select any item in your scene, not just the camera.

6. Select the camera (**<C>**). If you didn't close the Object Properties window, it will change to reflect the properties of whatever item you have selected. In this case, it should now display the Camera Properties instead. If you did close the Object Properties window, simply press **<p>** to open the Camera Properties window. Under the Stereo and DOF tab, set the Focal Distance to **11.1189**, as shown in Figure 4-25.

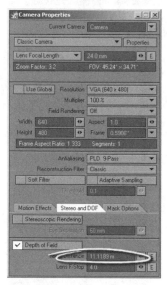

Figure 4-25: Set the new focal distance.

7. Click on **Render | Render | MB Preview** (**<Shift>+<F9>**) and see how things look now that we have set the Focal Distance to focus on the middle object. Look closely at the effect. Hmmm.... The last issue we have now is that everything appears to be *in focus*!

8. To adjust the amount of distance in front of and behind the middle object that stays in focus (which is what *depth of field* actually means), we need to adjust the Lens F-Stop value. Open the

Camera Properties window again, and under Stereo and DOF, set the Lens F-Stop to **0.1**. The smaller this value, the faster things appear to go blurry or out of focus. Press **<Shift>+<F9>** to preview the effect.

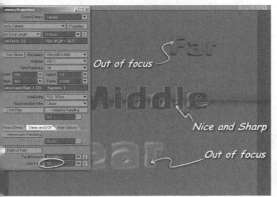

Figure 4-26: A more pronounced depth of field effect.

Note

In the real world, the F-stop adjusts the amount of light entering the camera lens. In LightWave, rather than light, it controls the sharpness of the image hitting our virtual film. The quality of the out-of-focus blurriness created in LightWave is controlled by how many passes of antialiasing you also have set up (with nine being the minimum). At times, you may find that you need more passes to give a nicer result.

So we saw just how easy it was to set up some basic depth of field effects. Now for something even cooler that will save you time, let's focus the camera on the far object. This time, however, let's do it *interactively*, without the need for tools like Range Finder.

9. Change the viewport to a **Top** view. If you look closely, you should notice a dashed circle around the camera. This shows us the focal distance from the camera. Open the Camera Properties window (if it's been closed) and then click and drag the left mouse button on the mini-slider next to the Focal Distance field (see Figure 4-27). As we adjust the value, the circle interactively changes to show us exactly where the focus will be.

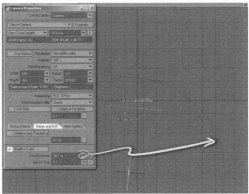

Figure 4-27: Drag the mini-slider and watch the circle visually show you where the focus will be.

10. Drag the mini-slider next to Focal Distance until the circle cuts into the **dof_objects:far** object, as shown in Figure 4-28. If you don't want to bother manually doing this, you can also just type **14.7 m** into the Focal Distance setting directly. Be sure to switch the viewport back to Camera View and then press **<Shift>+<F9>** to see how the far object now appears in focus (Figure 4-29).

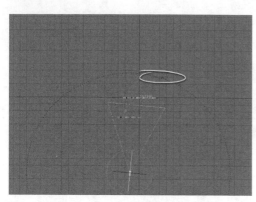

Figure 4-28: Get the circle to cut into the far object.

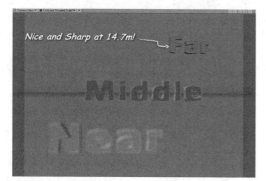

Figure 4-29: The effect is obvious, as the far object is now in focus.

Note

The Focal Distance circle can only be seen in the *orthographic views* (that's top, bottom, front, back, left, or right). It doesn't appear in any other viewport type. In Chapter 25, we look at how we can use LightWave's ability to control values with mathematical expressions to create an automatic focus for the camera. If you feel adventurous at this early stage in the book, go take a peek to see some more ways to set up the depth of field in LightWave!

Mask Options

The last tab at the bottom of the Camera Properties window, Mask Options, is a relatively simple one. Its sole purpose is to allow you to specify a rectangular area for the viewable part of the final output. Anything outside this area is painted out with a colored border.

Figure 4-30: The Mask Options tab.

One reason you may want to use a mask is so that you can create a *letterbox effect* — where you place a thick border at the top and bottom of the render to simulate the appearance that the image was filmed in a wide-screen format for cinema. This can give your creations a cool cinematic feel.

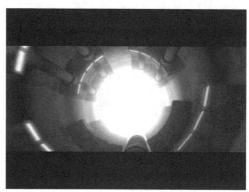

Figure 4-31: Nothing says cinematic like a letterbox effect.

To use a mask, you must *enable* it by clicking on the **Use Mask** check box in the Mask tab of the **Render | Render Globals** window. It is here in the Render Globals window that you can also set the color of the mask and the default (global) size.

The options in the Mask Options tab of the Camera Properties window allow you to use the mask size specified in the Render Globals window or to override it with new settings.

- **Use Global** will use the mask size specified in the Render Globals window. Unchecking this option allows you to override the global size settings and specify new Left, Top, Width, and Height settings.

This needs to be activated to use any camera mask options in LightWave.

Figure 4-32: Choose Use Mask from the Render Globals window to activate the mask options.

If you want to specify the mask settings on a camera-by-camera basis (rather than having each camera use the global settings), simply leave the Use Global button in the Camera Properties | Mask Options tab unchecked. Doing so will allow you to define new Left, Top, Width, and Height settings.

- **Mask Left** and **Mask Top** define the top-left pixel in the final output where the visible region of the image will start.

- **Mask Width** and **Mask Height** define the rectangular size of the visible area of the final output.

Limited Region

For those of you who've used previous versions of LightWave, you may have used the **Limited Region** option to create letterbox effects. Limited Region lets us specify a region in the Camera View that LightWave will render. It's a great tool for targeting smaller areas of a complex render to test quickly.

In LightWave v9 this option has been removed from the Camera Properties window. **Render | Render Globals** is the new home for this option, and we'll be looking at this option in detail in Chapter 7. However, I felt that since it is an integral part of the camera system also, it was worth mentioning here. The keyboard shortcut to activate Limited Region hasn't changed from previous versions of LightWave, and is still <l> for those of you wondering.

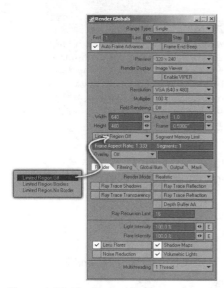

Figure 4-33: The Limited Region settings on the Render Globals window.

- **Limited Region** (<1>) is a pop-up menu that allows you to specify a smaller portion of the frame to render. Limited Region can only be adjusted while looking through the Camera View (represented by a yellow dotted rectangle, initially set to the edges of the camera viewport). There are

two types of limited region to choose from. **Limited Region Borders** will render full-sized frames; however, everything outside the limited region area will be masked off in black. **Limited Region No Border** will crop the area normally masked out by the Borders option, thereby giving you an image whose dimensions are exactly the size of your limited region. (Continue to press <1> to cycle through the three menu options.)

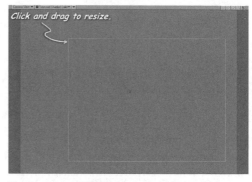

Figure 4-34: While looking through the Camera View viewport, adjust a limited region by clicking on the dotted yellow lines that appear and drag them to resize. Click and drag inside the limited region area to reposition the rectangle.

Perspective Camera Type

The overview we've just been through covered the basics of most camera properties in LightWave. In fact, it covered the Classic Camera type, which is the default camera type in LightWave, from head to foot. Let's look at the next most common camera you may find yourself using in LightWave — the Perspective Camera.

At first glance, this looks no different from the Classic Camera. In fact, it's not — at least in terms of the settings (which we won't look at in detail here since we just discussed them in the previous section).

Figure 4-35: The Perspective Camera settings.

Where it does differ is in how it creates the 3D image.

The Perspective Camera renders imagery in a more advanced manner by *ray tracing* everything from top to bottom of the image in one go (shadows, reflections, volumetric haze, and other effects). The Classic Camera, on the other hand, renders the opaque polygons first, then transparent polygons, followed by effects like volumetric lights (covered later in Chapter 10) one after the other in separate passes. Figure 4-36 shows an example of the two camera types rendering the same scene at roughly the same time. Note how the Classic Camera has already rendered the polygons, and has just started to create the effect of haze from a light in the scene. The Perspective Camera, however, is drawing everything line by line as it traces its way down the image.

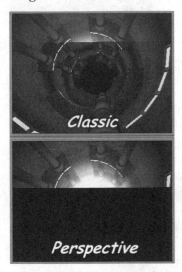

Figure 4-36: The Perspective Camera renders everything in one pass.

Why Use the Perspective Camera?

The Classic Camera renders *polygons*, which can cause hidden geometry to be rendered by the camera even though it is never seen in the final image. The Perspective Camera renders *pixels*, which avoids the issue by firing out rays and only seeing the pixel color returned from that location. Perspective doesn't render unseen polygons. For complex scenes, Perspective will render faster than Classic.

Take care, however, as simple scenes can actually be slower to render with the Perspective Camera. It's well worth testing the render times by swapping between Classic and Perspective camera types to see if there's any render speed benefit from using one or the other. By the way, if you're curious, the image in Figure 4-36 was actually slower to render with the Perspective Camera by around 5 seconds. For this scene, I would use the Classic Camera.

> **Note**
>
> Ray tracing requires polygons to have a surface area. Since one- and two-point polygons do not have a surface area, the Perspective Camera cannot see them. As mentioned earlier, when creating star fields or other effects with one- or two-point polygons, always use the Classic Camera.

Orthographic Camera Type

Orthographic simply refers to a flat view of something. We know what orthographic means from Modeler's viewports — the Left, Right, Top, Bottom, Front, and Back views are all orthographic.

In Layout, we now have a camera that can also *render* orthographically. Of course, when we say orthographic, we don't just mean a view from a particular side (like the above-mentioned views); we mean removing the perspective distortion created normally by the camera and creating images that literally have no depth. Figure 4-37 shows two renders from the same camera angle and location. However, note the effect that the Orthographic Camera has on the feeling of depth in the render. It's been flattened out completely.

This makes the Orthographic Camera ideal for creating technical imagery for use in architecture, sprite graphics for 2D video games, and schematic diagrams or blueprints for products.

To set up the Orthographic Camera, simply specify whether you want to render using a horizontal or vertical size, and then set the size in meters. Confused why a camera may have a physical size? To better understand how this all works, let's sneak back into another technobabble session and see.

Rendering in Parallel

Since we covered the technical concept of 3D cameras at the beginning of this chapter, let's examine just what this camera is doing so that we can understand how to best use it. It's actually quite simple — we know that sending out the rays through our field of view will create the effect of perspective. Well, if we were to instead send out the rays in a straight line from the surface of, say, a rectangular area, then there would be no perspective at all!

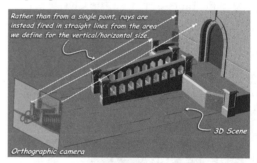

Figure 4-38: Orthographic cameras project rays in straight lines, creating an image with no perspective distortion.

The area that the rays are fired out from is defined by setting the **Horizontal Size** or **Vertical Size** in the Camera Properties window. When we change to the Orthographic Camera type, the effect is shown in any viewport set to Camera View. Seeing

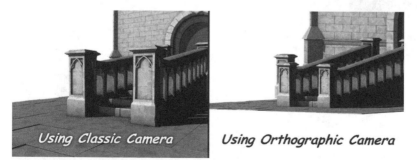

Figure 4-37: Note the change in depth perception between a standard and orthographic view of the same scene.

through the camera this way makes life much easier when setting things up.

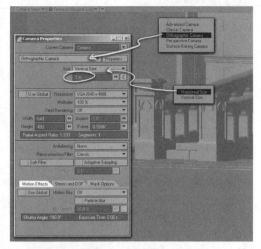

Figure 4-39: Setting up the Orthographic Camera.

Obviously when rendering a picture, there are two dimensions to any image: horizontal and vertical. In the Orthographic Camera, we can only set one of these options. So how does LightWave know how big the other dimension should be? No need to worry — the other dimension is simply calculated from the Frame Aspect Ratio setting (discussed earlier in the chapter). The rectangular area is the area of the final image we will be creating, and each ray is fired out from the location of each pixel in the image.

We're starting to see something clever happening here: LightWave's newly engineered camera system seems to be controlling the way that these rays are shot out for the image we're creating. We learned earlier that firing from a point outward creates a perspective effect. Now we've discovered that firing directly outward in a straight line from a rectangle (rather than a point) flattens the effect. That whole concept leads us into the monster of all LightWave cameras....

Advanced Camera Type

Welcome to the most complex, flexible, and powerful camera type in LightWave v9: the Advanced Camera! With great power, however, comes great responsibility, and a mild case of utter confusion for most new users! Luckily though, we know a little about how cameras work in LightWave from the technobabble we discussed earlier, which is going to make this tool a lot easier to grasp. The Advanced Camera lets us specify pretty much every aspect of how LightWave sees the virtual world around it, giving us an immense amount of flexibility. It does this by letting us customize all those essential details that make a CG camera work: where the rays fire from and in what direction they go once they leave the camera.

Figure 4-40: The Advanced Camera window.

Note

Because of the complex nature of this camera, we can't see it in the Camera View of Layout. It's too complex to recreate in real time, so it can be a little more difficult to judge what we can expect to see when using it initially.

Where Have the Settings Gone?

When you change Camera Type to Advanced, the Advanced Camera window pops up. But if you close this window... well, it's gone. So how do you redisplay this big window of information? That's what that **Properties** button we see next to our Camera Type pop-up is all about. Click this to reopen the Advanced Camera window.

Obviously, that's a pretty big window of settings that we can tweak and toy with. We could almost write an entire chapter dedicated to this camera. For now, though, let's just take a peek under the hood and learn a little about how each property works.

Where It All Starts — the Ray Start

As we know, the 3D camera has to send its rays from somewhere. The top section of the Advanced Camera window lets us set this up.

Figure 4-42: The Ray Start section.

• **Ray Start** lets us specify a location for the rays to start from. This could be any item in a scene (camera, light, or object), the location on the surface of an object using a UV texture map (we look at UV maps in Chapter 11), perhaps the X and Y location on a flat plane (i.e., the concept used for the Orthographic Camera), or a custom location anywhere in the virtual 3D universe.

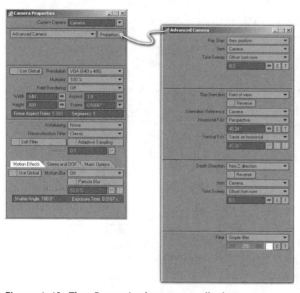

Figure 4-41: That Properties button actually does something.

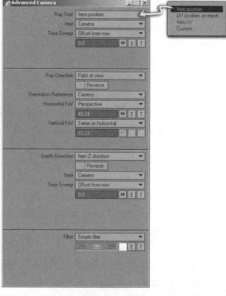

Figure 4-43: A handful of options are offered to let us modify the location from which our camera rays are generated.

Note

When we change the Ray Start setting, the other settings on the window also change to reflect the type of information required for that position. For now, let's stick to the defaults that the Advanced Camera starts out with.

Figure 4-44: The Ray Direction section.

- **Item** lets us select the item in our scene that this Ray Start will fire from.

- **Time Sweep** lets us change the time in an animation when we want to read the location of the ray starting location (which can create extremely cool effects, especially if this Ray Start location happens to be animated.) We'll look at an example of using this later in this section.

Note

Did you spot the "E" and "T" buttons next to the Time Sweep setting? We'll see these a LOT when working in LightWave. Often they'll appear next to values for properties of a tool or feature. Clicking E will open up the Graph Editor window, which lets us animate any value over the course of time. (We'll be looking at the Graph Editor later in this chapter when we get into animation basics.) By clicking on T, we open up the Texture Editor window and can control the value using LightWave's extensive texturing system. We'll be looking at texturing later on in Chapter 6.

Where It Goes To — the Ray Direction

Once our camera starts to render, it shoots out rays from the starting location. With the Classic and Perspective Cameras, rays are sent out in a spread defined by the field of view. We know that the Orthographic Camera fired the rays in straight lines from the rectangular area we defined in its properties. In the Advanced Camera, we can spread out the rays in any way we like!

- **Ray Direction** defines the direction rays will take once they leave the ray start location. Like the Ray Start setting, this can be a number of possible locations, from items to UV maps. The default option is Field of view. We'll take a look at additional options available for this setting.

- **Reverse** will flip the direction of the rays; instead of firing outward from the ray start location, they fire from the direction back toward the ray start. This makes the camera effectively look back at itself.

- **Orientation Reference** lets us specify a direction for the rays to fire based on the rotation of an item in a scene. Often we'll use the camera itself, but we could use any item's rotation to determine in what direction the camera rays need to fire.

- **Horizontal FoV** lets us specify the horizontal field of view angle. By default, this is set to Perspective and works like a standard camera. The field of view is determined by the angle setting below the pop-up. This pop-up also lets us change the field of view to work orthographically or view around the ray start location in a cylindrical or spherical direction.

- **Vertical FoV** lets us specify the vertical field of view angle. This can be tweaked just like the horizontal FoV, or we can specify that this work the same as the horizontal FoV.

How Far Away It Is — The Depth Direction

Measuring the distance of items from the camera is important for effects such as depth of field. Like Ray Start and Ray Direction, we can also completely modify the way that this is calculated! Well, it's not called the Advanced Camera for nothing!

Figure 4-45: The Depth Direction section.

- **Depth Direction** defines the direction rays will take to calculate the depth of the items from the camera. By default, Item Z direction is used to measure the depth in front of a selected item (from the Item pop-up just below).

- **Reverse** will flip the direction in the same way that the option did for Ray Direction.

- **Item** lets us select the item in our scene from which our depth is calculated. By default, this is always the camera.

- **Time Sweep** works the same way as it did for Ray Start, allowing us to read the location of the item at a different time in our animation.

Seeing through Rose-Colored Glasses — The Filter

The Filter is a system to process the color of the rays being rendered. Think of this as the CG equivalent of a lens filter on a real camera that modifies the color of light passing through the lens.

Figure 4-46: The Filter section.

- The **Filter** pop-up lets us select what kind of filter to apply: Simple filter, which filters the color of each pixel, or Mixing filter, which gives us the ability to filter the red, green, and blue components of the color of each pixel independently.

Since the Advanced Camera is so different from any other camera in LightWave v9, it's well worth taking a little time to look at a couple of the basic concepts here. We'll start by looking at how we can get some clever effects with the advanced capability to customize the field of view.

1. Load the scene **Scenes\Chapter 04\advanced_fov.lws** from the companion DVD. This scene places our camera in the middle of an ancient temple in some past civilization. Select the camera, and open the Camera Properties window (**<p>**) for it. Change its Camera Type to **Advanced Camera**. The Advanced Camera window, shown in Figure 4-47, will pop up.

2. Let's use the advanced capabilities of the camera to create an extreme fish-eye lens effect. That is, imagine the scene is viewed from the inside of a bubble that shows the scene around itself. Change Horizontal FoV to **Spherical** and set the angle below it to **360** degrees. Note that the Vertical FoV option will gray out since the lens is spherical.

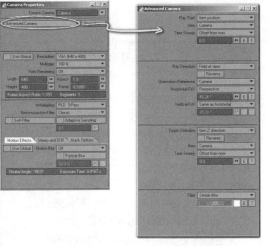

Figure 4-47: Switching to the Advanced Camera.

3. For now, let's close the Advanced Camera window. In the Camera Properties window, set the Antialiasing pop-up to **PLD 3-Pass** so that we can remove any jaggies from our final image. (If you have closed this window, simply select the camera and press <p> to reopen it.) To make sure we can see the resulting image, check that **Render | Render Globals | Render Display** is set to **Image Viewer.** This is a pop-up window that displays our 3D image when LightWave has finished creating it. Press <F9> and let's check out the result in Figure 4-51.

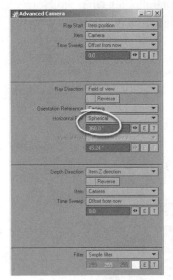

Figure 4-48: Set up the Advanced Camera for an extreme fish-eye view.

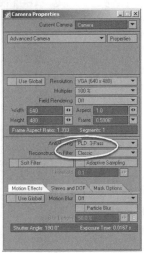

Figure 4-49: Remove those jaggies with PLD 3-Pass.

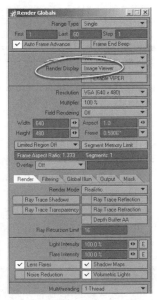

Figure 4-50: Make sure that Image Viewer is active.

117

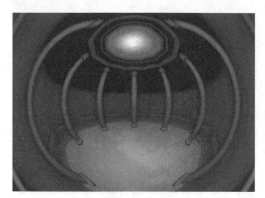

Figure 4-51: Extreme fish-eye view with the Spherical FoV.

Mac-specific Note

On the Mac, OS X's Expose feature may be using the <F9> keyboard shortcut, making it not work in LightWave. The solution in this case is to simply modify the settings for Expose to not use <F9> or simply click the Render | Render Frame button on the toolbar (avoiding the keyboard shortcut altogether).

4. A little extreme, perhaps? However, it's not often we know what life looks like from all around the camera in the same image! Perhaps we want to make a less extreme fish-eye lens, one that shows what is in front of the camera. Simply open up the Advanced Camera

Figure 4-52: An extreme fish-eye lens, but a little more acceptable at 180 degrees.

properties window again by clicking the **Properties** button on the Camera Properties window and change the Horizontal FoV angle to **180** degrees. Press <**F9**> to see how it looks.

So we can create cool fish-eye effects very quickly and easily, even rendering around and behind the camera. How about creating something cool but perhaps less extreme? Let's create a panoramic image that looks around a full 360 degrees.

5. Change Horizontal FoV to **Cylinder** and set its angle to **360**. For the Vertical FoV setting, choose **Same as horizontal**. Unlike Spherical, Cylinder treats the camera lens in a similar way that we might tilt and pan with a tripod in the real world, spinning the camera about its axis. It's still seeing around the entire camera in a single image, but it doesn't create that bubble-like distortion that the Spherical FoV does.

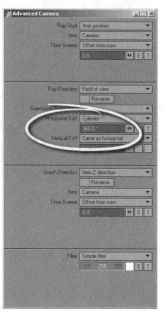

Figure 4-53: A change to Cylinder for our FoV.

6. Before we create our image, let's change the Width to **800** pixels and Height to **400** pixels in the Camera Properties window. I've found that panoramic views tend to be twice as wide as they are high. Press <**F9**> to check out the result.

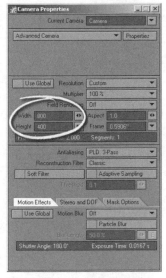

Figure 4-54: Set the image size to twice as wide as it is high.

Figure 4-55: The panoramic image.

Very cool! In Chapter 12, we learn how we can use images like this to fake the environment around our 3D worlds. This image may be useful later on, so **File | Save RGBA** to store it away for future use if you wish to. I tend to save images using the LW_PNG24 (.png) format.

So, while changing the lens' field of view is definitely more advanced than any kind of camera we've probably ever used in LightWave (or any other 3D application for that matter), there's still more to look at. As I mentioned earlier, I could write a whole chapter dedicated to this camera, but we'll just look at the essential information that will get us on the road to discovering the power hidden inside LightWave!

1. Load the **Scenes\Chapter 04\time-sweep.lws** scene file from the companion DVD. The scene contains a block of mini-skyscrapers. There's not much to this scene, as we can see in Figure 4-56.

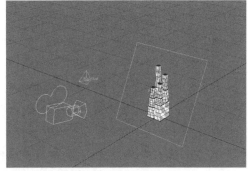

Figure 4-56: A simple but oddly interesting-looking scene.

There are a couple of other items that we can also see here. One is a small pyramid-shaped item labeled "Ray Start." The other is a large flat square and has the word "Ray Direction" in the center. (In Figure 4-56, the text is a little obscured by the skyscrapers.) These items are called *nulls* — a special non-rendering type of object that we can use for a huge number of things. In fact, we'll learn all about how to create and use these nulls later in Chapter 12.

If we click the Play button in the lower-right corner of the Layout interface, we also see that these null items appear to be spinning around the mini-skyscrapers over the 60 frames of the scene. We're going to be using these items in the Camera Properties window, and the animation of them is going to give us some pretty clever options too. Let's check this out.

Figure 4-57: Click Play to see the null objects rotating around the skyscrapers.

2. Select the camera and open the Camera Properties window (<**p**>). Change the Camera Type to **Advanced Camera**. Once the Advanced Camera window appears, make sure that Ray Start is set to **Item position** and Item is set to **null_RayStart**. This is the small pyramid-shaped null in the scene and is going to be the location from which the camera rays fire. Change Ray Direction to **Through item XY** and set Ray Direction Item to **null_RayDirection**. This will make this rectangular object the shape through which the rays will fire from the Ray Start location, defining the "field of view" for us!

3. Press <**F9**> to render an image to see how this new "null"-based camera looks. Nothing looks too out of the ordinary. The camera, however, is now using the null_RayStart null object as the camera location, and the null_RayDirection null object to define the field of view. Very cool! The camera is now controlled through two completely unrelated objects in the scene.

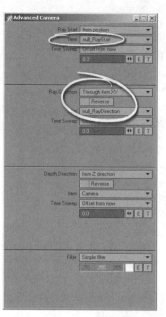

Figure 4-58: Setting the Ray Start and Ray Direction properties.

Figure 4-59: The render using nulls — nothing out of the ordinary.

4. Let's do something completely crazy. Set the Ray Start Time Sweep to **Range down image start now**. Set the value below this to **2.0** seconds (which is the time needed for 60 frames of animation at 30 frames per second). Set the Ray Direction Time Sweep to **Same as Ray Start Time Sweep**. Press <**F9**> and take a look at the result.

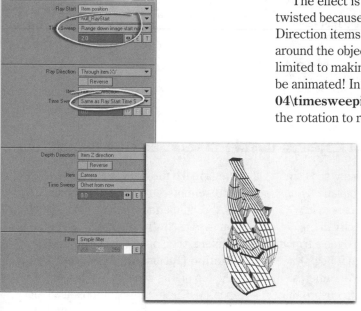

Figure 4-60: Advanced time sweeping — totally twisted results.

The effect is that the image appears twisted because the Ray Start and Ray Direction items happen to be rotating around the object. This effect is not just limited to making still images; it can even be animated! In the scene **Scenes\Chapter 04\timesweeping_ F.lws**, I've modified the rotation to repeat forever, and also have a few slow down and speed up sections along the way to vary the rotation a little. To see the effect, check out the render I made from this scene in **Renders\ Chapter 04\timesweeping.mov** (set QuickTime to loop this video as it repeats seamlessly).

There's a lot more that the Advanced Camera is capable of. Now that you have explored how to change some basic parameters and how they work, I'll leave the discovery of the power available in the Advanced Camera to your creative mind and the LightWave manual.

Now that's very freaky! The Time Sweep setting lets us tell the camera to *sweep* through time and work out where the camera is at that time when rendering a particular line or pixel in the image. The option **Range down image start now** tells the camera to start creating the first line of the image at whatever frame it happens to be on at the time. The value below of **2.0** seconds simply says to create the bottom line of the image two seconds later in time. The rest of the image is spread out (or *swept*) over those two seconds.

> **v9.2 Note**
>
> LightWave v9.2 features an additional camera type called Real Lens. For information on the Real Lens camera, check out the Depth of Field and Motion Blur Preview video in the LightWave 9.2 Videos folder on the companion DVD.

Surface Baking Camera Type

The Surface Baking Camera will render the surface of a selected object and record the result into an image based on a UV map. This is a great way to *bake* complex textures and lighting directly into an image

that can be painted back onto an object. These textures are ideal for creating characters for a game engine, and are a great way to speed up a complex architectural walk-through animation.

Tracking the Subject with the Camera

Ever been to an air show with a video camera and wanted to film an old biplane flying across the airfield? Without a tripod, it's hard to keep the subject perfectly in the view of your shot. Sometimes even a tripod doesn't make it easy (but often it helps).

While we're on the subject of cameras, there are times where I want to ensure that the camera keeps track of a subject in a project, no matter where it moves. LightWave has a tool to automatically make the camera follow a target. Here's how it's used:

1. Open the scene **Scenes\Chapter 04\follow_me.lws**. In this scene, a rogue satellite orbits quickly across in front of the camera, zooming in from one side and out the other.

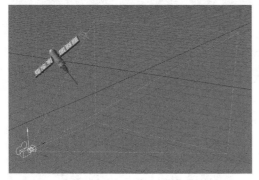

Figure 4-61: A fast-moving satellite whips past the camera.

2. Let's make the camera track the satellite, reminiscent perhaps of those early NASA animations you may have seen on the Discovery Channel. Select the camera, then open the **Windows | Motion Options** window (<**m**>). At the top of this window is a Target Item pop-up. Click on the pop-up and select the **null_Satellite** item from the list.

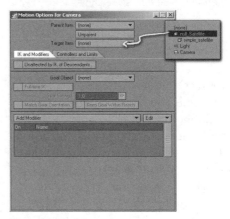

Figure 4-62: Set up the camera targeting.

3. Close the Motion Options window. Notice how the camera is now targeting the satellite! LightWave creates an orange dashed line between the camera and its target to let us know that the camera is targeting an item (without having to open the Motion Options window to find out).

You may have realized that null_Satellite is not the 3D satellite model, but a null object created specifically for attaching the satellite object to. (In 3D terminology, attaching one item to another is called *parenting*.) This null is then animated (the satellite is parented (attached), so it obviously moves along with it). Why do this? Well, simply to give us a system where we can modify the animation of the satellite

object on its own without interfering with the original motion. In this exercise, I rotated the satellite to give it a subtle spin, while the null took care of tilting and moving it. This concept is known as *hierarchical animation*. While it may sound complicated at first, it will all make sense later on in Chapter 12 where we cover this topic in much more detail.

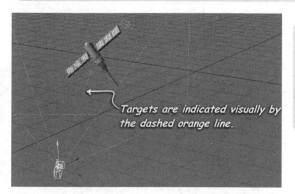

Targets are indicated visually by the dashed orange line.

Targeting an item is not limited to just the camera. In fact, we can make any item in LightWave target another by simply selecting it, opening the Motion Options window, and setting a target item.

Figure 4-63: The camera now targets and follows the moving satellite.

Animation in LightWave

I like to think of LightWave as my virtual film production facility. Modeler is our workshop where we build the props, create the scenery, and set up the actors and costumes. Layout is our virtual film studio. Here, as we say, is where we make the magic happen!

Now that we know all about the camera equipment we use to film our productions, let's look at how we get this magic to happen. This section explores the basic tools that LightWave uses to control the movements of items within an animation.

Key Frames (Keys)

The concept of *key frames* comes from traditional animation (animation drawn on paper). The animator draws the *primary* poses, the ones that define the action, and assigns the drawings positions on a *dope sheet* (a spreadsheet that shows the position in time of every drawing within a scene). After the animator is happy with the action, the scene goes on to other artists who fill in the drawings between the key drawings (creatively called *in-betweens*).

A *key frame* in LightWave is a record of an item's (object, bone, light, camera, etc.) position, rotation, and/or scale. A key frame is recorded in LightWave when you change an item's scaling, rotation, or position (if you have Auto Key Create active) or by using Create Key to manually create a key frame. In this section, we'll get a little practice using both techniques.

How do animators know how much time (how many frames) to put between their key frames? With experience, many animators gain a feel for how much time is needed; however, in general, most use a stopwatch to time either how long it takes for us to do an action physically or how long the action takes to play out in our imaginations. One of the problems with stopwatches is that they don't give timings in frames (working in 30 FPS (NTSC), 25 FPS (PAL), or 24 FPS (film)), feet/frames, SMPTE, or whatever. To resolve this, Tim Albee created a little utility in Flash (included on the DVD that came with this book) that serves as an animation timer and unit-conversion utility. It's a handy piece of software for any animator, traditional or otherwise.

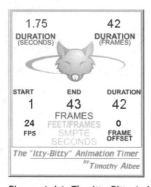

Figure 4-64: The Itty-Bitty Animation Timer.

The Itty-Bitty Animation Timer looks simple but packs a lot of power. Click on the icon at the center to begin timing how long you hold the mouse button down. Click **Frames**, **Feet/Frames**, **SMPTE**, or **Seconds** to see your time displayed in that format. You can also manually enter any value for any field and press <**Return**> to update the calculations.

(This is how you change your FPS or add a frame offset if you're timing part of an action that doesn't start on frame 0.)

> **Note**
>
> You can find more information on the Itty-Bitty Animation Timer, along with a whole slew of other plug-ins, programs, and utilities, in Chapter 27.

Auto Key

I mentioned Auto Key earlier — but what exactly does it do? Creating key frames in LightWave is pretty easy, but when projects get complex it can quickly become repetitive and time consuming to manually create key frames. That's where Auto Key comes into the picture. If the Auto Key button (<**Shift**>+<**F1**>) is enabled, any move, rotation, or scale will be recorded for us automatically. The **Create Key** button simply turns the Auto Key feature on and off; however, the settings that let us specify how Auto Key creates key frames are found in the General Options panel (<**o**>).

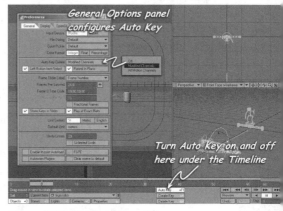

Figure 4-65: The Auto Key settings.

By default, Auto Key will only create a key on the channel we adjust (i.e., if we move an item on its Y-axis, it only adds or updates the Y key frames). You can change the Auto Key Create setting to **All Motion Channels**, which will create a key frame on every channel.

Be aware before making the decision to use Auto Key that every time you adjust anything in Layout, it records the changes. The danger is that an accidental mouse click can quickly add unwanted key frames or change key frames you've carefully laid out, ruining all your hard work. If you're particularly new to animation, often it's safer to deactivate Auto Key and set the key frames manually using Create Key.

Anyway, let's check out just how we animate, and what cool tools are available to us in LightWave.

1. Make sure that you start with a clean Layout by clearing the scene if necessary. Load the **Objects\Chapter 04\logo.lwo** file from the companion DVD. This loads up a multi-layered object that we will use for creating a simple little "flying logo" animation for a fictitious company called Robo Productions. (You might recognize the mascot from Chapter 3.)

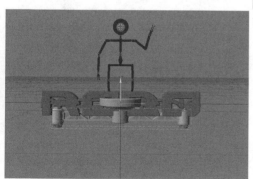

Figure 4-66: The logo model loaded into Layout.

2. Before we get too carried away, let's make sure that Layout is set up to give us a good, efficient working environment. Like Modeler, we can have

multiple viewports in Layout as well. When animating, sometimes it's nice to be able to view the scene from various angles. Open the **Edit | Display Options** window (**<d>**). Near the top of the window, we have the **Viewport Layout** pop-up. This lets us reconfigure the location and sizes of the viewports in Layout. Click this and select the **1 Left, 2 Right** configuration. I like this setup as it gives me one big viewport at the left and two smaller ones on the right that I can use for whatever I need. Of course with experience, you'll develop your own working preferences in Layout.

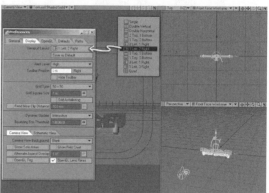

Figure 4-67: Set up three viewports in Layout.

Note

If you like this setup, then click the **Save as Default** button below the Viewport Layout field to set this to be the default startup for Layout from now on. (You can always come back and change it later, but this will save having to set it up each time.)

3. Because this is a logo, we'll want to make sure that we respect the title safe zones so that the logo fits the screen comfortably. In the Display tab (**<d>**) of the Preferences window, activate **Show Safe Areas**. I also like to use

Show Field Chart. Safe Areas defines the area in the Camera View in which our items will be seen for TV broadcast. The inner border indicates the boundary inside which the text and logos will be guaranteed to be seen on TV. The Field Chart is a set of crosshairs in the Camera View that I find extremely useful for lining up items.

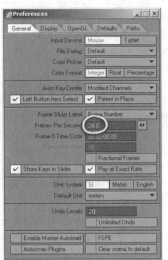

Figure 4-69: Set the Frames Per Second setting to 24 on the General tab.

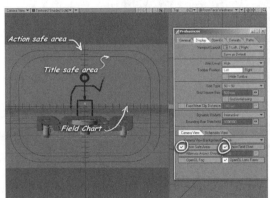

Figure 4-68: Choose Show Safe Areas and Show Field Chart.

4. I've also decided to work at a setting of 24 frames per second (film), so make sure that you've got this set under **Edit | General Options | Frames Per Second.** (If the Preferences window is still open, simply click on the General tab to bring up the General Options.)

> **Note**
>
> Internally, LightWave records all animation in *time* format (seconds). If we decide later that we should have been working at 30 frames per second for NTSC TV, simply change the Frames Per Second setting, and all the frames of our animation will automatically be adjusted to the correct locations for the new rate!

5. Our animation will be around 2.5 seconds (which at 24 frames per second is 60 frames), so enter **60** as the End Frame in both the Time Slider and the Render | Render Globals | Last settings.

> **Note**
>
> 60 frames is usually the default that LightWave uses anyway. If so, then you probably don't need to change anything; however, it's always safe to check (especially once you start doing a lot of work and things start to change between sessions in LightWave).

6. You'll notice that the object looks a little jumbled here. That's because it's comprised of four different layers all sitting in the same place. When you load an object comprised of multiple layers into Layout, each layer is treated as a separate item. Click on the **Objects** button (<O>) at the bottom of the screen to make sure we're working with objects in Layout. To make picking items easier, we can bring up the **List Manager** window by clicking

on the small button to the right-hand side of the Current Item pop-up (as shown in Figure 4-70). The List Manager gives us a nice floating window that can sit on the desktop for quickly selecting items in the scene.

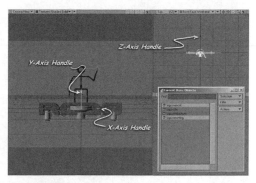

Figure 4-71: Move the objects upward on the Y-axis.

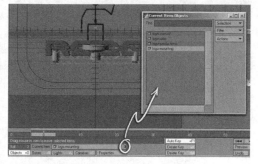

Figure 4-70: The List Manager window.

7. Let's adjust a few things here to get the scene set up properly. Make sure that the Time Slider is on frame 0. In the List Manager, select the **logo:mounting** object, then press **<Ctrl>** and click on **logo:mascot** to select both of these objects. Make sure that the **Modify | Move** tool is active (**<t>**) and then move the objects upward on the Y-axis. This can be done either by clicking and dragging on the *green* handle (the up arrow in the viewports) or by holding down the right mouse button and dragging. (Right-click gives us the ability to move on the Y-axis when working in 3D views like Camera View.) Move the items up the Y-axis approximately **150mm** or judge the distance by eye until it looks like Figure 4-71. (The field chart, seen as crosshairs in the camera viewport, comes in handy in this respect!)

> ### Note
>
> Clicking and dragging on an item's handles will restrict movement, rotation, or scaling to one axis. It makes precise positioning much easier, especially when working in a Perspective viewport. (Make sure you have **Edit | OpenGL Options | Show Handles** active.) To see exactly how much you're adjusting items, you can view the values in the Quick Info text boxes at the bottom of the toolbar (Figure 4-72). If you need to be more precise, you can type the numeric value directly into these boxes, but be warned — numeric changes are only applied to the first item you selected (in the case of multiple selected items). You will need to select each item one by one to enter any numeric values across a selection.

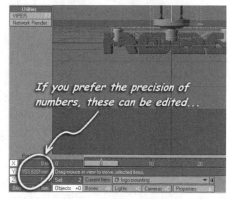

Figure 4-72: Use the numeric controls for more precision.

8. Once that's done, make sure that you record this change by clicking **Create Key** (<**Return**>). Make sure that Create Key At is **0** and that the For pop-up says **Selected Items**, then click **OK** (<**Return**>) to record the move for both of the items.

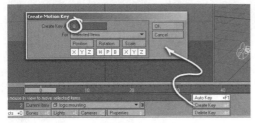

Figure 4-73: Create a key frame for the two items we just moved.

9. At last, we're going to get into some actual animation! With logo animation, often it's easiest to set the *finishing location* of the object as the first thing we do. Move the Time Slider to frame 30 (let's make the logo come to rest halfway through the animation) and select both the **logo:robo** and **logo:productions** objects in the List Manager. Move the objects toward the camera on the Z-axis (the blue handle if you wish to use it) so they sit in front of the mascot and mounting, and then down a little. Moving on the Z-axis is done in Camera View by simply holding the left mouse button and dragging the mouse up and down. Once they're positioned about the same as in Figure

4-74, click the **Create Key** button (<**Return**>) and create a key frame for both items at **frame 30**.

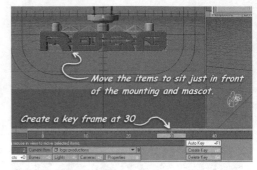

Figure 4-74: Move the words forward and down a little at frame 30.

10. Select the **logo:productions** object in the List Manager, and then move it down so it sits below the **logo:robo** object nicely. Click **Create Key** and update this item at **frame 30**. When a change is made at an existing key frame, we need to recreate the key frame again to update it. (Of course, this is where Auto Key saves time, but for now, let's ignore it while we're picking up the basics.)

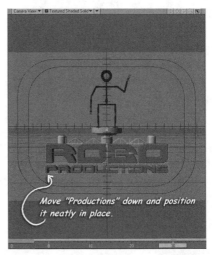

Figure 4-75: Move the Productions text down below the robot.

If you scrub the Time Slider between 0 and 30, you'll see the logos have some very minimal animation on them already; however, since we've only updated where the logos end at frame 30, we now need to adjust where they start so that they appear more appealing and interesting.

Note

Don't hesitate to flip back through Chapter 2's section on Layout if you need to. There's a lot to remember here! Learning is a skill that is developed through practice!

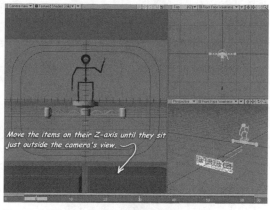

Figure 4-77: Move the logos back just out of view.

11. Let's set the Time Slider back to the start at frame 0. This can be done either by sliding the Time Slider manually or by clicking the Rewind button, as shown in Figure 4-76.

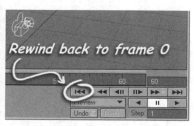

Figure 4-76: Click to rewind to the start frame.

12. Use the List Manager to select both the **logo:production** and **logo:robo** items, then move them back toward the camera on the Z-axis until they sit just outside the Camera View (Figure 4-77). Click **Create Key** at frame 0 to record the updated position of the two logo items. Scrubbing the Time Slider back and forth between frames 0 and 30 should now show the logo flying in from behind the camera and finishing below the company mascot. Congratulations! We've just created an animation in LightWave!

Note

When items are animated, we see their path displayed in the viewport with each key represented by a marker on the path as shown in Figure 4-78. This feature can be activated (or deactivated if you don't want to see it) from **Edit | OpenGL Options | Show Motion Paths**.

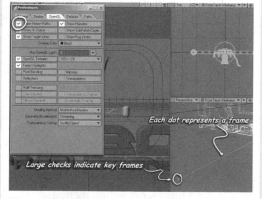

Figure 4-78: Motion paths in Layout.

13. Let's give the text a little "twist" as it settles at frame 30. Select the **logo:robo** item on its own, and activate the **Modify | Rotate** tool (<**y**>). Rewind to frame 0 (if you're not already on frame 0), and then let's enter the values numerically, just for a little more precision. Pressing <**n**> will highlight the value for H at the

129

bottom of the toolbar (Figure 4-79).
Type **25.00** for the value here, and then
press <**Tab**> to enter the value and
skip down to the P value text box. Type
–40.00 here and press <**Return**> to
finish. Remember to press **Create Key**
at frame 0 to update these changes for
the item.

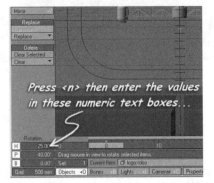

Figure 4-79: Entering the values numerically in
Layout.

14. Repeat the process for the **logo:pro-
duction** item, this time entering an
H value of **–25.00** and a P value of
40.00 (so that the logo:production
object twists from the opposite direction). Create the key frame at 0 to
update the item.

So we've got a basic "flying logo" animation up and working; however, the two
words fall in a straight line at a fairly constant speed. It would be nice to perhaps
give them a little acceleration as they fly in,
and then have them slow down and settle
into the last frame. Tweaking such details in
an animation leads us to one of the animator's main tools of the trade — the Graph
Editor.

> **Note**
>
> Like modeling, animation should be built on
> a solid foundation. Start simple. Make sure
> the most basic of moves is working for you
> before getting too carried away with adding
> the details.

"Motion" Graph Editor

Just above the Scene Editor pop-up menu
on the upper-left side of the Layout interface is the Graph Editor button. Clicking on
it (or pressing <**Ctrl**>+<**F2**>) will open
the "Motion" Graph Editor for your
selected item. (The Graph Editor controls a
lot more than just motions now, though at
one time that's all it did, and so us "old-tim-
ers" still sometimes call it by its original
name: Motion Graph.)

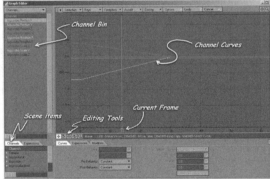

Figure 4-80: The "Motion" Graph Editor.

Every aspect of an item's motion and every
"envelopable" attribute is controlled
through this interface. When it's open,
press <**a**> to Zoom All and <**A**> to Zoom
Selected if you want to view all the information for your item's channels. (There's so
much here that I'm just going to hit the
high points and leave the details to the
LightWave manual. LightWave's manual
covers the Graph Editor in immense detail
and is well worth taking the time to read
through!)

- On the left side, the **Channel Bin** shows all the aspects that LightWave is tracking for the currently selected item. Click on one channel to view and edit it in the Graph area, or <Shift>+click or <Ctrl>+click to select more than one channel to view and modify at once.

- Double-click on an item under the **Channels** tab (this is the tab found *below* the Channel Bin) to change which item's curves you are viewing (without having to close the window, select the new item, and reopen the Graph Editor). <Shift>+ double-click to add an item's channels to the list you are currently viewing.

- The **Graph area** is where you right-click and drag to create a bounding box for selecting multiple key frames or left-click and drag to modify them. (The same hot key and mouse combinations you're used to in Modeler will work here as well to zoom and scroll the view.)

- Just below the Graph area are the Graph Editor's tool buttons. From the left are **Move Keys**, **Add Keys**, **Stretch Keys**, **Roll Keys**, and **Zoom**. (Left-click and drag affects the selected keys' *values*, while <Ctrl>+left-click and drag affects the selected keys' *frames*.)

In Figure 4-81, we are looking only at the "curve" for the X position for the item named **logo:robo**. The other channel curves are also visible; however, their gray appearance means that they are not

currently editable (we can't tweak them until we select them in the Channel Bin on the left; consider them as *background layers* in the Graph Editor). Notice how rolling the mouse cursor over a key frame pops up a small box that shows us information about the key.

Below the Graph Editor tools are three tabs where all the numeric controls reside. We'll only be looking at the **Curves** tab here, since this is where we tweak the way a channel's motion curve works. The Expressions tab lets us modify the way channels work through mathematics; this is a little too technical to delve into so early in the book, and hence is covered in much more detail in Chapter 25. The Modifiers tab allows us to modify the way channels work through specialized modification tools; this is covered in more detail later in Chapter 12.

Let's check out what the Curves tab is all about.

Figure 4-82: The Curves tab controls.

Note

To edit the details of a key frame in the Graph Editor, click on it to select it in the Graph area. The key frame dot will turn yellow, and the Curve controls will become active.

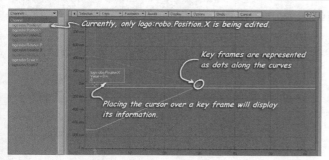

Figure 4-81: Graph Editor at work on the X position.

Frame is an input field that shows on what frame your currently selected key frame is located. **Value** tells you the channel's selected key value (an angle, percentage, or other kind of numeric value related to the channel).

Think of these options as a way to numerically "fine-tune" key frames. For example, if we decide that a key frame is at the wrong location, we can select it and simply enter in a new frame number to adjust the keys. Let's try our hand with the Graph Editor.

1. I felt that the **logo:robo** object was a little slow in getting to its final resting place. Let's use the Graph Editor to move the keys at frame 30 back to, say, 10. If the **logo:robo** wasn't the item selected when you opened the Graph Editor, simply double-click on it under the Channels tab on the bottom left of the Graph Editor. This should populate the Channel Bin with the logo:robo channels.

2. Click on the first channel in the list, **logo:robo.Position.X**, hold down <**Shift**>, and then click on the last channel (**logo:robo.Scale.Z**) to select all the channels for editing. Once selected, press <**a**> to fit all the channels into the Graph area.

3. Right-click and drag a selection marquee over the last keys in all channels as shown in Figure 4-86. Once selected, simply enter a new Frame value of **10** and press <**Enter**>. All the selected keys should now move from frame 30 to frame 10.

You may have noted that the Channel Bin is taking up a lot of the Graph Editor window, making the Channels tab area below it quite confined. If we move the mouse cursor to the area just above this Channels tab, it will change to a size-drag cursor, as shown in Figure 4-83. Left-click and drag to change the height here. To make this section wider, we can also move the mouse over the vertical line on the right (as shown in Figure 4-84) until the cursor changes, then left-click and drag to widen this section.

Figure 4-83: Vertically resizing the Channel Bin and Channels tab area.

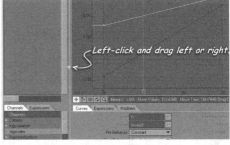

Figure 4-84: Horizontally resizing the Channel Bin and Channels tab area.

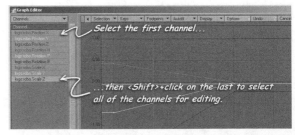

Figure 4-85: Select all the channels you want to edit, then press <a> to fit them into the Graph area.

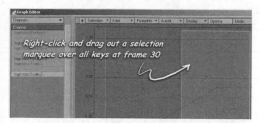

Figure 4-86: Mass select all the keys at frame 30.

Note

You may have noticed that the Value input had *(mixed)* in its text box. This indicates that your selected keys are not all the same. Setting a new value to replace *(mixed)* forces all the selected keys to that new value. The same happens if you select keys on different frames, and can be a great way to line up keys on different channels.

I mentioned earlier that it would be cool to give the logo a little acceleration as it came into the shot. Changing the speed for a channel (which is simply the number of frames it travels over in a given time) is done through the settings on the right side of the Curves tab.

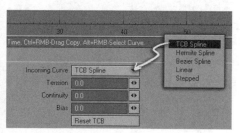

Figure 4-87: Speed controls for curves in the Graph Editor.

• **Incoming Curve** tells LightWave how to handle the curve segment that is directly to the *left* of the selected key. Layout gives us a few ways to tweak the look of the motion curves.

   • **TCB Spline** is LightWave's default setting, and it gives good results most

of the time, without having to worry about tweaking the curves much. (Tension, Continuity, and Bias all affect the shape of the curve, based on values from –1 to +1. Of these, I have only ever found myself needing to use Tension, and then only to put in a value of +1 to get an item to ease into or out of its keyed position.)

   • **Hermite Spline** gives you little "handles" that extend from the key, allowing you to visually control the shape of the curve. (It isn't quite as controllable as a Bezier spline.) <Alt>+dragging on one of these handles will let you split it from its partner, so it is not a mirror of the handle on the other side of the key. Double-clicking on a handle that has been split will get it to once again mirror the angle of the handle on the other side of the key.

   • **Bezier Spline** also gives you handles, but you can move the position of these handles a great distance relative to their respective keys, giving you a lot more control. (<Alt>+double-clicking on these handles splits and reunites the handles with their partners, just as with Hermite Spline handles.)

   • **Linear** gives you a straight line in-between from the previous key frame.

   • **Stepped** holds the value of the previous key until the moment before the stepped key, so it goes right from one value to the next without any kind of in-betweening. (It looks similar to a traditional animation "pencil test" before it goes to the assistant animators who put in the "missing" frames.)

How can we get logo:robo to appear to come into the shot quickly, then appear to decelerate as it comes to rest? We just need to change the **Incoming Curve** behavior. Let's get things happening here.

1. While all the channels are still selected (if you unselected them, simply click on the top one in the Channel Bin, then <**Shift**>+click on the bottom again), right-click and drag a marquee to select the first key frames of all the channels.

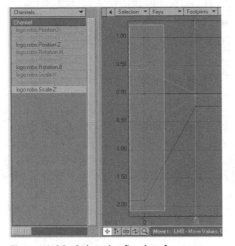

Figure 4-88: Select the first key frames.

2. For simple motion like this, I usually just use the default **TCB Spline** curve. Enter a Tension of **–1.0** to give the key frames at 0 some acceleration. Note how the shapes of the curve change. Acceleration occurs when the curve is steep, as shown in Figure 4-89.

3. Let's deselect all the keys. To do this, simply right-click once in an empty area of the curve area. Right-click and drag a marquee to select the end keys at frame 10 and let's make the logo decelerate as it settles into place. For these keys, change the Tension to **1.0**. Note again how the shapes of the curves change to indicate deceleration.

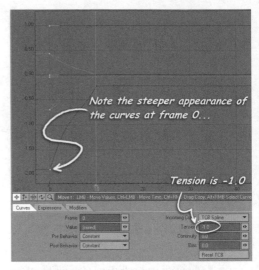

Figure 4-89: Tension of –1.0 accelerates.

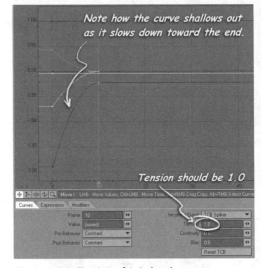

Figure 4-90: Tension of 1.0 decelerates.

The Graph Editor is an essential tool for animation. It's where all the fine-tuning of animation happens to get things to move correctly, speed up or slow down, or even repeat themselves. Let's look at how we can make the mascot behind our logo a little more interesting by having it slowly rotate on its platform at a constant speed. We do all of this in the Graph Editor too.

4. The rotation of the mascot on its platform is going to be around the Heading axis. We can edit this single channel, and even set up key frames for it directly in the Graph Editor. Under the Channels tab, let's expand the logo:mascot item's channels (click the triangular widget to the left of the name). Scroll down the list and double-click on the **Rotation.H** channel. This will place this single channel into the Channel Bin for editing.

Sometimes it's easier to work on animation in the Graph Editor when there's less clutter from the other channels being displayed in the background. We could select one channel at a time for editing like we did above, but working this way would obviously be very inefficient and slow. Luckily, there's an option in the Graph Editor under the Display pop-up menu called **Hide Background Curves** that will take care of this for us.

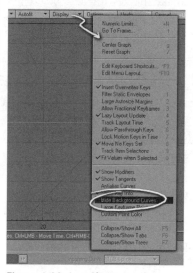

Figure 4-92: Less clutter can be a good thing.

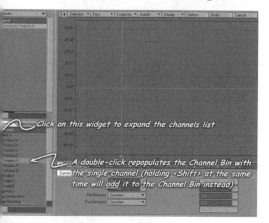

Click on this widget to expand the channels list

A double-click repopulates the Channel Bin with the single channel (holding <Shift> at the same time will add it to the Channel Bin instead)

ure 4-91: Editing a single channel at a time.

5. Create a new key frame for the rotation of the logo:mascot.Rotation.H channel. To do this, press <**Return**>. This will pop up the Create Key dialog to let us precisely set the frame and value. Since this animation is being done at 24 frames per second, let's set a Frame of **24** and a Value of **90°**. Click on **OK** to create the new key frame. If I want to precisely control the speed or rotation, setting a value at the one-second mark in a scene often gives me a good way to get exact control. In this case, I want the mascot to rotate at *90 degrees per second*.

Pressing <Return> will open the Create Key dialog when working in the Graph Editor.

Figure 4-93: Creating a key numerically in the Graph Editor.

6. Let's take a look at another way we can add key frames in the Graph Editor. Press <a> to see the whole curve for the logo:mascot.Rotation.H channel, then activate the **Add Key** tool from the toolbar. Once activated, the cursor will change appearance as shown in Figure 4-94. Let's move the cursor around frame 15, then click where we would like the key frame to be created (don't worry where for now, as we'll be deleting this extra frame anyway).

Figure 4-94: We can manually add keys.

7. We've added a new key frame manually. Add Key is a very useful tool when creating more complex curves in the Graph Editor. If the key frame isn't quite right, we can also fine-tune it using the properties found under the **Curves** tab. Obviously, we don't really want this new key frame here, so let's look at another ability of the Add Key tool. Hold the <**Ctrl**> key and then click on the new key frame we created around frame 15. This will delete the frame instantly for us.

8. If we now look at the curve for the channel, it starts at frame 0, but then stops at frame 24 where it holds at 90 degrees. I'd like this mascot to constantly rotate for the length of my animation at the *90 degrees a second* speed. To do this, let's look at the **Pre Behavior** and **Post Behavior** settings on the Curves tab. These let us specify the behavior of the channel before its

first key frame and after its last key frame (respectively).

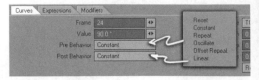

Figure 4-95: Repetition can be controlled below the Value input.

There are a few options found in these pop-ups:

• **Constant** (as shown in Figure 4-95) holds the value of the *first key* for "infinity" before the first key frame begins and/or the value of the *last key* for "infinity" after the last key frame.

• **Reset** sets the value of the graph to 0 when it has no more keys with which to work.

• **Repeat** plays the series of keys over and over again, *ad infinitum*.

• **Oscillate** "ping-pongs" the animation set by the keys, reversing it when it reaches the end and playing it forward once again when it returns to the beginning.

• **Offset Repeat** repeats the motion but with everything shifted by the difference between the first and last keys (this would make our curve into an infinite set of "stairs").

• **Linear** continues the curve infinitely, projecting it at an angle established by the last two keys (or first two keys, if we're talking about Pre Behavior).

9. Tell this channel to continue in its nice constant motion forever by setting Post Behavior to **Linear**. As this is a straight line, Linear seems the most appropriate option. Zoom out to show a bit more of the graph (press the keyboard shortcut <,> about three times)

and see how it works. The result is shown in Figure 4-96.

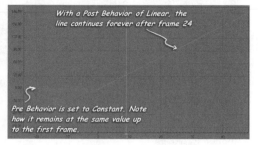

With a Post Behavior of Linear, the line continues forever after frame 24

Pre Behavior is set to Constant. Note how it remains at the same value up to the first frame.

Figure 4-96: Linear Post Behavior continues forever.

Knowing what the Curves tab controls do will give you the core tools you need to modify and get the animation looking the way you want. We've touched on the essential knowledge here, but as you know, there are obviously a lot more options and tools in the Graph Editor to explore and learn! I'd encourage you to explore the features yourself, and also check out the excellent documentation in the manual.

Graph Editor Warning!

There is one thing to be very aware of, and that is that the Graph Editor has one level of Undo (<**Ctrl**> + <**z**>). Take extreme care when working on critical projects in the Graph Editor if you're prone to accidentally clicking and dragging things.

Although the Undo may be limited, let's look at one more essential feature that can save your bacon in case of extreme Graph Editor crash-and-burn situations.

Figure 4-97: Footprints options.

The **Footprints** drop-down (located along the top row of pop-up menus as shown in Figure 4-97) lets you choose one of three options: Leave Footprint, Backtrack Footprint, and Pickup Footprint.

Leave Footprint places a bit of a "ghosted" image of how your curve looked when you left the footprint. You can use this as a visual reference to help you as you tweak. If you totally mangle things, you can use **Backtrack Footprint** to get back to the way things were (a complete undo of all changes you made). If you like how things are, you can choose **Pickup Footprint** to remove it if it's no longer required.

Note

Footprints only last until you close the Graph Editor window, use Pickup Footprint, or select a different item's curves.

Let's check out the Footprints options for quick-fixing a crazy situation like, well, accidentally clicking and dragging the mascot rotation way out of whack!

1. We should still have the logo:mascot.Rotation.H channel in the Graph Editor Channel Bin. If not, refer back to how we selected that single channel by double-clicking it under the Channels tab in the previous section.

2. Let's choose **Footprints | Leave Footprint** (<**F**>). Nothing may appear to happen, but trust me — the simple linear motion has been recorded as a snapshot.

3. Let's make a mess now. Right-click once in an empty part of the curve area to unselect any key frames, and make sure that the Graph Editor's Move tool (<**t**>) is active (the cross-hair button at the start of the Graph Editor toolbar). Left-click and drag upward anywhere inside the curve area of the

Graph Editor. The curve will move upward. Let go of the mouse button, then hold down <Ctrl>, left-click, and drag to the right to shift the key frames sideways. Yipes!

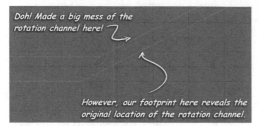

Doh! Made a big mess of the rotation channel here!

However, our footprint here reveals the original location of the rotation channel.

Figure 4-98: Move the graph around.

Note

In Modeler, having nothing selected when using any of the tools affects all the geometry. The same can be said of the Graph Editor. Having nothing selected in the Graph Editor will make any tool we use affect *everything*, as we've just seen!

4. Once the curve was moved in Figure 4-98, we would then see the footprint that was created much more clearly. Let's use the footprint as a way to restore the graph to its original state after the whacked-out move we just did. Select **Footprints | Backtrack Footprint** (<B>) to make the curve return to its former glory! Now that we've finished, click **Footprints | Pickup Footprint** (<R>) to remove the footprint.

Close the Graph Editor and let's check out the animation. The Play controls are situated on the bottom right of the Layout interface (as shown in Figure 4-99). To make sure that the animation plays back at the real speed, you may need to check that **Edit | General Options | Play at Exact Rate** (<o>) is enabled, as shown in Figure 4-100.

Note

All the controls, buttons, and gizmos in the Graph Editor may seem like overkill, but believe me, everything here has a purpose. Although you may not need one of these bits of functionality much, when you do need it, you'll be thankful it's there. Bear in mind that this is only scratching the surface. The Graph Editor is the animator's most trusted and versatile tool. Its spline types, handles, footprints, etc., let you have the minimum number of keys to hold your animation in place.

Click "Play"

Figure 4-99: Play the animation.

Figure 4-100: Play at Exact Rate option.

Previews

If you have a slow computer or a heavily complex scene, not like this simple flying logo we're working on but something really heavily detailed, your scene won't look good at all when played using the animation controls. You'll have to make a preview first.

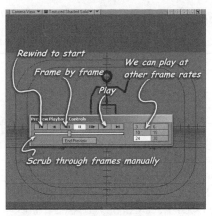

Figure 4-102: Preview VCR-style controls pop up and play back in the left viewport.

1. Click on the Preview pop-up at the bot-tom right of the interface and select **Make Preview** from the options (Fig-ure 4-101). A dialog will appear that lets us specify the range of frames over which to make the preview. Make sure that First frame is set to **0** and Last frame is set to **60**, with a Step of **1** (i.e., every frame) and then click **OK**.

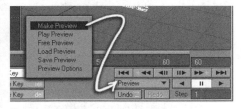

Figure 4-101: Creating a preview.

2. Layout will create a preview in the left viewport of the animation, and then pop up a VCR-style playback control that we can use to view our animation playing back in real time. We can play the preview back at a variety of frame rates (on the right side of the controls), and use the slider to scrub back and forth through the preview manually.

3. Once we've watched the preview, click **End Preview** to exit the Preview playback.

Layout keeps the last preview we make in memory. If you exit the Preview playback, simply select **Play Preview** from the pop-up to watch it again. If you decide you don't need this preview any more, selecting **Free Preview** from the pop-up will clear it from memory. (You'll need to choose **Make Preview** to create it again if you free it.) You can also choose **Save Preview** to store the preview as a movie file to disk, and use **Load Preview** to load and play back a saved preview.

Overall, it's not too bad. We have the robot now spinning endlessly in the background thanks to the Post Behavior in the Graph Editor. The Robo text comes flying in and settles quickly, but perhaps it's a little too quickly. That Productions text may also be a tad too slow as well. Maybe a little timing "adjustment" is needed here…

Adjusting Timing

Let's take a look at a few different ways in which we can tinker with timing to refine our animation. We learned earlier that we could use the Graph Editor. The Graph Editor is a great tool of course; however, it would require selecting keys in multiple channels to adjust them, and could lead to a lot of hard work. LightWave ships with two tools just to move the timing around quickly — the **Dope Track** and **Dope Sheet**.

The Dope Track can be accessed from the main interface, and is designed as a quick and easy way to move the key frames around for the selected item. Its cousin, the Dope Sheet, is more complex and can be found in the Scene Editor. It lets us adjust key frames on a scene-wide basis. Both offer a slightly different set of tools for adjusting the timing of your animations.

Dope Track

Let's do some fine-tuning using the Dope Track. Move the mouse over the gray bar just above the main Timeline until it changes to a white up-arrow (Figure 4-103) and click once. This will open the Dope Track, as shown in Figure 4-104.

You'll notice that a second timeline appears, complete with a duplicate set of key frames. The difference between these keys and the ones found in the main Timeline, however, is that they can be

Figure 4-103: Watch for the cursor to change to a white up-arrow.

Figure 4-104: The Dope Track, open and ready to use.

dragged to different locations, cut, copied, pasted, and "baked" to create keys for the in-between frames. The Dope Track is an editable version of the Timeline!

Let's adjust the Productions text to come in quicker, to help match the Robo text timing a bit better. We don't want it identical, perhaps three to four frames behind instead to let it settle in after.

1. Select the **logo:productions** item, and then click on frame 30 in the Dope Track. When a key is selected, a small white box will appear at the top of it.

Figure 4-105: Key 30 selected in the Dope Track.

2. Let's move the key back to frame 13. To drag the key, left-click on this white box and hold down the left mouse button. Drag the key back toward frame 13 — you'll see the frame number displayed on the key as you drag. Once you reach frame 13, release the mouse to drop the key at its new location.

Figure 4-106: Drag the key back to 13.

In animation, just as in film and video editing, timing is crucial. The difference of a few frames can literally make or break a scene. That's why features like the Dope Track are so vitally important. They make it easy to fine-tune the timing of elements in our scene. Let's take a look at some of the other features available in the Dope Track.

Key frames can be added to the Timeline simply by double-clicking. The values for the new key in the Dope Track will be taken from those found at the *location* of the Time Slider below it. Let's use a clever little technique for making the Productions text settle a little more softly, perhaps with a subtle bounce to remove the perfect "stop" that it currently makes.

1. Select **logo:productions** (if it's not already selected). We want to simply repeat the last key frame again about four to five frames later. We know the last key is at 13, so press **<f>** to bring up the **Go to Frame** dialog and enter **13**. Click **OK** (**<Return>**) to adjust the Time Slider.

Figure 4-107: We can move the Time Slider numerically.

2. Place the mouse cursor over frame 17 in the Dope Track, and double-click to copy frame 13 at frame 17. Play back the animation (or make a preview) to see how the extra frame gives us a little bounce to the way the Productions text settles at the end.

Figure 4-108: A new copy of 13 now at frame 17.

Note

The subtle bounce effect is caused by the way that LightWave calculates the motion through the three keys. When there were only two key frames, the motion was linear. A third key creates a curved motion and causes a subtle "dip." We can see this effect more clearly in the Graph Editor. Often this "dip" is an artifact (issue) for many animators that gets fixed through tweaking the curve values, except in this case, we're taking advantage of it.

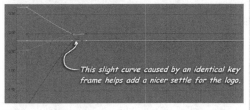

This slight curve caused by an identical key frame helps add a nicer settle for the logo.

Figure 4-109: Using the curve artifact for subtle secondary motion.

The Dope Track also features "markers" that can be placed to identify specific locations. They can even be labeled to provide greater clarity as to the purpose of each marker.

1. Holding the **<Shift>** key down, double-click in the Dope Track timeline at frame 17 where we just created the new key. A marker will be created.

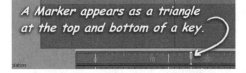

A Marker appears as a triangle at the top and bottom of a key.

Figure 4-110: A marker appears at frame 17.

2. Drag your Time Slider over to frame 17. You'll notice that the marker changes from white to yellow.

3. Right-click on the Dope Track and select **Set Marker Text** from the pop-up menu. In the dialog that appears, type the text **Production Settled**. This will remind us that on this key frame, the Productions text has settled here. Click **OK**.

Figure 4-111: A pop-up menu for the Dope Track.

4. A marker label now appears in the info field to the bottom left of the Timeline.

Figure 4-112: The marker text appears in the info field.

At this point we can drag our key around from frame 17 and still have a visual reminder of its original location in the form of the yellow marker. These markers are always present in the Dope Track, no matter what item you have selected. They're also handy as indications where certain events occur in an animation, which can prove invaluable when working out the timing of other items in a scene.

What if we no longer need a marker? Well, let's remove this marker from the Dope Track for now.

1. Move the Time Slider to frame 17. The marker will turn yellow. This tells us that we can perform functions on this marker.

2. Right-click anywhere in the Dope Track to activate the pop-up menu. Choose the **Delete Marker** option.

Our animation is looking better, but there's still room for improvement. Let's edit the keys so that the Robo text settles its motion and rotation slightly offset from each other and see how it looks.

Wait, the Dope Track only lets us slide the main key frames around. We'll need to use the Graph Editor to edit the channels — or will we? Let's check out another cool feature of the Dope Track.

1. Select the **logo:robo** item. Right-click anywhere on the Dope Track and scroll all the way to the bottom of the pop-up menu that appears. Select **Channel-edit Mode**. You'll notice that the key frames on the Dope Track are no longer represented by solid yellow lines. Instead, they are made up of three small bars colored red, green, and blue. These correspond to the individual X, Y, Z, or H, P, B channels of our object.

Figure 4-113: Channel-edit mode in the Dope Track.

> **Note**
>
> The Dope Track is context-sensitive. That means that the colored bars correspond to X, Y, Z if we happen to have the Move or Scale tool active. When the Rotate tool is active, they correspond to the H, P, and B axes instead. Only the keys for the corresponding tool will be displayed.

2. Select the **Modify | Rotate** tool (<**y**>) so we can adjust the rotation keys. Take a look at the keys in the Dope Track. The three bars tell us that there are key frames here for Heading, Pitch, and Bank on both frames 0 and

10. Let's modify the H and P rotations to offset them. Take a look at the Quick Info section at the bottom of the toolbar. Do you see the H, P, and B buttons?

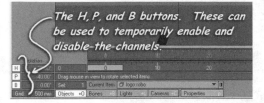

Figure 4-114: The H, P, and B buttons.

3. Even if a channel is present (i.e., key frames exist for it), you can limit the Dope Track's ability to tweak it by deselecting its button in the Quick Info display. Try turning on and off the different channels to see how they affect the Dope Track. When you're finished, turn on the **H** channel only and let's adjust it using the Dope Track.

Figure 4-115: Activate only H to lock the others out of the Dope Track.

4. Select frame 10 in the Dope Track and drag it to 13. Note how the Timeline now shows a key at both 10 and 13. We haven't moved the keys for the P or B channels since we locked them down by turning them off. When we dragged frame 10 in the Dope Track, we simply dragged the keys for the H channel only.

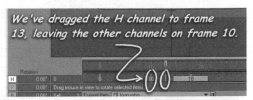

Figure 4-116: The H channel dragged to frame 13.

5. Turn both **P** and **B** back on, and note how their keys are still at frame 10.

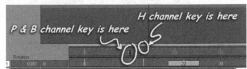

Figure 4-117: Keys at 10 for P and B.

Note

Keep in mind that the settings I give you here as we tweak things are just a guide. Feel free to experiment with different locations for each key frame. Remember, you are the artist. The look and feel of this animation is entirely up to you!

Dope Sheet

Our animation is just about finished; however, I still would like to fine-tune the speed and timing for both the Robo and Productions text. Let's take a quick look at the Dope Sheet. Press **<Ctrl>**+**<F1>**, or choose **Scene Editor | Open** from the toolbar. The Dope Sheet can be found on the tab at the right side of the Scene Editor (see Figure 4-118).

Think of the Dope Sheet as a "spreadsheet" of key frames in an animation. In traditional animation, dope sheets are often used to identify where key drawings need to be in the time line. In Layout, it's where all the key frames exist in the scene.

143

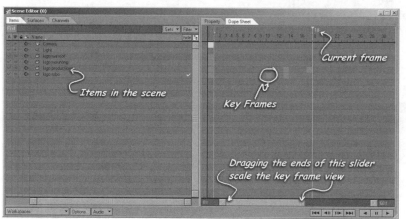

Figure 4-118: The Dope Sheet.

The blocks in the Dope Sheet represent key frames (all key frames, no matter what channel they exist in). By default, the blocks for objects appear in blue, the blocks for cameras appear in green, and the blocks for lights appear in magenta. You can click on any block to select it, or click and drag to define a range. Once a key frame or range of frames is selected, you can move and scale it at will.

1. Click on the blue box at frame 10 in the Dope Sheet for the **logo:robo** item to select it. Yellow borders will appear around the left, right, and top of the frame as shown in Figure 4-119. These

denote the boundaries of the current selection.

2. Click and drag to move the key to frame 20. Notice in Figure 4-120 that a gray box has been left on the key's original frame. This gray box acts as a marker, making it easy for you to return the key to its starting position should you find the change unsatisfactory.

3. You'll also notice that there are play-back controls at the bottom right of the Scene Editor. Press **Play** to preview your animation. If needed, minimize

Figure 4-119: The key frame selected.

Both the vertical and horizontal location are also highlighted with the selected key...

Figure 4-120: Drag the key to frame 20.

A gray square marks the original location of the key frame.

the Scene Editor or move it out of the way, but do not close it just yet.

Moving this key frame didn't really help anything at all, simply making the Robo text settle a little too late for my liking. Let's return it to its original position (the gray box).

4. Bring up the Scene Editor again. Since we did not close it, the frame we moved should still be highlighted.

5. Click and drag the key frame until it rests over the gray box at frame 10.

So far, we've been adjusting key frames for all channels just as we did in the Dope Track. It's also possible to adjust the key frames for individual channels. The **C+** icon to the left of each item allows you to expand an object to see its individual channels, as shown in Figure 4-121.

The red, green, and blue blocks here are simply larger versions of the ones we saw in the Dope Track. The key frames for

individual channels can be moved, cut, copied, pasted, and scaled. Let's scale the time a little to slow down the motion of the text objects. Collapse the channels (click the **C–** icon in the Dope Sheet), as we want to scale all the channels simultaneously.

1. Left-click on the **logo:productions** first key frame at 0. <**Shift**>+left-click on frame 18 for **logo:robo**. This selects the entire range of keys for both the logo:productions and logo:robo items. (See Figure 4-122.)

Note the solid yellow bar on the far left and right sides of the selection. Dragging this bar allows you to interactively scale the selection.

2. Click the yellow bar on the right side of the selection and drag it right until it lies on frame 22. This stretches the time for the key frames, as we can see by the way the key frames move and space themselves apart.

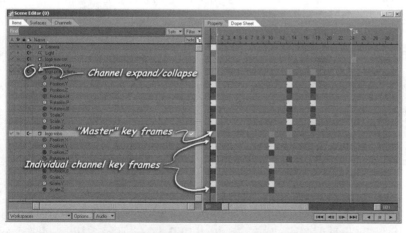

Figure 4-121: The Channel-edit mode of the Dope Sheet may look like a Tetris game gone awry, but it really offers a powerful way to adjust the key frames of elements in your scene.

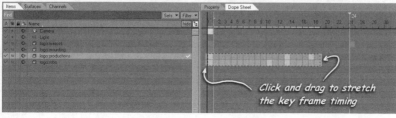

Figure 4-122: Selecting the keys for both Robo and Productions.

Figure 4-123:
Interactively scale
the keys to frame
22.

Click and drag right

Like the single key, gray squares
indicate the original selection area.

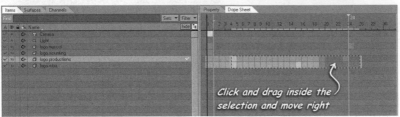

Figure 4-124:
Dragging the keys
four frames right.

Click and drag inside the
selection and move right

3. Clicking and dragging inside the selection will let you drag everything. Click and hold down your left mouse button over any selected block *between* the yellow edges. Now drag to the right until the first yellow edge rests at frame 4. Note that the gray blocks still show the original position of your key frames.

So we not only used the Dope Sheet to scale the length of the animation for each of our logo components, but also shifted the whole lot to give a four-frame start before the items appeared in the Camera View.

4. Finally, click any portion of the Dope Sheet that does not contain an item (such as a camera, object, or light) to deselect the range.

If you haven't done so recently, this would be a great time to save your scene!

Final Touches

The last thing I want to do here is compose the shot for the logo a little better so that we can get a much more dynamic camera angle. After I finished animating this scene, I wasn't too happy with the rather uninspired view of the default camera in LightWave. To quickly finish up this project, let's just keyframe the camera at a better position and angle.

1. Rewind the scene back to frame 0 (using the knowledge we've gained from this chapter). Select the camera, and let's move the camera into

position. We're going to do this numerically, so make sure you first turn on **Modify | Move** (<**t**>) and then press <**n**> to highlight and edit the X numeric value in the Quick Info area at the bottom of the toolbar. Enter **–935 mm** for X, press <**Tab**>, and enter **–370 mm** for Y. Press <**Tab**> once more and set the Z value to **–1.7 m**. Press <**Return**> to finish and click **Create Key** for frame **0** to record these changes for the camera.

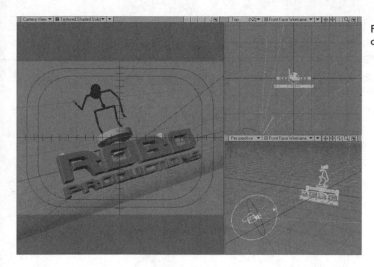

Figure 4-125: The final camera composition.

2. Let's rotate the camera. Turn on **Modify | Rotate** (<**y**>) and press <**n**> to enter the numeric values for the rotation. Following the same process as in the first step, set H to **30.00**, P to **–15.00**, and B to **–20.00**. Don't forget to keyframe the camera again. Your scene should look similar to Figure 4-125.

If you've already saved your scene, then save it again now that we've updated the camera and pat yourself on the back for a job well done!

> **Note**
>
> My finished scene can be loaded from **Scenes\Chapter 04\logo_F.lws** if you're curious about anything in this chapter and want to see what your resulting scene should look like.

Conclusion

Whew! That's a lot of knowledge to digest, but luckily this is a book, and books can be referred back to as many times as you need until the knowledge becomes second nature. We've been through the filming equipment of Layout, our virtual film studio. We've seen some pretty clever stuff, and we've even learned a bit of technical info about how 3D cameras work, taking us a step closer to understanding the way our tools work on the inside.

We've looked at the tools we need to direct our virtual actors, and started creating our own movies. At its core, animation is nothing more than manipulating an item's changes in *position*, *rotation*, and/or *scale* over time. All LightWave animations consist of moving, rotating, and/or scaling an object, bone, light, camera, or special effect, creating key frames that record these changes over time, and using the Graph Editor to hone the shape of the curves that LightWave uses to store the motion data.

What you've learned in this chapter has shown you the basic tools used by *all* CG animators, whether flying spaceships through minefields, creating explosions, or animating mortal combats. We'll build on this basic knowledge as we work through the rest of this book. So take the time to become comfortable with the concepts we've discussed. When you're ready, move on to the next chapter where we'll take our first look at lighting in 3D.

Chapter 5

Basic Skills: Lighting

Lighting is, beyond the shadow of a doubt, the most important factor in making anything look good in 3D. While we can't exclude texturing and image composition as important factors in creating great 3D art, lighting is what defines the mood, feel, and emotion of the scene at hand. Think about how a particular scene might feel if it were lit incorrectly — say, a dark alleyway with bright yellow lights and no shadows instead of the creepy reds and greens from the neon signs of the street or a gentle evening on the back porch lit with a global white light instead of the soft pinks of the setting sun.

Figure 5-1: Just a simple amount of adjusting the lighting in LightWave can make a huge difference.

Lighting Terminology 101

Because lighting is so extremely important to how every form of visual art impacts its audience, it's a great idea to explore as many different types of lighting as you can. Go through your art history books and see how masters like Rembrandt and Caravaggio handled lighting. Take a class on black-and-white photography (where the focus is light, not color). Take a class on theatrical lighting, or volunteer at your local community theater as an assistant lighting technician. Watch documentaries and listen to DVD commentaries for information that may be discussed on lighting approaches in films and movies.

The more angles you can approach your work from, the better your work will look. (Besides, learning new things is fun!)

For those of you who want a few simple pointers to help you get started, this chapter covers some terms and concepts that will be useful for your CG lighting journey into LightWave. With excellent resources for lighting specifically in LightWave such as *LightWave v9 Lighting* by Nicholas Boughen (Wordware Publishing), we're just going to give you a taste here and let books like Boughen's explain the "hows" and "whys" of it all.

Key Light

A *key light* is the name given to the main source of light in a scene. For a room, it may be the light coming through the window. On a stage, it may be the spotlight shining down on the performer. Your main source of light is your key light.

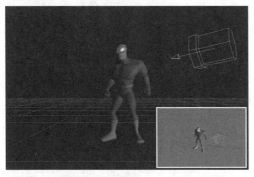

Figure 5-2: The key light is the main source of light in the scene.

Fill Light

A *fill light* is like a booster light that is used to lighten up areas that are too dark. You'll usually find the fill lights set up on the side and direction opposite the key light (Figure 5-3). Sometimes a fill is not needed, for example, if something needs to be in dark shadow (such as the face of a monster in a horror movie perhaps). Sometimes a fill is needed when there is not enough light, so that the viewers can see the bad guy

sneaking up from the shadows behind the hero in a movie.

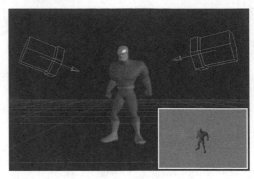

Figure 5-3: The fill light adds extra light in areas where the key light could not.

Rim Light

A *rim light* is an intense light (often much brighter than the key light) that is usually placed behind the characters or items in a scene to give them an extremely bright edge, or rim (Figure 5-4). Usually this is used to help avoid losing the silhouette or form of the character and keep characters from fading into their backgrounds. In green screen and blue screen work, sometimes this kind of lighting is added to help keep the edges of the actors "crisp" against the colored backdrop and allow for cleaner chroma keying (i.e., where the colored background is replaced with alternative

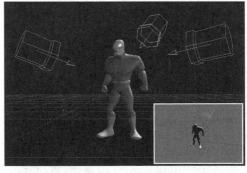

Figure 5-4: The rim light helps break the character away from the dark background.

footage, such as a CG environment in a sci-fi episode).

Three-Point Light Rig

A *three-point light rig* refers to a lighting setup that includes a key light, fill light, and rim light (Figure 5-5). You will hear this term a lot in CG circles and on forums, and it is sometimes recommended as a "good way" to light things in 3D. In my experience, this is not always true. In fact, I hardly ever set up such a lighting system — I only add lights as I feel the need for them arises, and sometimes it's a mix of a key and a few fill lights, but no rim light. Knowing the right light for the job will become second nature as you become more experienced with lighting in LightWave.

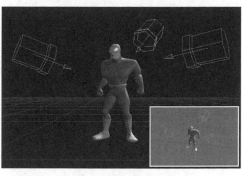

Figure 5-5: Key, fill, and rim lights make for a typical three-point light rig.

The best way to learn is through doing, so let's work through some basic lighting concepts and tools in LightWave by applying lighting to a simple scene.

Step 1: Load the Base Scene

Load **Scenes\Chapter 05\ch5_still_ life.lws** from the companion DVD and press **<F9>** to give it a render (Figure 5-6).

What do you think of the render? It's not too great. In fact, it's rather dull and uninteresting to look at. There is no real light set up in the scene; just the default settings that LightWave creates for us when we start any new project. Let's continue and see just what we can do here to improve upon this.

Figure 5-6: The default lighting shows a definite need for some improvement.

Step 2: Lighting Intensity

The setting we're interested in looking at first is Ambient Intensity. LightWave's Ambient Intensity generates a pervasive, directionless light source. What does that mean in plain English? Well, Ambient Intensity can be thought of as a brightness adjustment for the scene. The more ambient light you pour into your scene, the brighter everything will become.

The Ambient Color and Ambient Intensity settings at the top of the Light Properties window (using the left mouse button, select the current light and press <p> to activate the Light Properties window) are shown in Figure 5-7. These two settings allow us to tweak the global ambient lighting, which is set at 5% by default.

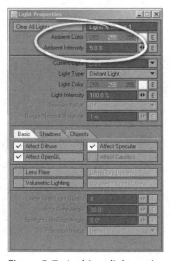

Figure 5-7: Ambient light settings.

LightWave's default of 5% Ambient Intensity is a good base setting. But just to illustrate its use, change this to 50% and do another <F9> test render.

The effects of the increased ambient light can be seen in Figure 5-8. This setting has its advantages and disadvantages depending upon the effect we're after; however, too much ambient light can have the effect of a less defined contrast on our renders.

Once you've seen the effects of Ambient Intensity, change this setting to 0%.

Note

Something I do with ambient light when I don't want to get rid of it entirely is to set Ambient Color to a color that is *complementary* (opposite on the color wheel) to the primary light color used in my scene and change the Ambient Intensity to something from 8% to 12%. This adds a nice bit of "richness" to the shadows, like the way shadows on snow on a sunny evening are a rich blue-violet.

Another use I sometimes make of the ambient settings is to color grade my renders. (Which is probably better left to a post-processing stage in a project; however, sometimes doing it directly in LightWave is more efficient for small projects when you don't have time (or don't want to post-process footage)). For instance, say the scene needed to have a more bluish feel to it and be darker because we were creating a more "nighttime" feel to the scene. Rather than spending more time tweaking the lighting, I'd set Ambient Color to an orange tint (which is complementary, or opposite, to the blues), then set Ambient Intensity to a *negative value*, something from –5% to –10%. As orange contains both green and red, these two colors would be subtracted from the overall render, leaving a blue tint to the whole image.

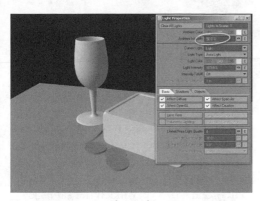

Figure 5-8: Boosting the Ambient Intensity setting brightens up the image substantially.

Let's look at one more group of settings that we may want to use to globally control the lighting in our scene. These settings can be found in our Render Globals window, which is accessed through **Render | Render Globals**.

Using the Light Intensity setting at the bottom of the window, you can *scale* every light in your scene at once. You can think of this as a way to adjust the contrast of your scene's lighting if you like. You can do the same thing with lens flares (the stars and sun dogs you see when you aim a film or digital camera at a light) with the Flare Intensity setting in the Render Globals window. (Used with *subtlety*, they can be great tools; used garishly, they can make an image look cheap.) You can also disable and enable all flares, shadow maps, and volumetric lights (lights where you can see the beam of light, such as sunlight filtering through a window).

We get into flares and volumetric lighting later on in the book, so don't worry too much at this stage about what these do. Just be aware that they exist for now.

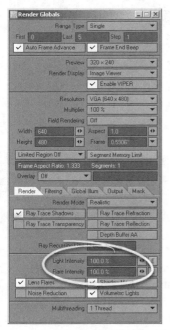

Figure 5-9: Global lighting settings in the Render Globals window.

Step 3: Changing the Light Type

If anything stood out in our test renders from the previous step, it was probably the rather unrealistic and uninteresting feel of the render. This alone tells us just how important lighting is in making 3D models look like something more than CG. To allow us to better light things in LightWave, we should have a basic understanding of the types of lights that we have at our disposal, and just how these differ.

LightWave currently has five types of lights available — the default being the distant light. Each of these lights behaves and lights in a different way. They also look different in the LightWave 3D interface.

Distant Light

The *distant light* is the default type of light that LightWave will create when you add a new light or create a new scene. A distant light is also known as a parallel, directional, or infinite light in some other applications. While it has an animatable location and rotation in LightWave, only the rotation of the light is important. It defines from which direction this light shines. There is no known "location" or source for this light (even though we can see where it is).

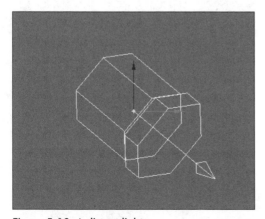

Figure 5-10: A distant light.

Point Light

A *point light* is also called an omni light in some 3D applications. It's a light that emanates from a central point. While you can rotate this light in LightWave, given that this light emanates in all directions from the center, it's the position of it that is more important. It defines the location of the light source, and looks very much the same as a light bulb you might have in your living room or in a lamp next to your bed.

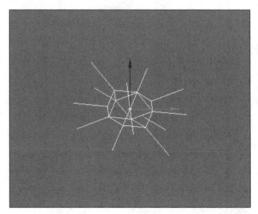

Figure 5-11: A point light.

Spotlight

A *spotlight* is one of the most popular light sources for many 3D artists, in that it shines both in a direction and from a location. This makes a spotlight easy to position and point in the direction that you need it. It behaves much like a light in the real world, such as a flashlight or studio lamp. It has some extra controls that other light sources do not, such as how wide the spread of light is (the cone size), as well as some options that make this light very flexible for many purposes.

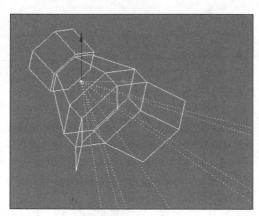

Figure 5-12: A spotlight.

Linear Light

A *linear light* is a line of light. Not only is its orientation and location important, its size is also relevant to the effect it produces. In a way, it is similar to a fluorescent tube you might have in your office, school, or hospital. Being able to scale the light means it has physical length (but not size as it's a single "line" of light), which will change the effect of the illumination and shadows it creates.

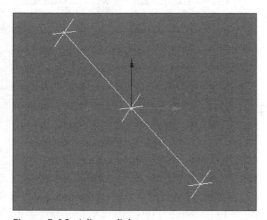

Figure 5-13: A linear light.

Area Light

An *area light* is a panel of light. It relates closely to the linear light, but is different in that it has a physical area from which the source of light is generated rather than a one-dimensional line. Light bulbs, fluorescent tubes, and even the sun have a physical scale that influences the effect of their illumination in reality. The area light mimics these light sources, making it a great light type for achieving realistic lighting in CG.

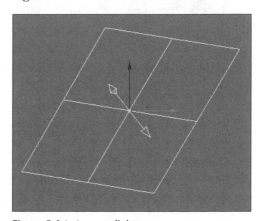

Figure 5-14: An area light.

Note

An interesting fact with CG lighting is that you can't actually see the light source in your renders (though we can see them represented in the user interface). This is because lights in the real world come from a source — usually a hot filament inside a gas-filled glass capsule. In CG, there is no need for such physical devices (as it's all clever mathematics doing all the work behind the scenes). This has both advantages and disadvantages, which we'll be looking at more closely later in the book.

Each light has a series of common parameters that can be accessed and adjusted through the Light Properties window of the light by selecting a light and pressing <p>, or selecting a light and clicking the **Properties** button at the bottom of the LightWave interface. Let's take a quick glance at what these properties mean and how they work. Most of the properties are self-explanatory and will be discussed as we work through this project; hence we won't be going into anything here in a lot of detail.

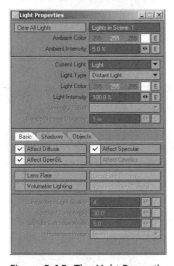

Figure 5-15: The Light Properties window.

• **Ambient Color** and **Ambient Intensity** allow us to tweak the global ambient lighting in a scene.

• **Current Light** allows us to select any of the lights in a scene from a drop-down list. Not only that, but we can also type a new name here for the selected light to rename it at any time.

• **Light Type** lets us change the light to one of the five standard types, as discussed earlier in this chapter.

• **Light Color** and **Light Intensity** work together to tell the light how bright and what color it is.

• **Intensity Falloff** and **Range/Nominal Distance** work together to let us fade out the light's strength as it gets farther from the source. In CG, light can travel forever;

in real life, it can't. We'll look at this setting in more detail in Step 6 of this project.

• Below these basic settings are three tabs: **Basic** for controlling the behavior of the light, **Shadows** to set the way shadows are generated, and **Objects** to select which objects the light should affect. We won't go into detail at this stage about the various options in each of these tabs, as we'll be looking more into these later on in both this chapter and the book when we will look at some more advanced techniques for lighting in LightWave.

Let's continue with our project here, and change the main light in the scene from the default distant light to a kind of light we'd have in the real world. Let's try a spotlight first and see how that looks.

a. With the light selected (by clicking on it or selecting it from the Current Item pop-up menu when Lights are the active Item type), press <**p**> to bring up the Light Properties window, as shown in Figure 5-16. Click on the Light Type pop-up and change the type to **Spotlight**. The viewport in the top left is set to Light View, which shows me what the light is seeing; the shaded circle around the outside of the circle shows me where the spotlight's light doesn't reach.

b. As you can see in Figure 5-16, some parts of our object are outside the circle and thus will not be lit correctly. I'll use this view while I adjust the position of the spotlight to get all items inside the circle before continuing.

c. I've changed the light's color from 255, 255, 255 (white) to a bit of a bluish tint and changed Light Type to **Spotlight**. Something else I'd like us to do is bring the Spotlight Soft Edge Angle up to **30.0°**, the same as the Spotlight Cone

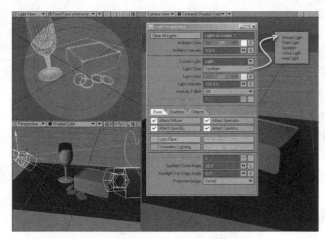

Figure 5-16: Change the light type to Spotlight.

of view as to what it "sees" and what is "hidden" from it. For most of my video work, I generally use a shadow map size of 1,024. It produces a good-looking shadow map for most instances, without eating a lot of my computer's physical memory while the scene renders.

The Shadow Fuzziness setting has always seemed a bit arbitrary to me. I've done a couple of quick test renders and found that 12 gives me the shadow softness I'm looking for.

You can save a little time in rendering a scene by activating Cache Shadow Map if a shadow-mapped spotlight doesn't move and nothing moves through its "beam." This uses the shadow map data generated by the first frame rendered for all the other frames in that render.

You can manually change the shadow map's "view" by deactivating Fit Spotlight Cone and fiddling with the Shadow Map Angle setting. The shadow map image that is created will be displayed in the Light View as a square inside the circle. While we don't need to worry about doing so for the current project, this can be important if your spotlight cone angle is spread across a large area. Wide cone angles can create inaccuracies in the shadow map, causing shadows to appear disconnected or offset from the subjects in the scene. Do an <F9> to render and see the effect of our shadow map!

Angle. This means that the spotlight will fade in intensity evenly from its center to its outer edge. (The dashed line in the Light View viewport responds when I change this input, showing me where the light begins to fade from its base intensity.)

d. Increase the Light Intensity to **125%**, and click on the **Shadows** tab so we can make the objects feel like they're "sitting" on something.

e. I'm not a fan of the sharp, hard-edged shadows that ray tracing "casts" from spotlights, so I'm not even going to go there. We're going to start right off with a Shadow Type of **Shadow Map**. Shadow maps are quick to calculate, they look good enough under most circumstances, and they let spots cast soft-edged shadows.

How "good" a shadow map looks is directly related to how large it is. It is, after all, only a 2D "bitmap" created from the light's point

Step 4: Why Do Things Look "3D"?

What makes something look "3D"? Just the fact that it *is* 3D isn't enough; an actor's face can look flat if it's not lit well by the crew's director of photography.

The general rule of thumb for making something look "3D" is to hit it with a warm (in terms of what color it is) light on one side and a cool light on the other side. One light should be much brighter than the other to form the key light source, and the other will act as the fill light source. And that's it, for the most extreme "basics" of lighting at least.

> **Note**
>
> One of the reasons I stress studying theatrical lighting so much is that a theatrical lighting director must make his set and actors look 3D, even to someone sitting in the cheap seats at the back of a 5,000-seat auditorium. All he has to do this with are spots in the auditorium aiming at the stage and banks of warm and cool lights hanging directly above the stage.
>
> Challenging? Yes. But theatrical lighting directors, over many, many years, have developed ways of making these limitations work and work well. The best way to know what they know is to work a few shows with them.

We're going to be adding another light and moving it around, and the easiest way to move lights is to have them target something; that way you don't have to move, then aim, move, then aim again, etc.

a. With your light still selected, press <m> to bring up the Motion Options window for that light.

b. In the Target Item pop-up menu, select **Still_Life**. Now the light will always have that item's pivot point centered directly in its field of view. This will very likely change the way our light is

pointing; hence we may need to move the light back a little to get our scene back inside the spotlight's circle.

c. Since the settings for our current light are pretty okay, rather than start from scratch for the new light, let's clone this light so the new one is an exact replica of the old. **Items | Add | Clone** brings up a little window where you can tell LightWave how many clones of that item you want. Let's just go for one at the moment.

> **Note**
>
> If you have more than one light set for Max OpenGL Lights in your OpenGL Display Options, you immediately see the effect of the new light in your shaded view(s). If you want accurate shading and appearance of your lights in LightWave, you can also activate the GLSL shading option for the Shading Method setting. This option, however, does require that you have a modern 3D video card capable of OpenGL 2.0 or greater.

d. Before we do anything else, let's make it easier for us to distinguish between these two lights. LightWave automatically tacks on a parenthetical number to items with the same name in a scene, but we can do more.

Change one of the view types (if you have multiple viewports active in Layout) to Schematic. We'll use Schematic view to rename our lights and change the way they are depicted in Layout (there are also other ways to do this, which we'll look at later on).

The Schematic view may seem scary at first, but it actually provides a fun, powerful way to organize and view the content in your scene. Every item is represented by a small colored bar. These bars can be moved around to your liking without affecting the actual object's position within Layout. While other organizational tools such as the Scene Editor provide you with a highly structured means for managing content, the Schematic view takes a more free-form approach, allowing you to arrange items as if they were strips of paper laid out on a large table.

e. We'll save the organization for another time. For now, simply right-click on the light labeled **Light (2)**. From the pop-up menu as seen in Figure 5-17, choose **Rename** and change the light's name to **Warm**, pressing **OK** when you are done. Then right-click it again and use the **Set Color** option to change its Sketch Color (the color with which it is depicted in Layout) to **Orange**.

f. After changing Light (2)'s name, the parenthetical after the first light went away since there weren't two items of the same name for you to keep track of. Still, let's change that light's name to **Cool** and its Sketch Color to **Blue**.

g. Bring up the Light Properties window if it's not already open. For the light named Warm, change its Light Color to a soft, warm ochre (**252, 218, 154**) and change its Light Intensity to **42%**. I've also set its Shadow Fuzziness to **24** to add a bit of visual variety and to give a bit of a visual cue to viewers that the lights on either side are not identical.

h. As shown in Figure 5-18, move Warm to the right of the still life and up (on the Y-axis) just a little.

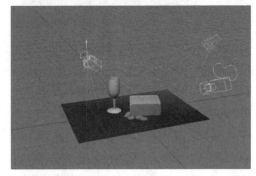

Figure 5-18: Warm on the right, Cool on the left.

Don't forget to do an <**F9**> to create a render and see the effect of our lighting setup.

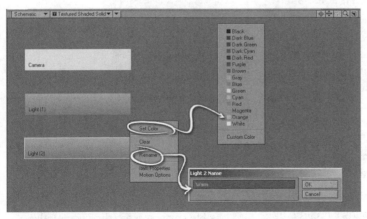

Figure 5-17: The Schematic view is just another way to manage scene items.

Step 5: Ray-Traced Soft Shadows

What if you want things to look more realistic? (Figure 5-19 looks neat, but it still has a flavor of 3D-ish-ness to it.)

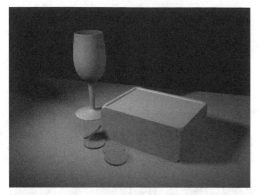

Figure 5-19: Our still life rendered with the warm and cool spotlights.

Recall that in Step 3 we discussed the types of lights available in LightWave. As we know, area and linear lights have a physical size; therefore it would be advantageous to assume things could be a little more realistic if we were to have LightWave figure out *exactly* what the shadows would look like when cast from a light that has some surface area to it, like a fluorescent tube or a light with a diffusing screen in front of it.

a. In the Light Properties window, set the Light Type of both your lights to **Area Light**. Because area lights tend to be a lot brighter than other kinds of lights, change the Light Intensity for Cool to **50%** and for Warm to **18%**. Double-check both lights to make sure Shadow Type is set to **Ray Trace**.

Do a quick render with **<F9>** to see the effect of the ray-traced shadows created by the area light.

v9.2 Note

In LightWave v9.2, the intensity of area lights has been revised to be consistent with other light types. If you're working in LightWave v9.2 or later, you shouldn't need to lower the Light Intensity as described in the previous step.

Note

Setting the Shadow Type to Ray Trace tells the *lights* that you want them to calculate exact shadows. LightWave's rendering engine still needs to know that *it* needs to pay attention to Ray Trace Shadows. *Be sure this is active on the Render tab of the Render Globals window* (accessible from **Render | Render Globals**).

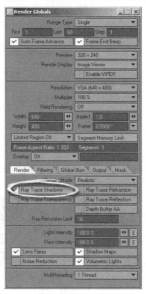

Figure 5-20: Make sure Ray Trace Shadows is selected.

b. Area lights cast light away from their visible surface area (the rectangular shape that you see in the interface of LightWave), so the larger the area, the softer the shadows. I want the Warm light, the least intense of the two, to cast very soft shadows. With Warm selected, activate the Size tool under **Modify | Transform | Size**. In the numeric input panel (in the lower-left corner of the LightWave window), enter **2 m** for all axes of the item's scale.

After tweaking the lights, let's give things another render with **<F9>**.

Figure 5-21: Note the soft falloff of the area light shadows.

Note

The finished scene for this step is **Scenes\ Chapter 05\ch5_still_life_arealight.lws**.

Step 6: Falloff (Atmosphere)

Even in a small room, the air absorbs "wavicles" of light, so the area of a wall nearest a lamp is significantly brighter than the wall on the opposite side of the room. One of the tools that we have to recreate this is the Intensity Falloff setting in each light's Light Properties window. Note that this option is not available for distant lights. As we know from what we learned about the light types in LightWave, a distant light is one that generates light from everywhere in a defined direction — it has no point source from which to "fall off" from.

When Intensity Falloff is set to Linear, the light's intensity falls off in a smooth, lin-ear fashion, falling to 0% at the distance set in the Range/Nominal Distance field. When the Intensity Falloff is set to Inverse Dis-tance, the light's intensity falls off in a parabola, and the value in Range/Nominal Distance shows the place where the light's intensity *will be what you set it at in the Light Intensity field*. (*Inside* that "nominal distance," the intensity of the light will *increase* along the same parabola of Inten-sity = –1 * Distance to Light.)

When the Intensity Falloff is set to Inverse Distance ^ 2, the formula creates a much steeper curve for the light's intensity (the effect of there being lots of stuff in the atmosphere to absorb the little wavicles of light).

a. Set both lights to have an Intensity Falloff of **Inverse Distance**.

161

b. While looking in a Top viewport, adjust the slider buttons in the Light Properties window (the ones to the immediate right of the Range/Nominal Distance field) so the dotted ring for the light passes through the approximate center of the still life (see Figure 5-22).

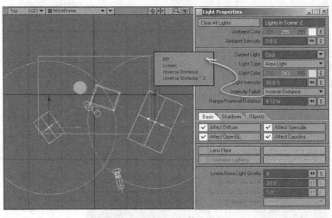

Do another <**F9**> to render. While the effect is subtle (see Figure 5-23) compared to the previous render, it does help make the lighting a little more realistic in the way that the light decays.

Figure 5-22: Setting the Intensity Falloff.

Figure 5-23: The darker, softer falloff of light from the Intensity Falloff tweaks we made.

> **Note**
>
> Intensity Falloff is a great option for getting a more accurate light simulation in your scenes. I often use Inverse Distance ^{2} to create the feel of a camera-mounted lamp, or a flashlight from a first-person perspective shot; the light is intense close to items directly in front of the camera, and quickly decays. Try this setting for your next mineshaft exploration or walkthrough of a dark haunted house.

Render Away!

In this chapter we got our first taste of lighting in 3D. We covered essential information, from basic terminology you'll run into in the world of lighting to the kinds of lights in LightWave and how to manipulate the global lighting in a scene, finishing up with applying some real-world attributes such as the decay of light (using Intensity Falloff) to make our lighting more realistic.

Now that you've sampled lighting in

LightWave, don't stop with what we've covered in this chapter. I strongly encourage you to experiment with the settings of the lights, including the light type, intensity, and colors, just to see what they do! Try adding an extra light or two as well, and test the results.

Lighting is a science unto itself, and well worth taking time to learn, master, and apply in LightWave.

Chapter 6

Basic Skills: Surfacing

Surfacing (also called texturing or shading in some 3D programs) is the art of defining an object's appearance. LightWave's surfacing tools allow you to simulate the properties of different materials, such as rock, wood, plastic, metal, or glass. LightWave has one of the most powerful surfacing systems on the market today. It is comprised of four distinct parts: primary attributes, textures, nodes, and shaders. Each of these can be used on its own or in conjunction with others to give you unprecedented control over the appearance of your objects.

UNSURFACED

SURFACED

Figure 6-1: Surfacing lets you change the appearance of your objects to mimic their real-world counterparts. Nearly any material imaginable can be simulated in LightWave.

LightWave's Surfacing System Components

Primary Attributes

The primary attributes are those that define an object's general appearance. Typically, they determine how a surface reacts to light. They include 13 basic properties, 10 advanced properties, and eight environmental properties. Every surface will require adjustments to some (but typically not all) primary attributes.

Textures

Textures allow you to use raster images (such as JPEG and TIFF files), computer-generated patterns (known as "procedurals"), and "gradients" (which allow surface properties to change according to conditions defined by the user) to add detail to your surfaces.

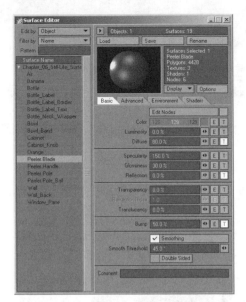

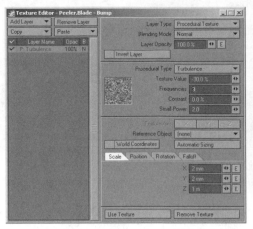

Figure 6-3: Textures allow you to add detail to a surface.

Figure 6-2: The primary surface attributes (found throughout the various tabs of the Surface Editor) let you adjust the basic appearance for a surface.

Nodes

Nodes allow you to link various attributes together in a hierarchical flowchart. They also provide access to LightWave's advanced shading routines, allowing you to create effects such as anisotropic specularity and sub-surface scattering. We'll cover nodes in more detail in Chapter 19.

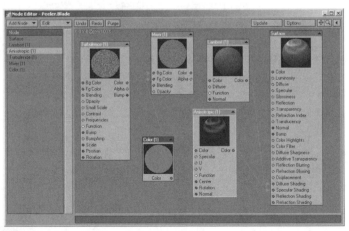

Figure 6-4: Nodes let you construct extremely complex and detailed surfaces.

Shaders

Shaders are utilities that give you enhanced control over a surface's primary attributes. Effects that are difficult or even impossible to create with the other surfacing techniques can often be achieved through the use of shaders.

In this chapter, we'll work through the process of surfacing a still life scene. But before we begin, let's address two simple questions: What are surfaces? and How do you apply them to your objects?

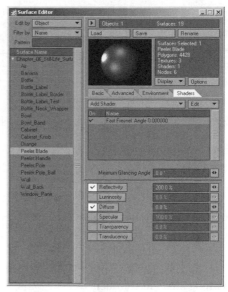

Figure 6-5: Shaders give you greater control over the primary attributes.

Surface Basics

A *surface* is a collection of unique properties that allow you to describe what an object looks like. It's similar to a recipe, telling you which ingredients — and how much of each ingredient — you should use. The ingredients, in this case, are specific attributes such as color, reflectivity, and transparency.

polygon. In most cases, surfaces are applied to groups of polygons that all have similar qualities. For example, on a character, the head, hands, arms, and legs might all be given the same surface called "Skin."

Surfaces are applied to polygons in Modeler as they are created. If you don't specifically assign a surface, Modeler will use its default surface, which is a basic light gray.

There are no hard limits on the number of surfaces you can have in an object. You can assign one surface for an entire object or you can assign a different surface to each

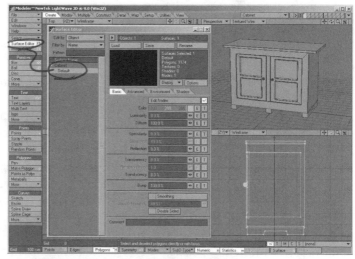

Figure 6-6: When you create polygons in Modeler, they are automatically given a "default" surface.

To assign a surface to a specific group of polygons, select them and press the Surface button at the bottom of Modeler's interface. This will bring up the Change Surface window.

The Change Surface window lets you assign surfaces to your object. You can choose from a list of existing surfaces or you can type in a new name to create a new surface. With new surfaces, you have the option to change the Color, Diffuse, Specular, and Smoothing attributes (which we'll talk about in just a bit). You don't have to adjust these settings when you create a new surface; if you prefer, you can adjust them later through the Surface Editor.

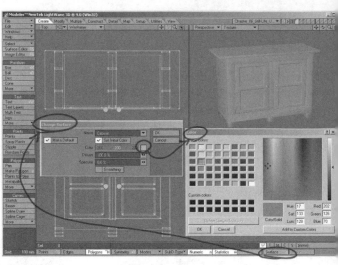

Figure 6-7: Click the Surface button (or simply press <q>) to bring up the Change Surface window. This allows you to assign a new or existing surface to your polygons.

Surface Editor Overview

The Surface Editor is the heart of LightWave's surfacing system. You can access it by pressing the <F5> keyboard shortcut or by clicking on the Surface Editor button on the main interface of both Modeler and Layout. From here, you can adjust the primary attributes, open Texture Editor windows, access the Node Editor, and apply shaders. (See Figure 6-8.)

By default, surfaces are listed as a subset of the object to which they belong. (The control for this is found in the Edit by

pop-up menu in the upper-left corner of the Surface Editor.) You can also list surfaces by scene. This will provide a single list containing every surface in your scene. If several different objects have the same surface name, you'll only see that surface listed once. This allows you to make changes to one surface and have it affect all the objects to which that surface is applied.

You can filter the Surface list by name, texture, shader, or preview. You can also type a string of text into the Pattern field

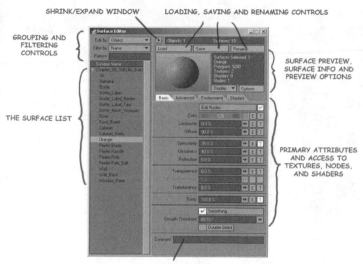

SHRINK/EXPAND WINDOW LOADING, SAVING AND RENAMING CONTROLS

GROUPING AND FILTERING CONTROLS

THE SURFACE LIST

SURFACE PREVIEW, SURFACE INFO AND PREVIEW OPTIONS

PRIMARY ATTRIBUTES AND ACCESS TO TEXTURES, NODES, AND SHADERS

Figure 6-8: The Surface Editor is the heart of LightWave's surfacing system.

COMMENT FIELD FOR SHORT NOTES ON EACH SURFACE

and the Surface Editor will only display surfaces whose names match that pattern. (See Figure 6-9.)

In the upper portion of the Surface Editor are controls that allow you to collapse and expand the size of the Surface Editor as well as load, save, and rename surfaces (Figure 6-10).

Just below the loading/saving buttons is the Preview sphere. It will update as you make changes to your surface to give you a

quick idea of what your surface will look like under the current lighting conditions. To the right of the Preview sphere is a window containing specific information about the surface(s) you have selected.

You can use the Display and Options buttons to determine exactly what the Preview sphere displays. You can also right-click on the Preview sphere itself to change these settings.

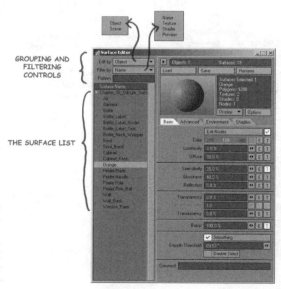

GROUPING AND FILTERING CONTROLS

THE SURFACE LIST

Figure 6-9: You can change how your surfaces are listed and which surfaces are displayed in the Surface list with the Edit by, Filter by, and Pattern settings.

SHRINK/EXPAND WINDOW   LOADING, SAVING AND RENAMING CONTROLS

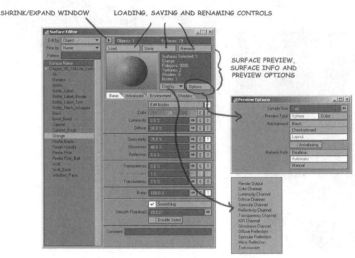

SURFACE PREVIEW,
SURFACE INFO AND
PREVIEW OPTIONS

Figure 6-10: You can load, save, and rename surfaces using the controls in the Surface Editor. You can also get a quick idea of what the surface will look like as well as detailed information about the surface through the Preview sphere and info display.

Below the Preview sphere are the controls you'll use to adjust the properties for each surface. Clicking on the name of a surface in the list on the left allows you to adjust the controls for that particular surface. You can <Shift>+click to select a range of surfaces or <Ctrl>+click to select non-sequential surfaces. This allows you to change the properties for multiple surfaces at the same time. At the very bottom of the Surface Editor is a Comment field where you can enter notes for each surface.

To the right of each of the first 10

controls on the Basic tab of the Surface Editor are three small buttons. The first is a left-right arrow. Dragging this allows you to adjust values with the mouse rather than having to enter numbers directly into each field. To the right of the arrows are two buttons labeled E and T respectively. The "E" button means you can assign an "envelope" for that setting to change it over time. The "T" button opens up the Texture Editor, where you can use images, procedural textures, and gradients to alter the values for each channel.

CLICK & DRAG TO
ADJUST VALUES

CLICK TO OPEN THE
ENVELOPE EDITOR

CLICK TO OPEN THE
TEXTURE EDITOR

THE SURFACE LIST:

SINGLE-CLICK TO
EDIT ONE SURFACE

<SHIFT> OR <CTRL> +
CLICK TO EDIT
MULTIPLE SURFACES
(SHOWN HERE)

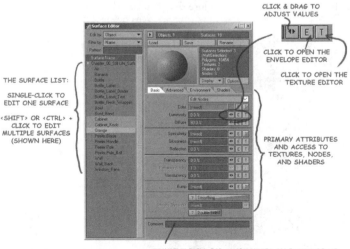

PRIMARY ATTRIBUTES
AND ACCESS TO
TEXTURES, NODES,
AND SHADERS

Figure 6-11: Click on the name of a surface to edit its properties. <Shift>+click or <Ctrl>+click to select and adjust more than one surface at a time.

COMMENT FIELD FOR SHORT NOTES ON EACH SURFACE

> **Note**
>
> To quickly get rid of an envelope or a texture (if you've clicked on the buttons just to see what they brought up and are now wondering how to deactivate the button), simply hold <Shift> while clicking on the button.

Copying/Pasting Surfaces and Using Presets

You probably noticed that there aren't any buttons on the Surface Editor that allow you to copy and paste settings from one surface to another. Like many features in LightWave, this one is hidden behind a right mouse button click. To copy the settings from one surface to another, simply left-click on a surface to select it. Then right-click and choose either Copy or Paste.

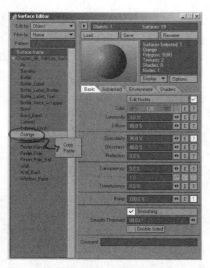

Figure 6-12: To copy or paste surfaces, simply left-click on their name in the Surface list, then right-click and choose Copy or Paste.

If you've created a surface that you think you might use again in the future, you can save it as a preset and load it from the Surface Preset window. This window (available from the Windows | Presets Panel menu option) gives you quick, visual access to dozens of generic surfaces provided by NewTek (as well as those you create on your own). Preset surfaces are available for everything from cowhide to vinyl. They are separated into different libraries, selectable through the pop-up menu at the top of the window (which shows the WorkSpace library by default).

Double-clicking on a preset will load its settings onto the currently selected surface in the Surface Editor. Right-clicking on a preset will open a menu tree where you can rename it, delete it, move it to another library, or create and manage libraries of your own.

If you want to add the surface you're working on to your currently active preset library, just press <s> when the Surface Editor's window is active. A preset will be created with an icon of the current sample sphere named the same as your currently active surface.

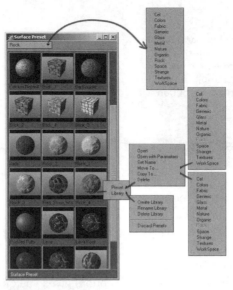

Figure 6-13: The Surface Preset window lets you choose from one of the pre-made surfaces that ships with LightWave. You can also store your own surfaces for later use.

Primary Attributes

The primary attributes are the properties that govern the general appearance of a surface. They can be found on the Basic, Advanced, and Environment tabs of the Surface Editor. When you begin surfacing, these are the attributes you'll likely adjust first. Let's briefly talk about the various settings. Then we'll get some hands-on experience as we begin a real-world surfacing project.

Basic Attributes

The Surface Editor lists 13 "basic" attributes that affect the look of each surface. The first 10 of these are known as "channels." You'll be working with these channels a lot, so let's get acquainted with them.

● The **Color** channel is used to change the base color of a surface. You can click on the color box to open a color picker. Alternately, you can drag left or right on any of the three numbers, representing red, green,

and blue (0 to 255), to adjust their values. Right-clicking on these numbers will toggle between RGB and HSV modes. Dragging in HSV mode allows you to alter the hue, saturation, and value (brightness) of the color.

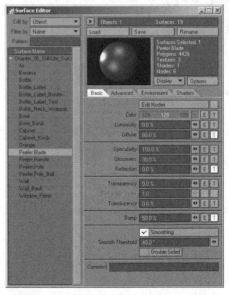

Figure 6-14: The Basic tab lists the most common attributes for each surface.

- The **Luminosity** channel determines the degree to which a surface is self-illuminating. For example, rocks generally don't emit light, so they would have a Luminosity value of 0. However, molten rock (lava) does emit light. Therefore, lava would be given a higher Luminosity value (such as 40 to 60). When you use Luminosity in conjunction with Radiosity (discussed in Chapter 10), your surfaces will actually become a light source and will illuminate the environment around them, just as they would in the real world.

- The **Diffuse** channel determines how much light an object reflects. Higher values mean the surface will reflect more light and in turn be brighter. Lower values mean the surface will reflect less light and typically be darker.

> **Note**
>
> There are two types of reflection on every surface. There's the reflection of *light*, which is called Diffuse, and there's the reflection of the *environment*, which is called Reflection. As a rule of thumb, the sum of the Diffuse and Reflection values should equal 100%. For example, if your Diffuse value is 80%, your Reflection value should be 20%. In some cases, Specularity is used instead of (or in conjunction with) Reflection. When this is the case, your Diffuse, Specularity, and Reflection values should add up to 100%.

- The **Specularity** channel controls the intensity of highlights that appear on the surface of your object. Specularity is a surface "cheat." In the real world, highlights are actually reflections of bright light sources such as the sun or a large open window. However, in LightWave, the lights we use in our scene aren't visible. You can point the camera directly at a light and you still won't see it. And neither will your reflective objects. In order to create reflections of the lights in your scene, you can use the Specularity settings.

> **Note**
>
> Since real highlights are reflections of bright light sources in the environment, the best way to create *realistic* highlights in LightWave is to model simple shapes (discs, rectangles, etc.) as your light sources and give them a unique surface with a high Luminosity value. Then use Reflection instead of Specularity on your normal surfaces, which will cause these modeled light sources to appear as bright reflections on your object.

- The **Glossiness** channel determines how big the specular hotspot will be. High Glossiness setting values produce a small, tight hotspot, while low numbers give a wide, soft highlight. If your Specularity value is at zero (meaning there are no specular highlights), this channel will be inactive.

- The **Reflection** channel controls how much of the *environment* is mirrored on the surface of your object. Under the Environment tab of the Surface Editor, you can set whether the surface truly reflects its environment, which is computationally intensive, or uses a reflection map to give a quick but convincing illusion of reflecting the world around it.

> **Note**
>
> To see accurate environmental reflections on the surface of your object, you must ensure that the Ray Trace Reflection option is checked in the Render Globals window.

- The **Transparency** channel determines the degree to which you can see through a surface. Higher values will make your object "invisible"; however, the surface will still show specular highlights and reflections. (To make an object truly invisible, you would use the Object Dissolve setting in Layout's Object Properties window.) Using Transparency in conjunction with the Color Filter setting on the Advanced tab of the Surface Editor, you can create tinted transparent objects such as colored plastic and stained glass.

• The **Refraction Index** channel determines how much the light is "bent" as it passes through transparent surfaces. This bending of the light is a natural phenomenon and different materials such as glass, crystal, air, etc., have different refraction indexes. Glass, for example, has a refraction index of roughly 1.5. Air has a refraction index of 1.0. You can find a list of refraction indexes for common materials in Appendix B at the end of this book.

• The **Translucency** channel measures how much light passing through an object will be "seen" on its other side (think of leaves glowing when backlit by the sun).

• The **Bump** channel determines the overall intensity of the textures applied to this channel. *This setting does not make your surface bumpy.* If you want your surface to be bumpy, you must use a texture map. This setting simply increases or decreases the overall bump effect, just like a dimmer increases or decreases the brightness of a light bulb. Negative numbers and numbers over 100% are allowed. (We talk more about textures later in this chapter.)

• The **Smoothing** option tells LightWave to render adjacent polygons as a single smooth surface rather than distinct, individual polygons. Smoothing works in conjunction with the **Smooth Threshold** setting to shade adjoining polygons. The default value is 89.5 degrees. This means that if two polygons meet at an angle of 89.5 degrees or less (basically just below a right angle), those polys will appear to blend

together. If polys meet at 89.6 degrees or more, there would be a sharp "crease" visible where they join. It can be tempting to just leave this setting at 89.5 and never change it; however, you can drastically affect the look of your surface by lowering this setting. If your object doesn't appear as crisp and defined as you'd like, try lowering the Smooth Threshold setting.

• The **Double Sided** setting makes the surface of a polygon visible from either side, regardless of which way its surface normal is facing.

Advanced Attributes

The Advanced tab of the Surface Editor offers access to properties that are needed on some, but generally not all, surfaces. Let's take a look at the settings on this tab.

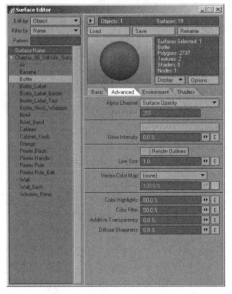

Figure 6-15: The Advanced tab of the Surface Editor window controls powerful but less used surface settings.

• The **Alpha Channel** and **Alpha Value** settings let you determine how this surface affects the alpha channel when you render.

In most cases, you can simply leave Alpha Channel at its default of Surface Opacity. In Chapter 10 we'll see how you can use the Shadow Density option to composite 3D objects with real-world photos.

• **Special Buffers** allows you to enter values that affect rendering image filters. We'll talk more about this in Chapter 7.

• **Glow Intensity** lets you determine how strong a surface will glow when used with the Glow options found in the Processing tab of the Effects panel in Layout. Adding a little glow to your objects, especially metallic objects, can add extra visual punch to your images. Glow also works well for broadcast graphics such as logo animations.

• **Render Outlines** allows you to render your surface in its wireframe state while still respecting the basic surface properties such as Color, Specularity, etc. This can be useful for high-tech looking graphics and is especially effective when blended with a full-color render in an image editing program. You can adjust the overall line thickness with the **Line Size** setting.

• Color maps allow you to add color at specific points on your model. If you've created a color map, you can apply it to your surface by selecting it in the **Vertex Color Map** pop-up menu. Doing so will cause the **Vertex Coloring** option to become active. You can use this setting to adjust the visibility of the color map. A setting of 0% will make the map completely invisible, while a setting of 100% will make it completely opaque, overriding any base surface color and tinting any textures you've applied.

The Vertex Color Map option only allows you to use one color map per surface. For more nuanced coloring, you can use weight maps and gradients. See the bonus video tutorial on the DVD for details on this powerful texturing technique.

• **Color Highlights** allows the specular highlight from lights in your scene as well as reflections from reflection maps (discussed in the next section) to take on the object's base surface color. This can be particularly useful on metallic and transparent objects, whose specular color tends to be tinted toward the surface's base color. Another handy use for Color Highlights is to limit the intensity of the highlights on your object. If you find that your highlights are blown out, try increasing this setting.

• **Color Filter** allows transparent objects to take on the base color of the surface. This can be particularly useful for things like colored glass or plastic. The higher the Color Filter amount, the more the transparent object will inherit the base surface color. I typically set a bluish color when surfacing transparent windows and then add a small percentage of Color Filter to keep the windows from completely disappearing in the render.

• **Additive Transparency** provides another way of adding color to transparent objects. Instead of simply tinting the transparent surface, this setting allows you to brighten the color of the objects seen through transparent surfaces. The base surface color will be added to the color of background objects, increasing their RGB and in turn their overall brightness. The Additive Transparency setting works in conjunction with the Transparency value on the Basic tab of the Surface Editor. Lower Transparency values will enhance the effect of Additive Transparency. Higher Transparency values will diminish the effect of Additive Transparency.

> **Note**
>
> In order to see the effect of Additive Transparency, the value you enter for Transparency on the Basic tab of the Surface Editor must be lower than 100%.

- **Diffuse Sharpness** tightens the falloff from light to dark over the surface of an object. Typically when a light shines on an object, it scatters evenly over the surface, creating a subtle falloff. Increasing this setting makes the falloff more distinct. This can be particularly useful on space scenes where the distinction between the light and dark sides of a planet or moon should be more pronounced.

Environment Attributes

Reflective surfaces will mirror their environment. But what happens if there is no environment (which is typically the case unless you've specifically modeled one)? Or what if your environment is sparse and you want to give the impression of fuller surroundings? The options in the Environment tab control the type of environment visible on reflective surfaces.

The upper half of this tab is dedicated to reflection. The bottom half offers identical settings, but applies them to refraction, which is the distortion that occurs when light travels through a transparent object.

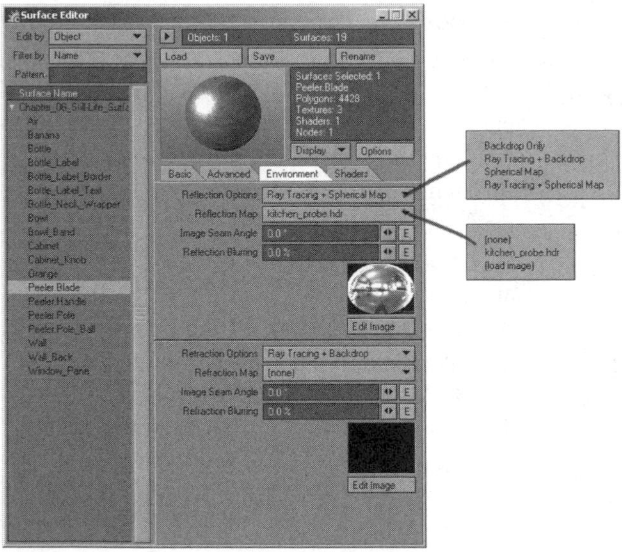

Figure 6-16: The Environment tab of the Surface Editor window allows you to determine the type of environment that will be visible on reflective surfaces.

- Under the Reflection Options pop-up menu, there are four options:

Backdrop Only will cause this surface to ignore objects around it and only reflect environments set in the Effects | Backdrop tab. This can be useful for certain effects, but in all my years of working with LightWave, I can only think of a few times I've actually used this setting.

Ray Tracing+Backdrop is the default setting. This will cause reflective objects to reflect objects around them as well as environments set up in the Effects | Backdrop tab. This produces the most realistic reflections, but it often comes at the price of longer rendering times.

Spherical Map is similar to Backdrop Only. It will ignore objects around the reflective surface and only reflect the image you choose from the Reflection Map pop-up menu. This image is presented as if it were wrapped around a large sphere encompassing your entire scene. This method doesn't require ray tracing and therefore renders quickly; however, it does not produce very realistic results, which limits its application.

Ray Tracing+Spherical Map will cause the reflective surface to show objects within the environment as well as the image you choose from the Reflection Map pop-up menu. Again, the image here is mapped to a virtual sphere that encompasses your entire scene. You'll never see this sphere. It only exists to give your objects something to reflect. This is a very effective solution in many cases and allows you to set up realistic-looking reflections without having to use the Effects | Backdrop tab options.

- If you're using a spherical map, you can adjust the location where the edges meet (known as the seam) by adjusting the **Image Seam Angle** parameter.

- Lastly, you can adjust the amount of **Reflection Blurring**. Most surfaces have tiny imperfections that cause their reflections to spread out, making them appear to be blurred. However, most objects in computer graphics lack these imperfections. You can manually add a tiny bump texture to recreate this effect. But an easier way is

to simply increase the Reflection Blurring amount.

> **Note**
>
> Reflection Blurring will cause your render times to increase and will also require higher antialiasing passes to look good. While the effect provides a subtle realism, it will be up to you to determine whether it is worth the price of longer render times.

All of the options on the Basic, Advanced, and Environment tabs make up the primary attributes. Remember, surfacing consists of primary attributes, textures, nodes, and shaders. We'll be looking at textures and shaders in just a bit, and nodes later in Chapter 19. At this point, let's apply what we've learned so far by working through a real-world surfacing project.

Still Life Surfacing 1 — Assigning Primary Attributes

Talking about surface settings is nowhere near as fun as *using* them. So in this section we'll have some fun by assigning primary attributes to the surfaces in a still life scene. We'll work through the process of surfacing several common materials, including wood, glass, metal, and porcelain. Later in the chapter, we'll also add textures and shaders to bring this scene to life.

> **Note**
>
> Before you begin surfacing your object, you should calibrate your monitor. What appears bright on your screen may look dark on someone else's. I recommend using the excellent calibration chart on Jeremy Birn's site: http://www.3drender.com/light/calibration.htm The calibration chart and instructions on its use are included on the DVD for this book, courtesy of Jeremy Birn.

1. Open Layout and set the Content Directory (**Edit | General Options | Paths**) to point to the content from the companion DVD. Load the **Chapter_06_Still-Life_Surfacing_v001.lws** scene for this chapter.

Scene Setup

Let's talk briefly about this scene.

1. Place your mouse over the topmost viewport (which should be showing the Camera View) and change it to a Perspective view. Then zoom out and swivel around the scene a bit.

I built a simple room in Modeler consisting of four walls, a floor, and a ceiling. Along the back wall is a cabinet. On top of it are some

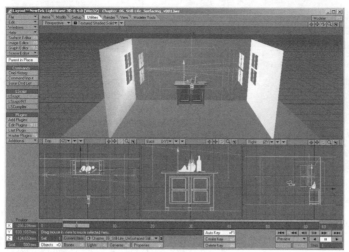

Figure 6-17: Load the Chapter_06_Still-Life_Surfacing _v001.lws scene from the DVD and switch the top viewport to a Perspective view. Zoom out and take a look at the objects in the scene.

bananas, a bowl of oranges, a wine bottle, and a vegetable peeler. On the left and right sides of the room, I've placed four rectangles. These will act as bright window panes that will appear in our reflective objects. Since the windows are our primary sources of light, I've placed area lights directly in front of them. I've also placed area lights at the ceiling and toward the back wall. These are used to simulate bounced light. The last light in the scene is a spotlight. Rather than directly contribute to the illumination of the objects, it is used to provide a swath of visible light across the scene through the use of volumetrics (which we'll discuss further in Chapter 10).

> **Note**
>
> Before I begin surfacing an object, I typically spend time setting up my lights. Once the basic lighting is done, I adjust the primary attributes for each surface. In most cases, this will require a bit of tweaking to the lighting, followed by more tweaking to the surfaces. This back-and-forth adjustment phase is something you should expect to do in your own projects, but since the purpose of this tutorial is to focus on surfacing, I've already set the lights up the way they will be in the final render.

2. Place your mouse over the topmost viewport again and change it back to a Camera View. Frame 0 of this scene shows the final composition. Subsequent frames show close-up shots that we can use to get a better look at each object. Drag the Frame Slider through the first seven frames (0 through 6) to see what each frame depicts. Then drag it back to frame 0.

> **Note**
>
> Frame 2 should depict one of the oranges on the cabinet. If you don't see the orange, open the Display tab of the Preferences window (press the <d> keyboard shortcut) and enable Fixed Near Clip Distance. Then set the distance to 35 mm.

3. Press the <F9> key on your keyboard to do a quick test render. None of the advanced rendering options are turned on yet, so things should render fairly quickly. When the render is finished, click the **Abort** button to close the Render Status window.

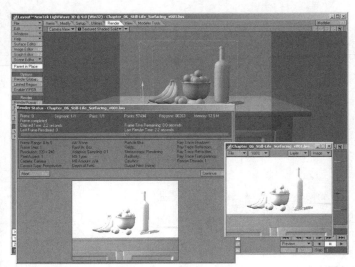

Figure 6-18: Press <F9> to do a test render.

Note

Rendering will open the Render Status window, which provides information on the rendering options currently in use. When your render is complete, the image will pop up in a new Image Viewer window. You'll be required to hit the Abort button before you can continue working. From here on out, I'll be expecting you to close the Render Status window (and optionally the Image Viewer window) after each <F9> render.

VIPER

We can begin applying surface settings right now, but our results will be contingent on the power of our OpenGL graphics card. To level the playing field, we can use LightWave's Versatile Interactive Preview Renderer, also known as VIPER. VIPER provides a degree of real-time rendering that makes surfacing tasks much easier.

1. Click the **Enable VIPER** button in the Render | Options menu. When you activate VIPER, you are telling LightWave to hold the next render in a special buffer. You can access this

buffer through the VIPER preview window and get immediate feedback on changes to your surface settings without having to re-render. Let's look at how to do this.

2. With VIPER enabled, press <**F9**> to perform another render (Figure 6-19).

Note

VIPER only captures the first rendering pass into its buffer. If you're going to use VIPER to preview your surface changes, you can save yourself time by turning off antialiasing in the Camera Properties window before you do your <F9> render.

Note

Rendering with VIPER enabled will slow down your rendering. Be sure to disable VIPER after you're done using it.

3. Open the Surface Editor. Then click the **VIPER** button in the Render | Utilities menu.

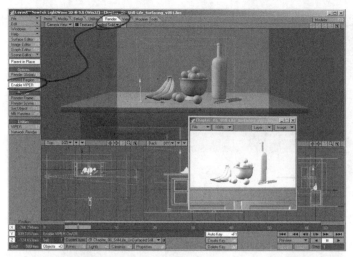

Figure 6-19: Enable VIPER. Then press <F9>.

Figure 6-20: Open the Surface Editor and then the VIPER preview window.

Note

VIPER is primarily a surface previewing system. If the Surface Editor isn't open, you may not see anything in VIPER's preview window. Be sure that you've got the Surface Editor open when you're going to use VIPER for changing surface settings.

Note

You may notice that VIPER's preview isn't as brightly lit as your actual render. VIPER doesn't always do the best job at previewing complex lighting setups, as is the case with this scene. You can compensate for this by temporarily changing the intensity of the wall and ceiling lights. They're currently both set to 30%. Increasing them to 100% will blow out your renders (so make sure you set these back to 30% before doing any final renders), but the image in VIPER will look much better.

The VIPER window may seem small and unassuming, but it has a number of powerful options. At the top you can change the preview window size and preview options. At the lower left you can adjust the rendering quality. At the lower right you can force a VIPER preview refresh, add a surface preset, and build a preview animation.

One of the less apparent functions is the ability to click on an object in the VIPER window and have that object's surface selected in the Surface Editor. Give it a try.

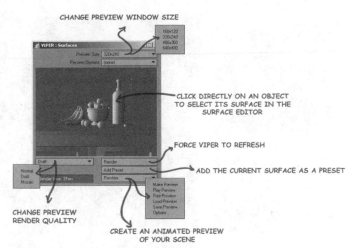

Figure 6-21: The VIPER window offers tremendous functionality.

4. Click on the bowl and the surface called Bowl will be selected. Click on the wine bottle and the surface called Bottle will be selected. This visual interactivity can save a tremendous amount of time as you work to surface complicated objects.

You'll notice that the resolution of the VIPER preview is pretty low. The window is also a bit too small to really see what we're doing. Let's change this.

5. Click the Preview Size pop-up menu in the VIPER window and choose a resolution of **640x480**. Then click the Resolution pop-up menu with the word Draft in it. Change this to **Normal**. This will make the window bigger, but it won't increase the resolution because we've only captured a 320 x 240 render into VIPER's buffer. Hence, we need to give VIPER more image data to work with.

6. Open the Camera Properties window (press the keyboard shortcut <**C**>

followed by <**p**>). Make sure the Resolution for the camera is set to **640x480**. Then change Multiplier from 50% to **100%**. Now press <**F9**> to render again (Figure 6-22). This will fill VIPER's buffer with a full 640 x 480 image. Then change Resolution Multiplier from 50% to **100%** (if it's not already set that way).

7. Close the Camera Properties window. Click the **Render** button in the VIPER window. VIPER will refresh and you'll notice that the image is much clearer. You'll also notice that at this size the refresh took a bit longer. As you work with VIPER, you'll want to work back and forth with the resolution settings to balance the quality and performance that works best for you.

Now that the preview is taking a bit longer, let's look at one more feature of the VIPER window. When you click on a surface in the Surface Editor (or directly in the VIPER window), VIPER will refresh. As it refreshes, *the surface you've selected will be drawn first*. Everything else will be blanked out. Once the refresh is completed, everything will appear again. You can use this

Figure 6-22: Change the VIPER preview size to 640x480 and the resolution to Normal. Then change your camera's resolution to 640x480 at 100%. Press <F9> to render.

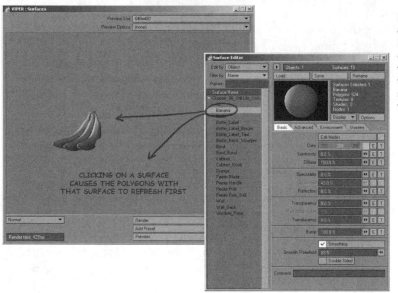

Figure 6-23: Clicking on a surface (either in the Surface Editor or the VIPER preview window) will cause that particular surface to refresh first.

feature to quickly tell whether you're making changes to the right surface and to identify which objects in your image use a particular surface.

Surfacing the Wood Cabinet

Let's begin surfacing. We can start anywhere, so let's begin with the cabinet.

1. Click on the surface called **Cabinet** from the list on the left side of the Surface Editor.

This cabinet could be made of anything. That's the fun part of surfacing. You get to decide what your objects are made of! I envision this as being a run-of-the-mill wood cabinet, so we'll surface it as such.

There are a lot of different types of wood. If I wanted to simulate something specific, such as oak or cherry, I could use an image map that accurately depicted the color and grain. But for this exercise, I simply want a generic brown wood.

180

2. Click the color box to open the Color Picker window. Choose a medium brown color such as RGB **161, 111, 061**. Then click **OK** to close the Color Picker window.

> **Note**
>
> New users tend to gravitate toward using extremely saturated colors. Most colors in the real world, however, are not that saturated. To make your work look more realistic, you should avoid using over-saturated colors. You can right-click on the RGB color numbers in the Color channel of the Surface Editor (just to the left of the color box) to switch to Hue, Saturation, Value mode. This lets you easily adjust the saturation while retaining the overall color and brightness.

3. Wood doesn't emit light (unless it's on fire, which fortunately this cabinet is not!), so leave Luminosity at **0%**.

4. Wood typically reflects most of the light that shines on it, so set Diffuse to **90%**.

> **Note**
>
> If you're having trouble determining the Diffuse value for a surface, use deductive reasoning. We already know that the values for Diffuse, Reflection, and Specularity (if it's used) should add up to 100%. If you look at an object and see that it has little to no highlight or reflection, then you can be fairly certain it has a higher Diffuse value. On the other hand, if you look at an object and it's got an intense highlight or is reflecting a lot of the environment, you can be fairly certain it has a lower Diffuse value.

In most cases, wood has a sheen to it. This sheen is a reflection of the light and generally comes from the wood having been polished to one extent or another. Highly polished wood creates an almost mirror-like surface, while less polished wood only shows faint highlights. If we wanted to create the highly polished look, we could

increase the amount of Reflection on our surface, but that's not the look I'm after. Instead, I just want some highlights to appear. So instead of Reflection, I'll use Specularity.

5. Since we're using Specularity instead of Reflection, we need to ensure that its value plus the Diffuse value totals 100%. Our Diffuse value is 90%. Therefore, Specularity should be **10%**.

6. Now that we've got some Specularity, we need to determine how broad the specular highlight will be. This is determined by the Glossiness channel. A high Glossiness value will create a small, tight highlight. A lower value will create a broad swath of light. I want something a little broader, so let's set Glossiness to **30%**.

7. Since our reflections are coming from the Specularity channel, we'll leave the Reflection channel set to **0%**.

8. Wood is opaque, so leave Transparency at **0%**. This also disables the Refraction Index, which is dependent on there being some amount of transparency in your surface.

9. Wood is not translucent. If you placed a light behind a piece of wood, the wood itself wouldn't light up. Therefore, leave Translucency at **0%**.

10. Bump is currently set to 100%. As I mentioned earlier, this setting works like a dimmer, increasing or decreasing any textures applied to this channel. Since we haven't applied any textures yet, this setting is currently moot.

11. Make sure Smoothing is enabled. And for now, let's leave Smooth Threshold at its default of **89.5** degrees. We may want to lower this later, but for now, the default should be fine.

12. The last setting is Double Sided. Since the polygons that make up this cabinet face outward and we're not going to open the cabinet doors to peer inside, we can leave Double Sided turned off.

Figure 6-24: Set the cabinet's surface properties.

Since the cabinet doesn't glow, isn't transparent, and doesn't reflect anything, we don't need to make any adjustments to the Advanced or Environment tabs.

We're done with the basic settings for the cabinet. That wasn't so hard, was it?

> **Note**
>
> Thinking your way through each channel is the trick to effective surfacing. You're free to simply play with the sliders until you get something you like, but you'll get better results faster by thinking about what each channel does and determining whether or not it applies to your particular surface.

Looking at the Surface list, I can see that there's a Cabinet_Knob surface. I added this so that I'd have the option to make the knobs metal, plastic, etc. But since the knobs don't show up in this render, it doesn't really matter what surface we give them. For fun, let's make them the same as the cabinet.

We could enter all the values for this surface just as we did before, but there's an easier way: Simply copy the Cabinet surface and paste it onto the Cabinet_Knob!

13. Right-click on the **Cabinet** surface in the Surface Editor and choose **Copy**. Then left-click on the **Cabinet_Knob** surface to select it. Finally, right-click on the **Cabinet_Knob** surface and choose **Paste**. Voilà! The cabinet's knobs now have the same surface settings as the cabinet.

Surfacing the Oranges

Let's move on to the oranges.

1. Click on the **Orange** surface in the list (or click on one of the oranges in the VIPER window). We'll work through the same process as we did with the cabinet, beginning with the Color channel.

2. Oranges are, well, orange. So click the color box and choose a nice orange color. I chose **255, 128, 000**.

> **Note**
>
> You'll notice that this color is highly saturated. As I mentioned before, you should try to avoid using highly saturated colors; however, this is one of those times that the color should really pop, so having a high saturation value won't be a problem.

3. Oranges don't emit light, so you can leave the Luminosity at **0%**. They do reflect most of the light that shines on them, so set the Diffuse to **80%**.

You may be wondering why I set the Diffuse value to 80%. The answer is simple. I know that oranges have a soft specular sheen. Since I want this sheen to be a little brighter than it was for my wood surface, I'm setting the Diffuse value a little lower.

Figure 6-25: Set the orange's surface properties. The VIPER window is beginning to show some nice results.

4. Oranges are slightly shiny. It's not a highly polished shine, but more like a soft sheen, so we'll use Specularity to simulate this. Since our Diffuse value was set to 80%, we'll set Specularity to **20%**. That way, Diffuse and Specularity add up to 100%.

5. Since the Specularity is going to give us a hotspot from the lights in our scene, we need to determine how large the hotspot will be. Oranges have a fairly soft, broad sheen. So let's set the Glossiness to **30%**.

6. Since we're using Specularity to simulate our reflections, we can leave the Reflection channel set to **0%**.

7. Oranges aren't transparent, so leave Transparency at **0%**. And you can't see the light shining through them, so leave Translucency at **0%**. Orange peels do have a bumpy texture to them which we'll add later. For now, leave the Bump value at **100%**.

8. Since our oranges are made up of fairly low-res spheres, we need to turn on **Smoothing** and set the Smooth Threshold to **89.5** degrees (which it should already be). Lastly, make sure the Double Sided setting is turned off so we don't waste rendering power calculating parts of the orange that we'll never see.

Surfacing the Bananas

Now that we've surfaced the oranges, let's move on to the bananas.

1. Click **Banana** in the Surface list to select it. I want these bananas to be at the stage where they begin to ripen. They should have a slight tinge of green, but also be showing some dark spots. We'll add the spots later. For now, click on the color box and choose a yellow-greenish color. I set my RGB to **183**, **183**, **051**.

2. Bananas should reflect most of the light that falls on them, so set your Diffuse to **90%**. Bananas aren't as shiny as oranges, but if they're fresh, they will have a slight sheen. So set your Specularity to **10%**. The sheen should be fairly broad. So set the Glossiness to **30%**.

3. Leave Reflection, Transparency, and Translucency at **0%**. Leave Bump at **100%**. Turn Smoothing on and leave Smooth Threshold at its default of **89.5** degrees. Finally, leave Double Sided off.

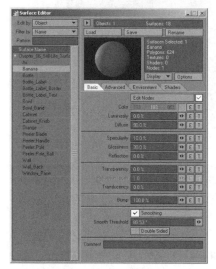

Figure 6-26: Set the banana's surface properties.

One of the things you'll notice about bananas is that their stems are typically a bit greener and their bottoms and tops are typically brown. We'll add these extra colors using textures later in this chapter.

Surfacing the Wall

Let's add some color to the back wall.

1. Click the **Wall_Back** surface (or simply click on the back wall in the VIPER window). Walls can be any color but I want this wall to be dramatic, so let's make it a dark red. Click the color box and choose a dark red color. I set my RGB to **125, 024, 024**.

2. Even though the wall is dark it still should reflect most of the light that shines on it, so set the Diffuse to **90%**. Most indoor paints have a degree of

gloss that acts as a protective coat. We could use Specularity to simulate this, but I want the gloss on this wall to actually reflect the objects around it, so leave Specularity at **0%**. This disables Glossiness, so we don't have to worry about it.

3. Turn Reflection up to **10%**. This will create crisp, sharp reflections, making the paint look really glossy. That's not really what I want. Instead, I want the wall to have soft reflections. There are several ways to achieve this. The easiest is to simply enable Reflection Blurring in the Environment tab of the Surface Editor, but this would dramatically increase our rendering time. So let's hold off on that for now. When we get further down the line, I'll show you how to create soft reflections with textures.

4. Leave Transparency, Translucency, and Bump at their defaults. The wall is totally flat, so turn Smoothing off. And we won't be seeing it from the back side, so leave Double Sided off.

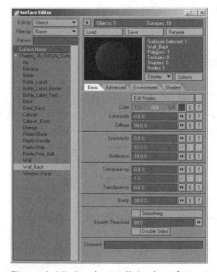

Figure 6-27: Set the Wall_Back surface properties.

We don't really see the other walls in our render. Since these walls already have the default light gray color, we can simply leave them as is and move on!

Surfacing the Bowl

Let's surface the bowl. As with the cabinet, this could be made of anything. It could be a glass bowl, a metal bowl, a plastic bowl. It's really up to you. I want this to be made out of porcelain.

I've created two surfaces for this object — one for the main parts of the bowl and another consisting of a few polygon loops around the outside, which will act as decorative bands. If you click on the Bowl or the Bowl_Band surface in the Surface Editor, you'll see the polygons that these surfaces are applied to as VIPER refreshes.

1. Let's start with the main part of the bowl. Click **Bowl** in the Surface list and set your RGB to **194, 203, 205**. This creates an off-white color with a tinge of blue in it.

2. Leave Luminosity at **0%** since the bowl isn't emitting light.

3. Set the Diffuse to **95%** since it should reflect most of the light that hits it.

4. Porcelain is shiny, so you might be tempted to use a high Specularity value. But remember that Specularity is a fake reflection of light; it's not a true reflection of the environment. Porcelain gets its unique look from environmental reflection, so leave Specularity at **0%**.

Now let's talk a little more about reflection. The amount of reflectivity on most surfaces appears to increase at glancing angles. In other words, when you look directly at a reflective surface, it appears *less* reflective than it does when it's pointing away from you. This phenomenon was discovered by French physicist Augustin Fresnel, and it is known as the Fresnel effect. We can recreate the Fresnel effect in LightWave through the use of gradient textures or shaders. We'll get to that later.

5. For now, set Reflection to **5%** so that it and the Diffuse total 100%. Leave all the other surface settings at their defaults and make sure that Smoothing is turned on.

Figure 6-28: Set the Bowl and Bowl_Band surface properties.

Now let's texture the bands for the bowl. Since the bands are made from the same basic material as the bowl, they will have similar properties.

6. Copy the Bowl surface and paste it onto the Bowl_Band surface. Now we'll give the bands a different color.

7. Set the RGB for the Bowl_Band surface to **090**, **123**, **206**. This gives these polys a nice medium blue color.

Surfacing the Peeler

Let's tackle the peeler. This object consists of several surfaces: the blade, the handle, the pole that connects the blade to the handle, and the ball at the end of the pole that holds everything together. We'll make each of these surfaces metal, but having them broken down separately gives us a greater degree of flexibility should we desire to add something like rust to the blade later on down the line.

Metal can be tricky to surface. Next to glass, it's one of the most difficult surfaces to recreate. Metal is highly dependent on its environment for its appearance. It makes use of the Fresnel effect and often requires anisotropic reflections in order to look right, so special textures and shaders are typically required. But don't worry! I put a peeler in this scene to teach you how to create great-looking metal quickly and easily.

1. Begin by selecting the **Peeler.Blade** surface. I want the color to be silver, so set the RGB to **089**, **089**, **089**. This is a darker gray, but it will brighten up once we add in the reflections.

2. Metal is not self-illuminating, so leave Luminosity at **0%**.

Metals typically have a strong reflection of their environment, which is what causes

their distinctive look. That means that our Reflection value is going to be fairly high. And since Reflection and Diffuse are linked, if we have a high Reflection value, we need to have a low Diffuse value.

3. As I mentioned earlier, metal makes use of the Fresnel effect, which means that the diffuse and reflection values will change based on the angle at which they're viewed. We'll tackle this later in the chapter. For now, simply set Diffuse to **75%** and Reflection to **25%**, bringing the total reflected light to 100%.

4. Leave Specularity, Transparency, and Translucency at **0%**. Leave Bump at **100%**. Turn on Smoothing and leave the Smooth Threshold at **89.5** degrees. Make sure Double Sided is turned off.

Since metal depends heavily on its environment, let's take a quick look at the options in the Environment tab of the Surface Editor.

5. Reflection Options should be set to **Ray Tracing+Backdrop**, which is the default setting. This will allow the surface to reflect the objects around it as well as whatever is set in the Effects | Backdrop tab. In most cases, this will yield the best results, but it can also be the most time-consuming in terms of rendering, as it relies heavily on ray tracing for its effect.

A slightly less realistic (but still very impressive) option is to use Ray Tracing + Spherical Map. This is especially true when you use an HDR image for your spherical map. (HDR images are covered in detail in Chapter 10.) Essentially, this setting allows your surface to reflect the objects directly around it and to use an image to simulate objects in the distance.

Note

Both the spherical map and the backdrop can use images to simulate detailed environments. (We cover environments in Chapter 12.) The main difference between a spherical map and a backdrop image is that a backdrop will be seen by all reflective objects. A spherical map image will only be seen by the surface it's applied to.

Note

HDR images contain multiple camera exposures in a single file. This gives them greater dynamic range that will help make our reflective objects look incredible. Whenever possible, you should try to use HDR images for your reflection maps.

Note

After copying the Peeler.Blade surface, you can <Shift>+click the remaining surfaces to create a multiple selection, then right-click and choose Paste to apply the copied settings to them all at once.

Even though we've got an environment for our peeler, it's a pretty sparse environment. Let's use an image to give the appearance that there's more to our scene than four blank walls and a couple of windows.

6. Change Reflection Options to **Ray Tracing+Spherical Map**. Then click the Reflection Map pop-up menu and choose the (**load**) option. Select the **kitchen_probe.hdr** image from your LightWave content CD (or download it from http://debevec.org/Probes/).

7. Since our entire peeler will be metal, we can use these same settings on its remaining surfaces. Copy the **Peeler.Blade** surface and paste it onto **Peeler.Handle**, **Peeler.Pole**, and **Peeler.Pole_Ball**.

That's it for now. Once we learn a bit more about textures, we'll come back to this surface and add gradients to make it ultra-realistic.

v9.2 Note

Metal and glass, two of the most difficult surfaces to simulate, can now be created with ease using the Material nodes in LightWave v9.2. For more information on creating metal and glass, check out the Materials - Conductor and Materials - Dielectric movies in the LightWave 9.2 Videos folder on the companion DVD.

Figure 6-29: Set each of the peeler surfaces with the same properties.

Surfacing the Bottle

The last visible object in our scene is the wine bottle. This object has four different surfaces. There's the bottle itself. This will be glass and we'll talk about surfacing it shortly. There's also the label, the label border, and the label text. Normally, we'd use an image map for the label, but for now, we'll show how you can use polygons with different surfaces to get the job done.

Let's start with the label. Labels are typically printed on paper, which can either be glossy or have a flat matte surface. We're going to make things simple and go with a flat matte surface.

1. Click on the **Bottle_Label** surface. Change the color to RGB **036**, **007**, **000**, which is a dark red.

2. The label doesn't emit light, so leave Luminosity at **0%**.

3. Since we're not going to use any reflection on this, we can leave Diffuse at **100%**. That means Specularity and Reflection can be left at their defaults of **0%**.

4. The paper isn't transparent, so leave Transparency at **0%**.

5. While you can see the light shining behind most paper (generally because it's so thin), this paper is applied to a bottle and we typically won't see light behind it. Therefore we're going to leave Translucency at **0%**.

6. This paper will be smooth, so we won't be applying any textures to it. That being the case, you can leave Bump at its default of **100%** as it won't affect anything.

7. The label does wrap around the bottle, so make sure that Smoothing is turned on. Leave the Smooth Threshold at **89.5** degrees and turn Double Sided

on. That way, if we ever turn the bottle around, we'll be able to see the label through the back side of the glass.

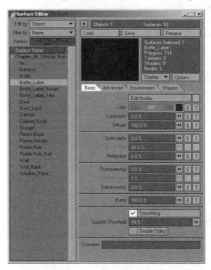

Figure 6-30: Set the Bottle_Label surface properties.

Now that the label is surfaced, we can see the text. Let's take a quick look at its surface.

8. Click on the **Bottle_Label_Text** surface. We can see that it's just the default light gray surface that Modeler assigns to new polygons. No problem here. We'll just leave it as is.

9. We can leave the **Bottle_Label_Border** at its defaults as well. With this setup, the border will be light gray, the label will be dark red, and the text will be light gray.

Now it's time to surface the glass for the bottle. You'd think that glass is simple — just make the surface transparent and you're done. But the fact that glass is transparent means that the light will bend when it passes through the surface. This bending of the light is known as refraction. It's one of the keys to getting realistic-looking transparent objects and it requires a bit of trickery to get it to work properly.

Every transparent object causes some degree of refraction. The degree of refraction is controlled by the Refraction Index setting. Air has a refraction index of 1.0. Water has a refraction index of 1.33. Glass has a refraction index of 1.5. See Appendix B for a list of refraction indexes for common materials.

Now bear with me. In order to understand how refraction works in LightWave, we have to talk about what's happening "under the hood."

When a light ray encounters a transparent surface, it checks the surface's refraction index to determine how much the ray should bend as it passes through the object. The light ray will continue on its bent path until it encounters a new surface with a different refraction index.

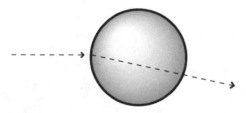

Light rays bend when they pass through a transparent surface

Figure 6-31: A light ray passing through a crystal ball.

Let's say you're surfacing a crystal ball. When a light ray that's moving through the air hits the outside of the ball, it will bend and head off on a different trajectory as it passes through the ball. When the ray exits the crystal ball, it should "unbend" because it's no longer moving through crystal — it's once again moving through air. But in LightWave, that doesn't happen.

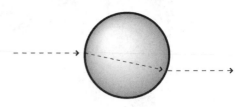

When the rays exit a transparent surface, they should no longer bend.

Figure 6-32: A light ray exiting properly.

Now keep in mind what I said earlier. A ray will continue on its path until it encounters a new surface with a different refraction index. We already know that by default, LightWave only sees one side of a polygon. That means that with a standard single-sided surface, the ray has no way of knowing when it has exited the crystal ball object and is once again traveling through the air.

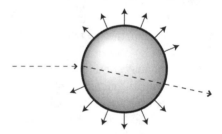

Since the surface normals all face outward, the light ray doesn't know that it has exited out of the transparent object.

Figure 6-33: A light ray exiting improperly.

You may think that you can remedy the problem by turning on Double Sided. This will certainly allow LightWave to see the back side of the object, but the polygons on the back side of the object will have the same surface settings (and therefore the same refraction index) as the transparent object, so the ray will just keep on heading down the wrong path.

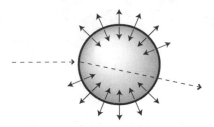

Even if the surface normals faced both in and out, the surface settings would still be the same. Therefore, the light would not change direction.

Figure 6-34: Turning on Double Sided will allow the ray to see the back side of the object, but it will still have the same refraction index so the ray won't change direction.

The solution to this problem is to use a copy of the object with a new surface, typically called "Air." The Air surface needs to be 100% transparent and have a refraction index of 1.0. Also, the normals for the Air polygons need to face the *opposite* direction of those of the glass surface.

With this setup, the ray will bend when it hits the outside of your transparent object. The ray will continue on its bent path as it travels through the object. When it reaches the back side of the object, it will encounter the Air surface. This lets the ray know that it is exiting the object and that it should no longer be bent.

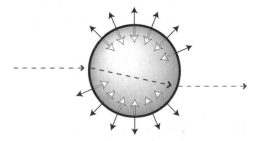

By using two objects with different surfaces and different normal directions, the ray will bend and unbend correctly as it enters and exits the object.

Figure 6-35: To correctly set up transparency, you must use two objects with different surfaces whose normals face opposite directions.

This may seem like a convoluted process, and it is, but it's a necessary one. Without the Air object's polygons, your transparent objects will not refract properly and you will never get realistic results.

So with all of that said, if you look at the Surface Editor, you will see that we've got the Bottle surface and we've also got an Air surface. I've already gone through the process of copying the bottle in Modeler, pasting a copy over the top of itself, flipping the normals, and giving the polys a new surface called Air. When you create transparent surfaces for your own objects, you'll need to go through the same process.

1. Let's set up the Air surface. You can leave all of the default settings just as they are, but the Transparency should be set to **100%** and the Refraction Index must be at **1.0**.

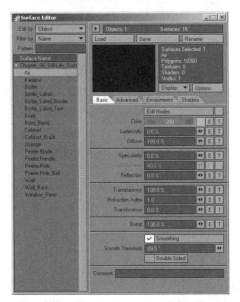

Figure 6-36: Set the Air surface properties.

Now for the bottle itself. Glass is reflective and transparent, and therefore it is subject to the Fresnel effect. We'll take care of setting that up later. For now, let's enter a few starting values.

2. Click on the **Bottle** surface. Since wine bottles are often colored, we'll give this a deep, dark blue color. Set your RGB to **000, 003, 026.**

3. The bottle doesn't emit light, so leave Luminosity at **0%**.

4. Enter **95%** for Diffuse. This will be adjusted for the Fresnel effect later.

5. We'll be using a Reflection setting on the glass, so leave Specularity at **0%**.

6. Since we set Diffuse to 95%, we need to set a starting Reflection of **5%**. That way, the total amount of light reflecting off our surface equals 100% of the light being cast onto it.

7. Set Transparency to **100%**. This will be modulated later via the Fresnel effect.

8. The refraction index for glass is 1.5, so set Refraction Index to **1.5**. (See Appendix B for a list of refraction indexes for common materials.)

9. Leave Translucency at **0%** and Bump at its default of **100%**.

10. Make sure Smoothing is turned on. Leave Smooth Threshold at **89.5** degrees.

11. We have the Air object's polygons facing inward and are changing the Refraction Index, so make sure that Double Sided for the Bottle surface is *not* checked.

Since our Transparency is set to 100%, the entire surface of our bottle is now invisible.

To reintroduce color into our bottle, we can use a combination of the Color Highlights and Color Filter settings on the Advanced tab of the Surface Editor.

12. There are no hard-and-fast rules for using these settings, but it's safe to say that the higher the value, the more the base color will appear in your transparent surface. I tinkered with this for a bit and settled on **20%** for Color Highlights and **40%** for Color Filter. Don't feel locked into using these settings. If you want more or less color in your glass, try increasing or decreasing the Color Filter setting accordingly.

> **Note**
>
> If you want to create clear glass with no color tint, set Color Highlights to roughly 20% but *leave the Color Filter setting at 0%*.

Since this surface uses Reflection, we have the option of using a spherical map in the Environment tab just as we did with the peeler. There's no harm in adding a spherical map as long as you use the Ray Tracing +Spherical Map option. The Ray Tracing option is the key. We need ray tracing in order to accurately reflect the objects and windows in our environment.

13. I'm going to skip the spherical map and just use the default of Ray Tracing + Backdrop for this bottle.

Looking at the VIPER preview window (or just looking at the camera's OpenGL viewport), it would appear that we're done. But there's one last surface we need to set up.

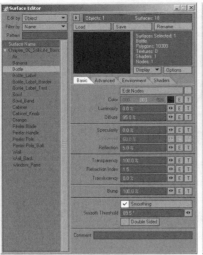

Figure 6-37: Set the Bottle surface properties.

Surfacing the Window Panes

As I mentioned when I first described the primary attributes, the best way to create realistic highlights for reflective objects is to avoid the Specularity channel altogether. Instead you should put simple geometry in your scene to mimic real light sources and give these polygonal light sources a highly luminous surface. *This trick is the key to getting photo-realistic reflections.* It may seem like extra work, but the difference it makes is undeniable.

In this scene, we've got four rectangles on either side of the room. We'll use them to simulate bright window panes. By increasing the Luminosity setting for the surface of these window panes, they will appear in the reflections on our objects and create highlights that would be impossible to recreate with the Specularity setting.

1. Click on the **Window_Pane** surface in the Surface Editor. Change the color to white (**255, 255, 255**) and increase the Luminosity to **1000%**. You can leave all the other settings at their default.

WITHOUT LUMINOUS OBJECTS IN THE ENVIRONMENT

WITH LUMINOUS OBJECTS IN THE ENVIRONMENT

Figure 6-38: The above bottles are identical. Both make use of the Fresnel effect (which we'll set up later). Both have the Color Filter set to 0% so that we can clearly see the glass without tinting. Both renders use Ray Trace Reflection and Ray Trace Refraction (enabled in the Render | Render Globals window). The only difference is the addition of luminous objects in the environment (as seen on the right). Placing luminous objects in your scene is the key to creating realistic

There's no magic formula for determining how luminous your objects should be. In some cases, 100% Luminosity will work just fine. In other cases, 200% to 500% will be best. Since we tinted the wine bottle, we need to increase the Luminosity quite a bit to ensure the windows still show up as reflections on our object.

Figure 6-39: Set the Window_Pane surface properties.

Figure 6-40: Press <F9> to render your scene and see your progress thus far. If you want a better preview of how things are shaping up, turn on the Ray Trace options in the Render Globals window before rendering.

2. Go ahead and close the VIPER preview window and press <F9> to render your scene. Not bad! Of course, it could be better. Open the Render | Render Globals window. Turn on **Ray Trace Shadows**, **Ray Trace Transparency**, **Ray Trace Reflection**, and **Ray Trace Refraction**. If you'd like, you can also open the Camera Properties window (select the camera, then press the <p> key to open the properties window) and add some Antialiasing. Then press <F9> to do another render (and go take a coffee break).

Adding in all of the goodies makes the render take a *lot* longer, but it also looks much nicer.

3. This would be a good time to save your object and scene. Go to Objects selection mode (press <O>). Then go to the File menu and choose **Save | Save Current Object**. Change the name of this object to **Chapter_06_Still-Life_ Basic_Surfaces.lwo**. This new object will contain all of the surface changes we've made. Now go to the File menu and choose **Save | Save As**. Call this new scene **Chapter_06_Still-Life_ Surfacing_Basic_Surfaces.lws**.

> **Note**
>
> If you're working directly off the DVD that came with this book, you will need to save the scene to your local drive since the DVD is write-protected.

Textures

You can accomplish quite a bit by adjusting the primary attributes for each surface. But looking at the render in Figure 6-40, it's clear that the primary attributes will only take you so far. The wood cabinet doesn't really look like wood. The wine bottle lacks realistic reflections. And the bananas look like they're made of yellow clay.

The problem with the primary attributes is that they do not provide control over surface *variations*. For that, you need to use textures, which you apply to your surface via the Texture Editor.

The Texture Editor can be opened by clicking on the "T" button next to any surface channel (such as Color, Diffuse, Transparency, etc.).

You can assign textures to each of the 10 channels in the Surface Editor. These textures will only affect the channel to which they were applied. For example, applying a texture to the Diffuse channel will cause variations to your surface's diffuse value. But that texture will not affect any of the other channels in your surface.

The Texture Editor makes use of LightWave's "layered" texturing system. Layers in LightWave work similarly to those found in image editing programs like Photoshop and Painter. Individual layers are stacked on top of one another and can be blended together to create complex compositions.

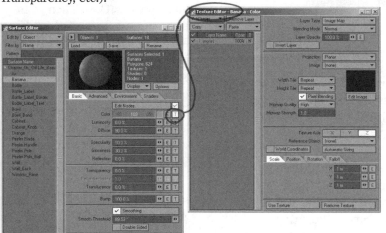

Figure 6-41: Click the "T" button next to a surface channel to open the Texture Editor for that channel.

Layer Types

There are three types of layers available in the Texture Editor.

• **Image Map** — This type of layer uses an image to affect the current channel. The image will be pasted onto the surface of your object (much like a decal) using one of

several "projection" methods. (See Figure 6-42.)

• **Procedural Texture** — A procedural texture is a computer-generated, resolution-independent, tileable texture. Procedurals can be used to simulate a wide variety of natural effects such as clouds, rust, dirt, etc. Most procedural textures are static, meaning that they won't change over time. But a few (like the Ripples procedural texture) are self-animating and will evolve over time without requiring any extra work on your part. (See Figure 6-43.)

- **Gradient** — Gradients are conditional textures. Their name is often misleading to newcomers who typically associate gradients with color blends. While you certainly can use gradients to do that in LightWave, that's really their least common function. (See Figure 6-44.)

Gradients are textures that follow a logical "*if…then*" formula. For example, *if* the polygons on the surface of an object are facing *toward* the camera, *then* use value A. But *if* they are facing *away* from the camera, *then* use value B. And *if* they're anywhere *in between*, *then* use a value between A and B. This type of conditional texturing opens the door for a wide range of effects and is the key to creating the Fresnel effect discussed earlier.

Image maps, procedural textures, and gradients can all be used together to affect one another. For example, you can apply an image map to your object and then overlay a procedural texture on top of it to vary and break up the color. You can then place a gradient on top of the procedural so that the color breakup only occurs when the light shines on the surface. Pretty powerful stuff!

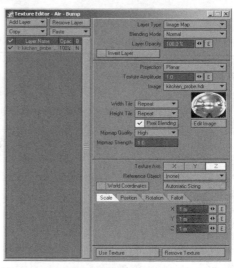

Figure 6-42: The Image Map layer type.

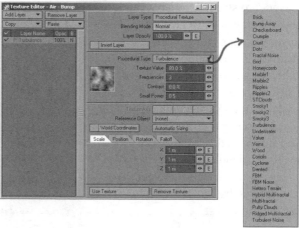

Figure 6-43: The Procedural Texture layer type.

Note

In this chapter, we'll be focusing on procedural and gradient textures. We'll take a detailed look at texturing with image maps in Chapter 11.

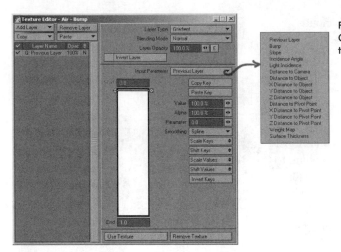

Figure 6-44: The Gradient layer type.

Blending Modes

Layers are stacked from bottom to top. When you add a layer, it will cover portions of the layers underneath it. If you want more of the other layers to show through, you can simply decrease the layer's opacity level or use a blending mode.

Clicking on the Blending Mode pop-up menu displays a list of the available blending modes. Each of these affects how the selected layer is displayed based on the textures *below* it in the list.

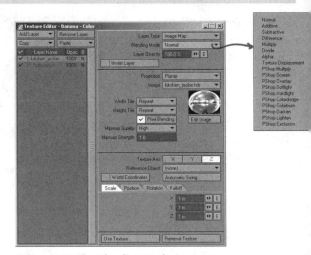

Figure 6-45: The Blending Mode pop-up menu.

Standard Blending Modes

• **Normal** displays the layer without any regard to the layers underneath it.

• **Additive** increases the brightness of your texture based on the values of textures below it.

• **Subtractive** decreases the brightness of your texture based on the textures below it.

• **Difference** is a variation on the Subtractive mode. Rather than adjust the

brightness of your surface, however, it adjusts its color and saturation. Dark colors in underlying layers will maintain the color and saturation in the selected layer. As the brightness in underlying layers increases toward a medium gray, the saturation of the selected layer will decrease. As the brightness of underlying layers goes from medium gray to white, the saturation of the selected layer will increase and the color will invert.

- **Multiply** will both increase and decrease the brightness of your texture based on the brightness of the texture below it. (Lighter values will increase the brightness of your layer while darker values will decrease it.)

- **Divide** is the opposite of Multiply, and will cause lighter values to darken the current texture layer (and vice versa).

- Blending modes that start with PShop work identically to those found in Photoshop and related image editing applications.

Note

I typically use the Normal, Alpha, and Texture Displacement blending modes; however, I occasionally play with the Additive and Multiply modes just to see how they affect my image. There's no hard-and-fast rule or "correct" blending mode. In most cases, it comes down to what you're trying to achieve. Don't get locked into a routine of only using one blending mode, though. You may find that you're able to achieve striking results by experimenting and thinking outside the box.

Alpha and Texture Displacement Blending Modes

There are two blending modes that differ greatly from the rest and are important for you to understand. These are the Alpha and Texture Displacement blending modes.

- The **Alpha** blending mode causes the current layer to affect the visibility of the layer directly *below* it.

  Alpha layers allow you to mask out portions of the layers below them and can be useful for blending two layers together in very specific manners.

- The **Texture Displacement** blending mode causes the current layer to affect the shape of the layer directly *above* it.

Displacement blending modes are great for breaking up the otherwise clean and orderly lines found in most procedural textures.

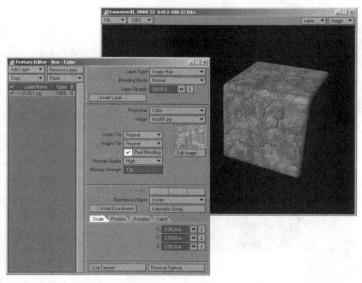

Figure 6-46: A standard image map layer applied to a box object.

197

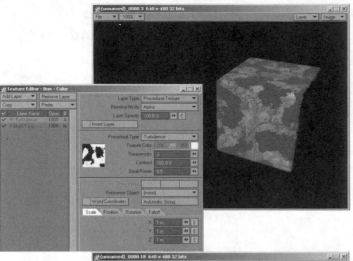

Figure 6-47: Adding a Turbulence procedural texture layer above the image map and changing its blending mode to Alpha effectively masks out areas of the layer below, allowing you to see the surface's base color (since there are no layers below it in the list).

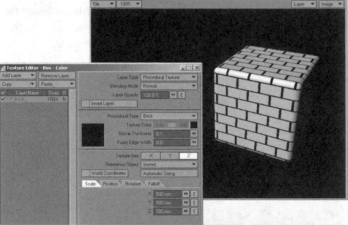

Figure 6-48: A Brick procedural texture has been applied to a box object.

Figure 6-49: Adding a Turbulence procedural texture layer below the Brick layer and setting its blending mode to Displacement allows the lower layer to disrupt the shape of the upper layer.

Layer Opacity

The visibility of an entire layer can be changed through its Layer Opacity setting, which defaults to 100%. This means any opaque portion of the current layer will completely cover the layers below it.

You can allow underlying layers to show through by lowering the opacity level. To blend multiple layers using just the opacity controls, you would need to lower the value for each successive layer.

> **Note**
>
> Image maps with embedded alpha channels will respect their transparency when used in LightWave. Additionally, most procedural textures have an opaque foreground color and a transparent background color. Changing the Layer Opacity setting for one of these layers will force the opaque portions of the layer to become more transparent.

The technique for achieving an even blend between multiple layers is to divide the total opacity (this would be 100%) by the layer number (starting from the bottom and working your way up). For example, the first layer would have a Layer Opacity setting of 100%, since 100/1 = 100. The second layer would have an opacity of 50%, since 100/2 = 50. The third layer would have an opacity of 33.33%, since 100/3 = 33.33.

By using multiple layers of image maps, procedural textures, and gradients in conjunction with the various blending modes and opacity levels, you can achieve remarkably complex surfaces.

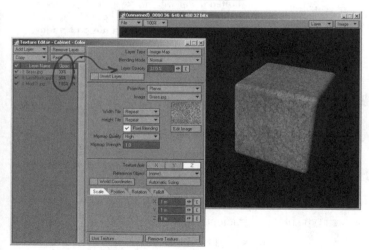

Figure 6-50: If you're only using the Layer Opacity setting to blend layers, each layer should have an opacity value equal to 100 divided by the layer position (starting from the bottom and working up). The opacity level of each layer is displayed to the right of its name in the Layer list.

199

Adding and Removing Layers

In the upper-left corner of the Texture Editor are buttons that allow you to add, remove, copy, and paste layers.

- The **Add Layer** pop-up menu allows you to add each of the specific layer types. Once added, these layers can be changed by using the Layer Type pop-up menu at the right side of the window.

- The **Remove Layer** button will remove the currently selected layer. This option is not undoable, so use this carefully.

- The **Copy** pop-up menu allows you to copy either the currently selected layer(s) or all the layers in the current Texture Editor. Multiple selection of layers can be achieved through the standard Windows conventions <Ctrl>+click and <Shift>+click. Being able to copy all the layers makes it easy to transfer your textures from one channel to another.

- The **Paste** pop-up menu allows you to replace the currently selected layers, replace all existing layers, or simply add the copied layers above the current layers in the list.

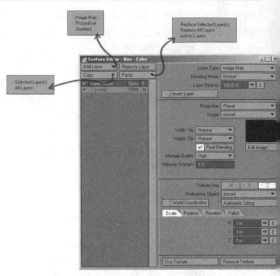

Figure 6-51: The controls in the upper left of the Texture Editor allow you to add, remove, copy, and paste layers.

> **Note**
>
> I often tinker with my layer settings to see what type of results I get. For me, the experimentation process is both fun and creative. When I find a combination of settings I like, I typically copy the entire set and then continue tinkering to see if I can get something better. If I find that I'm not happy with the results, I simply choose Paste | Replace All Layers to get back to my "safe" settings.

Working with Layers

The Layer list provides a tremendous amount of information about each type of layer.

- The check mark at the far left of each layer enables or disables the layer. This is similar to turning on and off the visibility in Photoshop with the Eye icon.

- Under the Layer Name column you'll find pertinent information about each layer. Image map layers appear with an "I:",

procedural textures appear with a "P:", and gradients appear with a "G:".

- After the Layer Type indicator comes relevant information about each layer. For image maps, the image name is shown. For procedural textures, the procedural type is shown. For gradients (remember, these are conditional "if...then" textures), the condition (called the input parameter) is shown.

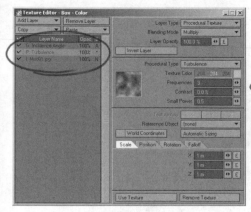

Figure 6-52: The Layer list gives a status readout of each layer in the Texture Editor.

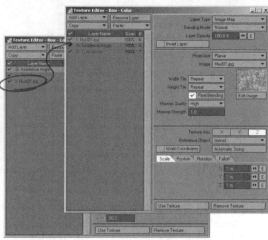

Figure 6-53: You can click and drag a layer to adjust its position in the stack.

- The next column shows each layer's opacity level.

- The final column (labeled "B") shows each layer's blending mode. We can see in Figure 6-52 that the bottom layer uses the Normal blending mode (N). The middle layer uses the Multiply blending mode (*). And the top layer uses the Alpha blending mode (A).

You can click and drag on any layer to adjust its order in the stack. Keep in mind that Displacement and Alpha blending modes will affect the layers above and below them respectively, so take care when reordering these types of layers.

- If you're happy with your changes, you can click on the **Use Texture** button at the bottom of the Texture Editor. To remove the entire texture stack from this channel, choose the **Remove Texture** button.

> **Note**
>
> You can also remove a texture stack entirely with a <Shift>+click on the "T" button in the Surface Editor.

Procedural Textures

Procedurals are resolution independent, computer-generated textures that you can apply to your surfaces. They can be enlarged or reduced at will without affecting the quality of the texture. They allow you to create everything from puffy clouds to alien skin. In most cases they don't require you to think about *how* they're applied to your object (which is typically the case with image-based textures). You just apply them, tweak a few settings, and go.

Note

Adobe's Photoshop gives you access to three procedural textures: Clouds, Difference Clouds, and Fibers. LightWave provides you with 33 different procedural textures, and there are dozens more available online! Best of all, LightWave's procedurals are dynamic. They can be edited and adjusted at any time! Procedurals give you access to a professional texture creation system right inside of LightWave, making them an incredibly powerful addition to the program.

Their ease of use makes procedurals a favorite texturing option for many users, but they do have a few drawbacks. Because they're generated by the software, they will increase your rendering time. Additionally, procedurals often have a "footprint" that makes them easily identifiable. You can produce amazing work with procedural textures, but you often need to put in extra effort to avoid their distinctive look.

Each procedural texture has its own unique properties. Let's take a look at one of the most common procedurals called Turbulence.

Note

LightWave v9 has drastically improved its support for OpenGL textures, including procedural textures. This allows you to see the effects of your work in the Color, Diffuse, Specularity, and Transparency channels without having to rely on VIPER. If you've applied a procedural texture to one of these channels but don't see the results in your Textured Shaded Solid viewport, open the Preferences window and click on the OpenGL tab. Enable all the Multi-Texturing options. Then turn on GLSLShaders under the Shading Method pop-up menu.

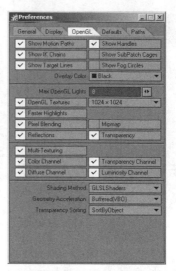

Figure 6-54: Be sure to enable Multi-Texturing and GLSLShaders to see the results of your procedural textures in the textured shaded viewports.

Note

In order to see the effects of procedural textures on the Transparency channel, you must increase the base value above 0%. Typically setting this to 1% will allow your transparency effects to show up in your viewports.

Note

The quality of your OpenGL display is determined by your computer's graphics card. A card with more power and RAM will be able to display more features. If you've turned on Multi-Texturing but still don't see textures on your objects, try lowering Max OpenGL Lights to 1. This will reallocate your graphic card's resources to display textures rather than dedicating them to your lights and can often solve the problem of textures not showing up in your OpenGL display.

The Turbulence Procedural Texture

Turbulence is a fractal noise texture. It works wonderfully for adding variety to the color of your object (used in the Color channel), adding dirt to your objects (used in the Diffuse channel), and making things less "perfect" (used in the Bump channel). You can think of Turbulence as the Swiss Army knife of procedural textures.

added a red procedural texture in the Color channel, the surface would appear mostly red with some of the underlying white base color showing through.

> **Note**
>
> When used in other channels (such as Diffuse, Specular, or Bump), the "Color" option for procedural textures is replaced with a "Value" option. Value allows you to determine the maximum intensity of the texture. A setting of 100 will give the brightest parts of the texture a value of 100, while darker parts of the texture will fall off proportionately. Negative settings can be used to invert the effect of the texture. For example, if you're using a procedural texture in the Bump channel and the texture protrudes *out* from your surface, you can use a negative Value setting to cause the bumps to press *in*.

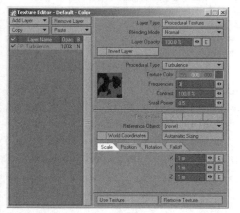

Figure 6-55: Turbulence is one of the most versatile procedural textures.

The first option the Turbulence texture gives you is **Texture Color**. This color gets applied over the top of your base surface color. So if you had a white surface and you

Using the **Layer Opacity** setting, traditional blending modes and Alpha layers can help limit the effect of the Turbulence texture on your object.

> **Note**
>
> Remember that you can click and drag on the RGB values to change them. Right-clicking on these values changes them to HSV, allowing you to do most of your color adjustments right in the Texture Editor without having to open the Color Picker window.

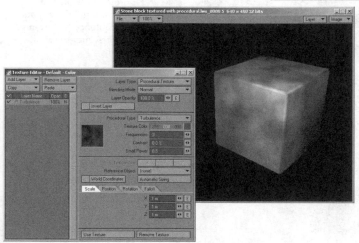

Figure 6-56: The Turbulence texture color gets applied on top of your base surface color.

The **Frequencies** option determines how detailed the Turbulence texture is. Smaller values will give a more blobby texture. (When combined with a higher contrast, this can be used to create the look of camouflage.) A higher Frequencies setting will require more processing time (and therefore longer renders), but will provide more detail to the texture.

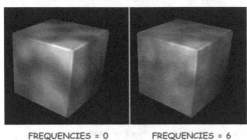

FREQUENCIES = 0   FREQUENCIES = 6

Figure 6-57: Frequencies determines the amount of detail in the texture.

The **Contrast** setting adjusts the falloff between the Turbulence texture and the colors underneath it. At its default of 0%, the texture will blend evenly with the colors in the layers beneath it. As you increase the Contrast value, the difference between the background and the Turbulence texture will become more apparent. Lower values work well when you want a subtle effect,

like dust covering a surface. Higher values work well for things like paint splats. You can even enter negative numbers. This will often create an overall wash of color with spotted regions of denser color.

> **Note**
>
> A great way to break up a solid color is to add a Turbulence texture and set the Contrast between –50 and –75. If you increase the Small Power setting (described next) to 2 and lower the overall scale (relative to the size of your model), you'll get a wash of color with spots of imperfection that will make the surface appear less "CG" and more realistic.

The **Small Power** setting determines how much fine detail is present in the texture. This setting is similar to Frequencies. Higher values will create more detail at the expense of render time; lower values create less detail but render quicker.

> **Note**
>
> I typically prefer to leave Frequencies at 3 and then vary the Contrast and Small Power settings. After I get the general look I want, I adjust Frequencies to see how that affects the overall texture.

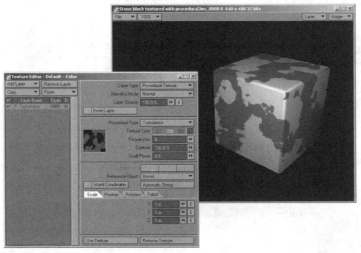

Figure 6-58: Contrast adjusts the falloff between the Turbulence texture and the colors underneath it.

Figure 6-59: Small Power determines how much fine detail is present in the texture.

Most procedural textures (including Turbulence) don't require you to specify a **Texture Axis** setting; they get applied evenly over the entire surface of your object. In these cases, the Texture Axis setting will be disabled. However, some textures require you to select a Texture Axis. Doing so will cause the texture to be "projected" down that axis and onto your object.

Note

You can achieve a nice noise/grain with the Turbulence texture. For color noise, choose a Texture Color setting that is slightly darker than your surface color. Leave Frequencies at 3 and Contrast at 0%, but increase Small Power to 2.0. Then adjust the overall Scale settings until the noise effect is small enough to suit your needs. If you apply this noise in the Bump channel and set the Texture Value to about 30%, you will get a nice, slightly imperfect finish to your surface, which will help avoid the unnaturally smooth qualities of computer graphics.

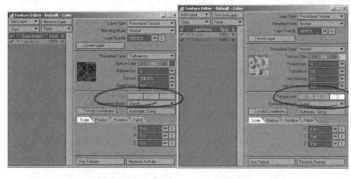

TURBULENCE PROCEDURAL:
NO TEXTURE AXIS REQUIRED

MARBLE1 PROCEDURAL:
TEXTURE AXIS REQUIRED

Figure 6-60: Most procedural textures are applied evenly over your object. When this is the case, the Texture Axis setting will be disabled. When this is not the case, you will be required to specify an axis to apply the texture to. The texture will then be projected down that axis onto your object.

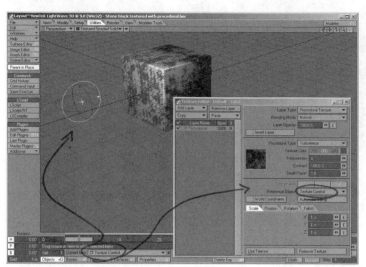

Figure 6-61: Reference objects (typically null objects) allow you to interactively adjust the size, position, and rotation of your texture.

The **Reference Object** pop-up menu allows you to choose an object that controls the size, position, and rotation of your texture. Null objects work extremely well for this purpose. Just hit <Ctrl>+<n> to add a null object. Name it **Procedural Control** (or anything else descriptive), then choose it as the reference object in the Texture Editor. When you move, size, or rotate the null object, the procedural will be affected. This makes the process of adjusting the size, position, and rotation of textures on your object interactive and (most importantly) easy.

When you're happy with your settings, you can choose (none) from the Reference Object pop-up menu. Doing so will enter the appropriate settings into the Texture Editor, allowing you to use the same null to adjust other textures.

The **Scale**, **Position**, and **Rotation** tabs all affect how the texture is applied to your object. The most important is arguably Scale, as this affects the overall size of the texture. You can manually enter these values, but using a Reference Object setting as described above will allow you to find the ideal settings quicker and easier.

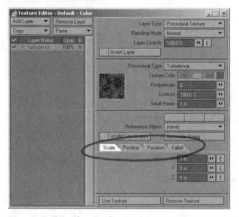

Figure 6-62: The Scale, Position, and Rotation tabs allow you to change how the texture is applied to your object.

As you can see, there are a lot of options available for this one simple procedural texture. Now consider the fact that there are 33 procedural textures in LightWave and dozens more available online. (Denis Pontonnier's fabulous RMan collection, included on the companion DVD, will add another 28 procedural textures to your arsenal!)

The LightWave manual does a good job of highlighting what each procedural does, but nothing beats hands-on experience. We'll use procedurals to improve our still life scene in the next section. But if you want to get your hands dirty right now, you can. Simply load the box.lwo object found in the Objects\Chapter 06 directory and start playing. I suggest starting with the Turbulence texture first. Then move on to the other textures. Make sure you've enabled Multi-Texturing to see your results in the OpenGL viewports and use a reference object to change their size, position, and rotation. Be sure to scrub the Timeline now and again. Procedural textures like Ripples and Underwater are self-animating and will blow you away!

Gradients

When I hear the term "gradient" I invariably think of colors blending together. Perhaps it's my art background. Or maybe it's my extensive use of the Gradient tools in programs like Photoshop, Illustrator, and Flash. I don't really know. But whatever the reason, it made it really hard for me to understand LightWave's Gradient layers.

I figured that gradients were simply there to add color blends to your surfaces. But I couldn't have been more wrong. Gradients in LightWave are *conditional* layers that apply a range of values to a specific channel based on unique criteria. Technically, the range of values does qualify these layers as gradients, but make no mistake, gradients in LightWave are not simply color blends.

Gradients are equations made up of three basic questions: *What? When?* and *How much?* Here's an example:

Let's say we want the specularity of a surface to vary based on how close the camera is to it. If an object is 10 meters from the camera, then its Specularity setting should be set to 25%. But if it's 1 meter from the camera, then its Specularity should be set to 100%. If it's anywhere in between, then the Specularity should be adjusted accordingly between 25% and 100%.

The gradient for this scenario would look like this:

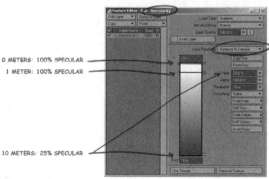

O METERS: 100% SPECULAR

1 METER: 100% SPECULAR

10 METERS: 25% SPECULAR

Figure 6-64: This gradient adjusts the surface's Specularity value as the surface gets closer to the camera.

The *"What?"* portion of the equation is the distance to the camera. Here, *"What?"* does not refer to *what changes* (that's determined

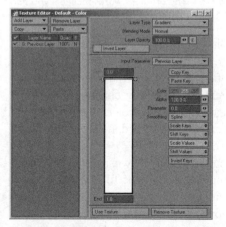

Figure 6-63: The Gradient texture layer.

by the channel the gradient is in), but rather what is *causing* the change.

The *"When?"* portion of the equation sets the limits to the equation. Here, it is "When this surface is anywhere from 1 to 10 meters away from the camera."

The *"How much?"* portion of the equation is "25% up to 100%."

A single gradient, then, can dynamically adjust the values of a channel based on *whatever* criteria you choose, *whenever* you choose, and by *however* much you desire. Imagine the possibilities!

Gradient Options

Let's take a look at the Gradient layer options.

The very first option we're presented with is **Input Parameter**. From this pop-up menu you can choose a variety of conditions.

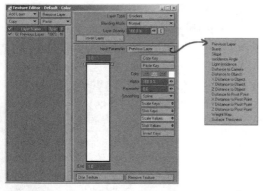

Figure 6-65: The gradient's Input Parameter setting controls the condition of the texture.

The Input Parameter is the key to the Gradient layer. It answers the *"What causes the value to change?"* portion of the equation. The effect a gradient has on your surface is based entirely on this setting. We'll talk about a few of the more interesting Input Parameter options in just a bit.

> ### Note
>
> The Input Parameter options change depending on where the gradient is being used. In the Surface Editor's Texture Editor, the Input Parameter list will have options such as Incidence Angle, Surface Thickness, etc. However, in the HyperVoxel Texture Editor, you'll find options such as Particle Weight, Particle Speed, and Time. Remember that gradients are *conditional textures*. When you see the option to use a gradient, be sure to check the Input Parameter menu for new options.

To the left of the Input Parameter pop-up menu is the **gradient workspace**. This is where you answer the *"When do things change?"* portion of the equation.

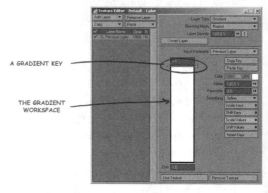

Figure 6-66: The gradient workspace lets you add keys to and delete keys from the gradient.

The line with the arrow on the left and box on the right is known as a "key." It defines a specific value for the gradient. Since this gradient is in the Color channel, the key represents a specific color. The first key in a gradient is always fixed in place and can't be moved.

You can add keys by clicking on a blank portion of the gradient. To select an existing key, simply click on the key's arrow or bar. To move a key, click and drag the key's arrow or bar. To remove a key, click the box on the right side of the gradient. To lock a key, right-click on its arrow. The arrow's

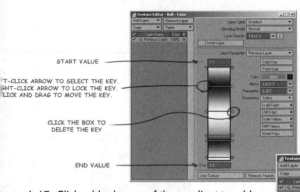

START VALUE

T-CLICK ARROW TO SELECT THE KEY.
GHT-CLICK ARROW TO LOCK THE KEY.
LICK AND DRAG TO MOVE THE KEY.

CLICK THE BOX TO
DELETE THE KEY

END VALUE

gure 6-67: Click a blank area of the gradient to add a
y. Click the box to remove the key. Click to select keys.
*l*ick and drag to move keys along the gradient.
*g*ht-click the arrow to lock the layer. The Start and End
*a*lues correspond to the chosen Input Parameter.

these values to another key, select it
and hit the **Paste Key** button.

Below the Copy Key and Paste
Key buttons is the **Color/Value** field.
You assign a color or value for each
key. In so doing, you answer the
"How much should things change?"
portion of the equation.

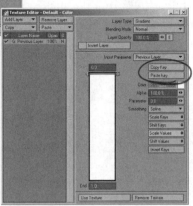

Figure 6-68: The Copy Key and Paste Key buttons
let you copy key values between one another.

direction will flip and you will no longer be
able to adjust any of its parameters.

Above and below the gradient workspace
are the Start and End values. These values
correspond with the Input Parameter option
you've chosen. Depending on which parameter you choose, one or both of these
values might be locked. For example, an
Input Parameter of Slope will prohibit you from adjusting the Start
and End values, because by their
very nature, Start and End define
the beginning and ending of a slop-
ing surface. But the Distance to
Camera parameter only has the
Start value locked. This is because
the Start value represents the position of the camera. The End value
can be changed at will, as it is up to
you to define how far away from the
camera the gradient values extend.

If this seems confusing, don't
worry. These are admittedly strange
concepts, but they'll make more
sense once we put them into practice, so hang in there.

To the right of the gradient workspace
are buttons for copying and pasting key values. To copy a key's settings, simply select
it and hit the **Copy Key** button. To apply

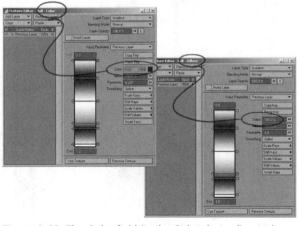

Figure 6-69: The Color field (in the Color channel) or Value
field (in all other channels) determines what gets applied to
the Input Parameter.

When you're working in the Color channel,
this field will depict RGB values and a color
box. Clicking this box allows you to choose
a specific color from your default color
picker. In all the other channels (Diffuse,

Specular, Bump, etc.), this will appear as a Value field. Here you can set the specific value for your channel based on the time set in the Gradient and the condition set in the Input Parameter.

The next field, **Alpha**, allows you to blend the gradient with textures below it in the stack. In many cases, you'll probably just leave this at 100%. But the ability to lower the opacity of a given key gives you unlimited options in your gradient textures.

Second, it allows you to change the position by typing in a new number.

Below the Parameter field is the **Smoothing** pop-up menu. This allows you to determine the interpolation of values between keys. The default of Spline works well in most cases. If you'd like a more abrupt change, you can set this to Step.

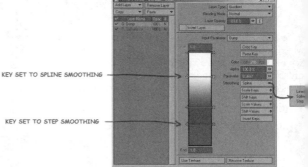

KEY SET TO SPLINE SMOOTHING

KEY SET TO STEP SMOOTHING

Figure 6-72: The Smoothing pop-up menu lets you choose how values between keys are interpolated.

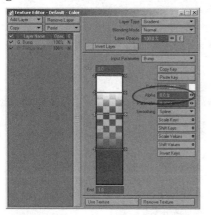

Figure 6-70: The Alpha field lets you lower the opacity of any key to blend its Value with the layers below it.

The **Parameter** field serves two purposes. First, it acts as a readout allowing you to see the exact position of the selected key.

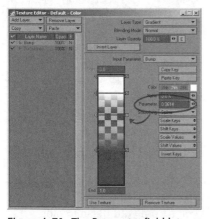

Figure 6-71: The Parameter field lets you enter a specific position for your keys.

The remaining controls in the Gradient layer affect the overall position and values of your keys. You can click and drag these up and down to affect all the keys in your gradient.

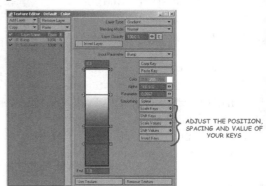

ADJUST THE POSITION, SPACING AND VALUE OF YOUR KEYS

Figure 6-73: The remaining buttons affect the overall position and value of your keys.

Common Input Parameters

Perhaps the most commonly used Input Parameter setting is Incidence Angle. Incidence (also referred to as the glancing angle) refers to the point at which you are looking straight on at an object. If the object's surface curves away from your point of view (as would happen if you were looking at a ball), the angle from the point of incidence to the farthest point away that is still visible (typically 90 degrees away since most people can't see beyond right angles) is known as the incidence angle.

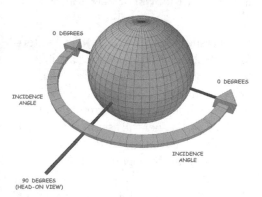

Figure 6-74: Incidence Angle is one of the most commonly used Input Parameter settings. It allows you to change values for a channel based on the angle of an object's surface in relation to your point of view.

In the real world, many surface properties change over the incidence angle. For example, on reflective surfaces, the amount of reflection *increases* with the angle of incidence, while the diffuse value *decreases* with the angle of incidence. On transparent surfaces, the amount of transparency also *decreases* with the angle of incidence.

As we discussed earlier, this phenomenon is known as the Fresnel effect (pronounced "Frah-nel"). Creating a gradient with an Input Parameter of Incidence Angle is an easy way to recreate the Fresnel effect in LightWave.

The Incidence Angle parameter isn't only for simulating natural effects. You can apply it to a gradient in the Diffuse channel to give your objects the appearance of having a hand-drawn edge.

Another common Input Parameter setting is Bump. This allows you to control the value of other channels based on the height of the texture found in the Bump channel. For example, if you painted a custom bump map (we'll cover this in Chapter 11) of a knife cut, you could fill the wound with blood by using a gradient with a Bump Input Parameter. By animating the depth of the cut, you would cause more blood to appear in the wound.

One of my favorite Input Parameter settings is Weight Map. By assigning specific portions of your object to a weight map in Modeler, you can use gradients to apply color and texture to those specific parts.

We'll use each of the Input Parameter settings described above when we add textures to our still life scene.

Shaders

In LightWave, shaders are utilities that provide specialized control over the look of your surface. There are nearly three dozen shaders that ship with LightWave. Let's look at the process involved in applying and using one of the most popular shaders: Fast Fresnel.

We talked about the Fresnel effect in the previous section on gradients. To recreate the Fresnel effect in LightWave, you can add a gradient with its Input Parameter set to Incidence Angle and then adjust the values so that they start and end accordingly. A glass surface would use the Fresnel effect in the Diffuse, Transparency, and Reflection channels. While it's not hard to create a gradient and copy it into multiple channels, changes to one will often require changes to all the others. The Fast Fresnel shader can simplify the process. In essence, it gives you the ability to control the gradients for multiple channels all from a single interface.

1. Load the still life scene that you saved at the end of the Assigning Primary Attributes tutorial (if it's not already open) or load the Chapter_06_Still-Life_Surfacing_Basic_Surfaces.lws file from the companion DVD.

2. Click on the **Bottle** surface. Then click on the **Shaders** tab in the Surface Editor. From the Add Shader pop-up menu, choose **Fast Fresnel**. Then double-click the shader in the list to access its options.

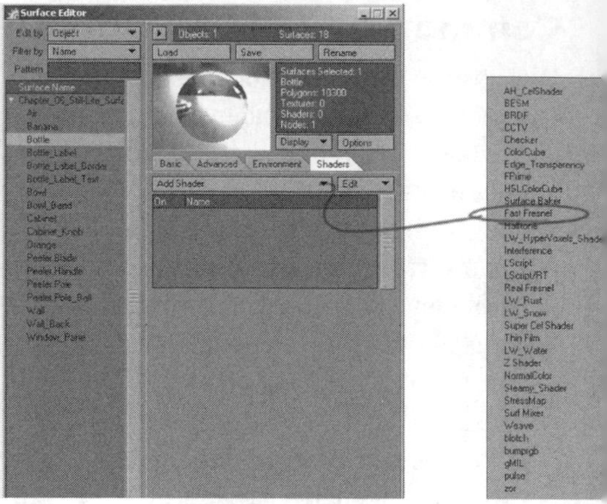

Figure 6-75: Add the Fast Fresnel shader to the Bottle surface.

Fast Fresnel uses the values you've entered for each channel's basic surface attributes for the minimum glancing angle (0 degrees or head-on view). For example, the Transparency for our bottle is currently set to 100%. Fast Fresnel will assume that when you look directly at the bottle (which is the minimum glancing angle), the transparency will be 100%. You can then use the settings in the shader to alter the value for the maximum glancing angle (90 degrees away from your point of view).

Figure 6-76: Fast Fresnel will modulate the value for selected channels between the numbers entered on the Basic tab and those entered into the shader.

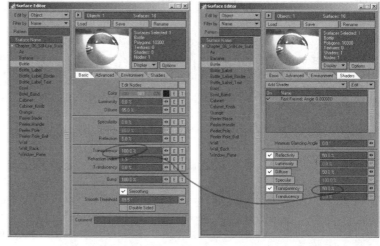

FAST FRESNEL WILL CREATE A GRADIENT BETWEEN THE VALUES
ENTERED ON THE BASIC TAB AND THOSE ENTERED INTO THE SHADER

3. Fast Fresnel enables the Reflectivity, Specular, and Transparency channels by default. Leave Reflectivity and Transparency active. Click the Specular check box to turn it off. Then click the Diffuse check box to turn it on (as shown in Figure 6-76).

4. Leave Minimum Glancing Angle at **0** degrees. Then set Reflectivity, Diffuse, and Transparency to **50%**. This will cause the Diffuse value to start at 95% and fall off to 50% as your viewing angle increases. It will cause the Reflection channel to start at 5% and increase to 50% as your viewing increases. And it will cause Transparency to start at 100% and drop to 50% as your viewing angle increases.

This will produce a fairly realistic glass for our scene. You can use these settings to simulate glass on other objects, but keep in mind that your reflective and refractive surfaces are highly dependent on their environment. If you're not getting the look you're after, you can always set up a spherical map in the Environment tab. Since our bottle exists in a real environment and we're using highly luminous "window pane" objects to enhance our reflections, we won't do that for this surface.

5. Open the Render | Render Globals window and turn on **Ray Trace Shadows, Ray Trace Transparency, Ray Trace Reflection**, and **Ray Trace Refraction**. Then press <**F9**> to see how the Fast Fresnel shader helps make the bottle look more like real glass.

Note

You can move the Frame Slider to frame 5 to get a close-up of the bottle.

WITHOUT FAST FRESNEL   WITH FAST FRESNEL

Figure 6-77: Without Fast Fresnel, our bottle looks good, but the reflections aren't right. With Fast Fresnel we get a more realistic-looking glass surface. The effect can be subtle (especially on this tinted glass) but as they say, the devil is in the details!

As you can see, shaders can really enhance the look of your surfaces and they can make repetitive tasks like managing Fresnel gradients much easier. There are dozens of shaders at your disposal. You can use the BESM shader to make your objects look as though they were hand-drawn. You can use the BRDF shader to add anisotropic highlights to your surfaces (helpful for creating the look of brushed steel). You can use the CCTV shader to apply a camera's view to the surface of your object. And you can use the StressMap shader to add wrinkles to a character based on its movement and deformation. These are just a few of the dozens of shaders in LightWave. Unfortunately we can't cover all of them here, but hopefully this introduction will take away some of the intimidation and encourage you to explore all the shaders at your disposal.

Still Life Surfacing 2 — Assigning Textures and Shaders

Now that we've taken a look at textures and shaders, let's put them to use and finish off our still life scene. We're going to move fairly quickly to finish off this tutorial, but I'll explain the key points and why we're doing things the way we are in more detail.

1. We'll start with the banana. To get a better feel for what we're working with, drag the Frame Slider to frame 1. Open the Render | Render Globals window and turn off the four Ray Trace options. Make sure your camera's Antialiasing is turned off and that VIPER is enabled. Then press <F9> to render.

2. Close the Render Status window and the Image Viewer. Open the VIPER preview window from the Render | Utilities menu. Change the Preview Size to **640x480** and the Resolution pop-up menu to **Normal**. Now click on the Banana surface in the Surface Editor list. This will cause VIPER to refresh.

Note

If you've got a more modern graphics card, you can turn on all the OpenGL settings in Layout's preferences window. This will allow you to see the effects of your procedural textures right in your OpenGL viewport.

Texturing the Bananas

Our banana has a good base color, but it could really use some spots.

1. Open the Color Texture Editor by pressing the **T** button to the far right of the Color options. The texture defaults to an Image layer type. Click the Layer Type pop-up menu in the upper-right corner of the Texture Editor and change this to **Procedural Texture**. Set the Blending Mode for this texture to **Multiply** and leave the Opacity at **100%**.

2. Click the Procedural Type pop-up menu and choose **Crust**. This will create a spotted texture over your surface. Change the Texture Color to a dingy

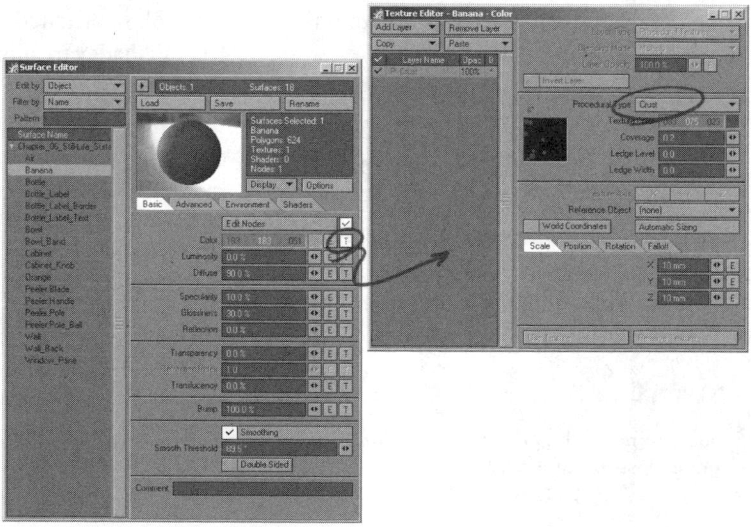

Figure 6-78: Add a Crust procedural texture to the banana's Color channel. Use the settings shown here as a starting point for your own experimentation with procedurals.

yellow-brown. I set my RGB to **083, 075, 023**.

3. Set Coverage to **0.2**, and Ledge Level and Ledge Width to **0**. Then change the Scale for X, Y, and Z to **10 mm**.

> **Note**
>
> As we work through the remainder of this chapter, I'll be giving you specific numbers to feed in for each texture. You may be asking yourself how I came up with these numbers. There's no real secret. In most cases, I just played with the settings until I got something I liked. There's nothing magic about them, so don't feel like you have to use these exact settings. In fact, I would highly encourage you to experiment and come up with your own settings. You're not going to break anything by playing around. And the time you spend tinkering will go a long way toward helping you to understand how to use the software. Besides, playing and having fun is what this is supposed to be about! So have fun!

part of most bananas is rough. Let's take care of this.

4. With the Color Texture Editor still open, click the Add Layer pop-up menu in the upper-left corner of the window. Add a new **Gradient** layer. Change the Input Parameter to **Weight Map** and from the Weight Map pop-up menu, choose **Bananna_Stem**.

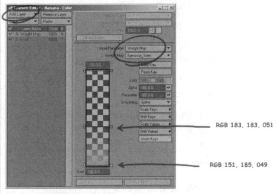

Figure 6-80: Add a new Gradient layer with a Weight Map Input Parameter. Choose Bananna_Stem as the Weight Map.

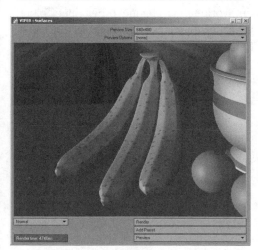

Figure 6-79: The VIPER preview window shows the effect of the Crust procedural texture.

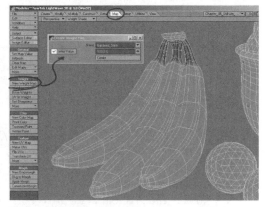

Figure 6-81: The weight map was created in Modeler by selecting polygons in the appropriate area and creating a new weight map for them.

Adding the Crust procedural added the necessary spots, but the banana still needs work. The very top and bottom of the banana should be brown, and the stem should be slightly more green. Also, the top

A weight map is an influence map created in Modeler by selecting some polygons and choosing the Map | Weight | New Weight Map command. This weight map allows us to use a gradient to add color to just these polygons without having to create a new surface.

5. Click a blank portion of the gradient workspace and add two new keys. (There should be a default key already placed at the top of the gradient.) Drag one of the new keys to the bottom of the gradient until its parameter is **100%**. Set the other to roughly **17%**.

6. Change the color for the keys at –100% (the top key) and 17% (the middle key) to RGB **183, 183, 051**. This is the base color for our banana. Then set the Alpha for each of these keys to **0%**, making them fully transparent.

7. For the last key, the one at 100% (the bottom key), give it a greenish color of RGB **151, 185, 049** and leave its Alpha at 100% (totally opaque).

Now let's talk briefly about what's going on in this gradient. The parameters for this gradient correspond to weight map values. Weight maps range from –100% to 100%. If you look back at Figure 6-81, you'll see that the value for the Bananna_Stem weight map (shown just below the Name field in the Create Weight Map window) is 100%. That means the polygons we selected will be given a weight map value of 100%. (We can use the other tools in the Map tab of Modeler to vary the values of this weight map, but that's beyond the scope of this tutorial.) All the remaining polygons for this weight map have a value of 0%.

Now look at the gradient in Figure 6-80. The bottom key is set to 100%. The polygons that have a weight map value of 100% will take on the greenish color for this key. The key at 17% has a color that matches the base color of our banana. This means that the greenish color will gradually fall off and blend with the underlying banana color. (Even though the Alpha for this key is at

0%, making it transparent, the greenish key at 100% will still attempt to blend into this transparent key's color, which is the same color as the banana.)

Almost all of the polygons except those in the stem of our bananas have a weight map value of 0%. So why did we set our middle key to 17%? By moving this key down, we've tightened the falloff for our color. It's purely a matter of aesthetic preference.

The top key in the gradient has the same parameters as the middle key. There are no polygons with negative weight map values, so this key shouldn't affect anything. I simply gave it the same parameters as the key below it to be safe.

When I'm setting up gradients for use with weight maps, I typically create this same setup. I create three keys: the first at –100%, the second at 0%, and the third at 100%. I then change the colors (or values if I'm working in a channel other than Color) for each key and begin adjusting their positions until I'm happy.

> **Note**
>
> You've probably noticed that when you added the gradient with the Input Parameter set to Weight Map, VIPER didn't register any of your changes. That's normal. When texturing with gradients and weight maps, you will need to do test renders in order to proof your work. For this reason alone, I *highly* recommend investing in Worley Labs' FPrime renderer. It's like VIPER on steroids and will completely change the way you work with LightWave.

8. Copy this Gradient layer by clicking on the Copy pop-up menu and choosing the **Selected Layer** option. Then click on the Paste pop-up menu and choose **Add to Layers**.

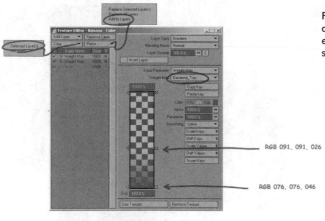

Figure 6-82: Copy the Gradient layer and paste a copy, adding it to the existing layers. Set its parameters as shown.

RGB 091, 091, 026

RGB 076, 076, 046

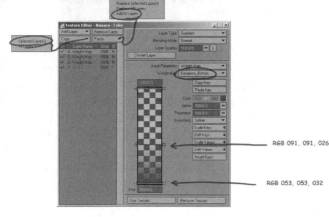

Figure 6-83: Copy the Gradient layer again and paste another copy, adding it to the existing layers. Then set its parameters as shown.

RGB 091, 091, 026

RGB 053, 053, 032

9. Set the values for this gradient as shown in Figure 6-82. Choose the Weight Map setting of **Bananna_Top** and the colors should be adjusted accordingly. This will add a dark color to the very top of the banana bunch.

10. Finally, copy this layer and choose **Paste | Add to Layers** to add a third gradient to the Texture Editor. Change its Weight Map to **Bananna_Bottom** and set its parameters as shown in Figure 6-83. This will add a dark color to the bottom of each individual banana.

11. Press <F9> and do a test render. Our bananas are looking much better!

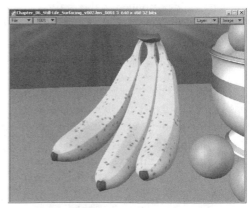

Figure 6-84: Do a test render by pressing <F9>. Our bananas are looking much better! Notice that the stems now have a slight tinge of green that blends into the yellow color of the banana, and the tops and bottoms of the banana are dark brown.

There's one last thing we should do to make this surface appear more realistic. The top of most banana bunches is a bit rough. But on our render it's unrealistically smooth. Let's fix that by adding a bump map.

12. Click the **Use Texture** button in the Color Texture Editor window to accept your color textures. Then click the **T** button to the right of the Bump settings in the Surface Editor to open the Bump Texture Editor.

13. Change the default layer to a **Procedural Texture**. Then add a Gradient layer on top of it. Set each of the parameters as shown in Figure 6-85.

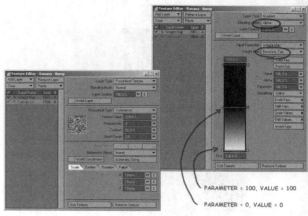

PARAMETER = 100, VALUE = 100
PARAMETER = 0, VALUE = 0

Figure 6-85: Add a procedural texture and a gradient with the settings shown here.

Let's talk briefly about what this setup is doing. The bottom layer is a Turbulence procedural texture. I've increased the Small Power and the Texture Value and slightly increased the Contrast. At a scale of 10 mm, this provides a nice bumpy texture. If we were to add this texture alone, the bumpy surface would be applied to the entire banana. But the bumps should only be applied to the top of the bunch. To limit their influence, we added the gradient.

The gradient uses the Weight Map Input Parameter, and the weight map we chose was Bananna_Top. The Blending Mode setting for the gradient is set to Alpha. That means that it will affect the visibility of the layer below it (in this case, the Turbulence procedural texture). By setting up three keys in the gradient just as we did in the Color channel, we can control the values for –100%, 0%, and 100% of the weight map.

In an Alpha blending mode, white areas will show the underlying texture. Black areas will not show the underlying texture. By setting the key with 100% weight map

to 100% Value setting (pure white), we are telling this gradient to ensure that any polygons with 100% of the Bananna_Top weight map influence will show the Turbulence texture below. The keys at 0% and –100% are both set to a Value of 0 (pure black). This ensures that the bumpy Turbulence texture does not appear on the polygons with 0% of the Bananna_Top weight map or less.

14. Click **Use Texture** to accept the changes to the Bump channel and press **<F9>** to render again. You'll see that the top of our banana bunch is now bumpy and a bit more realistic.

That wraps up the texturing for the banana. If you'd like to see my results, you can load the Banana surface from the Surfaces\Chapter 06 folder on the companion DVD.

> Note
>
> Using weight maps and gradients is a powerful way to texture your objects. If you'd like a more in-depth look at this process, I have included a full-length video tutorial called "Texturing with Weightmaps and Gradients" on the DVD that came with this book.

Now that we've added textures to the banana, let's move on to the bowl and bowl band.

Texturing the Bowl

The settings for the Bowl object and its decorative band are essentially the same. The only difference is the color we used. Therefore, we can make the changes to one surface and simply copy the settings to the other.

1. Drag the Frame Slider to frame 3, which focuses on the Bowl object. Open the Render Globals window and turn on **Ray Trace Reflection**. (All the other Ray Trace options should be off.) Press <**F9**> to do a preview render (Figure 6-86).

2. When the render finishes, close the Render Status window but *don't* close the Image Viewer that shows the finished render. Instead, simply minimize it. We'll use this window later to compare our before and after results.

3. Click on the Bowl surface in the Surface Editor list. The bowl is reflective, which means it's subject to the Fresnel

> **Note**
>
> You can close the VIPER preview window for now. VIPER is able to preview image-based reflections (such as spherical maps used in the Environment tab of the Surface Editor) but it cannot preview ray-traced reflections. Since our Bowl surface relies heavily on ray-traced reflections of the environment, VIPER won't be of much use to us here. Instead, we must do test renders to check the results of our work.

effect. We've already seen how we can use the Fast Fresnel shader to accomplish this. To make things interesting, let's see how we can do the same thing with gradients. In the process, we'll see how the use of gradients gives us more control than is offered by the Fast Fresnel shader.

4. Click the **T** button next to Diffuse to open its Texture Editor. Change the default layer from Image Map to **Gradient**. Set the Input Parameter setting to **Incidence Angle**. The first key will already be positioned at a Parameter of 0. Place three additional keys at the locations shown in Figure 6-87.

Figure 6-86: Drag the Frame Slider to frame 3. Turn on Ray Trace Reflection and do an <F9> preview render.

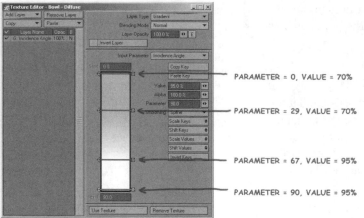

Figure 6-87: Add a gradient to the Diffuse channel of the Bowl surface and set its Input Parameter to Incidence Angle. Create three additional keys as shown here.

PARAMETER = 0, VALUE = 70%

PARAMETER = 29, VALUE = 70%

PARAMETER = 67, VALUE = 95%

PARAMETER = 90, VALUE = 95%

5. Give the first key in the gradient (Parameter = 0) a Value of **70%**. Move the second key to a Parameter of **29** and give it a Value of **70%**. Move the third key to a Parameter of **67** and give it a Value of **95%**. Then move the last key to the very bottom of the gradient (Parameter = **90**) and give it a Value of **95%**.

Let's talk about why we set the gradient up this way. We know that in order to create the Fresnel effect, reflection must increase as our viewing angle decreases. (See Figure 6-74 for a refresher on this.) Since the Reflection and Diffuse settings are linked, if the Reflection setting *increases*, Diffuse will *decrease*. Therefore, our Diffuse gradient should start high and end low.

The bottom key (Parameter = 90) represents our head-on viewpoint. It is set to 95%. This matches the value we originally entered for the Diffuse channel on the Basic tab of the Surface Editor. The top key (Parameter = 0) represents the farthest distance away from our head-on viewpoint. It is set to 70%. This means there will be a 25% drop in Diffuse over the surface of our object.

Note

As I mentioned earlier, most of the values used here were derived from playing with the settings until I got something I liked. You don't have to use four keys to create the Fresnel effect for this surface, but I found that for this object, it created nice results.

We could create the Fresnel effect with nothing more than the two keys described above. But I wanted to squeeze the gradient so that it held its initial value (95%) longer and arrived at its ending value (70%) earlier. To accomplish this, I created two extra keys as shown in Figure 6-87.

Note

Since we're using a texture to control the Diffuse channel and none of the keys in this gradient are transparent (Alpha = 0), the values we use here will completely override the value we entered on the Basic tab of the Surface Editor.

6. We can use the same gradient we've created here for our Reflection channel. Copy this layer, then choose **Use Texture** to close the Texture Editor. Open the Texture Editor for the Reflection channel. Click the Paste pop-up menu

and choose **Replace Selected Layer(s)**.

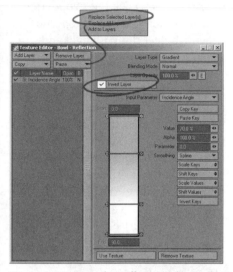

Figure 6-88: Copy the Diffuse gradient and Paste | Replace Selected Layer(s) into the Reflection channel.

7. The key positions for the gradient don't need to change, but the Values should be the exact *opposite* of those in the Diffuse channel. We could change each key in the gradient by hand, but there's an easier way. Simply activate the **Invert Layer** option in the Texture Editor by clicking on it. This will cause the values for all keys to be inverted. For example, if the first key in the Gradient is 70%, its inverted value will be 30%.

Note

Invert Layer and Invert Keys (found at the bottom right of the gradient workspace) do very different things. Invert Keys will flip-flop the *position* of the keys in the Gradient (determined by their parameter). Invert Layer will invert the *value* of the layer (which in this case is defined by the Value for each key).

8. Now that our gradients are set up, press <**F9**> to do another test render. Click **Abort** to close the Render Status window. If your Image Viewer window is still minimized, restore it to its full size.

Note that the Fresnel effect causes the reflections to really increase toward the edges of the bowl, making it look like there's a glaze over the entire surface.

When the Image Viewer window is in focus (meaning that you've clicked on it to make it active), you can use the Page Up and Page Down buttons on your keyboard to flip through the images stored in the Image Viewer buffers. This is a great way to compare the subtle changes between two images. You can also save images directly from the Image Viewer window by clicking the File pop-up menu in the upper-left corner of the window and choosing Save RGBA. We'll cover rendering and saving images more in Chapter 7.

WITHOUT THE FRESNEL EFFECT GRADIENT   WITH THE FRESNEL EFFECT GRADIENT

Figure 6-89: Press <F9> to do another test render. Then use the Page Up and Page Down keyboard shortcuts to compare the renders in the Image Viewer window.

Note

If you're going to use the Page Up and Page Down keys to flip through renders stored in the Image Viewer window, make sure that the Image Viewer is in focus first. If it's not and any of Layout's other windows are in focus, the Page Up and Page Down keys will activate real-time scene playback. If this happens, just click on the Pause button in the lower-right corner of Layout to stop the playback.

Texturing the Cabinet

Now let's do some much-needed work to the cabinet.

1. Open the Render Globals window and turn off Ray Trace Reflection. (All of the Ray Trace options should now be off.) Move the Frame Slider to frame 6. This gives us a nice general close-up of the cabinet that will help us in creating our wood grain.

2. Make sure VIPER is enabled. Then press <F9> to do a test render. When it's finished, close the Render Status window and the Image Viewer window. Open the VIPER preview window. You'll notice that the cabinet surface is extremely dark. So dark, in fact, that it will be nearly impossible to use VIPER. To correct for this, we need to temporarily adjust the lights in our scene.

3. Switch to Lights selection mode by clicking the button at the bottom of the interface. Then click the **Properties** button to open the Light Properties window. Select the **Wall** light and change its Light Intensity value to **100%**. Do the same for the **Ceiling** light as well. Close the Light Properties window and press <**F9**> to perform another test render. When it finishes, close the Render Status window and the Image Viewer window. Then bring up the VIPER preview window and press the **Render** button. VIPER will refresh and you'll notice that the wood surface is much easier to see.

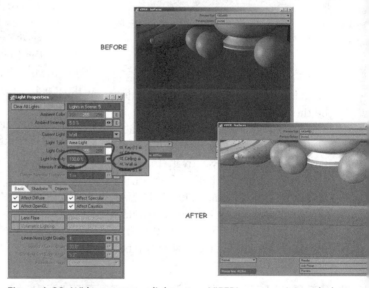

Figure 6-90: With our current light setup, VIPER's preview is too dark to texture the cabinet. Increase the Light Intensity for the wall and ceiling light to 100%. Press <F9> to do another test render. Then press Render in the VIPER window to see the results.

I'd like to add some dents and dings to this wood to make it look a little battered and beaten. I also want to add some wood grain. We'll produce both with procedural textures.

4. Click on the Cabinet surface in the Surface Editor. Then open the Texture Editor for the Bump channel. Change the default layer to **Procedural Texture**. From the Procedural Type pop-up menu, choose **Dented**.

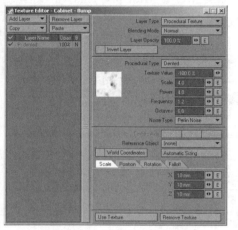

Figure 6-91: Add a Dented procedural texture to the cabinet's Bump channel.

5. Leave the Texture Value at **80%**. (Figure 6-91 shows the Texture Value at –100%. We'll change this to –100% later. For now, leave it at 80%.)

6. Set Scale to **4.0**, Power to **4.0**, Frequency to **1.2**, and Octaves to **6.0**. Leave the Noise Type at **Perlin Noise**. Then change Scale to **10 mm** for X, Y, and Z.

If you look at the VIPER preview window, you'll see the Dented texture applied to the cabinet's surface. But there's a problem. The bumps are raised up, making it look like a crusty texture covering the surface.

To fix this, we need to adjust the Texture Value. Remember, Texture Value determines the maximum intensity of a procedural texture. Positive numbers will cause the texture to rise up from the surface. Negative numbers will cause the texture to cut into the surface. A Texture Value of 0 will eliminate the effect of the texture altogether.

7. Change the Texture Value to –100% and take a look at what that did in VIPER's preview window. It's much better! But it's a little extreme. It looks like the cabinet has taken a beating. We could adjust this by increasing the Texture Value to something like –80%, but let's look at another way.

8. Click the **Use Texture** button to accept the changes to the Bump Texture Editor. Looking at the Surface Editor, we can see that the Bump value is set to 100%. As we've discussed earlier, this setting works like a dimmer. You can globally increase or decrease the effect of all textures applied to the Bump channel with this setting. Let's

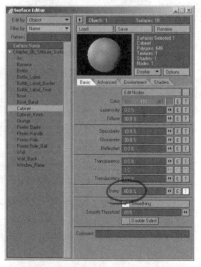

Figure 6-92: Use the Bump setting on the Surface Editor to lower the intensity of the bump texture.

223

take some of the edge off. Lower the Bump value to **60%** and take a look at the VIPER preview. You can still see the bumps, but the effect is much more subtle.

9. Now let's add some grain. Open the Color Texture Editor and change the default layer to **Procedural Texture**. From the Procedural Type pop-up menu, choose **Wood**. Set the Texture Color to RGB **014**, **011**, **007** (a dark brown). Set Frequencies to **3**, Turbulence to **1.0**, Ring Spacing to **0.02**, and Ring Sharpness to **3.0**. Change the Texture Axis to **X** and leave the Scale

at **1 m** for X, Y, and Z. Then take a look at the VIPER preview window.

> **Note**
>
> You'll notice that we needed to assign a texture axis for the wood. The Texture Axis setting here determines the direction the wood grain will run. I want the grain to run left to right, so I choose the X-axis.

10. That wood grain is really intense and it looks horrible! Let's tone it down. Change the Blending Mode setting for this layer to **Multiply**. This will cause the wood grain to blend into the brown surface color a little better. Then lower

Figure 6-93: Add a Wood procedural texture to the Color channel with the settings shown here.

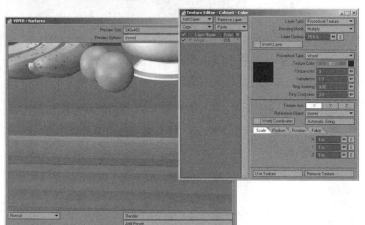

Figure 6-94: Change the Blending Mode to Multiply and drop the Layer Opacity to 15% to tone down the overall wood grain.

the Layer Opacity to **15%**. This gives us a much fainter (and much nicer) wood grain.

At this point, our grain is okay, but it's not great. One of the main problems is that the wood grain is really straight. In the real world, wood grain moves, bends, and swirls. We need to disrupt our wood grain so that it's a bit more natural. To do this, we'll use a texture displacement layer.

11. Add a new procedural texture (which by default will be a Turbulence texture). Drag this layer below the Wood layer. Change the Blending Mode to **Texture Displacement**. Leave Layer Opacity at **100%**. Change the Texture Color to pure white (**255, 255, 255**). Increase Frequencies to **4**. Leave Contrast at **0%**, and set Small Power at **0.5**. Then change the X Scale to **10 m**, but leave Y and Z at **1 m**. (See Figure 6-95.)

Texture Displacement layers must be positioned directly *below* the layer they affect. If it helps, you can think of it like a mouse running under a rug. If the mouse runs on top of the rug, there will be no noticeable difference in the rug's shape. But if the mouse runs under the rug, it will bulge up

and displace. That's how texture displacement layers work.

Most of the settings for the texture displacement layer are at or just above their defaults. But if you look at the Scale setting, you'll notice that we've really increased the value for the X-axis. This causes our fairly uniform texture to stretch out on the X-axis (the same axis we chose for the grain of our Wood texture). For kicks, change the Scale of the X-axis back to 1 m and look at the results. The wood grain now looks strange and almost marbled. You can play with the Scale settings for this layer to see how they affect the texture. When you're ready to move on, set X back to 10 m and Y and Z back to 1 m.

The wood grain for our cabinet looks pretty good, but it's lacking fine details. Let's add some noise to break things up.

12. Add a new **Turbulence** procedural texture and make sure it's placed on top of the Wood texture. Change the Blending Mode to **Multiply** but leave the Layer Opacity at **100%**. Set the Texture Color to RGB **081, 040, 000** (a dark brown). Leave Frequencies at **3** and Contrast at **0%**. Increase the Small Power to **2.0**. Then set the X, Y, and Z Scale to **10 mm** each (Figure 6-96).

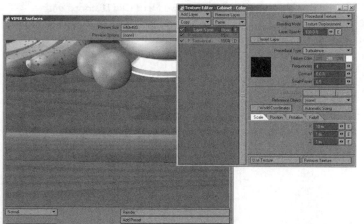

Figure 6-95: Add a new Turbulence procedural texture. Change its Blending Mode to Texture Displacement and drag it under the Wood texture. Then adjust the layer settings.

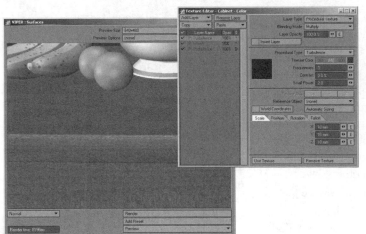

Figure 6-96: Add a new Turbulence procedural texture. Change its Blending Mode to Multiply and adjust the layer settings as shown here.

Increasing Small Power to 2.0 adds a lot of detail to the Turbulence texture. Decreasing the Scale setting (in relation to the size of the cabinet) creates a beautiful noise pattern. Setting the color to a dark brown and the Blending Mode to Multiply allows this colored noise to affect the color of the wood grain below it. You may feel that the noise is too strong. If so, simply adjust the Layer Opacity setting until you find something you're happy with.

We've now got a really nice wood pattern. Of course, it could still be improved, but I'll leave it to you to play around with the settings. What's important to note is that this entire texture is being generated right in LightWave. No image maps are being used. As you're likely beginning to realize, procedural textures can do some amazing things!

13. Before we move on, be sure to copy the Cabinet surface and paste it onto the Cabinet_Knob surface.

Texturing the Oranges

Now let's add some textures to our oranges.

1. Drag the Frame Slider to frame 2. This is the close-up shot of our orange. Make sure that VIPER is enabled in the Render tab. Press <F9> to do a quick render so that VIPER's buffers will be filled with the new image. Then close the Render Status window and the Image Viewer.

> **Note**
>
> If you don't see the orange on frame 2 in your OpenGL viewport, open the Display Options panel (keyboard shortcut <o>). Activate Fixed Near Clip Distance and change the value to 35 mm.

2. Bring up the VIPER preview window and click on the **orange** to select it in the Surface Editor. The overall color is fine, but the surface is too smooth. Let's add some bumps. Open the Bump Texture Editor. Change the Layer Type setting to **Procedural Texture** and choose **Turbulence** from the Procedural Type pop-up menu.

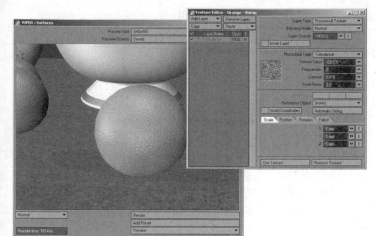

Figure 6-97: Add a Turbulence procedural texture to the Bump channel for the Orange surface. Adjust the layer settings as shown here.

3. Leave the Blending Mode at **Normal** and the Layer Opacity at **100%**. Change the Texture Value to **–60%**. Leave Frequencies at **3** and Contrast at **0%**, but increase Small Power to **2.0**. Then change the Scale for X, Y, and Z to **5 mm** each.

As we've seen before, using a high Small Power with a low Scale produces a nice noise pattern. And as we've also seen with the cabinet surface, using a negative Texture Value causes the texture to cut into the surface rather than project away from it. Are you beginning to see how powerful and versatile the Turbulence texture is?

Our orange looks pretty great as is, but there's one more thing we can do to make it look even better. If you look closely, you'll notice that the specular sheen covers the entire surface of our orange evenly, including the depths of our bump textures. In reality, the sheen would fall across the outer surface, but would diminish as it goes into the bumpy divots. We can create this effect with a gradient in the Specularity channel.

4. Open the Texture Editor for the Specularity channel. (You don't have to close the Bump Texture Editor first. Clicking the T button to open another Texture Editor will accept your

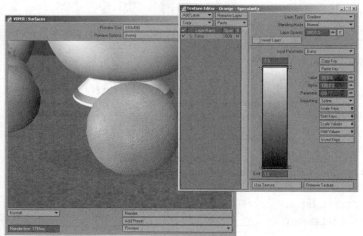

Figure 6-98: Add a gradient to the Specularity channel for the orange surface. Set the Input Parameter to Bump and adjust the layer settings as shown here.

changes in the current window and open the new one in its place.) Change the default layer to **Gradient** and set its Input Parameter to **Bump**. A default key will appear at the top of the gradient. Add a second key and drag it to the very bottom.

The Bump parameter allows you to adjust values based on the height or depth of the textures in the Bump channel. The range is from 0 (representing the lowest intensity in the Bump texture) to 1 (representing the highest intensity in the Bump texture).

The bottom key (at the 1.0 position) on this gradient will control the Specular value at the most intense point in the Bump texture. Since we used a negative texture value for the Bump channel, this key will determine the specularity at the bottom of the divot, as that is the most intense point of the texture.

The top key (at the 0.0 position) on this gradient will control the Specular value at the least intense point in the Bump texture. With this Bump texture, that will be anything that's not in a divot.

5. If you look at the Basic tab in the Surface Editor, you'll see that we set the Specularity to 20%. So click on the first key in this gradient and give it a Value of **20%**. Now click on the last key in the gradient (at 1.0) and give it a Value of **0%**. This will cause the specularity to be 20% over the entire surface of the orange. But when the surface begins to dip into a divot, the specularity will diminish, eventually falling off to 0.

If you want to get a better idea of how this effect is working, increase the Value for the first key to 100%. Then drag the bottom key up to about the halfway point. If you look at the results in the VIPER preview window, it will be overwhelmingly clear how this gradient works. You can continue tweaking this if you'd like. When you're ready to move on, return the settings to those described above.

Texturing the Peeler

Now let's texture the peeler. As with the bowl, the peeler makes use of ray-traced reflections. Since these don't show up in VIPER, we'll have to use test renders to make sure everything looks right. Currently, our test renders are blown out because we increased the Light Intensity setting of our wall and ceiling lights. Let's reset these to 30% each.

1. Open the Light Properties window and change the Light Intensity for the Wall and Ceiling lights to **30%**. Then close the Light Properties window. In order to get accurate reflections, we need to turn on Ray Trace Reflection. Open the Render | Render Globals window. Activate **Ray Trace Reflection** and ensure that all the remaining Ray Trace options are turned off.

2. Drag the Frame Slider to frame 4 so that the peeler is shown in the frame. Now press <**F9**> to do a test render.

> **Note**
>
> You may notice that your test render for this frame takes a while to complete. That's because the bottle is also in the shot. If you want to temporarily speed up the rendering, you can deactivate the Fast Fresnel shader for this surface and set its base Reflection Value to 0. This will disable reflection for this surface and in turn speed up the render. Just be sure to reactivate these settings when you're through.

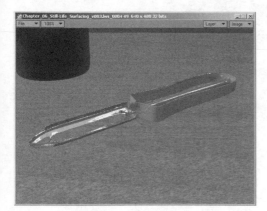

Figure 6-99: Drag the Frame Slider to frame 4. Enable Ray Trace Reflection and press <F9> to do a test render.

3. It's not bad, but it could benefit from the Fresnel effect to help modulate the reflection. Click on the **Peeler.Blade** surface in the Surface Editor. Click on the Shaders tab and add the **Fast Fresnel** shader. Activate Reflectivity and Diffuse, but turn all the other options off. Set the Reflectivity value to **90%** and the Diffuse value to **10%**. Then copy this surface and paste it onto the **Peeler.Handle**, **Peeler.Pole**, and **Peeler.Pole_Ball** surfaces.

4. Press <F9> to do another render.

The Fast Fresnel shader really helped the reflections, but there's still something that's not quite right. The reflections are almost too pure. They don't look quite right. The reason for this is that most metal has tiny imperfections that cause the reflections to spread out. There are a variety of ways to do this. You can add a Turbulence procedural texture to the Bump channel of the surface. By giving it a high Small Power and a very small Scale (around 1 mm or less for X, Y, and Z), you can simulate these imperfections. You can also use a post-processing filter (discussed in Chapter 7). But an easy way to accomplish this is to add a

small amount of Reflection Blurring to the surface.

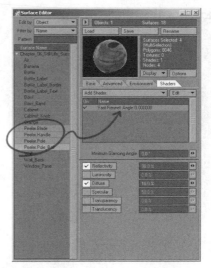

Figure 6-100: Add the Fast Fresnel shader to the Peeler.Blade surface. Set the Reflectivity to 90% and the Diffuse to 10%. Then copy this surface to the remaining Peeler surfaces.

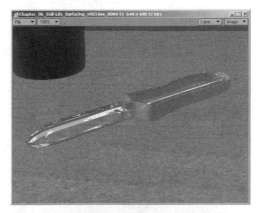

Figure 6-101: Do another test render. You can see that adding the Fast Fresnel shader helped bring out the reflections, especially on the blade.

5. High amounts of Reflection Blurring can drastically increase your rendering time, but lower amounts can produce good results without taking all day to render. Click on the **Peeler.Blade** surface. Then click on the Environment tab. Increase Reflection Blurring to

30%. Copy this surface and paste it onto the other peeler surfaces.

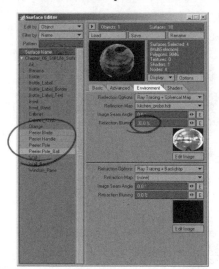

Figure 6-102: Add 30% Reflection Blurring to each of the peeler surfaces.

6. Press <**F9**> to do another test render. If you've got a little extra time, go ahead and enable Ray Trace Shadows in the Render Globals window as well.

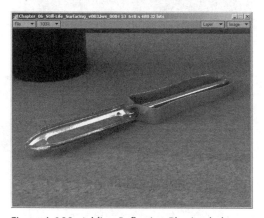

Figure 6-103: Adding Reflection Blurring helps soften the reflections, creating a more realistic-looking surface. Here, Ray Trace Shadows has been enabled to show you how great our metal surface really looks!

Adding the Reflection Blurring really makes a noticeable difference! (The soft ray-traced shadows from the area lights don't hurt either!) We've now got a great-looking metal surface. Let's move on to the back wall and we'll wrap up this tutorial.

Texturing the Back Wall

We're nearly done with our still life. The last thing to do is enhance the look of the back wall. Currently, the wall has two noticeable problems. The first is that its texture is perfectly smooth. The second is that its color is perfectly flat. Most walls have some amount of texture that breaks up their surface. They also tend to have slight color variations from day-to-day wear and tear. Let's add these effects.

1. We're going to use VIPER again, and the preview is going to be dark. So open the Light Properties window and increase the Light Intensity setting for the Wall and Ceiling lights to **100%.**

2. Drag the Frame Slider back to frame 7. This is a close-up shot of the wall so that we can see the fine details. Make sure the VIPER window is enabled. If you've enabled any of the Ray Trace options, turn them off in the Render | Render Globals window. Then press <**F9**> to perform a test render.

3. Close the Render Status window and the Image Viewer window. Bring up the VIPER preview window and click on the **Wall_Back** surface. So far it's nothing but a flat, dark red color. Open the Bump Texture Editor.

4. Change the default layer to a **Turbulence** procedural texture. Leave the Blending Mode set to **Normal** and the Layer Opacity at **100%.** Change the Texture Value to **60%.** Leave Frequencies at **3** and Contrast at **0%.**

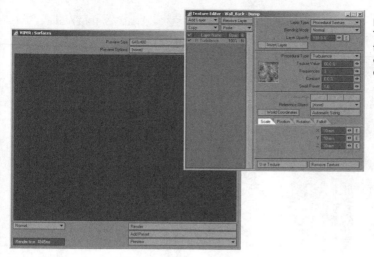

Figure 6-104: Add a Turbulence procedural texture to the Bump channel of the Wall_Back surface and change the settings.

Increase the Small Power to **1.0** and set the Scale for X, Y, and Z to **10 mm**.

5. Click on the **Use Texture** button to close the Bump Texture Editor. The texture looks good, but it's a little strong. Back out on the Surface Editor, drop the Bump value down to **30%**. This gives us a very subtle bumpy surface.

> **Note**
>
> Subtlety is often the key to realism. One of the most common mistakes made by new users is exaggerating the settings. This typically results in garish results. You may be tempted to increase the Bump amount until it's overwhelmingly noticeable. While there's nothing wrong with increasing the setting to suit your taste, if you're aiming for realism, you'll achieve better results by practicing restraint and adding subtle details. While the eye may not consciously notice them, the brain will unconsciously register them, especially when they're absent (at one end of the extreme) or exaggerated (at the other).

6. Now let's add some color variation. Open the Color Texture Editor and change the default layer to a **Turbulence** procedural texture. Leave the Blending Mode set to **Normal** and the Layer Opacity at **100%**.

7. Set the RGB to **074, 019, 019**. This is a slightly darker red than we're currently using for our wall. Leave Frequencies at **3**. Change Contrast to **–65%** and increase Small Power to **2.0**. Then set the Scale for X, Y, and Z to **10 mm**. (See Figure 6-105.)

You'll notice that the color for the wall is now speckled as if it's had a sponge paint coat applied. The variation in color comes from the use of a negative number in the Contrast field. Negative Contrast values will coat your surface with an overall wash of color while letting speckled areas of light and dark poke through. This can be very effective at "dirtying up" a surface. If you feel like the surface is too speckled and you'd prefer a more subtle "wear and tear" look, simply lower Small Power to **1.0**. This will generate less detail for the texture and produce fewer speckles.

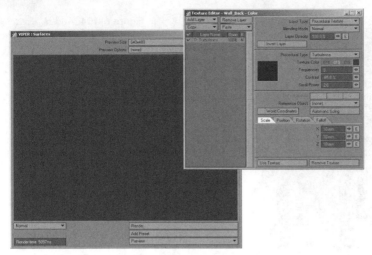

Figure 6-105: Add a Turbulence procedural texture to the Color channel of the Wall_Back surface and change the settings.

8. Click on the **Use Texture** button to close the Color Texture Editor. The surfacing and texturing of our still life is now complete. Close the VIPER preview window and disable VIPER in the Render tab. Then reset the Light Intensity for the Ceiling and Wall lights back to **30%**. Finally, drag the Frame Slider back to frame 0.

9. In order to ensure that we don't lose our work, we must now save the object. Remember that surface settings are saved with the object, not the scene. Activate Objects selection mode by clicking the button at the bottom of the screen. This ensures that we can save the currently selected object.

> **Note**
>
> Always remember that your surface settings are saved with your object! There's nothing like investing an entire day fine-tuning your surface settings and textures, only to lose them because you didn't save your object (or wrongly assumed they would be saved with your scene file).

10. Click the **File | Save | Save Current Object** menu option. Give this finished object the name **Chapter_06_Still-Life_Final.lwo**.

11. Since we saved our object with a new name, we must also save our scene. Click the **File | Save | Save Scene As** menu option. Call this new scene **Chapter_06_Still-Life_Final.lws**.

You can find the final surfaced and textured object and scene files on the book's companion DVD.

12. Let's render this scene so you can show off your hard work. Open the Render | Render Globals window. Activate all of the Ray Trace options. Then lower Ray Recursion Limit to **8**. Finally, enable the **Volumetric Lights** option at the bottom of the Render tab.

13. Activate Cameras selection mode and click on the **Properties** button to open the Camera Properties window. Make sure Resolution is set to **640x480** (or higher). If you've got the time, turn on Antialiasing. Nine-pass PLD should produce a good render without taking all day.

Figure 6-106: Save your object and scene. Adjust the Render Global settings as described above and add 9-Pass antialiasing in your Camera Properties window. Then press <F9> to render. Your results should look like this.

14. Close the Camera Properties window and press <**F9**> to render your final still life image.

Conclusion

We've covered a lot of ground in this chapter, but believe it or not, we've only scratched the surface of what you can do in LightWave! You may have had little or no experience with surfacing when you started this chapter. But by now, you should have enough experience with primary attributes, textures, and shaders to take on your own surfacing projects. (A good way to hone your skills would be to surface the LightBot you created in Chapter 3.)

If you need more practice, go back through the relevant portions of this chapter. Take time to experiment and play. When you're ready, move on to the next chapter (the last in our Basic Skills section) where we'll learn the secrets of great rendering!

Chapter 7

Basic Skills: Rendering

Over the previous six chapters we've explored the LightWave interface, learned the basics of 3D modeling, delved into the art of 3D filmmaking, studied the basic properties of light, and examined how to give our objects unique surface properties. In this chapter we'll wrap up our Basic Skills section with a look at the fine art of rendering.

We've touched on some of the concepts of rendering earlier. But in this chapter, we'll go further by looking at the key options that affect your final image. In the process, you'll see how to work smarter, not harder, to achieve great results in less time. Let's begin by explaining just what we mean by the term "rendering."

What Is Rendering?

Rendering is the process of transferring what LightWave's camera sees to a digital image that can be saved to your hard drive. It is the equivalent of snapping the shutter of a camera to capture a still picture or pressing the Record button on a video camera to capture a moving sequence.

In the strictest terms, rendering is an activity performed by the computer. But when we talk about rendering in LightWave, we're typically referring to one of three different things:

- Preparing an image to be rendered.
- Initiating the rendering process.
- Waiting while LightWave generates images for us.

Once you initiate the rendering process, there's not much to do but sit back and wait while LightWave generates your images.

Therefore, it may not seem like there's much you need to know about the rendering process. But the truth is there's more to rendering than sipping coffee and watching the computer chew through your scene. The work you do *preparing* a scene to be rendered (which I call the "art of rendering") has a tremendous impact on the overall quality of your final image and the time it takes LightWave to produce it.

Take a look at Figure 7-1. The image on the top looks nearly identical to the one on the bottom; however, the render times are anything but equal. The image on the top took 26 minutes to render. The one on the bottom only took 13 minutes. So how did I get the image on the bottom to render in half the time while still maintaining the overall image quality? Would you believe all it took was adjusting a single setting?

Figure 7-1: Your rendering options can have a tremendous impact on the time it takes for LightWave to generate an image.

It's not uncommon for users to suffer from unnecessarily long render times. That's why the art of rendering is so important. In the real world of deadlines, knowing how to gain control over your renders can make or break your career. If you can produce the same caliber of work as the guy down the street, but you can knock it out in half the time, who do you think the client will hire?

Before we get into the nuts and bolts of rendering, let's address a rather obvious question: How do you actually render something?

Initiating a Render

It's always easier to learn something when you have a concrete example to work from. So before we go any further, let's load a scene from the DVD.

1. Open the scene called **Chapter_07_ Still-Life-Spots.lws**. This is a variant of the finished still life scene from Chapter 6.

2. To initiate a render, simply press one of the four buttons found in the **Render | Render** menu. Each of these buttons allows you to start a different type of render.

Figure 7-2: Open the Chapter_07_Still-Life-Spots.lws scene from the DVD. You can initiate a render by clicking on one of the Render options found in the Render tab.

- **Render Frame** (<F9>) will render a still image from the current camera. (If you have multiple cameras in your scene, the last camera you selected will be used for your render.) The frame to be rendered is determined by the location of the Frame Slider in your scene. The Render Frame option is the most common rendering option and is often referred to as an "F9 render" after its keyboard shortcut. It is ideal for generating quick test renders as well as finished images.

- **Render Scene** (<F10>) will render a range of images from the current camera. The range can be set in the Render Globals window. This is the second most common rendering option and is typically used for rendering animations (such as AVI or QuickTime) and image sequences (such as TGA or TIFF for use in a compositing application).

- **Sel Object** (<F11>) will render just the selected object from the current camera on the frame indicated by the Frame Slider. While not as common as <F9> and <F10> renders, this option is useful for generating tests with specific objects. (Multiple selection of objects is allowed.) For example, if you have an object with detailed procedural textures applied to it (such as

the cabinet in this scene), you can test various levels of antialiasing (see Chapter 4) without having to wait for LightWave to calculate the other objects in your scene.

- **MB Preview** (<Shift>+<F9>) will generate a preview of your camera's Motion Blur and Depth of Field settings. Unlike the previous three rendering options, MB Preview will not generate an image that can be saved to disk. Rather, the results of this option will appear in your camera's OpenGL viewport. (See Chapter 4 for an explanation of how to use the MB Preview render.)

3. Move the Frame Slider to frame 0 and press <F9> to initiate a still frame render. When you initiate one of the main render types (Render Frame, Render Sequence, or Sel Object), the Render Status window will appear.

The Render Status Window

The Render Status window provides you with valuable information on the status of your render. Let's take a look at the information provided in this window.

Figure 7-3: The Render Status window gives you valuable information about the current render, including the options you've set and an estimated time to complete the frame or animation.

Note

When you initiate a render, LightWave will examine the various parameters you've set. If it sees a potential issue, it will warn you and provide options on how to proceed. For example, if you attempt to render a still frame but haven't told LightWave how to display the final image, you will be asked whether or not you want to enable Image Viewer. There are several different warnings that can pop up, depending on your circumstances. In most cases you can simply accept LightWave's recommendation and trust that the program is looking out for your best interest.

The Render Status window is split into two halves. The top half provides information about the current frame being rendered. The bottom half provides information about the specific rendering options that have been enabled.

Figure 7-4: The top portion of the Render Status window gives information about the current frame being rendered.

The first line at the top of the Render Status window provides details about the frame being rendered. We can see that we are currently rendering frame 0.

This frame will render as a single segment. If the memory required to render this frame exceeds the amount set in the Render Globals window, LightWave will split the render into smaller segments and stitch the results together at the end to form a single image.

To the right of the segment display, we can see the current/total number of antialiasing passes. (We discussed antialiasing in Chapter 4 and we'll touch on it again later in this chapter.) If antialiasing is enabled in the Camera Properties window, the frame will be rendered in multiple passes to smooth out jagged edges. In this case, antialiasing has not been enabled, so only the first pass is rendered.

I can see that there are currently 63,756 points and 98,076 polygons being rendered on this frame, and that 14.6 MB of RAM is required.

The second line on the Render Status window tells us what LightWave is processing at any given time. When the render is finished, this will display "Frame completed."

The third line in the Render Status window provides us with a readout of the elapsed time and the frame time remaining. This information is updated in real time, giving you a good estimate of how long it will take to see the finished image.

The fourth line indicates the last frame that was successfully rendered and how long it took to render it. This number can be useful for comparing render times when testing various rendering options such as shadows, reflections, and motion blur.

Below the written information in the top half of the Render Status window is a progress bar, which graphically depicts the status of each frame.

The lower half of the Render Status window provides a wealth of information about the advanced rendering options that have been enabled. This allows you to easily ascertain whether or not an option is active without having to cancel the render and check the settings.

We'll take a more detailed look at the main options listed here later in the chapter. For now, the only thing I want you to note is the shade of the display text. The color of the text in this portion of the Render Status window is context sensitive, just like Modeler's Statistics panel. When an option is disabled, it is listed in light gray. When it is enabled, it is listed in black.

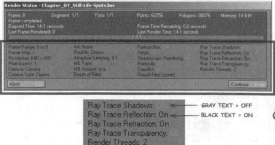

Advance is turned off, Preview is turned off, and Render Display is set to **Image Viewer**. Then close the Render Globals window.

Figure 7-5: The lower half of the Render Status window gives detailed information on the advanced rendering options in use.

At the bottom of the Render Status window are two buttons, Abort and Continue. During the rendering process, only the Abort button will be active. You can click the Abort button at any time to cancel a render in progress.

If your render has completed, both the Abort and Continue buttons will be active. For single frame renders (Render Frame or Sel Object), both buttons will produce the same results by exiting the Render Status window.

4. Click on the **Abort** button to exit the Render Status window. The finished image should be visible in the Image Viewer. Minimize this window for now but don't close it.

Render Status for Sequences

When rendering a sequence, the Render Status window provides nearly identical information to that which is offered for single frame renders. However, there are a few notable differences.

1. Click on the **Render** menu tab and open up the Render Globals window. We'll take a detailed look at the options in this window later in this chapter. For now, make sure that Auto Frame

Figure 7-6: Disable Auto Frame Advance and Preview in the Render Globals window, but leave Image Viewer on.

2. Press <**F10**> to initiate an image sequence render for this scene, then look at the Render Status window.

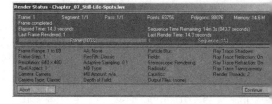

Figure 7-7: The Render Status window offers additional information when rendering an image sequence or animation.

Rather than displaying the frame time remaining, the top half of the Render Status window now provides information on how long it will take to finish rendering the entire sequence.

The progress bar for a sequence is also different. Rather than a single bar, we now have two. The one on the left indicates the progress of the current frame being rendered. The one on the right indicates the progress of the entire sequence.

When rendering a sequence, the functions of the Abort and Continue buttons become a little clearer. Clicking Abort cancels any render currently in progress. If your current frame has finished rendering, clicking Abort exits the Render Status window. Clicking Continue causes LightWave to render the next frame in the sequence.

3. Click on the **Abort** button to exit the Render Status window once the first frame of this sequence finishes

rendering. The Image Viewer will display the results of the render.

Note

You may be wondering if you have to click Continue after each image in order to render a complete sequence. You don't. LightWave will *automatically* advance to the next frame as it renders when Auto Frame Advance is enabled in the Render Globals window. I deliberately had you turn this option off so that there was actually a purpose for the Continue button. In most cases (especially when rendering image sequences), you'll want to make sure this option is turned on.

Let's take a look at the Image Viewer, LightWave's powerful display utility.

Image Viewer

When you render an image, it will typically appear in LightWave's default display utility known as Image Viewer. There's more to this little utility than meets the eye, and in this section we'll look at some of the cool things you can do with it.

You should already have the first frame of the scene displayed in the Image Viewer window.

The first and most obvious function of the Image Viewer is to display pictures. You can get detailed information about the image you're viewing simply by looking at Image Viewer's title bar.

The first bit of information gives us the name of the scene that we're working on. In this case, it's Chapter_07_Still-Life-Spots.lws. The underscore and the number that follows give us

the frame number we've rendered (using a four-digit numbering system). So 0000 is frame 0. Frame 1 would be 0001, frame 2 would be 0002, etc.

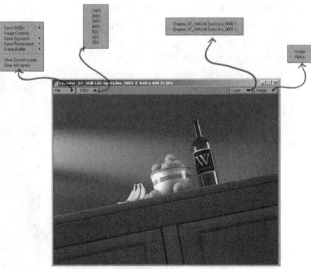

Figure 7-8: The Image Viewer utility allows you to view images, compare renders, and save files in a variety of formats.

To the right of the frame number is the layer number. Image Viewer can hold multiple images in its buffer, making it particularly useful for comparing different renders. In this case, since we've rendered two images (the first with <F9> and the second with <F10>), the layer number is 2.

Next to the layer number is the physical dimension of the image. Here, the render is 640 x 480 (as shown in Figure 7-8). And the last bit of information in the title bar is the bit depth of the image. Here, we're viewing a 24-bit image with an 8-bit alpha channel, giving us a 32-bit image.

Below the title bar are four pop-up menus. The one on the far left is the File menu. From this menu you can save your images, adjust the size and exposure of your image, transfer the image to a display buffer (for viewing on an external monitor), and clear layers from memory.

Let's take a look at how to save an image.

1. Click on the **File** pop-up menu. The first option is Save RGBA. This allows you to save the current image as an RGB with an optional 8-bit alpha channel. Common formats include JPEG, PSD, PNG, and TIFF. You can even save your file as a high-dynamic range image by

choosing the Radiance format. This format allows you to save your image in the full 128-bit range rather than the more common 32-bit range of standard RGB files. The Radiance format can be a good choice for still images as it allows you to adjust the overall exposure of your image without losing valuable image data.

I typically save my renders in the LW_PNG32(.png) or LW_PShop32(.psd) format. The PShop32 format is a Photoshop file with an alpha channel for portions of your image that don't contain geometry. The PNG32 format provides the same functionality, but it automatically applies the alpha channel to the image, thereby making any "blank" areas of your scene (where there is no geometry) transparent. This is a great format to use for flying logos or illustrations that will be composited in an application like Photoshop or After Effects.

In our scene, there are no major blank areas, so saving in either format would produce the same basic results. If you're not sure what constitutes a "blank" area, you can check the alpha channel that LightWave saves with its 32-bit images.

Figure 7-9: Click the File pop-up menu and choose one of the formats under the Save RGBA menu to save your render.

2. Click on the **Image** pop-up menu and choose the **Alpha** option.

Figure 7-10: Click the Image pop-up menu and choose Alpha to see the alpha channel that will be saved with any 32-bit file.

Most of the image is white, indicating that these areas are completely opaque. But if you look closely, you can see a few small dots of black around the bottle where there is heavy refraction.

3. Switch back to the RGB image by clicking the pop-up button again and choosing **Image**.

Suppose you want to inspect some of the detail in this image or scale down an image that's larger than the current window size. You can do this with the options in the Resolution pop-up menu. Currently, this menu shows 100%, indicating that we're viewing the image at its actual size.

4. Click the pop-up menu and set the size to **400%**. You'll notice that the size of the Image Viewer window did not change, but that the image within the window is now four times as large. There are no slider bars on this window, but that doesn't mean you can't pan around the image.

Figure 7-11: Click the Resolution pop-up menu and choose 400% to zoom in on the details of your image.

5. Press and hold the <Alt> key on your keyboard and then click and drag within the Image Viewer window. The image will pan within the Image Viewer window. Pan around your image until the top of the bottle comes into view.

Note

If you'd like to make the window larger or smaller, you can simply grab one of the outside edges of the window and click-drag it to resize it.

You may have noticed that if you click and drag in the Image Viewer window without pressing the <Alt> key modifier, you get a strange-looking cursor and a bunch of numbers in the Image Viewer title bar.

Figure 7-12: <Alt>+click and drag to pan around images that are larger than the current window size. Click and drag without <Alt> to get information about the pixels in your image.

The first two numbers represent the X and Y position of your cursor within the overall image. The last four numbers represent the red, green, blue, and alpha values of the pixel directly under your mouse. This can be extremely helpful for sampling a particular color so that you can note its RGB, but it's also helpful for noting the alpha value of any pixel in your image.

6. Click and drag around your image. You can see that in most cases, the alpha value is 255, or pure white. But if you click and drag over the lip of the bottle, you'll notice that the alpha drops down around 20. At 0, the alpha would be completely black, yielding 100% transparency in the alpha channel. At 20, the pixel is nearly transparent, but it still retains a degree of opacity.

Note that the RGBA values range from 0 to 255, which are the limits for a standard 32-bit file (24-bit color plus an 8-bit alpha). LightWave doesn't calculate color in 32 bits — it calculates it at a whopping 128 bits! You can access renders in this bit range and even make adjustments to them (although your monitor will still be limited to

displaying in 24 bits). Let's take a look at how to do this.

7. Open the Render Globals window from the **Render | Options** menu. Click the **Render Display** pop-up menu and change it from Image Viewer to **Image Viewer FP.** This allows you to use a floating-point version of Image Viewer and access a wider dynamic range.

Figure 7-13: Changing your Render Display setting to Image Viewer FP allows you to examine and process your renders in their full 128-bit dynamic range.

8. Close the Render Globals window and drag the Frame Slider to frame 1. Then press <**F9**> to render. When your render finishes, the display will pop back to 100% and your finished image will appear. It may not look like much has changed, but if you look at the title bar, you'll notice that the image we're seeing is available in 128 bits. You'll also notice that your layer number dropped back to 1. Or did it?

9. Click on the **Layer** pop-up menu. You'll see three layers listed. The layer number appears at the far right of the

list. You'll see a 1, a 2, and a 1 again. Image Viewer keeps a running list of the images in its buffers and it delineates between 32-bit images and 128-bit images. We have two 32-bit images, which are listed first. Then we have a 128-bit image. It's listed last, but its layer number is 1 because it's the first 128-bit image we've rendered.

Figure 7-14: The Layer pop-up menu lists all the renders Image Viewer is storing in memory. The 32-bit images are listed first, followed by 128-bit images.

You don't have to click the Layer menu to flip through the images in Image Viewer's buffer. If the window has focus (meaning it's been selected), you can use the Page Up and Page Down keys on your keyboard to cycle through your renders.

Using Page Up and Page Down is a great way to compare two different images. But let's look at another nifty feature of Image Viewer for comparing images. First, let's get an image that's significantly changed from frame 0.

10. Drag your Frame Slider to frame 60 and press <F9> to render. You should now have two images stored at 128 bits.

11. Click on the **File** menu and choose the **Image Controls** option. A small window will open, containing a list of the images Image Viewer is storing in memory.

> **Note**
>
> It's important to note that Image Viewer holds renders in a temporary buffer. If you close Image Viewer, these images will be lost. Make sure you save any renders you want to keep before closing Image Viewer.

This window (shown in Figure 7-15) is similar to Modeler's Layers palette. The FG and BG columns represent foreground and background images. By default, the current image is the foreground image and it will have a check in the FG column. You can also designate a background image by clicking in the BG column next to its name.

12. Click the BG column next to the first 128-bit image (directly above the currently selected FG image). Once you have a foreground and background

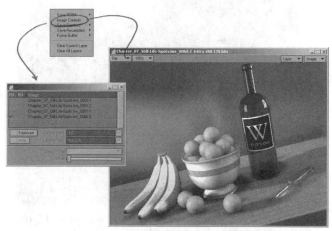

Figure 7-15: The Image Controls window lets you compare two images and adjust the exposure of 128-bit renders.

image, the Blend Mode pop-up menu at the bottom of the window will become active.

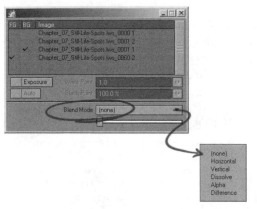

Figure 7-16: The Blend Mode pop-up menu lets you determine how to blend the foreground and background images.

13. The Blend Mode menu is currently set to (none), indicating that there is no blending between the foreground and background. Click this menu and choose **Horizontal**. Doing so activates the Blend slider.

The Blend slider determines what amount of each image is shown. When the slider is all the way to the left, only the foreground image will be shown. At the halfway point, both the foreground and background images will be visible. When the slider is all the way to the right, only the background image will be displayed.

Try out the other blending modes to get a feel for how they work. These options can be very useful in comparing differences in lighting, color, and camera composition.

14. Click on the 128-bit image for frame 60 in the Image Controls list to make it the foreground image and uncheck any background image. When you're working with 128-bit images, the Exposure option becomes available. Clicking the **Exposure** box activates the controls that allow you to change the White Point and Black Point settings (Figure 7-18).

By altering the white and black points, you can adjust the dynamic range of your renders. And because the changes are happening at a higher bit rate, your image won't suffer from the "clipping" that normally accompanies continued image adjustments at lower bit depths.

Figure 7-17: The Blend slider determines the amount of foreground and background images that are visible.

Figure 7-18: When working with 128-bit images, you can enable the Exposure controls to adjust the dynamic range of your renders.

Note

If you've ever adjusted the levels for an image in a program like Photoshop, you're probably aware of the clipping that can happen when you alter a picture's dynamic range. Repeated adjustments can create a posterized effect on your images. But by working in a higher bit depth, you can adjust your range at will without fear of negative impacts on the final picture.

Our render has a decent dynamic range, but let's punch it up a bit just to see how the Exposure controls work.

15. Activate the Exposure controls. Lower White Point to **0.85**. This will brighten the image. Then increase Black Point to **150%**. This will darken the image. The net effect is an increase in the overall contrast of our render.

16. Once you've adjusted the range of your image, click and drag around the Image Viewer window and note the numbers that appear in the title bar.

If you recall, our 32-bit images listed our pixel color as an integer ranging from 0 to 255. But when we're dealing with floating-

point images at 128 bits, the pixels are not listed as integers but rather as percentages.

17. Click and drag over the white highlight hitting the left side of the bowl. You'll notice that the pixels here exceed 100%. When you see values over 100%, it means that there is additional information in the image and even though your monitor is showing it as white, there is information here that you can access by tinkering with the Exposure controls.

Figure 7-19: The pixel colors displayed for a floating-point image are listed as percentages rather than integers.

18. Change the Black Point setting to **1000%**. At 1000%, the lower-right corner of the image appears black, as shown in Figure 7-20. But if you click and drag over this portion of the cabinet, you'll notice that the percentage is not 0 — it's in the 10s and 20s. Your 24-bit video card cannot display the full spectrum of the color and brightness in this image, but that information is still there and can be brought out via the Exposure controls.

19. Set Black Point back to **150%** and close the Image Controls window.

If we want to save this adjusted image, we can using the Save Exposed command.

Click on the **File** menu and choose the **Save Exposed** option. Then choose an appropriate file format.

Hopefully, you're beginning to see what a powerful tool the Image Viewer can be. Let's take a quick look at a few of the other options in the File menu before moving on.

If you're happy with your image but want to save it out at a larger or smaller size, you can do so using the **Save Resampled** command. You have the option to save in all of the formats available with Save RGBA and Save Exposed. But after choosing a format and giving the file a name, LightWave will pop up a Resample Image window, as shown in Figure 7-21.

Figure 7-20: Even though an image may appear as pure white or pure black, checking it in Image Viewer will tell you whether there's additional information in the render that can be brought out with the Exposure controls.

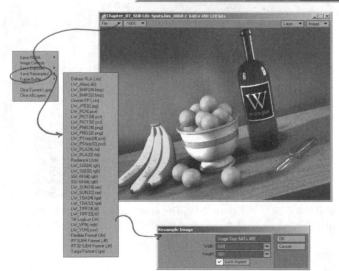

Figure 7-21: Save Resampled allows you to save your image at a different size than its original render.

You can see the original image size along with fields for adjusting the width and the height. If the **Lock Aspect** option is checked, a change to one field will automatically result in a change to the other.

> **Note**
>
> Keep in mind that LightWave's fields can perform basic math. If you want an image that's half the size of your current render, simply type "/2" for the Width, make sure Lock Aspect is turned on, and hit the Tab key. The width of your image will be divided in half. If you want to scale your image up, use an asterisk (*) followed by the amount you want to enlarge the image.

If you have an external monitor, you can send one of your images to it using the controls in the File | Frame Buffer menu. (This can be helpful for checking how your renders will look on TV rather than a computer monitor.) You can also use the options in this menu to display images and renders in one of LightWave's viewports. We'll take a look at how to do this later in the chapter.

The last two options in the File menu allow you to clear images from Image Viewer's buffer. You have the option to clear the current layer or to wipe out all layers.

That's it for our look at Image Viewer. And you probably thought it was only good for viewing pictures!

Render Globals Window

We've touched on some of the options in the Render Globals window in other chapters. In this section we'll take a more detailed look and discuss how the settings here can help give you full control over your renders.

> **Note**
>
> You'll be accessing the Render Globals window often as you work. For this reason, I highly recommend assigning a keyboard shortcut for it. I typically assign it to <Ctrl> +<F10>, which reminds me that I'm "controlling" the "F10" render options. (See Chapter 2 for a refresher on how to assign keyboard shortcuts.)

There are so many options in this panel that it may seem overwhelming, so before we get into the meat of it, let's try to make sense of what we're looking at.

The settings in the Render Globals window can be broken down from top to bottom into four distinct sections. The first section controls which frames to render.

The second section controls how frames are displayed during and after a render. The third section controls the global camera settings. And the fourth section controls the advanced render settings.

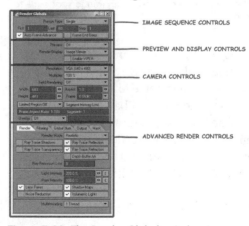

Figure 7-22: The Render Globals window is broken down into four distinct sections.

Let's take a detailed look at each of these sections.

Image Sequence Controls

When you press <F10>, LightWave will render your scene. But how do you define the length of your scene? And what if you only want specific frames to be rendered? The options in this section allow you to address these and other issues.

• The first option here is **Range Type**. The available settings are **Single**, **Arbitrary**, and **Keyframe**.

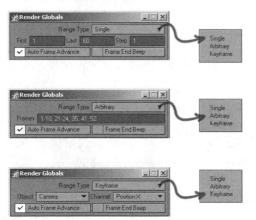

Figure 7-23: The Range Type options let you determine which frames in an image sequence to render.

Single is the most common Range Type setting. It allows you to define a simple range from one frame to another as indicated by the First and Last frame fields.

The **Step** field determines which frames in the range will be rendered. When Step is set to 1, each frame will be rendered. When Step is set to 2, every other frame will be rendered. When Step is set to 3, every third frame will be rendered, and so on.

> **Note**
>
> Here's an old (but useful) rendering trick for you. By inverting the range (i.e., First Frame = 60 and Last Frame = 1) and setting the Step to –1, you can make LightWave render the sequence in reverse.

Setting the Range Type to **Arbitrary** allows you to specify any combination of single frames and frame ranges to render. This can be particularly useful when you only want to render specific portions of your scene, such as the beginning and the ending but not the middle. Each frame or range must be separated by a comma. For example, Figure 7-23 shows that we have chosen to render frames 1 through 10, 21 through 24, and 35, 41, and 52.

Setting the Range Type to **Keyframe** allows you to render only the frames that have keys set for a specific object. This can be useful for rendering storyboards that depict how your object will change at key intervals throughout an animation.

The **Object** pop-up menu allows you to select the item whose key frames will be used to determine the frames to render. The **Channel** pop-up menu allows you to select the channel (typically one of the Position, Rotation, or Scale channels) on which to look for key frames.

• Below the Range Type controls are two options: **Auto Frame Advance** and **Frame End Beep**. Auto Frame Advance allows you to render an image sequence or animation without having to click Continue after each frame completes. Frame End Beep causes your system to produce an audible "beep" when each frame finishes rendering.

The Frame End Beep is a useful but annoying feature that I normally turn off. But thanks to Jon Tindall/Binary Arts, I'm now getting plenty of use from this option. Jon released a clever little plug-in (PC only) that lets you change the default "beep" to any sound file you like. Now you can have Homer Simpson (or even Jessica Simpson) alert you to the fact that your render is finished. Jon was kind enough to allow us to include this plug-in on the book's companion DVD. See Chapter 27 for more information on this delightful utility.

Preview and Display Controls

The options in this section allow you to see how your render looks while it's being rendered and after it has finished rendering.

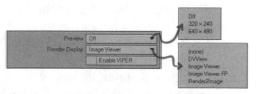

Figure 7-24: The Preview and Render Display options allow you to see how your render looks while it's being rendered and after it's completed rendering.

The Preview pop-up menu allows you to activate a display window that will appear at the bottom of the Render Status window. The size of the preview window can be set in this pop-up menu.

The Preview option is extremely useful in the early stages of development when you're working out lighting and surfacing issues. Rather than waiting for an entire frame to finish, you can see it being rendered right before your eyes.

Using this feature will slow down your render slightly, but the benefits are often worth it, especially on lengthy renders. There's nothing like waiting 45 minutes for a single frame to complete, only to realize that something is not as it should be. Using the Preview option allows you to catch problems early on. When you're sure everything is set properly and you're ready to render your final animation, it's best to turn this feature off.

The Render Display option allows you to determine how your image is displayed

after it is rendered. If you're rendering a still frame, it's best to turn this option on. (If this option is set to (none) and you attempt to render a still image, LightWave will prompt you with a warning and ask you if you'd like to enable Image Viewer.) If you're rendering a finished animation, you'll likely want to turn this off as it will unnecessarily slow down your render.

The options in this pop-up menu allow you to turn off the display (none), send it to a third-party DV display device (DVView), display it using LightWave's Image Viewer (Image Viewer FP), and render to a temporary image buffer for use with the Visor tool (Render2Image).

The last option in this section allows you to enable or disable VIPER. This option performs the same function as that found in the Render | Options menu on the main interface. Turning it on will cause the next <F9> render to be captured into VIPER's buffer. This option will slow down your render slightly, so make sure it is turned off before rendering an entire animation.

Camera Controls

The next section in the Render Globals window contains global camera controls. For the most part, the options here are identical to the ones found in the Camera Properties window. (See Chapter 4 if you need a refresher on these options.) You can set the size of the rendered frame from a set of presets using the Resolution pop-up menu. You can scale the presets up or down using the Multiplier pop-up menu. You can enable or disable Field Rendering with its respective pop-up menu. And you have controls for independently setting the width and height as well as the pixel aspect and frame aspect ratios.

CAMERA PROPERTIES

RENDER GLOBALS

Figure 7-25: The camera controls in the Render Globals window are virtually the same as those found in the Camera Properties window. The only difference between the two is the addition of the Limited Region, Segment Memory Limit, and Overlay controls.

Since the camera controls appear in two places, you might be wondering which one is the correct one to use. Should you set your options in the Render Globals window or in the Camera Properties window? The answer is simple: *It's up to you*.

I typically use the global camera settings when I'm doing test renders. This allows me to quickly adjust the resolution multiplier when testing out computationally expensive effects like ray tracing, radiosity, or caustics without having to jump back over to the Camera Properties window and adjust it there.

You can also use the Render Globals window to define one master setting that every camera in your scene can use. For example, if you've got multiple cameras, rather than feeding identical settings in for each one, you could configure the Render Globals window and simply check the **Use Global** button in the Camera Properties window.

Don't let the replication of these settings confuse you. They're just there to give you more options and greater flexibility while working. If you find it easier to work with the settings in the Camera Properties window, you can safely ignore the camera settings in the Render Globals window altogether.

One thing to keep in mind about the Render Globals camera settings, however, is that it includes three options not found in the main Camera Properties window: **Limited Region**, **Segment Memory Limit**, and **Overlay**. These settings can be very useful, so let's take a look at what they do.

Limited Region

The Limited Region pop-up menu allows you to render only a portion of the overall image seen by the camera. This is useful for speeding up test renders by only focusing on a small portion of a larger image.

Limited Region has three options: Off, Borders, and No Borders. When turned off, the entire camera frame will be rendered. The Borders option will render the frame at its specified size, but everything outside of the limited region area will be blanked out. The No Borders option will crop the image to the area specified.

When either Limited Region Borders or Limited Region No Borders is active, a

LIMITED REGION OFF

LIMITED REGION BORDERS

LIMITED REGION NO BORDERS

Figure 7-26: The Limited Region options allow you to render a portion of the overall image.

dotted yellow box will appear, surrounding the outside of the frame in the Camera View viewport. Click and drag the sides or corners of the dotted box to adjust the size of the limited region.

You can also activate the Limited Region controls directly from the Render tab under the Options menu. When the Limited Region button is not highlighted, the feature is turned off. The first click on this button will turn on Limited Region Borders. Clicking on it a second time will activate Limited Region No Borders. Clicking it a third time will turn Limited Region off.

Segment Memory Limit

Segment memory is the amount of RAM available to LightWave when rendering each frame above and beyond the amount of RAM used for geometry and image maps. The default value is 32 MB, which should suffice for most purposes.

> **Note**
>
> You can see how much memory each frame requires by looking in the upper-right corner of the Render Status window. See Figure 7-4 for an example.

If you're rendering a high-resolution frame size (such as HD video or print), LightWave may exceed the amount of RAM you've allotted. When this happens, Layout will render the frame in smaller chunks called "segments." Once the entire frame has finished rendering, each segment will be stitched together to form a single image.

Rendering in segments allows you to render extremely large frame sizes;

however, it will increase the time it takes to render each frame.

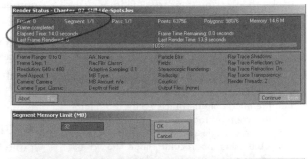

Figure 7-27: Segment memory determines how much RAM LightWave can use during a render. If you don't have enough RAM, LightWave will render in segments, which will increase the time it takes to render each frame.

If you notice that your frame is rendering in multiple segments (as indicated in the Render Status window), you should increase the amount of RAM LightWave can access. You can do this by clicking on the Segment Memory button.

Clicking on the Segment Memory Limit button will pop up a small requester where you can type in a new number representing the megabytes LightWave can use. When you click OK, you will be asked whether or not this should be the new default. If you're working on an odd scene that requires excessive amounts of RAM, you may wish to leave the default as is. In this case, you would respond "No." But if you find that your scenes are frequently rendering in multiple passes, it would be a good idea to set a new default.

Proper management of your Segment Memory Limit settings is one of the subtle tricks to lowering your render times. Make sure that whenever possible, you're only using a single segment for each rendered frame.

> **Note**
>
> Some image filters (which we'll discuss later in this chapter) require the frame to be rendered in a single segment. If you are having trouble using a particular image filter, check to make sure that you're only using one segment for your entire render.

Overlay

The Overlay controls allow you to superimpose text and time/frame information over your rendered frames.

This feature is especially handy when producing test animations, as it allows you to pinpoint specific frames for editing or adjustment. It also allows you to add text such as your studio's name or a copyright notice to each frame.

The Overlay pop-up menu has five options:

- **Off** — This is the default setting. It turns the Overlay feature off. No information will be superimposed over the finished frame.

- **Frame Number** — This will cause the current frame time (registered in frame numbers) to be superimposed in the lower-right corner of the frame.

- **SMPTE Time Code** — This will cause the frame time (registered in hours : minutes : seconds : frames) to be superimposed in the lower-right corner of the frame.

- **Film Key Code** — This will cause the frame time (registered in feet + frames) to be superimposed in the lower-right corner of the frame.

- **Time in Seconds** — This will cause the current frame time (registered in seconds) to be superimposed in the lower-right corner of the frame.

When any of the Overlay options are activated, a field to the right of the Overlay pop-up menu will also be active. Any information you type into this field will be displayed in the lower-left corner of each rendered frame.

Advanced Render Controls

The last section in the Render Globals window deals with advanced render controls. These controls have the greatest impact on how long it takes to render a frame.

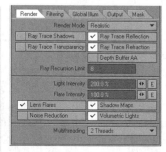

Figure 7-28: The Overlay controls let you superimpose custom text and time information on your finished renders.

Figure 7-29: The advanced render controls occupy the bottom of the Render Globals window and have the greatest impact on how long it takes a frame to render.

The settings in this section are broken down over five tabs:

- **Render** — The settings in this tab control high-end rendering features such as ray tracing, lens flares, and volumetric lights.

- **Filtering** — These settings control the use of antialiasing and motion blur.

- **Global Illum** — These settings control high-end lighting tools such as radiosity and caustics.

- **Output** — These settings control how files are processed when you render a scene.

- **Mask** — These settings enable and control the use of image masking.

Let's take a look at each of these tabs in a little more detail.

Render

The settings found in the Render tab are arguably the most important in the entire Render Globals window. You'll likely find yourself adjusting these settings on a regular basis, so let's take a good look at what's here.

The first setting we encounter is Render Mode (Figure 7-30). This pop-up menu controls the level of detail seen in the final render. There are three modes:

- **Wireframe** — In this mode, all objects will be rendered as wireframe meshes. The color of the wireframe is determined by the base surface color for each object.

- **Quickshade** — In this mode, textures and advanced surface and rendering options (such as smoothing, shadows, and reflections) will be ignored. Each poly

will be rendered as a flat color determined by the surface that is applied to it.

- **Realistic** — This is the default mode. In this mode, all advanced surfacing and rendering options that have been enabled will be used in your render.

Wireframe and Quickshade modes can be extremely useful for testing animations, where the *motion* of items in your scene is more important than their appearance. Wireframe mode can also be useful for producing "technical" looking renders, especially when it's combined with the Realistic mode in a compositing program.

Directly below the Render Mode pop-up menu are the Ray Trace options. Ray tracing allows LightWave to perform high-level calculations to produce realistic-looking shadows and reflections.

We looked at **Ray Trace Shadows**, **Ray Trace Reflection**, and **Ray Trace Refraction** in Chapter 6. These settings are fairly obvious. They allow LightWave to calculate accurate shadows, reflections, and refractions. Be aware that enabling these settings will also cause your render times to soar.

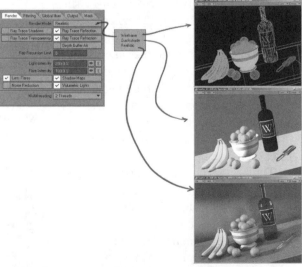

Figure 7-30: The Render Mode pop-up controls the level of detail seen in the final render.

The purpose of **Ray Trace Transparency** sounds fairly obvious; however, in practice, its use is a little more esoteric. You might expect this to be used for calculating transparency. But LightWave will calculate transparency just fine *without* this setting enabled. Instead, this setting allows volumetric effects (which we'll discuss in Chapters 10 and 14) to appear behind transparent surfaces.

Enabling the **Depth Buffer AA** option will cause any antialiasing passes to affect your depth buffer in addition to your final render. The depth buffer is a grayscale image that represents distance from the camera. It can be used to simulate depth of field effects and for compositing layers in an application like After Effects or Fusion.

Figure 7-31: The Ray Recursion Limit setting can have a dramatic impact on your render times.

> **Note**
>
> We'll discuss how to use the depth buffer when we look at the Photoshop PSD Export filter later in this chapter.

Ray Recursion Limit is a simple but powerful setting. It determines how many times a ray will bounce between reflective surfaces. Imagine two mirrors facing each other. The reflection would bounce back and forth into eternity. In the real world, this reflection happens at the speed of light. But in LightWave, each reflection back and forth requires additional rendering time. The Ray Recursion Limit setting tells LightWave to only allow a ray to bounce back and forth off of other reflective surfaces a given number of times.

The default for this setting is 16, and will produce good results in most situations, but it will also create unnecessarily long render times in others. Consider the case mentioned at the beginning of this chapter, which is shown again here in Figure 7-31.

We have two nearly identical images. But one took 13 minutes to render and the other took 26 minutes. By simply lowering the Ray Recursion Limit, I was able to cut my render time in half.

It's best to adjust this setting after everything else in your scene has been completed and you're getting ready to produce your final render. Start off with an extremely low value, such as 2. Then press <F9> to do a test render. Leave the Image Viewer window open, then increase the Ray Recursion Limit and render again. Keep increasing the Ray Recursion Limit until the changes between renders become minimal. Then use the lowest acceptable Ray Recursion Limit to achieve the results you want.

Below the Ray Trace settings are the global lighting settings (shown in Figure 7-32).

Figure 7-32: The light settings on the Render tab allow you to make global adjustments to the lights in your scene.

• **Light Intensity** — This setting allows you to increase or decrease the overall lighting in your scene. If you've set up your lights just the way you want but find that the lighting is a little too hot, you can lower the Light Intensity in the Render Globals window and every light in your scene will decrease in intensity. Conversely, if you find that your image is a little too dark, you can raise this setting and increase the overall lighting.

You'll notice in the Chapter_07_Still-Life-Spots scene that the Light Intensity was set to 200% (see Figure 7-32). This scene was originally lit with area lights in LightWave v9.0, which were a bit brighter than other lights. (The discrepancy in area light intensity has been resolved in LightWave v9.2.) When I switched to spotlights, the overall intensity was lost. Rather than having to tweak each light to compensate, I simply increased the Light Intensity value in the Render Globals window.

• **Flare Intensity** — Lens flares are the visible light sources that appear around selected lights in your scene. (We'll talk more about them in Chapter 10.) Like the Light Intensity setting, the Flare Intensity setting allows you to increase or decrease the brightness of lens flares in your scene.

• **Lens Flares** — This check box globally enables or disables the use of lens flares in your scene.

• **Shadow Maps** — This check box globally enables or disables the use of spotlight shadow maps in your scene.

• **Noise Reduction** — This check box enables or disables the use of Noise Reduction in your scene. When it is enabled, it will apply a smart blur to the Diffuse channel of each of your surfaces. This can help smooth out the noise that results from the use of area lights and radiosity (discussed in

more detail in Chapter 10), but will soften the look of your render.

> **Note**
>
> Lowering the quality of area lights in the Light Properties window and turning on Noise Reduction here in the Render Globals window can be a great way to speed up renders without having a major impact on the overall quality of your image. This is especially true when using a moderate degree of antialiasing, as each pass will help smooth out the blockiness associated with lower light quality levels.

• **Volumetric Lights** — This check box globally enables or disables the use of volumetric lights. In the Chapter_07_Still-Life-Spots scene, a volumetric light is used to cast a swath of visible light from the upper left to the lower right of the screen. While it's a nice effect, it does increase the render time. You can disable all volumetric lights and speed up your renders by unchecking this option.

The last option in the Render tab is Multithreading.

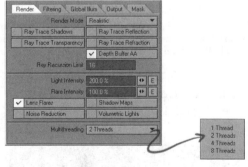

Figure 7-33: The Multithreading pop-up menu allows you to designate the number of CPUs in your system that LightWave will use for rendering.

The **Multithreading** pop-up menu allows you to specify how many CPUs LightWave will use when rendering. LightWave will attempt to automatically set this based on the CPUs it recognizes in your system. But you are free to change it as you see fit.

Some users report that they get better results using two or more threads on a single CPU system. In my experience, this is largely determined by the scene you are working on. In most cases, you can simply leave this at the default setting. But it's worth noting that you may be able to get better performance by using a different number of threads.

Filtering

The options in the Filtering tab allow you to apply a smoothing algorithm to your render to eliminate "jaggies" and refine detailed textures. They also allow you to apply motion blur to your renders.

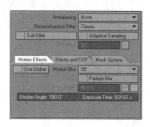

CAMERA PROPERTIES   RENDER GLOBALS

Figure 7-34: The Filtering tab contains Antialiasing and Motion Blur options. These options are identical to those found in the Camera Properties window.

The options in this tab are identical to those found in the Camera Properties window. (See Chapter 4 for an in-depth look at these settings.)

Changing the antialiasing settings in the Render Globals window will automatically apply the same settings to every camera in your scene. Likewise, changing the antialiasing settings for any camera will apply those settings to the Render Globals window.

The only difference between the Camera Properties window and the Render Global | Filtering tab is the Use Global button, as seen in Figure 7-34. When you set Motion Blur options in the Render Globals window, you are defining parameters that can be used by any camera in your scene. But each camera can override these and use custom settings.

If you want to use the Motion Blur settings defined in the Render Globals window, just check the Use Global button in the Camera Properties window. If you want to define your own motion blur settings, simply *uncheck* the Use Global button.

Global Illum

The Global Illum tab contains options for controlling advanced lighting techniques, specifically radiosity (also known as global illumination) and caustics.

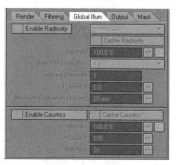

Figure 7-35: The Global Illum tab contains advanced lighting options.

v9.2 Note

Radiosity received a major overhaul in LightWave v9.2. For details on the new global illumination options, check out the Radiosity video in the LightWave 9.2 Videos folder on the companion DVD.

Radiosity allows light to bounce off of objects, causing both color and illumination to bleed onto the environment around them. This is how light behaves in the real world, and as such, renders using radiosity often appear "photo-real." While radiosity renders are beautiful, that beauty comes at the high price of extra-long render times.

Caustics are the visible patterns of light caused by refraction. When you look at the swirling patterns of light at the bottom of a swimming pool, you are seeing caustics.

Since both radiosity and caustics deal with lighting, we'll hold off on discussing them here. Instead we will cover them in more detail in Chapter 10.

Output

The options in the Output tab control how files are saved when you initiate an <F10> (Render Scene) command.

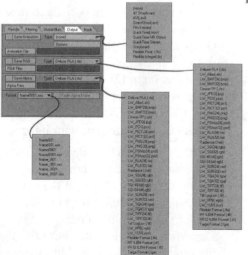

Figure 7-36: The Output tab contains file saving options for rendering scenes.

There are three types of files that you can save (and you can save all three simultaneously if you wish): Save Animation, Save RGB, and Save Alpha.

LightWave is an animation application, so you might think that the Save Animation option is for saving your animations while Save RGB is for saving your stills. But that's not exactly the case. Here, the term "Animation" refers to one file containing all the frames in your scene. (I call these "video" or "movie" files.) The term "RGB" refers to an image sequence where each frame in your scene is saved as a separate file. Both Save Animation and Save RGB are designed to save the rendered frames in your scene. They just differ in how they go about doing so.

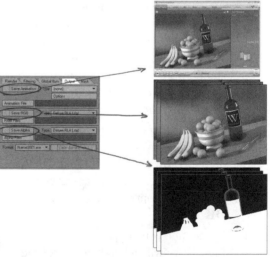

Figure 7-37: Save Animation saves out movie files, Save RGB saves out sequences of images, and Save Alpha saves out sequences of alpha channel images.

The Save Alpha option allows you to save out the transparency information for each frame. This option will only save image sequences.

The process of saving animations, RGBs, or alphas is nearly identical. First you activate the save option. Then you select a file

257

format. And last, you set a filename and save to location. Let's look at how to save out an animation file.

1. Click on the **Save Animation** box so that it is checked. This tells LightWave that we want to save a video file when we render our scene. Now we need to determine what type of video file to create. Click on the **Type** pop-up menu. The most common types are AVI and MOV, but esoteric formats such as QuickTime VR and Flexible Float can also be selected. Choose **QuickTime (.mov)**.

2. At this point, we need to customize the settings for this format. If you're saving out an AVI, this would include choosing a codec and setting compression options. Click on the **Options** button. A new window will appear. Here you can configure the QuickTime settings as you see fit. The default settings should work well in most situations. When you've configured QuickTime to your liking, click **OK**.

3. The last thing we need to do is choose a file name and save to location. Click on the **Animation File** button. Navigate to a folder on your hard drive and enter an appropriate name. Then click **OK**.

4. Now, when you press <F10>, LightWave will generate a QuickTime movie from your scene.

The steps for saving out RGB and alpha image sequences are basically the same, so we won't cover them here. Instead, we'll talk about the practical use of the settings in this tab.

As a rule of thumb, you should never save your renders directly to an animation. You should always save out an RGB image sequence first and then compile these still images into an animation in a separate pass. The reason for this is simple: If LightWave crashes during your render (which is rare but does happen), your entire animation file will likely become corrupt and unusable. This only has to happen once (especially when you're fighting a deadline) to realize what a bad idea it is to render directly to an animation file.

So let me save you the agony. Don't render to an animation file. Render an RGB image sequence. Then use LightWave to compile the still images into an animation. Let's look at how to do this:

Converting a Still Image Sequence into an Animation

1. Open the Chapter_07_Still-Life-Spots.lws scene file from the book's companion DVD.

2. On a relatively fast computer, this scene will take around 15 minutes to render. To speed things up, let's change the Render Mode setting. Open the Render Globals window and click on the **Render** tab. Click the **Render Mode** pop-up menu and change it from Realistic to **Quickshade**.

3. Now set up the Output options to save an RGB image sequence. Click on the **Output** tab. Click the **Save RGB** box so that it is checked. Change the Type pop-up menu to **LW_JPEG (.jpg)**, which will save out high-quality JPEG files. Click the **RGB Files** button and choose a location to save your images.

4. Enter a name into the File Name field of the Save RGB dialog box and place an underscore (_) symbol at the end. This will clearly separate your file name from the frame number that LightWave appends to it. Click **OK**. To the right of the RGB Files button, you

should see a sample of how your images will be named.

5. Press <F10> to render the scene.

6. When the render has finished, open up a new instance of Layout.

7. In this new instance of Layout, open the Image Editor from the left side of the interface or press the <F6> keyboard shortcut.

8. Press the **Load** button and navigate to the folder where you saved your image sequence. Click on the first frame in the sequence and press **OK**. A thumbnail of the first image will appear in the Image Editor.

9. Currently, LightWave sees this as a solitary image and not an image sequence. We need to change that. Click on the **Image Type** pop-up menu from the Source tab of the Image Editor. Change it from Still to **Sequence**. You can now drag the slider under the thumbnail in the Image Editor to get a preview of your animation.

10. Take a look at the information to the right of the thumbnail in the Image Editor. Note the size. It should be 640 x 480. Now close the Image Editor.

11. Open the Camera Properties window. Make sure the camera's Resolution is set to **640 x 480**. Then close the Camera Properties window.

12. Click on the **Windows** menu and choose **Compositing Options** (or press the <Ctrl> + <F7> keyboard shortcut). This will open the Compositing tab of the Effects panel. We'll take a more detailed look at compositing in Chapter 10 when we learn how to integrate 3D objects with photographic backgrounds. For now, click on the **Background Image** pop-up menu and

select the image sequence you just loaded. This will composite the rendered image sequence with what our camera sees. Since there's nothing in our scene for the camera to see, the only thing that will appear is the background footage.

13. Open the Render Globals window. Click on the **Output** tab and check the **Save Animation** box to activate it. Choose an animation type (typically either an AVI or MOV file) and configure it with the Options button for the appropriate codec and compression settings. Then click on the **Animation File** button. Choose a location to save the animation and give it a file name. Then click **OK**.

14. Everything is now set up and all that remains is to render. Press <F10>. Since there is no foreground geometry to render, LightWave will zip through the background images and compile them into a new animation very quickly.

15. When rendering is finished, navigate to the folder where you saved your animation and inspect the results. If needed, you can go back and reconfigure the compression and codec settings.

This process may sound tedious and convoluted, but once you've done it a few times, you'll find that it's really a simple and straightforward process. And hopefully it has opened your eyes to what can be accomplished by using footage in the background. On more than one occasion I've used LightWave to transcode video from one format to another. It works wonderfully for converting AVIs into QuickTime and vice versa.

There are two more options on the Output tab that we need to take a look at. The Format pop-up menu determines how LightWave appends the frame number and file format extension to your saved images. The default is "Name0001.xxx." This will save the name of your file immediately followed by a four-digit number, a period, and a three-digit file format extension.

In step 4 above, I had you add an underscore to the file name. But you can force LightWave to add this underscore automatically. Simply click on the Format pop-up menu and choose the Name_001.xxx option. It's worth noting that you can also force LightWave to remove the three-digit file format extension by choosing an option without the ".xxx" on the end.

The last option is Fader Alpha Mode. LightWave was originally included with NewTek's Video Toaster and used for broadcast graphics. When using Light-Wave's renders with an external video keyer, the native alpha channels don't always produce ideal results, so the Fader Alpha Mode was added. In all my years of working with LightWave, I've never had a need for this. But if you're using an external keying device to composite graphics over live video, you should check this option. Otherwise, leave it off.

Mask

The last tab in the Render Globals window is Mask. This tab provides options for masking out a portion of your image and is often used to create a "letterbox" style render on a 4:3 aspect ratio image.

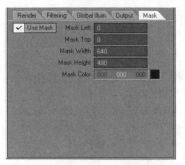

Figure 7-38: The Mask tab allows you to cover portions of your rendered image with a flat color.

To use a mask, you must click the Use Mask button. The options here allow you to define global settings that will apply to all cameras in your scene unless they are specifically overwritten (by unchecking the Use Global button in the Mask Options tab of the Camera Properties window). See Chapter 4 for more information on using the mask options.

Closing Thoughts about the Render Globals Window

We've just spent a good chunk of time talking about the options in the Render Globals window. There are a lot of options here, so you may feel a little overwhelmed. That's natural. But it's important to get a handle on these settings as they are the key to effectively managing your render times. Before moving on to the next section, load the Chapter_07_Still-Life-Spots.lws scene and tinker with the various settings we've discussed so far. Make your own mental notes about what each setting does. Frame it in terms that you understand. Knowledge is power and what you learn by working with these settings will empower you to tame the unwieldy rendering times that often plague new users.

The Effects Panel

Let's talk about the Effects panel. This simple window provides access to a host of powerful options. You can access the Effects panel by clicking on the **Windows** menu and choosing either **Backdrop Options**, **Volumetrics and Fog Options**, **Compositing Options**, or **Image Processing**. Each of these menu items will open the Effects panel with their respective tab selected. I find it easiest to just hit <Ctrl>+<F5>. That opens the Effects panel with the Backdrop tab active, and from there you can quickly navigate to the other tabs in the window.

The **Backdrop**, **Volumetrics**, and **Compositing** tabs provide control over the appearance of your 3D world. We'll cover these concepts in greater detail in Chapters 10 and 12, but I'll summarize them for you here.

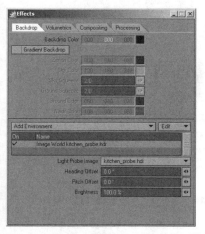

Figure 7-39: The Backdrop tab of the Effects panel allows you to alter the appearance of the environment, such as changing the default black backdrop color and adding virtual skies.

In the **Backdrop** tab, you can change the default black background to any solid color or gradient. You can also add environment generators such as Image World (which will wrap a picture inside a virtual sphere around your entire scene) or SkyTracer (which lets you create beautiful cloudy skies).

In the **Volumetrics** tab, you can add fog and apply volumetric rendering tools to create dust, smoke, fire, or water. (See Chapters 12 and 14 for more on volumetric effects.)

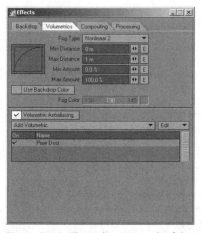

Figure 7-40: The Volumetrics tab of the Effects panel allows you to add fog and apply volumetric tools to create effects such as smoke, dust, and fire.

In the **Compositing** tab, you can layer images in front of and behind the objects in your scene. (We used some of the options in this tab earlier when we converted a rendered image sequence into an animation file.)

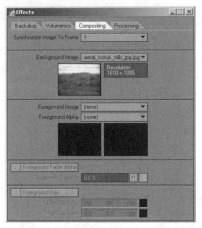

Figure 7-41: The Compositing tab of the Effects panel allows you to layer images between the objects in your scene.

The Backdrop, Volumetrics, and Compositing tabs all have one thing in common: They alter the appearance of your 3D world. But the last tab in the Effects panel, Processing, is quite different. It doesn't alter the 3D world but rather your renders of the 3D world. And since this chapter is all about rendering, it is important that we discuss some of the options in this tab in more detail.

The Processing Tab Options

The Processing tab of the Effects panel can be broken down into four basic parts. The first section deals with color and brightness settings. The second section provides glow controls. The third section allows you to add pixel filters, and the fourth section allows you to add image filters. We'll briefly touch on the first three sections and then spend the bulk of this section dealing with the fourth — image filters — as these offer some of the greatest control over your final images.

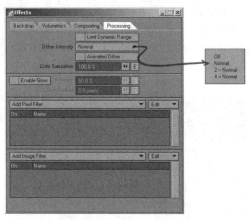

Figure 7-42: The Processing tab of the Effects panel allows you to alter your final rendered image.

Color and Brightness Settings

The first section in the Processing tab allows you to adjust the brightness and color of your rendered image.

• **Limit Dynamic Range** — This will prohibit extremely bright areas in your render from exceeding 100%. If you recall our discussion of Image Viewer earlier in this chapter, we saw that LightWave renders images in 128-bit depth. When using Image

Viewer FP, bright parts of our image could easily exceed 100%. In some cases, these extremely bright areas can be difficult to antialias properly. Limiting the dynamic range can help improve the antialiasing, but it comes at the cost of losing brightness values above 100%.

- **Dither Intensity** — When you're working with an image that has a limited color range (such as in a gradient that has two similar colors of blue), "banding" effects (where each step from one color to the next is visible) can appear. To limit banding, LightWave can "dither" the pixels between areas of like colors. This helps blend colors together more naturally.

In most cases, the default setting of Normal will produce excellent results. If you would like to make the dithering effect more pronounced, you can change this setting to 2 x Normal or 4 x Normal. If you don't want any dithering at all, you can set this pop-up menu to Off.

- **Animated Dither** — Increasing the Dither Intensity setting can create a more "noisy" image in large flat areas of color. When you're animating a scene, the dithering pattern can become noticeable. Activating the Animated Dither option will change how the dither is applied to each frame and create a more natural appearance. When used with the higher 4 x Normal Dither Intensity setting, it can create the appearance of film grain in your animations.

- **Color Saturation** – Computer-generated images have a tendency to be oversaturated, which gives them an artificial appearance. Lowering the Color Saturation setting by about 20% can be a subtle yet effective way to increase the

realism in your scene. (You'd be surprised at how much this can help.) This effect can be animated by clicking on the E button and using the Graph Editor to change the value over time.

Glow Controls

Each surface in an object has the ability to radiate a glow based on its surface color. We'll cover the process of setting up glowing surfaces in Chapter 10, but here's a quick run-through of the options found in the Processing tab.

- **Enable Glow** — In order to get surfaces to glow, you must first activate the Enable Glow option.

- **Intensity** — This is a global intensity control and it is animatable. You can increase or decrease the glow intensity of all surfaces (or at least those that have some amount of glow specified in the Advanced tab in the Surface Editor) with this value.

- **Glow Radius** — This is how far the glow will spread away from the actual surface of an object. Like Intensity, this value can be animated.

Pixel Filters

Pixel filters are utilities that affect an image during the rendering process. They differ from image filters, which affect an image after the rendering process has completed. Most of the pixel filters in LightWave are considered "legacy tools." They exist only to provide support for earlier versions of LightWave. But there are notable exceptions. Perhaps the most important pixel filter is SasLite, which is a hair and fur simulator. We'll take an in-depth look at this utility in Chapter 20.

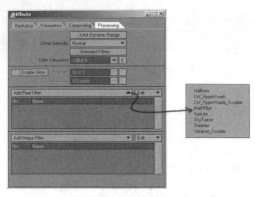

Figure 7-43: Pixel filters are utilities that affect an image during the rendering process.

Image Filters

Image filters are effects that are applied to your image once the rendering process is finished. In many ways, they are similar to Photoshop filters. Image filters can be used to adjust color, brightness, and hue; they can add film grain or blur the image; and they can create stylized images such as sketches or embossing. For these reasons, it may be tempting to think of image filters

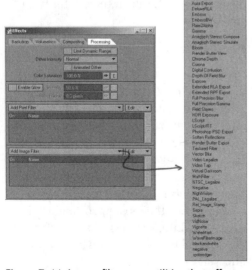

Figure 7-44: Image filters are utilities that affect an image after it has been rendered. Think of them as Photoshop filters on steroids.

as convenient albeit unnecessary post-process tools. However, image filters can accept input from LightWave surfaces, which makes them much more powerful than Photoshop filters. We'll see how this works when we examine the Corona filter in the next section.

The LightWave reference manual does a good job of covering each of the filters (including each of their options), so we won't attempt to cover every single detail here. Instead, I will touch on some of the more useful filters and give you a taste of how they can be used to enhance your renders.

Image filters are added by clicking on the **Add Image Filter** pop-up menu and selecting a filter from those shown. You can access a filter's options by double-clicking on it once it's been added. You can add more than one filter (and even more than one instance of the same filter). You can rearrange filters that have been added by dragging and dropping them in the same manner that you arrange texture layers in the Texture Editor.

Corona

This wonderful little utility allows you to add halos or light blooms around bright parts of your image. In the real world, when a camera snaps a picture showing a very bright surface, excessive amounts of light enter the camera lens, causing those areas to glow. Corona gives you this ability within LightWave.

The interface for Corona can seem a little scary, so let's quickly run through it and then we'll put it into action.

The Corona window is divided into three sections. The top section allows you to identify which parts of your image will be affected by the filter. The middle section allows you to specify how intense the effect

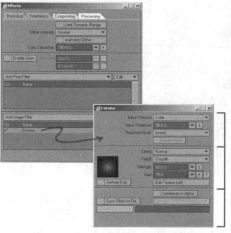

WHAT BLOOMS?

HOW MUCH BLOOM?

SAVE THE BLOOM AND
AFFECT THE ALPHA CHANNEL?

Figure 7-45: The Corona image filter allows you to create halos around bright portions of your image.

Adding the Corona filter added bloom, which is most noticeable around the bananas and oranges. That's nice, but I'd really rather it be around the reflections in the bottle and the bright spot on the left side of the bowl. We can achieve this by tweaking Corona's settings.

will be. The bottom section allows you to save the effect to a file and determine whether or not it contributes to the image's alpha channel.

1. Open the **Chapter_07_Still-Life-Spots.lws** scene and drag the Frame Slider to frame 60. Then press <F9> to do a test render.

2. The image looks nice, but it's a little bland. Press <Ctrl>+<F8> to open the Effects | Processing panel. Click on the **Add Image Filter** pop-up menu and choose **Corona**. The filter will appear in the list. Now press <F9> to perform another render.

3. Double-click the **Corona** filter in the list to open its options window. We can see that Input Channel is set to Color. This means that Corona will look for the brightest colors in the image and add a glow to them.

4. I only want Corona to be applied to the reflective objects in this scene, so click on the **Input Channel** pop-up menu and choose **Reflectivity**. Then lower the Input Threshold to **80%**.

The Input Threshold setting works like a trigger. When the value of the Input Channel setting (in this case Reflectivity) reaches a certain level (determined by the Input Threshold) the surface will bloom. By lowering the Input Threshold we are telling Corona to be less "picky" about how much

Figure 7-46: Load the Chapter_07_Still-Life-Spots.lws scene and add the Corona image filter. Move the Frame Slider to frame 60 and press <F9> to render.

WITHOUT CORONA

WITH CORONA

265

Figure 7-47: Open the Corona properties by double-clicking on it in the list. Then change the Input Channel to Reflectivity and lower the Input Threshold to 80%.

reflection is needed in order for the surface to bloom.

5. Press <**F9**> to render.

We can see that this gave us a nice glow around the bright window reflections in our bottle, but it also caused the blade of the peeler to blow out, which really isn't what I want. If I lower the settings to compensate for the peeler, I'll lose the nice settings on the bottle. So I need a way to tell Corona to affect the bottle and not the peeler. Fortunately, Corona gives us a relatively easy way to do this.

The Threshold Mask pop-up menu allows us to restrict the Corona effect to a specific channel (such as color, reflectivity, etc.). Among the list of channels is an

option called Special Buffer. Special Buffer is a generic "trigger" that tells Corona (and other image filters that utilize it) to look at the Special Buffer values assigned to each surface. If the Special Buffer value is 0, then Corona won't be applied to that surface. But if the Special Buffer is 1, the Corona filter will be applied. Let's see how to set this up.

6. Click the **Threshold Mask** pop-up menu and choose **Special Buffer**. Then open the Surface Editor and click on the **Bottle** surface. Click on the **Advanced** tab and then click on the **Special Buffers** button. A Special Buffers Options window appears.

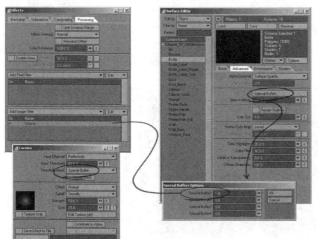

Figure 7-48: Set the Corona Threshold Mask to Special Buffer. Then set Special Buffer1 for the Bottle surface to 1.0.

The Special Buffer tends to confuse people, but it's really not that hard to understand. There are four Special Buffer slots. These slots target the first four image filters that are added in the Effects | Processing panel. So the value you enter for Special Buffer1 will be accessible to the first image filter that appears in the list. The value you enter for Special Buffer2 will be accessible to the second image filter in the list, and so on.

Currently we only have one image filter in our list, so the only Special Buffer that matters at this point is Buffer1. And as I mentioned earlier, when Corona checks for Special Buffers, it's looking at each surface for a value of 1.0. A value of 1.0 says, "Hey, Corona! You should be applied to me!"

7. Enter **1.0** for Special Buffer1 and click **OK**. Then press <F9> to render again.

You can see that the bloom now appears only on the bottle surface. If we want the Corona effect applied to other surfaces, we simply need to change their Special Buffer1 value to 1.0. Easy, huh?

Figure 7-49: Using the Special Buffer option allows us to only apply the Corona effect to the surfaces we desire. Here we have limited the Corona effect to the bottle surface.

8. Let's add the Corona effect to the bowl. Click on the **Bowl** surface in the

Surface Editor. Then click on the **Special Buffers** button in the Advanced tab. Enter **1.0** for Special Buffer1 and press **OK**.

9. Since the bowl consists of two surfaces, Bowl and Bowl_Band, we should add the effect to the band as well. Click on the **Bowl_Band** surface and enter **1.0** for its Special Buffer1. Click **OK**, then press <F9> to render again.

You'll notice that nothing seemed to happen. The reason for this is that the Input Threshold that we've set for the Corona filter is too high. Remember, the Input Threshold corresponds to the Input Channel. The Input Channel in this case is Reflectivity. The bowl is reflective, but it's not as reflective as the bottle and therefore it isn't being affected due to the high Input Threshold.

10. Open the options window for the Corona filter in the Effects | Processing panel. Lower the Input Threshold to **10%** and press <F9> to render.

You can see that the side of the bowl now has a nice, bright bloom, but if you look closely, you'll realize that we've lost most of the effect on our bottle. In reality, the effect is still there, but because we've lowered the threshold, it's being applied differently due to the change in the Input Threshold. Let's correct this.

11. Close the Corona options window. Make sure that Corona is still selected in the Image Filter list. Then click on the **Edit** pop-up menu and choose **Copy**. Click on the **Edit** pop-up menu again and choose **Paste**. A second instance of Corona will be added to the Image Filter list.

Figure 7-50: Lower the Corona Input Threshold to 10% and render again. You can see that the side of the bowl now has a nice, bright bloom.

Now that we've got a second instance of the Corona filter (with the same settings), we need to tell the Bottle surface to look to it rather than the first instance.

12. Open the Surface Editor. Click on the **Bottle** surface. Go to the Advanced tab and click on the **Special Buffers** button. Currently, we have 1.0 entered for Special Buffer1. This is telling the first instance of Corona to apply to the Bottle surface. But we want the second instance of Corona to affect this surface, so change Special Buffer1 to **0**. This eliminates the effect of the first Corona filter. Then change Special Buffer2 to **1.0**. Click **OK**.

13. Open the options window for the second instance of the Corona filter. Change the Input Threshold to **80%**. While we're here, let's also increase the intensity of the effect. Change Strength to **65%**. Then press <**F9**> to render.

We now have a beautiful bloom effect applied to the bowl and the bottle. Getting the Corona applied to the right portions of the image is the biggest challenge in using this tool, but as you can see, by using the Special Buffer feature, we can handpick which surfaces the effect is applied to.

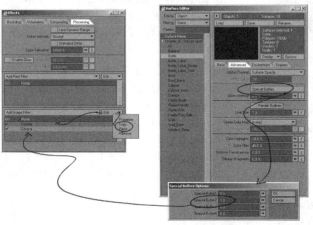

Figure 7-51: Copy the Corona filter and paste it in to create a second instance. Then change the Bottle surface's Special Buffer1 to 0.0 and Special Buffer2 to 1.0.

Figure 7-52: Increase the Input Threshold of the second Corona instance to 80%. Then increase the Strength to 65%.

You can continue to experiment with the settings found in the Corona options window if you'd like. Try changing the Effect and Falloff settings. The options in these menus allow you to tailor how the effect is applied and can have a tremendous impact on how the effect looks.

Applying Corona in Post Production

It's often best to apply Corona in post production rather than having it "baked" into your final render. While it requires a bit more work to set up, this approach gives you greater control over the look of your render and also allows you to use this great filter with third-party renderers like FPrime. (See Chapter 27 for more information on FPrime.) Let's take a look at how to apply Corona in post.

1. The first step is to render out a "clean" pass of your scene without the Corona effect applied. If you've already set up Corona, simply uncheck each instance of it in the Image Filter list to disable it. Then render your scene to an image sequence as described earlier in this chapter.

2. The second step involves setting up the Corona filter to save the effect to a file we can use in post production. Open the Corona options window by double-clicking on it in the Image Filters list. The bottom section of the Corona window contains a check box labeled **Save Effect to File**. Click this to activate it. Then click the **Save As** button and choose a name and location for the effect files to be saved. Finally, choose a file format. In most cases, JPEG files work just fine, although you can choose any format you like.

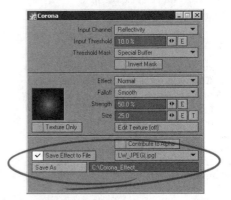

Figure 7-53: To add the Corona effect in post production, enable the Save Effect to File option in the Corona options window.

3. The third step is rendering the Corona pass. If you disabled Corona in the Image Filter list in order to render your clean pass, be sure to reactivate it again. Now this can be a bit confusing, so pay close attention. The Corona effect is saved through the Corona filter. It is not saved through the Render Globals | Output options. Therefore, you do not (moreover should not) have these settings enabled during your Corona pass. Open the Render Globals window and click on the **Output** tab. If any of the output options are enabled (such as Save Animation or Save RGB), disable them. Now press <**F10**> to render your scene. LightWave will warn you that you don't have any saving options enabled and ask you if you want to proceed. Just click the **Yes** button to continue. When LightWave finishes, you should have a separate image sequence containing the Corona effect over a black background.

although you can accomplish the same thing with other popular compositing programs.)

Import both the **clean pass** and the **Corona pass** as image sequences. Create a new composition and add both sequences to it. The clean pass should be on the bottom and the Corona pass should be above it. Finally, change the blending mode for the Corona pass to **Screen**.

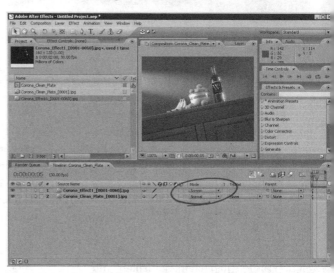

Figure 7-54: Combine the clean pass and the Corona pass in a compositing program and set the blending mode for the Corona pass to Screen.

4. The fourth step involves combining the files in a compositing program. (In this example, I'm using After Effects,

Your composition will now show the Corona effect as it would look if it were rendered in LightWave. You can try out different blending modes and also adjust the dynamic range of the Corona sequence to adjust the overall look of the effect.

Digital Confusion

In Chapter 4, we saw how we could use LightWave's Depth of Field (DOF) setting to create a limited area of focus. The problem with depth of field is that it typically requires high levels of antialiasing in order to look good.

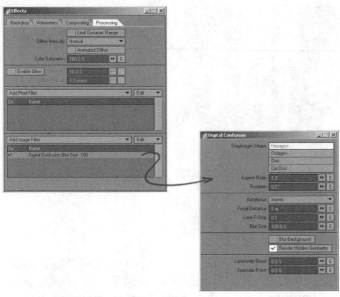

Figure 7-55: Open the Chapter_07_Still-Life-Confusion.lws scene and add the Digital Confusion image filter.

The Digital Confusion window, as shown in Figure 7-55, is broken down into four parts. The first section determines the appearance of the effect. The second section determines the amount of the effect. The third section determines what will be affected, and the fourth section corrects any loss to brightness that might occur from using the filter.

I tend to leave the top settings (which deal with the appearance of the effect) alone until I've got the proper amount set. So how do we determine the proper amount? The first thing we need to do is determine where the effect will take place. Which area should be in focus? From there, it's a trial-and-error game to determine the amount.

Digital Confusion gives us the option to enter an exact focal distance. But it also gives us an Autofocus option, which is easier and much more fun to use.

A nice alternative to LightWave's true DOF is to use Digital Confusion. The term digital confusion refers to the "circle of confusion" used in traditional photography to measure depth of field.

It's important to note that Digital Confusion will never achieve the same levels of quality or realism as true DOF. But in many cases, it can produce perfectly acceptable results in less time.

1. Load the **Chapter_07_Still-Life-Confusion.lws** scene. This is a simple variation on the Still Life Spots scene we've been using throughout this chapter. Move the Frame Slider to frame 60. Press **<Ctrl>+<F8>** to open the Effects | Processing panel. Click on the **Add Image Filter** pop-up menu and choose **Digital Confusion**. Once the Digital Confusion filter has been added to the list, double-click on it to open its options window.

2. Close the Digital Confusion options window. Click on the **Items** tab at the top of the Layout interface and click on the **Add | Null** button.

3. The Build Null Object window appears. Enter the name **Focus** for this null and press **OK**. Then move the Focus null up and center it on the frontmost orange. Make sure that you center the null in at least two viewports so that it is truly centered on the orange.

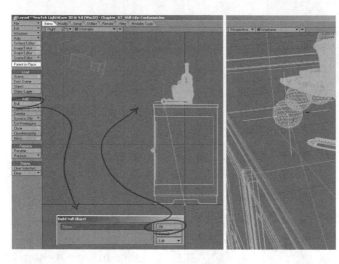

Figure 7-56: Add a null called Focus and center it on the frontmost orange in the scene.

You may notice that the Focus null has a dotted line running from it to the origin (as seen in Figure 7-56). This dotted line is a motion path and indicates that the null will move over the course of the animation. When we created the null, LightWave placed it at the origin and created a key frame for it at frame 0. Since the Frame Slider was at frame 60 when we moved the null up to the orange, LightWave created a new key frame, which is now causing the null to move over the course of the animation.

4. The Focus null should remain fixed throughout the animation. To ensure this, make sure the Frame Slider is on frame 60. Then press the **Create Key** button below the timeline. The Create Motion Key window appears. Enter **0** into the Create Key At field and press **OK**. This creates a key at frame 0 with values identical to those on frame 60. The motion path for the Focus null should disappear, indicating that it no longer moves throughout the animation.

5. Open the Digital Confusion options window. Click on the **Autofocus** pop-up menu and choose the **Focus**

null that you just created. The Digital Confusion filter will always focus on this object. No more guessing. No more trial and error. Wherever this null object is placed, that will be the center of focus.

Now that we've determined where the focus should be, we need to determine how much the areas away from this point will be blurred. This is controlled by the Lens F-Stop setting. The lower this number, the more shallow the depth of field, and consequently the more pronounced the blur. This number defaults to 0.1, but 0.1 will provide different results with different scenes. This value is dependent on the size and scope of your overall scene. In our case, 0.1 is much too low.

6. Increase the Lens F-Stop setting to **1.0**. Then press <**F9**> to render.

This creates a great depth of field effect that renders in a fraction of the time it would take for normal DOF. If you like, you can continue adjusting the settings in the Digital Confusion options window, but remember that subtlety is often the key to realism. Extreme DOF effects are

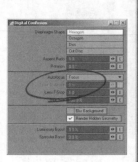

Figure 7-57: Set Autofocus to the Focus null object. Then change the Lens F-Stop setting to 1.0 and press <F9> to render. This creates a nice depth of field effect.

interesting but can often shout "Look at me! I'm a 3D render!"

Photoshop PSD Export

Oftentimes when you've finished rendering an image, you will need to do some amount of post-processing work in a program like Photoshop or After Effects. Unfortunately, there's only so much you can do with a flat image. But what if you had the ability to control the various attributes of an image after it has been rendered? With the Photoshop PSD Export filter, you can.

1. Open the **Chapter_07_Still-Life-PSD.lws** scene from the companion

DVD. Then press **<Ctrl>** + **<F8>** to open the Effects | Processing panel. Click on the **Add Image Filter** pop-up menu and choose the **Photoshop PSD Export** filter. Once it has been added to the list, double-click the filter to open its options window.

There are dozens of options in the PSD Export window, and we could spend an entire chapter detailing each of the options for this one filter. I'll leave the full exploration of this tool to you. But I will show you some of the cool things you can do with this great tool.

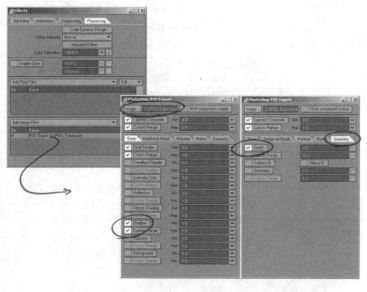

Figure 7-58: Open the Chapter_07_Still-Life-PSD.lws scene and add the Photoshop PSD Export filter. Open the options window for the filter by double-clicking on it. Then set the options as shown here.

Each of the options here allow you to export a different channel, which will appear as a separate layer in the final Photoshop file. By default, Layered Composite and Custom Range are checked, as are Final Render and Custom Range on the Basic tab.

2. Activate the **Shadow** and **Custom Range** options on the Basic tab. Then switch to the Geometry tab and enable **Depth**. Lastly, click on the **Image** button in the upper-left corner of the window. Choose a location on your hard drive to save the Photoshop file and give it a name. Then press <**F9**> to render.

3. Your render will proceed as normal, but once it's finished, the PSD Exporter will kick in. When the render has finished, the Image Viewer window will appear as normal. Exit the Render Status window and close the Image Viewer. Then navigate to the folder where you saved your image and double-click on the file.

> **Note**
>
> I will be using Photoshop for the rest of this section; however, most image editing applications such as Paint Shop Pro and the open-source GIMP offer functions similar to what I describe below.

4. Once the file has been loaded into Photoshop, open your Layers palette. You will see 11 layers, each labeled as to what they contribute. You'll also notice that only the lavender colored layers are visible. By adjusting the levels and opacity for each of these layers, you can retroactively affect your image in ways that would be difficult or impossible to do otherwise.

Figure 7-59: Open the exported Photoshop file. You'll see layers for each channel and how they contribute to the overall render.

At the bottom of the Layers palette you'll find two blue colored layers, one for Shadow and one for Depth. The Shadow layer allows you to determine the amount of shadow falling across an image. The Depth layer allows you to determine how far objects are from the camera. Let's look at how we can use each of these layers to adjust our render.

5. Click the eyeball icon to turn on the visibility for the Depth layer. Then click on the **Depth** layer and press <**Ctrl**> +<**a**> to select all. This copies the Depth layer to the clipboard.

6. Click on the **Channels** tab to the right of the Layers tab. Click the page icon in the lower-right corner of the palette to create a new alpha channel. Press <**Ctrl**>+<**v**> to paste the Depth layer data into this new alpha channel. Press <**Ctrl**>+<**d**> to deselect. Click on **RGB** at the top of the Channels tab to return to RGB mode. Then click on the **Layers** tab and turn off visibility to the Depth layer.

We now have the depth data from our render in an alpha channel (see Figure 7-60). This enables us to create masks that will allow us to position layers *behind objects* in our render. Let's see how this is done.

Figure 7-60: Copy the Depth layer and paste it into a new alpha channel.

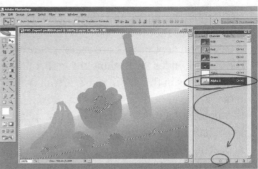

Figure 7-62: Create a selection from the Depth alpha channel.

7. Open the **Wood.jpg** file from the content CD that came with LightWave. Copy this layer and paste it into your Photoshop document. Then position the layer just below the Final Render layer. We're going to make it appear as if our back wall is made of wood.

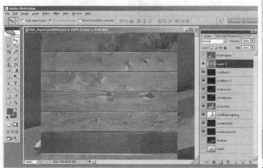

Figure 7-61: Copy the Wood.jpg file from the LightWave content CD and paste it into the Photoshop render document. Position it just below the Final Render layer.

8. Click on the **Channels** tab again. Click on the alpha channel containing the Depth map. Then click on the dotted circle icon to create a selection from this channel.

9. Switch back to the **Layers** tab and click on the **Final Render** layer. This will pop you back into RGB mode. Turn on the visibility for the Final Render layer. Then click on the **Add Layer Mask** icon at the bottom of the Layers palette (circled in Figure 7-63). This creates a layer mask using the Depth alpha channel data.

Figure 7-63: Select the Final Render layer and turn on its visibility. Then click the Add Layer Mask button. This will add a mask using the Depth alpha channel's grayscale values.

You can see that the wood layer is beginning to show through, but only slightly. If you look closer, you'll notice that the wood layer is actually more opaque at the bottom than it is at the top. The reason for this is that Photoshop considers lighter areas to be opaque and darker areas to be transparent.

275

Remember, we added the mask to the Final Render layer (not the wood). So the lighter areas in the depth mask are making more of the Final Render layer show through, and darker areas in the depth mask are allowing more of the underlying layers to show through. But if more of the wood is appearing closer to the camera and less is appearing farther away from the camera (where the wall is), this is the opposite of what we want. So we need to invert the mask.

10. Click on the small picture icon of the mask for the Final Render layer. Then press <Ctrl>+<i> to invert it. The wood will become much more prominent toward the top of the wall.

> ### Note
> Make sure that you select the picture icon for the mask and not the picture icon for the image. You should see a white border around the picture icon when it is selected.

11. I don't like the fact that the boards are running horizontally. I want them to run vertically. Select the wood layer and press <Ctrl>+<t> to active the Free Transform tool. Rotate the layer 75.5 degrees. Then move it up so that it completely covers the red wall.

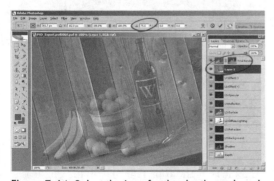

Figure 7-64: Select the icon for the depth mask and press <Ctrl>+<i> to invert it. Then select the wood layer. Rotate it 75.5 degrees and move it up to completely cover the red wall.

The wood looks good, but it fades right into the still life. It needs to be pushed back behind these objects. To do this, we need to adjust the levels for the depth mask.

12. Click on the picture icon for the depth mask to select it. Then press <Ctrl>+<l> to open the Levels window. Drag the white triangle on the right side of the histogram to the left. You will see the wood layer appear to recede behind the still life items, but that the wood at the top left of the image begins to fade out. To compensate, move the black triangle on the left side of the histogram to the right until the wood becomes solid. Adjust the white and black triangles until the wood is positioned behind the objects and appears to be solid. I found the levels of **47**, **1.0**, and **50** to work for me.

Figure 7-65: Select the picture icon for the depth mask. Adjust its levels until the wood layer pops behind the still life items in the scene.

It will be difficult to push the wood far enough back so that it sits right behind the cabinet. But so long as it's behind the bottle, the bowl, and the bananas, we're in good shape. Let's clean up the wall a bit.

13. Turn off the wood layer, then select the **Final Render** layer. Drag your

Photoshop window out so you can see the canvas around the image. Then use the Polygonal selection tool to select an area that encompasses the entire cabinet, as shown in Figure 7-66.

Figure 7-66: Select the Final Render layer and then draw a polygonal selection that encompasses the entire cabinet.

14. Select the picture icon for the depth mask (which should now be nearly black and white). Then choose **Edit | Fill** and fill the area we just selected with white. This makes the cabinet and anything on it fully opaque. And since this layer is above the wood layer, it will make the still life objects appear to be in front of the wood.

Figure 7-67: Select the depth mask for the Final Render layer and fill the selected area with white.

15. Deselect. Then turn on visibility for the wood layer. Set the blending mode to **Multiply** and drop the Opacity setting to **65%**. This allows the wood to take on some of the color of the back wall as well as its shading.

Figure 7-68: Turn on visibility for the wood. Change the blending mode for the wood layer to Multiply and set Opacity to 65%.

The wood is now fairly well integrated into our render. But let's do one last thing to help sell the effect.

16. Drag the Shadow layer from the bottom of the Layers panel to the very top. Turn on visibility for this layer. Then, with the layer selected, press <Ctrl>+<i> to invert the layer. Change the blending mode to **Color Burn** and set Opacity to **25%**.

Figure 7-69: Move the Shadow layer to the top of the list and make it visible. Invert this layer. Then set the blending mode to Color Burn and Opacity to 25%.

Adding the shadow layer boosts the shadows being cast from the still life objects onto the wood wall and makes them appear as if they are really part of the scene.

As you can see, the Photoshop PSD Export filter opens all kinds of doors for creative post processing. But it's not limited to stills. You can use the PSD Export filter for animations as well.

Using the PSD Export Filter for Post Production

We've just seen how we can utilize the layers from the PSD Export filter to affect a still image. But the same concepts can be applied to animations. Once you've applied the PSD Export filter and configured it to suit your needs and save a layered file (as described above), you can simply render your entire animation. When you are finished, you will have a sequence of PSD files. These files can be imported into a program like After Effects and adjusted just as we did with Photoshop.

The key to using the PSD sequence in post production lies in how you import your files. In After

Effects, you must choose to import the PSD sequence as a composition.

Once the sequence has been loaded, you will see a new composition in your Project bin. Double-click on this composition to open it. You will see each of the layers arranged just as they would appear in Photoshop with the proper blending mode already set. Unlike Photoshop, however, each of the layers in this composition actually consists of multiple frames grouped into a layered composite.

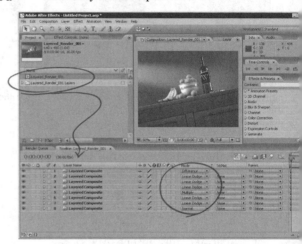

Figure 7-71: Once you've imported the PSD sequence, open the resulting composition. You're now free to adjust your layers as you see fit.

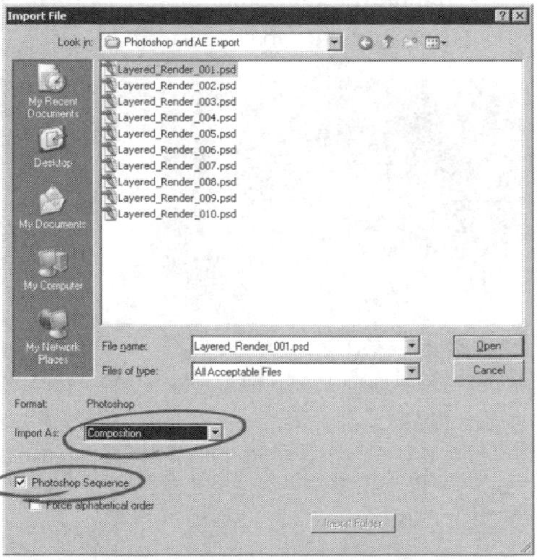

You are now free to adjust each layer as you see fit.

Sketch

One of the great aspects of working with LightWave is that it allows you to create photo-realistic renders. But what if you want to create something more stylized? You can create anime-style cel shading with either the BESM or Super Cel Shader surface shader utilities. But these tools must be applied to every surface in your scene and, while they offer a ton of features and can produce terrific results, they require a

Figure 7-70: To use the PSD Export filter in After Effects, import the sequence as a composition.

lot of work to set up. Fortunately, we can create cartoon-style renders quickly and easily with the Sketch filter.

The LightWave manual covers all of the settings for the Sketch tool in detail. Rather than repeat that information here, I'm going to touch on what the major settings do and then spend the rest of this section showing you how to use this great tool.

1. Open the **Chapter_07_Still-Life-Sketch.lws** scene from the DVD. This is a modified version of the still life that we've been using throughout this chapter. Make sure the Frame Slider is set to frame 60, then press <**F9**> to render.

As you can see in Figure 7-72, there's not much here. I've removed the textures from most of the surfaces and changed the lighting to use a point light with hard ray-traced shadows.

2. Open the **Effects | Processing** panel and add the **Sketch** filter from the Add Image Filter pop-up menu. When the filter has been added, double-click on it in the list to open its properties. Then press <**F9**> to render.

Figure 7-72: Open the Chapter_07_Still-Life-Sketch.lws scene and render frame 60.

3. Once you've rendered your scene, close the Render Status window and click in the large black area at the top of the Sketch options window. You'll see a thumbnail preview of your render appear. This preview allows you to see the changes you make to many of the Sketch options without requiring you to continually re-render.

The Sketch filter is designed to draw black lines around the contours of the objects in your scene. By defining areas of contrast, you can effectively manage the lines and

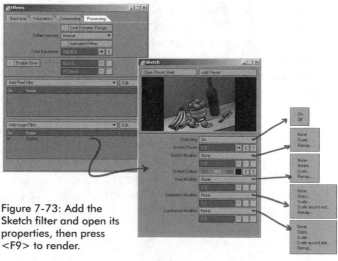

Figure 7-73: Add the Sketch filter and open its properties, then press <F9> to render.

where they are drawn. Let's take a look at the options the Sketch tool gives us.

The first option is the **Sketching** pop-up menu. It is set to On by default, although you can turn it off to see what your render looks like without the filter applied.

The next option is **Sketch Power**. This works like a combination of contrast and line density. Essentially, it determines how much the filter affects your image. Higher numbers cause the filter to be more selective about where the sketch lines are drawn. Lower numbers make it less selective and hence the lines will appear on more of your image.

You can choose to animate the Sketch Power option over time. You can also use a texture (such as a gradient) to affect the Sketch Power setting.

The **Sketch Modifier** option works like a multiplier for Sketch Power. You can turn the modifier off, set it to Scale (which will multiply the effect by the number you enter below the pop-up menu), or remap the effect to an expression.

You can envelope the Sketch Modifier to animate it over time and you can apply a texture to it as well. We'll see how this can be helpful shortly.

The **Sketch Colour** option allows you to change the color of the line. Note that this, too, can be enveloped or have a texture applied to it.

The last three options allow you to adjust the hue, saturation, and luminance (brightness) of your image. The options in each of the pop-up menus (seen in Figure 7-73) provide a slightly different way to perform the adjustments. For example, the Steps option (in both the Saturation and Luminance menus) will posterize the effect based on the number you enter into the

field below the menu. But the Scale option multiplies the effect by the number you enter below the menu.

By varying these options, you can create a dizzying array of effects. Let's take a look at how to set up a cel-shaded render.

Creating a Cel-Shaded Render with the Sketch Filter

1. We'll begin by setting the amount of Sketch Power. Remember, Sketch Power controls both the contrast and the placement of the lines created by the Sketch filter. The default is **1.0**. For our purposes, this should be just fine.

We'll leave the Sketch Modifier and the Sketch Colour as they are for the time being and instead make some changes to the Hue, Saturation, and Luminance settings.

2. Click the **Hue Modifier** pop-up menu and change it from None to **Rotate**. This lets us rotate the hue from –1.0 to 1.0. A value of 0.0 will have no effect whatsoever. Set the value in the field below the pop-up menu to **0.025**. This will shift the hue slightly toward green.

3. Now let's adjust the saturation. Click on the **Saturation Modifier** pop-up menu and change it from None to **Scale**. Enter a value of **5.0** below the menu. This will increase the overall saturation for our image.

4. Finally, let's change the brightness of our image. Click on the **Luminance Modifier** pop-up menu and change it from None to **Steps**. This will posterize the image, creating distinct areas of shading. Enter **8.0** in the field below the pop-up menu.

5. Press <F9> to render and check your results.

You can see that we're starting to get that cel-shaded look, but there are some notable problems. First and foremost is the fact that the shadows have dark outlines around them. That's not good. Also, if you look closely, you'll notice that the highlights and bright areas on the bottle now have a thick black outline. Again, not good. Let's remedy this.

Figure 7-74: Set the Sketch parameters as shown and then press <F9> to render.

6. Click on the **Sketch Modifier** pop-up menu and change it from None to **Scale**. This allows us to boost the effect of the line. But we don't want to boost it uniformly. We want to kill the lines around the edges of the shadows and around the highlights of the bottle. This will require us to use a gradient.

7. Click on the **T** button below the Sketch Modifier pop-up menu to open its Texture Editor. Change the default texture layer to a **Gradient** and set its Input Parameter to **Luminance**. Setting the Input Parameter to Luminance allows

us to modify the sketch effect based on the brightness of the underlying image.

8. Create three keys in the gradient with the parameters and values as follows: For the first (top) key, its Value should be **4.0** and its Parameter should be **0.0**. For the second (middle) key, its Value should be **0.0** and its Parameter should be **0.4**. For the third (bottom) key, its Value should be **0.0** and its Parameter should be **1.0**. This tells the Sketch filter that where the image isn't very luminous (bright), the Sketch Power should be scaled by a factor of 4. But where the image is luminous, the Sketch Power should be scaled by 0.

Figure 7-75: Set the Sketch Modifier to Scale and add a gradient texture with its Input Parameter set to Luminance and its key values as shown here.

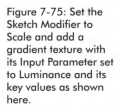

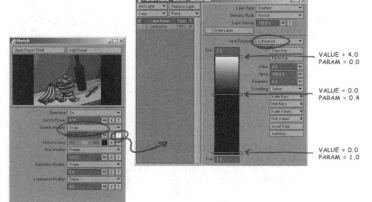

9. Press <**F9**> to render and inspect your results.

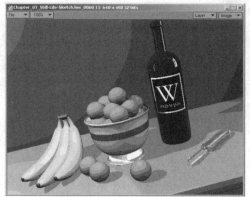

Figure 7-76: Adding the Sketch Modifier gradient took care of the bad outlines around the shadows, but it also removed the good lines around the geometry.

You can see from Figure 7-76 that by adding the Sketch Modifier gradient texture, we were able to remove the sketch lines around the shadow and the bright areas of the bottle. But in the process, we got rid of all of the lines. Fortunately, there's an easy way to get them back, but it doesn't involve the Sketch filter.

10. Close the Sketch Modifier Texture Editor, the Sketch options window, and the Effects | Processing panel. Switch to Objects selection mode (<**O**>) and then open the Object Properties window (<**p**>).

11. Click on the **Current Object** pop-up menu and choose **Cabinet**. Then click on the **Edges** tab. The options here allow us to add a stroke to various portions of our objects.

12. Activate the first four check boxes in this tab: **Silhouette Edges**, **Unshared Edges**, **Sharp Creases**, and **Surface Borders**. Leave Other Edges

unchecked and all of the other settings at their defaults.

13. Click on the **Current Object** pop-up menu and choose **Oranges-Bowl**. Activate the first four check boxes on the Edges tab for this object just as you did for the Cabinet.

14. Repeat this process for the Peeler and the Banana objects.

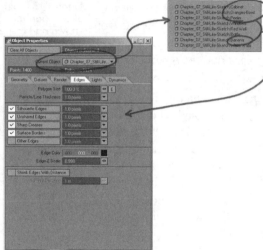

Figure 7-77: Open the Object Properties window and activate the edge options shown here for the Cabinet, Oranges-Bowl, Peeler, and Banana.

15. Open the Camera Properties window (<**C**> followed by <**P**>). Make sure your Camera Type is set to **Classic** (as of LightWave v9.2, edges won't render in any camera other than Classic). Set Antialiasing to **PLD 9-Pass**, and set Reconstruction Filter to **Box**. Activate **Adaptive Sampling** and leave Threshold at its default of **0.1**. Then press <**F9**> to render.

We've now got a beautiful cel-shaded render with minimal fuss.

Figure 7-78: Turn on the camera antialiasing options shown here and press <F9> to render. You can see that we've now got a beautiful cel-shaded image with gorgeous lines.

WaveFilterImage

Before we wrap up our discussion of image filters, let's take a quick look at WaveFilter-Image. WaveFilterImage is the Swiss Army knife of image filters. It allows you to make a number of image processing adjustments to your image from one easy-to-use panel. It's not showy, but what it does, it does well.

1. Open the **Chapter_07_Still-Life-Spots.lws** scene from the DVD. Move the Frame Slider to frame 60. Open the Camera Properties window and set Antialiasing to **PLD 5-Pass**. Set Reconstruction Filter to **Box** and turn

on **Adaptive Sampling**. Then press <F9> to render.

2. The native render is nice, but it could be even better with a few small adjustments. Open the Effects | Processing panel and add **WaveFilterImage** from the Add Image Filter pop-up menu. Then double-click on it to open its properties window.

Note

If you have any image filters applied from previous exercises, go ahead and remove them so that we can focus our attention on the WaveFilterImage utility.

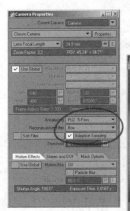

Figure 7-79: Open the Chapter_07_Still-Life-Spots.lws scene. Turn on the antialiasing options shown here and then press <F9> to render.

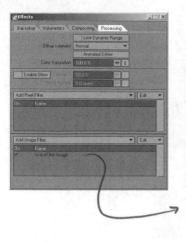

Figure 7-80: Add the WaveFilter-Image to the Image Filter list and open its properties.

Most of the image processing functions you'll ever need can be found in this panel. You can blur and sharpen your image. You can blend the edges of objects. You can adjust the saturation, invert the colors, limit the dynamic range (high and low colors), and reduce the palette through posterization or color reduction. You can add film grain and you can even translate the image, flipping it horizontally or vertically. And those are just the options in the Image tab.

We won't cover all of the options in this panel. Most of them are self explanatory and the ones that aren't are covered in the documentation. It's enough to know that this filter lets you do common image processing and manipulation.

Let's put it to use to make our render look that much better.

3. Click on the **Sharpen** check box to activate it and then set its value to **10%**. Then click on the **Saturation** box and lower its value to **70%**. Next, click on the **Film Grain** box and set it to **40%**.

Figure 7-81: Set the Sharpen, Saturation, and Film Grain values.

Adding a little film grain can really help reduce the overly perfect "CG" look common to computer graphics. The key to using the Film Grain option effectively is to use it subtly. If you notice the film grain, you're probably using too much.

At the bottom of the window you'll see a box with four patterns in it. This is the WaveFilterImage's default preview and is

Figure 7-82: Press <F9> to render. This fills the Wave-FilterImage buffer. Then change the preview pop-up menu to Last Render.

useful for getting an idea of how the filter will affect your render. But you're not limited to using this default image. If you press <F9> after adding the WaveFilterImage, you can click the Preview pop-up menu and choose the Last Render option to see the effects as they will be applied to your render.

4. Press <F9> to render your image. When the render is finished, change the Preview pop-up to **Last Render**.

The lower saturation and added film grain have helped remove some of the CG feel, but in the process, the image lost some of its punch.

5. Click on the **Color** tab. Click on the **Contrast** button to activate it. Set Contrast to **120%** and leave Center at **50%**. You'll see the changes in the small preview in the lower-left corner of the window.

6. Click on the **Gamma** button and set its value to **1.1**. Then press <F9> to render again.

If you've left Image Viewer open, you can compare this latest render to the original one by using the Image Controls as we discussed earlier in this chapter. You'll quickly see that with some simple adjustments, you can take your renders to a whole new level.

Figure 7-83: Adding some contrast and adjusting the gamma makes the image "pop."

Visor

Now let's turn our attention to Visor. Visor is a utility that allows you to preview images inside a Layout viewport. Let's take a look at this amazing tool.

1. Open the **Chapter_07_Still-Life-Spots.lws** scene if it's not already open.

Visor is considered a "custom object." Therefore, we need to apply it to an object in order for it to work. We can choose any object in our scene, but I prefer to use a null.

2. Click on the **Items** tab, and from the Add menu, choose **Null**. The Build Null Object window appears. Enter **Visor** for the name and hit **OK**. Activate Objects selection mode and then hit **<p>** to bring up the Object Properties window.

3. Click on the **Geometry** tab of the Object Properties window. Make sure that the Visor null object is the current object. Then click the **Add Custom Object** pop-up menu and select **Visor**.

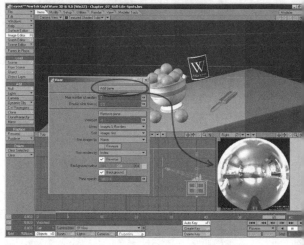

Figure 7-85: Open the Visor properties by double-clicking on Then click the Add pane button. A Visor preview window will appear in the lower-right viewport.

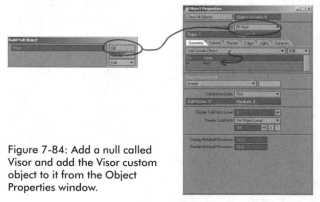

Figure 7-84: Add a null called Visor and add the Visor custom object to it from the Object Properties window.

4. Double-click on **Visor** to open its settings. We'll talk about the various

options in just a moment. For now, click on the **Add pane** button. Once you do so, a Visor preview will appear in the lower-right viewport.

The image currently being displayed is the kitchen_probe.hdr that is used for reflections on the bottle. You can view any image that you can load into LightWave within a Visor preview pane, and you can even use it to view renders. We'll see how to do this shortly. But first, let's address a fairly obvious question: Why would you want to view images in a viewport in the first place?

Layout's Image Viewer already does a great job of viewing images and renders. So why use a utility that places images into a viewport? Space. If you haven't already noticed, LightWave has a lot of panels and windows. There's the Surface Editor, the Image Editor, the Scene Editor, the Graph Editor, the Texture

Editor, and all of the Properties panels. Even on a dual-monitor system, you can quickly run out of space. And if you're on a single monitor setup, you're constantly opening and closing windows. Being able to view previews directly in a viewport is all about space.

There are also some very practical reasons to view images in a viewport. If you're working on texturing an object, it can be extremely helpful to have a reference image open while you work. The same holds true for lighting. When you're trying to match the lighting of a particular photo, having that photo open for comparison is invaluable.

The Visor preview is incredibly flexible and can be customized in a number of ways. Let's take a look at the options available to us.

Figure 7-86: The Visor options let you customize the operation and appearance of the Visor window.

The first option in the Visor window is the Add pane button. As we've already seen, this allows us to add a preview to one of our viewports. But it's interesting to note that you can add more than one pane.

5. Click on the **Add pane** button once again. It won't appear as if anything has

happened. That's because the second pane was added on top of the previous one. Click on the slider to the right of the Viewport option (which is currently set to –1) and drag it to the left. You'll see this second preview move one viewport to the left.

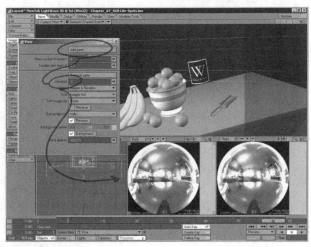

Figure 7-87: Click the Add pane button again. Then drag the Viewport slider to the left to move the second preview to a new viewport.

Using the options in the Show pop-up menu, you can customize each preview pane to display images (imported pictures such as textures and reference photos), renders, or a combination of the two. By default, Visor will display both images and renders.

Using the Sort menu, you have the ability to determine what types of files Visor shows first. You can choose to display images first or renders first.

For both images and renders, you can determine how the files are sorted using the options in the Sort images by and Sort renders by menus. And if needed, you can even reverse the order by clicking on the appropriate Reverse button.

Since we've got two preview panes, let's set one to view only images and the other

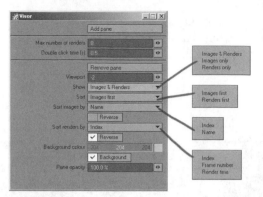

Figure 7-88: You can determine exactly what Visor displays with the options in the Show and Sort menus.

in the preview pane on the right. The handles on the left pane will disappear, indicating that it has been deselected.

8. Double-click **Visor** in the Object Properties window to open its settings window.

9. Click on the **Show** pop-up menu and choose **Renders only**. The preview will turn blue, indicating that there are no renders currently available.

to view only renders. The left Visor preview is currently active. Let's make this our images-only preview.

6. Click on the **Show** pop-up menu and choose **Images only**. You can leave all of the sorting options at their defaults; however, you're welcome to play with these settings if you'd like.

7. To change the settings for the original preview pane, we must select it. This can be a bit tricky. Click in the upper-left corner of the right Visor viewport. The Visor preview pane should become active, as indicated by the presence of small gray boxes (resizing handles) at its four corners.

If you accidentally deselect the preview pane, don't worry. Simply click on the Current Item pop-up menu on either the main interface or the Object Properties window and select the Visor object again. Both preview panes will be selected and will display sizing handles at their four corners. Click on one of the handles

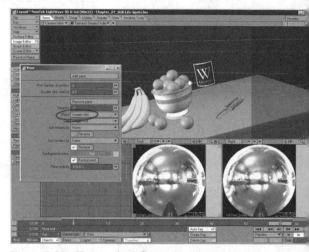

Figure 7-89: Change the left image pane to show images onl

Figure 7-90: Select the right image pane. You will know it is selected when you see resizing "handles" at its four corners. Then set it to show renders only.

Now, you may be thinking to yourself, "Hey! I already rendered. Why doesn't Visor see my render?" Visor requires that all renders be sent to a special frame buffer called Render2Image.

10. Close the Visor window and open the Render Globals window. Select the **Render Display** pop-up menu and choose **Render2Image**.

Figure 7-91: Open the Render Globals window and choose Render2Image for the Render Display

With the Render2Image display selected, our renders will be fed directly into Visor's preview and will bypass the Image Viewer altogether.

Let's create a render for the Visor preview. To speed things up, let's lower the resolution of the camera a bit.

11. Open the Camera Properties window and set Multiplier to **50%**. This will give us an image that is 320 x 240, which will render quite a bit faster.

12. Move the Frame Slider to frame 0 and press <**F9**> to render. When the render finishes, click **Abort** to exit the Render Status window. Once you do so,

the new render will appear in the Visor preview.

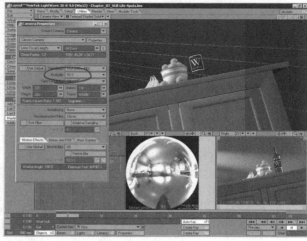

Figure 7-92: Set the resolution Multiplier to 50%. Then move the Frame Slider to frame 0 and press <F9> to render.

13. Move the Frame Slider to frame 30 and press <**F9**> to render. When it finishes, exit the Render Status window and move the Frame Slider to frame 60. Once again, press <**F9**> to render.

CLICK AND DRAG TO SORT THROUGH YOUR RENDERS/IMAGES

Figure 7-93: Render frame 30 and frame 60. Then select the Visor object. By clicking and dragging the image slider, you can move through your rendered images.

289

We now have three images stored in Visor's buffer. We can flip through these images with the controls in the Visor viewport.

14. Click on the **Visor** object to select it. Both preview panes will become active. Click on one of the handles in the Render only preview pane to select it. You'll notice a dark gray rectangle with a lighter gray box in its center. This is the image slider. Click and drag on the small gray box to move through the images stored in Visor's buffer.

15. Drag the image slider all the way to the right. This will display the first image we rendered (frame 0). As you move through your images, Visor will shrink the previous image and make the incoming image larger. By setting the image slider halfway between two images, you can preview two images at once. Let's do this using a larger viewport.

16. Open the Object Properties window and double-click on **Visor** to open its settings window. Click and drag the Viewport slider until the Renders only preview pane is in the top viewport (Figure 7-94).

The preview pane is a bit too small for this viewport. Let's resize it.

17. Click on the resizing handle in the lower-right corner of the preview pane and drag it until the render fills the window from top to bottom. Then click and drag on the gray box at the center of the preview pane to reposition it.

Move the pane to the center of the viewport.

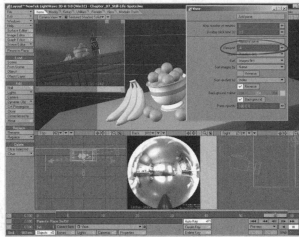

Figure 7-94: Open the Visor window and change the Viewport control to move the Renders only preview pane to the top viewport.

Figure 7-95: Resize the preview pane and move it to the center of the viewport.

18. Now click and drag the image slider in the preview pane until the two images are of equal size. You'll notice that the images are still fairly small. Resize the preview pane so that it fills the entire upper viewport. As you can see, Visor's preview panes are extremely

flexible and can be customized to fit any size in any viewport.

What happens if you're happy with one of your renders and would like to save it? There are no saving options available in Visor. So do you have to re-render your image? Absolutely not! When you render an image to the Render2Image display, it is stored as a temporary file in RAM and dropped into the Image Editor. You can access all of your Visor renders from this window.

19. Open the Image Editor. You'll see three files with an exclamation point followed by the word Render, a number, and the resolution of the file. These are Visor's renders, which are being held in RAM. Double-click on any of these renders. It will open up in Image Viewer, as shown in Figure 7-92. Now you can save the image to the format of your choice.

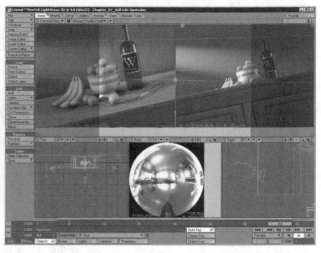

Figure 7-96: Drag the image slider until the two renders are the same size. Then resize the preview pane so that it fills the entire upper viewport.

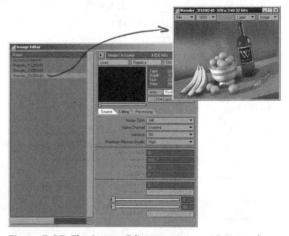

Figure 7-97: The Image Editor stores your Visor renders. Double-click on any render and it will open in Image Viewer.

Note

Keep in mind that Visor stores its files in RAM. If LightWave crashes (or you simply close the program), you will lose any unsaved images it is keeping track of. Be sure to save your images directly to disk when creating final renders.

Before we wrap up this look at Visor, let's examine one of the lesser-known (and yet extremely powerful) options that Visor gives us.

Creating an Image Viewer History

We have seen throughout this chapter how useful Image Viewer can be. But it has one major shortcoming: When you close the Image Viewer window, any renders it has stored in memory are lost. Wouldn't it be nice if Image Viewer had a history that

allowed you to access renders even
if the window were closed? Well, you
can create one. Let's see how.

1. Close the Image Editor and the
   Image Viewer. Open the **Chap-
   ter_07_Still-Life-Spots.lws**
   scene from the DVD (if it's not
   already open). Open the Render
   Globals window and set Render
   Display to **Image Viewer**.
   Move the Frame Slider to frame
   0. Then press **<F9>** to render.

2. When the render finishes, click
   Abort to close the Render Status window.

Figure 7-98: Open the Chapter_07_Still-Life-Spots.lws scene.
Move the Frame Slider to frame 0 and set Render Display to
Image Viewer. Then press <F9> to render the frame.

Our render is now displayed in the
Image Viewer. If we close this window, we'll lose the render. But we can tell
Image Viewer to send the rendered image
to a Visor buffer. Doing so will place a copy
of the image into RAM and it will be accessible from the Image Editor. Let's see how
to do this.

3. Click on the **File** menu in the
   upper-left corner of the Image Viewer
   window. Select **Frame Buffer** and
   choose the **Render2Image** option.

LightWave can send renders to a variety of
frame buffer devices. Traditionally, you
would use these to preview renders on a
broadcast color-calibrated monitor. But
with the advent of Visor, we now have the
option to send our images to a temporary
RAM buffer.

Image Viewer has two methods for sending renders to a frame buffer. You can
manually send them or you can automatically send them. Right now, Image Viewer
will only send images to the buffer when
you specifically tell it to do so. Let's do this
now.

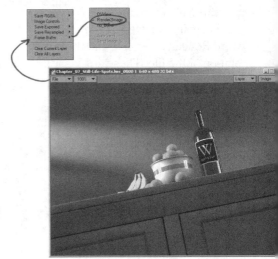

Figure 7-99: Choose File | Frame Buffer and select
Render2Image.

4. Click on **File | Frame Buffer** and
   choose **Send Image.** Your render has
   now been recorded as a temporary file
   and can be accessed from the Image
   Editor. Open the Image Editor and take
   a look.

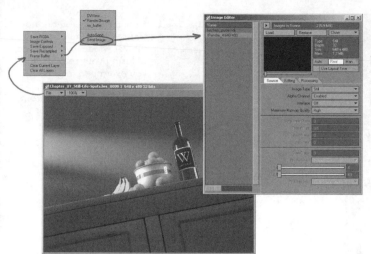

Figure 7-100: Choose File | Frame Buffer and select Send. This tells Image Viewer to send the current image to the Visor frame buffer. The image will then be available in the Image Editor.

By using the manual send option, you can temporarily store any image from the Image Viewer without having to store it. But if you want to create a true history, you can use the Auto-Send option.

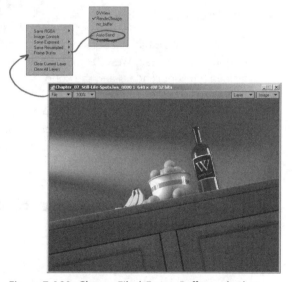

5. Click on **File | Frame Buffer** in Image Viewer and choose **Auto-Send**. Now, whenever you render, your image will be sent to the Visor buffer.

6. Move the Frame Slider to frame 60 and press <**F9**> to render. The finished render will appear in the Image Viewer window. It will also be listed in the Image Editor. You are free to close the Image Viewer window. If you need to open your image again, simply double-click on it in the Image Editor.

Figure 7-101: Choose File | Frame Buffer and select Auto-Send. Move the Frame Slider to frame 60 and press <F9> to render.

> **Note**
>
> Remember that files in Visor's buffer are not stored on the hard drive, nor will they be saved with the scene. They are stored in temporary RAM and will be lost when the program closes. Be sure to save any images you wish to keep before exiting LightWave.

Figure 7-102: You are now free to close the Image Viewer window without fear of losing your renders. If you ever need to get back to one of your renders, simply double-click it from within the Image Editor.

Conclusion

In this chapter, we've taken a detailed look at the rendering process. We've explored the various types of renders and the options that have a tremendous impact on the time it takes to produce a rendered image. We've examined the Image Viewer and Visor utilities and seen how they can be used to enhance your workflow. And we've touched on several key image filters that can be used to enhance your finished render.

Rendering is more than pushing a button. It is a series of intelligent decisions that you make to ensure you are in control of the render rather than it being in control of you.

Closing Notes on the Basic Skills Section

This is the last chapter in the Basic Skills section. By now you should be getting a handle on how to work with LightWave. I'm sure you're eager to move on to the more advanced sections in this book. But can I make a recommendation? If you're just getting started, don't move on just yet. Instead, go back and reread Chapters 2 through 7. The only way to master something is to practice. Repetition builds familiarity. Familiarity builds efficiency. And efficiency allows you to spend your energy focusing on *what* you want to do rather than *how* you're going to do it.

If you're just getting started with LightWave, you've probably only caught about 40% of what we've covered in the Basic Skills section. So do yourself a favor. Go back and read through these chapters again and spend time working with the tools and exercises therein. I guarantee that if you do, you'll be a stronger LightWave user than the person who hastily pushes through to the next chapter.

With that said, when you're ready, move on to Chapter 8, where we'll begin our Intermediate Skills section with another look at Modeler.

Intermediate Skills: Modeling

Working in LightWave is all about problem solving. In this chapter we're going to explore more than two dozen tools that can help you solve some of the more common modeling problems. Since we'll be covering so many tools, we won't spend a great deal of time on any of them. But rest assured, we'll get the essential information across and provide plenty of details where needed.

Let's begin by looking at a few tools that can help you create sophisticated geometry more easily.

EPSF Loader

EPSF is an acronym for Encapsulated Post-Script File. EPS files are vector graphics produced by programs like Adobe Illustrator, Photoshop, and Flash. They are common in the graphic art community and typically used for sharing logos and clip art between various programs.

Using **File | Import | EPSF Loader** allows you to bring EPS files into LightWave. This tool can be extremely helpful when creating broadcast graphics for TV where it's common to create "flying logo" animations.

> **Note**
>
> There are two requirements for using the EPSF Loader:
>
> • **Your EPS file can only consist of vector art.** Make sure that you convert fonts, stroked line weights, and any other effects to pure vector outlines. In Illustrator, the best way to do this is to use the Object | Expand Appearance command. (You may need to run this command twice in order for it to completely convert your artwork to outlines.)
>
> • **Your EPS file must be saved in Illustrator 8.0 or earlier format.** The EPSF Loader will not recognize files from newer versions of Illustrator. If you're using more recent versions of Illustrator, Flash, etc., make sure you save the file in Illustrator 8.0 or earlier format.

To use EPSF Loader, you must first convert your art to outlines and save the file in Illustrator 8.0 (or earlier) format.

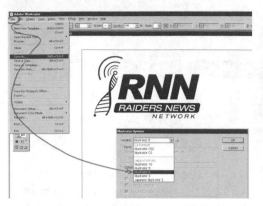

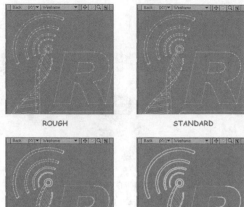

ROUGH   STANDARD

FINE   SUPER FINE

Figure 8-1: EPSF Loader allows you to bring logos and other vector art into LightWave. Make sure your art is converted to outlines and saved in Illustrator 8.0 (or earlier) format.

Figure 8-3: The Curve Division Level setting allows you to determine how many points will be used on the polygons created with the EPSF Loader.

In Modeler, choose the **File | Import | EPSF Loader** option. A window will appear allowing you to choose the file and set several options.

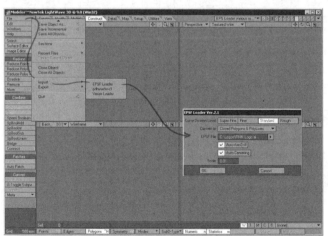

Figure 8-2: The EPSF Loader options determine how LightWave converts vectors into polygons.

The **Curve Division Level** buttons allow you to determine how many points will be used to create polygons from curved shapes in your EPS file. The Standard setting will work in most cases, but if you plan on rendering close-up shots, you may want to

consider using either the Fine or Super Fine settings.

The **Convert to** pop-up menu lets you choose what type of geometry your EPS curves will be converted into in Modeler.

- **Closed Polygons & PolyLines** turns any closed shape into a polygon and every line (single path) into a connected series of two-point polygons (polylines).

- **Closed Polygons** turns everything into polygons, even open-ended lines.

- **PolyLines** turns everything into systems of two-point polygons.

- **Spline Curves** turns all the lines of both open and closed shapes into LightWave's default spline curves. (We'll cover splines in more detail later in this chapter.)

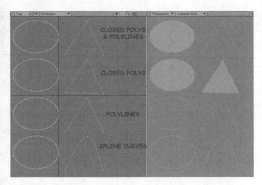

Figure 8-4: The Convert to menu geometry choices.

In most cases, using the default, Closed Polygons & PolyLines, will work just fine, but the other options here can be useful when the artwork isn't prepared just right. For example, if your logo has an open path that should have been closed, you can simply choose the Closed Polygons option in the EPSF Loader rather than having to make the change to the EPS file itself.

Below the Convert to menu is the **EPSF File** field. Clicking on the blue arrow to the right of this field allows you to navigate to and select the EPS file you wish to load.

- **Auto AxisDrill** will look for compound paths within an EPS file and attempt to drill holes in the polygons it generates to accurately recreate the appearance of the artwork. This feature can be particularly helpful with text objects. Letters such as "O" and "A" are not solid shapes. They have holes in them. Activating the Auto AxisDrill option will cut the holes out of these objects during the file import.

- **Auto Centering** automatically centers the imported geometry at the origin. I've never found a reason to turn this option off.

Note

If you get an error telling you that the "Internal buffers are too small" when using EPSF Loader, try turning off Auto AxisDrill. This error typically occurs when there are multiple overlapping objects in your EPS file. By turning off Auto AxisDrill, the object will usually import successfully. You can then drill the object manually to finalize the artwork. (See Chapter 3 for a discussion on the Drill tool.)

Note

If Auto AxisDrill gives you an error (typically "Buffers are too small"), it may be the result of trying to drill several complex polygons into one another. There is a known problem with Modeler when drilling complex polygons. There are two things you can do to resolve this. The first is to only use one drilling polygon at a time. For example, if you want to drill the word "BOX" into a rectangle, first drill the B, then the O, then the X. Second, you may need to cut the polygon being drilled, sectioning it off into smaller pieces. For example, if you have trouble drilling the word "BOX" into a single polygon, use the Knife tool (discussed later in this chapter) to section it off into three separate polygons — one for each letter. The simpler you can make things for the Drill tool, the more likely your chance of success.

AUTO AXISDRILL OFF   AUTO AXISDRILL ON

Figure 8-5: Auto AxisDrill will drill polygons to recreate the look of compound objects (such as certain text letters) in your EPS file.

- **Scale** resizes the imported geometry to LightWave's conventions of measurements. (With the default setting of 0.01, an 8.5" x 11" EPS file comes in at just over 2 m tall.) As with Auto Centering, I've never had a need to change the default setting.

When you've got all your options set, click **OK** to import the EPS file. You are now free to use the rest of Modeler's tools (such as Extrude and Bevel) to create dynamic 3D objects from your 2D artwork.

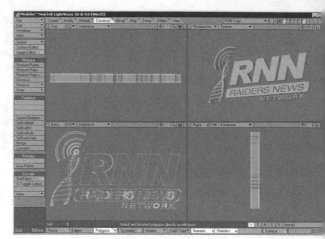

Figure 8-6: Once imported, you can use Modeler's tools (such as Extrude and Bevel) to create dynamic 3D objects from your 2D artwork.

Note

Remember LightWave's self-imposed limitation of 1,023 points per polygon when you're importing Encapsulated PostScript files! If you're having problems with things coming in as a "cloud" of points instead of as polygons, it means that LightWave is trying to create more points on a poly than it will "allow" itself to have. You can decrease the Curve Division Level setting, or, in your vector-based illustration program, cut your image up into a series of different-colored bands. Each color in the illustration will import as a separate polygon.

Primitives

Gemstone

The **Create | Primitives | More | Gemstone** tool makes quick work of creating diamonds, emeralds, rubies, and other faceted stones. Simply activate the tool, then click and drag in one of your viewports to create the stone.

You can interactively adjust the overall size of the gemstone by dragging the blue box that surrounds it while the tool is active. You can also adjust the height of its crown and pavilion by dragging the blue handles at the top and bottom of the stone.

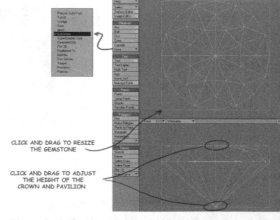

CLICK AND DRAG TO RESIZE THE GEMSTONE

CLICK AND DRAG TO ADJUST THE HEIGHT OF THE CROWN AND PAVILION

Figure 8-7: The Gemstone tool lets you create perfectly cut stones. You can interactively adjust the size and the height of the crown and pavilion.

The Numeric panel contains additional options that give you full control over the look of your gemstone. We won't cover each of the options, but let's take a look at a few of the more important ones.

- **Symmetry** — This determines the number of facets in the crown of the jewel.

- **Girdle** — This determines the space between the crown (at the top of the gem) and the pavilion (at the bottom).

- **Table** — This determines the diameter of the flat disc at the very top of the crown.

Figure 8-9: Always make sure you enable the Make Air Polys option so that your gemstones will render properly. (You must have Ray Trace Reflection and Ray Trace Refraction enabled in Layout's Render Globals window to see the effect of Air polys in your object.)

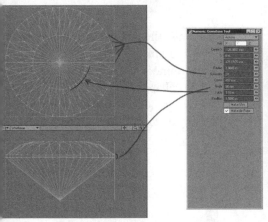

Figure 8-8: The Numeric panel contains important controls that allow you to alter the look of your gemstones.

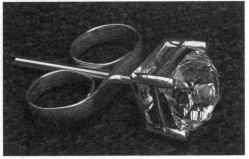

Figure 8-10: Gemstones are easy to create and look great when rendered.

- **Make UVs** — If you have already created and selected a UV map (see Chapter 11 for a discussion on UVs), you can activate this option to create UV data for the stone.

- **Make Air Polys** — This one is really important. As we discussed in Chapter 6, Air polys are necessary for transparent refractive surfaces to render properly. Enabling this option will create a duplicate set of polygons with a different surface whose normals face opposite those of the gemstone. *Unless you have a good reason to deactivate it, you should always make sure this option is active.*

Star Sphere

Stars are a staple of sci-fi space animations, but they can also be used to enhance typical dusk and night scenes as well. The basic idea is simple. You encompass your scene in a dense sphere of single-point polygons. When your camera moves or pans around the environment, the single-point polygons will create a great-looking star field with realistic parallax (where stars closer to the camera will appear to move faster than ones farther away).

Figure 8-11: The Star Sphere tool lets you create hundreds of stars with different "magnitudes" that allow you to vary their brightness in order to simulate distance.

When you run the **Create | Primitives | More | Star Sphere** tool, a window will appear allowing you to determine the number of stars to create at each "magnitude." The polys created at each magnitude will be given a different surface, allowing you to alter their Diffuse value to simulate varying distances.

You can adjust the size of the star sphere by changing the **Sphere Size** setting. You can also determine whether or not the object will be collapsed into a single layer or spread out over nine layers (one for each magnitude) by enabling the **Multilayered Object** check box.

When you press **OK**, Modeler will create a new Star Sphere object.

Curves

Hot Key Block

<Ctrl>+<p> Make Open Curve

So far, we've been working with three types of items in Modeler: points, polygons, and edges. In this section, we're going to introduce a new type of object: curves.

Curves (also called splines (*spatial lines*) or rails) are vector objects that smoothly flow from one point to the next. They are technically considered polygons, but unlike polygons, they cannot be assigned a surface and will not show up in your renders. Therefore, curves work best as an aid in the construction of other objects and not as final objects themselves.

There are typically three ways to use curves in LightWave:

● To form complex 2D shapes that can be extruded into 3D objects.

● To act as guides for other modeling tools.

● To construct a "cage" that can be "patched" to create complex objects.

In this chapter, we'll take a look at the first two ways to use curves. Later, in Chapters 17 and 18, we'll explore the third way as we learn how to model a realistic head with splines.

Make Curve

One of the easiest ways to create a curve is to create a few points (or select a few existing ones) and run the **Create | Curves | Make Curve | Make Open Curve** tool.

Close any object you may have open so that you're starting fresh. Press the < + > key on the numeric keypad to activate the **Points** tool. Then create four points in the Back viewport in a zig-zag pattern (where points alternate higher and lower). Remember that you can create multiple points simply by clicking with the right mouse button where you want each point to be created.

Click on the **Make Curve** menu at the bottom of the Create tab and choose **Make Open Curve** (or press <Ctrl> + <p>).

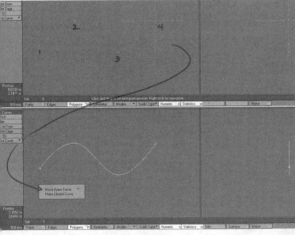

Figure 8-12: The Make Open Curve tool will create a spline curve from selected points.

The curve object will smoothly flow from one point to the next. It would take dozens of points to create a curve that's this smooth on a regular polygon. Yet with splines, we only need a handful of points.

You can move the points in the curve to adjust its overall shape. The position of points in a spline curve is the main key to controlling its shape.

The Make Open Curve tool is extremely powerful, but you may have noticed that there's no way to create an enclosed shape with it. To create a closed shape, use the **Make Closed Curve** option from the **Create | Curves | Make Curve** pop-up menu. This will generate a spline curve whose end point is connected to its starting point.

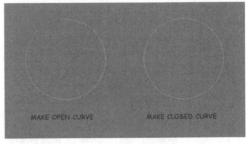

Figure 8-13: The Make Closed Curve tool will create a spline whose end point connects back to its start point.

Curve Start/End Points and Control Points

When you're working with curves, it's important to keep in mind that they have a designated beginning and end.

The beginning point on a curve is indicated by a small diamond, which can be seen when the curve is selected. In and of itself, neither the beginning nor ending point is that important. But certain modeling tools

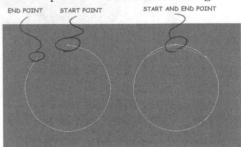

Figure 8-14: The beginning point on a curve is designated by a small diamond, which can be seen on the curve when it is selected.

that use curves (such as the Rail Extrude tool) factor the beginning point into their calculations. So it can be helpful to know which end of the curve you're dealing with.

> **Note**
>
> If you don't see the diamond indicating the beginning of the curve or the dotted lines of its control point handles (mentioned below), make sure that the Show Normals option is turned on in the Display Options window.

> **Note**
>
> You can flip a curve with the Flip tool (keyboard shortcut <f>). Flipping the curve will swap its beginning point with its end point.

You can also designate the first or last point on any curve as a "control point" to help adjust the shape of the curve. If you're familiar with vector drawing programs like Illustrator, Freehand, or Flash, you can think of control points as the tangent handles you find on a typical path.

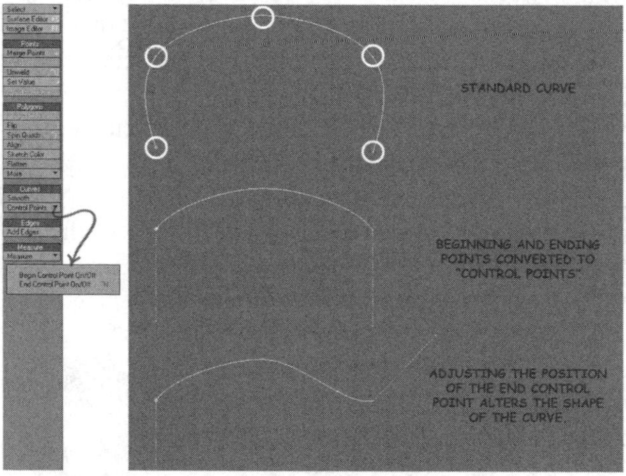

Figure 8-15: Turning the control point on for either the beginning or ending point of a curve lets you use the point to adjust the curve's overall shape.

Create five points as shown at the top of Figure 8-15, then press <Ctrl>+<p> to create an open curve.

Navigate to the **Detail** tab. From the **Curves** menu, choose the **Control Points** pop-up menu and activate the **Begin Control Point On/Off** option. Click the **Control Points** pop-up menu again and choose the **End Control Point On/Off** option.

The points on either end of your curve have now been designated as control points. They are no longer officially a part of the curve itself. Rather, they exist for the sole purpose of giving you greater control over the shape of the curve. Select the control points on either end of the curve and move them to adjust its overall shape.

You can easily determine whether or not a point is a control point by the presence of a dotted line pointing away from the end of a solid curve (as seen in the middle and bottom of Figure 8-15). You can disable the control point status for the end point in a curve by simply selecting the appropriate option from the Control Points pop-up menu again.

Freezing Splines

If you've created an open or closed curve and would like to convert it into a polygon, you can do so by "freezing" its shape using the **Construct | Convert | Freeze** tool (Figure 8-16). The resolution of the resulting polygon (the number of points used to create a smooth arc) is determined by the Curve Divisions setting in Modeler's General Options window.

When you freeze a curve, Modeler will create a standard polygon whose starting point is connected to its ending point. This can be beneficial if *you're already working with a closed curve shape*. But if you're working with an open curve (as seen in Figure 8-17)

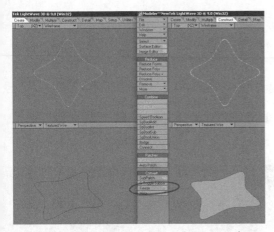

Figure 8-16: You can convert a curve into a polygon by using the Construct | Convert | Freeze tool.

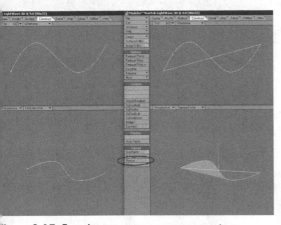

Figure 8-17: Freezing an open curve can create a polygon that crosses over itself.

and simply want to give it some depth, freezing is not the solution. Instead, you should simply extrude the curve as seen in Figure 8-18.

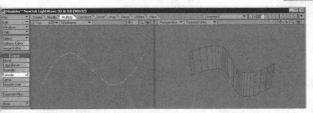

Figure 8-18: Simply extruding the curve is the simplest way to give it depth.

Using Splines to Create Complex 3D Shapes

Using spline curves to form complex 2D shapes that can be developed into 3D objects is one of their primary functions. In this section, we'll take a quick look at this process.

In the video tutorial from Chapter 3 (LightBot_Part_08.mov), it took nearly 15 minutes to model the hand for our LightBot using standard polygons. But by using splines, we can create the same model in less than a minute. *Yes, less than a minute.* (I actually timed myself!)

1. Open the Display Options (<**d**>) window and load the **LightBot Hand.jpg** file from the Images\Chapter 08 directory of the companion DVD into the Back (BottL) viewport. Set the Image Resolution to **1024** and lower the Brightness and Contrast settings so that we can see the geometry we create on top of the image. Press **OK**. Then zoom in to the clamp part of the hand.

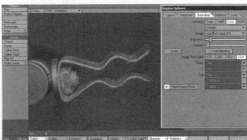

Figure 8-19: Load the LightBot Hand.jpg image into the Back viewport and zoom in so that it fills the viewport.

The clamp is symmetrical, so if we create one half, we can use the Mirror tool later to quickly complete the object.

2. Press the < + > key on the numeric keypad or go to the **Create | Points** menu and activate the **Points** tool. Starting at about the bottom center of the clamp (shown on the far left side of Figure 8-20), create several points that follow the basic contour of the clamp. (I used a total of 10 points, circled in Figure 8-20.) Then press <**Ctrl**> + <**p**> to create an open curve.

Our clamp now has depth, but it's lacking thickness. Let's take care of that.

> **Note**
>
> The technique for creating "thickness" shown here is not limited to your use of spline curves. It will work for virtually any hollow 3D object.

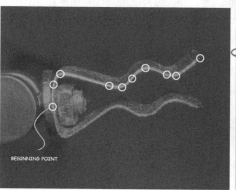

Figure 8-20: Lay down points as shown here and press <Ctrl>+<p> to create an open curve.

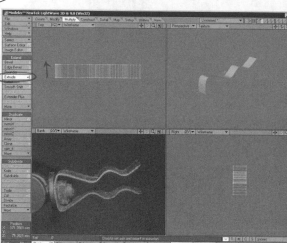

Figure 8-21: Extrude the curve to give it some depth.

3. Move the points around if necessary to adjust the shape of the curve. When you're happy with the shape, copy it and paste it into a new layer. This leaves the original on Layer 1 as a backup.

4. Now let's give this shape some depth. Switch to **Polygons** selection mode and select the spline (if it's not already selected). Go to the **Multiply** tab and click on the **Extend | Extrude** tool (or use the <**E**> shortcut). Place your mouse in the Top viewport and using the middle mouse button (or the <Ctrl> key modifier), click and drag to extrude the curve to give it some depth. I found that 50 mm seemed like a good amount, but you can be the judge of that.

5. Switch to **Polygons** selection mode and lasso select all of the polygons in the clamp. Press <**Ctrl**> + <**c**> to copy them. Then press the minus key <−> to hide the selected polys.

6. Press <**Ctrl**> + <**v**> to paste the copied polys back in place. Then press <**f**> to flip their normals, as shown in Figure 8-22.

7. Select the flipped polys. Then go to the **Multiply** tab and select **Multishift** from the Extend menu. Make sure that both the Shift and Inset pop-up menus are set to **Contour** in the Numeric panel. Then shift the selected polys about 6 or 7 mm, making sure you do not inset them (inset should be 0 m).

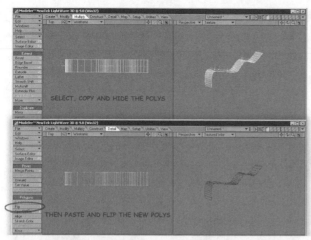

Figure 8-22: Select the clamp polys and copy them. Then hide them. Paste the copied polys into the same layer as the hidden polys. Then flip them to switch the direction of their normals.

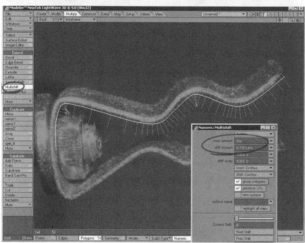

Figure 8-23: Use the Multishift or Smooth Shift tool to shift the polys.

Note

If you want to ensure you don't inset your polygons, you can use the Smooth Shift tool instead of Multishift. Smooth Shift works similarly to the Multishift tool, but it lacks the ability to inset the polys, making it ideal for this type of task.

8. Drop the Multishift tool and deselect the polys. Then press the Backslash key <\> to unhide the hidden polygons. Finally, use the **Merge Points** tool (<m>) to join the polygons together. (See Figure 8-24.)

9. Delete the poly at the bottom-left side of the clamp. Then activate the **Multiply | Duplicate | Mirror** tool. Position your mouse at the lower-left edge of the clamp (where you just deleted the poly). Click and drag in the Back viewport to mirror the polygons. In the Numeric panel, turn on **Free Rotation**. Then adjust the mirror line in the Back viewport until you get something similar to what you see in Figure 8-25.

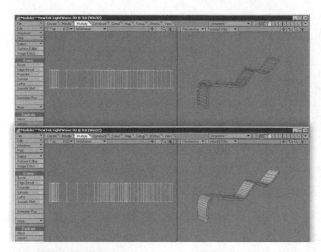

Figure 8-24: Deselect the polys and unhide the hidden polys. Then merge points to create a solid shape.

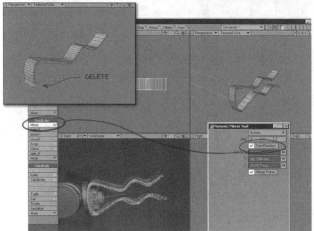

Figure 8-25: Delete the poly at the bottom-left side of the clamp. Then use the Mirror tool to mirror the clamp from top to bottom.

10. Zoom in to the area where the two halves of the clamp join together. It's likely that the points in this area don't overlap. Select the points on the bottom and move them up so that they're close to their counterparts. They don't have to be exactly on top of them.

11. Hold down the <**Shift**> key and lasso select all the points that should be connected (circled at the top of Figure 8-26). Then press <**m**> to run the Merge Points tool. Change the Range from Automatic to **Fixed** and enter a Distance that's large enough to encompass the gap between the disconnected

points. If you turn on the grid and check the grid size in the lower-right corner of Modeler's interface, you can get a good idea of what to enter into the Distance field. (See Figure 8-26.)

12. Press **OK** to fuse the points and connect the top half of the clamp to the bottom. Zoom out and inspect your work.

This new clamp is much better than the one we built in the Chapter 3 video tutorial. And it took a lot less time as well.

The technique shown here (roughing out a 2D shape, then giving it 3D depth and thickness) is one of the main uses of spline

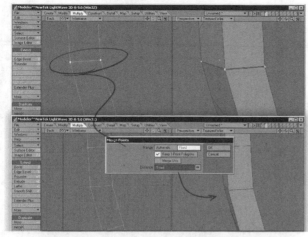

Figure 8-26: Zoom in to the area where both halves of the clamp come together. Move the points so that they almost overlap. Then deselect them and run the Merge Points tool to fuse them together.

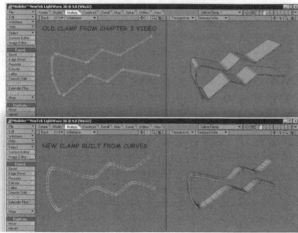

Figure 8-27: Compare the old clamp built in Chapter 3 to the one we've created here.

curves. But it's not the only one. As we get further into the chapter, we'll see how splines can be used by other tools to create complex objects in a snap!

Point Translation Tools

If you've been working with Modeler awhile, you may have noticed that you're required to move points around quite a bit. So far, you've seen how you can move an individual point by selecting it and then repositioning it with the Move tool. This works, but when you have dozens of individual points that all need tweaking, the constant select, move, deselect process can be tedious. Fortunately, there's a much easier way.

Hot Key Block
<Ctrl>+<t> Drag
<;> Drag Net
<G> Snap Drag

Drag

The **Modify | Translate | Drag**
tool allows you to move individual
points *without selecting them first!*
You simply activate the tool, place
your mouse over the point you want
to move, then click and drag.

You can use the Drag tool in any
viewport, including the Perspective
viewport. And it works extremely
well with Symmetry mode, allowing
you to fine-tune the shape of your
objects quickly and easily.

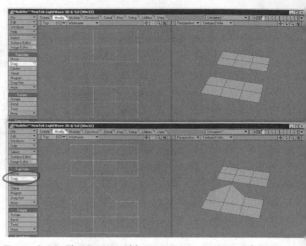

Figure 8-28: The Drag tool lets you move points without
selecting them first.

Drag Net

The **Modify | Translate | Drag
Net** tool is similar to Drag. It allows
you to move points around without
selecting them first. But while the
Drag tool works on individual points,
the Drag Net tool works on groups
of points within a given radius.

The effect of the Drag Net tool
falls off from the center of its area of
influence to its outer edge. Therefore, points at the center will be
affected more than those at the outside edge.

You can right-click and drag to
interactively adjust the size of the
area of influence. Placing your
mouse over a point, then left-clicking and dragging will affect it and the
points around it (within the area of
influence).

The Drag Net tool is particularly useful
when working on subpatch objects (discussed in Chapter 15) because it provides a
fast way to move groups of points in a very
organic manner.

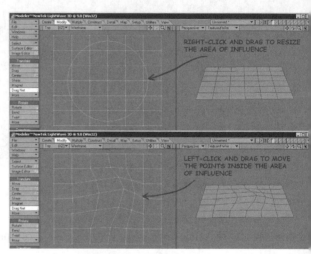

Figure 8-29: The Drag Net tool lets you move groups of points
within a user-defined area of influence.

Drag Net has a sister tool called Magnet,
which can be found in the Modify | Trans-
late menu. It operates similarly to Drag
Net, but allows you to define a fixed area of
influence. We'll see how the Drag Net and
Magnet tools can be used to reshape
objects in the Chapter 8 video tutorial.

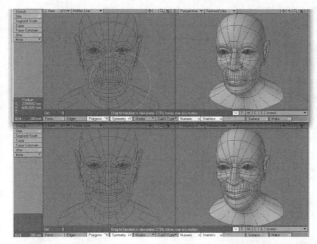

Figure 8-30: The Drag Net tool is particularly useful when used on subpatch objects and in Symmetry mode where a single click-drag can have a major impact on the appearance of your object.

Snap Drag

The **Modify | Translate | More | Snap Drag** tool is one of Modeler's hidden little gems. It allows you to drag individual points and snap them to other points in the active foreground layers.

The **Drag Set** pop-up menu in the Numeric panel is the key to using the Snap Drag tool effectively. There are thee options that affect which points are moved:

- **One Point** allows you to drag a single point on an object. This is identical to the function of the standard Drag tool, but with the added benefit of being able to snap to other points.

- **Connected Points** allows you to drag groups of polygons that share common points. This is useful when you have two objects and want to snap one to another (as seen in Figure 8-31).

- **All Points** will move all the points in the current foreground layers. This mode is similar to the standard Move tool with the added benefit of being able to snap to other points. (You can limit the points that move by selecting them first.)

Figure 8-31: The Snap Drag tool lets you snap points in the foreground layer(s) to one another.

The **View Alignment Only** check box allows you to prevent snapping in all three dimensions. Take a look at Figure 8-32.

The top image shows a point (circled in the orthographic viewport) that I want to align with the point immediately to its left. With View Alignment Only turned off, dragging in the orthographic viewport causes this point to snap on top of the other point (as shown in the middle image). But with View Alignment Only turned on, dragging in the orthographic viewport allows me to snap in only the two dimensions of the viewport in which I'm dragging.

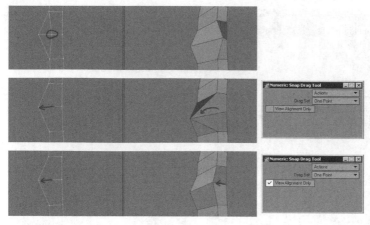

Figure 8-32: The View Alignment Only option affects the ability of a point to snap along the axis perpendicular to the viewport in which you drag.

Rotation Tools

Bend

The **Modify | Rotate | Bend** tool allows you to incrementally rotate polygons along a user-defined axis. Let's see how this is done.

1. Create a tall rectangular box with roughly 30 segments as shown in Figure 8-33.

> **Note**
>
> In order to get a smooth bend, your object must have a sufficient number of segments. If you need to add more segments, you can do so with the Knife tool, which is discussed later in this chapter.

2. Click on the **Modify | Rotate | Bend** tool (or press the <~> shortcut).

Bending is a two-step process. First, you must define the range and axis for the bend. Then you must create the bend.

3. Position your mouse at the bottom center of the rectangular box in the Back viewport. Click with your right mouse button and drag up. The direction you drag defines the axis along which the bend will occur. By dragging up, we are telling Modeler that the bend will take place along the Y-axis.

4. You will see a blue symbol appear as you drag your mouse. This symbol defines the range of polygons that will be affected by the Bend tool. The polygons at the narrow end of the range will bend the least and those at the wide end will bend the most. Drag your mouse all the way to the top of the box (as seen in Figure 8-33).

5. Now we can bend our object by left-clicking and dragging in the viewport that looks down along the axis we defined earlier. How do you know that you're using the correct viewport? Take a look at Figure 8-33. You'll notice that the top of the range forms a blue cross in the Top viewport. The viewport containing this cross is the one in which you should click and drag.

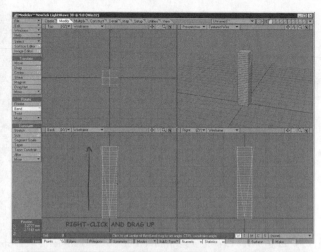

Figure 8-33: Create a tall box with enough segments to create a smooth bend. Activate the Bend tool and define the axis and range by right-clicking and dragging.

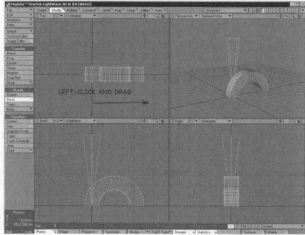

Figure 8-34: Left-click and drag in the viewport that looks down on the axis you defined earlier.

What happens if your object is at an angle and the cross doesn't appear in any of the orthographic viewports? Simply rotate your Perspective viewport until you see the cross shape. Then click and drag to bend your object in the Perspective viewport.

You can limit the bend simply by changing the start and end points on the range.

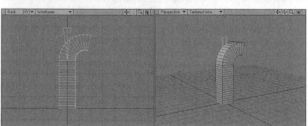

Figure 8-35: Changing the start and end range positions allows you to achieve different bend results.

Twist

The **Modify | Rotate | Twist** tool rotates polygons around a user-defined axis. Note that this is different from the Bend tool, which rotates *along* a specific axis.

You use the Twist tool in the same way that you use the Bend tool. First you must define an axis and range. Then you can proceed to twist your polys. As was the case with the Bend tool, you will need a sufficient number of segments in your object for the Twist tool to work well.

Create another tall rectangular box with roughly 30 segments just as you did before. Activate the Twist tool and position your mouse over the bottom center of the box in the Back viewport. Then right-click and drag up to define the axis and range as shown in Figure 8-36.

Now we can twist our object by left-clicking and dragging in the viewport that looks down along the axis we defined earlier. As was the case with the Bend tool, we can determine the proper axis simply by looking for the blue cross formed by the range symbol.

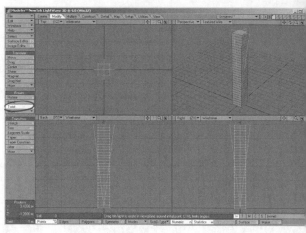

Figure 8-36: Create a segmented box as shown here. Activate the Twist tool and right-click and drag to define an axis and range.

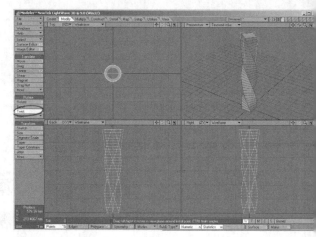

Figure 8-37: Left-click and drag in the viewport that looks down the axis you defined earlier.

> ## Note
>
> Bending and twisting your polygons is a quick way to produce non-planar polygons. (See Chapter 3 for a discussion on non-planar polys.) Make sure you check the Polygon Statistics panel and correct any non-planar polys that could present errors at render time.

Transformation Tools

Hot Key Block
<**J**> Jitter
<**M**> Smooth

Taper

The **Modify | Transform | Taper** tool allows you to resize your polygons along a user-defined axis. The same rules that apply to the Bend and Twist tools also apply to the Taper tool. Namely, tapering is a two-step process that involves defining a range/axis and then actually performing the taper.

Create a tall rectangular box with roughly 30 segments as seen in Figure 8-38. Click on the Modify | Transform | Taper tool to activate it. Position your mouse over the bottom center of the box in the Back viewport and then right-click and drag up to define the axis and range shown in Figure 8-38.

Position your mouse over the Top viewport. This is the viewport that looks straight down the axis we defined (as indicated by the blue cross from the range symbol). Left-click and drag to taper the box.

With the Taper tool still active, take a look at the Numeric panel. (Press the <n> keyboard shortcut if the Numeric panel isn't already open.) There are two settings here that can have a tremendous impact on the way your tools work: the Shape buttons and the Shape sliders.

Adjusting the Shape controls will change the way tools like Bend, Twist, and Taper affect your object. Press each of the Shape buttons to see it interactively alter the range you've defined. Then click and drag both of the Shape sliders. The sliders allow you to ease the effect of the tool in and out at both the start and end of the range.

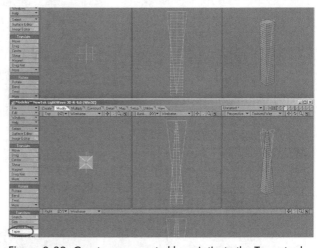

Figure 8-38: Create a segmented box. Activate the Taper tool and right-click and drag to define an axis and range. Then left-click and drag in the Top viewport to perform the taper.

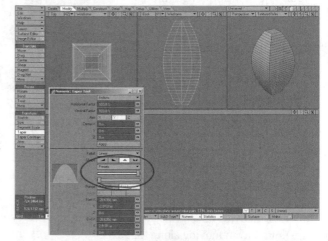

Figure 8-39: The Shape settings in the Numeric panel allow you to make complex modifications with the Taper, Bend, and Twist tools.

The only thing you need to know about the Shape controls is that they must be adjusted *before* you left-click and drag, not after. They will not automatically update geometry that you've modified earlier with a different Shape setting.

Jitter

The **Modify | Transform | Jitter** tool (keyboard shortcut <**J**>) will randomly move the points in your object, creating an organic unevenness to it. This can be used to quickly create rough landscapes or to break up the perfect symmetry on a character model.

When you run the Jitter tool, you will be presented with a requester that allows you to change how the points will move and by what amount.

The **Type** pop-up menu options let you choose how the points are moved. I typically leave this at Gaussian, which will produce a nice, random movement to the points in your object. We won't go through each of the settings in the Type menu here (they're covered in detail in the LightWave manual) but I will say that in the past 10 years, I've only changed Type once or twice. Take that for whatever it's worth.

The **Radius** settings allow you to define the outside distance that points are allowed to move. Points will move random amounts along the positive and negative side of each axis for which you specify a non-zero number. Leaving an axis at 0 will prohibit the points from moving along that axis.

Smooth

If you're working with an object and find that a fairly dense point mesh is causing unwanted bumps on your surface, you can use the **Modify | Transform | More | Smooth** tool to average them out.

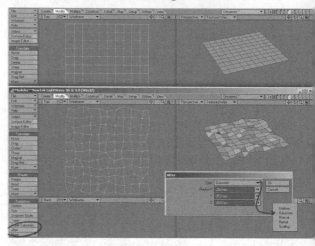

Figure 8-40: The Jitter tool lets you randomize the position of points in your object.

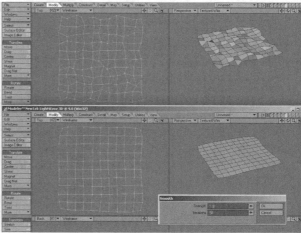

Figure 8-41: The Smooth tool lets you average the position of points in your object.

When you run the Smooth tool, you will be presented with a requester containing two options: Strength and Iterations.

You would expect a higher Strength value to create a smoother object. But in my experience, the higher the Strength value, the more chaotic your results will be.

I find that I get the best results by leaving Strength between 0.5 and 2.0 and increasing the Iterations between 10 and 50.

Extension Tools

Hot Key Block
\<L> Lathe
\<Ctrl>+**\<r>** Rail Extrude

Rounder

The **Multiply | Extend | Rounder** tool is a powerful edge beveling and point rounding utility.

Rounder is essential for creating realistic models. In the real world, the corners and edges of every object (no matter how sharp they might appear) are slightly rounded. This rounding produces a glint along the object's edge when the light catches it. Unfortunately, 3D software makes it easy to create corners and edges that are infinitely sharp. These edges don't catch the light like real objects do. When rendered, they have the distinct look of "computer graphics."

Rounder has two modes. You can toggle between them at any time during the tool's use. In the first mode, Rounder bevels points (called a chamfer in some 3D applications). In the other mode, it rounds the edges of polygons.

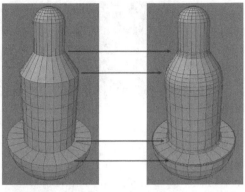

Figure 8-42: Rounder makes edge beveling quick and easy.

ROUNDER'S "POINTS" MODE   ROUNDER'S "EDGES" MODE

Figure 8-43: Rounder allows you to bevel points (also called a chamfer) as well as the edges of polygons.

To use Rounder, first select one or more points, edges, or polys. Then choose whether or not you want to round points or edges, click in any viewport, and drag your mouse. Dragging up and down increases and decreases the bevel size. Dragging left and right increases and decreases the number of bevel segments.

The key to using Rounder effectively comes from how Rounder "sees" your selection. Take a look at Figure 8-44.

> ### Note
>
> Rounder only works on 3D objects. It will not work on a single 2D polygon. When working with Boolean objects, make sure that you have merged points first or Rounder will give you an error!

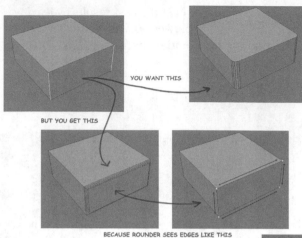

YOU WANT THIS

BUT YOU GET THIS

BECAUSE ROUNDER SEES EDGES LIKE THIS

Figure 8-44: Rounder sees everything in terms of point selections (regardless of whether you have points, polygons, or edges selected). This simple fact is the key to using Rounder effectively.

If you select two edges of a box as shown in the upper left of Figure 8-44, you would expect Rounder to produce the results you see in the upper right. But that's not what you'll get. Instead, all four edges are rounded as seen in the lower left. The reason for this is simple: *Rounder doesn't see edges.*

Rounder has an Edges mode, but it doesn't truly understand Modeler's edges. Instead, Rounder sees all selections (points, polygons, or edges) as point selections. The image at the lower right of Figure 8-44 shows what Rounder "sees" when you select two edges. As you can tell, there's a big difference between four points and two edges. Four points effectively creates four edges, not two.

Since Rounder only sees point selections, you may find it helpful to stick to point selections. (I find it easier to predict the results when I'm working with point selections.) In order to get the results seen in the upper right of Figure 8-44, you need to round one edge at a time, as shown in Figure 8-45.

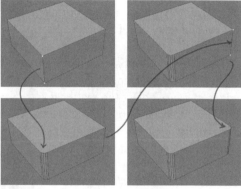

Figure 8-45: To round adjacent edges, you must do so one at a time.

Rounder is an incredible tool with a wealth of options available in its Numeric panel. Let's run through these options.

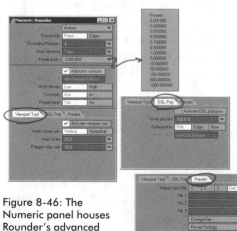

Figure 8-46: The Numeric panel houses Rounder's advanced options.

- **Round only** allows you to toggle between point rounding and edge rounding modes.

- **Rounding Polygons** determines the number of bevel segments to use. Higher numbers will result in a smoother-looking bevel.

- **Inset distance** determines the size of the bevel.

- **Adjacent surfaces** tells Rounder to apply the surface from the surrounding polygons to the new geometry. If you uncheck this box, you can specify a new surface name in the New Surface field.

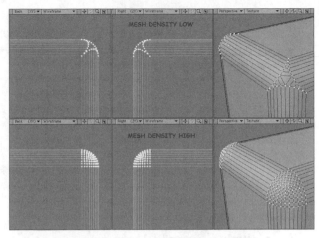

Figure 8-47: Mesh density settings at Low and High.

- **Mesh density** determines the resolution of the mesh at the corners of your object. Low uses a minimum number of polygons; however, the rounding effect is compromised. High creates a wonderfully smooth corner, but generates more polygons in the process.

- **Convexity** determines whether the corner bevel pulls the new polygons in or pushes them out. You won't see this in Edges mode as often as you will in Points mode.

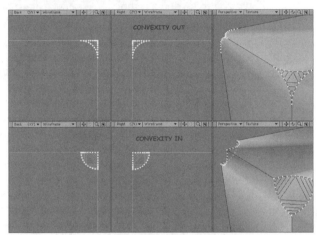

Figure 8-48: Convexity settings set to In and Out.

- **Project Inset** uses a complicated set of algorithms to determine how the rounding will occur at the physical edge of your object. There is no "right" setting for this. In practice, if you find that the rounding is giving you unsatisfactory results, try turning this setting on and off.

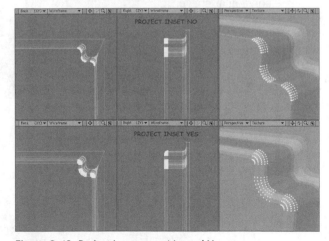

Figure 8-49: Project Inset set to No and Yes.

At the bottom of the Numeric panel are three tabs.

- **Viewport Tool** allows you to adjust settings that deal with Rounder's interactivity controls.

- **OGLPoly** provides settings for correcting OpenGL rendering errors.

- **Presets** allows you to store and recall your favorite settings.

Lathe

The **Multiply | Extend | Lathe** tool allows you to sweep a template polygon or spline curve around a user-defined axis to create a solid object.

In Figure 8-50, a spline curve (shown on the left) has been created to form the profile of a goblet. By using the Lathe tool, we can "sweep" this shape 360 degrees around the Y-axis to create a complete 3D object.

To use the Lathe tool, simply generate your template polygon or curve.

Then press <L> or go to the **Multiply | Extend** menu and choose **Lathe**. Position your mouse over the location where you want the lathe action to be centered. This will typically be the inside edge of your template object. Left-click and drag to define the axis for the Lathe tool to sweep around. (If you create your object in the Back viewport, you will typically drag down to lathe around the Y-axis.)

In many cases, you'll choose to sweep your template polygon at its inside edge (as seen in Figure 8-51). But if you center the

action away from the template, you can create looping objects like springs, phone cords, and even spiral staircases.

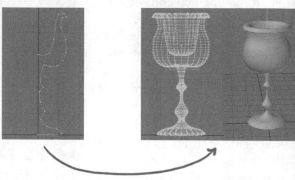

Figure 8-50: The Lathe tool lets you create solid objects from a template poly by spinning them around a user-defined axis.

CREATE YOUR TEMPLATE AND ACTIVATE THE LATHE TOOL

POSITION YOUR MOUSE WHERE THE ACTION WILL BE CENTERED

LEFT-CLICK AND DRAG TO DEFINE THE AXIS.

Figure 8-51: Using the Lathe tool is a simple three-step process. Create your template and activate the Lathe tool. Then position your mouse at the center of the action. Finally, click and drag to define the axis for the tool to work on.

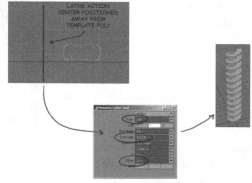

Figure 8-52: By centering the action away from the edge of your template and using the Numeric panel options, you can create looping objects in a snap.

The Numeric panel for the Lathe tool gives you additional controls that allow you to create complex looping objects in a snap. The primary controls here are Sides, Start/End Angle, and Offset.

- **Sides** — This determines the resolution of the final object by controlling how many instances of your template polygon are used in the Lathe operation.

- **Start/End Angle** — These settings determine the range of the effect. By lowering the Start or End Angle below 360 degrees, you can create an incomplete lathe as seen in Figure 8-54. By increasing these settings beyond 360 degrees, you can create a looping effect as seen in Figure 8-52.

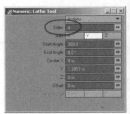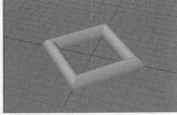

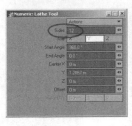

Figure 8-53: The Sides setting determines the resolution of your lathed object.

Figure 8-54: The Start/End Angle setting determines the range of the lathe operation.

Note

You can enter mathematical formulas into any Modeler data entry field. If you want to spin your template around 8.5 times but don't want to do the math yourself, you can simply enter 360*8.5 into the End Angle field and Modeler will calculate the result for you.

- **Offset** — This moves the template poly from the Start Angle to the End Angle by the amount you enter here.

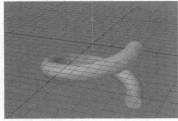

Figure 8-55: The Offset setting will move the template poly from the Start Angle to the End Angle by the amount you specify.

Note

When you work with the Lathe tool, you may find that your polys appear flipped. If this happens, simply hit the <f> key to flip their normals while the Lathe tool is still active. (You do not need to drop the Lathe tool first.)

Rail Extrude

The **Multiply | Extend | Rail Extrude** tool allows you to extrude a template polygon along the length of a background spline curve. This opens the door for the creation of all kinds of flowing shapes, from stylized hair to octopus tentacles. Let's take a look at how to use this tool to create part of the decorative stand for the mirror seen in Figure 8-56.

1. Load **Mirror.jpg** (from Images\ Chapter 08 on the DVD) into Modeler's Back viewport and lower the Brightness and Contrast slightly so that you can see the geometry you create over it.

2. Position your mouse over the bottom center of the stand (circled in Figure 8-56). Use the **Points** tool to create a sequence of points following the curve of the mirror's stand. Then press <Ctrl>+<p> to make an open curve. Adjust the curve if necessary using the **Drag** tool (discussed earlier in this chapter).

Figure 8-56: Load the Mirror.jpg file into the Back viewport. Create a new spline that follows the shape of the mirror's stand.

3. When you're satisfied with the spline you've created, switch to a new layer and place the layer with the spline curve in the background.

4. Use the **Ball** or **Disc** tool to create a small circle in the Right viewport. Then move the circle so that it is positioned at the beginning of the background spline.

5. Resize the circle if necessary so that its diameter is roughly that of the mirror's stand (shown in the Back viewport of Figure 8-57).

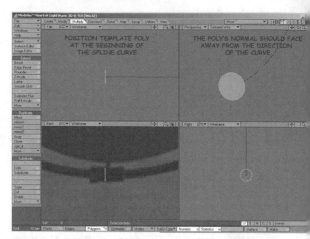

Figure 8-57: Create a circle in the Right viewport. Size it to roughly the diameter of the stand and position it at the beginning of the spline curve (placed in the background).

> **Note**
>
> The Rail Extrude tool requires your template poly to be positioned (and rotated if necessary) so that it lines up perfectly with the direction of the background spline. If you aren't getting the results you expect from this tool, make sure that your template poly is aligned and rotated properly and that it is positioned just behind the start of the background spline curve.

6. The normal for this circle should be facing away from the direction of the spline. If necessary, flip the poly.

7. With the template poly in the foreground and the spline curve in the background, run the **Multiply | Extend | Rail Extrude** tool. A configuration window will appear with the following options:

    •   **Automatic** segmentation will let LightWave use its best judgment in determining how many "slices" to make and where they should be so the extrusion most closely follows the background curve.

- **Uniform Lengths** lets LightWave distribute the specified number of segments so they are all equidistant along the curve's length.

- **Uniform Knots** tells LightWave to distribute the specified number of segments with relation to the placement and number of knots (points) on the background curve.

- **Oriented** tells LightWave to rotate the poly, aligning it to the curve as it is extruded.

8. Leave Segments at **Automatic** and make sure that **Oriented** is checked. In most cases, this will produce the best results with the least amount of fuss. Press **OK**. Modeler will extrude the circle over the length of the spline. Your results should be similar to those seen in Figure 8-58.

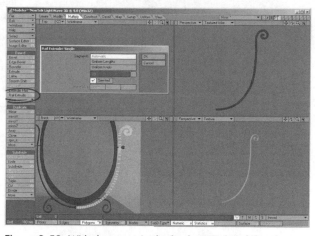

Figure 8-58: With the curve in the background and the template poly in the foreground, run the Rail Extrude tool. Leave Segments at Automatic and make sure Oriented is checked. Then press OK.

> **Note**
>
> If parts of your extruded object look funky, it's likely due to points in the spline curve being too close together. Whenever you get unwanted results with the Rail Extrude tool, the first thing you should do is closely inspect the number and position of points in your curve. If two points are in close proximity (especially at the beginning or end of the spline), delete them and try running the tool again. In my experience, this turns out to be the culprit 90% of the time.

Magic Bevel

The Rail Extrude tool is great for creating complex extrusions, but you may have noticed in the previous section that the size of the extrusion was constant over the length of the spline. In our mirror stand, we want it to taper as it comes to an end (as seen in Figure 8-59).

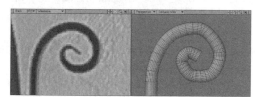

Figure 8-59: The end of the stand should gradually taper, but the Rail Extrude tool (used in the previous section) kept the diameter constant over the length of the curve.

Unfortunately, there's no way to taper the extrusion with the Rail Extrude tool. But we can recreate the effect with the **Multiply | Extend | More | Magic Bevel** tool.

The Magic Bevel tool is a powerful tool with a dizzying array of options. Unfortunately, we can't cover them all here due to space limitations. But we can show you the essentials to help get you started on the right foot.

1. Zoom in to the curly end of the stand you created with the Rail Extrude tool in the previous section. Locate a ring of points positioned around the area where the stand begins to taper. Select them, then press <p> to create a new polygon.

2. Switch to **Polygons** selection mode. The new polygon should be selected. Cut it and paste it onto a new layer as shown in Figure 8-60.

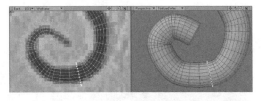

Figure 8-60: Select the circle of points located where the tapering begins. Create a new polygon from them. Then cut this circle and paste it to a new layer.

By creating a circle polygon from the existing points on our object, we can ensure the shape we create with Magic Bevel will perfectly line up with our Rail Extruded object.

3. Run the **Magic Bevel** tool from the **Multiply | Extend | More** menu. A small blue circle will appear at the center of the polygon.

4. This blue circle is a handle. We'll use it in just a bit to drag out a bevel. First, open the Numeric panel (if it's not already open).

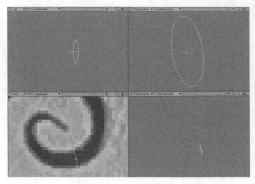

Figure 8-61: Run the Magic Bevel tool. A small blue circle will appear at the center of your polygon.

5. The Operation pop-up menu at the top of the Numeric panel should be set to **Extrude**. In this mode, the Magic Bevel tool will extrude and taper your polygon when you click and drag on the blue handle. The other modes in this menu allow you to customize the shape of the bevel after it has been extruded.

6. Make sure that **Spline**, **Uniform**, and **Align To Path** are checked. The Spline setting will calculate the extrusion using a smooth curve rather than linear segments. This makes it easier to see and adjust the shape of your bevel after it has been extruded. (Note that the Spline setting does not enable you to extrude *along* a curve, as was the case with the Align to Rail tool. It simply uses a curve in its calculations to help smooth out the placement of bevel segments.) Uniform will create equally spaced segments. Align To Path ensures that the template polygon will be rotated as necessary.

Toward the bottom of the Numeric panel are three options: **Precision**, **Scale**, and **Spin**. These options have a tremendous impact on how you use the Magic Bevel tool.

- **Precision** — In my experience, this is one of the most important settings. It determines how many new segments are created as you click and drag the blue handle on your polygon. Lower Precision settings will create more segments. Higher settings will create fewer segments. There is no "right" setting. You will have to tinker with this to get a setting that "feels" right for how you move your mouse.

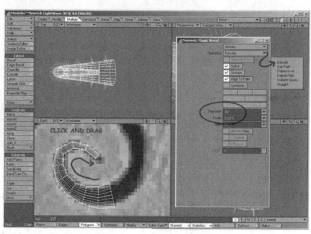

Figure 8-62: Open the Numeric panel. Make sure Operation is set to Extrude. Then set Precision to 40. Click and drag the blue handle in the Back viewport to extrude the polygon. Finally, lower the Scale setting to taper the polygon over the length of the extrusion.

Note

Unfortunately, adjusting the Precision setting after you've extruded your shape will not retroactively adjust it. The Precision setting only affects your next extrude. If you extrude and find that you're getting too many segments, simply undo, increase the Precision, and try again.

- **Scale** — This adjusts the amount of tapering on your extruded polygon. You can adjust this at any time and see the results on your object. This makes it easy to extrude first, then adjust the scale afterward.

- **Spin** — This will rotate the polygon from its starting point to the end of the extrusion. This can be helpful for correcting the orientation of your template poly if it rotates unexpectedly as you extrude it.

7. Set Precision to **40**. That should allow you to drag out the bevel at a reasonable pace and not create too many unnecessary segments.

8. Place your mouse over the blue handle in the Back viewport. Click and drag, following the curve of the mirror stand.

9. Once you have the basic shape, adjust the scale so that it tapers properly. I

found that setting Scale to **83%** gave me the results I wanted.

10. When you're satisfied with the results, drop the tool and deselect the polygons.

11. Switch back to the Rail Extruded shape you created in the previous section. Select the polygons that should have tapered in but didn't. (All the polygons to the left of the circular polygon you created at the beginning of this section.) Copy the Magic Beveled tip into this layer and press <**m**> to merge points.

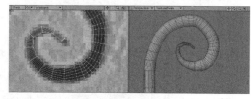

Figure 8-63: Delete the old polygons and paste the Magic Beveled polygons into their place. Then merge points to create a single object.

Duplication Tools

Note

If nothing is currently selected, you can quickly select everything in your foreground layers by pressing `<">` (double quote). This is the keyboard shortcut to invert your selection. If nothing is selected, inverting the selection will cause everything to be selected.

Clone

The **Multiply | Duplicate | Clone** tool allows you to duplicate objects. It includes an impressive range of options for offsetting, scaling, and rotating each successive clone. Unfortunately, the tool is not interactive, which means you can expect a lot of trial and error if you're trying to do anything fancy.

Let's take a look at the most simple and straightforward uses for this tool.

1. Open the **Chain.lwo** object from the Objects\Chapter 08 folder on the companion DVD. It consists of a single link; however, we can use the Clone tool to quickly create an entire chain.

The link in the Chain object is oriented along the X-axis. Therefore, if we wanted to create a long chain, we would need to clone it along the X-axis. But before we can do so, we need to know how far to move each copy so that the chain appears to be linked together.

Modeler has several tools to measure distances, but to be honest, I find it easier to move a copy of my object and note the distance in the Quick Info display than to fiddle with the measuring tools. Let's take a look at how this is done.

2. Lasso select the chain link, making sure all its polygons are selected.

3. Copy the link and paste it back into the foreground layer. It will be pasted right on top of the selected polys.

4. Activate the Move tool (keyboard shortcut `<t>`) and, holding down the `<Ctrl>` key (or clicking the middle mouse button), drag your mouse to the right until the left side of the selected link juts up to the right side of the unselected link, as shown in Figure 8-64. Keep your mouse button held down. Do not release it. When the object is in position, look at the Quick Info display in the lower-left corner of Modeler's interface and note the amount of movement on the X-axis. This is the amount we need to enter into the Clone tool.

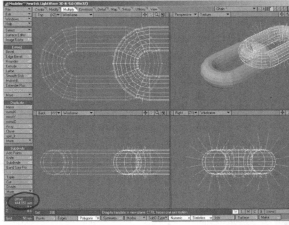

Figure 8-64: Open the Chain.lwo object. Select all the polygons. Copy and paste them into the foreground layer. Th move them as shown here. With your left mouse button still held down, note the amount of movement along the X-axis i the Quick Info display in the lower-left corner of Modeler's interface.

5. Drop the Move tool and press the **Delete** key to get rid of the selected polys. Now that we've got our offset amount, we're ready to clone our object.

6. Press <c> to open the Clone window or go to the **Multiply | Duplicate** menu and choose **Clone**. Enter the amount of movement you saw on the X-axis into the **Offset X** field. For the Chain object, it should be roughly **444 mm**.

7. Increase the number of clones as you see fit. For this example, I've entered **11**. That will produce a chain with 12 links (11 clones plus the original).

Every link in a chain is rotated 90 degrees from the one before it. We can easily accomplish this with the Rotation controls in the Clone window. The H, P, and B fields refer to heading, pitch, and bank; however, they assume that your object is oriented along the Z-axis. Therefore, we have to readjust our thinking accordingly. (This is where the problematic lack of interactivity in the Clone tool becomes apparent.)

Normally a rotation from side to side would be considered a rotation around an object's bank. However, since the Clone tool assumes an object is oriented along the Z-axis, it would not be the bank we need to adjust, but rather the pitch.

8. Enter **90** for the Rotation P field. Then press **OK**. The link will be rotated and cloned 11 times, creating the chain shown in Figure 8-65.

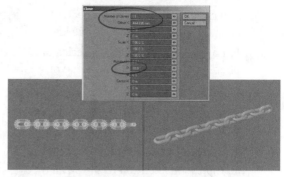

Figure 8-65: Delete the selected polys and run the Clone tool. Enter the amount you noted in the Quick Info display into the X field. Then enter 90 into the Rotation P field. Increase the number of clones to 11. Finally, press OK.

Point Clone Plus

The Clone tool works wonderfully when you want precise, predictable clones. But what about those times when you want your clones to be randomized, for example to place rocks of various sizes over a landscape? In instances such as this, the **Multiply | Duplicate | More | Point Clone Plus** tool is indispensable. Let's look at how we can use this tool to quickly add leaves to a barren tree.

1. Open the **Tree.lwo** object from the Objects\Chapter 08 folder. Let's talk briefly about this object. On Layer 1, I

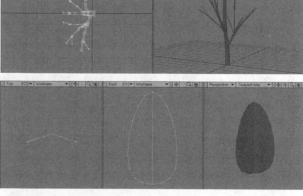

Figure 8-66: Open the Tree.lwo object. The first two layers contain the tree and a single leaf.

have created a simple tree object. On Layer 2, I have created a simple leaf.

2. On Layer 3, I have created a series of spheres that form the basic shape of the canopy. Once the rough shape was in place, I selected all the spheres, copied them, and pasted them back in place. I then used the **Modify | Translate | More | Move Plus** tool with the right mouse button to shrink all the spheres in place.

3. Finally, I copied these smaller spheres, pasted them in again and used the Move Plus tool once more to reduce them in size. This gave me a set of three spheres for every one that's visible. These extra layers help fill out the canopy and give it a sense of depth.

4. I copied the finished canopy into Layer 4 and used the **Construct | Reduce | Remove | Remove Polygons** tool (see the "Remove Polygons" section later in this chapter) to kill the polygons but leave the points. I then used the Jitter tool to randomize the position of the points. The Point Clone Plus tool will use these points to turn a single leaf into a beautiful canopy.

> **Note**
>
> Remember that points will only be visible in one of the wireframe modes. If you don't see the points in Layer 4, try switching one of your viewports to a wireframe mode.

5. Click on Layer 2 (the leaf). Copy this object and paste it into a blank layer. Then place Layer 4 (the canopy points) in the background. Click on the **Multiply | Duplicate | More | Point Clone Plus** tool. A configuration window will appear.

At first, this window may seem overwhelming. But if you look closely, you'll see that it simply gives you the option to randomize the rotation, size, scale, and centering for each axis.

6. The first thing we'll do is randomize the rotation of our leaves. We can set a minimum and maximum rotation for each axis. Leave the Min H, P, and B at **0**. But change the Max H, P, and B to **90** each. This allows each leaf a maximum rotation of 90 degrees.

We should also vary the size of each leaf. If we wanted control over each axis, we could enter Min and Max settings in the Random

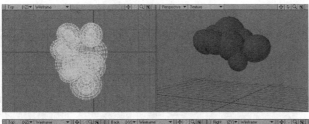

Figure 8-67: The third layer contains the canopy polygons. The fourth layer contains the points from the canopy that have been jittered to randomize their position.

Scale fields. But if we simply want an overall variation in size, we can just use the Random Size fields.

7. Enter **0.75** for the Min Random Size and **1.25** for the Max Random Size. This allows each leaf to be slightly larger or slightly smaller than our original.

8. If we wanted to randomly offset each leaf from the point to which it gets cloned, we could enter values into the Random Centering fields. But for this object, that won't really be necessary, so leave these fields at **0**.

9. The X, Y, and Z Axis buttons allow you to choose to which side of the axis the object will be cloned. In most cases, you can simply leave these at **Center**.

10. Press **OK**. The template leaf will be cloned 6,384 times (one clone for each point in the background layer) and randomly sized and rotated.

The result will be a beautiful array of leaves as seen in Figure 8-69.

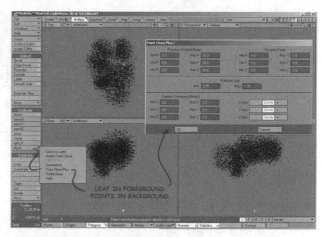

Figure 8-68: Place the leaf in the foreground and the canopy points in the background. Run the Point Clone Plus tool with the settings shown here.

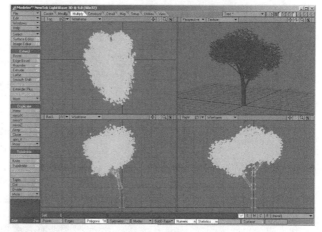

Figure 8-69: Using Point Clone Plus we are able to create a rich canopy of leaves in a matter of seconds.

Subdivision Tools

Knife

The **Multiply | Subdivide | Knife** tool allows you to slice through any object, creating new segments in the process. It will not cut an object in two (resulting in the creation of two separate objects); rather, it divides a single object into two separate halves. It is particularly useful whenever you need to add segments to a polygon or object.

To use the Knife tool, simply select it from the Multiply | Subdivide menu or choose the <K> keyboard shortcut. Position your mouse on one side of your polygon or object where you want the slice to begin. Then using your left mouse button, click and drag across your object.

Note

Always make sure you slice completely through your object when using the Knife tool. Partially cut objects can quickly lead to non-planar polygons that display unusual artifacts when rendering.

Note

You can constrain the Knife tool by holding down the <Ctrl> key before you click and drag. Alternately, you can click and drag with your middle mouse button to constrain the slice to a straight line.

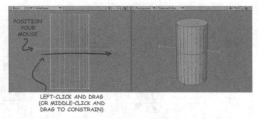

Figure 8-70: You can use the Knife tool to add extra segments to your objects.

With the Knife tool still active, you can create additional cuts by placing your mouse over the blue cut line, then clicking and dragging with your right mouse button to move the cut line to a different position on your object.

Figure 8-71: You can create additional cuts by placing your mouse over the blue cut line and right-clicking and dragging the cut to a new location.

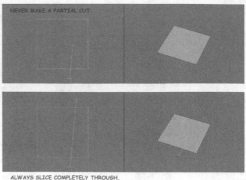

Figure 8-72: Always make sure you slice completely through your entire polygon or object. Never make a partial cut. It will only lead to trouble later on.

Divide

It's not uncommon to find yourself in need of an extra point along the edge of a polygon. While you can use the Multiply | Subdivide | Add Points tool to add points to the edges of your polygons, trying to add a point to the exact center of an edge with this tool can be difficult at best. But the **Multiply | Subdivide | Divide** tool allows you to do this very easily.

Simply select an edge (or the two points that make up an edge) and click on the **Divide** button. The edge will be divided into two equal halves with a new point at the center.

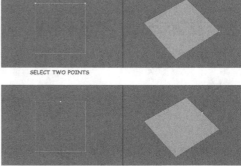

Figure 8-73: Use the Divide tool to add a new point at the center of a polygon's edge.

Note

The Divide tool is particularly useful when used in conjunction with the Connect tool (discussed later in this chapter).

Band Saw

Earlier in this section we saw how the Knife tool allows you to add segments to your objects. The beauty of the Knife tool is that it's simple, fast, and will cut through anything. But if you need to make precise cuts at specific locations, the Knife tool is a marginal choice at best. The **Multiply | Subdivide | More | Band Saw** tool, however, allows you to cut segments into quad polygons with exacting precision.

The one limitation of the Band Saw tool is that it only works with quad polygons. In many cases, however, you will be working with quads, so this is not the major limitation it may seem.

Note

Under the Multiply | Subdivide menu there is a tool called Band Saw Pro. This tool works almost identically to the Band Saw tool, but has the "benefit" of real-time feedback. In my experience, this real-time feedback causes the tool to be sluggish and unresponsive. For this reason, I'm going to show you the Band Saw tool. Once you understand it, you can experiment with the Band Saw Pro tool to determine which tool you like better.

To use the Band Saw tool, you must select two quad polygons running along the direction you wish to cut. Then choose **Band Saw** from the **Multiply | Subdivide | More** menu. The BandSaw window will appear, as shown in Figure 8-74.

The interface for the Band Saw tool can seem foreign and daunting at first. But it's really quite simple. The white strip at the center represents your polygon. The lines in this white strip represent the cuts that will be made to your polygons. By default, there will be one cut, but you can easily add or delete cuts and edit them to position them precisely where you want them.

The thing that's important to understand is that the white strip is not an indicator of the shape of your polygon. It simply provides a visual representation of the top and bottom of the band that will be cut. Take a look at Figure 8-75.

If you make a vertical selection, then the Band Saw strip will correspond to the left and right edge of your polygons. But if you make a horizontal selection, the Band Saw strip will correspond to the top and bottom of your polygons. You may find it helpful to imagine the strip being rotated 90 degrees.

Let's talk briefly about the other options in this window.

At the top of the window are the **Edge to select** controls. This option allows you to determine whether the left side of the

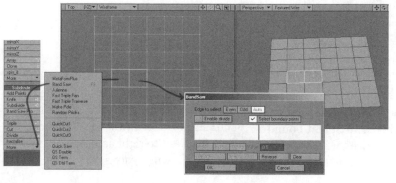

Figure 8-74: Select two quad polys running along the direction you wish to cut. Then select the Band Saw tool.

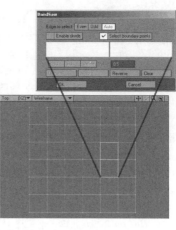

FOR HORIZONTAL SELECTIONS:
IMAGINE THE BAND SAW STRIP
ROTATED 90 DEGREES RUNNING
FROM TOP TO BOTTOM.

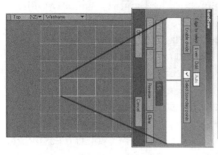

Figure 8-75: The white strip in the BandSaw window determines where the cuts will be made. If you make a horizontal selection, you may find it easier to imagine the Band Saw strip running from top to bottom rather than left to right.

Band Saw strip corresponds to the left side of your polygon or the right side. In most cases, you can simply leave this set to **Auto**. (In all my years of modeling, I don't think I've ever changed this.)

The **Enable divide** button tells the Band Saw tool that you want to use it to make a cut to your object. If you leave this unchecked and press OK, Band Saw will simply select all of the quad polygons in either direction of the two you initially selected. (In the old days (before the Select Loop tool), the Band Saw tool was one of the few tools that allowed you to quickly select a band of quad polys.)

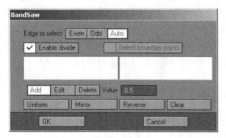

Figure 8-76: Clicking the Enable divide button allows you to change the slices in the white Band Saw strip.

If you don't have the Enable divide button activated, you can choose to **Select boundary points**. This will cause the points on either side of the band to be selected when

you press OK. (You may need to switch to Points selection mode to see the point selection.) When you activate Enable divide, this option will no longer be available.

The remaining controls determine how cuts are placed in the white Band Saw strip. Most of these will be ghosted until you click the Enable divide button.

The **Add**, **Edit**, and **Delete** buttons are modes. When the Add button is active, you can click anywhere in the white strip to add a new slice. When the Edit button is active, you can click and drag any slice to move it to a new location. (Clicking a slice will select it and its color will turn from blue to red.) When the Delete button is active, you can click on any slice to remove it from the white strip.

The **Value** field tells you the location of the selected slice. The range is from 0.0 (the far left side) to 1.0 (the far right side). A value of 0.5 is in the exact center of the band.

The **Uniform**, **Mirror**, **Reverse**, and **Clear** buttons allow you to adjust the position of slices already positioned on the white strip. Uniform will equally space slices from left to right across the entire strip. Mirror will create a copy of the

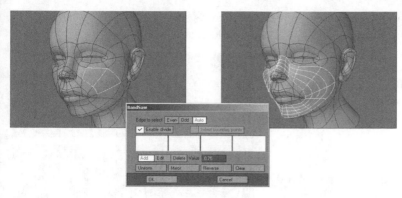

Figure 8-77: Band Saw works great on regular polygonal objects. But it works best on subpatch models.

selected slice on the opposite side of the halfway point. Reverse will flip the slices on the entire strip from left to right. (This can be helpful if you specify a slice on one side of the white strip but find that it gets applied to the wrong side of your band. If this happens, simply undo and run Band Saw again. Then click on the Reverse

button.) The Clear button will remove all slices, leaving only the default slice in the center of the strip.

The Band Saw tool is great for slicing cuts into standard polygonal objects. But its true power is only realized when it is used on subpatch objects. (We discuss subpatch objects in detail in Chapter 15.)

Construction Tools

Hot Key Block

\<k\> Remove Polygons

\<l\> connect

Remove Polygons

In certain circumstances, it can be beneficial to eliminate your polygons but keep their points. (This is often the case when you want to convert the points of your object into single-point polygons or you want to use the points with a tool like Point Clone Plus.) The **Remove Polygons** tool, which can be found in the **Construct | Reduce | Remove** menu, allows you to do this.

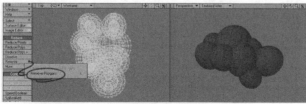

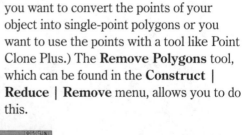

Figure 8-78: The Remove Polygons tool allows you to eliminate polygons while keeping their points.

The keyboard shortcut for Remove Polygons is <k>. You may find it helpful to think of it as "k"illing your polygons.

There are no options for the Remove Polygons tool. Simply run it and your polygons will disappear, leaving only their points behind.

Band Glue

The **Construct | Reduce | More | Band Glue** tool is the antithesis of the Band Saw tool. Rather than adding segments to your object, it removes them.

To use the Band Glue tool, simply select a sequence of quad polygons that you wish to merge, then run the Band Glue tool. Each band of polygons running perpendicular to your original selection will be merged. Bands that are parallel to your original selection will be left intact.

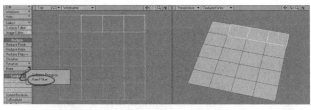
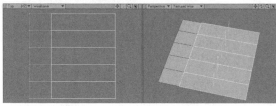

Figure 8-79: The Band Glue tool merges sequences of quad polygons.

Bridge

The **Construct | Combine | Bridge** tool allows you to connect polygons by creating new geometry to "bridge the gap" between them. The Bridge tool can be used for everything from tunneling through objects to connecting hands and feet to a

character's arms and legs. Let's take a quick look at how it is used.

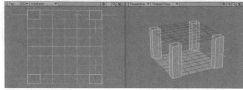

Figure 8-80: The Bridge tool allows you to connect separate polygons together.

Using the Bridge tool is easy. Simply select two groups of polygons on separate objects, then click on the tool. Bridge will attempt to intelligently connect the polys together and will eliminate the source polygons. This ensures that you don't end up with geometry accidentally hidden inside your object.

One of the great things about the Bridge tool is that it doesn't require you to use polygons with the same number of points. Nor does it require you to use the same number of polygons. The Bridge tool will do its best to simply connect any two shapes together.

> ### Note
>
> When you connect objects with differing numbers of points, the Bridge tool may leave behind points that are not connected to any polys. Simply select them using the Statistics panel (as described in Chapter 3) and delete them.

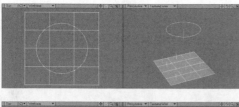

Figure 8-81: Objects with disparate numbers of points and polygons can easily be connected together using the Bridge tool.

Connect

The **Construct | Combine | Connect** tool allows you to create a new edge between two points on a polygon. This gives you the power to quickly reshape the polygons in your object and correct non-planar polys.

Take a look at Figure 8-82. The top image shows a highly non-planar polygon. We can correct this by simply connecting the two sets of points on either side of the object.

To use the Connect tool, simply select two points on opposite edges of a polygon and click on the Connect button. A new edge will be created. Using the Divide tool we discussed earlier in this chapter, you can quickly add new points to your polygons

and then connect them with the Connect tool.

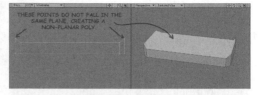

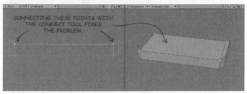

Figure 8-82: You can use the Connect tool to create an edge between two points on a polygon. This can often be helpful for correcting non-planar polygons.

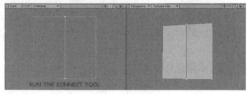

Figure 8-83: Select two points on a polygon and press the Connect button to create an edge between them.

Detail Tools

Unify Polygons

Undoubtedly, there will come a time in the course of your career when you look down at your Quick Info display and realize to

your astonishment that there are far more polygons selected than there should be. You check your point count, but everything seems normal. And yet you have more polygons than you should.

In almost every case, the culprit turns out to be duplicate polygons whose points have been merged together. It happens to the best of us and it can be nearly impossible to fix by hand. Fortunately, we have a tool that can quickly solve our problem. It's called **Unify Polygons** and it can be found in the **Detail | Polygons | More** menu.

When you accidentally copy and paste your object into the same layer, then merge points later on, you will end up with two copies of your object fused together. To correct this, simply run the Unify Polygons command. This will eliminate any polygons that exist in the same space whose points have been merged together.

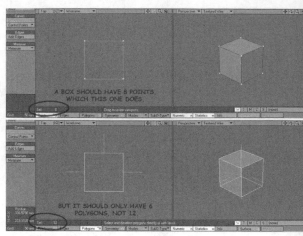

Figure 8-84: A box should have eight points and six sides. This box has eight points and 12 sides. Obviously, there's a problem.

Figure 8-85: The Unify Polygons tool will eliminate any polygons that occupy the same space whose points have been merged together.

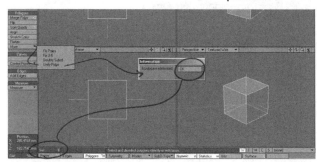

Add Edges

The **Detail | Edges | Add Edges** tool lets you draw edges onto your object. This allows you to restructure the "flow" of your objects' polygons and add localized detail where it's needed.

When you activate the Add Edges tool, small blue dots will appear on the edges of every polygon. These blue dots are control points. They can be moved anywhere along the polygon's edge (and even restricted or snapped if you desire).

Adding a new edge is as simple as playing "connect the dots." Simply click on the first blue dot where you want your new edge to begin. Then click one of the blue dots on an edge opposite from it. You can

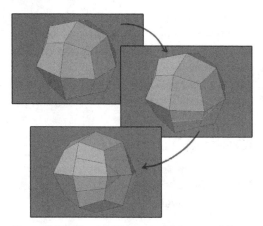

Figure 8-86: The Add Edges tool lets you add new edges to your object, allowing you to add localized detail and restructure your polygon's "flow."

continue clicking from dot to dot to define a continuous edge.

If you're happy with your new edge and would like to make another, you can either drop the Add Edges tool and then reactivate it, or simply click once with your right mouse button. This will accept your work while keeping the tool active, allowing you to start defining a new edge elsewhere on your object.

The Numeric panel contains a wealth of options that let you customize how the Add Edges tool works. Let's take a quick look at these options.

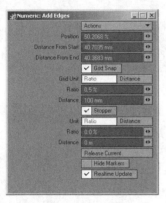

Figure 8-87: The Numeric panel offers additional control over the Add Edges tool.

Note

The settings in the Numeric panel are simply there to give you a greater degree of control over the Add Edges tool. Don't let the myriad of options intimidate you. You can use all of the edge tools quite effectively without ever opening the Numeric panel. Just know these options are available should you need them.

- **Position**, **Distance From Start**, and **Distance From End** are all methods of determining the placement of the currently selected control point. You can adjust these interactively by clicking on one of the control points and dragging it along its existing edge.

- **Grid Snap** enables you to constrain the motion of the control points. Without

Grid Snap, they will freely move along their existing edge.

- **Grid Unit** allows you to select a method of constraint for the motion of your control points. You can snap to a ratio or a distance.

- **Ratio** looks at the edge on which the control point lies and lets you constrain its movement based on a percentage of the source edge's length. Setting this to 50% will constrain your control point to the center (50% of the current edge's length) or either end (0% or 100%).

- **Distance** allows you to determine an exact size for the grid snap. You can enter any size you'd like; however, if the size is larger than the length of the edge on which the control point lies, the control point will jump to either end of that edge.

- **Stopper** allows you to restrict the motion of the control point to a limited area. The settings used to define that area are similar to those used to define the Grid Snap.

- **Unit** allows you to choose a method for defining the Stopper area. **Ratio** sets the restriction area to a percentage of the length of the source edge on which the control point lies. At 50%, this will lock the motion of the control point entirely. **Distance** allows you to set a distance from the beginning and end of the source edge to restrict the control point's motion.

- **Release Current** clears the most recently created edge.

- **Hide Markers** turns off the control points. This can make it easier to see the new edges you've created.

- **Realtime Update** shows the creation of your edges in real time. If your graphics card is a little older or begins to bog down, you can turn this off to get better feedback.

View Tools

Center Pivot

Each layer in Modeler has its own pivot point. When you bring an object into Layout, the pivot point for each layer will be used as its center of rotation. If your pivot point is off center, it can make rotating your object difficult and unpredictable. To remedy this, Modeler has a **Center Pivot** tool, which can be found in the **View | Layers** menu.

You can see the location of your layer's pivot point by activating the Pivot tool. The pivot will appear as a three-dimensional blue cross. To center your pivot, simply click the Center Pivot button.

You can also use the Center Pivot tool to center the pivot point around selected geometry. This can be extremely helpful when you want to position the pivot point at the center of a specific location (such as a robot's knee joint). Simply select the points, polygons, or edges you want the tool to center the pivot point around and click the Center Pivot button.

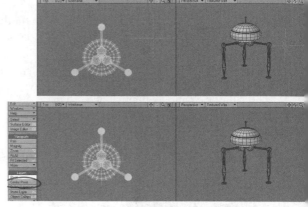

Figure 8-88: The Center Pivot tool will move the pivot point for the foreground layer to the center of the geometry on that layer.

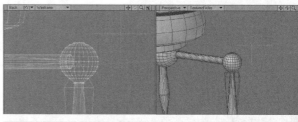

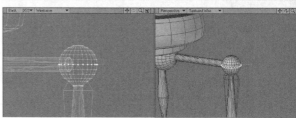

Figure 8-89: You can center the pivot around selected points, polygons, or edges by selecting them first.

Tutorial

The tools introduced in this chapter give you the ability to model faster and take on projects that are much more complex. To help ground you in the use of these tools and to see how they can be used with the tools you learned earlier in Chapter 3, you'll find a comprehensive video tutorial for this chapter on the companion DVD.

This extensive tutorial will show how to model a cordless phone with smooth flowing shapes — all without the use of subpatches! Along the way, you'll pick up tips and tricks that will help you solve common modeling problems. And you'll develop workflow patterns that will help you in the coming chapters.

As always, the emphasis is on honing your skills, not rushing through to the end. So watch the video through first to get a

Figure 8-90: Think subpatches are the only way to create smooth, curving objects? Think again! This phone was built using the tools covered in Chapters 3 and 8. You'll learn how to model it in the Chapter 8 video tutorial, which can be found on the companion DVD.

feel for how the work is done, then follow along on your own.

Conclusion

In this chapter we've added over two dozen tools to your Modeling arsenal. The tools described here can help you solve a variety of common (and often time-consuming) modeling problems. They will supercharge your productivity and take the drudgery out of many tedious tasks.

Before moving on, be sure to spend some time getting a feel for how these tools work and can be integrated into your own workflow. Then move on to the next chapter, where you'll hone your modeling skills by building a house from the ground up.

Intermediate Modeling Exercise: Architectural Modeling

Introduction

In this chapter we'll dive into the art of architectural visualization. This is a growing market for CGI, and many LightWave users have found it both rewarding and lucrative. But even if you never plan on making renders of high-rises for a living, the work involved in constructing a 3D building is perfect for honing your modeling skills.

This chapter will cover the steps needed to create a 3D home from a 2D floor plan. You'll be using most of the tools you've learned thus far and you'll be picking up a few new ones along the way.

This is an intermediate modeling project; therefore, it's important for you to be comfortable with tools and techniques discussed in Chapters 2, 3, and 8 before getting started.

Each step in this tutorial will be described in detail in this lengthy chapter. In order to keep things as concise as possible, I won't be listing every single action.

For example, if I tell you to make a box in the Top viewport, I expect you to:

1. Navigate to the Create menu.

2. Locate and activate the Box tool.

3. Position your mouse in the Top viewport.

4. Click and drag to make the box.

5. Drop the Box tool.

If there's a specific reason *not* to drop a tool or deselect points or polys, I'll let you know. Otherwise, these types of actions will simply be implied. Additionally, in order to keep the image count under control, the figures in this chapter will show the major steps, but there are minor steps you'll be required to do that are not depicted in the illustrations. Be sure to pay close attention to the text as you go.

Plug-ins

LightWave comes with an extremely well-rounded set of tools, and many users find that they never have need of plug-ins in their work. I'm not one of them. Plug-ins often make difficult tasks much easier and I have no hesitation in using them. Anything that makes me more productive, I'm for. There are literally thousands of plug-ins for LightWave and many (if not most) of them are free.

Architectural modeling requires a fairly high degree of precision. To achieve this, we'll be relying on two outstanding plug-ins from the Japanese developer Pictrix. Both of these plug-ins can be found on the DVD that comes with this book or directly from the Pictrix website at http://www.pictrix.jp/lw/index_2.html.

- **SP Polygon** is a real-time polygon creation tool. It allows you to make regular polygons as well as curves and polylines. But its greatest attribute is its ability to align and snap points to one another during the creation process. This makes it easy to create polygons with precise right angles.

- **SP Move** is an advanced version of Modeler's own Snap Drag tool. It allows you to move points and polys and snap their vertices to one another. What distinguishes SP Move from Snap Drag, however, is that it allows you to snap to points in the background. Furthermore, SP Move offers visual feedback as to which axis you're snapping to. This tool will shave hours (if not days) off your architectural modeling projects.

You'll be using these tools frequently throughout this chapter, so you'll probably find it helpful to create dedicated buttons or assign special keyboard shortcuts for them. See the "Menu Layout Customization" section in Chapter 2 for a refresher on how to create buttons for custom tools.

There are video tutorials for this chapter on the book's companion DVD that outline the basic use of each of these plug-ins. Before you begin working through this tutorial, be sure to watch the videos so that you have a better understanding of their use.

> **Note**
>
> You'll find a number of other outstanding plug-ins on the companion DVD. See Chapter 27 for a list of some of our favorite plug-ins.

New Tools

In addition to the Pictrix plug-ins, there are two additional LightWave tools that you'll find useful: Magnify and Pan. These tools replicate the actions of the icons in the upper-right corner of each viewport; however, learning their keyboard shortcuts will make your job much easier, especially on a project such as this.

Magnify

The **View | Viewports | Magnify** tool allows you to quickly zoom in to and out of your workspace. The keyboard shortcut is <Ctrl>+<Alt>. Hold down these two keys at the same time, then click your left mouse button and drag left and right. Dragging right zooms in. Dragging left zooms out.

Pan

The **View | Viewports | Pan** tool allows you to move around any orthographic viewport. This is critical for navigating around your model when you're zoomed in close. The keyboard shortcut is the <Alt> key. Hold <Alt> down and then left-click and drag in one of your orthographic viewports.

Hot Key Block	
<Ctrl>+<Alt>+left-click and drag left and/or right	Magnify
<Alt>+left-click and drag	Pan

Notes

As an American, I can't help but think in measurements of inches and feet. Even though I've adapted to using the metric system when modeling, there are still some things I can't help but think of in English measurements. For example, I think of the average ceiling height being 8 feet, not 2.4384 meters. Fortunately, Modeler allows us to work in the metric system so that we can keep the advantages of a base 10 system and simply input English values when needed. For example, you can keep your **Display Options | Units** set to **Metric** or **SI** and simply enter feet (ft) or inches (in) in any numeric field when needed. Modeler will automatically do the conversion for you. Keep this in mind as you work.

We'll be working off of a floor plan image to build our house model. Floor plans can be easily found on the Internet. Sometimes they will have detailed measurements telling you the exact size of each room; other times they will not. For this exercise, we'll work with a floor plan without measurements. This will be a "worst-case" scenario, but I'll show you how you can deduce the actual size of the house without floor plan measurements later on.

We'll be using the **Multiply | Extend | Multishift** tool quite a bit throughout this process. Unless otherwise noted, the **Inset** and **Shift** pop-up menus should both be set to Contour and the **Group Polygons** option should be checked.

Before we begin, it's worth noting that there's a bug in Modeler that can crop up when you're using the Boolean or Drill functions. The error message will say "Internal Buffers Too Small For Requested Operation." If you get this message when you attempt to perform a Boolean or Drill operation, save your work and close down Modeler. Then open Modeler, load your object, and try again. This usually fixes the problem.

Building the House

Constructing a home is not a difficult task, but it can be time consuming. If this is your first time building a 3D home, you should expect it to take the better part of a day to complete (if not longer). Therefore, be sure to save often. You may find it helpful to save a new version after each step.

I've placed object files containing the key steps on the companion DVD in the Objects\Chapter 09 folder. This will allow you to jump to any stage of development should you want to skip earlier steps in the process. These files can also be used to compare your results with mine.

You'll also find Multishift presets in the Multishifts\Chapter 09 folder. These presets are simply there to save you time, but I'd encourage you to experiment with your own shifts as you go. More on that later. Let's get started!

Step 1: Lay Out the Floor Plan for the Outer Walls and Rooms

The first step is to create polygons for the perimeter of the house and each of the rooms. We'll use these polygons to create the walls (both inner and outer) for the house.

1. Make sure Modeler's configuration is set to a quad view and the top left viewport is set to Top. Open the Display Options window and load the **floor plan.jpg** image from the Images\Chapter 09 folder into the TopL viewport. Then size it to **10 m**. Turn on **Pixel Blending**. Turn down the Brightness

and Contrast. Then set the Image Resolution to **1024** so that we get nice clean lines.

> **Note**
>
> If you'd like, you can simply load in the Floor Plan for Step 1.cfg background preset from the Setup\Chapter 09 folder.

> **Note**
>
> We'll be using the Pictrix plug-ins from here on out. Be sure you've installed the plug-ins and watched the video tutorials on their use before you begin. You can find the tutorials in the Video Tutorials\Chapter 09 folder.

2. Click the **Maximize** button in the Top viewport to go full screen. Use the **SP Polygon** tool to create a polygon that encompasses the outside perimeter of the floor plan. This polygon will form the outside walls. Be sure to watch the tool as you work to ensure that the points are aligned to one another and create perfect right angles. (See the video tutorial on SP Polygon for more information about its use.)

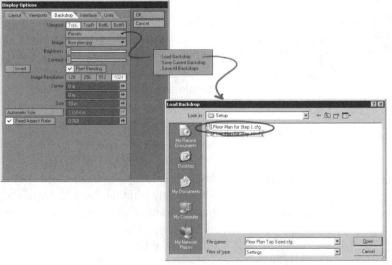

Figure 9-1: Load the floor plan.jpg file into the background for the TopL viewport and configure the settings as shown here.

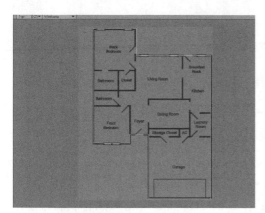

Figure 9-2: Use SP Polygon to create a poly around the perimeter of the home.

3. Go to a blank layer. Place the perimeter poly you created in the background, then use SP Polygon to make a box for the front bedroom. Be sure to watch the SP Polygon tool to ensure the points of this room snap to the perimeter polygon. You should see an XZ or XYZ when the point you place is lined up with other points in the foreground or background.

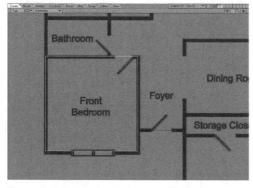

Figure 9-3: Place the perimeter poly in the background and use SP Polygon to create a poly for the front bedroom.

4. Cut this room and paste it into a separate layer. This layer will be a repository for each of the room polys you create.

5. Place both the front bedroom poly and the perimeter poly in the background and use SP Polygon to create another room (it doesn't matter which one). Again, make sure it snaps to the points in the foreground and background so that you end up with perfect 90-degree angles. When finished, cut and paste it to the layer with the front bedroom.

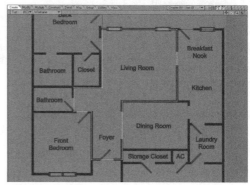

Figure 9-4: Place the perimeter poly and the front bedroom poly in the background and use SP Polygon to create a poly for another room.

6. Repeat this process until each room shown in the floor plan is complete. The more rooms you add, the easier it will be to snap the points together.

7. When finished, exit full-screen mode, place all the polygons in the foreground, and check the points in the orthographic viewports to ensure they all fall in the same plane. For example, all the points that make up the rooms should be at the same position on the Y-axis. If they are not, your foundation will be off and it will create problems later.

8. Also check to ensure that the rooms line up perfectly with the outside perimeter poly and that there are no gaps between any of the rooms. If there are, select the points along the errant edge and use the Stretch tool (with Action

Center: Selection) with the middle mouse button (or the <Ctrl> key modifier) to bring them in line with one another on a single axis. Keep an eye on the Quick Info display in the lower-left corner of the interface. When its Scale percent reaches zero on one axis, you can be certain that all the points are in line with one another.

> **Note**
>
> You can also use the Point Info panel to check the point locations and set them to a specific location. For example, if some of the points vary on the Y-axis, you can quickly place them all at the 0 coordinate. Select all of the points in your object, press <i> to bring up the Point Info panel, and look at the X, Y, and Z fields at the bottom of the panel. If you see "(mixed)" in any of these fields, it means the selected points have differing values. Simply click in the field you want to change (in this case the Y field) and enter 0. Then press OK. All of the points in your object will now be placed at the 0 coordinate on the Y-axis.

> **Note**
>
> From here on out, you should enter and exit full-screen mode whenever you see fit.

9. Delete any stray points that exist on polygon edges that are not at a corner. (This can happen at the front entrance, for example.)

10. Check that the walls line up to the background image as much as possible. Select whole groups of points and move them if necessary.

11. Place the perimeter poly in Layer 1 and the room polys in Layer 2. Then save your model.

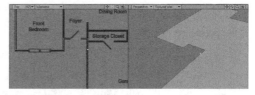

Figure 9-6: Delete any stray points along poly edges, then place the perimeter poly in Layer 1 and the room polys in Layer 2.

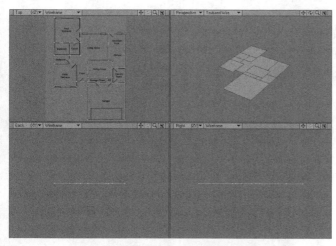

If you'd like to compare your results with mine, you can load the Step 1 object from Objects\Chapter 09 on the companion DVD. Remember that all the steps we'll be working through in this chapter are included on the DVD for you to review if necessary.

Figure 9-5: When all the rooms are finished, check to make sure all the points fall in the same position on the Y-axis.

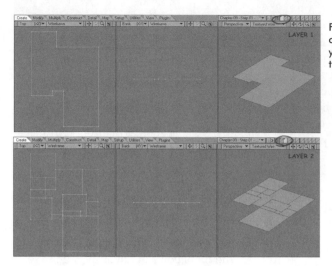

Figure 9-7: The results from Step 1 can be seen here. Compare this to your own work and make sure they're the same before continuing to Step 2.

Step 2: Bevel the Inner Wall and Rooms by Equal Amounts

The next step is to bevel the polygons for the perimeter and rooms by equal but oppo-site amounts. This will create an even thickness for the walls. Since we're not working with known dimensions, we'll have to "eyeball" the thickness of the walls and hope for the best.

1. Change your Perspective view type to Textured Wire so you can see a solid view of your polys along with their wireframe edges.

2. Select the perimeter poly. Then use the Bevel tool to inset it by **–50 mm**, as shown in Figure 9-8. Keep an eye on the Quick Info display or the Numeric panel. There should only be a value for Inset. Shift should remain at 0.

3. We want to keep the poly that has been inset but get rid of the rest. With the perimeter still selected, cut it, then delete the leftover polys and paste the perimeter back into place. This gives us a copy of the perimeter that is 50 mm larger all the way around.

4. Select the room polys and use the Bevel tool to inset them **+50 mm** (Figure 9-9).

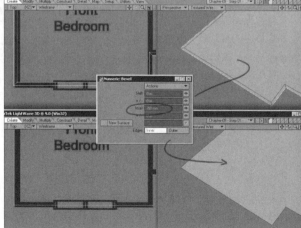

Figure 9-8: Bevel the perimeter poly with a 0 Shift and a –50 mm Inset. Then cut the selected perimeter poly, delete the unselected polys, and paste the perimeter poly back in place.

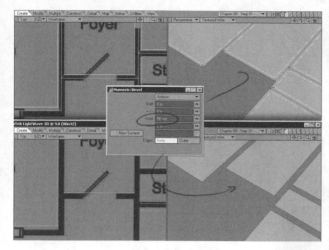

Figure 9-9: Bevel the room polys with a 0 Shift and a +50 mm Inset. Then cut the selected room polys, delete the unselected polys, and paste the room polys back in place.

5. We want to keep the room polys that have been inset but get rid of the rest. With the room polys still selected, cut them, delete the leftovers, then paste the room polys back into place. This gives us copies of the room polys that are 50 mm smaller. Combined with the perimeter poly, we now have 100 mm of space from the perimeter to the rooms. This means our walls will be 100 mm thick.

When Layer 1 and Layer 2 are placed in the foreground together, the result should look like Figure 9-10.

Figure 9-10: When the perimeter and rooms layers are both selected, there will be space between them. This space will form the walls of the building.

> ## Note
>
> In rare cases, polygons created with the SP Polygon tool will go bad. The easiest way to spot this is to watch your polygons as they're being beveled. If one appears to have its normals flipped or if it appears to bevel out when it should be beveling in, you know you've got a problem. I've yet to figure out what causes this problem, but it may be the result of creating the polygon in a counter-clockwise (rather than clockwise) fashion. The solution is simple: Just delete the bad poly and remake it. In almost every case, this fixes the problem.

Step 3: Drill (Tunnel) the Rooms into the Larger Floor Plan

To create the walls, we simply need to subtract the room polys from the perimeter poly. This can easily be done with the **Construct | Combine | Drill** tool using the **Tunnel** option.

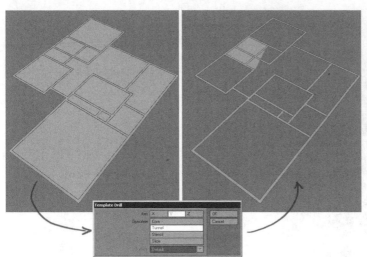

Figure 9-11: Drill the rooms into a copy of the perimeter using the Tunnel option. This creates a 2D wall structure. You may see OpenGL errors after drilling.

1. Copy the perimeter polygon and paste it into a new layer. Drill the room polys into the perimeter poly using the **Tunnel** option. This creates a 2D template that we can extrude to create 3D walls.

2. You'll want to keep the original perimeter polygon (the one that you didn't drill) and room template polys. The perimeter will be used as the floor for our home and the room polys will be used to create the ceiling.

Drilling the room polys into the perimeter will often result in OpenGL shading problems. It will appear as if some of the polygons haven't been cut out even though they actually have. These OpenGL problems typically come from complex polys whose points are not connected together in a way that LightWave fully understands. The solution is to add and connect points on your polygon until the OpenGL display is fixed.

If you have OpenGL shading problems, follow these steps:

    a. Make sure that no points are currently selected. Switch to Polygons mode, and select the perimeter poly.

    b. Activate the **Multiply | Subdivide | Add Points** tool. This tool allows you to add points to a polygon by clicking directly on its edge.

    c. Add four points on the left side of the perimeter and right side of the front bedroom as shown in Figure 9-12. You should see the OpenGL issues disappear.

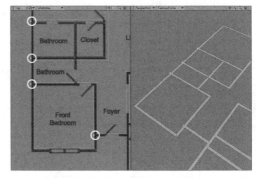

Figure 9-12: To fix OpenGL errors, you need to add points to your poly.

    d. Just to be sure everything is kosher, connect the points as shown in Figure 9-12.

    e. Select two of the points and click on the **Construct | Combine |**

Connect tool. Then repeat for each of the remaining points.

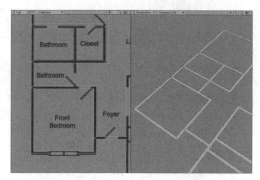

Figure 9-13: Just to be sure the OpenGL errors are taken care of, you should connect the points with the Connect tool as shown here.

Now let's consolidate the model and clean up some of the leftover building materials.

3. Place the original perimeter poly in Layer 1 if it's not already there. Give it a surface called **Floor.**

4. Go to the layer with the room polys that you used as the drilling template (this should be Layer 2). Assign these a surface called **Ceiling.** Then cut them and paste them into Layer 1 with the Floor surface.

5. Layer 2 should be empty. Cut the wall template that you drilled earlier and paste it into Layer 2. Then delete anything else that's left over on any other layer.

6. Save your model.

Step 4: Create Doorway Polygons

Now that we've got the wall template built, let's create polygons for the doorways. The doorways are simply the openings in the wall leading in and out of each room. The templates we create in this step will be

used to cut the doorways out of the walls and to create the doorframes later on.

1. Using the **Box** tool, create a rectangle in the Top viewport for the door located at the main entryway and size it according to the floor plan background image. Don't extrude the box at this time or give it height. Just keep it 2D in the X and Z.

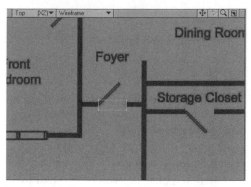

Figure 9-14: Create a poly for the front doorway.

2. Select this poly and copy and paste it back into place. Then move it to the opening for the front bedroom door.

You'll notice that the front bedroom door opening is smaller than that of the main entryway. There are actually two common door sizes in this home. The doors on the left half of the house (left of the main entryway) will match the front bedroom doorway with the exception of the back bedroom closet. The doors on the right half of the house (right of the main entryway) will match the size of the main entryway with the exception of the AC (air conditioning) closet and the dining room.

3. Resize the poly you moved to the front bedroom to fit its doorway.

4. You now have two doorway template polys. Use these to create the remaining doorway polygons. Copy and paste

347

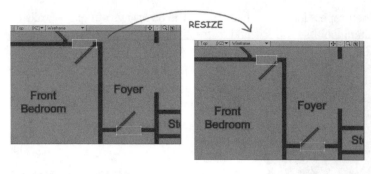

RESIZE

Figure 9-15: Copy and paste the front doorway poly and move it to the front bedroom. Then resize it to fit.

them, then move them into place, rotating as necessary.

Don't forget to include openings for rooms that don't specifically have doors (such as the dining room). Speaking of which, the left entry of the dining room is 200% as wide as the front door.

You may notice that some of the door openings aren't exactly the same size as the two main templates. If you really want to get picky, you can resize the doorway template for each room as you see fit. But to keep things simple, let's stick with the two main templates and only resize the three exceptions (the back bedroom closet, the dining room, and the AC closet).

When you're finished, you should have all your doorway template polys on the same layer.

Step 5: Extrude the Walls

Now let's extrude our 2D wall template to create the 3D walls of our home.

1. Check to make sure that the normal for your wall template poly is facing up along the Y-axis. If it's facing down, press the <f> key to flip it.

2. Use the **Extrude** tool to extrude the wall template approximately –2 meters along the Y-axis. The height of the walls at this stage isn't important since we don't know the measurements of the floor plan. I used two meters because it looks good for a start and it gives us enough height to easily select the points at either the top or bottom of the walls later on.

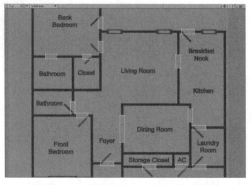

Figure 9-16: Copy and paste the polys to create the remaining doorway templates.

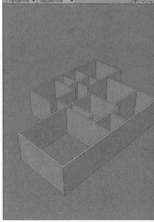

5. Save your model.

Figure 9-17: Extrude the walls roughly –2 meters along the Y-axis. Then assign them a Walls surface.

3. Assign the walls a new surface called **Walls**. Then save your model.

Step 6: Round the Wall Corners

Walls typically come together at a sharp right angle, but by now you should know that in the real world, very few things are perfectly sharp. Most walls have a little bit of joint compound that rounds them slightly. We can soften the corners slightly and ensure that they look more realistic by using Rounder.

1. Copy the extruded walls to a new layer. We'll round the corners of this copy, but we need to keep the unrounded version for use later on.

2. Only the walls on the inside of the house need rounding (although you're welcome to round the outside ones if you desire). Begin by selecting the two points that make up the upper-left corner of the back bedroom. Since these points share the same X and Z coordinates, it's easiest to select them in the Top viewport.

3. Activate the **Rounder** tool and bring up the Numeric panel. We want to round the edge where the walls meet at a 90-degree angle, so make sure your Round only option is set to **Edges**. We don't need a lot of polygons in the corners, so lower Rounding Polygons to **2**.

4. Inset distance will determine how round the walls are. In some homes, the wall joints are fairly round. In others, the corners are almost razor sharp. You can use any Inset distance you

think looks good. For this tutorial, I'm going to use **10 mm**.

5. All of Rounder's other settings can be kept at their defaults: Mesh density = Low, Convexity = Out, and Project Inset = Yes.

6. Once you've entered these settings, left-click and drag slightly in one of the orthographic viewports. This will activate the tool and apply the settings. (You can also activate the tool by clicking on the Actions pop-up menu in the Numeric panel and choosing Activate.)

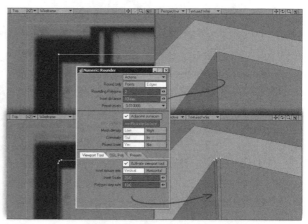

Figure 9-18: In the Top viewport, select the two points that make up the upper-left corner of the back bedroom. Use Rounder to round the points with the settings shown here.

Getting a feel for how much you need to click and drag in order to activate Rounder takes a bit of practice. If you click and drag too much in one of the viewports, Rounder will adjust its settings, so keep an eye on the Numeric panel to make sure that Rounding Polygons remains at 2 and Inset distance remains at 10 mm.

7. Now that this edge has been rounded, deselect the points. Select the points for another corner and activate Rounder again; it will run with the

settings you previously used. Deselect these points and repeat this process for each of the inside walls.

Rounding can be a tedious process. See the following tips to help things go quicker and easier.

8. Once you have rounded all of the inside walls, save your model.

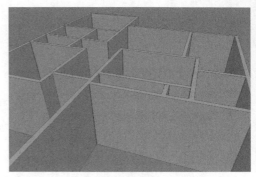

Figure 9-19: Round each of the remaining corners of the house.

Tips

• You can round more than one edge at a time, but you must make sure that the edges aren't directly to the left or right of one another. Rounding edges diagonal from one another typically works well and won't give you troubles.

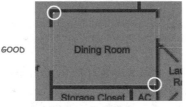

Figure 9-20: If you want to speed up the rounding process, you can select multiple edges. Just make sure they aren't directly connected to one another. Selecting edges diagonal from one another works well.

• If you have trouble rounding an edge, make sure you don't have multiple layers selected. Rounder hates that.

• It's okay if your edge branches out (see Figure 9-21). But it's a good idea to check

these areas in the OpenGL preview to ensure nothing is wrong.

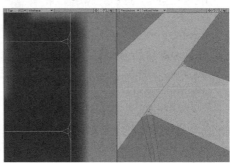

Figure 9-21: Some rounded corners will branch out, as seen here. This is completely normal, but you should still check the OpenGL display to be certain everything looks right.

• Use the Zoom and Pan keyboard shortcuts to quickly move around your workspace.

• It really helps to assign a keyboard shortcut to Rounder. I find <R> works for me.

• Pay close attention to the Inset distance setting in the Numeric panel as you work. If you accidentally drag your mouse too far when activating the tool, you will increase the Inset distance.

• You can choose a 10 mm Inset distance by choosing the 0.010000 preset from the Preset insets pop-up menu.

Step 7: Create the Molding Template

Most homes have floor molding (also called "baseboards"). Technically, molding can be either at the top or bottom of a wall. Since we'll be adding both, we'll refer to the bottom as the "molding" and the top as the "cornice" (which we'll get to later).

There are countless molding designs. Some are smooth and simple, while others feature intricate bevels. We'll use a fairly standard design with a few smooth arcs to form simple bevels. To do this, we'll create a profile of the molding using a spline.

1. Go to a quad viewport layout. Place the walls in the background and zoom in to the bottom of the walls. Molding comes in a variety of sizes, so there's no set rule for how big it should be. And since we don't know the dimensions of the house, we have to eyeball the size so that it looks good in proportion to the walls and floors. (We can always adjust the size later if necessary.)

2. Create a spline in the Back viewport similar to the one seen in Figure 9-22. (Mine is approximately 60 mm high.) This shape represents the profile, or cutaway, of our molding strip. It will act as a template that we can extrude later into a full 3D shape.

Make sure that you create a closed curve, not an open one, and remember that the closer two points are to one another, the sharper the curve will be in that area.

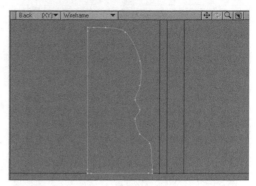

Figure 9-22: Create a closed curve in the Back viewport roughly 60 mm high as seen here, or load the Molding Spline.lwo file from the companion DVD.

> **Note**
>
> The SP Polygon tool that you used earlier can also be used to create open and closed curves. While I still prefer the manual method (old habits die hard), you may find it more to your liking so it's worth giving it a try.

Now that you've got your molding spline, you could simply extrude it; however, this would result in an extremely complex object with far more polygons than we need. And remember, this molding will go around every room of the house. We need it to be detailed, but efficient at the same time. Therefore, rather than extruding this curve, we'll use it as a template to create a lower-resolution polygon with fewer points.

3. Click on the **Construct | Convert | Freeze** tool to convert the spline into a single polygon. You'll notice that it has an outrageous number of points. You can manually delete the points you don't want, but there's a way to make this task a little easier.

> **Note**
>
> If you don't want to create a molding spline template, you can load mine from the DVD. It's in the Objects\Chapter 09 folder and is called Molding Spline.lwo.

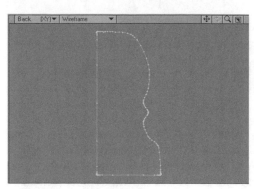

Figure 9-23: Freeze the spline so that we can control how many points are used in our molding strip.

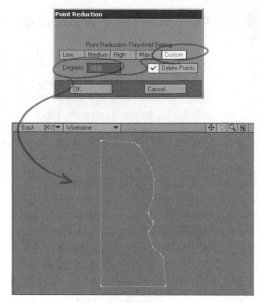

Figure 9-24: Use the Reduce Points tool with a Custom setting of 10 degrees to remove unnecessary points from the polygon.

4. Click on the **Construct | Reduce | Reduce Points** tool. The Point Reduction window will open. You can test out the different presets if you like, but I found that I needed something between Medium and High. If you're using the curve that I created, set Point Reduction Threshold to **Custom**, enter **10** for the Degrees and leave the **Delete Points** option checked. Then press **OK**.

The Reduce Points tool does a nice job of narrowing down the points while keeping the overall shape, but in many cases you'll still want to do some manual cleanup. That's certainly the case here.

The left edge of the molding template will form the back edge of the molding strip, and the bottom edge of the molding template will form the bottom edge of the molding strip. I want these edges to line up flush with the wall and the floor, so I need a perfect 90-degree angle at the lower-left corner. And since the upper-left corner will be up against the wall (where it won't really be seen), it doesn't need extra points (which will yield extra polys) either.

5. Zoom in to the lower-left corner and delete all but one of the points. Then

pan to the upper-left corner and delete all but one of the points.

Now the points that make up the left side of the template are not straight. No problem. We can use SP Move to correct this.

6. Activate the **SP Move** tool and right-click and drag on the upper-left point until it snaps into alignment with the point below it and also the point to its right. Then right-click and drag the bottom-left point until it snaps in line with the point above it and to its right. You should now have a straight edge from the back to the top and bottom.

7. Check the template poly in all viewports. When you snap points in only two dimensions, the possibility exists that the point will no longer line up in the third dimension. If any of your points are off, simply use the Stretch tool in the Top or Side viewports to squeeze all the points together until

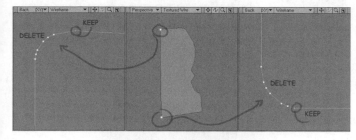

Figure 9-25: Manually delete the extra points on the left side (top and bottom) and adjust them with the SP Move tool until they are straight and form right angles, as shown here.

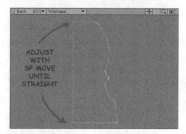

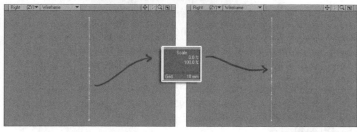

Figure 9-26: Check to make sure the points are planar in the Right viewport. If they are not, stretch them together until they are.

they're back in line with one another. The best way to do this is to stretch along a single axis (using the <Ctrl> key or middle mouse button) until the Scale is 0% (as seen in the Quick Info display).

Now that the molding template is complete, we can extrude it. When you extrude, you must do so away from the direction that your polygon's normal is facing. Otherwise, the normals on the extruded polys will be flipped.

8. Make sure the normal for the molding template faces toward the –Z-axis. (Select the template poly and press <A> to fit it to the viewport. Then look in the Top viewport. The normal

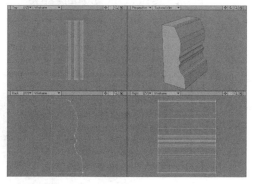

Figure 9-27: Extrude the molding template along the Z-axis by about 50 mm.

should be pointing toward the –Z-axis. If it isn't, flip the template poly by pressing the <f> keyboard shortcut.)

9. Use the **Multiply | Extend | Extrude** tool to extrude it along the

+Z-axis about **50 mm.** The exact length isn't important.

We're going to create what I call "molding blocks." These are two strips of molding that come together at a right angle. You can place these blocks at the corner of every room and then bridge their ends together to create complete molding strips.

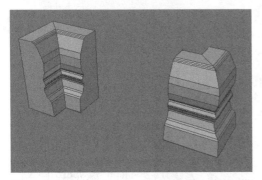

Figure 9-28: These are the "molding blocks" we'll be creating. One juts in and the other juts out.

10. There are two types of corners in our home: ones that jut in and ones that jut out. We need to create molding blocks for both, so select the molding strip you created, copy it, paste it back into place, then move it down along the –Z-axis so that it is positioned below the first one in the Top viewport.

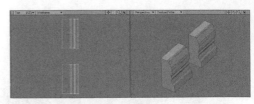

Figure 9-29: Copy the molding strip and move it down along the –Z-axis in the Top viewport.

To create the molding blocks, we need to cut each molding strip at a 45-degree angle. We'll do this by Boolean Subtracting boxes that we'll place on either side of each molding strip. Let's create those boxes now.

11. In the same layer as the molding strips, create a perfect square in the Top viewport. Rotate it 45 degrees in the Top viewport so that it's shaped like a diamond.

12. Select the square and extrude it along the Y-axis so that it forms a tall rectangular box. It should be taller than the molding strips.

13. Size the box so that it's about twice the width of the molding strip. Then move the box so that it covers the top of the upper molding strip. Make sure that the top and bottom points of this box are on the *left* side of the molding strip, as shown in Figure 9-31.

Figure 9-30: Create a box in the Top viewport and rotate it 45 degrees. Then extrude it along the Y-axis so that it's taller than the molding strips.

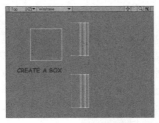

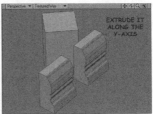

14. Copy this box and move it down so that it covers the bottom of the lower molding strip. Move it to the right until its top and bottom points are on the far *right* side of the molding strip, as shown in Figure 9-31.

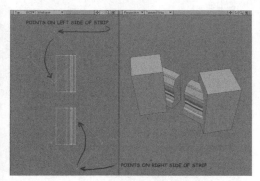

Figure 9-31: Position the box on the left side of the top molding strip. Copy it and place it on the right side of the lower molding strip.

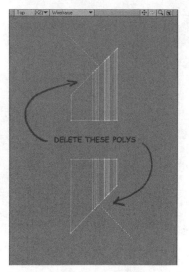

Figure 9-32: Select the top of each box and Speed Boolean Subtract. Then select the polygons at the 45-degree angle on each molding strip and delete them.

Since the centers of these boxes are on either side of the molding strips, they will cut through them at different angles.

15. The diamond-shaped boxes and the molding strips should be in the same layer. (If you inadvertently put them in separate layers, cut them and place them into a single layer now.)

16. Select the top polygon on each diamond-shaped box. Then run Speed Boolean Subtract by clicking on the **Construct | Combine | SpBoolSub** button.

17. The Boolean operation will leave a polygon at a 45-degree angle on each molding strip. Select this polygon and delete it.

Now we can use the Mirror tool to complete the molding blocks.

18. Select the top molding strip. Run the **Mirror** tool from the **Multiply | Duplicate** menu. In the Numeric panel, turn on **Free Rotation**. Then click and drag with your middle mouse button (or hold down the <Ctrl> key and click and drag with your left mouse button) until you have a copy at a 90-degree angle.

> **Note**
>
> It's important to constrain the Mirror tool with the middle mouse button (or <Ctrl> key modifier) in this instance. If your mirror is not exactly 90 degrees, you'll have trouble lining the mirrored parts up to one another.

19. Repeat this process for the lower molding strip. When you're finished, you should have four molding strips and it should be fairly obvious how they connect together.

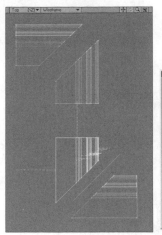

Figure 9-33: Select and mirror each molding block at a 45-degree angle.

20. Select the mirrored polys for the upper molding block. Use the **SP Move** tool with the left mouse button to snap these to their counterparts. Make sure that you see a blue XYZ, indicating that the snap is occurring in all three dimensions. Then repeat this process for the lower molding block.

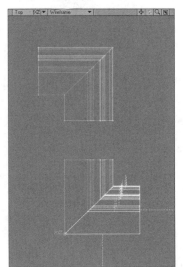

Figure 9-34: Use SP Move to snap each block to its counterpart. You'll know it's perfectly snapped when you see the small blue XYZ letters appear.

You now have two molding blocks, but each block is still comprised of two separate parts. We need to merge the points so that the two parts are joined together into a single object.

> ### Note
>
> If you use the spline template I provided, you should see 31 points merged for each molding block (so a total of 62 points for both). If you don't get that many being merged, check to ensure that the polygons line up perfectly. Select a few points at the joint and press <A> to zoom in. If the points don't line up perfectly, you probably didn't mirror the molding strips at a perfect 45-degree angle. Delete the mirror and start again. Mirroring at a perfect 45 degrees and using SP Move with XYZ snap will make everything line up perfectly.

The last thing we'll do is move the ends away from the 45-degree joint. This will make it easier to lasso select the ends later on.

21. Select the poly at the end of each molding block and move it away from the joint. You don't need to move it too far — just enough so that when you're zoomed out pretty far you'll be able to lasso select just the end.

Figure 9-35: Merge the points so that each block is a complete object. Then move the ends out to make them easier to lasso select later.

22. You now have two molding blocks — one for corners that jut in and one for corners that jut out. Place them on separate layers so that you don't confuse the two. Then delete any extraneous building materials and save your model.

Step 8: Place Copies of the Molding Blocks into Position at Each Corner of the Floor Plan

Now that we have molding blocks, we need to place them into position at the corners of our walls. If you look at the joint of the molding block, it creates a perfect 90-degree angle. And if you recall, we kept a copy of our extruded walls (before rounding). These walls form perfect 90-degree angles. Therefore, if we place this copy of our walls in the background, we can use SP Move to easily snap copies of our molding blocks into place.

1. Put the inner-facing molding block in the foreground and the extruded floorplan *without* the rounded corners in the background.

2. Move and rotate the molding block until it's positioned roughly in the corner of a wall.

3. Use **SP Move** to snap the molding block to the corner of the floor plan. Make sure it snaps fully to the XYZ.

4. Select this molding block. Copy and paste it into place. Then move and rotate it to another corner and use **SP Move** to snap it into place.

5. Repeat this process for each corner of every inner wall. When you're finished with the corners facing in, select the outer molding block and repeat the process for the corners facing out.

6. Check to make sure that you've got molding blocks for each corner. It can be easy to miss some corners, so double-check before moving on.

7. When all the molding blocks are in place, check to ensure that they are all level. None should be higher or lower in the Y-axis than the others. When you're satisfied, save your model.

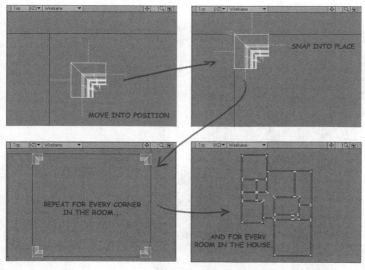

Figure 9-36: Position molding blocks at the corner of every wall. Use SP Move to snap them into position.

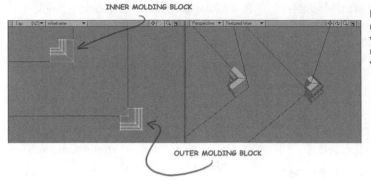

INNER MOLDING BLOCK

OUTER MOLDING BLOCK

Figure 9-37: Use an inner molding block where the walls jut in and an outer molding block where the walls jut out.

Step 9: Connect the Molding Together with the Bridge Tool

Now that the molding blocks are in place, it's a fairly simple matter to connect them together.

1. Zoom into the Top viewport so that you can see two opposing molding blocks. (You may want to open the Top view in full screen so that you've got plenty of space to work with.) Lasso select the end of one block. Then hold down the <Shift> key and lasso select the opposite end. Make sure that only two polys are selected. Check the Quick Info display to ensure this.

2. Now run the **Construct | Combine | Bridge** tool to connect the ends together into one long molding strip. Deselect the bridged polys.

Note

If your bridged polys look twisted or weird, it's probably because the polygons you selected aren't directly across from one another. Zoom out and make sure your polys are in a direct line and that you're not trying to connect corners that belong in other rooms. If that doesn't fix the problem, undo and check how many polys you have selected. Only two polys should be selected when you run the Bridge tool.

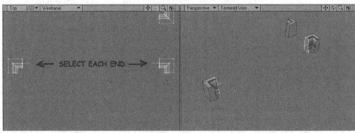

←— SELECT EACH END —→

Figure 9-38: Select the ends of two opposing molding blocks and use the Bridge tool to connect them together.

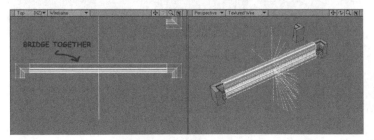

BRIDGE TOGETHER

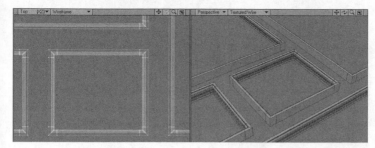

Figure 9-39: Bridge the molding blocks for each room in the entire house.

3. Repeat this process until the molding blocks for every room have been bridged together.

4. Exit the Top viewport and open the Right viewport full screen.

5. Place the molding in the foreground and the extruded *unrounded* walls in the background. Use the **SP Move** tool to move the molding until it is flush with the bottom of the walls.

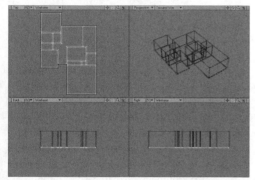

Figure 9-40: Place the unrounded walls in the background and snap the molding to the bottom of the walls.

6. Finally, apply the surface name **Molding** to the molding. Then cut and paste it into the rounded wall layer. You can now exit the Right full-screen viewport and delete the unrounded walls. You'll no longer need them.

Step 10: Scale the Home to a Realistic Size

We may not know the dimensions of our floor plan, but that doesn't mean we can't figure out how big our house should be. By using some common measurements, we can size our model and get it fairly close to its actual size.

Most homes have 8-foot ceilings. A quick check at HomeDepot.com also tells me that doors are typically 36" x 80". These two dimensions are all we need to deduce the size of our home.

1. Create a rectangle in the Back viewport. Using the Numeric panel, enter **8 ft** for Height. This will be the gauge for our 8-foot walls. The width of this polygon doesn't matter, so you can just make it a couple of meters wide.

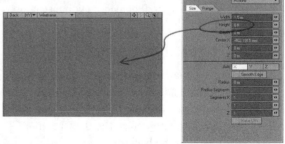

Figure 9-41: Create a rectangle in the Back viewport that's 8 feet high and roughly 1 or 2 meters wide.

2. Create another rectangle that's 36 inches wide by 80 inches high. This will be our door reference poly.

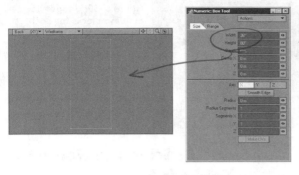

Figure 9-42: Create another rectangle in the Back viewport that's 36" x 80".

3. Place the door reference poly in the foreground and the walls with the molding in the background. Move the door reference poly to the front door area. You'll notice that the reference poly is nearly as wide as the entire hallway. But if you check the floor plan image, you'll see that the door should only be about half the size of the hallway. Therefore, we know that our home is currently too small.

Figure 9-43: Move the door reference poly to the front entryway and place the walls in the background. You'll notice that the door is nearly as wide as the entire foyer. That means our house is currently too small.

4. We're going to size everything we've created so far. Place the walls, floor/ceiling, and doorway template polys (the ones you created in Step 4) in the foreground. Then place the door reference poly in the background.

5. Switch to **Action Center: Mouse**.

6. Activate the **Size** tool (keyboard shortcut <**H**>) and place your mouse over the center of the door reference poly.

7. Use the **Size** tool to scale the building up until the doorway poly for the front entrance that you created in Step 4 roughly matches the width of the door reference poly in the background. It should be approximately 207%.

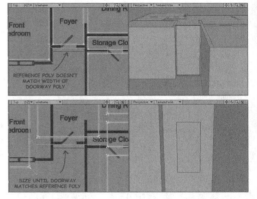

Figure 9-44: Switch to Action Center: Mouse and use the Size tool to increase the scale of the house until the front entry doorway poly matches the door size reference poly.

The overall size of the house is now correct in the X-axis and Z-axis. With that being the case, we can size the walls accordingly.

8. Place the walls, the floor/ceiling, and the doorway polys in the foreground and the 8-foot wall reference poly in the background.

9. Move everything on the Y-axis until the floor is roughly at the bottom of the 8-foot box.

10. Switch to **Points** selection mode. Lasso select the points at the top of everything in the foreground. Then use the **Move** tool to move them until they are at the height of the 8-foot wall, as seen in the Back or Right viewports.

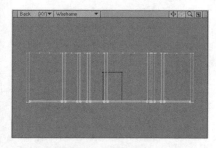

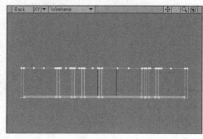

Figure 9-45: Place the walls, floor/ceiling, and doorway template polys in the foreground and move them so that the walls are at the base of the 8-foot poly. Lasso select the points at the top and move them down so they are level with the top of the 8-foot poly.

11. Congratulations! Your house is now very close to its actual size. Save your model.

Note

Now that you've sized the house, it will no longer match up to the floor plan background image. You should change the size and position of the background image in the Display Options and then save it as a preset so that you can use it later on. If you loaded my backdrop preset in Step 1, you can simply load in the Floor Plan for Step 10.cfg background preset from the Setup\ Chapter 09 folder.

Step 11: Create the Door and Doorway Polygons

Now that the walls and moldings are complete and the house has been sized to realistic proportions, it's time to begin working on the doorways.

It's easy to think of a doorway as just an opening in a wall, but doorways are actually a bit more detailed than that. They typically have a frame around them. And inside that frame there is typically a doorjamb at the center that separates the frame into two sides. We'll be creating all of these parts over the next few steps. The process is fairly simple. We start with the largest part and work our way inward. But first, let's consolidate our model.

1. Select the ceiling polys and use **SP Move** to snap them to the top of the walls. Then select the floor polys and use SP Move to snap them to the bottom of the walls. Place the ceiling, walls, moldings, and floors in the first layer. Move the doorway polygons (the ones you created in Step 4) to Layer 2. Then delete the 8-foot ceiling reference poly and the door size reference poly.

2. Place the doorway polygons into the foreground and the wall polys in the background. Then open the Display Options and turn off the floor plan background image.

3. You will probably notice some areas where the doorway polys don't fully cut through the wall in the background or that the doorway polys are too close to the edge of a wall. Select each poly and adjust it with the Move and/or Stretch tools so that it completely passes through the wall on both sides and that the doorways are not too close to any corners.

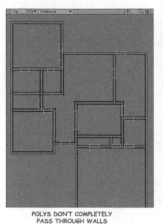
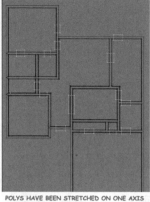

Figure 9-46: Your doorway polys may not completely pass through the walls and in some instances (such as the hall bathroom) they may not be centered properly. Move and/or stretch the polys so they pass completely through the walls in the background.

POLYS DON'T COMPLETELY
PASS THROUGH WALLS

POLYS HAVE BEEN STRETCHED ON ONE AXIS
TO ENSURE THEY PASS THROUGH WALLS

Note

You'll probably notice that some doorway polys line up with one another. These will likely be "off" by the same amount. You can make quick work by multiple-selecting these polys and moving/stretching them at the same time.

Note

If you switched to Action Center: Mouse to resize the floor plan, be sure to switch back to Action Center: Selection when stretching doorway polys.

6. We've been calling these "doorway" polys because they're positioned at the doorways. But we'll actually be using them to create both the door*way* and the door*frame*. As I mentioned earlier, we're starting with the largest part and working our way inward. The largest part is not the doorway, but the frame that goes around it. So the polys we just extruded will be used to create the doorframes. Now we need polys that are slightly smaller for the actual doorway.

4. Once the doorway polys have been adjusted as needed, activate the **Extrude** tool (keyboard shortcut <**E**>). Using the Numeric panel, enter **–80**" in the Y field and press **Tab** to accept the value (Modeler will convert from English to metric units automatically). This will extrude the doorways down by 80".

5. Drop the Extrude tool and move the doorway polys down until they are just below the bottom of the floor plan. About 10 mm below should be just fine.

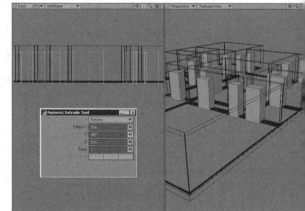

Figure 9-47: Extrude the doorway polys by –80". Then move polys so they are roughly 10 mm below the bottom of the walls.

7. Copy the polys you extruded and paste them into another layer. Place the originals in the background.

8. Activate the **Modify | Translate | More | Point Normal Move** tool. This tool resizes geometry based on the average of the object's poly normals. It allows you to make objects larger or smaller while keeping the position relatively unchanged. It's typically used to make things thicker or thinner. In this case, we will use it to shrink the size of the doorframe polys without moving them away from their positions in relation to the walls.

9. Using the Numeric panel, make sure Mode is set to **Selected Points**, enter **–200 mm** in the Move box, and press **Enter** to accept the value. This will scale all the doorframe polys in by 200 mm to create doorway polys.

10. Copy the doorway polys to a new layer. Lasso select all the points that make up the bottoms of the doorways. Place the walls in Layer 1 in the background.

11. Use the **Move** tool to move the selected points down so they are well below the bottom of the walls. This will ensure that we cut completely through the lowest point of the house when we

Boolean the doorways out of the doorframes later on.

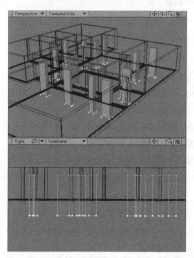

Figure 9-49: Copy the doorway template boxes to a new layer. Place the walls in the background. Select all the points at the bottom of these boxes and move them down below the walls.

12. Assign the surface name **Doorway** to the doorway template boxes and assign the surface name **Door Frame** to the doorframe template boxes. Then save your model.

13. Before moving on to the next step, copy the doorframe boxes and paste them into a fresh new object. Save this new object as **Door Frame Boxes**. We'll be using it later.

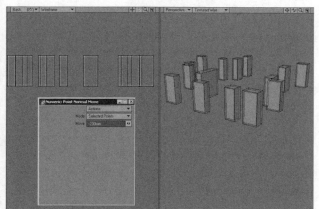

Figure 9-48: Copy the doorframe template boxes and use Point Normal Move to shrink them by –200 mm to create doorway template boxes. The originals are shown here in the background for comparison.

Step 12: Solid Drill the Doorframes

Now that our template polys are built, we can start constructing the doorframes.

1. Use the Polygon Statistics panel (keyboard shortcut <**w**>) to select the walls in Layer 1. (See Chapter 3 for more info on using the Statistics panel to select points and polygons.) Copy the wall polys you selected and paste them in a new layer. Then place the doorframe boxes in the background.

2. Use the **Construct | Combine | Solid Drill** tool to stencil the walls with the surface called **Door Frame**. If

you get an error, check to make sure the bottoms of your doorframe polys are situated slightly below the walls. If they're too close, you may get an error.

3. Save your model.

> **Note**
>
> The Solid Drill tool works similarly to the regular Drill tool. The main difference is that the Solid Drill tool requires you to use a 3D cutting object in the background and the position of that cutting object is very important. It must intersect the object you want to drill. That's why it was important for our doorframe boxes to completely pass through the walls. If they did not, the doorframe would not cut through both sides of the wall.

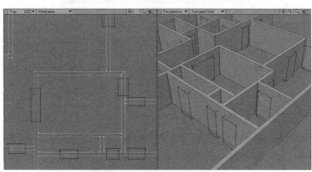

Figure 9-50: Copy the walls to a new layer. Place the Door Frame Boxes object in the background. Use the Solid Drill tool with the Stencil option to cut the doorframes into the walls using a surface called Door Frame.

Step 13: Multishift the Doorframes

We've just cut polygons into our walls that we can use to create the doorframes. And by stenciling them with a specific name (Door Frame) we can now easily select them with the Statistics panel.

1. Use the Statistics panel to select the doorframe polys.

Doorframes can be either simple or fairly elaborate. We're going to keep ours simple. We could simply shift the doors out using either the Smooth Shift or Bevel tool (with no Inset). But remember that most, if not all, geometry should be beveled. So instead of just pushing the doorframes out, we'll bevel them in slightly, then shift them out, then bevel them in slightly again.

2. You can do this with the **Multiply | Extend | Multishift** tool (as described below) or you can simply load in the **Door Frames.ss** Multishift preset from the Multishifts\Chapter 09 folder.

3. If you want to do it yourself, use the Multishift tool to inset the doorframe polys by **4 mm** and shift them by **3 mm**. This creates a bevel between the frame and the wall. Then insert a new shift (click on the **Insert Shift** button in the Numeric panel) and shift the polys an additional **27 mm** (the total will be 30 mm in the Multishift Numeric panel). Then insert another shift. Inset the polys by an additional **5 mm** (the total inset should now be 9 mm) and shift the polys by an additional **6 mm** (bringing the total to 36 mm). Then drop the tool and deselect your polys.

> **Note**
>
> When you use Multishift to create a series of bevels, the inset amount and shift amount shown in the Numeric panel is a total for the current and all previous shifts. For example, if the first shift is 5 mm and then you insert a shift and shift 5 mm more, the second shift will display 10 mm.

4. Once you've beveled and shifted the doorframes, save your model.

Figure 9-51: Use the Statistics panel to select the doorframe polys you stenciled into the wall. Then Multishift them as shown here or simply load the Door Frames.ss Multishift preset from the companion DVD.

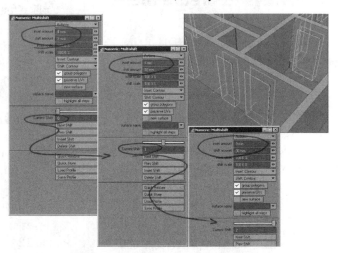

Step 14: Boolean the Doorways

We're working our way from the outside to the inside — from the largest part to the smallest part of the doorway. We just created the doorframes. Now we need to carve the doorway out of it. We'll do this with the Boolean tool.

1. Place the walls in the foreground and the doorway polys in the background. (Remember that the doorway polys are the boxes that are slightly smaller than the doorframe boxes.)

2. Run the **Construct | Combine | Boolean** tool with the Subtract option to remove the doorways from the doorframes (Figure 9-52).

3. Merge points to connect the doorway cutouts to the doorframes. Then save your model.

Step 15: Multishift the Doorways to Create the Doorjambs

With the doorway now cleared out, the walls are starting to look much better. But they still need a slight bevel on the inside and they also need the doorjambs. We'll create them in this step.

1. Use the Polygon Statistics panel to select just the doorway polys. Then activate the **Multishift** tool.

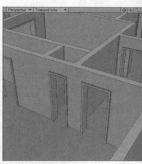
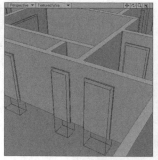

Figure 9-52: Use the Boolean Subtract tool to cut the doorway box templates out of the doorframes. Then merge points to connect everything together.

2. Use the **Multishift** tool to bevel the doorways in by about **2** or **3 mm** (for both the shift and inset). This keeps the edge of the doorframe from being unrealistically sharp. Then insert a new shift (click on the **Insert Shift** button in the Numeric panel) and simply inset the polys by about **118 mm** (the total will show up as 120 mm in the Numeric panel). Don't shift them. This puts the doorway poly in just about the right place for the doorjamb.

3. Insert a new shift. Shift the polys out an additional **1 mm** and inset them an additional **2 mm**. This creates a bevel where the doorjamb meets up with the doorway.

4. Insert a new shift and simply shift the polys about **12 mm**. Don't inset them. This gives the doorjamb some depth.

5. Finally, insert another shift. Inset and shift the polys about **2 mm**. This bevels the doorjamb in slightly. The total inset amount for the last shift should be **124 mm**. The total shift amount for the last shift should be **17 mm**.

6. Drop the Multishift tool and deselect the polys.

> **Note**
>
> You can follow the steps outlined below to create the doorjamb or simply load the Doorjambs.ss Multishift preset found in the Multishifts\Chapter 09 folder on the DVD.

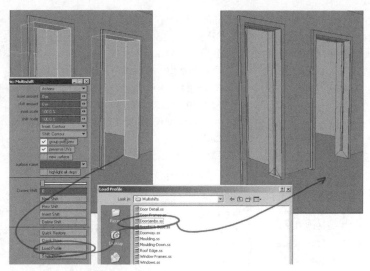

Figure 9-53: Select the doorway polys with the Statistics panel. Then use Multishift to create the doorjamb as described above. Alternately, you can load the Doorjambs.ss preset as shown here.

The doorframe, doorway, and doorjamb are now finished, but if you look closely, you'll see that the doorjamb doesn't come flush to the floor. We can correct this quite simply by trimming off the areas we don't want.

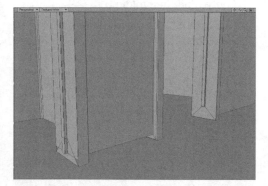

Figure 9-54: The doorjamb doesn't come down to the floor. We can fix this by simply trimming off the area we don't want.

7. Place the original walls in the background (the ones in Layer 1 that haven't had the doorways cut out of them).

8. Switch to **Points** selection mode. Lasso select all the points that make up the bottom half of the walls. This should include all the points that make up the doorways, doorframes, etc.

9. Move these points way down below the bottom of the walls seen in the background.

10. Activate the **Multiply | Subdivide | Knife** tool. Position your mouse roughly at the location of the bottom of the walls in the background. Use the Knife tool with the middle mouse button (to constrain it to a straight cut) and slice completely through the walls in

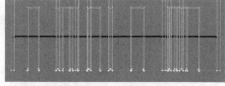

Figure 9-55: Place the original walls (in Layer 1) in the background. Lasso select the points on the walls with the doorways cut out and move them way down below the originals in the background. Then use the Knife tool to slice through the polys at the base of the walls in the background.

the foreground. You may want to zoom in to ensure your slice is positioned exactly at the base. If you do, make sure you zoom out again to ensure your slice goes through the entire house.

11. Now we could just delete all the polys on the bottom half of the slice we just created, but we don't want to lose the wall "caps" — the polys at the bottom of the wall whose normals point toward the –Y-axis. We need these in order to properly create the garage later on. So use the Statistics panel to select the walls. Then hide the unselected objects (keyboard shortcut <=> (equal sign)). Lasso select the polys at the very bottom of the walls (again, the ones whose normals run along the Y-axis) as shown in Figure 9-56. Cut them. Then unhide everything (keyboard shortcut <\>).

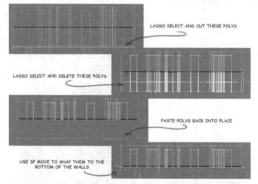

Figure 9-56: Select the walls using the Statistics panel. Hide the unselected polys. Select the wall caps (first image) and cut them. Unhide everything. Select the walls on the lower half of the cut (second image) and delete them. Paste the wall caps back into place (third image). Then use SP Move to snap them to the bottom of the walls (fourth image).

12. Lasso select all the polys on the bottom half of the slice you created with the Knife tool. Delete them. Then paste the wall "cap" polys back into

place. Lasso select them and use the **SP Move** tool to move them up until they snap to the bottom of the walls. Use **Merge Points** with Automatic settings to join the polys together. The bottom of the doorframe and wall is now clean again and comes flush to the ground.

> **Note**
>
> If you have any stray points left over after deleting the bottom of the walls, use the Point Statistics panel to select any points connected to 0 polygons and then delete them.

13. Go back to Layer 1 and use the Statistics panel to select the walls that haven't had the doorways cut out of them. Delete them. All that should be left in this layer is the floor/ceiling polys and the molding.

14. Use the Statistics panel to select the molding. Cut it and paste it to a new layer.

15. Place the floor/ceiling polys in the background and the walls with the doorways cut out of them in the foreground.

16. Select all of the points that make up the bottom of the walls.

17. Use **SP Move** to move these points until they line up perfectly along the Y-axis with the floors. Then drop the SP Move tool and deselect your points. Inspect the walls. They should line up perfectly with the ceiling polys and floor polys in the background.

18. Copy the walls and paste them into Layer 1 with the floors and ceilings. Then save your model.

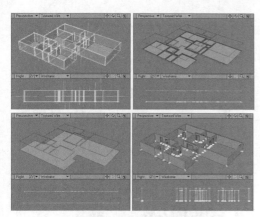

Figure 9-57: Select the walls in Layer 1 and delete them (upper-left and upper-right images). Select the molding and cut and paste it to a new layer, leaving just the floors and ceiling in Layer 1 (lower-left image). Select the points on the bottom of the walls and use SP Move to snap them to the floors in Layer 1 (lower-right image).

Step 16: Boolean the Molding to Create Door Openings

We created the molding for each room by bridging each corner block together. But now that we have doorways, the molding runs right through them. We need to trim the molding so that it ends where the doorframes are.

1. Place the doorframe template boxes in the foreground. These polys currently have the surface called Door Frame. Assign a new surface for them called **Molding Cap**. This will make it easy to select these polys later on.

2. Place the molding in the foreground and the doorway template boxes in the background.

3. Use **Boolean Subtract** to cut out the doorway areas from the molding.

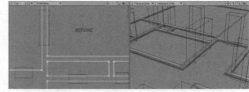

Figure 9-58: Boolean Subtract the doorway template boxes from the molding. Then Merge Points.

4. Finally, run the **Merge Points** command on the molding to join the ends created by the Boolean operation to the original sections of the molding. Then save your model.

Step 17: Bevel the Open Ends of the Molding

The ends of the molding come to an abrupt end. They should be beveled slightly.

1. With the molding in the foreground, use the Statistics panel to select the Molding Cap polys. These will be the polys at the end of the molding that the doorway template boxes trimmed away.

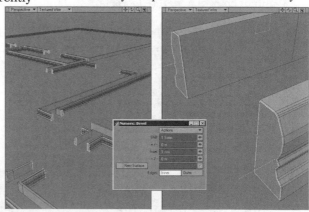

Figure 9-59: Select the Molding Cap polys and bevel them with a Shift of 1.5 mm and an Inset of 1 mm.

2. Use the **Bevel** tool to bevel the ends of the molding. Shift them about **1.5 mm** and Inset them about **1 mm**.

3. Deselect the Molding Cap polys and assign all the molding polys the same surface name of **Molding**.

4. Cut the molding and paste it into Layer 1 with the walls, floors, and ceilings. Then save your model.

Step 18: Create a Basic Door Shape

We have doorways but we don't have doors. Over the next few steps we'll take care of this. We'll begin by creating a simple door shape.

1. Place the walls in the background and zoom into the area of the front door in the Back viewport.

2. Use the **Box** tool to create a rectangle in the Back viewport that fills the area of the doorway inside the doorframe. This will be our door.

3. Drop the Box tool and move the 2D door to the outside of the doorframe. Make sure that its normal faces toward the –Z-axis (the outside of the house).

4. Extrude the door along the +Z-axis until it comes up to the doorjamb.

5. Select the front and back polys of the door (but not the sides).

6. Use the **Bevel** tool to shift and inset the front and back sides of the door slightly by about **4 mm**.

7. We now have a simple door that fills the doorframe. Save your model.

Step 19: Multishift Door Detail and Save as a Preset for Later Use

Most home doors have decorative panels. They look like squares and rectangles that have multi-step bevels. Although there are a number of ways to achieve this, I prefer using the Multishift tool.

1. Create a box in the Back viewport about **200 mm** square. It should be about one-third the width of the door poly.

2. Use the **Multishift** tool to create several bevels and insets. There is no rule for how these bevels should look — it's purely an artistic decision. When you're happy with your bevel, save the Multishift profile to your hard drive for use later.

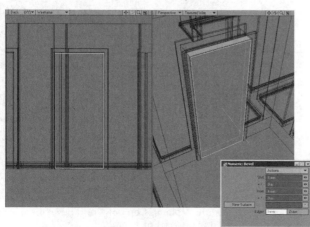

Figure 9-60: Create a box in the Back viewport that fills the front doorway. Extrude it along the Z-axis and fit it in the doorframe. Then bevel the front and back faces by 4 mm.

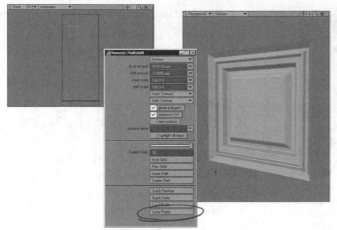

Figure 9-61: Create a box in the Back viewport about one-third the width of the door. Use the Multishift tool to create a series of bevels. Then save the results by clicking on the Save Profile button in the Multishift Numeric panel. We'll use this preset later.

Note

Be sure to add the .ss extension to your profile when you save it. If you don't add the extension, the file will not appear when you try to load it later.

3. If you'd like to use my settings, you can simply load in the Door Detail.ss profile from the DVD.

Note

The poly we created to make our multi-step bevel preset is roughly one-third the size of the door. This is roughly the same size as the polys we'll use to add detail to the door. We created the poly at this size so that we could simply apply the preset later on to the door details. If our box were bigger or smaller, we would likely have to resize the effect using the inset scale and shift scale options in the Multishift Numeric panel.

Step 20: Create the Door Details

Now that our multi-step bevel preset has been created, we can add detail to the door. We'll do this by drilling several template polys into the door and then applying the Multishift preset we saved in the previous step.

You can create any combination of template polys to add detail to your door. For this lesson, I'm going to create six panels. There will be three on the left half of the door and three mirror copies on the right.

The first thing we need to do is find the center point of the door. This will allow us to position the template polys correctly on the left side and it will also act as a guide for using the Mirror tool later on.

1. Select the front face poly of the basic door and copy it to a new layer.

2. Select the two points at the top of the door and use the **Multiply | Subdivide | Divide** tool to add a point directly between them.

3. Select the two points at the bottom of the door poly and use the **Divide** tool to add another point directly between them.

4. Select the two new points and use the **Construct | Combine | Connect** tool to connect them. We now have a division at the halfway point on the door.

5. Place the poly with the vertical division in the background. In a new layer, create a box and two rectangles on the left half of the door division.

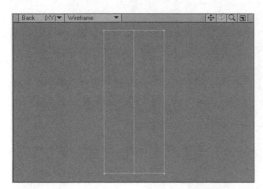

Figure 9-62: Copy the front face poly of the door and paste it into a new layer. Use the Divide tool to add points to the center of the top and bottom edge. Then connect these points using the Connect tool.

6. Use the **Mirror** tool to mirror these over to the right side of the door. Place your mouse over the center division when mirroring so you know you're mirroring at the halfway point.

7. With the detail polys in place, put the actual door (the one without the division) in the foreground and the detail polys in the background.

8. Drill the detail polys along the Z-axis into the door using the Stencil option with a new surface called **Door Details**.

9. Use the Statistics panel to select just the Door Detail polys.

10. Activate the **Multishift** tool and load the profile you saved earlier. This will bevel each of the detail polys into the door.

11. Deselect any polys. Then assign a new surface for the door called **Doors**.

12. You can now delete the door detail template polys and any other extraneous construction materials. You should have the walls, floors, ceiling, and molding in Layer 1. Move the finished door to Layer 2. Then save your model.

Figure 9-63: Create a box and two rectangles on the left side of the door (slightly offset from the center). Then Mirror them over to the right side of the door.

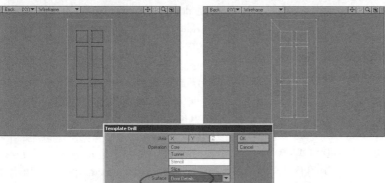

Figure 9-64: Drill the detail polys into the door using the Stencil option. Change the Surface setting in the Template Drill window to Door Details.

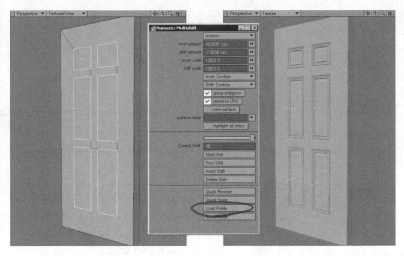

Figure 9-65: Select
the Door Detail polys.
Run Multishift and
load the profile you
saved in Step 19.

Step 21: Create the Doorknob

Our door looks great, but it's missing door-knobs. Let's fix this. We'll start by creating the doorknob base.

1. Place the door in the background and zoom in to the area where the door-knob should go, about halfway down the door and toward the left edge.

2. Make a disc in the Back viewport that's centered between the multi-step bevel details and the far left edge. It should be roughly **60 mm** in diameter and its normal should face the –Z-axis.

3. Extrude the disc along the +Z-axis about **10 mm** to give it some thickness. (See Figure 9-66.)

4. Select the disc that you originally created (the one that faces the –Z-axis). Use the **Bevel** tool (or Multishift if you prefer) to shift it about **3.5 mm** and inset it about **15 mm**. (See Figure 9-67 images A and B.) Keep the Bevel tool active and the disc selected for the next few steps.

5. With the Bevel tool still active, right-click to create a new bevel. Then shift the disc about **8 mm** but don't inset it.

6. Right-click again to create a new bevel. Inset the disc about **2 mm** but don't shift it.

7. Right-click one more time to create a new bevel. Shift the disc back about **–6 mm**. (See Figure 9-67 image C.)

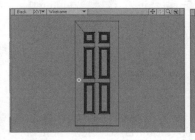
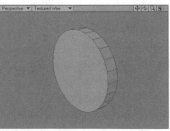

Figure 9-66: Create a disc
roughly 60 mm in diameter
and positioned on the left
side of the door. Extrude it
along the Z-axis by 10 mm.

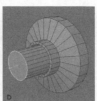

Figure 9-67: Select the front disc and bevel it as described above and shown here.

This completes the base, but *don't drop the Bevel tool just yet.* We still need to create the pole that connects the knob to the base.

8. With the Bevel tool still active and the disc still selected, right-click to create a new bevel. Inset the disc about **1 mm** but don't shift it at all. This puts some space between the base and the knob.

9. Right-click to create a new bevel. Then shift the disc out about **25 mm** but don't inset it at all. (See Figure 9-67 image D.)

> **Note**
>
> If you'd like, you can simply load in the Doorknob Base.ss Multishift profile and apply it to the front poly of the disc you extruded earlier. You've got to love Multishift's ability to save and load profiles!

We now have a base and the pole. They're admittedly rough, but we'll use Rounder to take care of that in just a bit. First, let's create the doorknob.

10. Go to a new layer and place the doorknob base in the background.

11. Place your mouse in the Back viewport and create a ball that's approximately **60 mm** in diameter. (Starting the ball in the Back viewport ensures that its pole will run along the Z-axis.) Then position the ball so that it's centered around the doorknob base in the background and located at the end of the pole jutting out from the base.

12. Make sure your Action Center is set to **Selection**. Place your mouse in the

Top viewport and activate the **Stretch** tool. Click and drag down with your middle mouse button (or hold down the <Ctrl> key modifier) to squeeze the ball along the Z-axis until it's a doorknob shape. A Horizontal Factor of **100%** and a Vertical Factor of **38%** should work just fine.

13. With the doorknob base still in the background, move the doorknob into position at the end of the base pole. Then assign it a surface called **Doorknob.**

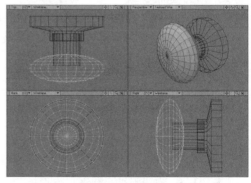

Figure 9-68: Create a ball for the doorknob and stretch it along the Z-axis.

Now let's finish things off by rounding the edges of the doorknob base. The base should be much smoother and have a more subtle flow to it. Right now it's got a lot of right angles.

14. Switch back to the doorknob base layer.

15. Select the ring of points shown in Figure 9-69 (either lasso select them or use the Select Loop command).

16. Run the **Multiply | Extend | Rounder** tool. Click and drag in the viewport to activate it. Set Rounding Polygons to 4 and Inset distance to **5 mm**. Then drop Rounder and deselect these points.

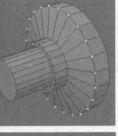

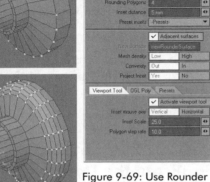

Figure 9-69: Use Rounder to round the edge with the settings shown here.

17. Select the next ring of points shown in Figure 9-70. Run **Rounder**. Click and drag very slightly in one of the orthographic viewports to activate the tool. Rounder will use the previous settings,

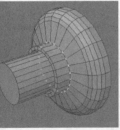

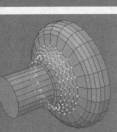

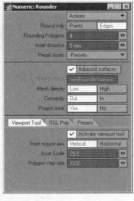

Figure 9-70: Use Rounder to round the edge with the settings shown here.

which is fine. Drop the tool and deselect the points.

18. Select the next ring of points shown in Figure 9-71. Run **Rounder**. This edge doesn't need nearly as much geometry. Click and drag in one of the orthographic viewports to activate the tool. It will use the previous settings. Lower Rounding Polygons to 2 and lower Inset distance to **500 um** (0.5 mm). Drop the tool and deselect the points.

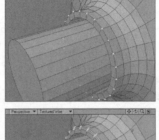

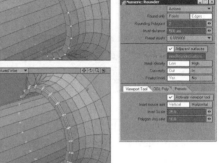

Figure 9-71: Use Rounder to round the edge with the settings shown here.

19. Finally, select the last ring of points shown in Figure 9-72. Run **Rounder**. Click and drag in one of the orthographic viewports to activate the tool with the previous settings. You don't need to change anything. Drop the tool and deselect the points.

20. The base is now complete. Assign it the **Doorknob** surface, then cut the base and paste it into the layer with the doorknob ball.

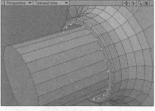

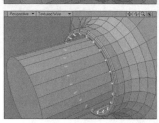

Figure 9-72: Use Rounder to round the edge with the settings shown here.

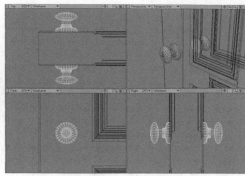

Figure 9-73: Mirror the completed doorknob and position it on the opposite side of the door.

Now let's position and duplicate the doorknob so there's one on either side of the door.

21. Place the completed door in the background. Move the doorknob until it's flush with the door on the Z-axis. Then position it in the Back viewport along the X-axis and Y-axis until it's where you'd expect the doorknob to be.

22. Activate the **Mirror** tool and position your mouse at the center of the door. Using your middle mouse button (or the <Ctrl> key modifier) click and drag in a horizontal line to create a mirror copy of the doorknob.

23. Drop the Mirror tool and zoom in to the mirrored doorknob. If necessary, select it and move it along the Z-axis so that it's flush with the door. (See Figure 9-73.)

24. Finally, cut the doorknobs and paste them into the layer with the completed door.

25. Your door is now complete. Delete any leftover construction materials that may be lying around. Then save your model.

Step 22: Position and Duplicate the Door

At this point we only have one door; however, there are nearly a dozen doors in the whole house. We need to duplicate this door.

There are a number of ways to duplicate objects. Copying and pasting is one way. But that's boring. I'm going to show you a little technique I like to use when I've already blocked out the basic position of my objects.

1. Open the **Door Frame Boxes** object that you saved earlier. These boxes were used to create the doorframes. They are sized and positioned just about where each door needs to be. Copy the Door Frame Boxes and paste them into a blank layer in your house object. Then place the walls in the background and double-check that they fit the doorways.

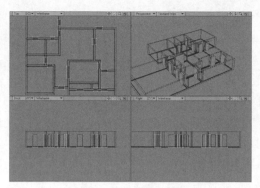

Figure 9-74: Open the Door Frame Boxes object that you saved earlier. Copy the boxes and paste them into a blank layer in your home model.

2. Place the doorframe boxes in the foreground and the single door in the background. Check the height of the boxes. They should be the same height as the door. If they're not, adjust their height accordingly.

Figure 9-75: Position the doorframe boxes so they are located at the bottom of the door. Then adjust the top of the boxes so they match the top of the door.

3. Click on the **Construct | Reduce | More | Collapse Polys** tool. This will convert each doorframe box into a single point positioned at the center of where the box used to be.

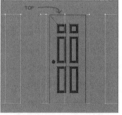

Figure 9-76: Run the Construct | Reduce | More | Collapse Polys tool to convert the boxes to single points.

4. Place the door in the foreground and the points from the collapsed polys in the background.

5. Select the **Multiply | Duplicate | More | Point Clone Plus** tool. A window will appear where you can configure the duplication options. Just leave everything at its default and hit **OK**. Copies of your door will be created at the position of every point in the background layer.

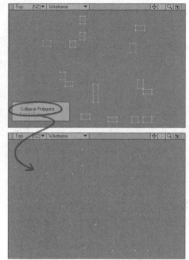

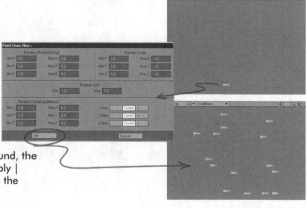

Figure 9-77: Put the door in the foreground, the points in the background, and run Multiply | Duplicate | More | Point Clone Plus with the default settings.

Cool, huh? Granted, we still have some work to do, but collapsing a group of pre-positioned polygons and running Point Clone Plus is a quick and handy way to replicate objects.

Okay. We have a few extra doors in places they shouldn't be. Let's get rid of them.

6. Select the doors into and out of the dining room and delete them. (Place the floor plan.jpg image in the background if you need to reference room names.)

7. Select the door going from the living room to the breakfast nook and delete it.

8. Select the door going from the back bedroom to the bathroom and delete it.

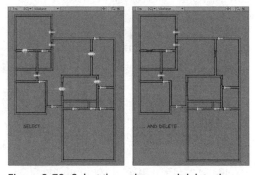

Figure 9-78: Select these doors and delete them.

9. Now inspect the floor plan image and note which doors need to be rotated 90 degrees. Rotate them one by one in the Top viewport.

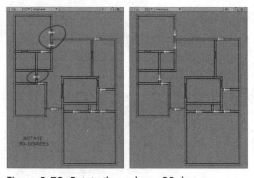

Figure 9-79: Rotate these doors 90 degrees.

Now if you look closely, you'll notice that not all doors fit their doorframes. Remember that the doors on the left side of the house are a bit smaller. To correct this, you'll need to resize some of the doors.

10. Zoom in to the front bedroom door. Select a few polys on the door. Then press <]> to select all the connected polys. The entire door (but not its doorknobs) should be selected. Hide the *unselected* geometry (keyboard shortcut <=> so that the door is the only object visible on the layer.

11. Make sure your Action Center is set to **Selection**.

12. Use the **Stretch** tool with the middle mouse button (or the <Ctrl> key modifier) to squeeze the door until it fits within the doorframe.

13. When the door is sized properly, swap the hidden polys with the visible polys (keyboard shortcut <|>). This should reveal the doorknobs and hide the door.

14. Lasso select the doorknobs, then unhide everything. This will leave the doorknobs selected and will show you the doors again.

15. Move the doorknobs into place. If you only moved and stretched the doors on one axis, you should simply be able to

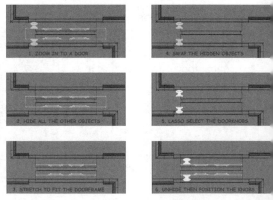

Figure 9-80: Follow these steps to fit each door into its doorframe.

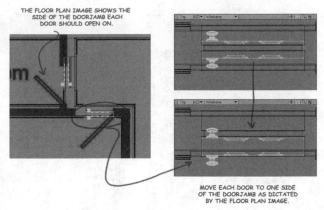

THE FLOOR PLAN IMAGE SHOWS THE SIDE OF THE DOORJAMB EACH DOOR SHOULD OPEN ON.

MOVE EACH DOOR TO ONE SIDE OF THE DOORJAMB AS DICTATED BY THE FLOOR PLAN IMAGE.

Figure 9-81: Using the floor plan image as a guide, move each door to the appropriate side of the doorjamb.

move the doorknobs along that same axis to position them in place.

16. Repeat this process for each of the smaller doors until every door in the house fits inside its doorframe.

Now we need to position each door on one side of the doorjamb. Doors always open on the side of the doorjamb they're placed on.

17. Select each door and move it to one side of the doorjamb. You can check the floor plan background image to get an idea of which way the doors should open.

18. Check that all the doors have been sized and positioned in the doorframes correctly. When everything looks like it fits into place, delete any leftover construction materials. Then save your model.

Step 23: Create the Cornice and Ceiling

Now let's create the cornice. This is a strip of molding that runs along the upper edge of each wall and juts up to the ceiling. We'll use a spline to define the profile of the cornice, but rather than extruding it and creating blocks as we did with the baseboard molding, we'll use a simpler technique involving Rail Bevel.

The Rail Bevel tool allows you to create multi-step bevels that match the shape of a spline you place in the background. This spline must be oriented along the Y-axis, and the number and proximity of points in the spline will determine the number and placement of segments in the bevel. Therefore we need to pay close attention to the spline we create.

1. Load **Cornice Spline.lwo** from Objects\Chapter 09 and copy it to a blank layer of your house object.

> **Note**
>
> Don't feel like you have to use this cornice spline. There's nothing special or magic about it. I just whipped it up to make things easy, but you're welcome to create your own if you'd like or you can use mine as a starting point for your own creation. Just be sure to size it relative to the height of the walls. It should be somewhere between 60 and 150 mm high.

The Cornice Spline object we're working with has a nice shape, but it needs more points in the arcing areas in order to work well with the Rail Bevel tool. We can manually add points or we can simply freeze the spline and then clean up the points we don't want. Let's go with the latter approach.

2. With the Cornice Spline in the foreground, click on the **Construct |**

Convert | Freeze button (or press the <**Ctrl**>+<**d**> keyboard shortcut) to convert the spline into a single polygon. You can see that it has a fairly large number of points. Let's get rid of some of the unnecessary ones.

3. Click on the **Construct | Reduce | Reduce Points** tool. The Point Reduction window will appear. Just as we did with the molding spline, let's use a custom setting. Click on the **Custom** button and enter **10** into the Degrees field. Then click **OK**.

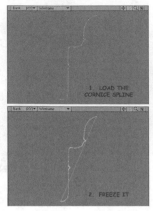

Figure 9-82: Load the Cornice Spline object. Use the Construc | Convert | Freeze command to convert it to a polygon. Use the Construct | Reduce | Reduce Points tool to eliminate unnecessary points. Then reselect the points and create a new open spline curve.

The Reduce Points tool did a nice job of filtering out unwanted points and leaving the ones in the curved areas, right where we need them.

4. Open the Back viewport full screen and press <**a**> to fit the foreground poly in the viewport. Switch to **Points** selection mode. Starting with the point at the very bottom, begin selecting the points on the polygon in order. You will probably need to zoom in to properly select the points in the curved areas. Be sure to use the Pan and Magnify keyboard shortcuts you learned at the beginning of this chapter.

5. Once all of the points in the polygon are selected, press <**Ctrl**>+<**p**> to create an open spline.

6. We now have both a spline and a polygon. Switch to **Polygons** selection mode. The spline will be selected. Hide it, then delete the polygon. Finally, unhide the spline. It's now ready to be used with the Rail Bevel tool. Exit full-screen mode and return to a quad layout.

7. Click on Layer 1 and use the Statistics panel to select the ceiling polys. Cut them and paste them into a new layer. Select the polys and check the direction of their normals. They should be facing down.

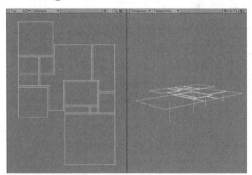

Figure 9-83: Cut the ceiling polys and place them in a new layer. Check to ensure that their normals face down.

8. Click on the layer with the spline in it and place the ceiling polys in the background. Move the spline until it rests on top of the ceiling polys in the background. This will give us a good indication of how the polys are

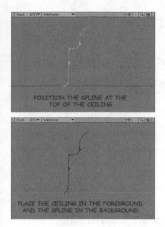

Figure 9-84: Move the spline up so that it rests at the top of the ceiling polys. Place the ceiling polys in the foreground and the spline in the background. Then use Rail Bevel to shift the ceiling polys up and in with the settings shown here.

matching up to the shape of the spline when we use the Rail Bevel tool.

9. Swap the foreground with the background (keyboard shortcut <'> (apostrophe)). Click on the **Multiply | Extend | More | Rail Bevel** tool. You can click and drag in the orthographic viewports to adjust the Shift and Inset for this tool, but I find this to be unintuitive and unwieldy. I tend to prefer using the Numeric panel with the Rail Bevel tool.

10. Enter **–100%** for the Shift and **135%** for the Inset, as shown in Figure 9-84. (Note that the Shift is a negative value and the Inset is a positive value.) You should see the ceiling polys match up to the background spline. (If you used your own cornice spline, you will likely have to adjust the values slightly to match.) When you're satisfied with the results, drop the tool.

11. Rotate your Perspective viewport so that you can see the faces of the polygons. The large flat areas are the ceilings. Everything else is the cornice. By using Rail Bevel on the individual room polygons, we've quickly created a cornice for each room in the entire house!

Figure 9-85: The completed cornice and ceiling.

Note

Creating the cornice with the Rail Bevel tool is a snap. You may be wondering why we didn't do that for the molding. The main reason is that the molding needed to be trimmed with the Boolean tool in order to clear areas for the doors. The Boolean tool works best on solid 3D objects like our molding block. Our Rail Beveled cornice, however, is not a solid object. It has no backing. For this reason, using the Boolean tool would produce "holes" at the end of the sections that get trimmed away. These holes are nearly impossible to fill. Therefore, the Rail Bevel technique works best on things like the cornice that won't be subjected to the Boolean tool later on.

12. In the Perspective viewport, select the flat areas that make up the ceiling of each room. Assign them the surface name **Ceiling**. Then **Invert** the selection (keyboard shortcut <">> (double quotes)) and assign the rest of the object the surface name **Cornice**.

The cornice is now complete. Let's line it up to the walls.

13. Place the cornice/ceiling in the foreground and the walls in the background. Use the **Move** tool with the middle mouse button (or <Ctrl> key modifier) to move the cornice so the top of it is level with the top of the walls.

> **Note**
>
> You can try to snap the cornice to the walls with SP Move, but with so many points to snap to in the background, it's easy to get the cornice/ceiling polys out of alignment. Therefore, I find it best to use the regular Move tool and just zoom in to ensure I'm getting things as close as possible.

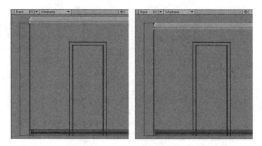

Figure 9-86: Move the cornice and ceiling down so they are flush with the top of the walls.

14. Once the cornice/ceiling polys are in place, cut them and paste them back into Layer 1 with the walls. Then save your model.

Step 24: Create Window Openings

In this step we're going to create the window frames. The process for creating window frames is very similar to creating doorframes. We'll create boxes and Solid Drill them into the walls. Then we'll Boolean openings out of them. In the next step, we'll create the actual windows.

1. Start by loading in the Floor Plan background preset you saved in Step 10. (This is the resized version of the floor plan that matches the resized model of the house.) You'll notice that there are window openings in the front bedroom, back bedroom, living room, and breakfast nook.

2. In the Top viewport, create a 2D box for the far left window of the back bedroom. The windows are designated by the *inside* set of lines. The *outside* set of lines represent the boundary of the window frames. As you create this box, make sure that it extends completely across the wall on both sides.

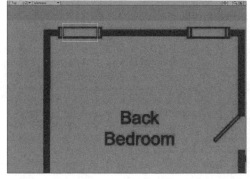

Figure 9-87: Create a box for the back bedroom window as shown here.

3. Copy and paste this window, then move the copy to the right and position it over the second back bedroom window.

4. Copy and paste this rectangle again for each of the remaining windows. All of the windows along the back of the house are the same size. When you get to the front bedroom window, you'll need to resize the poly to fit this larger window area.

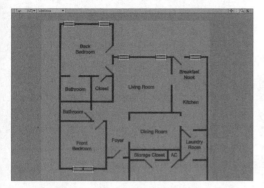

Figure 9-88: Copy the first window box and paste it to create boxes for the remaining windows.

Now that we have 2D polys for the windows, we need to give them depth (or in this case height). Since we don't have a front elevation image, we'll have to guess at the size. In my home office, the window is 38 inches high. That seems like a reasonable height to use for the windows on our 3D house.

5. Check the Perspective display to ensure that the normals for the window polys are facing up. (If they aren't, press <f> to flip them.)

6. Use the **Extrude** tool to extrude the window polys −38" along the Y-axis, as shown in Figure 9-89. Then assign the window boxes a surface called **Window**.

7. Move the window boxes so that their tops are roughly level with the tops of the doors. You don't have to get it perfect. Just get it close and that will do.

8. Copy the window boxes to a new layer. Place the originals in the background. Then use **Point Normal Move** to resize the copies to match the window frames in the background Floor Plan image. (I Point Normal Moved mine about 320 mm.)

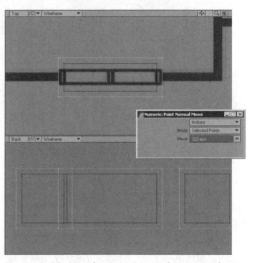

Figure 9-90: Use the Point Normal Move tool to size copies of the window boxes up to fit the window frames.

9. Once you've sized the boxes to match the window frames, assign them a surface called **Window Frame**.

10. Use the Statistics panel to select the walls in Layer 1. Cut and paste them to a new layer.

11. Place the walls in the foreground and the Window Frame boxes in the

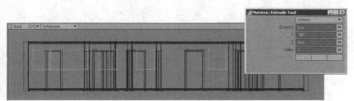

Figure 9-89: Extrude the window boxes −38 inches along the Y-axis. Then position them so they are level with the top of the doors.

background. Use the **Solid Drill** tool with the **Stencil** option to cut the window frame shape into the walls. Be sure to select the **Window Frame** surface when you're using the Stencil option of Solid Drill so that the polygons that get cut will inherit this surface.

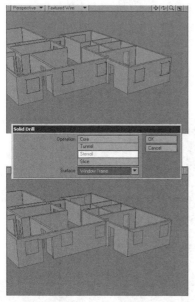

Figure 9-91: Stencil the Window Frame boxes into the walls using the Solid Drill tool.

Just as the doorframes needed to be beveled, then shifted and beveled again, so do the window frames.

12. Use the Statistics panel to select the Window Frame polys you just drilled into the walls. Activate the Multishift tool. Inset and shift the polys **2 mm** each. Then insert a new shift. Shift the polys out by **20 mm** but don't inset them. Insert another shift. Shift the polys an additional **4 mm** and inset them **2 mm**. Then drop the Multishift tool. (See Figure 9-92.)

> **Note**
>
> If you'd like, you can simply load the Window Frames.ss Multishift preset from the Multishifts\Chapter 09 folder.

13. Now let's cut the window boxes out of the window frames. Place the window box polys in the background.

14. Click on the **Boolean** tool and use the **Subtract** option to cut holes in the window frames. Then run **Merge**

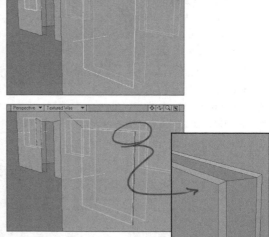

Figure 9-92: Use the Multishift tool to bevel and shift the window frames.

Points and use the Automatic settings to join the parts together.

We can now see through the window frames, but the inside edge of the frame is too sharp. Let's bevel it.

15. Use the Statistics panel to select the window polys. These are the ones that were created during the last Boolean operation.

16. Activate the **Multishift** tool to shift and inset the polys by **5 mm**. This creates a nice bevel on the inside of the window frame.

17. Delete the Window Frame template boxes but keep the Window boxes. We'll use them in the next step.

18. Cut the walls with the window frames and paste them back into Layer 1. Then save your object.

Step 25: Create Window Panes

Now that we've got window frames, let's create some windows. We currently have window boxes that are sized to fit the window frames. We can use these as a starting point for the creation of our windows.

1. The box for each window currently has a side that faces into the house and a side that faces out of the house. For each window box, select the side that faces out. Once they are all selected,

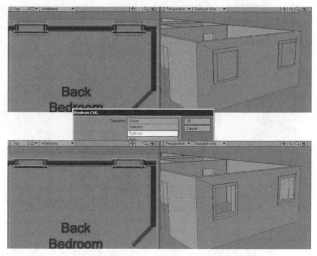

Figure 9-93: Boolean Subtract the window boxes from the window frames.

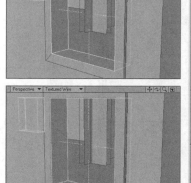

Figure 9-94: Use Multishift to bevel the inside of the window frames by 5 mm.

press <">> (double quotes) to invert the selection. Then delete the selected window box polys. This gives us one poly for each window.

Most windows are made up of several smaller windows separated by a thin frame. Let's create these.

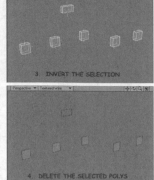

Figure 9-95: Select the outward-facing poly for each window box. Invert the selection, then delete the selected polys.

2. Click on the **Multiply | Subdivide | Subdivide** tool. The Subdivide Polygons window will appear. Choose the **Faceted** option and click **OK**. Each window polygon will be divided into four smaller polygons.

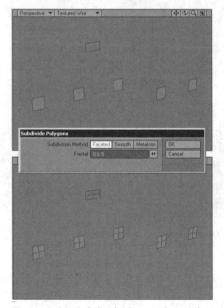

Figure 9-96: Subdivide the window polys with the Faceted option.

3. Select all the polys. An easy way to do this when nothing else is selected is to simply hit <">> (double quotes). This inverts the selection. If nothing is selected, it will cause everything to become selected.

4. Activate the **Bevel** tool and inset the polys by about **25 mm**. This creates the basic frame. With the Bevel tool still selected, right-click to create a new bevel. Shift the polys by **–6 mm** and inset the polys by **6 mm**. This gives the frames a little bit of depth.

5. Drop the Bevel tool but don't deselect the polys. At this point only the innermost polys on each window should be selected. These will be our window panes. Assign them a surface called **Glass**. Open the Surface Editor and give the Glass surface a transparency of **95%**. This is not a permanent surface setting. Rather, it simply makes the Glass polys look a bit more like glass in the OpenGL preview.

6. Invert the selection so that the frames are selected. Assign them a surface called **Window Pane Frame**. Then deselect your polys.

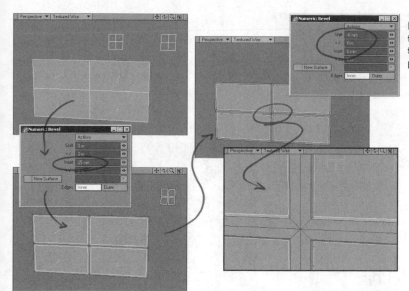

Figure 9-97: Bevel the subdivided polys to create the window pane frames.

We now have an outward-facing window. We need a mirror copy for the inside.

7. Lasso select the polys for the front bedroom window. Use the **Mirror** tool with the middle mouse button to create a mirror copy across the X-axis.

8. With the Mirror tool still active, click and drag on the starting point of the blue mirror line. This allows you to change the position of the mirrored polys. Drag down until the mirrored copy *almost* touches the original. Then drop the tool and deselect your polys.

9. Repeat this mirroring process for each of the remaining windows. Note that many of the windows along the back of the house can be mirrored/moved at the same time.

10. Now we need to center each window in its window frame. Select the entire window for the front bedroom (both inward- and outward-facing sides). Place the walls in Layer 1 in the background. Turn off the Floor Plan background image so that you can

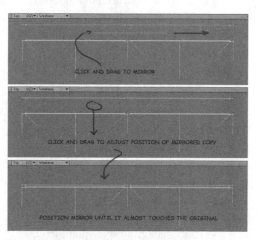

Figure 9-98: Mirror the front bedroom window and position it so that it almost touches the original. Then repeat for each additional window.

clearly see the window frame. Then move the front bedroom window until it's centered in the frame. Be sure to check the centering in the Right viewport. Since it isn't cluttered by the cornice or molding, it is easier to get an idea of when your window is truly centered.

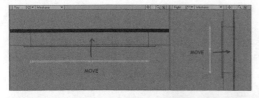

Figure 9-99: Center the front bedroom window in the window frame. Then repeat this process for each additional window.

11. Repeat this for the back windows.

12. Once the windows are positioned correctly, cut them and paste them into Layer 1 with the walls. Then save your model.

Step 26: Make the Garage

This house has a garage but currently no way to get a car into it. Let's fix that. The process of creating a garage door is similar to creating doors and windows. We'll cut a hole in the wall. Then we'll create a garage door.

1. Place the Floor Plan image in the Top viewport background (or just load in the preset you saved in Step 10).

2. Create a box in the Top viewport for the garage opening. Its width should match that shown on the Floor Plan image in the background. (See Figure 9-100.)

3. Extrude the box along the Y-axis so that it extends below the floor. That way we can be sure that it will cut clearly through the wall.

4. Move the box along the Y-axis so that its top is in line with the top of the doorframe.

5. Assign the surface **Garage** to the box. That way when we Boolean the wall, the polys that remain will have this surface.

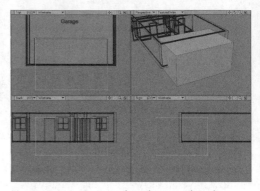

Figure 9-100: Create a box that matches the garage opening in the Floor Plan image. Its top should be in line with the top of the doors and its bottom should extend well below the walls.

6. Cut the walls from Layer 1 and paste them into a new layer. Place the garage box in the background.

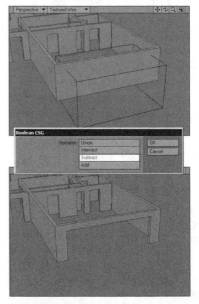

Figure 9-101: Boolean Subtract the garage box from the walls.

7. Boolean Subtract the garage box out of the wall. Then run the **Merge Points** tool with the Automatic settings. (If you see any stray points (not connected to any geometry) after the Boolean operation, just delete them.)

8. The garage opening needs a bit of a bevel. Use the Statistics panel to select the garage polys. Then use **Multishift** to shift and inset them by **7 mm**. Drop the Multishift tool and deselect the polys.

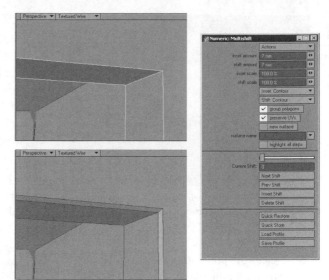

Figure 9-102: Use the Multishift tool to bevel the garage opening by 7 mm.

9. Go back to Layer 1 and use the Statistics panel to select the molding. Then place the garage box in the background and use the Boolean Subtract tool to cut the molding away from the garage entrance. Merge points. Finally, select the ends of the molding that have the Garage surface (created from the Boolean operation) and bevel them by **2 mm** for both shift and inset.

The garage opening is now complete. It's time to create the garage door.

10. Create a new layer and place the walls with the garage opening in the background.

11. In the Back viewport, create a box that fits snugly within the garage opening. With the Box tool still active, increase Segments Y in the Numeric panel to **8**.

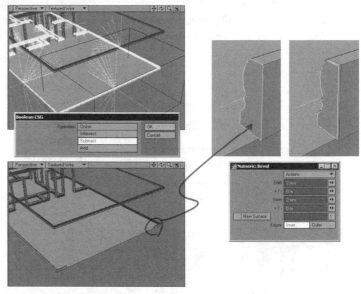

Figure 9-103: Boolean Subtract the garage box from the molding in Layer 1. Then bevel the ends of the molding by 2 mm.

This will create a rectangle with eight individual segments. These segments will be used to create detail panels on the garage door.

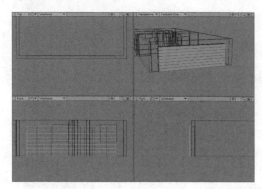

Figure 9-104: In the Back viewport, create a box that fits snugly in the garage opening and has eight horizontal segments.

12. Select the points that make up the interior segments of the box. Then use the **Stretch** tool with the middle mouse button to squeeze them together along the Y-axis. Finally, move these points down so that the first small segment is located about one-third of the way from the top.

13. Switch to **Polygons** selection mode and select the smaller segments. Then use the **Bevel** tool to shift them by **–25 mm** and inset them by **25 mm**.

The basic garage door is complete, but it's still missing windows in the upper third of the door. You can create any number of windows in this area. For this exercise, let's create six of them.

14. Go to a new layer and place the garage door in the background. Create a rectangular box in the upper third of the door. It should be small enough that five copies will fit across the width of the door. (Be sure to set Segments Y back to 1 so that you create a single-polygon box.)

15. Move the box to the left side of the garage door and center it between the top and the first detail panel. Don't make it flush with the door. It should be off to the right a bit.

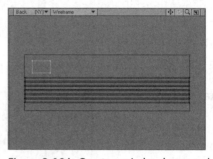

Figure 9-106: Create a window box template poly and position it as shown here.

We need to create five copies of this box evenly spaced across the door. To do this, we'll use the Clone tool. But first we need to know how much to offset each clone.

16. Using the middle mouse button to constrain its motion, move the box to the

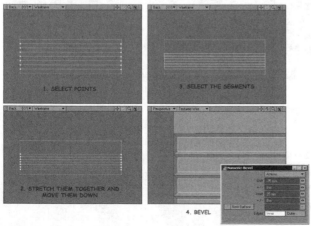

1. SELECT POINTS

2. STRETCH THEM TOGETHER AND MOVE THEM DOWN

3. SELECT THE SEGMENTS

4. BEVEL

Figure 9-105: Select the points for the segments. Stretch them together and position the first segment about one-third of the way from the top of the box. Select the segments and bevel them as shown here.

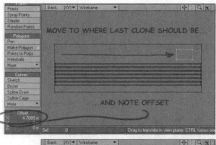

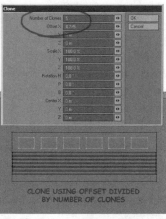

Figure 9-107: Move the window template to where the last copy should be placed and note the offset distance. Then use the Clone tool to create five copies across the distance you just noted.

right and position it where the last box should be but don't let go of the mouse button when you get it there! Once the box is in place, take a look at the Quick Info display and note the X Offset amount. In my case it's about 4.7 meters. Let go of the mouse button and undo the move to return the box to the left side of the garage door.

Now that we know the distance, we can easily create our clones.

17. Run the **Clone** tool (keyboard shortcut <c>). Enter **5** for the number of clones. For the Offset X setting, enter the distance you just moved your poly, then /5. In my case it would be **4.7/5**. Modeler will divide the distance and give you the proper offset. Press **OK** to accept the Clone tool settings and create the clones.

18. If needed, move the five boxes until they're visually centered left to right on the garage. We now have our window templates in place.

19. Place the garage door in the foreground and the windows in the background. Use the **Drill** tool with the **Stencil** option to cut the window templates into the door along the Z-axis. The Drill Stencil option will allow you to specify a surface for the newly cut

Figure 9-108: Drill Stencil the window boxes into the garage door using the Garage Window Frame surface.

polygons. Type **Garage Window Frame** into the Surface field and press **OK**.

Now that we have the basic frame shapes, let's detail them just as we did with the window pane frames earlier.

20. Select the window frame polys you just drilled and use the **Multiply | Subdivide | Subdivide** tool with the **Faceted** option to divide them. Keep these subdivided polys selected.

21. Use the **Multishift** tool to bevel the polys as a group. Shift them by **–10 mm** and inset them by **10 mm**. This gives our frame a little bit of depth. Keep the polys selected.

22. Now use the **Bevel** tool to inset (but not shift) the selected polys individually by approximately **25 mm**. This will complete the window pane frame. The polys that are selected will be the glass.

23. Assign the **Glass** surface to the selected polys. Then drop the Bevel tool and deselect the polys.

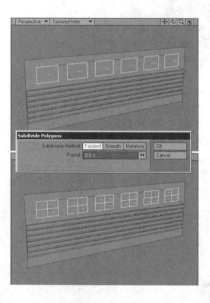

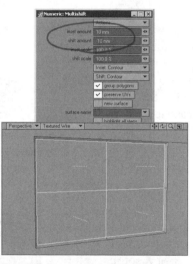

Figure 9-109: Subdivide the garage windows with the Faceted option. Then use Multishift to bevel the polys as a group.

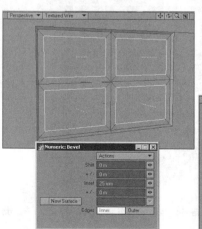

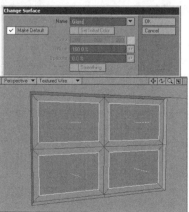

Figure 9-110: Bevel the polys with an inset of 25 mm. Then assign them the Glass surface you created earlier.

24. Hide the glass polys. Then select and hide the garage window frame polys.

25. Assign the surface **Garage Door** to the remaining polys. Then unhide the hidden polys.

26. Place the walls with the garage opening in the background. Position the garage door in the garage door opening.

27. Cut the garage door and paste it into the layer with the walls that have the garage door opening. Finally, cut the walls and garage door and paste them back into Layer 1.

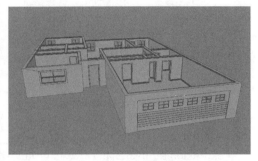

Figure 9-111: Position the garage door so it fits in the garage door opening of the walls. Then move the walls and the garage door back to Layer 1.

28. Save your model.

Figure 9-112: Create a box in the Top viewport with a single horizontal division. It should cover the main area of the house and extend over the walls evenly on all sides. Then move the points at the center division up about 2 meters to create a 20-degree pitch.

Step 27: Make the Roof

Our house model is nearly complete. The last major step is to create the roof. Most roofs are pitched (they rise at the middle and slope down either side) and many have small perpendicular extensions that jut out to cover things like the garage or room additions. This is the type of roof we'll create for our home model.

1. If you've got the Floor Plan background image in the Top viewport, turn it off. You won't need it any longer.

2. Place the walls in the background. In the Top viewport, create a box that covers the main portion of the house and extends beyond the walls evenly on each side. The box should have a horizontal division running down the center (increase Segments Z to **2** in the Numeric panel).

3. Place the walls in the background and the roof box in the foreground. In the Right viewport, move the box down so that it's flush with the top of the walls.

4. Select the two points that make up the middle edge and move them up about **2 meters** to create a pitch of approximately 20 degrees.

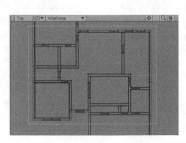

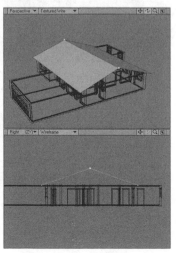

Now we have the main roof polys created. It's time to block out the perpendicular extensions for the back bedroom and garage.

5. Go to a new layer and place both the roof polys and the walls in the background. Create a box that runs from the center of the roof and extends over the back bedroom. It should have a vertical division running down the center, so drop Segments Z back to **1** and increase Segments X to **2**. It should extend evenly over the left, right, and back of the back bedroom.

6. Use the **SP Move** tool to snap this poly to the left side of the roof in the background.

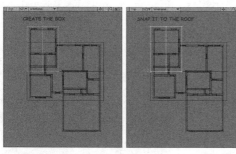

Figure 9-113: Create a box in the Top viewport with a single vertical division. It should cover the back bedroom and extend over the walls evenly on all sides. Then use SP Move to snap it to the left side of the roof in the background.

7. Repeat this process for the garage. Make a new box that starts at the pitch and extends over the front of the

garage. It should extend over the garage evenly on all sides. Then snap it to the right side of the roof.

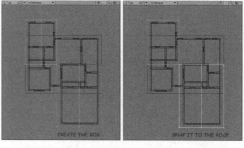

Figure 9-114: Create a box in the Top viewport with a single vertical division. It should cover the garage and extend over the walls evenly on all sides. Then use SP Move to snap it to the right side of the roof in the background.

We'll use these boxes as templates to note where points should be placed on the roof so that we can properly construct the extensions.

8. Place the roof in the foreground and the extension templates in the background. Add points along the back edge, the center pitch edge, and the front edge of the house to match the points on the template polys. You don't have to be exact in your placement at this point. Just add the points to these edges for now.

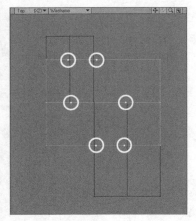

Figure 9-115: Add points to the roof where the extension polys are as shown here.

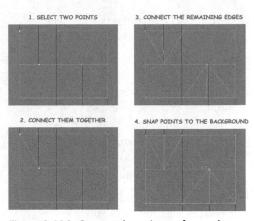

Figure 9-116: Connect the points to form edges as shown here, then snap them to the points in the background.

Now we need to connect the points on the front and back edges to those on the horizontal pitch edge.

9. Select the two points shown in Figure 9-116 and press <1> (lowercase L) or use the **Construct | Combine | Connect** tool to create an edge between them.

10. Repeat this process for the other points you just added. Your results should match those shown in Figure 9-116.

11. Once the points have been added and connected together, use the **SP Move** tool with the right mouse button to snap the points to their counterparts in the background.

12. Select the points on the front and back edges shown in Figure 9-117. Use the **SP Move** tool to move these up in the Back or Right viewport until they are the same height as the pitch. You should see SP Move indicate that they are snapped in line along the Y-axis.

Note

Another nice way to add edges to the roof is to use the Add Edges tool. Rather than adding points and connecting them together, simply place the template polys in the background and run the Add Edges tool. Connect the blue dots to form an edge. Then while the tool is still active, right-click to accept the edge and connect two more dots to form another. Repeat this process until all the edges are complete. Then simply snap the points to the background template with the SP Move tool. There is almost always more than one way to do something in LightWave. Finding the way that works best for you is key to developing your own workflow.

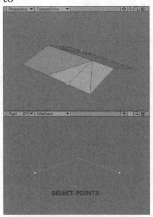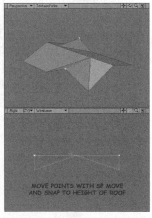

Figure 9-117: Select the points shown here and use SP Move to move them straight up until they snap to the height of the roof.

We have now created the perpendicular extensions for the roof, but they don't jut out to cover the bedroom or garage. Let's fix that.

13. Place the roof in the foreground and the extension templates in the background. Select the three points along the front edge and the three points along the back edge that make up the extension.

14. Run the **Multiply | Extend | Extender Plus** tool. This will add a new edge, but you won't see it until you move it away from the original.

15. Activate the **Stretch** tool and use your middle mouse button (or the <Ctrl> key modifier) to push the new edges away from the house.

16. Drop the Stretch tool and select the three points along the back edge. Use the **SP Move** tool to snap them to the edge of the template in the background.

17. Repeat this for the points along the front extension of the garage.

The basic shape of the roof is now complete; however, the roof still needs a few adjustments. If you look closely you'll see that the roof sticks out more on some edges than others. That's not a huge problem, but it's kind of sloppy. Let's adjust the edges so that they come in closer to the house and are fairly equal all the way around.

18. Go to Layer 1 and use the Statistics panel to select the **floor**. Copy it and paste it to a new layer.

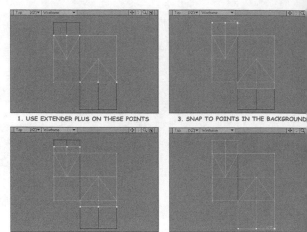

1. USE EXTENDER PLUS ON THESE POINTS   3. SNAP TO POINTS IN THE BACKGROUND

2. STRETCH VERTICALLY   4. SNAP TO POINTS IN THE BACKGROUND

Figure 9-118: Select the points shown here and use Extender Plus to add a new edge. Use the Stretch tool to move the edge out. Then snap each edge to the points in the background.

The floor represents the outside perimeter of our home. If we want the roof to extend evenly on every side, we can use the Bevel tool to inset the floor poly, which can then be used as a guide for where our points ought to be.

19. Activate the **Bevel** tool and inset (but do not shift) the copy of the floor poly by **–900 mm**. That's roughly three feet on every side, which is a reasonable overhang.

20. Place the roof in the foreground and the inset floor poly in the background. Select the points along each edge of the roof and use **SP Move** to snap them to

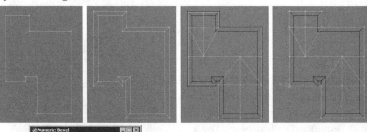

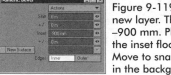

Figure 9-119: Copy the floor and paste it to a new layer. Then use the Bevel tool to inset it by –900 mm. Place the roof in the foreground and the inset floor in the background. Then use SP Move to snap the edges of the roof to the edge in the background.

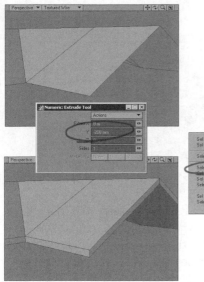

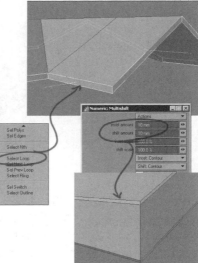

Figure 9-120: Extrude the roof by –200 mm on the Y-axis. Then select the trim and use Multishift to bevel it by 10 mm.

the edges of the inset floor poly in the background.

21. Now let's give this roof some depth. Activate the **Extrude** tool and extrude the roof by **–200 mm** on the Y-axis.

We now have a 3D roof, but the transition from the slope to the trim around the edge is too harsh. We need to bevel the trim.

22. Select two polygons along the trim and then run the **Select | Select Loop** command. All of the trim polys should be selected.

23. Use the **Multishift** tool to shift and inset the trim by **10 mm**.

24. The roof is now complete. Assign it a surface called **Roof**.

25. Now let's move the roof so that it lines up with the house. Place the roof in the fore-ground and the walls in the background.

26. Move the roof along the Y-axis until it almost touches the top of the walls. You don't want

the roof to be floating too far above the walls, nor do you want it to be poking through the top of the ceiling. It should almost rest on the walls. This will take a bit of trial and error. Spin around in the Perspective viewport and check the house from the bottom looking up. You're looking for areas where the roof is cutting through the cornice. If you see this happening, you need to move the roof up. You might also find it

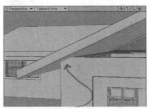
ROOF IS TOO LOW AND CUTS THROUGH CORNICE

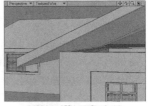
ROOF HAS BEEN MOVED UP AND CORNICE IS NOW VISIBLE

Figure 9-121: Position the roof so that it rests slightly above the walls. If the roof is too low, it will cut through the cornice as it slopes down toward the walls of the house.

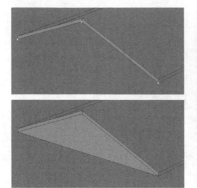

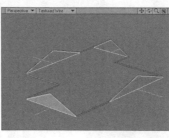

Figure 9-122: Select the roof trim and hide the unselected polys. Then select the points in each triangular area of the roof and make polys from them.

helpful to Shift-select Layer 1 occasionally to see how the roof and walls look when they're both in the foreground.

27. Now it's time to create the triangles that bridge the walls to the roof. Select the loop of polys that make up the trim of the roof. Then hide the unselected polys.

28. Select the points that form the bottom of each triangular area in the roof and make polygons from them. You may find it easiest to do this with the Perspective viewport in full screen.

29. Keep the roof hidden for now, leaving only the roof trim visible. Then cut the triangles and paste them into a new layer.

We need to snap the triangles to the walls; however, there are too many polys around the walls to make this easy to do with SP Move. Let's hide some of these polys.

30. Click on Layer 1 and use the Statistics panel to select the walls. Then press the < = > key to hide the unselected objects.

31. Go back to the layer with the triangles. Place it in the foreground and place both the walls and the roof trim in the background.

32. Use **SP Move** to snap each triangle flush with the outside wall. This is easiest to do in the Top viewport. Select a triangle, run **SP Move**, grab the top point of the triangle, and move it in toward the wall. You should see it snap in both the X-axis and Z-axis once it reaches the wall.

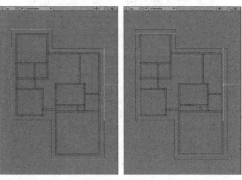

Figure 9-123: Place the triangles in the foreground and the walls and the roof trim in the background. Then use SP Move to snap the triangles to the walls.

33. Go back to the roof layer and unhide the rest of the roof.

The triangles are flush with the walls, but if you place them both in the foreground you'll see that the left and/or right edge of every triangle sticks out over the wall. Not good.

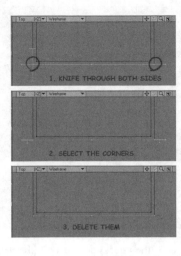

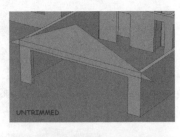

Figure 9-124: Place the triangles in the foreground and the walls in the background. Knife through the triangles where they intersect with the walls. Then delete the ends of each triangle created by the Knife tool.

34. Place the triangles in the foreground and the walls in the background. Select the triangle that goes over the garage. Zoom in to it in the Top viewport. You will see that it extends over the wall in the background.

35. Use the **Knife** tool to create vertical slices on the left and right sides of the triangle where it intersects the wall in the background. Remember that you can constrain the Knife to a vertical cut by clicking and dragging with the middle mouse button (or holding down the <Ctrl> key modifier). Also, keep in mind that if you don't get the cut in the exact spot, while the tool is still active, you can left-click and drag on the blue Knife line (anywhere but the ends) to move the entire cut to a new location.

36. Once you've sliced the left and right side of the triangle, select each side and delete them. (See Figure 9-124.)

37. Repeat this process for each of the remaining triangles. Anywhere the triangle extends beyond the wall, trim it off.

38. When you've finished trimming the triangles, assign the **Walls** surface to them.

39. Cut the triangles and paste them into Layer 1 with the walls. Inspect them in the Perspective and orthographic viewports to ensure that they line up with the walls. When you're satisfied, unhide the hidden geometry in Layer 1.

40. Go to the layer with the roof. Cut it and paste it into Layer 1 with the walls. The house is now complete! Delete any leftover construction materials and save your model.

Figure 9-125: The completed house.

Step 28: Finalize

The last step is to finalize the home, making it ready to bring into Layout for lighting, surfacing, and animation.

Let's begin by resting the home on the ground and creating a ground plane.

1. Place both the home and the doors in the foreground. Then click on the **Modify | Translate | More | Aligner** tool. The Aligner window will open. Mode should be set to **World**. This allows us to align to Modeler's origin. The X, Y, and Z buttons should be set to **c**. This will center the objects to the origin. We want to center the X and Z, but we want the home to be resting on the ground. The bottom of the house should be at 0 on the Y-axis and everything else should be above it. Therefore, leave X and Z at "c" and set the Y button to "+". This will position the geometry on the positive side of the Y-axis. Then click **OK**.

The home will now be centered and rest firmly on the ground.

2. Now let's create a ground plane for the home to rest on. Go to a new layer and place the house in the background. Create a box in the Top viewport that encompasses the entire home. Make sure that its normal runs along the Y-axis. Assign it the surface name **Ground**.

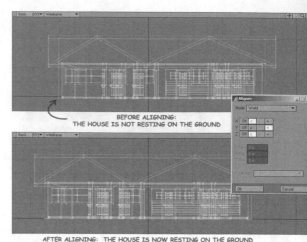

Figure 9-126: Place Layer 1 (the house) and Layer 2 (the doors) in the foreground. Then run Aligner with the settings shown here to rest the home on the ground and center it in X and Z around the origin.

3. Now let's center this ground plane and rest it on the ground. Press the **<F3>** key, which is the keyboard shortcut for the Modify | Translate | More | Rest On Ground command. The Rest On Ground window will appear. Make sure Rest Axis is set to **Y**, the Center X, Y, and Z Axis buttons are selected, and Sense is set to **+**. Then click **OK**. The ground plane will center itself

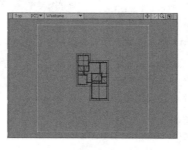

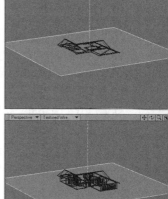

Figure 9-127: With the house in the background, create a ground plane in a new layer. Then press <F3> to rest it on the ground.

around the origin in X and Z, and be resting on the ground. Cut it and paste it into Layer 1 with the house.

> **Note**
>
> You may be wondering why we didn't use the Rest On Ground tool for the house and doors. The answer is simple: The Rest On Ground command will not work on multiple selected layers. If you want to affect objects in multiple layers, you must use the Aligner tool.

Now let's set the doors up to be animated. Doors rest on hinges that allow them to swing. We didn't model any hinges, but we can simulate their effect on the doors by placing them on individual layers and adjusting their pivot points.

To place each door on its own layer, you could simply select one door, cut it, go to a new layer, paste it, and then go back to the layer with the rest of the doors and repeat the process. But here's a slightly easier method.

4. Lasso select one of the doors (including the doorknobs). Then invert the selection. Cut the selected doors and paste them to a new layer. Then repeat this process. Instead of selecting a door and moving it to a new layer, you're selecting a door and moving everything else to a layer. This allows you to keep the large group on the current layer so that you're not having to pop back and forth as much. It's not a huge time-saver, but every little bit helps!

Once all the doors are on their own layers, it's time to adjust their pivot points so that they will rotate properly in Layout.

5. Click on the first door layer. Press <a> to fit it to all the viewports. Then place the house in the background.

6. Click on the **View | Layers | Pivot** tool. In the Top viewport, position your mouse on the outside of the door and opposite the doorknob, then click. The pivot for this layer will jump to your mouse. Position the pivot where the door's real hinges would be — to the right and outside of the door slightly.

You don't have to adjust the pivot in the Y-axis. You can if you want, but it won't affect the quality of the rotation at all.

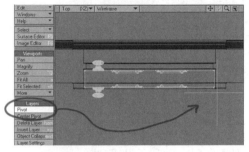

THE PIVOT POINT ACTS LIKE A HINGE ALLOWING US TO ROTATE THE DOOR IN LAYOUT

Figure 9-128: Zoom in to the door on each layer and place its pivot point as shown here.

7. Repeat this process for the remaining doors.

8. When the pivot has been set for each door, go back to Layer 1 and set the pivot point to the center of the house.

The last thing we should do is name our door layers. This will make it easy to select the appropriate items in Layout.

9. Click on Layer 1 and press <a> to fit it to all the viewports. Then click on the **Windows | Layers Panel** option. The Layers panel will appear.

10. Click the white triangle to toggle open the layers for your object. Double-click on the first layer and name it **House**. Then click on the second layer and click the check mark in the B column for the House layer. This will place a

401

door in the foreground and the house in the background, allowing you to see which door you're dealing with.

11. Double-click on the foreground layer and give it a name. I typically name door layers for where they go to. For example, "Laundry to Garage" or "Hall Bathroom."

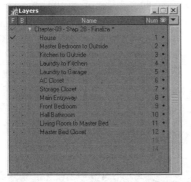

Figure 9-129: Use the Layers panel to name each layer for easy selection in Layout.

12. Once all of the layers are named, save your object. Your 3D house is now complete!

Figure 9-130: The finished home, textured and lit in Layout, ready for tenants to move in!

Conclusion

In this chapter we capitalized on the tools and techniques covered in previous chapters to create a detailed 3D home. There was a lot of repetition in this lesson and, while it may have been tedious at times, the repetition has helped to solidify the techniques, hone your skills, and sharpen your workflow. All of which go toward making you a better modeler.

With the information you've learned so far, you should be able to tackle just about any polygonal modeling job that comes your way. Remember that the trick to modeling is defining the objects you see in terms of the tools you know. A soda can is not a soda can. It's a disc that's been extruded and then beveled at the top and bottom. When you see the world in terms of LightWave tools, there will be no limit to what you can accomplish.

Now let's move on to Chapter 10, where you'll learn some great techniques for lighting things like the home you just built.

Chapter 10

Intermediate Skills: Lighting

When people in the industry talk about *production value*, they are referring to whether the work looks like it was done "professionally." Is *each* and *every* part of its process brought up to the highest level appropriate for the story? "Low budget" does not have to look low budget. Just because you're filmmaking on a shoestring doesn't mean it has to look that way! There are hundreds, if not thousands, of simple, little things you can do to "kiss the details" and make your work read with a high production value.

One thing that can raise production values in your own projects is lighting. As we discussed earlier in Chapter 5, lighting is without a doubt one of the most important factors in making our CG look great, hence it's one area that will greatly influence the production value of your projects. In this chapter we'll look deeper into LightWave's arsenal of lighting and effect tools that we can use to help raise the bar on the work we do, whether it be integrating CG into live footage, or just making our own animation look that much slicker!

Essential Lighting Concepts

In reality, lighting is a complex beast. Not only do we have a direct source of light (such as the sun, for example) but we also have a lot of ambient light bouncing about, illuminating the world around us. Ambient light comes from other indirect sources (such as the sky) and light being reflected off other surfaces (like the walls of buildings

and the ground). It's this insane complexity that we need to recreate if we want to produce renders that are more realistic, especially if we are working with CG and live-action integration.

Luckily for us, LightWave has the tools we need to do this easily.

Radiosity

By default, LightWave uses a *local illumination* model. By that, we mean that we give the scene some light sources and it uses those to shade and render by just tracing the light rays from the light to the objects. This lighting approach is fast and often

looks great, but it doesn't mimic the way light really works. Local light hits the surface of an object and that's kind of where it stops (unless the surface happens to be transparent); it doesn't travel anywhere else after that like light does in the real world. The result is something like Figure 10-1. Note how dark the room is, with only the surfaces hit by the light being seen.

Figure 10-1: A simple local light shining through an arched window.

Radiosity is a *global illumination* model. It's all about that concept of bouncing light around, much in the same way light behaves in real life. Let's load up a scene and tweak it to create a more realistic lighting system through radiosity!

v9.2 Note

Radiosity received a major overhaul in LightWave v9.2. Not only are there new Radiosity modes, but there are also new ways to tweak the performance. For details on the new global illumination options, check out the Radiosity video in the Light-Wave 9.2 Videos folder on the companion DVD.

1. Load the scene **Scenes\Chapter 10\window_room.lws.**

This scene will create the image we saw in Figure 10-1. On my computer, it took roughly 3.7 seconds to render. Let's get the light to bounce around as we would expect it to in reality and see if we can create a render that gives us a more realistic effect.

2. Open the **Render | Render Globals** window, and click on the Global Illum tab. Activate **Enable Radiosity** and change Rays Per Evaluation to **3 x 9**. Leave the Type as **Monte Carlo** and then press **<F9>**, but be prepared to wait… Radiosity is a slow and computationally expensive process!

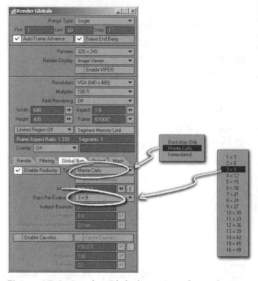

Figure 10-2: Render Globals settings for radiosity.

Note

Radiosity works by firing out rays from the surfaces of objects to sample and analyze the lighting bouncing off of other surfaces in the scene. The quality of this is set through the Rays Per Evaluation option. The higher the number of rays, the higher the overall quality of the shading, but the render time is hugely increased at the same time! I've often found **3 x 9** to be a good base setting to achieve a decent result without hitting huge render times.

3. After a long wait, you should have an
    image like Figure 10-3. On my com-
    puter, the render time soared from 3.7
    seconds to a whopping *4 minutes and
    15 seconds*. However, note how the
    areas that were in shadow now look a
    lot brighter and more natural from the
    light rays that have been bouncing
    around the room. Nice, but very slow!

Figure 10-3: The radiosity render.

Improving Radiosity Performance

Radiosity may be slow, but performance
can be tuned to get better results through
a variety of options so that we can use
this more realistic lighting solution in our
projects. In this section, we'll look at a
few of the options we have.

Tweaking

We noted that Rays Per Evaluation set
the quality of the radiosity in our scene.
Dropping the Rays Per Evaluation setting
will greatly improve the rendering time,
but at the expense of a grainier, noisier-
looking render. Never fear! On the **Ren-
der | Render Globals | Render** tab
there is a button called Noise Reduction.
Activate this option, and mix in a few
Antialiasing passes (found under the

Figure 10-4: Activating Noise Reduction and setting
Antialiasing.

Filtering tab on the Render Globals window) to help improve the appearance of
lower quality radiosity. For this technique to
work effectively, ensure that the Adaptive
Sampling option, below the Reconstruction
Filter option, is *not* active (as shown in Figure 10-4).

Re-rendering the window_room.lws
scene with Rays Per Evaluation set to 2 x 6,
Noise Reduction activated, and PLD-3 pass
antialiasing resulted in Figure 10-5. The

405

Figure 10-5: Faster radiosity.

Figure 10-6: Interpolated radiosity.

time wasn't super fast; however, it took only 3 minutes and 4 seconds, rather then our previous 4 minute 15 second delay, and doesn't look half bad either! We shaved over a minute from the render time compared to using 3 x 9 passes!

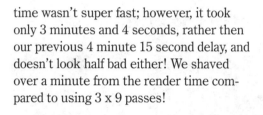

> **Note**
>
> When multiple passes of antialiasing are used, the radiosity shading is recalculated for each pass. This makes any grainy noise appear *differently* in each pass. Noise reduction helps smooth these over, and then at the end of the rendering, these variations are blended to create the final result.

Interpolation

Another way to tune up radiosity is to use the Interpolated type. This type of radiosity creates a preprocessed solution for how the radiosity shades the surface of the items in your scene by only sampling random areas of the surface rather than the entire surface itself. Let's change this same scene to use **Interpolated** radiosity, set Rays Per Evaluation to a much higher quality, like **10 x 30**, and set Tolerance to **1.0**. (This tells LightWave how accurate it needs to be when calculating the lighting solution. A value of 0.0 makes LightWave favor fully

evaluating each sample, creating a more accurate but somewhat slower lighting solution. A value of 1.0 makes LightWave favor an interpolated value using the precalculated samples, creating a slightly less accurate but faster lighting solution.)

What a huge difference! From 3 minutes 4 seconds to only 25.2 seconds. Interpolated radiosity can be super fast, but be aware it can also generate some pretty ugly artifacts (resembling a fractal noise type pattern). I recommend if using this type of radiosity that you experiment with Tolerance and Minimum Evaluation Spacing (the smaller this number, the noisier I've noticed the result appears to get).

Fake It!

Radiosity is a more accurate and realistic lighting concept, but it's often a computationally expensive one that adds immense amounts of time to rendering. It should be used with caution if you have a deadline to meet, or faked by simply adding extra local lights where the extra light is needed.

Let's look at how we can fake this effect using extra lights instead, and then compare how these look and perform.

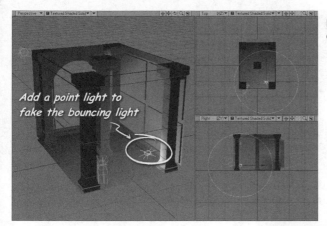

Add a point light to fake the bouncing light

Figure 10-7: Adding an extra light.

1. Reload the scene again from **Scenes\Chapter 10\window_ room.lws**

2. If we examine how radiosity behaved in Figure 10-3, we can see how parts of the room were illuminated by the light bouncing around. This bouncing light seemed to primarily emanate from the rear wall behind the camera, spilling light forward and onto the backs of the pillars. Let's add an extra light to fill where the areas of the scene are in shadow. I often use simple distant lights, but for more "localized" areas like this, often a point light can be a better source. To prevent local lights from spilling around the scene and filling it with too much light, don't forget to specify some falloff. (See Chapter 5 for a refresher on this if you've forgotten how.)

3. When adding these lights, I'll use colors similar to those found on the walls or areas that the light is bouncing off (in this case, use a color of **255, 238, 221** for a warmish tone from the outside sunshine), and give low Light Intensity values (start with **30%**). Once the feel is about right, press

Figure 10-8: The local lighting setup.

<F9> and compare the look with the radiosity version.

Render speeds are pretty impressive compared to radiosity (only 4 seconds), but often they don't recreate the subtleties of global illumination, such as the soft shadowing in edges and cracks. However, these can be shaded back onto polys using a technology known as ambient occlusion; while it does slow things down a little more while rendering (Figure 10-9 took 1 minute and 17 seconds, compared to the original 4 seconds), it's nowhere as slow as radiosity and looks pretty good!

Figure 10-9: Local lighting combined with ambient occlusion shading.

Ambient occlusion refers to the blocking, or *occluding*, of the overall ambient light by surrounding geometry. The way this works is to simply analyze whether a spot on the surface is anywhere near geometry such as on outcropping walls, in a groove, or under other close-by geometry, and then shade it depending upon how much of this geometry is getting in the way of any light that might be coming in from around it. Note that this causes edges and grooves in an object to start to appear to collect grime. This is why ambient occlusion can also be used to create the effect of grime and dirt on an object!

> **Note**
>
> Here's something for you to check out later on as you come to grips with LightWave v9: LightWave's node-based surfacing system (covered in detail in Chapter 19) contains a Diffuse shader node specifically designed to produce this ambient occlusion effect. The scene Scenes\Chapter 10\window_room_ambOcclusion_F.lws contains a version of the object with this shader applied. After reading Chapter 19, I would highly recommend coming back and checking out how this works by examining the texture settings for the room model in this scene.

High Dynamic Range Imagery

Another way to use radiosity to create uber-realistic renders is to make it use *reality* as a light source — or at least an image of reality! This can be done using an image format known as HDR (which stands for High Dynamic Range). Unlike a traditional image that you may be used to viewing on your computer where each pixel is a simple color value, an HDR image instead stores the intensity information for the color of each pixel. Each of the red, green, and blue values can range from 0% to 10,000%, depending upon how much light was coming from that pixel at the time.

HDR images are created by analyzing a variety of identical photos taken using different exposure settings on a camera, then compiling the variations in exposure into what should be close if not accurate information about how bright areas of the photo are in terms of light.

> **Note**
>
> Some digital cameras allow you to *auto bracket* the exposure amount. What this feature does is simply create three images for each photo taken by creating one that has a slightly lower exposure setting and one slightly higher. (Often the amount of +/– exposure can be set on the camera if it has this feature.) This is a handy feature for collecting variations in images if you plan on creating your own HDRI later on.

By wrapping one of these images around a scene as a backdrop in LightWave, radiosity can use the brightness and color of each pixel of the image and treat it as though it's a source of light!

Let's look at how this HDR can create more realistic lighting for us.

1. Open the scene **Scenes\Chapter 10\hdr_render.lws** from the companion DVD.

2. Rendering this normally won't show us much, as seen in Figure 10-10. We need to add in our HDR image and tell LightWave to use it.

Figure 10-10: The render is not too exciting.

3. For this step, we'll need to access the free content supplied with LightWave. Let's open the Image Editor, and load in **images\HDR\Building_Probe.pic** from the classic content that ships with the software. Please note that this is not available on the companion DVD; you must have the full version of LightWave to access this image.

> **Note**
>
> This image may not be loadable or even visible in the file browser window since .pic is not a file extension that LightWave may recognize. However, this is quickly remedied. In Windows, change the Files of type setting to All Files. In OS X, the same thing can be achieved by simply changing the pop-up next to Enable to All Documents.

This will load in an Angular map, or what is more commonly known as an *HDR probe*. This image has been shot using a reflective ball to create a rough approximation of the surrounding environment. In a way it behaves like a poor man's wide-angle lens. We can use this image and wrap it around our scene so that radiosity can use it.

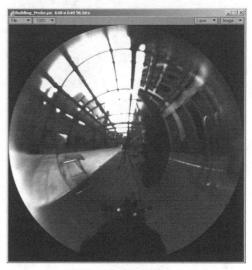

Figure 10-11: The HDR probe image.

4. Let's add it to the backdrop. Select **Windows | Backdrop Options** (**<Ctrl>+<F5>**) and add the **Image World** environment plug-in in the Backdrop tab. Image World will unwrap this HDR probe image and rewrap it around the scene for us. Open the Properties panel of Image World, and select the **Building_Probe.pic** image from the Light Probe Image pop-up. You can now close the Backdrop tab.

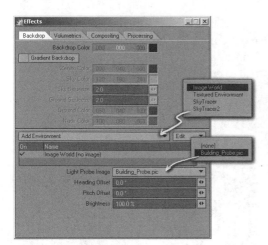

Figure 10-12: Adding Image World.

5. Let's deactivate the light that's currently in the scene. Select the light, open up its Properties window and uncheck the Affect Specular and Affect Diffuse options to disable the light from affecting our render.

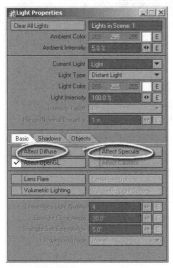

Figure 10-13: Disable the light's effect on the scene.

6. Select **Render | Render Globals | Global Illum** and activate **Enable Radiosity**. Set Type to **Backdrop Only**. Set Rays Per Evaluation to **3 x 9**.

Be sure to activate the **Noise Reduction** option on the Render tab, then press <F9> to render and see the effect of the HDR image.

Figure 10-14: The HDR lighting effect.

The HDR is providing the equivalent of the actual lighting we would receive if this object happened to be sitting in the actual location the photo was taken.

HDR can be used like this to light an entire scene. However, you may have noted how grainy things can get with HDR images. Large, detailed HDR images don't always make for the best or most accurate lighting solution since LightWave can read pixels slightly differently each frame when the image is complex. Often it's not a bad idea to use small-sized and sometimes heavily blurred HDR images to soften up the noisiness of the HDR image itself so that LightWave only sees the overall lighting, and not all the image detail that it doesn't really need. There is a filter in the Image Editor that can be used to post-process HDR images called Full Precision Blur.

To add this filter to an HDR image in LightWave, open the **Image Editor** (<F6>) and select **Full Precision Blur** from the Add Filter pop-up found under the Processing tab.

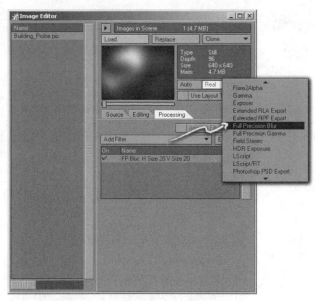

Figure 10-15: HDR images can be processed with Full Precision Blur before being used for lighting.

You may need to edit the amount of blur by opening this filter's Properties panel (double-click on Full Precision Blur in the filter list). In Figure 10-16, I set both the Horizontal Size and Vertical Size values to **32** (the maximum the filter allows) and then pressed <**F9**> to test it.

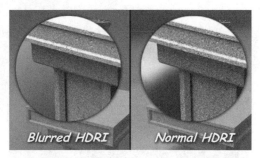

Figure 10-16: Note the less grainy, blurred HDRI result with the same scene.

To rescale and edit HDR images, many image manipulation tools such as Adobe Photoshop CS2 and Ulead Photo Impact now have features to create and tweak them. The man responsible for a lot of research into HDRI, Paul Debevec, also developed a tool called HDRShop, which can be downloaded and used for non-commercial or academic use free of charge (Version 1, that is) at http://www.hdrshop.com/.

There are many commercial and free sources of HDR images available. Check out the Photography section of http://www.unparent.com for a fantastic collection of HDR probe images from artist Keith Bruns.

Mix and Match Lighting Techniques

While radiosity and HDR are slick, we can also mix in local illumination (lights) to add to the look of a scene. For instance, radiosity may be used to simply create the ambient lighting in a scene, but a distant light might be used to add the key light source. If you recall when we were looking at **Render | Render Globals | Global Illum**, we could edit the Intensity value of the radiosity. This can be used to help balance it with other lighting.

Also, radiosity only affects diffuse shading of objects. A light may be used that adds specular highlights to a surface by setting Affect Specularity on and deactivating the Affect Diffuse option entirely (Figure 10-17). By tweaking the light's color and intensity, we can easily control the highlights in a scene.

Figure 10-17: A light set to Affect Specular.

Clay-look Rendering

While we're on the theme of global illumination, it seems fitting to also mention that a popular way to show off modeling work is to create a clay-style render of it. This is usually done with objects surfaced using a simple flat color (often just a shade of gray), then using a Backdrop Only type radiosity with either a flat white backdrop or a gradient backdrop (if we want to simulate the effect of top-down lighting). The backdrop will give us even shading over the entire object, giving our object a very clay-like appearance.

1. Load your model (or scene) into Light-Wave. In my example, I quickly created a teapot in Modeler (using **Create | Primitives | More | Teapot** if you're interested in making your own).

Figure 10-18: A classic object.

2. Open **Windows | Backdrop Options** and add the environment plug-in called **Textured Environment**.

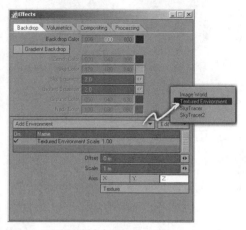

Figure 10-19: Add the Textured Environment plug-in.

3. Click the **Texture** button to open the Texture Editor. Change Layer Type to **Gradient**, set Input Parameter to **Pitch**, and make two keys — one at the top with a white color and one at the bottom with a black color. This will create a top-down illumination effect for the render. Close the Texture Editor.

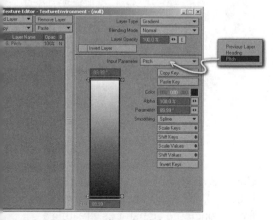

Figure 10-20: Set a gradient backdrop.

4. Open **Render | Render Globals** and activate **Enable Radiosity**, then set Type to **Backdrop Only**. Deactivate the Affect Diffuse and Affect Specular options of any lights in the scene, then press <**F9**> and you should get a clay-style render as seen in Figure 10-21.

Figure 10-21: A clay-style rendered object.

> **Note**
>
> Both HDRI and clay-style backdrops can leave unwanted backdrop imagery in your renders, especially if the only use of these backdrops was for calculating lighting. If you want to replace the backdrop after rendering has completed with a flat color, or fill it with black, simply create a simple image with the color you want to use. Press <**Ctrl**>+<**F7**> to bring up the compositing options, and load the image you created as the background image. When you render the scene again and the render has completed, the background will be replaced with the color image.
>
> This image can be as small as 1 pixel in size, as LightWave will stretch the image to fill the background. A tiny image of this size takes almost no memory, especially important should you be working with complex, memory-hungry scenes in LightWave.

Caustics

Another advanced effect for lighting is caustics, which simulates the reflection and refraction of light rays off one surface and onto another. Caustics are seen everywhere — the dancing patterns of light around the bottom of a glass of water as it sits on a table, the moving patterns of light at the bottom of a swimming pool, the bright spot on a surface when we focus light through a magnifying glass. Let's see how we can create this same effect with LightWave.

1. Load the scene **Scenes\Chapter 10\caustics.lws**.

2. Press **<F9>** to check out the scene as it is now. It's not a bad render. The gemstones are clear and reflective; however, in reality they'd probably be generating a lot of caustic patterns as they reflect and refract the light passing through them.

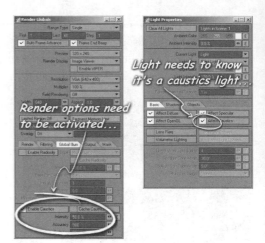

Figure 10-23: Setting up the caustic render options.

Intensity sets the strength of the caustics effect on the surfaces in the render, and Accuracy sets the quality of the effect. Softness, which we didn't touch, will smooth the effect if it happens to be too noisy. We'll leave this setting at its default for now.

4. Once the values have been set, press **<F9>** and watch what happens.

Figure 10-24: Caustics at work.

Figure 10-22: Something's missing here.

3. Select the light and open its Properties window. Make sure that the option **Affect Caustics** is active, then open the **Render | Render Globals** window. Under the Global Illum tab, check **Enable Caustics**, set Intensity to **50%**, and set Accuracy to **500**.

Caustics are generated! The light is refracted, reflected, and focused on the surface through the gemstones, creating a richer and more vibrant render!

I recommend you experiment with the settings here as it's a great way to learn how to tune caustics to get the best look for your projects. For instance, set Intensity to **100%** and check out the difference when you render this with **<F9>**.

Atmospherics

Atmosphere is essential to adding that level of extra realism or quality to your work. When we refer to atmosphere, we are often talking about the mist, dust, or haze we see around us — the dust in the air of a dark room that creates a visible beam of light from the sun shining through the window or a light bulb in a dark alleyway with a soft glow around it from the moisture in the damp air. Often these effects are not consciously noticed; however, when they're missing from a CG render, they create that "something is missing" feeling.

All these effects we see in everyday life can be recreated in LightWave, and can take your CG up a level in terms of quality.

Glow Effect

While the Glow Effect is a *post-process* filter (an image filter effect applied *after* a frame is rendered) and not actually created

through LightWave's lighting system, it is still an effect worth mentioning because of how it simulates something that is often associated with lighting and atmospherics.

Glow Effect isn't something to be restricted to "recreations of reality." Glow Effect cranks up the cool factor on flying logos, web graphics, and all kinds of design-oriented applications. It can even be used to imitate volumetric lighting (a subject we'll be covering later in this chapter).

Figure 10-25: Glowing text.

The only difference between the two versions of the text in Figure 10-25 is that the one on the right uses Glow Effect. Let's see how we can use glow to add some production value to a simple light bulb scene.

1. Load **Scenes\Chapter 10\Warm_ glow.lws**.

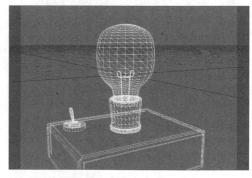

Figure 10-26: A simple light bulb scene.

2. A quick **<F9>** render (with the camera's Antialiasing level set to **Enhanced Low** in the Camera Properties window) shows us what we've got to start with (see Figure 10-27).

415

Figure 10-27

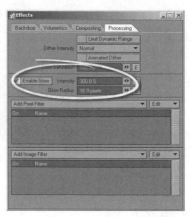

Figure 10-28: Cranking up the glow.

This shot works; however, just because we think it looks okay doesn't mean a little production value boost wouldn't go amiss!

We'll want to tweak our light bulb's surface (Bulb_Glass) and use the Glow option to bring the energy of light to life. The Glow Effect is a two-part process. It must be activated both on the Advanced tab of the Surface Editor (a percentage that acts as a "multiplier" for the global settings — and need not be restricted to 100% as its maximum) and on the Processing tab of the Effects panel, where Enable Glow must be active and the Intensity and Glow Radius values must be set.

3. Select **Windows | Image Processing** (<**Ctrl**> + <**F8**>) and select **Enable Glow,** then set Intensity to **300%**, and Glow Radius to **16** pixels (for an NTSC-size frame). This is an old trick I picked up a long time ago. I started using it because at first, you couldn't set an individual surface's Intensity setting above 100%. I still use it because it produces a beautiful effect with lots of diversity among the glowing surfaces in a single scene.

4. With the global glow settings cranked to the level we've got them in Figure 10-28, we need just a touch of Glow Intensity on the surface to make it start doing its magic. Set Glow Intensity for the object's Bulb_Glass surface to **10%** (Figure 10-29). Do an <**F9**> render and see how just a little glow can greatly improve the realism of a simple light bulb.

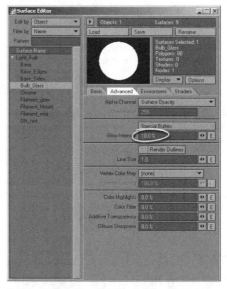

Figure 10-29: Set the Glow Intensity value to 10%.

Figure 10-30: A little glow goes a long way.

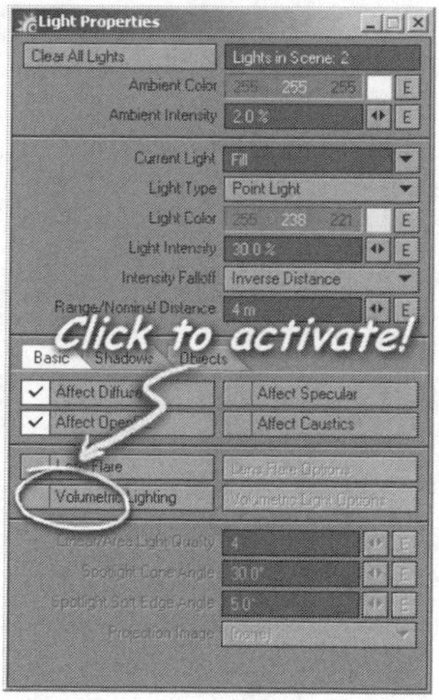

Figure 10-31: Activate volumetrics for a light in the Light Properties window.

Volumetric Lighting

LightWave incorporates the ability for lights to appear to illuminate particulate matter in its virtual atmosphere (like morning light streaming in through a misty forest). This effect is called *volumetric lighting*. In this section, we'll look into how we can set up and use volumetric lighting to create some spectacular effects. Note, however, that these effects can often be slow to render due to the more complex mathematical calculations the computer needs to make. Later on, we'll also look at some ways in which we can improve the performance and still get the same type of effect in our work!

Switching on volumetric lighting is easy; simply activate the **Volumetric Lighting** option on a light's Properties window.

When a light has volumetrics active, the viewport will indicate the area of volume with a white wireframe. Different types of light generate different volumetric areas, as shown in Figure 10-32. Note that two lights — linear and area — don't have the ability to generate volumetric effects due to their more complex nature.

Figure 10-32: Different light types give off different volumetric shapes.

Clicking on the Volumetric Light Options button opens up an options window that lets us change the way the light's volume appears. Here, we can tweak the volumetric effect to get the look we're after.

> **Note**
>
> Using the VIPER tool (<F7>) is a fast way to preview changes we make to the volumetric settings of any light. You'll find this tool mentioned throughout the book.

The volumetric atmosphere is illuminated by the light, and also influenced by the color of the light. After all, a volumetric is the effect of light traveling through our virtual atmosphere. Lower levels of light will

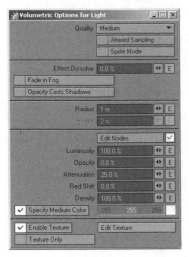

Figure 10-33: Volumetric Options window.

obviously be weaker and that means the light won't travel as far.

- **Quality** defines the amount of precision that LightWave will apply when calculating the effect. The higher this setting, the slower (but more accurate) the effect will be.

- **Jittered Sampling** adds a little noise into the precision mix, making rendering a little quicker but at the expense of being a little grainier in quality.

- **Sprite Mode** is a clever little option that makes rendering super fast by simplifying the volume to a flat slice through the middle of the effect. However, while fast, this does simplify the appearance a lot, which doesn't work well with some things like shadows in the light. We'll look at this option later on in a little more detail.

- **Effect Dissolve** makes the effect much fainter. This is a nice way of fading a beam of light without affecting the appearance of the overall effect itself.

- **Fade in Fog** fades the volumetric effect when inside fog in a scene. Chapter 12 will cover fog in more detail.

- **Opacity Casts Shadows** causes the particulate matter in the atmosphere to influence the volumetric shadows cast by a light. Think of it as thick dust obscuring the light.

- **Radius/Cone Start** is the width of the atmosphere around the light for a point or distant light. In the case of a spotlight, it's the distance in front of the light where the volume starts.

- **Height** is the length of the volume in front of the light. A point light ignores this since it's a spherical area; however, distant and spotlights both use this to indicate how far in front of the light the atmosphere exists.

- **Edit Nodes** allows us to control the volumetric atmosphere through LightWave v9's new node-based surfacing system. You can learn all about how this tool is used in Chapter 19, where it is discussed in detail.

- **Luminosity** controls how much each particle in the atmosphere is influenced by light hitting it. The higher this value, the brighter the particle will get when light hits it.

- **Opacity** controls how solid the particles in the atmosphere are. The higher this value, the less light passes through the particle. This value affects the shadowing option we mentioned earlier.

- **Attenuation** is how the light falls away, or fades out, as it travels through the atmosphere. The higher this value, the faster light will fade out.

- **Red Shift** works along with Attenuation and changes the wavelength of the light as it travels. A positive value here starts to influence the color of the light toward red as it makes its way through the atmosphere. A negative value starts to remove red, and makes the light go toward a blue tint.

Note

The reason the sky is blue is because the wavelength of light passing through the Earth's atmosphere is attenuated and changed, eventually becoming blue in color. LightWave can simulate this concept through the Red Shift value.

- **Density** sets how much particulate matter is in the atmosphere. The higher this is, the thicker and denser the volumetric becomes.

- **Specify Medium Color** lets us set a color for the matter in the atmosphere.

The bottom three options in the window let us use textures inside the volumetric effect to help simulate smoke clouds, dust, and other such effects. By default, any texture is applied within the volume itself. By selecting **Texture Only**, we can force the volumetric to appear only where our texture is. This is great for creating a variety of visual effects such as rocket booster exhaust or laser beams.

Let's create something with volumetrics and see how it can benefit our production values. How about creating dust for the room that we used earlier to demonstrate radiosity?

1. Load the scene **Scenes\Chapter 10\ window_room_volumetrics.lws**. This is the scene we looked at earlier, except I've modified the position and angle of the camera for a more dynamic shot.

2. Let's select the light and open its Properties window. Check **Volumetric Lighting**, and click on the **Volumetric Light Options** button to set it up.

3. Set Height to **13.76 m**, Luminosity to **50%**, and Attenuation to **10%**. Give Red Shift a **–10%** value to shift the light toward a cooler blue color inside the room. Set Density to **50%** to lessen the amount of dust in the air, and set Quality to **Low**. Finally, let's activate **Jittered Sampling** to help speed things up a little. Press **<F9>** and do a render to see how things look.

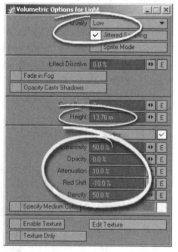

Figure 10-35: Set up the volumetric lighting.

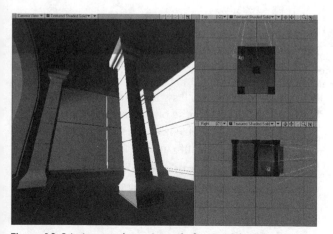

Figure 10-34: A more dynamic angle for our volumetrics.

Figure 10-36: The room before and after volumetrics.

A little dustier!

Using Sprite Mode

As mentioned earlier, we can use volumetric Sprite mode to generate much faster rendering, but at the expense of the volumetric being simplified to a slice from the middle of the effect. As you can see in Figure 10-37, this can have a big impact on the appearance of the volumetric effect if we have shadows or textures in the volumetric, so it's not suited for every situation.

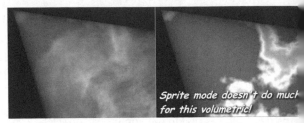

Sprite mode doesn't do much for this volumetric!

Figure 10-37: Bad sprite mode — textures and shadows don' look good!

Textures *can* be tweaked to look better by toning them back (so they're not as intense as original settings may have required). However, should we be lighting a street scene, where multiple volumetric beams of light are needed to sell the illusion of street lamps, Sprite mode can be a godsend!

Note

To see the effects of Sprite mode as shown in Figure 10-37, load the scene Scenes\Chapter 10\Bad_Sprite_mode.lws. Select the light, open the Light Properties window (<p>), and then click on the Volumetric Light Options button. The pattern in this volumetric is created through a simple Smokey 2 procedural texture. (Click on Edit Texture to view the settings.) I recommend that you use VIPER (<F7>) to preview this light in real-time, and then tweak settings such as the Sprite mode option to see the differences for yourself.

Faking Volumetric Lighting

While I'm sure you'll agree that volumetric lighting is very cool and looks great, it is slow to render. When working on a commercial project with a tight deadline you won't always have the luxury of using such tools, yet the project may call for such an effect. When this happens, you can always fake the effect using geometry and textures. Let's check out how this can be done easily.

1. Load **Scenes\Chapter 10\fake_ beam.lws**. I've created a 1 meter tall cone-like object to be our "shaft of light" and thrown a bit of animation on it (so it'll swing from right to left over the course of our scene). But everything else is at the default and up to us to put into effect.

2. The first thing we've got to do is change the default surface on that cone of light to something that looks a bit

less like automotive primer. Change the following settings for the surface:

a. Set Color to **216, 240, 254**.

b. Change Luminosity to **100%**. (It's a shaft of "light," right? It's supposed to be "perfectly lit" under all lighting circumstances.)

c. Set Diffuse to **0%**. (If it's "perfectly lit," it doesn't need to scatter light from its surface.)

d. Transparency should be set to **100%**. (Won't this make it impossible to see? Yep. But we're going to do some special tricks with its Texture channel, so hold tight.)

e. Activate **Smoothing** and **Double Sided**.

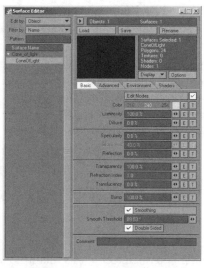

Figure 10-38: Setting up the light surface.

3. Now, we're going to make our shaft of light visible. Open the Texture Editor window for the Transparency channel, and set Layer Type to **Procedural Texture**. Set Procedural Type to **Value** (this is a procedural texture that is just a flat, featureless expanse of whatever value we enter for it), and enter **42%**

for its Texture Value. Under its Falloff tab, enter **125%** for its Z-axis, and set Type to **Spherical**.

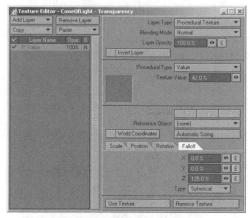

Figure 10-39: Using a Value procedural.

This will force the effective value for the surface's transparency to be 42% at the object's origin, then falling off to the setting we entered in Figure 10-38 (100%) at a rate of 125% per meter. So, in just under a meter from its origin, the shaft will be 100% transparent! Doing a quick <**F9**> at frame 0 shows us what we've got.

Figure 10-40: The transparent cone.

4. Now, very few light beams (other than perhaps a laser) are as "hard-edged" as the render in Figure 10-40. So, let's soften the edge of our cone by adding

421

the **Edge_Transparency** shader under the Shaders tab. Set its Edge Transparency to **Transparent** and its Edge Threshold to **1.0**. (Effective values for this shader range from –1 to 1. While an Edge Transparency of Transparent is good for things like shafts of light, Opaque is handy for creating things like soap bubbles and similar things that are more opaque around their edges.)

Figure 10-42: Warm glowing light beam.

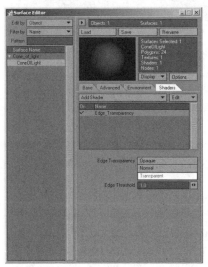

Figure 10-41: Adding the Edge_Transparency shader.

5. By setting **Enable Glow** with an Intensity of **300%** and a Glow Radius of **16** pixels and then setting the Glow Intensity for the surface to **18%**, we crank up both the *intensity* and *realism* of our shaft of light. Do an <**F9**> to check this out.

Now, because I pride myself on being an unabashed smart aleck (and can never leave anything well enough alone when there's the possibility of making something *better*), I want us to go back into our Transparency Texture channel and add some "niftyness" that will make it look like our beam is catching little puffs of moisture.

6. Going back into the Transparency channel's Texture Editor window, select **Add Layer** and set the new layer's Layer Type to **Procedural Texture**.

   a. Set Blending Mode to **PShop Overlay** (which will blend the brightness of the values generated with the layer(s) below it in the Layer list).

   b. Check **Invert Layer**. This will flip-flop the effect of this texture, reversing the lights and darks.

   c. Set Procedural Type to **Dented**. (This is my personal favorite "mathematical playground" that at the time of publication produces different results on Macs and PCs; PC users should be aware that their shaft of light won't match the figures in this section.)

d. Set Scale to **8**, Power to **2**, Frequency to **0.977**, and Octaves to **6**. (I've read the manuals, and I still don't fully understand what effect each of these settings has on the *exact* result of the texture. Mostly, I just fool around until I find something I like, watching the effect on the "render ball" on the main surface window and doing quick renders using **Rendering | Render | Sel Object**.)

e. Check **World Coordinates**. This will "lock" the texture to the "world," which means that when the beam moves, it will appear to pass through smoke that is hanging in the air, *completely independent of the beam*.

f. On the Scale tab, set X, Y, and Z all to **400 mm**.

g. Now, on the Position tab, click on the little **E** button to open the Graph Editor where we will create an "envelope" that will let this texture *move through space over time*!

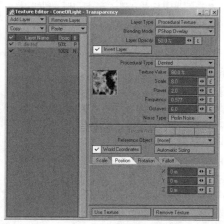

Figure 10-43: Adding a little smokiness to the air.

7. With one of the Position channels active (it doesn't matter which one, as we'll be copying and pasting it to all the others), activate the **Add Keys** button and click somewhere near frame 48. Don't worry if it's one or two frames off — precision isn't too critical at this stage as the next step will correct this.

Figure 10-44: Adding a key to the motion.

8. With the newly created key frame still selected, enter **48** for Frame and **84.722 mm** for Value. (From frame 0 to frame 48, the texture's position along the Y-axis will change by +84.722 mm.) Pre Behavior and Post Behavior should both be set to **Linear**, so the rate of change defined by the keys at frame 0 and frame 48 continues *indefinitely* both *before* and *after* our two key frames.

9. Right-click on the channel you have been working on and choose **Copy**. Then, right-click on the other two channels, in turn, and choose **Paste** to get the texture moving along *all three axes*.

423

Extra misty action!

Figure 10-45: Our misty light source.

You'll see how the clouds of mist move through the beam while the beam holds still and how as the beam moves, it appears to move through the mist, just as it would in real life.

This combination of tricks looks sharp and holds up well under most situations. It breaks down when the camera is looking directly down the shaft of the beam. Just be aware of this if you use this trick, and plan your scenes accordingly.

Lens Flares

Lens flares generate the effect we often see in photos where a strong light has been caught in the shot and causes a variety of artifacts to appear (often rings and halos). Most filmmakers and photographers regard lens flares as something to avoid, but in the

CG world, we never get these naturally because our computer camera is not made from intricate mirrors and lenses, and CG light sources don't tend to have a visible source (such as a glowing filament or a gas giant burning at the center of the solar system). Having the ability to create this imperfection gives us a level of realism by removing that "artificial CG" appearance from our art.

Before you start getting excited, heed a word of warning: As soon as computer software, both 2D and 3D, began to produce lens flares, the industry saw a flood of flares. After a while, even the lay public could tell which program was used to generate a particular lens flare. Don't get me wrong — lens flares are most definitely cool and can do a lot to increase the production value of a render, but because our audience is more educated, we must be more *subtle* in the application of our tricks.

Lens flares assume their base coloring from the color you have set for the light itself. You activate a flare for an individual light by checking **Lens Flare** in its Light Properties window, and you change its settings by clicking on **Lens Flare Options** to open the window seen in Figure 10-48.

Figure 10-46: Activating a lens flare.

You can see lens flares in real time in Layout by having **OpenGL Lens Flares** active under the Display tab of the Preferences window (<d>), but be aware that if you don't have a "full GL" graphics accelerator, even a single GL lens flare will make graphics updates dreadfully slow. (For Figure 10-47, I started up Layout with an empty scene, and moved the one light to the top center of the Camera View viewport. I then activated Lens Flare, set Light Intensity to 100%, and activated the Lens Reflections options found under the Reflections tab.)

The Lens Flare Options window is where you set the options that affect the look and feel of your lens flares. (Central Ring and Red Outer Glow are the two default settings that most clearly identify a flare as coming from LightWave.)

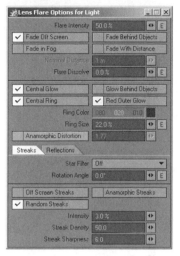

Figure 10-48: Lens Flare Options window.

• **Flare Intensity** is a measure of how "overpowering" the flare is. (A setting of 450% nearly obliterates everything else on the screen.) It also affects the size of the lens flare.

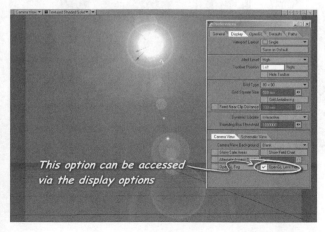

Figure 10-47: OpenGL lens flares.

- **Fade Off Screen** will let your flare "ramp up" as it gets closer to being on screen for an added touch of reality.

- **Fade Behind Objects** will reduce your flare's intensity when it goes behind objects. Without this option active, a flare will appear to shine through an object.

- **Fade in Fog** will reduce your flare's intensity when it is "submerged" in LightWave's fog effects.

- **Fade With Distance** will let the flare diminish in intensity the farther it gets away from the camera, with the **Nominal Distance** being the distance from the camera where the flare is at the intensity set in the Flare Intensity field.

- **Flare Dissolve** will let your flare become fainter without reducing its size (unlike the Flare Intensity setting).

- **Central Glow** is the soft glow of the flare, colored by the light's base color.

- **Glow Behind Objects** sets the glow of the flare behind any object that comes between the light and the camera. Using this setting, you can simulate atmospheric glows at some distance from the camera or place effects behind logos.

> **Note**
>
> Without Glow Behind Objects checked, the flare is rendered on top of everything in the scene, *regardless of its relative Z position from the camera.* Of course, using Fade Behind Objects is another way of preventing a lens flare from being rendered on top of everything else if you don't need to see it glowing behind an object.

- **Central Ring** and **Red Outer Glow** are the two things that just scream, "Hi! I'm a LightWave lens flare!" They make a ring around the flare and tint the flare with a ruddy hue. (**Ring Color** and **Ring Size** control the hue and size of the Central Ring, respectively.)

- **Anamorphic Distortion** "stretches" the whole flare along the camera's X-axis, similar to what happens when lens flares are recorded while shooting on film with an anamorphic lens. (In a nutshell, anamorphic lenses "squish" a "wider" field of view onto a "narrower" strip of film. They are often used when filming a movie to be seen in 2.34:1 aspect ratio on 35mm film, which normally records in 1.85:1.)

Figure 10-49: A flare glowing behind text.

Figure 10-50: Anamorphic lens flare effect.

There are a number of additional options in the **Streaks** tab.

- **Star Filter** behaves as if you'd screwed a "star filter" onto your camera (for those misty, dreamy high school prom type photos). Its pop-up menu gives you access to many different starring effects, all controlled by the (envelopable) **Rotation Angle.**

Figure 10-51: Adding a star filter to the flare.

- **Off Screen Streaks** lets the "streaks" that your flare casts be seen, even when your flare is off-screen. (This is, of course, affected by your Fade Off Screen setting.)

- **Anamorphic Streaks** gives you those blue horizontal line streaks you've seen in *Aliens* when the plasma cutter opens Ripley's escape pod and in *The X-Files* when the flashlights shine. These kinds of streaks are often seen when something has been filmed with a Panavision lens.

Figure 10-52: Anamorphic streaks.

- **Random Streaks** are the fine, numerous "spiky streaks" that help give the impression of something being painfully bright.

The **Reflections** tab offers access to a multitude of settings to recreate the sun dogs that appear when light catches within the multiple layers of camera optics. (I'd suggest using these settings sparingly, creating your own custom combinations of elements instead so this effect doesn't look canned.)

Figure 10-53: Lens reflections.

Let's go back to the fake volumetric light scene we were working on in the previous section of this chapter. If you didn't save this scene, don't panic! You can load it from **Scenes\Chapter 10\fake_beam_F.lws**.

1. Before we begin, make sure that you set the current frame to 0 by dragging the frame slider to the beginning. Select the light in the scene. Using the Motion Options (<**m**>) window, set the light's Parent Item to your cone of light object. Make sure the light is keyed at the top of the cone using the Move tool, then reset its position to 0,0,0 with **Modify | General | Reset**.

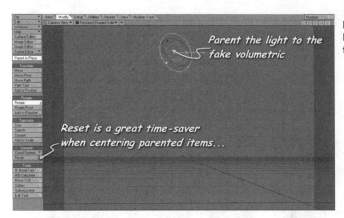

Figure 10-54:
Parent the light to
the cone.

2. Activate **Lens Flare** for the light, and open the Lens Flare Options window. Deactivate Central Ring and Red Outer Glow. Activate **Anamorphic Distortion** and **Anamorphic Streaks**. (Leave everything else as is.)

3. An <F9> gives you something you might see hovering over a rural landscape on *The X-Files*.

Figure 10-55: The X-Files are back!

One of the best ways to use lens flares is to work them into your scene in such a way that the viewer isn't even aware that a lens flare is being used. (Huh?) That's right! When you have a flare that is just a Central Glow with a high Intensity and a fairly high Flare Dissolve, the flare serves more to add a bit of "light bloom" to the entire scene,

giving the same feel that lights do when "catching" in a faint hint of haze. This faint hinting is indicative of the elusive quality of subtlety that runs through all I try to convey to an up-and-coming artist. Anyone can tell the difference when shown a render "with" and a render "without," but on its own, it doesn't jump out at the viewer because it just looks good.

Lens flares aren't just for "realistic" works. The addition of *two* lens flares in the center of the work in Figure 10-56 lets us add a hot outer red glow, but also makes the effect more intense all over. Flares render very quickly, so don't be afraid to use as many flares as it takes to get the exact look you're trying to create.

Figure 10-56: Extra lens flare for boost.

Artificial Shadow Details

If you recall in the radiosity section of the chapter, we used a room where light was cast through an open archway. However, say we wanted to create a shot looking from the window inward, and we wanted to add in the shadows of, say, a tree that was just outside the building. That means we need to model a tree, then set it up so that the shadows cast the way we want. Hmmm… This could be tricky, and time consuming as well. Well, it would be if it weren't for the fact that LightWave can use image maps to fake the necessary shadows through a spotlight.

> **Note**
>
> This effect is similar to the real-life way in which production crews may use color gels or gobos in front of a light to generate the necessary mood or effect. A gobo is simply a cut-out shape that is placed in front of a light and casts shapes by shadowing the light. This is the same effect we're about to create with an image map instead.

1. Load the scene **Scenes\Chapter 10\ look_from_window.lws**.

2. Press <**F9**> to create a render, and take a look at how this appears. Well, it's there, but where's the shadow of the tree we thought was growing outside?

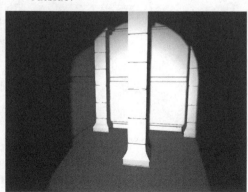

Figure 10-57: No tree?! Yipes!

3. Let's select the light and open its Properties window. Under Projection Image, load the image **Images\Chapter 10\tree_gobo.png** and then close the Properties window.

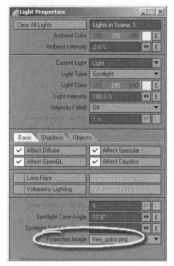

Figure 10-58: Adding a gobo image to the spotlight.

If we change the viewport to Light View, we can see where our new tree_gobo image will be projected through our light. This can make positioning and pointing the light source to get the gobo effect we want a little easier.

Figure 10-59: Become one with the gobo.

4. Press <F9> to create a render. Voilà! Instant shadows without the need for the geometry!

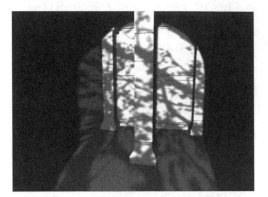

Figure 10-60: The tree has appeared!

Compositing

Compositing packages such as Digital Fusion, After Effects, Shake, and Combustion are fantastic production tools. They allow us to take a mixture of layers such as rendered objects and photographic backdrops, and blend and tweak them to produce amazing effects and sequences. The downside of these tools: They're often expensive and require that you learn yet another application.

Luckily for us LightWave owners, we have the ability to composite elements together without having to open up another piece of software if we don't want to. In fact, LightWave comes with a lot of post processing tools that allow us to not only composite, but also filter and tweak the output of renders until we're happy.

Let's take a look at a typical example of how we can use LightWave to not only render but also composite 3D items into a photographic backdrop.

CG Elements onto a "Live-Action Plate"

1. Let's start by loading up the scene **Scenes\Chapter 10\Compshot_ setup.lws.** This opens a simple scene containing an armed and angry-looking robo droid that we want to integrate into a live photographic backdrop.

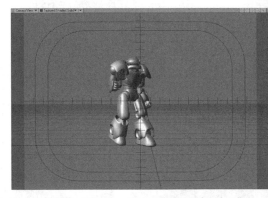

Figure 10-61: A scene with a waiting robo droid.

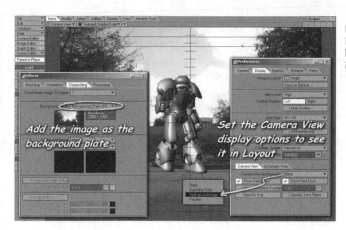

Figure 10-62: Displaying the background image.

2. The first step to getting anything composited onto a live-action plate is to load that plate into **Windows | Compositing Options | Background Image** (<**Ctrl**>+<**F7**>). (Either select the plate, if Background_Plate.jpg is already in the list, or choose **(load image)** and select **Images\Chapter 10\Photos\Background_Plate.jpg** if it isn't in the list.) You can get a really good feel for how this composite will look by choosing **Background Image** in **Preferences | Display | Camera View Background** (<**d**>). Your camera viewport will show your objects over your background image.

3. Let's start by working out the camera so that it matches the background plate. To assist in getting the alignment correct, let's use the grid in Layout. Open the camera's Properties window, and set Lens Focal Length to **18 mm.** (If the pop-up below the camera type says Zoom factor, simply change it to Lens Focal Length instead.) This is roughly the same as the real camera used to take the

background image. The camera should also be approximately **1.8 m** up on Y (roughly the height of the photographer), and moved **2.1324 m** on X and **–6.6589 m** on Z. The camera should also be rotated **–7.2 degrees** on H and **–4.70 degrees** on P (Bank should be **0.0**). You should note at this stage that the grid appears to be "laying" on the ground in the photo. If your scene is set up the same as mine, the black line should be running perfectly along the paving in the background (as shown in Figure 10-63).

Figure 10-63: Getting the camera about right.

Note

While we can roughly guesstimate the position of the camera in terms of how tall the photographer may have been, without having any record of detailed measurements of the background plate itself (like distance to items, etc.), then there is always going to be a little "fudge factor" necessary to match things. One tip that I've found useful when trying to match photographic background plates, especially digital photos, is that we can often gain a lot of information about the camera used from the image's EXIF data. EXIF (Exchangeable Information File Format) is information that many digital cameras will insert into JPG or TIF images that they record on their memory cards. Most modern image applications can display this information, and often the camera zoom will be recorded in here. In Figure 10-64, we can see the EXIF information for the background plate we're using (as displayed by the excellent freeware IrfanView application (http://www.irfanview.com).

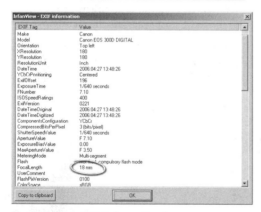

Figure 10-64: EXIF information for our background plate.

4. Let's modify the light in the scene to closely match the angle of the main source of light. While it's primarily the overcast sky, as shown in Figure 10-65, there are clues we can use to identify the location and direction. First, change the light to an area light so that we can create the soft shadowing we see in our image. Using the power of

guesstimation, we can use clues in our background plate such as angles of shadows, etc., to get the light approximately the same. Set the light's rotation to **–93.0** on H and **71.6** on P. Let's knock back the light's Intensity to **50%**. Because an area light has "physical" size, let's make sure that the source is located above our robot by moving it numerically to **1.6192 m** on X, **4.84 m** on Y, and **2.7709 m** on Z.

Shadows and highlights are clues to lighting!

Figure 10-65: Typical clues indicate the light comes from the right.

v9.2 Note

The intensity of area lights has changed in LightWave v9.2. If using an Intensity of 50% does not yield satisfactory results, feel free to increase the value as you see fit.

The light creates the key source from the sky; even though it's overcast, there is still a direction it comes from. What about matching the color of the environment to get the ambient bouncing light we discussed earlier looking realistic? Well, let's

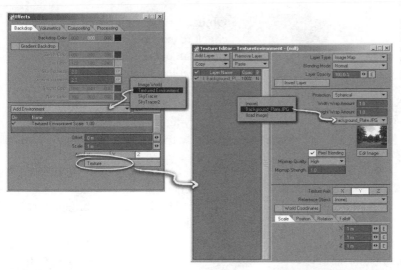

Figure 10-66: Fudging the environment using the background plate.

use a little fudge factor here to simulate this.

5. Open the **Windows | Backdrop Options** tab (<**Ctrl**> + <**F5**>) and choose **Textured Environment** from the Add Environment pop-up. Double-click on this tool to open its Properties panel, then click the **Texture** button to open the Texture Editor. Change Projection to **Spherical**, select **Background_Plate.jpg** as the image, and set Texture Axis to **Y** to wrap this image around our scene. (It's not 100% accurate, but it'll do as a fake ambient lighting solution.)

6. Open **Render | Render Globals | Global Illum**, and activate **Enable Radiosity**. Set Intensity to **130%** and Type to **Backdrop Only**. Activate **Ray Trace Shadows** under the Render tab. This should suffice to produce some fairly "close" lighting for our object. Press <**F9**> and let's see how it looks.

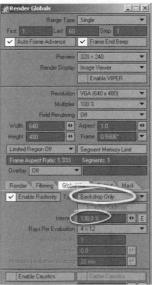

Figure 10-67: Set up radiosity, and press <F9> to see the result.

Note

Adding a backdrop and using radiosity is one of LightWave's "secret weapons" in integrating CG and live-action plates, allowing us to add more complex lighting to the objects based around the images we're compositing over.

Figure 10-68: Our composited robot... But wait!

What's the big thing that stands out as being "wrong" when you look at Figure 10-68? *The object isn't casting any shadows!* Compositing shadows onto things seen in photographic plates is a bit of a multi-part process with the tools that are a part of LightWave's basic toolset. (There are plug-ins that streamline shadow compositing, most notably Worley Labs' G2, which does many other things for your rendering as well, including letting you see changes to your render in real time.)

But here, we're going to show you how to composite shadows using the basics of LightWave *right out of the box*, without having to own a separate compositing program or buy additional software.

First, we've got to have something that "catches" the shadows cast by the robot. This "shadow catcher" is just a simple bit of geometry that *mimics* the general shape and position of the things seen in your plate. (You'd be surprised at how general this "shadow catcher" can be and still look good.)

7. Load in **Objects\Chapter 10\ shadow_catcher.lwo**. This object is a very simple plane, given that the area around the robot is pretty flat. Move it **2 m** along Z to ensure it sits nicely below the robot character. Under its

Object Properties | Lights tab, check to exclude **Radiosity** and **Caustics** from being calculated for that object; it'll save lots of time when rendering. (The only light that needs to interact with our shadow catcher is our primary light source. You may find it easier to match your shadow-catching objects to their respective landmarks on the plate when they're viewed as wireframes and not as opaque, solid objects. This can be set through the Scene Editor.)

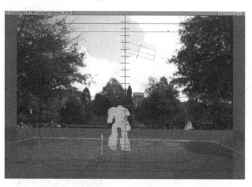

Figure 10-69: Shadow catcher, loaded and ready.

When you first load shadow_catcher.lwo, it has a default surface on it, with its Transparency bumped up to 80%, so it will receive shadows *and* still show the background image through it. This lets me fine-tune the positioning of the shadow catcher, the lighting, and the objects that are casting the shadows. When everything is as it should be (and everything should be fine in our scene if we've tweaked according to these steps), move on and get everything ready for a final render.

8. As shown in Figure 10-70, set the Shadow_catcher surface Color to **000, 000, 000** (black) and its Transparency to **0%**. On the Advanced tab, set Alpha Channel to **Shadow Density** (which is what will let us composite the black of

the object's surface color onto our plate). As final preparation for generating an image that can be composited onto the plate, we need a completely *black* background. ("Premultiplying" our foreground image with black helps the computer deal with the rather touchy process of seamlessly blending the edges of our foreground image into that of our background.) Replace your **Windows | Compositing Options | Background Image** with **Images\ Chapter 10\black.png**. (This is necessary to hide the environment we're using for the radiosity.)

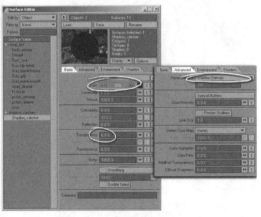

Figure 10-70: Setting up the shadow catcher.

9. Do an **<F9>** to render the image. Once our completed foreground plate is rendered, it's almost ready for compositing onto our background plate. To work with a single frame, as we are here, under the Render Display's File menu choose **Save RGBA | LW_PNG32 (.png)** (see Figure 10-71). PNG (Portable Network Graphics) files are the most compact file type that holds both the image channel (24 bits) and its alpha channel (another 8

bits), making a total of 32 bits per pixel in a *single file*. If you wanted to save a series of frames, perhaps if you were doing this for a movie, you would select **Render | Render Globals | Output | Save RGB** and set the file format to a 32-bit file format (possibly even save out the alpha separately, just in case your compositing application needs the alpha as a separate file).

Figure 10-71: Our foreground plate, rendered.

Looking at Figure 10-71, you may also be wondering where the shadows are. They're there, but they're black, the same color as our background image. When we take a look at our alpha channel, which is what is used to "cut out" our foreground elements, we see that the shadows are there, but they're *white* (see Figure 10-72). In a LightWave alpha channel, what is white is *opaque* and what is black is *transparent* (some programs have this reversed). So, the white shadows on the alpha channel will make the black of the foreground plate's image channel opaque where the shadows are!

435

Figure 10-72: The alpha channel reveals the missing shadows.

10. Now, to piece the background and foreground together, save your scene, and then clear your scene (or start another instance of LightWave), so we can have a completely "virgin" space in which to work our "magic." In that empty scene's Image Editor, load **Images\ Chapter 10\Photos\Background_ Plate.jpg**. Also, load the render of the foreground elements that you saved in Figure 10-71 (you can use mine, if you wish: Renders\Chapter 10\CompFG _F.png). With your foreground "plate" selected, choose **Clone | Instance** to create a "referential copy" of the image.

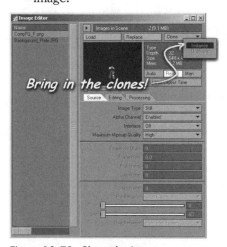

Figure 10-73: Clone the image.

11. Finally, with the *instance* selected, choose **Alpha Only** for Alpha Channel. (This "splits" the 32-bit image into one image that has the colors of the foreground elements and another image that has their alpha "mask.") Then, under **Windows | Compositing Options** (<Ctrl>+<F7>), choose **Background_Plate.jpg** for Background Image, choose your (original) foreground image for Foreground Image, and choose your instanced image that has been set to Alpha Only for Foreground Alpha.

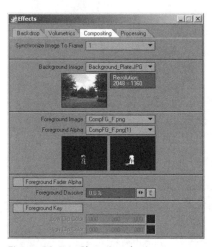

Figure 10-74: Choosing the images.

Figure 10-75: The final render.

Better Integration

Obviously, the shadows may not perfectly match our source footage. The main issue is they're just too dark compared to the shadows in the background plate. This is usually where making the decision to render the ground shadows as a *separate pass* to that of the object is a much better idea. With the shadows as a separate layer, we can tweak the opacity and coloration of the shadows until we're happy with it. In fact, let's quickly see how we can do that with LightWave.

12. If you didn't save your foreground scene, then load the **Scenes\Chapter 10\Compshot_setup_F.lws** from the DVD. This is my completed composite setup scene. To create a shadow pass on its own, select the robot and set its **Properties | Render | Alpha Channel** option to **Constant Black**, and activate the **Matte Object** option. Matte Object will force the surface of the object to take on a flat color and ignore any shading. Make sure that the Matte color is set to black (**000, 000,**

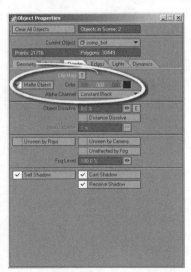

Figure 10-76: Prepare to render out a ground shadow pass.

000). Setting the alpha channel to **Constant Black** will paint out the robot from the alpha channel itself. (As you recall from looking at the shadow, white indicates anything solid in an alpha channel.)

13. Render the image. Note how the whole image now looks black; however, displaying the alpha channel reveals that the shadow is there, and that the robot has been removed from the alpha channel as well as the color. Save this render as a LW_PNG32 image called **CompGS_F.png** (for Ground Shadow).

Figure 10-77: Robot go bye-bye.

14. Let's do something similar now, but remove the ground shadow and only render the robot. To do this, deactivate the robot's Matte Object option, and set the Alpha Channel option back to **Use Surface Settings**. For the Shadow_catcher, check its **Properties | Render | Unseen by Camera** option to prevent it from being rendered. Create a render and save this image as an LW_PNG32 image called **CompRobot_F.png**.

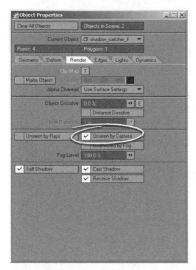

Figure 10-78: Set Unseen by Camera for the shadow catcher.

15. Clear the scene and load the **Background_Plate.jpg**, **CompGS_F.png**, and **CompRobot_F.png** files into the Image Editor. Now, given that we have three layers to composite, we can't use LightWave's simple two-layer approach offered by its compositing options. For

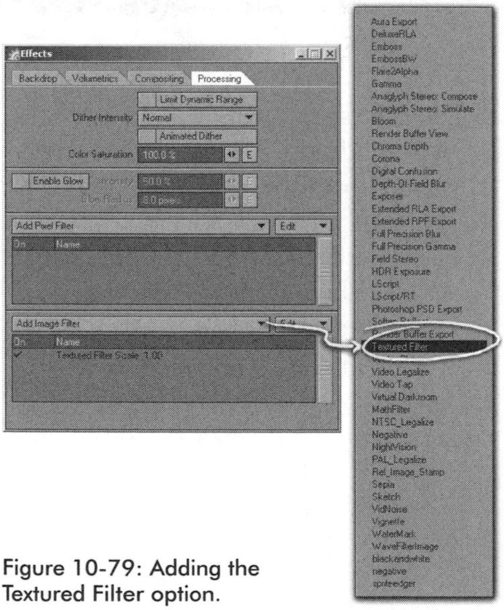

Figure 10-79: Adding the Textured Filter option.

this we'll have to slip into the Processing tab of the Effects panel (**Windows | Image Processing**), and choose **Textured Filter** from the Add Image Filter pop-up, as shown in Figure 10-79.

Textured Filter is an image filter that lets us manipulate and layer elements and effects using LightWave's Texture Editor tool. It gives us an immense amount of post processing capability, only a little of which we'll be touching on in this exercise.

16. Let's double-click on **Textured Filter** to open its parameters, then click the **Texture** button to open the Texture Editor panel. Using the Texture Editor to post-process images and renders opens up all kinds of possibilities, but for now, let's just set Image to **Background_Plate.jpg**.

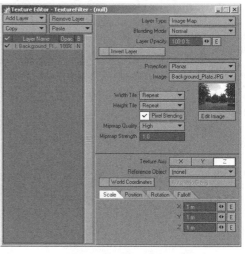

Figure 10-80: Set up the background image first.

17. Choose **Add Layer | Image** to create a new image layer. Select the **CompGS_F.png** image to add the shadows to the background plate.

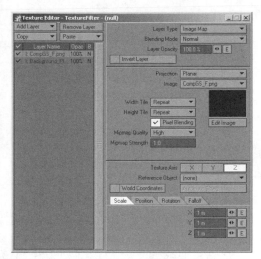

Figure 10-81: Adding the ground shadows.

18. Finally, let's choose **Add Layer | Image**, and this time select the **CompRobot_F.png** image. The three layers should now be layered and ready to render by pressing <**F9**>.

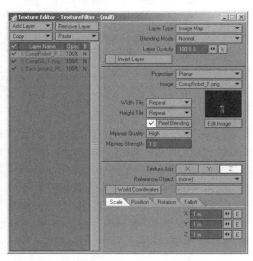

Figure 10-82: Chucking in the robot for good measure.

So, what's the point here? We learned how to layer multiple images, but we get the same result as the two-layered approach!

19. Well, I felt the shadows were too dark compared to our background plate. With the shadows as a separate layer, all we need to do is set the opacity of the shadow layer to **50%** and render. Instant tweakability of those ground shadows!

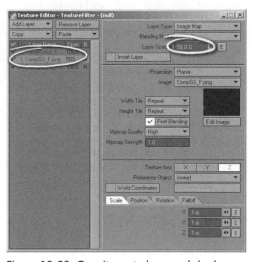

Figure 10-83: Opacity controls ground shadow darkness.

20. Press <**F9**> and let's check out our handiwork!

Figure 10-84: The final render, with lighter shadows.

Note

It's times like this, when you're compositing your render onto something shot on film, that you'll want to render your foreground elements with the camera's "filmic" soft filter. You may also want to add some "film grain" to the foreground elements using either the WaveFilterImage or Virtual Darkroom filters (both of which are found under **Windows | Image Processing | Add Image Filter** (<**Ctrl**>+<**F8**>).

Virtual Darkroom is an amazing tool. It does much more than add film grain. It actually *simulates* the ways that certain films, processing techniques, and photographic papers would record the image that LightWave renders. Image processing modifies your final renders and, because of this fact, it's a much better idea to *not* apply this filter directly to your renders, but instead use this filter on a prerendered series of frames

(saved using an image format like Flexible Format (.flx), Radiance (.hdr), SGI 64-bit (.rgb), SGI 48-bit (.rgb), Tif LogLuv (.tif), or Cineon FP (.cin) that supports LightWave's ability to create images in high dynamic range color, rather than in 24-bits-per-channel, television-color-depth images).

Virtual Darkroom isn't the most intuitive tool for most users, but does come with a plethora of presets that can be applied. It can be used (to a degree) to "color grade" your footage, giving it the unearthly feeling of *Minority Report* or the look of footage shot in rural America in the '70s (the Kodak Gold 100 preset gives this look quite nicely). It even has settings for black and white film, letting you make your work look like it was unearthed from some esoteric, archive film vault.

Conclusion

So you've picked up some techniques to make your work look polished, slick, and professional — just like the pros use. (Heck, these techniques *are* what we use!) I imagine you're pretty darn excited, thinking of all the doors these techniques can open up for you. (I know I'd be.) Honestly, I think you're absolutely right to be excited! You're now standing on a knowledge base where you can see that all you'd hoped to accomplish with LightWave is indeed within your range of ability. The really awesomely cool thing about this is knowing just how much more is still out there, *just waiting to be discovered by you* — and shared with others!

The true understanding of knowledge is to know just how much is out there for you to know. That's the really exciting thing about this whole 3D gig! "Learning to learn" means that everything out there that you *don't* know is an adventure just waiting to be explored. That's exciting as heck! You're *never* going to know all there is to know about LightWave (not anymore — it's just too big). There will always be new things to explore and learn and help you create visions of things you've always wanted to see and no longer will wait for someone else to create for you!

Chapter 11

Intermediate Skills: Projection Mapping

In Chapter 6 we took a detailed look at surface properties. We learned that the appearance of a surface is determined by four basic properties:

- Primary attributes (Color, Diffuse, Specularity, etc.)
- Textures (images, procedurals, and gradients)
- Nodes
- Shaders

We learned that textures allow you to add variation to a surface's primary attributes. For example, by adding a Turbulence procedural texture to the Diffuse channel, you can vary its ability to reflect light, making

the surface appear old and weathered. We spent a good deal of time in Chapter 6 talking about procedurals and gradients, but we only briefly mentioned the use of images. We'll remedy that in this chapter.

Over the course of this chapter you'll learn the fundamental principles of *projection mapping* (the technique used to apply an image to the surface of your polygons). We'll look at *Standard projections* as well as *UV projections* and we'll take the mystery out of each. We'll also look at some of the more helpful UV tools at your disposal. Then we'll put these concepts into practice by learning how to texture a Russian MiG-29 fighter jet.

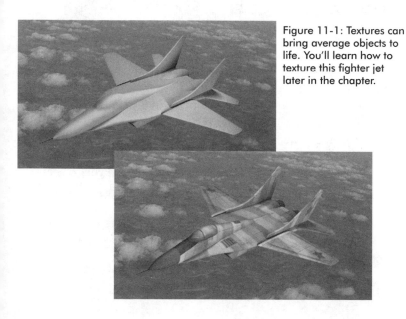

Figure 11-1: Textures can bring average objects to life. You'll learn how to texture this fighter jet later in the chapter.

Images vs. Procedurals

There's a debate that's been going on in the LightWave community for as long as I can remember. Some argue that the only way to get photo-realistic results is to use images. Others argue that you can get them using procedurals. Personally, I don't understand the point of this argument. LightWave gives you access to both, so use both. Don't favor one over the other. Use what works best for the texturing task at hand.

As a general rule of thumb, when you simply want to add natural, random variations, procedurals offer a fast, flexible solution. Since they're generated dynamically, you can change them on the fly without having to go back and spend time fixing things in a paint program. However, when you want your surface to have specific colors, shapes, or patterns at *precise* locations on your object, then you're better off using images.

The two are not mutually exclusive. In many cases you can use procedurals to add wear and tear to pristine images. This gives you a tremendous amount of flexibility when texturing.

IMAGE-BASED TEXTURES • PROCEDURAL TEXTURES = GREAT TEXTURES

Figure 11-2: As a general rule of thumb, images are best for adding *specific* colors and patterns such as the design of this box. Procedurals are best for adding *random* colors and patterns such as the bumps and dents. The two are not mutually exclusive, but rather can be used together to enhance your overall texturing capabilities.

The Advantage of Images

One of the main advantages to images is that they allow you to add a tremendous amount of detail with little effort. This is especially true when using photographic images. Achieving a comparable level of detail with procedurals requires the use of many layers and a hefty investment of time tinkering with their settings.

Another advantage to using images is that they have a negligible impact on render times. Procedural textures have to be calculated when you render. The more procedural textures you add, the longer it will take to render your scene. Image-based

textures allow you to add detail without significantly impacting your render time.

Perhaps the greatest advantage to using images is that they allow you to add a personal touch to the look of your objects. Procedural textures often have a recognizable "footprint" that can give your models a distinctly "3D" look. A hand-painted texture map, however, will give your objects a certain warmth and a look that's distinctly your own.

So how do you get images onto your model? It's simple. You *project* them.

Projections

The process of placing an image onto the surface of your object is called *texture mapping*. An image (texture) is applied (mapped) to specific polygons by "projecting" it onto their surfaces. It is very similar to the process of projecting a movie onto the screen at the theater. If you keep this simple analogy in mind, it will make it much easier to understand the concepts we'll be exploring throughout this chapter.

When you add an Image Map layer in LightWave, you are telling the program that it should create an invisible movie projector and point it toward the surface of your model. The settings found in the Image Map layer allow you to position and orient the invisible projector so that the image will fit perfectly on the surface of your object (which is akin to the movie screen).

When you click on the Projection pop-up menu, you'll find a list of six different projection types. Each projection type gives you a different way of shining the image onto your object's polygons. The available projection types are:

- Planar
- Cylindrical
- Spherical
- Cubic
- Front
- UV

The first five projections use similar techniques, but the last one, UV, works a bit differently. Therefore, you can break the six projections down into two categories: "Standard" and "UV."

If it helps, you can think of Standard projections and UV projections like the differences between VHS and Beta (for the over-30 crowd) or HD-DVD and Blu-Ray. Both do the same thing. They just do it a bit differently.

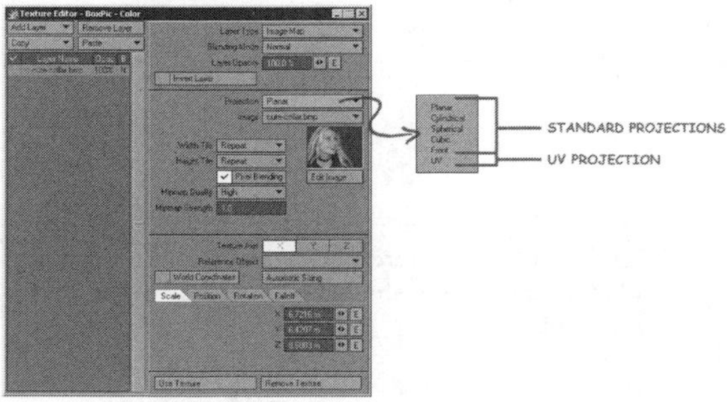

Figure 11-3: Adding an Image Map layer in LightWave creates an invisible movie projector that you can shine on the polygons of your surface.

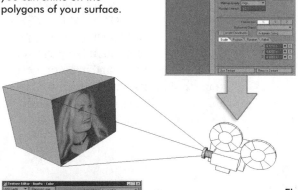

Figure 11-4: There are six projection types, but in reality there are only two categories: Standard (which includes the first five projections) and UV (the last projection).

STANDARD PROJECTIONS

UV PROJECTION

Projection Space

Both Standard projections and UV projections work by pointing a virtual projector at the surface of your object. The difference between them lies in *where* the projector is placed.

Standard projections place the image projector in the 3D space surrounding your object. (This is typically called "world" space.) UV projections place the projector above a hidden 2D space called "UV," which is only visible by changing one of your viewports in Modeler to UV Texture.

world. The projector can be placed in any position and rotated in any direction. And it can project an image with any aspect ratio, be it perfectly square or a thin, narrow rectangle.

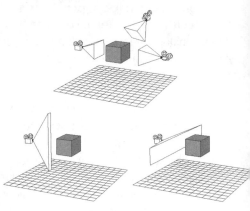

Figure 11-6: Standard projectors can be positioned and rotated anywhere in the space around your model and they can cast an image with any aspect ratio.

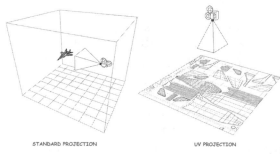

STANDARD PROJECTION   UV PROJECTION

Figure 11-5: Standard projections put the virtual projector in the 3D space surrounding your object. UV projections place the virtual projector above a secret 2D space that's only visible when one of Modeler's viewports is set to UV Texture.

In this section we'll talk about how projections work in both standard 3D and UV 2D space. Textures can be applied to your object in either Modeler or Layout; however, in order to help you understand the differences between Standard projections and UV projections, we'll focus our attention on the application of textures in Modeler. The differences between the two categories are a bit more obvious there.

"Standard" 3D Space

The virtual projector for any of the *Standard* projection types is oriented in relation to your object's position/rotation in the 3D

Let's say that you have a box that's positioned 2 meters above the ground in Modeler. When you create an Image Map layer (which creates a virtual movie projector), you must position the projector 2 meters above the ground in order for it to properly shine its image onto the box. (Fortunately there's an easy way to do this, which we'll look at in just a bit.)

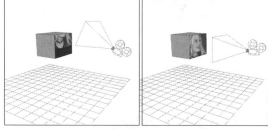

Figure 11-7: Standard projectors must be positioned or rotated to properly shine their images onto your object' polygons.

Once the projector has been set in place, if the box were to move down so that it rested on the ground, what do you think would happen? Would the texture move with it? No.

If you position a projector at a specific location and shine its image in a specific direction, it will continue to be positioned at that location and shine in that direction *even if the object it's supposed to be shining onto moves*. This is critical to understand. Standard projectors are not tied to the position of your object until you enter Layout (at which point they are "parented" to the object). At that time you are free to move and rotate the object, and the texture will move and rotate with it. However, if you move the object in Modeler, the texture will stay where it was, because the projector doesn't automatically move with it.

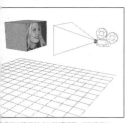 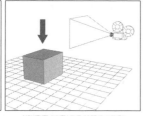

THE PROJECTOR IS ORIENTED CORRECTLY IN FRONT OF THE OBJECT...

HOWEVER WHEN THE OBJECT MOVES, THE PROJECTOR STAYS IN PLACE.

Figure 11-8: Standard projectors are not linked to the position, rotation, or scale of your object. If you move your object, the projector will not move with it and your texture will no longer appear properly on your object. Projectors are only linked to objects once they're loaded to Layout.

"UV" 2D Space

The virtual projector for the UV projection type shines down on a 2D space called "UV." The projector cannot be moved, rotated, or scaled. And unlike Standard projectors, the image shone by a UV projector will always be square.

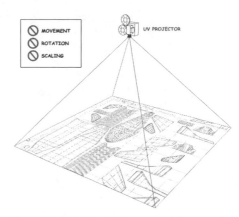

Figure 11-9: UV projectors cannot be moved, rotated, or scaled and the image they cast will always be square.

UV space typically scares the hell out of new users, but it shouldn't. I'm convinced that the main barrier to understanding UVs is the name. It's too cold and technical. Moreover, whenever I hear "UV" I invariably think of suntan lotion (perhaps because I grew up in Arizona). UV offers tremendous texturing abilities, so don't let the cryptic name intimidate you.

The letters "U" and "V" actually refer to the coordinate system used in the hidden 2D space. The U coordinate represents left and right. The V coordinate represents up and down. I don't know why they didn't just call it "XY," but that's what it is. UV is XY. There is no Z, because it is a 2D space.

The UV coordinates run from 0 to 1 and the space is measured as a percentage of the distance from the lower-left corner to the upper-right corner of the UV space. You can see the boundaries of the UV space by turning on the grid in Modeler's Display Options. I recommend turning the grid on whenever you're working with UVs in LightWave.

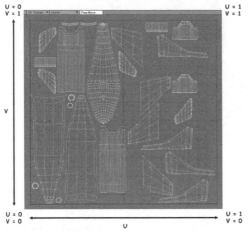

U = 0, V = 1 (top left)   U = 1, V = 1 (top right)

U = 0, V = 0 (bottom left)   U = 1, V = 0 (bottom right)

V (left axis)   U (bottom axis)

Figure 11-10: UV refers to the coordinates used in the 2D space. You can see the space by turning on the grid.

So what is the point of having a hidden 2D space in a 3D program? Simple. Wrapping a flat 2D image around a complex 3D object can be difficult. But if you could somehow unwrap that 3D object and lay it out flat on a 2D surface, texturing would become a whole lot easier. And that's what the UV space and UV mapping techniques are all about.

The process of unwrapping a 3D object is called "skinning," "pelting," or simply "unwrapping." LightWave has a number of tools that can help you with this, and we'll look at them shortly. For now, let's focus on the difference between standard 3D space (as described above) and UV 2D space.

As mentioned earlier, *standard* texture projectors are oriented in the 3D space around your object. They must be positioned in relation to your object in order to properly shine their image on it. But UV projectors are locked down. They never move, never get scaled, and never get rotated. They are fixed in place and always focus their image onto a square screen.

When you move polygons in front of this square screen, the image will appear on them. It's very similar to what happens when someone walks in front of the screen at a movie theater. The image will project onto the person rather than the screen.

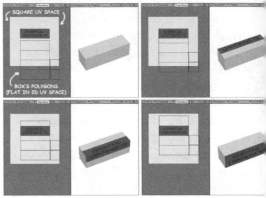

Figure 11-11: UV projectors cast their image onto a square screen. When polygons are moved in front of that screen, they pick up whatever part of the image is being shone there.

If you apply a UV texture to an object in Modeler and then move it around, the texture will move, rotate, and scale along with it. This is the exact opposite of what happens when using Standard projections. But why?

Remember, Standard projectors exist in the 3D world alongside your object. But UV projectors exist in an entirely *separate* world. The polys in the UV world are only remotely linked to the 3D world. When you move, rotate, or scale polys in the 3D world, it has no impact on the polys in the UV world. Therefore, if you apply a UV texture to your object, that texture will stick to your object regardless of where you move it in the 3D universe. *The only way to shift the texture around is to move the polygons within the UV space.*

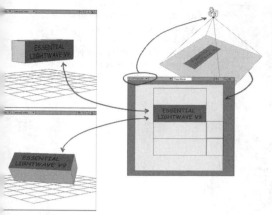

ure 11-12: Altering the position, orientation, or scale
an object in the 3D world will not affect the polys in
UV world. They will remain fixed in place, as will the
projector. Therefore, when you move, rotate, or scale
object with a UV texture applied to it, the texture will
k to the polygons.

Getting Polygons into UV Space

In order to get polygons into the UV world, you must open a portal so that the object's polygons can exist in both the 3D world and the UV world at the same time. You can do this by clicking on the **Map | Texture | New UV Map** button in Modeler.

To see the UV world, you must switch one of your Modeler viewports to UV Texture. And, as I mentioned earlier, you'll probably also find it helpful to turn the grid on. If you don't, you won't be able to see the boundaries of the UV canvas.

Once you're able to see the UV world, you need to specify which UV space you want to peer into. You do this by choosing an existing UV map from the pop-up menu in the lower-right corner of the interface. Click on the "T" button to specify that you want to select a UV Texture map, then select the UV from the list. Any foreground polygons that have been assigned to that UV space will be visible.

You can also use **Windows | Vertex Maps Panel** to select and modify any available UVs.

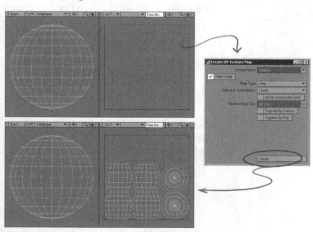

Figure 11-13: The New UV Map tool opens the Create UV Texture Map window in which you can create a new UV space and transfer polygons into it.

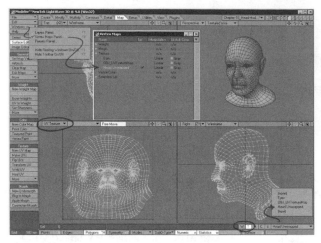

Figure 11-14: You can view the UV world by changing one of your viewports to UV Texture. You can change which UV space you're looking at via the Vertex Maps panel or the menu at the bottom of the interface.

The UV Texture Viewport

The UV Texture viewport allows you to peer into UV space. Since this is not an alternate 3D view, but rather an entirely different space, it's worth talking about how things operate here.

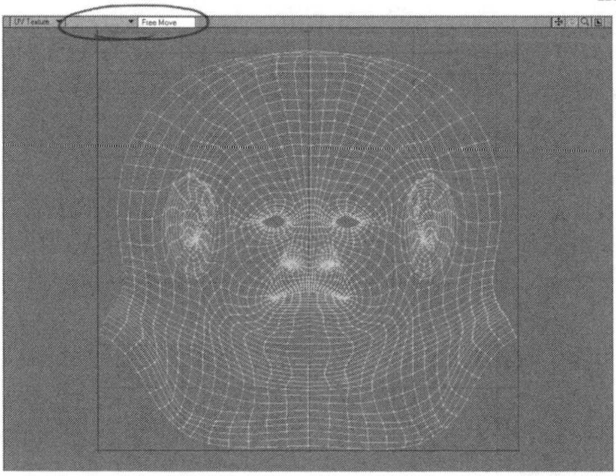

Figure 11-15: The UV Texture viewport offers several features not available with the other viewport types.

At the top of the viewport, you'll notice two new commands. The first (to the right of the Viewport selection pop-up) is an **Image** pop-up menu. From here you can select an existing image or load a new image

to see how it will be projected into UV space.

As I noted earlier, UV space is perfectly square. Therefore, all of your UV images should be created with a 1:1 aspect ratio. I typically stick to the power of 2, creating images at a size of 1024 x 1024, 2048 x 2048, or 4096 x 4096 pixels.

To the right of the Image pop-up menu is the **Free Move** button. This allows you to move individual polygons (and groups of polygons) in the UV space as if they were distinct objects.

As you probably know, when you attempt to move polygons whose points are connected to other polys in the 3D world, they remain connected. Activating Free Move allows you to select the polys and move them, effectively

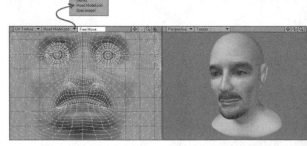

Figure 11-16: Images can be loaded into the UV Texture viewport, allowing you to see what part of the texture will be shone onto specific polygons.

cutting them loose in the UV Texture viewport. (Note that the polys are actually still connected in the 3D world.) This allows you to reposition groups of polygons (often called "islands") to make the best use of the UV space. Without this option on, the only way to move connected groups of polys is to unweld their points in the 3D world and then move them in the UV space.

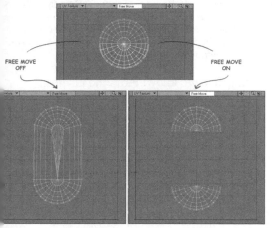

11-17: The Free Move tool lets you move *ups* of polygons in the UV space as if they were *tinct* objects.

Being able to break apart connected groups of polys is just one of the differences between UV space and 3D space. But there are others. Many of the tools you rely on in the 3D world don't work in UV space. For example, Symmetry mode, which is essential for working with symmetrical objects, is disabled in the UV world. Tools like Snap Drag and plug-ins like SP Move don't work in UV space. Then there's the issue of discontinuous polygons.

Continuous and Discontinuous Polygons

The entire point of a UV map is to take a 3D object and unwrap it so that it can be spread out flat on a 2D canvas for easy painting. Unwrapping involves separating polys from one another along one or more edges in the UV space. In the 3D world, however, the polys on either side of the unwrapped edge remain connected. Therefore, the polygons are considered *continuous* (connected together) in the 3D world but they are considered to be *discontinuous* (not connected together) in the UV world.

When you look at your polygons in the UV Texture viewport, you will notice that some of the vertices are red and some are white. The white vertices indicate that the polygons connected to them are continuous. The red vertices indicate that the polygons connected to them are discontinuous.

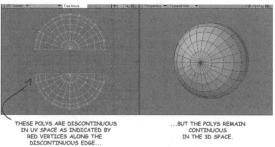

THESE POLYS ARE DISCONTINUOUS IN UV SPACE AS INDICATED BY RED VERTICES ALONG THE DISCONTINUOUS EDGE...

...BUT THE POLYS REMAIN CONTINUOUS IN THE 3D SPACE.

Figure 11-18: Discontinuous polys are indicated by red vertices in the UV Texture viewport.

In earlier versions of LightWave, discontinuous polys caused three problems that harried users and made many avoid UVs altogether. The first notable problem involved the inability to move certain polygons. Fortunately, the addition of the Free Move button in the UV Texture viewport resolved this during the LightWave 8 development cycle.

449

The second problem came from the way that subpatch geometry was handled. The effect of subpatching (discussed in more detail in Chapter 15) would appear in the 3D world but not in the UV world. The new Subpatch Interpolation modes (also introduced in the LightWave 8 development cycle) did a nice job of fixing this. (We'll talk more about subpatch interpolation later in this chapter.)

The third problem is still ongoing. It comes from the fact that Modeler tries to keep polygons continuous whenever possible. It often happens when running one of the standard UV tools and results in polys being connected to others in different parts of the UV space. This problem is easy to work around as we'll see later on.

If you're feeling a little disoriented by UVs, don't worry. We'll spend a good deal of time working with them later in the chapter. For now, there are only two things you

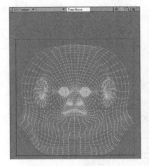

Figure 11-19: Modeler attempts to keep polys continuous whenever possible. This can result in polys being connected in strange ways in the UV Texture viewport when you perform certain actions. We'll see how to work around this later.

really need to know: First, the image projected into UV space is fixed in place. And second, you don't move the projector to shine the image properly onto your polys, but rather move the polys into the area in which the projector's image is already shining.

Standard Projection Types

Now that we've gotten a basic feel for the different projection types, let's take a more detailed look at how they work and the options they offer. We'll begin with a look at the Standard projection types.

Planar

Planar projections are the most common type of Standard projection. They work just like a movie projector casting an image onto a screen at the theater. Planar projections work wonderfully on any relatively flat surface. Tables, benches, walls, and floors are good examples of where planar maps can be used. Slightly curved surfaces can also use planar maps, so long as the polygons don't deviate too much from the specified projection axis.

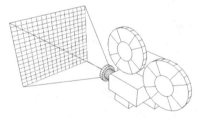

Figure 11-20: Planar projections are the most common type of Standard projection and can be used for a wide range of texturing needs.

Cylindrical

Cylindrical projections are similar to Planar projections; however, the projector has the ability to wrap the image around a single axis. Think of the way that a soda can label wraps around the can, or the way the tread wraps around a tire. A Planar projection would cause the texture to stretch as it moves away from the single projected axis. A Cylindrical projection, however, allows the texture to wrap around an axis so that no distortion occurs.

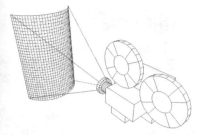

Figure 11-21: Cylindrical projections allow you to wrap your texture around a single axis.

Spherical

Spherical projections are similar to Cylindrical projections; however, where Cylindrical projections allow the texture to wrap around *one* axis, Spherical projections allow it to wrap around *two*. Think of a map of the world wrapping around a ball to create the appearance of planet Earth. The texture is wrapping around the object's longitude and latitude.

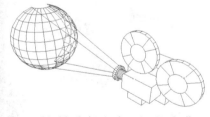

Figure 11-22: Spherical projections allow you to wrap your texture around two axes.

Cubic

Cubic projections are similar to Spherical projections; however, where Spherical projections allow the texture to wrap around *two* axes, Cubic projections allow the texture to wrap around *three* axes. Think of a cardboard box or a wooden crate. You can project the same image onto all sides of the box. If you want to add variation, you can

simply add a second Image Map layer and use a Planar projection to add a different image to one or more of the sides of your object.

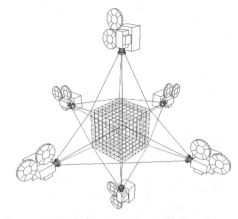

Figure 11-23: Cubic projections allow you to project a single image around all three axes.

Front

Front projection is a special type of Planar projection. The virtual projector is placed directly in front of the camera within Layout and casts its image onto the specified surface in front of it. This is often used for in-camera compositing. For example, by placing simple geometry in your scene and shining a front projected image of your real-world background footage onto it, you give the impression that your 3D objects are integrated with items in the real world. A UFO can emerge from behind a real building, or a 3D car can cast a shadow onto the real ground.

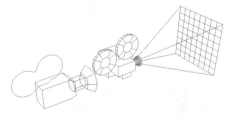

Figure 11-24: Front projections allow you to position a virtual projector directly in front of the camera in Layout.

Standard Projection Options

Each Standard projection offers a number of options that allow you to customize how the image is mapped onto the object's surface. Many of these options exist for each of the projection types. Rather than repeat them for each type, I'll simply describe the common features here.

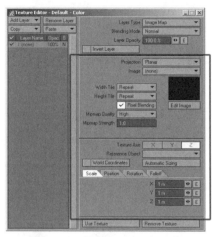

Figure 11-25: The Standard projection types offer a variety of ways to customize how the image is cast onto your object's surface.

Image Pop-up Menu

This pop-up menu allows you to choose any image that has been loaded into the program. You can also load an image by

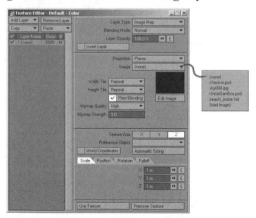

Figure 11-26: The Image pop-up menu.

choosing the (**load image**) option from the menu.

Width/Height Tile

The Width and Height Tile options determine how the image behaves when its size is smaller than the physical area of the polygons it's being projected onto. Think of a projector that's too close to the screen. Its image won't fill the entire screen area. The settings for Width Tile and Height Tile determine how the unused portions of the screen are treated.

Reset

The Reset option causes the image to be placed on the surface like a decal. When the image comes to an end at the top, bottom, left, and right, the underlying texture (or base surface color if there is no other texture) will be seen.

Figure 11-27: The Reset Tile option places a single copy of your image on your surface.

Repeat

Repeat is the default setting for Width Tile and Height Tile. It causes a new copy of the image to be placed right after the old one, which means the image will tile across the surface, allowing you to use a small, seamless image to lay down a large, complex area of texture. You can quickly create repeating floor patterns, wallpaper, fabric, brick, etc. Then you can also overlay this with a procedural texture to add natural variation and disguise the obvious repeating pattern.

Figure 11-28: The Repeat Tile option (set here along the Width) places consecutive copies of the image across your surface.

Mirror

The Mirror option is similar to Repeat; however, once the image repeats, it will also be flipped, creating a mirror image. Since the pixels at the edge of the image will perfectly line up, it can be used to create a "poor man's" seamless image.

Figure 11-29: The Mirror Tile option places consecutive copies of the image, flipping each to create a mirrored image effect. Compare the effect of the Mirror tiled image seen on the right with the Repeat tiled image on the left.

Edge

The Edge option will cause the pixels at the edge of the image to be repeated across the rest of the surface. It may seem useless at first, but imagine that you want to create something like the French flag. Rather than creating an image that covers the entire surface area of your flag, you could create one that's the exact width but only a single pixel high. The edges would then stretch out to create color over the entire surface. This allows you to use a smaller image, thereby conserving memory.

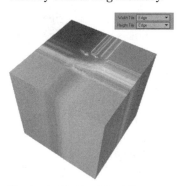

Figure 11-30: The Edge Tile option repeats the color of the pixels at the edge of each side of the image across your surface.

Pixel Blending

Pixel Blending allows LightWave to smooth pixels together when the camera gets close to the image. If you turn this off, your textures will be pixelated when the camera gets too close to them. Turning on Pixel Blending is similar to setting Photoshop's image resizing to Bicubic or Bilinear. It allows the image to appear smoother when it's enlarged.

PIXEL BLENDING OFF   PIXEL BLENDING ON

Figure 11-31: Pixel Blending allows LightWave to smooth textures that get close to the camera.

Mipmap Quality/Mipmap Strength

Mipmap is a type of filter that's designed to reduce image graininess as your camera moves away from an object by adding a slight blur to it. In many cases it can filter out noise and give you cleaner renders with lower levels of antialiasing. You can set the Mipmap Quality option to Off, High, or Low. When it's set to High or Low, you can adjust the overall strength of the filter with the value in the Mipmap Strength field.

Mipmapping can be a mixed blessing. In some cases it can eliminate the need for extra antialiasing to smooth out noisy textures. In other cases it can blur out the subtle details. On more than one occasion

THE ORIGINAL FRAME SIZE SHOWS HOW FAR THE OBJECT IS FROM THE CAMERA

I've traced texture problems back to Mipmap, especially with ZBrush-generated normal and displacement maps.

Mipmap is turned on by default. If you find that your textures lack the detail you know you've added, try turning this setting off. You can disable it on a texture-by-texture basis within the Texture Editor. You can also turn it off for all textures by changing the Mipmap settings in the Image Editor.

Image Preview/Edit Image

When you're using an Image Map, you will be presented with a small thumbnail picture of that image. This gives you a visual indication of the image you're working with. Directly below this image is the Edit Image button. Clicking on it will open the Image Editor window, where you can perform a number of adjustments.

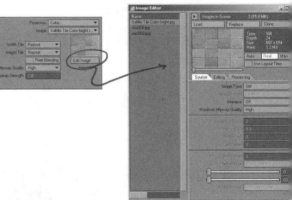

Figure 11-33: The Image Editor window.

Texture Axis

Most of the Standard projections give you the ability to define a texture axis. For Planar projections, this allows you to determine the direction the virtual projector is pointing. For Cylindrical and Spherical projections, it allows you to determine which axis the texture should

MIPMAP OFF   MIPMAP ON (HIGH)

Figure 11-32: Mipmap adds a slight blur to objects as they move away from the camera.

be wrapped around. Note that the Cubic projection doesn't allow you to define a texture axis because by its very nature it projects along all three axes at the same time. Similarly, the axis of a Front projection is automatically determined by the direction of the camera.

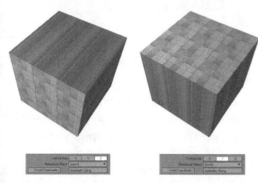

Figure 11-34: The Texture Axis buttons determine which direction a Standard projector is facing and what axis the texture should wrap around.

Reference Object/Camera Pop-up Menu

In order to help you position textures on your object, you can assign an object from the Reference Object pop-up menu. This will typically be a Null object, although any object in your scene will work. Moving the reference object will move the texture on your surface. Likewise, rotating or scaling

the reference object will rotate or resize the texture. This gives you a very interactive method for placing Standard projection textures on your object. When you're using a Front projection type, the Reference Object pop-up menu changes to a Reference Camera menu. This allows you to select the camera you would like to use for your Front projections.

World Coordinates

As I mentioned earlier, the virtual projectors for Standard projection types are fixed in space. If you position a projector in Modeler and then move your object, the texture won't move with it. However, when you bring the object into Layout (or simply apply a texture therein), the projector becomes linked to the object, allowing you to move, rotate, and scale the object with the texture following suit.

By default, projectors in Layout are linked to their objects. However, you can *unlink* them by clicking on the World Coordinates check box. This will give you the same effect as if you were moving the object in Modeler. The projector (and the image it's shining) will stay in place and the model will be able to move around it.

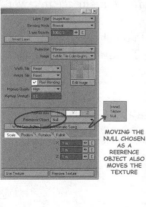

Figure 11-35: The Reference Object menu lets you choose which object will be used to aid in the position/rotation/scale of textures. For Front projections, you can select a camera from this menu.

MOVING THE NULL CHOSEN AS A REFERENCE OBJECT ALSO MOVES THE TEXTURE

Figure 11-36: The World Coordinates option allows you to unlink Standard texture projectors from their objects, thereby recreating the effect of a projector in Modeler.

Why would you ever want to do this? In most cases you wouldn't. But by disconnecting the texture from the object you can create a number of special effects. The immediate impression this gives is that the object is moving *through* its texture. It's as if the texture were a part of the environment. This is often used to create fake volumetric lights. (See Chapter 10 for more on this.)

Automatic Sizing

Automatic Sizing allows you to automatically adjust the position, rotation, and scale of your virtual projector so that the image it's casting will fit perfectly on the polygons of your surface. It does so by looking at the outside perimeter of all the polygons that share the surface in question and then positioning the projector and sizing the image to fit accordingly. In most cases, if you set up your image properly, you only need to choose a Texture Axis option and click the Automatic Sizing button to get your textures projected properly onto your object.

Width/Height Wrap Amount

Cylindrical and Spherical projections wrap their image around your object. When you choose either of these projection types, you will be given the option to specify how many times the image should repeat around the texture axis. The default is 1.0, which will wrap the image completely around the surface one time. Increasing this number allows you to repeat the image to create interesting effects. You can enter a negative number to flip the direction in which the texture is mapped.

You may think that setting this value to a fraction, such as 0.5, will only cause the texture to wrap halfway around the object; however, this is not the case. There is no way to limit the amount of wrapping within the Cylindrical or Spherical settings. If you want to adjust how far the texture will wrap, you must limit your surface to fewer polys, change the canvas size of the image in a program like Photoshop, or use an Alpha layer in the Texture Editor to mask portions of the image.

Figure 11-37: The Automatic Sizing button adjusts the position and size of a Standard projector to fit the surface onto which the texture is applied.

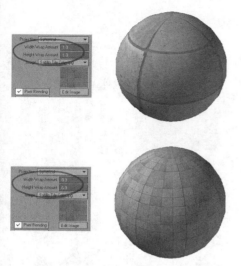

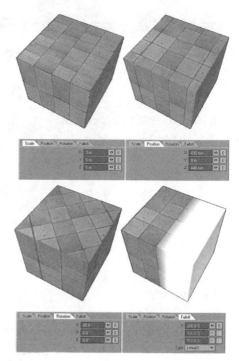

Figure 11-38: The Width/Height Wrap Amount settings determine how many times a texture is repeated when it's wrapped around a cylindrical or spherical object.

Figure 11-39: The Scale, Position, Rotation, and Falloff tabs let you change the size, location, orientation, and visibility of the texture.

Scale/Position/Rotation/Falloff

The first three tabs at the bottom of the Texture Editor allow you to change the size, position, and direction that the virtual projector is pointing. In many cases, you can simply press the Automatic Sizing button and never need to make adjustments to these settings. In other cases, you can set up a reference object (such as a Null object in Layout) and adjust these values interactively. But if you want to manually adjust these settings, you can do so here.

The last tab, called Falloff, provides several methods for fading your textures. The options for Falloff Type include Cubic, Spherical, and Linear along the X, Y, or Z.

The values can be keyframed by setting up an envelope in Layout. You can use numbers higher than 100%, and you can also use negative numbers to reverse the direction of the fade.

I typically don't use the Falloff settings to blend my surfaces together as the Falloff options don't have a whole lot of control over where or how soft the fade is. In most cases, you can achieve better texture compositing by painting a black and white image and applying it to a layer with an Alpha blending mode.

Creating a Standard Projection

The process of creating and applying a Standard projection map is fairly straightforward. Let's take a look at how to texture the floor of the house we built in Chapter 9. Since the floor is flat, we can use a Planar projection.

1. The first step is to zoom in to the polys of the surface that you'll be applying the texture to. This is best done with the Statistics panel in Modeler. Then you should maximize the viewport that faces the polygons. In the case of the Floor, it would be the **Top** viewport. Finally, press <A> to fill the viewport with the selected polys.

2. The next step is to capture an image of the selected polys. The easiest way to do this is to perform a screen capture. It sounds low-tech, but I do this all the time and it works great for most objects. (Of course, it helps if your screen is set to a larger size such as 1280 x 1024 or higher.)

3. Once you've done a screen capture of the polys in Modeler, you simply paste the image into your paint program. In Photoshop, if you perform a screen capture and then press <Ctrl>+<n> to create a new document, the size of the document will automatically match that of the screen capture.

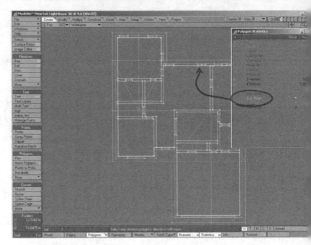

Figure 11-40: To create a texture for the floor of the house yo built in Chapter 9, you would begin by selecting all the polys with the same surface, then maximize the viewport that best faces them and fit them to the size of the viewport.

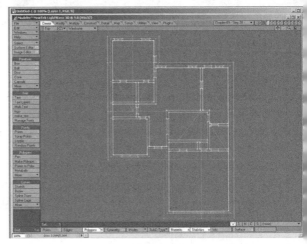

Figure 11-41: Once the polygons for your surface are maximized in the viewport, press the Print Screen button on your keyboard to capture the image to your computer's memory. Then paste the screen capture into your paint program.

4. After the image has been placed in your paint program, you need to crop it to the outside boundary of the polygons onto which the image will be applied. This is an important step, so don't overlook it. Cropping to the boundaries of your surface allows you to simply click on the Automatic Sizing button in the Texture Editor and never have to worry about getting the image to fit properly on your polygons.

Choose the appropriate axis (for the Floor polys this would be the Y-axis), then simply press the **Automatic Sizing** button. The image will be applied to your object and will fit precisely.

From here you can apply other maps (such as bump maps or diffuse maps) to increase the surface's realism. You can also add procedurals and gradients to help add surface variations.

> **Note**
>
> The method described here allows you to paint different textures on specific areas of your map. But if you simply want to apply a repeating image across your entire surface (such as wood panel or ceramic tile), you don't need to go through this process. Simply open the Texture Editor and apply the tileable image to the various channels of your surface. You can adjust the size and Width/Height Tile settings to determine how your image repeats across the entire surface.

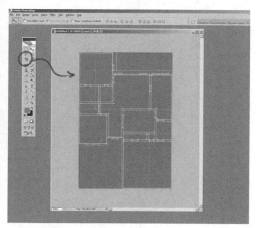

Figure 11-42: Crop the image to the boundaries of the surface you'll be texturing.

5. Once the image has been cropped, you're free to paint on it. You can add tile floors in some rooms and carpet in others. You have complete freedom to use whatever photos and custom painted imagery you like.

6. Once you're finished, you can save the image and load it into LightWave. Open the Surface Editor, click on the **Floors** surface, and add a new Image Map texture to one of the primary attribute channels (Color, Diffuse, Specular, etc.).

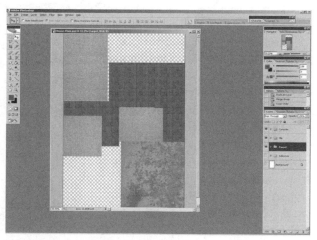

Figure 11-43: Paint the texture using any combination of photos and hand-painted imagery. Then save the file without the screen capture showing.

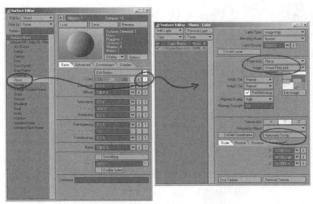

Figure 11-44: Open the Surface Editor in LightWave and open the Texture Editor for one of the primary attribute channels (such as the Color channel). Make sure Projection is set to Planar. Select the appropriate axis (here it would be the Y-axis) and press the Automatic Sizing button.

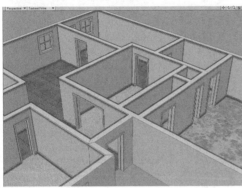

Figure 11-45: The texture will be applied to your object and visible in any textured viewport.

UV Projection Options

When you want your polys to have a presence in the UV world, you must transfer them there by creating a new UV map or adding them to an existing UV map. You create a new UV map by selecting your polys (if no polys are selected, then all of them will be added to the UV map) and choosing **Map | Texture | New UV Map** or clicking the **T** button in the lower-right corner of Modeler's interface and choosing **(new)** from the pop-up menu to its right. Doing so opens the Create UV Texture Map window.

When you create a new UV map, you are creating a parallel 2D world that will exist alongside the 3D

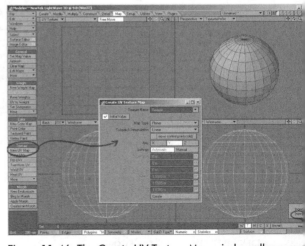

Figure 11-46: The Create UV Texture Map window allows you to create a new UV space and add polygons to it. It can be called up from the New UV Map button or by choosing (new) from the UV Texture pop-up menu in the lower-right corner of the interface.

world. You can define a number of properties for the UV world and choose settings for how objects are brought into it with the options found in the Create UV Texture Map window. In this section we'll take a look at each of these options in detail.

Texture Name

Since each UV map is a unique 2D space, you need a way to distinguish between them. The best way to do this is to give each one a descriptive name. You can call your UV space anything you want. The default name is "Texture," but it's often helpful to call it something that matches the geometry you'll be putting into it, such as "Zorgon's Head" or "Battle Cruiser Tail Fin." If you'd like to add geometry to an existing UV space (rather than typing in a new UV name), you can click on the arrow button to the right of the Texture Name field and select it from the list.

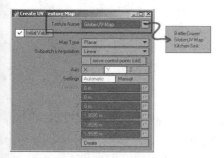

Figure 11-47: The Texture Name option lets you assign a name for your new UV map. The arrow button to its right lets you choose an existing UV map to add geometry to.

Initial Value

In most cases you'll want to create a UV space and immediately transfer polygons into it. But should you ever desire to create a UV space and then transfer polygons into it later, you can do so. The Initial Value check box allows you to do this. When the box is checked, Modeler will create the UV

space and transfer any selected polygons into it. If you uncheck this box, a blank UV space will be created, allowing you to add polygons to it later.

Figure 11-48: The Initial Value option lets you add geometry to the new UV space. When this is unchecked, the UV space will be created but no geometry will be added to it.

Map Type

When you click the Map Type pop-up menu, you'll see a list of familiar options. The options here include Planar, Cylindrical, Spherical, and Atlas. It may be tempting to think of these as UV counterparts to the Standard projection types; however, that would not be accurate. The options in the Map Type menu do not define how the virtual projector casts its image onto your object. Rather, they determine how the object will be *unwrapped* (if at all) when it is transported into the 2D UV space.

It's important to understand that the Map Type option does not describe the type of UV map. There are no different types of UVs like there are different types of Standard projections. UV space is UV space. The Map Type simply describes how the currently selected geometry will enter that space. You can change the Map Type at any time and it will not affect the existing geometry in the UV; it will only affect how new geometry is added to it. You can use a Cylindrical map to add geometry, then switch to an Atlas map and add more geometry. You choose the Map Type that's most

461

appropriate for the type of geometry you're adding to the UV at that time.

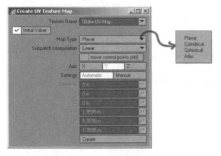

Figure 11-49: The Map Type options determine how an object will be unwrapped when it's brought into the UV space.

Planar

The Planar map type doesn't unwrap your object. Rather, it captures the shape of the geometry by looking at it from one of the three standard axes (X, Y, or Z). This is typically useful for capturing flat surfaces that have not been rotated to odd angles in space. Keep in mind that once an object has been captured, it can be transformed (moved, rotated, scaled, etc.) in the regular 3D world and it will not affect the polys in the UV world. For this reason, it can be helpful to create Planar UVs early on in the modeling process before modifying your geometry.

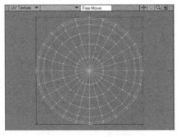

Figure 11-50: The Planar map type does not unwrap your object but rather captures its shape from one of the standard axes.

Cylindrical

The Cylindrical map type unwraps your geometry along a specific axis. If you think of how a Standard Cylindrical projection wraps your texture around an axis, just think of a UV Cylindrical map as the reverse process. It *unwraps* around that axis. Any polys that are not in line with the unwrapping axis will be distorted, squashed, or simply appear as a thin polyline in the UV space.

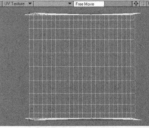

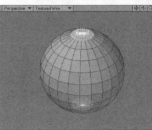

Figure 11-51: The Cylindrical map type unwraps your object around a specific axis. Note that polys that move away from the selected axis (such as the polys shown selected here) appear squashed in the UV space.

For example, if you were to use a Cylindrical map type to unwrap a soda can, the sides would unwrap just fine, but the geometry at the top and bottom of the can would seem to disappear. In reality, they're transferred into the UV space, but they will appear as a single polyline. To properly map these polys, you would need to clear them from the map (using the **Map | General | Clear Map** tool) and add them back into the UV map using the Planar mapping option. Remember that the Map Type settings are simply a means for transferring polys into your

UV space. You can use more than one map type to add polys to a single UV.

Spherical

The Spherical map type is similar to the Cylindrical option. It unwraps your object along a given axis, but it accounts for the fact that some polys will bend away from the specified axis and will attempt to leave room for them in the UV space.

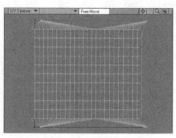

Figure 11-52: The Spherical map type unwraps your object around a specific axis, but also accounts for geometry running perpendicular to that axis. Notice how the top and bottom of the sphere are no longer squashed in the UV space as they were when using a Cylindrical map type.

Atlas

You'll notice that there isn't a Cubic map type for UVs. Rather, UVs have the cryptic-sounding "Atlas" type. This map type attempts to capture flat areas within your model and group them together in the UV space. These groups are often referred to as "islands." The Atlas map type will create multiple islands, and the results will look as though you had added multiple Planar UVs to a single map.

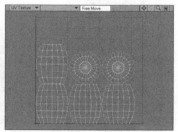

Figure 11-53: The Atlas map type unwraps your object by capturing large flat areas and laying them out within the UV space.

Atlas maps are a good choice for quick, brainless unwrapping. But the highly discontinuous nature of Atlas UVs can make them difficult to paint on, which usually defeats their purpose. I typically use Atlas maps when creating UVs for surface baking (in which the software "paints" your surface details to an image map) or occasionally for use in external 3D paint programs like ZBrush.

Planar, Cylindrical, and Spherical UV Map Type Options

Whether you're using a Planar, Cylindrical, or Spherical map type, the options given to you are the same. Let's take a look at the features available for these types of maps.

Move Control Points (Old)

In previous versions of LightWave, subpatch polygons reverted to standard polygons when they entered UV space. This resulted in the polygons being stretched in the UV space, which caused distorted textures back in the 3D world. To counteract this, you could tell Modeler to move the control points of the mesh in the UV space so that the shape was more consistent with the subpatched polys in the 3D world.

With the introduction of LightWave 8.2, we gained new Subpatch Interpolation options (described later in this section). These options overcame many of the problems inherent with using UVs with subpatch objects. The option to move control points is still there, but it is noted as "old" since there are more modern solutions to the problem.

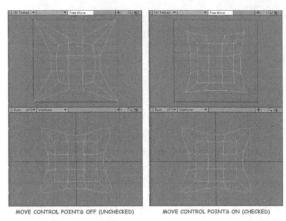

MOVE CONTROL POINTS OFF (UNCHECKED)   MOVE CONTROL POINTS ON (CHECKED)

Figure 11-54: The Move Control Points (old) option was a method used for dealing with subpatch geometry prior to the introduction of the Subpatch Interpolation options in LightWave 8.2. It attempted to more closely match the linear UV geometry to the subpatch shape.

Axis

The Axis setting allows you to determine how the polygons are transported to the UV space. In a Planar map, it will simply capture the polys facing the specified axis. In a Cylindrical or Spherical map, it will determine the axis around which the object will be unwrapped.

Figure 11-55: The Axis setting determines how an object is captured (with Planar UVs) or the axis it is unwrapped around (with Cylindrical and Spherical UVs).

Settings: Automatic/Manual

When you transfer polygons into UV space, you can let Modeler determine how the polygons should be laid out, or you can manually determine the

layout. In most cases, you can simply leave this set to Automatic and you'll get great results. This is especially true with Cylindrical and Spherical map types. However, for Planar mapping, you may wish to set this to Manual.

With a Planar map type, choosing Automatic will cause Modeler to fit the polygons into the entire UV space. This often results in your polygons losing their aspect ratio. For example, a long rectangle will be stretched into a perfect square. Changing Settings to Manual will allow the polygons to retain their aspect ratio.

When you change Settings to Manual, you'll find that the Center and Size fields become active. The Center options determine where the polygons will be placed within the UV space. The Size options determine the size of the UV space. Note that the Size options do *not* change the size of the polygons. They change the size of the UV space. If you have a box that is 1 meter and you enter 10 m for the X, Y, and Z Size settings, the UV space will be 10 meters square and your 1-meter box will fit

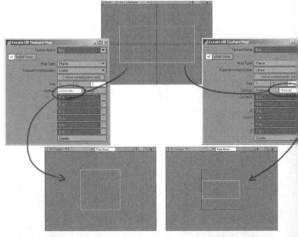

Figure 11-56: The Automatic and Manual settings determine how the polygons fit within the UV space. Choosing Manual works best for Planar maps as it helps maintain polygon aspe ratios.

in one-tenth of the available space. If you have a 1-meter box and you enter 100 mm for the X, Y, and Z Size settings, the UV space will be 100 mm square and your 1-meter box will be 10 times the size of the available space.

When I'm creating Planar UV maps, I typically switch to Manual mode and then enter 1 m for all the Center and Size fields. Then I hit the Create button to create the UV space and resize my polygons to fit accordingly.

Atlas UV Map Type Options

When you choose to use an Atlas map type, you will be presented with an entirely different set of options than are available for Planar, Cylindrical, or Spherical UV map types. In this section we'll take a look at the Atlas UV map options.

Figure 11-57: The Atlas map type offers a different set of options than those available for Planar, Cylindrical, or Spherical maps.

Relative Gap Size

When you create an Atlas map, Modeler will break the polys into distinct groups (called "islands"). The amount of space between each island can be adjusted with the Relative Gap Size setting. The default is 20%, which tends to work well, but if you're trying to cram a lot of polys into a single UV space, this may not give you much room. Therefore, you may opt to

lower this setting in order to maximize the space better.

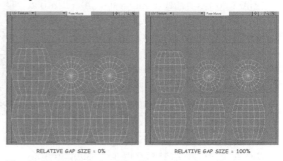

RELATIVE GAP SIZE = 0%   RELATIVE GAP SIZE = 100%

Figure 11-58: Relative Gap Size determines the amount of space between UV islands when using the Atlas map type.

Segment by Surface/Segment by Part

If you've "grouped" polygons together by assigning them surface names or if you've created distinct parts (using the **View | Selection Sets | Create Part** tool), you can tell the Atlas map to create islands for the polygons within these groups. This gives you a bit more control over how the Atlas map type transfers your geometry into the UV space.

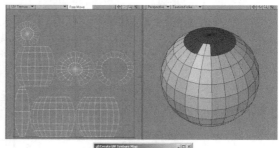
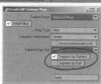

Figure 11-59: The Segment by Surface/Segment by Part settings attempt to create islands based on the boundaries between surfaces or parts.

Subpatch Interpolation

When you convert a polygonal object into a subpatch, its vertices will pull toward each other. (Subpatches are discussed in more detail in Chapter 15.) In LightWave 8.0 and earlier, subpatch objects were depicted as unsubpatched objects in UV space. This often resulted in stretching, distortion, and texture inaccuracies, especially when there was a large difference between the look of the subpatch object and its non-subpatched polygonal "cage."

When LightWave 8.2 was released, Modeler gained the ability to depict subpatches in UV space. This helped resolve many longstanding UV problems, but it also created an interesting dilemma. Since subpatches pull their open edges inward, how should discontinuous polygons be handled? After all, most of the edges are only discontinuous in the UV space, not in the 3D world. To remedy this, a new set of options was introduced. Now when you create a UV for a subpatch object, you have the ability to define how the edges should be handled. This is done by choosing a mode from the Subpatch Interpolation pop-up menu in the Create UV Texture Map window. In this section we'll take a look at the different interpolation options available to you.

Linear

In Linear mode, all polygons in the UV space are treated as standard polygons, regardless of whether or not they are subpatches in the 3D world. This is the way UV space worked prior to LightWave 8.2. If you're creating a UV map for a non-subpatched object, you should choose this mode. If you're creating a UV map for a subpatch object, you should try one of the four remaining options.

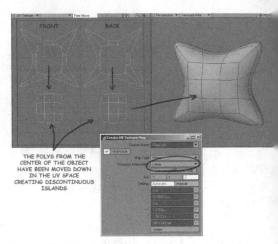

THE POLYS FROM THE CENTER OF THE OBJECT HAVE BEEN MOVED DOWN IN THE UV SPACE CREATING DISCONTINUOUS ISLANDS

Figure 11-60: When you use the Linear interpolation, subpatch polygons will be viewed as regular polys in the UV space. Notice how the polygons in the UV Texture viewport differ greatly from those in the Perspective viewport.

Subpatch

In Subpatch mode, any subpatched polygons in the 3D world will be represented as subpatches in the UV world. Traditional polygons, however, will appear as standard polygons in the UV space. If you toggle subpatches on or off in the 3D world, they will update in the UV world as well.

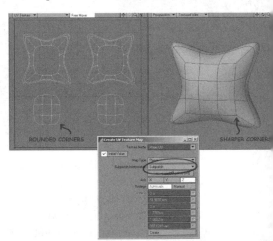

ROUNDED CORNERS   SHARPER CORNERS

Figure 11-61: When you use Subpatch interpolation, a subpatch polygons will be treated as subpatches. Notice how the edges of the discontinuous islands are rounded. They do not match the sharper corners of the continuo polys in the Perspective viewport.

This mode works quite well; however, the edges of discontinuous polygon islands will stretch inward, which is contrary to how they appear in the 3D world. This can lead to texturing inaccuracies on discontinuous polygon islands.

Linear Corners

Linear Corners mode provides a hybrid between Linear and Subpatch modes. It retains subpatches, but the corners of discontinuous polygon islands will be sharp, as if they used the Linear mode (or were not subpatched).

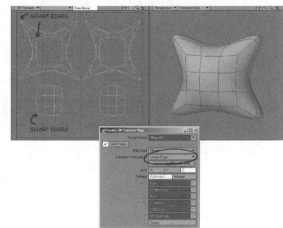

Figure 11-63: When you use Linear Edges interpolation, subpatch polygons will be treated as subpatches, but the edges of the polygon islands in the UV space will be sharp.

Across Discontinuous Edges

The Across Discontinuous Edges mode provides what is perhaps the best interpolation for subpatch objects. Subpatch polygons are depicted as subpatches (just as is the case in the Subpatch mode), but the edges of discontinuous islands will maintain a continuous appearance. This

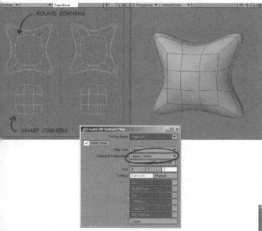

Figure 11-62: When you use Linear Corners interpolation, all subpatch polygons will be treated as subpatches, but the corners of discontinuous polys will be sharp.

Linear Edges

Like Linear Corners, Linear Edges mode provides a hybrid between Linear and Subpatch modes. It retains subpatches, but the edges around islands in the UV space will be treated as if they were not subpatched.

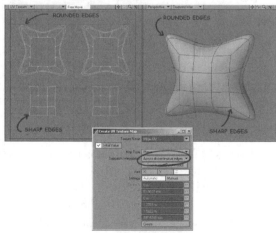

Figure 11-64: When you use Across Discontinuous Edges interpolation, subpatch polygons will be depicted as subpatches, but the edges of UV islands will not change in the UV space. Notice how the polygons in the UV Texture viewport closely match those in the Perspective viewport.

makes them look more like their counterparts in the 3D world.

With five different modes, you may feel a little overwhelmed. If I can give you a rule of thumb, it would be this: For non-subpatched objects, use Linear interpolation. For subpatched objects (or combinations of subpatch and non-subpatch objects), use the Across Discontinuous Edges option. This ought to suffice for the majority of circumstances. But don't rule out the other modes. They are there should you ever find that you need them.

Changing the Subpatch Interpolation Method

If you ever need to change your Subpatch Interpolation mode, you can do so by choosing **Windows | Vertex Maps Panel**. Toggle open the Texture option by clicking on the white triangle and you will see a list of available UV maps. You will also see a Sel Interpolation column. Click on this column

to the right of the texture map you'd like to change and select a new interpolation type. If you have the UV Texture viewport visible, you'll see the change take place immediately.

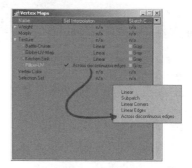

Figure 11-65: You can change the Subpatch Interpolation mode for a UV map via the Vertex Maps panel.

Note

Right-clicking on a map listed in the Vertex Maps panel gives you the ability to rename, delete, copy, and set the value for your UV map.

Creating a UV Projection

In the previous section we examined the options available for creating a new UV space and the different methods for adding geometry to it. Once all the geometry has been added to a UV, you must capture the UV space, put it into your paint program, and create your textures. We'll go over this process in detail later in the chapter. If you'd like to experiment with UVs now, you can follow the process described here.

The process for capturing the UV space is similar to that used when capturing polys for Standard projections. Maximize the UV Texture viewport, turn on the grid, and press <a> to fit the UV space in the viewport. Then press the Print Screen

button on your keyboard and paste the image into your paint program.

You can also use the **File | Export | Export Encapsulated PostScript** option to save your geometry in a resolution-independent EPS file. (This technique will be covered in more detail in the tutorial at the end of this chapter.)

Once you've finished painting your texture, you can load it into LightWave. Add an Image Map layer in the channel of your choice (Color, Diffuse, etc.) and set Projection to UV. Then select the UV space you created earlier. Finally, choose the image you loaded. You will see the texture applied to your object.

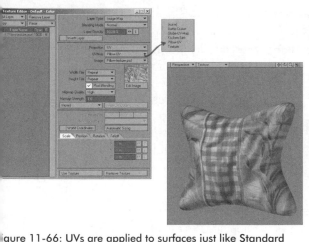

You'll notice that there is no Automatic Sizing button for UVs. In addition, the Scale, Position, Rotation, and Falloff tabs are disabled for UV projections. Remember that the virtual projector for a UV cannot be moved, sized, or rotated. It is locked in place (see Figure 11-9 for a reminder). Therefore, these options are unnecessary for UV projections.

Figure 11-66: UVs are applied to surfaces just like Standard Projections. The only difference is that you must tell LightWave which UV space to project the image into.

UV Tools

LightWave's Modeler offers a wealth of tools to help you create and edit UV maps. In addition to the native tools, there are many advanced plug-ins that make working with UVs a breeze. We'll explore the most essential UV tools and plug-ins in this section.

New UV Map/Make UVs

The **Map | Texture | New UV Map** tool brings up the Create UV Texture Map window we examined earlier. From this window you can create a new UV space and

fill it with the geometry in your foreground layers. If you deselect the Initial Value button, you can create a blank UV space without any geometry.

If you opt to create a blank UV space, you can use the **Map | Texture | Make UVs** tool to fill it with geometry. The Make UVs tool opens the Assign UV Coordinates window, which offers nearly all of the same options that are found in the Create UV Texture Map window. The only difference is the absence of the Initial Value button.

You can use either of these tools to create UV spaces and to add geometry to existing UV spaces. There's virtually no difference between them other than the ability to create a blank UV space with the New UV Map tool.

Clear Map

Thus far we've spent a lot of time talking about how to get geometry *into* UV space. But what if you want to remove it? The **Map | General | Clear Map** tool allows

NEW UV MAP   MAKE UVs

Figure 11-67: The New UV Map and Make UVs tools allow you to create UV spaces and add geometry to them.

you to remove polygons from the currently selected UV space. Simply select the polygons you wish to eliminate and then hit the Clear Map button. They will disappear from the UV space (but they will remain intact in the 3D world).

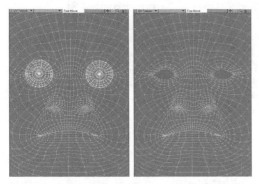

Figure 11-68: The Clear Map tool lets you remove geometry from the UV space. Here, the eyeball geometry (shown selected on the left) has been removed from the UV (as seen on the right).

It's important to note that UV maps are actually vertex maps. While you typically associate UVs with polygons, Modeler is keeping track of the actual vertices. Attempting to clear a polygon that shares points with other polygons in the 3D world will clear all of the polygons connected to it.

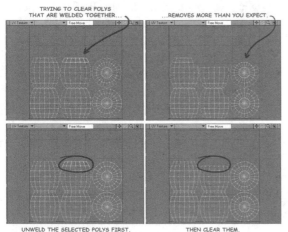

Figure 11-69: In order to remove only the selected polygons, you should run the Unweld command before clicking on the Clear Map button.

In order to safely remove only the polys you want, you should first unweld their vertices by clicking on the **Detail | Points | Unweld** button or simply pressing the **<Ctrl>+<u>** keyboard shortcut. Unwelding ensures that each polygon is treated as a distinct object. As such, it does not share points with other polygons and can be cleared without affecting any of the polys around it.

Flip UVs

Flipping UVs can be an efficient way to texture symmetrical geometry. For example, by flipping one half of a symmetrical object in the UV space and overlaying the UV islands, your image will be applied to both sides of the symmetrical object at once. The **Map | Texture | Flip UVs** tool allows you to do this.

Running the Flip UVs tool brings up a window that asks which direction you'd like to flip the polygons along. You can choose U (Horizontal), V (Vertical), or both (Horizontal and Vertical).

When using this tool, it's important to remember that Modeler will attempt to connect discontinuous polygons. This often results in polygons located in one part of the UV space being connected to others in a completely different part of the UV space. The result often looks like a bad stitching job and can cause shock and horror when you first see it. But don't panic! There's a simple solution.

As I noted earlier, UV maps are simply vertex maps. If you unweld the points of your object, each polygon will be treated as a distinct object and Modeler will not attempt to stitch them together in the UV space. Therefore, before using the Flip UVs tool, you should select all of the polygons that you want to flip and run the **Detail | Points**

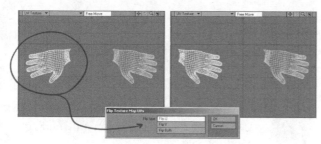

Figure 11-70: The Flip UVs tool lets you flip UV geometry in the UV space. Once flipped, the UV islands can be positioned on top of one another. This will cause both objects to receive the same texture, allowing you to save time when texturing.

| **Unweld** tool. If you're working with a subpatch object, it will appear to go haywire in the 3D world, but don't worry — it's only temporary.

Once you've flipped the polys, you can merge the points by pressing <**m**> or clicking on the **Detail | Points | Merge Points** tool using the Automatic settings. Your points will be reconnected and your object in the 3D world should look just as it did before.

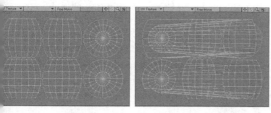

Figure 11-71: Be sure to unweld the points of the polygons you want to flip. Otherwise, Modeler will try to keep them continuous and you'll end up with a jumbled mess like the one seen on the right.

Transform UV

The **Map | Texture | Transform UV** tool allows you to move, size, and rotate the polygons in your UV space. You can easily use the traditional Move, Rotate, and Scale tools in the UV space to accomplish the same thing, but the Transform UV tool allows you to do so with a bit more precision and it can perform all these operations at once.

When you click on the Transform UV button, the Transform UV Values window appears. You can activate any of the options by clicking on their buttons on the left side of the window. Doing so will make the fields for that option active, allowing you to change them. You'll notice at the bottom of the window a Center option. This allows you to change the center of the scale and rotate transformations.

I typically use the Transform UV tool in conjunction with Pixologic's ZBrush. ZBrush doesn't allow your object to have more than one UV map; however, you can work around this by placing additional geometry outside the standard UV space. Using the Transform UV tool, you can easily offset your geometry by 100%, 200%, 300%, and so on. This ensures that your geometry will be placed one full UV space

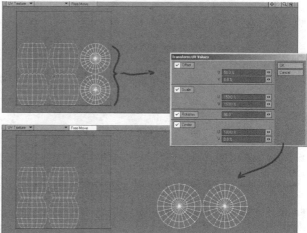

Figure 11-72: The Transform UV tool lets you move, rotate, and scale polygons in the UV space at the same time.

471

outside of the main UV boundary and will work properly in ZBrush. (If you'd like more information on using LightWave with ZBrush, please see my LightWave-ZPipeline Guide, which is available on the Pixologic website.)

Note

As was the case with the Flip UVs tool, it's best to unweld your geometry before using the Transform UV command. This will ensure that Modeler does not attempt to connect discontinuous polys during the transformation.

Heal UV

Use the **Map | Texture | Heal UV** tool to make continuous polygons out of discontinuous polygons. This tool works by analyzing the selected polygons and trying to join their vertices to the nearest points in the UV space. There are no options for this tool. Simply select the discontinuous polygons you want to join together and run it. Since you don't have a lot of control, your results can be hit or miss. Therefore, you should always try to position the discontinuous polygons as close to one another as possible before running this tool.

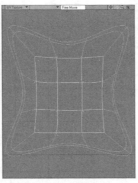

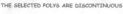
THE SELECTED POLYS ARE DISCONTINUOUS.   RUNNING HEAL UV CONNECTS THEM TO
NEARBY POLYS AND MAKES
THEM CONTINUOUS.

Figure 11-73: The Heal UV tool converts discontinuous polygons into continuous polygons by joining them with polys nearby.

UV Spider

Creating a UV map for a flat, straight line of polygons is typically not a problem. But what happens when your polygons twist or bend? If your object is made up of quads, you can use the **Map | Texture | More | UV Spider** tool to straighten out winding bands of polys.

To use the UV Spider, select two polygons running along the band you want to unwind, then run the tool. You'll be presented with the UV Spider options window.

Figure 11-74: UV Spider creates a straight sequence of polys from a winding band of quads. The options in the UV Spider window allow you to determine how the polys are unwrapped.

The first option is the Vertex Map field. You can enter a name for a new UV map or add your geometry to an existing UV map by clicking the arrow to the right of the field.

The next option is the Select Edge pop-up menu. The options are Odd, Even, or Auto. Personally, I find the terms "Odd" and "Even" too cryptic to bother with. Just make sure you select two polygons in the direction you want to unwind, and then leave this set to Auto.

Below the Select Edge menu is the Direction pop-up menu. This menu allows you to determine how the band will be oriented in the UV space. You can choose to have your bands run horizontally by choosing the U option or vertically by choosing the V option.

Below the Direction pop-up menu are four fields for the U and V Start and End. These fields allow you to limit the placement of the polygons as they're added to the UV space.

There are two basic ways to use the UV Spider. If you're running it on a single band of quads, you can simply select two or more polys in the band, run the UV Spider tool, and accept the defaults. Then you can move, size, and rotate the polys in the UV Texture viewport as necessary.

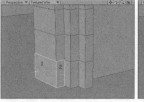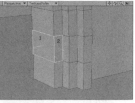

SELECT EACH SUCCESSIVE BAND IN THE SAME ORDER

Figure 11-77: Be sure to select each successive band in the same order as the previous one.

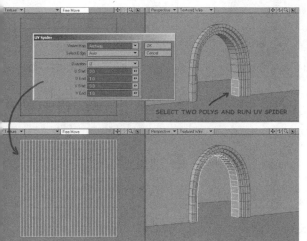

SELECT TWO POLYS AND RUN UV SPIDER

gure 11-75: To straighten a single band of quads, just select
o or more polys in the direction you want to unwrap and run
e tool with the default settings. Then adjust the size of the
lys in the UV space as necessary.

If you want to unwrap a more complicated object, however, you will need to run the tool *multiple* times, working row by row with polys *perpendicular* to the flow of your object.

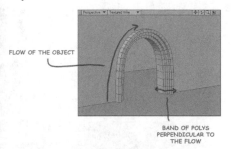

FLOW OF THE OBJECT

BAND OF POLYS
PERPENDICULAR TO
THE FLOW

Figure 11-76: To unwrap a more complicated object with multiple bands of quads, you must select bands of polys perpendicular to the flow of your object and run UV Spider on them one at a time.

You begin by selecting two polys on a row perpendicular to the flow of your object. Then run the UV Spider. Repeat this process for each successive row, making sure you select the next two polys in the same order as the first two. This will ensure that the first poly of each band will line up in the UV space.

Each time you add a new band, it will be layered on top of the previous ones. When you're finished, you will have a number of bands lying directly on top of each other. At this point you need to line up each individual band to create a sequence of polys. Unfortunately, there's no easy way to do this. You have to do it by hand.

Currently the bands fill the entire UV space. Therefore, if you divide the number of bands by the available space, you can determine how large each band needs to be. For example, in the arch seen in Figure 11-78, there are 32 bands. That means that if each band is approximately 3% of the available space, when the bands are stacked on top of one another they will almost fill the entire UV space.

At this point you simply need to select each band and move it on top of the previous one. The first band should stay fixed in place. The second will be stacked on top of it, and the third on top of the second. When you're finished, the entire UV space will be

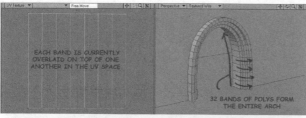

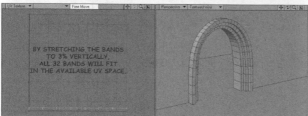

Figure 11-78: Scale the bands so that they can fit in the available space when stacked on top of one another.

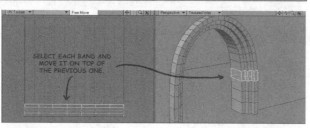

Figure 11-79: Select each band and move it on top of the previous ones until the entire UV space is filled.

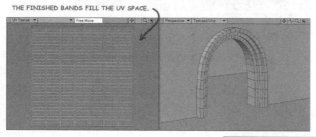

filled with bands of polys as shown in Figure 11-79.

You can now paint a texture for your UV geometry as described earlier. In Figure 11-80, a photo is used to make the arch appear to be fashioned out of bricks. The geometry was stretched in the UV Texture viewport and moved so that the geometry would line up with the mortar of the bricks in the image.

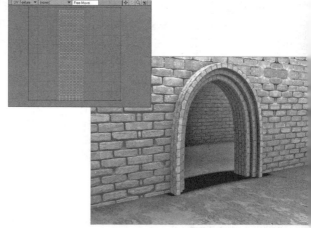

Figure 11-80: When you apply a texture to your UV, the imagery will now follow the flow of your object. Notice how the bricks follow the flow of the arch.

The "Nifty" PLG Plug-ins

LightWave's native UV tools typically require a lot of work to get the job done. Just look at how much work it took to unwrap the archway with the UV Spider. And once your objects are unwrapped, the native tools don't offer any way to correct for mesh distortion or make the best use of the available UV space.

Fortunately, there are a handful of plug-ins that resolve the shortcomings in the native tool set and make UV creation a breeze. These plug-ins rival the tools found in programs like Maya, XSI, and Modo. Best of all, they're free. Once you start using them, you'll probably never go back to the default UV creation tools again.

The PLG UV plug-ins can be downloaded directly from http://home-page2 .nifty.com/nif-hp/index2_english.htm. You can also find a copy of them on the DVD that came with this book. In this section we'll take a look at four of the PLG UV tools and the options available in each. We'll be using these tools throughout the tutorial at the end of this chapter, so I would recommend creating buttons for them on the main interface. (See Chapter 2 for a refresher on how to do this if you've forgotten.)

Make UV Edit

The Make UV Edit plug-in is a powerful unwrapping tool that gives you complete control over the unwrapping process. This type of tool is sometimes referred to as a "pelt" mapping tool in other 3D packages.

Figure 11-81: The Make UV Edit plug-in is a powerful pelt mapping tool that gives you complete control over the unwrapping process.

The options may seem overwhelming at first, but the process is actually quite simple. You begin by entering a new name for your UV Map just as you would with Modeler's native New UV Map tool. Then you define the seams along which your object will be unwrapped by selecting a series of edges. If you click on one edge, then hold down the Ctrl key and click on another edge farther down the loop, all of the edges between the first and last will be selected. You can make multiple selections and you can select edges on any objects in the foreground layers. Once your unwrapping edges are selected, you simply press the **Make UV** button and your object will be unwrapped.

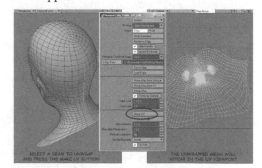

Figure 11-82: Using the Make UV Edit tool is simple. Just select an edge to unwrap along and press the Make UV button.

Selecting edges can be a bit tricky. To make things easier, you can turn off the Hide Handle option. This will place small blue dots at the center of each edge, giving you a much better idea of where you need to click in order to select the edge. Turning this option on will slow down your OpenGL display speed, so be sure to turn it off when you don't need it.

Figure 11-83: Turning off the Hide Handle option will place blue dots on each edge, indicating where you should click to select it.

If you find that you've accidentally made a mistake in your selection, you can simply hit the Undo Selection button. If you want to clear the selection altogether, you can click on the Actions pop-up menu and choose Reset.

If you'd like to select an entire edge loop, you simply select one edge and then use the Advance Edge button. The Advance Threshold Angle field can be used to help select edges that run over extreme angles or to limit the selection if you find that it's going too far. The default is 70 degrees, which works well in most cases.

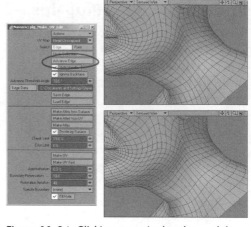

Figure 11-84: Clicking on a single edge and then clicking the Advance Edge button will select all edges in a loop as long as they don't exceed the Advance Threshold Angle setting.

Selecting an entire edge loop will cause the Make UV Edit tool to isolate the mesh enclosed by the selection when it creates UV geometry. This is a great way to section off portions of your object.

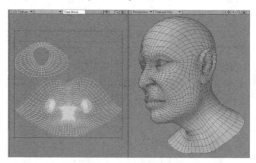

Figure 11-85: Selecting a complete edge loop will create separate islands for the geometry on either side of the loop. Here the head has been sectioned off from the neck.

If you've made a complex edge selection, you can save it for later use. Simply click on the Edge Data button and choose a location on your hard drive to save the settings. Then click on the Save Edge button. You can use the Load Edge button to load in edge data as well. Just click on the Edge Data button and then locate the Edge Data file. Then click the Load Edge button and the selection will appear on your object.

Figure 11-86: Complex edge selections can be loaded and saved.

If you'd like to make a custom Atlas map, you can choose Make Atlas from Surface, Make Atlas from UV, or Make Atlas. The Make Atlas button will trace the edges that it deems best and select them. Once selected, you can add or remove edges simply by clicking on the center of the edge in question.

The Divide by Surface option will ensure that new UV islands are created for any polys that have a different surface. This is similar to the Segment by Surface option found in LightWave's New UV Map tool. You can use this setting on its own or in conjunction with a custom edge selection to provide added control over how your object is unwrapped.

When your selections have been made (or you've simply sectioned off your object by assigning different surfaces), you can click on either the Make UV or Make UV Fast button. The Fast option will process your results faster at the cost of accuracy.

It may take some time to generate your UV map. Be patient; there's a lot of complex work being done. If you find that you'd like to speed things up, you can increase the Approximation setting. As with the Make UV Fast button, the higher the Approximation value, the less accurate your results will be.

If you're not happy with the results, you don't need to undo. Just select or deselect one of the edges on your object. This will clear the map and allow you to generate a new one. This provides a simple means for testing out various unwrapping configurations.

As you can see, the Make UV Edit tool is extremely powerful and offers tremendous control over how your object is unwrapped. We'll be using this tool extensively in the upcoming tutorial.

Align Chart Direction

When you create UVs with the Make UV Edit tool, it's not uncommon for the resulting UV mesh to be rotated slightly. The Align Chart Direction tool will attempt to correct this rotation. (The PLG UV tools refer to UV islands as "charts.") There are no options for the tool. Simply select the polygons that you want to correct (or make sure no polys are selected to correct all objects in the UV space) and run the tool.

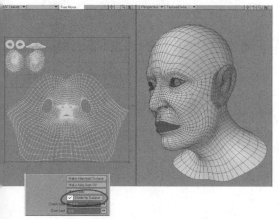

Figure 11-87: The Divide by Surface option will create new UV islands for each surface.

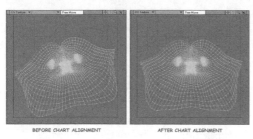

Figure 11-88: You can straighten UV islands with the Align Chart Direction tool.

Relax UV

When you unwrap an object, the conversion from 3D to 2D will invariably cause some amount of distortion to the shape of the polygons in the UV space. The easiest way to identify distortion is to apply a checkerboard pattern to your object. Ideally, the pattern should appear consistent across the entire surface. You shouldn't see areas where the squares vary in size or the pattern stretches. If you do see these things, you can use the Relax UV tool to fix the problem.

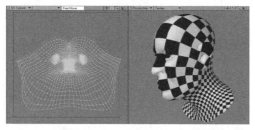

Figure 11-89: Applying a checkerboard pattern lets you identify areas of distortion within the UV map. The squares should be roughly the same size and should not stretch. You can see here that this model has a tremendous amount of distortion.

Note

I recommend applying a checkerboard pattern to the Color channel of your object's surface after creating your UVs. You can find a basic checkerboard image in the Images\Chapter 11 directory.

When you "relax" a UV, you are attempting to reconcile the difference between the shape of the polygons in the 2D UV space and those in the 3D world. Running the Relax UV plug-in brings up an options window with the following settings.

Figure 11-90: The Relax UV tool settings let you customize how the tool attempts to remove UV distortion.

Max Iteration

Max Iteration is the number of times the tool will attempt to reduce UV distortion. The default is 1000, which works well in most situations. If you find that the tool hasn't done a good enough job of reducing distortion, you can increase this value. If you find that the tool is running too slowly or that it inadvertently *increases* the amount of distortion, you can reduce this value.

As the tool works, it will check its ability to relax the UVs. If you've set Max Iteration to 1000 and the tool finds that it can't do anything more by the 500th iteration, it will stop early and won't waste time on the remaining iterations.

Area Weight

There are eight numeric buttons next to Area Weight that provide increased deformation correction by scanning a larger area of your mesh. The higher the number, the longer it will take to relax the UVs. Personally, I've found that I get the best results by using higher values. I typically start off by setting Area Weight to 8 and checking the results. If I find that the distortion amount increases rather than decreases, I lower Area Weight and/or adjust Max Iteration.

Fill Hole

Many of the PLG UV tools have a "Fill Hole" option. These tools define "holes" as areas inside the mesh that do not contain geometry. For example, in the letter "O" the area that forms the outer portion of the letter would be considered a "boundary" and the area that forms the inside of the "O" would be considered a "hole." Turning on the Fill Hole option will cause the plug-in to process the hole areas a bit differently. In some cases this gives better results. I would recommend starting with this option turned on. If you find that areas such as eye sockets and mouths aren't relaxing properly, turn this option off.

When you've set your options, simply press OK. Relaxing can take a bit of time, so be patient. When the calculations are complete, you should see a notable reduction in deformation over the surface of your object.

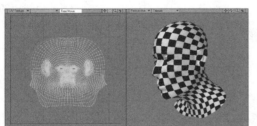

Figure 11-91: After relaxing the UVs, the checkerboard pattern is more consistent, indicating that distortion has either been greatly diminished or removed altogether.

> **Note**
>
> If you find that the amount of distortion has *increased* over the surface of your object, check for large areas that may be better separated, such as hands or feet or even the inside of a character's eyes or mouth. Oftentimes, moving them to another area in the map can help focus the tool on the key areas and eliminate the distortion.

> **Note**
>
> By selecting points along an edge of your object, you can restrict the effect of the Relax UV tool. This can be useful for ensuring that open edges (such as the neck on a head model) aren't affected by the tool's operation.

Pack UV Chart

Oftentimes when you're creating UVs for your object, the geometry will not make the most of the available UV space. (This is especially true for Atlas maps.) Other times, you may want to size the various UV islands relative to their counterparts in the 3D world. You can do these things with the Pack UV Chart tool.

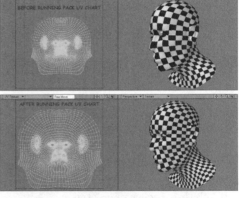

Figure 11-92: The Pack UV Chart tool allows you to make the most of the available UV space.

When you run this tool, a window will appear with the following options.

Figure 11-93: The Pack UV Chart options determine how the polygons fit in the UV space.

Adjust Scaling to 3D Mesh

This option ensures that the proportions of the objects in the UV space are consistent with the proportions of the object in the 3D world. For example, if you have a box that's 1 meter and another that's 2 meters, checking Adjust Scaling to 3D Mesh will ensure that the boxes remain proportional to one another as they are scaled within the UV space.

Gap Size

The Gap Size setting determines the amount of space between UV islands. The default is 128. Higher numbers increase the processing time but will pack the space tighter and leave less room between UV islands. The default value of 128 is quick and typically does a nice job. Personally, I've never found a need to change it.

Rotate Chart

The Rotate Chart option allows the plug-in to rotate UV islands to best fit within the

available space. If you've aligned objects using the Align Chart Direction tool, you should turn this setting off. If you're using an Atlas map (where the geometry is likely already rotated) or simply want to ensure that the tool is able to utilize the space as efficiently as possible, turn this setting on.

Optimize Scaling

This setting allows the plug-in to fit the UV islands into the available UV space as efficiently as possible.

When you've adjusted the settings to suit your needs, hit the OK button and the geometry in your UV space will be redistributed.

With these four plug-ins you can tackle most texturing jobs with ease. I'll prove that to you now.

Texturing Tutorial

We've spent a good deal of time grounding ourselves in the concepts and tools involved in texturing. Now let's put that knowledge into practice. In this tutorial, we'll texture a Russian MiG-29 fighter jet. I'll walk you through the process of creating and editing UVs and talk briefly about how to paint maps in a program like Photoshop. The actual painting will not be covered step by step (since that's largely a series of aesthetic choices and not technical in nature), but I'll give you enough detail to understand how the work is done.

1. Let's begin. Open Modeler and change one of

your viewports to **UV Texture**. Then load the **Mig29-Untextured.lwo** object from the Objects\Chapter 11 folder.

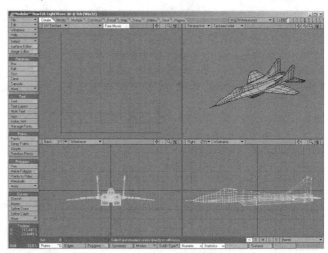

Figure 11-94: Load the Mig29-Untextured object into Modeler and switch one of your viewports to UV Texture.

Note

The various stages of creating UVs for the model can be found in the Objects\Chapter 11 folder on the DVD that came with this book. You can load these objects at any time to compare your results with mine or to pick up midway through the tutorial.

This is a simple model that was built using a combination of spline modeling (see Chapters 17 and 18) and subpatch modeling (see Chapter 15). It has the basic form but it lacks quite a bit of detail. By texturing it, we can add detail and turn this into a much more professional-looking model.

Before I begin texturing, I like to break the model into its basic components. This gives me a better idea of how the model was formed and allows me to make better choices about how it should be textured.

2. Change your Perspective viewport to **Textured Wire** (if it's not already set that way). Select a few polys around the cockpit. Then hit <]> to select all the connected polys. The entire fuselage will be selected. Press <"> to invert the selection. Then cut these polys and paste them into Layer 2, leaving the fuselage in Layer 1.

Figure 11-95: Select the fuselage. Invert the selection. Cut the selected polys and paste them into Layer 2, leaving the fuselage in Layer 1.

3. Select a few polys on the hull of the ship (which runs down the center of the craft). Select the connected polys, invert the selection, cut the selected polys, and paste them to Layer 3, leaving the hull in Layer 2.

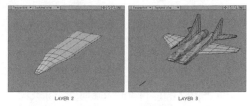

Figure 11-96: Select the hull. Invert the selection. Cut the selected polys and paste them into Layer 3, leaving the hull in Layer 2.

4. Select the left and right wings. Invert the selection, then cut and paste everything else to Layer 4, leaving the wings on Layer 3.

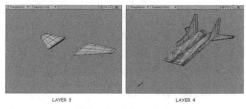

Figure 11-97: Select the left and right wings. Invert the selection. Cut the selected polys and paste them into Layer 4, leaving the wings in Layer 3.

5. Repeat this process for the left and right fins (also known as vertical stabilizers), then repeat for the horizontal stabilizers. This will leave you with the two "engine boxes" (I don't really know what these are called) and the needle nose. Select the needle nose, then cut it and paste it to Layer 7.

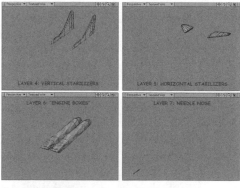

Figure 11-98: Place the remaining parts on separate layers as shown here.

The various parts of the MiG should now be spread out over seven layers. If you look closely, you'll see that most of the objects that make up the fighter jet are relatively flat. They have a distinct top and bottom (such as the hull) or left and right (such as the fins). That means that we could use Standard projection maps instead of UVs to texture them. But that would be too easy and wouldn't give us as much of an opportunity to learn about UVs, which more people seem to have trouble with. So we'll skip the Standard projections and use UVs instead.

If you'd like to see the work done so far, you can load the Mig29-Layered object from the Objects\Chapter 11 folder on the DVD.

Making the UVs

Let's begin with the fuselage in Layer 1. In the old days I would have used a Cylindrical map type to unwrap this object. But the bulge in the cockpit and the tapering at the tail would have produced a lot of UV distortion and required a good deal of time tweaking the UVs to remove it. Thank God those days are over. We're going to use the Make UV Edit plug-in to unwrap the fuselage rather than using a Cylindrical map type.

1. Currently this object is in Subpatch mode. Press the **Tab** key to toggle subpatches off so that we can easily see the exact shape of the polygons we're working with.

> **Note**
>
> The Make UV Edit tool works fine with subpatch objects, but it selects edges based on the polygonal "cage" (the shape of the object when it's not subpatched). This can make edge selection difficult if there's a big difference between what the object looks like when it's subpatched and when it's not subpatched. For this reason, I recommend turning off subpatches when working with this tool.

Since we're not using one of LightWave's automated unwrapping map types, we need to make a decision about how the fuselage should be unwrapped. When you unwrap your object, it will create a seam on either side of the discontinuous edge in the UV space. If you paint over the seam on one side and don't pick the stroke up at the exact same place on the opposite side, the texture will appear to be out of alignment. Seams are a natural byproduct of UVs. Therefore, when you're determining how an object should be unwrapped, you should really be thinking about the place where a seam would be least noticeable.

Looking at our fuselage, it seems reasonable to believe that the underside of the fuselage will be seen a lot less than the top. Therefore, the seam should run along the belly of the ship. Hence, we can define an unwrapping edge along the bottom of the fuselage, running from front to back.

2. Activate the **Make UV Edit** tool and bring up the Numeric panel. In the UV Map field, enter **Mig29**. We'll place all of our geometry on this single UV. Leave Select set to **Edges**. Then uncheck the Hide Handle option. Once you do so, your model will be covered with blue dots.

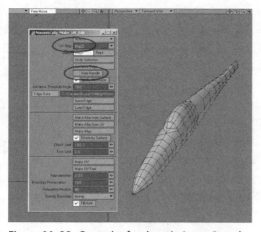

Figure 11-99: Go to the fuselage in Layer 1 and turn off subpatches. Then activate the Make UV Edit tool. Enter Mig29 for the texture name and turn off the Hide Handle option.

3. Zoom in on the front of the fuselage and select the edge shown in Figure 11-100. Press <a> to fit the model to your viewport (thereby zooming out). The edge will still be selected.

Figure 11-100: Zoom in to the front of the fuselage and select the edge shown here.

4. Zoom in on the back of the fuselage. Hold down the <Ctrl> key and select the edge shown in Figure 11-101. All the edges between the first and the last will be selected. Zoom out and check to make sure that the selection runs in a straight line along the bottom of the fuselage.

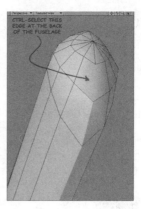

Figure 11-101: Zoom in on the front of the fuselage and select the edge shown here.

5. Once you've checked that the edge runs straight down the bottom of the fuselage, click on the **Make UV** button in the Numeric panel. After a moment, you'll see the unwrapped fuselage appear in the UV Texture viewport. Cool, huh? Drop the Make UV Edit tool. The UV for the fuselage is now complete.

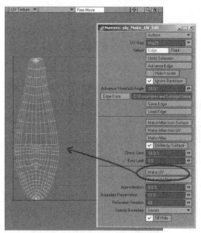

Figure 11-102: Click on the Make UV button and the fuselage of the ship will be unwrapped and appear in the UV Texture viewport.

That wasn't so hard. In fact, it was downright easy. Let's move on to the hull.

6. Switch to Layer 2 and press <a> to fill the viewport with the model. Then

press the **Tab** key to turn off subpatches.

> ### Note
>
> When you click on Layer 2, the UV geometry for the fuselage in Layer 1 will disappear. Don't worry! You didn't lose the UV. If you click back to Layer 1 you'll see that the geometry for the fuselage is still there. The UV space will only show the geometry that is currently in the foreground layers.

The hull is basically a flat shape. You can see that there's an edge that runs right around the middle of the object. This is a natural edge to unwrap around as it will provide a distinct top and bottom in the UV Texture viewport.

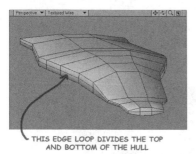

Figure 11-103: The hull can easily be divided into top and bottom halves. This makes for a natural unwrapping seam.

As we learned earlier, if you select an entire edge loop, the object will be divided into two parts in the UV Texture viewport. Therefore, if we create a selection around the center of the hull, it will give us one UV island for the top and another for the bottom.

7. Activate the **Make UV Edit** tool. The UV Map field should still say "Mig29," indicating that we'll add the geometry for this object to the same UV space as the fuselage.

8. The Hide Handle option should still be unchecked. If it isn't, uncheck it now so

that you can see the edge handles. Then select any edge that runs along the center of the hull.

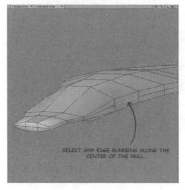

Figure 11-104: Select a single edge anywhere along the center of the hull.

We want the entire edge loop to be selected. Fortunately, there's an easy way to do this. Check the Advance Threshold Angle setting. It should currently be set to its default of 70 degrees. That means that if you use the Advance Edge button inside the Make UV Edit tool to select the edge loop, the selection will follow along the loop until it reaches any polygons with an angle greater than 70 degrees. At that point it will stop the selection.

9. Looking at the hull, we can see that some angles are greater than 70 degrees. In fact, some exceed 90 degrees, so a setting of 70 degrees is too small. Change the Advance Threshold Angle to **95** degrees. This will ensure that the selection will go around right angles. Then press the **Advance Edge** button. The entire edge around the hull will become selected (Figure 11-105).

10. Spin your model and inspect the edge selection. You may notice that the back of the hull has a selection all the way around it, as shown in Figure 11-106.

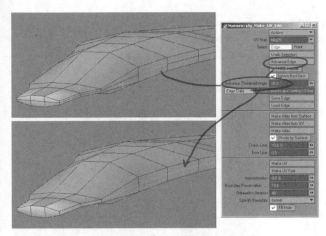

Figure 11-105: Change the Advance Threshold Angle to 95 degrees and press the Advance Edge button. The edge loop around the hull will be selected.

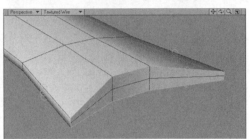

Figure 11-106: You may notice that the selection goes around the top and bottom on the back of the hull (as shown here) rather than straight through.

In some cases where the edge of your object exceeds 90 degrees (as it does on the back of the hull), the Make UV Edit tool will choose to follow the path of least resistance, meaning it may choose to follow a less extreme angle even though it means deviating from an established edge loop. When this happens you must manually correct the selection or remake it from scratch. That's what we'll do here.

11. Click the **Undo Selection** button. This will undo the Advance Edge action you just performed but will leave you with the selection you made originally. Change the Advance

Threshold Angle to **89.5** degrees. This ensures that the selection will not go around right angles. Then click the **Advance Edge** button again. You'll see that the edges along the sides and front of the hull have been selected but none of the edges along the back got selected. We must manually select these edges to complete the loop.

12. Click the three edges along the back of the hull as shown in Figure 11-107. With the selection complete, we're ready to make the UV.

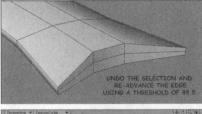

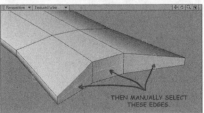

Figure 11-107: Click on the Undo Selection button. Change the Advance Threshold Angle to 89.5 degrees and click the Advance Edge button again. Then manually select the remaining edges in the loop as shown here.

13. Click on the **Make UV** button. You'll
    see the hull added to the UV space.
    Notice that there are two geometry
    islands in the UV Texture viewport.
    One contains the geometry for the top
    of the hull and the other for the bottom.

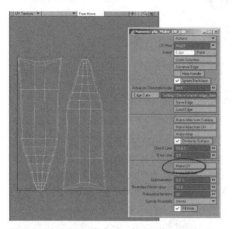

Figure 11-108: Click on the Make UV button and
the hull will be added to the Mig29 UV map.

14. Drop the Make UV Edit tool and click
    on Layer 3. This layer should have the
    wings in it. The wings are currently
    subpatched. Hit the **Tab** key to toggle
    subpatches off.

The wings are a lot like the hull. You can
see that there's a clear edge running around
the center of each wing. We'll use this as
our dividing point.

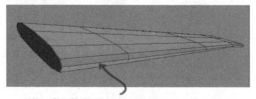

THIS CENTER EDGE LOOP MAKES A NATURAL SEAM

Figure 11-109: Each wing can be divided into top
and bottom, just like the hull. This makes the
center edge loop a logical place for our seam.

15. Activate the **Make UV Edit** tool. The
    UV Map name should still be Mig29

486

and the Advance Threshold Angle
should still be set to 89.5. Click on one
of the center edges for the right wing
(which would be the pilot's left wing).
Then press the **Advance Edge** button.

SELECT AN EDGE.

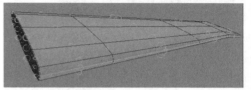

THEN PRESS THE ADVANCE EDGE BUTTON.

Figure 11-110: Select an edge along the center of
the wing and press the Advance Edge button.

16. Spin your model in the Perspective
    viewport and check the edge selection.
    It's likely that the edge loop will not be
    complete around the entire object since
    there are angles in the wing that
    exceed 90 degrees.

17. Click on any edge in the loop that
    wasn't selected and press the **Advance
    Edge** button again.

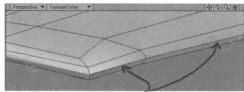

SELECT ANY EDGE THAT DIDN'T GET SELECTED.

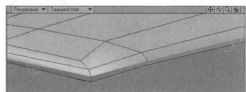

THEN PRESS THE ADVANCE EDGE BUTTON AGAIN.

Figure 11-111: Manually select any edge that
didn't get selected and press the Advance Edge
button again.

18. You may notice that the edge deviates from the edge loop as it moves around the inside of the wing. If this happens, manually deselect the errant edges. Then manually select the edges around the center of the wing. Remember that you can hold down the Ctrl key to manually select a range of edges.

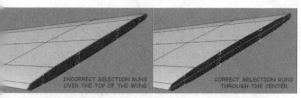

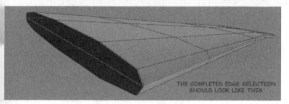

ure 11-112: Check the edge selection around the inside of wing. If it deviates from the center edge loop, manually select and then reselect the edges to complete the loop.

19. If we press the Make UV button now, we'll get three UV islands: two for the wing that we just unwrapped and one for the wing we didn't. In order to properly unwrap both wings, we need to repeat the edge selection on the other wing. Go ahead and do that now.

Figure 11-113: Select the center edge loop on the opposite wing.

20. When you're finished and both wings have complete edge selections, press the **Make UV** button but don't drop the tool. Keep it active.

Take a look at the UV Texture viewport. You'll see the top and bottom of each wing

and four small strips of polygons at the top of the UV space. (See Figure 11-114.) What are these and how did we get them?

If you select the small polys in the UV space and then look at your Perspective viewport, you'll see that these are the polygons with the black surface on the inside of each wing. But why are they separate from the rest of the wing?

By default, the Make UV Edit tool will create a new UV island for each surface in your object. Our wing has two surfaces (one for the wing and another for the inside edge of the wing). And since our selection sliced through the center of the wing, there were two halves for each surface. Therefore, we ended up with a top and a bottom for the main wing and a top and a bottom for the inside of the wing. Technically, there's nothing wrong with this; however, I want to keep everything together so I have fewer seams to deal with.

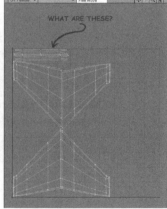

Figure 11-114: Press the Make UV button and look at the UV Texture viewport. What are the four small polygon strips shown here?

21. The tool should still be active. Click on any unselected edge in the Perspective viewport. This will clear the UV from

Figure 11-115: Clear the existing UV by selecting and deselecting an edge. Uncheck the Divide by Surface option and click the Make UV button again.

Figure 11-116: The fins can easily be divided into left and right halves, making the center edge loop a natural unwrapping seam.

the UV Texture viewport. Then reclick the edge to deselect it. Uncheck the Divide by Surface button in the Numeric panel and press the **Make UV** button once again. You should now see four islands in the UV Texture viewport: two for the tops of the wings and two for the bottoms. The wings are now complete.

> **Note**
>
> Now that you understand the function of the Divide by Surface option, you can use it on your own objects. In fact, you can take it a step further. Just assign surfaces to your object and run the Make UV Edit tool with the Divide by Surface option checked. You don't have to make an edge selection at all. Just hit the Make UV button and the boundaries between surfaces will be used as edge selections by the plug-in.

22. Let's move on to the vertical stabilizers (also called "fins") in Layer 4. They're subpatched, so press the **Tab** key to toggle subpatches off, then take a look at the wireframes. Just like the hull and wings, there's a clear division running down the center of each fin.

23. You should be familiar with the unwrapping process by now. Go ahead and use the **Make UV Edit** tool to select the edge all the way around the center of each fin. Then press the **Make UV** button to add the fins to the UV space. Your results should look like those in Figure 11-117.

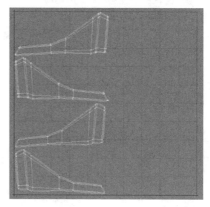

Figure 11-117: Unwrap the fins just like you did the wings. The results should look similar to those shown here.

24. With the vertical stabilizers complete, let's move on to the horizontal stabilizers in Layer 5. Press **Tab** to turn off the subpatches and then inspect the wireframes. You can see an edge

clearly dividing each stabilizer. Use the **Make UV Edit** tool to select the edge around the center of each stabilizer and then press the **Make UV** button to add them to the Mig29 UV space. Your results should look like those in Figure 11-118.

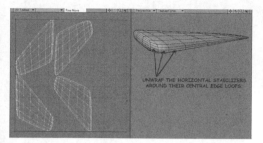

Figure 11-118: Unwrap the horizontal stabilizers in the same way you did the vertical stabilizers. Your results should look similar to those shown here.

25. We're almost finished creating our UVs. The last two objects are the "engine boxes" in Layer 6. Click on Layer 6 and press **Tab** to turn off subpatches. Then swivel around the mesh in the Perspective viewport to get a feel for how it's built.

Note

If you get a message saying that only polys with more than four points can be subpatched when you press the Tab key, just ignore it. The engine boxes consist of both regular polygons and subpatches. The Tab key simply toggles between the two. In this case it is attempting to turn off the existing subpatches and turn on subpatches for the regular polygons. However, subpatching doesn't work on polygons with more than four points (CC SubD's do, but subpatches don't) so you'll see this message. We'll talk more about subpatches in Chapter 15.

The engine boxes are a bit more complex than the other objects we've dealt with so far. Looking at the objects, we can see that they are box-shaped on one end and

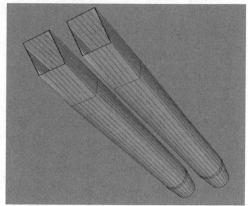

Figure 11-119: The "engine boxes" are complex objects that transition from boxes to discs over the length of a cylindrical tube.

disc-shaped on the other. The shapes blend together to form a long cylindrical tube. When I first looked at these objects, I had no idea how I should unwrap them. I knew that I wanted the cylindrical tube to unwrap along its length. And since the top of the tube isn't visible, I knew that I needed to unwrap along this part of the mesh so that the seam would not be visible.

I determined that the cylindrical tube should be a distinct island. I also decided that the front box shape and the rear disc shape should each be distinct islands. Armed with this knowledge, I set out on a trial-and-error process. I won't lie to you: I didn't get it right the first time and I don't have some "magic" reason for the choices I made. I simply looked at my mistakes after each attempt and tried new things to correct them. It took several tries before I finally found a configuration that gave me the results I was looking for.

When you're trying to unwrap complex objects, you will likely go through a similar process of trial and error. There's nothing wrong with this. Don't expect to get things right the first time. Most of us (myself included) don't. But be persistent and don't give up when you make mistakes. Perseverance is a virtue.

26. Follow the images in Figures 11-120 through 11-122 to create the edge selection for the engine boxes. If you prefer, you can simply load the edge_ data file from the Setup\Chapter 11 folder.

> **Note**
>
> For clarity, only one engine box is shown here; however, you should make the same selection on both objects.

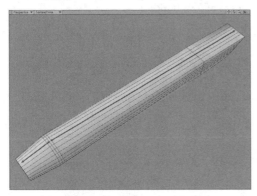

Figure 11-120

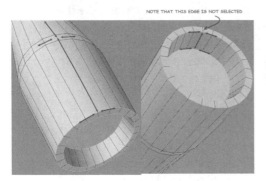

Figure 11-121

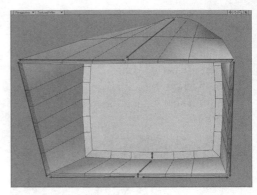

Figure 11-122

27. Be careful when selecting the perimeter of the box area as the edges are packed together, which can make selection difficult. Be sure to zoom out and check the selection once you're finished to ensure you haven't selected any unwanted edges. When you're satisfied, press the **Make UV** button. The UVs will be added to the Mig29 UV space and your results should be similar to those in Figure 11-123.

Figure 11-123: The unwrapped engine boxes should look like this in the UV Texture viewport.

Congratulations! You've finished creating the UVs for this object. Now it's time to test them for deformations and correct any problems.

Testing and Correcting UVs

When geometry is unwrapped and added to the UV space, it is not uncommon for the shape of the polygons in the UV Texture viewport to deviate from their counterparts in the 3D world. When this happens, you'll often find areas where the texture distorts. This distortion can range from mild to extreme and can have a major impact on the appearance of your textures. Therefore, it's a good idea to test your UVs for deformation before you begin painting texture maps.

The best way to test UVs for deformation is to project a repeating pattern into the UV space. A checkerboard works well. The squares are evenly spaced and don't vary in size, making it easy to spot places where the texture is deforming.

In order to see the checkerboard, we must add an Image Map texture to our surface.

1. Open the Surface Editor. You'll see three surfaces for this object: Mig-29 is the main surface and is used by most of the polygons we created UVs for. Mig-29 Needle-nose is the surface for the pole projecting from the nose of the plane. Since this is so small, we didn't bother creating textures for it (although you're welcome to do so if you'd like). Wing-Inside is for the black

polygons on the inside edge of the wings. Since they're rarely seen (being largely covered by the hull), they've simply been given a black color.

2. Click on the **Mig-29** surface and open the Texture Editor for the Color channel. The default layer will be set to Image Map. Change Projection from Planar to **UV**. This will cause a UVMap pop-up menu to appear just below the Projection menu. Choose the **Mig29** UV that you created earlier. Then click on the Image pop-up menu and load the **checker.psd** file from the Images\ Chapter 11 folder on the DVD.

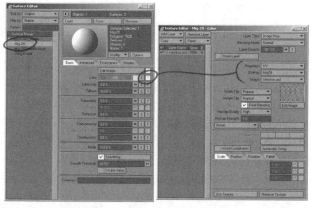

Figure 11-124: Create a UV projection for the Color channel of the Mig-29 surface. Select the Mig-29 UV you added your geometry to and load the checker.psd file from the Images\ Chapter 11 folder.

Let's talk briefly about what we've just done. By adding an image map and setting its projection to UV, we've told Modeler to create a virtual projector and to shine its image into the square UV space. Any polys that happen to be in that space will be covered by a portion of the image, just like a person walking in front of a movie projector will be covered by a portion of the movie.

Since most of the polygons have the Mig-29 surface and we created UVs for just about every part of the model, a checkerboard pattern will appear over most of the model. This looks cool (in a retro-'80s sort of way), but what are we looking for? We're looking for squares that deviate in size or shape. We're also looking at the seams to make sure they're not horribly noticeable or in places they shouldn't be.

3. In order to ensure that we're seeing the most accurate results, we should turn subpatches back on. Place Layers 1 through 6 in the foreground and press the **Tab** key. You can ignore any message that comes up about polygons with more than four sides not being able to be subpatched.

When we used the Make UV Edit tool to create our UV space, it chose a Linear subpatch interpolation. (The Make UV Edit tool doesn't have the option to change subpatch interpolation, so every UV it creates will have a Linear interpolation.) Since the MiG will be subpatched, we should change the Subpatch Interpolation type.

4. Open the **Windows | Vertex Maps Panel**. Toggle open the Texture option. You will see Linear in the Interpolation column. Click this and change it to **Across discontinuous edges**. We're now ready to examine our object for distortion.

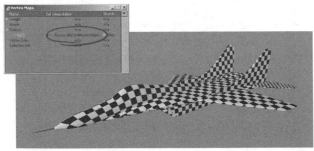

Figure 11-125: Place Layers 1 through 6 in the foreground and press Tab to convert the polygons to subpatches. Then use the Vertex Maps panel to change the Subpatch Interpolation type to Across discontinuous edges.

5. Click on Layer 1 and you'll see the fuselage. Change your Perspective viewport to **Texture** so that you can see the checkerboard pattern applied to it without wireframes. The texture looks good and is relatively free of distortion. (This is largely due to the advanced unwrapping performed by the Make UV Edit tool. For fun, try creating a Cylindrical UV map and compare the results.) Even though the results are good, you can still see some areas where the checkerboard pattern is stretching, such as the nose of the plane. To fix this, we'll use the Relax UV plug-in.

Figure 11-126: The nose of the plane shows a slight amount of distortion. Anytime you see distortion you should try to minimize it with the Relax UV tool.

6. Activate the **Relax UV** tool. Leave Max Iteration set at 1000. Change Area Weight to **8** and leave the Fill Hole option checked. These are the settings I start off with on every object. If they don't successfully remove the distortion, I typically increase the Max Iteration to 2000 and work my way up from there.

7. Press **OK**. After a few seconds you'll see that the texture has been smoothed out and the distortion has been minimized. That's all you need to do!

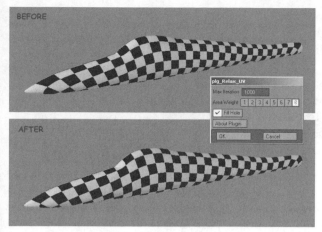

Figure 11-127: Using the Relax UV tool helps minimize UV distortion. Notice how the stretching in the nose has been reduced.

Let's move on to the next layer. Click on Layer 2 and take a look at the checkerboard pattern. The texture looks pretty even and the UVs probably don't need to be relaxed, but we'll go ahead and run the Relax UV tool on them anyway.

8. Activate the **Relax UV** tool. It should pop up with the previously used settings of 1000 for Max Iteration, Area Weight of 8, and Fill Hole checked. Press **OK**. You'll see a slight change to the checkerboard pattern.

Figure 11-128: Run the Relax UV tool with the same settings as before. You may only see a slight change, as is the case here.

9. Repeat this process for each additional layer. In each case you should notice a slight change to the checkerboard pattern and any distortion should be minimized or removed.

10. When you've finished relaxing the UVs for each object, click on Layer 6 and look at the checkerboard pattern on the engine boxes. You'll notice that the seam is visible on the top of the texture. This seam is made more apparent by the fact that the texture is cocked at an angle.

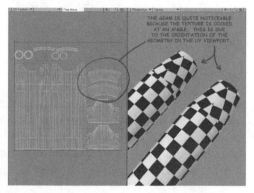

Figure 11-129: The squares on the engine boxes are cocked at an angle due to their orientation in the UV Texture viewport.

This isn't a result of distortion. Rather, it's due to the way the geometry is laid out in the UV Texture viewport. If you select a few of the cone polys in the Perspective viewport and look at which ones are selected in the UV Texture viewport, you can see that the polys are arranged in an

493

arc. This arc is what's causing the problem. If the polys were straight, the checkerboard pattern would be straight as well. Let's take a look at how to correct this.

We can correct each cone shape individually, but since they're identical, we can easily overlap the polys in the UV Texture viewport and correct them all at once.

11. Select the lower polys as shown in Figure 11-130 and move them up so that they're directly over the polys above them. (If you zoom in you may notice that the polys don't fit exactly. This is a result of the relaxing process and is nothing to worry about. Just get the polygons close.) When you're satisfied, zoom out so you can see the entire UV island.

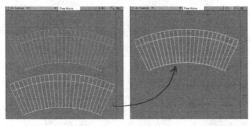

Figure 11-130: Select the bottom arc of polys and move them up so they overlap those above them.

12. Select the points along the uppermost edge. Change your Action Center mode to **Selection** and activate the **Stretch** tool. Then click and drag downward

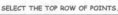
SELECT THE TOP ROW OF POINTS.

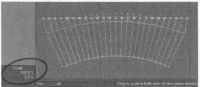

STRETCH UNTIL THE VERTICAL FACTOR IS 0%.

with your middle mouse button (or hold down the Ctrl key and drag) until the Vertical Factor (seen in the Quick Info display at the bottom-left corner of the interface) is **0%**. This will ensure that all of the points are level.

13. You may notice that the points intersect those below them. With the points still selected, use the **Move** tool to move them up so that they're out of the way of the other points below them. Then drop the Move tool and deselect the points.

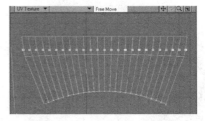

Figure 11-132: Move the points up so they do not intersect those below them.

14. Select the next band of points and repeat the process of stretching them until they are level. Your results should look like those in Figure 11-133.

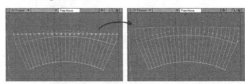

Figure 11-133: Select the next band of points and stretch them so that they line up.

Figure 11-131: Select the top row of points and stretch them with a 0% Vertical Factor so that they line up.

15. Finally, select the lowest band of points and repeat the stretching process again. When you're finished, all of the points should be level across the U (horizontal) axis. Your results should look like those in Figure 11-134.

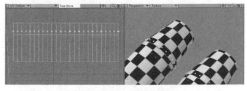

Figure 11-136: Select the middle band of points and stretch them slightly horizontally so that they line up with the top and bottom rows of points.

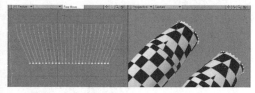

Figure 11-134: Select the bottom band of points and stretch them so that they line up.

You can see in Figure 11-134 that the checkerboard pattern is no longer rotated at such an awkward angle but there's still a lot of stretching in the texture. Let's fix that.

16. Select the points along the bottom edge. Using the **Stretch** tool, click and drag to the right with your middle mouse button until the points are spaced almost evenly with those along the top edge. Your results should look like those shown in Figure 11-135.

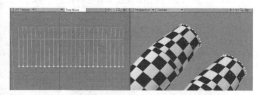

Figure 11-135: Select the bottom band of points and stretch them horizontally so that they line up with the top row of points.

17. Now select the middle band of points and use the **Stretch** tool to space them out slightly as well. If you need to, adjust the points along the bottom again until your results look like those shown in Figure 11-136.

These simple adjustments really helped. You can now see in Figure 11-136 that the

checkerboard pattern flows more naturally along the surface of the cone.

18. This would be a good time to save your object.

Optimizing the UV Space

The UVs are now complete and the distortion has been checked and corrected. We're just about ready to begin painting, but there are a few more things that need to be done.

1. Place all seven layers in the foreground. Cut the model, click on Layer 1 so that it's the only one in the foreground, then paste the model into place. This does two things. First, it puts the individual pieces back together again so that we can animate it as one object in Layout. And second, it allows us to clearly see the ungodly mess in our UV space. (If you don't see the geometry in the UV Texture viewport, make sure the Mig29 texture is selected from the pop-up in the lower-right corner of the interface.)

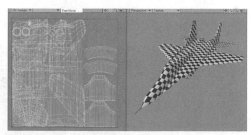

Figure 11-137: Select all the layers, then cut the geometry and paste it all into Layer 1. Notice the mess of polygons in the UV Texture viewport!

When we created our UVs, we did so with geometry that was placed on separate layers. With no other geometry to consider, the Make UV Edit plug-in filled the UV space as it saw fit. But when all of our geometry is placed in the same layer, it overlaps, creating a jumbled mess. We need to separate each island in the UV space. Fortunately, the Pack UV Chart tool will allow us to do this very easily.

2. Activate the **Pack UV Chart** tool. In the options window, check the **Adjust Scaling to 3D Mesh** option. This ensures that the geometry in the UV Texture viewport will be scaled relative to its size in the 3D world. It prevents parts like the horizontal stabilizers from being sized larger than the wings, for example.

3. Leave Gap Size set to **128**. The default usually works well and you'll likely never need to change it.

4. Uncheck the Rotate Chart option. This ensures that the various parts of the model will stay oriented properly and not be rotated in order to maximize the available UV space.

5. Check **Optimize Scaling** to ensure that the entire UV space is filled as efficiently as possible. Then click **OK**. After a few seconds you'll see each island scaled and positioned in the UV space.

Since the Pack UV Chart tool uses so many unseen variables, your results may look different than mine. That's okay. The important thing is that you end up with no overlapping geometry.

6. Save your model.

Congratulations! The UV work for the MiG-29 is now complete. You have successfully unwrapped the object, fixed the distortion, and fit everything into the UV space. You now have geometry that can easily be painted on in a program like Photoshop. But just how do you get the geometry into Photoshop?

Exporting the UV Template

There are two main ways to get geometry into your paint package. The easiest method is to simply save a screen capture of the full-screen viewport and paste the result into your paint program. This works well for most objects, but when you want to create high-resolution textures, it's not necessarily the best option.

For high-res textures, the best approach is to export the UV Texture viewport as an EPS file. This will create a resolution-independent file and allow you to rasterize it at any size. Let's take a look at how to do this.

1. One of your viewports should still be set to UV Texture. If it's not, change one of them now. Then click on the

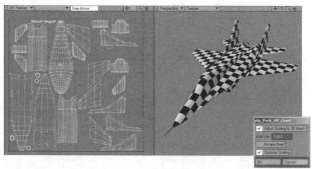

Figure 11-138: Run the Pack UV Chart tool with the settings shown here. Your results will look similar (but not necessarily identical) to those here.

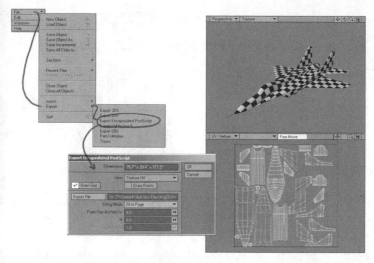

Figure 11-139: Make sure one of your viewports is set to UV Texture. Then run the Export Encapsulated PostScript command.

File | Export | Export Encapsulated PostScript option. The Export options window will appear.

2. Change the View pop-up menu to **Texture UV** as shown in Figure 11-139. This will ensure that only the UV Texture viewport is exported. Check the **Draw Grid** option but uncheck the Draw Points option. This will ensure that the grid is drawn but that the points that make up the grid are not exported as vector shapes.

3. Click on the **Export File** button and choose a location to save your file. You can leave Sizing Mode set to its default of Fit in Page and leave the Page Size set to its default of 6 inches for both the width and height. Then click **OK**. Your EPS file will be saved to your chosen location.

You can load this EPS file into most paint programs for texturing. When you do so, keep in mind that your texture should be perfectly square so that it will project properly in the UV space. Also, while it's not mandatory, many people (myself included) prefer to work with resolutions in the power of 2. I typically use a 2048 x 2048 or

a 4096 x 4096 file size, although I'll occasionally use a 1024 x 1024 image for objects that won't be close to the camera.

Painting Textures

Painting textures for 3D models is a creative and liberating process. Since you're not bound by the limitations of 3D, you can add as much detail as you like. In fact, the more detail you add, the better your textures and objects will look.

The techniques involved in painting a texture map from start to finish are beyond the scope of this chapter; however, I will outline the steps I use so that you can get a better understanding of how the overall texturing process works. Before we begin, let's talk briefly about the purpose of textures.

Textures serve two basic purposes. The first is to add structural detail. The second is to tell a story. I call the first type "structural textures" because they are used to simulate geometry that could have been modeled but was not (typically because it would produce an unwieldy amount of polygons). I call the second type "narrative textures" because they tell a story about your object's history. They let you know how the object has been used and what it has gone through.

Structural textures are typically added to the Bump channel. They may also appear in the Transparency channel or used as clip maps or displacement maps (found in the Object Properties panel in Layout). Narrative textures are typically added to the Color, Diffuse, and Specular/Reflection channels. You should consider the types of textures you need (both structural and narrative) before you begin painting.

Think about the MiG-29 model we've been working with. It is missing large parts (such as flaps) and small parts (such as panels and rivets). It can definitely use structural textures to simulate these details. The MiG-29 also has colorful patterns (typically camouflage) and will undoubtedly exhibit some degree of wear and tear. These details are best created with narrative textures placed in the Color and Diffuse channels.

Once you know the types of detail you need to create (both structural and narrative), you can begin painting.

The first thing you should do is import your UV reference, whether it's pasting a simple screen capture or loading an EPS that you've exported from Modeler. The larger the texture, the more detail you'll be able to add. I typically use 2048 x 2048 resolution maps unless my object will appear close to the screen, in which case I will increase the resolution to 4096 x 4096.

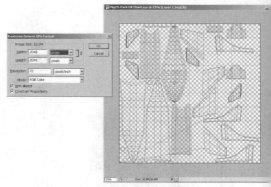

Figure 11-140: The first step in texturing is to import the UV geometry as a reference into your paint program.

Once the UV reference has been loaded, I find it helpful to label the parts of my object. This makes it easy to identify what you'll be painting over. I select a few polys in Modeler and then check what's selected in the UV Texture viewport. Then I add a label to those parts in Photoshop. I repeat this until all the major parts are labeled.

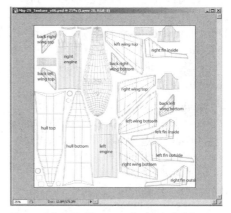

Figure 11-141: You may find it helpful to label your geometry so that you can easily determine what you're painting onto.

I like to add the structural details first as they typically act as a guide for the narrative textures. Structural textures are usually bump maps. When painting a bump map, you should fill a new layer with a 50% gray canvas and then place your reference

UV in a layer above it so that you can see where you're placing your strokes. Any pixels lighter than 50% will cause the surface to rise up and any stroke darker than 50% will cause it to recede.

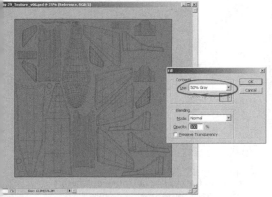

jure 11-142: When creating a structural texture pically a bump map), begin by filling a blank layer th 50% gray and placing the reference file over the cture so you can see what portion of the model you're inting on.

For characters, the bump map will typically contain things like pores, small wrinkles, surface bumps, etc. For planes, tanks, and other machines, the bump map will often contain panels (or panel divisions), rivets, scratches, and mild damage.

Note

You can typically find schematics on the Internet that will assist you in placing panel markings for common vehicles and aircraft. Just type the name of the craft into Google's Image Search along with the word "schematic" and you should get several hits.

There's no easy way to place panel markings. I find that it's best to study one small area of a reference image and then attempt to replicate it on your texture map. The panels of most craft usually fit together like puzzle pieces. If one is off, it will become apparent as you create the panels around it. For this reason, it's a good idea to create

panel markings with vector lines, which are easily editable.

Figure 11-143: Panel markings are best created with editable lines such as vectors. This allows you to easily adjust their position and shape.

When your object has symmetrical parts, you can simply create the details for one part and then duplicate and transform them to create the textures for the opposite side.

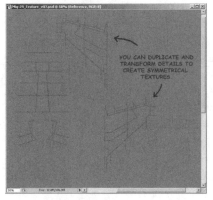

Figure 11-144: You can duplicate and transform the textures on one part of your model to quickly create symmetrical details.

When all the structural details are in place I load the object into Layout, set up a few lights, and position the camera so that the model can be clearly seen. Then I create test renders to get a feel for how the details actually look on my model. (I use Worley's FPrime plug-in, which provides real-time rendering in order to see how my textures look, but you can do the same thing without the plug-in by simply creating several test renders.)

Figure 11-145: Once the structural details are in place, you can set up a basic scene to see how they look on your model. Then take note of any areas that need adjusting and correct the problems in your paint program.

I keep an eye out for areas with problems and then make my adjustments in Photoshop. I work back and forth between Photoshop and LightWave as necessary until everything looks right.

Once the structural details are complete, I paint the narrative textures, starting with the color map. When you're painting colors, it's important to remember that you shouldn't be painting any shadow information. You're simply painting in raw color data. Shading is best handled by the Diffuse channel.

The color textures for the MiG-29 are fairly simple. They consist of some camouflage, a black color for the nose of the plane, a few stars, and the cockpit.

I didn't model the cockpit, so I painted a little detail in the Color channel that allowed me to fill the canopy with a tinted light to dark gradient. If I were working on a more realistic model, I would have modeled the cockpit and the interior of the

plane, but this level of detail wasn't necessary for the intended purpose of this object and the painted detail worked just fine.

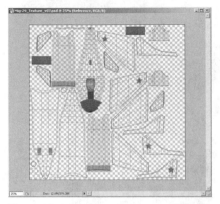

Figure 11-146: When the structural details are complete I turn to the narrative details, starting with the color map.

Trying to paint camouflage in the UV space can be extremely difficult. In order to get the appearance of a continuous brushstroke covering each part of your object, you must paint over one edge of a UV island and pick up the stroke on another UV island so the two line up in 3D space. This is not an easy task. Rather than struggling with the UV map, you can simply use a Standard projection.

Since the MiG-29 is composed primarily of a single surface, a Planar map can be used to paint over the entire object at once. And since the plane is largely flat, the stretching that normally occurs when your

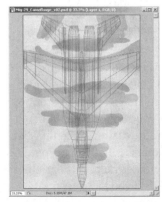

Figure 11-147: Don't feel locked into using your UV map. You can use a Standard Planar projection for details like camouflage.

texture moves away from the specified projection axis won't be a problem.

I added the Planar projection of the camouflage to the Color channel. Then I saved my UV color information from Photoshop as a PNG file with no background. LightWave understands the transparency in a PNG file and will respect it. This allows you to use multiple layers without having to spend time tinkering with the various blending modes.

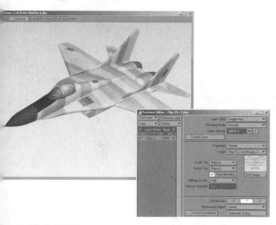

Figure 11-148: You can use any combination of standard projections and UV projections to get the results you're looking for. Here, a Standard Planar Projection was used for the camouflage and the Mig29 UV was used to add the cockpit, nose, and stars.

Once the color texture is complete, I usually create a diffuse texture. The Diffuse channel determines how much light a surface reflects. Placing a texture in the Diffuse channel allows you to shade portions of your surface and is great for making a surface appear worn or dirty.

I often begin the work of creating a diffuse map by copying portions of my bump map. Since dark colors in the Bump channel recede and dark colors in the Diffuse channel appear darker, using portions of the bump map in the Diffuse texture can enhance the depth in your bump map. I also paint custom wear and tear marks in the

Diffuse channel. On the MiG, I painted faint streaks that help create the look of dirt and oil across the surface.

Figure 11-149: The diffuse map allows you to add shading to your surface and can help create the look of wear and tear.

For this object, I didn't paint reflection or transparency maps, as they weren't needed, but the process for creating both would be the same as the techniques used for the bump, color, and diffuse maps. I also didn't paint details that wouldn't be seen in the final render. If they won't be seen, there's no point in spending time on them. Working smart when you paint textures is just as important as working hard.

Figure 11-150: The final render with the Bump, Color, and Diffuse textures applied, placed over an aerial photo.

501

At this point the texturing is "complete." Of course, a lot more work can be done to enhance these modest textures. But now that you understand the basic process, I'll leave that up to you.

Conclusion

In this chapter we've taken a detailed look at the concepts of texturing in LightWave. We examined how Standard projections and UV projections work. We explored the UV space in depth and talked about LightWave's core tools for working with UVs. We also looked at the essential UV plug-ins you need to make quick work out of your texturing projects. Finally, we walked through a complete texturing project and touched on the basics of painting texture maps.

Hopefully this chapter has inspired you and taken the mystery out of texturing in LightWave. I would encourage you to paint your own maps for the MiG-29 model, making them as detailed as you can imagine. You'll quickly see that good textures are a key component in a successful 3D scene and can bring average-looking objects to life.

Chapter 12

Intermediate Skills: Environments, Hierarchies, and Motion Modifiers

In this chapter we're going to look at a collection of essential concepts in LightWave. Environments give our scenes something more than a simple black background and bring our virtual worlds to life, where hierarchies let us create complex interconnecting parts of objects such as robots or wheels on cars. Motion and channel modifiers help add automatic motion and time travel (keep reading!) to make our animations slicker.

These are essential skills we'll need as we create our amazing projects, animations, and virtual worlds in LightWave!

Environments

What lies beyond the edges of our CG cityscape? What do we see when we point the camera up into the virtual sky above that CG forest, or target an empty location in outer space? Unless we've created the atmosphere, the immense infinite depth of space, or the distant landscapes ourselves, there's nothing there but a void of bits and bytes in the memory of your computer.

That's where the power of using environments comes into play, letting us create a world beyond the crafted 3D world. Imagine taking a 360-degree photograph of the world around you, then replacing reality by painting the photo on the inside of a gigantic ball that surrounds you completely. Well, that's what an environment in LightWave is: an infinitely sized ball that surrounds the virtual world in which we're creating our pieces of art.

However, unlike a simple image that is painted inside a ball, this environment can be animated, reflected, refracted, and even used as a global source of lighting (which we discovered back in Chapter 10).

Setting Up an Environment

Environments in Layout are accessed through **Windows | Backdrop Options**. By default, the environment is represented by the **Backdrop Color**.

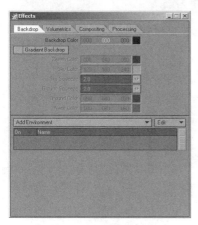

Figure 12-1: The Backdrop options.

Gradient Backdrop

We have the ability to use simple color gradients to represent sky and ground in this window. A gradient backdrop gives us a quick way to create simple sky tones, and in fact can be used along with some of the other environment tools later on to add background coloration. To use a gradient backdrop, just activate it!

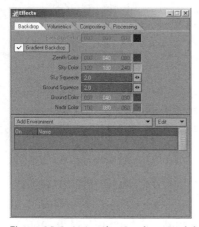

Figure 12-2: Using the Gradient Backdrop option.

The gradient can be tweaked easily by adjusting the colors and options.

- **Zenith Color** is the color of the environment seen directly above the camera.

- **Sky Color** is the color at the base of the horizon.

- **Sky Squeeze** controls the gradient spread between the Sky and Zenith colors. The higher the value, the more Zenith color is present and the tighter the squeeze along the horizon. (Various levels of squeeze are shown in Figure 12-3).

Figure 12-3: The effect of squeezing the gradients.

- **Ground Squeeze** controls the gradient spread between the Ground and Nadir colors. It gives the same effect as we've seen for the sky, except obviously for the ground.

- **Ground Color** is the color of the ground just below the horizon.

- **Nadir Color**, the opposite of Zenith color, is the color of the environment directly below the camera.

Environmental Plug-ins

LightWave ships with a small collection of environmental plug-ins designed for creating more complex environments than just colors or gradients. These can be accessed from the **Add Environment** pop-up. Let's look at these additional tools in a little more detail.

Image World

Image World, as we learned back in Chapter 10, is a tool we can use for unwrapping angular maps (those HDR probe images, which are the poor man's fish-eye images taken by pointing the camera at a chrome ball). Image World unwraps this fish-eye view of the world into something that is then mapped back as an environment. We've already touched on this subject in Chapter 10 by using an HDR image as an environment for lighting. As a reminder, let's start Layout and add an environment using Image World.

1. Open up Layout and start with a fresh new scene (if Layout is already open, simply **File | Clear Scene** (<**N**>)). Activate VIPER (<**F7**>) so that we can preview the Image World environment. Open the Image Editor (<**F6**>) and load **images\HDR\Building_ Probe.pic** from the classic content that ships with LightWave. (This is the high dynamic range image we used back in Chapter 10 for creating lighting.)

2. Click on **Windows | Backdrop Options** and add the **Image World** plug-in from the Add Environment pop-up. Double-click on **Image World** to open its properties and set the Light Probe Image option to **Building_ Probe.pic**.

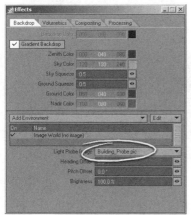

Figure 12-4: Setting the HDR probe for Image World.

3. We're now using the HDR probe image as an environment. Animate the camera, panning around by going to frame 60 and setting the rotation of the camera to **360** on Heading. Make a preview in VIPER to see the environment at work.

Figure 12-5: Making a preview in VIPER is a quick way to check out an environment at work.

> ## Note
> Want to see just what Image World does with an image? Layout's amazing new Advanced Camera technology can be used to not only see the effect of any environment in LightWave, but also to create unwrapped HDR maps for other uses in texturing and other things (where we don't want to use Image World). Setting the Advanced Camera to be a 360-degree by 180-degree cylindrical camera and then rendering (<F9>), we can quickly create an unwrapped spherical image map as seen in Figure 12-6. Refer back to Chapter 4 for a refresher on LightWave's camera system if you need to.

505

Figure 12-6: Rendering around the whole scene with the Advanced Camera.

Figure 12-7: Backdrops, VIPER, and the Preset shelf.

While VIPER is a quick way to check out an environment, it can't perform complex rendering like the Advanced Camera can. We need to <F9> to see this effect.

If you are using LightWave's Image Viewer window to see your rendered images and want to maintain the more complex HDR information, you need to set the Render | Render Globals | Render Display pop-up to **Image Viewer FP** (FP means full precision (high dynamic information for each pixel)). After the render window pops up, simply choose **File | Save RGBA**, and save the image in HDR format using one of the image formats such as Radiance (.hdr).

Textured Environment

Textured Environment uses LightWave's powerful Texture Editor to create the environment. It opens huge doors for us in terms of creating amazing environmental backdrops, or compiling layers of imagery! Let's look at how we can use the textured environment to quickly create some great backdrops for our projects.

Let's use Textured Environment to add a quick environment using a spherical sky map to an otherwise bland cityscape.

1. Load the scene **Scenes\Chapter 12\ The_city.lws.** This is a simple scene with a black environment color and a generic cityscape object. A quick render reveals how unexciting it is.

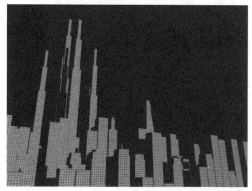

Figure 12-8: The bland cityscape on its black backdrop.

2. Let's add a spherical environment image map to add some life to our scene. Open **Windows | Backdrop Options** and choose **Textured Environment** from the Add Environment pop-up.

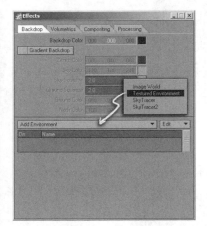

Figure 12-9: Add the Textured Environment plug-in.

3. Double-click on **Textured Environment** to open up the properties for the plug-in. Click the **Texture** button to open the Texture Editor. Select the **(load image)** option from the Image pop-up, and load **skymap_clearsky-sunset.png** from Images\Chapter 12\ Environments. Set Projection to **Spherical** and Axis to **Y.** Do an <**F9**> to test the result.

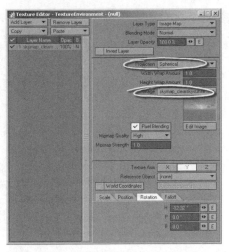

Figure 12-10: Adding the spherical environment map.

Figure 12-11: The rendered result, now with trendy sky map!

That was easy. With all of the power of the Texture Editor, there's no end of things we can create as backdrops. Creating wildly splattered paint backdrops can be as simple as applying a multicolored gradient over the top of a Turbulence procedural, outer space can be imagined through a tiny Crust procedural with Turbulence for nebulae... The only limit to what you can create is your own imagination!

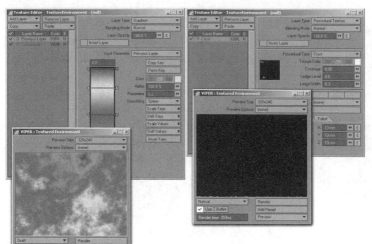

Figure 12-12:
Psychedelic paint
or crusty star field
— take your pick.

SkyTracer2

SkyTracer2 is an atmosphere simulator. It renders sun, moon, clouds, haze, and more. While we won't go into deep detail on this tool, let's look at how we can quickly create a cloudy sky for our animations using SkyTracer2.

1. Create a new scene in Layout. Let's make sure we have VIPER active with <F7> and then select **Windows | Backdrop Options**. Select **SkyTracer2** from the Add Environment pop-up. Double-click on **SkyTracer2** to open its properties window.

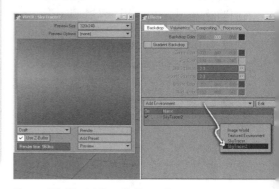

Figure 12-13: Adding SkyTracer2.

2. As we can see in the VIPER window, there's a lovely gradient, but not much sky going on. Click on the SkyTracer **Clouds** tab, and then choose **Enable Clouds** from the Low Altitude Clouds tab. This will add in some low, thick

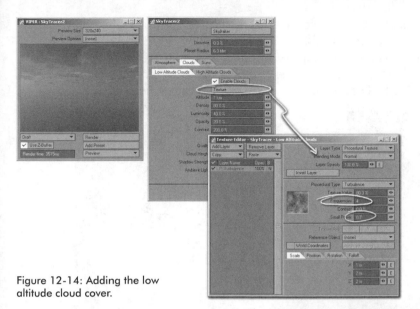

Figure 12-14: Adding the low altitude cloud cover.

cloud cover. We can tweak the look of the clouds through the **Texture** button if we wish. Once I press the Texture button, I usually edit the Turbulence settings in the Texture Editor to something like Frequencies of **4** and Small Power of **0.7** to get a little more detail in the cloud appearance.

> **Note**
>
> The High Altitude Clouds tab adds thin, wispy backdrop clouds and can be activated also if you want to.

3. We can change the Cloud Height option to create thinner clouds by setting this value to **50 m**. Because SkyTracer2 is an actual simulation of atmospherics, the thinner clouds allow more light to pass through also, and hence creates a lighter appearance. It also speeds up the render time a little as well.

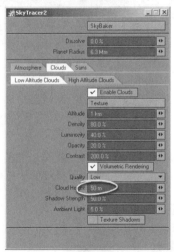

Figure 12-15: Changing cloud height.

4. Let's just take a quick peek at setting up the sunshine. When SkyTracer2 is added to a scene, a special light is also added called SKT_Sun. This light's only purpose is to act as the direction that the sun is shining from. SKT_Sun is controlled by a date/time/position tool that can be accessed through the **Sun Position** button. While this is

clever, it's not exactly the most convenient way to set up a sun. Luckily, however, you can use any light source you want with SkyTracer2, so swap the SKT light out for the **Light** option.

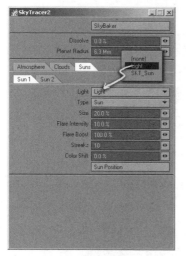

Figure 12-16: Changing the sun's light source.

5. SkyTracer2 uses the rotation of the light source to determine where in the sky it's coming from. (Essentially the same concept as a distant light.) Let's rotate the light **180.00** on Heading and **2.00** on Pitch to place it just above the horizon line, and in front of our camera.

Figure 12-17: Adjusting the light's rotation creates a nice-looking sunset.

This creates a nice, soft pink sunset feel to our sky.

If you want to, feel free to tweak the other sun parameters to see how they work. To create richer, intense sunset skies, try setting Size to **100%** to increase the sun's size. As we can see in Figure 12-18, suddenly we get a much richer, more dramatic effect from simply increasing the sun's size.

Figure 12-18: Big change from simple tweaks. The dramatic sunset.

Just to see the difference in effect, try switching the sun to be a moon instead. SkyTracer2 will illuminate the atmosphere as though it's now evening and not midday. While it may look okay initially, I've found that often it's necessary to tweak the **Atmosphere | Atmosphere | Thickness** setting to up to a quarter as much to get the coloration of the night sky to behave correctly, as shown in Figure 12-19. When the atmosphere is too thick, the light can shift toward a reddish tone, which is definitely not realistic.

SkyTracer2 is a nice kit and worth spending a little time playing around with.

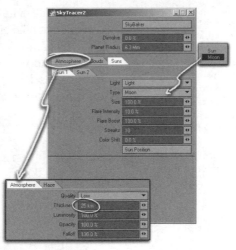

Figure 12-19: Now it's a moon.

Note

SkyTracer2 is a great tool, but as we discovered, it can slow things down immensely. Did you notice that the top of the SkyTracer window has a button called SkyBaker? Clicking this option allows us to render out various image maps (including HDR probes) and then use the images in place of the more time-consuming mathematics required by SkyTracer2. Often I will bake out any cool skies to a sphere and then use Textured Environment to apply them back into a scene as we did earlier in the chapter. As an image, the sky renders almost instantaneously and it's worth doing if you plan on making use of skies a lot in your projects.

Using Background Images

It's possible to place images into the backdrop using **Windows | Compositing Options** and selecting an image as a background. This image will be stretched to fill the image, and will appear in any gaps where there is no geometry, overwriting the environment behind it.

We used this option back in Chapter 10 when working through the compositing process. In Chapter 10 we placed a photograph behind a 3D character to create the illusion that the character was part of the photograph.

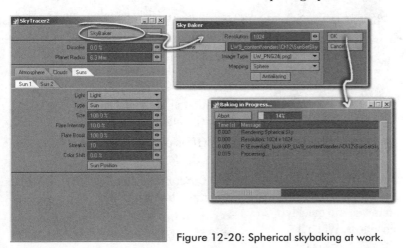

Figure 12-20: Spherical skybaking at work.

Fog

In the real world, atmosphere is everywhere. Even on the clearest of days, there's always some small amount of haze in the air, whether it's the bluish color of those mountains in the distance or the thick moist haze surrounding the islands of the Adriatic in the scorching heat of the day. Adding atmosphere to any scene can greatly add to its production value (as we learned in Chapter 10), and using fog in LightWave is one of those tools that simulates this effect quickly and effectively.

Figure 12-21: Hot, clear day in the Adriatic (off the coast of Croatia). Note the thick haze surrounding the outer islands.

By fading the surface appearance of objects toward a fog color based on the surface's distance from the camera, we can quickly add the illusion of atmosphere. While it doesn't work like real fog as there is no

"volume" of mist in the CG air, it is a very effective fake effect and works very quickly. To use fog in a scene, we simply activate the **Windows | Volumetrics and Fog Options | Fog Type** by setting it to something other than Off.

Figure 12-22: Fog options.

Note

Lens flares and various other effects in LightWave can also be affected by fog for more realistic renders, such as for recreating the glow of the lamps on the sides of a carriage rushing through the thick pea soup of a London street. We'll look at these in this section.

Fog settings are fairly simple to understand.

- **Fog Type** controls the fade effect of fog — how it fades from a minimum amount through to its thickest. The small chart to the left of the settings gives us a graphical visualization of the Fog Type so that we can see how the effect will work.

  - **Off** is obvious in that it just disables the fog.

  - **Linear** fades the fog linearly from minimum to maximum.

  - **Nonlinear 1** fades the fog linearly at the start, but eases in to create the illusion of thickness increasing with distance.

• **Nonlinear 2** fades the fog in thickly and quickly.

• **Realistic** is a new mode for LightWave v9 that creates a more natural appearance to the way the fog behaves. It also allows fog to work correctly with transparent, reflective, and refractive properties.

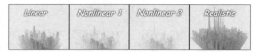

Figure 12-23: Fog types in action.

• **Min Distance** is the distance from the camera where the fog begins to fade toward the maximum. By default, this is set to 0 m, or from the camera itself. Increasing this value means that the fog won't start to thicken up until items are at this distance.

• **Max Distance** is the distance from the camera where the fog is at its thickest.

• **Min Amount** is how thick the fog is from the camera to the Min Distance point.

• **Max Amount** is how thick the fog gets at its maximum.

• **Use Backdrop Color** will take the environment color at the same pixel, and then apply it to the amount of fog being added to the item in the scene. We'll look later at just how useful this option can be!

• **Fog Color** is a flat color used for the fog effect. Ideally, this color should match the environment if you want to simulate realistic fog, but can be anything really. For example, you may want to use the default light blue/gray tone here to simulate the

subtle haziness of the far-off mountains in a scene.

Where's the Fog?

LightWave has a couple of handy display tools. These tools help us set up and get the fog happening visually without relying upon the unartistic approach to using numbers and parameters.

OpenGL Fog

In the Camera View, we can see the effect of fog in real time. If you can't see anything in the Camera View after activating the fog, press <d> to bring up the Display Options, and make sure that **OpenGL Fog** is active, as shown in Figure 12-24.

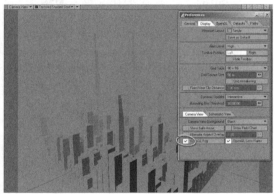

Figure 12-24: OpenGL Fog in action.

Fog Circles

In any orthographic view, the minimum and maximum distances for fog can be viewed as dotted circles around the camera itself. If no circles are visible, then press <d> and select the OpenGL tab. Make sure that the **Show Fog Circles** option is active, as shown in Figure 12-25.

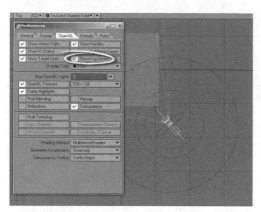

Figure 12-25: Show those fog circles.

Let's take a quick look at the fog tool and see how it works.

1. Start by loading up the scene **Scenes\ Chapter 12\foggy_street.lws**. This scene contains a simple street lit by streetlights. Something weird is going on! A huge dented-up old shiny chrome ball appears to be rolling down the street. Let's see how we can make this scene a little creepier with a little fog! In Figure 12-26, you'll see that the reflections are visible in the Layout viewport. To make your view look like Figure 12-26, simply check the **Reflections** option in the Edit | OpenGL window.

Figure 12-26: Street Wars: Attack of the chromes.

2. Do an **<F9>** and let's check out what the scene looks like without any fog (as shown in Figure 12-27). Now let's see how things look once we throw in a little fog. Open **Windows | Volumetric and Fog Options** and activate the fog by setting Fog Type to **Nonlinear 1**. Set Max Distance to **75 m** and activate the **Use Backdrop Color** option to make the fog blend in with the background. Do another **<F9>** to see the difference from the non-fog version.

Figure 12-27: No foggification. Hmmm.

Figure 12-28: Now with fog.

3. Not bad! But there is a small issue: The fog gets thicker in the distance, but the lights are still burning bright. Select one of the lights in the scene, and then open the Light Properties

Figure 12-29: Tweaking the lens flares to work with the fog.

window by pressing <p>. Open the Lens Flare Options window, and activate the **Fade in Fog** option. Change the Flare Intensity setting to **100%**. Once the flares start to fade in the fog, the original 30% becomes too weak and loses the visual impact.

> **Note**
>
> The Lens Flare Options window is *non-modal*, allowing it to stay open while we work, and will update and display the details for the *currently selected light*. We can use the <Up Arrow> and <Down Arrow> keys to switch between lights in the scene quickly, and just tweak the Lens Flare options as they appear in this window. It's just one of the many ways to improve your speed and workflow in LightWave!

Hierarchy

Ever sing that song about how "the leg bone's connected to the hip bone, and the knee bone's connected to the leg bone"? Well, as geeky as this may sound, this is a song about the hierarchical relationship between parts of a skeleton. Each bone is connected to a previous bone and keeps the skeleton connected together so that, for instance, if the upper arm lifts, then the other parts that are connected to it also move.

In LightWave, we have the ability to create connections like this; in fact, it's a day-to-day necessity in most projects. Hierarchy is all about relationships between things, and in LightWave we work in what is referred to as a *parent-child hierarchy* system.

Where's My Baby!?

It can sound a little overwhelming at first — *parent, child, hierarchy*. Those are techy-sounding buzzwords, but in reality it's no different than a person walking a dog. The dog is *parented* to the person by its leash; while the dog stays attached to the person through the leash, it can still do its own thing like run about, sniff trees and lamp posts, and do all the other activities dogs do. Yet the leash keeps these two attached. The dog follows the person (parent) when the leash is pulled around. (Well, some dogs do, that is!)

When an item in LightWave is connected to another, it is known as being *parented* to it. What this means is, from now on wherever this parent item goes and whatever this parent item does (stretch, rotate, and the like), then this item will follow and inherit these actions, as well as still being able to do its own thing. This item is now the child of the parent item. It's related in more ways than just being simply attached to it!

We don't have leashes in LightWave, but we can connect items together pretty easily in a number of ways. Let's take a look at creating a hierarchy for an item, such as a modern desk lamp. The lamp's heavy base will be the parent. Its various hinged parts and the light on top will all need to be connected — or *parented* — in a hierarchical order if we want to be able to fold and unfold the lamp for animating later on.

1. Start up Layout (if it isn't running already) and load the object **Objects\ Chapter 12\Desk_Lamp.lwo**. This desk lamp is made up of four pieces, which we're going to connect together using parenting.

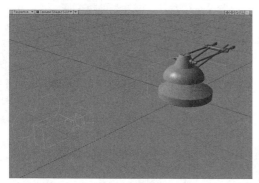

Figure 12-30: Load in the Desk_Lamp.lwo model. There are four parts that need to work as one.

2. Before we start building our hierarchy, let's make sure that the pivots of each part are in the right place. The *pivot* is the location at which items rotate, and it's important that these are set up properly, given that the lamp parts need to rotate from hinged locations.

Switch the viewport display to a **Left (ZY)** display view and set the viewport to display in **Front Face Wireframe** mode (as shown in Figure 12-31). This will make placing the pivot location easy to see.

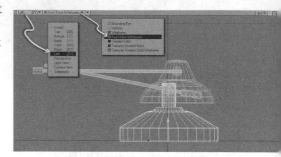

Figure 12-31: Setting the display for the viewport.

3. Let's go through each object (except the Desk_Lamp:Base, as its pivot is okay) and set up the pivot points. Start with the selection of the **Desk_Lamp: Lamp** object, and then select **Modify | Translate | Move Pivot**. Move the pivot location to the center of the rod that runs through the lamp, as shown in Figure 12-32. (If you want to numerically set the pivot location, set **294.7788 mm** on Y and **–37.948 mm** on Z.)

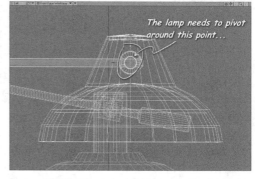

Figure 12-32: Move the pivot location to here.

4. Next, select the **Desk_Lamp:Upper_stand** and set its pivot to the center of the hinge as shown in Figure 12-33. Like the lamp, you can also set this numerically by setting Y to **293.593 mm** and Z to **421.0347 mm**.

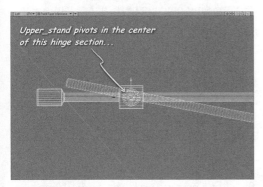

Figure 12-33: Upper_stand pivot.

5. Finally, let's set up the **Desk_Lamp: Lower_stand** object as shown in Figure 12-34. (The numeric values are Y = **215.8497 mm** and Z = **–3.1254 mm**.) We don't need to modify the Desk_Lamp:Base object as its pivot is in the correct place to begin with. Once finished, we're ready to go!

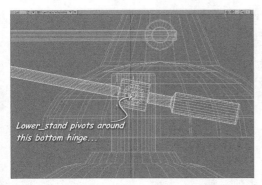

Figure 12-34: Setting the pivots for the Lower_stand object.

Note

Parenting snaps an object's pivot location to the pivot location of the parent item. This is, however, only true if the option Parent in Place is *not active*. The Parent in Place button, found on the toolbar just under the Scene Editor pop-up, will parent an item but retain its current position and prevent the snapping that usually occurs. While useful, there will be times when you may *want* to snap an item to the center of the parent. In this case, either deactivate Parent in Place or, once parented to another item, keyframe the item's location to 0,0,0.

Parenting items can be done in a handful of different ways in LightWave. I'll show you a couple of ways that we can apply parenting items.

6. First of all, let's select **Desk_Lamp: Lower_stand**. Open the **Windows | Motion Options** window and select **Desk_Lamp:Base** from the Parent Item pop-up (Figure 12-35). This is the simplest approach to parenting in LightWave. If you click on the Parent Item pop-up again, you'll see that the Desk_Lamp:Lower_stand is now displayed in this list indented below its parent item, as shown in Figure 12-36.

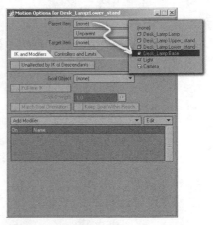

Figure 12-35: Setting the parent item to Desk_Lamp:Base.

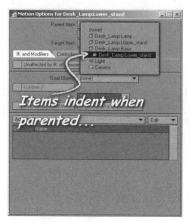

Figure 12-36: Note the way that parented items indent in the list.

Lamp:Lower_stand that we parented to the Desk_Lamp:Base. If we look at Desk_Lamp:Base, we'll see a small triangular widget to the left of it. Click on this to expand the children of the Desk_Lamp:Base object and voilà! Our missing piece is here, as we can see in Figure 12-38.

Note

The Scene Editor is like a spreadsheet of all the items in a scene, and it's a great workflow tool for changing parameters en masse, sliding and stretching animation frames around, and parenting items to each other quickly.

7. Here's another more visual method of parenting, and probably one you'll use more than any other in LightWave. Click on **Scene Editor | Open** to open up the Scene Editor window (Figure 12-37). You'll notice that we're missing one item here: the Desk_

8. Let's parent the Desk_Lamp:Upper_ stand to the Desk_Lamp:Lower_stand. In the Scene Editor, click and hold down the left mouse button on the **Desk_Lamp:Upper_stand**, and then drag up and over the Desk_Lamp: Lower_stand object until a line appears

Figure 12-37: The Scene Editor.

Figure 12-38: Expanding the Desk_Lamp:Base to see its children.

below the Desk_Lamp:Lower_stand as shown in Figure 12-39. Once the line appears, release the mouse button to parent the objects together. Once parented, you should see a triangular widget appear next to Desk_Lamp: Lower_stand, and the Desk_Lamp: Upper_stand appear indented below it.

9. Lastly, let's select the **Desk_Lamp: Lamp** object in the Scene Editor, then left-click and drag the item up and onto the Desk_Lamp: Upper_stand to parent them (Figure 12-40). Release the

mouse button once the line appears below the Desk_Lamp:Upper_stand object and we're finished building our desk lamp hierarchy (Figure 12-41), and it's ready for posing or animation!

Now that the desk lamp is connected together as a hierarchy, select each part and try rotating it around its pitch axis to see how its child objects stay connected. To move and position the entire lamp, simply move the parent of everything — Desk_ Lamp: Base.

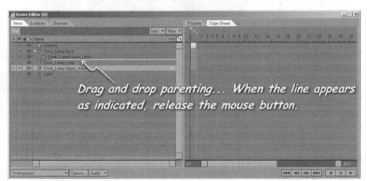

Figure 12-39: Click and drag until a line appears.

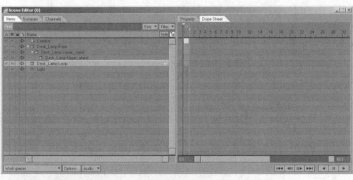

Figure 12-40: Parenting the Desk_Lamp:Lamp to the Desk_Lamp:Upper_stand.

Figure 12-41: The parented hierarchy is visually apparent in the Scene Editor.

Nulls

Null, nil, zilch, nothing all mean the same thing... Except in the world of CG, where a *null* is an incredibly useful non-rendering nothing object. Whether it's being used as a control in an animated character, providing a handy location for the camera to follow around, or defining the location in virtual space to create a planetoid, the null is every LightWave artist's "Swiss Army Knife" tool!

Its use comes through the fact that it doesn't have any solid form, hence it can't be rendered, cast shadows, or interfere in any way with your final rendered work (it is indeed *null* — not there). But it is still a valid item in your scene. It can be animated (moved, rotated, scaled), and even parented or attached to things as well as referenced by other items and plug-ins.

In LightWave v9, the null object has had a facelift. As shown in Figure 12-42, when we create a new null (<**Ctrl**>+<**n**>) we're presented with a Build Null Object window. Clicking the **Edit** button reveals a whole new range of controls that allow us to change the look and display of this item in Layout (as seen in Figure 12-43).

Figure 12-42: The initial Build Null Object window.

The settings to change the look of the null are all pretty self-explanatory.

- **Shape** lets us give the null its own visual appearance in the interface. There are eight different shapes to choose from, and a None setting if we don't want the null to be represented by a shape.

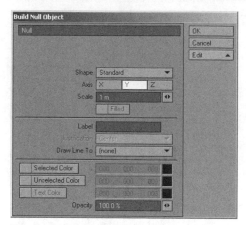

Figure 12-43: A facelift for LightWave v9!

- **Axis** defines the orientation of the shape.

- **Scale** lets us size the shape of the null.

- **Filled**, if it's available on the selected shape, will make it a solid, flat color.

- **Label** can be used to display some text next to the null, which is helpful when using nulls as controls for other items.

- **Justification** sets the location of the text in relation to its center.

- **Draw Line To** will draw a dashed line from the null to a selected item, which, like the label, allows us to point out possible relationships with other items in a scene.

- **Selected Color, Unselected Color,** and **Text Color** give us the option to customize the display colors of our null.

- **Opacity** sets how solid the null appears in the interface. Setting this to something like 50% creates a partially transparent null, which is sometimes ideal if you happen to be using a filled shape.

Figure 12-44: Various new ways to show off your nulls.

Let's see how we can use a null to create a tool that creates a perfect circular motion for the camera. Note that this is just one of *hundreds* of possible uses of a null, and we'll be using the null object later on in the book for a lot of other tasks (so keep your eyes peeled.)

1. Open the scene **Scenes\Chapter 12\look_at_me.lws**. This is a simple scene with a camera looking straight at a classic teapot.

2. Let's add a null with **Items | Add | Null** (<Ctrl>+<n>). Give the null the name **Camera_Control**, then click on **Edit** to open the display options for the null. Let's set Shape to **Ring**, set Scale to **300 mm**, give it a Label of **Camera_Control**, and set Draw Line To to be the **Camera** (so we get that visual reference to the item the null relates to). Click **OK** to create this new null.

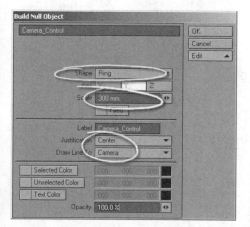

Figure 12-45: Add in the camera control.

3. Select the camera. Open the **Windows | Motion Options** window and let's parent the camera to the Camera_Control null.

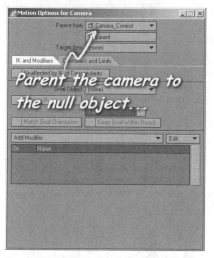

Figure 12-46: Parent the camera to the new control null.

4. Move the frame slider to frame 60, then select the **Camera_Control** null and set its rotation to **360** on Heading. Create a key frame at **60** to record this rotation. Move the frame slider back to 0, and set the rotation to **27.10** on the Pitch. Be sure to keyframe the null again, then play back the animation. We should now have a clean, perfect circular motion. The null is doing all the work of moving the camera for us!

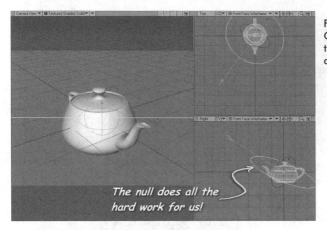

The null does all the hard work for us!

Figure 12-47:
Camera in motion,
thanks to the handy-
dandy null.

Note

If you are still unsure of exactly what went on here, then imagine a crane with a long boom in a movie studio. We connect the movie camera to the end of this crane boom and then control the camera's physical motion through rotating and pivoting the crane. In LightWave, the null provides the pivot location of the "crane." We can use nulls to create virtual camera rigs to give us control over the motion and movement of the camera in a way that's cleaner and easier than animating the camera directly.

No doubt about it — nulls are uber-flexible tools. They're invisible to the render, but they're very visible to the user where it counts! Keep your eyes peeled throughout the book to see just how many times we'll make use of these all-in-one tools of the trade.

Motion Modifiers

Animating by hand is fun, but things can be hard if we're trying to create realistic or complex motions such as making items avoid each other or travel across the surface of a rolling landscape. Motion modifiers are all about modifying or even completely replacing the animation of an item. Light-Wave can modify the rotation of an item based on the path that it travels along, or it can use one of a handful of motion modifier plug-ins to create more specialized motion and even travel through time, as we'll be seeing later in this chapter.

To modify the motion of any item, select it and then open the **Windows | Motion Options** window.

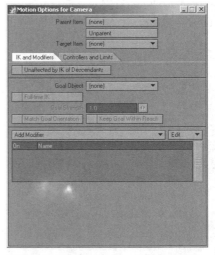

Figure 12-48: The Motion Options window.

This window lets us apply a variety of motion modifying controls and tools. We'll be looking at some of the features in the Motion Options window in upcoming chapters, but for now, let's look at a few of the new key tools and how we can best use them to create amazing animation.

Align to Path

Have you ever tried to animate the swerving and turning of a car driving along a racetrack? Unless you key the vehicle at the right spots, it can be a little tricky to keep it from looking a little floaty, and well, it's just time consuming to do something that you probably would assume to be simple. Help, however, is at hand with LightWave's ability to align an item along a path. This option has been available in LightWave for some time, but has been vastly improved in LightWave v9 to be more accurate and give better control. Let's give it a whirl!

1. Load the scene **Scenes\Chapter 12\follow_path.lws**. It's an exciting shot from a possible upcoming sci-fi epic. While it's looking pretty cool, there's something not quite right with that spacecraft and the ways it's flying into the shot. The problem is that the ship feels like it's *sliding in*, not flying

Figure 12-49: Here comes the ship into frame, but not facing in the direction it's traveling.

in. This is because the object doesn't face the path it's traveling, and instead always points along the Z-axis.

2. Let's select **Space_ship.lwo** (from Objects\Chapter 12) and then open the **Windows | Motion Options** window. We're going to use the **Align to Path** options here to get the ship at least facing the right way as it flies along. Click on the **Controllers and Limits** tab, and then select **Align to Path** from both the Heading Controller pop-up and the Pitch Controller pop-up.

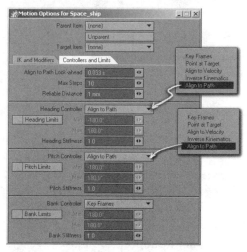

Figure 12-50: Aligning the direction of the ship along its path.

Note

The old pre-LightWave v9 method of aligning an item to its path is still available, but has been renamed *Align to Velocity* instead (which better describes the way it is calculated).

Play back the animation. The ship now turns and tilts correctly as it travels along its journey through the buildings. However, when flying vehicles turn, they often bank into the turns. Let's add this quickly to add the final touch to this animation.

3. Go to frame 30, select the Rotation tool <y>, and then set the angle to **–39.00** for Bank. Go to frame 55 and set Bank to **59.00**, then go to frame 83 and set Bank to **–24.00**. Now play this animation back to see the improvement!

Figure 12-51: Banking into the turns.

> **Note**
>
> Did your changes not "stick" when you set them? Make sure you remember the golden rule of creating key frames to record changes in animation. Or use the handy Auto Key option instead!

There is a rendered animation you can look at in **Renders\Chapter 12\follow_ path.mov** if you want to see the sequence in its full rendered glory. In Chapter 10, we talked a lot about production value, and how lighting plays a large part in the quality of our final production. I used this advice myself, and changed the light in the final version of this exercise to an area light. This created much nicer shadows and helped sell the sunset feel of the scene much better than the default lighting. I also set **Render Globals | Limited Region Borders** to narrow the height of the image, and add a cinematic feel to the final render by creating a letterbox effect. Check out **Scenes\Chapter 12\follow_path_F.lws** to

see these simple changes that help raise the production value of this simple piece of work.

> **Note**
>
> Sometimes Align to Path can generate odd jitters and shakiness in an object's motion. Simply tweaking the setting for Reliable Distance to something larger than the default 1 mm (like 100 mm, for example) can eliminate these small issues.

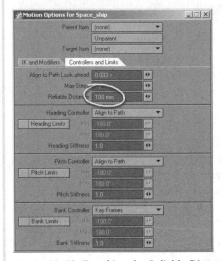

Figure 12-52: Tweaking the Reliable Distance parameter to smooth the motion.

Sticky

Something very slick and cool that's been added in LightWave v9 is the new motion modifier called Sticky. The name pretty much gives it away: Sticky is all about making sure items remain attached to the surface of other items. Until now, this could have been exceptionally complex should you want to create jeeps driving over rough terrain, or yachts sailing across the ocean. Let's see just how simple this tool is to use, and how cool this effect is!

1. Load the scene **Scenes\Chapter 12\floating_by.lws.** The scene is a simple boat motoring its way across a simple displaced mesh. Obviously the boat eats its way through the waves unrealistically, and isn't even facing the correct direction… Well, we could say this looks like a sticky problem. (Or a problem for Sticky, to be more exact!)

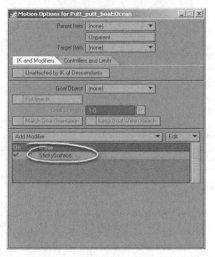

Figure 12-54: Make the ocean surface sticky.

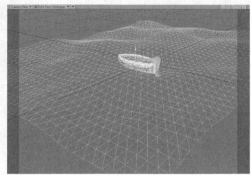

Figure 12-53: Half submerged, an unseaworthy ship if ever we saw one!

2. Select the **Putt_putt_boat:Ocean** object, open the **Windows | Motion Options** window, and select **StickySurface** from the Add Modifier pop-up. StickySurface lets us specify the items that we want sticky objects to attach themselves to; in this case, the ocean surface.

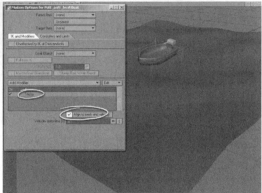

Figure 12-55: Tell the boat to stick to the ocean, and we're done!

3. Select the boat object, open the **Windows | Motion Options** window, and select **Sticky** from the Add Modifier pop-up. Double-click on **Sticky** to set some basic parameters. Activate the option **Align to mesh and velocity**, and then close the Motion Options window. Play the animation and watch!

> **Note**
>
> I've rendered the animation to **Renders\ Chapter 12\Sailing_by.mov** if you want to see how well Sticky takes care of moving the boat across the surface of our surging water. This final version of the scene is available in **Scenes\Chapter 12\floating_by_F.lws.** Note how I slightly modified the textures of the ocean and added in a null to allow me to add some pseudo-froth to the wave caps. (Hint: It's all controlled through the Luminosity channel.) It's worth a look-see if you're curious.

The possibilities are endless as to how we can use this tool — a simple boat on the ocean like this example, perhaps more complex interactions between bugs running across that CG corpse for the next big horror flick you are working on, or maybe that clothes iron running along the surface of the product logo for that next TV commercial.

Figure 12-56: Landing gear in action.

Cyclist

"Set driven key" is probably a term that you have heard used by many animators. But how many of you know exactly what this means? *Set driven key* simply means the driving (or playback) of one animation's key frames through the actions of another. For instance, you can animate the squash and stretch of a bouncing ball based on the Y-axis of the ball, or perhaps control the expanding and bulging of muscles based on the rotation and bending of limbs. How about unfolding the landing gear of a starship when the bay doors open or close? Controlling parts of an animation through the actions of another is a fantastic way to automate complex animation, and that's what Cyclist is all about! Rather than talk, let's do.

1. Load the scene **Scenes\Chapter 12\cyclist_this.lws**. This scene contains a 30-frame animation of the nose landing gear opening on some kind of vehicle. This simple sequence is constructed of various moving parts: doors opening, a wheel dropping down, sliding collars moving down the gear strut, and hydraulic rods moving forward.

Let's consider how time consuming reanimating all of these pieces would be each time we wanted to raise or lower the gear here. This is where we'd greatly benefit from being able to play this sequence back and forth through a simple control system. Let's set up this sequence to be controlled through a null item. As we learned earlier, the null is the animator's Swiss Army knife. Here we'll use one as a control that we can animate to drive the landing gear.

2. Choose **Items | Add | Null** to add the null item. Give it the name **GearControl** and expand the Edit options. Set Shape to **Ring** and Axis to **X**. Enter the text **Gear Controller** as the Label and then click **OK** to create the null. On frame 0, move the GearControl null to **–6 m** on the X-axis. It won't matter too much where you place the null. We just need to place it somewhere easily accessible by the animator that's not going to make it difficult to use.

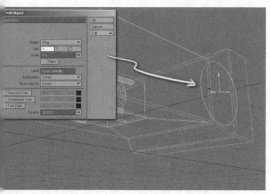

Figure 12-57: Adding a null.

3. Select the **Landing_Gear:Strut** and open the **Windows | Motion Options** window. Add the **Cyclist** plug-in as shown in Figure 12-58. Double-click on **Cyclist** to bring up the Cyclist — Animation Control window, and set the Cycle Controller pop-up to **Gear-Control**. Change the pop-up to the right of Cycle Controller to **Pitch Angle**. Set the Controller Range From value as **0.0** and the To value as **90.0**. Make sure that the End Behavior pop-up is set to **Stop** and click **OK** to close the window.

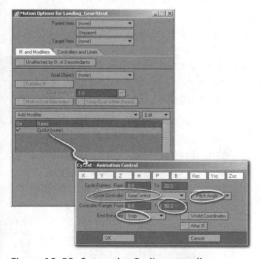

Figure 12-58: Set up the Cyclist controller appropriately.

If we play back the 30-frame sequence we'll notice an error: One part of the landing gear has stopped working! Cyclist now overrides the keyframed animation, instead playing back frames 0 to 30 for the Landing_Gear:strut item based on the pitch rotation of the GearControl null. We set up Cyclist to play back the animation as the Gear-Control rotated from 0 degrees to 90 degrees. All we need to do now is repeat the process for all the other items in the scene that are animated.

Let's speed things up, like we did in the "Fog" section, by taking advantage of the concept of non-modal windows and the ability to switch between items quickly with the <Up Arrow> and <Down Arrow> keys. The Windows | Motion Options window is non-modal. Make sure that it's open for the Landing_Gear:Strut item, and then select the **Cyclist** plug-in in the list. Click on the **Edit** pop-up as shown in Figure 12-59, and select **Copy**. This will copy Cyclist and all of its settings.

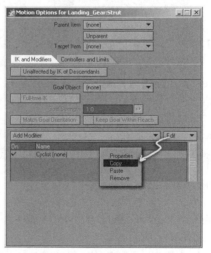

Figure 12-59: Copy Cyclist and all its settings.

Leave the Motion Options window open. As it's non-modal, it will update to display the settings for each item as we select it.

527

4. Press the <**Down Arrow**> key to select the **Landing_Gear:Collars** item. On the Motion Options window, click on the **Edit** pop-up and select **Paste** to add the Cyclist plug-in. The settings that we applied to the Landing_Gear:Strut are added automatically (note that GearControl appears next to Cyclist in Figure 12-60), saving us time in tweaking options and helping make our workflow faster!

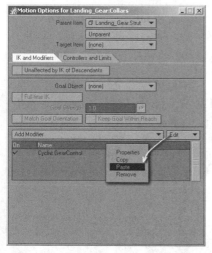

Figure 12-60: Paste Cyclist onto the collars.

5. Press the <**Down Arrow**> again and select the **Landing_Gear:Hydraulics** item, pasting the Cyclist plug-in into the Motion Options window as we did for the previous item. Press the <**Down Arrow**> twice to select the **ShipNose:LeftDoor** and paste Cyclist. Press the <**Down Arrow**> one last time to select the **ShipNose: RightDoor** and paste Cyclist again. We've finished setting up our automated control of the landing gear!

Playing this animation will reveal nothing. Everything is now under the control of the GearControl null, and plays back when we

rotate it on its Pitch axis between 0 and 90 degrees. Let's test it out and see just how easy it is to animate the gear for this sequence.

6. Change the last frame on the slider to **120**. Select the **GearControl** null, and then use the Rotate tool. At frame **40**, rotate the GearControl null to **90** on the Pitch and keyframe it. Copy this key frame again at frame **60** by clicking on **Create Key** and setting the Create key at value to **60**. Click **OK** to generate the key frame. On frame **80**, rotate the Pitch back to **0** degrees and keyframe it here. Play this animation back and note how easily we can control the gear moving in and out, as well as how by simply animating the null faster or slower we can also change the speed of the gear animation.

Timewarp

Have you seen those films where the down-and-out kid finds a device that lets him move so fast it's as though everybody around him is frozen in time? No? Well, meet Timewarp, the motion modifier that can warp and manipulate time around the camera and create effects like bullet time, speed up, slow down, and even reverse time during a render!

Sounds like amazingly cool fun? It is! See for yourself.

1. Load the scene **Scenes\Chapter 12\ Shuriken_BulletTime.lws**. A deadly ninja throwing star whips toward the camera. But imagine how much more dynamic this could feel if we were to see it moving past the camera in slow motion just before the strike. Let's see how we can use the amazing new Timewarp tool to achieve this.

2. Let's first enable Fractional Frames. This option in LightWave allows us to create and use key frames between whole frames, and given that Timewarp allows us to use this fractional time, it is recommended that this be enabled. To enable Fractional Frames, open the **Edit | General Options** window and activate the **Fractional Frames** option as shown in Figure 12-61.

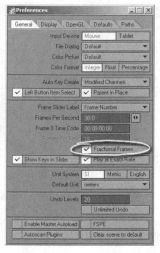

Figure 12-61: Activating Fractional Frames.

3. Timewarp is a motion modifier that is applied to the camera in the scene. Select the camera, and then open the **Windows | Motion Options** window. Choose **Timewarp** from the Add Modifier pop-up.

> **Note**
>
> Important! Timewarp modifies the time in a scene, and therefore you can only add *one* instance of Timewarp to a scene! If you have more than one camera, only one of these can have Timewarp.

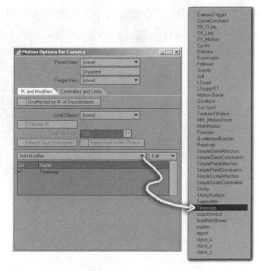

Figure 12-62: Adding Timewarp.

4. Double-click on **Timewarp** to open its properties window. To animate the time effect, we simply need to map the rendered frame to the animation frame using the Graph Editor. Click on the **E** next to **Frame warp** to open the Graph Editor, and let's see how this works. Frames along the graph horizontally are the rendered frames that we are going to create. The value of a key vertically indicates the frame in the animation that will be rendered at the current frame. As shown in Figure 12-63, the Frame warp graph works by remapping the animation frame to the frame that is being rendered. By manipulating which frame in the animation is mapped to which frame that is rendered, we can manipulate the way time is rendered — not only faster and slower but backward!

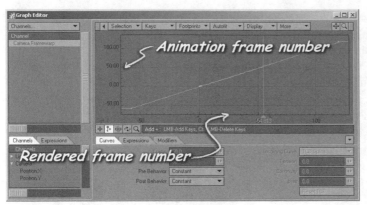

Figure 12-63: Timewarping maps the rendered frame to any frame in the animation.

5. Let's plan ahead and create a slow-motion effect for the ninja star just before the strike happens. I've identified that frames 50 to 55 look ideal for this effect to slow down, then have the effect suddenly kick back in from frames 56 to 60 as the star makes its deadly strike. Let's create this in the Graph Editor by creating a new key at

frame 50 and setting its value to also be 50. I've found that the cleanest way to do this is to press <Return> while in the Graph Editor, and type the values in numerically as shown in Figure 12-64.

6. Repeat the process again and create a key at frame 55, set to a value of 55. This will create the keys we need for

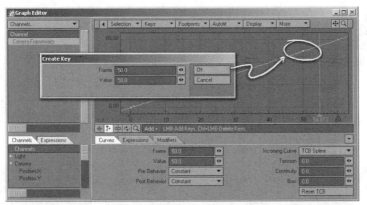

Figure 12-64: Normal speed up to frame 50.

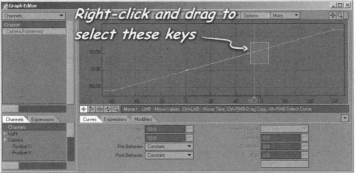

Figure 12-65: Selecting frames 55 and 60.

the start and end of the slow-down sequence. All we need to do now is simply select frames 55 and 60 in the Graph Editor by right-clicking and dragging a marquee over the two frames as shown in Figure 12-65.

7. Once selected, make sure that you have the Move tool active in the Graph Editor, then hold <**Ctrl**> and left-click and drag the keys along the Graph Editor approximately 30 frames to make the five frames between 50 and 55 last one second. It's as simple as that!

> **Note**
>
> If dragging isn't your thing, you can select the key on frame 60 and numerically set its key frame to 90, as shown in Figure 12-67. Select the key at frame 55 and numerically enter a new key frame value of 85.

8. Before we finish, let's select all the keys in the Timewarp graph (right-click and drag a marquee over all the items) and change Incoming Curve to **Linear**. This will straighten out all the lines, creating a more dynamic, snappy

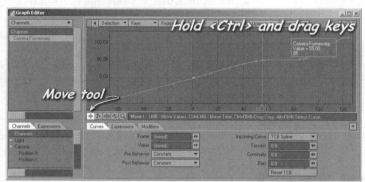

Figure 12-66: Drag the frames along about a second (30 frames) to stretch time.

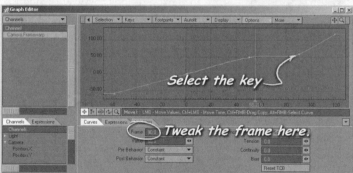

Figure 12-67: Numerically moving the keys.

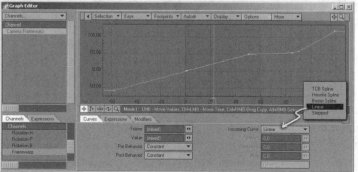

Figure 12-68: Linear motion to create snappier timewarping.

531

change from fast to slow and back to fast.

9. Let's check out the effect in Layout. Close the Graph Editor. The Timewarp window should still be on screen. (If it's not, select the camera and open the **Windows | Motion Options** window again, then double-click on the Time-warp plug-in.) Click the **Preview** button at the bottom of the Timewarp window (Figure 12-69). Change Last frame to **90** (where frame 60 now resides) and then click **Play >** to see the result in real time.

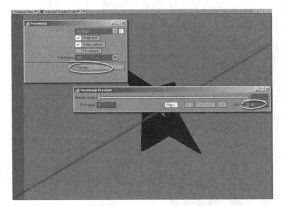

Figure 12-69: Previewing our timewarp.

Before doing any rendering, it's *very important* that we change not only the last rendered frame but also the last frame on the Frame Slider to your timewarped last frame (as we're rendering a different number of frames to the animated ones). If we don't change the Frame Slider, Timewarp will get stuck on the last frame and keep rendering the same frame over and over.

In this project, I'm rendering 90 frames for my 60-frame animation (see Figure 12-70). You can check out the difference between the original animation and the timewarped version in **ninja_normal.mov** and **ninja_slowdown.mov** in the Renders\Chapter 12 folder.

Figure 12-70: Be sure to set the last frame to the timewarped version.

Note

Timewarp works by manipulating the Frames Per Second settings as it renders. You may have spotted the Sub frames setting on the Timewarp properties window. This value is used to determine how much precision to use when creating the warping effect. (A value of 10 means that each frame will have 10 in-between frames.) When rendering, things can appear odd. The Frame Slider can start to expand like crazy to a huge number of frames; however, this is how Timewarp works, so don't panic!

There is one thing you need to watch out for: Timewarp will reset Frames Per Second after the render is finished. If we decide to abort a render partway through, Timewarp won't reset this. Instead, things can become a little weird and not play back correctly. No need to worry; simply check the **Edit | General Options** window and

Figure 12-71: Resetting Frames Per Second.

set **Frames Per Second** back to what it should have been. Your animation will be back to its normal self in no time.

This is just a small taste of what Timewarp can do. Try deactivating **Warp Camera** to enable the camera to move at normal speed around your slow-motion scene for that bullet-time effect. Deactivating the **Warp Blur** option lets us see the motion blur frozen in time. If you want to

see how these options work, check out **Scenes\Chapter 12\Trapped_in_time_Flws**. For those who just want to see the motion blur effect slowed down in time, I've rendered this scene out in **Renders\Chapter 12\trapped_in_time.mov**.

Timewarp is going to add a lot of fun to rendering animation in LightWave, if not create an overdose of bullet-time effects and gags!

Channel Modifiers

Where motion modifiers alter the actual animation of an item in LightWave, channel modifiers simply modify the motion of channels in the Graph Editor, which gives us control over the animation of individual channels for more specialized effects such as the flickering illumination of a light source or a soft wave motion on the Y-axis of a boat.

Let's try our hand at applying one of these channel modifiers, just to become familiar with what they are and how they work.

1. Open the scene **Scenes\Chapter 12\candleLight.lws**. This scene contains a simple candle sitting in a dark room. I've already prerendered this animated scene in **Renders\Chapter 12\candlelight.mov**. The main issue here is that candles tend to flicker as they burn. Our CG candle unfortunately has a constant illumination that just doesn't work and appears unrealistic.

2. Let's give the candle a little more realism by making its light fluctuate and flicker over time. We'll do this by adding a channel modifier to the intensity of the light that sits in the candle. Select the light, then click on Properties (<**p**>) to bring up the Light

Properties window. Click the **E** button next to the Light Intensity setting to bring up the Light.Intensity channel in the Graph Editor.

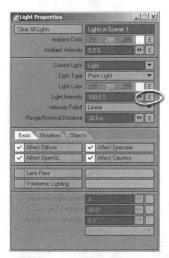

Figure 12-72: Let's edit the light illumination by clicking E.

3. Click on the Graph Editor's Modifiers tab, then select **Noisy Channel** from the Add Modifier pop-up as shown in Figure 12-73. The Noisy Channel modifier adds random motion to the animation of whatever channel we apply it to; in this case to the illumination.

533

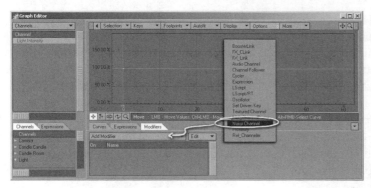

Figure 12-73: Adding some noise to our illumination channel.

Notice in Figure 12-74 how channel modifiers display their modifications as dotted curves in the Graph Editor. This gives us a good idea of what the modifier is doing to our channel. When a channel is modified in any way, a small dot is displayed to the left of the channel as indicated by the arrow.

4. To fine-tune the flickering (by default, it's modifying the light intensity up or down by up to 100%), double-click on

the **Noisy Channel** modifier to display its settings, and change Scale to **0.2** (which is 20%) as shown in Figure 12-75.

To see the effect of this modifier, I've rendered the animation in **Renders\Chapter 12\candlelight_flicker.mov**. The scene is also available in **Scenes\Chapter 12\candleLight_F.lws**.

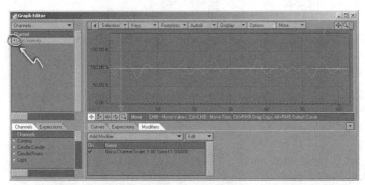

Figure 12-74: Modified channel.

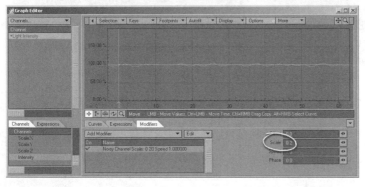

Figure 12-75: Lessen the flickering intensity to a maximum of 20% difference.

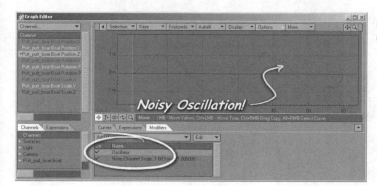

Figure 12-76: Adding multiple modifiers.

Note

Channel modifiers modify the animated data on a channel. We can add multiple channel modifiers to the list, and each will modify the result of the previous modifier to create more complex animation! For instance, adding the Oscillator modifier will create a sine wave motion to a channel, but adding a Noisy Channel modifier to this will apply a random noise to the oscillation as shown in Figure 12-76.

There's a handful of cool modifiers here. Let's take a quick look at one of the cool new offerings in LightWave v9 to help get the creative juices flowing!

Proximity

Ever needed to avoid something in your way? How about a low-flying aircraft avoiding collision with a bridge across the ravine it happens to be flying down? LightWave v9 ships with a special motion modifier just for tasks like this! Proximity will work out the distance from another item and allow us to manipulate a channel based on this detection.

Let's look at how we can quickly make an item avoid objects in its path using this tool.

1. Load the scene **Scenes\Chapter 12\avoid_bridge.lws**. A small aircraft flies along a valley toward an old stone bridge in the European countryside;

however, the pilot must be asleep since he doesn't avoid the bridge, and instead flies through it! In this example, we'll give the pilot a little assistance by using Proximity to improve his plane's autopilot capabilities.

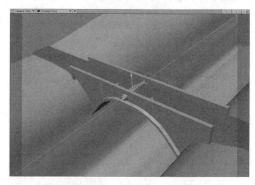

Figure 12-77: Watch out! Flying while asleep can be bad for your health.

2. Select the **TheBridge:Aircraft** object, then open the Graph Editor (**<Ctrl>+ <F2>**). We'll need to get the aircraft to duck underneath the bridge if we hope to ensure this pilot survives. Select the **TheBridge:Aircraft.Position.Y** channel and then click on the **Modifiers** tab in the Graph Editor. From the Add Modifier pop-up, select the **Proximity** modifier (Figure 12-78).

Proximity calculates the distance of an item from the surface of another. This distance is what we'll use to make the aircraft adjust

535

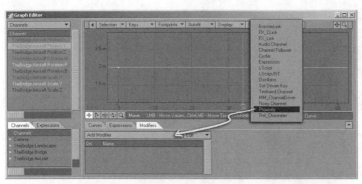

Figure 12-78: Adding Proximity to the Y channel.

Figure 12-79: The Y channel gets the distance value. Not quite the effect we're after.

when it gets close. By default it uses the distance directly as the modified value for the channel (Figure 12-79). Not quite the effect we want. Let's set up Proximity to correct this.

> **Note**
>
> If you can't see the Y channel as shown in Figure 12-79, press <a> while in the Graph Editor to view all the channels in their entirety.

3. Double-click on the **Proximity** modifier to open up its properties window. Change Target to **TheBridge:Bridge** and change Distance Modifier to **Remap…**. Remapping lets us read the distance of the aircraft to the bridge, then remap this information to a height value at which we want the aircraft to fly.

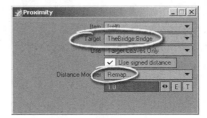

Figure 12-80: Set up the Proximity properties.

4. Click the **T** button below Remap… to open the Texture Editor for remapping purposes. Change Layer Type to **Gradient**, and set Input Parameter to **Proximity Distance**. Change the End value to **5.0** (as the aircraft starts around 5 or more meters away from the bridge) and then add a key at the bottom of the gradient with a Parameter of **5.0** and a Value of **2.0** (2 meters being the original height of the aircraft).

5. Add a third key in the gradient and set it to a Parameter of **2.0** and a Value of **2.0** so that the aircraft is still at its original height when it's 2 meters away from the bridge. Finally, make the aircraft a little more aerobatic and set the top key's Value to **1.5** (so that it just swoops under the bridge).

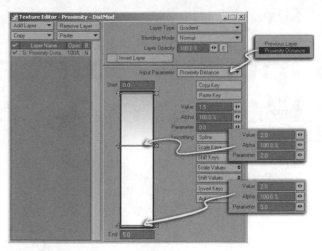

Figure 12-81: Setting the gradient.

> ### Note
> You may wonder why we're using three keys. After all, we could have just used two: a key at 2.0 and the top key to make the aircraft dip under the bridge. The third key is simply needed to help make the motion smoother. Two keys is not enough to define a smooth curve in LightWave, and the result would have been a linear path between the two keys. Feel free to delete the bottom key and see for yourself (but create it again to get the smooth motion back).

To check out my final scene, simply load **Scenes\Chapter 12\avoid_bridge_F.lws**. When looking at this scene, I also added an **Align to Path** controller for the Pitch to the aircraft, just to add a finishing touch to the animation.

Conclusion

We've created cool backdrops for our scenes with images using mathematical textures and sky simulators. We've learned how LightWave lets us connect things together into a hierarchy, and how we can get assistance in making some of the animation tasks we do every day a bit easier and more accurate. We even looked at how to travel in time and saved a sleepy pilot

from collision. But we've only scratched the surface here.

As you're aware by now, LightWave is a truly feature-packed beast! Dig deep, experiment and toy with these amazing tools, and most importantly learn and expand your skills and knowledge to create those CG masterpieces.

Chapter 13

Intermediate Skills: Particle Animation

Imagine someone said, "Create a virtual fireworks show for me in LightWave." (Perhaps like the one shown in Figure 13-1.) How would you do this? Fireworks generate thousands of hot little sparks of burning magnesium, gunpowder, and various combustible materials. To create such effects, we'd need a way to simulate all those little sparks. What about creating hundreds of soft flakes of snow gently drifting down from the sky or perhaps handfuls of candy-coated chocolate flying around a room? These kinds of things would be nearly impossible to create without the help of a particle system, so it's extremely lucky for us that LightWave comes with such a tool!

Particle animation is the basis behind many of the amazing effects we see on our favorite TV shows and movies — effects like missile smoke trails, hot sprays of sparks, huge space explosions, streets filled with colored rubber balls, turbulent waterfalls, and scorching fireballs. Any effect that is created through complex amounts of moving matter is ideal for a particle system. In this chapter, we are going to explore LightWave's excellent real-time particle system, as well as look at some of the features and the tools we can use to animate them.

> **Note**
>
> Particle animation is generated by simulating the motion of the particles using a variety of settings and rules. This kind of animation is often termed "procedural animation." We hear the term procedural also being used for those mathematical kinds of textures like fractals as well. When terms are shared about like this, it's not surprising that many people find themselves getting a little confused.

Figure 13-1: How would you create virtual fireworks like this without particles?

Step 1: Creating Particles

Particles are nothing more than singular points that are dynamically emitted from an object. Not surprisingly, an object that emits particles is also called an emitter. Particles have weight, air resistance, size, and even a lifespan that we can control the length of. When combined with some environmental behaviors like gravity, and given some initial motion when they are emitted, particles can behave like the sparks in fireworks, water in a fountain, or even light flakes of snow falling from the sky with very little work. LightWave takes care of working out how the particles should move, behave, and even interact with their surrounding environment.

Let's work our way through a simple particle effect to give us a feel for creating particles in LightWave. In this example, let's examine how we might go about creating a simple snowfall.

1. Start with a fresh, new scene. Choose **Items | Add | Dynamic Obj | Particle** to open the Add Particle Emitter dialog.

2. Enter the name **Snow** and accept the Emitter Type of **HV Emitter** (see Figure 13-2).

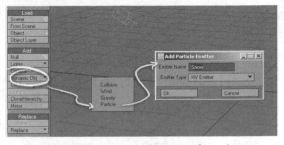

Figure 13-2: Add a new particle emitter from the Dynamic Obj pop-up.

A little box will appear in the middle of the viewport when you click **OK**. This represents the place where the particles will be emitted. An FX_Emitter panel will also appear, containing a number of interesting parameters that can be tweaked to control the particle effects.

Note

An emitter can be one of two kinds in LightWave: HV or Partigon. An HV Emitter (the default) will emit non-renderable null particles that can be used for attaching renderable information to, albeit other objects (which we'll look at in Chapter 22) or volumetric effects (which will be covered in Chapter 14). The other type of emitter is a Partigon emitter. This type emits renderable, single-point polygons that can be textured using the Surface Editor. Partigons are useful for simple effects, like sparks from a laser or anything that only requires a very simple appearance.

Step 2: The Anatomy of an Emitter

A particle emitter has many attributes, or parameters, that can be set to tell the emitter how its particles should move and behave. After we added the emitter in step 1, not only did an emitter appear, but the FX_Emitter panel popped up, containing all the emitter's parameters. Let's take a look at what everything in here means, and tweak a few settings along the way to set up our emitter.

The parameters are broken up into eight tabs across the panel. While we won't go into immense detail on every single option, we will look at the general options that are important to all particle effects.

Generator

How many particles are going to be born, from where, and how often? These are details that the emitter needs to know. The Generator tab lets us tell the emitter how life for all the particles begins. We can also limit the emitter so it only creates a certain amount of particles, much like a fireworks rocket only has a certain amount of gunpowder inside before it runs out.

1. For our new particle emitter, let's set a Birth Rate of **10**, and set the Generate by pop-up immediately below to be **Frame**. This means that 10 particles will be created every frame by our emitter. As this is a gentle snowfall, I didn't want to have too many flakes being generated quickly.

2. Set the Generator Size X and Z to **5 m** and the Y to **100 mm**, and set Particle Limit (the maximum number of particles that this particular emitter can generate) to **3000**.

At 10 particles per frame, our emitter should last for 300 frames of animation before it stops creating particles, which should be more than enough for whatever we want to do with these effects later on. We can fine-tune these values later should we decide to use this particle emitter in a shorter or longer animation. We've created a 5 by 5 meter area that's quite thin, so it should provide plenty of sky area for snow to fall from.

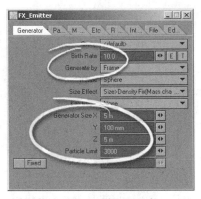

Figure 13-3: Set up the particles we want to emit.

Particle

The Particle tab is where we tell the emitter the general specifications for each particle it creates: the weight, size, and air resistance that affects it as it travels in our virtual 3D atmosphere. We can also specify just how long we want each particle to live.

Interestingly, there is no real-world value for some of these settings. Particle Size lets us set things in meters, and Life Time (frame) is in frames of animation. Particle Weight, however, is purely a value that LightWave will use when calculating the amount of influence some effects, such as gravity or wind, will have on a particle.

3. Let's tweak the particle settings in our new emitter to give all the particles a little uniqueness. Set Particle Weight to **0.3** (since snow is quite light), and set the **+–** value to **0.1** (which will make our particles "weigh" from 0.2 to 0.4 units). Since this unit setting is not relevant to any real-world measurement, it's not uncommon to need to fine-tune these values later.

4. Set Life Time (frame) at the bottom to **0**. This will make each particle "live" forever (or the length of our animation at least).

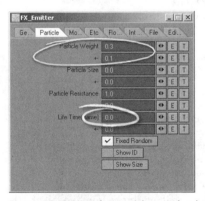

Figure 13-4: Vary the particles randomly with a little difference here and there.

Motion

The Motion tab tells the emitter how much initial movement and energy a particle has when it's generated. The X, Y, and Z velocities let us give the particles energy on a particular axis, and below those settings we even have the ability to influence the particles to be emitted toward another item in the scene.

By default, this initial energy will be related to the local axis of the emitter. This means rotating the emitter will spray the particles around like a garden hose! However, sometimes we just want the particles to travel in one direction, no matter where the emitter is pointing. A smoke plume would be a good example; if the emitter were attached to another item that was moving about, having the smoke go in directions other than upward would look a little odd. This is what the World

Coordinates button at the top of the tab is all about.

Once things are moving, particles that follow straight lines can be a little boring, and even unrealistic. Luckily, there are yet more settings we can play with here to get things looking less CG. Explosion is a setting that forces the particles outward from the center of the emitter, while Vibration is a random setting that gives each particle a unique direction and speed to travel when it's created.

5. We want our snow to simply drift down from the sky; however, a little randomness in direction will help break up any obvious CG appearance to the particles. Set Vibration (m/s) to **3** (meters per second).

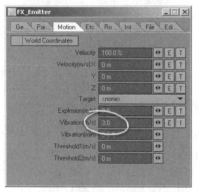

Figure 13-5: A little randomness in vibration will help vary our flakes.

> **Note**
>
> What is cool is that all these settings on this tab can work together. For instance, giving some motion in the Y-axis and also some Explosion amount can be used to force particles to spray outward and also upward like a fountain.

Etc

The Etc tab contains other influencing parameters for particles, such as gravity and whether they are influenced by the movement of the emitter (if it happens to be animated, that is).

6. Because snow falls downward, we'll need to include a little gravity. Set the gravity in Y to be **−9.8**, which is the equivalent of Earth's gravitational pull.

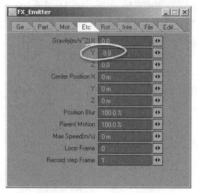

Figure 13-6: Gravity sucks (downward, that is).

> **Note**
>
> One setting that is often useful to tweak is the Parent Motion value. By default this is set to 100%, which forces particles to pick up the velocity and direction of the emitter at the point where they were created. It's great if you want to spin an emitter and have it spray particles outward like a sprinkler. However, that's not always something you might want. For example, if an emitter happens to be emitting smoke from the tail of an asteroid, we often want the smoke to be "left behind" as the asteroid travels along and not move at the same speed. In that case, we'd set Parent Motion to something very tiny, or even nothing.

Rotation

The Rotation tab lets us tell the emitter how we would like particles to orient themselves when they are moving, and is one of the cool new features added in this latest release of LightWave.

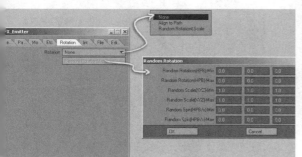

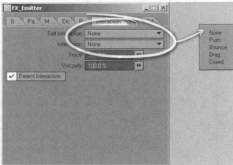

Figure 13-8: Play nicely with the others.

Figure 13-7: LightWave v9 gives us powerful new rotation capabilities for particles.

With the Rotation option set to None (the default), particles tend to follow the rotation of the emitter itself. This setting causes each particle to rotate like the emitter, which can be quite strange but useful for effects where you want all your particles to move in the same direction simultaneously. The other options are Align to Path (which obviously aligns the particles along the path they are traveling) and Random Rotation&Scale. This last option is extremely cool in that clicking the button below the Rotation selection will let us specify not only random rotation values, but also options to randomly scale and stretch the particles. This option is perfect for creating complex systems such as asteroids.

Interaction

The Interaction tab is all about telling particles how to treat their neighbors. If particles get close to one another or collide, this tab lets us tell the particles just what they should be doing. We can specify how we want particles to behave when

interacting with each other, but also how we'd like them to play with the kids from different emitters as well.

File

The File tab lets us save and load both the particle emitter settings and the motion of all the particles to disk (which we'll use later on).

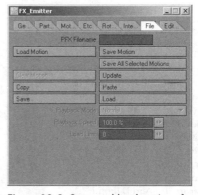

Figure 13-9: Save and load settings from the File tab.

EditFX

Finally, the EditFX tab lets us edit the paths of particles and delete ones we don't like. These tools are designed to let us hand-animate and modify particles on a one-by-one basis and are great for repairing any odd particle behaviors after we've let

LightWave simulate them. We'll look at these tools later in the book when we start to play more with the dynamics of LightWave.

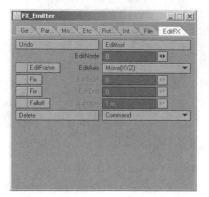

Figure 13-10: Edit the motion and delete unwanted particles using the Edittool options.

So, we've looked at the settings and we've tweaked a few things. We're almost done here…

7. Move our emitter to **4 m** on the Y-axis to get it to sit up and out of the camera view (Figure 13-11). When you scrub the Frame Slider, you see particles "falling" from our emitter. When you're done with all that, set End Frame to **200**.

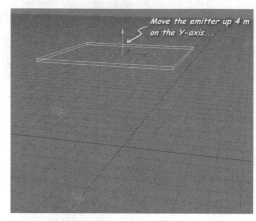

Figure 13-11: Get that snow to fall from the sky, not the floor.

Note

Particle emitters are not limited to the simple box shapes we've used in this tutorial. We can emit particles from geometry and even from other particles themselves. (See the scene **Scenes\Chapter 13\ cg_Fireworks_ display.lws** for an example of particles emitting other particles.) Adding an emitter to an object is done through the object's Properties window Dynamics tab and selecting an emitter from the Add Dynamic pop-up. To edit the particle emitter properties, double-click on the emitter in the list box. It displays the same options are we've just looked at in the FX_Emitter panel. We can tell the particles to emit from the object itself by selecting Object-Surface from the Nozzle option, as shown here.

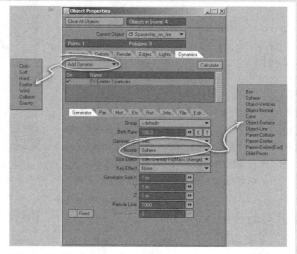

Figure 13-12: Emitting from geometry is not that different from the simple emitter we created.

Step 3: A Particle Needs Friends

Particles on their own are pretty cool, but bunch them together with a few playmates and they can be even better! What we're talking about are other dynamics tools that let us influence and turn our particle effects into something much more. These dynamics are wind, gravity, and collisions, and act as influencing forces that prod, push, and pull particles around after they've been emitted.

- **Wind** and **Gravity** pull and push particles about in some pretty cool ways, and can be used to swirl smoke or guide water flow down a ravine.

- **Collisions** can get in the way of particles, and can be made to get particles to bounce off them, stick to them, and even be deleted on contact.

> **Note**
>
> If you recall, the FX_Emitter panel has an Etc tab that also contains a Gravity option. This option controls a gravitational pull on the motion of particles. The Gravity dynamic is similar, but more like a gravitational "area" in 3D space that can be used to influence the motion of the particles in some interesting ways (like a black hole or a magnetic vortex).

Let's give our particles a couple of playmates to help give our snow a more realistic feel. Since snow is made of flakes, they occasionally appear to float as they fall, sometimes picked up by small air currents and swirled about. Let's create this effect by adding a friend to play with the particles.

1. Select **Items | Add | Dynamic Obj | Wind**. Give it the name **Float Effect** and click **OK**.

2. In the FX_Wind panel that appears, Wind Mode should be set to **Vortex**, and Falloff Mode should be set to **OFF**.

Set Power to **50%**. On the Vector tab in the panel, set Wind X to **1 m** and Wind Y to **0 m**.

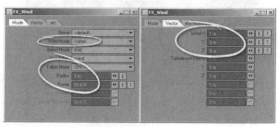

Figure 13-13: Set up the FX_Wind dynamic to create our gentle air currents.

If we play the animation again, it's looking a little nicer as some particles had a little snakey motion to them (the effect is also relative to how heavy the snow is).

> **Note**
>
> Sometimes you will use more than one wind effect in LightWave to create more dynamic effects with your particles. The Etc tab on the FX_Wind panel not only gives us options to save any favorite settings we may create for a wind, but using the **Full Wind Evaluation** option allows us to visually see the effect of how other winds influence the current wind. While this project only has a single wind, I've put together an example in Figure 13-14 that shows three completely different winds at work together.
>
> We can also change the way in which LightWave displays the wind. Activating **Draw All Wind** displays the entire area of a wind object (including the area where the wind has no effect). This can appear quite busy, and often it's just nicer to leave this off so that we see just the "windy" areas, and not everything. How this wind is drawn in LightWave is controlled by the options at the bottom of the panel. Usually we'll leave Draw Style set to Auto and the grid settings at their defaults of 8. If we require a denser view of the wind effect, we can increase these grid numbers as required.

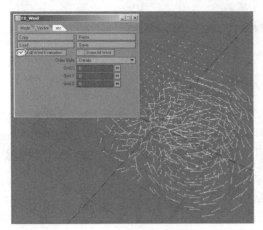

Figure 13-14: The cumulative effect of multiple winds can be previewed in LightWave v9.

It might be nice to also catch the snow on the ground. Let's create a virtual ground plane by adding a second playmate — this time a Collision dynamic.

3. Select **Items | Add | Dynamic Obj | Collision**. Give the object the name **Ground** and click **OK**.

4. Much like our emitter, we're presented by an FX_Collision panel that lets us modify the parameters of our collision object. Change Type to **Plane** (which will make it an infinite plane along the XZ-axis) and Mode to **Stick**. Set Radius/Level to **–1 m** to sit the collision area below the emitter.

5. We want the snow to land and stick to the ground. To prevent any kind of slipping or sliding around on the collision object, set the Fix power value to **1.0**. (This will help stop snow from subtly sliding when it lands, or being shifted by the Wind dynamic.)

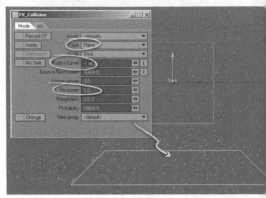

Figure 13-15: Setting up a ground plane for snow to land on.

6. Play the animation in LightWave and see how it looks. While it may not be the most photo real of snowfalls, the important thing here is that it *feels and looks* like a snowfall, and we can always change things and improve on them with very little effort. This is one of the many reasons computer animation is so great to work with!

Step 4: PixieDust

We may have created a simple snowfall animation, but snowflakes are soft, white particulate material.

As we learned in Step 1, there are two kinds of emitters we can create. The one we chose was an HV Emitter, an emitter that produces non-renderable null particles. That means if we do a test render by pressing <F9>, we'll see that nothing actually appears, unless we attach some kind of rendering mechanism to make them visible.

New to LightWave v9 is the PixieDust volumetric, which is perfect for simple fireworks, soft sparkles, soft snowflakes, and, well, pixie dust effects! PixieDust is a volumetric rendering tool, which quickly allows for thousands of particles to be rendered as simple soft points. While this tool is not as technical or flexible as HyperVoxels (which we will be looking at in the next chapter), it is perfect for our needs in this simple project.

1. Select **Windows | Volumetrics and Fog Options** (or press <**Ctrl**> + <**F6**>). Click the **Add Volumetric** pop-up, and select the **PixieDust** volumetric.

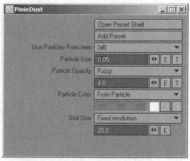

Figure 13-17: PixieDust options panel.

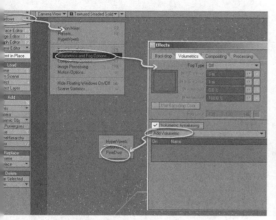

gure 13-16: Selecting a volumetric rendering echanism for rendering our particles.

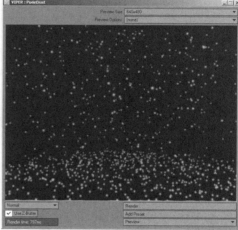

Figure 13-18: At last, the ski season has started!

2. Press <**F7**> to open the VIPER preview window. VIPER is LightWave's preview render tool that you may have run across when surfacing a 3D object, and it's a very fast way to preview the effects of PixieDust without creating numerous test renders using <**F9**>. The VIPER title bar should indicate that it is previewing PixieDust.

3. Double-click on the **PixieDust** volumetric in the list box to bring up its options panel (Figure 13-17).

4. Select the **Snow** emitter from the Use Particles From Item pop-up.

Create a preview in VIPER to see the result of PixieDust in making our particles visible (Figure 13-18).

Unique Particle Settings

One feature of PixieDust worth looking at is its ability to create unique attributes for particles based on when in the animation they were generated. For example, let's say we want the snowflakes to become larger as time goes on. (A bit odd, but you never know what Mother Nature can do in the virtual world!) This we can do using some of the features offered to us in PixieDust. If you closed the PixieDust panel, reopen it by double-clicking on the PixieDust volumetric again on the Volumetrics tab (<**Ctrl**> + <**F6**>).

5. Click the **T** next to Particle Size to open the Texture Editor. Change Layer

547

Type to **Gradient**, and set Input Parameter to **Relative Particle Birth Time**.

6. Set the gradient key at 0 to **0.05** (the default particle size). Add a second key at the bottom of the gradient and change its Value to **0.5**.

Create another preview in VIPER and see the effect this has on the size of our PixieDust particles. (See Figure 13-20.) The final scene, including this modified PixieDust particle size, can be loaded from **Scenes\Chapter 13\SnowScene_pixiedust.lws**.

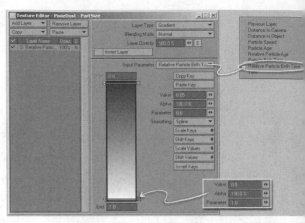

Figure 13-19: Set up the gradient to alter the snowflake size as time goes on.

> **Note**
>
> VIPER is a context-sensitive tool. What exactly does this mean? Well, VIPER can pre-view cameras, surfaces, or volumetrics in LightWave, but *only* if we've got the panel or tool currently active. When loading the PixieDust scene, we may need to activate PixieDust to kick VIPER into action. To make sure VIPER renders PixieDust, ensure that you open the Volumetrics tab (<Ctrl>+ <F6>) and double-click on the PixieDust volumetric.

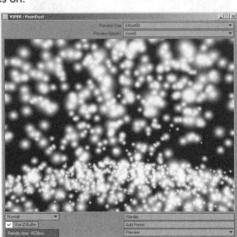

Figure 13-20: The effect of ever-increasing snowflake size.

Conclusion

We've covered particles and their settings and capabilities in some detail in this chapter. We also looked at adding a few extra dynamics to our scene to modify and manipulate our particles. We've only just scraped the surface in terms of what's possible with particles, and I'm sure you'll agree that the particle system is an area where not only can you create great effects, but also have a lot of fun just playing around with it!

We also took a quick look at visualizing particles using the PixieDust volumetric shader to create a soft, almost ethereal appearance. By using gradients to control parameters, we could use PixieDust's extra input parameters to create unique per-particle effects. While PixieDust is fine for simple effects like soft snow, in the next chapter we'll be looking at a more powerful volumetric visualization system called HyperVoxels that can create more realistic effects.

Chapter 14

Intermediate Skills: HyperVoxels

Having just come from playing with particle simulations in the previous chapter, you're probably hyped up and ready to push things one level further in terms of making those particles look pretty! Well, in this chapter we're going to show you one of the cool features in LightWave that is key to creating effects like fire, smoke, and water — HyperVoxels.

So, what exactly is a *voxel*? Well, it's a pixel with *volume* (a <u>vo</u>lumetric pi<u>xel</u>). In LightWave, voxels are represented by small spheres, which can be formed and shaped through the use of procedural textures, or in LightWave terms, *hyper*-textures. *HyperVoxels* are tools for rendering gases, fluids, or solids based on volumetrics rather than polygons. But what in the world is *volumetrics*? In plain English, it's the math/science/study of how stuff moves within and fills a certain space (aka volume). These little doodads known as HyperVoxels are pretty darn powerful and versatile.

How Are HyperVoxels Used?

If you've just read the previous chapter on particle simulation, you're probably thinking that HyperVoxels are destined for use on particles, perhaps those HV Emitter particles in particular. (Ah! Now "HV" is starting to make sense!) Yes, you'd be correct. However, HyperVoxels can be applied to anything with a point or points in it. A null object has a center point and is ideal for simple singular HyperVoxels (for example, if you want to create a planet or a simple fireball explosion). The points on an object can also be used, for instance, if you want to use HyperVoxels to create the blobby welding along the joints of an armor-plated tank. And of course we know all about particles, and how they can be animated in so many ways, from pouring like water to swirling snowstorms!

The HyperVoxels Window

HyperVoxels can be used to create three types of volumetric objects: surfaces, volumes, and sprites. Each of these objects is specialized for creating various types of effects, and we'll look at each in this chapter as we create some cool effects. Let's take a quick look at the HyperVoxels window, which can be activated through the **Windows | HyperVoxels** option.

> **Note**
>
> The HyperVoxels window is also accessible through the Effects panel, which can be found by selecting Windows | Volumetrics and Fog Options, or by pressing <Ctrl>+<F6>.

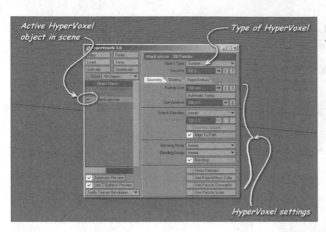

Figure 14-1: The HyperVoxels window.

The HyperVoxels window's tabs control the settings:

● **Geometry** — The basic size of each HyperVoxel.

● **Shading** — The surface appearance (textures and shading) of each HyperVoxel.

● **HyperTexture** — A procedural displacement map that affects the shape of the HyperVoxel.

What each setting does and how we should use it will be explained as we work our way through the chapter, so let's get started and find out more.

VIPER: Our Workflow Assistant for HyperVoxels

Throughout this chapter, we'll be using the VIPER tool. While we looked at VIPER back in Chapter 6, here we'll discuss some of the VIPER settings that are relevant when working with HyperVoxels.

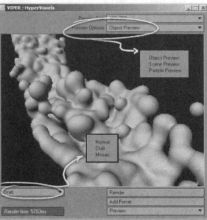

Figure 14-2: The VIPER interface when working with HyperVoxels.

Note

VIPER is a context-sensitive tool. This means that it displays the results for the selected tool (displayed in the VIPER window title bar). In Chapter 6, we used it to display changes we made in the Surface Editor. When we have HyperVoxels active, it will display any changes we make to the HyperVoxels. If we activate VIPER without any active HyperVoxels or surfaces, we won't see much!

Rendering Modes

HyperVoxels can be rendered in VIPER quickly by using the Draft mode, which gives us a fast preview of how they'll look before we do any rendering. And unlike when working with the Surface Editor, VIPER doesn't require you to do an initial <F9> test render before it starts to display HyperVoxels.

The Mosaic mode will do a three-pass refining render and is great for a fast "rough" preview of what your HyperVoxels will look like, especially if they take a while to render in the VIPER window.

> **Note**
>
> Mosaic mode is good for still previews as it gives us an initial low quality but faster visualization of the changes we make to our HyperVoxel settings. However, it won't make any improvement in performance while creating previews, simply due to its three-stage refining nature.

Preview Options

When working with HyperVoxels, the **Preview Options** setting at the top of the VIPER window plays an important role.

- **Object Preview** shows us the selected HyperVoxel object only. If you plan on working with complex scenes containing a lot of different HyperVoxel objects, this setting will show you just the one you are working on.

- **Scene Preview** shows us all the HyperVoxel objects in a scene, so you can see the effect of everything together. Note that this can be very slow if there are a lot of things happening.

- **Particle Preview** shows us a single HyperVoxel from the selected object. If you're refining a candy-coated chocolate, then this would be the best option rather than showing the entire bowl of candies.

HyperVoxel "Surfaces"

HyperVoxels, by default, start life as *surface* type voxels. This creates a "skin" around each point/particle. When we have many HyperVoxels within close proximity to each other, they tend to blend into each other, creating a seamless blob or shape. This makes surface-based HyperVoxels ideal for simulating materials like water, mercury, rock, lava, and the like.

Let's take a look at how this works by creating our first HyperVoxel-rendered particle simulation.

1. Start out by loading the scene **Scenes\ Chapter 14\waterflow.lws**, which contains a very simple particle simulation flowing into a kitchen sink object. Play the animation to see it in action

(Figure 14-3). While we're getting started, also press <F7> to activate and display the VIPER window.

Figure 14-3: Our simple particle scene in action.

2. Let's activate **Windows | HyperVoxels**. From the HyperVoxels

window, click on **WaterFlow** and click the **Activate** button at the top to enable it. A small check should appear next to the WaterFlow object name. By default, HyperVoxels will give the particles their own "best fit" size for the Particle Size value. Change the Particle Size to **10 mm**.

active objects in the HyperVoxels window. (Note that I said *uncheck* and *not* Deactivate (the button at the top of the HyperVoxels window). Unchecking disables HyperVoxels temporarily, while the Deactivate button completely removes it from the object (and any settings you may have created).

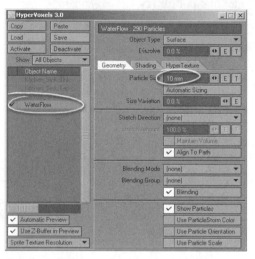

Figure 14-4: Activate the particle object in the HyperVoxels window.

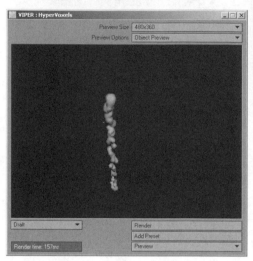

Figure 14-5: Blobby HyperVoxel action should appear in VIPER.

3. VIPER should update in real time to show us the appearance of our Hyper-Voxel water. If needed, scrub to a frame in the animation where there are lots of particles to get a better idea of what this looks like, and click the **Render** button on the VIPER panel. We should see a blobby mass appear where the particles once were.

4. Sometimes it's nice to be able to see at least a representation of the geometry in VIPER, combined with the Hyper-Voxels, so that we can get an idea of how the HyperVoxels will integrate with the other parts of the scene. To do this, first make sure you uncheck any

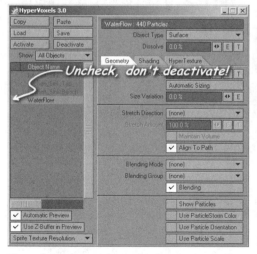

Figure 14-6: Be sure to uncheck, or temporarily disable, any HyperVoxel objects.

5. Also disable any camera options for antialiasing and lower the render size of the camera to save a little time creating this simple preview for VIPER to use. (It doesn't make sense to waste time rendering at high quality just for VIPER.) This scene contains fairly reflective objects, so unchecking **Ray Trace Reflection** on the Render Globals window may also be advantageous, but not necessarily required if you don't mind the extra few seconds of rendering time. Once you've done this, simply press <**F9**> to quickly render the scene. Once the render is complete, it should appear inside VIPER along with the HyperVoxels. If it doesn't, make sure that the option **Use Z-Buffer in Preview** is activated on the HyperVoxels window.

settings we are familiar with from the standard Surface Editor. Let's change the surface Color to a bluish tint of **183, 219, 255**. Adjust the Diffuse value to **50%**, Specularity to **10%**, Glossiness to **50%**, and Reflection to **10%**. Finally, set Transparency to **100%** and Refraction Index to **1.333**.

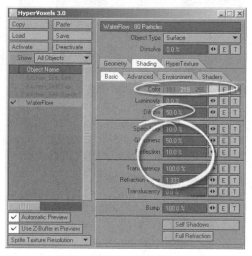

Figure 14-8: The surface settings in the HyperVoxels window.

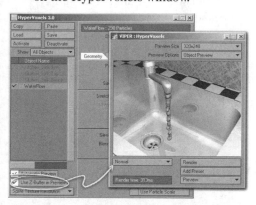

Figure 14-7: HyperVoxels can be previewed alongside a representation of our geometry.

6. Now we need to make this blobby mass look more like water, and to do that we will need to adjust the appearance of the HyperVoxels surface settings. This can be done through the Shading tab on the HyperVoxels window (as shown in Figure 14-8). It should look familiar since it contains all the same kinds of

> **Note**
>
> Here's an interesting observation that's worth noting: Water has no color! It looks blue because it's usually reflecting the sky. Don't believe me? Ask yourself why a glass of sea water doesn't look bright blue when in a glass. You may have noted that I set a blue color (and a low Diffuse value) for the surface for my water. Obviously you wouldn't do this if you are striving for true realism, but for this example we're creating our own artistically licensed water, and adding a little color can enhance the CG a little more.

The HyperVoxel water will now appear *black* in the VIPER window, as shown in Figure 14-9.

Figure 14-9: The water looks black in VIPER.

Don't panic! When we set Refraction Index higher than 1.0, we forced the HyperVoxels to refract the only thing VIPER could see — the black backdrop color! That's simply because VIPER is a preview tool, and is actually incapable of rendering real reflections or refraction in the scene. This can make life a little harder when working with transparent surfaces such as water; however, we can create fake reflections and refractions that VIPER can display fairly easily.

7. Select the **Environment** tab, set Reflection Options for the HyperVoxel to **Spherical Map**, and then from the Reflection Map pop-up, select **skymap_clearskysunset.png**. This will give the HyperVoxels something to reflect, which can be displayed in VIPER as well.

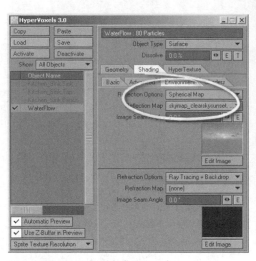

Figure 14-10: Faking reflections for our HyperVoxels.

8. While we could repeat the same spherical map setting for the Refraction Options setting, this would simply cause the water to change from black to brown, refracting the image map and not the background geometry. Instead, try this handy tip: Set Refraction Options to **Spherical Map**, but leave Refraction Map as **(none)**. This forces the transparent HyperVoxels to refract

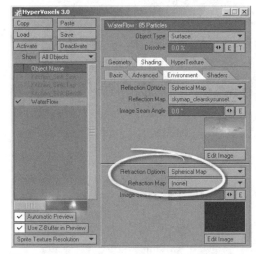

Figure 14-11: Setting a non-refractive option for the HyperVoxels.

nothing, appearing transparent as we might expect water to be!

9. One property of transparent surfaces like water and glass is that they become less transparent and more reflective as they appear more on-edge to the camera. This effect is called the *Fresnel* effect, and LightWave has a shader that can help us create this visual property very easily. Under the Shaders tab of the surface settings, select the **Fast Fresnel** shader from the Add Shader pop-up.

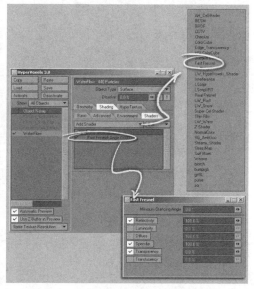

Figure 14-12: Add a Fast Fresnel shader.

You may think that Fast Fresnel isn't really doing much; however, this is purely because of the way that VIPER displays the water. Remember, VIPER is only a preview tool. To see what the water will really look like, we'll need to render it.

10. Make sure that you switch the HyperVoxel's Refraction Options setting on the Environment tab to **Ray Tracing+Backdrop**. This will ensure that the HyperVoxels can refract the

surrounding scenery. VIPER will make the water appear black, but don't let that disturb you. Go back and reactivate any Render Global options you may have unchecked (such as Ray Trace Reflection) and do an <F9> at frame 85 to see how the water and kitchen sink look together. (VIPER does not render, and hence won't give us a true representation of the transparency and reflection at work.) It looks better (as shown in Figure 14-13), but one can't help but feel that perhaps its blobby nature isn't quite "water-like."

Figure 14-13: This water has lost its marbles, or at least it's trying to look like some!

HvDeform

HyperVoxels are great, but they don't always look right as we learned from our water experience above. For instance, the water flowing into the kitchen sink may look like some kind of liquid, but it breaks apart into small spheres rather than the pool of water we might expect to see as it settles into the sink. A pool of water is formed through the tension of the surface of the water creating a smooth skin and is one of the things that we'd need to see if we expected this water to appear more realistic in LightWave.

LightWave v9 ships with an excellent tool called HvDeform that is designed to deform the shape of HyperVoxels, making it ideal for creating the effects we need. We're going to use this to improve the appearance of our water and give it a more realistic appearance as it starts to fill the sink.

1. HvDeform has some particular requirements that need to be set for it to work correctly. While we're still in the HyperVoxels window, under the Geometry tab, set the Stretch Direction pop-up to **Velocity**. Set Stretch Amount to **–100%**, and make sure that **Maintain Volume** is unchecked and **Align To Path** is checked.

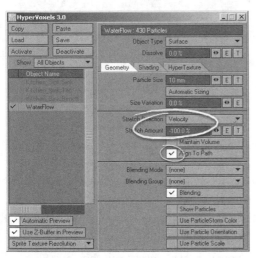

Figure 14-14: Set up some necessary options so HvDeform will work properly.

> **Note**
>
> The settings we've just applied to our HyperVoxels, such as the negative Stretch Amount, may not make much sense; however, these settings are purely for the HvDeform tool to work properly. Why? That would be an answer we'd have to ask the programmer of HvDeform!

2. Select the **Kitchen_Sink:Sink** object (the object our particles are flowing into). Open its Object Properties window (**<p>**), click on the **Deform** tab and choose **HvDeformSurface** from the Add Displacement pop-up. This lets the HvDeform tool see the surface of the sink so that it can use it to deform the HyperVoxels as needed.

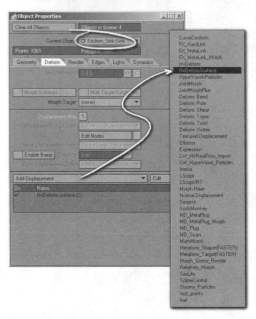

Figure 14-15: Add HvDeformSurface to the kitchen sink.

3. Select the **WaterFlow** object from the Current Object pop-up at the top of the Object Properties window and then double-click **HvDeform** from the Add Displacement pop-up.

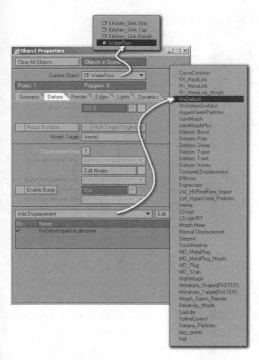

Figure 14-16: Adding HvDeform to our water.

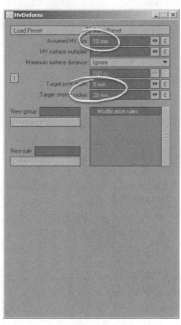

Figure 14-17: Set up the basic HvDeform settings.

4. The HvDeform panel is where we will need to set up things so that HvDeform can do its magic. Set Assumed HV size to **10 mm** (the same as the HyperVoxel), HV surface multiplier to **1.0**, Target pool depth to **5 mm**, and Target stretch radius to **20 mm** (as shown in Figure 14-17). The target values tell the HvDeform effect how to squash or stretch the HyperVoxel where needed, effectively changing it from a blob to a puddle.

HvDeform can't do anything without a little hand-holding. While we've told it the size ratios to stretch and squash the Hyper-Voxels by, it still doesn't know when or why it should. This is where we need to create a set of rules to teach it how.

5. Type **in_the_Sink** into the New rule input box, and press **<Return>** to create a new modification rule. This rule will appear in the Modification rules list box. Left-click on the rule in the list to bring up the options for this rule. Select **On surface** from the Fraction pop-up. Change Thickness to **Squash** (so that the water pancakes into a pool when it lands in the sink) and Orientation to **Surface normal** so that it sits correctly on the sink surface. We'll also expand the volume of the liquid to fill more area, so let's change Size to **Custom**, and enter **15 mm** as the value.

557

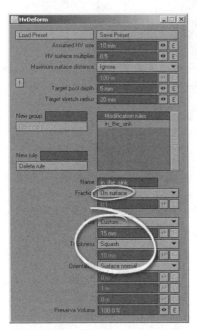

Figure 14-18: Setting a rule helps flatten and smooth the water in the sink.

> **Note**
>
> You can see the effect of this tool in VIPER. However, you may need to first scrub the Time Slider back and forth a frame or two to update the tool before it will update in VIPER.

6. Scrub to frame 120, then press the **Render** button on the VIPER window to see the deformed HyperVoxels. You'll notice that VIPER seems to have stopped displaying the liquid coming from the tap, and only shows the HyperVoxels sitting in the sink itself. That's because HvDeform has only been told to work out how to draw the HyperVoxels that are sitting on the sink surface.

Figure 14-19

7. To make sure we can see the liquid coming from the tap, enter **pouring_in** into the New rule input box and press **<Return>**. Left-click once on **pouring_in** to display its options. Set this rule to use a Fraction setting of **Remainder**, and set Size as **Assumed HV size**, Thickness as **Same as size**, and Orientation to **Velocity&Normal transition**.

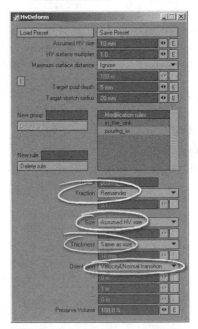

Figure 14-20: Adding the pouring_in rule.

The water now pools as it lands on the sink surface. It no longer has the original marbles look we get without using HvDeform.

Figure 14-21: Get ready to wash those dishes!

This is just a very basic look at HvDeform, but it gives you an idea of how it works and how it can be used to fine-tune the appearance of HyperVoxels in LightWave. HvDeform is not limited to surface-type HyperVoxels either (though they would be the most obvious type to use it with), and it offers a number of other features and functions for even more complex and realistic results. This tool is well worth taking the time to dig deeply into the LightWave manual to learn.

To Blend or Not to Blend

As we've seen with HyperVoxel surfaces, things tend to blob together. This is great for those mercury/liquid type effects, but what if you need to create something like a flow of candy-coated chocolate? We obviously don't want all those candy pieces to start melting together when they get too close! What about asteroids, rock falls, and other such effects where it would be nice to have loose matter rather than blobby or flowing liquid? Luckily for us, HyperVoxels has a setting on its Geometry tab especially for deactivating that blobbing effect. Simply uncheck the **Blending** option to prevent HyperVoxels from combining when they get close together, as shown in Figure 14-22. Simple as that!

If you recall from the previous chapter, we also mentioned that particles could have their very own rotation controls. In fact, we said that they could have their own random rotation and scale. We can also tell Hyper-Voxels that we want to take advantage of this information to create more complex visual effects by activating the options **Use Particle Orientation** and **Use Particle Scale** (see Figure 14-23).

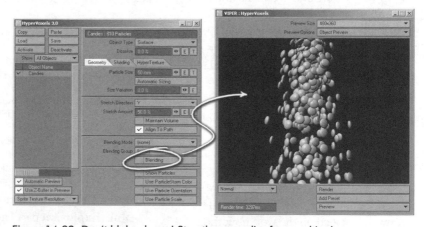

Figure 14-22: Don't blob, please! Stop those candies from melting!

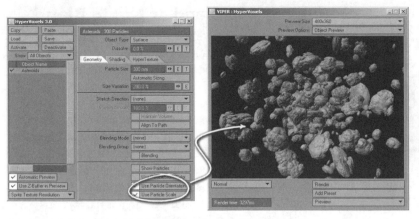

Figure 14-23: Complex individual spinning space junk in no time!

HyperVoxel "Volumes"

The second type of HyperVoxel we can create in the HyperVoxels window is a *volume*. A volume is something like a gas or cloud, and is great for creating effects such as fire, smoke, trees, and many other such effects. While we can apply HyperVoxels to particles to create motion and dynamic simulations, we can also use a single null and some of the HyperVoxel options to create spectacular explosive cloud effects.

Let's take a look at creating an effect for a scene where an alien force of some kind has fired a laser beam into the side of a large building in some imaginary city. Obviously, the intense heat of the evil alien ray would vaporize the plaster, metal, and other building materials, creating huge clouds of dense material.

1. Begin by loading the scene **Scenes\ Chapter 14\Building_hit_by_ aliens.lws**. This scene contains some simple geometry and a premade particle simulation, as shown in Figure 14-24. Open up VIPER <**F7**> so that we can speed up the workflow, then press <**F9**> to capture the background geometry into VIPER.

Figure 14-24: The scene ready for the visual effects guru (you) to add the final touches.

> ### Note
>
> You might be concerned that VIPER did not display anything, even after you did the <**F9**> to render the scene. This is normal, and is nothing to worry about. As mentioned at the start of the chapter, VIPER is context sensitive. We'll need to add HyperVoxels to the scene to see anything displayed within it.

2. Open the HyperVoxels window (**Windows | HyperVoxels**), then select the **MainExplosion** particle emitter and activate it. Change its Object Type to **Volume**. Under the Geometry tab, set

Particle Size to **100 mm** and give it a Size Variation of **200%** to add some random variation to the size of each HyperVoxel. Uncheck the **Align To Path** option, as this causes the HyperVoxels to turn and twist when they change direction — not something we'd expect to see in an explosion.

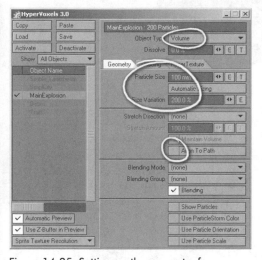

Figure 14-25: Setting up the geometry for MainExplosion.

Because this is an animation, viewing the HyperVoxels at frame 0 won't give us much to look at in VIPER. Scrub through the timeline to the last frame, and check out how things look in VIPER (you may need to click the Render button to update VIPER). We should have a huge cloud of debris and dust hovering over our building in the center.

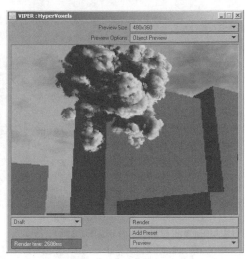

Figure 14-26: Your visual effects are starting to look promising!

3. Let's tweak the appearance of this cloud a little to make it more appealing. Under the Shading tab, let's change the way the light affects our HyperVoxels. Click on the **Advanced** tab. Let's also change the way that HyperVoxels are lit by changing the Illumination pop-up to **Rayleigh**. Rayleigh tells HyperVoxels to be lit up by favoring any light that is penetrating the volume from behind it, rather than in front. Since the main light for our scene happens to be coming from one side, this

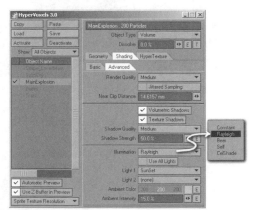

Figure 14-27: Changing the way light affects the volumetric HyperVoxels.

Figure 14-:28 Beer versus Rayleigh.

gives the HyperVoxels a darker but softer appearance that in my opinion looks a lot better for a dust cloud (see Figure 14-28).

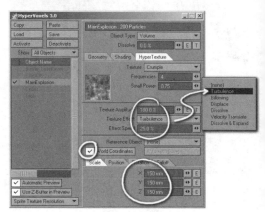

Figure 14-29: Setting a HyperTexture for our volume.

> **Note**
>
> If you happen to have a fairly slow computer, change both Render Quality and Shadow Quality to Very Low. These settings control the overall quality of the volumetric appearance, and in many cases we can lower these values for faster rendering speeds while we work. Before we render, we can always come back and increase these if we wish.

4. Under the HyperTexture tab, change the Texture Effect pop-up to **Turbulence** and set an Effect Speed of **25%** just to give the HyperVoxels a little secondary animation. Change Scale to **150 mm** all round, and activate **World Coordinates**.

Texture Effect adds motion to the HyperTexture within the HyperVoxels using a variety of effects. A Turbulence effect simply pushes the HyperTexture toward the camera. The Effect Speed tells the HyperTexture how fast it's moving. This is a percentage of the Default Unit found on the General Options (<o>) window (in most cases, it should be meters). An Effect Speed setting of 25% would move the HyperTexture at 250 mm per second.

At this stage, create a preview in VIPER if you want to see how the effect looks when it's animated.

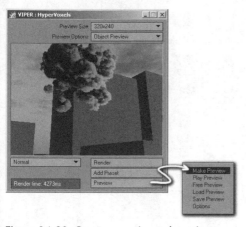

Figure 14-30: Create an animated preview to see the HyperVoxels in action!

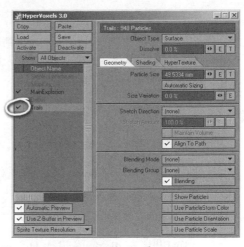

Figure 14-31: Activate the Trails emitter.

Note

The Texture Effects setting can be used to help embellish and create a variety of visual effects. The one I find the most useful, however, is Velocity Translate. What this does is move the HyperTexture in the direction and speed of each HyperVoxel. When used with complex particle simulations for sand or dust, it can be used to create the illusion of finer particulate matter within the HyperVoxel.

5. Let's go back to the HyperVoxels window and activate the **Trails** emitter. This emitter creates the dust clouds left behind by chunks of the building that have broken away and fallen to the ground.

6. Set the Trails HyperVoxels to an Object Type of **Volume** also, and like the other emitter, uncheck the **Align To Path** option. Let's set these particles to be something a little smaller. Set a Particle Size of **20 mm**, with a Size Variation of **100%**. As the debris falls, we'd expect the dust trails left behind to slowly expand as the dust breaks up and spreads in the air. Let's set the HyperVoxels to do that by clicking the **T** button next to Particle Size and changing Layer Type to **Gradient**. For this gradient texture, Input Parameter must be **Relative Particle Age**. Add a key at the bottom of the gradient with a Value of **300%**.

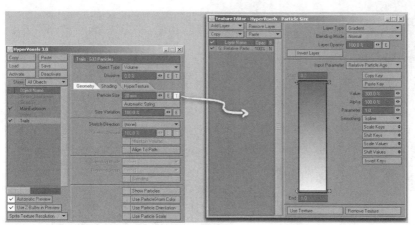

Figure 14-32: Expanding dust clouds from debris using a gradient in particle size.

7. I felt that this emitter should create thinner dust and matter, so we'll want to "thin it out" compared to our previous emitter. On the **Shading | Basic** tab, let's drop Thickness to **5%**.

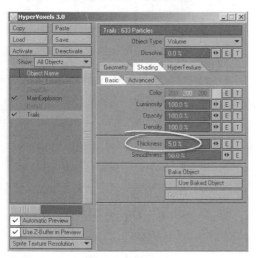

Figure 14-33: Let's thin out those dust trails.

8. We're done. If we want to preview both emitters in VIPER, then change the Preview Options setting to **Scene Preview** (as discussed at the start of the chapter) before making the preview shown in Figure 14-34.

Note

Thickness tells the HyperVoxel the rate at which the particulate matter that forms the HyperVoxel thickens to become too solid to see through. LightWave will stop calculating a HyperVoxel if its thickness reaches 100% (as it wouldn't make too much sense to keep going). By tweaking the Thickness value, you can fine-tune the rendering speed of Hyper-Voxels; however, make sure you don't also change the look that you were trying to achieve in the process!

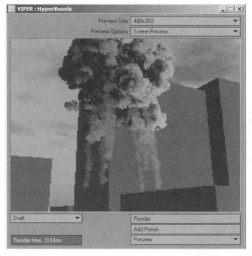

Figure 14-34: We've finished the effects; roll on the next shot!

Obviously, this effect would benefit from a little camera shake from the initial impact. For those wanting to see such a scene, load my finished scene from Scenes\Chapter 14\ Building_hit_by_aliens_F.lws. I've also created a final render in Renders\Chapter 14\Building_hit_by_aliens.mov. Enjoy!

HyperVoxel "Sprites"

Something you can do that greatly reduces the time LightWave needs to render Hyper-Voxels is to not render the *whole* volume but to render only a "slice" of it. LightWave doesn't need to calculate the whole volume, only a tiny fraction of it — a *plane* that runs directly through its *center*, always aiming at the viewer (camera or viewport angle). We learned about another tool in LightWave that does this called PixieDust back in Chapter 13; however, unlike PixieDust, HyperVoxels can be textured, blended together into more complex forms, and the light used within a scene.

As an example of the difference in appearance, change the Object Type setting of the previous explosion to Sprite mode and see for yourself (Figure 14-35). It's not as detailed or volumetric in appearance, but we can use sprite HyperVoxels to generate less dense volumetric effects such as fog, fine sand, or dust.

There are definitely some things we can do with this simpler Sprite mode to make some very cool effects, so let's do something without the aid of particles this time and see just how this simpler HyperVoxel can be used to great effect!

1. Start with a new scene running at 24 FPS. Set the End Frame to **120** (for *both* the scene itself and within the Rendering Options). Add a null, naming it **HV_Sprite**. Set its Y position to **800 mm**. Then, under the camera's Motion Options, set the camera's Target Item to **HV_Sprite**. To give us something a bit more exciting in the "background department," under **Windows | Backdrop** (<**Ctrl**>+<**F5**>), activate **Gradient Backdrop** and set the Zenith Color to **020, 000, 047**, both the Sky and Ground Colors to **098**,

Figure 14-35: Sprite mode explosion. A slice from the center.

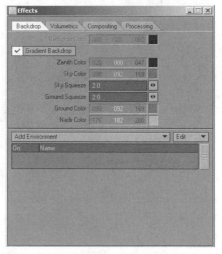

Figure 14-36: Setting a gradient backdrop.

565

092, 169, and the Nadir Color to **176, 182, 200** (see Figure 14-36).

2. Next, activate HyperVoxels for HV_Sprite. Bring up the presets for HyperVoxels (**Windows | Presets** (**<F8>**)), then select the **Generic** library. Double-click on **Sand_Explosion** to load in its settings, changing its Particle Size to **2 m** and its Object Type to **Sprite**. When you check **Show Particles**, you get much more than a linear representation of the voxel — you get a real-time image of the sprite, *complete with OpenGL transparency* (see Figure 14-37). (To increase the detail of the

sprite, choose a higher resolution from the Sprite Texture Resolution pop-up menu; this will impact your graphics accelerator, however.)

3. You can increase the quality of your rendered voxel by *increasing* the number of slices (found on the Shading | Basic tab). Comparing the rendered results in Figure 14-38, there is a marked increase in detail, and the render time is still light-years away from the lengthy render we would have were we to set our Object Type to Volume.

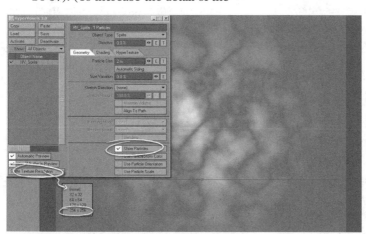

Figure 14-37: Show Particles gives us a visual reference in OpenGL.

Figure 14-38: Quality difference with slices (1 and 7 in this case).

4. Now, let's do something really cool. Under the Geometry tab, set Particle Size to **20 m**, Stretch Direction to **Y**, and Stretch Amount to **4%** (this will "squish" our voxel down to 4% of its natural spherical shape along the Y axis). You may as well uncheck **Show Particles**, since the effect we're creating isn't "captured" by the Show Particles engine.

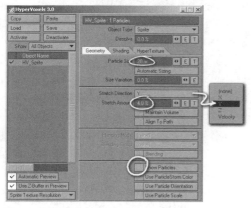

Figure 14-39: Setting the geometry for our HV_Sprite.

5. Under the **Shading | Basic** tab, set Color to **200, 200, 200**, Luminosity to **100%**, Opacity to **0%**, Density to **80%**, and Number of Slices to **1**. Then, under the HyperTexture tab, set Texture to **Dented** (and double-check that Scale is **4**, Power is **3**, Frequency is **0.8**, and Octaves is **6**). Set Noise Type to **Gradient Noise** (just a different kind of "fractal engine" powering our Dented procedural texture). Set Texture Amplitude to **150%**, Texture Effect to **Turbulence**, and Effect Speed to **50%**.

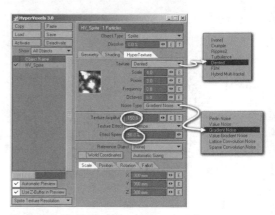

Figure 14-40: Setting HyperTexture options.

(Be sure your settings match the text in steps 4 and 5; if they don't, your render won't match Figure 14-41.)

Figure 14-41: Making something really cool!

A render shows something that looks like high-altitude clouds. What we've done is quickly fake volumetric ground fog (the misty, wispy stuff that hovers in quiet hollows on nights when the moon is full). You can move through this ground fog, and you can set the fog's *exact* position above the ground by positioning the null. It won't catch shadows very well, but if you ever try "real" volumetric ground fog, you'll appreciate the time-in-render-land this hack provides.

If you want to see how this fog moves, then press <F7> to bring up VIPER and make a preview for a quick look at the effect in action. You'll see that you've not only created some nifty fake ground fog, but you'll realize this hack can also be used to recreate the way clouds roil in time-lapse photography! (Effect Speed is the setting that controls the speed of the roiling.)

Scenes\Chapter 14\HV_Sprite_ 01_F.lws is the scene that created Figure 14-41.

But that's not all we can do with Hyper-Voxel sprites! Ever want to create your own forest in a flash? Well, with Hyper-Voxels, you can!

1. Load the scene **Scenes\Chapter 14\ hillside.lws**. This loads in a generic hillside with a backdrop sky map.

2. Let's plant a few seeds for our trees to grow from first. To do this, we're going to use some simple particles that we'll randomly generate on the surface of our hillside. Select the **Hillside** object and open its Object Properties window <**p**>. Under the Dynamics tab, choose **Add Dynamic | Emitter** and click on it in the list to display its parameters. Set Birth Rate to the number of trees we want to plant (in this case, start with **300**), and Particle Limit to the same number. Set Generate by to

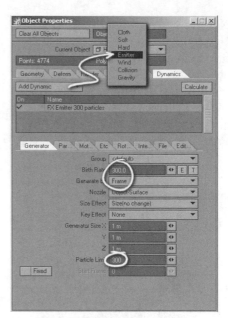

Figure 14-42: Adding a particle emitter to the hillside.

Frame to make sure we plant all our seeds in the first frame.

3. Make sure our trees stay alive by setting Life Time (frame) to **0** on the Particle tab. Also, uncheck **Fixed Random** to make the particles a little more random. We should see small particles dotted all over the hillside (Figure 14-43). Now that our seeds are planted, let's grow some trees!

Planting particles to grow our trees!

Figure 14-43: The seeds are planted; we're ready to grow the forest!

4. Open the Image Editor and load **HV_tree_sprite.png** from Images\ Chapter 14. This image is a simple tree with an embedded alpha channel so that it can be cut out cleanly. You'll see that the tree image appears in the top half of the image. This is because HyperVoxels will draw the image centered on the sprite. We move it to the top half so that the bottom of the trunk starts where the particle is planted (as shown in Figure 14-44).

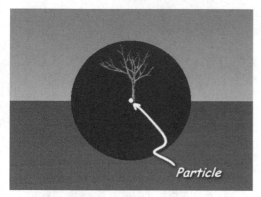

Figure 14-44: How the image gets aligned with a particle when using sprites.

> **Note**
>
> HyperVoxels are spherical in nature, so any image maps used for sprites need to have some edge around them to prevent them from becoming clipped and appearing as a circular shape.

5. Bring up the HyperVoxels window (**Windows | HyperVoxels**), and then activate the **Hillside_v001** object as a HyperVoxel. Set Object Type to **Sprite**, Particle Size to **500 mm**, and Size Variation to **150%** so that we get different sized trees randomly.

6. Under the **Shading | Basic** tab, check the **Orient Slices to Ray** option. Then under the **Shading | Clips** tab, add the **HV_Tree_sprite.png** image as a clip, making sure that we set Alpha to **Embedded** (see Figure 14-45). Lastly, under the HyperTexture tab, make sure that the Texture pop-up is set to (**none**) so that we remove any possible noise on the sprite.

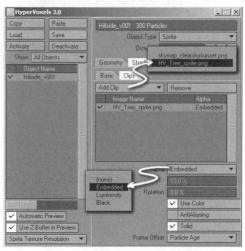

Figure 14-45: Setting up the image as a sprite clip.

7. If we want to see our forest in the viewport, activate the **Show Particles** option to see the basic trees appear. Voilà! Instant forest.

> **Note**
>
> A really cool thing about HyperVoxel sprite clips is that you can load in *more than one* clip onto an HV object. Each clip will be assigned, in turn, to the next point of the HV object's point order. In the above example, we could have a collection of tree images that we could use to create a more varied forest.

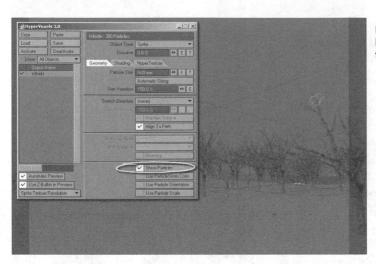

Figure 14-46: Activate Show Particles to see the forest in the viewport.

Assuming you have a few nice clips of some flame and smoke sequences, you could (using particles) also create the same fire effect as seen on the Balrog in *Lord of the Rings: The Fellowship of the Ring*. And (just to plant ideas in your head) using Particle Age as the clip's Frame Offset and LightWave's ability to have collisions "spawn" new particles, you could have non-looping clips of explosions "do their thing" when a projectile impacts its target!

For something even more complex, if you have clips of splashing water and create a particle simulation of water flowing where splash particles are spawned when the water particles collide with objects, you will have recreated the "two-and-a-half-D" used to create the breathtaking water effects seen in feature films such as *Tarzan* and *The Road to El Dorado*.

To find out how to have particles react with one another and with objects in your scene, dive into the LightWave manual. It's all there for you, just waiting to be unearthed!

Conclusion

We've covered quite a bit of ground in this chapter. I'm sure you'll agree that Hyper-Voxels combined with particles are a powerful tool for creating special effects, and that this chapter has only touched on what's possible. Hopefully you are sufficiently inspired to go and try some of your own ideas!

By exploring these simulations and appreciating the levels of detail their mathematics create — details no one person could ever envision in their entirety — you have hopefully touched upon one of the greatest truths: Knowing the answer is not important. Knowing how to solve the question is.

Closing Notes on the Intermediate Skills Section

This is the last chapter in the Intermediate Skills section. With the new modeling, lighting, texturing, and animation skills you've picked up in this section, you should be feeling a lot more confident with the software. Of course, repetition is often the key to success, and that's certainly the case here. If you really want to master LightWave, take time to apply the concepts and practices you've learned in this section. Then when you're ready, move on to the Advanced Skills section where we'll cover character modeling, rigging, animation, and much more!

Chapter 15

Advanced Skills: Subpatch Modeling

The use of subpatches (sometimes also referred to as modeling with *subdivision surfaces*) has become an extremely popular modeling technique for creating stream-lined shapes and organic forms. A *subpatch* is just a regular four-sided polygon that has been subdivided into smaller four-sided polygons. How many depends upon the value set for Subpatch Divisions (level of detail) in the General Options (<o>) window. (Three-sided polygons will also subpatch, but not as nicely.)

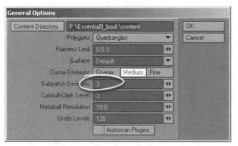

Figure 15-1: The Subpatch Divisions setting can be altered in Modeler.

Pressing <Tab> activates **Construct | Convert | SubPatch**, which tells LightWave to handle all your quads as subpatches. (I hesitate to say that the polys are "converted" into subpatches because the polys technically remain exactly as they were and are directly referenced in the interpreting of the subpatch surface. Pressing <Tab> again turns the subpatches right back into the polys you were looking at before.)

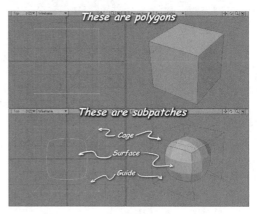

Figure 15-2: The anatomy of a subpatch in Modeler.

By default, LightWave viewports show a subpatch's:

- Cage — The "ghosted" representation of the polygon(s) that define the subpatch.

- Surface — The subpatch surface; what will actually be rendered in Layout.

- Guide — A ghosted line drawn from the surface to the point on the original poly that "controls" (influences) it.

Personally, I prefer to disable cages and guides for all viewports using the Display Options (<**d**>) window, as they tend to slow down the performance of Modeler and also make the display a little busy for my liking. Right up to LightWave 6.5, these features were the only way to select a point for editing on a subpatch surface. When objects start to become complex, this would often make accurate editing a little frustrating. With LightWave 7.0, NewTek implemented the ability to edit points by clicking directly on the subpatch surface itself, which made for a huge improvement in subpatch modeling workflow!

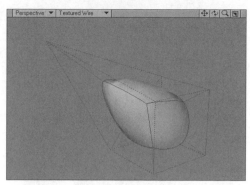

Figure 15-3: A subpatched object behaves a lot like digital clay.

Note

Take care when increasing Subpatch Divisions in Modeler. To display the model, these extra subdivided polygons need to be created and drawn by the computer as though they physically existed in the model to begin with. A high Subpatch Division can create huge numbers of tiny polygons that slow Modeler's performance and make modeling difficult. When Subpatch Divisions is set to a level of 3, each subpatched polygon is divided into 3 x 3 (9) smaller polygons. A level of 4 becomes 4 x 4 (16) smaller polygons, and so forth. As you can imagine, if your model happened to be built from 25,000 polygons *before* subpatching, a level of 3 would increase the number of polygons to display up to 225,000!

Saying that a subpatch is "just" a polygon diced into tinier ones in no way, shape, or form gives even an inkling of how fantastic subpatching is. When an object is subpatched, a new subpatch surface is calculated that smoothly flows within the object's original geometry (termed the *subpatch cage*). Each of the points of the original poly exerts *influence* over how the subdivision surfacing algorithm creates the smooth surface of the subpatch. The subpatch surface behaves a lot like stretchy, digital clay.

When and When Not to Subpatch

When is a good time to use subpatching? How about when modeling a sports car or 3D character, where creating the smooth and sleek shapes can be a complicated task to do by hand? By modeling a low-polygon representation (*cage*) that closely resembles the shape of the model, subpatching takes care of the complexity of smoothing the model for us.

Figure 15-4: Objects like this character, with its smooth, organic shape, make good candidates for subpatching.

These types of models often require smooth, flowing surfaces, and make ideal candidates for subpatching. Imagine the complexity of trying to model the smooth complex surface *without* subpatching and you'll quickly appreciate the beauty of subpatching!

Another benefit is that subpatching not only helps simplify the modeling process when creating characters, but also helps achieve a better look for your model when

deforming it in Layout. (We'll be looking at how this works in more detail later in Chapter 23.) Subpatch surface models can also have their resolution dialed up or down, not only while you're modeling but while you're animating as well! In Layout's Object Properties window, you set the resolution at which your subpatch model will be displayed and the resolution at which it will be rendered. (In Figure 15-5, that's a huge difference of 16,064 polygons!) You can animate with a very speedy, low-poly mesh and render with the ultra-polished, 18,072-poly mesh without having to change a single setting when it's time to render!

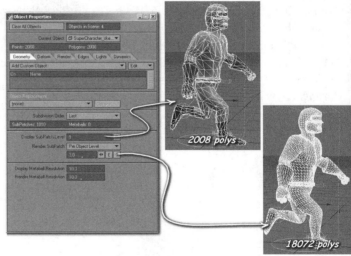

2008 polys

18072 polys

Figure 15-5: The Display SubPatch Level and Render SubPatch settings can be different in Layout!

What about modeling machines, or perhaps architecture? Sure, we can subpatch some parts to get a smooth, curved surface, but panels that have been cut or grooves that have been inset may need sharp edges to look right. One downside of subpatching is that everything often becomes smooth, or "blobby" in shape. As we'll see in the next section, we can add in more geometry to sharpen edges (using a tool such as Band Saw, which is covered in Chapter 8); however, sometimes we may need to cut complex panels into an object using tools such as Drill and Bevel. Cutting detail like this into a subpatched object can break the subpatching altogether, or cause the surface to change its smoothness. We could alternately model this detail using more polygons to allow the subpatching to work, but that adds to the modeling complexity and time. Is that time worth it, just to use subpatching on an object that can be modeled faster without?

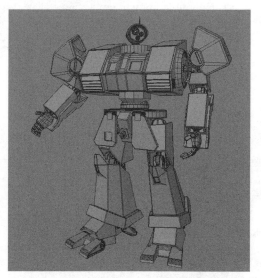

Figure 15-6: Hard-bodied objects might not be good candidates for subpatching.

Of course, these aren't strict guidelines, and some people prefer to model their hard-body objects using subpatching. But these are things that you should at least think about when planning your modeling approach to decide if subpatching is really the best or most efficient way of modeling your project.

> ## Note
>
> Sometimes using subpatching to create the starting geometry for a model is a great idea, even if you don't plan on using subpatching to create the final model. Subpatch models can be converted into polygons in Modeler using **Construct | Convert | Freeze** (<**Ctrl**>+<**d**>). When freezing, the Subpatch Divisions value in the General Options (<**o**>) window is used to determine how many polygons to create. To create a "subpatchable" ball, change Subpatch Divisions to **2**, create a default box, and then subpatch (<**Tab**>) and freeze (<**Ctrl**>+<**d**>). This will create a simple low-poly ball made from quads, and can be a great starting point for modeling an object such as a character's head.
>
>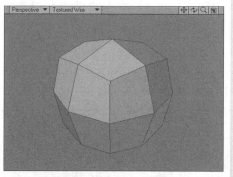
>
> Figure 15-7: Freezing a subpatched box generates a ball created from quads, a good starting point for character modeling.

Less Is More

Before starting out modeling with subpatches, it's important to get one fact clear: Subpatching creates a smoother, denser mesh based on the structure of the geometry you model initially. How you construct your model will heavily influence how the subpatch surface appears, and also how many new polygons are generated for animation and rendering.

When a subpatch surface is calculated, every corner is analyzed to calculate the curves of the subpatch surface. Corners that have points closer together create smaller, sharper-looking curves. Corners where the points are spread farther apart create broader, softer-looking curves. As we can see in Figure 15-8, we can use this simple knowledge to create rounder or sharper curves for a simple box.

Corners that are too close to each other or geometry that is very dense can create denting, or pinching artifacts, on the subpatched model. When there is too much geometry, keeping a model smooth while modeling can become very difficult.

Adding geometry is an important part of the modeling process. With subpatching, we know that smaller distances between corners makes curves sharper. This has the disadvantage that as we add detail to an object, it starts to lose its curve and will require some modifying to smooth it as we work. However, knowing in advance that this is the case will save us plenty of headaches later on.

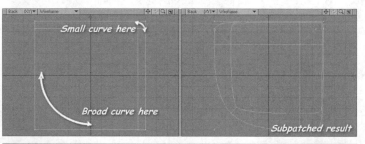

Figure 15-8: The effect of varying distances between edges on a subpatch surface.

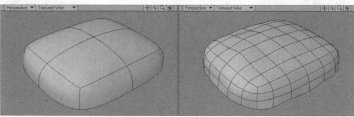

Figure 15-9: Geometry that's too dense is harder to keep smooth.

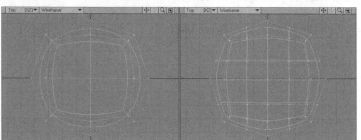

Figure 15-10: Adding geometry causes us to lose some of our nice subpatch roundness.

Subpatching should *not* be considered a replacement to using the Smoothing option in the Surface Editor. If a model is already quite detailed and high-poly to begin with, subpatching will only serve to push that polygon count exponentially and could cause modeling, rendering, or animating issues later on.

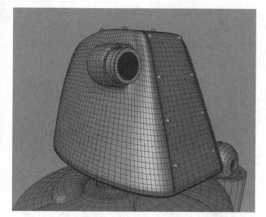

Figure 15-11: A high-poly model that is already smooth is not a good subpatch candidate.

The golden rule of "less is more" applies strongly to any subpatch modeling you plan on doing. Keep your models as simple as possible, while still creating the basic structures needed to get the subpatch surface detail.

Let's see how we can use this knowledge to produce a subpatched model with a mix of both soft and hard curves, using a simple low-poly model.

1. Start up a fresh copy of Modeler. Before you start, let's get your viewports looking the same as mine. Make sure the display type for the Perspective viewport is set to **Textured Wire**. If you haven't already, open the Display Options window (<**d**>) and click on the **Viewports** tab, then activate the

TopR viewport's **Independent Visibility** option. When active, most of the controls below will become available. Disable **Show Cages**, **Show Guides**, and **Show Grid**.

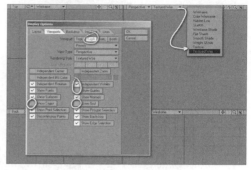

Figure 15-12: Tweak the display options for the TopR (Perspective) viewport.

2. Let's start the model with the **Create | Primitive | Box** tool (<**X**>) and press <**n**> to open the Numeric panel. This should create a default box 1 m in size and centered neatly in the middle of each viewport. If it doesn't, click on **Actions | Reset** to reset the numeric values to their defaults. Close the Numeric panel, then press <**Return**> to finish creating the box. Press <**Tab**> to subpatch the box.

3. The box now looks a lot more like a small ball. To get the box back into shape, let's slice in a few extra polygons. For this, I'll be using Band Saw Pro. This tool operates in exactly the same way as Band Saw, which we looked at back in Chapter 8, except that it is more interactive and gives real-time feedback. Select the top and front polys to define the direction for Band Saw Pro to take, as shown in Figure 15-13, then activate **Multiply | Subdivide | Band Saw Pro.**

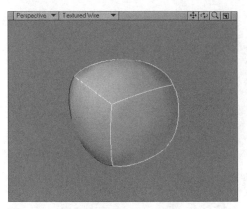

Figure 15-13: Select the top and one side poly to prepare for Band Saw Pro.

By default, Band Saw Pro will slice through the center of the box (providing the **Enable divide** option is checked), creating a cylindrical shaped object. (As you know, adding more geometry to the object changes how the subpatch surface is calculated.) However we want to create a box, not a cylinder, as we can see in Figure 15-14.

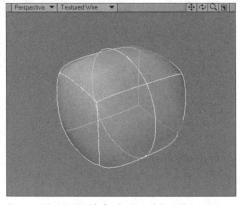

Figure 15-14: By default, Band Saw Pro cuts through the center, creating a cylindrical shape.

Note

Band Saw Pro (and Band Saw) will remember any alterations that you made to the settings when the tools are next used. To reset the tool to its default of cutting through the center, click on the **Clear** button.

4. Open the Numeric panel (<**n**>) for the Band Saw Pro tool, make sure that Operation is set to **Edit**, and change Value to **5%** to move the slice to one end of the box. The smaller gap between the side of the box and the new cut at 5% creates a sharper subpatch curve. We'll need to also slice the other side of the box, so click on Band Saw Pro's **Mirror** button to create a second cut at 95%. Once cut, close the Numeric panel, and press <**Return**> to finish.

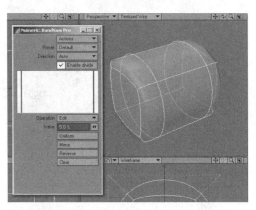

Figure 15-15: Slicing the edges of the box.

The box still looks very much like a cylinder because we've only added geometry in one direction around the box. To reshape the rest of the box, we'll have to repeat the Band Saw Pro tool two more times.

5. Deselect all the polygons (</>) that we've just created, and select two of the top polygons that run along the cylindrical surface, as illustrated in Figure 15-16. Once selected, activate **Multiply | Subdivide | Band Saw Pro** again. (The numeric options we changed in step 4 should still be in place.) The cylindrical shape should instantly change to more of a box!

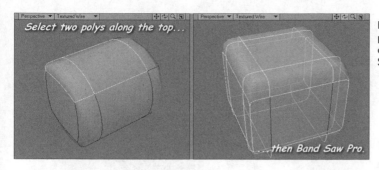

Figure 15-16: Selecting two polygons that run along the cylindrical surface and Band Saw Pro again.

6. We're not quite finished. Press <**Return**>, then deselect the polygons (</>). Let's press <**Tab**> to unsubpatch the box. You'll see that we have sliced in two directions, but not the third, as shown in Figure 15-17. Let's get that step out of the way.

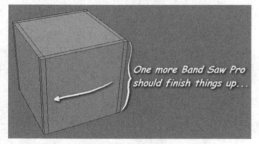

Figure 15-17: We're still one slice short of finishing the basic box.

7. Select two polygons on the front of the box, then **Multiply | Subdivide | Band Saw Pro** to finish slicing the box. Press <**Return**>, deselect the polygons (</>), and press <**Tab**> to resubpatch the box. Our subpatch box is now box-shaped!

So why create a box this way? We could have done this without the need for subpatching. We used this technique for two reasons. First, we've created a box with slightly rounded edges that give the box a nicer, less CG quality. Second, I plan for this box to become a six-sided die, with rounded dots that are sunken into the box.

To set up the box for adding the dots to create a die, we'll want to subdivide the middle poly of each side of the box into a 3 x 3 grid. To do this, we're going to repeat what we did in steps 4 to 7, but with a little adjustment in our Band Saw Pro settings.

8. Let's start by defining the direction for Band Saw Pro by selecting two center polygons running from back to front on the top of the box as shown in Figure 15-19. Activate **Band Saw Pro**, and press <**n**> to open the Numeric panel. To get a nice 3 x 3 grid for our dots, we'll want to make three *evenly spaced* slices. Click on the **Uniform** button; this will evenly space the two cuts for

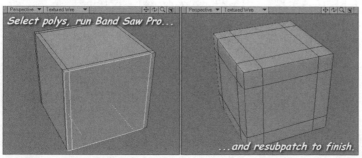

Figure 15-18: Select the two front polygons, Band Saw Pro, and resubpatch.

us! Press <**Return**> and deselect the polys (</>).

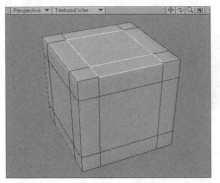

Figure 15-19: Select the two top center polygons.

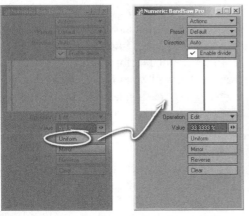

Figure 15-20: Click Uniform to spread Band Saw Pro's slices evenly.

9. Repeat step 8 for the two remaining directions around the box to slice in the rest of the grid pattern that we need. If the subpatch box makes this look a little confusing, deselect all the polygons and press <**Tab**> to unsubpatch the box if it's easier for you. Once you've finished, press <**Tab**> to resubpatch the box.

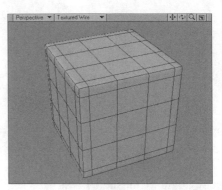

Figure 15-21: The box now sliced and diced!

10. Using the Perspective viewport, hold down the <**Shift**> key and carefully select the polygons that will become the dots of the die (Figure 15-22). Rotate the viewport (*not* the object) to see each side of the die, and repeat the process until you do all six sides.

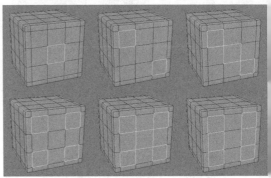

Figure 15-22: Selecting the polygons for each "face" of the die from the new 3 x 3 grid.

Once all the polys for dots are selected on each side of the die as shown in Figure 15-23, we're ready to continue.

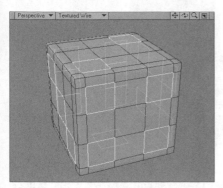

Figure 15-23: All dot polys selected.

11. Activate the **Multiply | Extend | Bevel** tool (**<b>**). Hold down **<Ctrl>** to constrain the Bevel tool, then left-click and drag slowly to the *left* to inset the new dots for the die. If you don't have a "steady" mouse hand when working with the Bevel tool, you can press **<n>** to open the Numeric panel. Set an Inset value of **40 mm** for the bevel. Leave all other values at **0 m**.

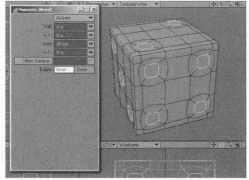

Figure 15-24: Bevel the dots into the die.

12. Once you've completed the bevel, right-click once to create a *new* bevel. Note how this new geometry alters the way the subpatch surface is calculated, making the dots appear much rounder. Left-click again, and drag the mouse slowly downward to drag the dots into the die. Again, you can use the

Numeric panel, but this time set Inset to **0 m** and Shift to **–40 mm**.

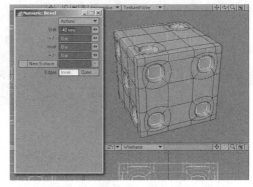

Figure 15-25: A second bevel is needed to sink the dots into the die.

13. Click on **Surface** at the bottom of the Interface (**<q>**) and give the selected polygons the Name **Dots**. Set this surface to a Color of **000, 000, 000**, with Diffuse of **100%** and Specular of **50%**. Make sure that **Smoothing** is active.

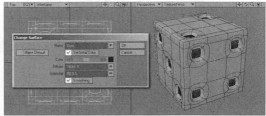

Figure 15-26: Our subpatched die, now with dots.

14. Note that like the first bevel we made, these dots appear quite "square." To finish the dots up, create one more bevel for the selected polygons, holding down **<Ctrl>** and dragging to the left just a little. As we noted in step 12, this extra bevel changes the subpatch surface calculation and creates a rounder result. Once done, press **<Return>** to complete the bevel, then deselect the polygons and save the model if you wish.

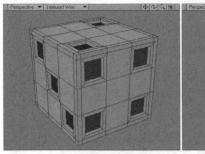

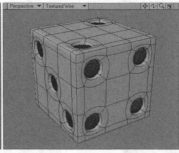

Figure 15-27: The finished die, in its polygon and subpatched states.

Press <Tab> to unsubpatch the die model temporarily and note how simple the geometry is. Subpatching has taken this simple model and created a great result without us having to worry about how we would otherwise model this object using traditional methods!

SubPatch Weight

Sharpening up the curves of a subpatch using extra geometry is one way to control the shape of a subpatch surface. Another way is through a special weight map called the SubPatch Weight. To edit the SubPatch Weight map, make sure that the **W** Vertex map selector is active, and select **SubPatch Weight** from the top of the weight map pop-up menu as shown in Figure 15-28.

Figure 15-28: Select SubPatch Weight from the pop-up.

Activate **Map | Weight | Weights**, then left-click on a point and drag to adjust the weight map tension. (Switching the display mode of the viewport to Weight Shade will display the tension in color (green being neutral or 0% tension). Dragging to the right increases the tension (sharpening), which in Weight Shade view becomes red. Dragging to the left decreases the tension (softening), which is displayed as blue in Weight Shade view.

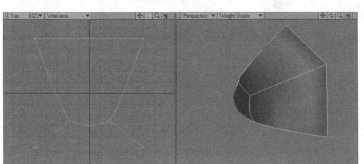

Figure 15-29: Subpatch weighting affects the tension or sharpness at points.

> **Note**
>
> Left-clicking and dragging on a point is great if you want to manually adjust the weighting of single points. To adjust the weighting on multiple points numerically, select the points and use **Map | General | Set Map Value** to numerically apply a value to all selected points. For more manual control, **Map | General | Airbrush** will allow you to paint weights onto the points. When using the Airbrush tool, left-click will increase the weight values, **<Shift>**+click will decrease the weight values, and **<Ctrl>**+click will decrease the values until they reach 0%. Right-click allows the size of the brush to be adjusted.

This weight map should be used carefully, as a weight of 100% (or more) drags the subpatch surface to a sharp corner (which is the same as if the point were not subpatched at all). This is ideal for creating sharp talons for claws perhaps; however, if you want a sharp edge instead (like the edges of the box for the die), then consider using extra geometry.

Alternatively, we could use *edge weighting* — a feature of the new Catmull-Clark subdivision system.

Catmull-Clark Subdivision

LightWave v9 offers the option to do *Catmull-Clark subdivision*, an alternative method for subdividing the polygons of our models based on work by Edwin Catmull (Pixar) and Jim Clark (Silicon Graphics). You may be wondering "Why would we need two ways to subpatch geometry?" Unlike the standard subpatch calculations in LightWave, Catmull-Clark subdivision can work with *n-gons* (polygons that have more than four sides), which eliminates the requirement of modeling exclusively with triangles and quads. Catmull-Clark has a slightly rounder appearance to its subpatch surface, and can also sharpen or soften

edges (something that standard subpatching cannot do easily without extra geometry as we've already seen).

> **Note**
>
> The Catmull-Clark Level can be set in Modeler under the General Options window (**<o>**). Be warned that Catmull-Clark generates a *lot* more polygons than the standard subpatching, hence a lower value is preferable here.

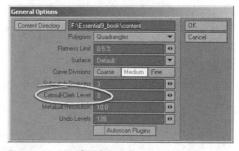

Figure 15-31: The Catmull-Clark Level can be altered under the General Options window.

How do we make use of this new subdivision system? To change which subdivision type to use, select it from the **SubD-Type** pop-up at the bottom of the Modeler interface, as shown in Figure 15-32.

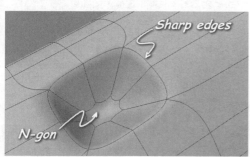

Figure 15-30: Catmull-Clark can subpatch n-gons, and also offers edge sharpening capabilities.

Figure 15-32: The subdivision system can be changed.

It's important to note that changing the SubD-Type won't change any *already subpatched* polygons to the new type. To apply the new subdivision type to subpatched polys, unsubpatch the polygons first, then resubpatch them to pick up the new subdivision type. It's also important to note that the number of polygons that Catmull-Clark subdivides polygons into is drastically different from those created by LightWave subdivision, as demonstrated in Figure 15-33. In Chapter 21, we'll look this issue and how the new Adaptive Pixel Subdivision features in Layout can be used to optimize and work with high amounts of subpatching.

> **Note**
>
> **User warning:** Whatever you do, don't let Catmull-Clark become a way to subpatch *bad* geometry. Catmull-Clark offers a great new option for subpatching, but it's not a way to get around bad modeling techniques and bad geometry that won't subpatch using the standard subpatch system.

Still a little confused over how to use the new Catmull-Clark system? Let's look at how this works by creating a simple coffee cup object, and demonstrate not only how to apply Catmull-Clark subdivision but also how to take advantage of the new edge weighting capabilities.

Either start a fresh Modeler session, or select **File | New Object** (<N>) to continue.

1. Let's start out with the **Create | Primitives | Disc** tool. Press <n> to open the Numeric panel. From the Actions pop-up at the top of the panel, select **Reset**. This will force all the values to reset to a series of defaults that we will be using in this exercise. Once reset, change Axis to **Y** and Sides to **8** to create an eight-sided cylinder. Close the Numeric panel and press <**Return**> to finish the tool.

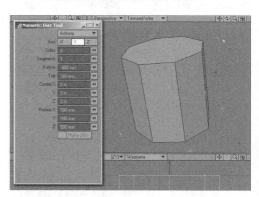

Figure 15-34: An eight-sided cylinder.

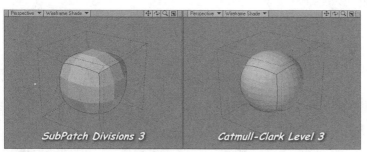

Figure 15-33: Catmull-Clark creates a larger number of polygons than LightWave's original subdivision.

2. From the SubD-Type pop-up, select **SubD Type: Catmull-Clark** to switch Modeler into the right subdivision mode, then press <Tab> to subdivide the cylinder. The cylinder, including the eight-sided n-gons on the top and bottom, is instantly subdivided using Catmull-Clark.

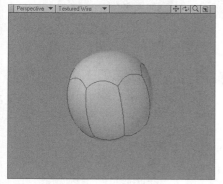

Figure 15-35: Subdivide the cylinder, eight-sided polys and all!

3. Like the die, we can sharpen up our Catmull-Clark subdivision by adding more geometry. Let's select the top

polygon (an n-gon), and then use **Multiply | Extend | Bevel** (<b>). Hold down <Ctrl>, left-click, and drag the mouse upward to extend the top of the cylinder, flattening it out (Figure 15-36).

4. Right-click once to create a new bevel, then left-click and drag the mouse to the left to inset the top a little. Right-click again, and bevel the poly back down into the cylinder about the same amount as we beveled up at the beginning. This will create a nice lip around the top of the cylinder. Right-click and bevel the poly down inside the cylinder once more to create the inside of our coffee cup. Your coffee cup should look similar to Figure 15-37.

Note

I'm using a visual approach to bevel and tweak the shape of the coffee cup here, adjusting polygons to something I think looks right. Often I won't use exact measurements or values (unless I'm creating something that needs to match a real-world object), which is why I'm not indicating any numeric options here. Take your time, move the mouse carefully, and remember to use the <Ctrl> key to constrain the operation of tools as you model.

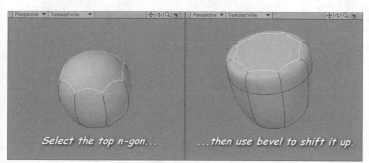

Select the top n-gon...   ...then use bevel to shift it up.

Figure 15-36: Bevel and shift the polygon upward to flatten the top of the cylinder.

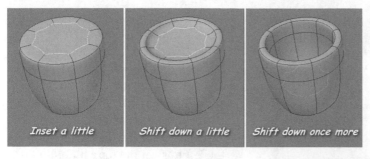

Figure 15-37: Three more bevels create the inside for our coffee cup.

Inset a little

Shift down a little

Shift down once more

Well, this is nice, but what if we wanted to make the edge at the top of the coffee cup a little sharper? We could create more geometry around the top of the edge, or we could use Catmull-Clark's ability to sharpen the edge instead! Let's see how this works.

5. Switch to **Edges** selection mode, and then select two of the outer top adjacent edges as shown in Figure 15-38. Now we need to select the entire edge around the top. The quickest method is to click on the **Select** pop-up near the top of the toolbar and choose **Select Loop.** Like Band Saw, Select Loop will use the two selected edges to define the loop that it selects.

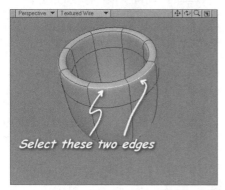

Figure 15-38: Selecting two edges.

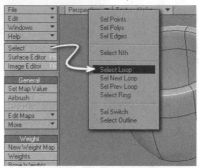

Figure 15-39: Select | Select Loop will select the rest of the edges that form a loop.

6. Select **Map | Weight | Set Sharpness** to enter a sharpening amount for this edge. We don't want to make this razor sharp, so enter **50%** for Value and click **OK** to set the sharpness. The edge becomes instantly sharper without the need for additional geometry!

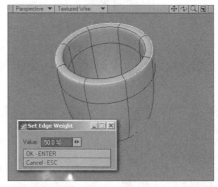

Figure 15-40: Subpatch edges, now 50% sharper.

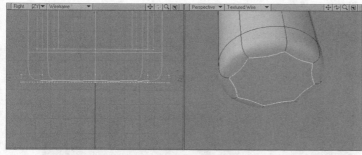

Figure 15-41: Extend the base using Bevel.

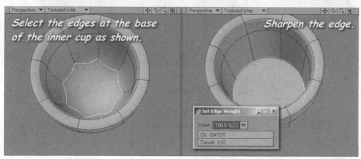

Select the edges at the base of the inner cup as shown.

Sharpen the edge.

Figure 15-42: Setting a 100% sharpness flattens the inside of the cup.

7. Switch back to **Polygons** selection mode (**<Ctrl>**+**<h>**). Select the polygon on the base of the cylinder, and use **Multiply | Extend | Bevel** (**<b>**). Left-click and drag upward to extend the polygon just enough to flatten the base.

8. Let's use edge weighting to flatten out the inside of the cup. Select the edges around the base of the inner cup, then **Map | Weight | Set Sharpness**. Set Value to **100%** and click **OK** to flatten the bottom edge to a perfect circle.

9. The cup now looks close to complete. We just need to add one more thing... a handle. Select one of the central side polygons, activate the **Multiply | Extend | Bevel tool** (**<b>**), left-click, and inset the poly by dragging the mouse to the left until it looks like Figure 15-43.

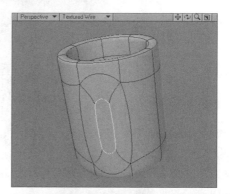

Figure 15-43: Select one of the side polys and inset it to create the start of a handle for our coffee cup.

10. Right-click to create a new bevel, then left-click and drag upward to push the handle out from the cup. Once things look like Figure 15-44, press **<Return>** to drop the Bevel tool and then deselect the polygon.

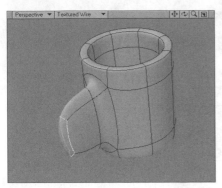

Figure 15-44: Extend a handle outward from the cup.

11. Select the polygons on either side of the handle, and bevel an inset to form the shape for the inside of the handle.

12. With both polygons still selected, let's create the hole by selecting the

Construct | Combine | Bridge tool. This will create a bridge, or join, between the two polygons, making our handle *hold-able*. Our Catmull-Clark coffee cup is now ready for some hot java.

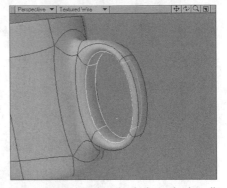

Figure 15-46: Create the hole in the handle using the Bridge tool.

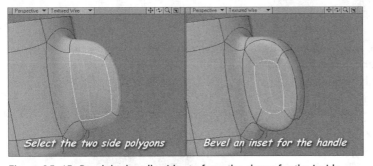

Select the two side polygons

Bevel an inset for the handle

Figure 15-45: Bevel the handle sides to form the shape for the inside.

Model for Intended Use

Know what you plan on using your created object for *before* you start modeling. If it's for animation and you plan on deforming the object with morphs, bones, or other such tools, it's critical you plan on creating your object cleanly, efficiently, and structured to best work for animation. For example, a character should be built to match the shape of the final subpatched

character's *virtual anatomy*. This will make life easier later on when we need to add animation controls to the object (see Chapter 23), and will influence the way the subpatch surface deforms when animated. We'll be looking more at character modeling in Chapter 16, but for now, just start creating those mindsets.

Your model should closely resemble the form of your subpatch version

Figure 15-47: Building a character to closely match its final subpatched shape.

An object that will not need to be deformed, such as a piece of furniture or a prop, can be modeled as a sculpture. There are no strict rules regarding the structure of the geometry, though keeping it as clean and tidy as possible is always a bonus!

The Box Method of Modeling

A box modeling approach is a great way to build almost anything, from characters to coffee cups. Starting from a simple box, we can sculpt, bevel, and slice detail to create a base polygon cage for subpatching. We used this box method earlier when we created the die; however, it's possible to create pretty much anything using this method. In Chapter 16, we'll be getting plenty of practice modeling a character using the box method!

The Point-by-Point Method of Modeling

Point-by-point modeling is a great way to sculpt more complex forms into a rough polygon structure that can then be refined through subpatching. This method simply means that we build up the model by creating polygons manually, and is sometimes also referred to as "detail-out" modeling. One of the downsides of this approach is that you need to have a *feel* for sculpting, as you are literally "sculpting" the location, orientation, and shape of the surface by hand. However, once grasped, this method can be used to create just about any model — including those that may be difficult to sculpt from a basic primitive.

We can generate polygons manually by pressing < + > to create points, then select them and press <**p**> to build the polygon. However, often it's faster to start with some basic geometry and extend extra polys from the sides of this initial geometry.

We'll take a look at how to use this approach to create the casing for an imaginary MP3 player. This device is molded from plastic, and hence has soft, rounded edges that make it a good candidate for subpatch modeling.

Create a fresh new object in Modeler and let's get started. Before we get too far, if you've just been playing with Catmull-Clark subdivision, be sure to change the SubD-Type pop-up back to **SubD Type: Subpatch**.

1. I've prepared a simple design as a guide for creating this MP3 player casing. Press <**d**> to open Modeler's Display Options window, and click on the **Backdrop** tab. Into the TopL viewport (which should be set to the default display of Top (XZ)), select **Image | (load image)** and load

mp3_background.png (Images\Chapter 15). Set Image Resolution to **256** and close the Display Options window.

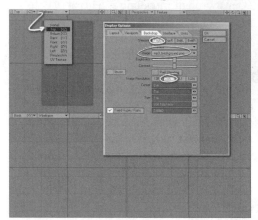

Figure 15-48: Load the mp3_background.png image into the TopL viewport.

2. Maximize the top-left viewport so that we have a single viewport to work in, and zoom in to make the backdrop fill the workspace.

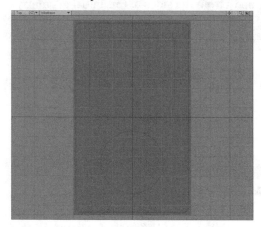

Figure 15-49: Zoom in to the viewport to get the backdrop as large as possible.

The screen and a circular cursor pad are the key features found on the front of this new MP3 player. These features only need to be created as holes within the case, ready to model in the details later if we wish to continue the project beyond this exercise. These holes must be modeled carefully so that they are part of a seamless subpatched surface, so point-by-point modeling is a good method for this. We'll start out creating the circular cursor pad and detail the object out from there.

3. Click on **Create | Primitives | Disc** and then press **<n>** to enter numeric options for the Disc tool. Set Axis to **Y**, Sides to **8**, Center Z to **–230 mm**, and Radius X and Z to **170 mm**.

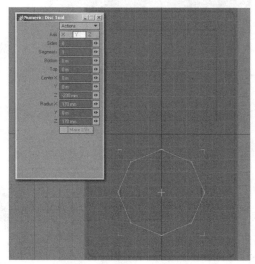

Figure 15-50: First create a disc for the cursor pad.

Hold on… we know that an eight-sided polygon won't subpatch without using Catmull-Clark. Don't panic; we're not planning on keeping this polygon. We're simply using it as a starting *shape* from which we'll be modeling a hole for the cursor pad to sit in. Let's continue.

4. Switch to **Edges** selection mode, and then select all the edges around the disc. Activate **Multiply | Extend | Extender Plus** (**<e>**) *once* only. Don't be fooled by the fact that nothing appears to change visually. Extender

Plus has generated new polys around the edges of the disc, even though we can't see any visible change. Using Extender Plus too many times will generate a lot of excess geometry that can cause issues later on.

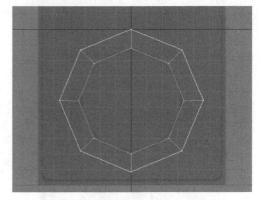

Figure 15-51: Stretch the new extended edges outward.

Note

If you've accidentally run Extender Plus numerous times and you're not sure how many times you need to undo to fix things, here's a quick tip on how to clean up the mess before it starts to affect your model. Start by first deselecting (</>) all the selected edges, points, or polygons, then press <m> to merge points. This will compact all the extra geometry together. Press <l> to unify all the compacted geometry. (Unify will delete any duplicate polygons that share the same points, which they all do after we merged points.) A message box will tell you how many polygons were deleted. Click OK. Duplicate edges that have been "cleaned up" this way usually leave a mess of two-point polygons behind. These don't render nicely, nor do they subpatch. To remove these, make sure you are in Polygons selection mode (<Ctrl>+<h>), and open the Statistics panel (<w>). Click the + symbol next to 2 Vertices, then delete the selected polys. Now you know how to do that, make sure you don't press Extender Plus too many times next time around and save yourself the effort!

5. Activate the **Modify | Transform | Stretch** tool (<h>) and place the mouse cursor in the center of the disc. Left-click and drag the mouse to the left and upward to stretch the new geometry we created using Extender Plus outward from the edges of the disc. We don't need to stretch these out too far (just enough to clearly see them), as we'll be straightening things up shortly.

6. Drop the Stretch tool using the <**Return**> key, deselect the edges, then reselect the two left edges of the new geometry. Reactivate the Stretch tool (<h>), line up the mouse cursor with the left side of the backdrop image's "screen," and hold down the <**Ctrl**> key. Left-click and drag the mouse to the left as much as necessary to straighten the edges in line with where we placed the mouse cursor.

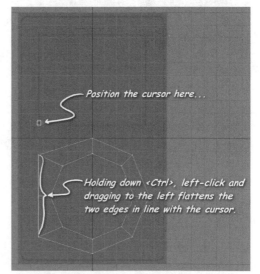

Position the cursor here...

Holding down <Ctrl>, left-click and dragging to the left flattens the two edges in line with the cursor.

Figure 15-52: Flatten the left edge using the Stretch tool.

Using the Stretch tool with the <Ctrl> key is a handy way to "flatten" or straighten up selected geometry. When dragging to the left, the geometry won't stretch beyond the location of the mouse cursor.

7. Repeat step 6 for the two right edges, this time aligning them with the right side of the background's "screen" area. Note that you should still click and drag to the *left* with the Stretch tool and *not right* to flatten these edges correctly.

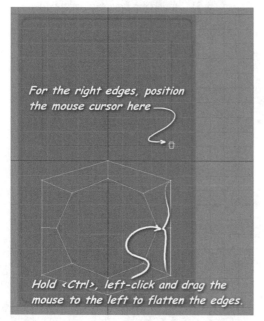

For the right edges, position the mouse cursor here

Hold <Ctrl>, left-click and drag the mouse to the left to flatten the edges.

Figure 15-53: Repeat step 6 for the right edges.

8. We need to also flatten out the top and bottom of the edges. Let's use the same Stretch tool method that we used in steps 6 and 7 for the top two and bottom two edges. The only difference here (other than positioning the mouse cursor at the top or bottom of the geometry) is that rather than clicking and dragging to the left, we should click and drag *downward* (for *both* the top and bottom) to get the Stretch tool to flatten the edges nicely.

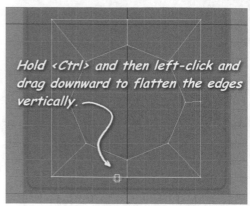

Hold <Ctrl> and then left-click and drag downward to flatten the edges vertically.

Figure 15-54: The same process applies for the top and bottom edges to flatten things out nicely.

With the outer edges flattened out into a nice clean rectangular shape, as shown in Figure 15-54, let's create the rest of the geometry to finish up this object.

9. Select the left and right edges, press <e> to extend them, then activate the Stretch tool (<h>). This time, place the mouse cursor in the center of the disc, and left-click and drag left to stretch the new geometry out to the sides of the backdrop image as shown in Figure 15-55.

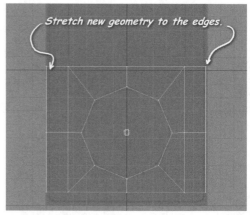

Stretch new geometry to the edges.

Figure 15-55: Extending the geometry out sideways.

10. Select the edges along the top of the new geometry. Press <e> once to extend the geometry, then activate the **Modify | Translate | Move** tool (<t>). Move the edge of the new geometry to the top of the backdrop image.

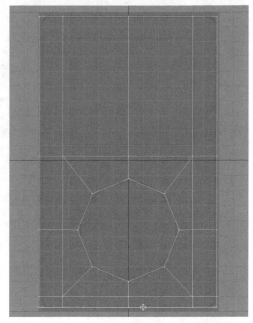

Figure 15-57: Extending the bottom of the geometry.

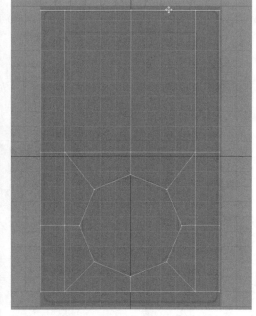

Figure 15-56: Extend and move the new top edges to the top of the image.

11. Repeat step 10 for the bottom edges, moving them to the base of the backdrop image (Figure 15-57).

We've got the overall shape finished. Let's set up the hole for the screen.

12. Make sure that the **Polygons** selection mode is active. Select the **Multiply | Subdivide | Knife** tool (<K>), and let's cut in the top and bottom of the screen area.

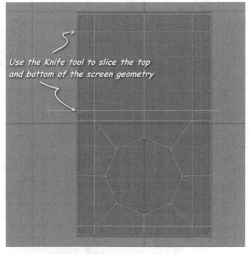

Use the Knife tool to slice the top and bottom of the screen geometry

Figure 15-58: Cutting the screen into place.

13. Let's get rid of the excess geometry for the screen and the cursor pad by selecting the polygons where we need these holes and deleting them, as shown in Figure 15-59.

593

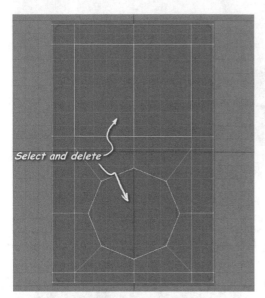

Figure 15-59: Select and delete these excess polygons. We're almost there!

Once deleted, press <Tab> and let's see how this looks subpatched.

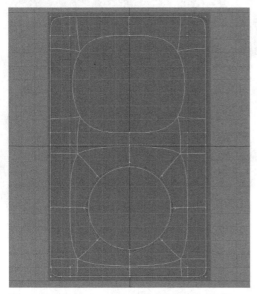

Figure 15-60: Subpatched, but doesn't look like it's quite there yet.

Not quite there yet. The screen needs to be much sharper on the corners. However, as we've learned in this chapter, we can control the sharpness by slicing in a little more geometry. We're close to finished, though. Press <Tab> to unsubpatch and let's continue.

14. Using **Multiply | Subdivide | Knife** (<**K**>), cut a thin slice across just below the top of the screen, followed by another just above the bottom.

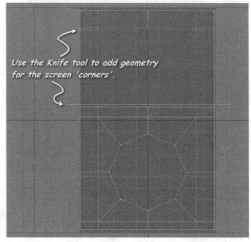

Figure 15-61: Cut a slice at the top and bottom of the screen to help sharpen the subpatching.

15. Cut two vertical slices right down and through the inside of the left and right of the screen as seen in Figure 15-62. This should give our screen area the sharper corners it needs. The downside is that these two cuts will cause us four small issues that we need to deal with.

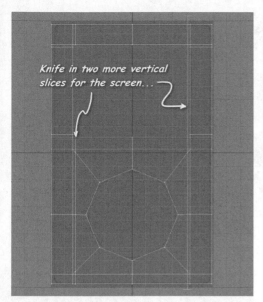

Figure 15-62: Two vertical slices should tidy things up nicely, but something else rears its ugly head.

five-sided polygon (n-gon) won't properly subpatch.

These types of situations aren't too difficult to deal with, however. One way is to delete the triangle and fix the hole by welding two of the points together, as shown in Figure 15-64.

Alternatively, we could use a tool in Modeler specially designed for such situations called the **Fix 3-5** tool.

16. Select all the 3-5 polys as shown back in Figure 15-63, then run **Detail | Polygons | More | Fix 3-5**. All the polygons are split into quads, perfect for subpatching, and saving us a few mouse clicks worth of effort to repair.

By slicing through some of these polys, we've managed to create ourselves a *3-5 situation*: a three-sided and five-sided polygon on each corner of the disc area! As we know, a

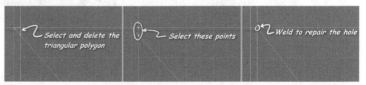

Figure 15-64: We can manually fix the problem by deleting the triangle and welding points.

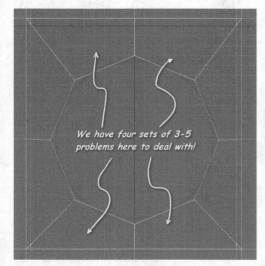

Figure 15-63: n-gon catastrophe caused by our vertical slicing!

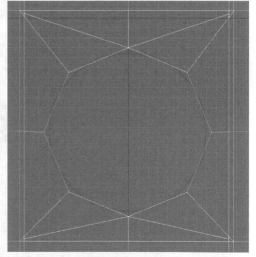

Figure 15-65: Running Fix 3-5 repairs the catastrophe for us!

17. Deselect all the polygons, and press <**Tab**> to see our nicely subpatched MP3 player front plate!

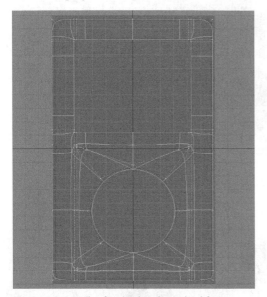

Figure 15-66: The finished, subpatched front plate.

All that's left is a little extending of the edges inside the holes and down the outside to create the final piece, ready for the details to be added. As we've been working so much with selecting edges, extending, and stretching, I'll leave these simple touches up to you to finish if you so wish. You can check out the tweaked version of the player in **Objects\Chapter 15\MP3_Front_E.lwo.**

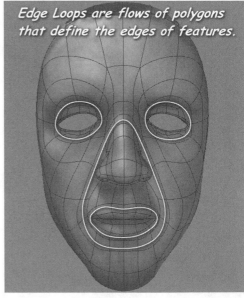

Figure 15-67: With a few simple edges extended and moved down.

Flow

Flow, or the path that polygons follow through a model, is important in subpatch models. The flow of polygons not only helps define the form of the subpatch surface when it's calculated, but is also vital for animated characters to deform naturally. As we've seen, tools such as Band Saw Pro and Select Loop also use the flow to work their way around a model's geometry.

Some of the more common types of flows are found in the facial areas of a character and are called *edge loops*, since they form a loop around the edge of particular details such as the eyes and mouth. Not only do they help form the structure of the face, but they also simulate the basic muscle structure around the face, helping make deformation appear more natural when animating. We'll look more closely at flow and

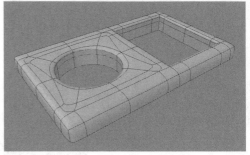

Edge Loops are flows of polygons that define the edges of features.

Figure 15-68: Edge loops form flow around the edges of details.

at how these loops are created in Chapters 16 and 18, where we build a subpatched superhero and a realistic human head. We'll also come back to flow and its importance in animation later in Chapter 23.

Modeler comes with tools to help work with the flow of polygons, giving you the ability to edit and build edges, and another extremely handy tool known as Spin Quads.

Spin Quads

Spin Quads, found under **Detail | Polygons | Spin Quads** (**<Ctrl>+<k>**) "spins" the shared edge between two selected quads. It's an important tool that we refer to again later in Chapter 23, where we use this tool to update a character for animation purposes. To use this tool, select two quads that share an edge, and then press <Ctrl>+<k> to spin the edge once. Three applications of Spin Quads should return the edge to its original starting position

Be sure to only use this tool on two quads at a time. Using Spin Quads on multiple quads together can get quite messy!

Cut

While the Band Saw (and Band Saw Pro) tool allows us to slice through polygons by following the flow, the **Multiply | Subdivide | Cut** tool (**<U>**) does the same, but instead follows a user-defined selection of polygons.

Using the tool is a piece of cake. First select the polygons you wish to cut in the order you want them to be sliced up. Once selected, activate the Cut tool, edit the options as necessary, and click OK.

Cut has all of the features found in Band Saw, plus some other options that make it ideal for working with subpatched objects.

- **maintain quads in corners** ensures that when cutting around a corner, the polygons are split to form quads and not n-gons.

- **square corner quads** should be used in conjunction with the maintain quads in

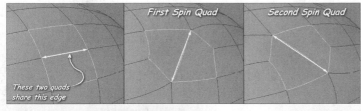

Figure 15-69: Spin Quads spins the shared edge between two quads.

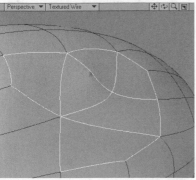

Figure 15-70: Use only two quads at a time to prevent this kind of mess from ever occurring!

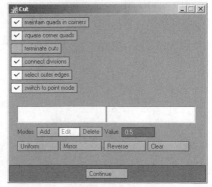

Figure 15-71: The Cut tool options.

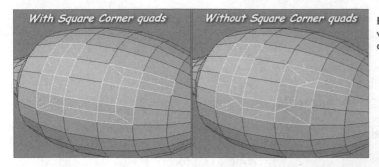

Figure 15-72: With and without square corner quads active.

corners option. When active, this option ensures that the cut through the corner is rectangular and not a four-sided triangle, as shown in Figure 15-72.

- **terminate cuts** adds an extra split on the ends of the user-defined selection, ensuring that the geometry is subpatchable and not made from n-gons.

- **connect divisions** is the option that ensures Cut will split the polygons. Without this option active, only the new points (and not the edges) are created, as shown in Figure 15-73.

- **select outer edges** tells the Cut tool whether it should affect the polygons on the end of the user-defined selection. For example, it specifies whether the terminate cuts option should split the user-selected polys on the ends, or whether it should select the next poly from the end as shown in Figure 15-74.

- **switch to point mode** changes selection mode from Polygons to Points once the

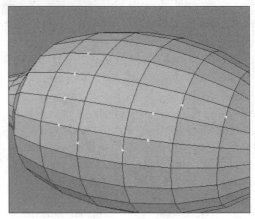

Figure 15-73: Connect divisions ensures that polygons are split with new edges.

cut operation has been completed. When Cut has completed its task, like Band Saw, it selects the newly created points along the newly cut edges.

The options at the bottom of the window work in an identical fashion to Band Saw, so we won't discuss them here.

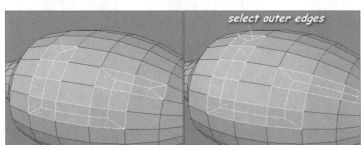

Figure 15-74: Select outer edges tells Cut to go one polygon beyond the ends of the selection.

Cutting Presets

One useful feature of the Cut tool is the ability to create three preset options: Quickcut 1, Quickcut 2, and Quickcut 3. These, along with the default setup for the Cut tool itself, can be defined using **Edit | Edit Modeler Tools**.

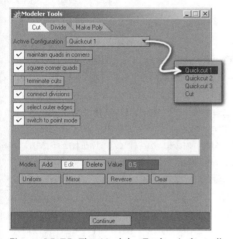

Figure 15-75: The Modeler Tools window allows us to set up some presets and defaults for the Cut tool.

To use one of these presets, select the Quickcut option of choice from the **Multiply | Subdivide | More** menu. Below the Quickcut options are four more handy quick cutting tools that can be used.

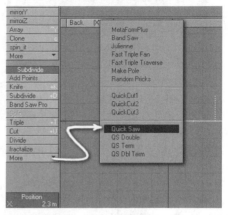

Figure 15-76

QuickSaw will slice through the center of all the selected polygons instantly. **QS Term** does the same thing, except it ensures that the ends are terminated so that they can remain subpatched. **QS Double** and **QS Dbl Term** both perform similar operations, but they slice each polygon in three, creating a central polygon that can be selected and edited for such details as grooves and insets.

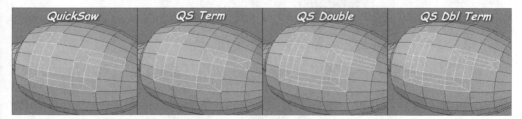

Figure 15-77: QuickSaw tools provide speedy ways of cutting geometry without the pop-up window of the Cut tool.

Fix Poles

When triangular polygons all meet at a central point, they create what is commonly known as a *pole*. Poles can create unsightly pinching, as seen in Figure 15-78 where I have subpatched a ball primitive as an example (a ball automatically generates poles). To intensify the effect, I modified the ball a little by pulling the central point inward. While we can avoid having this kind of geometry with careful planning, should such things arise, then luckily for us there's a tool in Modeler designed to help!

To minimize the effect, select all the polygons around the pole, then activate **Detail | Polygons | More | Fix Poles**. The effect is minimized by creating an extremely tiny edge very close to the center of the pole.

Note

If you can still see any minor issues after using Fix Pole, running it again can help. While this can almost completely remove any artifacts, the extra geometry can also cause the pole to flatten out and lose its subpatch smoothness.

Fix 3-5

As you know, the standard subpatch system won't work with n-gons. While we can switch to Catmull-Clark subdivision to deal with this, we can also repair some n-gons using the Fix 3-5 tool. As we saw while working on our MP3 player, we can be left with three-sided and five-sided (or n-gon) polygons after knifing through geometry. (Deactivating the Cut tool's maintain quads in corners option will also create 3-5 geometry, as seen in Figure 15-80.) Activating **Detail | Polygons | More | Fix 3-5** converts the polygons to subpatchable quads.

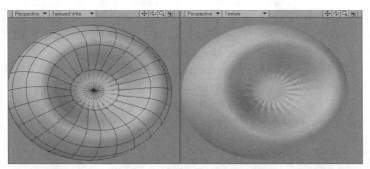

Figure 15-78: Poles can create nasty pinching for subpatched objects.

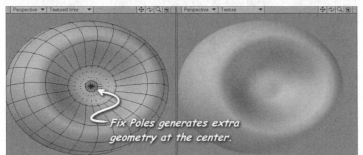

Figure 15-79: Minimizing the pinching using Fix Pole.

Fix Poles generates extra geometry at the center.

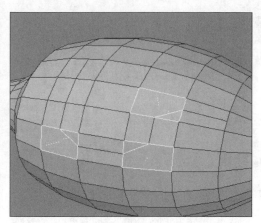

Figure 15-80: Deactivating the Cut tool's maintain quads in corners option causes 3-5 problems!

Extender Plus

We've already touched on **Multiply | Extend | Extender Plus** (<e>) back in Chapter 3. I've repeated it here because I felt it's worth noting what a fantastic tool this is for creating new subpatch geometry! For fast modeling, this tool is a godsend, allowing you to unintrusively create new geometry on the fly while keeping your tool of choice always active!

> **Note**
>
> In the past, creating new geometry in this way was done by activating the **Smooth Shift** (<F>) tool, then clicking once without moving the mouse to create new geometry. While it worked, the Smooth Shift approach meant dropping whatever tool you were using, and added a few more mouse clicks to the whole workflow process. Extender Plus eliminates the need to drop the current tool you're using.

> **Note**
>
> If you do not select any polygons, the Fix 3-5 tool will analyze the entire mesh and repair any 3-5 situations that it finds. This can take some time, so it's recommended that you select the polygons before running this tool.

Conclusion

Subpatches open up a whole new level for both modeling *and* animating. By creating simpler base geometry, modeling complex meshes can now be done in a fraction of the time it would take to noodle all those minute polys. Animating with a cast of subpatch characters means we can obtain more organic, smoother deformations for our animation. As we'll discover later in Chapter 21, we'll also be able to optimize the speed at which we can work and render using LightWave v9's ability to have separate subpatch quality settings for the display and render. Now that we understand subpatching and how it's used, let's move on to the next chapter to put this newfound modeling ability to the test, creating your very own subpatched superhero character!

Chapter 16

Advanced Modeling Exercise 1: Modeling a Stylized Character

Let's take the skills we learned from the previous chapter on subpatch modeling, and extend them out to create a simple superhero-style character in Modeler.

I've found that it's easy for artists to get swept away in the minutiae of the work, not wanting to move on until what they've done looks "perfect." There are three issues I have with this way of working. One, it makes for a very slow working process.

Two, human perception is *referential*; we can't easily tell what's "right" and what's "wrong" without something with which to compare it. Three, when you come back to a piece, even after only half an hour, you see things that you missed before. By letting the rough forms have time to air out a bit, you are allowing yourself the ability to see where you can make things better.

Step 1: Starting with the Body

1. Start out using **Create | Primitives | Box** (**<X>**) to create a box. Open the Numeric panel (**<n>**), and set Width to **1 m**, Height to **2 m**, and Depth to **750 mm** to create a rectangular box. Make sure the box is centered (by setting Center X, Y, and Z all to **0 m**). The box should also have two segments each on X, Y, and Z. Once the box has been created, apply a Surface (**<q>**) with the name **Suit**, and let's get going.

2. In the Top view, select the points on the corners of the box. Activate the **Modify | Transform | Stretch** tool (**<h>**), then place the mouse cursor into the middle of the box and click-drag to stretch the points into a

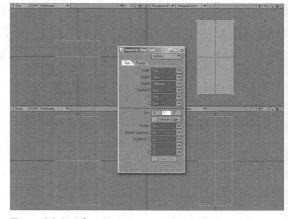

Figure 16-1: A box is a great starting point.

simple tube shape. This will help ensure that we start out with a more anatomically pleasing form at the beginning of the project.

Note

I often model by eye rather than use accurate scale. What's great about CG in general is that it's modifiable! You're never forced into getting it right as you go, and if you make a mistake, well, it's easy to undo or tweak. Once the character is modeled, I can scale the character to a more realistic size if I need to.

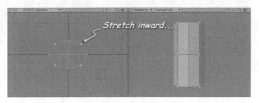

Figure 16-2: Starting out with a tubular box.

Note

By default, modification tools in Modeler should work from the mouse cursor location as the action center. If you find that this is not the case, you can modify this behavior from the Modes pop-up found on the bottom of the Modeler interface. The default should be set to the option Action Center: Mouse (<Shift> + <F5>).

3. **Construct | Convert | SubPatch** (<Tab>) the box, then select the top polys and Stretch (<h>) these out to create a wide chest area (something we'd expect to see on any decent superhero). Select the lower polys,

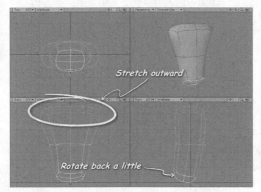

Figure 16-3: Molding the form a little more.

place the mouse cursor in the center of the box, and Rotate (<y>) to bend the hips back (as shown in Figure 16-3).

4. Make two slices using the **Multiply | Subdivide | Knife** tool (<K>) between the upper and lower halves of the box. Once these cuts are in place, select the top polys and Stretch (<h>) them back to shape the upper chest area a little more. Select the points (or edges if you prefer) around the torso and Stretch them to sculpt the body into form as shown in Figure 16-4.

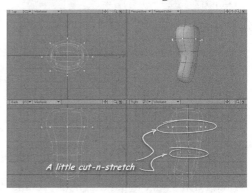

Figure 16-4: Slice and sculpt that body.

5. We're almost done here with the basic body shape. Select the upper four polygons and Rotate (<y>) them to create the flat shelf we often see at the top of the chest (Figure 16-5). This gives us a nice, simple torso to work with for our new character.

Figure 16-5: Finish up with a rotate and we're getting close.

6. Lastly, let's also shift in the polys that will form the base of the neck of our character. We could do this in a number of ways; however, for this I'm going to use the uber-bevel-shifting tool, **Multiply | Extend | Multishift**. Inset the neck polys about 50% of the way into the base polys. Make sure that the **Group Polygons** option is also checked in the Multishift Numeric panel (<**n**>); otherwise, Multishift will bevel each poly individually.

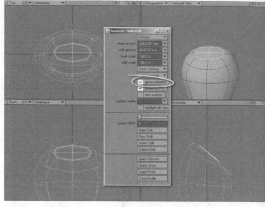

Figure 16-6: Making space for the neck.

Note

Multishift operates identically to the way the Bevel tool does (assuming at this stage in the book that you're extremely familiar with the Bevel tool, that is). To shift (i.e., extend) polygons outward, left-click and drag the mouse up. To inset the polygons, left-click and drag the mouse to the left.

Step 2: Adding a Little Detail to the Body

While I don't want to get caught out adding those details that can often drag out projects like this, I do want to add just a little more body sculpting to finish up the basic body before we continue. Let's add some simple pectoral details and a little more geometry to allow us to add some basic details.

1. Select a couple of the polygons that sit above or below each other on one side of the body as shown in Figure 16-7.

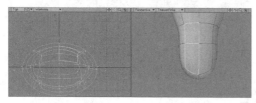

Figure 16-7: Select two neighboring polygons on the same side of the object.

(It doesn't matter which polygons you select, as long as you select two *neighboring polys* on that *same side* of the object.)

2. Select the **Multiply | Subdivide | Band Saw Pro** tool. Bring up the Numeric panel (<**n**>) for Band Saw Pro. Make sure that you check the **Enable Divide** option. This should cut an extra edge vertically through the polygons running down one side of the body as shown in Figure 16-8. If the cut doesn't appear through the center of the polygons, click the **Clear** button on the Numeric panel to reset the cut to the center of the polys (indicated by the red line in the Numeric panel).

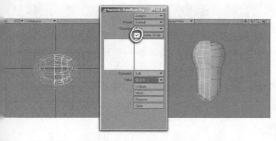

Figure 16-8: Band Saw Pro — slice and dice time!

3. Repeat the process by selecting two neighboring polygons on the *other side* of the body and activating the Band Saw Pro tool again. Adding extra geometry is needed to give us enough geometry for sculpting in a few more details, as well as preparing the body for modeling in other parts of the anatomy.

4. Once the geometry has been created, select the two inner edges (using the Edges selection mode) up in the chest area, and use the Stretch tool (<h>) to bring those in and up a little. Move them forward just a tad to create simple pecs for the body.

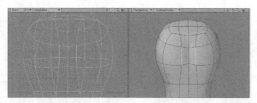

Figure 16-9: Adding the pectorals.

5. Select three edges at the top of the back, and use the Move tool (<t>) to move those inward to form the shoulder blades and create the sunken spine.

Figure 16-10: Sink the spine in to create the shoulder blades.

6. Let's prepare the upper chest for the arms by extending the shoulders out a little. Select the top four polys on each side of the body, then use **Multiply | Extend | Extender Plus** (<e>) to create new geometry. You can activate Symmetry mode for this step (<Y>), then use the Move tool (<t>) to bring the new polys out, then in a little as shown in Figure 16-11.

> **Note**
>
> While Symmetry mode works much better if your model is *a perfect mirror* across the X-axis, it can also be used to mirror the actions of tools on whatever is selected at the time, even if the geometry *is not perfectly symmetrical.* This makes it handy if you simply want to move selections on two sides of an object in opposite directions.

Figure 16-11: Select and extend out some shoulder detail.

7. Lastly, Extend (<e>) the selected polys again and move them out to form some basic arm detail. Stretch (<h>) them in a little to taper the arms. We'll finish up here for now and come back later to finish up the arm detail.

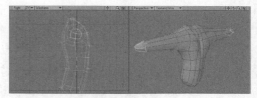

Figure 16-12: Extending the arms.

Step 3: Legs and Feet

Next we'll jump down and get the legs out of the way. We'll be creating one leg at a time, so ensure that you *do not* have the Symmetry option active for this step. This is a stylized character, so we're going to create short, disproportionate sized legs to give the character a little more of a cartoon-ish appearance. It will also help increase the effect of his upper body build.

1. Select the four polys on the bottom left half of the body. Extend (<e>) these and then Move (<t>) them down a little. Once there, use the Drag tool (<Ctrl>+<t>) to drag and shape the edges to form a nicer, rounder-looking leg.

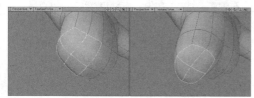

Figure 16-13: Start the first leg.

2. Extend (<e>) the polys again, and as we did for the arms, move them down to where the bottom of the leg should be, then Stretch (<h>) them in to taper the legs a little (Figure 16-14). Use your best judgment on this. After all, the beauty of modeling in CG is that we have the ability to make changes easily afterward if we decide we need

to reproportion the anatomy of our superhero a little more.

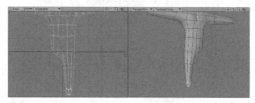

Figure 16-14: Extend the leg down.

3. Once you're happy, select the four polys for the other side of the character and repeat to create the other leg.

4. Use the Knife tool (<K>) to make a slice for the knees through the middle of both legs, then select the points (or edges if you prefer) and move them a little forward to create a bent appearance.

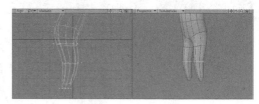

Figure 16-15: Create a slice for the knees and bend them slightly.

The basic legs are done. Obviously, they're extremely simple at this stage, but let's not dwell on details just yet until we've nutted out the main character itself.

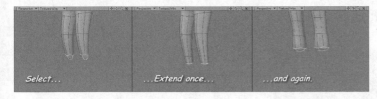

Figure 16-16: Get the feet in place.

5. Let's select the base polys of both legs, Extend (<**e**>) them, and Move (<**t**>) them down just a little to form the ankle. Extend (<**e**>) a second time and left-click and drag to move them down to form the rear of each foot (as we see in Figure 16-16).

Note

Did you notice how we *didn't* need to reactivate the Move tool after the second extend? The Move tool was still active, which meant we could instantly adjust the new extended geometry. The reason for this is that Extender Plus is a *command*, and not a *tool*. What's the difference? Simply that a tool requires user interaction, i.e., the Move tool uses the left-click and drag of the mouse while it's turned on. To stop the user interaction from moving geometry, turn off the tool. A command, on the other hand, just does a single task once when it's activated, then exits. Not having to switch out of one tool to extend geometry, then switch back to the tool to continue is just one way we can work faster.

6. Select the four polys at the front of each leg as shown in Figure 16-17. These will form the basic feet of our character. Extend (<**e**>) and move these out, using a little Stretch (<**h**>) to taper and shape the toes at the end. Again, visually judge how long the feet should be. These feet will be simple boots, and like the proportions of the legs, we're going to leave them quite small and cartoony.

Figure 16-17: Creating simple feet.

Step 4: Arms

We have the legs and basic body, but the arms need a little TLC to bring them up to scratch. Let's finish up the basic arms so that we can say at least we have a close-to-complete form for our new superhero!

1. Let's use Knife (<**K**>) to slice in some elbows on each arm, followed by an extra slice between the elbow and each end of the arm as shown in Figure 16-18.

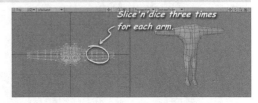

Figure 16-18: Slice up the arms with three slices each.

2. Select the points around the elbows (or edges if you prefer) and then Stretch (<**h**>) them inward, and move them

607

toward the back of the character to give them more form.

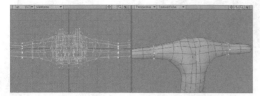

Figure 16-19: Finish up the elbows quickly.

Step 5: The Head

A character can't see where he's going without a head, so let's give him one. As with most superheros, we're not going to see much of his face as he'll be wearing his super suit to hide his real identity from the public. However, like any good superhero, we'll give him a strong chin and mouth so he can at least talk to the police commissioner coherently!

1. As shown in Figure 16-20, select the rear four polys on the center top of the object and Extend (<e>) them to create geometry for the neck. Move the extended polys up and flatten them out using the Stretch tool as we've been applying it throughout this chapter.

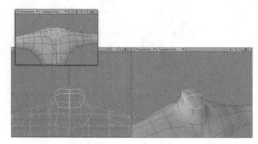

Figure 16-20: Adding the neck.

2. Extend (<e>) these polys again, move them up just a little, and Stretch (<h>) them outward to form the

bottom of the head itself. Extend (<e>) again and move the polys up to form a simple head shape, then select the point in the top middle and pull it up to round the top of the head, as shown in Figure 16-21.

Figure 16-21: Creating the basic head.

3. Use the Knife tool (<K>) and slice the head through the middle to add extra geometry (Figure 16-22). Once that's done, let's select the 14 polys on the front of the head, Extend (<e>) them, and Move (or Stretch if you prefer) them out to form the face and chin geometry (Figure 16-23).

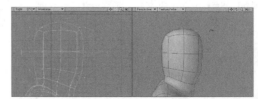

Figure 16-22: Slice through the head to add detail.

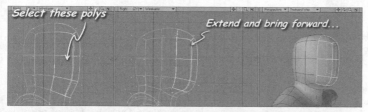

Figure 16-23:
Extending out the
face area.

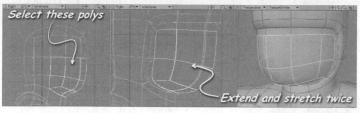

Figure 16-24:
Select and extend
the lower face
inward.

4. Communication is key in crime fighting, so as our superhero needs a mouth, it would make sense that we uncover the bottom of his face mask. Select the bottom 16 polys that form the chin area of the mask (as shown in Figure 16-24) and then Extend (<e>) and Stretch (<h>) them inward *twice* to form the face area.

Figure 16-25: The jutting chin.

5. No superhero would be super without that hard chin, so select the two edges in the middle of the chin and Move (<t>) them out and down a little to square up the side profile, then select the two edges above those (approximately where the mouth will be) and move them back to make the chin point outward a little, as we can see in Figure 16-25.

6. Let's select and move down the cheek area of the face mask a little to make things look a little better (Figure 16-26).

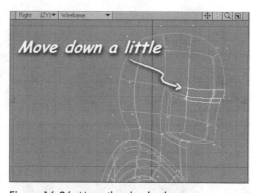

Figure 16-26: Move the cheeks down.

7. Now let's add the mouth. Select four polys at the front of the face and Extend (<e>) them, using your artistic judgment to stretch them inward to form a simple mouth as we can see in Figure 16-27. This gives us a nice starting point to detail out from.

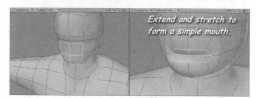

Figure 16-27: Build a basic mouth shape.

Note

Does your mouth look odd? For some reason, do the lips not look right? It could be that you're running into a problem I like to call "Monkey Mouth." I gave it this odd name to describe the problem of the mouth jutting out forward, in a way not too dissimilar to how monkeys at the zoo sometimes purse their lips forward. If you run into this problem, you have modeled the mouth on your character too flat, and not followed the shape of the face (which is normally curved). Another common problem is that the corners of the mouth may be lined up across the face too much. If you look at your own mouth, you see that the corners pinch inward. Selecting the points on the corners of your CG mouth and pulling them back "into" the face can help fix this issue nicely.

8. Extend (<e>) again and Stretch (<h>) the polys vertically to form a little more detail in the mouth (Figure 16-28, left). As shown in the middle of Figure 16-28, Extend (<e>) and move back, carefully Stretching the polys back into the head to start creating the inner mouth. Extend (<e>) once more and stretch the polys back to form the inner mouth (Figure 16-28, right). A little dragging (<Ctrl>+<t>) of points to sculpt the shape, and the inner mouth is done.

9. Use <}> repeatedly to "select-connect" the attached polys of the mouth until you get to the lips as shown in Figure 16-29. Move the selection up and back just a tad to get the mouth aligned better with the face.

10. Select the two middle edges below the mouth (Figure 16-30) and move them down to better form the lower lip (which is often the fatter of the two). Select the two polys of this lower lip, and then **Multiply | Subdivide |**

Figure 16-28:
Inner mouth
action.

Figure 16-29:
Align the mouth a
little better with
the face.

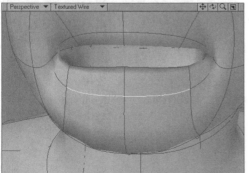

Figure 16-30:
Sculpt the lower
lip.

Band Saw Pro them to create the extra geometry that we need to shape the lips better, as shown in Figure 16-31.

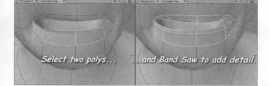

Figure 16-31: Band Saw Pro to create extra geometry.

11. As we can see in Figure 16-32, select the middle two edges and move them out and down to sculpt the lower lip, then use the two edges above them to further round the lower lip.

Figure 16-32: Use the other edges to round and soften the lower lip.

12. Let's give the character a sterner super pout by selecting the lower chin region and rotating (<**y**>) it into a pout-type expression as in Figure 16-33. **Multiply | Subdivide | Band Saw Pro** another strip around the eye line as indicated in Figure 16-34 and then sculpt the points to form a simple nose and eye indentations subtle enough to remain a "mystery" to all those he helps!

Figure 16-33: Finish the pouting super-expression.

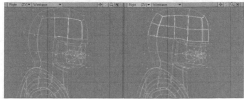

Figure 16-34: Band Saw Pro another strip around the eye line.

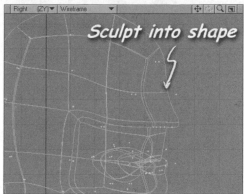

Figure 16-35: Sculpt some basic facial shape.

13. Select all the polys of this lower face, and let's give them a surface named **Skin**. Set Color to a light skin tone of **251**, **231**, **183**, Diffuse to **75%**, and Specularity to **5%**.

Figure 16-36: Give the face area a surface.

14. Last of all, we'll need some way for our hero to see what's in front of him. Let's add a visor. Start by selecting the four edges along the centerline for where his eyes would be.

611

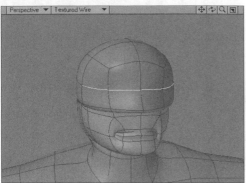

Figure 16-37: Select these edges.

15. Let's generate some geometry here for the visor. With the edges selected, let's use the **Multiply | Extend | Edge Bevel** tool (**<Ctrl>** + **<b>**) to split this edge into two.

Figure 16-38: Creating necessary detail for the visor.

16. Select the four front polys in this new area of detail, and Extend (**<e>**) them to create the visor area. Using Stretch (**<h>**), adjust the polys until the visor looks like it fits snugly into his suit. Once it's looking nice and snug, press

<q> and name these polys **Visor**. Give them a dark purple color (I've used **128, 0, 128,** but feel free to adjust this to your own taste) and a little specularity.

Figure 16-39: Snug as a bug in a... Well, a visor in a super suit!

17. Finally, let's just give the visor nicely formed edges by simply Extending (**<e>**) one more time. If need be, some subtle stretching can be used to tweak the shape a bit and we're done!

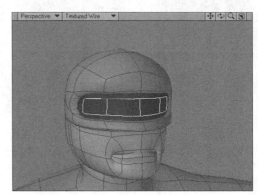

Figure 16-40: Extend and finish! Now he can super-see where he's super-going!

Step 6: Super Gloves

The last stages of the character modeling are to simply create a pair of gloves (and give the character hands!) and maybe a simple belt to help give his outfit some detail.

1. Let's start in a new layer (just to make life a little easier for working on this new part) and start with a box (<**X**>) with **2** segments on X, **3** segments on Z, and **1** segment on Y. This box will obviously be smaller than the character, so set Width to **500 mm**, Height to **207.4773 mm**, and Depth to **500 mm**. Position the box roughly at the end of the arm as shown in Figure 16-41. We'll be creating a simpler four-fingered hand here, rather than a more realistic five-fingered hand.

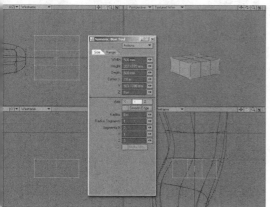

Figure 16-41: Start out with another box.

2. Select the front three polygons of the box, then Bevel (<**b**>) them a little out and inward to form the first joint to the palm. Right-click the mouse to create a new bevel, and bevel the fingers out to where they should end. Like everything, use your best judgment visually, as we can always tweak these

later! At the ends, simply rotate the polys to taper and shape the tips.

Note

Traditional animation started drawing the "three finger plus thumb" hand for one main reason — budget. It was much cheaper to have an artist draw one less finger, and most people could accept hands with three fingers just as well as they could with all four. Because of this, we can also get away with it in CG and nobody really asks why! Of course, it's not hard to model five fingers, but why make more work for ourselves if we don't have to?

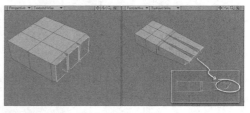

Figure 16-42: Quick fingers.

3. Fingers wouldn't work too well without knuckles. Cut the fingers in thirds with the Knife tool (<**K**>) to create the knuckle positions (Figure 16-43), then make cuts again on either side so that we can create the knuckle detail quickly by selecting the center points (or edges) and moving them up a little (Figure 16-44).

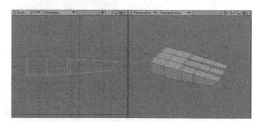

Figure 16-43: Cut the knuckles in.

613

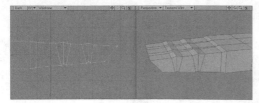

Figure 16-44: Creating the knuckles.

Note

I often taper the cuts on either side of the knuckles as you saw in step 3. This is simply because knuckles usually are quite broad on top, yet have a tighter crease underneath where the skin folds over. Having this angled cut helps create this effect in our CG model.

4. Use the Drag tool (<**Ctrl**> + <**t**>) to modify and sculpt the hand, ready for the thumb to be created as shown in Figure 16-45.

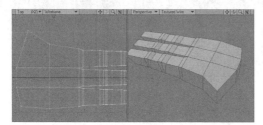

Figure 16-45: Sculpt the hand a little more into shape.

5. Select the poly for the thumb and quickly Bevel (<**b**>) it out to form the thumb itself. Like the fingers, Rotate (<**y**>) the tip and Knife (<**K**>) in a single knuckle about halfway along (Figure 16-46). Once you're done, you can Subpatch (<**Tab**>) the hand to see how it looks.

6. Complete the glove by selecting the back three polys, then Extending (<**e**>) and Stretching (<**h**>) them about five times to form the back of the glove (Figure 16-47). Select the points

on the end of the glove, then Rotate (<**y**>) them to create a sleeker end to the super gloves (Figure 16-48).

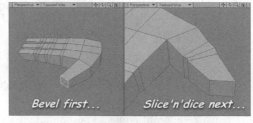

Figure 16-46: The hand with thumb and fingers.

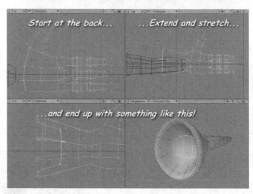

Figure 16-47: Extend roughly five times to create the back of the glove.

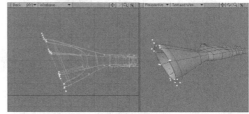

Figure 16-48: Sleeker back end.

We can make the glove look a lot better by adjusting the finger size and orientation. If we look at our own hands, we see that the fingers are not the same length (the middle finger being the longest), and that often our fingers are splayed apart a little. Let's do that to add a final bit of polish to the glove.

7. Select the polys for the little finger, then activate the **Modify | Transform**

| **Size** tool (**<H>**). Position the mouse cursor where the little finger joins the hand, then left-click and drag to shrink the little finger until it's about 80% to 85% of the size of the middle finger (Figure 16-49).

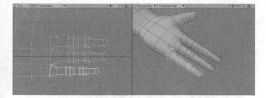

Figure 16-49: Resize the little finger.

8. While the polygons are still selected, Rotate (**<y>**) the little finger outward in the Top viewport.

Figure 16-50: Rotate the little finger outward for a slightly more natural appearance.

9. Deselect the little finger completely and select the index finger as shown in Figure 16-51. Repeat steps 7 and 8 for the index finger, making sure to only size the finger down 90% to 95% of the size of the middle finger, and rotate it splayed out in the opposite direction, as shown in Figure 16-52.

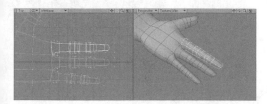

Figure 16-51: Select the index finger polys.

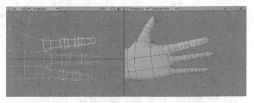

Figure 16-52: Size and rotate the index finger.

10. Position and size the glove so that it fits over the end of the arm (making sure to position it so that the wrist appears in the correct location). You may also need to Stretch (**<h>**) the end of the arm to fit it nicely, as shown in Figure 16-53. Once it fits, use the **Multiply | Duplicate | Mirror** tool (**<V>**) to duplicate the other glove.

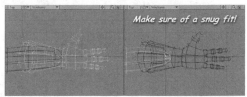

Figure 16-53: Making the glove a good fit.

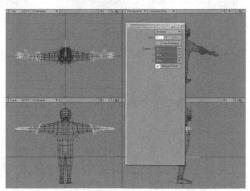

Figure 16-54: Two hands are better than one.

11. Finally, give the gloves a surface name (**Glove**). I've used a dark red (**178, 0, 0**), with a little specularity to sell the shiny material they're made of.

615

Figure 16-55:
Surface the gloves.

Step 7: Finishing Touches

This last stage is simply a quick detailing and surfacing exercise, where we'll make sure all the necessary surfaces are set up, as well as add in a belt we can detail later if we wish.

1. Select the polygons around the waist of the character, and make a slice just below the top edge to form an edge we'll use for the belt.

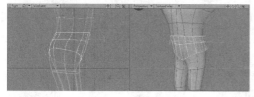

Figure 16-56: Adding a super belt.

2. Use the **Multiply | Extend | Multi-shift** tool to inset the belt a little. Right-click to create a new shift, then adjust and shift the polys outward to form the thickness of the belt. Finally, right-click to generate a third shift, and inset a little to finish the belt off. If things don't look right when using Multishift, bring up its Numeric panel (<**n**>) and ensure that Shift is set to **Point Normals**, and Inset is set to **Contour.** This should ensure the belt shifts nicely.

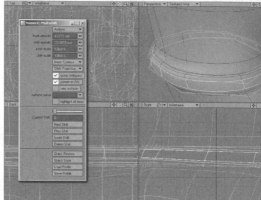

Figure 16-57: Extend the belt using Multishift.

3. Drop the Multishift tool (<**Return**>), then use **View | Selection | Expand Selection** (<}>) twice to reselect the rest of the belt. Press <**q**> and give the belt a surface name of **Belt**, coloring it appropriately.

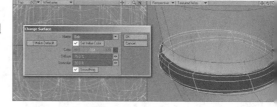

Figure 16-58: Select the belt and surface it.

4. Now let's just tidy up the super boots a little. Create a slice halfway up the shins using the Knife tool (<**K**>), then select all the polys from there down. Press <**q**> to name the surface **Boots.**

ure 16-59: Finishing up the boots.

And we're finished creating our very own stylized superhero character! Obviously, there's still plenty of work you can do to polish and detail this character even further, but the skills we've used while creating this character can be used to create literally any kind of character you can imagine.

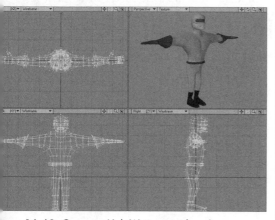

ure 16-60: Our new LightWave superhero!

Note

If you'd like to load the character I modeled for this exercise, he can be found in Objects\ Chapter 16\SuperCharacter_F.lwo. If you load him in, you'll notice that he's facing along the positive Z-axis (versus "looking" along the negative Z-axis, as he was while modeling him). When I'm modeling, I don't get all concerned with which way my character is facing; I'm all about getting the job done well and quickly. However, when I'm *animating* a character, I *always* have him facing along the positive Z-axis (as do 98% of all other technical directors). So, for SuperCharacter_F.lwo, I've already rotated him 180 degrees around his Y-axis at X=0, Z=0, so he's facing the "proper" way.

How did this convention of characters facing along +Z get started? It's the way LightWave likes to think when working out targeting or aligning items along their path. The +Z-axis is called the *facing direction*, and it's this direction that LightWave considers to be the starting direction of 0 when it needs to autorotate things. I can only speak for myself, but when I started getting into rigging some complex character setups, I found that I could "trust" IK more readily for what I was doing if I had the character facing along +Z. With the improvements to how LightWave handles rotations and pivots, this isn't quite as important as it was then, but I stick with the convention because it has come to make sense to me. I don't have to think about it when I'm working; I *expect* things to be a certain way.

Conclusion

Nearly all character modeling follows the same basic steps outlined here. When building my own characters, I always start with a base like this; something that has only as many segments as needed to hold the geometry in place. Often, I'll save my base for later, just in case I want to have a "stand-in" model if my scene becomes so thick with objects that animating slows to a crawl.

For making my final, "super-mega-ultra" high-res models, I take this base, whose proportions I know are correct, and start working at it like a sculptor chiseling away at a rough-hewn marble likeness. Because I know the *proportions* are good, I can lose myself in the details for days, knowing that what gnarly stuff I've done won't have to be scrapped because I wasn't paying attention to the rest of the character.

I suppose what we're doing here could be called "deductive modeling," which is modeling from the *general* to the *specific*, just like Sherlock Holmes' reasoning in solving a mystery. Because we've created such general forms to work with, with only a few more hours of working, you can quickly turn this base into nearly any bipedal, humanoid character imaginable!

Chapter 17

Advanced Skills: Spline Modeling

In Chapter 8 we took our first look at the use of splines (also called "curves" or "rails") as a modeling tool. In that chapter I mentioned there are three primary uses for splines:

- To form complex 2D shapes that can be extruded into 3D objects.

- To act as guides for other modeling tools.

- To construct a "cage" that can be "patched" to create complex objects.

We covered the first two uses in Chapter 8. In this chapter, we'll begin our study of the third use, which is typically referred to as "spline modeling." Spline modeling can seem intimidating at first, but in reality it is no more complex than any other modeling technique you've learned so far.

Spline modeling is simply a way of creating a "patch" of polygons between three or four adjoining curves. This allows you to define complex shapes that bend in more than one direction. It is perfect for creating smooth flowing surfaces and is commonly used in the automotive, aircraft, and architectural design industries.

Spline modeling is similar to subpatch modeling. In fact, the two often go hand in hand (as we'll see throughout the next chapter). The advantage to using splines is that they allow you to quickly map out large curved shapes and they give you the ability to visualize an object's finished form early on in its development.

Spline modeling is not without its pitfalls, however. There are rules to be followed and deviating from them can quickly cause problems. In this chapter, we'll take a quick look at the basics of spline modeling. We'll identify the rules and get a feel for how patching works. Then, in the next chapter, we'll put this information to real-world use by building a high-quality head model.

The "Rules of the Game"

Splines are powerful modeling tools, but there are several rules that you need to follow when using them for patching:

- Spline patches can only be generated from areas bounded by three or four curves.

- The ends of each curve must be welded to the curves around them.

- The order in which you select the curves to be patched affects how Modeler creates the patch.

- "Automated" patching rarely works.

Let's jump right in and take a look at how spline patching works.

Three-Curve Patches

In order to keep us all on the same page while we're working with these tools, I've created a couple of examples to work from. Load the **SplinePatchExamples.lwo** object from Objects\Chapter 17. On the first layer, you'll see the spline "cage" shown in Figure 17-1. Notice that this object uses three curves and that the points on the ends of each curve have been welded together.

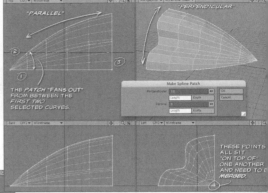

Figure 17-2

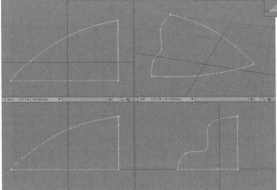

Figure 17-1

As I mentioned earlier, patches can be generated from areas defined by three or four curves. You'll get different results when using three curves than you will using four curves. When patching areas that are defined by three curves, Modeler creates polygons that fan out from the point where the first two curves you select intersect. You can attain completely different patch shapes by selecting your curves in a different order. See Figures 17-2 through 17-4.

Selecting the curves in the order shown in Figure 17-2 and then using **Construct | Patches | Patch** (or the <Ctrl>+<f> keyboard shortcut) brings up a dialog box in which you can adjust how the patch will be created. Let's take a quick look at what these settings do.

Perpendicular and Parallel

The Perpendicular and Parallel settings determine how many polygons are used to build the patch. When you're working with a cage built from three splines, the Perpendicular setting determines the number of polygons that fan out from the place where the first two splines you selected intersect. The Parallel setting determines the number of polygons that run along the length of the first two splines.

Length

The Length setting tells Modeler to evenly space the specified number of polygons along the length of the curves in the cage.

Knots

The Knots setting tells Modeler to space the specified number of polygons according to the distribution of points on the selected curves. Areas with more points will receive a higher distribution of polygons. This can give you a little more control over the placement of polys, but it also requires you to think about the placement of the points in your spline, which can get rather confusing.

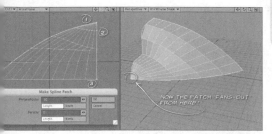

ure 17-3: Altering the order in which the curves are
ected changes the place from which the patch "fans
," making a marked difference in how the patch
ks.

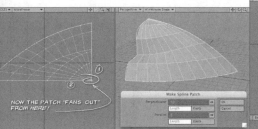

ure 17-4: Same settings, different order, different
ch results.

By changing the setting for the Parallel segments to Knots (and selecting the curves in the same order as we did in Figure 17-2), the "long" curves now have their segments weighted according to the locations of the curve's points.

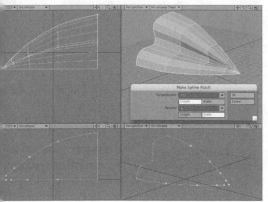

ure 17-5

By altering the position of the knots and using the Knots setting for defining our Parallel segments, we can adjust the way our segments are placed over the resulting surface. (LightWave interpolates its segmentation in a "connect-the-knots" fashion.)

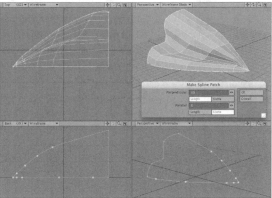

Figure 17-6

Note that the direction in which you select the curves (clockwise or counterclockwise) determines the direction of the normals on the resulting polygon patch. When you select splines in a clockwise fashion, the normals will face downward. Selecting the splines in a counterclockwise fashion will cause them to face up. This is the exact opposite of what happens when you create polygons from individual points.

Ultimately, it doesn't really matter which way (clockwise or counterclockwise) you select your splines — the Patch tool will work just the same. Any polygons that aren't facing the right way can easily be flipped using the **Detail | Polygons | Flip** command. And if some polygons are facing the wrong way but others aren't, you can use the **Detail | Polygons | Align** tool to make them all face the same direction. Personally, I have a hard time remembering to

select splines in a counterclockwise fashion, so I just select them in a clockwise order and then end up flipping the polygons when I'm done.

Four-Curve Patches

Patches defined by four curves work almost exactly the same as ones defined by three curves. The end points of each curve must still be welded to the curves around it, and the order in which the curves are selected still controls what the Patch tool thinks of as "parallel" and "perpendicular." The one thing that really differs when using four curves is that the segments won't "bunch up" in a corner. They spread themselves out from one curve to another. This makes them a bit more predictable (and easier to work with) than patches defined by three curves.

Click on Layer 2 of the **SplinePatchExamples.lwo** object and you'll find a funky shape to play with (as seen in Figure 17-7). Note that there are four adjoining splines creating a single bounded area.

By selecting the curves in the order shown in Figure 17-8, Perpendicular now refers to the polys that extend away from the first curve selected, and Parallel refers to polys that run along the length of the first curve selected.

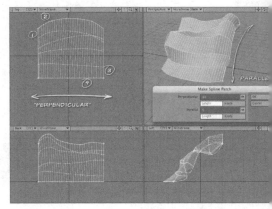

Figure 17-8

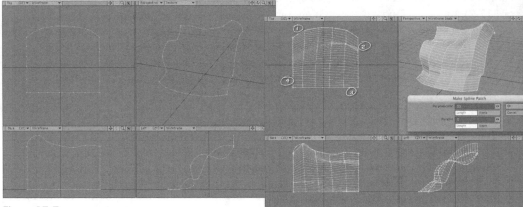

Figure 17-7

Figure 17-9: Same settings, different order, different patch.

The selection order, the number of knots you use, and the settings chosen for the Perpendicular and Parallel segments can have a great impact on the results you get when modeling with splines. Take a look at Figure 17-10. There are two patch areas. The same settings were used on each area, but the selection order was different, and thus the polygons between the patches don't line up.

ure 17-10: The same patch settings were used on two acent areas; however, the spline selection order was ferent on each, causing the polys in the patched areas not line up.

In most cases, you'll want to ensure that the number of polygons in each patch line up with those around it. This ensures that you can create a single, continuous mesh from the results, such as those shown in the Perspective viewport of Figure 17-11. (Subpatches have been turned on in this example).

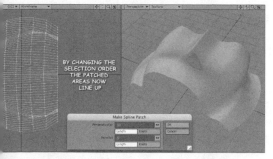

ure 17-11: When the patched polygons line up, you n create a single continuous mesh that can then be opatched (as shown in the Perspective viewport here).

Note that when you patch multiple areas, each patch will be a distinct object and its points will not be connected to the polygons from other patches. Therefore, when you're finished patching a spline cage, you should run the **Merge Points** tool (press the <m> keyboard shortcut) with the Automatic settings to ensure that all overlapping points are welded together. This step is important, especially if you plan on subpatching your object later on.

> ## Note
>
> Under the Construct | Patches menu, you may have noticed the Auto Patch tool. This is supposed to "automatically" patch all the curves in your spline cage at once. It sounds great in theory; however, in my experience, this tool never produces the results you want. And as I'm sure you can see with even the simple examples we've gone over so far, spline modeling outcome can vary widely, even when patching the most modest of cages. You're welcome to try out the Auto Patch tool, but in most cases, I think you'll find that it's simply faster to manually select your splines and patch them by hand.

Conclusion

In this chapter we've taken our first look at the basics of spline modeling. We talked about the rules that govern spline patching and seen how curve selection order and patch settings have an important impact on your results. While brief, the information we've covered here has laid the groundwork for the detailed tutorial in the next chapter.

If you're still feeling a bit intimidated by splines, don't worry. I'm about to show you how easy they are to use. When you're finished with the tutorial in Chapter 18, you'll have the skills needed to tackle any spline modeling project.

Chapter 18

Advanced Modeling Exercise 2: Modeling a Realistic Human Head

Splines are wonderful modeling tools and I hope you're beginning to see just how powerful they can be. Splines are often used to model objects with large complex surface areas, such as vehicles and aircraft. In this chapter, we'll be using splines as the basis for creating a realistic human head model.

This chapter provides a detailed explanation of the process. It is a long chapter, but don't let that intimidate you. Each step is broken down and discussed in detail, making it easy to follow. That said, however, I expect you to have already worked through the previous modeling chapters and to have a basic understanding of the spline modeling rules outlined in Chapter 17.

Figure 18-1: The head model built in this chapter with textures applied.

We'll get into the actual modeling shortly, but first let's talk about the things that make a good head model.

Poly Count and Flow

I've seen hundreds of head models and dozens of tutorials showing how to build them. There are as many techniques for building a head as there are people building them. But regardless of how the head is constructed, there are two inherent qualities it must possess in order for it to be "successful." Contrary to what you might think, looking good is not one of them. Rather, the most successful head models are those with a reasonably low polygon count and an ideal polygon flow.

Poly Count

The best modelers are always striving to create their objects with the fewest number of polygons possible. This isn't just an obsessive-compulsive drive; it's a practical quest. The more polygons an object has, the longer it will take to render. Even with the most modern processors, a high-poly subpatch object will hit the render engine harder than a low-poly object. But the quest for minimal polygons isn't just about render time. It's much more practical than that. You see, when you subpatch an object, you are actually interpolating geometry between each point in your object. (See Chapter 15 for more information on subpatch modeling.)

Take a look at Figure 18-2, which shows two subpatched objects. The object on the left is a simple rectangle with a single cut running down the center. Moving the points at the center of this rectangle creates a smooth arc from one end of the object to the other. This arc is caused by the interpolation of geometry that occurs when an object is subpatched. Now take a look at the object on the right. It is the same rectangle; however, in this case there are six more cuts running through it. Moving the middle points on this object still results in an interpolation of geometry, but since the points on either side of those being moved are now closer together, the arc is tighter and more pronounced. Understanding this simple truth is the key to effective subpatch modeling. The more polygons you have in a given area, the more pronounced the effect will be on the movement of points in that area. Take a look at Figure 18-3. Keeping in mind what you saw in Figure 18-2, you can imagine what would happen if you moved the points on either of these objects. Undoubtedly, the object on the left would enable you to make broad changes (similar to the object on the left in Figure 18-2). Small movements to the points on this object would not have a drastic impact on its overall shape. That's not true for the

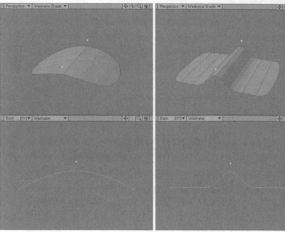

Figure 18-2: A low poly count enables broader changes to your model.

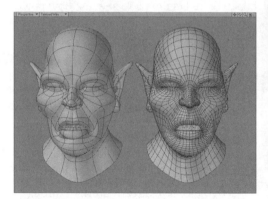

Figure 18-3: The more polygons your object has, the more time consuming it will be to edit. You should always work toward eliminating unnecessary polygons in your object.

object on the right. Even a minor adjustment to this object's points would result in a noticeable change in its form. Therefore, the more polygons you have, the more time-consuming it becomes to make basic adjustments to your object. You should strive to work with as few polygons as possible in order to achieve the overall form. Then you can add geometry in specific areas when more detail is needed.

Learning to control the poly count and understanding where and when it's appropriate to add more geometry is a skill that takes time to develop. But suffice it to say that as you model, you should strive to keep your poly count as low as possible.

Poly Flow

The other quality that makes a good head model is good polygon flow. Flow is a difficult concept to grasp, especially for those new to organic modeling. In essence, it is the deliberate layout of polygons into overlapping bands or loops that, when fully realized, mimic the natural flow of muscles under the skin.

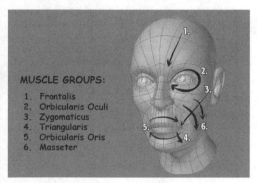

MUSCLE GROUPS:

1. Frontalis
2. Orbicularis Oculi
3. Zygomaticus
4. Triangularis
5. Orbicularis Oris
6. Masseter

Figure 18-4: Basic muscle flow of the human head.

Keep in mind what we mentioned back in Chapter 1. When you model, you are simulating reality. Whether it's a wineglass, a sports car, or a human being, you are building a simulation of a real-world object. In the case of organic models such as animals and people, you are simulating the features that make up their outward appearance, typically muscle and bone. It is important, then, to study in great detail the forms you are attempting to simulate. When you see an amazing character model posted on a web forum, it isn't by accident. The best character modelers are those who have a solid grasp of human anatomy.

Unfortunately, an introduction to anatomy is beyond the scope of this chapter, but

I would encourage you to pick up an anatomy book or attend a figure drawing class if you intend to pursue character modeling. And I would strongly encourage you to visit http://www.fineart.sk and http://www.3d.sk. These two sites offer the most comprehensive set of resources for character modelers that you can find.

The need for ideal polygon flow doesn't stem from a purist compulsion. Like polygon count, it is a practical requirement. Consider this: Character models are rarely built to hold a single pose or a solitary facial expression (like Michelangelo's sculpture of David). On the contrary, they are built to be animated and posed in a variety of fashions. Now, keep this in mind. If a real face can make expressions (i.e., smiling or frowning), it can do so because of the layout of muscles in the face. Therefore, if your 3D model's polygons do not mimic the flow of muscles in a *real* face, it will be difficult to create realistic expressions in a *simulated* face. You will find yourself fighting the model to get so much as a smirk. It becomes imperative, then, to build a model with great flow.

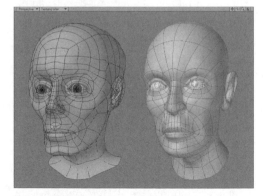

Figure 18-5: Bad polygon flow (left) can cause pinching and creasing in odd places, making it difficult to achieve a "natural"-looking object. Good polygon flow (right) follows the object's musculature, making it easy to create good-looking objects.

In Chapter 15, we talked about point-by-point modeling (also known as the detail-out approach). The advantage to the detail-out approach is that it is a WYSIWYG process. You have immediate feedback on the model at each stage of development. The problem with the detail-out approach is that point-by-point construction makes it

frustratingly difficult to develop good flow (especially for beginners) and it often yields objects with a high poly count. Spline modeling, however, avoids these pitfalls, allowing you to visualize the flow of your polygons and to selectively adjust the resolution of each patch for optimal poly count.

Spline Modeling Pitfalls

Spline modeling, while elegant and efficient, is not without its problems. As we've seen in previous chapters, there are rules that need to be followed. And even when the rules are followed, the occasional "Curves Do Not Cross" error will appear (seemingly for no reason at all). Moreover, spline modeling's greatest strength can also be its biggest weakness, especially when dealing with organic models. While splines make it easy to visualize the flow of your polys, you must have a solid understanding of flow in

the first place to build them correctly. You also have to be extremely careful when specifying your Perpendicular and Parallel patch settings to avoid creating polygons that do not line up properly from patch to patch. And as if all of that weren't enough, the cold hard truth is that some objects are not well-suited for spline modeling. These drawbacks cause many modelers to steer clear of splines altogether. But you're in luck. I'm going to show you several tricks to work around these pesky problems.

Spline Modeling Tips and Tricks

The major pitfalls of spline modeling can be avoided by following these simple tips and tricks.

- **Tip #1: Use splines for their strengths, not their weaknesses.** It sounds obvious, but you'd be surprised at how many people don't get this. Splines work best as a visualization tool, allowing you to establish the overall form of your object quickly and easily. They do not work well for creating intricate details. But I see people attempting this all the time. They build spline cages with an incredible amount of detail and expect to simply patch it and be done. It sounds great in theory, but it rarely works out in practice. So rather than using splines as a be-all and end-all,

use them for what they're good for, namely, building the overall form of your object. Then use the other tools at your disposal to model in the details.

- **Tip #2: Build quad cages.** It's best to build your cage so that every region is bounded by four splines. I call this a "quad cage." It consists of splines for the top, bottom, left, and right for each area in your cage, both large and small. Building a quad cage is perhaps the most critical component of spline modeling and I'll be teaching you more about it as we go.

- **Tip #3: Use simple patches.** One of the most time-consuming aspects of spline modeling is determining the proper Parallel and Perpendicular patch settings. Figuring this out is like some sort of twisted game. You have to remember which spline you selected first in order to establish how the Perpendicular and Parallel patches are constructed. And then you have to ensure that the patches line up properly to those around them. It's a hassle, but here's a simple solution: *Use the same patch settings for the whole object*. If you construct your splines properly (by making sure your patched areas are roughly the same size), you can use the same patch settings for your entire object. This can save you loads of time and frustration down the line.

Keep these simple tricks in your back pocket and they will make your spline modeling job much easier.

Now that we've covered the basics, we're ready to start modeling. Here's an outline of what we'll be doing:

1. First we'll build the spline cage. I'm going to show you how to construct a cage with great flow using the tricks outlined above. Once built, this cage can be saved and used over and over again to quickly knock out other head models.

2. Next, we'll patch the splines, add a few details, and learn how to reduce the number of polygons to obtain an optimal poly count.

3. Lastly, we'll construct the remaining details using tools you're already familiar with.

Fire up Modeler and let's get started!

Creating the Cage

It's helpful (and often necessary) to use a reference image when building your spline cage. You can find the images for this chapter on the companion DVD. In the Setup\Chapter 18 folder, there is also a Backdrop config file. Bring up the Display Options window (<d>) and click on the **Backdrop** tab. From the Presets drop-down menu, select **Load Backdrop** and load the **Spline_Head_Back-drop.cfg** file from the Images subfolder for this chapter.

> ### Note
>
> If you get an error telling you that not all backdrop settings could be restored when you load the backdrop config file, make sure that your viewport layout is set to the default quad view as discussed in Chapter 2.

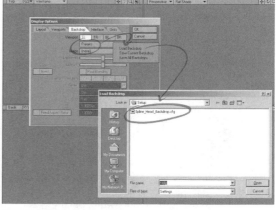

Figure 18-6: Load the Spline_Head_Backdrop file, which we'll use as a reference for building the spline cage.

Once your images are loaded, zoom in to the eye on the right (which is the character's left eye). Oftentimes, finding the best place to start a spline cage can be difficult. I chose the eye as a starting point because it can easily be divided into four sections (top, bottom, left, and right), and that provides a good starting point for building a quad cage (see Tip #2 above).

1. Begin by laying down three points over the top of the eye in the Back viewport. Then, with the points still selected, use the **Create | Curves | Make Curve | Make Open Curve** tool (or press <**Ctrl**>+<**p**>) to generate your first spline. Finally, use the **Drag** tool (or a similar tool for moving points) to adjust the spline in the Right viewport. Keep in mind that the eye bulges out in the center, so your middle point should stick out farther than the points on either side.

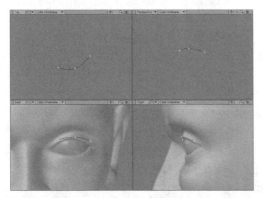

Figure 18-7: Create the first spline over the top of the eye.

Note

Don't feel that you have to adhere to my particular workflow. I find that laying down points and then converting them into splines gives me the control that I want, but if you're more comfortable using the Sketch, Bezier, or Spline Draw tools, go right ahead. It's not important how you arrive at the end result as long as you are comfortable with the process used to get there.

Note

The most basic curve consists of a starting point, an ending point, and a "controlling" point somewhere in between. You can build your splines with as many points as you like, but keep in mind that the more points you have, the more difficult it will be to adjust the overall shape of the spline.

Note

As we build our splines, many of them will jut up against each another, creating harsh angles between them. This is nothing to worry about. There's no need to rebuild your splines. We'll be fixing these harsh angles after we've completely built our cage.

Note

You'll notice as we proceed that the splines I lay down don't strictly adhere to the reference image. *Remember Tip #1!* At this stage, we're only interested in getting the basic form. We'll be doing plenty of fine tuning to the model after we patch it. So do yourself a favor. Don't waste time trying to precisely match the reference image. Focus on the overall form. Getting it close is good enough for now. The actual refining stage comes later.

Note that this spline does not extend over the top of the entire eye. Rather, it covers about 70% to 80% of the total area. This is done to ensure that the splines on either side of the eye are roughly the same size as those on the top and bottom. Remember Tip #3. We want to create patches that are roughly the same size. If some are significantly smaller, the polys created by patching this area will get crammed together, resulting in an unpleasant pinching effect that's difficult to remove in the final object.

2. Create three more points in the Back viewport along the bottom of the eye and press <**Ctrl**>+<**p**> to convert them into a spline. Then shape the spline in the Right viewport as you did in step 1. The middle point on this spline should stick out farther than the end points, but not as much as the middle point for the top of the eye.

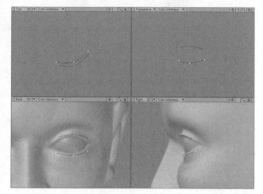

Figure 18-8: Create the second spline along the bottom of the eye.

Note

Shaping the spline in at least two of the three viewports is something you will always need to do. From here on out, I'm going to describe the creation of each spline, but I will expect you to make the adjustments necessary in each viewport.

3. Create a single point at the outside corner of the eye, then deselect it. Now select the outside point on the top spline, followed by the point you just created, and finally the outside point on the bottom spline. Press <**Ctrl**>+ <**p**> to create a new spline.

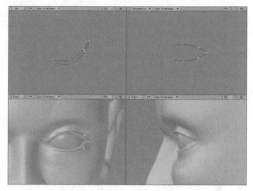

Figure 18-9: The third spline is created by using two existing points from our other splines and a new point at the outside corner of the eye.

4. Create a single point at the inside corner of the eye, then deselect it. We're going to repeat the procedure of step 3 for the left (inside) part of the eye. Select the point on the inside top spline, then the point you just created, and the point on the inside bottom spline. Then create a new spline by pressing <**Ctrl**>+<**p**>.

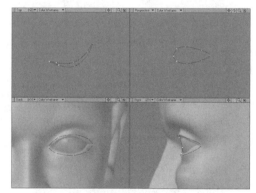

Figure 18-10: The fourth spline is created in the same manner as the third by using two existing points and a third new point at the inside corner of the eye.

You've just completed the outline of the eye using four separate splines. Take a moment to spin around in your Perspective viewport and check for anything that looks out of place. The outline should bulge out at the center and taper in and back on the sides. Inspecting your splines like this should become a habit. Check it from multiple angles and don't be afraid to move points that seem out of place. Oftentimes you'll find that the Perspective viewport will reveal problems that would be difficult to identify in the orthographic views alone.

Now that we've got an initial outline, it's time to branch out.

5. Create three more points over the top of the eyebrow and convert them into a spline.

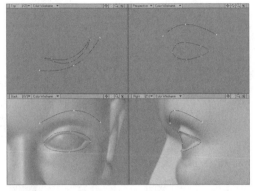

Figure 18-11: Create a new spline over the eyebrow.

6. Create three points under the eye (about the same distance below as the eyebrow spline is above), then convert these into a spline. The inside point for this spline should rest at the base of the nose and the outside point should rest on the cheekbone.

7. Add a new point where the top of the nose and the eyebrow meet. Move it back slightly on the Z-axis, then deselect it. Select the inside point from the eyebrow spline, the point you just

created, and the inside point from the spline below the eye. Press <**Ctrl**>+ <**p**> to create a new spline and adjust its shape as needed.

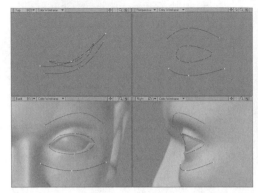

Figure 18-12: Create a new spline under the eye.

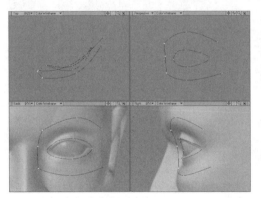

Figure 18-13: Create a new spline running along the inside of the eye.

8. Add a new point at the outside of the eye behind the eye socket cavity. Deselect this point, then reselect the point on the outside of the eyebrow, the new point you just created, and the point on the outside of the cheekbone spline. Press <**Ctrl**>+<**p**> to create a new spline.

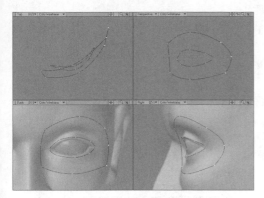

Figure 18-14: Create a new spline along the outside of the eye.

As we did before, spin your view around in the Perspective viewport to check for anything that looks out of place.

We've now got two sets of splines radiating out from the eye of our model. The area enclosed by these splines forms a loop, also known as an "edge loop." When we patch the splines in this loop, the resulting polys will follow the basic musculature of the orbicularis oculi shown as the dark polys in Figure 18-15.

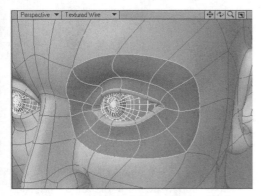

Figure 18-15: The orbicularis oculi edge loop.

9. Let's go ahead and patch them now. Select the splines of the outer loop in a counterclockwise fashion and click on the **Construct | Patches | Patch** tool

or press <**Ctrl**> + <**f**>. Accept the defaults of 10 Parallel and 10 Perpendicular and press **OK**. If you get a "Curves Do Not Cross" error, press <**m**> to ensure that the points in your splines are merged together properly. Figure 18-16 shows the results.

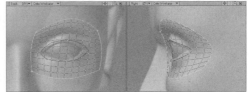

Figure 18-16: The results of patching the outside splines.

Wait a minute! This is just a grid-like mesh. We were expecting a nice clean edge loop. What happened? Well, here's the problem. Even though we built our splines with four sides (as described in Tip #2), the outer splines have no way of knowing that they should be *bounded* by the inner splines. When we patched the outer splines, they generated polys that ran right over the inner splines. That's definitely not what we want. In order to resolve this, we need to link the outside splines to the inside splines so that we can patch the region *between* them.

10. Go ahead and undo the spline patch, then add three points in a roughly horizontal line about the center of the eye. They should mimic the points in the splines above and below them. In other words, the middle point should stick out farther than the ones on the left and right. Deselect these, then select the points shown in Figure 18-17 and create a new spline.

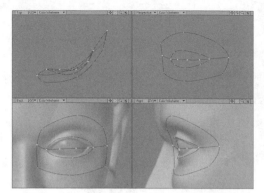

Figure 18-17: Create a new spline that runs from the bridge of the nose to the outside edge of the eye.

11. Select the points shown in Figure 18-18 and create a new spline.

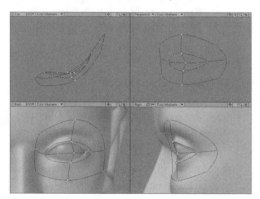

Figure 18-18: Create a new spline from these existing points.

Let's take a look at what we've got. By adding these two extra splines, we've partitioned off sections of this edge loop. That's good. But we no longer have a quad

cage. That's bad. It may *look* like we have a quad cage, but in reality, each area is made up of six separate splines.

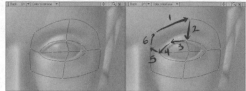

Figure 18-19: It looks like we've sectioned our edge loop with four splines, but in reality, each area is made up of six separate splines.

We can resolve this by partitioning our edge loop with a few more splines, and in the process we'll begin to expand our cage.

12. Zoom out and create a new point in the center of the forehead, just a bit above the bridge of the nose. Select the remaining points as shown in Figure 18-20 and create a new spline.

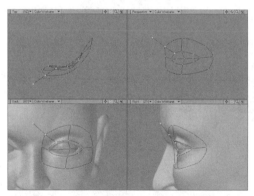

Figure 18-20: Expanding the spline cage.

13. Create a new point at the center of the nose, about the same distance from the bridge as the point you created in step 12. Then create a second point slightly off to the right and down a bit. This second point will act as a constraint, allowing us to shape the spline better to fit the nose. Finally, select the remaining points shown in Figure 18-21 and create a new spline.

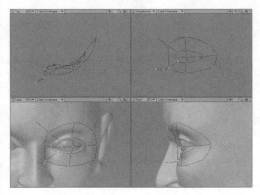

Figure 18-21

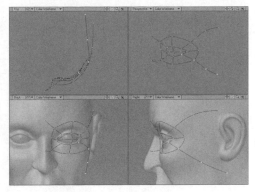

Figure 18-23

14. In the Right viewport, create two more points as shown in Figure 18-22. The first should be placed at the temple region of the head, and the second should be placed above and in front of the ear. Deselect these points, then reselect them in the proper (sequential) order and create a new spline.

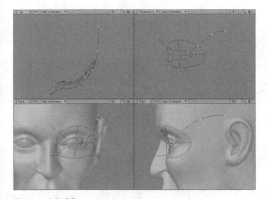

Figure 18-22

15. Again, in the Right viewport, create two more points as shown in Figure 18-23. The position of these points should loosely mirror those created in the previous step.

Go ahead and inspect your cage in the Perspective viewport, correcting anything that looks out of place.

Let's talk briefly about what we've just done. The primary purpose of these four splines was to partition our edge loop into a quad cage. We've successfully done that. But we've also used them to expand the entire spline cage and set new boundaries. The two additional splines on the inside reach to the center of the nose and forehead. The two on the outside reach to the edge of the face. As we proceed, we'll continue to build the spline cage around half of the face. Once the face half is complete, we'll build the cage out to encompass the back of the head and neck. Then we'll patch the cage and mirror it across the X-axis to create a full head. It sounds like a lot of work, and if you're new to the art of modeling, it will certainly seem so. But trust me when I tell you that with practice, the process becomes second nature and can be done in a snap.

Let's get back to expanding our spline cage. We already have splines extending from four of the points in our edge loop. Let's continue building splines off of the rest of the points in the loop.

16. Add one point at the center of the bridge of the nose, then select the point to its right and create a new spline.

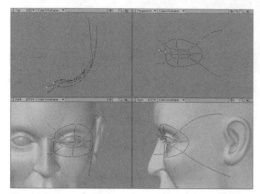

Figure 18-24

17. In the Right viewport, add two points between the splines created in steps 14 and 15. Select the points as shown in Figure 18-25 and create a new spline.

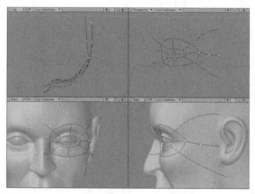

Figure 18-25

18. Create two more points as shown in Figure 18-26, then select the three points shown in the figure and create a new spline. Note that the spline does not run straight up the forehead, but rather it veers off to the right and back. We are doing this in order to space our splines evenly apart (see Tip #3).

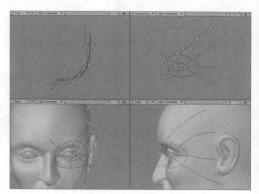

Figure 18-26

19. Now for the tricky spline. Add three points as shown in Figure 18-27. The first gets placed below the center of the eye and slightly to the right of the nostril. It also gets placed out farther on the Z-axis to account for the bulge of the cheek. The next point gets placed below and slightly behind the first one (as seen in the Right viewport of Figure 18-27). The third point gets placed just above the lip.

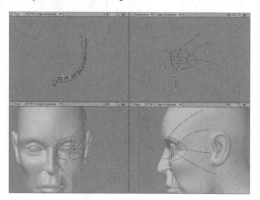

Figure 18-27

Spin your model around in the Perspective viewport and check for anything that appears to be out of place.

At this point the cage may seem a little unruly. Don't panic! Keep in mind the simple tips I gave you. Tip #2 says that we should build quad cages. We did that at the start by creating an edge loop out of four distinct splines and then expanding and dividing the cage from there. We now need to create an even larger edge loop that encompasses most of what we've built so far. We'll do this by building a new quad cage.

20. In the Right viewport, create a number of points along the profile of the background image. These points should run from the top of the forehead to the top of the upper lip. Select the points in sequence and create a spline similar to the one shown in Figure 18-28. This will become the left spline of a quad cage (see Tip #2).

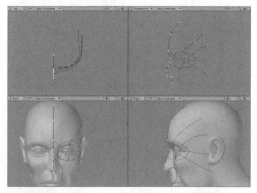

Figure 18-28

Note

The number of points you'll need to create the spline in step 20 will depend on the reference image you're using. (I created nine new points and used three existing ones, giving me a total of 12 points in my spline.) Ultimately, the number doesn't matter as long as you have enough to capture the basic shape. Keep in mind that you can always add points to a spline by using the **Multiply | Subdivide | Add Points** tool and you can delete them by simply selecting the point and hitting the Delete key.

21. Add a single point as shown in Figure 18-29. Place it above the eye and between the profile spline and the spline extending from the center of our edge loop. Then select the points in order and create a new spline. This will become the top of our quad cage.

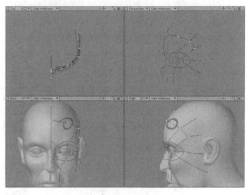

Figure 18-29

22. Add three more points over the top of the lip. Be sure to adjust the points in both the Back and Right viewports so that they follow the curve of the lip back toward the cheek. Select all of the points shown in Figure 18-30 and create a new spline. This will become the bottom of our quad cage.

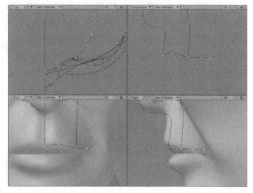

Figure 18-30

23. Finally, add the three points circled in Figure 18-31. The first should be placed above and behind the corner of the mouth. The second should be placed slightly above, to the right and behind the first. The third should be placed above, to the right and behind the second. Once you've created these three points, select all of the points and create a new spline. This will become the right spline in our quad cage.

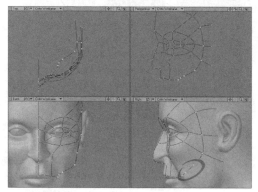

Figure 18-31

Check your model by spinning it around in the Perspective viewport and correct any errors you might find.

We're making good progress. We've built a quad cage with four new splines (top, bottom, left, and right) that forms a new edge loop. This loop runs over the brow, behind the eye, down across the cheek, and over the upper lip and tip of the nose. Of course, we now have a number of regions bounded by more than four splines (violating Tip #2). It's time to correct this.

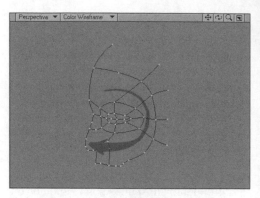

Figure 18-32: Our new edge loop.

24. Create a new point at the top of the forehead between the first point in the profile spline and the first point in the spline to its right (see Figure 18-33). Select the remaining two points shown highlighted in Figure 18-33 and create a new spline.

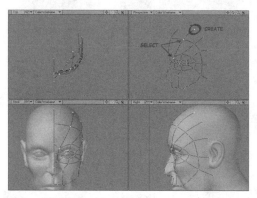

Figure 18-33: Partition off this region with a new spline to create a quad cage.

25. Take a look at Figure 18-34. This next spline is a little tricky, but don't let that intimidate you. We're going to create a spline that runs from the outside edge of the nose, down over the nostril, and ends at the upper lip. As was the case when creating our profile spline, the number of points we use isn't extremely important as long as you

have enough to define the general shape. In my example, I'm using five new points (and two existing points) to define the spline. The first gets placed on the outside of the nose, just above the nostril. The second gets placed toward the front of the nose just above the nostril. The third is placed toward the front of the nose just below the nostril. The fourth goes right under the nostril, and the fifth is positioned right on the lip toward the back of the nostril. As always, select the points in order (including the existing points shown in Figure 18-34) and create a new spline.

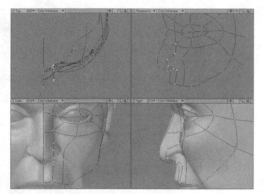

Figure 18-34

26. Create three more points as shown in Figure 18-35. The first should be placed at the outside of the cheekbone. The second and third should be placed toward the inside of the cheek.

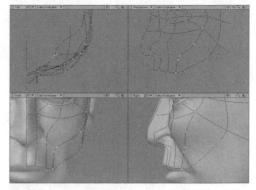

Figure 18-35

Step back and take a look at what you've got. It's starting to come together! We've successfully partitioned the cage so that each area is bounded by four splines, making a successful quad cage. Now it's time to add splines around the outside edge of the face.

27. Select the three points that run over the top of the forehead as shown in Figure 18-36 and create a new spline. Keeping Tip #2 in mind, this will become the top spline in a new quad cage.

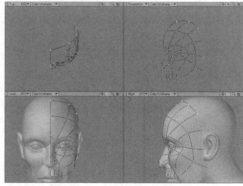

Figure 18-36

28. Select the four points running down the side of the head as shown in Figure 18-37 and create a new spline. This

becomes the side spline of our quad cage.

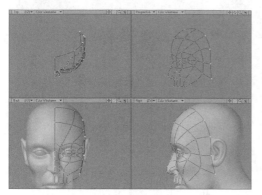

Figure 18-37

shown highlighted in the figure and create a new spline.

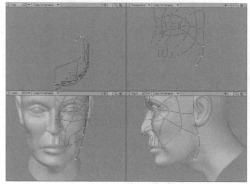

Figure 18-38: Add a second side spline to define the rest of the jaw.

Spin your model around in the Perspective viewport and check for any problem areas. Since the cage is starting to take shape, it will be much easier to spot areas where the splines don't curve naturally.

We've now completed the upper portion of the face. You can see that the splines we created in steps 27 and 28 are beginning to form a new edge loop running over the forehead and down the side of the face. Unfortunately, the lower part of the face (consisting primarily of the jaw and lower lip) has yet to be defined.

We already have splines for the top and right sides of a new quad cage. In order to complete the quad cage we started in steps 27 and 28, we need splines for the bottom and left sides of the face. There's just one problem. If you look at the Right viewport, you can see that the jaw actually runs farther down the side of the face than our current side spline does. In other words, our side spline is not long enough. We could create a bottom spline that runs up to the side, but that would violate Tip #2. Therefore, we need create a *second* side spline.

29. Create two more points as shown in Figure 18-38. Select the three points

30. Create two more points as shown in Figure 18-39. The first should be placed at the center of the chin (as shown in the Back viewport) and underneath the jaw (as seen in the Right viewport). The second should be placed straight down from the corner of the mouth (when looking in the Back viewport) and centered between the first point and the last point of the spline created in step 29. Create a new spline. This will act as the bottom of our quad cage.

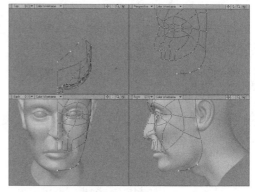

Figure 18-39: Note the placement of the points, especially in the Right viewport.

Since we now have top, right, and bottom splines, we need to complete our quad cage with a left spline.

31. In the Right viewport, create four new points as shown in Figure 18-40. These should start at the lower lip and run down the profile, ending at the center of the chin. The points should be positioned at the very center of the head in the Back viewport. Select the five points shown in Figure 18-40 and create a new spline.

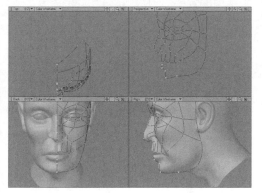

Figure 18-40

Spin your model around in the Perspective viewport and check for anything that looks out of place.

We've expanded our spline cage, but the area around the mouth is still open. Let's close that off. Considering that we already have a top spline (created in step 22), it makes sense that we should create splines for the bottom, left, and right to complete a quad cage. However, there's no need to patch the region inside the mouth. As such, there's no need for a left spline. You can create one if you like, but it won't be used. Hence, we simply need splines for the right and bottom.

32. Create the bottom two points at the edge of the mouth, as shown in Figure 18-41. Select the three points shown

highlighted and create a new spline. This will be the right side of our quad cage.

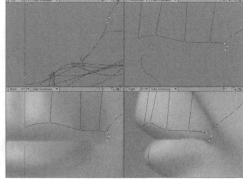

Figure 18-41: This small spline defines the corner of the mouth.

33. Create two more points on the bottom lip as shown in Figure 18-42. Then select the points shown highlighted and create a new spline. This will be the bottom of our quad cage.

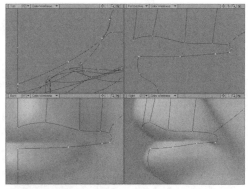

Figure 18-42

By adding these two splines, we've created the inside boundaries for our face, but we're now in violation of Tips 2 and 3. The area over the nose and cheek is much larger than the other regions in our cage, and the area around the jaw consists of more than four splines. We need to address both of these issues.

34. Select the existing points under the nose and over the cheek as shown in Figure 18-43 and create a new spline. (If you don't have the points needed to create this spline, you can add them by selecting each spline and using the Multiply | Subdivide | Add Points tool.) This becomes the top spline of a new quad cage.

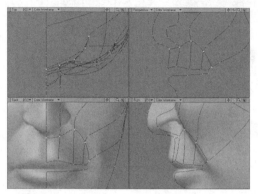

Figure 18-43

35. Create two more points at the outside of the mouth as shown in Figure 18-44. Select all of the points shown highlighted and create a new spline. This becomes the right spline in our quad cage.

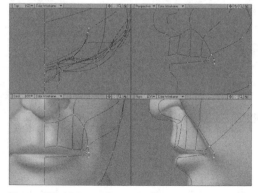

Figure 18-44

36. Create two points along the bottom of the lower lip as shown in Figure 18-45. Select the points shown highlighted and create a new spline. This becomes the bottom spline in our quad cage. Since the profile spline already exists, it will act as the left spline, completing the quad cage for this area.

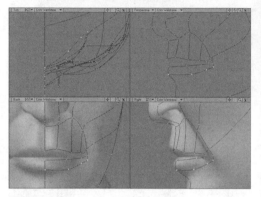

Figure 18-45

We've partitioned off the area under the nose and around the cheek, but it wouldn't hurt to break the area into smaller sections.

37. Create a single point at the top of the nostril, where it indents and joins the tip of the nose. Then select the existing points as shown in Figure 18-46 and create a new spline. This becomes the top of a new quad cage.

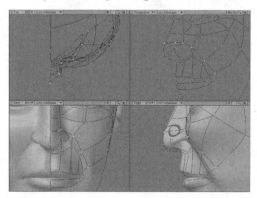

Figure 18-46

You'll notice that this new spline is not evenly spaced between those around it. As a result, we have created a narrow region running over the tip of the nose and down the side of the face. This narrow region will produce the extra polygons we need to define the muzzle region of the face.

38. Create two more points radiating out from the corner of the mouth as shown in Figure 18-47. Select all of the points and create a new spline. This becomes the side of our quad cage.

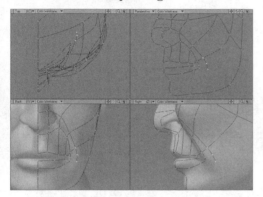

Figure 18-47

39. Create two more points below the lower lip as shown in Figure 18-48, then select all of the points in order and create a new spline. This becomes the bottom spline in our quad cage. Once again, with the profile spline acting as

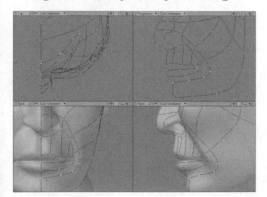

Figure 18-48

the left spline, this completes our quad cage.

Spin around your model and check for anything that looks out of place. If you haven't done so recently, now would be a good time to save your model.

You can really see the face starting to take shape! But we still have areas that consist of more than four splines (specifically around the jaw and chin areas), so we must partition these to create quad cages.

Looking at Figure 18-49, we can see that two distinct edge loops converge at the jaw. We need to section off the jaw so that each of these loops can continue along their own distinct path.

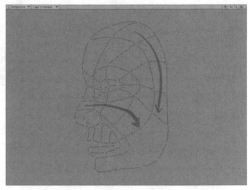

Figure 18-49: Two edge loops converge at the jaw, requiring us to divide the area with a new spline.

40. Create three new points that follow the jaw line as shown in Figure 18-50. Select each of the highlighted points shown in the figure and create a new spline. You can see that each loop from Figure 18-49 now has its own path to follow.

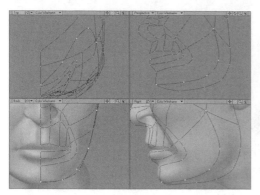

Figure 18-50

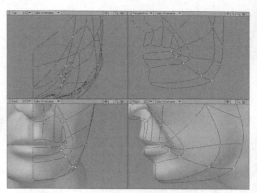

Figure 18-52

Spin your model around and check for anything that appears to be out of place. Looking at the cage, two things are pretty clear. First, we're almost done with the face. And second, we're violating Tip #3. Although the jaw now consists of a quad cage (where each region is bounded by four separate splines), the areas to be patched are much larger than those around them. We'll finish the face by partitioning these areas.

41. Select the existing points shown highlighted in Figure 18-51 and create a new spline.

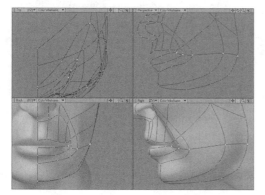

Figure 18-51

42. Select the existing points shown in Figure 18-52 and create a new spline.

43. Select the existing points shown in Figure 18-53 and create a new spline.

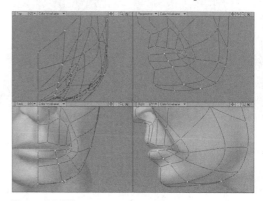

Figure 18-53

Zoom out and take a look at your spline cage, correcting anything that seems out of place. The face is now complete. All that remains is to build splines for the back of the head and neck, but if you've made it this far, that will be a piece of cake.

We can use the existing cage as a starting point for building the remaining splines. But with no ending point to guide us, it's difficult to determine where each spline should go. Therefore, we must develop a basic framework to help guide the placement of each new spline. This framework can be created from an outline of the head and neck.

Take a look at Figure 18-54. The head and neck can be broken down into one large quad cage. There are distinct top, bottom, left, and right sides. At this point, most of the left side and part of the top already have splines in place. We simply need to complete the remaining splines to form a quad cage around the entire region.

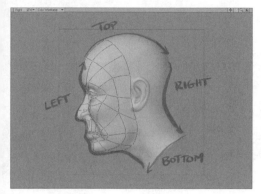

Figure 18-54

44. Create three more points at the center of the head that run over the top toward the back of the skull. Deselect these points. Select the four points shown in Figure 18-55 and create a new spline. This completes the top spline in our quad cage.

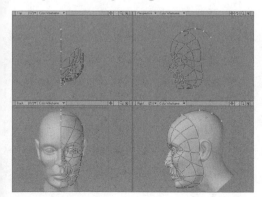

Figure 18-55

45. Create five more points running down the back center of the head. Select all

of the points shown in Figure 18-56 and create a new spline. This becomes the right spline in our quad cage.

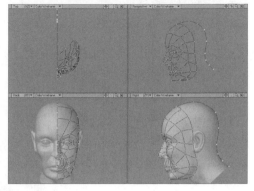

Figure 18-56

46. Create six new points around the neck running from the back to the front. Then select all of the points shown in Figure 18-57 and create a new spline. Make sure that you adjust the points for this spline in both the Back and Right viewports to ensure that the spline forms a semicircular shape. This becomes the bottom spline in our quad cage.

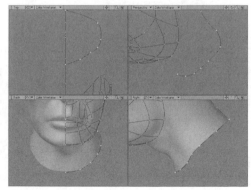

Figure 18-57

47. Create a single point about halfway up the center of the neck. Then select the points shown in Figure 18-58 and

create a new spline. This becomes the left spline, completing our quad cage.

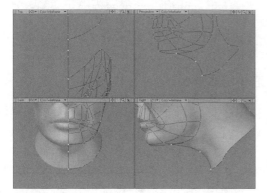

Figure 18-58

Having completed the framework, we can wrap up our spline cage by playing "connect the dots." The existing splines on the face end at an edge loop that runs over the forehead, down the side of the head, and under the chin. Each of these splines can be connected to the framework created in steps 44 through 47 (see Figure 18-59).

Figure 18-59: The remaining splines can be created by connecting those in the face to those outlining the head and neck.

We could build each of these splines as we've done in the past by creating "in-between" points, then selecting the points in order and pressing <Ctrl> + <p>. However, our spline cage has become fairly complex and this will make it difficult to position the in-between points on the back of the head. As a result, we're going to use a different technique for building these splines.

48. Select the two circled points in Figure 18-60 and press <**Ctrl**> + <**p**> to create a new spline.

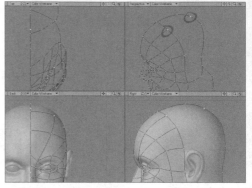

Figure 18-60

I mentioned at the beginning of this tutorial that the most basic spline consists of three points. Two act as end points. The third acts as a controlling point, allowing you to adjust the shape. We've just created a two-point spline which, if you look at carefully, is perfectly straight. It needs a *third* point to alter its shape.

49. Switch to Polygons selection mode. The spline you just created should be highlighted. Navigate to the **Multiply | Subdivide** menu and select the **Add Points** tool. Click on the center of the spline to add a third point. Then use the **Drag** tool (keyboard shortcut <**Ctrl**> + <**t**>) to adjust the shape of the spline. Make sure you rotate around your object in the Perspective viewport to check the shape of this new spline.

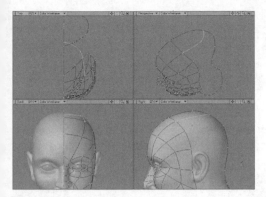

Figure 18-61: Add a third point to this spline and adjust its shape using the Drag tool.

Note

You probably noticed that the region we defined in steps 48 and 49 has only three sides (see Figure 18-62). Sometimes, no matter how hard you try, it's impossible to create a quad cage. This is one of those times. In circumstances like this, you should do your best to position the three-sided cage in a part of the model that will rarely be seen (as we've done here).

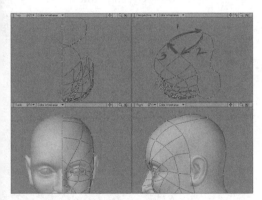

Figure 18-62

50. Continue connecting the dots and adding control points to create four more splines as shown in Figure 18-63. Be sure to check your model in the

Perspective viewport after you shape each new spline. Remember that the back of the head is rounded at the top but tapers as it approaches the neck. Your splines should reflect this. If you feel that you need additional control points to help maintain the shape of the splines, feel free to create them. (I've added extra points to two of the splines shown in Figure 18-63.)

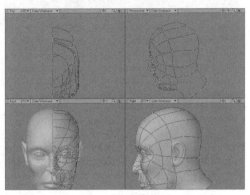

Figure 18-63

Note

You'll notice that we are skipping over the ears at this point. Ears can be created with splines, but the process of linking them into a larger spline cage can be tricky. As such, we're following Tip #1 by using splines to create the overall form. The detailed process of creating the ears will be covered in the final section of this chapter using traditional modeling tools.

At this point, we have another instance where two edge loops converge at a large empty space (see Figure 18-64). We need to partition this space just as we did before so that each loop can continue on its own path.

Figure 18-64: Two edge loops converge at the neck, requiring us to divide it with a new spline.

51. Select the two end points shown in Figure 18-65 and create a new spline. Then use the **Add Points** tool to add a central control point. Use the **Drag** tool in the Back viewport to move this point to the left slightly, creating a subtle arch in the neck.

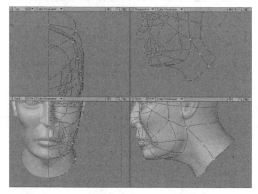

Figure 18-65

We have a nearly perfect quad cage, but the back of the head and the neck are comprised of areas that are much larger than the rest of our cage. We must not forget Tip #3! These areas should be divided into smaller sections so that the same patch settings can be used on the entire model.

52. Select the points shown in Figure 18-66 and create a new spline running down the back of the head. Then add a new control point to the area circled in Figure 18-66.

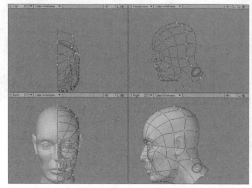

Figure 18-66: Keeping Tip #3 in mind, we must section off these large areas by creating a new spline. Be sure to create a new control point for the spline as circled here.

53. Create the three remaining splines under the jaw shown in Figure 18-67 using the techniques you learned earlier.

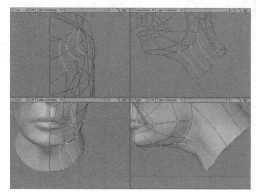

Figure 18-67

54. The last thing we need to do is section off the neck so that its surface area is not so large. Select the existing points shown highlighted in Figure 18-68 and create a new spline.

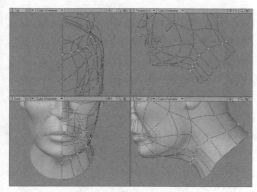

Figure 18-68: Divide the neck area into two halves with this new spline.

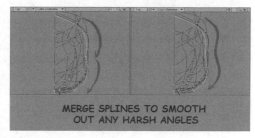

MERGE SPLINES TO SMOOTH
OUT ANY HARSH ANGLES

Figure 18-69

55. Spin your model around in the Perspective viewport and move any points that seem out of place. If you feel that you need more control over your splines, you can add points to help adjust their shape. When you're finished, save a new version of your model.

Before we wrap up this section, there are a two more things we should do. The first is to run a Merge Points operation on our model. As I mentioned earlier, the number one cause of the "Curves Do Not Cross" error is splines whose points are not welded together. By running a Merge Points operation, we can ensure that any stray points are fused together and preemptively ward off this infamous error message.

56. Press the <m> key to bring up the Merge Points window. Accept the default settings and press OK.

The second thing we should do is merge a few of these splines. Take a look at Figure 18-69.

The image on the left shows two splines that follow the same path from the top of the eye to the back of the head. At the point where these splines meet, there is a sharp dip. This dip isn't a major problem and

won't affect our ability to patch this region; however, it will have a subtle effect on the overall shape of our model. As such, it's a good idea to merge these splines together.

57. With the two splines selected, press <Z> to merge them into a single spline. The image on the right in Figure 18-69 shows the effect of merging these splines together. Note that the slope is now much more gradual.

You can continue working through your spline cage at this point, merging the splines that, like those above, follow the same basic path but meet at sharp angles. The splines highlighted in Figure 18-70 are just a few of the ones I would recommend merging.

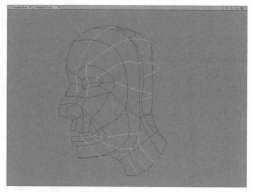

Figure 18-70: Merge these splines to refine their overall shape.

Note

Merging splines can be beneficial to the overall shape of your cage, but it can also be detrimental if taken too far and can ultimately affect your ability to patch the cage. For example, merging the profile splines that run from the front of the head to the back will cause major problems when you try to patch your cage. As you merge your splines, keep in mind Tip #2: Build quad cages. Try to keep the top, bottom, left, and right splines distinct from one another. Merging a top spline with a right or left spline could have adverse effects. If you find that you are getting erroneous patches (or patches that don't fit the area you're attempting to fill), try splitting large splines into two or more parts. You can do this by selecting the spline, then switching to Points mode, selecting the point where you'd like the split to occur, and clicking on Multiply | Subdivide | Split or pressing <Ctrl>+<I>.

Congratulations!! Using the tips and tricks outlined at the beginning of this section, you've built a very complex spline cage. This cage is not only efficient, but it has exceptional flow, one of the most crucial factors of a good head model.

Note

At this point, I recommend saving your object with a name such as "Generic Spline Head Cage." One of the great things about modeling with splines is that a basic cage can be used over and over to create similar objects. In this case, a variety of head models can be created from this one basic cage.

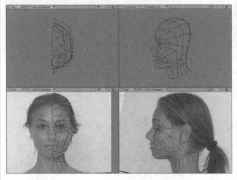

Figure 18-71: The cage we've just built can be quickly modified to create other head models.

In the next section, we'll patch the cage and modify the results to ensure optimal poly count. When you're ready, save your object with a new name and let's begin.

Patching Tips and Tricks

We've done a lot of work to get to this point, but this is where our initial investment really pays off. Under normal circumstances, patching our cage would involve the tedious and painful process of determining how many Perpendicular and Parallel divisions to use for each section of our cage. No more! Since we've built a quad cage and partitioned it into similarly sized segments, we can use the same patch settings for the whole object, making it a relatively easy procedure. *Easy*, however, does not mean *foolproof*. There are a

number of problems that can plague the patching process. Therefore, before we get started, I'm going to share a few more tips and tricks with you.

• **Tip #1: Patch in the Perspective viewport.** Trying to select splines in one of the orthographic viewports can be cumbersome. To make your life easier, I suggest working directly in the Perspective viewport. Click the Maximize Viewport button to work full-screen within this view.

- **Tip #2: Patch in Wireframe mode.**
As you patch your cage, each region will be filled with polygons. Unfortunately, Modeler treats *splines* as polygons. If your view type is set to one of the shaded views (i.e., Smooth Shade, Flat Shade, or even Textured Wire), Modeler will attempt to select the polygons on top first and will skip over the polygons on the bottom. As such, it can be particularly difficult to select your splines, especially as you get further along in the process. Therefore, I suggest working in the Color Wireframe mode. When in the wireframe modes, Modeler does not respect polygon order and will select everything your mouse moves over, not just the polygons on top.

- **Tip #3: Use contrasting sketch colors.** The biggest pitfall of working in one of the wireframe modes is that it can be difficult to distinguish between your splines and your polygons. To make this process easier, give your spline cage one color and your polygon wireframes another. Here's how: Go to the Detail menu and under the Polygons heading, click on the Sketch Color tool. From the pop-up menu, select Black as the sketch color and click OK. Changing the sketch color here will cause our spline cage to be black when viewed in the Color Wireframe mode. Now bring up the Display Options panel by pressing the <d> keyboard shortcut. On the Layout tab, change the Default Sketch Color setting to white. By changing the default sketch color, we are telling Modeler to use white wireframes for all of our newly created geometry. This division of color will help us determine which polys are splines and which are

patches when viewed in a wireframe render style.

- **Tip #4: If at first you don't succeed, patch, patch again.** The number one problem that people run into when spline modeling is the enigmatic "Curves Do Not Cross" error. Often this results from splines whose points aren't welded together properly. *But sometimes it happens in spite of the fact that everything has been done correctly.* I see questions like this posted online all the time: "My points are welded but I'm still getting the 'Curves Do Not Cross' error… What's wrong?" I honestly don't know. Sometimes Modeler is weird like that. But I can tell you this. If you go back and select your splines in a different order (even reverse order), it will often work. I've run into a number of cases where selecting top (1), left (2), bottom (3), and right (4) will give me an error, but selecting in a different order, for example left (2), bottom (3), right (4), and top (1), will work. I can't explain it. I can only tell you that it works. It's very likely that you'll be seeing the "Curves Do Not Cross" error when you patch your head model. If that happens, refer back to this tip.

- **Tip #5: Don't worry about spline selection order.** To get the normals of your polygons facing out, you must select your splines in a counterclockwise order before you patch them. But as we've seen in Tip #4, there may be times when this results in a "Curves Do Not Cross" error. Therefore, don't worry about the order in which you select your splines. It's easy to correct polygons whose normals are facing the wrong direction after the fact. For now, simply patch and have fun.

Patching the Cage

Let's begin patching the cage. Make sure that you've set your spline color to black and Default Sketch Color to white as described in Patching Tip #3. Then maximize the Perspective viewport and change the view mode to **Color Wireframe**. Hit <a> to "fit all" so that our cage fills the screen as shown in Figure 18-72.

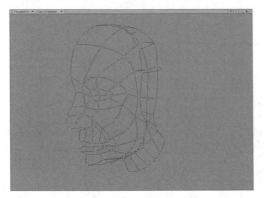

Figure 18-72: We're ready to begin patching!

You can begin anywhere you'd like, but the area around the eye is a nice place to start.

1. Select four splines in a clockwise or counterclockwise order and press <**Ctrl**>+<**f**> to bring up the Make Spline Patch window.

> **Note**
>
> You can access the Make Spline Patch window from the Construct | Patches | Patch menu item, but I recommend using the <Ctrl>+<f> keyboard shortcut as it will save you a good deal of time.

2. The default for a spline patch is 10 perpendicular and 10 parallel divisions distributed over the length of the splines; however, 10 divisions is far too many for the cage we've built. Change each of these settings to **2**. Leave the distribution set to its default (**Length**)

and click **OK**. The splines will be patched with four new polygons. Deselect the splines. Figure 18-74 shows the results of this new patch.

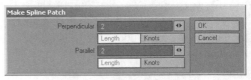

Figure 18-73: The proper patch settings.

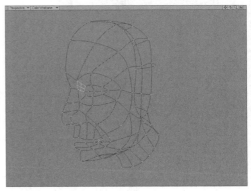

Figure 18-74: Our first patch.

3. Continue patching the edge loop around the eye.

If, as you select your splines, you happen to select a few polygons from one of your patches, don't worry. The Make Spline Patch tool will ignore any non-spline objects. If you get a "Curves Do Not Cross" error at this point, there are several things you should do:

a. Make sure that you have four splines selected. (Press <i> to bring up the Info panel and count the number of curves listed.)

b. Make sure that you've selected your splines in a clockwise or counterclockwise order.

c. Double-check that the points of each spline are welded together.

If this doesn't resolve the problem, see Tip #4 above.

The results of patching this area are shown in Figure 18-75.

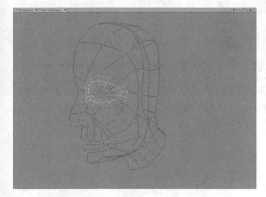

Figure 18-75: The patched edge loop.

4. Continue working around the face of your cage, adjusting your view as needed in the Perspective viewport.

Note

Don't patch the inside area of the eye. We'll build the inside of the eye with regular modeling tools later in the chapter.

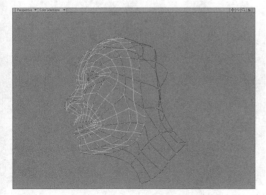

Figure 18-76: Continue patching the face section of the cage.

5. When you've finished with the face, start patching the neck.

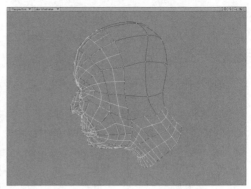

Figure 18-77: After you finish with the face, patch the neck.

6. Finally, work your way up the back of the head.

Take a look at Figure 18-78. I've nearly completed patching the head model, but the region shown on the left side of the figure is giving me a "Curves Do Not Cross" error when the splines are selected in the order shown. I checked to make sure that four splines were selected in a counterclockwise order and that all their points were welded together properly. Having worked through the obvious solutions, it's now time to try Patching Tip #4. By selecting the splines in the order shown on the right side of Figure 18-78, I no longer get an error message.

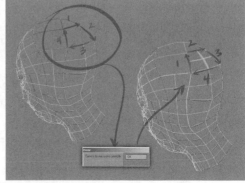

Figure 18-78: This region will not patch properly, but following Patching Tip #4 enables me to work around the problem.

7. The last area to patch should be the triangular region at the top back of the head shown in Figure 18-79. Since there are only three splines here, the order in which these splines are selected will affect the polygon layout of our patch. In all honesty, you can select them in any order you desire, but to be consistent with the work we'll be doing throughout the rest of this chapter, select them in the order shown in Figure 18-79.

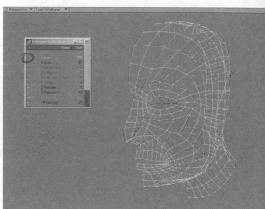

Figure 18-80: Select the polygons created by patching the cage. Cut and paste them into a new layer.

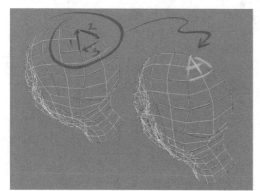

Figure 18-79: Patching the triangular region in the order shown on the left yields the polygon layout on the right.

8. Spin your model around in the Perspective viewport to check for any unpatched areas in your cage. When your whole cage has been patched, bring up the Statistics panel by pressing the <w> keyboard shortcut. If any splines are selected, deselect them. Then press the "+" icon to the left of the word "Faces." This will select all of the polygons in your head model. Cut these and paste them into a new layer, leaving just the spline cage in this layer. Then save your object.

9. Exit the full-screen Perspective view and return to Modeler's normal quad view. Then change your Perspective view type from Color Wireframe to **Textured Wire**. If you see any blank or incorrectly colored areas in your model (and you know that you successfully patched those areas), it's likely that the normals for the polygons have been flipped. Select these errant polygons and from the **Detail | Polygons** menu select the **Flip** command (or press the <f> keyboard shortcut).

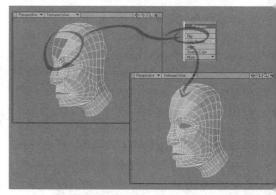

Figure 18-81: Flip any polygons whose normals are facing the wrong direction.

Congratulations on successfully patching your spline cage!

Mirroring the Head

Now let's move on to mirroring the head. We can now mirror the object to complete the basic head, but before we do that we need to run the Merge Points command again. As it stands, each individual patch is a separate object. You can see this for yourself by selecting any single polygon and tapping the <]> (right bracket) key to select the connected polygons. No more than four polygons will ever be selected because each patch is its own distinct object. In order to fuse the patches together into one large object, we need to merge points.

1. Press the <m> key to bring up the Merge Points window. Accept the defaults and press **OK**. A message should appear saying that roughly 300 points have been eliminated.

Now we can go ahead and mirror our object. To successfully mirror the head, we need to ensure that the points running down the center are positioned *exactly* at 0 on the X-axis.

2. Click the **Maximize** button for the Back viewport. This takes us to a full-screen view. Tap the <a> key to fit the object in our viewport as shown in Figure 18-82.

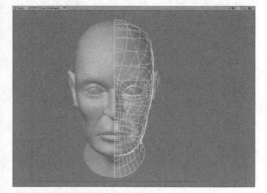

Figure 18-82

We need a way to select all of the points running down the center of our object, but as you can see, there are a lot of points in this region. Selecting them all by hand would be a nightmare. To remedy this, we'll use Modeler's Volume Select tools.

3. Press <Ctrl>+<j> *twice* to active Inclusive Volume Select mode. (Pressing <Ctrl>+<j> once would activate Exclusive Volume Select mode.) Volume Select mode enables us to drag a bounding box around the polys or points we want affected. The Inclusive option means that anything partially inside the bounding box will still be selected. Drag out a bounding box as shown in Figure 18-83.

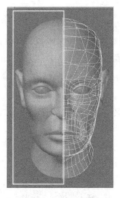

Figure 18-83: Using the Inclusive Volume Select tool, drag out a bounding box that reaches just inside your model.

4. From the **Detail | Points** menu, select the **Set Value** tool (or press the <v> keyboard shortcut). Set the Axis to **X** and the Value to **0**. Then press **OK**.

The points at the center of your object should now rest at 0 on the X-axis. To check this, select several of the points along the center of the head and press <i> to bring up the Point Info panel. The Y and Z values should say "(mixed)" but the X value should be 0 (see Figure 18-84). Exit the Point Info panel and deselect your points. Then exit full-screen mode, return-ing to Modeler's default quad view. Finally, switch back to Polygons selection mode.

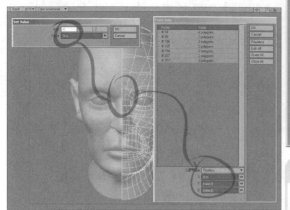

Figure 18-84: Use the Set Value tool to ensure that the points in our Volume Select region are positioned at 0 on the X-axis. You can check these points using the Point Info window.

Figure 18-85: The Numeric panel with the proper settings for the Mirror tool.

Note

If any of your points were not aligned to the 0 mark on the X-axis, you may notice "tears" in the object when we activate Subpatch mode. If you find that this is the case, you will need to isolate the problem points and weld them together.

We'll wrap up this section by mirroring our object to complete the basic head model.

5. From the **Multiply | Duplicate** menu, select the **Mirror** tool. Then press the <**n**> keyboard shortcut to bring up the Numeric panel. (If the Numeric panel is already open, select the Activate button from the Actions pop-up menu.) Bringing up the Numeric panel auto-matically activates the tool with the settings shown in Figure 18-85. With your head model successfully mirrored, you can now close the Numeric panel and press the **Spacebar** to drop the Mirror tool.

Voilà! You're now looking at a completely spline patched head model! Granted, it still needs work, but at this point you have suc-cessfully spline patched a head. Take a bow!

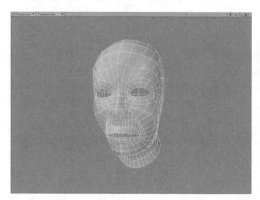

Figure 18-86: The basic spline-patched head, ready to be detailed.

Basic Detailing

Our head model has great flow, but it's lacking a number of details. In this section, we'll start adding some of those details. We'll also do some basic refinements so that our head model looks less like an alien and more like a human. Once we have the necessary geometry in place, we'll move on to the process of optimizing our mesh.

Let's set up our workspace by making it more conducive to modeling a subpatch object. We no longer need white wireframes to distinguish polygons from splines, so let's change the color to something with more contrast, such as black.

1. Deselect any polys that may be currently selected. From the Detail tab, open the **Polygons** menu and choose the **Sketch Color** tool. Set the Sketch color to **Black**. Then bring up the Display Options window by pressing the

\<**d**\> keyboard shortcut. Since we'll be creating new geometry, we should change the Default Sketch Color here so that the wireframe color for all new geometry will match our existing model.

While we're in the Display Options window, let's also set up our viewports. I've found over the years that the best way to refine a subpatch object is to have two Perspective viewports open at the same time. One of these should have a wireframe shaded view of the model and the other should have a smooth shaded view. The wireframe shaded view enables you to see the underlying mesh and easily make changes. The smooth shaded view gives you an unencumbered picture of the model (free from distracting wireframes), allowing you to clearly see the changes you are making to your mesh.

2. Click on the **Viewports** tab of the Display Options window. Click on the **TL** button to affect the top-left viewport. Change View Type to **Perspective** and Rendering Style to **Texture**. Uncheck all of the Independent options as shown in Figure 18-87, then click on the **TR** button to change the top-right viewport. The View Type should already be set to **Perspective**. Change Rendering Style to **Textured Wire** and make sure that the Independent options are deselected (again, as shown in Figure 18-87). Exit the Display Options window.

Until now, our model has been a standard polygonal object. At this point, we are going to activate Modeler's real-time subdivision surface mode, which will smooth out the rough edges and enable us to easily adjust the mesh. As was mentioned in Chapter 15,

657

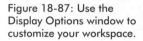

Figure 18-87: Use the Display Options window to customize your workspace.

Modeler has two subdivision surface modes: Subpatch and Catmull-Clark. You can use Catmull-Clark SubDs if you like, but our object is composed primarily of quads, which means there's no real advantage to using them over Subpatch SubDs. Since subpatches are a bit more responsive than CC SubDs, I'll be using them for this exercise.

3. Press <Tab> to activate subdivision surface mode. We're now ready to begin modeling.

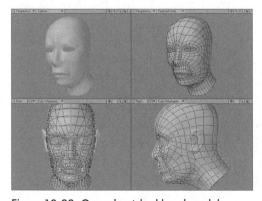

Figure 18-88: Our subpatched head model.

Take a look at look at Figure 18-88. The smooth shaded (no wireframes) view in the top left shows a number of areas with problems. The region between the brows is pinching too much. Also, the area where

the nose meets the upper lip needs to be defined more so that we can build the nostrils. Let's start by addressing these problems.

4. Activate Symmetry mode by pressing <Y> or clicking on the **Symmetry** button at the bottom of the interface. Using the **Drag** tool (or a similar shaping tool), adjust the points at the center of the brows so that they are flush with the points around them. Then select the innermost point on the brow and move it out slightly so that the crease in the forehead is smoothed out.

5. Grab the points where the nose meets the lip and move them up to help define the bottom of the nose. Then select the two points around the nostril region and move them out and back slightly. Figure 18-89 shows the points to move (top) and the effect of moving them (bottom).

Figure 18-89: Smooth out the forehead and tighten up the bottom of the nose.

Let's add a little extra geometry to the eyes so they don't look like paper cutouts.

6. Select one or two of the points running along the loop at the inside of the eye. Then click on the **Select** pop-up menu (just below the Help pop-up menu) and

choose **Select Loop**. All of the points around the inside of the eye will be selected.

Figure 18-90: Select the points around the inner edge of the eye socket.

7. Navigate to the **Multiply | Extend** menu and choose the **Extender Plus** tool. The geometry around the inside of the eye will automatically be extended.

8. Click the **Modes** button at the bottom of the interface and change your Action Center to **Mouse**.

9. Activate the **Stretch** tool (keyboard shortcut <**h**>) and position your mouse over the center of the eye on the positive side of the X-axis. (This is the left eye of the model.) Stretch the new points down and in slightly. Then activate the **Move** tool (keyboard shortcut <**t**>) and in the Right viewport, move the points slightly back into the head. Figure 18-91 shows the results.

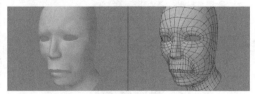

Figure 18-91: Extend the points, then size them down and move them back slightly.

Now let's work on the nose by adding a basic nostril. Select the four polygons (there will be a total of eight selected if you've got Symmetry turned on) shown in Figure 18-92.

10. Click on the **Multiply | Extend | Extender Plus** tool. This will add a new edge all the way around the selected polys.

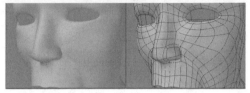

Figure 18-92: Select the four polys shown in the top image, then click on the Extender Plus tool to get the results shown in the bottom image.

11. Sculpt the nose as shown in Figure 18-93. The points around the tip should be moved outward. The points at the top and bottom of the nostril should be moved up slightly. This will round the outside of the nostril and create a slightly concave shape underneath.

Figure 18-93: Sculpt the nose region and refine the nostrils.

Looking at our model again, it appears that the skull of our character no longer seems to fit the reference image. Let's fix that.

659

12. Select the polygons that make up the top of the head, shown at the top of Figure 18-94.

13. Activate the **Stretch** tool and position your mouse just above the center of the ear in the Right viewport.

14. Hold down the <**Ctrl**> key (or use your middle mouse button) and drag your mouse to the right, stretching the head horizontally about 107% or until it more closely fits the background image.

Zoom out and take a look at what you've done so far. These small changes have made big improvements. In order to make

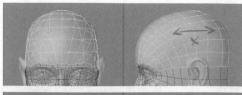
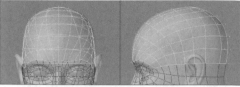

Figure 18-94: Stretch the top of the head slightly so that it more closely matches the reference image.

the rest of our changes, however, we're going to need a serious reduction in polys.

Polygon Reduction

So far, we've achieved the first goal of head modeling — developing good flow. But the second goal of minimal polygon count is still unmet. You may have noticed as you worked through the steps in the last section that even minor adjustments to the vertices of your model had a serious impact on its overall appearance. Trying to work with this number of polys can be a real nightmare and often makes the detailing process unnecessarily time consuming. In this section we'll work through the process of reducing the number of polygons, leaving us with an object that is easier to edit.

> **Note**
>
> Reducing the number of polygons will have a drastic effect on the appearance of our model. Don't panic when you see that the reduction is making things look *worse* rather than *better*.

Modeler has several automated polygon reduction tools, but frankly, they don't work that well. I've found that I can get much

better results by simply merging key bands of polygons. The primary tool for this is Band Glue, found under the Construct | Reduce | More menu.

1. Click the **Maximize** button in the top-right Perspective viewport to enter full-screen mode. Press the <**a**> key to fit your model to the viewport. If you spin your model around, you will see consecutive bands that, if merged together, would not cause problems to

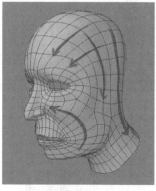

Figure 18-95: The polygons on either side of these arrows can be merged together to create one new band.

the mesh. Figure 18-95 shows arrows running down the center of several of these bands.

2. Select the two polygons shown on the left side of Figure 18-96 and activate the **Band Glue** tool. The result of this operation can be seen in the image on the right.

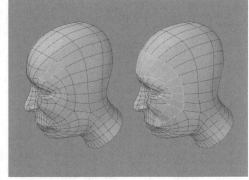

Figure 18-98

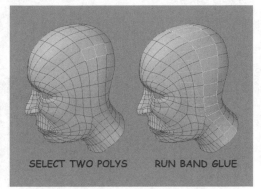

SELECT TWO POLYS   RUN BAND GLUE

Figure 18-96: Select the two polygons on the left and run Band Glue to merge them together. The image on the right shows the results.

3. Continue running Band Glue on the groups of polygons shown in Figures 18-97 through 18-109.

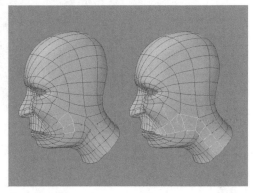

Figure 18-99

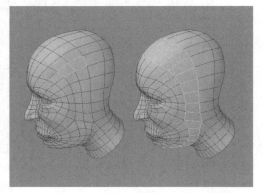

Figure 18-97

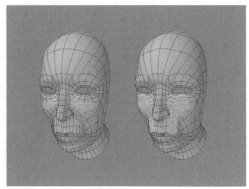

Figure 18-100

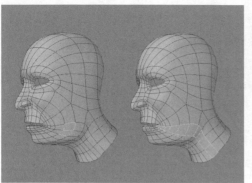

Figure 18-101

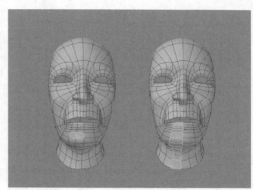

Figure 18-104

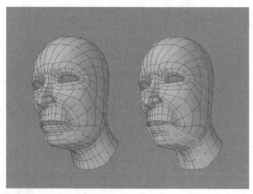

Figure 18-102

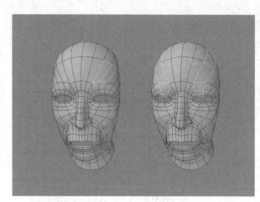

Figure 18-105

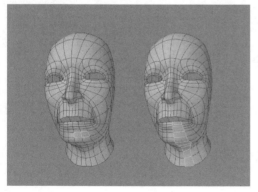

Figure 18-103: Be sure to turn off Symmetry when selecting the polys in this figure.

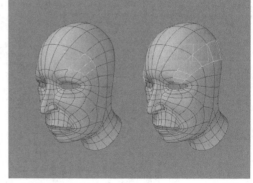

Figure 18-106

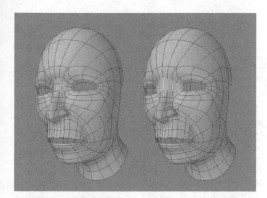

Figure 18-107

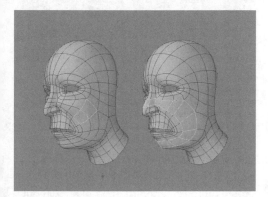

Figure 18-108

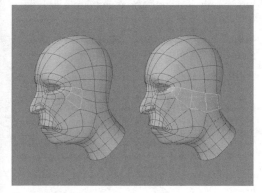

Figure 18-109

4. The last step is to eliminate the triangles at the top of the head. You should have already turned Symmetry off when selecting the polygons in Figure 18-103. Select the polygons shown in the upper-left corner of Figure 18-110. Since there are only four points on the outside perimeter of these two polygons, we can safely merge them into one single quad. Press <**Z**> to merge the polygons as shown in the upper-right corner of Figure 18-110.

5. Now repeat the process for the two polys on the opposite side of the X-axis as shown at the bottom left of Figure 18-110.

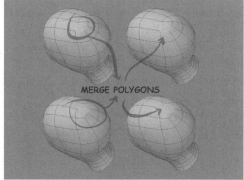

Figure 18-110: Select the two polys on either side of the X-axis and merge them together.

Zoom out and take a look at your model. It's kind of ugly, but this is where the fun really begins! You've done the hard work and achieved the two most important goals in head modeling: great flow and minimal polygons. Now it's time to play. Save your model and move on to the final phase: advanced detailing.

663

Advanced Detailing

One of the most difficult concepts to grasp for those new to organic modeling is that most models look awful until they're about 93% complete. It shouldn't be surprising, really. When you think about it, people all over the world share identical features (eyes, nose, mouth, ears), but the subtle differences in size and shape determine whether a person is considered ugly or beautiful. Nevertheless, I frequently see people in online forums asking for tips on how to improve their models when quite often there's nothing wrong. At least not technically. Oftentimes, the problem is that they've hit the 90% mark and given up in frustration. They've come to a point where all of the geometry is in place and they've developed a reasonable flow with an acceptable number of polygons, but their model still looks bad. Almost without fail, the solution in these cases is to push past the 90% mark. You'd be surprised at how quickly things can come together, especially if you've done everything right from the start.

If you've followed the technical directions in this chapter, I can tell you that you've done everything right. You have created a head model with great flow and minimal polys that is 85% complete. In the next few minutes, we will bring that up to the 90% mark. The biggest challenge before you, then, is whether or not you're willing to push past the 90% mark.

We are nearing the completion of our head model and there is little left for me to teach you. It is up to you as the artist to take what you have learned and apply it in a manner that expresses your artistic vision. As I mentioned earlier, this is where the fun really begins. This is where I let go of the bike and you begin to pedal on your own. I'll still be here to guide you, but I encourage you to begin making this model your own. Experiment and play, for that is the true joy of modeling.

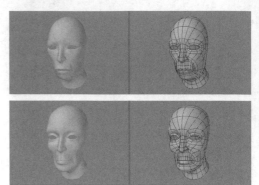

Figure 18-111: Technically there's no difference between these two models, but the one on the bottom looks a lot better because its points have been adjusted to create a more aesthetically pleasing form.

Take a look at Figure 18-111. There is virtually no difference between the model shown on the top and the model shown on the bottom. They both have the same number of polygons and the exact same polygon flow. Yet one looks markedly better than the other. This is due to the subtle difference in size and shape that I spoke of earlier. By simply moving points and sizing polygons, you can have a significant impact on the appearance of your model. Let's start detailing.

The four prominent areas of change are the eyes, mouth, cheeks, and jaw/chin. You should spend time working on each of these areas.

1. The eyes are currently too boxy. Begin by sculpting them with one of the modification tools. (I prefer the Drag tool, but you can also use the Dragnet, Magnet, or even Move tools.) You should work toward creating a more almond-like shape. Be sure to turn on

Symmetry so that the changes you make to one side of your model will be reflected on the other as well.

2. When you're finished shaping the eye, select the ring of points highlighted in Figure 18-112 and pull them back in toward the face. Doing this causes the inner two rings of points to jut out, giving the appearance of eyelids.

3. Grab the outside point also highlighted in Figure 18-112 and move it down and out slightly. This point acts as the upper support for our cheekbone. By moving this point around, you can make drastic changes to the shape of your character's face.

4. Continue refining the points and polygons around the eye to match the bottom two images shown in Figure 18-111.

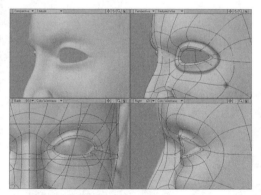

Figure 18-112: Move the highlighted ring of points back on the Z-axis to create the appearance of eyelids. Then adjust the highlighted point for the cheekbone.

5. Reshape the three bands of points radiating out from the side of the nose as shown in Figure 18-113. The first (top) band should be moved up and out. This band defines the overall shape of the cheek and acts as the lower support for the cheekbone. The second (middle) band of points defines the outer muzzle

of the face. The third (lower) band enhances the middle band. Adjusting the points in the third band determines how strong of a crease you'll get where the cheeks meet the muzzle of the face.

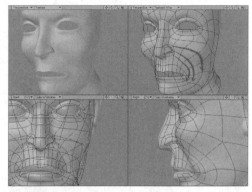

Figure 18-113: Adjust these three bands of points as shown, distributing them more evenly to define the cheeks and muzzle.

6. Redistribute the points below the lower lip as shown in Figure 18-114 to shape and form the jaw.

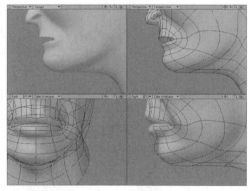

Figure 18-114: The points below the lower lip can be reshaped to form the chin and jaw.

7. Select the lower set of points that form the upper lip as highlighted in Figure 18-115. Activate the **Stretch** tool and position your mouse in the Back viewport over the lowest point in the group. Hold down the <**Ctrl**> key (or

press the middle mouse button) to con-strain the motion, and drag down until the points are roughly in line with one another. Then, with the points still selected, move them up slightly so that the mouth region is open.

8. Continue to shape the points in and around the mouth so that they create the oval-like shapes seen in Figure 18-115.

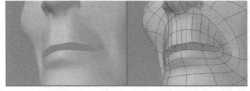

Figure 18-115: Even out the points of the upper lip and continue to shape the points around the mouth.

9. Select the innermost ring of points that make up the mouth and, from the **Mul-tiply | Extend** menu, run **Extender Plus**.

10. Shape the points in the mouth region as shown in Figure 18-116.

Figure 18-116: Extend the ring of points around the inside of the mouth. Then shape the points as shown.

11. Make sure that **Symmetry** is turned on and select the four polygons shown in Figure 18-117.

12. Click on the **Extender Plus** tool. A new band of geometry will be created.

13. Sculpt the nostril as shown in the bot-tom image of Figure 18-117.

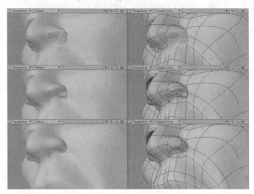

Figure 18-117: Select these four polys. Run Extender Plus, then shape the nostril as shown.

14. Select the four innermost polygons from the nostril and run **Extender Plus** again. With the four polygons still selected, activate the **Move** tool and move them up into the nose as shown in Figure 18-118.

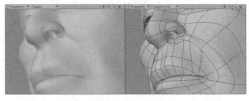

Figure 18-118: Run Extender Plus on the inner polys of the nostril and move them up and into the nose.

Zoom out and spin your model. From here, you should continue adjusting the mesh, watching the changes that take place in your smooth shaded viewport. If your model doesn't look like the background image, don't be concerned. The most important thing is that you resolve any issues with the overall appearance. If the model looks good to you, then it's a success. Continue refining until you're happy. Then continue reading to build the remaining details.

We're down to the last two details: the eyes and the ears. Let's start with the eyes.

1. Deactivate Symmetry. Then go to an empty layer and activate the **Ball** tool by pressing <**O**>. In the Back viewport, drag out a circle over the eye on the right side of the head. Hold down the <**Ctrl**> key to constrain the Ball tool. Position your mouse over the Right viewport and drag to create a perfect sphere. The size of this sphere should be roughly the size of the eye shown in the background image.

2. Select the polygons that make up the back half of the eye and press <**Delete**> to remove them. Since we won't ever be seeing the back of the eye, we can safely eliminate the extra geometry here.

3. Create a new surface for this object (keyboard shortcut <**q**>) called **Eye.**

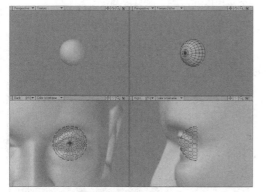

Figure 18-119: Create a sphere for the eye and delete the back half of the object.

The eye is covered by a transparent surface called the cornea. The cornea bulges out slightly at the center. It is this bulge that catches the light, creating a glint that gives the eye a "lifelike" appearance. Let's create the cornea.

4. Copy the eye object to a new foreground layer and place the original in the background. From the Modes button at the bottom of the interface, change your Action Center to **Selection**.

5. Activate the **Size** tool and drag your mouse, resizing the eye by about 1% so that it is slightly *larger* than the original.

6. Select the two bands of polys at the center as shown in Figure 18-120. Activate **Extender Plus** to create a new edge around the perimeter of the selected polys. Then use the **Move** tool to move the two selected bands of polys out slightly.

7. Use the **Size** tool to scale the polygons down to about 85%. Then deselect the polys.

8. Give this object a new surface (keyboard shortcut <**q**>) and call it **Cornea.**

9. Cut the cornea object and paste it into the layer with the eye. It will fit snugly against the eyeball.

10. Finally, use the **Mirror** tool to mirror the eye across the X-axis.

Figure 18-120: Use the Extender Plus, Move, and Size tools to create the cornea.

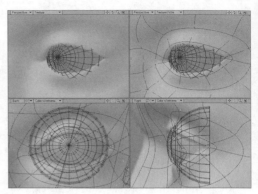

Figure 18-121: Reshape the eye socket to better fit the eye.

At this stage, you will need to shape the area around the eye socket so that it fits snugly over the eyeball.

11. Place your head model in the foreground and your eye objects in the background. Activate **Symmetry** mode and then begin sculpting. If you can see the background layer poking through your mesh (as in Figure 18-121), you need to either move the eye back slightly or reposition the polygons in the face to accommodate it. Sculpting this area can take time, so be patient and pay close attention to detail.

Before you finish with the eye, make sure that the points that make up the inner ring of the eye socket get pulled back into the eye, past the cornea. *If these polygons do not pass through the cornea, you can end up with rendering errors.*

With the eyes finished, it's time to move on to the ears. When new users are asked what they consider to be the most difficult part of the head to model, the ear is almost always at the top of their list. Ears are not that hard to model, as you'll soon see. They are, however, very detailed and require that you pay close attention to the overall form. As you model, you should focus your attention on *what* you are modeling more than *how* you are modeling it. The most important question to keep in mind is not "Am I following the steps correctly?" but rather "Am I making this look like an ear?"

1. Begin by selecting the four polygons shown in Figure 18-122.

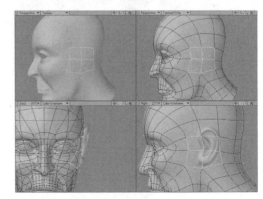

Figure 18-122: Select these four polygons to begin modeling the ear.

2. Activate the **Extender Plus** tool.

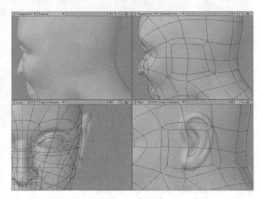

Figure 18-123: Run Extender Plus on these polygons to add extra geometry.

3. Reshape the polys into the basic form of an ear. The back of the ear should begin to bulge out away from the head as shown in Figure 18-124.

> **Note**
>
> Sculpting the ear requires frequent movement around the Perspective viewport. Since the ear is a highly detailed form, be sure to check it from all angles as you continue modeling.

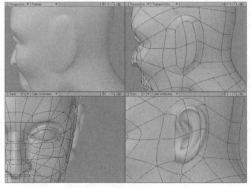

Figure 18-124: Shape the polygons to resemble an ear.

4. Select the four polygons at the center and also the eight polygons forming the loop around them. Run **Extender Plus** on these as you've done in the past.

5. Change your Action Center to **Mouse** and use the **Stretch** tool to resize the polygons that are still selected after the Extender Plus operation in the previous step.

6. Use the **Drag** tool to continue reshaping the ear. The point at the very center of the four polygons should be dragged in to create a concave surface. Then drag this same point toward the back of the head slightly, as shown in Figure 18-125.

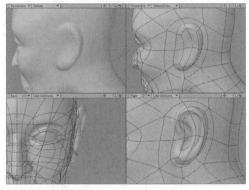

Figure 18-125: Run Extender Plus on the 12 polys that currently make up the ear, then size them and continue sculpting.

7. Select the 12 polygons we extended in step 4 and run **Extender Plus** on them again.

8. In the Back viewport, use the **Move** tool to move these 12 polygons away from the head slightly. Then use the **Stretch** tool to resize them as shown in Figure 18-126.

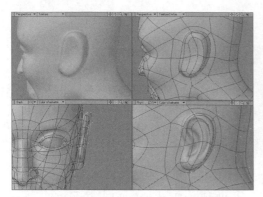

Figure 18-126: Run Extender Plus on the 12 polys again, move them away from the head, and resize them slightly.

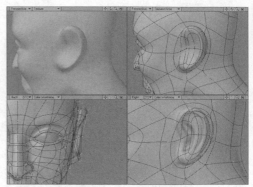

Figure 18-128: Run Extender Plus on the four polygons at the center of the ear.

9. Continue reshaping the ear as shown in Figure 18-127. The points at the center on the left side of the ear should be flush with the rest of the head. The center point from our original four polygons should continue to be pushed back into the ear to form a concave shape.

11. Adjust the polygons that form the outermost loop around the ear. By dragging the points at the top of this loop down, you can begin to distinguish the ear from the rest of the head.

Figure 18-129: Move the points at the top of the ear down to separate it from the head.

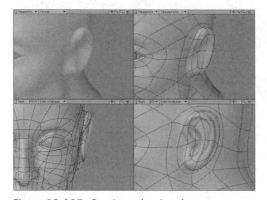

Figure 18-127: Continue shaping the ear.

12. Resize the inner four polygons and move them up slightly. The points at the top of these four polygons should be pushed into the ear slightly. The points on the bottom should be pulled out as shown in Figure 18-130.

10. Select the original four polygons at the center of the ear and run **Extender Plus** on them again.

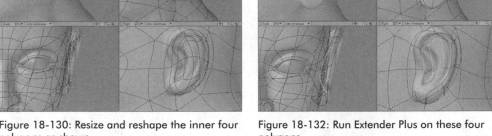

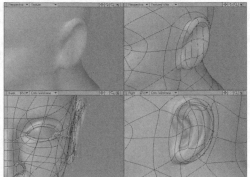

Figure 18-130: Resize and reshape the inner four polygons as shown.

Figure 18-132: Run Extender Plus on these four polygons.

13. Continue reshaping the entire ear as shown in Figure 18-131.

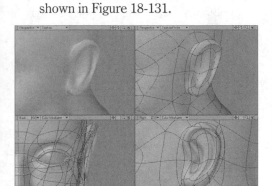

Figure 18-131: Continue shaping the ear.

14. Select the four polygons inside the ear as shown in Figure 18-132 and run **Extender Plus** on them as we've done in the past. Then, with these four polygons still selected, use the **Drag** tool to reshape them as shown in both the top and bottom images of Figure 18-133.

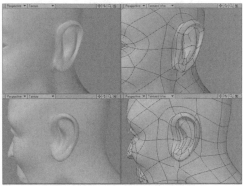

Figure 18-133: Spend time shaping the polygons you just extended to resemble the images shown here.

15. Continue shaping the ear as shown in Figure 18-134. Then select the two highlighted polygons.

Figure 18-134: Continue shaping the ear as shown in the top image, then select the two highlighted polygons in the bottom image.

671

We're going to redirect the flow of these polygons to better fit the ear.

16. Navigate to the **Detail | Polygons** menu and press the **Spin Quads** button (or press the <**Ctrl**>+<**k**> keyboard shortcut). Then continue shaping as shown in Figure 18-135.

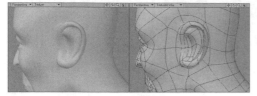

Figure 18-135: Run the Spin Quads tool once on the selected polygons. Then continue shaping the ear.

17. Select the two polygons shown in Figure 18-136 and run **Spin Quads** on them as well.

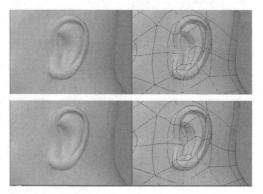

Figure 18-136: Run the Spin Quads tool on the selected polygons. The image on the bottom shows the results.

18. Select the two polygons shown in Figure 18-137 and run **Spin Quads** on them.

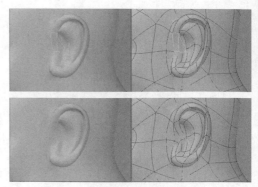

Figure 18-137: Run the Spin Quads tool on the selected polygons. The image on the bottom shows the results.

19. It's time to eliminate a few of these polygons. Select the two polys shown in Figure 18-138. Press <**Z**> to merge them.

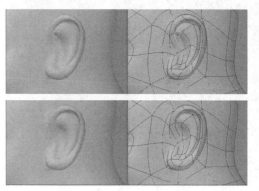

Figure 18-138: Merge the selected polygons. The image on the bottom shows the results.

20. Now select the two polygons shown in Figure 18-139 and merge them.

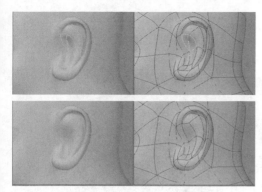

Figure 18-139: Merge the selected polygons. The image on the bottom shows the results.

21. Select the polygons shown in Figure 18-140 and run **Extender Plus** on them.

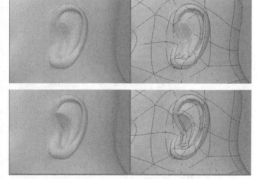

Figure 18-140: Run Extender Plus on the selected polygons. The result of the extender operation can be seen in the bottom image.

22. Reshape the polygons you just extended as shown in Figure 18-141. By pushing them into the head slightly, you can begin to distinguish between the inner folds and outer folds of the ear.

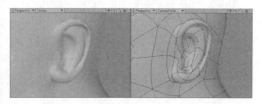

Figure 18-141: Reshape the polygons as shown.

23. Shape the polygons at the front of the ear in the places where they connect with the head as shown in Figure 18-142. By forming a small indention, we can begin the process of building the ear canal.

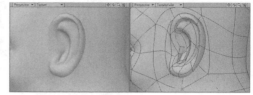

Figure 18-142: Reshape the ear as shown.

24. Select the two polygons shown in Figure 18-143 and press <**Z**> to merge them.

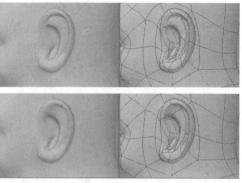

Figure 18-143. Merge the selected polygons. The results are shown in the image on the bottom.

25. Reshape the ear as shown in Figure 18-144.

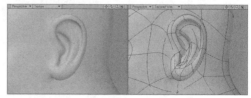

Figure 18-144: Reshape the ear.

We're just about through with the ear. The last few steps require quite a bit of sculpting work, so be sure to move about your

Perspective viewport often to get a good look at what you're doing. Also, it may help to select the polys you wish to adjust and tweak them individually in the orthographic viewports.

26. Select the three polygons shown in Figure 18-145 and run **Extender Plus** on them as we've done in the past.

27. Activate the **Stretch** tool and from the Modes button, set your Action Center to **Mouse**.

28. Position your mouse in the Back viewport just to the left of the selected polygons (still highlighted from the Extender Plus operation). Hold down the <**Ctrl**> key and drag left to flatten out the polygons.

29. Position your mouse in the Right viewport over the three selected polygons and resize them as shown at the bottom of Figure 18-145.

30. Move the three selected polygons back into the head slightly to form the ear canal.

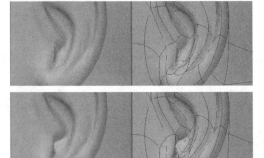

Figure 18-145: Run Extender Plus on the selected polygons and reshape them as shown. Then push the selected polys slightly into the head.

31. Continue shaping the ear by rounding it and making sure that it stands out from the head properly. If you need to, change your upper-left Perspective

viewport back to a Top view and rotate the ears slightly so they stick out a bit more.

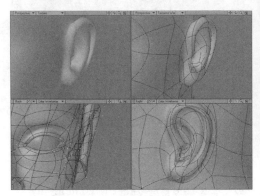

Figure 18-146: Reshape the ear as necessary to ensure that it stands out from the head.

From here, you can continue to reshape the ear to your satisfaction. Figure 18-147 shows the completed ear.

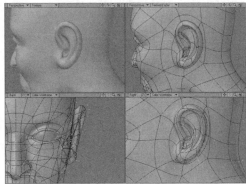

Figure 18-147: The finished ear.

Zoom out and take a look at what you've got. If you find that it's not quite to your satisfaction, I encourage you to continue working with it. Being willing to push past the point of mediocrity is often what turns a good model into a great one.

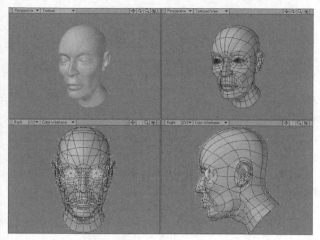

Figure 18-148: The finished head.

Conclusion

We've covered a tremendous amount of ground in this chapter, from the proper techniques of building a spline cage to the skills involved in refining the mesh and adding complex details. In the process, we've constructed a world-class head model that can be used as-is or refined even further in a program like ZBrush.

The techniques you've learned in this chapter are not just for characters. They can be used to build cars, planes, or nearly any other complex flowing shape. There will always be challenges before you, but now that you've worked through the process of building a head model, you should have the knowledge and skills needed to take on any modeling project.

Chapter 19

Advanced Skills: The Node Editor

With this new release of LightWave comes a whole new tool for creating textures and surfacing effects that will literally blow your creative mind once you realize just what it's capable of. Its name is the Node Editor (also known as Nodal to some LightWave beta testers and third-party developers), and it provides an additional way in which you can design and apply surfaces to your objects using a much more advanced "node" building concept.

Does this mean we're suddenly doomed to having to learn a completely new method to create textures in LightWave? Absolutely not! What's fantastic about this new tool is that it's integrated directly into LightWave's existing Surface Editor <F5>, which still works in the familiar way we're used to, making it a seamless part of the

workflow. However, the sheer power we gain through being able to plug all kinds of effects into other things will make you want to switch to this system once you see what it is capable of.

Does the sound of connecting nodes sound daunting and confusing? Rest assured, this chapter will have you excited and instill in you a whole new passion for surfacing and texturing in LightWave v9!

v9.2 Note

LightWave v9.2 has expanded the power of nodes with a new set of materials. Material nodes allow you to create realistic metal, glass, skin, and other complex surfaces with ease. For more information on the new Material nodes, check out the various Material videos in the LightWave 9.2 Videos folder on the companion DVD.

Layers vs. Nodes: What's the Difference?

Let's take a look at creating a cool texture the standard way in LightWave. For example, let's look at creating a scraped-up paint-on-metal texture using simple procedural textures.

1. Load the scene **Scenes\Chapter 19\ theCrate.lws** of a typical sci-fi type crate object into LightWave. This crate currently has no textures on it; however, we're about to change that. Open VIPER using **<F7>** and then press

<F9> to render the object into the VIPER buffer.

2. Let's create a generic scraped paint job on the crate. Open the Surface Editor **<F5>** and set the color to **122, 129, 003** to give it a rather military-grade olive drab green. Click on the **T** button to open the Texture Editor for the color and set up a Turbulence procedural (default option) to generate the scratched paintwork. Set its color to a

mid-level gray of **192, 192, 192**, Contrast to **100%**, Frequencies to **6**, and Small Power to **0.8**. Change the scale to **700 mm** all around (as shown in Figure 19-1). Now select the layer and click **Copy | Selected Layer(s)** to copy this procedural into the clipboard.

Figure 19-1: Setting up a Turbulence procedural for metallic scraped-ness.

3. Change the default Diffuse to **80%**. Open the Texture Editor for the Diffuse channel and select **Paste | Replace All Layers** to paste the Turbulence texture. Set its Value to **40%** and click **Use Texture** to close the Texture Editor.

4. Set the default Specularity to **10%**. Open the Texture Editor for the Specularity channel and select **Paste | Replace All Layers** to paste the Turbulence layer here. Set its Value to **50%**. Click **Use Texture** to close the Texture Editor, and then set the Glossiness to **20%**.

5. As per the other channels, let's also paste the Turbulence texture into the Reflection channel and set its Value to **25%** to make the scraped metal a little more reflective.

6. Finally, let's paste the Turbulence into the Bump channel and change its value to **–10%** to give the scraped metal surface a little bit of texture. We use a negative amount of bump here to ensure that the scraped metal looks scraped, and not lumpy.

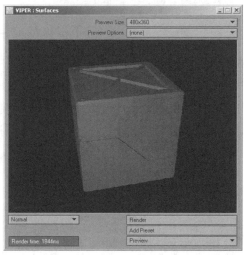

Figure 19-2: The crate is now looking decisively scraped up.

Note

If you want to keep this texture for later use, or just so you can play with it and improve upon it, either add it to the Preset shelf <F8> or click the Save button at the top of the Surface Editor <F5>. Alternatively, you might just want to save the object with a new filename.

Not bad for a simple layer copied and pasted across several channels. However, what if I was to now say, "The scale is a little too large; you'll need to make it smaller." Every channel that has a procedural texture would need to be edited and *manually resized*. That could be a lot of work if we were to create something more complex with rust, and other procedurals and layers to control multiple channels.

Making It Nodal

Now, let's hold the <Shift> key and click on all the "T" buttons that are active to clear the settings we just made. This time let's see how we can create a similar surface with the new Node Editor.

Let's start up the node-based surfacing system!

1. Click the **Edit Nodes** button at the top of the Surface Editor's basic parameters section to open the new Node Editor panel. It's as simple as that!

For every nodal surface, there will always be a master node that represents the surface itself. This contains a list of the standard surface parameters for color, reflections, transparency, shading, and more. These items, called inputs, are what we will be connecting nodes to. We are essentially creating more nodes and connecting them to these inputs to control parts of the surface (see Figure 19-3).

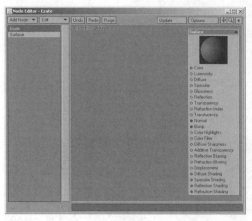

Figure 19-3: The main parameters of the surface.

2. Let's select **Add Node | 3D Textures | Turbulence** to add a Turbulence procedural node to our surface. Double-click on this node to open up its options panel.

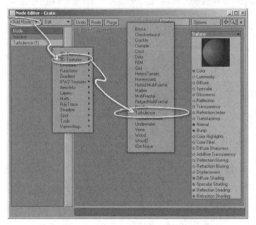

Figure 19-4: Adding a node from the Add Node pop-up.

Note

We can also adjust a node in a pop-out panel that can be accessed by clicking the widget as shown in Figure 19-5.

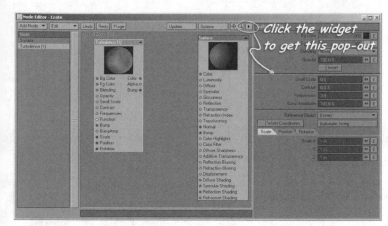

Figure 19-5: Access a node's parameters using the pop-out.

3. Change the foreground color to gray (**192, 192, 192**). Set the background color to our olive green of **122, 129, 003**. Set Contrast to **100%**, Frequencies to **6**, and Small Scale to **0.8**. Change the Scale values to **700 mm** all around again. Note that there's also a Bump Amplitude value here that we will change to **–10%**. These are essentially the same values we used in our surface previously.

> **Note**
>
> You may find that some parameters have slightly different labels in the Node Editor. The Turbulence node has a Small Scale value, whereas the layer-based Turbulence has a value called Small Power. While these values have different labels, they do exactly the same thing for the Turbulence texture.

Now what? You may feel a little intimidated if you've never worked in a node-based system before; however, it's actually much simpler and a lot more powerful than you could have ever imagined.

4. Left-click on the Color output on the Turbulence node, hold and drag, and connect the line you drag out to the Color input on our master node, Surface. Let go and a connection should appear that indicates the color of the

Turbulence is now being fed into the Surface's Color channel.

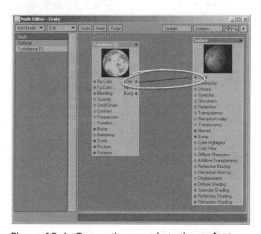

Figure 19-6: Connecting a node to the surface.

> **Note**
>
> You can quickly disconnect an input at any time by simply clicking once on the arrowhead itself. This removes the connection and can make for a faster workflow when creating nodal surfaces.

While we're on the topic of node connectivity, it's interesting to note that nodes have five different types of inputs and outputs. Each is specially color-coded to make it easy to identify what kind of information on a node is being offered.

679

- **Green** represent Scalars. These are numbers that can contain decimal places. For instance, a percentage is represented by a scalar. 1.0 is the same as 100%, and 0.4 is the same as 40%.

- **Red** represents Colors, which are comprised of three numbers that represent the red, green, and blue values of the color.

- **Blue** represents Vectors, which are three values indicating position or direction in 3D. These can be used to identify which way a polygon or item may be facing, or where in the 3D universe it might be sitting.

- **Purple** represents Integer values, which are whole numbers such as 1, 2, 3, and so on. Obviously, for more precision, we'd use Scalars. Integers are useful with some nodes that return a "switchable" value (such as a drop-down selection on their properties window) where the values indicate each option in a list.

- **Yellow** represents a Function, which is a special type that translates one value into another based on some clever rules.

So, what about the other parameters? In the layer-based system, we had to copy and paste the Turbulence layer over and over to get these into each channel; however, it's much easier in the node-based system.

5. The Diffuse channel, or in the nodal system, the Diffuse input, needs to be set to 40% where the fractal metal pattern is. Let's add another node to set this value. Click **Add Node | Constant | Scalar** and set its parameter to **0.4** (which is the decimal equivalent of 40%).

6. Now, determining the Diffuse value is not quite as simple as in the "classic" layer system, in that we have to think cleverly about how to "calculate" the

fractal pattern. Just to see how fancy we can get, let's create a little calculation network by adding a **Math | Scalar | Multiply** node, and connecting the Scalar node to B and the Turbulence Alpha output to the Multiply A input. This will create a fractal pattern that uses a maximum value of 40% in the pattern.

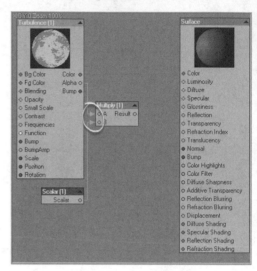

Figure 19-7: Creating a 40% diffuse fractal.

If we were to now connect the Result output of the Multiply node directly to the Diffuse input node, the non-metal areas of the surface would become black. Why? The Alpha output of the Turbulence node lets us read the opacity values for the Turbulence pattern. Where there is no turbulence, the opacity is 0 (black). Where the turbulence exists, the opacity is non-zero (gray to white). When 0.0 is multiplied by 0.4, we get 0.0! A 0.0% Diffuse means the surface will become completely black where the turbulence doesn't exist. We'll need to adjust this before we continue.

We know from our previous layer example that we had set a default Diffuse value of 80%. Therefore, if we want to make sure we get the same result, perhaps we need to do a little more math. How can we make those 0.0 values become 0.8 (80%) from the Multiply node, and keep that 0.4 (40%) value where the Turbulence pattern appears?

Simple. We just subtract the Multiply result from a value of 0.8! A Multiply result of 0.0 subtracted from 0.8 will be 0.8 (no change), and a Multiply result of 0.4 subtracted from 0.8 is... well, also 0.4! Let's see this at work.

7. Let's add a **Math | Scalar | Subtract** node to the mix. Set up the Subtract parameter's A to be a value of **0.8** (the same as 80%), then connect the Result output of the Multiply node to the B input of the Subtract node. Connect the Result output of the Subtract node to the Diffuse input and we get a Diffuse value of 0.8 (80%) with only 0.4 (40%) where the Turbulence pattern appears! Perfect! A Diffuse value that works the way we need it to!

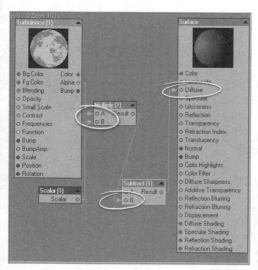

Figure 19-8: All that, just to see a working Diffuse pattern!

8. Let's create the Specularity channel values. This time let's see if we can make the process a little easier. We need a default of 10% (0.1) with 50% (0.5) where the fractal metal is. Well, we've already created a multiplication node that contains a fractal of 0.4, so let's add a **Math | Scalar | Add** node, set the A value for the node to **0.1**, and then click and drag the output of the Multiply node to the B input of the Add node.

Hold on? Did we just do that? Yes! We can connect the outputs of any node as many times as we like to as many other node inputs. What a time-saver! Of course, this then creates a 0.1 value with an *added* 0.4 where the fractal is (giving us the 0.5 we need for the metal surface).

9. Now connect the output of the Add node to the Specular input.

Note

If you don't connect anything to an input on a Surface node, it uses the default settings found in the Surface Editor. This is why we do not need to create anything to control the Glossiness input.

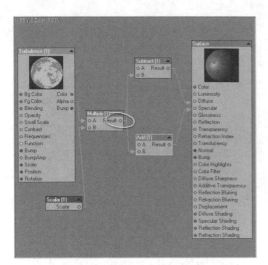

Figure 19-9: You can share node outputs.

10. Let's do the Reflection channel now. This should be easy as the base reflection is 0. Let's add a **Math | Scalar | Multiply** node to the mix, set its A parameter to **0.25** (which of course is 25%), and then plug the Turbulence Alpha output to the Multiply B input (again, sharing the output with the other nodes). Connect the Multiply node output to the Reflection input of the surface.

11. The final input is the Bump channel. Don't panic. We don't need to add any more nodes because most texture nodes, like Turbulence, actually have their own built-in Bump output! If you recall, we already set this up at the start, so let's just connect the Bump output from Turbulence to the surface's Bump input.

Our nodal surface is now done! We can see the structure of the node network for this surface in Figure 19-10.

Let's save this node-based surface for playing with later. We can use all the usual methods as we would for normal surfaces (save the object, save the surface from the Surface Editor <F5>, or create a preset in the preset shelf). But what if we instead decided we liked the clever way we created the diffuse settings? Perhaps we would love to be able to insert this setup again into other surfaces to save time. Well, we can also export sections of our nodal surface out as a .node file.

12. Select the Turbulence layer by clicking on it once, then <Ctrl>+click on each node that we want to export. Once all the nodes are selected, select **Edit | Export Selected** to save the surface.

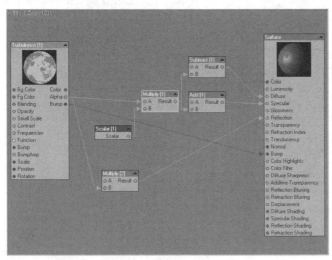

Figure 19-10: Our first nodal surface.

Nodal Panel Workflow

One of the things you might have noticed while creating the surface in the Node Editor is that it can become busy and difficult to read as more and more nodes become connected and added. Luckily for us, the Node Editor works using the same intuitive interface that we're used to in LightWave, and has a few options we can use to get our workflow humming while working in it.

While we won't cover everything to do with using the Node Editor here, let's look at a handful of handy methods for its use.

Hide What You Don't Need

The triangle widget at the top of each node (see Figure 19-11) expands and collapses the inputs and outputs of the node. If you are finished working with a node, collapse it to give yourself a little more screen space.

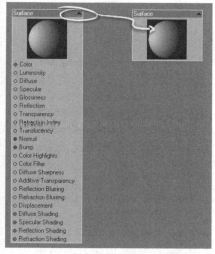

Figure 19-11: Click the widget to hide or show the inputs and outputs.

Note

We can't select any outputs from a node while it's collapsed; however, we can still drag a connection onto a collapsed node. When the mouse button is released, a pop-up of all the inputs of the collapsed node is displayed so you can quickly connect to it.

Figure 19-12: Drag and drop connections onto collapsed nodes if you like working with less clutter.

Note that you can't disconnect a connection from a collapsed node; you'll need to expand it to do that.

Make It Meaningful

Sometimes node networks can become monsters and you can quickly forget what some of the nodes you added were needed for. Use descriptive names for your nodes so that you will remember their use. For example, select the Turbulence node by clicking on it, then use **Edit | Rename** and give this node a more descriptive title like ScrapeUp rather than Turbulence, as shown in Figure 19-13.

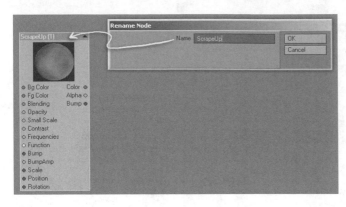

Figure 19-13:
Rename nodes for
easier recall.

See It All

Although we can hide and display our nodes using the traditional viewport widgets, sometimes even that does not clear the screen enough to show all the nodes clearly. Another way to display the entire node network is to press <**F**> to zoom out and fit the network to the panel. It's important to note, however, that we can't change or make connections if the network is not displayed at 100%.

Why Use the Node Editor?

So, other than giving us what appears to be a more "convoluted" approach to surfacing, how exactly will the Node Editor improve the way we texture in LightWave?

Let's use the following example to illustrate. I've decided I want to adjust the look of the Turbulence pattern across the surface because I decided it is too big, or perhaps not detailed enough. You remember how we'd have to do this in the old layer system, right? Each surface parameter with a texture layer would need to be manually tweaked to change its size.

In the Node Editor, we see there's just *one* turbulence to adjust, as everything is

"plugged into" this one node! Just adjust the parameters of the Turbulence node, and it's done. There is no need to go through and manually tweak values across layers in several channels of the Surface Editor just to update a complex surface. That's already a *huge* time-saver if you want to recycle your cool surfaces and need to tweak the overall scale!

What else? Well, how about making the crate surfaces look better by telling them how the materials that make up the surface should behave when rendered? That takes us into the next section in this chapter.

The Lowdown on Node Editor Nodes

In this section, we'll take a quick look at just some of the many nodes available and how they work in the Node Editor to give us uber-creative power in our surfacing. Let's start with a group of powerful new nodes that will change the way you texture your objects — Shader nodes!

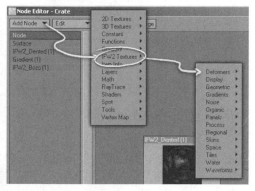

Figure 19-14: Third-party developers can extend the Node Editor's options.

Shader Nodes

One of the coolest features of the Node Editor is its ability to create more realistic surface shading behaviors using a collection of Shader nodes, which are found under Add Node | Shaders.

If you open up one of these pop-up lists under Shaders you may be confused by some of the obscure names such as Oren Nayar, Minnaert, and Cook-Torrance.

Possibly brands of tasty biscuits you might have with your cup of coffee? You may be familiar with these and other names, however, as they are methods 3D software can use to calculate the shading of surfaces on an object.

What is exciting about having access to all these new ways to calculate the way the surface is rendered is that it opens up so many new doors to creating spectacular surfaces for your models! The key to making the best use of these new tools, however, is understanding just what they do, and where you might best use them.

Let's change the behavior of the specularity of the surface on our crate by applying a shader to render it a little differently.

1. Add a **Shaders | Specular | CookTorrance** node.

This shader calculates the specularity by treating the surface as though it has an extremely low level of "roughness" to it (sometimes referred to as being covered in "micro-facets," or microscopic bumps). In reality, pretty much everything from skin to metal has this roughness to some degree. This shader attempts to generate a more realistic specular shading result using this concept, or as it's more accurately described, lighting model.

2. Edit this node's parameters by setting Glossiness to **20%**.

3. Disconnect the current Specular input from the Surface node and reconnect it to the Specularity input of the CookTorrance node. Now connect the Color output of the CookTorrance node to the Specular Shading input at the bottom of the Surface node. The bottom four inputs (see Figure 19-15) are

specially designed for the new shaders and will probably become a common part of your surfacing workflow in LightWave.

Figure 19-16: With the new node-based shading system, we have more flexibility in the shading capabilities available to us.

Figure 19-15: Connecting the shaders to the right places.

The shading in VIPER should now look different. It appears brighter, more like it has a higher amount of Diffuse perhaps; however, this is the Cook-Torrance shader applying a whole different "model" of how Specularity (not Diffuse) should be rendered in LightWave. Shaders give us the ability to get completely different surface qualities that we just can't get with LightWave's default surfacing system. (Compare the difference in Figure 19-16.)

Shaders are just one reason that the nodal shading system is going to rock your world!

Note

To use these shaders, you should connect their output to the appropriate *shading input* on the Surface node; these are the bottom four inputs we saw in Figure 19-15. However, like everything in LightWave, just because a shader calculates a specific attribute of a surface doesn't mean you can't try connecting it to a different input (including the input of other shaders). It's often using tools for things they weren't originally intended that we reveal new ways to solve the many challenges we meet when working in CG!

So what exactly do these cool shaders do?

Diffuse Shader Nodes

Diffuse shaders calculate the way that the color of the surface appears when light shines on it. With this in mind, when using a shader you should consider connecting any nodes that control the color of the surface to the Color input of the Diffuse node instead (and not the Surface node Color input).

Each shader calculates the shading in a different way, and each of these shaders works well for certain types of surfaces.

Lambert

Figure 19-17

Lambert is the standard method used by LightWave for shading surfaces. It's generally good as a starting point for most surfaces; however, it tends to consider the surface to be smooth and reflect light equally all over, making it much better for simulating plastics or similar types of bright materials. You can, of course, soften or roughen up the surface by tweaking other attributes (such as Bump); however, you may wish to use a different shader to create more accurate surface shading if you are trying to achieve a particular look.

Minnaert

Figure 19-18

Minnaert is a shader that works in a similar way as Lambert, except the shading becomes darker on the surface that faces toward the camera. This causes this shader to behave in a way similar to the way light hits materials like velvet or perhaps the ocean at night as moonlight spreads across the surface.

Occlusion

Figure 19-19

Occlusion is a shader specifically for creating "ambient occlusion" shading. Ambient occlusion simulates the effect of ambient light being *occluded* (blocked or obscured) from a surface by other geometry surrounding it. This shader can create the effect of not just ambient shadows, but also grime in grooves and around the edges of geometry. This is a quite specialized shader, and often is not one you'd use on its own. By combining the results of this shader with others, effects such as rust stains or verdigris (the corrosion you see on old copper sculptures) can be created easily.

Oren Nayar

Figure 19-20

Oren Nayar is another shader that works best on surfaces that are matte or have a roughness to them. This shader is great for creating surfaces such as the rubber on a tire, clay, the sandy surface of a desert, or any other surface that is generally not too polished or smooth. While it may look similar to Minnaert, Oren Nayar tends to be darker on lit surface areas, rather than those that face the camera as Minnaert does. Both shaders produce similar effects, so experimenting with the two types is worthwhile to see which works best for you.

Translucency

Figure 19-21

Translucency shading creates a surface that favors back illumination, such as the light you see through leaves and curtains. Like the Occlusion shader, this shader works best in combination with others.

Theta

Figure 19-22

Theta is an advanced translucency shader, and uses a more complex ray tracing solution to determine the amount of back lighting than the Translucency shader. When light is coming from behind the surface and is directly in line with the camera view, the back lighting will be much more intense than when the light is to one side of the camera view. This makes Theta ideal for simulating thin surfaces such as an eggshell or the membranes in a bat's wings.

Specular Shader Nodes

Specular shaders calculate the specular highlighting of the surface. Like the Diffuse shaders, each shader can be used to create a certain look that works better for different surface types.

Anisotropic

Figure 19-23

Anisotropic shading follows fine grooves or scratches along surfaces, often resulting in specular highlights that are spread across a surface in the direction of the grooves and scratches. Typical examples where this type of effect is noticeable are brushed metals, waxed and polished car paint, compact discs and vinyl records, and of course, hair with its hundreds of strands.

Phong

Figure 19-24

Phong is a traditional method for calculating specular highlighting, and is the method used by LightWave as its default calculation. It creates round highlights that have fairly soft edges, and works on most types of surface. However, as with Diffuse shaders, it's worth investigating the other options to achieve the surface appearance you're after. Phong is ideal for plastics and glossy painted surfaces.

Blinn

Figure 19-25

Blinn calculates specular highlights in a similar fashion to Phong shading; however, it tends to keep the specular highlight shape sharper and rounder. This can be ideal for hard surfaces such as glass, chrome, and other smooth, polished surfaces.

Cook-Torrance

Figure 19-26

Cook-Torrance is designed to consider a surface as being covered in microfacets, or extremely tiny dents and bumps. Imagine having an extremely low level of "roughness" to the surface and you have the concept behind Cook-Torrance. It is an effect usually achieved with traditional specularity by setting a low Glossiness value. You might consider using this shader for metallic surfaces or for shiny leathers and vinyl.

Reflection Shader Nodes

Reflection shaders calculate the way that reflections on the surface are computed. This may include blurring and tinting of reflections themselves, or something much more complex such as *dispersion*, the phenomenon of splitting light into its color spectrum. LightWave v9 also includes Ani-reflections, a shader that calculates reflections using anisotropy.

As you'd expect, this extra functionality means more mathematics and complex calculations. Note that using these shaders means your rendering time may increase.

> **Note**
>
> Reflection shaders won't do much on their own. The surface needs some reflection value applied to its Reflection input to work.

Subsurface Scattering Shader Nodes

Subsurface Scattering (or SSS as it's sometimes known) calculates the effect of the absorption and dispersion of light into the material that the surface is made of. You may have heard of this type of shader being used to create more realistic human skin, where light gets trapped within the epidermis and gives a subtly brighter and warm pinkness to the look of the skin. Subsurface Scattering can also help create a more

realistic appearance for any light-permeable material, such as wax, fruit, milk, and more.

> **Note**
>
> This shader system needs to measure the distance the light penetrates into the material of your object. There are two shader nodes here: Kappa, which is designed to simulate this and is pretty good for most surfaces, and Omega, which is more complex and attempts to accurately calculate Subsurface Scattering based on the physical aspects of your geometry. To use Omega correctly, you'll have to create an internal structure below the surface. The quickest way to do this is to simply copy your original model, flip its polys, and texture it as 100% transparent with a refraction index of 1.0.

Let's see how Subsurface Scattering can be applied to skin and the effect it creates.

1. Load the scene **Scenes\Chapter 19\ SimpleHead.lws**. This will give us a head with some simple lighting. If we do an <**F9**> to render, we'll see it looks okay, but it's nothing to write home about (Figure 19-27).

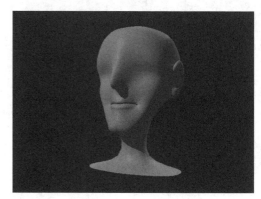

Figure 19-27: A fairly dead appearance to the head.

2. Let's open the Surface Editor <**F5**>, select the **Skin** surface, and then click **Edit Nodes** to open the Node Editor. The first thing we need to do is create

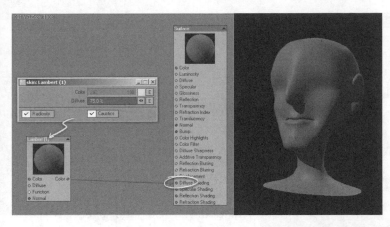

Figure 19-28:
Start out by
creating a simple
skin tone Diffuse
shader.

some generic shading using a **Shaders
| Diffuse | Lambert** node. Edit its
parameters to give it roughly **75%** Diffuse, and a soft pale skin tone of **242,
225, 198**. If we connect this to the Diffuse Shading input of the Surface node
and press **<F9>**, it doesn't look any
better... yet... (see Figure 19-28).

3. Add a **Shaders | SubSurfaceScatter
    | Kappa** node. Kappa lets us simulate
    the effects of Subsurface Scattering
    much more quickly than Omega, which
    calculates more accurate (but much
    slower) scattering. As shown in Figure
    19-29, edit the parameters of Kappa to
    give it a soft pink color of **255, 166,
    166**, a Range of **50 mm**, and Samples
    at **3 x 9**. The Samples setting dictates
    the quality of the effect; however, the
    higher this number, the slower the rendering. Leave Mode as **Backward**
    (this tells Kappa to favor lighting from
    behind).

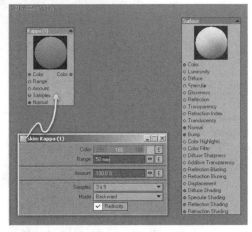

Figure 19-29: Set up the Kappa node for our
subsurface with a nice soft fleshy pink.

If we were to now connect Kappa directly
into the Diffuse Shading input of the Surface node and press <F9>, we won't quite
get the effect we had hoped for (as shown in
Figure 19-30). This is because Kappa only
calculates the overall effect of Subsurface
Scattering, not the "addition" of it to the
skin itself. To get Kappa working, we'll simply need to combine it with the Lambert
node to produce the final result.

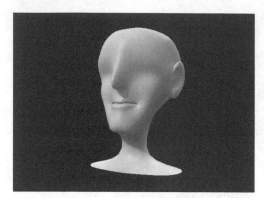

Figure 19-30: Kappa on its own makes for a pink face, but not much else.

Transparency Shader Nodes

Transparency shaders calculate the way that refractions appear when looking through transparent surfaces. *Refraction* is the effect of bending light in a transparent surface as it passes from one medium (most commonly the air) through another (such as water or glass). The amount that the light bends is set through the IOR (Index of Refraction) value.

These shaders also include the ability to create blurring and tinting effects, which can be used to create the appearance of frosted glass and other such surfaces. Transparency shaders can also create dispersion effects (as we read about back in the "Reflection Shader Nodes" section), creating the effect of *chromatic aberration* (the rainbow effect we sometimes see in crystals, prisms, and other such surfaces). Of course, with the added complexity of generating such effects comes extra calculation time when rendering, so make careful use of these new tools to prevent excessive render times.

4. Add a **Math | Vector | Add** node. We need a Vector Add node because we'll be combining colors, and colors contain three values for red, green, and blue (the same number of values in a vector). Once the node appears, simply connect the Color output of the Kappa shader to the A input and the Color output of the Lambert shader to the B input, then the Add node's Result output to the Diffuse Shading input on the surface. Do an <**F9**> and admire how more alive our skin now looks (Figure 19-31).

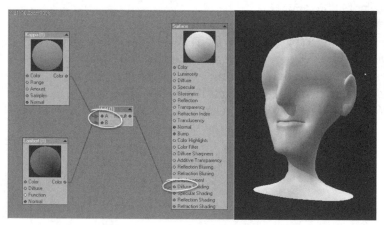

Figure 19-31: It's alive! The skin with subsurface scattering to bring out the pinkness below.

Note

Like the Reflection shaders, Transparency shaders won't do much if there is no transparency in your object.

As you learned in just that short overview, shaders are very cool and let us achieve more realistic or even stylized appearances for our surfaces, and are worth trying.

2D Texture Nodes

A 2D texture is one that is generated and applied to a surface in exactly the same way that any image map we might load from disk might be. In fact, to use image maps in the Node Editor, you'll find an Image node for just such a purpose. 2D textures also contain a specialized node for using normal maps.

What Is This Normal Map?

A bump map is a texture map in which the brightness of pixels in the map are used to create the illusion of the geometry having more detail than what has been modeled. It does this by shading the surface as though it's covered in the textures found in the bump map. A normal map, on the other hand, records the "physical" normal information for each point on the surface. By using a highly detailed model, a normal map can be created to store the normal directions of the surface of an object. This information can then be applied to a lower-polygon model, fooling the renderer into calculating the shading and lighting as if the surface were made of more complex detail. This is precisely why it's a popular concept for the games industry.

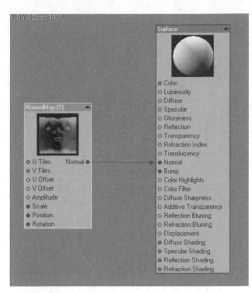

Figure 19-32: Plugging in a normal map is an easy task.

Note

Because normals are stored as vectors (these vectors indicate which direction a spot on the surface is facing), this information in an image is stored in the R,G, and B channels, which is why a normal map looks a bit psychedelic when viewed in an image editor.

3D Texture Nodes

3D textures are the procedural textures we're all used to using in the "classic" LightWave surfacing system. All our favorites, such as Turbulence (which we used earlier in surfacing the crate), are also found as 3D textures in the Node Editor, and we also have a lot more control over the parameters that create these procedurals. This is something we never had in the older surfacing system, and is a good reason to be very excited about node-based shading!

Gradient Nodes

Another node that is worth taking time to play with is the node version of the gradient, which you are probably familiar with from the traditional layer system. Let's see exactly what makes this node better than its layer counterpart.

1. Load the **Objects\Chapter 19\Eyeball.lwo** object into Layout. This is a simple ball object, but with the power of nodal gradients, we're going to convert it into an eyeball! Open VIPER with <**F7**> and then do an <**F9**> to capture the render into the VIPER tool. Remember, VIPER is LightWave's workflow friend.

> **Note**
>
> Did you finish rendering but did not see the display in VIPER? VIPER is a context-sensitive tool. It changes its display based on whatever tool is currently active, so if you are wondering just where your nice render is, try opening the Surface Editor to kick VIPER into action.

2. Let's open the Surface Editor <**F5**>, select the **Eyeball** surface, and click on the **Edit Nodes** button to access the Node Editor panel. Let's start by selecting **Add Node | Gradient | Gradient** to add a Gradient node to the surface.

3. Connect the Color output of the Gradient to the Color input of the Surface. Double-click on the Gradient node, and let's edit the parameters.

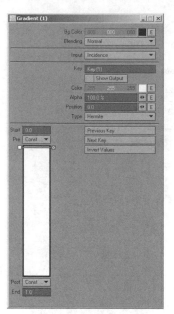

Figure 19-33: The Gradient node's parameters panel.

> **Note**
>
> Not all nodes can be edited through the pop-out panel on the right of the Node Editor as shown back in Figure 19-5. Gradients are one example.

4. Set the Gradient's Input to **Incidence**. This tells the node we're going to texture based on the angle of the surface to the camera. Let's change the first key's color to **255, 255, 255** (white), and set Type to **Step**, as shown in Figure 19-34.

Figure 19-34: Set up the first key of the Gradient.

5. We'll need to add two more keys. Set the first one about three-quarters of the way down the gradient and give it a color of **160, 080, 080**. (Feel free to

use whatever color you like here, depending upon what planet this eyeball has come from.) Its Type should be set to **Step**. Add the next key just above the bottom of the gradient, with a color of black (**000, 000, 000**) and Type to **Step** also.

So now we have a simple, flat colored eyeball. This is something that we could do in the old layer system, so why use the Node Editor? Well, watch and learn about another cool feature that the node-based system offers, making the gradients here something special.

6. Select each of our keys in the gradient and activate the option **Show Output** (as shown in Figure 19-36). Look at what happens to the Gradient node in the node network. We have *three new inputs* for each key in the gradient that we can attach other nodes to! Here, we can control the keys in the gradient in ways we only wished for in the old layer system!

Figure 19-35: Setting up the simple eyeball gradient.

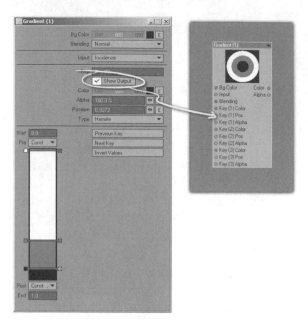

Figure 19-36: Nodes give the artist more control through key inputs.

7. Eyeballs are not made up of flat colors, so let's use **Add Node | 3D Textures | FBM** and set Bg Color to **255, 255, 255.** Set Fg Color to **157, 000, 000,** check the **Invert** option, and set Small Scale to **0.8,** Contrast to **90%,** and Frequencies to **4** (see Figure 19-37). This will create a white surface with soft red veins running over it. This is the texture we'd like to have for the white of

our eyeball, or Key(1). Simply connect the Color output of this FBM node to the Key (1) Color input on the Gradient.

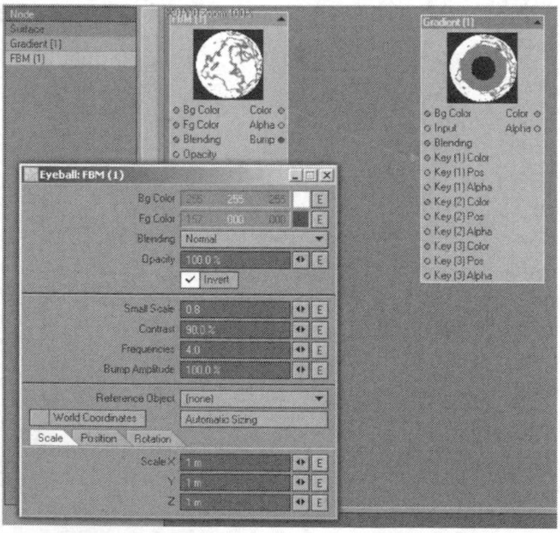

Color in the Node Editor doesn't mean a single, flat color! As we saw here, we can attach a multicolored node to the Color input of *anything,* including keys in our gradient!

> **Note**
>
> VIPER should update to show the white of the eyeball with veins. If things look incorrect, double-check the keys in your gradient and make sure that all your keys are set to a Type of Step. This will prevent the keys from blending and keep the nice, hard edges between eyeball, iris, and pupil.

8. Let's do the iris next with **Add Node | 3D Textures | Marble.** Use a couple of shades of the iris color you prefer, then set Vein Spacing to **.1,** Distortion to **0.05,** Noise Scale to **0.01,** Frequencies to **1.0,** and Axis to **Z.** Set the

Figure 19-37: Setting up the vein-covered white of our eyeball.

scale to **2m** all around as shown in Figure 19-38, then attach the Eyeball: Marble's Color output to the Key (2) Color input to apply this texture to our iris. While it's not a realistic iris pattern, it does help make the iris look a little better than a flat color.

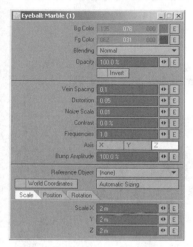

Figure 19-38: Setting up a pattern for the iris.

9. Open up the Gradient node, and let's just soften up the blend between the white of the eyeball and the iris. Select the first key and change its type to **Hermite**, then slide it down until it's a little above the iris key. If we look at VIPER, we should see the iris now has a softer edge (see Figure 19-39).

10. Let's make the eyeball seem a little more real by adding a new key at the top of the gradient. Set its color to **255, 096, 086** for a soft pinky-red, and drag it so it sits a little farther down from the top. As we can see in Figure 19-40, we now have a much nicer look with a little soft coloration on the edges.

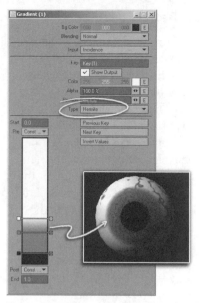

Figure 19-39: A quick tweak of the key location and type, and we soften things up quickly.

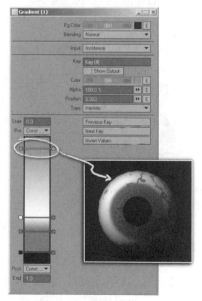

Figure 19-40: Add a little pinkness to the edges and we're done!

Making It Better

Of course, there's more you can do here to further improve on the eyeball. For instance, the pink at the top of the eyeball shouldn't paint over the veins as it does in this exercise. This could be fixed by simply copying and pasting the FBM node and changing the copied node's Bg Color from white to the pink color we set for the new key. Be sure to select Show Output for the top key, then attach the Color output of the new FBM node to the Color input of the new key instead. Other improvements could also include adding some reflectivity, specularity, and so forth. I'm leaving these small challenges up to you as a way to get into the node-based system and experiment.

As we saw, the gradient function in the Node Editor opens up a lot of possibilities for us in terms of what we can achieve. Not only can we create standard gradients like we are used to in the "classic" layer system, but with the ability to "plug in" information, textures, and more to the node, we've suddenly got a huge amount of control in how the gradient works! There's plenty of power in gradients. Imagine the ability to paint image maps of cliffs, rocks, and grass onto a landscape based on the slope as one obvious example to get your creative juices flowing.

Function Nodes

Functions are nodes that read information, then remap the values and return these new values from whence they came. Function nodes have a special use, and should only be used with other nodes that have a Function input.

Where would you use a Function node? Well, one use is with the Shader nodes, which we looked at earlier in the chapter.

Let's say, for instance, you wanted to change the way the diffuse shading was calculated so that the brightest shading was the mid-tones, with the dark and bright values fading out.

1. If you load up the Crate scene we looked at in the beginning of the chapter with its default gray surface, then select **Add Node | Shaders | Diffuse | Lambert** and hook it into the Diffuse Shading input, you should get something in VIPER that looks like Figure 19-41.

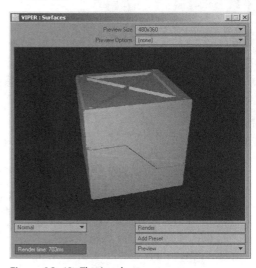

Figure 19-41: The Lambert crate.

> **Note**
>
> Lambert is the default shading that LightWave uses internally, so it should look the same as a layer-based render. However, as we know, nodes offer us a lot more control and options that will take our texturing to a level higher than what was possible in the old texturing system!

2. Let's see what happens if we **Add Node | Functions | Sine** function. Double-click on it and change Phase to **0.75**. Note that the highest point in the little graph on the node panel now sits

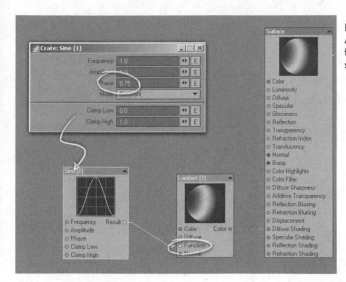

Figure 19-42: Adding a Sine function to a shader.

in the middle, with each end going to the bottom (or 0). Connect the output of this function node to the Function input on the Lambert shader node (Figure 19-42).

The Sine function now remaps the shading so that the mid-tones are boosted to 100% and the extremes are 0%. Compare the shaded areas between the first surface and the one using the new Sine function in Figure 19-43.

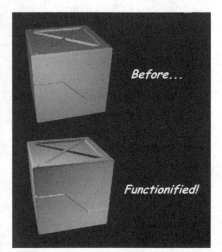

Figure 19-43: Before and after functionification.

Note

If you preordered your copy of LightWave v9, you would have received a copy of the excellent Vue 5 Infinite environment modeling and rendering package from e-onsoftware.com. If you are familiar with how Vue's filter options work to remap a texture's values, then you should be able to quickly understand what a Function node is. If you're now familiar with the Node Editor's functions, you can also apply this mindset to Vue 5 if you didn't understand it before.

Item Info Nodes

Item Info nodes read information from objects, lights, and cameras in the scene. This information can then be used to control other nodes. A Light Information node, for example, could be used to change a node's color based on the brightness of the light. Imagine a chameleon effect where a light might cause a character to take on the surface of another object.

Layer Nodes

A Layer node works exactly the same way as a layer in the traditional Texture Editor, allowing you to create (or copy) your favorite layered textures into a single node. This node is a great way to duplicate older non-nodal textures in the Node Editor. Once in the Node Editor, you can take advantage of the new shaders to further enhance your texturing.

Math Nodes

We touched on Math nodes at the beginning of the chapter. These are mathematical calculation nodes that you use when you want to process information from a node (or nodes) and calculate a result for use in another node. Vector nodes are great for not only working with colors (adding them together, for example), but also processing 3D information such as normals or coordinates from Item Info nodes. Scalar nodes work with single values, and include a special Logic node that can be used to test two values and return a true or false result, allowing for "smart" decisions in texturing!

RayTrace Nodes

RayTrace nodes allow you to shoot a 3D ray into the scene from any location and return information about what it hits. There are two types: RayCast and RayTrace. RayCast is the simpler of the two, returning only the distance the ray traveled before it hit something. RayTrace returns the color that the ray hit as well.

> **Note**
>
> You can use the World Spot and Normal information in the Spot Info nodes (discussed next) as inputs to these RayTrace nodes, and use them to query the distance of another surface from the current one being shaded. This obviously opens up many ideas and possibilities for surfaces that react to proximity of other objects or to simulate radiosity-type effects.

Spot Info Nodes

A Spot Info node lets us read information about the pixel or spot on the surface currently being shaded. This includes its position in 3D space, the location from which the ray hitting the surface came, how far the ray traveled, and lots of other fun information that can be used to manipulate other nodes. This information is extremely valuable when we start to look at how we can displace and deform the geometry of an object using node-based effects.

Tool Nodes

Tool nodes are translator and converter nodes that can create data from various inputs into other types. For example, the Color tool can adjust the Hue, Saturation, Brightness, and Contrast from various node inputs. A good example of this may be where you wanted to create a hue shift in a color based on the incidence angle of the surface, such as you might see on some fancy car paint job.

Vertex Map Nodes

Vertex Map nodes let us read and use morphs, weight maps, and color maps to control other nodes. In the case of morphs, we can also control the amount of morph through a node input.

Using Nodes for Displacements

While the node-based system will most likely spend most of its life being used for surfacing, it's not limited to it! The Node Editor offers us a lot of power in terms of deforming geometry in LightWave; much more than we've ever had before. Let's take a quick look at how this can be used to create some great results in LightWave v9.

1. Load the object **Objects\Chapter 19\SubD_Ball.lwo** into Layout. Open its properties panel <**p**> and set its Display SubPatch and Render SubPatch subdivision levels to **15**.

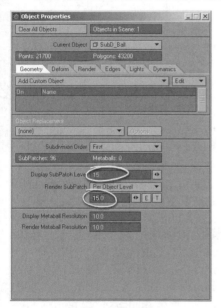

Figure 19-44: Set subdivision values.

2. Go to the Deform tab and activate the **Edit Nodes** check box, then click the **Edit Nodes** button to open the Node Editor panel.

3. Let's convert this ball into one that's made of bricks. Select **Add Node | 2D Textures | Bricks2D** to add the 2D brick node. Edit its parameters so that

Mapping is **Spherical**, the Axis is **Y**, and U and V Tiles are **5**.

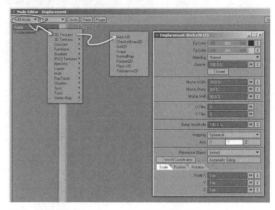

Figure 19-45: Setting up the Bricks2D Displacement node.

4. We want the bricks to displace outward from the surface of the ball, giving the effect of the ball being created from them. To do this, we'll need to add a **Spot | Spot Info** node so that we can find the direction along which the polys should displace. Let's also add a **Math | Vector | Multiply** node and then connect the Alpha output of Bricks2D to one of Multiply's inputs, the Smoothed Normal output from the Spot Info node to the other Multiply input, and finally the Result output of Multiply to the Displacement node.

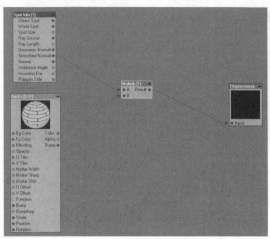

Figure 19-46: Plugging in the network.

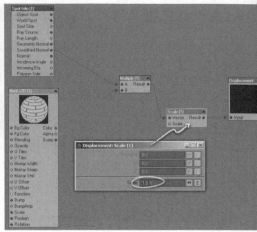

Figure 19-47: Scale the displacement.

> **Note**
>
> What's happening here is that we're asking the Spot Info node to tell us in what direction each point on the surface is facing, then multiply it by the occurrence of the brick texture if it exists at the same spot in our 3D texture. The mortar of the bricks texture is black. This is the same as multiplying by 0, or no displacement.

5. Because the Spot Info is a value between 0 and 1 in the X, Y, and Z axes, this is causing the bricks to extend an extra 1 m from the ball. This is huge, and obviously will need to be toned back. Let's disconnect the Displacement input temporarily and add a new **Math | Vector | Scale** node. Attach the Multiply result to the Vector input on the Scale node, then tweak the parameters of the Scale node and set Scale to **1%**. This will scale the intensity of the brick displacement (see Figure 19-47). Attach the Result output of the Scale node to the Displacement node input.

6. To complete the look of the brick ball, let's copy the same Brick2D node into the surface settings to get a true brick appearance to the final object. Select the Bricks2D node in the node panel, then **Edit | Copy** to copy this node into the clipboard. Close the Node Editor window for Displacement; we're finished with this for now.

7. Open the Surface Editor <**F5**>, click the **Edit Nodes** button to open the Node Editor window, then **Edit | Paste** to paste the Bricks2D node so that it can be used to texture the object. Let's add a **3D Textures | Turbulence** node to the texture, and give it a couple of shades of orange-brown with a Bg Color of **174, 087, 000** and a Fg Color of **130, 053, 002** as shown in Figure 19-48. Set the scale for the Turbulence to **200 mm** all around. Attach the Turbulence node Color output to the Fg Color input of the Bricks2D node to give it a nice brick-like surface.

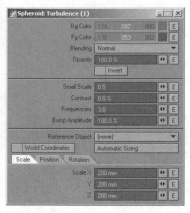

Figure 19-48: Set up the Turbulence node.

Figure 19-50: Crisp? At over three-quarter of a million polys, you'd hope so!

8. Finish up by adjusting the Bricks2D Bg Color to a medium gray of **125, 125, 125** to give the mortar a little color. Pose up the ball and light it nicely, then do an **<F9>** to see how it looks.

The finished scene can be loaded from **Scenes\Chapter 19\Brick_Ball_F.lws**.

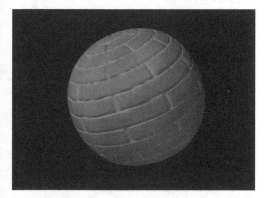

Figure 19-49: The final bricky-ball.

> **Note**
>
> The quality of the displacement is directly related to the density of our model, hence there are a few artifacts in our brick ball that we can see around the top and bottom of the ball. This can be improved by increasing the subdivision levels from 15 to something higher, such as 30, but at the expense of memory and a little extra rendering time (see Figure 19-50).

In Chapter 21, we'll be looking at some of the new, more powerful features of LightWave v9 that can really push what we can do here even further by using more adaptive approaches to how dense a mesh should be.

If you haven't already noticed, one of the main differences between LightWave's traditional displacement and node-based displacement is that node-based displacement is truly three-dimensional. Traditional displacement techniques in LightWave have often been mostly one-dimensional. That means the displacement lets us deform the points on an object along the X, Y, *or* Z, but not all three at the same time — unless we get clever with how we create our displacement textures (or use the Normal Displacement modifier that ships with LightWave).

If that wasn't enough displacement fun for you, let's quickly use displacements to add detail to the simple head object we textured earlier using SSS.

1. Load the scene **Scenes\Chapter 19\ SimpleHead_Displaced.lws**. This is almost identical to the scene we used back in the section on Subsurface Scattering, except this scene contains a version of the same head model that has been UV mapped. Select the

SimpleHead_UV.lwo object and open its properties panel. Set the subdivision settings for the object as we did for the brick ball, with both values set to **15**.

2. Click on the **Deform** tab and activate the node displacement options. Then bring up the Node Editor panel and add a **2D Textures | Image** node. Edit this node's parameters and load the image **Images\Chaper 19\DisplacementMaps\SimpleHead.tif**. This is a ZBrush-generated displacement map designed to add details to the face. Change Mapping to **UV Map**, and select **OBJ_UVTextureMap** for the UV Map.

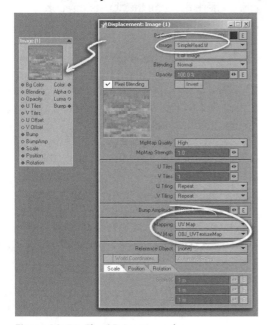

Figure 19-51: The 2D Image node.

3. As per the brick ball exercise, let's add a **Spot | Spot Info** node, a **Math | Vector | Multiply** node, and finally a **Math | Vector | Scale** node to the mix. We also need to add one more node — a **Math | Scalar | Subtract**

node. Let's connect the Luma (a form of "brightness" calculated from grayscaling a pixel's color) output of the Image node to the Subtract A input. Edit the parameters for the Subtract node and set the B value to **0.5**.

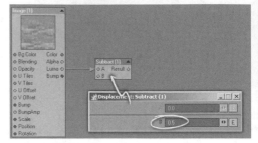

Figure 19-52: Subtracting 50% from the image's Luma value.

> **Note**
>
> The reason we need to subtract 0.5 (or 50%) from the image map is because the base, or "no-displacement" gray value in the image is equivalent to 50% already (that medium-gray that makes up the majority of the image map). This subtraction "equalizes" the image so that darker grays are negative (or indented) and lighter grays are positive. If we don't do this, then the mid-gray value will displace the surface outward, creating a chubbier face.

4. As before, let's mix up a displacement cocktail with our ingredients, connecting the Smoothed Normal output from Spot Info to the Multiply A input, the Subtract Result output to the Multiply B input, then the Multiply Result output to the Scale Vector input. Of course let's also set the Scale percentage to something small for now, like **10.0%** (we can tweak this later to intensify the effect if necessary). Finally, hook the Scale Result output into the Displacement node and we're done!

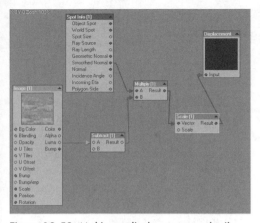

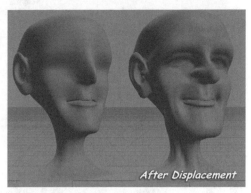

Figure 19-54: Our displaced character.

Figure 19-53: Making a displacement cocktail.

Using Nodes for Volumetric Lighting

Another place we'll find nodes is in the Volumetric Options for Light window. (We saw this back in Chapter 10 when we discussed volumetric lighting. Now that we know more about nodes, let's make use of them!) This opens up a ton of cool possibilities in creating amazing volumetric effects.

1. Start by loading **Scenes\Chapter 19\ VolumetricLighting.lws**. This should load a simple scene containing just a single light with a small volumetric setting. This light is going to become something a little more combustible by using nodes to control the volumetric effect.

2. Select the light, open its properties panel, and open the Volumetric Options window. The basic size is set up in the scene, but pressing <**F7**> to activate VIPER shows it's not exactly a burning inferno just yet (see Figure 19-55). Set Attenuation to **40%** to get the volumetric to fade away a little more. Disable the Enable Texture and Specify Medium Color options, as we won't be needing these.

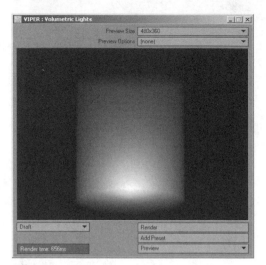

Figure 19-55: Not the scorching inferno we'd hoped for... yet!

3. Click on **Edit Nodes** to open the Node Editor window. As with surfacing, we get a master node for the volumetric light options (called NodalLight); however, what suddenly becomes clear is just how powerful this can be! By default, all these inputs had previously only been adjustable through the Graph Editor, and that meant the whole effect was affected en masse for the light in question. By having this node level of control, we suddenly open up full control to the volumetric matter inside the

light, not just the whole volumetric effect at once. Let's start by adding a **3D Textures | Turbulence** node. This will form the base of our fire effect.

4. Edit the parameters of this node. Set the scale to **500 mm** for X, **500 mm** for Y, and **1 m for** Z. Note that the Z-axis is the up direction (as the light comes from the top, it faces along the Z-axis). Fire, of course, is an animated effect, so to ensure that these flames move, let's edit the Position Z-axis using the Graph Editor. As shown in Figure 19-56, let's add a key at frame **20**, and set it to **1 m**. Set Post Behavior to **Linear** so that it keeps going forever.

5. Let's connect the Turbulence output to the NodalLight Density input. This will control the density of the volume inside the light using the Turbulence texture. If you create a preview and play it back in VIPER, you'll note it looks a little too soft and wispy (see Figure 19-57). Gas and smoke are often soft and wispy, but flames usually have some kind of form to them. Let's continue and see how we can improve on this.

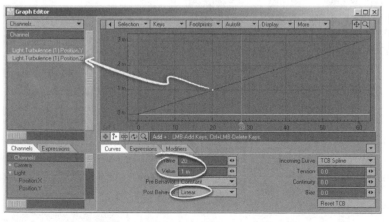

Figure 19-56: Animate the moving flames.

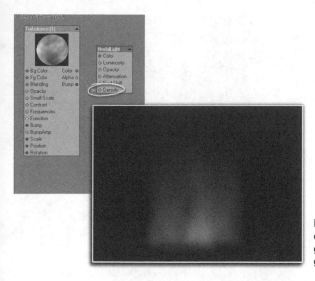

Figure 19-57: Soft and wispy is for girly smoke and gas animations!

6. So what would define our flames better? Perhaps we should increase the contrast of the Turbulence, but let's adjust it near the tips and keep that nice soft, less-defined look for the base of the flames. To do this, add a **Gradient | Gradient** node. Set its input to **Z**

Coordinate. Add an extra key just underneath this key as I've done in Figure 19-58, and then set the top key's Alpha value to **0%** and the bottom key's Alpha value to **100%**. Connect the gradient's Alpha to the Turbulence node's Contrast input.

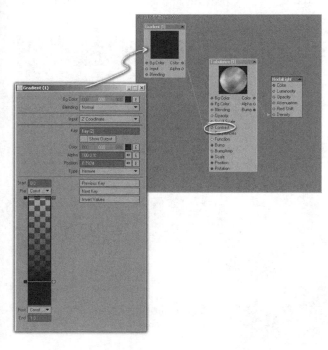

Figure 19-58: Contrast control gradient for the Turbulence.

Note

The Alpha value in a gradient is traditionally used to blend the gradient color value of each key with the Bg Color. Because Contrast is controlled through a percentage (or "Scalar" in node-speak), it makes sense that the Alpha values be used here (which is also represented as a percentage (Scalar)).

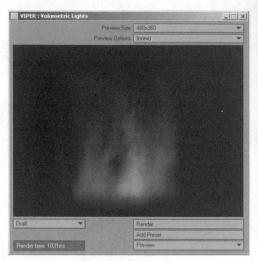

What we've done here is create the effect of the flames starting to break up as they travel and dissipate in the air (Figure 19-59), which is much better than the rather soft, wispy look we had before! And if you hadn't already realized, controlling the contrast dynamically like this is something that hasn't been possible before nodes became available.

Figure 19-59: High contrast for the flame tips.

7. Just to finish up the flame volumetric, it would be very cool if we could give the flames a little swirl and twist as they travel upward. Let's add a second **3D Textures | Turbulence** node, and set its Fg Color to **255, 255, 255** and the Scale to **2m** all around. Attach the Color output of this node to the

Rotation input of the first Turbulence node. The range of gray values from the color are changing the rotation of the flame's Turbulence texture as it passes up and through it. Do a VIPER preview and let's admire the flames in action!

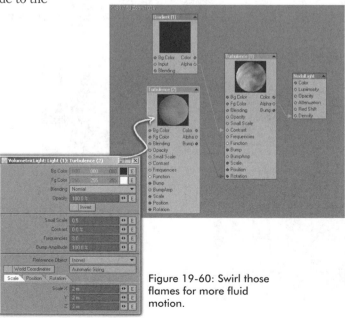

Figure 19-60: Swirl those flames for more fluid motion.

Obviously this is looking pretty good now, but it would be really cool if we just finished this up with a little color to get those flames looking like, well, flames! This means a little color and intensity control to get that heat happening.

8. Add another **Gradient | Gradient** node. This time, set its End value to **2.5** (roughly the height of the volumetric), then add a second key near the bottom. We'll be using both the Color and Alpha values of these keys to control the fire. Set the top key to a color of **255, 202, 097**, and its Alpha to **300%** (as this is the base of the fire). Set the bottom key to a dark red of **076, 000, 000**, and leave its Alpha at **100%** (see Figure 19-61). Connect the Gradient's Color output to the NodalLight Color input, and the Alpha output to the NodalLight Luminosity input as shown in Figure 19-62.

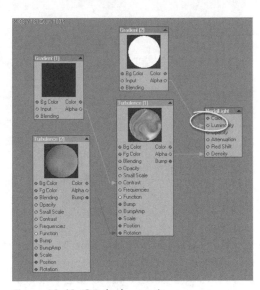

Figure 19-62: Get the heat on!

We're finished! Make a VIPER preview and admire our mini-inferno!

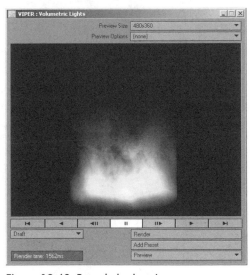

Figure 19-63: Burn, baby, burn!

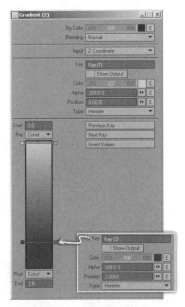

Figure 19-61: Making it hot with color.

If you want to see my finished scene, it can be loaded from **Scenes\Chapter 19\ VolumetricFire_F.lws**. The render is also available as **Renders\Chapter 19\burn-babyburn.mov**.

Conclusion

Hopefully you've been inspired by some of the very cool things available through this powerful new node-based system in LightWave v9. It's exciting, it's powerful, and it's going make a huge impact on the quality of your work produced in LightWave!

Like everything in LightWave, the best way to master node-based systems for shading, displacements, and lighting is to be creative and experiment with the new tools. While there are new light shading models for surfacing you can use on their own, be adventurous and see what blending two lighting models into one may look like by using some of the Math or Tool nodes to combine them, or experiment with remapping some shading using the various functions. Start creating mountains with the powerful new gradients that apply different rock bump maps and patterns in addition to changing color. Maybe use the Anisotropic shaders to create more realistic CD/DVD textures, or that extra-cool metallic robot casing.

The Node Editor is new, and it's extremely exciting! Don't forget to save and share your discoveries with the rest of the awesome LightWave community.

Chapter 20

Advanced Skills: Hair Simulation with SasLite

In this chapter, we'll take a detailed look at SasLite, the powerful hair and fur simulator that comes with LightWave. This chapter is included courtesy of Robin Wood, the artist who wrote the SasLite documentation for the LightWave [8] manual.

> **Note**
>
> The head built in Chapter 18 is also used in this chapter. This model uses the kitchen_probe.hdr image, which is available with the classic content CD that came with LightWave. Be sure to place a copy of that image in the Images\Chapter 20 directory before working through this chapter.

> **Note**
>
> SasLite is a simplified version of Sasquatch, the comprehensive fur and hair simulation system from Worley Labs. The name "SasLite" often gives users the impression that this tool is limited in its functionality and that you must purchase the full version of Sasquatch for any serious fur or hair work. I own the full version of Sasquatch, and I can tell you that I actually prefer SasLite for most of my fur and hair work. Not only is it *a lot easier* to use than Sasquatch, the fact that every LightWave user has access to it means you can share scene files without worry. In this chapter, we'll show you just how powerful SasLite really is by adding hair to the head model we built in Chapter 18.

An Introduction to SasLite

SasLite is a wonderful tool that allows you to add fur and hair to your objects. It works as both a displacement plug-in and a pixel filter. As such, you need to enable it in two different places in order to see the effect.

Let's jump right in and see how it works.

1. Load the **Furball.lws** scene from the companion DVD (Scenes\Chapter 20). This scene consists of a simple 1-meter ball, a key light, and a fill light.

2. With the ball object selected, open the Object Properties panel by tapping

<p>, and click on the **Deform** tab, where the Displacement plug-ins are stored. Click on **Add Displacement**, and choose **SasLite** from the list. (See Figure 20-1.)

3. Double-click on **SasLite** to open the Sasquatch Lite options panel. For now, just change the Fiber Color setting to something you like, and leave everything else at the default values. (See Figure 20-2.)

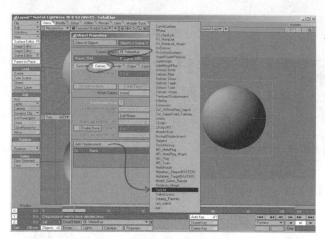

Figure 20-1: SasLite in the Add Displacement list.

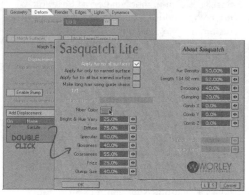

Figure 20-2: The Sasquatch Lite panel.

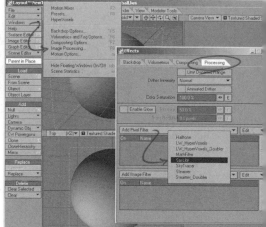

Figure 20-3: SasLite in the Add Pixel Filter list.

4. Press <Ctrl>+<F8> (or go to **Windows | Image Processing**) to open the Processing tab of the Effects panel. You'll see places to add two kinds of filters to your rendered image: pixel filters and image filters. Since SasLite is a pixel filter, that's the one you want. Click on **Add Pixel Filter** and choose **SasLite** from the list.

5. Double-click on the filter name to open its options panel. Click **Self Shadowing** to enable it, and close the panel by clicking **OK**.

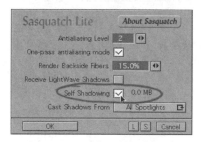

Figure 20-4: Enable Self Shadowing.

6. Press <F9> to render a single frame. Congratulations! You've used SasLite and made your first fur ball!

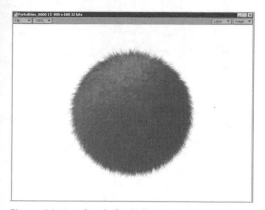

Figure 20-5: A lovely fur ball!

Figure 20-7: Same fur ball, but now the shadows are working.

7. But we're not going to stop here, because I want to show you something else. Press <L>, then <p>, (or click on **Lights** and then **Properties**) to open the Light Properties window. Make sure the key light is selected, then change it from a Distant Light to a **Spotlight**. You should see some difference in the Open GL shading of your sphere, but not a whole lot.

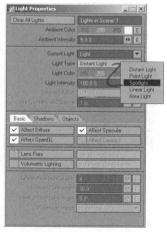

Figure 20-6: Change the light to Spotlight in the Light Properties window.

8. Press <F9> now, however, and you'll find that the sphere is considerably darker. This is because the fibers are now self-shadowing.

SasLite, like its older brother Sasquatch, works best with spotlights. That's something that you will want to remember. (If you need to prove it to yourself, turn off Self Shadowing in the Pixel Filter options (<Ctrl>+<F8>) and do another <F9> render. You'll find that the fibers look almost exactly the same as they did when we were using a distant light. In other words, even though we had Self Shadowing selected in the SasLite Pixel Filter options, the fibers weren't really shadowing themselves because we were using a distant light.)

So, to sum it up, if you want to use SasLite, you'll need to do the following three things:

● Choose **SasLite** from the Add Displacement pop-up menu in the Object Properties window.

● Choose **SasLite** from the Add Pixel Filter pop-up menu in the Processing tab of the Effects panel.

● Change the Light Type setting for all lights in the scene to **Spotlight** so that SasLite can shade the fibers properly.

Remember these three simple steps and the rest of the work is simply tinkering with the options!

Beyond the Basics

So much for a fur ball. What if you want to make something other than tribbles or dust bunnies? Say that you wanted to make a rug. No, not a toupee (although we will be doing that a bit later). I mean a flat rug, like the kind you find on the floor. Are you surprised that SasLite can be used to create a rug? Don't limit yourself to thinking of this as merely a "hair and fur" generator. SasLite makes fibers. It can simulate anything that's composed of strands — rugs, grass, seaweed, peach fuzz, centipede legs, cobwebs — anything that consists of one or more filaments.

Now it's worth noting that whatever color you choose for your fibers applies to the entire instance of SasLite. (There is a percentage variable for color, but it varies both brightness and hue, and is entirely random in its application.) So, in practical terms, if you want to use more than one fiber color on an object you have to assign different surfaces to that object, and different instances of SasLite for each surface.

> **Note**
>
> Be aware that you are limited to eight instances of SasLite in a given scene, so if you need more than that, you'll have to make several renders and composite them in post. (The full version of Sasquatch can use an unlimited number of instances.)

Since surfaces are applied on a per-poly basis, all you need to do is make the pattern for your rug using polys, and assign different surfaces and different instances of SasLite for each color.

This is really quite simple to do, especially if you want the fibers to be similar all over the object. Let's take a look at how it works using a rug with a simple design as an example.

Creating a Rug

1. Find the **StarRug.lwo** object on the companion DVD (Objects\Chapter 20) and load it into Modeler. When working with odd-shaped polygons (typically any n-gon) and SasLite, you'll need to do a little prep work in order to get things to work properly. (If you want to skip this part, you can. The StarRugEnd.lwo object doesn't need these modifications.)

When SasLite puts fur on a poly, it won't reliably follow concave curves. In other words, if you can draw a straight line between any two points of a poly, and part of that line falls outside the poly, the fur may follow that line. You can see what I mean by looking at Figure 20-8.

Figure 20-8: SasLite can't follow the outline of this poly, which results in undesirable ruggage.

To fix this, it's necessary to split the poly so that you can't draw such a line.

2. Switch to Points mode. Select two inside points that aren't next to each other, as shown in Figure 20-9. Then tap <1> (lowercase L) or go to **Construct | Combine | Connect** to split the poly.

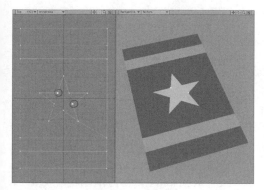

Figure 20-9: Select these two points, and split the poly.

3. Deselect the points and switch to Polygons mode. (If you have a mouse with extra buttons and you can assign keystrokes to them, you'll save a world of time if you assign the Deselect function to one of those buttons, by the way.)

4. Select the polygons that make up the star. Then go to **Multiply | Subdivide | Add Points**, and add a point to the "split" line you just made. It should be near the center of the star.

Figure 20-10: Add a point to the polys, as shown.

5. Tap the <**Spacebar**> to drop the Add Points tool, and select one of the inside star points and the new central point. Connect (keyboard shortcut <1>) the poly again as shown in Figure 20-11.

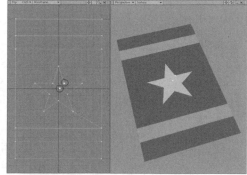

Figure 20-11: Connect the poly again using these two points.

6. Drop those points, and repeat this step for each of the remaining two inside corner points of the star. When you're finished, you should have a line going from each of those points to the middle point.

7. Select that point and tap <**F2**> (or go to **Modify | Translate | Center**) to center it. Then tap <**Ctrl**>+<**t**> (or go to **Modify > Translate | Drag**), hold down the <**Ctrl**> key to constrain the movement, and drag it down until the five polys that make up the star look about the same size.

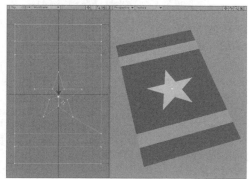

Figure 20-12: Center the middle point for symmetry.

8. Now SasLite will read the star correctly, but it will still render fur over the entire ground that the star sits on. So, once again, select the large poly that makes this background, and split it into smaller polys that have no concave curves.

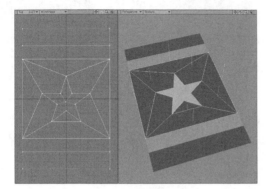

Figure 20-13: Split the ground into polys that will render correctly too.

9. When you're finished, send the object to Layout (or if you skipped the previous steps, load the **StarRugEnd.lwo** file from Objects\Chapter 20). Change the light to a **Spotlight** (choose **Lights** (<L>), **Properties** (<p>), and change the light type.) Then select the rug and rotate it so that you can see it in a Camera viewport. Make sure it's well lit by the spotlight.

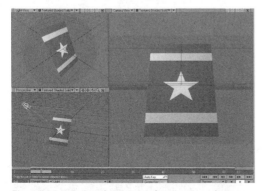

Figure 20-14: Set the rug up for easy rendering.

10. Open the Surface Editor. When you're assigning fur to surfaces in SasLite, you need to type in the exact name of the surface. It's easier to do this if the Surface Editor is open and you can see the name. SasLite does not use a drop-down list for selecting surfaces, but you can use a wildcard character, "*" (asterisk), to select several surfaces at once. So "*hair" would apply the displacement to surfaces named Leghair, Chesthair, Tailhair, and Backhair (but not Face Hair — it's case sensitive), which saves time.

11. Open the Object Properties panel. Click on the **Deform** tab and choose **SasLite** from the Add Displacement menu. Double-click on it to edit the parameters. The first thing we need to do is make sure that this instance will only be applied to one of the colors (surfaces) on the rug. So, at the top, click in the box to enable **Apply fur only to named surface**.

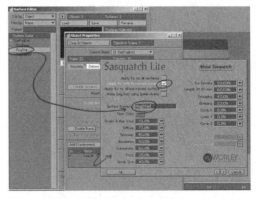

Figure 20-15: With the Surface Editor open, it's easy to pick which surface you want the fur applied to.

12. When you do, the Surface Name(s) text field will be enabled. Looking at the list of surfaces in the Surface Editor, pick one and type that name into the field. I'm going to use **RugStar**. If I type it

correctly and hit the <**Tab**> key, the little green numbers will now read 1/3. If they say 0/3, check your typing. (The first number tells you how many surfaces are using this instance of SasLite. The second tells how many surfaces there are in this object.)

Figure 20-16: Check the numbers to make sure that you typed correctly.

13. Pick a color that goes with the star for the Fiber Color option. I'm choosing **yellow**. (If you pick a color that's similar to the surface color, you can get away with less density, which saves rendering time.)

14. Now it's time to tweak the fibers in the rug. I'm setting Bright & Hue Vary quite low (**5%**) because I don't want much variation in the yarn colors used. Diffuse is high, and Specular and Glossiness are low because it's yarn and I don't want it to be shiny. Coarseness is high, because yarn tends to be fairly thick. Frizz is 0% because I want the fibers to be straight. Clump Size is low because I want the rug to look fairly new.

15. Fur Density is 100% because I don't want to see "holes" in the fibers of the new rug. Length is around 25% because I'm making the rug "real size"; at that percentage, the fibers will be about 15 mm, which is the length of those on the rug I have here. Drooping and Clumping are very low because of the "new" look I'm going for. Finally, I've set Comb Y to **90%** so the fibers will stand up tall.

Note

The Comb values are relative to the model's orientation in Modeler, not the way it's sitting in Layout. This means the fibers will grow away from the polys, even though we've rotated the rug.

16. You can match the numbers shown in Figure 20-17, or you can choose your own, of course.

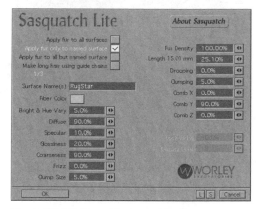

Figure 20-17: The settings used for the rug pictured.

17. When you're finished, click **OK**. You should see SasLite Seen on RugStar in the Add Displacement area of the Object Properties panel.

Figure 20-18: SasLite applied to a surface.

18. Tap <**Ctrl**>+<**F8**> (or go to **Windows | Image Processing**) to open the Processing tab of the Effects panel. Click on **Add Pixel Filter** and choose **SasLite** from the list, as you did before. Make the fibers self-shadowing so you can see them in the test renders. You know how to do that.

717

19. Tap <**F9**> (or go to **Render > Render Frame**) to see what you have. (It may take several moments to apply SasLite, depending on the speed of your computer.) If you like the results, then move on to the next step. If you don't, then feel free to tweak the settings until you do.

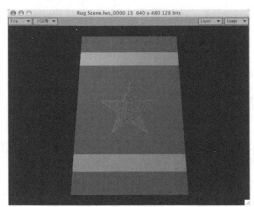

Figure 20-19: Fibers on the star!

20. Once you're happy with the fibers, you need to assign the same settings (except for color) to the other two materials. To do that, just click the SasLite Seen on RugStar line with the right mouse button and choose **Copy** from the pop-up menu that appears. Click again, and choose **Paste** to create another instance with the same settings. **Paste** again so you have three instances.

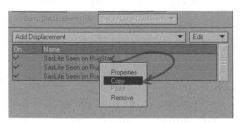

Figure 20-20: Copy and paste the displacement, one per surface.

21. Then simply click on each setting to open it, type in the name of the surface, and choose a new color. The rest of the settings can remain the same. When you're finished, you should have three instances, each showing a different surface.

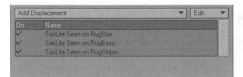

Figure 20-21: Three colors, three instances.

22. Render (<**F9**>), and you'll have a rug with three colors of fibers. You can, of course, obtain textural variation by adjusting any of the other parameters. You might also want to enable **Receive Shadows**, as was done here, in the SasLite Pixel Filter panel. Play with it some, and have fun!

Figure 20-22: The finished rug in its natural habitat.

There's Nothing Plain about This Grassy Plain

In the previous example, we used a separate instance of SasLite for each surface. You can also use multiple instances of SasLite on the same surface to add extra punch to your renders. For instance, you can easily make a field of mixed grass and weeds.

1. Load the **GrassyPlain.lws** file (Scenes\Chapter 20), and let's see how that's done. Everything is set up and ready for you here; all you need to do is add the plug-ins. Choose **SasLite** from both the Add Pixel Filter list in the Image Processing panel and the Add Displacement list in the Deform tab of the Object Properties window, as always.

2. Open the filter, and let's make grass. There's only one surface, so we can just leave the default setting (**Apply fur to all surfaces**) on. Then choose a grass color and set the parameters. You can see what I used in Figure 20-23.

As you will notice, you can push some of the parameters beyond 100%. In this case, I chose 200% Coarseness and 150% Fur Density.

> **Note**
>
> Coarseness is internally linked with Length. As you make the fibers shorter, such as the grass here, they automatically become finer, as well. (Think of them scaling in all three dimensions.) You won't see the numbers change, but it's happening, and those wispy grass blades won't give you good coverage. The answer, of course, is to crank up the Coarseness value. In SasLite, the maximum Coarseness is 400%.

If you decide to overdrive the Fur Density as I did, that increase will cost you in render time. Often, you can get the appearance of denser fibers by using the same surface color and fiber color. You can see that here, where the distant hills have some green areas and some brown areas. The grass looks thicker where the ground is green.

3. It still looks rather sparse and homogeneous, though. It's easy to give it more coverage and more variety, however, by adding another instance of SasLite. **Copy/Paste** the plug-in, as you did with the rug, and choose slightly different parameters for the second instance. Figure 20-24 shows what I used.

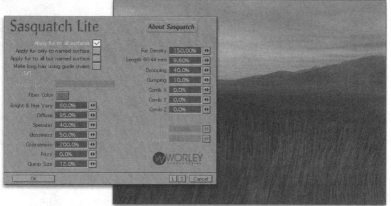

Figure 20-23: Settings for the grass.

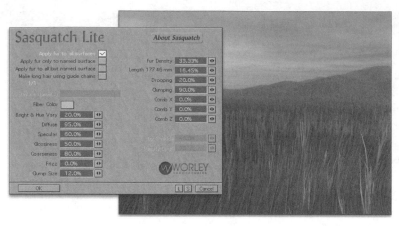

Figure 20-24:
Settings for the
second instance.

You can keep going, making more interesting and realistic grass, up to the eight instances that SasLite allows. I'll leave that for you to do. Have fun!

Hair's Where It's At!

Of course, you might also want to use SasLite to make fur and hair!

Say you wanted to add a beard and mustache to the head that you made in Chapter 18. There is no mapping of any kind in SasLite; the entire surface that the displacement is applied to will have exactly the same length, density, combing, and everything else. (The full version of Sasquatch does not have this limitation.)

So how can you make something like a beard, which needs a smooth variation in hair length? Simple. You don't apply the fur to the skin polys at all. Instead, you copy and paste those polys, put them *under* the skin, and apply the fur to them. It will grow right out through the skin with no problem since it doesn't care in the least if there's another surface beyond the polys it's assigned to.

Shall we see how it's done?

1. Open the finished head model from Objects\Chapter 20 called **Chapter-18_Head-Model_FINAL.lwo**.

2. Copy all the polys where you would expect the beard to grow, and paste them into a new layer. Put that layer in the foreground, and the head in the background. Name the new layer **Beard** and make it the child of the Head layer.

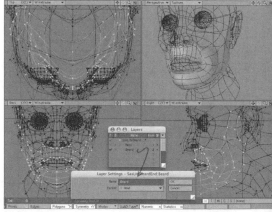

Figure 20-25: The beard polys in the foreground, with the head in the background.

3. Trim up the beard polys; in other words, split them, remove points, or whatever you think you should do to

shape them as much like a "beard wig" as possible. The hairline will exactly follow whatever you make here, so take your time and be careful with it.

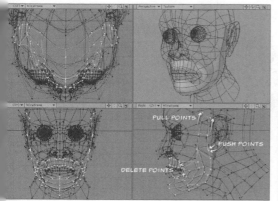

Figure 20-26: Reshape the polys so they have the line you want the beard to have.

4. When it looks pretty good, assign it a new material (<**q**>), call it **Beard**, and make it a color that will contrast with the skin color. Tap <**H**> to get the Size tool (or go to **Modify | Transform | Size**) and make it a little smaller, so it lies under the head polys. Put both layers in the foreground, and check from all angles to make sure that you can't see any of the beard through the skin. When you are satisfied with it, save it with a new name called **SasLiteHead-Setup.lwo**.

5. Open Layout, and load the **SasLite-Setup.lws** scene from Scenes\Chapter 20. This is a simple scene with a three-point light setup. (See Chapter 5 for a discussion of three-point lighting.)

6. Open the **SasLiteHead-Setup.lwo** object that you just saved. Make sure the head is selected (not the beard), then rotate it about 22 degrees on the heading so that it is not facing the camera straight on.

7. Apply the **SasLite** displacement to the Beard layer and add the **SasLite** pixel filter in the Effects | Processing panel, as you've done in the past. Leave the settings for both at the defaults for now; you'll have plenty of time to tweak them in a moment. Tap <**F9**> to get a quick render so you can see how the basic shape looks.

Figure 20-27: First test render of the beard with the default settings.

Now, most men trim their beards around the sideburns, so they won't grow straight out like this. You can't vary the length of SasLite fur, but you can pull the polys deeper into the head so that the hair will appear to be shorter near the sideburns.

8. Return to Modeler, make sure that **Symmetry** is active, put the head in the background once more, and begin to pull those points away from the surface. I use the Drag tool (<**Ctrl**> + <**t**> or **Modify | Translate | Drag**) to do this, but you can use any method that you prefer. You are aiming for something like what you see in Figure 20-28.

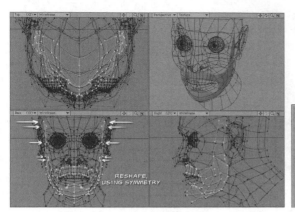

Figure 20-28: Pull the polys into the head where you want the hair to be shorter.

9. When you think it's right, return to Layout and do another test render. Continue this process until you have the basic shape of a beard.

Figure 20-29: A basic beard shape, still with default settings.

10. Now, it's time to tweak the settings. Open the SasLite settings from the Object Properties window. Begin by checking **Apply fur only to named surface**, because even though we only have one surface now, we're going to be adding more. That will enable the Surface Name(s) field. As always, you need to remember exactly what you named the surface. This time it's easy,

so type **Beard** into the field. (Case does matter, by the way.) When you do, the little green numbers should change to say 1/1. If they don't, then you've made a spelling mistake.

Figure 20-30: Check the numbers here to make sure the plug-in is being applied to the correct number of surfaces.

11. SasLite doesn't give you separate control of the hue and brightness; it's all one control. So, if you want a lot of variation in the brightness, choose a low saturation. Otherwise, you're likely to get very different colors as well. (Which may be what you want. If that's the case, go for it!)

12. Human hair, even beard hair, tends to be fairly glossy, so leave the Diffuse low, pump up the Specular, and give it a medium Glossiness value. Beards are fairly coarse, so make that on the high side. Choose the Frizz that seems best (more for a wilder beard, less for one that's more groomed). The same goes for Clump Size. The lower the value, the more the beard will look like it's been combed recently. The higher the value, the more you'll be making a Wild Man of the Mountains!

13. Give it medium Density and Length, with quite a bit of Drooping (otherwise, it's likely to look too spiky). Clumping, like Clump Size, will make it look clean or less than clean, depending on the value. (Higher for matted, lower for a neat beard.)

14. Combing influences the direction the hair grows. (It's also dependent on the

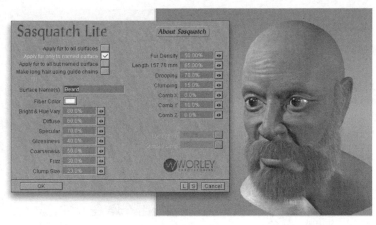

Figure 20-31: The values used for the beard shown, with Self Shadowing enabled.

Drooping value and the direction of the poly normal.) We're using quite a bit of Drooping, so the hair will leave the face and head downward. Let's use a small amount of combing on the positive Y-axis to give the hair a bit of a lift and make it just a tiny bit bushier. Think of it as backcombing. (Giving it a negative value will make it less bushy, if that's what you prefer.)

See Figure 20-31 for the values I used if you want to copy them.

15. Render this and see how it looks. (You may want to add shadowing so you can see what you're really getting if you intend to use it in the finished render. Fur can look very, very different with and without it.) If you're reasonably happy with the results so far, it's time to refine it further.

Refining the Beard and Mustache

Mustache hair tends to grow out from the philtrum (the groove in the center of the upper lip), often leaving the middle without hair at all. Since you can't vary the combing on a surface with SasLite, the only way to achieve that is to separate the Mustache surface from the Beard surface, and divide it into two pieces. So we'll do just that.

1. In Modeler, select the polys that form the mustache and hide the rest (tap the < = > key). Then select the half on the positive X-axis and give it a new surface name, say **lMustache**. Tap <"> (double quote) to invert the selection, and name the other side **rMustache**.

(These correspond to the model's right and left side, not yours.)

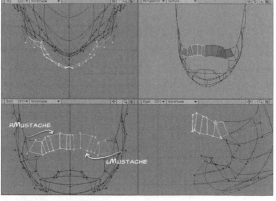

Figure 20-32: Divide the surface into three: the beard and the two halves of the mustache.

2. Return to Layout and open the Object Properties window if you've closed it. Click with the right mouse button on the line that says SasLite Seen on Beard, and choose **Copy** from the pop-up menu that appears. Right-click again, and choose **Paste**. That will give you two identical copies of the displacement.

3. Open one of them and change Surface Name(s) to **lMustache**. Lower the Length and Drooping values to **60%**. Then change the Comb X value. Make it pretty high. (I used **80%**, and also lowered the Comb Y value to **5%**.)

Figure 20-34: The beard and mustache.

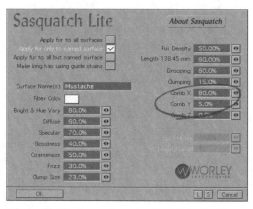

Figure 20-33: New values for the left half of the mustache.

4. Click **OK** to close the panel, and use the copy/paste trick again to make another copy. Change the parameters of the copy so that it's applied to the **rMustache** surface, and put a minus sign in front of the Comb value (for instance, –80%). That will send the hairs along the –X-axis, or toward the right cheek and away from the center of the face.

5. Render to see what you have now.

6. If the break along the philtrum is too pronounced, go back into Modeler, select the points on either side of the center line, and bring them closer to the center. You might also want to split the mustache so it can conform better to the shape of the lip.

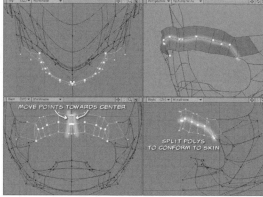

Figure 20-35: Modify the beard geometry further if needed.

7. Keep refining and making test renders until you have the beard and mustache you are looking for. Don't be afraid to add another couple of surfaces to blend the density, put in streaks of a different color, etc. You can have up to eight instances of SasLite in a scene. (If you

want more, you can render your scene in a couple of passes and put them together in post, or upgrade to the full version of Sasquatch, which provides unlimited instances.)

8. For this beard, I added a **BeardThin** surface on either side of the lower lip (just a couple of very small polys) and a **BeardWhite** surface to give him a couple of gray streaks. I also turned on **Receive LightWave Shadows** in the SasLite Pixel Filter options.

Figure 20-36: Finished beard.

9. Save your object (overwriting the SasLiteHead-Setup.lwo file). Then save the scene as **SasLite-Beard.lws**. My copy of this scene is available on the companion DVD.

If you want a step-by-step breakdown of the work done on the beard, you can inspect the SasLiteBeard.lwo file on the DVD. Each step listed here corresponds to a layer in the model.

When you're finished and it's just what you want, you can cut the beard polys, if you desire, and paste them inside the head. (The SasLite displacements will be on the Beard object, not the Head object, so you'll have to copy/paste them to the head if you do this.) The extra polys make it a bit trickier to animate the head (you'll have to include them in your endomorphs), but they will let you add believable hair, beards, mustaches, fur, etc., to your models.

You can use the same principles anytime you want to vary the length of SasLite fibers. For example, if you want grass to grow higher on the banks of a river, a werewolf's fur to bristle along his back, or a soldier to have a crew cut, all you need to do is make subsurface polys, and pull them back for shorter fibers or push them toward the surface for longer ones.

You can do the same thing for eyebrows, eyelashes, and the hair on the character's head, but there's another way to accomplish these effects that we have yet to explore. Instead of using subsurface fur patches, we can use long hair guides, which are also supported, in a limited fashion, in SasLite.

Creating Hair with Long Hair Guides

Long hair guides are two-point poly chains (two-point polys that share a point with another two-point poly) that direct the flow of the fibers. To work in SasLite (or the full version of Sasquatch for that matter), it's necessary for the point on the "root" end to have a different surface than the rest of the chain. (That's how the plug-in determines which end is which.) They are usually

named "Hair" and "Root" to keep things simple.

SasLite will generate a lock of hair that follows the general direction of the guide. The number of hairs in that lock, their length, and how closely they follow the guide is determined by the number and placement of polys in the chain, and the settings in SasLite.

1. Let's start with the hair on our model's head. Load the **SasLiteHead-Setup.lwo** file into Modeler (if it's not already open).

There are several methods to do this, the "point" of all of them being to spend less time creating the guides than it would take to actually grow the hair. Making hair guides can be grueling, but it doesn't have to be. The more control you want, or the more complex the hairstyle, the more guides you'll need. The process I'm about to show you isn't the easiest, but it will show you a way to make a whole lot of guides reasonably quickly, without using any third-party plug-ins. You won't normally need quite this many, but just in case you do, here's a good way to get them.

2. Begin by lassoing all the polys that could have hair growing from them. Then tap the <}> (right curly bracket) key to run Expand Selection and get the surrounding polys too. (Because of the way that subpatches work, the curve changes when polys are abruptly removed. By grabbing the polys next to the ones that you actually want, you can ensure that doesn't affect the polys you need.)

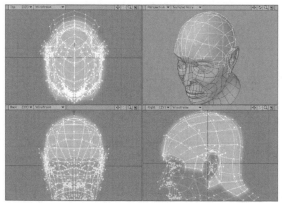

Figure 20-37: Select the scalp polys and the ones next to them.

3. Paste those polys into a new layer. For this particular method, we're going to use a lot of points to grow hair guides from, so tap <Ctrl>+<d> (or go to **Construct | Convert | Freeze**) and freeze the polys, which will make faces from the "virtual" polys in the subpatches. Tap the <**Tab**> key to subpatch those polys, and freeze again. (If you don't think you need as many guides, then you might want to freeze only once, or change the subpatch level (in either direction) before freezing.)

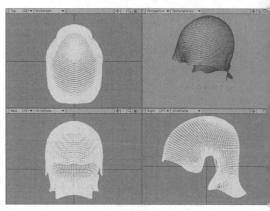

Figure 20-38: The poly-rich mesh that results from double-freezing.

4. We don't need the polys, just the points. So tap <**k**> (or go to **Construct | Reduce | Remove | Remove Polygons**) to "kill" the polys. That will leave you with a bunch of points that aren't connected to anything. Copy the whole bunch and paste them into another layer. Now begin to lasso and remove sections to form the actual hairline. As always, it helps if you have a reference. If you accidentally get too many, you can grab them from the previous layer and paste them in here. Just tap <**m**> to merge the points so you won't have to worry about multiple overlapping point

problems. Keep going until you are happy with it.

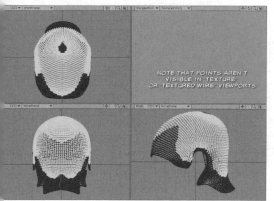

Figure 20-39: Trim the extra points away from the hairline. (The original points are shown in the background for clarity.)

5. When you're satisfied, tap <m> to merge points. (Even if you haven't copied points from another layer, it's good to do this just to be safe.) Then reduce the size of the wig slightly so it fits inside the scalp (<H>), and then tap <J> (or **Modify | Transform | Jitter**) and jitter the points a tiny bit (about 2 cm on all three axes should work) so it looks more like hair roots and less like transplants. Name this layer **Roots**. (You can name layers in the Layers panel found under the Windows menu.) You can delete the points from the previous layer now, if you feel so inclined, or save them "just in case."

6. We're going to rail extrude the two-point polys, but right now, we've only got points. Rail Extrude doesn't work on points. Therefore, we must convert our points into polygons. Go to the **Create** tab and click on **Polygons | Points to Polys**. Now that these points are considered polygons, we can assign a surface to them. Tap the <q> key to bring up the Change Surface window. Give these single-point polygons a surface called **Root**.

7. Copy all of the Root single-point polys and paste them into another layer, and name this layer **Hair Building**. Tap <q> again, and change the surface to **Hair**. We'll extrude the Hair polys and then merge them with the Root polys later on. This will give us the proper guides needed by SasLite (and the full version of Sasquatch).

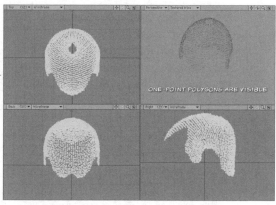

Figure 20-40: The Roots layer, all ready to grow hair!

8. Select the single-point polys that make up the hairline (as seen in Figure 20-41). Place them into an empty layer and call this empty layer **Hairline**. We're going to style them more carefully in a few minutes, but it's easier if the bulk of the hair is done first. (Depending on the style of the hair, these points could be along a part, just in the front, on the side, or wherever the scalp shows.)

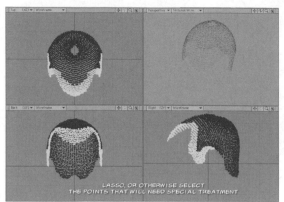

Figure 20-41: Put the Hairline polys in another layer for more careful treatment.

9. Open an empty layer, and put the Hair Building layer in the background. Beginning at the center, or where the part is, start to make a series of spline curves. (You can use whichever of the curve tools you are most comfortable with.)

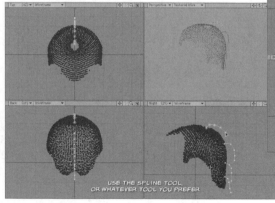

Figure 20-42: Begin to make curves to describe the bulk of the hair.

We are going to use Rail Extrude to extrude the one-point polys, which will automatically make two-point poly chains from them. The spline curves we just created are the rails the polys will be extruded along.

In SasLite, the actual hairs may appear to be a little shorter than the hair guides, so bear that in mind while you are making them.

10. Work from the hairline at the collar to the front so you can make each curve slightly overlap the one below it. This will keep the hair falling naturally, instead of having fibers diving under the ones below.

11. Make two to five curves, and then begin to copy/paste them, and move them around the head, rotating so that they will follow the line you want the hair to have. The more curves you use, the smoother the hair will be, but be aware that there are limits to how many splines Rail Extrude can handle before it simply tells you there are too many. (If you reach those limits, you can divide your hair into smaller sections to extrude, of course.)

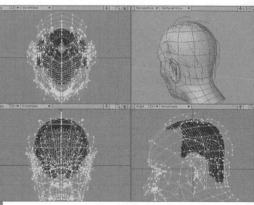

Figure 20-43: The head, with enough splines to describe the main hair mass.

12. When you have enough to describe the basic shape of the hair, somewhere between 5 and 20 or so, depending on the hairstyle, put the curves in the background and the Hair Building layer in the foreground. Tap <Ctrl> + <r> (or **Multiply | Extend | Rail Extrude**) to open the Rail Extrude: Multiple panel.

13. Choose **Length** for the Segments setting, make them **Uniform**, and choose around **5** or **6** segments. (There are limits to how many vertices SasLite allows, and they add up quickly.) Leave Strength at **2**, and disable both **Oriented** and **Scaling**.

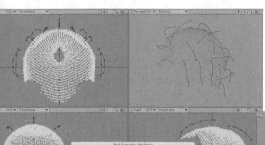

Figure 20-44: The Rail Extrude: Multiple panel.

14. Click **OK**, and you'll have a bunch of two-point poly hair guides! Name the layer **Wig**. We'll be collecting the hair here as we build it.

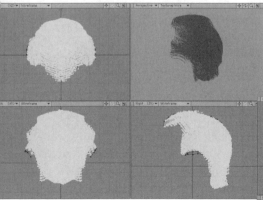

Figure 20-45: The bulk of the hair guides, made in a snap!

Now, of course, there are things that can go a little weird at this step.

The most common problems are the guides swirling in odd directions, piling up in ridges, and/or leaving bald spots when viewed against the head. Most of these are caused by the same thing: not enough curves for the number of one-point polys being extruded. (Although I've found that sometimes, for some reason, you can also fix the swirling problem by undoing and deleting the last point on the curve. So if you're pretty sure there are enough, you might want to try that.)

To fix them, of course, either add some curves or extrude a fewer number of one-point polys at once.

Figure 20-46: Ridges that leave bald spots can be corrected by adding four curves.

If a lot of the hair is below the surface, then your splines might be too close to the head. Undo, select all the points on the spline

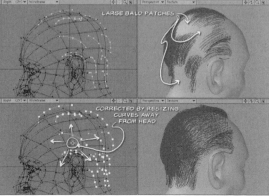

Figure 20-47: If the splines are too close to the head, the guides will be inside it, not outside.

except the end points, and use the Size tool (<h>) to make it all larger.

15. Now, if you want to shape it as you go, which is easier from my point of view (but also requires more steps), cut the hair. (That sounds like barber talk, but I really mean to cut using the <Ctrl>+ <x> shortcut, of course.)

16. Open the **Roots** layer and paste the hair in. Tap <m> to merge points, and accept the defaults. That will merge each chain with its root. Select the **Hair** material (using the Statistics panel (<w>)) and tap the <]> key (or go to **View | Select | Select Connected**) to get the roots as well. Cut again, and paste back into the **Wig** layer. Now you can tweak the hair to your heart's desire, without any fear of the guides becoming disassociated from their roots. Go ahead and do that, shaping it until you are happy with it. The Magnet tool works well for this, but of course you can use any tool you are comfortable with.

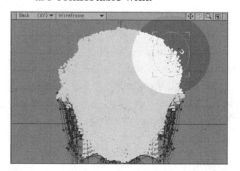

Figure 20-48: Styling the hair with the Magnet tool.

17. Once you are happy with that part of the hair, it's time to work on the front and the hairline. This is done the same way, except that you work on only a small section at a time, which gives you much better control and allows you to style the hair with (relative) ease.

By small, I mean small. The trick is to keep the sections to 20 or 30 of the one-point polys at a time.

18. If the portion of the hairstyle you're working on is symmetrical, select a group from the **Hairline** layer in one of the side viewports (Right or Left) so you get both sides, cut it, and paste it into an empty layer. Then make two or three splines, as if you were modeling the outermost hairs (and perhaps a middle hair) from that group. Mirror those splines across the X-axis, and tweak the mirrored ones a tiny bit so it's not too symmetrical. (I use the Drag tool (<Ctrl>+<t>) for that, because I'm a control freak, but you might want to use Jitter.)

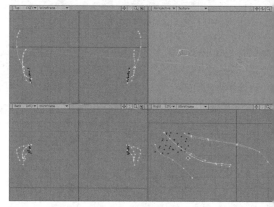

Figure 20-49: Symmetrical groups of one-point polys and rails.

19. Then Rail Extrude the points, using more segments if you can afford it. If they haven't gone wonky (that's a technical term), put the guides and the head in a foreground layer, and take a look. If they don't penetrate anything they shouldn't (like the ears), and if they are standing out from the scalp, move on to the next step. You don't have to be exact, since you can style the section with the Modify tools, but the closer

you are, the easier that will be. Just don't make yourself crazy with it.

Figure 20-50: Extruded guides, viewed against the head.

20. If the style isn't symmetrical it will take a little longer, because you'll have to grab the one-point polys one group at a time. You might find, though, that it's still easier to copy the curves and tweak them from group to group than it is to build a whole new set of curves.

Once again, I find it's easiest to work from back to front, with the finished hair piece and the roots you are currently working with in the background.

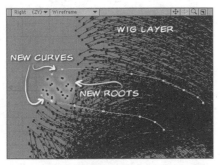

Figure 20-51: Making the rails for another section of hair.

Note

If you want to have the best, thickest hair you can have, then make sure you have more points at the tip than you do at the root, and extrude by knot, not length. SasLite uses the placement of points on the guide when it determines how to "grow" the hair. The more the points are concentrated at the tip, the thicker and longer the hair will grow.

21. As you finish each section, if you are using the style-as-you-go method, cut it and paste it into the **Roots** layer, merge the points, select the **Hair** surface, hit **Select Connected**, and paste it back into the **Hair Building** layer. Then, with that layer in the foreground and the Wig layer in the background, tweak the hair until you are satisfied with the shape. (Don't forget to add Minoxidil, to make the hair healthy and strong.*) Once it looks good, cut it again and paste it into the Wig layer. As I mentioned before, this method has more steps and may take more time, but for me, it gives much better results (with a lot less stress).

[* Don't go looking for the Minoxidil button. It's a joke! If you didn't get it, take a break right now.]

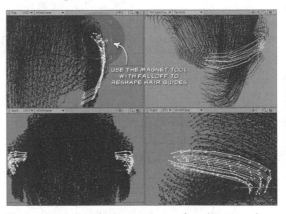

Figure 20-52: Tweaking a section and working into the wig.

While you are styling, remember that these are hair guides, not hairs. Every one of them will turn into multiple hairs when it's rendered with SasLite. Complete coverage isn't necessary, or even particularly desirable. It's better to make hair guides that are a little offset, with an even amount of room between them.

22. If you aren't using the style-as-you-go method, then just cut each section as you finish it, and paste it into the **Wig** layer.

23. Once a section is pasted into the Wig, open the **Hairline** layer, cut the next section of roots, paste it into the **Hair Building** layer, and make curves for it. (You might want to save all the curves, or you might want to delete them. It's up to you.)

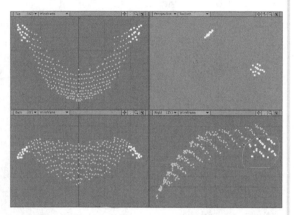

Figure 20-53: As each section is finished, select the next group of one-point polys.

All of this will probably take a while, especially if you haven't done this kind of thing before. But eventually you'll have a full head of hair guides, ready to convert into realistic hair.

24. If you aren't using the style-as-you-go method, select all the one-point polys in the **Root** layer, paste them into the **Wig** layer, and merge the points now. If you decide that you want to style it, go ahead.

If you want to practice making the guides some other time, and just want to use them for now, you can find the SasLiteHair-End.lwo model on the DVD. (On the other hand, if you really want to dissect the procedure, there's a model called SasLiteHairGuides.lwo there too, which has layers for each step of the process.)

25. When you decide that your wig is as good as you can get it without a test render, then it's time to do exactly that! If your wig is too large for SasLite to handle (25,001 polys, remember), you'll have to split it.

Splitting Hairs to Work with SasLite Limits

Lasso the section you want to remove, and then tap the <]> key to select all the connected polys. (Anything without a root isn't going to work, remember, so you need to keep the whole length of each individual guide together.) Cut the section and paste it into another layer. Each layer will need to have its own instance of SasLite. Good thing you can copy/paste the options, huh?

How you split it, of course, is up to you. In the image, since it's a wig for a balding man, I'm splitting it so that I have the possibility of an additional hairline. It's always a good idea to split it in some fashion that allows extra versatility, if you can.

When it's as ready as can be, save the head and load it into Layout.

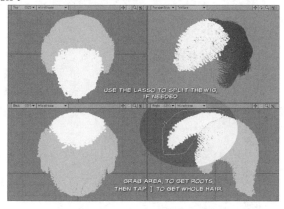

Figure 20-55: If you need to split the wig, try to do it so you get extra versatility out of it.

Rendering the Hair

1. As always, you will need to apply the **SasLite** displacement to the Wig layer in the Object Properties window, as well as the **SasLite** pixel filter in the Processing tab of the Effects panel.

2. Open the options for the plug-in, and choose **Make long hair using guide chains** from the list on the left. Once again, you'll need to type the name of the surface into the Surface Name(s) field. Unless you make a typing error, you should see the green numbers change, so the correct number of surfaces is displayed on the left. (In this case, 1/2. The second surface is Root.)

3. Set your parameters however you want them. Figure 20-56 shows what I'm using for this particular model, if you want to copy them.

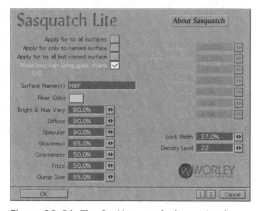

Figure 20-56: The SasLite panel when using long hair guides.

4. Once that's done, you need to make a test render and see if your hard work is resulting in the hair you envisioned. But if you render now, you'll see the polychain hair guides as well as the hair. That's probably not what you want.

So, with the Object Properties window still open, click on the **Render** tab, and set Object Dissolve to **100%**. That won't have any effect on SasLite, but it will cause LightWave to ignore the guides when it renders. (Don't forget to disable the shadowing as well to save render time.)

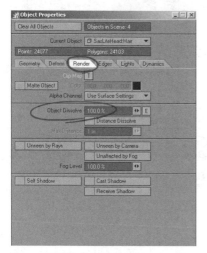

Figure 20-57: Set Object Dissolve to 100% to hide the long hair guides.

5. Tap <**F9**>, and see what you've got. If you need to go back and tweak the guides, do that and make another

render. Keep going, checking from all the sides that will be visible in your final render, until you have what you want. (Don't be afraid to copy and paste sections of guides to duplicate them if there's a thin spot in the hair. Just be aware of the SasLite limits when you do.)

The whole process can take an hour or more, but the results are well worth it. (Besides, if you get a nice wig, you can often reuse it for other characters with a minimum of restyling.)

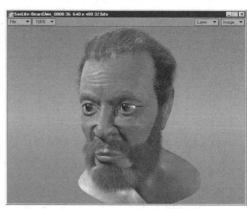

Figure 20-58: The finished wig-and-beard combo.

Long Hair Guides, the Sequel!

We're going to use another method of dealing with long hair guides to give this guy some eyelashes. This one is a lot faster, at least for me, but it does use a couple of third-party plug-ins. The good news is that you can download them from the web for free.

1. Select a couple of polys from the eyelid, where you want the eyelashes to grow. Then go to **Select | Select Loop** to get the "rim" of the whole lid. Tap the <}> (right curly bracket) key to expand the selection to the loops above and below that, so that there won't be distortion when they are isolated (just like we did for the head). Copy and paste into a new layer.

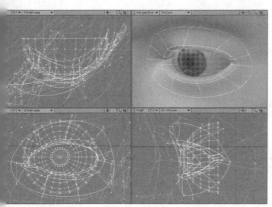

Figure 20-59: Select the polys for the lashes, and the es next to them.

2. Freeze the polys (<**Ctrl**>+<**d**>). Select two of the polys on the new edge, just as you did before, and **Select Loop** again. Then **Smooth Shift** the whole loop (<**F**>), but don't resize or move it in any way. Just click in a viewport and drop the tool. Deselect the polys, then tap <**m**> to merge the points. That will leave you with several rows of two-point polys.

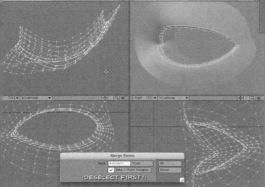

Figure 20-60: Select the edge loop, Smooth Shift, deselect, and Merge Points.

3. Usually those are something that you just delete, but we're going to use a

free plug-in from D-Storm called **Poly2Curves** to make them into a spline, which we'll then use to rail clone a lash. (You can download the plug-in from the D-Storm plug-in site at http://www.dstorm.co.jp/english/index.htm.)

4. Select the **2 Vertices** polys from the Polygon Statistics panel (click the + in the line), tap <**"**> (double quote) to invert the selection, and delete the polys. We don't need them any more. (It will look like you've selected everything, but you really haven't. Check the Statistics panel after deleting and you'll see the two-point poly chains are left.)

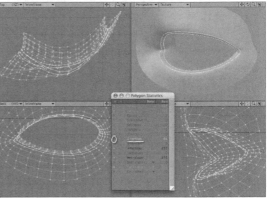

Figure 20-61: Select the two-point polys from the Statistics panel.

5. Select the "extra" one (whichever one you choose), and delete it. Then run the **Poly2Curves** plug-in from the **Utilities | Plugins | Additional** menu. (See Chapter 27 for details on adding plug-ins.) That will make each poly into its own tiny little curve. Merge them into one long curve by tapping <**Z**> (**Detail | Polygons | Merge Polys**).

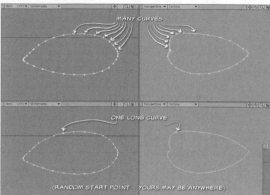

Figure 20-62: A string of little curves converted into one long curve.

6. With the curve still selected, tap the <**Spacebar**> to toggle to Points mode, select the two points in the corners of the eyes, and tap <**Ctrl**> + <**1**> (**Multiply | Subdivide | Split**) twice to split the curve into two pieces.

Figure 20-63: Select these points, and split the curve.

7. Use the <**Spacebar**> to toggle back, and you should see three of the little diamonds that Modeler uses to show the beginning of a curve: the two you just made, and the one that resulted from merging the polys.

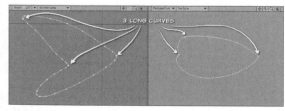

Figure 20-64: Three curves.

8. Click on whichever lid has only one spline to deselect it. That will leave both splines on the other lid still selected. Tap <**Z**> again to merge those two splines, and you'll have two curves that perfectly match the eyelids, all ready to go!

Figure 20-65: Merge the remaining two curves.

9. Take the top eyelid curve and paste it into an empty layer. Delete any points that go too far into the corners of the eyes, where you don't want lashes to grow. Select the curve, copy it, and paste it back into the same layer, so you have two curves.

10. Reshape the curve that's still selected. I use the Stretch and Magnet tools, but you can use any tools you find most convenient. You're making a curve that describes the "trim line" you want the lashes to have. Remember that the actual hairs will look shorter than this, so make it a bit farther from the lid than the desired lash length. Make sure that both of these curves start at the outer edge of the lid. (The diamond should be at the outer corner when the curves are selected.) If they don't, tap the <**f**> key to flip them.

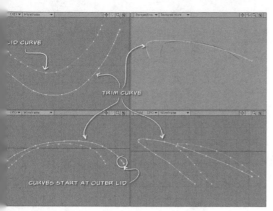

Figure 20-66: Upper lid, eyelid, and trim curves.

11. When you are pleased with them, put them in the background and open a new foreground layer. (The fastest way to do that is to click on another layer as background, and then Invert Layers using the <'> (single quote) key.)

12. Draw a third curve, in the shape you want the lash to have, and orient it so that it appears to grow from the outer corner of the eyelid. Match it to the curves as closely as you easily can, with the diamond that shows where the lash curve starts placed behind the curve, into the eyelid. (It doesn't have to be exact, but close is nice.) If you need to readjust the "trim" curve, then do so. (See Figure 20-67.)

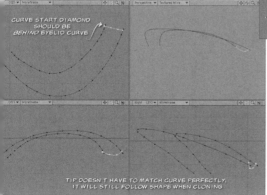

Figure 20-67: Position the first lash on the eyelid curve.

13. After you are happy with all three curves, put the lash curve layer in the foreground and the layer with the lid and trim curves in the background. Then go to **Multiply | Duplicate | More | Rail Clone...** to open the Rail Clone: Multiple panel. (See Figure 20-68.)

14. Choose whether you want to make clones by Length (evenly spaced) or Knots (weighted according to where the points are in the lid and trim curves), choose **Uniform** so you can determine how many clones there will be, and type in the number of lash guides you want, minus one. (You already have one, remember?) Leave **Oriented** and **Scaling** both enabled so the lash will change orientation and size as it conforms to the rails, and click **OK**.

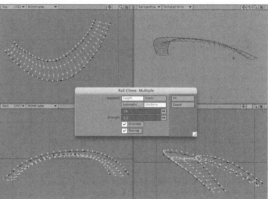

Figure 20-68: The Rail Clone: Multiple panel.

Presto! Perfect lashes, all set to go. But they are curves, and you need polychains with roots. Fortunately, there is a plug-in for that, called CurveToPolychain, written by Terry Ford. (In fact, there's more than one, but this is the best I'm aware of. It's available for both Mac and PC. Thanks to Richard Brak for compiling the Mac version and to Terry for allowing us to use it in this book.) You can find it on the companion DVD, or download it for free from http://www.aooe58.dsl.pipex.com/htm /frameplugins.shtml.

15. Run the **CurveToPolychain** plug-in. (If you haven't made a button for it, look in the Utilities | Plugins | Additional menu.) Type in the name for the Chain surface and one for the Root surface, or choose them from the drop-down menus. Then choose your segments and so on as you have for the last several plug-ins. Disable **Replace curves** if you want the polychains to be made in a new layer (in case you want to preserve the original curves). Disable **Merge/Unify poly chains** if you don't have any that overlap. (If there's nothing to merge and you leave it enabled, it's possible that Modeler will crash.)

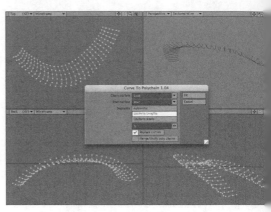

Figure 20-69: CurveToPolychain panel.

16. Click **OK**, and there you go!

17. Repeat the process for the bottom lid, mirror both sets of lashes across the head, and you're done.

18. Take them into Layout, apply **SasLite**, and render to see how they look. Tweak if necessary. You know the drill by now!

Eyelash Settings and Refinements

The values I used are shown in Figure 20-70. Coarseness and Frizz are high because these tiny chains make very fine hair, and lashes look more realistic to me if they aren't too straight. A high Lock Width spreads them out more around the guides, both vertically and horizontally, so they don't have the all-lined-up look of artificial lashes.

For close-ups, or more realistic lashes, you can add points to the rails where you want them to grow more thickly. (Do this before you copy them to make the trim curves, of course, to save work.) Then clone using Knots, not Length, to get a more realistic distribution of lashes.

You might also want two sets of guides, one on top of the other, if you need

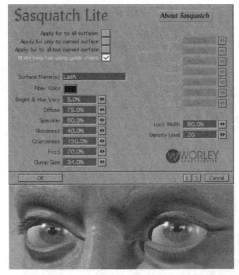

Figure 20-70: The SasLite panel, and the lashes it makes.

extra-heavy lashes; for instance in a glamour shot, where you want the model to appear "made up." That will enable you to control the length and clump size more easily.

Making Eyebrows

Eyebrows can be created using either fur or long hair guides. We're going to use long hair guides so that I can show you one more technique for creating them.

1. We are going to begin, once again, by selecting the area of the face that contains the polys the brow will grow from, and one poly out from that in all directions (<}>).

2. Paste the selection into another layer, then tap <o> to open the General Options window, and change Subpatch Divisions to 5. (That should give you enough points, without giving you too many.) Now freeze (<Ctrl>+<d>) the polys.

3. Tap <k> to kill the polys, so there's nothing left but points, and use the lasso to draw the brow in those points. The "brow" should light up, leaving the rest unselected. Take a look, and refine the selection if you are so inclined. When it's perfect, tap <">> (double quote) to invert the selection. Take one more look, refine if necessary, and delete the selected points. That leaves you with just the brow points.

jure 20-71: Choose the points for the eyebrow guides ▸m the frozen group.

4. Mirror them, so you have brow points on both sides of the face, and give them a little jitter. (Very little in the Z-axis, if you head is set up like most (facing down the Z-axis); you don't want them to wander away from the skin.) Hide the points on your left (select and <->).

5. Put that layer in the background, a new layer in the foreground, and draw an eyebrow hair in the middle of the brow. You just need one, but don't forget to shape it in all three dimensions. Mirror it, so you'll have a hair for the other brow, too. (If you're using the Numeric panel to make sure that your mirror is at 0 on all three axes, all you need to do is choose **Activate** and hit <**Return**> twice. The panel will use the same parameters as the last time.)

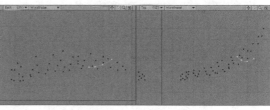

Figure 20-72: Make a single hair in the middle of the brow.

6. Hide the hair on your left, make sure the points are in the background, and go to **Multiply | Duplicate | More | Point Clone Plus...** to open the Point Clone Plus+ panel. This allows you to make clones of the hair wherever you have a point in the background layer.

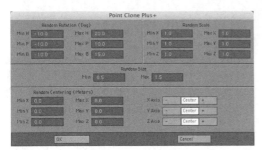

Figure 20-73: The Point Clone Plus+ panel.

7. Since this is an older man, I'm going to give him sort of wild brows. So, I'm setting a **Random Rotation** value in all three axes. Not much, but some. Put negative values in the Min fields and positive values in the Max fields.

8. I don't want the scaling to change, so I'm leaving all of those at the default, but I do want some size difference. The values for Random Size are multiples of the size, so 1.0 is no change, 0.5 is half the size it was, and 2.0 is twice the size. (Think of them as percentages.) I'm going to go 50% (**0.5**) in both directions. Leave the rest of the settings at the default, and click **OK**. Instant hair curves!

9. Tap < | > to toggle hidden, so the curve clones are hidden and the lone curve isn't. Tap <'> (single quote) to invert foreground and background, and then < | > again so the left side points are visible.

10. Invert again, to put the hair in the foreground and points in the background, and run the plug-in once more. It will remember the last settings used, so you don't have to. Unless you didn't use symmetrical settings, of course. In that case, you'll have to mirror the values. In other words, if you used a Min H of **–10** and a Max H of **20**, you'll need a Min H of **–20** and a Max H of **10**.

11. There you go! Unhide everything. You should have two unique eyebrows. Similar, but different enough to be realistic. Run **CurveToPolychain**, and you're ready to take it into Layout for testing.

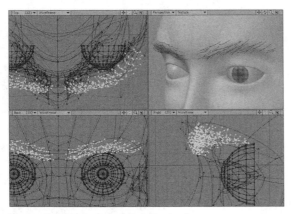

Figure 20-74: Bushy eyebrow curves!

Tips for SasLite Eyebrow Settings

You should be familiar enough with the settings by now that you can choose your own parameters. You might want to push the Coarseness value beyond 100%. You might also want a very small Clump Size and a very large Lock Width so the hairs look like they are growing individually. If you are interested, you can see the parameters I used by checking the SasLiteHead.lws scene on the companion DVD. You can also look at each step by opening the SasLite-Eyebrows.lwo model and checking out the layers.

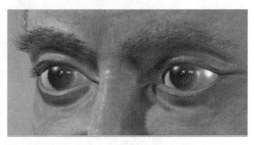

Figure 20-75: The finished brows and lashes.

Figure 20-76: The finished head.

Those three methods should give you a good jumping-off point for deciding how you want to make long hair guides. You can mix and match them, of course; for instance, Rail Extrude using a handful of guides for a lower layer of hair (for coverage), and then get a spline from the head, and use Rail Clone to make the hairline hairs. Or use Point Clone Plus for a short, spiky style, or use the spline and several circles around the head to gather the hair into a ponytail.

Or you can make straight guides, take them into Layout, and use dynamics to shape them. (Things like Wind, Collision, and Gravity allow the hair to flow naturally, without the drudgery of shaping each guide manually.)

The point is, you can do this. It's not as scary or difficult as you may have been led to believe, and the results can be fantastic.

Conclusion

In this chapter we've seen how SasLite can be used for everything from shag rugs to human hair. SasLite is a tremendous tool for creating all manner of hairy and furry objects. Hopefully, this chapter has taken some of the fear and intimidation out of this amazing tool. Now it's time to let your imagination run wild and try it out for yourself!

> **Note**
>
> Once you start using SasLite, it can be hard to stop. If you find yourself becoming a fur fanatic, I would encourage you to purchase the full version of Sasquatch. It has a wealth of additional features not found in SasLite that will allow you to take your fur and hair simulation to an entirely new level!

Chapter 21

Advanced Skills: Adaptive Pixel Subdivision

LightWave was one of the first 3D packages to offer a subdivision surface system. Originally a simple modeling tool for refining a mesh into a denser, smoother one, what was known at the time as "Metaforming" gave the artist the ability to create more organic geometry from simpler forms. When LightWave 6 came out, subdivision surfaces had become something else, and offered the artist the ability to not only model simple geometry, but now animate this same simple geometry and freeze it down in either display or render time (or both).

The system was limited to freezing down a mesh to one overall density. While this worked great 99% of the time, there were times where this would generate huge amounts of additional geometry that weren't needed.

With the release of LightWave v9, technology has stepped forward once again! **Adaptive Pixel Subdivision** is what its

Figure 21-1: Simple geometry to more organic geometry.

name suggests — adaptive! We still have the good old subdivision surfaces we've come to love over the years, but now we have the ability to completely control the level of subdivision in various ways, creating more complex geometry where it's needed.

Catmull-Clark vs. Subpatch

In Chapter 15, we looked at the newly added ability to use not just one, but two different ways in which a mesh can be subpatched.

Subpatch format is LightWave's native format. It uses points on corners to smooth and shape things; however, this only allows us to use three or four-sided polys. Anything higher (or lower) doesn't work.

Catmull-Clark format calculates the subdivision using edges. The advantage of this is that it can subpatch n-gons — polygons with more than four sides! Because it uses edges, it can also sharpen edges without losing form, and generates a smoother look than the Subpatch format.

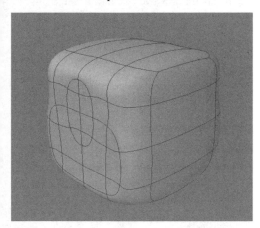

Figure 21-2: Catmull-Clark subdivides n-gons with ease.

The reason I mention these again in this chapter is that both of these systems subdivide geometry; however, the way they calculate the subdivision is very different. Catmull-Clark creates a much more complex mesh using the same subpatch values we may have used for the older system. This can lead to crazy amounts of polygons being created and crashing your machine if you don't take care!

The best way to show the difference is to look at the wireframe densities of two identical objects, each using a different subdivision system.

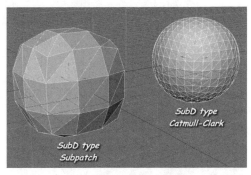

Figure 21-3: Two identical objects with a subpatch level of 3, but different types of subpatching.

Note that in Figure 21-3, both items use a subpatch level of 3. However, while the Subpatch version of the object subdivides each polygon into nine smaller polygons, the Catmull-Clark version subdivides each polygon into 64 smaller polygons. As you can see, Catmull-Clark objects are subdivided quite a bit more, even when they use the same subpatch level. The division of Subpatch polygons is calculated by taking the square of the subpatch level. For example, a subpatch level of 3 would be calculated as 3^2, or 3 x 3, which equals 9. But the division of Catmull-Clark polygons is calculated by taking 4 to the power of the subpatch level. Hence, a subpatch level of 3 would be calculated as 4^3, or 4 x 4 x 4, which equals 64.

That's a massive difference, and one that you should be aware of when setting subpatch levels for rendering. However, it's also a great reason to start looking at the new system offered up by LightWave v9.

743

Adaptive Subdivision at Work

Adaptive Pixel Subdivision gives us a third way to subdivide a mesh. In previous versions of LightWave, we simply set the Render and Display subpatch levels, as shown in Figure 21-4. It was an easy way to subpatch, but it meant the entire object got the same amount of subpatching. If we needed a close-up of a head, for example, cranking up the subpatch level to get a smoother appearance was easy, but it sometimes meant creating thousands of extra polys that were never in the shot.

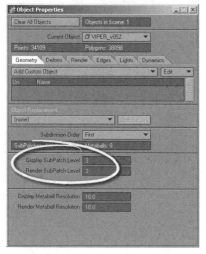

Figure 21-4: In previous versions of LightWave, the geometry of a subpatched object was set with two values.

Now in LightWave v9, we have more options. More efficient subpatching means better management of memory and higher-quality results. As we can see in Figure 21-5, we have a *selectable* method for Render subpatching.

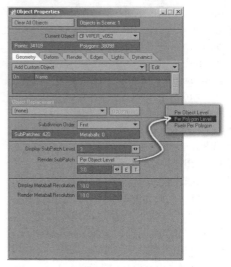

Figure 21-5: LightWave v9's new subpatch options.

Note

The Display SubPatch Level setting still uses the old approach of a single, non-adaptive value for setting the subpatch density. Adaptive Subdivision needs to calculate subdivision density based on whatever types of rules we may specify, and it's something that can't always be worked out in real time (and if it was, it would seriously bog down the performance of Layout).

So what kind of control do these new modes give us? Let's take a quick look.

Per Object Level

This mode is exactly the same as the previous versions of LightWave, where all the polygons in an object are subpatched at the same density. However, unlike the previous versions, LightWave v9 adds the ability to control this overall subpatch density through either envelopes or textures.

In fact, it's a great way to control the level of detail (LOD) for our subpatched objects. High levels of detail aren't really necessary when the object is far away from the camera. Let's look at a simple example of how we can control the LOD here.

1. Load the scene **Scenes\Chapter 21\lod.lws**. This scene contains a simple subpatched sculpture toward which the camera moves. The subpatch level remains the same throughout the animation, but obviously it would make sense to have fewer polygons when the item is farther away from the camera and more when it is closer.

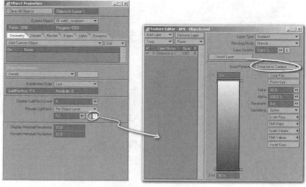

Figure 21-7: Distance to camera gradient.

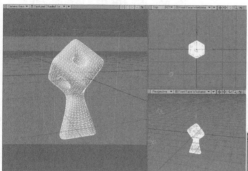

Figure 21-6: A sculpture of immense detail.

Note

To see the density of the subpatch object as seen in Figure 21-6, set the viewport to display using Texture Shaded Solid Wireframe. This displays the texture object with the subpatched wireframe mesh edges over the top.

2. Select the **subD_sculpture** object, and open its Object Properties window (**<p>**). Click on the **T** below the Render SubPatch setting to open the Texture Editor, and change Layer Type to **Gradient**. Input Parameter needs to be set to **Distance to Camera**. Set the

Value for the top key to **10.0**. Add another key at the bottom of the gradient, setting its Parameter to **10 m** and Value to **1.0**.

3. Make sure the Frame Slider is on frame 0, and then do an **<F9>**. Check out the polygon count in Figure 21-8. At a distance of 10 m or more from the camera, the level of detail of this object will be a subdivision of 1.0.

Figure 21-8: This far away we don't need so many polygons.

4. Now adjust the Frame Slider to frame 40 and do an **<F9>**. Note the change in polygon count! The detail starts to be added as the object gets closer to the camera.

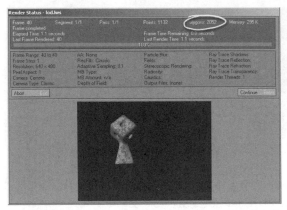

Figure 21-9: At frame 40, things start to get more detail.

5. Do another <F9> at frame 60. We can see just how the subdivision levels have been cunningly controlled by this gradient!

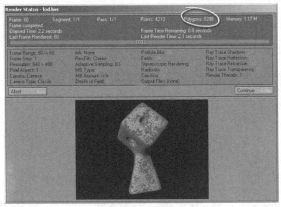

Figure 21-10: Frame 60 — meaty detail now!

Per Polygon Level

While we could control the quality of the mesh dynamically in Per Object Level mode, it did mean the entire object's subdivision was changed. In this second mode, Per Polygon Level, each and every polygon can have its *own* subpatch level! Imagine being able to get denser subpatching where we want it on an object. For example, the edges of a UFO could contain more detail

than the hard flat top of the ship. The ears, nose, and smaller areas of a character could have more geometry where it was needed, or perhaps the edges of a bouncing ball could be denser based on the angle to the camera.

Here's a quick demonstration to show you just how this works.

1. Load the scene **Scenes\Chapter 21\detail_teapot.lws**. This scene contains a simple subpatched teapot object, set up to render the edges of each polygon. This way, we can see the density of the teapot in our rendered images. At this stage, the object still uses the old Per Object mode, and it's set to a pretty low subpatch value of 1.0. Press <F9> and let's check out the mesh density.

Figure 21-11: Overall density is low.

Can you see the issue here? A common problem with subpatching is that we need a subpatch level high enough to prevent the edges from becoming faceted and jaggy like they are here, which screams that this is low-quality CG. While this is a simple example, the issue becomes more important when rendering close-ups of an object, or at resolutions for print and film work where faceted edges would make clients cringe.

The only way to improve this would of course be to increase the density of the subpatch level, but increased subpatch levels mean a ton of extra polys, which not only eats up our precious memory but also increases the render times.

The teapot has a specially painted weight map that targets the areas in need of more detail. Let's see how we can use the new adaptive capabilities of LightWave to generate a more efficient setup.

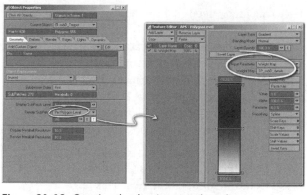

Figure 21-12: Creating the density control gradient.

2. Let's select the **subD_Teapot** object, and open its Object Properties window (**<p>**). Set the Render SubPatch mode to **Per Polygon Level** and then click on the **T** button to open the Texture Editor. Change Layer Type to **Gradient**. Set Input Parameter to **Weight Map**, then select the **TP_subD_details** map from the Weight Map pop-up. Add a key in the middle of the gradient, and set its Parameter to **0%** and Value to **1.0**. Add a key at the bottom of the gradient and set its Parameter to **100%** and Value to **10**.

3. Let's do another **<F9>** and see what this does. While the curved forms of the teapot are denser, the main body of the teapot is less dense as extra geometry is not needed here.

Figure 21-13: Very cool! More detail where needed, less where not.

This is just *one* way of creating an adaptive mesh. We have full control over the subpatch density through painting weight maps and using gradients.

Creating a Landscape

Let's look at another great use for Per Polygon subdivision — creating dynamic and exciting landscapes!

Landscapes can span vast areas, and to get enough detail we may need hundreds of thousands of polygons. How about dynamically controlling the amount of geometry based on the distance from the camera? Like our Per Object Level example, there's not much sense in rendering distant mountains containing thousands of polys. Let's see how a Per Polygon subpatch system can help control the level of detail for a single landscape mesh.

This mode needs a mesh built from a handful of polygons. A heavily subdivided single polygon can work great as a base for creating a landscape, but it won't be too much use given that the subpatch level is set to Per Polygon. Build that landscape, however, from a 20 x 20 grid of subpatched geometry, and now we're cooking! Let's check this out.

1. Load the scene **Scenes\Chapter 21\ dynamic_landscape.lws**. This is a simple scene with a basic subpatched object, just yearning to become something landscapey! The object is set up at a subdivision level of 10 to give it plenty of additional geometry, and also has rendered edges active so that we can see the density in our render.

2. Let's start by converting this item to something more than a flat shape. Select the **SubD_Landscape** object and open its Object Properties window (**<p>**). Select the **Deform** tab and click the **T** next to Displacement Map to open the Texture Editor.

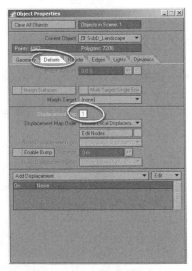

Figure 21-14: Set up a displacement map.

3. Change Layer Type to **Procedural Texture** and then select a Procedural Type of **Dented**. Set its Texture Value to **0.2**. Set the texture size under the Scale tab at the bottom of the Texture Editor to **500 mm** all around, and the Position to **X = 0 m, Y = 795 mm**, and **Z = –200 mm**. Finally, set the Rotation to **H = 90** and **P = 90** degrees. Click the **Use Texture** button to close the Texture Editor. This should give us a pretty cool-looking mountainscape to play with.

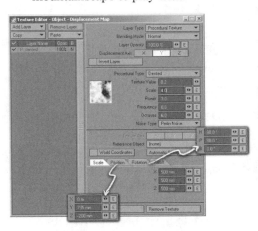

Figure 21-15: Setting up the procedural.

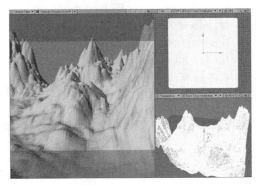

Figure 21-16: The new landscape, ready to roll…

4. Now, let's do a quick **<F9>** and check out the density of the landscape mesh. Not bad, but it's got an even density, even in the far-off mountains!

Figure 21-17: Rendered, but an even density.

Perhaps the foreground landscape could do with a little more detail, but that would entail upping the subpatch level from its current setting of 10. It would be nice to perhaps triple this value to give the landscape some real form, but this would hugely increase the overall density of the object. In Figure 21-18, I did a quick render after increasing the subpatch levels to 30. We can see from the render information just how dense this has become, and worse still, just how much of my precious RAM was required to create this mesh!

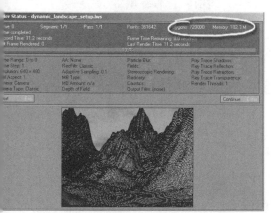

Figure 21-18: Upping the subpatch level to 30 eats RAM!

In reality, we'd only want to see the detail when the landscape got close to the camera. A great excuse to put the new Adaptive Subdivision to work! If you've tried this yourself just to see how a setting of 30 behaved, make sure that you return the subpatch levels back to 10 before continuing.

5. Let's select the **SubD_Landscape** object, open its Object Properties window (**<p>**), and change the Geometry | Render SubPatch setting to **Per Polygon Level**. Click on the **T** next to the value to open the Texture Editor, and then change Layer Type to **Gradient**. Set Input Parameter to **Distance to Camera**, and then set the Start key's Value setting to **30**. Change the End of the gradient from the default value of 10 m to **500 mm** (because the landscape mesh isn't to a realistic scale), as shown in Figure 21-19. Add another key into the gradient and set its Parameter to **500 mm** with a Value of **5.0** to lower the density as the landscape gets farther away from the camera.

6. Press **<F9>**. Let's see the difference this makes for our landscape.

Check out the use of memory as well as creation of extra geometry in Figure 21-20. Per Polygon Level is a great solution for some of those dense landscape and CG world projects, allowing much larger sized landscapes with more detail to be created without the huge memory requirement.

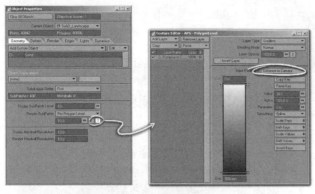

Figure 21-19: Density control based on distance to camera.

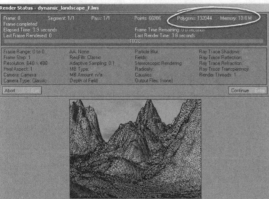

Figure 21-20: The new density.

resolution for a print job, and letting LightWave dynamically subdivide the polygons to make sure your objects in your print res render look nice and slick. This is what Pixels Per Polygon is all about.

Figure 21-21: Set Subdivision Order to Last for Pixels Per Polygon to work.

Pixels Per Polygon

The **Pixels Per Polygon** option subdivides the geometry so that each polygon covers approximately an area no larger than a specified amount of pixels in a rendered image. Making this value smaller will create more geometry. For example, subdividing at a level of one pixel per polygon will subdivide so that each pixel in your render is represented by roughly a polygon.

Now this is something very cool: Imagine creating a complex subpatched object that gets smoother as the item becomes larger in the rendered image. Imagine rendering a TV res frame at a much higher

Note

This mode doesn't work properly unless you set Subdivision Order to Last. Subdivided objects set to First are treated as static objects and not dynamically updated.

Let's look at an example of Pixels Per Polygon in use.

1. Load the scene **Scenes\Chapter 21\ppp_asteroid.lws**. A lone asteroid is flying through space toward the camera. The asteroid is a simple SubD mesh, but has a node-based displacement attached to it to give it extra detail.

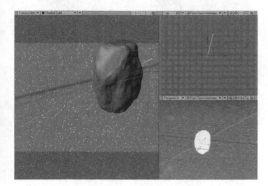

Figure 21-22: A lone asteroid.

The asteroid has been subpatched at a level of 3 (which is equivalent to 27,648 polygons), and stays this level throughout the animation. Obviously, when the asteroid is tiny in the distance, it's a waste of memory and render time to create a lot of polygons that we never see. Let's see how we can use Pixels Per Polygon to optimize the asteroid at a distance, and increase the quality of the asteroid as it passes close to the camera.

2. Select the **subD_asteroid** object, and open its Object Properties window (**<p>**). Change the Render SubPatch setting to **Pixels Per Polygon** and set the value to **32**. This will subdivide the asteroid's polygons by determining the size in the render. Each polygon will be subdivided until it meets the 32 pixels-per-polygon ratio.

Figure 21-23: Render SubPatch set to 32 pixels per polygon.

3. Leave the Object Properties window open so that we can see the Points and Polygons count as shown in Figure 21-24. Make sure that the Frame Slider is set to frame 0, then press **<F9>** and watch the value change as the object is subdivided to match the polygons-per-pixel ratio (see Figure 21-25).

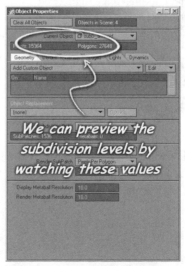

Figure 21-24: The Properties window shows us the object's size in polys.

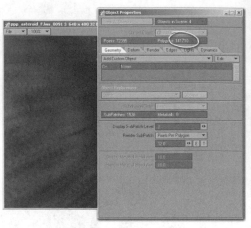

Figure 21-25: At frame 0 the asteroid is tiny, as is the polygon count.

Figure 21-26: Frame 91 shows extreme subdivision close-up.

4. Scrub through to frame 91 in the animation where the asteroid gets extremely close, then do another <F9> and watch the polygon count again. Quite a difference!

Once the frame is rendered, the polygon count quickly returns to its original display level. As you can see, we didn't have to worry about controlling the density by hand for this project and have let LightWave make sure that there is enough geometry for the asteroid to look its best.

> **Note**
>
> If we must use a Subdivision Order of First to create extra geometry for displaced objects, we obviously can't use Pixels Per Polygon due to its requirement to have a Subdivision Order of Last. Instead, consider using the Per Object or Per Polygon modes, and controlling the density with a texture or envelope.

Conclusion

We learned in this chapter that we now have adaptive ways to subpatch our objects. Finally, we're able to dynamically create more detail where we need it and less where we don't, thereby saving not only render times, but precious memory for those huge projects where every byte of RAM is critical. We can also make sure those low-res renders look great at print resolution, and that there's plenty of geometry to ensure that objects don't go all jaggy and faceted when they get close. Now is your chance to create your own virtual world or add detail to that old complex model with more efficiency.

Chapter 22

Advanced Skills: Dynamics

One of the most highly touted features of LightWave is Dynamics, which was added back in version 8. Dynamics consist of hard and soft body simulators, particle emitters, natural force generators, collision objects, and effect linkers, each with the ability to interact with the others. The attention given to these tools is well deserved. Dynamics effects allow you to imbue your objects with real-world physical properties such as weight, air resistance, and gravity. They allow you to create everything from realistic-looking clothes to debris-filled explosions. Complex effects that would take hours to animate by hand can now be done in a matter of minutes. In this chapter, we'll look at these incredible tools and cover the essential information you need to get started using them.

An Introduction to Dynamics

When we talk about dynamics, we are referring to the simulation of real-world physical properties within an artificial 3D environment. As strange as it may seem, to a 3D application such as LightWave, a leaf is just as heavy as a car and concrete is as permeable as water. That's because 3D applications cannot differentiate between objects. It's all just points and polygons in the eyes of the program. Therefore, if we want to simulate real-world phenomena, we have to tell our software about the unique characteristics of each object. We have to tell LightWave that a leaf is light, a car is heavy, water is permeable, and concrete is not. We do this by adding a dynamic property to an object that we wish to give dynamic properties. This can be done by opening the Object Properties window (<**p**>) and clicking on the **Add Dynamic** pop-up menu on the Dynamics tab. Left-click on any dynamic in the list to display its properties.

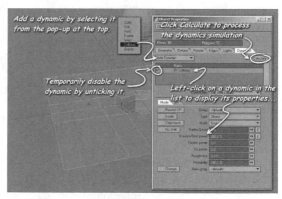

Figure 22-1: Dynamics options for items in Layout.

There are seven types of dynamic properties.

Personal Dynamics

The first four are what we'll refer to as "personal dynamics." They directly affect the *individual* object to which they are applied. Back in Chapter 13, we looked at one type of personal dynamic — a particle emitter. Particles are great, but they're just one part of the overall dynamics system in LightWave. There are four dynamics in this personal grouping.

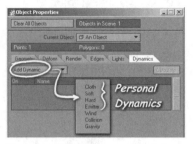

Figure 22-2: The four personal dynamics.

Cloth

Don't let the name fool you: ClothFX isn't just for clothing. This is LightWave's full-featured soft body dynamics engine, capable of simulating everything from the billowing of a superhero's cape to the violent splash of water on the surface of a pool.

Soft

SoftFX is a soft body simulator well suited to producing "secondary animation" for your objects. For example, you could animate a character running, and then apply SoftFX to get the stomach to jiggle and bounce in response to the motion.

Hard

HardFX is LightWave's rigid body dynamics engine. It allows you to simulate hard objects such as metal and stone. You can use HardFX to create the explosion of a spaceship or the breaking of a window as a baseball crashes through it.

Emitter

The Emitter dynamic turns your object into a particle emitter. Adding this dynamic property to your object gives you more options than the stand-alone emitters we looked at back in Chapter 13, such as the ability to generate particles from the object's points or to cover the entire surface of an object with particles.

Social Dynamics

There are three dynamics tools that we will refer to as "social dynamics." They affect the behavior of *other* dynamic objects within the scene. We also looked a little at these back in Chapter 13, where we saw how they added some influencing forces to give our particles some life.

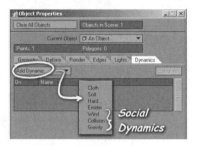

Figure 22-3: The three social dynamics.

Wind

The Wind dynamic allows you to apply a repelling force to your object. As a social dynamic, Wind does not affect the object to which it is applied. Rather, it affects the other dynamic objects around it. For example, you could add Wind to the model of a fan, causing any hard, soft, or particle objects to be pushed away when they pass in front of it.

Collision

The Collision dynamic operates as an indicator to other dynamic objects. It tells hard bodies, soft bodies, and particles that they cannot pass through the polygons of the collision object. For example, if you applied HardFX to a ball and dropped it onto a ground plane, it would simply pass through the ground and continue falling. However, adding the Collision dynamic to the ground would cause the ball to bounce off its surface.

Gravity

The Gravity dynamic is similar to the Wind dynamic. It is a force that can be tied directly to an object. But where Wind is generally used as a repelling force, Gravity is used as an attracting force. It causes personal dynamic objects to be pulled toward it.

The Dynamics Community

When you add a dynamic property to an object, you are telling it what behavioral tendencies it will have. In essence, you are giving it a personality. Taken this way, the process of building a dynamics simulation can be seen as a form of social engineering. You begin by building a community — a *dynamics community* — where each object is given a personality and told how it should react to the other objects within the community.

Knowing the difference between the various dynamic properties (or personalities) is important. But knowing how they work *together* is equally (if not more) important. You see, when you assign a dynamic property to an object, you are really asking LightWave to perform a simulation of physics on the object. Physics is science that deals with matter (hard objects, soft objects, particles) and energy (wind, gravity, collision). But more specifically, physics deals with the *interactions* between the two.

Assigning a dynamic property to your object is not enough. You need to understand how each of the properties work together in order to produce a successful simulation.

Think about Newton's Third Law of Motion. It states that for every action there is an equal and opposite reaction. In terms of the dynamics community, we would say: *For every personal dynamic, you should also have a social dynamic to which it is accountable.*

Consider this: When you place a can of soda on your desk, the can doesn't fall straight to the ground because it collides with the desk. To build this as a dynamics simulation, you would apply HardFX to the can of soda and Collision to the desk. One without the other would cause the simulation to fail, but together they produce the desired results. You should keep this rule in mind as you build your dynamics community. When you add a personal dynamic, make sure that you have a social dynamic somewhere in your scene to which it is accountable. This brings me to the most important issue of all: When is it right to build a dynamics simulation and, more to the point, when is it not?

Communal Groups

Dynamics in LightWave can be associated with each other in groups. Groups allow dynamics to work together and not interfere with other dynamics in a scene. Say for instance you wanted a Wind effect to affect the flow of a curtain, but you didn't want it to affect the flow of a stream of particles being used to simulate a heavy rainstorm outside. We could group the curtain and wind together so that they worked exclusively.

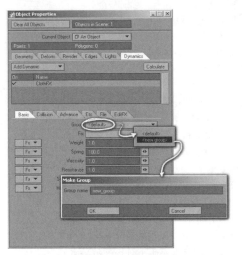

Figure 22-4: Grouping a dynamic is as simple as assigning it to a group.

There is one overall super group called *default* that makes the dynamic affect all groups, so you can still keep smaller groups working by themselves, but affect all of them by making global dynamic effects part of this uber-group, *default*.

Dynamic Decisions

Dynamics can be incredibly powerful, but they are far from foolproof. Just as people can be temperamental, so can dynamics.

There have been numerous occasions where making a single adjustment has sent my entire simulation into chaotic fits. And since every simulation is different, the problem can be difficult to troubleshoot. The important thing to consider, then, is whether or not it's worth the time to set up a dynamics simulation. You must ask yourself, "Can I do this by hand faster or easier than the time it's going to take to set up and tweak a simulation?" If I'm animating a basketball player shooting hoops, it would be easier for me to animate the ball by hand than it would be to set up a simulation. But if I were animating a pool hall junkie shooting a game of eight-ball, that would be a different story. Animating the complex interaction of each ball on the pool table while accurately replicating its rotation and constantly changing velocity would be time consuming to say the least. But it can be done with dynamics in a matter of minutes. So let this serve as sage advice to you. Dynamics are a lot of fun and can produce incredible results, but you don't want to find yourself in a production environment about to miss your deadline because you opted to use dynamics on an animation that could have been done just as easily by hand.

Applied Dynamics

In the following sections, we're going to look at some of the dynamic properties we can apply to items: ClothFX, SoftFX, and HardFX. Emitters were covered in detail back in Chapter 13; however, we'll also be using these to demonstrate a few of our other social dynamics such as Collision and Wind effects. We'll also be looking at how we can link items to dynamics, and how we can edit and fine-tune our simulations. These simulations will give you a taste of the power these tools offer.

Most dynamics have a lot of properties that can be tweaked. We'll only be looking at the options essential to the project we're working on. The manual and the online help system provide detailed information on each of these tools and you should refer to them when you need more information on a specific setting.

The knowledge you gain over the next few pages can be expanded upon to create many of the complex animations that you see in movies and on TV.

FX Browser

Although we won't be using this tool throughout this chapter, I did feel it important to make you aware of the FX Browser. This tool, accessed through **Utilities | Plugins | Additional | FX Browser**, provides a *central control center* through which you can add, edit, and calculate all the dynamics within a scene from one window.

The benefits of using this tool are that it can calculate the dynamics for individual groups in a dynamics community, rather than en masse as normal. It also provides options for calculating the dynamics in the background, and can save all precalculated motion files with one mouse click. Personally, I do not use this tool unless I'm working on a scene containing a fairly complex dynamics community. For most setups, I've found it often easier to just use the Dynamics tab on the Object Properties window (<**p**>). However, for complicated projects, this tool is of great value!

Anyway, bring up Layout and we'll begin our journey...

Collision Effects

Collisions are perhaps the most frequently used social dynamic, and it's not uncommon to have more than one of them in a simulation. Collision can cause dynamics to react when they touch, but they can also be told to trigger an event that can then be used to activate another dynamic effect. Let's take a look at how we can apply collision dynamics to give an object an "impactable" quality.

1. Load the scene **Rockface.lws** from Scenes\Chapter 22. This scene contains a simple rock face object, something we might expect to see torrents of icy cold water flowing over. Well, we don't have water, but how about some particles instead?

2. Add an **Items | Dynamic Obj | Particle** object to the scene to add some particles. Give it the name **WaterFlow** and click **OK** to create the emitter.

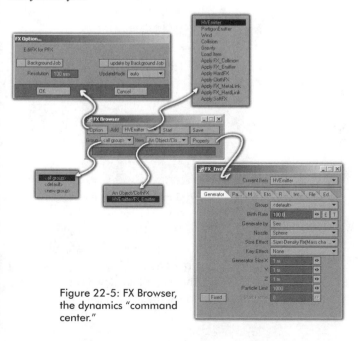

Figure 22-5: FX Browser, the dynamics "command center."

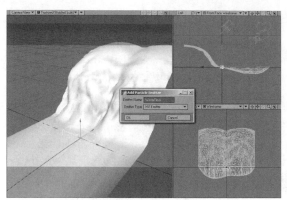

Figure 22-6: Adding the WaterFlow emitter.

3. The FX_Emitter properties window will pop up. Let's change a few of the settings for the WaterFlow emitter so that it behaves a little more like a torrent of water rushing from a spring high up in the mountains. Under the Generator tab, change the Birth Rate to **25.0**, and Generate by to **Frame**. We're going to tweak the Generator Size to **3 m** along the X-axis. Change the Size Effect option to **Size(no change)** to prevent any changes in the size of the emitter influencing the flow of particles. Lastly, increase the Particle Limit to **5000** to ensure we don't run out of water!

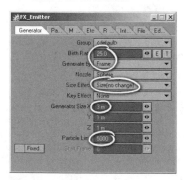

Figure 22-7: Tweaking the generator details for WaterFlow.

4. Under the Particle tab, let's change Particle Resistance to **0.0** to ensure the torrent of particles keeps flowing smoothly without any drag slowing them down. Change Life Time(frame) to **0.0** so that all particles live forever.

Figure 22-8: Create flowing water particles.

5. Let's change some settings under the Motion tab. Change the Velocity(m/s) for Z to **–5 m**. This gets our water flowing. To break up the particles so they become a little more chaotic and realistic in their motion, change Vibration(m/s) to **3.0**.

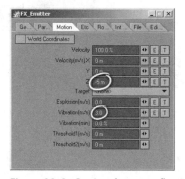

Figure 22-9: Getting the water flowing.

6. The last tweak we need to apply to our FX_Emitter is under the Etc tab. Set the Gravity(m/s^2) for Y to **–9.8 m** so that the water falls down the rock face, and doesn't float in midair.

Figure 22-10: A little gravity to help make water flow down the rock face and not float in the air.

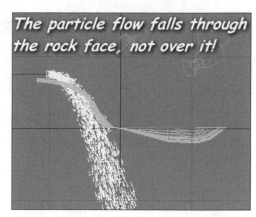

The particle flow falls through the rock face, not over it!

Figure 22-12: The rock face isn't solid, as far as LightWave is concerned!

7. Use the Move tool (<t>) to place the particle emitter at the top of the rock face (see Figure 22-11). If you want to position it exactly as I have, then you can tweak the numeric details using a Y value of **7.5 m** and a Z value of **10 m**. Make sure to create a key frame for the particle emitter at frame 0 to keep it in place.

8. Let's teach the **rockface** object that it is indeed impenetrable by selecting it, then opening the Object Properties window (<p>). Select the **Dynamics** tab, and select **Collision** from the Add Dynamic pop-up.

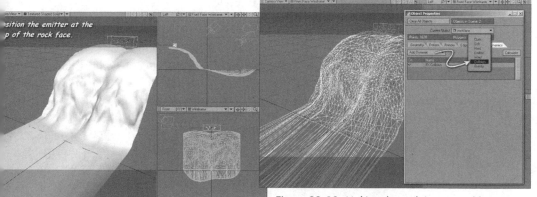

Figure 22-11: Setting the particle emitter at the top of the rock face.

Figure 22-13: Making the rock impenetrable.

Playing this scene works, but there's a small problem — the water particles fall through the rock face and not over it! (See Figure 22-12.) As we mentioned previously, this is because LightWave doesn't know that these polygons are actually constructed from a solid mass, nor that they should be impenetrable by our water flow.

Note

One of the cool things about basic particle dynamics like this in LightWave is that we can click the play button and tweak settings in real time, seeing the changes reflected in the viewport as the animation plays. Obviously, for more complex simulations with other dynamics or inter-particle interaction in the scene, this isn't possible in real time and needs to be calculated to be seen.

9. Left-click on **FX Collision** in the dynamics list box to display its properties.

The defaults are close to what we will use; however, let's add some tweaks to make things work right. Change Bounce/Bind power to **120%**, which will decrease the amount of bounce the particles will have when they hit the surface (a setting of 200% is a little too extreme for the water flow). The surface is rock, and we want the particles to flow a little less perfectly than they currently do. Give the surface a Roughness of **25%**, which will jitter the direction of each particle as it bounces off the surface of the rock. That should do it.

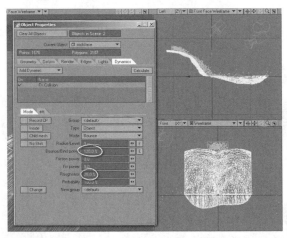

Figure 22-14: Getting the rock face to behave "solidly" for our particles.

Play the animation. The particles now collide and flow more realistically over the rock face! If you're feeling adventurous, go back to Chapter 14 and try your hand at using HyperVoxels to create a cool water effect for the particles. Don't forget to save the scene if you want to play with it later on.

Now that we've created our simulated waterfall, let's stop for a moment and think about how long it would have taken you to animate each of these particles by hand. You'll begin to realize just how powerful dynamics can be! The settings for a collision object play a large part in determining how it interacts with other dynamic objects in your scene. As we examine the remaining dynamic types, we'll spend more time talking about collision objects and their various settings. For now, however, we'll wrap up this discussion with a few helpful hints.

- A collision occurs when the *points* of an object come in contact with the *polygons* of another object. For this reason, it's best to have more points in the object that collides (often a personal dynamic) and fewer points in the object it collides with (the collision object).

- The Collision property works best when the object it's applied to is made up of quads. If you find that the collision detection is failing, even on simple geometry, try rebuilding the collision surface so that it is comprised of four-point polygons.

- Collision detection works differently depending on the type of object you're using. When the Collision dynamic is applied to a regular polygonal object with the default Type of Object, a *bounding box* will be used to determine the collision area. This works well in some cases, but not so well in others. Take, for example, Figure 22-15. You would expect the ball to fall through the hole in the ground, but it won't. Instead, the ball will fall *onto* the hole and bounce. To remedy this, we either need to change the collision Type for the ground to Object-Advanced, or convert our ground to a subpatch object. (Collision detection for subpatch objects is determined by the actual shape of the polygons in the object.)

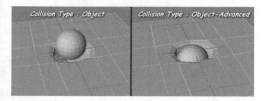

Figure 22-15: Ball falling into hole — or is it?

• A collision object containing huge amounts of geometry will increase calculation times. If a mesh happens to be close in form to a ball, box, or flat plane, it's faster to use a collision object Type that roughly resembles the geometry in this respect. Rather than adding the collision property to the object, create a new **Items | Dynamic Obj | Collision** object and move, stretch, and rotate it to match the object as closely as possible. Collision types like ball, box, and plane calculate a lot faster than a dense mesh of polygons (and can often be a little more accurate as well).

If you follow these hints, you should be able to avoid most situations that cause collision detection to fail.

Wind

We've looked at some of the basics of wind back in Chapter 13. LightWave v9 ships with a very cool new type of Wind dynamic called Animation Path wind. This Wind dynamic lets the animator lay out and animate a path for the wind to flow along, and then use this to influence personal dynamics within the scene. Let's take the opportunity to look at this cool new feature of LightWave v9, using particles to show the influence of this dynamic property.

1. Load **inner_journey.lws** from Scenes\ Chapter 22. A microscopic camera floats along the inside of a vein in a simple medical reconstruction scene.

2. The purpose of a vein is to convey fluids or materials, and to show this we'll use particles. Let's start out by adding some particles to flow inside this vein. Create a new **Items | Dynamic Obj | Particle**. Give it an Emitter Name of **Cells** and click **OK** to create the emitter.

3. Under the Generator tab of the FX_Emitter window, set Birth Rate to **10** and Generate by to **Frame**. Change the Generator Size to **300 mm** for X, Y, and Z.

Figure 22-16: Setting the particle emitter generator.

4. Click on the FX_Emitter **Particle** tab. Let's lighten up the particles by setting Particle Weight to **0.1**. Leave Particle Resistance at its default of **1.0**; however, set the **+-** below Particle Resistance to **0.25** to give each particle a random amount of resistance between 0.75 and 1.25. It's this resistance value that controls how influenced a particle will be by the wind dynamics in the scene, and randomizing it will help break things up and make them behave a little more naturally. Change Particle Size to **0.01**, and activate **Show Size** so that we can see the particles in the viewport.

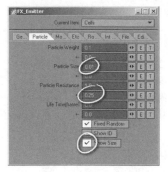

Figure 22-17: Setting the particle attributes.

If we play this animation, not much happens. The particles start to appear, but they're not flowing along the vein. To fix this, we'll use a Wind dynamic to influence the particle motion.

5. Add an **Items | Dynamic Obj | Wind** to the scene. Unless I'm planning on creating multiple wind dynamics in a scene, I'll leave this with its default name of **Wind**. In the FX_Wind window, set Power to **150%** and change Wind Mode to **Animation Path**. When asked to "Make Path Items?" click **OK**. This will create a couple of null objects, each named "handle" and parented to the wind. These nulls define key points along a curve that the wind uses as its path.

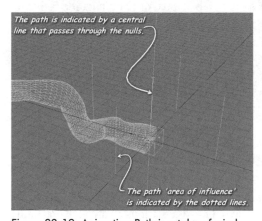

Figure 22-19: Animation Path is a tube of wind.

Playing this animation will get our particles influenced and moving, but obviously not in the right direction! For this next step, switch to a single viewport set to **Left (ZY)** so that we can align the wind's path using the profile of the vein object.

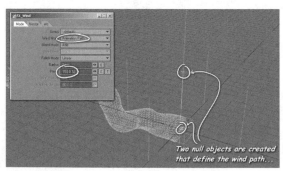

Figure 22-18: Creating the Animation Path wind.

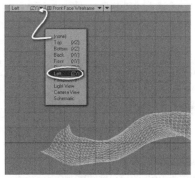

Figure 22-20: Switch to a single left viewport.

6. Select the null object **handle (2)** (the one above the wind emitter). Using the Move tool (<t>), move the null across and down to sit inside the vein as shown in Figure 22-21. Don't forget to keyframe the null in place at frame 0. (Or activate the Auto Key tool (<Shift>+<F1>) to take care of it for us. Just make sure the Time Slider is at frame 0 when you adjust the null when using Auto Key to prevent unwanted animation in the path!)

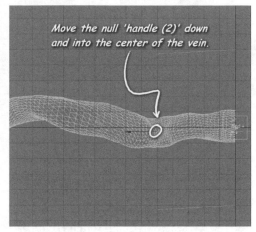

Figure 22-21: Move the null down and across to start the path.

Obviously, the path is a little more complex than a simple straight line between two nulls. We'll need to add some more handles to the animation path.

7. With **handle (2)** still selected, **Items | Add | Clone** the null (<Ctrl>+<c>) to create the next path handle. The clone becomes the selected item. Use the Move tool (<t>) to move the null along the vein as seen in Figure 22-22, and keyframe it in place at frame 0.

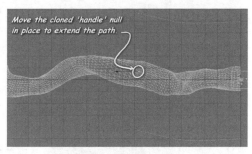

Figure 22-22: Adding a new handle to define more "path" for the wind.

8. Repeat step *7 three* more times and move the nulls to create a path that follows the vein (Figure 22-23).

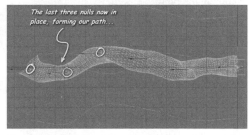

Figure 22-23: The path now laid out.

Note

Cloning the last handle in a path is the easiest way of extending the path; however, the Animation Path wind effector simply uses any child objects as control points. By selecting any control and unparenting it, we can remove it from the path completely should we decide we no longer need it. Likewise, any item (null, object, camera, or even a light for that matter) can be parented to the wind effector to include it as a control point along the path.

9. Switch the viewport to a **Top (XZ)** view, and move each of the handles to lie along the center of the vein as shown in Figure 22-24. Again, unless using Auto Key, don't forget to keyframe each null at frame 0 to lock it in place.

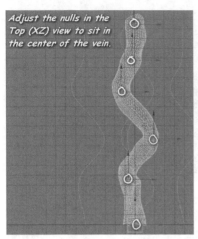

Adjust the nulls in the Top (XZ) view to sit in the center of the vein.

Figure 22-24: Move the handles in the top view to complete the path.

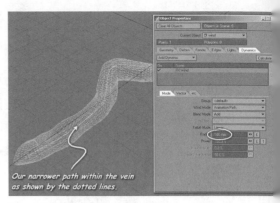

Our narrower path within the vein as shown by the dotted lines.

Figure 22-25: Narrow the radius.

The animation path is now ready to pull the particles along the vein. Play the animation and watch as the particles follow the vein. Let's just polish this up by making sure that the particles don't float outside the vein too frequently. We can do this by narrowing the path itself. A few straying particles won't hurt for this simple project; however, if you're concerned about making sure everything stays within the confines of the vein, use your new knowledge of collision dynamics to give the vein some impermeable qualities. (There's a simple challenge for you!)

10. Select the **Wind** dynamic, open its Object Properties window (<**p**>), and then click on the **Dynamics** tab. Left-click on the **FX Wind** dynamic to display its properties, then set Radius to **100 mm**. This should make the particles flow nicely through the middle of the vein.

We can narrow the overall wind using its Radius property; however, the path can also be widened and narrowed by simply keyframing a handle null's size. Likewise, rotating a handle null will adjust the curve of the path. The bank axis can be used to add a little twist to the flow as well if you wish. Indeed, one of the cool things about the Animation Path wind is that its handle nulls can be animated, changing the path over time. Paths don't need to remain static, and can be rotated, scaled, and moved to create anything from torrents of water rushing along twisting hydro slides at a fun park to the immense forces of nature pulling debris up into spinning tornadoes!

HardFX

HardFX is a personal dynamic that gives objects a rigid structure. You should apply HardFX to objects that need to interact with other objects while retaining their basic shape throughout the simulation. For example, HardFX can be applied to a set of bowling pins. The pins must be able to interact with the bowling ball and each other, but they must also retain their shape (i.e., not bend or stretch as a result of collisions). Another perhaps not so obvious effect is to simulate dry leaves being blown around. After all, dry leaves tend to be quite stiff and brittle.

One thing that HardFX is particularly good at is breaking rigid objects into pieces, even though they may be in a single object layer! Let's look at how this works.

1. Load the scene **Sanctum.lws** from Scenes\Chapter 22. In this scene ancient booby traps try to protect whatever secret lies deep within an ancient temple. A hammer swings to smash away one of the walkways, but if we look closely, it's not doing a very effective job!

Figure 22-26: The ancient booby trap doesn't do much for protecting anything.

What we need here is a way to create the complex animation needed for creating the smashing effect of the walkway by the booby trap. To do this we'll need to create a small dynamics community.

2. Select the **Inner_sanctum:walkway** object (the bricks that the booby trap is trying to smash) and open the Object Properties window (<**p**>). Under the Dynamics tab, apply an **Add Dynamic | Hard** dynamic to the object.

Once added, click on the HardFX dynamic in the list to bring up its properties. Let's take a look at what we've got to play with here in HardFX, and how it's going to let us smash up this walkway.

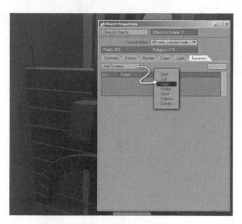

Figure 22-27: Click on Add Dynamic and choose Hard from the list.

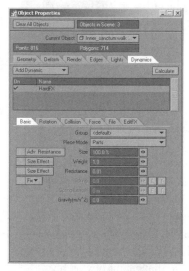

Figure 22-28: HardFX properties.

I'll quickly review just those settings that we need to know about for this project. Some of the other settings here are covered in more detail later in this section, while the manual provides an excellent resource for coming to grips with the rest.

● **Piece Mode** is important as it tells HardFX how to deal with an object. In this section, we'll be using the default setting of Parts. A Part in an object is determined by geometry that shares the same points (i.e., geometry that is connected together).

HardFX will analyze and find each of these Parts, treating them as though they were separate objects when calculating its simulation. For the Inner_sanctum:walkway objects, each brick in this object is created from an individual block, making HardFX see them as separate parts.

• **Weight** sets the mass for the object, which is important in calculating the momentum of the dynamics simulation. Heavier objects tend to pick up more momentum, while lighter objects have less. The **Size Effect** setting to the left makes HardFX distribute the weight through the parts of an object based on their proportions. This is a great way to make smaller parts appear lighter in a complex object.

• **Resistance** controls air resistance. This has a dampening effect on the momentum of objects, slowing them down over time. It also controls how much influence wind dynamics will have on the object as well. As with Weight, the **Size Effect** setting will distribute the resistance across the parts in a complex object, with smaller objects having less resistance than the larger ones.

• **Gravity** of course is essential if we want our dynamics to behave naturally and show that they have a bit of weight.

3. Most of the default values on the Basic tab are fine for this project; however, let's change Gravity(m/s ^ 2) to **–9.8** (the equivalent of Earth's gravity) so that bricks will fall once they're smashed by the booby trap.

4. Click the **Calculate** button, and check out the simulation so far. Hmmm. The whole wall just slides down as it's being influenced by the gravity. We'd rather see only the bricks that were smashed by the booby trap fall away.

Let's move to the Collision tab and see what we can do to correct this.

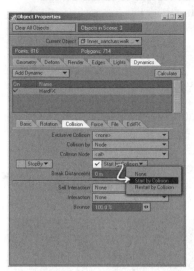

Figure 22-29: Setting Start by Collision to prevent premature gravitational pull on the walkway.

5. Click on the **Start by Collision** pop-up and select the option **Start by Collision**. This option will only calculate the dynamics for a part when it has been collided with, making sure that bricks don't fall away until they've been smashed by the booby trap.

Let's look at some of the other settings on this tab while we're here:

• **Exclusive Collision** allows us to ignore all but a specific collision object in a scene. In this option we could select the Inner_sanctum:boobytrap if we had multiple items in the scene set up as collision dynamics. In this case we don't, so let's leave this as <none> for now.

• **Collision by** specifies how the parts in the Inner_sanctum:walkway will detect collision. By default, a setting of Node uses all the points in each part as collision detection points. Depending on the complexiy of the object, this can be quite slow when an object has a complex level of geometry.

Changing the option to Box or Sphere will be much faster, but could be less accurate if the parts are complex in shape or form.

> **Note**
>
> When using the Collision by option of Sphere, each sphere is controlled by the Size option on the Basic tab (Figure 22-30).
>
>
>
> Figure 22-30: How changing the size changes the collision area.

- **Collision Node** sets what surfaces or vertices are included in the collision detection process. When geometry becomes complex, lowering the number of vertices required when determining collisions can increase calculation speed.

- **StopBy** is a pop-up, much like Start by Collision, that stops the dynamics calculations based on certain rules. StopByEvent stops calculating after an Event Mode collision has occurred with the part. StopByStabilizer will stop calculating after the part has a minimal amount of movement (or appears to have stabilized its motion).

- Below Start by Collision is a setting for **Break Distance(m)**. The collision distance between the part and the collision object needs to be farther apart than this value for the Start by Collision to occur. The default of 0 m will be used most of the time here.

- **Self Interaction**, **Interaction**, and **Bounce** all set internal collision between the parts in the dynamic and with other dynamics. Only Sphere and Box collision detection types are available here.

6. Click the **Calculate** button again. This time the Inner_sanctum:walkway object doesn't move at all, even when the booby trap smashes its way through it. As mentioned at the start of this section, we need to build a dynamics community. As part of that community, we need to add a Collision dynamic to the scene (in this case, adding it to the booby-trap object).

7. Select the **Inner_sanctum:boobytrap** object from the Current Object pop-up on the Object Properties window. Click on **Add Dynamic | Collision** to add Collision dynamic properties to the booby trap.

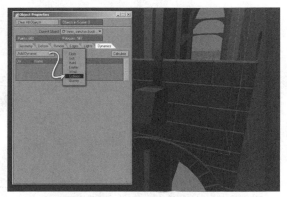

Figure 22-31: Select the boobytrap object, then add a Collision dynamic to it.

8. Click on **FX Collision** in the list to display its properties, then change Bounce/Bind power to **100%**.

9. Click **Calculate** and watch our simulation at work. Hmmm. Something isn't quite right here. Only a handful of the bricks are being smashed (Figure 22-32).

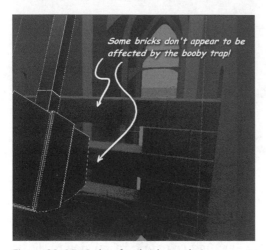

Figure 22-32: Only a few bricks are being smashed; the others seem to ignore the collision object.

The reason this is happening is simple: The bricks are using Node as their collision detection points. The arm of the hammer is smaller than the width of the bricks it passes through, hence it misses touching the nodes (the points) of the bricks.

Note

You'll recall from the end of the collision section that we mentioned a collision occurs when a point on a personal dynamic intersects with the polygon of a Collision dynamic.

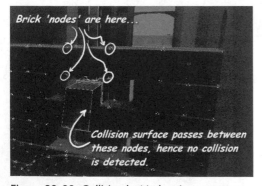

Figure 22-33: Collision by Node misses contact with the narrower booby trap on some bricks.

10. Let's correct this by making the collision object's detection area a little bigger. If you've closed the Object Properties window for the Inner_sanctum:boobytrap object, reopen it (<p>) and click on **FX Collision** under the Dynamics tab to display its properties.

11. Change the Radius/Level value to **1 m**. This forces the collision to be detected up to one meter around the collision object's surface, in essence creating a "larger" collision object without having to modify the object itself.

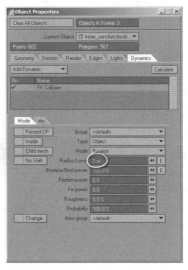

Figure 22-34: Tweak the Radius/Level to make the booby trap a little larger.

12. Click **Calculate** and see the difference. More bricks are smashed away, looking more exciting and dynamic! While the collision is no longer physically accurate (the collision area is larger than the physical "size" of the booby trap), what's important in the end with any animation is what we see through the camera view.

Figure 22-35: More brick smashing with a larger booby trap collision.

There's just one more adjustment to make to this dynamics simulation. I noted a few of the bricks on the side of the walkway dropped straight down without any kind of spin or rolling that you'd expect for objects smashed by a large hammer.

Some bricks in the wall seem to fall down unnaturally.

Figure 22-36: Some bricks just don't work here.

13. To finish up the effect, let's give the bricks some initial spinning and motion. Select the **Inner_sanc-tum:walkway** object, make sure its

Object Properties window (<**p**>) is open, then left-click on the HardFX dynamic under the Dynamics tab to display its properties.

14. Select the **Force** tab of the HardFX properties. The Force tab lets us give our parts some initial energy and rotation. Set Velocity(m/s) for the Z axis to **–2 m** to force the bricks to fly toward the camera when they're collided with. Set a Rotation(c/s) of **50%** to give the bricks a little spin and roll.

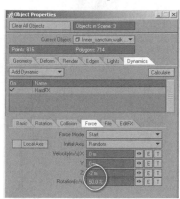

Figure 22-37: Setting some force parameters.

15. Save the scene, then click **Calculate** to see the final simulation at work. All the bricks now behave more dynamically. Obviously there's plenty of room for improvement here, but the effect works and is a great starting point for your own creepy dungeon projects!

Figure 22-38: Dynamic dungeons!

Saving Simulations

Once you've simulated and finalized your dynamics in LightWave, saving the scene ensures that the settings you set up for the dynamics community are saved as well. However, when a scene is reloaded later on, the dynamic animation needs to be recalculated before it can be viewed, or even rendered!

That's where the File tab in a dynamic's properties comes in. For the project we've just worked through, select the **Inner_sanctum: walkway** object and click on the **File** tab for the **HardFX** dynamic. Click on **Save Motion** to export the simulation we just calculated to a file.

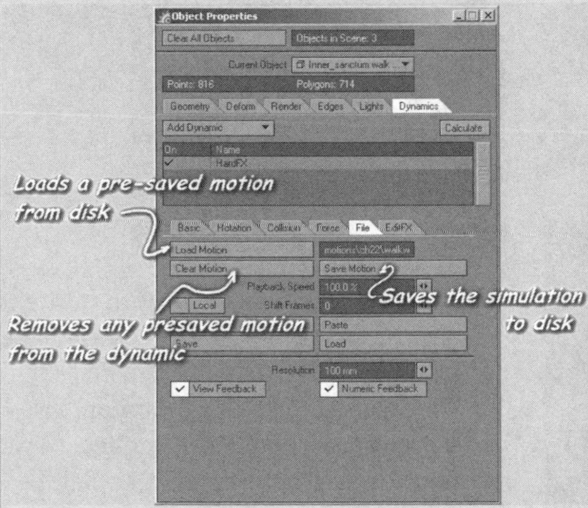

again! HardFX is reading the simulation calculations from a file instead of requiring us to recalculate the simulation.

Note how all the HardFX options are now ghosted out and disabled. To edit and recalculate the simulation, simply click on **Clear Motion** under the File tab to remove the file playback. Resave the motion once you're happy with your updates, and of course save the scene!

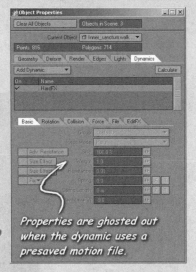

Figure 22-40: When playing back a simulation from a file, all properties are ghosted out.

Figure 22-39: Click on the File tab for more options.

The saved motion is automatically applied to the dynamic. Save the scene file once again to make sure that this updated setting is saved. Clear the scene and then reload the scene again; the dynamics animation plays without the need to calculate

Note

When preparing scenes for rendering on a network, or render farm (see Chapter 26 to learn more about what this is) it's *critical* that each and every dynamic you are using is being driven by a *saved motion*. Without a saved motion, each render will be created as though the dynamics are waiting to be calculated (i.e., doing nothing).

HardFX Rotation

We've seen how HardFX can break and smash up items; however, it can also be used to just control the rocking and rolling motion of items. In this next example, let's see how we can use HardFX to animate a hanging sign in the middle of a howling storm.

1. Load the scene **Scenes\Chapter 22\swing_sign.lws**. A dark and stormy night blows wildly, and lightning flashes as we stand under the sign of a local inn, "The Cats Eye." Playing the animation reveals that the sign isn't exactly blowing around. That's something we're about to let dynamics take care of for us.

2. Let's start by adding in some gusty wind. Select **Items | Dynamic Obj | Wind** and add a wind effector. Leave the Wind Effector Name as **wind**, and click **OK**.

3. The FX_Wind window will appear to let us configure the wind effector. Change Wind Mode to **Turbulence** and Falloff Mode to **OFF**. With no falloff, the wind doesn't die away as it gets farther from the wind effector, saving us having to position and set up the wind closer to the sign.

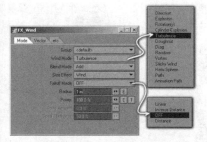

Figure 22-41: Configure the wind effector properties.

4. Under the Vector tab, we can fine-tune the animated turbulence effect. The Turbulence Size scales the size of a procedural texture that runs through the wind. For now, let's leave the default size of **1 m**. The Turbulence Vector sets the movement of the procedural texture "through" the wind. Set X and Y to **0 m** (no motion), and then set Z to **200 mm**.

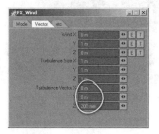

Figure 22-42: Setting the wind vector information.

> ### Note
>
> We can also randomize a wind under the Mode tab by adjusting the Power value using either an envelope (possibly using a motion modifier like Noisy Channel) or a texture (and applying an animated procedural texture). Mixing some randomness into the strength of the wind as well as the animated Turbulence under the Vector tab can help create a more natural wind effect. For now, I'll leave that as a challenge for you to experiment with later after we're done here.

5. With wind in place, the last thing we need to do is set up the sign so that it can be affected by this turbulent wind. Select the object **Hanging_sign:sign** and open its Object Properties window (**<p>**). Click on the **Dynamics** tab, and then add **Hard** from the Add Dynamic pop-up. Left-click on the **HardFX** dynamic in the list to display its properties. Let's configure the properties so that HardFX can take care of

picking up that breeze and swinging
the sign for us.

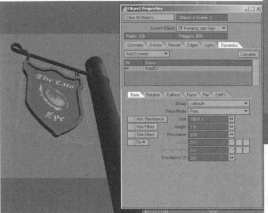

Figure 22-43: Double-click on HardFX to display its
properties.

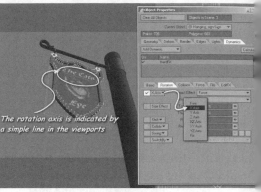

The rotation axis is indicated by
a simple line in the viewports

Figure 22-44: Limiting the rotation to one axis.

6. We only need to change one property
on the Basic tab. Set Resistance to **1.0**.
This setting indicates the amount of air
resistance for the HardFX dynamic.
When a dynamic is moving, this value
creates a drag factor that helps
decrease its momentum with distance.
When using wind effectors, this value
also sets how influenced a dynamic is
by any wind dynamics.

7. Click on the **Rotation** tab. These are
the settings that are going to do all the
work for us! Under the Axis pop-up,
select **X Axis** to limit the rotation to
one axis. When this is selected, a line
is displayed in all the viewports to indicate the axis orientation.

8. You probably noticed that this axis happens to be a little far down. The sign
should rotate around the rings from
which it hangs. To correct this, we can
shift the pivot location by changing the
Shift pop-up to **Y Shift**. The axis line
now becomes a dot to indicate the
pivot location of the object.

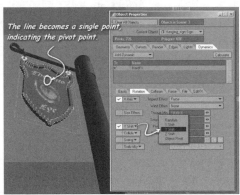

The line becomes a single point,
indicating the pivot point.

Figure 22-45: Preparing to shift the pivot.

9. Change the Pivot Shift value to **170%**.
This will move the pivot to about the
right location. The change is also displayed in the viewports, as seen in
Figure 22-46.

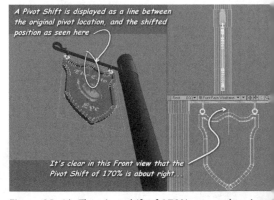

A Pivot Shift is displayed as a line between
the original pivot location, and the shifted
position as seen here

It's clear in this Front view that the
Pivot Shift of 170% is about right...

Figure 22-46: The pivot shift of 170% moves the pivot
about the right location.

10. Lastly, we need to tell the dynamic object to swing in the wind. Change the Swing pop-up to **Swing(Wind)**. Leave the Spring value at **100.0**.

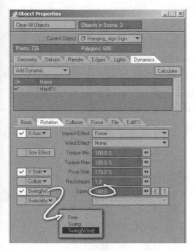

Figure 22-47: Swing that signage.

11. This is the most important step of the whole process: *Save the scene!* Before testing dynamics or complex setups in LightWave, it's a good idea to first save things in case the computer crashes while calculating. Once saved, click the **Calculate** button to watch the sign start to blow about in the wind! As with the previous HardFX section, there's plenty of room for improvement here, but it's a good starting point for creating this kind of effect. I've taken the

liberty of prerendering the sequence. The movie can be viewed in **Renders\ Chapter 22\swinging_sign.mov**.

Figure 22-48: Stormy night at The Cats Eye.

The Rotation options in HardFX can be used to create some pretty cool effects for items that don't need to smash apart, such as a hand brushing over the clothes hanging in a wardrobe that causes the clothing to gently swing on their hangers, or perhaps a set of wind chimes gently swaying outside the back door. As with every example in this book, these are just the essential starting blocks to get you familiar with the tools. Take time to experiment with the values and see how they change the animation.

ClothFX

ClothFX is a personal dynamic that gives your object elastic qualities. You should apply ClothFX to objects that you want to deform naturally and organically. For example, ClothFX can be used to simulate clothing that stretches and folds over a character's body. But ClothFX isn't just for clothing. It can be used to leave footprints on the ground where a character walks or create bullet holes in a wall from the impact of bullets. It can be used on the surface of a pond to create ripples and waves. It can even be used to simulate the motion of hair or the dangling of chains! ClothFX is an extremely powerful tool that can yield an impressive array of results.

In this section we'll look at a couple of effects we can create with ClothFX, starting with the most obvious: creating cloth!

Start up a fresh Layout or clear the scene if you have one loaded. (Make sure to save it first, however!)

1. Load **skirt_walk.lws** from Scenes\ Chapter 22. A mysterious female walks past the camera. Who is she, and why is her skirt made from an unnaturally stiff material? That's the dilemma that we're here to solve!

Perhaps a little too much starch in her laundry?

Figure 22-49: The unnaturally stiff skirt of our mystery woman!

Note

The animation here was created using *bones*, which are deformation tools that allow us to bend the leg geometry seamlessly. How these work, and how to create your very own walking animation, is covered in Chapters 23 and 24. For now, don't worry about how the walking animation was created, and let's concentrate on adding the dynamics to the skirt.

2. Select the **Legs_skirt:Dress** object. This object should be made from a cloth-like material that flops and sways as the character walks. Let's give it that quality by opening up the Object Properties window (**<p>**). Under the Geometry tab, leave the Subdivision Order set to **First**, and make sure both Display SubPatch Level and Render SubPatch are set at **3.0** for now. Add the **Cloth** dynamic from the Add Dynamic pop-up under the Dynamics tab.

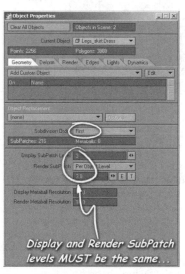

Display and Render SubPatch levels MUST be the same...

Figure 22-50: Make sure that the Subdivision settings are set as illustrated.

3. Click **Calculate** under the Dynamics tab. The skirt will be calculated as cloth, but won't behave the way we'd expect it to. You can see the effect in Figure 22-51. The object moves at the start, but very quickly stops as the legs walk through and away from it. This is because every vertex in the Dress object is now under the control of the ClothFX dynamic, completely ignoring the effect of key frames or animation (apart from the initial motion at the start of the animation).

Rules when Working with Subpatch Objects and Dynamics

Before we get any deeper into dynamics, realize that we're working with sub-patched objects in this scene. Dynamics applies its mathematical genius to the *vertices* of an object, and understanding how the subdivision settings on the Geometry tab of the Object Properties window affect dynamics simulations is important knowledge to have.

The **Subdivision Order** determines how much geometry the dynamics system sees when running a simulation. A setting of First converts the objects before any effects or animations occur. This creates denser geometry for the object that's ideal if we want to create detailed, wrinkled cloth.

A setting of Last will use the raw low-polygon geometry for simulation. The simulated geometry is then subpatched to a denser mesh to create the final result. This is ideal if we want to create smooth, flowing fabrics.

It's also important to realize that if we use a Subdivision Order of First, we must have the same subpatch density for both the Display SubPatch Level and Render SubPatch settings. Dynamics runs its simulation using the Display SubPatch Level density. We can't use different densities, or the new Advanced Pixel Subdivision options we learned about in Chapter 21. Any change between the calculated simulation mesh and the final rendered mesh will make it nearly impossible for dynamics to correctly determine which vertex receives what simulation information.

If you plan on rendering a complex cloth simulation but need to render it at high subpatch levels, consider creating a denser base mesh in Modeler and using a Subdivision Order of Last. This will ensure that your simulation works every time, and still gives you the flexibility of being able to render at any specified subpatch density.

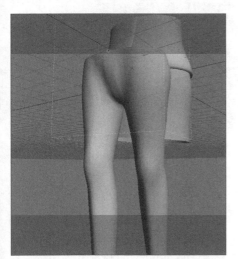

Figure 22-51: Calculating the cloth makes the skirt and legs drift apart.

4. Left-click on **ClothFX** in the Dynamics list box to bring up its properties.

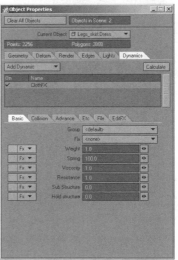

Figure 22-52: ClothFX dynamic properties.

ClothFX has plenty of options and values to tweak here. Some of these will be familiar from dynamics we've looked at previously in this chapter. For now, we'll just be adjusting the *essential* parameters. The manuals that ship with LightWave go into a lot of detail about what each and every parameter does, and are well worth taking some time to read.

5. Start by changing the Fix pop-up to **dress_fixed/pointset**. *Fixing* points makes them *unaffected* by the ClothFX dynamics, allowing them to keep their shape and be controlled by our key-framed animation instead. This pointset (more commonly referred to as a *selection set* in Modeler) contains all the points above the skirt, so that the top of the skirt stays attached to the character as it moves. The points of the skirt, however, are still treated as cloth and will "hang" from the fixed points.

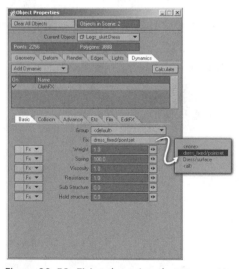

Figure 22-53: Fixing the points that we want to remain in place.

Note

Setting up points in a model to be *fixed* is as simple as selecting them in Modeler and creating a unique *vertex map (vmap)* — a weight map, selection set (pointset), or UV map — for them (see Figure 22-54). Alternatively, if the points belong to a group of polygons you'd like to fix, give these polygons a unique *surface name*. All surface names are also included in the Fix list. Also of interest is that these vmaps can be used to scale the effect of various parameters on a ClothFX object by selecting them from the Fx pop-ups we see to the left of various parameters.

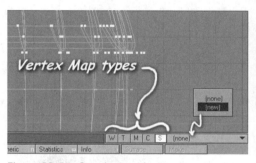

Figure 22-54: Creating a unique vertex map in Modeler.

Figure 22-55: The Fx pop-ups let us use vertex maps to control parameters within a ClothFX dynamic.

There are a lot of other properties under the Basic tab we can adjust here, but where do we even begin to create realistic cloth? Luckily for us, there's an easy way to get started!

6. Click on the **Etc** tab, and select a material type from the Preset pop-up at the bottom of the panel. This pop-up provides some generic types of materials we can simulate with ClothFX and is often a good starting point if you are new to working with ClothFX. From this pop-up, let's select **Cotton (thick)**.

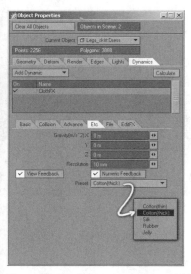

Figure 22-56: Select a preset to quickly set up the basic parameters for ClothFX.

Note

There may only be a small handful of ClothFX presets here, but by using the Save and Load buttons found under the File tab of the ClothFX properties, we can quickly build up a library of our own presets! All dynamics offer the ability to save and load their properties, meaning we never have to remember the values we used to create our favorite effects.

7. While we're in the Etc tab, let's also set Gravity(m/s ^ 2) for the Y axis to **–9.8 m** (the equivalent of Earth's gravity). This will ensure that the cloth "hangs" downward.

8. Click on **Calculate** and let's see how the cloth behaves. It's folding and wrinkling, and looking very cloth-like. Perfect! Well, no, not quite. It's completely ignoring the legs and cutting straight through them. Let's see how we can prevent the cloth from passing through the legs by creating another member of our dynamics community — a Collision dynamic.

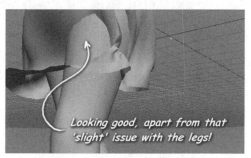

Looking good, apart from that 'slight' issue with the legs!

Figure 22-57: Wrinkling cloth at last. Well, except for those legs....

Note

When working with deformed objects (such as the legs that were animated using bones), things can appear a little misleading in the viewport display when using Textured Shaded Solid. The selection box for the object can be in a completely different location than where the object appears to be. This is because bones are deforming, or displacing the geometry away from the object's location (i.e., they are not actually moving the object, just its "skin" of polygons). I've set my viewport for this next step to Textured Shaded Solid Wireframe so that the wireframe is highlighted when the object is selected. (You can also use Frontface Wireframe mode if you don't need to see the surfaces.)

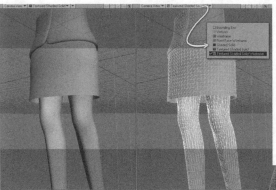

Figure 22-58: Altering the viewport display can help with seeing your selected object easily.

9. Select the **Legs_skirt:Legs** object, and open the Object Properties window (**<p>**). Under the Geometry tab, make sure that Subdivision Order is set to **Last**. Because the geometry is being deformed by bones, a Subdivision Order of Last creates a smoother skin over the deformed polygons, and hence a more organic appearance to the legs.

10. Left-click on the Dynamics tab, and let's select the **Add Dynamic** pop-up. Select **Collision** from the list. When the Collision dynamic is added to the legs, a raw wireframe of the original geometry should appear in the viewport (see Figure 22-59).

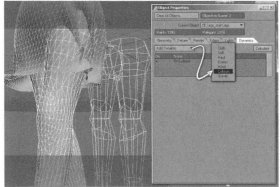

Figure 22-59: Adding Collision to the legs.

11. If we want to ensure that the collision is calculated using subpatched geometry and not the raw low-polygon cage, left-click on **FX Collision** in the dynamics list to display its properties. Change Type to **Object-Subdiv**. The wireframe should update in the viewport to show the denser subpatch geometry.

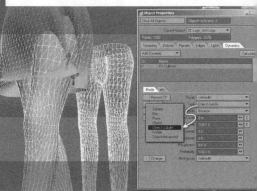

Figure 22-60: Changing the collision type to Object-Subdiv.

12. Select the **Legs_skirt:Dress** object again. You can do this quickly from the Current Object pop-up at the top of the Object Properties window (Figure 22-61). Once selected, the ClothFX dynamic should appear in the dynamics list box. Left-click once on **ClothFX** to display its properties, then under the Collision tab, change the Collision Detect pop-up to **Dress/surface**. This will ensure that only the points in the skirt are analyzed for collision with the legs (Figure 22-62).

> ### Note
>
> A Collision Detect setting of <all> would also work here, but limiting the detection to just the skirt lowers the number of points that LightWave will need to check for collision (speeding up calculations a little).

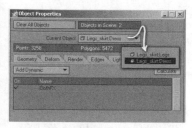

Figure 22-61: Select the skirt object.

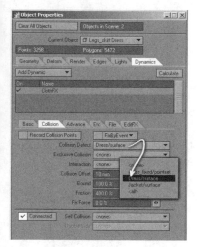

Figure 22-62: Making sure the cloth can detect the legs.

13. Click **Calculate** and let's check out how things are working. You'll notice that the calculation seems to take a little longer now that we have more detection happening, but still only takes a short time before it's finished. Play back the animation and check out how well the skirt now reacts and sways when the legs move.

With just some basic presets and a few simple tweaks, we've created a cool cloth simulation for some simple clothing. The only issue that I have with this is perhaps the cloth looks a little too wrinkled and floppy. Let's go back to our cloth settings and learn a little about how some of the properties can be used to fine-tune the behavior of our skirt.

14. Under the ClothFX properties Basic tab, let's tweak a few options. Change Weight to **5.0**. This will create a heavier cloth that should hang better and sway less. To decrease the amount of wrinkling, raise Viscosity to **3.0**. Viscosity absorbs some of the surrounding motion of the cloth, creating a thicker appearance to the cloth so that it doesn't fold and wrinkle so much as it swings around.

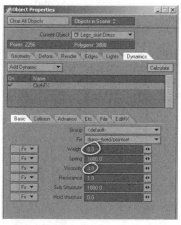

Figure 22-63: Tweak the Weight and Viscosity settings to thicken the fabric.

When cloth is heavier, it will stretch more as it's pulled by gravity and any other dynamic forces in the scene. Let's make sure that the skirt remains the same length by limiting the amount of "stretchiness."

15. Under the Advance tab, change Stretch Limit to **0.1%** to minimize the stretching of the skirt. Once set, click **Calculate** and we're about done!

> **Note**
>
> Don't be fooled. A Stretch Limit value of 0% will not stop stretching. Instead, it will *deactivate* the Stretch Limit effect completely. To minimize stretching, use a tiny value that's higher than 0%.

Well, we did it! We created a cool cloth effect for a skirt. It can probably be tweaked even further, so feel free to experiment with the settings and see how the calculated simulation looks.

> **Note**
>
> Like everything 3D, there is often more than one way of achieving the same result. This can be said of the settings in ClothFX also. In this section, we used Viscosity to create the appearance of thick cloth, but we could have used a variety of other settings and tweaks to get a similar result. (For example, the Layout manual includes a note under the section about the Advance tab on how to use the Compress Stress option to create thicker materials.) The key to getting what you want will be through trying things out, learning what combinations of options will do, and seeing what produces the result you're after.

16. Once you're happy with the animated cloth, the last thing we need to do before we finish up with the scene is to click on the File tab for ClothFX and click the **Save Motion** button to save the animated cloth to disk. Once the motion is saved, we no longer need to click Calculate to see the cloth in action. ClothFX will instead read back the animation from the disk file.

17. Be sure to also save the scene file after saving the ClothFX motion so that the next time you load the scene, ClothFX knows to use the saved motion. If you decide you need to tweak the cloth later, clicking the **Clear Motion** button under ClothFX's File tab will remove the saved motion and let you edit the dynamic settings.

Don't close the scene just yet. We're going to use it to learn a little about how we can fine-tune and fix simulations.

Editing Dynamics

All personal dynamics have an EditFX tab in their properties that can be used to manually adjust and fine-tune the vertices in a simulation (or individual particles in an emitter). While dynamics usually behave themselves fairly well, sometimes we may need to tweak the motion of a particular area of cloth that just isn't working. For example, say that the leg was cutting through the skirt at a particular point in the animation. That's where the EditFX tools come in, and allow us to drag and adjust the cloth to correct small issues.

Let's look at how we can quickly select and edit points in our ClothFX simulation. There's nothing visibly wrong here, but let's see how we can use these tools. I'm pretty happy with how this animation worked out (**Renders\Chapter 22\skirt_walk.mov**), so make sure you save your scene first before you use this tool!

1. Select the **Legs_skirt:Dress** object and open the Object Properties window (**<p>**). Left-click on **ClothFX** under the Dynamics tab to display its properties, click on the **EditFX** tab, then click on the **Edittool** button to activate the editing features.

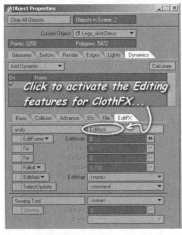

Figure 22-64: Activate the editing features of ClothFX.

2. When active, all the points within the dynamic will be highlighted. Left-click on one of the points and it will be selected, displaying its node number (the numeric ID of the point) and motion path as shown in Figure 22-65. A point (referred to as a *node* by the dynamics system) can be selected by left-clicking on it or by entering its node ID number in the EditNode box under the EditFX tab. When a node is selected manually, its node ID is automatically shown in the EditNode box.

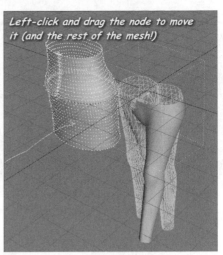

Figure 22-66: The whole mesh moves!

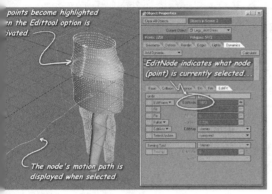

Figure 22-65: A node selected on our cloth object.

So now that we have a node selected, how do we edit it?

3. Left-click on the node in the viewport, and drag the mouse. We're editing the dynamics. But what the?! The whole mesh is moving, not just the single node! Let go of the mouse button and click the **undo** button under the EditFX tab to undo what we just did.

> **Note**
>
> Be warned! EditFX can only undo the previous edit. There are *no multiple undoes*.

Due to the nature of cloth, it would seem a little crazy to limit the Edittool to just tweaking individual "nodes" one by one. Of course, it's just as crazy to adjust the whole mesh as a single entity! Don't panic. Luckily, the tool gives us the Falloff and EditSize settings to define an *editing region* to give us more control. Any node that falls within a spherical area around the selected node set by the EditSize value will be adjusted. How much each of these other nodes is influenced by the editing tool is determined by the Falloff setting. By default, the Falloff is set to All. This is why the entire mesh moved when we edited it.

4. Click on the **Falloff** pop-up and select **Soft** to give the Edittool a nice, soft falloff. Nodes close to the selected node get most of the editing adjustment, and those farther away get less. Change EditSize to **0.5**. The area of the Edittool influence is displayed as a wireframe sphere, as shown in Figure 22-67.

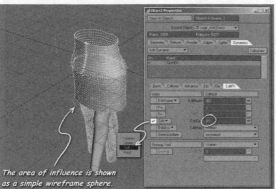

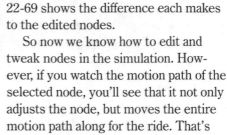

The area of influence is shown as a simple wireframe sphere.

Figure 22-67: Setting up a small area of influence for the Edittool.

Note

The Edittool is similar to the Magnet and Dragnet tools in Modeler.

5. Left-click and drag the selected node in the viewport. Now only the nodes within the falloff area are affected! Be sure to release the mouse button and click the **undo** button to restore the cloth.

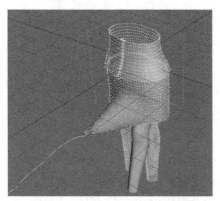

Figure 22-68: Edited nodes after setting up some falloff.

Try each of the options under Falloff to see how they work. (Remember to click undo each time to restore the cloth before trying another option.) Figure 22-69 shows the difference each makes to the edited nodes.

So now we know how to edit and tweak nodes in the simulation. However, if you watch the motion path of the selected node, you'll see that it not only adjusts the node, but moves the entire motion path along for the ride. That's where we need to look at some of the Edittool options to control *what* gets adjusted.

6. Click on the **EditFrame** pop-up. This option lets us specify what parts of the motion path get adjusted by the Edittool. We already know what All does. If we just want to edit a single frame, select Current to edit the current frame directly. If we want to edit the current frame and all the previous frames, select Before. To edit the current frame and all the ones up to the last frame, select After. If we want to make sure we can only edit a range of frames, click the two **Fix** buttons below EditFrame, and then set the range by setting the **EditStart** and **EditEnd** values. Any frames on either side of these two values become locked, preventing accidental editing.

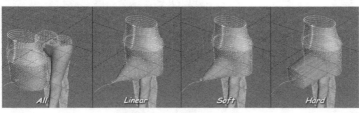

Figure 22-69: Each Falloff option behaves differently.

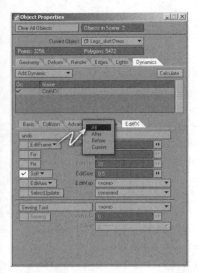

Figure 22-70: We can adjust what frames in our motion are affected by the Edittool.

That's sorted the frames we're editing. What about if we want to limit the editable nodes to just the skirt so we don't accidentally tweak the jacket?

7. Click on the **EditMap** pop-up and select the **Dress/surface** map. We can use vertex maps to limit the effect of the Edittool. In Figure 22-71, we can see the difference between using an EditMap on the dynamics and not using one. We can also limit the editing to a single axis by selecting it from the **EditAxis** pop-up.

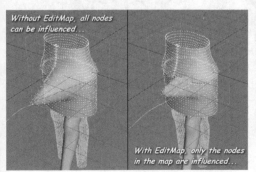

Figure 22-71: How the EditMap pop-up helps protect parts of the dynamic from being adjusted.

That's the core essentials of the EditFX toolset. You'll find these tools in all the personal dynamics. Some of the dynamics will have different options (for instance, HardFX has the ability to tweak rotations, among a few other parameters) but the basic operation of the tools are the same as we've covered here.

Worth also mentioning is the **command** pop-up. This pop-up has two options. Smooth will smooth the motion path of the selected node, which can be very useful after we've edited a dynamic. Makepath, on the other hand, is extremely useful for animation. When activated, it will bake the motion of the selected node onto a null object. This creates a keyframed item that follows the ClothFX surface. This null then becomes an indispensable tool for tracking the node. Typical uses for this would be parenting metal buttons to a piece of clothing or perhaps a boat floating on a dynamically generated ocean! In fact, you could use ClothFX just to generate some cool dynamic motions, then use Makepath to create a series of animated paths for other items to use or reference.

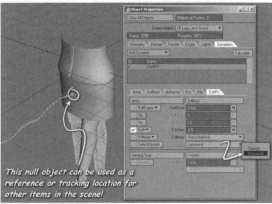

Figure 22-72: The Makepath command creates a null with the same motion as the selected node.

ClothFX — Sewing Tool

The last section at the base of the ClothFX EditFX tab contains the **Sewing Tool** button. As its name implies, when ClothFX is calculated, nodes that have been modified with this tool get "sewn" (attached) to each other. The Sewing Tool can do a couple of very cool things. One is that it can sew a cloth dynamic to *any other object* in the scene (e.g., sewing the cape of your superhero to the actual superhero). When a cloth object is sewn to another item, the sewn points become attached and behave as though they are *fixed*. The other thing that is cool is that these sewn nodes can be triggered to either be cut apart or sewn together by an event. That could mean ripping the curtains from a shower railing or perhaps closing up a zipper.

Let's check out this tool.

1. Load **the_bathroom.lws** from Scenes\ Chapter 22. This is a typical bathroom scene we might find in a future project. Play the animation and you'll see the curtain rings are animated, but they aren't connected to the curtain. Let's fix that situation right now.

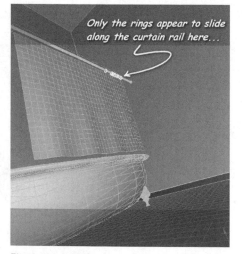

Figure 22-73: The curtain rings are a happening thing. Pity the curtains can't say the same.

Make sure that the Time Slider is set back to frame 0, then let's continue.

2. Let's attach the curtain to the rings using the Sewing Tool. Start by selecting the **bath_v003:curtain** object, opening the Object Properties window (**<p>**), and clicking on the **Dynamics** tab. Add a **Cloth** dynamic to the curtain from the Add Dynamic pop-up. Left-click on **ClothFX** in the list to display its properties, then click on the **Etc** tab. Set Gravity(m/s $^\wedge$ 2) for the Y axis to **–9.8 m**, and select **Cotton(thick)** from the Preset pop-up. Under the Advance tab, let's change the Stretch Limit to **0.5%**.

3. Switch Layout to a single viewport, set it to **Perspective**, then zoom and pan in closely to the curtain rings and top of the curtain so that we can easily see the points we need to sew here (Figure 22-74).

Figure 22-74: Zoom in close for a clear view of the rings and curtain.

4. If you closed the Object Properties window, select the **bath_v003:curtain** object and reopen it again (**<p>**). Select the **ClothFX** dynamic under the Dynamics tab, and click on the **EditFX** tab. To begin sewing, click on the **Sewing Tool** button. Right-click on the first point on the curtain, as shown in

Figure 22-75. This selects the point (or *node* as dynamics refers to them), ready to be sewn to another node. The node ID number should also appear in the EditNode field. The ID number for this node should be **627**.

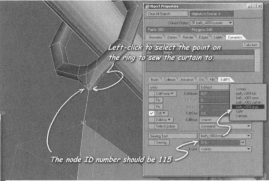

Figure 22-76: Selecting the curtain ring point to link (or "sew") the curtain to.

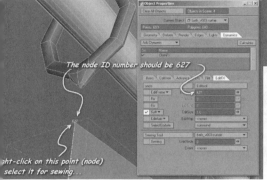

ure 22-75: Selecting the first point, ready for sewing.

5. To sew the node to the curtain ring above it, change the item pop-up to the right of the Sewing Tool button to **bath_v003:rings**. Rotate and adjust the Perspective viewport as needed to see the center point at the bottom of the first ring better, then left-click on the point as shown in Figure 22-76. This selects this point (node) as the LinkNode (its ID number should be **115**). This is the node that the EditNode will be linked (sewn) to. A line will appear to indicate the link between the two points.

6. After we have the correct points selected, check **Sewing** to make the connection between these two points. Once sewn, you can change the Event pop-up to **Cut by Event** so we can break this link later on (say, if we happened to want the curtain to be torn away by a character falling out of the bath). The curtain is now sewn to the first ring!

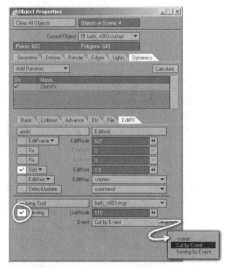

Figure 22-77: Sew the two points together, then set an event.

Note

At this stage, the points have *not* been sewn, just selected. If you have accidentally selected the wrong point on the ring, don't worry! Simply left-click on the correct one. The same can be said of the curtain. If you accidentally select the incorrect node, just right-click on the correct one.

7. Let's do the next ring. The same process applies. First, activate the **Sewing Tool**, then right-click on the curtain node (the ID number should be **635**) and left-click on the ring node (the ID number should be **173**). Check the **Sewing** option, and select **Cut by Event** from the Event pop-up. Figure 22-78 shows the second ring being sewn.

and check the connection in the viewport to make sure that this is correct before clicking on **Sewing**.

Figure 22-79: Enter the node details directly, but it pays to check in the viewport prior to sewing.

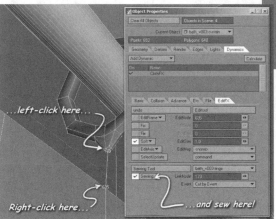

Figure 22-78: The second ring being attached.

> **Note**
>
> You may have already realized that sewing only allows us to sew two nodes at a time. It's a pretty easy process, but can be quite time consuming and monotonous when there are large numbers of points to be sewn. Luckily for us, there are only nine rings!

8. We can also sew nodes numerically under the EditFX tab using ID numbers directly. After activating the **Sewing Tool**, select the correct values in both the EditNode and LinkNode boxes, click on **Sewing**, then set **Cut by Event** from the Event pop-up. Let's do this for the next ring. The EditNode should be **643**, and the LinkNode should be **231**. It pays to just zoom out

9. You can repeat the process for the remaining rings, either manually or in the viewport. If you want to numerically sew nodes, the following ID numbers should finish up the rest of the rings:

   - EditNode **651** to LinkNode **289**
   - EditNode **659** to LinkNode **347**
   - EditNode **667** to LinkNode **405**
   - EditNode **675** to LinkNode **463**
   - EditNode **683** to LinkNode **521**
   - EditNode **691** to LinkNode **57**

> **Note**
>
> We can edit any pair of sewn nodes by clicking on the **Sewing Tool** button under the EditFX tab. Each time this is clicked, it will select the next pair of sewn nodes in order. When the last pair is reached, the selection will loop back to the first pair. This gives us a way to edit our handiwork should we need to change something. When selected, both node ID numbers and the Event option can be altered, or the nodes can be unsewn altogether by unchecking **Sewing**.

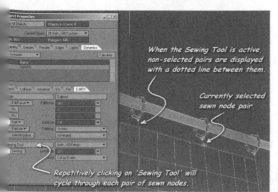

When the Sewing Tool is active, non-selected pairs are displayed with a dotted line between them.

Currently selected sewn node pair.

Repetitively clicking on 'Sewing Tool' will cycle through each pair of sewn nodes.

Figure 22-80: Repetitively clicking on the Sewing Tool button cycles through each pair of sewn nodes for editing.

10. Once we've finished up with the rings, switch back to a camera view, and then click on **Calculate** to see the result.

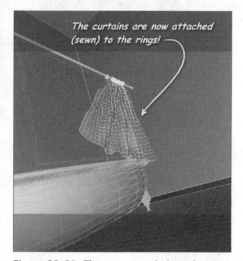

The curtains are now attached (sewn) to the rings!

Figure 22-81: The sewn curtain in action.

So what about this Cut by Event we set up? Perhaps after that last flick of the curtain, the force weakened the connection to the rings and the curtain should gradually break away from the rings near the end of the animation. Let's do this, just so we can become familiar with using those events to do something cool!

11. Add an **Items | Dynamic Obj | Collision**. The name isn't important for this project (though do change it if you want to). Click **OK** to create the collision object. Under the FX_Collision properties, change the Mode pop-up to **Event**. To cut the curtain from the rings, touch each sewn point with the collision object to trigger the cut.

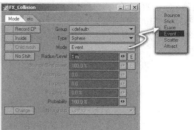

Figure 22-82: Add an event collision object.

Note

An Event collision simply generates a trigger for the ClothFX tool to cut the connection. It has no impactable effect on the cloth, hence it won't cause any kind of change in the cloth's behavior on contact other than to break the connection between the sewn nodes.

12. Move the collision object in line with the railing at frame 0. Repeat this key at frame 200, and then move the collision object along the curtain rail, creating a last key frame at 300. This should pop the curtain off the rings gradually.

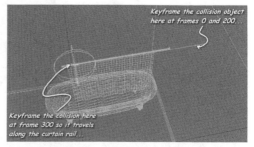

Keyframe the collision object here at frames 0 and 200...

Keyframe the collision here at frame 300 so it travels along the curtain rail...

Figure 22-83: Key the collision object at frames 0, 200, and 300.

13. Once done, click **Calculate** and check out the results! Of course, there's plenty of room for improvement in this small project. One would be to convert the **bath_v003:tub** object into a Collision dynamic so that the curtain drops into it (and not through it). I'll leave this up to you if you feel like a small challenge.

SoftFX

SoftFX is a personal dynamic that gives your object elastic qualities similar to those in ClothFX. The primary difference is that SoftFX is designed to be used on objects that need to return to their original state (meaning their size, shape, and orientation). ClothFX is not. For example, the belly of a fat character jiggles as gravity and momentum pull on the soft tissues; however, the jiggling dies off, returning the body to its original form once the character stops moving. SoftFX also has features that enable cyclical deformations, making it possible to automate many effects, including the expanding and contracting of a character's chest as it breathes.

1. Start out in Layout, and load the scene **Scenes\Chapter 22\jello_boy.lws**. Meet Jell-o-boy! A happy-go-lucky candy snack character bouncing toward the camera. Perhaps a part of a TV commercial for candy, or maybe a new kind of superhero?

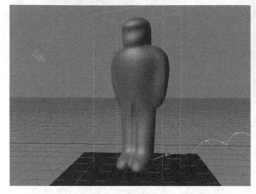

Figure 22-84: Meet Jell-o-boy. A candy hero, or simply in the wrong scene at the right time?

Play the animation through a few times. Jell-o-boy takes a few jumps and stops just in front of the camera. There's a little squash-and-stretch being used here, but let's give the character some gelatinous secondary animation with SoftFX.

2. Select the **jell-o-boy** object and open the Object Properties window (**<p>**). Click on the **Dynamics** tab, then add the **Soft** dynamic from the Add Dynamic pop-up. Click **Calculate** and let's check out what this does to our object.

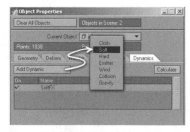

Figure 22-85: Add SoftFX to Jell-o-boy.

You can see that the original motion of the character has been exaggerated and the object appears to bounce up and down a little more than it did without SoftFX. Even when the character stops at frame 30, it continues to wobble back and forth, its motion dampening over time.

As a personal dynamic, SoftFX is subject to the laws of the dynamics community. And in the dynamics community, every personal dynamic must be accountable to a social dynamic. However, at this point, we only have one personal dynamic in our scene. There are no social dynamics, only a bit of motion. Ah, but there it is. You see, motion *is* a social dynamic. It's a user-defined social dynamic that every personal dynamic will respond to. SoftFX still responds to collisions, gravity, and wind, but it's uniquely designed to respond to motion. Let's see what changing the parameters here will do.

3. Left-click on SoftFX to display its properties. Under the Input tab, change Motion Force to **500%** and recalculate. Play the animation, and watch how the increase has caused the motion to be even more exaggerated.

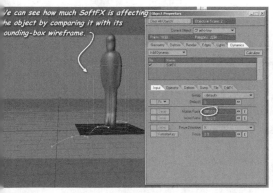

Figure 22-86: Increase Motion Force to increase the influence of motion on the object.

Note

After the initial calculation, SoftFX seems to update the animation in Layout without the need to click the Calculate button a second time! This isn't always the case, however. When other dynamics are involved that create various influences on SoftFX, you'll need to click Calculate. If the animation didn't update in Layout, simply click Calculate again.

4. So, it's nice being able to give Jell-o-boy some rubber band-like wobbling; however, let's see what we can do to set up SoftFX for some actual "usable" effects. Return Motion Force to **100%** and let's continue. Click on the **Operator** tab. The settings under this tab work hand-in-hand with the Motion Force from the Input tab, controlling the dampening of the motion. Note how Operator1 Map is set to **<all>**, making it affect the entire object. Here we can tweak the *wobbliness* of the SoftFX motion-driven effects.

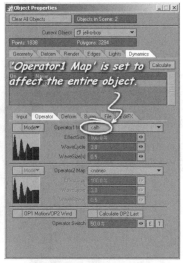

Figure 22-87: The Operator tab controls the wobbliness factor of SoftFX.

5. Let's change Operator1 Map to **FX_bendy/weightmap**. FX_bendy is a gradient weight map that starts at 0% at the feet and ends at 100% at the head. As seen in Figure 22-88, after the weight map is selected, the vertices in the object are colorized to show the effect of the weight map, with blue indicating 0% and red indicating 100%.

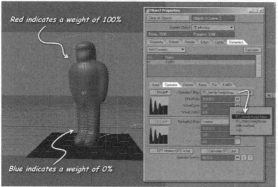

Figure 22-88: FX_bendy used as the Operator1 map.

6. Click **Calculate** and watch the animation again. FX_bendy is now scaling the motion effect, making the head and body wobble like a piece of rubber! Very cool indeed, and a bit more usable than the default as the feet now stay in place as we'd expect them to.

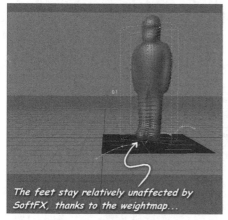

Figure 22-89: The feet stay in place now that the motion effect is controlled by the weight map.

So how exactly does all this operator stuff work? It's worth taking a little time here just to tweak the settings and watch how they change the overall effect.

7. Click on the **Mode** pop-up. This setting lets us change the way the weight map effect is applied to the vertices in the object to increase the effect, or invert them completely. Let's change Mode to **Square**.

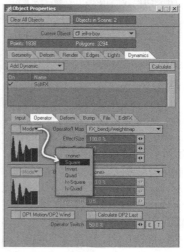

Figure 22-90: The Mode pop-up offers us a few options.

Square does not refer to the shape of the motion (as in square, rectangle, or triangle). Rather, it describes the application of the deformation. Square here is a mathematical term, as in $E=mc^2$. It amplifies the deformation of our object by multiplying the weight percentage by itself. This causes the top to receive significantly more deformation than the bottom.

> **Note**
>
> Try all the different settings to get a feel for how they change the effect. The settings Invert, Iv-Square, and Iv-Quad will invert the weight map values, which can be quite amusing as it makes Jell-o-boy wobble from his head down!

8. Let's change the dampening effect of the SoftFX motion. Change Wave-Cycle to **2.0**. This value controls the number of "jiggles" that the object will make after it stops moving. Change WaveSize(s) to **0.3**. This value indicates the time over which the "jiggle" motion will play out. Click **Calculate** and see how the jiggles stop more abruptly.

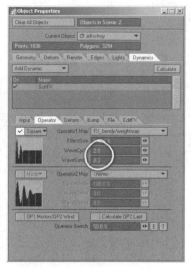

Figure 22-91: Setting up the operator values to lower the jiggliness.

Note

These changes for the wave settings are visually displayed in the small graph to the left of the settings, as seen in Figure 22-91. The graph helps us visualize the dampening effect of SoftFX.

9. The effect feels a little extreme in the middle of the animation, as it gets amplified with the bouncing motion. Let's scale this back to something less extreme and a lot more natural by setting EffectSize to **20%**. Check out the animation again and see how this looks a lot better!

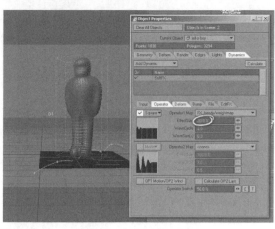

Figure 22-92: Toning back the EffectSize.

We're almost finished adding some secondary effects to our character. Let's look at one more cool feature we can use to give our character a bit of "puff" after all that hard bouncing around!

10. Click on the **Bump** tab. In this tab we can make our object bulge and contract. We'll look at another cool use in the next section; however, for now let's change the Make Wave by pop-up to **<all>**. This will create a cycling wave through the whole object, causing it to contract and bulge as though air were being pumped in and out of the object.

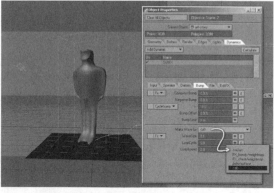

Figure 22-93: Is this wave sucking the life out of Jell-o-boy? Stay tuned for more....

11. Change the FX pop-up to **FX_chest/ weightmap.** This is a simple weight map centered in the chest of the character, and will be used to isolate the wave effect in this area. Change WaveSize to **0.01.** This value sets the distance the chest will move out from its default location. Leave LoopCycle at its default of **5.** LoopCycle sets the number of waves that are generated when we are generating a wave from a specified area in the object; however, for a Make Wave by setting of <all>, the LoopCycle value won't really make much difference to the overall effect. LoopSpeed controls the speed of the waves. Leave this at **2** for now, for a fast, out-of-breath effect. Click **Calculate** and play the animation.

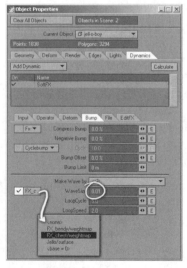

Figure 22-94: Making the wave effect appear in the chest.

Voilà! We've created a simple breathing effect for the character so that when he stops he appears to be out of breath! (The effect of eating too much sugar, no doubt!) By changing the WaveSize, we can decrease the amount of movement of the chest.

Changing the LoopSpeed will increase and decrease the breathing rate. Since both of these values can be controlled through envelopes in the Graph Editor, we could increase and decrease poor old Jell-o-boy's health over the course of the animation.

That's just a taste of what SoftFX can do for both characters and those rubbery objects in our animation. However, let's look at one more cool SoftFX application that can be combined with collision dynamics in a scene.

SoftFX — Compress Bump

In this quick little project, we'll use SoftFX to create the illusion of a heavy aircraft pushing down and forcing the tires of its landing gear to bulge. We will only be using a few settings here. Like all the dynamics available in LightWave, we don't need to use all of the features of the tool to create great effects!

1. Load the scene **Scenes\Chapter 22\ come_in_for_landing.lws.** The undercarriage is down; after a few bumps, a mysterious small aircraft comes to a stop. One thing that's going to help improve the scene and give the mysterious aircraft a feeling of being heavy here is obviously a little tire bulging as the wheel hits the ground. Let's check out how SoftFX can create this effect in near-to-no time!

2. Click on **Items | Dynamics Obj | Collision** to add some ground for our tire to contact. Give this collision object the name **ground.** When the FX_Collision properties window appears, change Type to **Plane,** and set Radius/ Level to **0 m.**

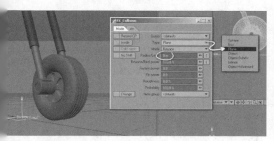

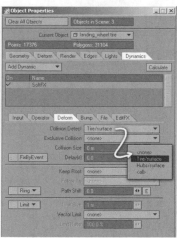

ure 22-95: Adding a ground plane for the tire to
d on.

Figure 22-97: Giving the tire the ability to impact
against the ground plane.

3. Select the **landing_wheel:tire** object,
then open its Object Properties window (<**p**>). Click on the **Dynamics**
tab, and add a **Soft** dynamic from the
Add Dynamic pop-up.

4. Left-click on **SoftFX** in the list to display its properties. We don't want
SoftFX to give the tire any flabby jiggle, just squash it against the ground.
Under the **Input** tab, set both Motion
Force and Wind Force to **0%** to prevent
unwanted jiggling by any social dynamics (such as motion or wind) in the
scene.

6. Click **Calculate** to check out the collision deformation. The tire now flattens
out as it impacts against the ground
collision plane; however, all the pressure and air inside the tire need to go
somewhere (see Figure 22-98).

*The tire impacts nicely against the ground,
but something's not quite right here...*

Figure 22-98: A nice flat bottom to the tire, but
no sign of that pressure being displaced from
within.

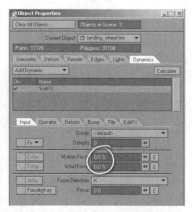

Figure 22-96: Turn off the force options to prevent
SoftFX from jiggling the tire.

Let's continue.

5. Click on the **Deform** tab, and set Collision Detect to **Tire/surface**. This will
ensure that the tire impacts against the
ground collision.

7. Click on the **Bump** tab, and let's give
Compress Bump a value of **250%**. This
setting tells SoftFX how much to bulge
geometry when it impacts (or bumps)
with any collision dynamics in the

scene; in this case, when the tire hits the ground.

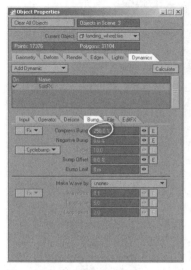

Figure 22-99: Add some Compress Bump to swell the tire up as it impacts with the ground.

8. Click **Calculate** and check out the secondary animation we've just added to the tire! Don't forget to click **Save Motion** under the **File** tab, and then *save the scene* to store the simulation for rendering later on.

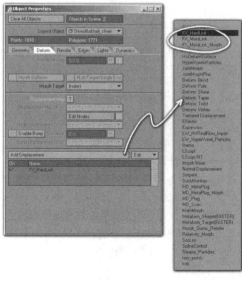

Compress Bump adds the additional bulging that helps sell the effect!

Figure 22-100: The bulge as we'd expect from the pressure of a heavy weight coming down on the tire.

Relational Dynamics

In addition to personal dynamics and social dynamics, there are also "relational dynamics" called *Effect Links*. Effect Links work on the *children* of dynamic objects, allowing them to inherit the properties of their parent. They are applied from the **Add Displacement** pop-up in the Deform tab of the Object Properties window.

While not true dynamics in and of themselves, Effect Links are often used to apply the dynamic properties of a simple object to a higher resolution mesh. This not only speeds up the calculation of complicated simulations, but it also opens the door for effects that would otherwise be difficult to achieve.

Figure 22-101: Adding a relational dynamic displacement.

HardLink

HardLink applies the dynamic properties of a parent object to its child using rigid body qualities. The obvious question is "Why would you want to do this?" Here's an obvious example: If you wanted to animate a chain, you might think of adding HardFX since chains are hard. But HardFX would only see the object in one of two ways: as an entire (solid) chain or as individual links. It would not understand that the links are actually connected to one another. Therefore, HardFX would not work for this simulation. ClothFX would keep the links together and allow the chain to dangle, but it would deform every point in the mesh, causing your links to stretch like rubber. What you need is a way to get the motion of ClothFX with the properties of HardFX. HardLink allows you to do this.

1. Load the scene **Scenes\Chapter 22\ FXHard_ball.lws**. A spiky demolition ball hangs from thick metal links, ready to swoop down and smash every building that gets in its way! However, playing this animation reveals no swooping action. Let's see how fast and easy adding the power of a dynamic swoop onto the chain can be!

2. Select the **DemoBall:dynamic** object. This object is a simple string of two-point polygons, each point aligned closely to the pivot rotation for each of the chain links in the other object layer. Open the Object Properties window (**<p>**), select the **Dynamics** tab and **Add Dynamic | Cloth**. Left-click on **ClothFX** in the list to bring up its properties and let's get started.

3. Set Fix to **FIXED_Topofchain/ pointset** from the pop-up list. We're not going to change a lot in here, other than setting Weight to **5.0** and the Fx

pop-up for Weight to **Cloth_weight/ weightmap**. This weight map scales the weights on each point, important for simulating the effects of a heavy ball versus the swinging and bouncing of a lighter chain.

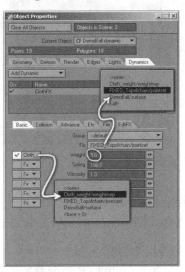

Figure 22-102: Set up the basics.

4. A chain is solid, and the links need to remain connected with each other. Under the ClothFX **Advance** tab, set the Stretch Limit to **0.001%**. We want to minimize the stretch as much as possible.

5. Under the Etc tab, set Gravity(m/s ^{2}) for the Y to **–9.8 m**, and we're finished with setting up the dynamics. Not much is going to happen if you click the Calculate button, so let's close the Object Properties window for now.

6. Select the **DemoBall:ball_chain** object and open the Motion Options window (**<m>**). Parent this object to the dynamic by setting Parent Item to **DemoBall:dynamic**.

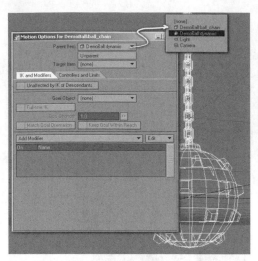

Figure 22-103: Parent the ball and chain to the dynamic.

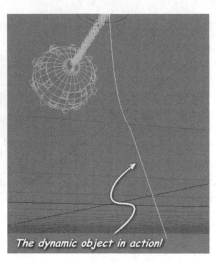

Figure 22-104: Click Calculate to see the dynamic swing in action.

7. Let's select **DemoBall:dynamic**, and then use the **Modify | Rotate | Rotate** tool (**<y>**) to rotate the Pitch up to **–90.00** degrees. Keyframe this rotation at frame 0 to lock it in place. When we calculate the dynamics, this will cause the dynamic to fall with gravity, giving the chain a bit of initial swing.

> **Note**
>
> If you're rotating the object but it appears to be frozen in the viewport, don't panic. If you've calculated the dynamics for this object, it's likely to still be under the influence of ClothFX. To remove any ClothFX motion from an object, open its Object Properties window (**<p>**), click on the Dynamics tab, and left-click on **ClothFX** to bring up its properties. Under the ClothFX File tab, click **Clear Motion** to remove the simulation from the object.

8. Open the Object Properties window (**<p>**) for the DemoBall:dynamic object, and click on the **Dynamic** tab. Click on **Calculate** to set the dynamic swing in motion.

That's a pretty cool-looking yellow line bobbing around, but not much is happening with that ball and chain! Let's fix that.

9. Select the **DemoBall:ball_chain** object and open the Object Properties window (**<p>**). Select the **Deform** tab, and select the **FX_HardLink** modifier from the Add Displacement pop-up. This will instantly activate and link the individual parts of the chain to its closest parent dynamic nicely.

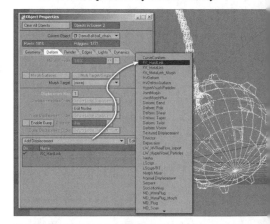

Figure 22-105: Activating FX_HardLink to get things swinging!

FX_HardLink has linked the rigid parts of our object to the dynamics in the parent item, DemoBall:dynamic, almost instantly. The nice thing about FX_HardLink is that you can update and recalculate the dynamic layer, and the changes are instantly reflected in the more detailed DemoBall:ball_chain object.

While this has given you a starting point, it's definitely not the *perfect* simulation of a swinging ball and chain. I encourage you to experiment with the settings in the dynamics. For instance, raise the Weight to see the change in momentum and swing effects (try a value of **50**), and remove the weight map to see the effect with and without this in place.

MetaLink

MetaLink functions similarly to HardLink, but rather than applying rigid body qualities to your child object, it applies soft body qualities. MetaLink is useful for those instances where you want to maintain the volume (or shape) of an object but still give it a degree of flexibility. For example, if you wanted to animate a rope rather than a chain, you could use ClothFX on a simple object (such as a two-point polygon chain) and apply MetaLink to the rope object. ClothFX will give you the motion you want, and MetaLink will help the rope to keep its basic shape.

Let's check out how we can get a little Indiana Jones-style action using MetaLink.

1. Load **jones_whip.lws** from Scenes\ Chapter 22. The camera is focused on some artifact in an ancient temple when suddenly the whip of an intrepid explorer catches onto the artifact! Well, at least that's the premise of this scene. Let's see how we can use dynamics to add the whip.

2. The scene is fairly simple. Like the HardLink example, MetaLink takes the dynamics of a parent item and uses it to deform a child item. In this scene, I've already set up the hierarchy. Select the object **jones_whip:dynamic**; this item controls the whip and needs a little dynamic attention.

3. Let's give the whip some dynamic motion. For this, open the Object Properties window (**<p>**), click on the **Dynamic** tab and add the dynamic **Cloth**. Left-click on **ClothFX** in the dynamics list to display its properties and let's begin.

4. A leather whip tends to be fairly thick and doesn't jiggle and wobble about; however, ClothFX tends to create this jiggling behavior when applying it to simple two-point geometry like this object. To minimize this, we'll be using a fairly high level of Viscosity, which will help dampen the jiggling motion. Under the Basic tab, start by setting Fix to **fix_whipgrip/pointset**. Set Weight to **10**, Spring to **200**, and Viscosity to **50**. Set Resistance to **0**.

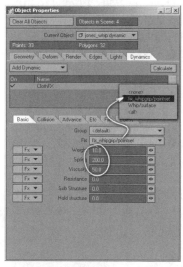

Figure 22-106: Setting up the basics for the whip.

5. Under the Collision tab, set Collision Detect to **<all>**.

6. A tightly bound leather whip won't tend to be overly elastic in nature. Under the Advance tab, let's set Stretch Limit to **0.001%** to minimize the stretching.

7. Finally, under the Etc tab, set Gravity(m/s ^ 2) for the Y axis to **–9.8 m**.

These settings won't magically create a perfect snapping whip, but they're exactly what we need to give the whip a rope-like action that's required for this scene. Do not click Calculate just yet; we've got one more thing we need to set up.

8. Select the object **jones_whip:artifact**. Open the Object Properties window (**<p>**) if it's not already open, and then add a **Collision** dynamic to this object.

9. Left-click on **FX Collision** and let's set up some basic properties. Type should already be set to **Object** (if it isn't, change it). Leave Mode as **Bounce**. Because the whip has a thickness to it, we'll probably want the dynamic to collide a small distance from the surface of this object, so set Radius/Level to **30 mm**. We'll also want to make sure that the whip not only collides but sticks to the collision object. Set Friction power and Fix power both to a generous **300.0** (Figure 22-107).

10. Now that that's in place, save the scene before we go any further! Once saved, click **Calculate** and let's check out the dynamics at work. The whip dynamic should wind itself around the artifact collision object.

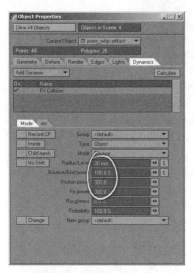

Figure 22-107: Making sure the whip has something to collide with.

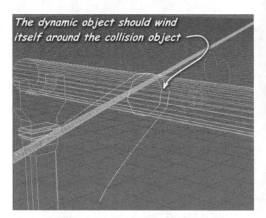

Figure 22-108: The dynamics at work.

11. If all looks good, click on **Save Motion** under the ClothFX File tab. Save the scene once again to make sure that we save this motion-driven dynamic setting. With that out of the way, we simply need to tell the whip object to use this dynamic motion.

12. Select the **jones_whip:whip** object. Open the Object Properties window (**<p>**) for this object (if it's not open already) and under the Geometry tab, make sure that Subdivision Order is set

to **Last**. We'll deform the object using the dynamic, but then subpatch the deformed geometry last so that the whip retains a nice smooth appearance.

13. This object is already parented to the jones_whip:dynamic object; therefore we simply need to apply our relational dynamics to give it some life! Click on the **Deform** tab, and select **FX_Meta-Link** from the Add Displacement pop-up. The whip should instantly deform to match the dynamics of its parent item.

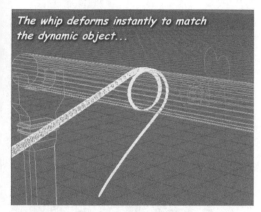

Figure 22-109: The whip is now deformed to match the dynamic simulation.

14. If all looks good, then select the **jones_whip:dynamic** object, open the **ClothFX** properties, and select **Save Motion** from the File tab. Once saved, make sure to save the scene again to store the link to the saved motion file.

I've added a few lights and added some motion blur to my final version. Check out **Scenes\Chapter 22\jones_whip_F.lws**, or watch **Renders\Chapter 22\jones_whip.mov** to see the result!

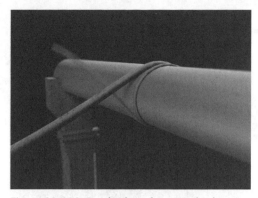

Figure 22-110: Da-da-dum-dum. Da-da-da.

> **Note**
>
> You may have noticed a *third* relational dynamic — FX_MetaLink_Morph — in the Add Displacement list. This isn't a third relational dynamic, but an enhancement to the FX_MetaLink tool's own functionality. FX_MetaLink on its own will override any morph animation that you may have in your object. To allow metalinked objects to also use morphs (should you perhaps have a morph that unravels the end of that piece of rope), combine the FX_MetaLink_Morph tool with the FX_MetaLink tool.

FX_DynamicLinker

As we've seen, relational dynamics gave us the power to relate child deformations of items to the motion of dynamics. Chains, hoses, ropes…. You name it, we can link it. What we can also do is link items to the dynamic motion of particles, our other dynamic system we looked at back in Chapter 13. Imagine connecting candy-coated chocolate to a waterfall or fountain of particles, or empty shells to particles ejecting out of the bolt of a machine gun.

1. Load the scene **Scenes\Chapter 22\pour_candy.lws**. This scene shows a simulation where particles pour out of a candy box. Of course there's a piece of candy sitting in the scene, but we'd rather it poured from the container

rather than sit on the ground, motionless.

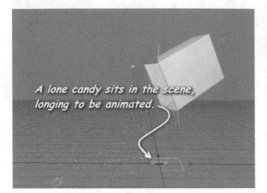

Figure 22-111: The static candy should be coming from the box.

2. Select the **candy** object, then activate the **Utilities | Plugins | Additional | FX_DynamicLinker** to connect our candy object to the particle system.

3. The ParticleFX DynamicLinker window will pop up. Make sure that Particles is set to use the particle emitter **Candy_stream**. Replace Object should be the **candy** object. Set the Rotation option to **align to path(hp)**, which will orient each candy to follow the particle's path. Clicking **OK** will create the necessary number of copies of the object necessary for linking to the particles (indicated in the **copy** setting).

> **Note**
>
> Lock Cloned Item will make each candy item locked, hence unselectable in the Layout viewports. If you want to edit or delete any of these items, you can still select them inside the Scene Editor (<**Ctrl**> + <**F1**>).

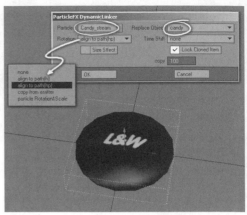

Figure 22-112: DynamicLinker properties.

4. Play the animation. Each particle now has an attached piece of candy!

Figure 22-113: Candy pouring out as expected.

> **Note**
>
> FX_DynamicLinker is smart. It *recycles* objects if their associated particles have died off and attaches them as necessary to other particles. Note that for this tool to work, you must have a particle emitter that is being driven by a presaved motion (a .pfx file) so that the tool can analyze and determine the optimal number of items to clone.

Conclusion

Combining multiple personal and social dynamics into a dynamic community is essential for creating visual effects such as explosions with smoke, dust and debris from that alien cruiser, or maybe leaves and dirt from the back of a land cruiser traveling through a mountain pass. As usual, we've covered a lot of ground in this chapter, but in reality we've only scratched the surface.

Dynamics are incredibly powerful tools. They are also a lot of fun to work with. Now that you've been introduced to the characters in the dynamics community, I encourage you to spend time becoming well acquainted with them. It's a relationship that will reward you greatly for the investment.

Chapter 23

Advanced Skills: Character Rigging

In the previous chapters we've examined the basic tools used to create *any* type of animation. In this chapter, we'll look at the tools designed specifically for *character* animation. The principles of character animation are the same in every major 3D package; it's just the way the tools are applied and the buttons you click that tend to change.

A Brief Introduction to Character Animation

Computer animation has come a long way over the past 20 years. Those who've been working in this field from the start will tell you how difficult it was in the beginning to get a simple character built, let alone animated. But today, 3D programs such as LightWave offer a number of highly advanced tools, giving you everything you need to bring your characters to life. And by definition, that's what animation is: the illusion of life. You create this illusion through the use of highly advanced technologies. Chief among these in LightWave are bones, forward kinematics, and inverse kinematics.

Bones and Rigs

Nearly all computer-based character animation is accomplished through the use of "bones." If this is your first experience with character animation, it's important to understand the difference between real bones (such as those in your arms, legs, hands, and feet) and 3D bones. In the real world, bones act as the framework for your body. That framework determines your overall shape. Think about it; without bones, you would be nothing but a large blob of skin sitting on the floor. But in the 3D world, that's not so. A character without bones does not go limp when it's taken out of Modeler and brought into Layout because its overall form is determined by its polygonal mesh. Like a stone sculpture, it's rather inflexible. So what purpose do bones serve in the 3D world? Well, here bones are used to deform a mesh by affecting the position, rotation, and scale of the points it's made from.

You can use a single bone to animate a character, or you can create a hierarchy of bones to allow for a greater range of motion. Generally speaking, the number of bones you'll need for any given character is directly proportional to the complexity of the animation you want to achieve. Sound confusing? Think of it this way: A single bone can be used to animate a hand waving back and forth. But if you want that hand to perform sign language, you'll need a lot more bones.

Having a structure of bones gives us a way to control and manipulate the geometry. This structure provides a control system that we refer to in LightWave as a *rig*. We'll look at what a rig is all about shortly, but for now, let's learn what these bones actually do. Knowing this will give us an appreciation for how we might use them later on.

Understanding Bones

Unlike the bones in your body, CG bones behave like small magnets, or force fields, inside a 3D object. These force fields play a game of tug-of-war with the points in your mesh, pulling and pushing them about. You might think this sounds a little hectic and crazy, right? Well, it would be complete anarchy if it weren't for the fact that the influence of each bone's force field diminishes as it gets farther away from the bone itself. Bones that strongly influence the points close to them tend to override the effect of others, winning this tug-of-war. By laying out bones carefully, we can isolate particular areas of a mesh from the influence of other bones.

Let's take a look at how this works. Open up a fresh Layout and let's get started.

1. Load **Simple_box_bones.lwo** (Objects\Chapter 23). This is a basic subpatched block object. We'll use this object to learn a little more about how bones work in Layout.

2. Make sure that Auto Key is *deactivated* (<**Shift**>+<**F1**>) so that we can tweak the bones safely. Auto Key will record any tweaks or adjustments we make. If I'm not planning on making an animation, I prefer to disable this option while I test my bones.

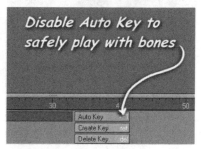

Figure 23-1: Deactivate Auto Key while "testing" bones.

3. Let's add some bones to the object in Layout, but before we do this, switch the viewport to **Top (XZ)** view and **Front Face Wireframe**. Creating bones only works while in an orthographic view. (Front Face Wireframe lets us see the bones inside the object.) The tools for creating bones are found under the Setup menu tab, so let's go there and click on **Draw Bones**. This tool lets us draw bones for the object by clicking and dragging in the viewport. Click and drag from the center of the object out to one of the corners of the object. Repeat this, dragging toward the other three corners to create a total of four bones, as shown in Figure 23-2.

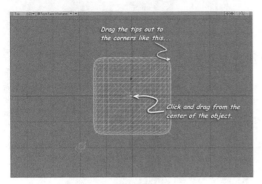

Figure 23-2: Draw bones in place.

4. Four bones have been created, but at this stage they are inactive (indicated by the fact they are displayed as dotted lines). Select all four bones, then click on **Setup | Modify | Orientation | Record Bone Rest Position** (<r>) to *rest* the bones. The bones will change from simple dotted lines to solid lines, indicating they're now active. This process of *resting* records the position, rotation, and size of each bone and where it exists inside this object when at rest (i.e., when the object is not deformed). This process is *very important*, as it lets Layout know where the force fields within the object will be generated.

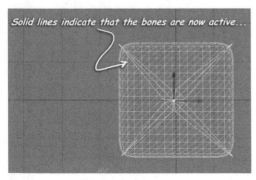

Figure 23-3: Rest the bones.

> **Note**
>
> Take *extreme care* when resting bones. Animating or modifying a bone in Layout, then pressing <r> can literally *destroy* a rig in seconds if you're not careful. This is just one reason why I have disabled the Auto Key option. To enable and disable a bone *without* resting it, press <**Ctrl**>+<**r**>. By clicking on the options found under the Setup | Bones pop-up, all the bones can be disabled and enabled with a simple mouse click.

5. Switch back to a Perspective viewport and set it back to a Shaded Solid or Textured Shaded Solid display. Select the camera or the object and suddenly the bones disappear with only their tips showing (see Figure 23-4). Click on the third pop-up (the triangle widget) on the top of the viewport to see more display options for the viewport, then select **Bone X-Ray** as shown in Figure 23-5.

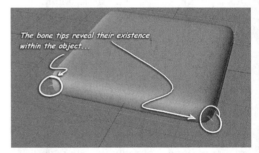

Figure 23-4: Bones be gone!

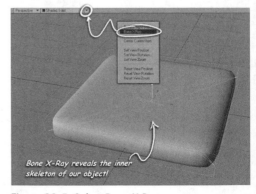

Figure 23-5: Select Bone X-Ray.

6. Let's check out how these bones work. Click on **Modify | Rotate** (<**y**>) and select one of the bones. Click and drag around to see how the bone deforms and bends the object. While the corner of the box deforms near the bone, we can also see how the bone is pulling at the other points in the object, as shown in Figure 23-6.

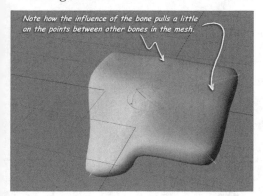

Figure 23-6: Bone deformation at work.

7. It's time to see just how this magnetic force field concept is behaving. Let's select the option **Bone Weight Shade** from the third pop-up on the top of the viewport.

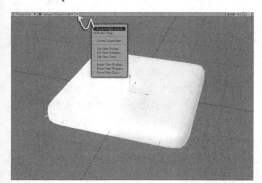

Figure 23-7: Select Bone Weight Shade.

8. Note that everything in Figure 23-7 has gone bright blue and white. It's a little tricky to see what exactly is going on here as the weight shading is actually

being affected by the lighting in the scene. To fix this, select the light in the scene, then open the Light Properties window (<**p**>) and deactivate the Affect OpenGL option.

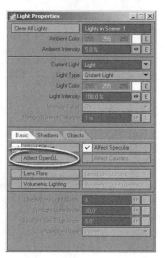

Figure 23-8: Deactivate the Affect OpenGL option.

You'll need to reselect a bone, but now things start to become a little clearer! The yellow color indicates where the bone's magnetic force field influences the mesh. Bright yellow indicates a lot of influence, while cyan indicates none.

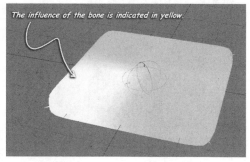

Figure 23-9: No lighting makes Bone Weight Shade much clearer.

So, now we can see the influence of bones on the mesh of an object using Bone Weight Shade view, but how do we modify or manipulate it?

9. With a bone selected, open the **Bones for Simple_box_bones** properties window (**<p>**), as shown in Figure 23-10. Note how the title bar of the properties window indicates which object the bones relate to, rather than just informing us that we're editing Bone properties. A small detail, but one that can be quite useful when trying to troubleshoot why bones aren't affecting the right object!

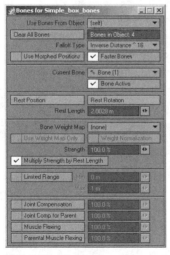

Figure 23-10: The bones properties panel for the object.

This panel lets us configure the way the bones in our object work. The speed at which the influence of the bones diminish is controlled by the Falloff Type pop-up at the top of the window. Note that the settings in this top section of the properties window are *global* to all bones inside the Simple_box_bones object, hence changing any value will apply to *every* bone here (not just the selected one).

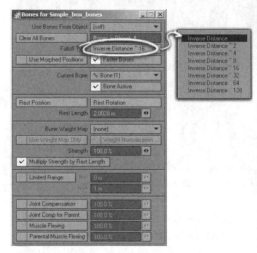

Figure 23-11: This section is global to all bones inside the object.

10. Change the Falloff Type pop-up to **Inverse Distance**, the first setting. This makes the influence of the bones very strong and slow to fade away. Note the change in the Bone Weight Shade display. The influence of our selected bone is hardly visible, not because it's weak, but because of the other three bones also pulling at the same points. Bone Weight Shade simply shows the effect of the *influence* of a bone on a mesh, not the *individual strength* of a bone.

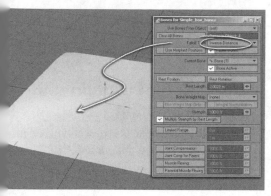

Figure 23-12: Inverse Distance influence.

11. Rotate the bone and see the difference made when all bones have a very strong influence on the mesh. Now let's change the Falloff Type (reopen the properties window if you've closed it) and set it to the highest setting of **Inverse Distance ^ 128**. The influence dies off much faster, allowing the other bones to hold their own areas in place a lot better. The influence of the bone appears to be very strong, as expected, now that the other bones don't interfere as much.

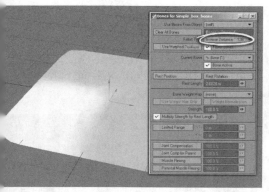

Figure 23-13: Inverse Distance ^ 128 allows bones to keep more influence closer to home.

Other Bone Influence Options

When we start to create complex rigs for characters, so many bones pulling and pushing points around in a mesh can actually start to slow down the performance of Layout. The option **Faster Bones** is designed to assist by only making each point in a mesh influenced by its *four closest bones*, rather than evaluating the influence from all bones within the object. This setting can usually be left active.

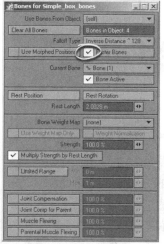

Figure 23-14: The Faster Bones option.

Setting the Falloff Type is one way to modify the influence of a bone in a mesh. The other way is to simply modify the size of the bone within the object. This is done through the **Rest Length** value. Combined with the options **Strength** and **Multiply Strength by Rest Length**, we can control the effect of a bone quite quickly by adjusting its size. In Figure 23-15, note how the

807

influence changes when the bone is adjusted to a tiny rest length and a huge rest length.

diminishes from the bone starting at the range's **Min** distance from the bone, and is completely gone by the **Max** distance.

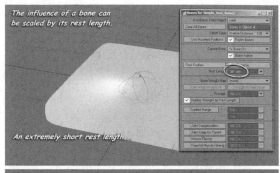

The influence of a bone can be scaled by its rest length.

An extremely short rest length.

An incredibly large rest length.

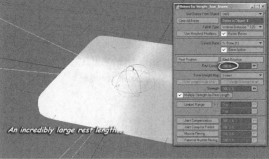

Figure 23-15: Rest Length and its cohorts at work!

Below these settings is yet another way to control the influence of bones. **Limited Range** lets us limit the range, or area, of a bone's influence. When active, the size of the range for the magnetic force field is displayed around the bone. The influence

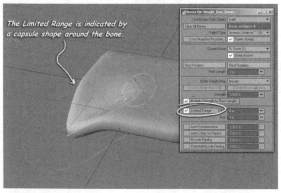

The Limited Range is indicated by a capsule shape around the bone.

Figure 23-16: Limited Range at work.

Joint Compensation and Muscle Flexing

By this point, we're pretty well versed in what bones do; we understand that bones are like force fields inside our object, and how they pull and push the points of our object around. While this is essential knowledge to have, it's also important to understand that the way geometry is constructed will determine how well an object will deform when it has bones applied to it. Let's continue our journey…

Clear the scene in Layout, and let's take a closer look at some of the things bones do to our 3D geometry.

1. Load **Simple_Arm.lws** from Scenes\ Chapter 23. This scene contains a very simple stumpy arm with a set of bones inside. The bones are all parented to each other, and form the arm's *rigging*, a control system set up for the animator to manipulate the arm itself. Let's make sure that we have **Modify | Rotate** (<y>) active and then select the second bone found in the forearm.

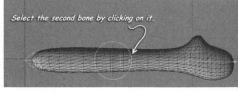

Select the second bone by clicking on it.

Figure 23-17: Select the second bone.

2. Rotate the bone around its Pitch axis (the green rotation handle) and check out how things look. Note how the

elbow area starts to squish in like a rubber hose! Not a great look, but a very common issue that we run across when working with bones.

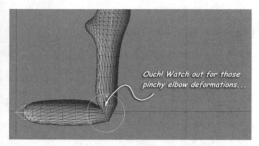

Figure 23-18: Rubber hose elbows.

Luckily, bones have options to help minimize this situation. At the bottom of the bone properties window are four options that set up joint compensation and muscle flexing. These options are designed to help keep the geometry from crimping or pinching, like we saw in Figure 23-18.

Figure 23-19: We have options to assist with minimizing that pinching effect.

At this stage, it's very important that you realize one simple fact: These four options *only work for rotation about the Pitch axis*, and not for rotation around either Heading or Bank. Later in this chapter, in the section titled "Skelegon Orientation and Handles," we'll look at how to set up bones to ensure that they rotate correctly. For now, just be aware of this limitation.

3. Activate both **Joint Compensation** and **Joint Comp for Parent** for the selected bone. Notice in Figure 23-20 how the geometry has been pumped back out to help retain the correct shape of the geometry around the elbow.

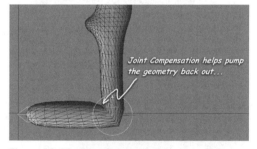

Figure 23-20: Joint Compensation at work.

4. Activate **Muscle Flexing** and **Parental Muscle Flexing**, then set the amounts of each to **200%**. These options simulate a simple muscle flexing effect by bulging the geometry, as

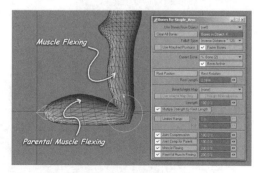

Figure 23-21: Muscle Flexing at work.

shown in Figure 23-21. While both the bone and its parent have some bulging going on here, the arm would obviously look a lot better if only Parental Muscle Flexing were used.

Subpatch Order

Something that also plays a big role in the way bone deformation affects geometry, given that most characters and objects we will work with are likely to be subpatched, is the order in which LightWave converts the subpatch polygons into renderable polygons.

1. Select the arm object, and then open the Object Properties window (<**p**>). By default, the Subdivision Order pop-up is set to **First**. When set to First, the subpatch geometry is frozen into its higher-density geometry *before* any deformations are applied. Bones then deform this denser geometry.

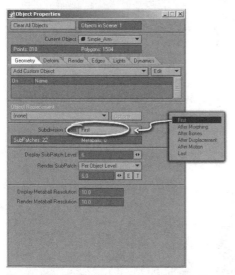

Figure 23-22: The Subdivision Order setting.

2. We can alter when LightWave will convert the subpatch geometry into denser polygons by changing this pop-up. Change Subdivision Order to

Last. In most cases, a setting of Last works great for characters and organic objects. Rotate the bone again to see how the change affects the way the elbow deforms.

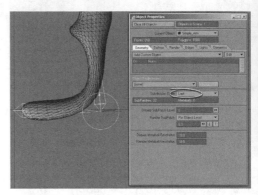

Figure 23-23: Change Subdivision Order to Last, then rotate the bone and see the difference.

What a crazy difference! The reason this now looks like a bent pipe and not an arm is simple. A Subdivision Order of Last tells Layout to subpatch the geometry *after* it has been deformed by the bones. However, as you saw in Figure 23-23, we've lost the form and appearance of the arm completely.

> ### Important Note
>
> At this stage you're probably wondering just why we'd change the Subdivision Order when it creates such a wacky result. While a Subdivision Order of First may have appeared to work better for the arm, it doesn't work well when we get into serious character rigging. Last is usually the pre-ferred setting as it creates a much smoother and cleaner organic result after bones and other tools have had their way with the model. To prevent this less than desirable bendy appearance while using a setting of Last, we'll need to plan our modeling approaches carefully.

Let's take a peek at why this is happening.

To see the original unsubpatched geome-try in Layout, make sure that the viewport is set to a shaded mode (Wireframe Shade,

Texture Wire, etc.) and activate **Show SubPatch Cages** under **Edit | OpenGL Options**.

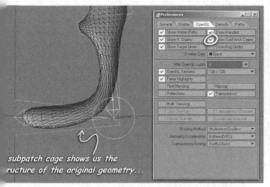

subpatch cage shows us the structure of the original geometry...

Figure 23-24: Activating Show SubPatch Cages shows the original mesh.

Did you see how the bones squeezed the points in the elbow in Figure 23-24, making the geometry taper inward toward the elbow? To correct this, we need to modify our geometry so that subpatching has more structure to hold the object's form better. A simple knife operation to create extra polygons before and after the elbow joint will ensure that the subpatching holds its form a lot better.

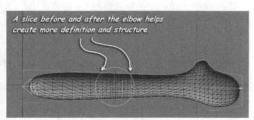

A slice before and after the elbow helps create more definition and structure.

Figure 23-25: A simple knife job helps define more structure when using bones and subpatching.

Combine this with a little joint compensation and we've removed that whole bendy-hose look completely, even though the Subdivision Order is set to Last.

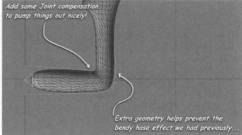

Add some Joint compensation to pump things out nicely!

Extra geometry helps prevent the bendy hose effect we had previously...

Figure 23-26: Mixing Joint Compensation with the knifed arm.

Holding Bones

We've learned about the influence and falloff of bones, and how they pull and push the points around in an object. As we understand it, the points closest to a bone will be more strongly influenced by that bone than the other bones inside an object. What about the parts of a model that are not close to *any* bone? Those points that sit midway between bones are open game to the bones around them, and this can have an adverse affect on how the mesh deforms if we're not careful.

Let's load **Simple_Arm.lws** scene file again (from Scenes\Chapter 23) and take a look at what we're talking about here.

Note

If you already have this scene loaded in Layout, you can reload the scene file and reset all your changes by selecting File | Load | Revert Scene to Last Saved. This option loads the last saved version of the current scene from disk. It makes for a fast way to restore a scene without having to clear it first.

1. Click on the first bone in the hand, and then use **Modify | Rotate** (<y>) to

rotate it around its palm. As seen in Figure 23-27, the thumb completely loses its form. Of course, since we know all about bones now, we can quickly identify the problem as being caused by the influence of the bones closest to these points playing their game of tug-of-war.

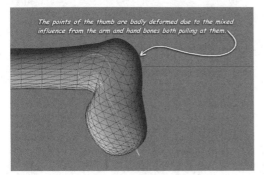

Figure 23-27: The thumb loses its form quickly.

2. Let's update the rig by placing an extra bone in the area where the thumb geometry resides. Doing this will add a more localized force field near these points, overriding the effect of the other bones. Using **Setup | Add | Draw Bones**, click and drag out an extra thumb bone as shown in Figure 23-28. Bones that we add to hold parts of a mesh in place are called, believe it or not, *hold bones*.

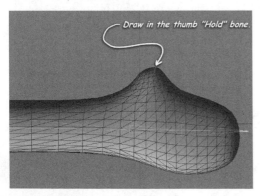

Figure 23-28: Drawing the thumb bone.

Note

Before continuing, make sure that the Parent in Place option (found just below the Scene Editor in the toolbar) is *active*. We'll be parenting bones to others while we work here, and Parent in Place will make sure that bones stay in place and don't move when they're parented.

3. This bone should be attached to the hand, so press <**m**> to bring up the Motion Options window for the new bone, and set Parent Item to the oddly named **Bone (3)_1**. Press <**r**> to rest this new bone.

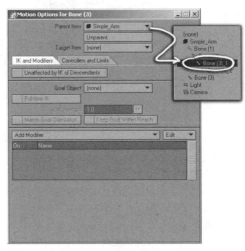

Figure 23-29: Parent and rest the new bone.

Note

When bones are created, they are given the default name of Bone. If you're lazy like me, you don't care what the bones are called as you go and you'll start to get rigs with bone names like we've just seen in step 3. It's a good idea to rename bones where possible so that the names are more meaningful. This can be done by selecting a bone, then clicking on **Items | Replace | Rename**. Alternatively, if you prefer to use the Scene Editor, select the bone and right-click to bring up a pop-up menu, than select the **Rename** option from the menu, as shown in Figure 23-30.

Figure 23-30: Renaming bones with the Scene Editor.

4. Select the hand bone again, rotate it, and watch the difference in the deformation (Figure 23-31). The new bone's influence is holding the points in the thumb, making sure it doesn't get distorted by the others.

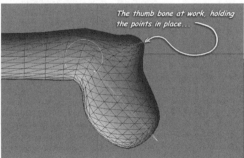

The thumb bone at work, holding the points in place...

Figure 23-31: The new thumb bone at work.

Hold bones are my personal preference for constructing a good bone structure (rig) for a character. LightWave does, however, offer another alternative system that we can use to control the influence of bones from interfering with other parts of the geometry. This system is called *weight mapping*, and is quite common in many 3D applications.

Weight Maps

In Modeler, we can create *weight maps* for points in a mesh. Each point can be given a weighting value (a percentage) that can then be applied to a bone to scale its influence on each point. For example, if we want to prevent a bone from influencing the points on the thumb, we'd make sure that the weight map the bone uses has a 0% weighting on the thumb points. This would scale the influence out, making the bone no longer have any effect in that area.

Let's reload our scene again to remove the hold bone we just created. Instead, we'll create and use weight maps to control the way that the arm and hand bones share the influence on the thumb geometry.

1. To use weight maps, we first need to create them in the model itself. Let's open up Modeler and edit the **Simple_Arm.lwo** object. In the Perspective viewport, let's change the display type to **Weight Shade** so we can see the weight maps when they are created (see Figure 23-32).

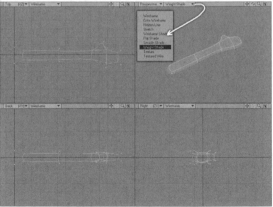

Figure 23-32: Editing the object and setting the Perspective viewport to Weight Shade.

2. Weight maps are saved within the object and relate to the points in a model. In this exercise I'm going to use

813

Polygons selection mode (<**Ctrl**> + <**h**>) and apply weight maps to the selected polygons instead. This applies the weight map to all the points that form the selected polygons. Select the arm polygons only (up to the wrist) as shown in Figure 23-33.

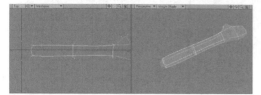

Figure 23-33: Select the arm polys only.

3.   Let's create a weight map. Make sure that the **W** button is selected on the bottom-right corner of Modeler and then from the pop-up menu at the end, select (**new**) to create a new weight map (see Figure 23-34). In the Create Weight Map window, change the Name to **wm_arm**, then click **Create** to generate the new weight map for the selection. Keep the Create Weight Map window open for now as we'll need it when we create more weight maps in a bit.

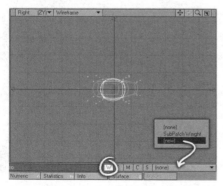

Figure 23-34: Create a new weight map for the arm polygons.

Figure 23-35: Enter the new weight map name, then click Create.

4.   The weight map is created! The Initial Value option, which is checked by default, ensured that a value of 100% was applied to all points of the polygons that were selected (if you want to create a weight map without applying any values, uncheck the Initial Value option). The Perspective viewport's Weight Shade display shows the weight map as a bright red color.

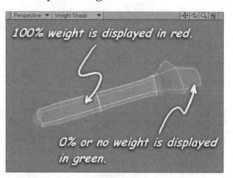

Figure 23-36: The new weight map is created.

> **Note**
>
> The Weight Shade display shows the currently selected weight map. Green indicates a value of 0%, red indicates a positive value, and blue indicates a negative value.

5.   Now let's turn our attention to the hand. While we could deselect the arm polys and select just the hand polys, my preferred method is to instead hide the selected polygons using **View | View | Hide Selected** (<**->**). Why, exactly, is this my preferred method? Simply because it ensures I don't accidentally reselect polygons or points

that have an existing weight map. It also means I can quickly spot any accidentally missed polys that should have been included, and gives me a good indicator for when I've completed all weight mapping in a mesh (i.e., when all the polys are hidden) (see Figure 23-37).

Figure 23-37: Hide the selected polys.

6. Now that the arm is hidden away, let's add a weight map to the hand. The Create Weight Map window should (hopefully) still be open on the desktop. If you accidentally closed the Create Weight Map window, simply reopen it by selecting *(new)* from the pop-up in the bottom-right corner of Modeler (like we did earlier). Set Name to **wm_hand**, and click **Create** to apply the new weight map to the visible hand polygons (see Figure 23-38).

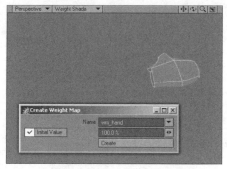

Figure 23-38: Create and apply the new wm_hand weight map.

7. Now press <\> to unhide the polygons and reveal the entire arm. One thing you may notice in the Weight Shade view is that the arm appears to no longer be weightmapped! Never fear! Weight Shade only displays the *currently selected* weight map. Changing the current weight map from the pop-up on the bottom right to wm_arm will change the Weight Shade display.

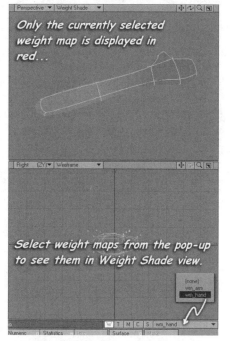

Figure 23-39: Unhidden polys, but where has the wm_arm weight map gone?

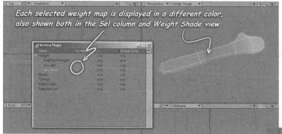

Figure 23-40: The Vertex Maps panel and the Weight Shade view show multiple selections of weight maps.

8. Let's save this version of the model back to the Objects directory as **Simple_Arm_Weighted.lwo**. (I've saved mine on the companion DVD as Simple_Arm_Weighted.lwo if you want to compare your weight maps with mine.) Close Modeler and return to Layout. Simple_Arm_Weighted should now be the name of the object in the scene (as the Hub should have updated the scene automatically).

9. Select the first bone at the start of the arm, and then press <**p**> to bring up the properties window. Begin by telling the first bone to have its influence weighted by the **wm_arm** weight map from the Bone Weight Map pop-up (Figure 23-41). Press the <**Down Arrow**> to select the second bone in the arm and apply the **wm_arm** weight map to this bone as well.

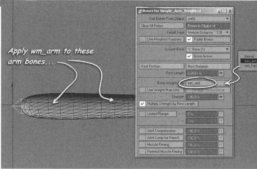

Figure 23-41: Set the first and second bones to use the wm_arm weight map.

10. Press <**Down Arrow**> again for the hand bone, and set its weight map to **wm_hand**. Press <**Down Arrow**> once more and set the second hand bone to also use the **wm_hand** weight map.

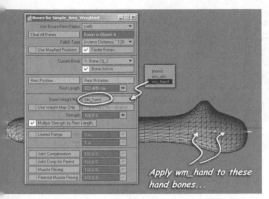

Apply wm_hand to these hand bones...

Figure 23-42: Set the hand bones to use the wm_hand weight map.

11. Rotate the hand bones and watch how the thumb appears to work fine when manipulating the hand.

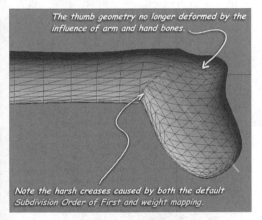

The thumb geometry no longer deformed by the influence of arm and hand bones.

Note the harsh creases caused by both the default Subdivision Order of First and weight mapping.

Figure 23-43: Weight maps keep the thumb in tow.

You may have noticed the way that the polygons now have a hard cut-off look at the wrist. This is primarily due to the weight map cutting the influence off at its edges, and of course the default Subdivision Order of First creating that denser mesh. This is just one reason why I prefer the hold bone method over using weight maps, as it keeps a softer, more organic appearance to deformation.

If you're feeling adventurous, I encourage you to play with the Subdivision Order setting, even using the Knife tool here and there to assist in keeping the form correct. Otherwise, we're ready to get into something a little more serious and fun: rigging up our character from Chapter 16!

Prepping for Rigging

We know that bones deform a mesh by dragging its points around, and the way that a mesh is modeled can play quite an important role in just how well (or badly) a model appears to deform when animated. In this section, we're going to use bones to rig the character we started modeling back in Chapter 16; however, before we do that, we'll need to apply a few small modeling tweaks to prep the mesh for rigging and deformation.

In this section, I'll assume that you'll be able to work out the tools necessary to tweak your own characters. I'll simply highlight the main changes that you may want to make to your own model. If you'd rather just jump into the rigging process and skip this section, then feel free to load my pre-prepped model from **Objects\Chapter 23\ SuperCharacter_prepped_F.lwo**.

Visual Quick Fix

The first thing I do is visually identify any odd-looking parts of the character that need to be tweaked. In this case, I felt that the armpits were missing completely. Without the armpits, the arms would be difficult to fold down to the character's sides. This was fixed by simply moving the points under the arms upward to correct the problem.

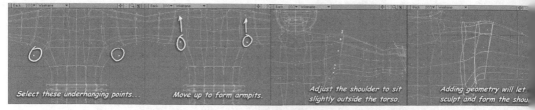

Figure 23-44: Fixing the armpits.

Maintaining Form: Limbs

As we discussed earlier when talking about how subpatch order affects the shape of the model, we'll want to apply the same simple updates to ensure that folds and bends in limbs retain their shape. In my model, I carefully added cuts above and below the elbows and knees to ensure that these will look correct when deformed.

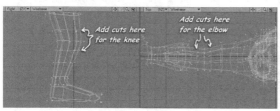

Figure 23-45: Adding cuts around limbs will help maintain form when using a Subdivision Order setting of Last.

While I was at it, I made sure to fine-tune and pump out the shape of the character. In general, subpatch models tend to start becoming "boxy" in appearance as we add more and more polys. When modeling, it's always a good idea to fine-tune as you go to keep things looking nice and "organic."

Something else worth checking is the shoulders. These should be located directly above the armpits and on the outside of the torso. I quickly sculpted and adjusted a little more geometry in this area to make sure we had geometry in place for the arms to hang from.

Figure 23-46: Creating the shoulders and placing the in the right location.

Flow

If we want to polish the look of the model, as well as make sure the polygon structure is designed to deform as nicely as possible, we'll need to adjust a little of its flow. Flow is the "visual" connection between neighboring polygons (how they appear to follow or flow into each other), and will play a part in making sure the character not only deforms nicely, but looks cool, too.

Figure 23-47: The "flow" of polygons in a model.

> **Note**
>
> Polygons that flow in a loop around the edges of geometry, such as details like the eyes or lips, are called "edge loops" (because of the fact they form loops around the edge of geometry). You'll recall we briefly talked about these, as well as flow in general, back in Chapter 15.

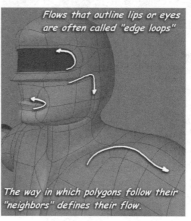

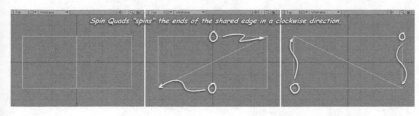

Figure 23-48:
What Spin Quads
does to the edges
of two quad
polygons.

As you probably noted in Figure 23-47, I've done a few things to fine-tune the flow of the shoulder and chest region. To define flow, the most important tool you'll use is the **Detail | Polygons | Spin Quads** (**<Ctrl>+<k>**) tool. We also looked at this tool a little in Chapter 15. Spin Quads takes two four-sided polygons and spins the edge that joins them, as shown in Figure 23-48.

To form the collarbone and flow the shoulders into the chest, I selected two polys on either side of the head as shown in Figure 23-49 and used Spin Quads (**<Ctrl>+<k>**) to change the flow of the polygons.

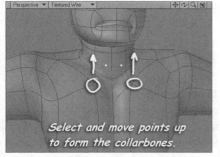

ure 23-49: Spinning some quads to get the polygon
w happening.

After changing the flow, I then moved two points up to bring out the collarbones.

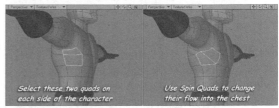

Figure 23-50: Select points and move or drag to sculpt the form better.

Lastly, I spun the quads under the arms to flow the arms into the chest.

Figure 23-51: One last flow tweak to finish the shoulders and arms.

Proportion

Finally, I did a quick review. I felt that while I'd designed the character to be a little cartoony, the balance of the character didn't quite feel right. The issue was mainly due to the fact the arms were way too long, and also perhaps a little too thick. After selecting the polygons of the left arm all the way up to the shoulder, I used the **Modify | Transform | Size** tool (**<H>**) to resize the arms by 90% from the shoulder until

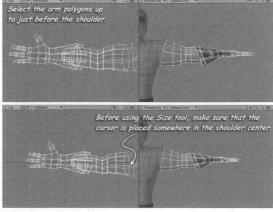

Figure 23-52: Scale the arms until they look in proportion.

819

things looked about right. I repeated the process for the right arm.

Once I was relatively happy that the character was prepped as far as I wanted to take it, I saved it so I could start rigging the character. Remember, one of the many nice things about 3D is that you can always go back and change things if they don't work. A little preparation, however, never goes amiss!

Rigging

Rigging is a term that you may have heard used when talking about sailing. *Rigging* refers to the complex structure of ropes and cables that form the control system for a ship's sails. In the CG world, rigging is no different; it refers to a system that lets us control the posing and animation of a character or object within Layout. We've learned all about the number one tool used for deforming and rigging our character — bones. Now let's look at what it takes to create a character rig using these bones.

Skelegons

The Bones deformation tool is found in Layout, hence bones are designed to be saved in scene files. However, it makes more sense that a bone structure should belong to a character. Modeler allows us to draw up bone locations and store these within characters as *skelegons* — a special type of polygon designed to lay out the structure of a skeleton within an object. We'll be using skelegons to draw up a skeletal structure that will later be used to form the rigging for the character in Layout.

So with that in mind, let's start up Modeler.

> **Note**
>
> It's very important at this stage to understand that skelegons are *not* bones. They are merely a design tool for laying out placeholders for real bones to be created later in Layout. Skelegons are a great way to keep the basic skeletal layout with the character to which it relates, and can be cut and pasted into other characters, saving immense amounts of time recreating skelegons from scratch.

1. Load the character model you created in Chapter 16 into Modeler. Using some of the concepts described earlier, make sure that you modify your model appropriately so that it will deform nicely. If you prefer, you can load mine from **Objects\Chapter 23\Super-Character_prepped_F.lwo**. We're going to be creating a skeletal structure using skelegons.

2. I often find skelegons easiest to set up by placing the character into the background and creating the skeleton structure in a new layer. Let's do that by setting layer 2 as our active foreground layer, and the first layer containing our character into the background. The skelegon tools are all found under the Setup tab. Click **Setup | Skelegons | Create Skelegons** and let's get started.

3. Creating the very first skelegon requires us to hold the left mouse button and drag out the shape. This is very important, so take care that you left-click and drag or you run the risk of creating an invalid skelegon. Let's do this in the Top viewport, starting just in front of the character and dragging back in a straight line until the tip ends inside the character's body. You'll note that a skelegon has a small triangular end; this is the pivot location, or the

rotation point, of the bone later in Layout.

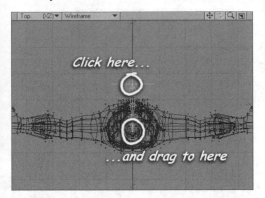

Figure 23-53: Drag out the very first skelegon.

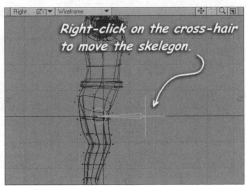

Figure 23-54: Adjust the first skelegon by right-clicking and dragging the cross-hair.

> ## Note
>
> It's important that we place the skelegon pivot in the correct location as we go. This location dictates the way that a bone will later rotate and, if at the wrong end of a bone, then limbs can start to go a little crazy! Luckily for us these are skelegons, which are polygons. If you ever draw a skelegon in the wrong direction, simply select it (using Polygons selection mode) and press <f> to flip the skelegon.

4. If we look at the other viewports, we'll notice that the skelegon probably doesn't lie at the correct location. This initial skelegon will be the main parent of the whole skeleton, and should be located just above the hips, where the *center of gravity* should be. Moving a skelegon can be done by left-clicking and dragging on the light blue cross-hair drag handle.

5. Once the initial skelegon is in place, let's draw the spine, neck, and head structure, this time in the Back (XY) viewport. Unlike the very first skelegon, to create connecting skelegons you simply place the mouse cursor at the location where you want your new skelegon to *end* and left-click *once*. Each skelegon you create becomes a *child* of the previous skelegon from which it came from.

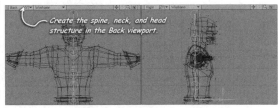

Figure 23-55: Draw the spine, neck, and head structure from the first skelegon.

I often keep my spine skelegons to the minimum needed — two or three bones — for the stomach, middle back, and chest area. There's not a lot of geometry in the model, so creating elaborate multi-boned spinal columns wouldn't really make much sense.

Skelegon Orientation and Handles

I draw these new skelegons in a different viewport for a good reason. The viewport we draw in helps dictate the direction of the Y-axis of the skelegon (the axis will be perpendicular to the viewport we're looking at, as indicated in Figure 23-56), and this in turn defines the orientation of the bone's rotational axes, or more importantly, the orientation of the Pitch axis. As we learned earlier, features such as Joint Compensation and Muscle Flexing rely on the Pitch to work.

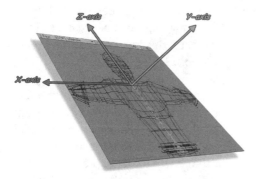

Figure 23-56: The viewport helps define the Y-axis of the skelegon.

Drawing in a particular viewport defines the Y-axis. If you forget, or accidentally draw in the wrong viewport, don't panic or undo all your hard work because we can actually edit this orientation. Look carefully at the skelegons and note the blue *drag handles* that are displayed. The circle at the end of each skelegon adjusts the tip of the skelegon, and any child bones after this are also moved. The blue cross-hair at the start indicates the parent of all skelegons in the chain, and lets us drag the whole chain of bones. The small sticks with circles at the tips are called the *bank handles*, and let us modify the bank orientation. It's this *bank handle* that we can use to orient how the

Pitch axis will be aligned. The bank handle is essentially defining the Y-axis.

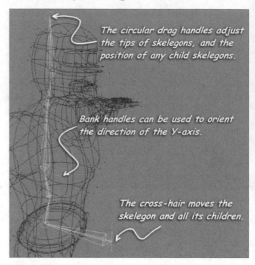

Figure 23-57: The drag handles of skelegons explained.

By left-clicking in the circle on the end of the bank handle, we can drag the bank handle around the bone. If the bank handle appears stubborn, try dragging it in a different viewport.

> **Note**
>
> The bank handle actually reorients the pivot of the child bone attached to the end of each skelegon, and not the skelegon itself. However, a tool in Layout called Record Pivot Rotation lets us apply this bank handle to the bone itself. We'll be looking at this tool and how it can be used in the next section.

6. Use the drag handles at the tips of the bones and place them where you'd expect the spine to actually be (so that they rotate realistically from the correct location in the body).

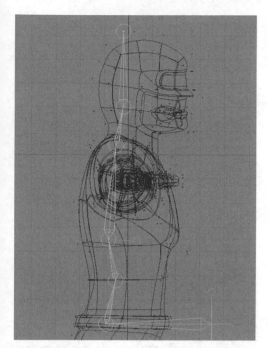

Figure 23-58: Lay out the spine appropriately.

7. Press <**Return**> to deactivate the Create Skelegons tool once finished. The spine is complete, so let's go and build the arm. The arm, or in this case, collarbone, comes out from the chest. We'll need to build the next skelegon starting from the end of the chest bone itself. Start by selecting the chest bone.

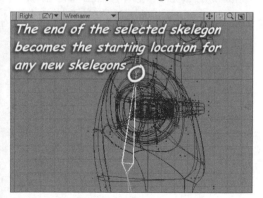

The end of the selected skelegon becomes the starting location for any new skelegons.

Figure 23-59: Select the chest bone.

Note

By default, skelegons will all have the same name of *Bone*. If you want to name your skelegons as you go, select a skelegon and click the Setup | Skelegons | Rename Skelgns button. Enter a name for the selected skelegon and click OK. Unfortunately, you can only rename one skelegon at a time. Alternatively, click on the Setup | Skelegons | Skelegon Tree button, which will give you a more structured display of the skelegons in Modeler (see Figure 23-60). Just double-click on a skelegon to rename it, or double-click on Weight Map to assign a weight map to the skelegon (if you have one in your model, that is).

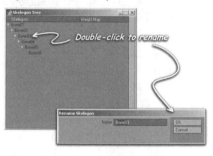

Figure 23-60: The Skelegon Tree window.

If you name a skelegon and weight map exactly the same (and when I say exactly, I do mean exactly!), then Layout will automatically apply the weight map to the bone for you. Personally, I'm no fan of the Skelegon Tree. I tend to do all my renaming in Layout once I have the bones in place (and only if I feel the need to rename them).

8. Activate the **Setup | Create Skelegons** tool, and simply left-click in the Top (XZ) viewport where you would like to place the end of the collarbone. The new skelegon will be created and parented to the end of the chest skelegon.

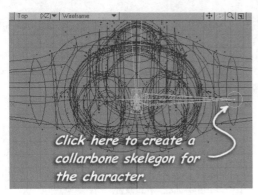

Figure 23-61: Draw a collarbone.

9. Now create an extremely tiny skelegon in a straight line just in front of the tip of this collarbone. In all my rigs I've found that adding a tiny bone into the joint areas, like shoulders and hips, gives me an extra controller I can use later on to prevent gimbal locking. *Gimbal locking* is a common problem caused by rotating an item 90 degrees on the Pitch, which in turn aligns the Bank and Heading axes, causing us to lose one axis of control.

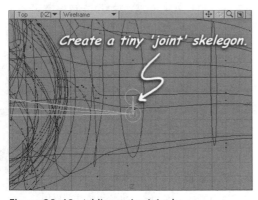

Figure 23-62: Adding a tiny joint bone.

10. Let's continue and build the arm. In the Back (XY) viewport, left-click on the elbow location to draw out the bicep skelegon, then click near the wrist to create the lower arm.

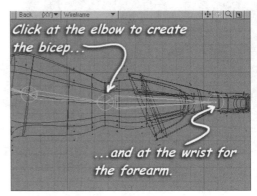

Figure 23-63: Adding the arm bones.

11. In the Top viewport, draw another small skelegon to represent the wrist (see Figure 23-64). Press <**Return**> to finish the arm. Select the two arm skelegons as shown in Figure 23-65, and then click the **Setup | Skelegons | Split Skelegon** button to convert these two into four smaller skelegons.

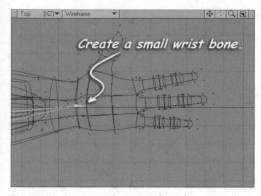

Figure 23-64: Draw the wrist, then deactivate the Create Skelegons tool.

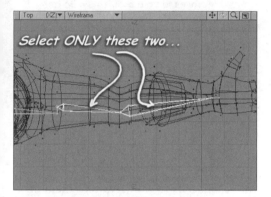

Figure 23-65: Select the arm skelegons.

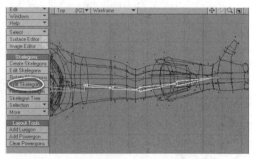

Figure 23-66: Use Split Skelegon to create four smaller skelegons.

Note

You may be wondering why we split those two arm skelegons. The answer is simple: So we can roll the wrist naturally. Your wrist is joined to the end of your arm and really can't roll on its own (the wrist joint doesn't allow it). In fact, it's easy to test by simply grasping your wrist hard with the other hand, then attempting to roll your wrist. You just can't do it. Instead, watch how your whole arm twists when you roll your wrist around. To allow us to create this same motion, we use multiple bones. This is the reason for so many bones in the arm. We'll take a quick look at using these later on.

12. Now that we have the arm completed, let's build the hand bones. These will give us control over the fingers and thumb so that we can make our character grasp items or form a fist to punch the bad guy's lights out! Select the wrist skelegon, as we want our fingers to be connected to this skelegon. In the Top (XZ) viewport, let's build the little finger by creating a skelegon that ends at the first knuckle of the finger, then click on each knuckle of the little finger until the finger rig is finished, as shown in Figure 23-67. Be sure to modify and tidy up the bones so that they sit in the center of each knuckle from the Top view. From the side, make sure the bones sit just above the center of the finger geometry.

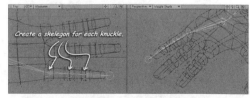

Figure 23-67: Drawing out the little finger.

13. Press <**Return**> to complete the finger. Select the wrist bone again, and repeat step 12 for the other three fingers and the thumb.

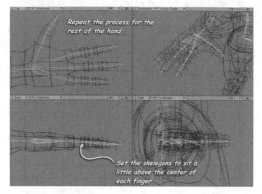

Figure 23-68: Repeat the process for each finger and thumb.

14. One thing we need to do here is correct the bank handle for the thumb, given that it rotates differently from the fingers. Select the first skelegon of the thumb (the one that starts from the wrist) then click on **Setup | Skelegons | Edit Skelegons**. We need to adjust the bank handles until the axis is pointing horizontally for the two upper skelegons, and around 45 degrees for the first skelegon (see Figure 23-69).

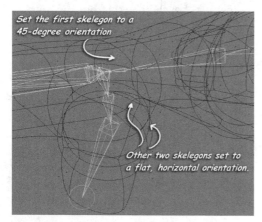

Figure 23-69: Adjust the bank handles.

> **Note**
>
> You may think the thumb has two joints, unlike the fingers with three, right? Strangely, that's a common misconception I run across. The first joint in the thumb starts out in the middle of your palm (just try it and see in real life!). If you also look closely at your real thumb, you'll notice that it's actually on roughly a 45-degree angle. In retrospect, the character could possibly do with a little more work to get the hand looking better. However, for now I'll use it as-is and leave that decision up to you if you feel the urge to improve on the model. I may go back and edit the model later on to tweak this if it proves to be a problem when animating. Again, the beauty of 3D is simply that we can change things when we feel like it!

After adjusting the bank handles, we're done with the hand. At this stage, it's probably a really good idea to save what you've done so far just in case things go bad, the power cuts out, or the cat pulls the plug out of the wall (it's happened before, trust me!).

15. That's a lot of work. Now for the other arm… Or if we were smart, we could instead select all the bones up to the collarbone (see Figure 23-70), and simply use Modeler's **Multiply | Duplicate | Mirror** (<**V**>) tool instead.

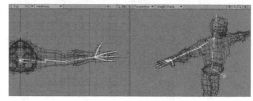

Figure 23-70: Select the arm bones first.

To make sure you mirror the arm cleanly, use the Numeric panel (<**n**>) to mirror. Set the Axis to **X**, Center to X = **0 m**, Y = **0 m**, and Z = **0 m**. **Merge Points** should be checked so that the mirrored arm becomes attached to the chest bone.

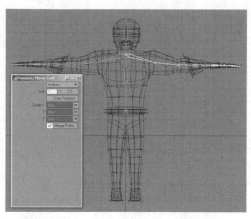

Figure 23-71: Use Mirror to create the other arm.

16. Let's create the hips and legs. This should be relatively simple. Start by selecting the very first bone we started with. The hips will hang from this bone. Once selected, click **Setup | Skelegons | Create Skelegons** and create a skelegon in the Back (XY) viewport that ends at the bottom of the crotch area.

Figure 23-72: The hip bone.

17. Draw the next skelegon out to where the hip joint would be (Figure 23-73) in the Back (XY) viewport. In the Top (XZ) viewport, let's add a small joint bone like we did for the shoulders (Figure 23-74).

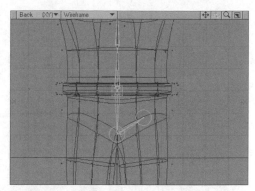

Figure 23-73: Draw a bone out to the hip joint.

Figure 23-74: Creating the tiny joint bone like we did for the shoulder.

18. In the Back (XY) viewport, draw a skelegon down to the kneecap, then a lower leg skelegon down to the ankle. Then add a small ankle bone.

Figure 23-75: Drawing the leg bones is relatively easy.

19. We now need to draw the feet. Did you notice we're missing a serious piece of prepping here? Polygons for toes! Luckily for us, this is CG, so adding this is extremely simple. Press <**Return**> to finish up with the skelegons for the moment (we'll come back and do the feet shortly). Swap the FG and BG layers using <'>, then using the Knife tool (<**K**>) let's slice

some geometry for the toes as shown in Figure 23-76.

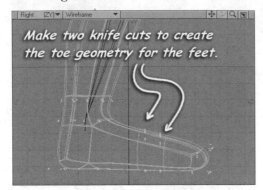

Figure 23-78: Adding the toe.

Figure 23-76: Slice and dice in some toes!

20. Swap the layers (<'>) to return to our skelegons again. Select the ankle skelegon and click **Setup | Skelegons | Create Skelegons**. In the Top (XZ) viewport, click in front of the character to create the skelegon, then adjust its tip in the Right (YZ) viewport until it sits at the back of the toe (the ball of the foot) as shown in Figure 23-77.

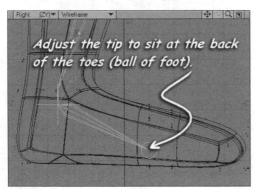

Figure 23-77: Adding in the foot bone.

21. In the Top (XZ) viewport, click at the tip of the foot to create the toe skelegon.

22. Remember the thumb in the previous section of this chapter, and how it was open game to the bones in the arm because it had no bone to hold its geometry in place? From experience, I know that the same problem will occur for the back of the foot, so let's add in a holding bone just to stabilize the foot. Select the main foot bone (the one from the ankle to the ball of the foot), and then click at the back of the foot in the Top (XZ) viewport to add the extra bone.

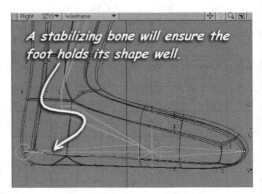

Figure 23-79: Adding the hold bone.

We're done with the leg! Excellent. All that needs to be done now is to simply mirror the leg as we did with the arm.

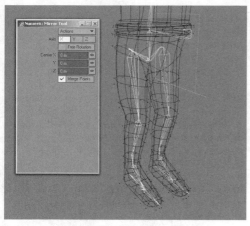

Figure 23-80: Mirroring the leg.

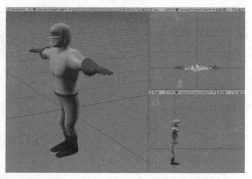

Figure 23-81: The character loaded and the light tweaked to see clearly.

The last thing I do now is to simply cut all the bones, then paste them into the model in layer 1. This will ensure that the bones are created inside the character itself. Once done, save the model and we're ready to check out the rig to make sure it's in working order before we get into any serious animation.

Skelegons to Bones

The skelegons have been laid out, but as we know, these are not bones but merely markers inside a model to tell Layout where bones should exist. Let's send our object to Layout and use these skelegons to create the rig for animation.

1. If you are still in Modeler, you can use the pop-up on the top right to **send object to Layout** once you have saved it. If not, simply open up a fresh Layout and load the object. The default light and camera show the character from behind. What I often do is rotate the light so it faces the character and makes it easier to see in the Perspective viewport.

> **Note**
>
> One light is never enough. Clone the default light and rotate it so that it faces the opposite direction on the Heading axis. Remember to keyframe the cloned light after adjusting its rotation. This will create a simple lighting setup to help us see the character more clearly in Layout from back and front.

2. To generate the bones using the skelegon structure we created in Modeler, click **Setup | Add | Cvt Skelegons.** A message should pop up to indicate how many bones have been created. If you've been following along with the book, there should be 67 bones. Make sure that you activate the **Bone X-Ray** display option for each viewport in Layout (if you happen to be running with more than one as we saw in Figure 23-81).

> **Note**
>
> If the Layout interface is too small to display the toolbar in its entirety, the skelegon conversion tool will appear under **Setup | Add | More | Convert Skelegons into Bones**. It's a little more verbose then the truncated Cvt Skelegons button.

829

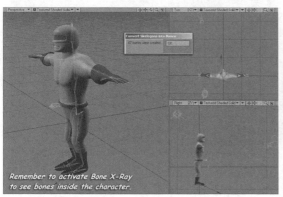

Remember to activate Bone X-Ray
to see bones inside the character.

Figure 23-82: Skelegons converted.

Layout has used the skelegons we created in Modeler to create the bones for the character. The next step is to just double-check that these bones are indeed going to work for us.

3. Before continuing, select the object and open its properties to set its Subdivision Order to **Last**. Select one of the bones, open its properties window, and set the Falloff Type to **Inverse Distance** ^ **128**. Make sure that you save the scene file before you continue.

Testing the Deformations

The first thing I do after creating the bones is to test them before I go any further into the rigging process. This lets me check that I have enough bones in place and that they are located in the right places for the mesh to deform fairly cleanly and as I expected. Make sure that Auto Key has been deactivated before you begin.

1. Select one of the upper leg bones and test it by rotating the leg back and forth. You may notice that the legs work, but the belt of the character just isn't working at all, bending and twisting around unnaturally. As we know, there's nothing in place around the belt

to hold the polygons in place, making this area of the model vulnerable for the bones to pull and push around.

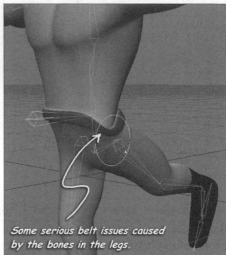

Some serious belt issues caused
by the bones in the legs.

Figure 23-83: The leg shows us some serious belt issues.

2. Select the neck bone and rotate the head about. Again, where there are no bones in the face area, there is nothing to hold it in place and it behaves like stretchy rubber instead.

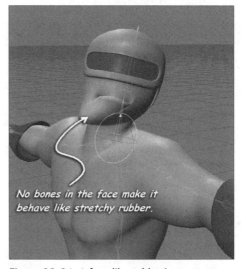

No bones in the face make it
behave like stretchy rubber.

Figure 23-84: A face like rubber!

3. Let's select the shoulder joint bones and use the Rotation tool to fold the arms down. Not having bones inside the muscular body makes the arms push and pull the body about just a little. The influence isn't as great as the other two regions and could be used as-is if we didn't mind a little squishiness here and there.

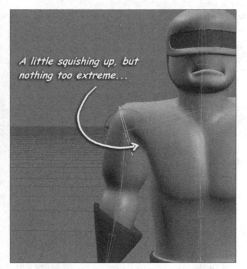

A little squishing up, but nothing too extreme...

Figure 23-85: The effect of the arms is there, but it's not as intrusive or noticeable as the other issues.

Deciding on a Deformation Solution

Now it's crunch time. How will we fine-tune the bone influences to prevent these deformation issues? We could create and use weight maps, or add extra hold bones. A decision needs to be made at this stage about which direction we should take.

Hold bones can give us more organic, soft deformation by letting the bones pull and push the points between them. We may, however, need to add a few bones to get the mesh to behave itself nicely. Weight maps, on the other hand, will let us define the borders of influence and control the blending of

bones on the geometry. We may not need to add in any extra bones at all, but we will need to paint in weight maps in Modeler and then tell all the bones what weight map they're going to be using.

While I'm a big fan of hold bones, I've decided that I'm going to opt for weight maps for this rig. Given it should be relatively easy to set up, it's also a great way to show you just how to best approach a character when working with weight maps.

Creating Weight Maps for a Character

The important thing to consider when creating weight maps is to *KISS* (Keep It Simple, Stupid). Bones can share weight maps, and it makes sense that we paint in weight maps for *regions*, not on a per-bone basis.

We should only need to create five regional weight maps in this character: Head, Body, Arms, Left Leg, and Right Leg. The arms are on opposite sides of the body and won't interfere with each other (hence can share the same weight map). The legs, on the other hand, are very close together and it makes sense for them to have their own weight maps to prevent them from pulling at each other's points.

1. Open Modeler and let's load the character (if it isn't already present in the drop-down at the top-right of Modeler). Let's just hide the skelegons for now by selecting one skelegon, then pressing <]> to select all the connected skelegons (they should all be connected to each other). Press <-> to hide the skelegons. Make sure that the Perspective viewport display is set to **Weight Shade** so that we can see the weight maps as we create them.

2. When creating weight maps, I like to start with the limbs first. Select all the polygons of the right leg, then create a new weight map by making sure the **W** button is active and selecting (**new**) from the pop-up at the bottom-right corner.

Figure 23-86: Select all the right leg polygons and create a new weight map.

3. Make sure that **Initial Value** is checked and the value is set to **100%**. Set Name to **wm_rightleg** for the leg weight map. Click the **Create** button. The polygons in the Perspective viewport should become bright red. Press <-> to hide the polygons from view.

Weight shade shows us the new weight map in glorious red...

Figure 23-87: Create the right leg weight map.

Note

Remember that windows like the Create Weight Map window are non-modal. We can leave this little window open and sitting on the desktop and use it to create each weight map as we progress through the character.

4. Select all the polygons of the left leg, then set Name to **wm_leftleg** in the Create Weight Map window. Click **Create**, and the left leg polygons should turn bright red in the

Perspective viewport. Press <-> to hide the polygons.

Figure 23-88: Finished the left leg.

Note

As a reminder (in case you've forgotten from earlier in the chapter), I'm hiding the geometry as I go because it prevents me from accidentally applying a weight map to the wrong part of the geometry (points can share multiple weight maps). As I gradually hide pieces of the character, it helps make the selection process easier with fewer polygons to choose from in Modeler.

5. Let's do the arms next. Select the polygons on both arms up to the shoulders as shown in Figure 23-89. Create a new weight map called **wm_arms**, and then hide the polygons.

Figure 23-89: Select and create the weight map for the arms.

6. The last "external" limb (of sorts) is the head and neck. Select the polygons for the head and neck as shown in Figure 23-90, create a **wm_head** weight map for these polygons, and then hide them.

ure 23-90: Select the head and neck, then create the
ight map.

7. Finally, we should be left with the body. Simply create the weight map **wm_body** and click **Create** to apply it to the remaining visible polygons. There's no need to hide these polygons given this is the last weight map we needed to create.

ure 23-91: Creating the body weight map.

Note

When we created the wm_body weight map, it was applied to the visible polygons. We didn't need to select the polygons because, as we know, when nothing is selected in Modeler, tools will affect everything in the viewport.

8. Unhide everything by pressing <\>, then save the model with a new filename. I often add the suffix _WM to the end of the name. (You can see my version of this model in Objects\Chapter 23\SuperCharacter_skelegons_F_WM.lwo.)

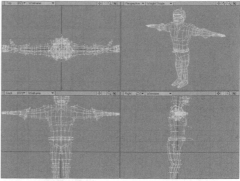

Figure 23-92: The character weightmapped and ready to go.

Now that we're done, let's go back to Layout and set up the bones to use these new weight maps. These will give us the control over the bones that we need to get our character deforming nicely.

Applying Weight Maps to Bones as a Group

One way to apply weight maps is to select a bone, then select the appropriate weight map from the Bone Weight Map pop-up.

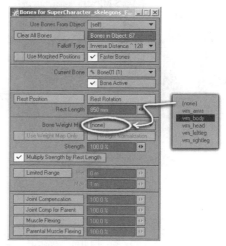

Figure 23-93: Applying a weight map to a bone in Layout.

There are 67 bones in our character. That's a lot of bones to apply weight maps to! Adding to this confusion, all the bones are called Bone and end with digits, which are not that easy to work with. Giving our bones a little clarity by naming them would be a good place to start, but renaming each and every one of the 67 bones can be time consuming. Instead, let's name the bones in their respective hierarchies.

1. Select the shoulder joint on the left arm as shown in Figure 23-94. Click on **Setup | Edit | Rename Hierarchy.** This tool will rename the selected bone and all of its child bones in one fell swoop! Leave the Name Edit Method as **Add Prefix**, and enter **LeftArm_** in the Prefix to add to Bone Names input box. Click **OK.**

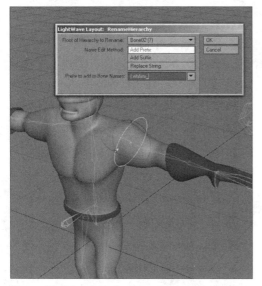

Figure 23-94: Select the left arm shoulder joint.

2. Select the shoulder joint on the right arm and repeat the process, this time changing the prefix text to **RightArm_**.

3. Select the left hip joint bone as seen in Figure 23-95, and rename the hierarchy using the prefix **LeftLeg_**.

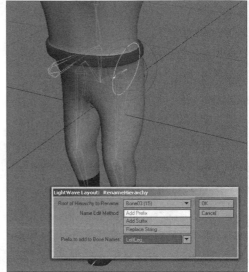

Figure 23-95: Rename the left leg hierarchy.

4. Repeat the process for the right hip joint. Of course, use the prefix of **RightLeg_**.

5. Let's select the neck bone and click on **Items | Replace | Rename** and give this bone the name **Neck**. Select the head bone and rename it **Head**. At this stage, it's a good idea to save the scene, just in case a power outage or some other disaster strikes!

6. I'm not going to worry too much about the other bone names. Renaming these hierarchies allows me to quickly identify the key groups of bones in the Scene Editor. This will make life a little easier when I use it to apply weight

maps en masse. So, let's do that. Open the Scene Editor (<Ctrl>+<F1>).

7. To view all the bones, right-click on the **SuperCharacter_skelegons_F_WM** object, and select **Expand Child Items (recursive)** from the pop-up menu.

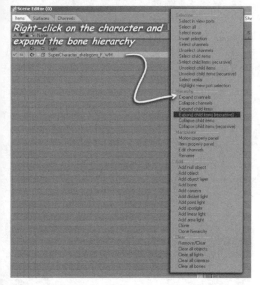

Figure 23-96: Expand the bones list recursively to view the complete skeleton.

8. Click on the **Property** tab (Figure 23-97) to switch from Dope sheet view to a scene properties spreadsheet view. This view allows us to tweak the properties of groups of items in our scene quickly.

ure 23-97: Scene Editor Property view.

9. Click on the **Bone Basic** pop-up, found directly below the Property tab, and change the view to **Bone: Influence**. This will change the spreadsheet view

to display all the properties related to the influence of bones, which includes the weight map information.

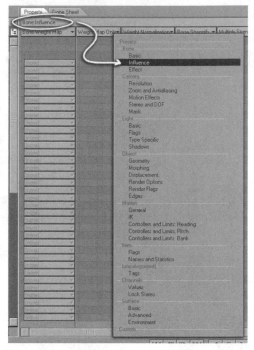

Figure 23-98: Change to Bone: Influence to display all properties related to the influence of bones.

10. Let's set up the RightLeg weight map next. To select a property on this spreadsheet, left-click in the small gutter that runs down the left-hand side of a column as shown in Figure 23-99. All the usual selection options that you may be used to in other parts of the LightWave interface apply here as well: <Shift>+click to select multiple items at once, or <Ctrl>+click to add to the selection.

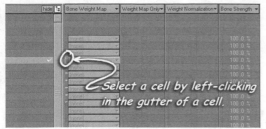

Select a cell by left-clicking in the gutter of a cell.

Figure 23-99: The Scene Editor cell selection.

Note

To completely deselect any item in a column, click once in a blank cell with no gutter (i.e., an item that does not have a relevant property in the spreadsheet). Alternatively, right-clicking in a gutter brings up a contextual menu that has the option to deselect all selected cells.

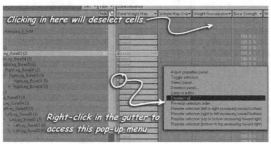

Clicking in here will deselect cells.

Right-click in the gutter to access this pop-up menu.

Figure 23-100: Clicking in a blank cell will deselect any selected items, as will right-clicking in the gutter and selecting the option Deselect all.

11. It can be tricky making sure you select the correct line in the spreadsheet, so I will often select the first bone in the item list on the left. Click in the gutter to the left side of the weight map of the selected bone, then hold <Shift> and click in the weight map gutter of the last bone in the **RightLeg_** hierarchy.

Click in the first RightLeg_ cell to select it…

…then <Shift>-click in the last to select the rest.

Figure 23-101: Select all the weight map rows for the right leg.

Note

You'll notice an Adjust Properties window pops up when you select any of the properties in the spreadsheet. This window gives you a way to modify the value for all selected properties (Figure 23-102).

Figure 23-102: The Adjust Properties window.

12. I've found that the quickest way to group set the weight map for the RightLeg_ bones is to *not* use this Adjust Properties window, but instead click on any of the selected cell's weight map pop-ups, then choose **wm_rightleg** from the list. All the selected weight maps will be updated instantly.

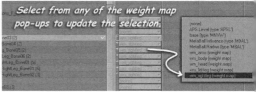

Select from any of the weight map pop-ups to update the selection.

Figure 23-103: Quickly adjusting the weight maps.

13. Repeat steps 11 and 12 for the LeftLeg hierarchy, setting their weight maps to **wm_leftleg**.

14. Skip down a little, and then select all the **RightArm_** hierarchy weight maps. You can include the **LeftArm_** hierarchy as well by first <Ctrl>+ clicking on the weight map for the first LeftArm_ item to add it to the collection, then <Shift>+clicking on the last LeftArm_ item's weight map to group select, and adding the LeftArm_ weight map cells to the selection.

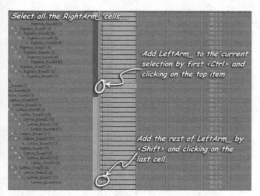

Figure 23-104: Mass selecting both arm weight map cells.

Note

When using weight maps, try to avoid leaving any bone *unweighted*. Weight maps scale the influence of bones and help prevent them from interfering with parts of a mesh. Because of the interfering nature of bones to push and pull points, as we've learned throughout this chapter, any bone without a weight map can suddenly gain control of areas of a mesh because its interfering neighbors are now being "kept in tow" by weight maps. If you discover a mesh going a little haywire with weightmapped bones, it's likely there's one or more that you have missed weighting.

15. Click on any of the weight map pop-ups, then select **wm_arms** to set the weight map for the entire selection.

16. At the bottom of the list, we have the head and neck bones. We can select both the weight map cells for these items very easily, and set the weight map to **wm_head**.

17. Lastly, find all cells that still indicate a weight map of (none). These bones are part of the body, so select and set each of these to use weight map **wm_body**.

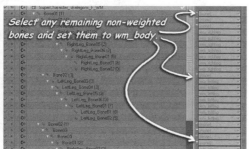

Figure 23-105: Setting any non-weighted bones to wm_body.

We're done setting up all the weight maps. Do a quick double-check to ensure that all bones have a weight map (there should be absolutely *no* (none) weight maps left for any bone).

18. This is probably the most important step of the process: Be sure to *save the scene* yet again before continuing.

Note

Using Save Scene Increment (<**S**>) rather than Save Scene (<**s**>) is a good idea and ensures that we keep backups of our rigs as we go. Nothing is worse than discovering that all that hard work has been destroyed by a simple corrupted scene file (and it does happen, trust me). Saving incrementally as we go is a good practice to get into, not only for making sure we don't lose our work, but also in case we hate something we've done and want to step back a stage to a previous version of a rig or scene.

Now that all the bones are weightmapped, our character should have much better deformation. Let's find out…

19. Select one of the upper leg bones and test it by rotating the leg back and forth. Now that the bones are weightmapped, the belt is not being pulled by the leg bones, and stays in place as expected.

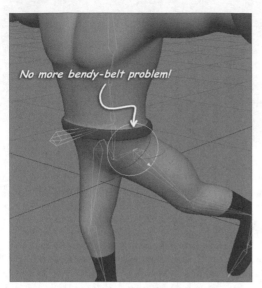

Figure 23-106: Weightmapped legs work much nicer.

20. Select the neck bone and use it to rotate the head about. No more floppy-face to worry about, as the face is no longer being influenced by the bones within the body.

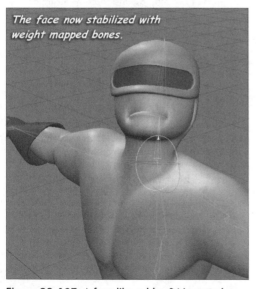

Figure 23-107: A face like rubber? No more!

21. Select the shoulder joint bones (those tiny bones at the end of the collarbones). Rotate the arm down. Like the rest, you have a much cleaner result! Even though the deformation didn't appear to be overly extreme, the weight map now gives the folded arm a better, more natural appearance.

Figure 23-108: The arm joints now behave better.

22. The last thing I'm going to do here is deactivate the main bone (that large one sticking out of the stomach). If you're wondering why, it's simply that this bone is merely needed as a parent for the entire skeleton to hang from. It's not really needed for deforming the character, and actually *interferes* by holding the front of the stomach in place. This prevents a more natural torso twist from the other bones. Select this bone and press <**Ctrl**>+ <**r**> to disable the bone.

At last, we've fine-tuned the bones and we're ready to animate. Or are we? When rotating bones, you probably noticed that not all bones are just like the others. In fact, some bones are suffering from major gimbal locking problems, making them incapable of rotating correctly. We'll want to repair some of these bones before we go forward.

Record Pivot Rotations

Remember how we adjusted some of the bank handles for skelegons in Modeler? I mentioned that these reoriented the pivot rotation of the *child* skelegon. I thought this was a good place to show that this is exactly what has happened by looking closely at the thumb of the character. If you recall, we reoriented the base bone of the thumb on a 45-degree Bank angle (or so we thought).

When we look at the thumb in Layout, it's the child bone (the next knuckle) that has the 45-degree orientation. The bones after the knuckle are oriented horizontally, and sure enough, the last bone has picked up this horizontal orientation.

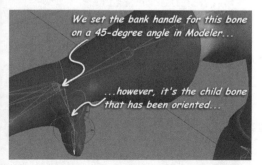

Figure 23-109: Bank handle rotations affect the child pivots.

So, what is the purpose of that bank handle? I mean, it seems odd that we should have to work through the parent skelegons one by one to correctly orient the child bones. Never fear, because we can in fact force the bones to use the bank handle orientation.

1. Select the base thumb bone. Let's force this bone to use the 45-degree bank handle we originally set up in Modeler by clicking on **Setup | Modify | Orientation | Record Piv Rot** (**<P>**). The thumb bone suddenly orients to the 45-degree angle we created for that skelegon.

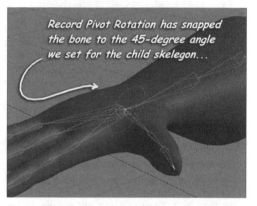

Figure 23-110: Recording the pivot rotation.

2. Using the **<Down Arrow>** key, we can cycle through the bones in the thumb, and use **<P>** to correct any oddly rotated bones. In Figure 23-111, I repeated the steps for the other two thumb bones to correct their orientation also.

Record Pivot Rotation was used here to tweak and adjust the other bones to match the bank handles...

This bone is not quite gimbal locked; however, it's enough to cause a problem for animation.

Completely gimbal locked!

Figure 23-111: The thumb bones now all aligned the way I like.

Figure 23-112: Some good candidates for Record Pivot Rotation include these gimbal locked bones.

Note

If you need to go back to the previous bone, use the <**Up Arrow**> key. Bones are selected in the *order that we created the skelegons* in Modeler. Manually cycling through bones using the arrow keys can be misleading, appearing to jump around from bone to bone, rather than flow from one to another in the hierarchy. We can make sure that bones are created in order by cutting and pasting back each skelegon, one by one, in Modeler. Once finished, use Merge Points to ensure all bones are connected together. Of course, this should be done before we get this far into the process. Personally, I don't mind the odd out-of-order sequencing (although it can be annoying in very complex rigs).

Note

Under Setup | Modify | Orientation is the option Remove RPR, which will remove the Record Pivot Rotation operations. Be warned, however, that this will wipe the changes from *all* the bones — not just the one that you have selected. When Remove RPR is used it also deactivates all the bones, and you will need to select and rest all bones to reactivate them cleanly.

A small issue arises when we reach the other thumb. The 45-degree bank handle is rotated the *same way* as the other hand. It should have been oriented in the opposite direction. This will have the unfortunate effect of the bone rotating in the wrong direction, and needs to be repaired.

3. Using the <**Down Arrow**> and <**Up Arrow**> keys, go through the rest of the skeleton looking for odd bones that have gimbal lock or are oriented oddly. Use <**P**> to reorient them. Note, however, that you *shouldn't* just do this for every single bone. Record Pivot Rotation can also mess up the rig!

4. As you'd expect, there's a tool to tweak this bank handle orientation directly in Layout: **Setup | Modify | Bone Twist**. When activated, a new controller is displayed with a yellow control handle that we can click on and drag to reorient the bank handle.

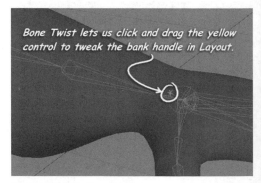

Bone Twist lets us click and drag the yellow control to tweak the bank handle in Layout.

Figure 23-113: Bone Twist.

5. Click on the yellow control handle and drag it down to rotate the bank handle until the green pitch ring looks correct. Press <y> to switch back to the Rotate tool (which takes care of deactivating the Bone Twist tool). To update the adjusted orientation, press <P> to record the updated pivot rotation. Press <r> to re-rest the bone. If the object deforms strangely after resting the bone, re-rest the child bones as well to correct the issue.

With the orientation of the bones now corrected, I like to do a mass-select of all the bones within the model, then press <r> to rest all the bones. Record Pivot Rotation and tools like Bone Twist can cause Layout to get a little messed up with where bones lay inside the object when a scene is next loaded back in. The effect is as though the skin has been ripped open and sets a lot of users into a little bit of panic (Figure 23-114).

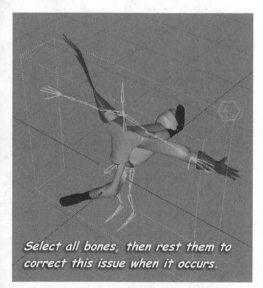

Select all bones, then rest them to correct this issue when it occurs.

Figure 23-114: Rest positions of bones gone haywire when a scene is loaded!

If you ever see such an issue, it's easily fixed by selecting all bones and resting them again. Of course, this will assume that your bones are all in the right places within your undeformed object. (Take care if you've animated your model in a scene!)

6. Select **File | Save | Save Scene Increment** (<S>) to save the scene.

Lock and Hide

We're in the home stretch now! With the bones deforming nicely and the rotations all tidied up, we're almost ready to start animating our character. Before we get to that stage, however, I like to spend a little time *dummy-proofing* my rigs to make my job easier. I do this by locking down any channels that I don't want to accidentally nudge or keyframe, and hiding any non-animating bones (such as the bones in the hand, hip, and so forth). Hiding bones means they can't be accidentally selected and saves a little sanity while working.

Just so you know, this step isn't an absolute necessity in the rigging process; however, when preparing rigs for other animators to use, it's essential for keeping those happy co-worker relationships!

Channel Locking

Locking channels is simple stuff. In fact, we've done it before in Chapter 4 when we locked down some rotation channels so that we could use the Dope Track's Channel Edit mode. If you recall, to lock any channel so it can't be modified, you simply click on the channel button in the Quick Info area at the bottom of the toolbar.

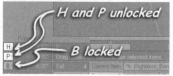

Figure 23-115: Locking channels is simple.

When animating bones, we'll spend a lot of time using the Rotate tool (and occasionally Stretch and Squash). There's very little requirement to move bones, and thus it would be a great idea at this stage to lock down each bone's motion channels for X, Y, and Z. This will prevent accidents from happening when we have the Move tool active. We can do this en masse using the Scene Editor (<**Ctrl**> + <**F1**>), and set things through the Property spreadsheet. All the channel lock states can be accessed by changing the Bone Basic pop-up to Lock States.

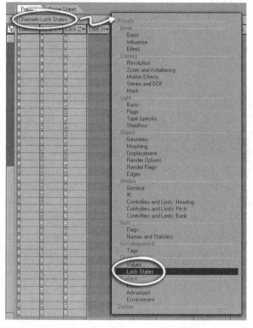

Figure 23-116: Select Channels: Lock States.

1. Select the cell for **Lock X** for the second bone in the hierarchy (let's leave the very first parent bone "movable"). Scroll down the list to the bottom bone in the hierarchy, then <**Shift**> and click in **Lock Z** for the last item. This will select all the cells across the three columns.

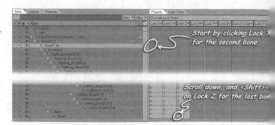

Figure 23-117: Select the motion channels to lock.

2. Click once in any of the selected cells. With so many channels to update, this may take a second or two. The cells should update and display as red pad-locked items (Figure 23-118). The motion channels for the bones are now locked off, preventing us from accidentally moving the bones about inside the skeleton.

Figure 23-118: The motion channels are now locked.

3. Close the Scene Editor, and go through the bones manually to lock down any rotational axis that we don't want to be used. Make sure that you activate the **Rotate** tool (<**y**>) and then use the <**Up Arrow**> and <**Down Arrow**> keys to cycle through the bones one by one. When I need to lock down channels, I simply click on the channel buttons (as we saw in Figure 23-115).

I'll highlight the bones where locking the rotation channels will help make our rig easier to work with.

4. The arms are first. As shown in Figure 23-119, the tiny bone in each shoulder is designed to drop the arms down by the character's side, and hence should only need to use the Bank axis. Disable both the Heading and Pitch axes.

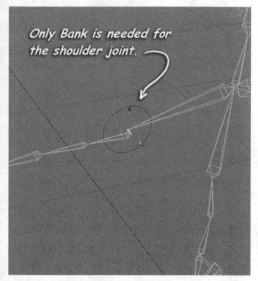

Figure 23-119: The small shoulder bone only needs to fold down on the Bank axis.

5. The upper arm bone that connects the arm to the shoulder only needs two axes active, Heading and Bank (since the shoulder takes care of the third axis control here). Disable the Pitch axis for this bone. While we're at it, the first lower arm bone is used to bend the elbow, and only needs the Pitch axis

active. (Elbows are called *hinge joints* since they can only rotate on one axis.) The Heading and Bank axes for this bone can be disabled.

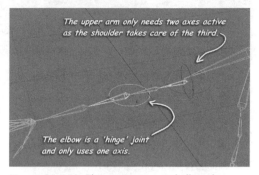

Figure 23-120: The upper arm and elbow bones.

6. The second upper arm and second lower arm bones are used to twist the wrist, and only need the Bank axis active. Disable both the Heading and Pitch axes here for these bones.

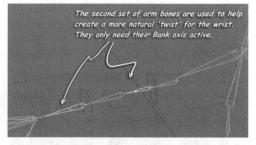

Figure 23-121: The two arm "twister" bones only need the Bank axis.

7. The finger bones are next. The knuckles of our finger and thumb are hinge joints, like our elbows, and should all be locked down to only use the Pitch axis (Figure 23-122). Disable the Heading and Bank axes for each of these bones.

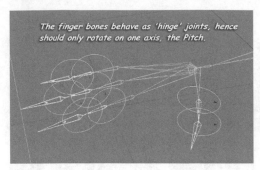

The finger bones behave as 'hinge' joints, hence should only rotate on one axis, the Pitch.

Figure 23-122: The knuckles are all hinge joints, and only rotate on a singe axis.

8. The very first knuckle, however, should also include a little sideways movement so that we can spread the fingers and twist the thumb. I left the Heading axis active, but disabled the Bank axis.

9. The small hip joint bones are used to swivel the legs outward (giving us a control that orients the knee), unlike the shoulder bone where it was needed to fold the arm down. These bones only require the Heading axis to be active, so disable both Pitch and Bank axes for the hip joints.

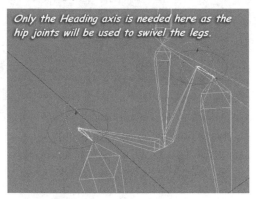

Only the Heading axis is needed here as the hip joints will be used to swivel the legs.

Figure 23-123: Lock down the hip joint to its Heading axis.

10. The upper leg has both the Heading and Pitch axis active; however, the Bank axis for this bone is disabled, as

this axis is controlled by the small hip joint.

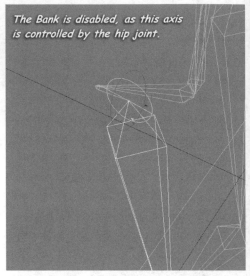

The Bank is disabled, as this axis is controlled by the hip joint.

Figure 23-124: The upper leg bone has its Bank axis controlled through the hip joint.

11. The lower leg bone is like the elbow — a hinge joint. It can't twist, so only its Pitch axis is left enabled. Disable both the Heading and Bank axes for this bone.

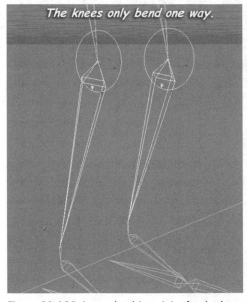

The knees only bend one way.

Figure 23-125: Lower leg hinge joint for the knee.

12. The last bones in the rig that I felt I needed to lock down were the toe bones. The toes are again a type of hinge, hence they only have a need for the Pitch axis. Disable the Heading and Bank axes for both of these bones.

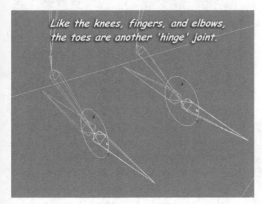

Figure 23-126: The toes are hinged, and thus only need the Pitch axis.

By locking down various axes, we limit the functionality of the bones. This can help make the use of the bone in the rig more obvious. When working in a team environment, this is often essential to prevent other animators from adjusting bones incorrectly. It also serves to prevent axes from being modified by other tools that may be applied during the process of animation.

Item Hiding

Now that the core bones in the rig are locked down to only rotate on their required axis, go through and select the bones that don't actually need to be animated at all, and hide them from view. Hiding bones makes them invisible in Layout, preventing us from accidentally selecting the wrong bone (something that can become quite frustrating — trust me!) and showing just the essential rig controls. This also keeps things clean and tidy. This can be done through the Scene Editor (<**Ctrl**> + <**F1**>).

Note

When using the Scene Editor, you need to select the character item, right-click, and select Expand Child Items (Recursive) to view all the bones. Here's a tip: If you are not concerned with seeing the full hierarchical structure of the rig in the Scene Editor, you can also deactivate the hierarchical view to show all items as a flat list (see Figure 23-127). This will display everything, saving that step of expanding each of the hierarchies within your character. (You will still need to expand the first level of the hierarchy, but not everything below it.)

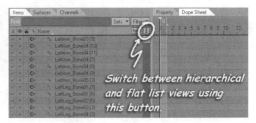

Figure 23-127: Viewing all the bones in a non-hierarchical, straight list.

13. Hide the two hip connection bones. Select the two bones in the viewport, then in the Scene Editor (<**Ctrl**> + <**F1**>), click on the dot icon next to each of the bones in the Visibility column. (We can easily identify which bones are selected by the small check mark next to them, as seen in Figure 23-128.) Deselect the bones (select another bone or item) and they will disappear from the viewport.

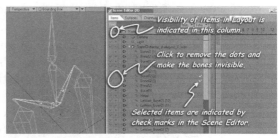

Figure 23-128: Hiding the hip bones.

Note

When a bone isn't visible, it also can't be accidentally selected in the viewport. If you decide later on that you need to select a hidden item, use the Scene Editor or select it from the Current Item pop-up. (You may want to rename the bones so that they can be easily identified by name.)

14. Repeat the hide process for the three bones in each hand, as shown in Figure 23-129. Again, let's hide the foot stabilizing bones as shown in Figure 23-130.

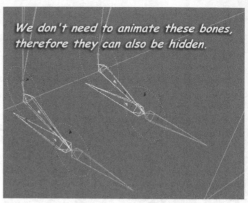

We don't need to animate these bones, therefore they can also be hidden.

Figure 23-130: The foot bones that we don't actually need to see.

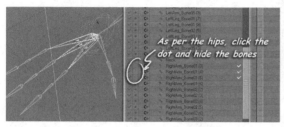

As per the hips, click the dot and hide the bones

Figure 23-129: Hiding the hand bones.

The bones are locked down, rotating nicely, and the unneeded bones are hidden. Looks like the character is now rigged and ready

to fight for justice! At this stage, make sure that you've saved your work using **File | Save | Save Scene Increment** (<S>), and pat yourself on the back for a job well done! You've created your first rigged superhero!

How exactly do we take this hard work and put it into motion to create cool animation? Let's look at the other tools of the trade…

Forward Kinematics and Inverse Kinematics

Every character rig employs a form of motion control known as kinematics. Okay, so what the heck is a "kinematic" and why would anyone care whether it's "forward," "backward," or somewhere in between?

Kinematics refers to the study of the mechanics of motion. Where 3D animation is concerned, kinematics defines the way in which you manipulate a system of hierarchical (parent/child) items. Of course, bones are a great example of a complex hierarchical system. Let's look a little deeper at these kinematics.

Forward Kinematics (FK)

Forward kinematics (most often referred to simply as FK) is the "old reliable" way of animating. To pose or animate the rig, FK simply means that we rotate and keyframe each bone manually. It's simple and reliable; however, its nature suggests it can be quite time consuming.

Start with a fresh Layout, and let's check out some simple FK animation with our rig. (If you still have the rig scene loaded, just use that (but be sure to save the scene first). If you would rather just use the rig I prepared, then you can load it from **Scenes\ Chapter 23\rigged_character_F.lws**.

Before we begin animating, I often like to save my scenes with a new filename. We want to keep the original rigged character scene as a *starting point* for creating animation, and it's very easy to accidentally overwrite our rigged character scene with an animated version. In this example, I'm going to save the scene as **FK_super-hero.lws**. As I work, I can then use Save Scene Increment (<**S**>) to make backups of my animation as I go.

Walk Cycle Using FK

Walk cycles seem to be the traditional starting point for many people wanting to learn character animation. It's the first thing they often try to do, and it seems appropriate that we should also use the walk cycle as our starting point. While it's a way to play with some FK animation principles, we can also use this exercise to discover some of the issues we'll run into when using FK for character animation. Before we start, let's look at the principles of a simple walk and what's involved with such an action.

Walking can be broken down into a series of repeating poses of a character. When we create a walk cycle, we're creating a stepping action that we repeat ad infinitum. Let's look at a basic two-pose walk to begin with. These two poses repeat, but simply change to the opposite feet for each step. A cycle usually starts and ends with the same pose, so to do this, we'll need to make two steps to bring the legs back to their original positions.

Figure 23-131: A simple two-pose walk.

The first pose is called our *contact* pose. It's where the feet are spread apart, both making contact with the ground. The distance between the feet determines the *stride length*, the distance that our character will move forward with each step. As the character moves forward, halfway through the step we get the second pose. This is called the *passing* pose, where one foot remains on the ground while the other lifts up and moves forward, passing it.

The feet are the most obvious things that move; however, also note how the body moves up and down as the legs bend and straighten during a walk. The arms also help counterbalance the body and move back and forth opposite the leg motion.

We won't be creating a hugely complex piece of character animation in this section. This is an extremely simplified walk concept, but as a starting point it gives us the basics we need to get things, well, walking!

1. Because walking tends to be seen from the side, it's often easiest to create the walk by working in a Right (ZY) view. Switch to a single viewport view in Layout (if you're using more than one, that is) and then set it to **Right (ZY)** so that it shows a side-on representation of the character (Figure 23-132). Note that I've also positioned and keyframed the character so his feet sit flat on the black center line (which I will use to represent where the virtual ground should be).

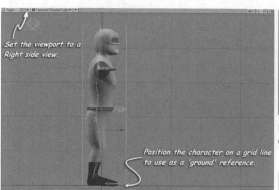

Figure 23-132: A single viewport showing our character from the side.

Figure 23-134: Tweak the character body position and legs until they sit on the ground.

2. Create the first pose — the *contact* — by rotating the upper leg bones in place. After posing each bone, click **Create Key** (**<Return>**) and record the change at frame 0.

Figure 23-133: Rotate the legs into the first contact position.

3. Notice how the legs now float above the line we set up as the "ground" reference. Select the character object and move the character down on the Y-axis until the front foot sits with its heel on the ground. Tweak the leg and toe bones in the rear leg until they also sit nicely on this ground reference. Don't forget to create a key frame for each adjusted item at frame 0 as you go.

4. Pose the arms in place next. For this, we should change the viewport to a **Perspective** view so that we can easily select each arm. The side view is okay, but it makes selecting each arm a little trickier.

Figure 23-135: Switch to a Perspective view so we can easily select the arms.

5. Rotate the arms down to the sides of the character using the Bank axis of the small bones in the shoulders (*not* the upper arm bones). Use the upper arm bones to swing the arms on their Heading axis so that they are spread out opposite the legs, as shown in Figure 23-136. Be sure to create a key frame at 0 for each bone as it's adjusted.

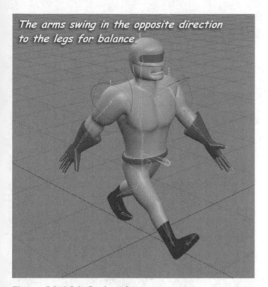

The arms swing in the opposite direction to the legs for balance.

Figure 23-136: Posing the arms.

So, the first pose is completed. It's pretty simple but usable. When we create a cycle, we need to not only start on this pose, but also end on it so we can repeat the walk seamlessly. One way to dramatically speed up the animation process is to just copy this pose from frame 0 to our last frame of animation. But before we can do that, we need to know how much time a step will take to complete. This is where mastering a few timing essentials is important.

We talked a little about timing back in Chapter 4, and I had mentioned that animators will often start to get a feel for it with experience and practice. I use some basic frame counts when roughing out animation as starting points to just how far apart key frames should be. In the case of a walk, think roughly half a second per step. I'll often use between 10 and 15 frames as my starting point. The beauty of 3D animation is that timing can be tweaked later if it's not quite right.

We're animating at 30 frames per second, so with each step taking half a second each, let's copy the key frames from frame 0 to frame 30. Also, change the last frame of the Timeline to 30 so that we can see the walk repeat seamlessly in Layout.

6. Select all the bones that we posed (there were only a few for legs and arms) and then click the **Create Key** button. Change Create Key At to **30** and click **OK**. This will create exactly the same pose at the start and end of the cycle (a one-second time frame at 30 frames per second). Also, select the character object and be sure to keyframe it at 30.

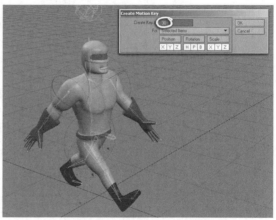

Figure 23-137: Copying the keyframed pose to frame 30.

7. We know that a walk cycle repeats the two-pose step sequence twice, with the second step using the opposite feet. Most importantly, make sure that Auto Key is *off* before you do this if you don't want to accidentally destroy your hard work! At frame 0, use the legs as a guide and pose the opposite leg over the top as shown in Figure 23-138. Click **Create Key** and keyframe these changes at frame 15.

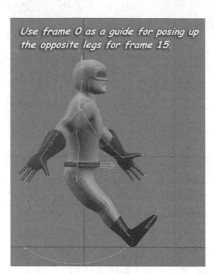

Use frame 0 as a guide for posing up the opposite legs for frame 15.

Figure 23-138: Posing the front leg to match the rear leg.

8. Scrub the Time Slider back to frame 0 to reset the pose. (Don't worry about the adjustments we made in step 7. Remember, we keyframed these at frame 15.) Repeat step 7 for the rear leg, this time posing it to match the front leg. Remember to keyframe it at frame 15 also. This will create the pose for the start of the second step.

9. Do the same steps for both arms also. Don't forget to also keyframe the character item to record its body position at frame 15.

Once finished, play the animation to see the basic starting block of our walk cycle. It's not there yet, but it's starting to look like "something." What's missing now are the *passing* poses. These poses occur at the halfway point between each of the *contact* poses. In this pose, the rear foot lifts and passes the other leg. Note that the front leg stays straight as it comes back, which in turn means the character's body should rise up at the same time.

10. Scrub to frame 7 (the halfway point between each step) and raise the character up so that the front leg (the one coming back) sits comfortably on the ground line. (Don't forget to create a key frame for the *character* at frame 7.) Since this pose is going to repeat again, create another key frame for the character at frame 23.

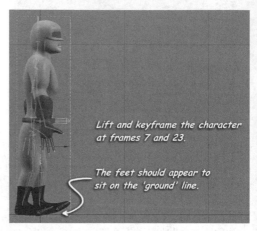

Lift and keyframe the character at frames 7 and 23.

The feet should appear to sit on the 'ground' line.

Figure 23-139: Raise the character so that the front foot stays on the ground.

11. At frame 7, pose the rear leg in a bent position so that the foot appears to be lifted, as shown in Figure 23-140. Make sure that you keyframe these bones at frame 7.

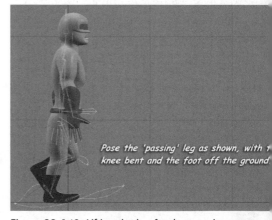

Pose the 'passing' leg as shown, with the knee bent and the foot off the ground.

Figure 23-140: Lifting the leg for that passing pose.

12. Scrub to frame 23, and make sure that you repeat the posing we did in step 11 for the opposite leg. Create key frames for the bones at frame 23.

13. Save the scene file using **Save Scene Increment** (<**S**>). Once saved, play the animation and see how it looks. It's not bad, but there are some things we need to tweak to polish this up. The toes will need some work to bend more naturally, and the position of the character's body may need some tweaking in the Graph Editor to ensure that the feet don't dip below the ground. The upper body should also have a little more motion to twist and bend the torso (as it currently looks quite stiff). When working with FK, this all must be managed by you, the animator.

As you can see, there are no "surprises" in this kind of animation; everything that's done must be done on purpose by the animator, and as such, it is a painfully slow way to work with a character's rig. One issue you may have noted is that the feet don't always sit on the ground, and require work to create the illusion that they do by adjusting the body motion or bending the legs (or both).

It makes more sense to find a way to lock the feet onto the ground, and that is just where using a system called inverse kinematics comes in.

Inverse Kinematics (IK)

Inverse kinematics (IK) is all about *chains*. Imagine a chain gate attached at one end to a post. On the other end is a hook that you can grab and move about. Between these two ends of the chain are the metal links. When either end is adjusted, the links rotate and bend, always hanging between the two end points.

In practice, an IK system consists of a chain of bones. The last bone in the chain acts as the *puller* (the hook at the end of the gate) for those higher up. The puller bone uses a *goal* object (this would be your hand), which it strives to remain in contact with. The goal is typically a *null* object, although it can be any object you choose.

For character animation, using IK for legs makes perfect sense. The leg bones form the chain, with one end connected to the hips, and the puller bone being the ankle. To ensure that the feet stay stuck to the ground, we give the ankles goal items that we place where we would like the feet to stay. IK therefore takes care of bending the legs to prevent the feet from sinking below the ground as we saw with FK.

"Standard" IK Basics

Let's take a look at the basics of "standard" IK. I'm saying "standard" here because the new IK Booster tool (which we'll discuss in the next chapter) provides a system that is as much of an advancement on IK as IK itself was on character animation back in the early '90s.

1. Load the scene file we saved for our rigged character. If you would rather use mine, it can be loaded from **Scenes\Chapter 23\rigged_character_F.lws**.

2. Let's start by adding in some *goal objects*. These will be used like virtual footprints, creating locations where we want the feet to stay. Click **Items | Add | Null** (<**Ctrl**> + <**n**>) and add a new null. Give it the name **LeftFoot**, and click the **Edit** pop-up to change its Shape to **Ball**, Scale to **500 mm**, and Label to **Left_Foot**.

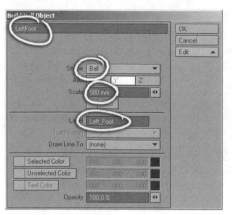

Figure 23-141: Create a goal object for the left foot.

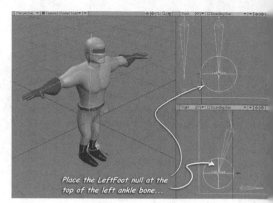

Figure 23-142: Moving the goal to the top of the ank[le]

> **Note**
>
> *Null objects* have to be the handiest little tools ever created for 3D (as we discussed back in Chapter 12). They are "place-holders," treated by LightWave with all the respect of a "real" object (i.e., one that has geometry), without taking up any memory or hard drive space. Null objects don't show up in a render or cast shadows and, like vampires, don't show up in reflective objects either.

Nulls are super handy when you want to create a "handle" to move a bunch of different objects, lights, and/or cameras at the same time, and they're perfectly suited for the job of being goal objects in an inverse kinematic system.

3. Move the **LeftFoot** null so it sits at the start of the left ankle bone and keyframe it in place at frame 0. Remember that a bone's pivot point is the one at the short triangle end of the bone. This is the location that will also try to remain in contact with the LeftFoot goal object later on.

> **Note**
>
> One way to always make sure you place your goal object at the correct end of a puller bone is to simply imagine the bone as an arrow. The small tip forms the arrowhead, and hence *points* to the goal object. Creating small visual "cues" like this can help immensely in giving you a way to recall how complicated processes or techniques work later on.

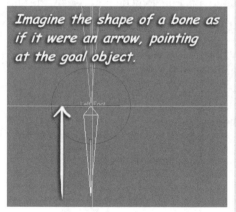

Figure 23-143: Imagine a bone as an "arrow" pointing to the goal object.

4. Repeat steps 2 and 3 and create a null for the right foot, giving the null the name **RightFoot** instead. Place it at the start of the right ankle bone. This gets our goal objects set up and ready for the IK system to use.

With the goals both in place, let's set up each leg to be controlled by inverse kinematics. Inverse kinematics puts the control of the rotation of the bones in the IK chain in the hands of the software, rather than using key frames as we did back in the FK exercise.

5. Select the small hip joint bone. This bone will form the "post" to which our IK chain is connected, and hence we need to tell Layout this is where the IK will begin. To do this, open the **Windows | Motion Options** window (<**m**>). For the hip joint bone, check the option **Unaffected by IK of Descendants**. This option marks this bone as the start where the IK chain begins.

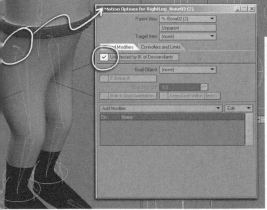

jure 23-144: Set up the hip joint bone as the start of e IK chain.

Note

The Motion Options window is *non-modal*, which means it can remain open while we work in Layout. As we select different bones in our character, their motion options will be displayed in this window so that they can be edited.

6. Select the upper leg bone (connected to the small hip joint), then click on the

Controllers and Limits tab of the Motion Options window. This panel lets us specify the way in which the rotation of the bone is handled in Layout. By default, all controllers are set to use Key Frames (FK). For this bone, let's change the Heading Controller and Pitch Controller to use **Inverse Kinematics** instead.

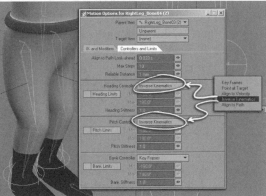

Figure 23-145: Set the Heading and Pitch Controller settings for this bone to Inverse Kinematics.

Each controller has a collection of other settings available to it. What do these other settings do? Let's look:

- The **Limits** check boxes let us limit the rotation of the axis to a particular angular range.

- **Min** and **Max** specify the range of rotation if Limits is checked.

- **Stiffness** adds a level of resistance to rotation when using inverse kinematics.

Do we need to set any of these other options? The answer for this exercise is simply "No."

Unless I'm locking down the limits of an FK bone, I've found I've never had to limit the rotation or tweak the Stiffness values at all. Limiting a bone's rotation, for instance, can actually cause issues with inverse kinematics. If a link in an IK chain can't rotate to meet the end points, this can cause other IK controlled bones to try to compensate, resulting in snappy behavior.

We only set the Heading and Pitch controllers for this bone to use IK. You may be asking why only two controllers, and not all three?

Number of Axes Solved

When you have two or more joints in an IK chain operating in 2D space, things tend to work quite well. But in three-dimensional space, the level of complexity of the calculations that IK must figure out rises dramatically. If you want things to work dependably, you're going to have to curb your demands on the IK system.

If you recall from earlier in the chapter, we locked down the rotational channels to those that I felt each joint should operate around. For instance, the upper leg might swing outward and bend forward, but the knee is a hinge joint and only works on a single axis. I've found that referencing "real life" while building rigs can help more than nearly anything else in making character setups that do what you'd expect them to do.

While the desire to use IK on "shoulder" or "hip" joints in order to solve for all three axes (Heading, Pitch, and Bank) is tempting, I find that often (though not always), this makes for a loose, "swively," and hard-to-control arm or leg. Quite often, character riggers will leave the Bank axis to be controlled manually by the animator through FK. (In this rig, I'm using a small joint bone to take care of this axis.) This lets the animator precisely control the position of the knee joint, just by rotating the hip joint.

A rule of thumb for good, solid IK chains in character rigs is that the *topmost item* (*parent*) can use IK to solve for a *maximum*

of two rotation axes. The *child item* in a character IK chain should use IK only for *one axis*.

> ### Note
>
> I don't recommend using "standard" IK on a bone chain consisting of more than two joints (for example, in a character's tail). It creates too many opportunities for the complex math to give you something you neither expect nor want. IK Booster (discussed in the next chapter) is the tool for the job if you have something like a tail, tentacle, whip, or rope you need to animate.

7. Let's select the lower leg bone. In the Motion Options window Controllers and Limits tab, let's set the single Pitch Controller to use **Inverse Kinematics**. As we know, this is a hinge joint and can only rotate around a single axis anyway.

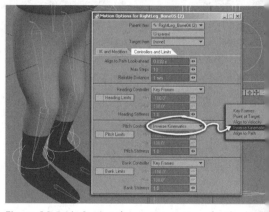

Figure 23-146: Setting the motion options for the lower leg to control the hinge-style knee action.

8. Select the ankle bone. This bone's rotations are not controlled by inverse kinematics; however, it is needed by the IK system to act as the *puller* bone — the other end of the chain. Click on the **IK and Modifiers** tab of the Motion Options window and select **Right_Foot** as the Goal Object. Check

the **Full-time IK** option and we're done! (Yes, really.)

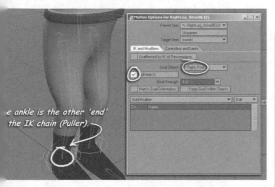

e ankle is the other 'end' the IK chain (Puller).

ure 23-147: Set up the puller bone and activate the chain.

> **Note**
>
> The Goal Strength option controls the influence of a goal item on the IK chain. The higher this value, the stronger the attraction influence of the goal on the puller of the chain. In most cases, I've found a value of 1.0 seems to work for most IK chains such as these legs. While this chapter covers the essential basics of building IK, it is possible to later add multiple pullers and multiple goals to create more complex chains. When this happens, the Goal Strength value can be used to increase and decrease the attraction of the various goals for fine-tuning the chain.

Did you notice that when IK is active, a line is displayed to indicate the start and end of the IK chain? (See Figure 23-148.) If you

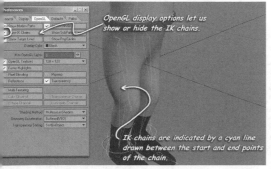

OpenGL display options let us show or hide the IK chains.

IK chains are indicated by a cyan line drawn between the start and end points of the chain.

gure 23-148: The IK chains are displayed as lines nnecting the start and end of each chain.

didn't see anything, you may need to check the **Show IK Chains** option on the **Edit | OpenGL** panel.

> **Note**
>
> What's the difference between full-time IK and IK that isn't "full-time"? Way back when IK was new, its calculations not yet streamlined, and 40 MHz was mind-bogglingly fast, the friendly folks at NewTek thought it would be a help for animators to have the option of only solving for IK when the chain's goal object was moved. This made IK a system purely for posing the links in a chain. Once posed, it was up to the animator to record that pose by keyframing each and every link. Essentially this made IK a great FK assistant, saving time for an animator in posing and positioning limbs and joints.
>
> *Full-time* refers to IK that is calculated constantly. The animator therefore only needs to animate the ends of an IK chain, and Layout takes care of animating the rest. Nowadays, CPUs are so fast, and the calculations for IK so optimized, there's *almost* no reason to not have all IK chains calculated *full-time*, all the time. I say "almost," because who knows... you may find a need for "part-time IK" you couldn't live without that nobody else has thought of. This philosophy of letting the users have all the options they might need is one major reason behind my strong respect for LightWave and for NewTek.

9. Repeat steps 5 through 8 for each of the bones in the other leg to finish up the IK rigging process, then save the scene as **rigged_character_IK.lws**.

> **Note**
>
> The visible IK chains are a good way to quickly spot any problems. If the IK chain lines don't look identical (as they are in Figure 23-149), double-check all the settings for your leg bones.

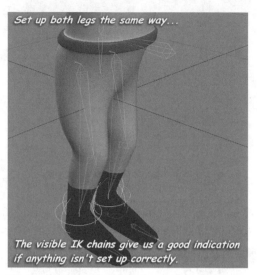

Set up both legs the same way...

The visible IK chains give us a good indication if anything isn't set up correctly.

Figure 23-149: Both legs are now IK enabled.

That's it! The legs are now controlled by IK and will attempt to hold the feet of each leg in place using the two goal nulls we created. See for yourself by moving the character object (which adjusts the position of the hips) and the nulls to see how well the legs update themselves.

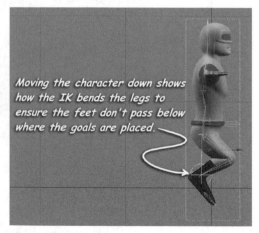

Moving the character down shows how the IK bends the legs to ensure the feet don't pass below where the goals are placed.

Figure 23-150: Moving the character down shows how IK is bending the legs to meet the feet.

Note

Is IK not working? This could be a possibility, especially if you've been working through this chapter continually since the beginning. Double-check **Setup | General | Enable IK** (<**Shift**> + <**F8**>). It's possible that IK calculations were temporarily disabled when you performed a Record Pivot Rotation command or used one of the bone tools such as Bone Twist. (You may remember the message box that popped up initially to tell us that IK had been disabled by these tools.) If so, simply reactivate **Enable IK** (<**Shift**> + <**F8**>) and things should kick into action.

Hold on! Let's look more closely at Figure 23-151. Moving the character up and down shows a small issue regarding the feet. The issue is that they dip into the ground, and that is simply because the rotation of the ankle is controlled by FK, or key frames. As we learned through the FK exercise, correcting this throughout an animation using FK could become time consuming. Luckily, IK has an option to help us resolve this small issue.

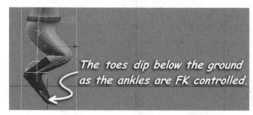

The toes dip below the ground as the ankles are FK controlled.

Figure 23-151: FK ankles cause the toes to dip below the ground.

10. Select the right ankle bone, open the **Motion Options** window (<**m**>) and check the option **Match Goal Orientation**. This option will force the ankle bone to match or lock to the rotation of the goal object Right_Foot. This may cause the foot to twist or flip, as seen in Figure 23-152, as the bone rotates to match the null.

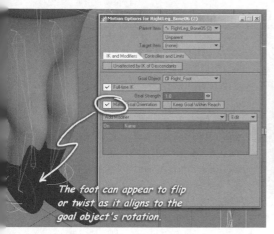

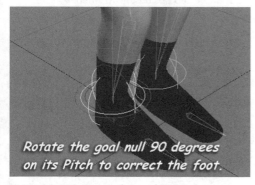

The foot can appear to flip or twist as it aligns to the goal object's rotation.

Figure 23-152: Forcing the ankle to match the goal null's orientation.

11. We need to rotate the goal null until the foot is corrected. In this case, simply rotating the goal 90 degrees on its Pitch flattened the foot back into position. This caused the foot goal to become gimbal locked; however, like bones, we can hit <P> and record its pivot rotation to correct this if necessary.

Rotate the goal null 90 degrees on its Pitch to correct the foot.

Figure 23-153: Rotate the goal by 90 degrees and key in place.

12. Repeat steps 10 and 11 for the other ankle, and save the scene once again using **Save Scene Increment**. Moving the character down now bends the legs, but the ankles are locked in place by matching the goal rotations.

This makes the goals not only responsible for positioning the end of the IK chain, but also for controlling the ankle rotation.

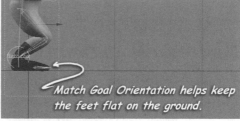

Match Goal Orientation helps keep the feet flat on the ground.

Figure 23-154: Match Goal Orientation keeps the feet flat on the ground, no matter how far we bend the legs.

Should We Use Keep Goal Within Reach?

You may have noticed the option Keep Goal Within Reach on the Motion Options window. This option attempts to snap the goal object to the puller item. Should the puller start to move away from the goal, the goal then moves and attempts to stay with the puller. I avoid this option when working with IK on legs in particular, as I find that it causes IK to jitter and also makes placing the goals less intuitive. However, that's my personal preference; other animators may find it makes life easier.

13. The IK is in place; however, to make sure we can adjust the whole rig and position it along with the IK goals, let's create one more null item (<Ctrl> + <n>). Call this null **SuperRig**, set its Shape to **Ring**, and give it a Label of **Super_Rig**. Position and keyframe the null at the bottom of the feet of the character. Parent the character object and the two IK goal nulls to this new SuperRig null, and save the scene one last time.

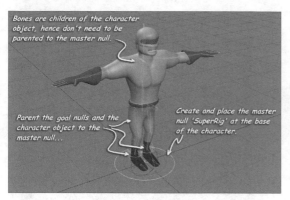

Figure 23-155: Adding a master control null for positioning the whole rig in a scene.

Layout has no concept that an IK chain is a leg, arm, or limb, and therefore only knows that it's a chain that must meet two end points. Sometimes it's incapable of determining the correct direction to bend a link and solves the IK by rotating in the opposite direction. Because the chain meets the end points, this is as correct as the other way as far as Layout is concerned. After all, it's all mathematics; software doesn't know that there are muscles, tendons, and soft tissues involved in these limbs.

This new null is not designed to do anything other than position the starting location of the entire rig. With this in place, we're ready to test out the new IK system!

Pre-Bending

Let's try something. Switch the viewport to a Right (ZY) view, and then let's move the character back and down to sit him on the ground (Figure 23-156). With IK in place, the feet stay locked to the ground, taking care of the whole "leg" side of things. However, as the character gets close to the ground, something odd happens. The knees pop backward. How painful would that be in real life!

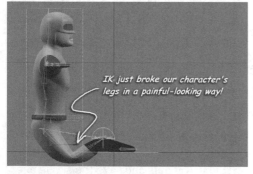

Figure 23-156: An uncomfortable sitting position.

> **Note**
>
> LightWave rotates items internally using the *Euler* (pronounced *oil-er*) rotation system. LightWave rotates an item by working out the rotation in order of Heading first, then Pitch, and finally Bank angles to get to the final rotation. When rotation on the Pitch axis reaches a +/– 90-degree angle, we get that issue of *gimbal lock* (as we saw for some of our bones while we were rigging) where the Heading and Bank axes become aligned. This rotational order can also cause a phenomenon known as *flipping* (items that appear to flip upside down) when we lose one of these axes through gimbal locking. This flipping can cause issues with IK, so it pays to take care when building your rigs to avoid reaching a +/– 90-degree Pitch angle on items if at all possible.

We've just seen one of the issues many animators run into with inverse kinematics, and probably the number one "freak-out" situation for new users trying their hand at setting up characters. However, the situation is easily resolved through pre-bending the bones into their *preferred rotational direction*, and keyframing them to train the IK to work things out the way we would like it to.

Note

Some users like the idea of simply limiting the rotation using the Limits options in the Motion Options window (Figure 23-157). By preventing items in the chain from going beyond their "natural" limits, ideally we should be able to resolve these issues. Right? Wrong. By limiting the rotation of items, we can actually increase the inaccuracy and behavior of the IK chain, causing it to snap and pop as it fights to work out the chain and compensate for links that are limited in their range. I never use limits when working with IK.

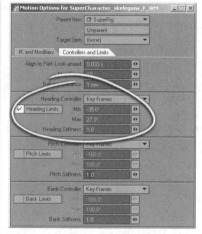

Figure 23-157: Adding limits to an item's rotation.

When solving IK, Layout can actually use keyframed rotations on each part of the chain as a determining factor for the *preferred direction* it should first try. Let's reset the character back upright, and try to train Layout to use a preferred direction when calculating IK. By doing this, we can get IK to behave itself almost all of the time!

1. Select the ankle bone and deactivate the Full-time IK option. When this option is active, it prevents the other items in the chain from being modified, and thus needs to be disabled first.

Note

Setup | General | Enable IK simply stops Layout from calculating IK in a scene. It doesn't unlock the control on chains caused by Full-time IK being enabled.

2. Select the upper leg bone and rotate it forward. Keyframe this at frame 0.

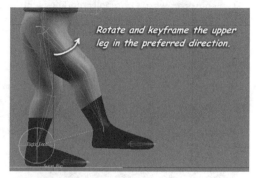

Rotate and keyframe the upper leg in the preferred direction.

Figure 23-158: Select the upper leg and rotate it in the preferred direction.

3. Select the lower leg bone and rotate it back. This is the preferred direction in which the knee should bend. Keyframe this rotation at frame 0.

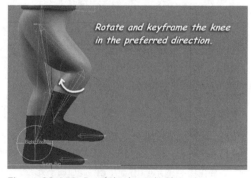

Rotate and keyframe the knee in the preferred direction.

Figure 23-159: Bend the knee back in the direction it should ideally be bent.

4. Select the ankle bone again, and reactivate **Full-time IK**. The leg will snap back in place.

5. Repeat steps 1 to 4 for the other leg.

The IK should still work as it did, except it should now behave itself and no longer pop the knee out painfully. We can test this by trying to make our character sit again. The knees should now bend correctly, no longer popping backward.

> **Note**
>
> The character wasn't originally modeled with performing the act of sitting down in mind, so don't expect to see great things when attempting to do so. Positions like this, however, are useful for fine-tuning the knee bending.

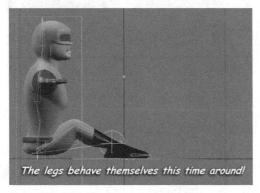

The legs behave themselves this time around!

Figure 23-160: The knees no longer pop.

If the legs do pop, then repeat the process and rotate the bones using a more extreme angle. Once things seem stable, make sure you save the scene!

"Standard" IK Rules

The following *rules* are more like *guidelines*, and summarize the essentials we've covered while setting up our character. Once you've mastered these rules, feel free to bend and break them as you see fit to suit the needs of your particular IK setup.

However, that being said, these rules have kept my characters moving smoothly and predictably through many productions. It's always best to learn the rules well

before you start seeing what happens by breaking them.

- IK is only dependable when solving rotations for a maximum of two items within an IK chain.

- On any item controlled by IK, let IK solve for a maximum of two axes.

- In a chain of two items, the child item should only use IK to solve for one of its axes.

- Always give your two-item IK chain a little "suggestion" in knowing which direction it should bend by pre-bending those items.

Walk Cycle Using IK

Now that the character is rigged with IK, let's recreate the simple walk cycle again, this time seeing how IK can help make animating the legs a lot easier. While we're at it, we may add a few more poses into the simple two-pose cycle to get a bit more personality into our walk. If you would rather try this exercise using the IK rig from the book, you can load my rig from **Scenes\ Chapter 23\rigged_character_IK_F.lws**.

Before we start, be sure to save the scene with an alternative filename, just to prevent accidentally overwriting the IK rigged character scene.

1. As we did in the FK exercise, let's switch the viewport to a Right (ZY) view. My rig should already be aligned to sit on the black center line. For your rig, simply select the **SuperRig** null to reposition the rig in place. Be sure to keyframe the SuperRig null at frame 0.

2. Start by creating the first pose — the *contact*. Using IK, adjust the IK goals for the feet to pose the legs. The rotation of the leg bones is taken care of for us by the IK system! You may need to rotate the IK goals to adjust the ankles,

and possibly tweak the toes where needed using key frames. Make sure you keyframe the IK goals at frame 0. If the legs appear above the ground line, move and keyframe the character object down until the feet sit on the ground.

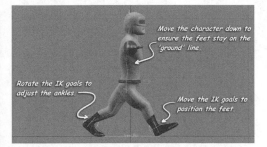

Figure 23-161: Rotate the legs into the first contact position.

3. Like we did in the FK exercise, pose the arms in place. I often prefer to leave the arms to use FK rather than IK. I find arms to be quite expressive, and IK takes away a lot of the creative control in posing the arms. Rotate the arms down to the sides of the character using the small joint bones in the shoulders. Use the upper arm bones to swing the arms so that they are spread out opposite the legs. Make sure you create a key frame at 0 for each bone as it's adjusted.

4. Select the bones we posed (there were only a few this time — upper arms and possibly toes) and then click **Create Key**. Change Create Key At to **30** and click **OK**. This will create exactly the same pose at the start and end of the cycle (a one-second time frame at 30 frames per second). Select the character object and IK goal nulls, and keyframe them at 30. Because the legs are controlled through IK, there's no need to keyframe the leg bones at all.

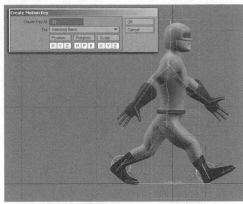

Figure 23-162: Copying the keyframed pose to frame 30.

5. We know that the walk cycle repeats the two poses twice; the second time simply by swapping to opposite feet. At frame 15, pose the legs to appear similar to frame 0 (except using the opposite legs) by adjusting the IK goals and the toe bones if applicable. With IK, there are fewer things to keyframe thanks to the legs automatically being taken care of. Don't forget to keyframe the IK goals, toe bones, and the character itself at frame 15.

6. Tweak and keyframe the arms in the opposite direction at frame 15. This will finish up the contact poses for the walk cycle. At this stage, **Save Scene Increment** (<S>). This will ensure that we don't lose work should the power cut partway through this exercise.

7. Let's scrub to frame 7. The front foot should be flat on the ground. If not, keyframe the IK goal for the foot moving back at frame 7 and raise the character up so that the front leg (the one coming back) appears to be straight. Unlike the FK walk cycle, we don't need to worry too much about the bones in the leg since they're being

taken care of by the IK! Don't forget to keyframe the character at frame 7. Since this pose is going to repeat again, you can also keyframe the character at frame 23.

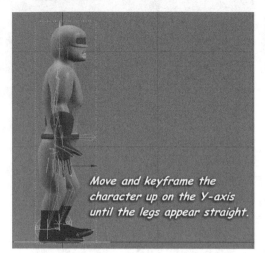

Figure 23-163: Raise the character so that the front leg is straight.

8. At frame 7, raise the IK goal for the rear leg to lift it as shown in Figure 23-164 and keyframe it in place. Also, rotate and keyframe the IK goal so that the ankle looks more natural.

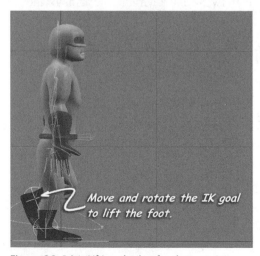

Figure 23-164: Lifting the leg for that passing pose.

9. Scrub to frame 23, and repeat what we did in step 8 for the opposite leg. Be sure to save the scene file using **Save Scene Increment**.

The animation is now at the stage that we had it with the FK exercise. Note how much easier it was to set up the legs using IK than it was using FK! Let's take this walk a little further and add in a few more poses to give the walk a little more personality.

In between the first contact and passing poses I'm going to add another pose: the *down* pose. This pose helps bring the illusion of weight into play. As the character steps forward in the walk, its body weight is caught by the front foot.

10. Scrub back to frame 0. Select the IK goal for the front foot and **Create Key** for this goal at frame 3. Scrub along to frame 3, and then adjust the rotation and position of the IK goal until the foot appears to sit flat on the ground. Create the key frame again at frame 3 to record this change.

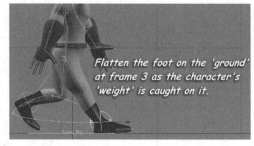

Figure 23-165: Adjusting the front IK goal to get the foot flat on the ground at frame 3.

11. Select the character object and move it down just a little. This drops the weight onto the front foot. Don't forget to create a key frame at 3 to record this update. While still on frame 3, adjust the rear foot's IK goal as well as the toe rotation to raise and flick the foot up, as

seen in Figure 23-166. Be sure to keyframe it, then scrub back and forth through frames 0 to 15 to see how this extra pose feels.

Figure 23-166: Adding the last details for the down pose.

It's a tiny detail, but it adds so much to the feel of the walk! If necessary, go back and tweak step 11 to exaggerate the feel of this pose, depending upon how cartoony or funky you want the walk to appear. When you're happy with the result, repeat the process to add the same down pose at frame 18 for the opposite leg.

Don't forget the most important part of 3D animation: Save the scene as you go!

While the down pose has helped add a little more "oomph" to our animation, there's one more pose that I'll throw in to get the walk to a stage where it's ready for you to take over and polish up further. This pose is in between the passing pose and the next contact pose, and is called the *up* pose.

In this pose, the character has pushed its body weight up and forward, ready to take the next step.

12. Scrub to frame 11, and move the character up until the rear leg straightens. Create a key frame to record this change.

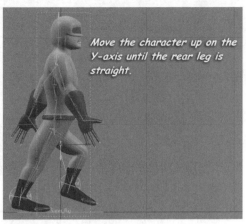

Figure 23-167: Move the body up at frame 11.

13. Select the front leg IK goal and adjust the position and rotation to be slightly farther forward, with the tip pointed upward a little. This leg is swinging forward in preparation to catch the character as his body weight comes back down. Keyframe the IK goal at frame 11.

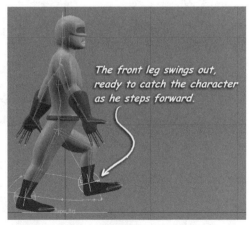

Figure 23-168: Swing that front leg out in preparation for catching the body weight.

14. Repeat steps 12 and 13 at frame 27 for the other leg. Once updated, save the scene using **Save Scene Increment**.

We're done! Play the animation and see how much better it feels with the two extra poses in place. Obviously, there's more work that can be done here. Getting the upper body to sway a little, bending the elbows of those swinging arms, and

relaxing those fingers a little more are all things that can help polish this walk. I'll leave these things for you to experiment and play with, using them to refine your character animation skills.

Conclusion

I can imagine that if you're new to character animation, rigging, or IK, all the information in this chapter may seem a bit overwhelming. Don't worry. In time, you'll find yourself talking about bones, IK, and FK as if they were the most natural things on earth. The important thing is not to be overwhelmed by the tools and options available.

While you may not at first completely understand the reasons things are done a certain way, you will find that once you've

gone through the process a few times, a lot more of it will make sense. Once you start actually *using* the rigs you've made, you'll experience a lot of "Ah, now I see why we did that" moments.

With these basic skills under your belt, you're already on your way to becoming a character animator; however, animation is an art form. Like any type of art, whether it's animation, music, or painting, plenty of practice is essential to becoming an expert!

Chapter 24

Advanced Skills: Character Animation with IK Booster

IK Booster is as much of an advancement to the art of character animation as IK itself was back in the early '90s. What exactly is IK Booster? It's a whole lot of things all wrapped up in a nice, neat little package. With respect to character rigging, it's best to think of it as something that can be used to add even more ease, power, functionality, and stability to IK systems.

The documentation that ships with LightWave v9 contains a large amount of information about the IK Booster tool, and it's well worth taking the time to read to see the power available with this awesome tool. This chapter will touch on the essentials necessary for using IK Booster for character animation, and will get you started working with IK Booster in no time!

Let's take a look and see just what it's all about.

Applying IK Booster

IK Booster can be applied to any object that has bones set up in a hierarchy. Let's familiarize ourselves with what IK Booster can do by creating a simple chain of bones.

1. Start Layout or clear the current scene (<**N**>). When testing IK Booster, let's work in a single viewport set to Top (XZ). Bones can only exist as child items of objects, so we'll need an object in our scene before we can move on. Let's do that by creating a null (<**Ctrl**>+<**n**>).

2. We could add a string of bones to the null by creating a new bone, then creating four child bones; however, there's a much easier way. Select the null object, then click on **Setup | Add | Bone** to add a bone to the null. (Don't worry about naming the bone unless you really want to.) Click **OK**; a single bone should appear, pointing along the Z-axis.

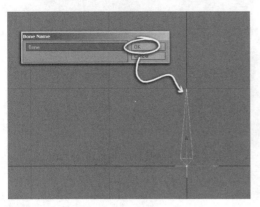

Figure 24-1: Add a bone to the null.

3. Let's convert this single bone to a chain of five smaller bones by clicking on **Setup | Detail | Bone Split**. The Bone Split window should pop up and ask how many new bones you wish to create. Change Number of New Bones to **5**, leave Mode of Fracture as **Colinear**, and click **OK** to split the one bone into five smaller bones.

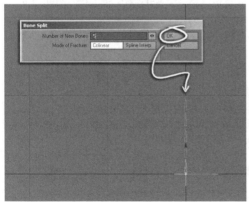

Figure 24-2: The bone split into five.

4. Select the null object, then activate **Modify | Tools | IK BoostTool** (**<Ctrl>+<b>**). Right-click on the *pivot location* of the null object (this will be the center of the null "shape" in the

viewport). A pop-up window will appear. Click the **Apply IK_Booster** option to add IK Booster to the hierarchy and we're good to go!

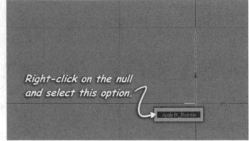

Figure 24-3: Apply IK Booster to the null.

Note

To apply IK Booster to an object and its hierarchy, you need to right-click on the *pivot point* of an object. Realizing this fact can save a lot of right-click frustration later on!

You'll notice a few things have suddenly changed (shown in Figure 24-4). For one, a series of circular control handles have appeared at the tips of each of the bones. Additionally, a square control handle has appeared around the null and, just above the Timeline, a new IK Boost Track has appeared.

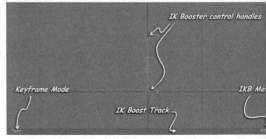

Figure 24-4: IK Booster ready to go!

IK Booster is a custom object function applied to the object itself. To remove it from an object, open the Object Properties for that particular object and either remove or disable (uncheck) the IK_Booster custom object under the Geometry tab. If you plan on using IK Booster again, disabling it will maintain all settings internally so that they kick back in when it's enabled again. If you never want to use IK Booster for this object, its preferable to completely remove it from the list using **Edit | Remove**.

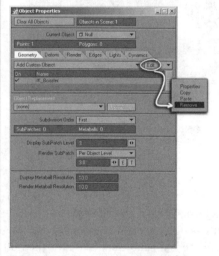

Figure 24-5: Removing IK Booster from the null object.

Let's look at how IK Booster allows us to modify and animate these bones.

IK Booster will keyframe all the bones that it adjusts if the Auto Key option is active. If you want to just play without storing the adjustments, make sure you deactivate Auto Key (<Shift>+<F1>) first.

5. Left-click on the control handle at the tip of the last bone to select it. The controller turns red to indicate it's currently selected. Left-click and drag the controller around with the mouse.

Wow! IK Booster poses and adjusts the bones as though they were all controlled by IK. And with reliable, non-flipping IK at that!

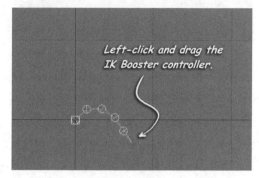

Figure 24-6: IK Booster makes bones IK-a-licious.

With IK Booster, you don't have to assign any goal objects and you don't have to tell LightWave to use IK for any rotation axes; you just grab any of the controllers and move them around! IK Booster handles "long chains" of hundreds of bones with speed and reliability. If you've got a whip, a tentacle, or a tail you need to animate, IK Booster lets you confidently use as many bones as you need to get the smoothest deformations possible.

You may have noticed that when you dragged the last controller a few things happened. For one, the controllers down the chain became highlighted to indicate that they were being updated and keyframed (if Auto Key was active, that is). What IK Booster updates and keyframes can be changed by right-clicking the Keyframe mode on the left side of the IK Boost Track, as shown in Figure 24-7.

Figure 24-7: Changing the Keyframe mode.

> **Note**
>
> Left-clicking on the Keyframe mode will cycle to the next option in the list. Of course, it's much quicker to simply right-click and pick from the list!

The other thing you may have noticed is that if you dragged the handle beyond the extent of the bones, the whole hierarchy, including the null, got dragged along for the ride! Yipes! It's usually about this stage that many users decide that IK Booster just isn't the tool for them. This situation, however, is not hard to remedy. What we have to realize is that IK Booster is no one-click wonder tool.

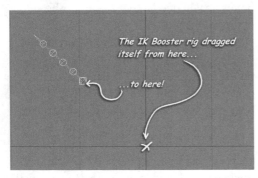

Figure 24-8: IK Booster dragged too far takes the rest of the hierarchy for a ride!

6. To prevent the null from being dragged along with the rest of the bones, we need to tell IK Booster that the IK chain is locked off at the start. Select the null's IK Booster controller (the

box-shaped handle), then right-click on it to bring up a pop-up menu. Select the option (**ikstop**) at the top of this menu to lock off the IK calculations at the null.

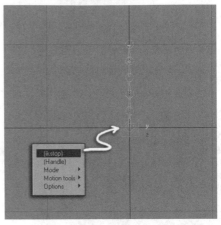

Figure 24-9: Prevent the null from being dragged around by locking it off using ikstop.

When a controller is locked off from being affected by the IK of its child items, its handle is displayed with a diamond inside. After setting ikstop for the null, reselect and drag around the last handle and see how the null no longer drags along with the chain.

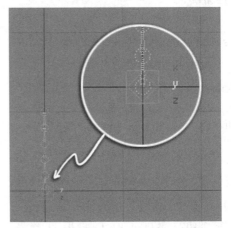

Figure 24-10: ikstop is indicated by a diamond inside the handle.

Note

Using the (ikstop) option is essentially the same as the process we learned about with standard IK, where we limited an IK chain by setting the start item's motion option to Unaffected by IK of Descendants.

That's all you need to do to apply IK Booster and start animating this chain of bones far more reliably than IK alone would let you! There's a lot more to IK Booster, however. Read on and let's dig deeper.

Understanding the IK Booster Controllers

IK Booster creates its own controllers for the items in the hierarchy. Unlike traditional FK, where bones needed to be rotated, IK Booster allows us to drag these controllers as though they were IK goal objects, updating the IK chain appropriately. On the other hand, *unlike* standard IK, we don't lose control of the rotation of the chain completely to IK Booster. Click on one of the other controllers in the middle of the IK chain, and let's find out why.

Channels

Next to the selected controller are three numbers, which represent the channels for Heading, Pitch, and Bank. Left-click and drag on any of these values to manually rotate the controller, giving us instant "tweakability" of any part of the IK chain.

We can do more than that. Recall back in Chapter 23 how we could lock down a channel by unchecking it in the Quick Info area below the toolbar? Here we can right-click on one of the channel values to get yet more options for managing the channels of a controller!

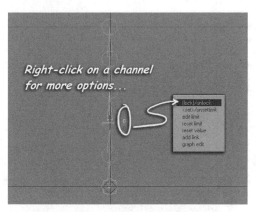

Figure 24-12: A channel's right-click menu gives us plenty of options for managing the channel.

Select the top option, **(lock)/unlock**, in this pop-up menu. This will lock and unlock a channel. When a channel is locked, its value is enclosed in parentheses to indicate its locked state. This channel is not only locked from accidental tweaking by us, but also locked from being affected by the IK calculations.

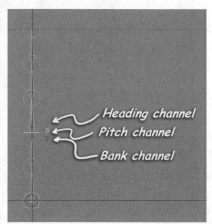

Figure 24-11: The channels can be left-clicked and dragged to manually rotate the controller.

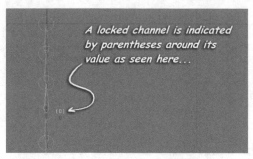

Figure 24-13: A locked channel is indicated by parentheses around its value.

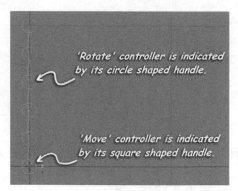

Figure 24-15: Different controller shapes mean different things.

We can also set or remove limits on the rotation of any channel by selecting the second option, **(set)/unset limit**. The minimum and maximum limits can then be edited using the pop-up option **edit limit**. When a channel has limits on its rotation, its value is enclosed between angle brackets (< >).

At any time, we can change the controller to move or rotate by right-clicking inside the controller to display the pop-up menu. Select the **Mode** option, and then change the operational mode of the controller.

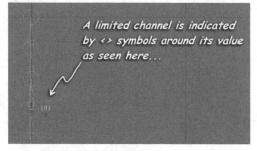

Figure 24-14: A limited channel is indicated by angle brackets (< >) around its value.

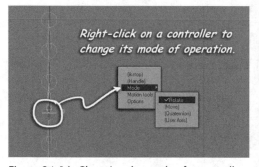

Figure 24-16: Changing the mode of a controller.

Controller Modes

Did you notice how the null had a box-shaped controller, while the bones each had circular controllers? A box-shaped controller indicates that this controller is for *moving* the item it's related to. The circular shape indicates the controller is for *rotating* the item it's related to.

> **Note**
>
> A movement controller doesn't display values for its channels; it only displays the axis letters x, y, and z. We can still tweak and lock down these channels as we did for the rotation.

Quaternion Rotations

If you followed the information in the section on pre-bending the bones for inverse kinematics in the previous chapter, you would have noted that LightWave makes use of Euler rotations to orient items such as bones. You may find it interesting to know that IK Booster allows for a new kind of angular mathematics that can help with the problems associated with Euler (such as gimbal lock): quaternion rotations.

You activate quaternion rotation for a controller within an IK Booster chain by selecting **Mode | Quaternion** from the controller's right-click menu.

You probably won't notice much more than a little "Q" appearing inside the controller, and that certain problem poses for your rigging may not be such a problem anymore. (Quaternion rotation only helps in dealing with the issues of gimbal lock; it is not a "magic bullet.")

Making Controllers More Accessible

Sometimes IK Booster controllers can become tricky to select. Controllers can be adjusted to float off the item they are controlling by right-clicking inside a controller and selecting **Options | Controller edit**. This places IK Booster into Controller edit mode.

Figure 24-17: Putting IK Booster into Controller edit mode.

While in Controller edit mode, left-click and drag inside a controller to adjust its position. A line visually indicates the link between the controller and its item.

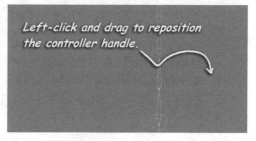

Figure 24-18: Dragging a controller about.

Right-clicking inside the controller while in Controller edit mode displays a different set of menu options.

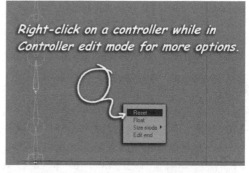

Figure 24-19: The Controller edit pop-up menu.

Reset will restore the controller to its original position and size. **Float** will leave the controller locked in place in the scene. When this option is deactivated, the controller moves along with its item.

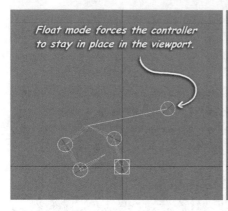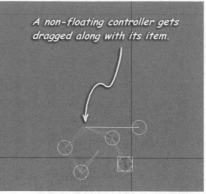

Float mode forces the controller to stay in place in the viewport.

A non-floating controller gets dragged along with its item.

Figure 24-20: A floating controller versus a non-floating controller.

Size mode allows us to change the size of the controller. **Edit end** switches Controller edit mode off.

> **Note**
>
> When rigs get complicated, it's sometimes helpful to be able to float some of the critical controllers to make them easy to access while animating.

The IK Boost Track

You saw how IK Booster created a new IK Boost Track when it was made active. This track packs a lot of punch for managing the key frames created by IK Booster. It's very similar to the Dope Track in that we can use it to manage key frames, but with a handful of IK Booster-specific functionality thrown on top.

Keyframe Movement

The IK Boost Track has capabilities similiar to the Dope Track (even when the Dope Track is inactive) for tweaking the keys in the Timeline. Let's try it out using a simple IK Booster scene file.

1. Load **Scenes\Chapter 24\ikb_track.lws**. This file contains a simple animated chain of bones with key frames that we'll update and manage with the IK Boost Track. Select the null object, and activate IK Booster (**<Ctrl>+<b>**).

2. To move key frames, left-click once in the IK Boost Track to place a center marker around which we will slide our key frames. The key frame will become highlighted in the IK Boost Track. Starting to sound confusing? Don't worry; it'll all become clear in a second.

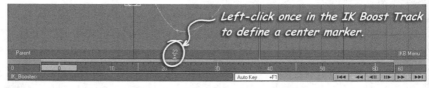

Left-click once in the IK Boost Track to define a center marker.

Figure 24-21: Left-click once in the IK Boost Track to define a center marker.

3. To move the keys on the *right side* of the center marker, left-click and drag in the IK Boost Track on the *right side* of the center marker. To move the keys on the left side of the center marker, well, left-click and drag in the IK Boost Track on the left side of the center marker! Now the use of the center marker should be starting to make sense. By strategically placing this marker at a key point along the Timeline, we can then shift frames on either side en masse without having to select anything first.

When we left-click and drag, the side we click in is highlighted, and two triangular indicators are displayed. The bottom one indicates the key frame origin where we initially clicked. The top one indicates the key frame move position on the Timeline.

hierarchy. To move the keys for only the selected controller, make sure that the Keyframe mode is set to Current item. To change Keyframe mode, left-click on the mode to cycle through to the next mode. Right-clicking on this option will display a pop-up list of the modes.

Once finished, left-click once on the center marker to remove it from the IK Boost Track.

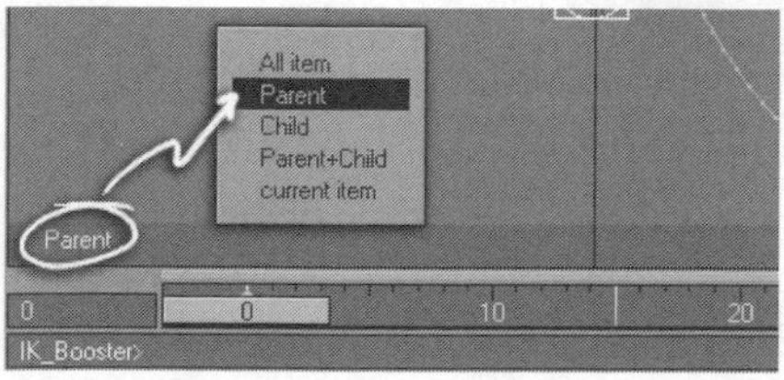

> **Note**
>
> When the Dope Track is made active (review Chapter 4 if you need a refresher on the Dope Track) while IK Booster is in use, it takes on the role of the IK Boost Track. The two menus (Keyframe mode and IKB Menu) also shift down to the left and right sides of the Dope Track. We can use the familiar select and drag capabilities of the Dope Track to adjust key frames.

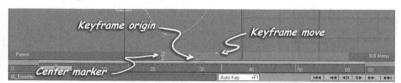

Figure 24-22: Dragging the keys.

You'll still need to use the upper IK Boost Track if you want to make use of its key frame adjustment options. The Dope Track doesn't have these capabilities, even when used as the IK Boost Track.

We're dragging key frames around, but perhaps not just for the selected item! The Keyframe mode on the left side of the IK Boost Track indicates which items are updated. The Parent mode moves the keys for the current controller and all of the parents before it in the

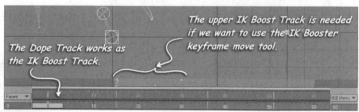

Figure 24-24: The Dope Track is used to manage and work with IK Booster.

Figure 24-23: The Keyframe mode defines which items are updated when using the IK Boost Track.

New Right-click Menus

The IK Boost Track has two right-click menu systems: a simple right-click and a right-click and drag menu. The one accessed with a simple right-click on a frame in the IK Boost Track itself opens a pop-up menu with options for the particular frame you right-clicked on. It is from this right-click menu that you can choose to delete a key frame, create one arbitrarily (without having to move or rotate an item), and more. Note that the action you choose is applied to the Keyframe mode choice at the left of the IK Boost Track. This could be for the current item, or it could be for all items, depending upon what this option is set to.

> **Note**
>
> Personally, I've found it's easier to pick individual key frames when using the Dope Track with IK Booster (as seen in Figure 24-25).

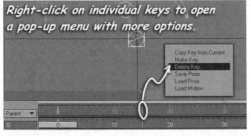

Figure 24-25: The right-click menu offers options for the frame you click on in the IK Boost Track.

The right-click and drag menu is used when you have a group of frames you want to affect at the same time. Right-click and drag over a range of frames, then release the mouse button to access another pop-up menu with options for managing the range of frames you selected. In Figure 24-26, I'm using the IK Boost Track (*without* the Dope Track) to show how the first and last frames in a selection are displayed on this track.

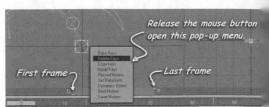

Figure 24-26: The right-click and drag pop-up menu you manage the selected range of frames in the IK Bo Track.

> **Note**
>
> When the Dope Track is active, the right-click menus work in there, and not in the upper IK Boost Track. Only left-click keyframe movement works in the IK Boost Track when the Dope Track is active.

Don't worry if you didn't quite drag over the correct range of frames, because most of the options in this menu display the start and end frames in their own options windows. For example, Figure 24-27 shows the Delete Keys window. The start and end frames can be edited here for more precise selection, as well as the Keyframe mode.

Figure 24-27: The right-click and drag menu options give you a chance to "fine-tune" the range of frames.

Bind Motion is worth noting, as its purpose is to duplicate the first frame of the selected range across all of the other keys in the range. This is one way that we can lock a particular item in place over a series of frames. It's important to note that there is no Keyframe mode selection on the Bind Motion window, so make sure that you select the mode prior to attempting to bind anything. To bind just the selected item in place, make sure the Keyframe mode is set to Current item prior to selecting and binding.

Motion Paths and Ghosting

Like the Move, Rotate, and Size/Stretch tools, IK Booster is simply another animation tool for creating key frames. Choosing **Edit | OpenGL Options** opens the OpenGL tab of the Preferences window, from which we can use the **Show Motion Paths** option to display the keyframed path in the viewports of Layout. As we modify things, the motion path will update to show the effect of the new key frames IK Booster creates.

Traditional animators often use an illuminated drawing table and special translucent paper so that they can see their

previous drawings as reference while animating. IK Booster also has a similiar feature it calls "ghosting." Make sure that IK Booster is active, then click on **IKB Menu | Options** to bring up the Options window for IK Booster. At the bottom of the window, change the Ghost Mode pop-up to **all bones**. Ghost Size specifies how many frames before and after the current key frame to display. Leave this at **10** and click **OK** to close the Options window. A simple wire frame representation of the previous and next poses of the IK chain is displayed.

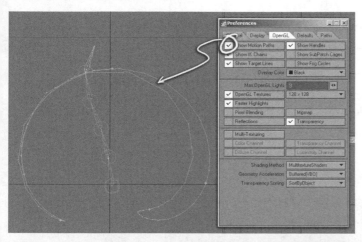

Figure 24-28: The OpenGL tab lets us view the motion paths of items in Layout.

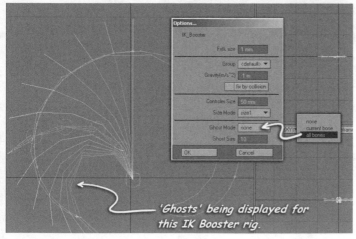

Figure 24-29: Ghosting at work, displaying the previous and next 10 frames of animation of the IK Booster chain.

'Ghosts' being displayed for this IK Booster rig.

So we've got the essential basics for using IK Booster. Now let's apply this to our rigged character from Chapter 23.

Applying IK Booster to a Character Rig

IK Booster can be used to add an extra level of control to our rig from Chapter 23. As we've already mentioned, IK Booster is no one-click wonder. Like any technical rigging task, there will always be some configuration required to get a stable IK Booster rig. Let's see how we can apply and configure IK Booster to our basic non-IK enabled rig.

1. In Layout, load **Scenes\Chapter 24\ rigged_character.lws**. This loads up the generic rigged character we were working with back in Chapter 23. We'll use IK Booster to enhance our rig here. Before we do, select the character and open the Object Properties window (**<p>**), then change the Display SubPatch Level to **1** to lower the display quality of our character while

we work. I've done this primarily to speed up Layout. When animating, it's more important to have a responsive rig than a visually pleasing one. Leave creating the cool visuals to the rendered output, not the workflow!

Note

Make sure that you deactivate Auto Key (**<Shift>+<F1>**). This will let us tweak and test our rig as we go, non-destructively.

2. Activate the **IK Booster Tool** (**<Ctrl>+<b>**) and then right-click on the pivot point of the character. Select **Apply IK_Booster** from the pop-up window, and we're set to go.

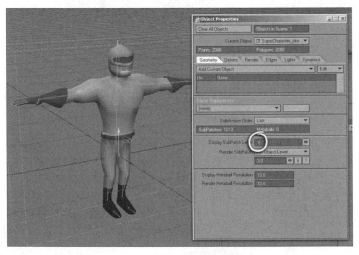

Figure 24-30: Lowering the Display SubPatch Level to help speed up workflow.

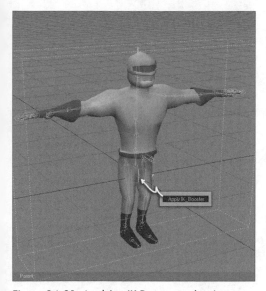

Figure 24-31: Applying IK Booster to the rig.

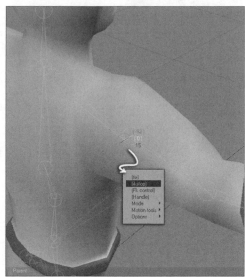

Figure 24-32: Lock down the right arm IK chain.

3. The first thing I do is go through and break my rig into smaller, individually controlled IK chains. I do this by treating each limb as a separate IK chain (each arm and leg). Start by selecting the controller at the start of the right shoulder (the small bone), right-click inside the controller (the dotted circle), and select (**ikstop**) from the pop-up menu to lock down the right arm (Figure 24-32). Repeat the process for the left arm.

Note

Recall how we did this in Chapter 23 when setting up IK for the legs, setting the first bone in each leg to Unaffected by IK of Descendants.

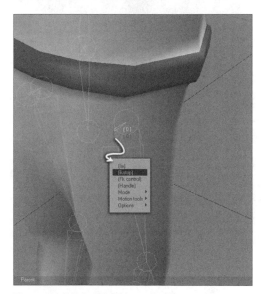

Figure 24-33: Locking down the legs.

4. Select the controller at the start of the right hip bone. Right-click and select (**ikstop**). Repeat this for the left hip.

This sets up the basic starting points of each limb. As we work our way through the setup process, we'll refine the settings to create a fairly stable IK Booster rig.

Controlling the Head through FK

I like to manually control some parts of the rig using FK, rather than let IK Booster control them through IK. The next step is going through each of these handles and setting them to be controlled through FK.

5. Start at the base of the neck (I prefer to control the head rotation manually), as shown in Figure 24-34, then right-click and select **(Fk control)**. When a handle is controlled through FK, a small "F" will appear in the middle of the handle.

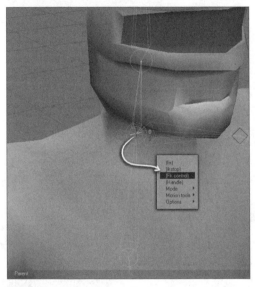

Figure 24-34: Setting up the head and neck for control via FK.

> **Note**
>
> FK prevents a controller from being included in the IK calculations. When we left-click and drag on the controller, it simply rotates the bone instead.

Configuring the Arms

If you recall from Chapter 23, we added four bones in each arm for a total of five each. Two of these were primarily there to act as a way to "twist" the arm nicely. We'll want to give FK control to these bones as it prevents them from being part of the IK chain, which would cause odd twisting in ways that can only be too painful to comprehend.

6. Let's select the second bone in the right arm. Right-click inside the controller, and select the option **(Fk control)** to place the rotation of this controller in our hands.

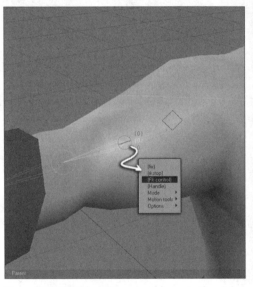

Figure 24-35: Select the second bone in the right arm, and set it to (Fk control).

> **Note**
>
> IK Booster respects and works alongside any settings we applied to our rig back in Chapter 23. When channels are locked, the value to the right of a handle is enclosed in parentheses. We can see in Figure 24-35 that both the Heading and Pitch channels are locked, as we'd set up back in Chapter 23.

7. Select the second lower arm bone (as seen in Figure 24-36) and right-click, then select (**Fk control**). I want the twist rotation of the arms to be a manually controlled process.

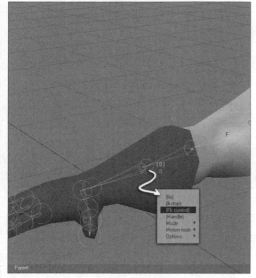

Figure 24-36: Select the second lower arm bone and set it to (Fk control).

Select the small wrist bone of the right arm, left-click, and drag it about to see how the arm behaves. Providing you've locked down the shoulder and set the twist bones to Fk control, it should work pretty well!

> **Note**
>
> Dragging the wrist about too much can cause the arm to occasionally pop and bend incorrectly. One of the beauties of IK Booster is that we can quickly "fix" such issues by adjusting the channels directly, as mentioned previously in the chapter. Unlike standard IK, IK Booster lets us pose and animate with both IK and FK techniques.

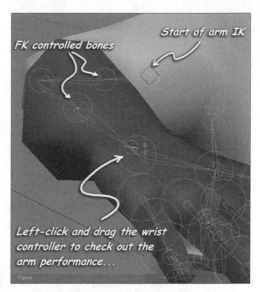

Figure 24-37: Left-click and drag the wrist of the right arm to check out the IK Booster at work.

Hand Configuration

Let's finish off the right arm and set the fingers to be controlled by FK. We'll also be looking at ways to simplify the control of finger bends and curls through some more clever features found in IK Booster.

8. Select the first bone controller in the first finger, right-click, and set it to (**Fk control**). Repeat the process for all the bones in the first finger, then continue until all the fingers have their controllers set to use FK mode as seen in Figure 24-38.

Note

The first thumb bone can be relatively difficult to select, since it connects to the wrist where the bones in the hand all tend to be connected. The quickest way to select this bone is to select the second bone in the thumb, as indicated in Figure 24-39, then press the <Up Arrow> key to select the previous bone.

Just be aware that using the <Up Arrow> won't always work for other rigs. The order in which bones are selected with the <Up Arrow> and <Down Arrow> is heavily dependent upon the order in which the skelegons were created (we discussed this briefly back in Chapter 23). The other way to select this bone would be to select it from the item list or from Scene Editor by name.

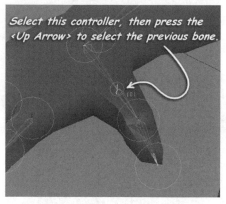

Figure 24-39: Selecting the second thumb bone and then pressing <Up Arrow> selects the first thumb bone easily.

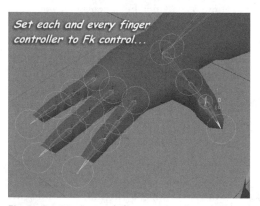

Figure 24-38: Set each finger controller to (Fk control).

9. Hmmm... If we left-click and drag the tips of any of the fingers, we can modify the arm IK chain! To prevent the fingertips from dragging the arm and hand about, select the first controller in each finger, right-click, and set it to (**ikstop**).

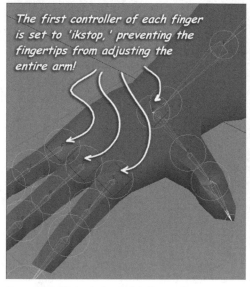

Figure 24-40: Lock down the fingers from dragging the hand and arm about.

Linking Channels in IK Booster

While we're working on the fingers, let's look at how we can control the curling of a finger from a single controller using another great feature of IK Booster: channel linking! In most cases, we'll be curling the hand into a fist, so adding this automated finger curl could help speed up our animation workflow.

> ### Note
>
> Consider what kind of performance or acting you have planned for your character before applying specialized setups such as this one for curling fingers. If you need more control over the expressiveness of your fingers, don't put systems in place that will limit your character's ability to perform.

10. Select the first controller in the index finger, as shown in Figure 24-41. We're not going to do anything with this controller other than to select it. All will become clear in the next step...

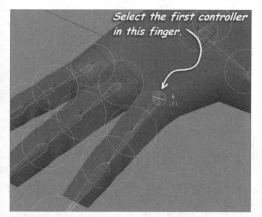

Figure 24-41: Select the first controller in the finger.

11. Select the second controller in the index finger, and then right-click on its Pitch channel value. Select the option **add link** from the pop-up menu to link this channel to the Pitch of the first controller. Aha! The importance of step 10 now becomes clear: The add link option links the currently selected channel to the same channel in the previously selected controller.

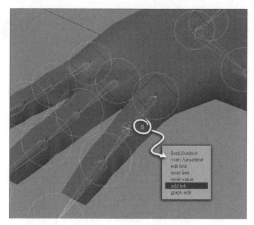

Figure 24-42: Select add link to link the Pitch rotation to that of the first controller of the finger.

When a controller's channel is linked to another item's channel, the word "link" is displayed next to it, along with a line showing the connection. We can see in Figure 24-43 that the second controller's Pitch channel is linked to the Pitch channel of the first controller. The small "P" at the end of the line indicates the Pitch channel is being "referenced" in the previous item by this channel.

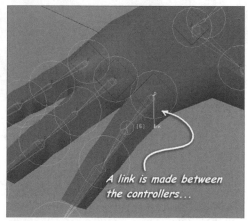

Figure 24-43: A linked channel is indicated visually.

Note

What if you accidentally link things incorrectly? Don't panic! Right-click on the word "link" next to the channel to display a pop-up menu. Select Remove and the link will be gone. We'll be looking at editing links using this menu in more detail shortly.

12. Select the third controller in the index finger, right-click on the controller's Pitch channel, and select **add link**. The Pitch channel will be linked to the Pitch channel of the second controller (which, of course, was the previously selected controller!). The link should appear as shown in Figure 24-44.

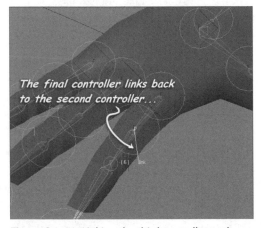

Figure 24-44: Linking the third controller to the second.

With all the finger controllers now linked on their Pitch channels back to the first, select the first controller, then left-click and drag on the Pitch channel value. The finger will curl! We're driving the second controller's rotation from this first one. The third controller is being driven by the second controller. Clever indeed!

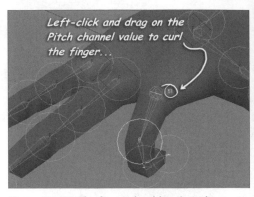

Figure 24-45: The finger should curl nicely.

Note

If you've successfully completed that finger, take a shot at setting up the other fingers the same way yourself. The only finger that won't be the same will be the thumb. You could link the two end controllers if you want to, or just leave the thumb without a curler. (I'll leave that decision up to you.)

Editing Links

Right-click on the word "link" next to the channel and a new pop-up menu will appear that lets us tweak the linkage details. Let's look at how to use these options to edit a link.

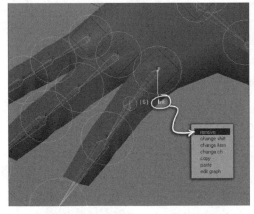

Figure 24-46: Edit a link by right-clicking on the word "link."

- **remove** is self-explanatory and will remove the link completely.

- **change shift** lets us delay the linked motion by a specified number of frames. When this option is selected, left-click and drag over the "link shift" text to adjust the value for the shift. A negative value adds a delay for the controller, making it lag behind the item it's linked to.

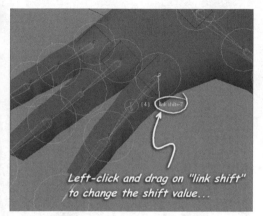

Figure 24-47: Adding a lag by using a negative shift.

> **Note**
>
> Adding some delay for links is a great way to create a little "swoosh" action in a rig. Examples include wagging a dog's tail, adding some snap to an intrepid explorer's whip, or swinging a vine in the jungle.

- **change item** is useful if you accidentally selected the wrong controller to link to at the start. The first step is to select the controller you *wanted* to link to. Reselect the controller you were just editing and right-click on the word "link" to open the pop-up menu, then select **change item**. The link will update to link to the controller you selected before clicking on this menu option.

- **change ch** will allow you to connect the link to any of the other motion channels

in the previous controller, rather than link to the same channel (which is used by default when the link is made). When the channel is changed, the new channel is displayed at the end of the link line, as shown in Figure 24-48.

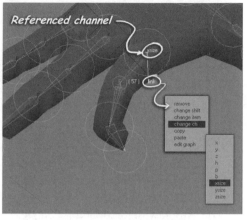

Figure 24-48: Changing the channel to link to.

> **Note**
>
> Driving a channel from a non-rotational channel is a great way to add some *anatomy* to a character. Imagine using the stretching of one bone to drive the movement or twisting of another in order to simulate muscles and tendons in your rig! That's just one possibility. Use your imagination to see where you might use links to automate parts of your rig!

- **copy** and **paste** are fairly self-explanatory, and allow us to copy and paste the link settings if we want to duplicate the same link on other channels.

- **edit graph** opens the Graph Editor for this linked channel. The channel link is controlled through a channel modifer (refer back to Chapter 12 if you need a refresher on what these are) called BoosterLink. Double-clicking on this modifier lets us directly edit the values more precisely

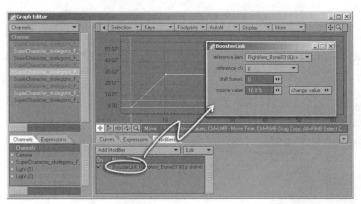

Figure 24-49: Editing BoosterLink settings directly through the Graph Editor.

(especially the Shift value, since dragging the value to set it can be a little tricky).

Let's continue…

13. Once the fingers and arm are set up, repeat steps 6 through 12 for the left arm. The process is identical; however, repetition with material this complex can be a great way to help absorb concepts, tools, and techniques.

14. Before we're finished with the arms, let's review one last part that needs ikstop-ing. That's the collarbones, the bones that form the connection from the top of the spine to the shoulder. If we don't ikstop these bones, raising the shoulder will also pull the rest of the spine about. That's something that's not really going to make things easy for us when animating…

However, like the thumb, the controller for these bones can be tricky to select. Use the same technique we applied for the thumb, and select the small shoulder bone, then press <**Up Arrow**> to pick the collarbone. Once selected, right-click on the controller and select (**ikstop**).

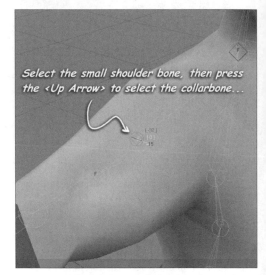

Figure 24-50: Pick the small shoulder bone, then press <Up Arrow> to select the collarbone.

15. Again, the most important step in every rigging job is to save the scene! Saving is critical when working on complex setups in LightWave. This step helps save our sanity should the computer crash after we've spent long periods of time fine-tuning complex setups like IK Booster!

Finishing Up with the Legs

The last things we need to set up are the legs. Once these are working reliably, we'll be ready to test out the IK Boosted rig, using it to create a simple animation.

16. Select the small right hip bone, right-click, and set this to (**Fk control**). This controller should be modified manually and used if we need to swivel the hip outward to point the knee.

17. All the other bones in the leg should have had their channels locked when we rigged this back in Chapter 23. It's not a bad idea, however, to just take a few moments to check. Select the controller for the upper leg bone and make sure that only the Bank channel is locked. Move down and select the lower leg, and make sure both the Heading and Bank are locked. (Remember that the knee is a hinge joint, and should only rotate on a single axis.)

18. Select the ankle controller and left-click and drag it about to check that the leg is behaving as expected. It behaves itself quite well, except in certain positions it may pop that knee backward as we see in Figure 24-52. With IK Booster, we can left-click on

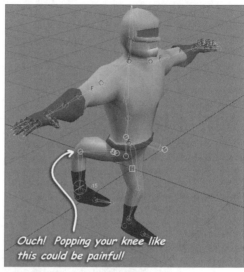

Ouch! Popping your knee like this could be painful!

Figure 24-52: Ouch! Popping that knee can be painful.

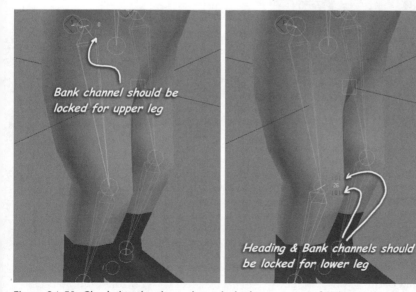

Bank channel should be locked for upper leg

Heading & Bank channels should be locked for lower leg

Figure 24-51: Check that the channels are locked as necessary for the two leg bones.

the knee controller's Pitch channel and "tweak" this by dragging the value, so it's not a huge issue. Let's see what we can do to prevent this from happening at all by setting some rotation limits.

19. Select the knee controller as shown in Figure 24-53, and then right-click on the Pitch channel and select **<set>/unsetlimit** to activate the rotation limits. The Pitch channel value should appear surrounded by angle brackets (< >) to indicate it has limits applied to it.

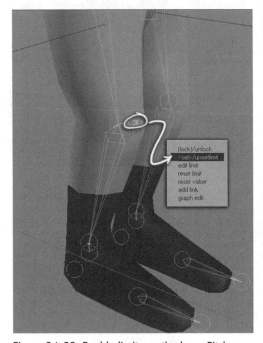

Figure 24-53: Enable limits on the knee Pitch channel.

20. Let's set the limits to prevent the popping. Right-click on the knee controller's Pitch channel again, and select **edit limit**. An Edit P Limits window will pop up in which we can change the rotational limits of the Pitch channel. Change min limit to **0** and max limit to **135**. The limited rotation range is

represented in the viewport as the unshaded portion of the rotation circle. Once the values are set, close the Edit P Limits window by clicking the X in the top-right corner. (There is no OK button in this window, so it needs to be closed manually.)

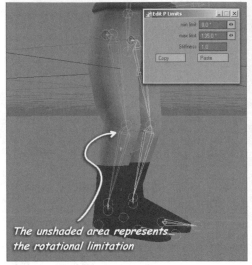

The unshaded area represents the rotational limitation

Figure 24-54: Limiting the knee.

Note

When entering values into panels or windows containing multiple input boxes, avoid using the mouse to click between input boxes. Simply clicking in another input box with the mouse doesn't guarantee Light-Wave will have accepted the value you entered. Instead, enter the value and then press the <Tab> key, as this will ensure that LightWave accepts the value and moves the cursor to the next input box automatically for you. I've learned from experience that it's a good habit to get into.

Fixing the Feet

The legs now bend and move as we'd expect. Select the controller on the back of the heel of the right foot and drag it around.

It moves the whole leg, but also causes the foot to wig out something crazy!

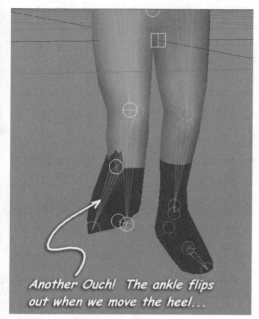

Figure 24-55: The foot wigs out because the rotation of the ankle is still controlled by IK.

There are a number of solutions we could employ here to solve this, but for this rig I'm going to go for the FK approach.

21. Select the ankle controller and right-click. Select (**Fk control**) to give us manual control of the rotation of the ankle. With this in place, we'll need to remember to use any of the foot controllers rather than the ankle to lift the foot off the ground. Left-clicking and dragging on the ankle will now control foot rotation rather than the leg.

22. There's one last foot controller that needs our attention. Let's select the toe controller (Figure 24-57), then right-click and set it to (**ikstop**) so that we can drag the tip of the toes without affecting the foot.

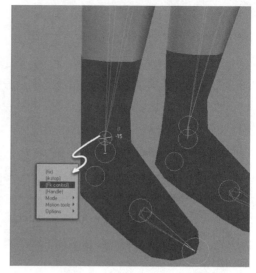

Figure 24-56: Select and set the ankle controller to FK.

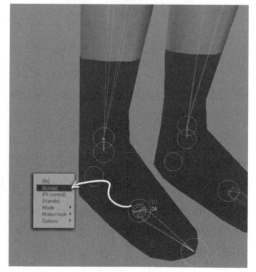

Figure 24-57: The toes set to (ikstop) so we can dip the toes independently.

23. The basic leg rigging in IK Booster is finished. As with the arm, repeat steps 16 through 22 for the left leg, then be sure to save the scene. As always, this is probably the most important step!

Well, that wasn't as painful as you probably expected it to be. The great thing about IK Booster is that it saves us a ton of extra work setting things up manually with the Motion Options window. IK Booster not only sets up IK behavior for our rigs, but it can also work side-by-side with existing standard IK rigging. It's possible to use IK Booster to enhance an existing IK-based rig as well. So, if you feel up to a challenge after this chapter, that's something worth trying.

Let's move on to seeing how we can use IK Booster's rigging and other features for animation.

Walk Cycle Using IK Booster

In Chapter 23 we did some basic walk cycle animation using both FK and IK rigging. Let's repeat the process with IK Booster to see how it differs in its approach to animation.

1. Make sure you have your new IK Boosted rig loaded and ready to go in Layout. If you'd prefer, use my rig from **Scenes\Chapter 24\ikboost_ character_F.lws**.

2. Before we get into the nitty-gritty of the animation, let's make sure we have a Right (ZY) viewport to work in, and move the character so the feet sit on a dark grid line as our ground reference. We've done this in Chapter 23, so this step should be a piece of cake.

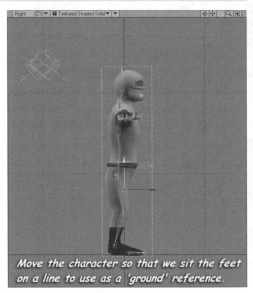

Move the character so that we sit the feet on a line to use as a 'ground' reference.

Figure 24-58: A Right (ZY) viewport and the character positioned in place.

3. Let's activate Auto Key (<**Shift**>+ <**F1**>) for this exercise, as it's essential if we want our tweaks with IK Booster to be keyframed. Once active, select the character and activate IK

Booster (<**Ctrl**>+<**b**>). We're ready to start!

Note

Did you notice how IK Booster's controllers are always visible, even when the viewport is in a shaded display view? Unlike in Chapter 23, we don't necessarily need Bone X-Ray active to see our rig for animation! While we *could* activate Bone X-Ray, seeing the bones can make things appear a little too busy in the viewport.

4. Make sure that the Time Slider is on frame 0, then select the heel controller on the rear foot and move the foot forward to pose the leg (use the other viewports to assist in making selection easier if needed). Select the heel controller on the frontmost foot and pose it back as shown in Figure 24-59. We can already tell how much smoother posing is going with IK Booster taking care of bending the limbs nicely.

Figure 24-59: Posing the legs using the heels of the feet.

5. The body needs to be moved down since the feet don't touch the ground. Select the square controller for the object, and move it down on the Y-axis. (The movement can be constrained by left-clicking on the Y channel of the controller and dragging the mouse to the left.) Position the body until the front heel sits firmly on the grid line we're using as our ground reference.

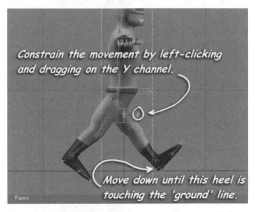

Figure 24-60: Move the character down until the front heel sits on the ground plane.

6. Switch the viewport to Perspective to make the arms easier to select and work with. Click on the right wrist and pose the arm forward as shown in Figure 24-61. (Make sure that the arms are posed in the opposite direction of the legs.) If you need to bend the elbow more than the IK Booster is allowing, click on the elbow, and left-click and drag on the Pitch channel to manually adjust the bend quickly.

Note

The ease of posing using IK along with the ability to fine-tune using FK is just one reason why IK Booster should be part of your animation toolkit!

889

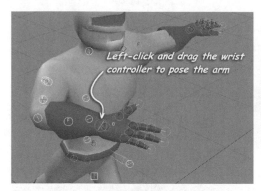

Figure 24-61: Pose the forward arm.

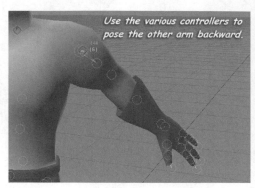

Figure 24-63: Tweak the other arm's pose.

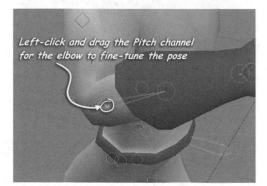

Figure 24-62: Tweak any elbow bending manually with the Pitch channel.

7. Let's loosen up those puppet-like hands by clicking on the first controller of each finger and use our cool linked finger setup. Left-click and drag the Pitch channel value of these controllers to curl each finger in a little (or a lot if you want to make a fist).

8. Repeat these steps for the other arm, this time posing it back. Note that the fingers could be curled here also if you want to give the character a more determined feel in its walk (with clenched fists). Use the wrist controller to pose the arm back, and fine-tune using the channels on the various controllers as needed.

Pose to Pose

In traditional animation, the lead artist will draw up the key poses for an animated sequence at key points, or *beats*, in the sequence. Another artist will draw the *inbetweens* (the frames of animation between each pose). In 3D, we create the key poses, and LightWave takes care of working out the inbetweens for us.

IK Booster is a great tool for creating animation using this pose-to-pose approach simply because, as we're learning here, it's a great tool for posing a character! But that's not all IK Booster can do. Let's look at how IK Booster offers tools to make working in a pose-to-pose fashion easy to manage!

When you have IK Booster applied to a character rig (even if you are using none of the other IK Booster features), you can save and load poses and motions for some or all of your rigging!

Let's save the pose at frame 0 so we can recycle it later on at frame 30 (or any other frame where this pose may need to be repeated).

9. Select the character controller (the square one), right-click, and select **Motion tools | Pose save**.... Click on the arrow to the right of File Name to choose a filename to save the pose to,

and make sure that Save Frame is set to **0**. Click **OK** to save the pose to disk. This will keep the pose for this controller and its child items (i.e., the whole rig) stored permanently on disk in case we need to recycle this pose for this or other projects.

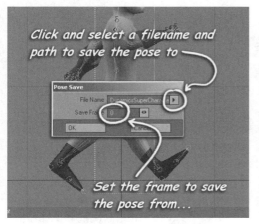

Figure 24-64: Saving the pose at frame 0.

Note

The controller Motion tools record the information for the current controller and all its children. This is why we selected the character controller, as the whole skeleton is parented to this one controller, therefore saving the pose for the entire rig. Poses aren't limited to the whole rig, of course. We could create some cool hand gestures, select the wrist controller, and save just those hand poses for use later on. Using this item-based way of saving/loading poses and motions, you can quickly build a library of clenched fists, martial-arts hand shapes, etc., that can be reused to save us literally hours of extra work later on! This means you can really take your time to get those complex poses perfect, knowing that you'll only have to create them once!

10. Let's reload this pose. Right-click on the character controller yet again, and select **Motion tools | Pose load**. Select the file for the pose we just saved and click **Open**. When the Pose Load window is displayed, set Load Frame to **30**. Click **OK** and the pose will be loaded in at frame 30.

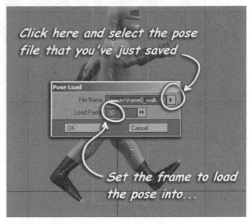

Figure 24-65: Loading the pose back into a different frame.

Note

IK Booster will let you load a pose or motion onto a different item in your hierarchy than the one you had selected, which can create some unpredictable results. Luckily, when saving a pose or motion, IK Booster will automatically use the name of the selected item as part of the filename (which you can change, but do take care if you decide to do so).

Let's continue on to frame 15...

11. Scrub the Time Slider to frame 15, and swap the arms and legs to create the other step in the walk. Use the heels and the wrists to pose things up quickly, and fine-tune using the channels in some controllers if you need to.

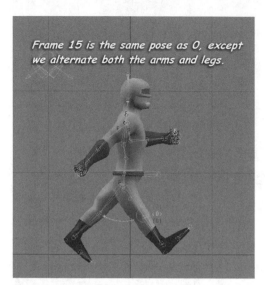

Frame 15 is the same pose as 0, except we alternate both the arms and legs.

Figure 24-66: Pose the arms and legs in the opposite directions at frame 15.

Once the key contact poses are done for frames 0, 15, and 30, let's add the passing pose to finish up the initial walk. The process is exactly the same as we learned in Chapter 23.

12. Scrub to frame 7, and let's move the character up to place its feet on the ground, and pose the back leg so it's in the passing pose.

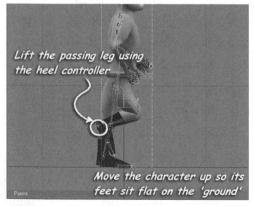

Lift the passing leg using the heel controller

Move the character up so its feet sit flat on the 'ground'

Parent

Figure 24-67: Frame 7 set up for the passing pose.

13. Repeat step 12 for the opposite leg position at frame 23.

Now we have a simple two-pose walk cycle in place using IK Booster. IK Booster's great posing capabilities helped smooth out the workflow and made setting this up relatively quick and easy. How about those other poses? Let's look at how we can throw in the down and up poses quickly before we tidy up any issues and call this animation complete.

At frame 3, we want to bring the weight of the character down on its front foot. However, adjusting the body will also slide the legs down with it. Let's see how we can adjust the character without making a mess of the legs.

14. Select the ankle controller on the front foot, right-click, and select the option **fix**. This will lock the controller from being moved about by the rest of the rig, essentially pinning it in place. Do the same for the other ankle. When controllers are fixed, their handles become solid shapes and not outlines.

If we scrub through the animation, the legs still move based on the key frames we created earlier. Let's see how fix will help out with the adjustments we plan on making to the body.

> ### Note
>
> Perhaps you wish you could have used the standard IK rigging to help hold those feet in place. One of the awesome features of IK Booster is just as its name suggests. It can be applied to a standard IK rigged character and be used to enhance, or boost, the amount of control we have as it does with our generic non-IK rig. IK Booster respects and uses any rigging controls we may have initially set up on our rig, making it a great complementary control system.

15. Scrub to frame 3, then select the character's controller. Move it down on the Y channel to create the down pose. Note how the feet stay locked in place and don't get pushed below the ground by the character!

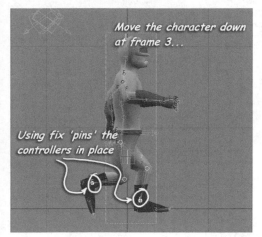

Figure 24-68: Move the character down at frame 3.

Repeat step 15 at frame 18 for the second down pose.

The up poses, as we know, are where the rear leg pushes our body up and forward, ready to take the next step.

16. Scrub the Time Slider to frame 11, then move the character controller as far up on the Y channel as it will go for the up pose. (The fixed controllers on the ankles will prevent it from going beyond the leg limits.) Repeat the pose again at frame 27. The body is done.

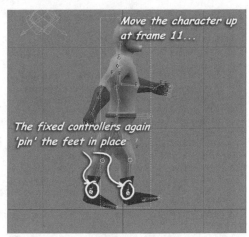

Figure 24-69: The up pose at frames 11 and 27 move the body upward.

All we need to do for these poses is swing that front leg out a little, and then go through and tweak any issues we see with the feet and we'll be finished! To get control back on the feet, right-click on each ankle controller and select **fix** to unpin the controllers.

17. Scrub back to frame 11. Select the front leg's heel controller, and move it forward and up a little to pose it ready for the next footstep. Repeat this pose again at frame 27 for the other leg.

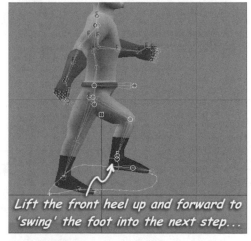

Figure 24-70: Swinging the leg forward a little, ready for the next step at frames 11 and 27.

18. Let's tidy up any issues with the toes. At frame 0, click on the tip of the rear toe and drag the controller at the tip of the toe up to bend it.

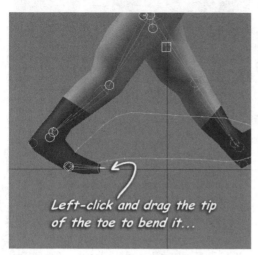

Figure 24-71: Bending toes by dragging the tips.

19. Scrub to frame 7, and let's reset the bent toe here. The quickest way to do this in IK Booster is to select the toe controller (the one in the center of the foot, not the one at the tip) and then right-click on the Pitch channel value.

Select **reset value** to quickly restore the rotation to its default value.

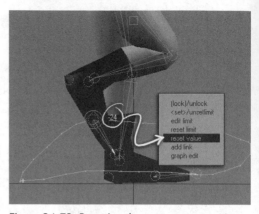

Figure 24-72: Resetting the toes.

20. Repeat steps 18 and 19 for the other foot on frames 15 and 23. Now save the scene and pat yourself on the back yet again for a job well done.

There are still a few small issues here and there with feet that don't always sit on the ground, but that I'll leave up to your new-found animation skills to fine-tune if you feel inclined to do so.

Conclusion

In this chapter and the previous one we've learned how to rig a character, how to apply IK and IK Booster, and created a walk cycle animation in FK, IK, and now IK Booster! Trying three different approaches to the same animation is a great way to learn the different workflows in each tool. This will help give you a basis to start building your own personal workflow, by letting you choose the tools and techniques that work best for you.

Rigging is indeed a complex, technical area of CG; however, if we want to animate our creations, it's a necessity. Chapters 23 and 24 have given you just a taste of the essential tools and skills you'll need to create awesome rigs for your characters, monsters, or machines. I hope that these chapters have given you the inspiration to delve deeper into this seemingly "black art," and to go out and learn from the many experts online in order to become an expert in your own right!

Chapter 25

Advanced Skills: Expressions

Ever wanted to simplify your animation by making some parts of your project "smart?" Expressions are clever little mathematical relationships between parameters in a scene. For instance, taking the movement of a spacecraft and relating it to the intensity of the engine glare could be a good example of where an expression may be used. LightWave has had expressions since LightWave 6, and they've been the mainstay tool of many animators and technical directors. In LightWave v9, they've been further enhanced with the inclusion of some new tools, so let's take a look under the hood and see what we can learn about using this system in LightWave.

Why Do We Need Expressions?

It's obvious that there are some things you really don't want to have to manually animate. For instance, say you have an army of robot warriors armed with machine guns. You are asked to animate this army shooting and fighting, but manually animating the firing of weapons for an entire army is going to be long and laborious, given that each weapon needs not only a particle effect for tracer fire, but a light source animated for that muzzle flash effect. This is where you could connect the animation of weapon fire components (like the particle emitter and the lights) to, say, the squeezing of the trigger of the weapon. Simply animating the triggers would take care of creating the extra animation needed for the weapons, saving you hours of hand animating particle bullets and flashes of light!

Maybe you want that walking character to perfectly step based on the distance and speed it is moving, the doors in your 3D shopping mall to open and close automatically when your characters walk through them, car wheels to roll perfectly, or the camera in LightWave to automatically create accurate focus for depth of field renders. All of these wants and needs are solvable in LightWave through the use of expressions.

LightWave's Native Expression System

LightWave v9 ships with not one, but two expression engines that you can use to drive your projects. In this section, we'll look at the native system that you may already be partially familiar with if you have used LightWave for a while. For those who are new to LightWave, the most common place to find expressions is in the Graph Editor (Figure 25-1) where we can directly link them to the individual channels of items to automate control.

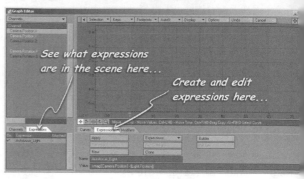

Figure 25-1: Expressions in the Graph Editor.

There are actually two Expressions tabs in the Graph Editor. The one we'll be working with most is found under the graph itself, between the Curves and Modifier tabs. The other Expressions tab, found next to the Channels tab, lets us see a list of all the expressions currently in our scene and how many channels they are attached to. By double-clicking on an expression name in this list, the channels being modified by this expression will be selected for editing in the Graph Editor. Extremely handy sometimes!

Note

There are also expression modifiers that can be applied to your items though the Windows | Motion Options window (Figure 25-2) and also within an object's Properties | Deform panel. These modifiers are more specialized for use in these particular areas, and also use a different syntax than the Graph Editor does.

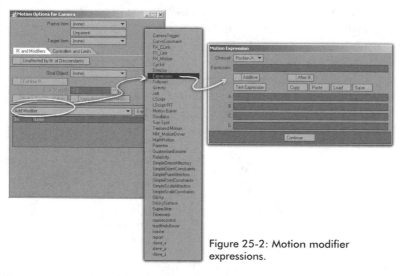

Figure 25-2: Motion modifier expressions.

Syntax of an Expression

You may have heard that expressions are clever little mathematical relationships between things. This probably already has some of you wishing that you could remember your high school mathematics! The nice thing is, while based on mathematics, expressions don't need to be complex beasts. In fact, an expression can be used to simply ask for information and not have any math in it whatsoever.

Understanding Basic Expression Math

Math in expressions is relatively simple to pick up. To perform simple math, simply use the format of:

value operator value

where *value* is a number or perhaps the location of an item in the 3D world, and *operator* is the math operation you want to perform. The basic mathematical operators you can use include:

*   multiplication, e.g., 25 * 33
/   division, e.g., 10 / 5
−   subtraction, e.g., 10 − 8
+   addition, e.g., 12+8

> **Note**
>
> When using the subtraction operator, be sure to include a space on either side of the − operator. This is because the − operator is also used to indicate a negative number, as in −25 or −100. Without spaces, expressions consider math like 10−25 as meaning "10 and −25," which will pop up an error message as this doesn't make sense.

Getting Information from LightWave

Expression syntax, the format in which you write these mathematical marvels, comes in two flavors. The first, called *LScript notation*, is how expressions started out in LightWave 6 using a programming-style format. This is also the format that is used in the expression modifiers we noted in the previous section. For example, to ask for the X coordinate of an item at the current frame in the animation, the syntax would be something like:

spaceship.pos(Time).x

> **Note**
>
> If you weren't already aware, LScript is short for LightWave Script, and is the programming language that was developed for creating plug-ins and tools for LightWave.

The second syntax, called *Channel notation*, uses square brackets placed around channels to evaluate expressions. This is the format that we often use when writing expressions in the Graph Editor. For example, the same expression we wrote above could also be written as a channel expression like:

[spaceship.Position.X]

In 99% of cases, we'll be using the Channel notation syntax, so it pays to become familiar with it.

Channel notation can only evaluate information from channels, and most information within LightWave is stored in what are termed *local* values. For instance, the position of a wheel on a car would be stored as the location in relation to the car body, and not where it exists in the 3D world of our scene. Of course, some information we want is created through the hierarchical link between items, or perhaps from modifier tools. These values are not stored in a channel, but calculated during animation. This is information that Channel notation can't always work out.

LScript notation, on the other hand, has the ability to also evaluate and return world-based information that is generated during an animation, and not locally inside an item. For example, when we say we are referring to the world coordinates of an item, we are referring to the *physical locations* of items within the virtual 3D world itself. Since Channel notation can only read this localized information, we sometimes find a requirement to use the LScript notation instead to resolve some things.

This example shows how an LScript expression can read the world X position of an item:

spaceship.wpos(Time).x

But There's More!

The expression system in LightWave is vast and there are many features and commands available to us for creating a variety of mathematical solutions. While we won't cover them all in this chapter, we will be touching on a few of the more essential ones. Later in this chapter, we'll also look at some great tools to help us build expressions.

Automatic Animation

Let's look at how we can use expressions to automate an animated clock. In this case, we'll look at how we can take care of rotating the second hand to keep accurate time.

1. Load the scene **Scenes\Chapter 25\ticktock.lws**. This scene contains an unanimated clock that we would like to keep realistic time throughout our animation. Obviously, manually animating this clock realistically is also something we could do, but that's more work and would require that we animate accurately for the number of frames per second at which our animation will play. These are all things that the computer is smart enough to work out itself and do perfectly!

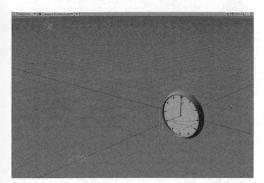

Figure 25-3: Tick-tock! A simple wall clock ready to wind up.

2. Select the object **clock:secondHand** and then open the Graph Editor (<**Ctrl**> + <**F2**>). Click on the Expressions tab (the one below the graph) and click the **New** button to create a new expression. Change the Name to **SecondTick**. This expression needs to simply rotate 1/60th of a full

circle every second. A circle is 360 degrees, hence to calculate the correct angle as time plays in LightWave, we simply use the mathematical expression below and type it into the Value text box.

Time * (360/60)

> ### Note
>
> Time is used in expressions to ask for the current time in an animation. This value is always returned in seconds. (At 30 frames per second, a single frame of animation is roughly 0.033 seconds.) As an animation plays in LightWave, this value increases per frame and is used in this expression to drive the rotation of the second hand.

3. Once the expression has been created and the math entered, it's ready to be used, or in LightWave terminology, applied. Let's make it control the clock

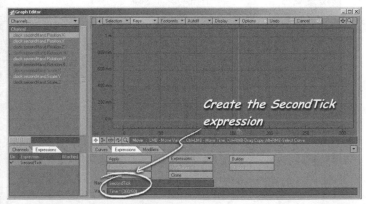

Figure 25-4: Creating the new expression to rotate the second hand.

Create the SecondTick expression

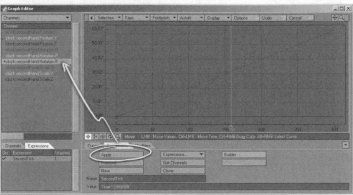

Figure 25-5: Link the expression to the Bank channel.

hand. Select the **clock:second-Hand.Rotation.B** channel from the Channel Bin on the left of the Graph Editor, then click **Apply** under the Expressions tab to attach the expression to the Bank rotation.

> **Note**
>
> We can see a dotted line appear in the Graph Editor, showing us the increasing effect of the expression. There is also a dot next to the channel name in Graph Editor to indicate that this channel is being modified by LightWave. You'll recall from Chapter 12 that the same thing occurs when using channel modifiers. Expressions are just another type of channel modifier — an expression is modifying the channel, after all!

If we play the animation, the second hand is moving, but it's a very smooth rotation because of the nature of the Time value being quite fine. In reality, a clock uses gears and cogs that click quite abruptly as they turn, and this often creates the effect of the clock hand skipping over to the next second rather than smoothly rotating as it does now.

4. Let's make the second hand correctly tick from second to second like we'd expect to see, and hence appear more realistic. This can be done by rounding up the Time value to the closest second. Simply edit the Second-Hand expression directly in the Value text box and change it to read:

integer(Time) * (360/60)

> **Note**
>
> When we apply the integer() command to Time, we are performing a process known as *typecasting*. In layman's terms, this is simply referring to converting one type of information into another (in this case, a number to an integer).

The dotted line in the Graph Editor updates to show us how this change is going to affect the Bank rotation (Figure 25-6). We've used the integer() command to convert the Time value from its number format (which can be something like 0.033 of a second per frame) to its closest integer. This means that Time is now a whole number, and any values in between are rounded up or down, creating a clock hand that skips from second to second, and not smoothly sliding its way around the clock face!

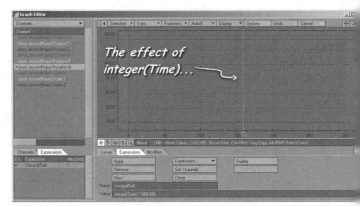

Figure 25-6: The updated ticking clock expression.

Sub-expressions

If you're eagle-eyed, you've probably noted that expressions are single lines of math. In fact, they're pretty simple stuff. But what about when we create more complex scenes containing lots of expressions that have the same chunks of math inside them? Could we perhaps strip out the repetitive mathematics into a single expression that all the other expressions could reference?

Think how we could save having to retype lines and lines of the same thing over and over if perhaps we could replace that math with a more descriptive word or command that made more sense.

That's where the concept of *sub-expressions* comes in. By placing commonly used mathematics into their own sub-expressions, we can simplify more complex projects and make things so much easier to manage. For example, imagine that we needed to calculate the mathematics of **Time/4** and use it in a variety of other expressions. We would create a new sub-expression called **DivTime** (short for *divided time*) and then enter the expression **Time/4**.

By the way, sub-expressions are *not* applied to channels. While they might be called sub-expressions, they are no different from any other expression. The difference is that they are simply there to be *referenced by other expressions*. Referencing a sub-expression is done by simply inserting the sub-expression name between two square brackets, as in this example where I'm adding the sub-expression to a number:

10+[DivTime]

The real beauty comes when you suddenly decide that the whole **Time/4** thing was actually incorrect, and should have been **Time/2** instead. Without sub-expressions like DivTime, imagine the editing you'd have to do if you had to update information in 10 or more expressions where this simple mistake had to be fixed. By simply updating **DivTime**, all the other expressions that reference it are updated instantly! Edit once, update many — a definite workflow time-saver!

Let's expand on our clock example by creating some sub-expressions that calculate the minutes and hours for us, then use these to rotate the minute and hour hands

of the clock. It's not the most optimal approach, but it does demonstrate how this is done. One thing it does offer us, however, is that it can make our expressions simpler to understand than just using raw numbers. Using sub-expressions with *meaningful names* can make it easier for us less-numerical artists to remember how our expressions work!

1. Open the Graph Editor (**<Ctrl>+ <F2>**). It doesn't matter what item is selected when you open the Graph Editor; we are simply going to be using it for creating some sub-expressions. As mentioned, sub-expressions don't get applied to channels (hence why item selection doesn't make a difference).

2. Under the Expressions tab (below the graph), click **New** to create a new sub-expression. Set Name to **TheMinuteAngle** and enter the following expression into the Value text box:

    (360/3600)

> **Note**
>
> To get the correct rotation of the minute hand, we simply want to make it 1/60th of the speed of the second hand. That would be something like saying rotate the second hand angle of 360/60, but divide it again by 60 to get (360/60)/60. What we have done is simplified the math by saying 360/ (60*60), which, if you check on a calculator, gives us the same result.

3. Take care to click **New** again to create another new sub-expression. (It's very easy to accidentally edit an existing expression in the Graph Editor without realizing.) Set Name to **TheHourAngle** and enter the following expression into the Value text box:

    (360/43200)

4. Let's use these new sub-expressions! Under the Channels tab on the left, find and double-click on the **clock: minuteHand** item (Figure 25-7) to bring up its channels in the Graph Editor. Make sure that we're on the Expressions tab (the main one below the graph) and click **New** to create a new expression with the name **MinuteTime**. Enter the following expression into the Value text box:

    integer(Time) * [TheMinuteAngle]

Once entered, select the **clock:minuteHand.Rotation.B** channel in the Channel Bin, and then click the **Apply** button to apply the MinuteTime expression.

5. Let's double-click on the **clock: hourHand** item under the Channels tab on the left, and repeat the process by creating and applying a new expression to the **clock:hourHand.Rotation.B** channel called

HourTime with the following expression:

integer(Time) * [TheHourAngle]

6. The clock is now fully functional; however, it fails in one area: We can't set the clock's starting time! By default, it will always start at 12:00. Let's edit all three of our Time expressions by adding the text: **Value +** at the start of each expression as shown below:

SecondTick:	**Value+integer(Time) * (360/60)**
MinuteTime:	**Value+integer(Time) * [TheMinuteAngle]**
HourTime:	**Value+integer(Time) * [TheHourAngle]**

7. Can we check that the clock works properly? Well, we can if we extend the number of frames enough to allow for a full hour to pass. However, at 30 fps,

Figure 25-7:
Select our minute hand so we can apply the expression.

this would require us to create an animation of 1,800 frames to see an entire minute go past, and 108,000 frames for a whole hour! Luckily for us, Time is based on the Frames Per Second setting of our animation, so to test the hands of the clock, simply change the Frames Per Second value on the **Edit | General Options** panel to something much smaller, like 1 frame per second.

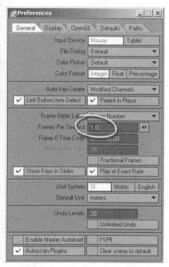

Figure 25-8: Setting the animation to 1 frame per second.

Note

One hour still requires 3,600 frames, and it's advisable to manually scrub the time bar to watch the clock at work (as each frame takes one second to tick over). To see the clock in action, check out **Scenes\Chapter 25\ticktock_F.lws**.

As you can see, expressions have saved us from having to animate the clock. This clock can be used in any scene and any animation. It takes care of itself, behaving realistically at the same time, and means it's one less thing for us to think about when creating our digital movies!

Expression Builder

Expressions can be a headache to create and write from scratch, so it's lucky for us that there's a tool available in LightWave to make things easier for us non-number crunching mortals. In a majority of cases, we'll be using the Channel expression system when working in LightWave (the expressions we set up from the Graph Editor). For those of us who do not consider math our strong point, there is a tool in the Graph Editor to help us called the *Expression Builder*. This is a nice, simple way to quickly create expressions, and includes not only the tools to create the expressions but help files and examples where such expressions can be used. Let's use it to create an auto-focus rig for the LightWave camera.

1. In a fresh new scene, let's select **Create | Add Null** and add a null called **FocusPoint**. Select **Windows | Motion Options** and set the Parent Item for the null to **Camera**. This will attach the null to the camera.

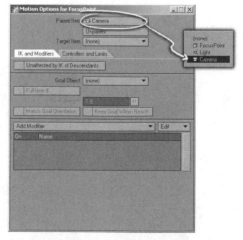

Figure 25-9: Parent the null to the camera.

2. Select the camera and open its Properties panel (<**p**>). Set the Antialiasing option to **PLD 9-Pass** and then select the **Stereo and DOF** tab at the bottom of the Camera Properties window. Activate the **Depth of Field** option, and then click the **E** next to Focal Distance to open the Graph Editor.

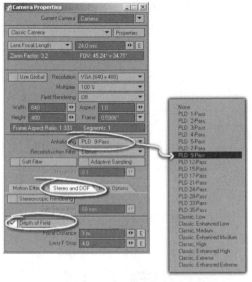

Figure 25-10: Set up antialiasing options, then envelope the focal distance.

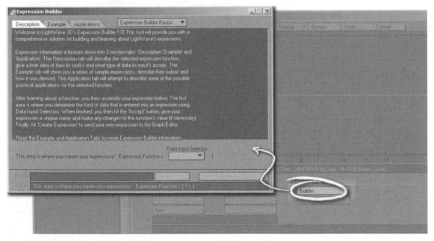

Figure 25-11: Opening up the Expression Builder tool.

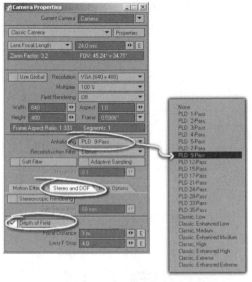

> **Note**
>
> In case you were wondering why I adjusted the Antialiasing setting, the depth of field options require an antialiasing level of 9 passes or higher to work.

3. Select the Expressions tab of the Graph Editor, and click on the **Builder** button to activate the Expression Builder tool.

4. The distance from the camera to the null is simply the measure of an invisible line between the location of each item, which is represented by a value called a vector. From the pop-up menu at the top of the Expression Builder window, select the **Vector Functions** menu item, then select the expression type **vmag(Distance, Standard)** from the list that pops out. This expression type will return a single value that represents the distance (or *magnitude* as it's known in math-talk) between two items in 3D.

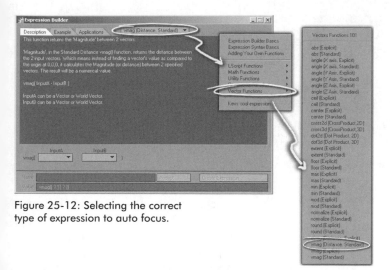

Figure 25-12: Selecting the correct type of expression to auto focus.

Note

One of the nicest features of the Expression Builder tool is the three tabs at the top: Description, Example, and Applications. These three tabs contain useful and interesting information about the expressions you are creating, examples of their use, and some applications where they can be used. It's worth spending a little time reading this information as it can greatly increase your understanding of the expression system in LightWave.

5. There are two input areas for this type of expression. To set these up, click on the **InputA** pop-up, and select **World**

Vector. When this is selected, a panel containing a list of items in the scene will appear. For this first parameter, select and expand the Camera channels (if they aren't already), then select one of the Position channels (in this case, just select **Position.X**) and click on the **Choose** button. For **InputB**, choose **World Vector** and select the **Focus-Point** null, then select the **Position.X** channel from the list for this item also.

6. Click the **Accept** button to generate the necessary expression notation. Once accepted, we can change the name of the expression to **AutoFocus** and click **Create Expression**. This last button creates and adds the expression to the Graph Editor. We're finished. Close the Expression Builder window.

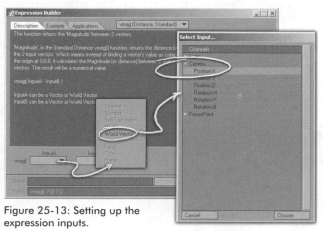

Figure 25-13: Setting up the expression inputs.

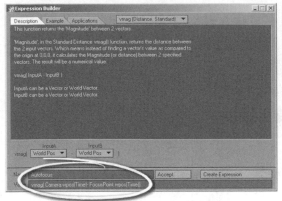

Figure 25-14: Creating the finished expression.

Note

Pressing <**Shift**>+<**F9**> while the viewport is set to Camera view will let us get a
preview of the depth of field effect quickly.

7. The last thing we need to do is simply
attach this expression to the camera's
FocalDistance channel. Select the
channel in the Graph Editor, and then
click the **Apply** button in the Expressions tab to apply the expression. A
small dot should appear next to the
channel once applied to indicate that
this channel is now being controlled by
the expression.

8. To use this rig, simply animate the
FocusPoint null moving along its
Z-axis to the location that you want the
camera to focus on. Simple as that!

9. To finish up this rig, let's add an additional tool to give us a better visual
representation of the focus effect. Add
another null to the scene, and call it
VIZFOCUS. Like the other null,
select **Windows | Motion Options**
and set the parent item for this null to
Camera. Make sure the null is perfectly centered in the camera. Select
Modify | Translate | Move, and
then click the **Modify | General |
Reset** button to zero out the location.
Keyframe the null here at frame 0.

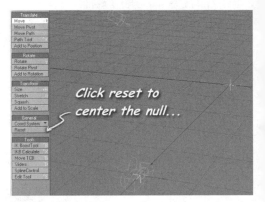

*Click reset to
center the null...*

Figure 25-16: Reset this null to be centered inside
the camera.

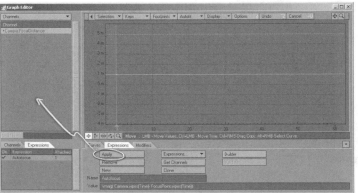

Figure 25-15:
Apply the
expression to the
camera's
FocalDistance
channel.

Note

VIZFOCUS should not be moved or adjusted in any way once it has been parented to the camera. It may be advantageous to perhaps lock the object in the Scene Editor or disable the axes from the Move tool to prevent accidentally moving it. This can be done quickly by simply activating the Move tool (<t>) and then un-highlighting the **X**, **Y**, **Z** buttons (next to the numeric info) by clicking on them at the bottom left of the toolbar.

10. Open the Object Properties window (<p>) for the VIZFOCUS null. From the Geometry tab, select the **Add Custom Object | Depth-Of-Field Display** modifier. Try animating the FocusPoint null back and forth and watch the display update accordingly (Figure 25-17). The shaded box area represents the area in which items will be in focus (the label Focus is also displayed at the center of this area), and dynamically updates when we alter various camera attributes, such as lens zoom or F-stop values.

Note

You will need to ensure that Auto Key is active for this tool to be interactive.

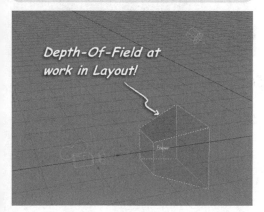

Depth-Of-Field at work in Layout!

Figure 25-17: The new auto focus depth of field display at work!

Note

Depth-of-field display is only shaded when the VIZFOCUS null is selected; however, it still displays and updates as a simple wireframe when unselected.

v9.2 Note

LightWave v9.2 provides enhanced Depth of Field previews that work great with rigs like this. For more info, check out the Depth of Field and Motion Blur Preview video in the LightWave 9.2 Videos folder on the companion DVD.

Relativity

Before there were expressions in Light-Wave, there was Prem Subrahmanyam, a very talented plug-in developer and LightWave artist who created a tool known as Relativity. Relativity was a breakthrough at the time, as it came along before expressions were added to LightWave. Relativity is often touted by its fans as being better than LightWave's own built-in expression system, so it's no surprise that LightWave v9 now includes this awesome system as part of the application!

How's This Different from LightWave Expressions?

There are a few differences between the built-in expression system and Relativity. For instance, Relativity is built around a collection of plug-ins (used in different parts of Layout), rather than being internalized like the built-in system. This does have an advantage in that it can see when Light-Wave has modified something, then take that into consideration before doing its own thing. Don't worry too much about the details at this point; we'll be looking at things more closely shortly!

Obviously, the syntax is different for Relativity as well. For instance, we've seen how the syntax of LightWave can retrieve the X coordinate of an item. Relativity's syntax works in a reverse manner, starting with specifying the X coordinate, and then asking which item it wants to read this from and at what time.

X(spaceship,t)

Gulp! This is starting to look quite scary! LightWave v9 now has *three* different expression notations to learn! This could get messy and deeply confusing! However, like the Expression Builder in the Graph Editor, we're in luck: Relativity contains several tools to take care of the technical stuff for us! What makes Relativity really cool is that it has been created with the artist, not the mathematician, in mind. Most of Relativity can be used without knowing anything about mathematics (though a little mathematical skill could greatly enhance your experience with Relativity).

Professors

Professors are clever little helpers for Relativity that make creating some of the more useful expressions a breeze by just asking you what you want to do. After answering the simple questions of a professor, the professor will create the mathematics as needed without you needing to pull out your cerebral calculator. There are many useful professors for creating rolling wheels, targeting other objects, controlling interconnecting gears. There's even a professor for building an expression!

Relativity — Wheel Rotator

In this short exercise, we're going to use Relativity to rotate the wheels of a car as it travels. Relativity is smart enough to work out the actual distance of the car no matter

how many turns and twists it takes, and it can also calculate orientation. Yes, Relativity can also work out whether you have put the car in reverse! This is hard if not almost impossible to do easily with LightWave expressions, but it's extremely simple for Relativity to do with almost no effort whatsoever!

1. Load **BroomBroom.lws** from Scenes\ Chapter 25. This will load a simple car rig scene in which the car rolls forward, stops, and then reverses. If you play this scene, you would notice that the wheels do not turn at all as the car moves. Sometimes an animator will attempt to manually animate the rotation of the wheels himself, which leads to the occasional slipping appearance of the tires on the road. However, this scenario is a common one, and an ideal situation for Relativity to automate and take control!

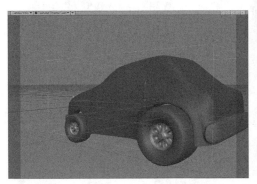

Figure 25-18: That's a fast car, which could be faster if only its wheels would turn!

2. Select the rear wheel object **speedy_ car:Rear_Fats** and bring up the **Windows | Motion Options** window. From the Add Modifier pop-up list, select **Relativity** and double-click on it to open the Relativity control panel, as shown in Figure 25-19.

3. These wheels roll on the Pitch angle. Next to the P: input on the Relativity panel, click on the **Ask a Professor** pop-up at the end of the text input box as shown in Figure 25-20. Select **Dr. Wheel Rotater** from the list.

4. The professor panel that opens (Figure 25-21) asks us for just two things. The first is to tell it the item that the wheel is connected to. Click the **Pick Item** button to open up the Pick an Item panel. In this scene, the wheels are *parented* to the body of the car. This means we can simply select the **Pick PARENT** button, then click **OK** to close the panel. The diameter of the wheel should be **1.0** (so you can leave it at its default), then click **OK** to exit the professor. Note how the text input box for the P: channel now contains the expression needed to roll these wheels! Relativity has taken care of working out the math for us.

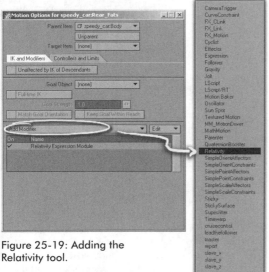

Figure 25-19: Adding the Relativity tool.

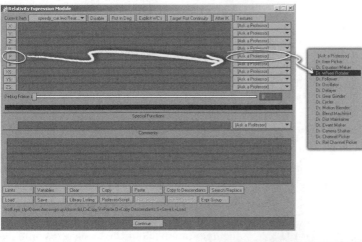

Figure 25-20: Asking a professor to rotate the wheels.

Figure 25-21: Set up the rotator.

909

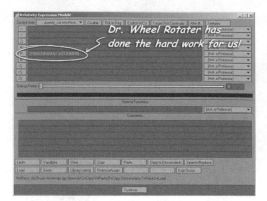

Figure 25-22: What a smart professor! The math is calculated for us!

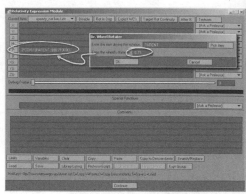

Figure 25-23: The setup for the Right_Front and Left_Front items.

5. Click **Continue** to close the Relativity panel. Play the animation and watch how our rear wheels now rotate nicely!

6. Repeat steps 2 through 4 for the items **speedy_car:Right_Front** and **speedy_car:Left_Front** to add the wheel rolling action to the front wheels. Note that the diameter of these wheels should be **0.71** (they're slightly smaller than the rear wheels).

7. We're done! Play the animation again and note how the wheels behave themselves, even rolling backward as the car reverses. The car has some slight acceleration and deceleration in its movement so that we can get an appreciation of the subtle control of the wheels offered by Relativity.

> **Note**
>
> While we tested the car using simple back and forth motions, Relativity's ODIST function will work out the actual distance no matter how many turns and twists we make. This function also recognizes the orientation of the object (hence the O in the name), correctly determining the wheel rotation if we decide to reverse the car as well. With Relativity, there are no excuses for inaccurate wheels on vehicles any more!

Conclusion

Automating parts of our animation, or adding control systems to areas of a machine, building, or character is a great way to simplify complex animation work for us. And as we've seen, we don't really need a Ph.D. in mathematics to drive it!

We've learned some of the basics of creating expressions in the Graph Editor, what certain kinds of data actually mean, and how the artist-friendliness of Relativity makes rolling wheels more accurate for our vehicles. Both systems are exciting and powerful stuff, and with some excellent documentation about these systems shipping with LightWave v9, it's well worth spending more time learning how to become expression control gurus in LightWave!

Chapter 26

Advanced Skills: Network Rendering

If computer graphics has an Achilles' heel, it's most likely to be rendering — or, to be more exact, the time it takes to render. All the complexities of the mathematics behind what makes the amazing visuals we create need to be processed, sometimes taking a while for even the fastest computers to think about.

As projects become more complex and we start to introduce some of the cooler effects and tools into our creative palette, things start to take longer and longer to render. What if we have a deadline to work against? In Figure 26-1, let's take the hypothetical concept that we're a one-person freelance company, and we've got an afternoon to produce a simple 300-frame animation for a client who needs it by that afternoon. Well, it's obviously going to take the day to create, animate, texture, and set up ready to render. And our test renders tell us it's around 30 seconds per frame to render. That doesn't sound like much, does it?

Aha! 9000 seconds (or 2.5 hours) in total is a little different than the "quick" 30 seconds a frame we had accidentally assumed would be fast to finish. And what happens if the client calls and says, "We need to get that footage ready for sending to tape in two hours." That sickening feeling in our stomach starts to kick in as we realize that we'll probably need an extra hour to finish the render (hoping that no crashes, power outages, or other issues pop up), then compile into a video file, burn to DVD, and courier out to our client (and pray that rush hour doesn't delay it).

This is where having a few extra computers on hand would have saved us that nauseating taste in the back of our mouth and the cold sweat and panic we suddenly went into after that phone call! Luckily, however, we just happen to have a couple of extra machines on hand. Now, if we networked these together, we could get, say, four renders going at the same time. Look at the difference in Figure 26-2. 37 minutes! And that, my friends, is what network rendering is all about — saving one's bacon, meeting deadlines, and keeping the stress levels at a minimum.

1 Computer
300-frame animation
30 seconds per frame

9000 seconds (2.5 hours!)

Figure 26-1: Do the math. The real render time needed for our project!

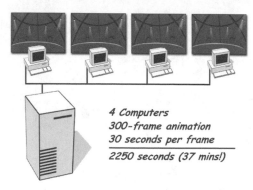

4 Computers
300-frame animation
30 seconds per frame
_____
2250 seconds (37 mins!)

Figure 26-2: Redo that math — now four times faster with four times the machines.

Note

A computer network that is set up to render is called a render farm, and each machine in this "farm" is referred to as a render node. You may have heard these terms mentioned online or in discussions with other artists at some time. It's amusing to note that e-on software, creator of the excellent Vue environmental animation and rendering software that you may own if you had preordered LightWave v9, has decided to call its HyperVue Network rendering nodes RenderCows — an obvious play on the render farm term!

ScreamerNet

LightWave ships with a small program called LWSN in its programs folder (Figure 26-3). What is this? Well, it's called ScreamerNet and is simply the rendering engine of LightWave on its own (with a few small bits of clever code to read and write files from a network). This program doesn't require a dongle to run either — and you can install it on up to 999 computers for the price of a single copy of LightWave! This makes it an amazing value for the money for people wishing to create rendering networks without investing thousands on additional software.

Figure 26-3: ScreamerNet icon.

lwsn.exe

ScreamerNet is a little different from the other applications in LightWave in that it is what is called a *console* application. It runs in a text window and operates through a series of parameters that are passed to it through the command line (or commandline text file for the Mac version). This makes it a little less intuitive to use for those who

are non-technical, but it's not hard to work out with a little patience.

Note

The PC and Mac versions of ScreamerNet work differently from each other due to the difference in the operating systems. I tend to mostly work with PCs; hence I apologize that most of this chapter will appear very PC-biased. Mac LWSN works in a very similar fashion, but due to differences in the operating system itself, a different approach will need to be taken to create the node setups on the server. There are plenty of excellent tutorials online, as well as great documentation that ships with LightWave for those of you who want to dig deeper than what this chapter covers.

ScreamerNet is actually quite simple to set up on a PC-based network, and can be done in about 10 to 15 minutes if you are PC savvy. Before you begin, let's start by looking at how the mechanics of a render farm work. While 3D usually requires high-spec'd workstations, a render farm network really relies on computers with fast CPUs, plenty of RAM, and the ability to talk via a network. With the price of hardware always dropping, building a cheap render farm can become a reality for many people.

Server

All render farms start out like any network. There should be one centralized computer that acts as a server. The purpose of the server is to simply be a "file location" for the rest of the network to talk with. This server computer will usually have a copy of LightWave installed on it, and also a copy of all the project files we've created in LightWave, ready for rendering. The server will also be the place where the other computers will render the images they create, so this computer should have plenty of hard disk space.

> **Note**
>
> While you can utilize Windows computers as servers, unless you buy a copy of Windows Server Edition with sufficient CALs from Microsoft (Client Access Licenses), most versions of Windows only allow for a *maximum of 10 connections* to talk with it. If your network is tiny, this may not be an issue. If you plan on creating a much larger network, you may want to consider using one of the many available Linux operating systems. This operating system is not for the faint of heart, but in most cases it's cheap and has no issues with network connection limitations.

Another solution is to source one of many excellent open-source file server setups such as FreeNAS (Free Network Attached Storage server) — http:www.freenas.org. Requiring around 16 MB of space once installed, this can be run from a USB memory stick if needed! Once running, it turns any computer into an instant file server.

Render Nodes

As expected, once you have a server, you then need more computers to talk to it to create the network. Each of these computers simply needs to be able to connect and read/write to the hard disk of the server. That's it. It's extremely simple. No software needs to be installed on the computer as it's going to run the LWSN program directly from the server itself.

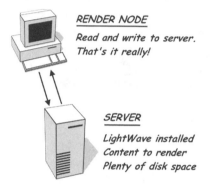

RENDER NODE
Read and write to server.
That's it really!

SERVER
LightWave installed
Content to render
Plenty of disk space

Figure 26-4: A network needs, well, networked computers!

Talk the Talk

Once we've got the tools and hardware in place, just how exactly does ScreamerNet work? Any render farm has two key components: the controller and the nodes.

Controller

There must always be a single computer that controls the render farm. This machine's task is to monitor how the render nodes are behaving and to send them more work when they're finished. In ScreamerNet, this is performed by reading and writing instructions to special text files that both the controller and the nodes work with.

Each node is controlled through a Job text file, which is where the controller program tells the node what it should be doing, such as render a frame, shut down, etc.

Nodes

Each render node on the network looks at the Job files from the controller and performs whatever it was asked to do. The node's job is to read scenes, objects, and images from the server, and render a particular frame from that scene. Once the frame is completed, it needs to be saved back to a location on the server.

Each node talks back to the controller using an Ack (short for Acknowledgement) text file. The controller uses this file to determine whether a node is waiting on a new job or if it's busy.

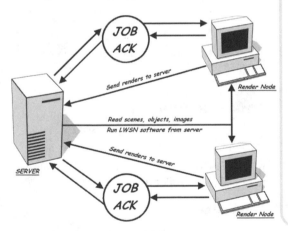

Figure 26-5: ScreamerNet chitchat.

> **Note**
>
> A render farm creates animation by rendering still image sequences. It doesn't render out to video files like AVI or MOV, simply because these types of files require each frame to be created in sequence and then compressed and added to a single movie file. Expecting a network of machines to "wait" for frames to complete before they can send their own back to the server, and expecting every machine to never crash either, would completely defeat the speed improvements that a network gives us, hence it's much more efficient to simply render still frames of animation.

> **Note**
>
> You can use LightWave to recompile an image sequence into an animation. Start with a new scene and set the resolution of the default camera to match your rendered image sequence. Then open the Image Editor and load in the first frame of the image sequence. Once the file has been loaded, check it in the Image Editor to ensure it has loaded the entire sequence and not just the first frame. Then open the Compositing tab of the Effects panel and specify your image sequence as the background image. Now open the Render Globals window and set the appropriate options to render out your animation (typically this will be an AVI or QuickTime file). Press F10 to begin the render. In a matter of seconds, LightWave will rip through hundreds of frames and compress them into an animation file ready to be proofed by your clients.

Become a Render Farmer

So now that we have a simple understanding of how ScreamerNet works on a network, put on those overalls, grab your milking bucket, and let's look at the steps to set up a render farm on a Windows network.

Note

This exercise is based around how I personally like to build *my* render farm setups. As with everything in the CG world, there are many approaches to the same subject.

1. On the server computer, create a new folder on your hard drive called **Screamernet**, then copy the Programs and Plugins folders from your LightWave installation here. Also, find the LWEXT9.CFG file for LightWave (which is usually saved inside the Documents and Settings folder of your machine) and copy it into the ScreamerNet folder as shown in Figure 26-6. To keep things clean here, I also like to create a folder called **command** (where the job and ack files will be stored), a folder called **Content** for all the LightWave projects, and a folder called **Renders** for the rendered images.

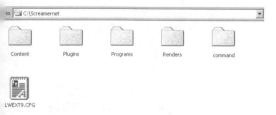

Content   Plugins   Programs   Renders   command

LWEXT9.CFG

Figure 26-6: Setting up a custom Screamernet folder.

2. Let's make sure that we set up the ScreamerNet folder to be shared on a network. Right-click on the **Screamernet** folder, select **Properties**, and make sure that the **Share this folder** option is active.

Figure 26-7: Set up sharing.

3. You will want to connect to this folder remotely from each workstation, so this step will need to be applied for *all* machines you plan on using in your network. There are two methods in Windows that we can use for this: using a mapped network drive letter or accessing through the machine's UNC name (UNC stands for Universal Naming Convention). This book isn't aimed at teaching Networking 101, so I'll go for the easier of the two for most people to grasp and use drive mapping. As shown in Figure 26-8, open a folder in Windows and select **Tools | Map Network Drive**. This will open a window that lets us specify both a drive letter as well as the location to map to. It's extremely important that you make sure you select the *same drive letter* on *every* machine you do this for, and then

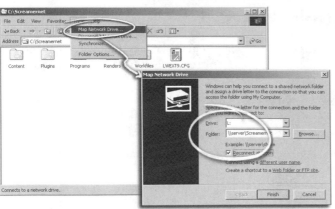

Figure 26-8: Map
the drive and
folder.

browse to the shared Screamernet
folder on the network. Ensure you set
Reconnect at Login so that you don't
have to repeat this step for every
machine again next time. I recommend
using **L:** as the drive letter (L for
LightWave of course!).

Why did we need the same drive letter on
each machine? Simple — because in the
next step we need to ensure all the render
nodes can load up the plug-ins needed to
render files correctly.

Note

I like to set things up using one machine to
get the ball rolling. To do this, I will often
map the network drive on the server back to
itself as the L: drive. This makes setting up
and testing settings on the server easy without having to run around the office and
work with another machine initially. Once
things work fine on the server, they're
almost guaranteed to work everywhere else.

4. Let's open up the LWEXT9.CFG file in
a text editor. This file tells LightWave
where to find the plug-ins it needs.

Note

You may wonder what is going on in
the config file. The text looks a little
odd, and there's a lot of doubled up
slash characters. LightWave uses
escaped character formatting. What
this means is that certain control characters are represented in text by
preceding a character with a backslash
(\) character. For example, a line feed
is represented as \n, a tab is represented as \t, and so forth. However,
this character is also used to delimit, or
separate, folders in a file path (such as
this config file), which means we need
to tell LightWave to treat it as a single \
character, and not try to interpret it as
some kind of escaped code. To tell
LightWave to use a single backslash,
we simply use a double backslash (\\).

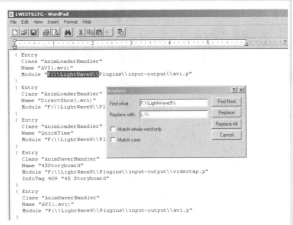

Figure 26-9: Quickly replace the paths in the LWEXT9
config file.

Because we copied this file from our LightWave installation, the plug-in files are set up to be loaded from somewhere on the computer that no render node can find. We need to replace the path for plug-ins to point to the new shared **L:\Plugins** drive path. That is why we need all the nodes to share the same drive letter.

Believe it or not, we're almost done. The last step in setting things up is to create a batch file (a DOS command script) that we can call from any of the nodes to start up the render farm. LightWave actually ships with such files, which you can look at yourself in the Programs folder you copied (it's called startlwsn_node.bat). However, let's write our own, and at the same time familiarize ourselves with how LWSN parameters work.

5. Create a new text file in a text editor. Enter the commands as listed in Figure 26-10 and save the file as **startnode.bat** into the **L:** folder.

6. The last step is to set up the nodes themselves. Go to the first computer you plan on using as a render node, and make sure that you've mapped the L: drive to the Screamernet shared folder on the server computer. Open the L:\ drive, and then make a shortcut on the desktop to the startnode.bat file we created in step 5. Right-click on the shortcut and select **Properties** to set up the render node ID number (each node must have its own *unique* number). Start with 1 for your first node, and make sure each node's shortcut is set to the next incremental number (1, then 2, 3, and so forth).

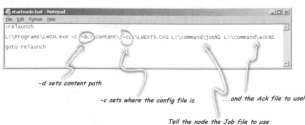

Figure 26-10: Creating our special batch command file.

Note

I've used a couple of batch file specialties in this short script to make things easier on the render farm management duties. The first is the use of a label called :relaunch at the start of the file and the goto relaunch command specified on the last line. These two lines will save us the hassle of walking around the office to reboot or restart nodes if they crash or stop. This works by forcing the computer to go back and try launching LWSN again if LWSN ever aborts for any reason.

The second is the use of %1 after the job and ack files at the end of the second line. This tells the script to use any value that is entered after the command startnode.bat and use it in place of the %1. If you're scratching your head over what I'm talking about now, don't worry — we'll explain this when we set up the nodes.

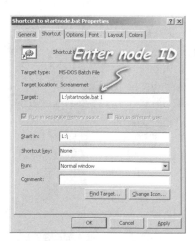

Figure 26-11: Setting up the node number in the shortcut.

Note

This number is what is used by the %1 I mentioned in the previous Note. The value is read and inserted into the script when it's run, saving us having to create a lot of separate files to start each of the nodes manually.

Note

It's possible to clean up a scene that wasn't cleanly content managed using the File | Content Manager tool. The Consolidate Only option will retrieve any external files for the scene loaded and pull them into the content directory for you. The other option, Export Scene, will let you export everything in your scene to a new, clean folder. This tool does have one issue: If you have multiple-layered objects in your scene, but at some stage you decided to clear one or more of the layers from the scene file, you may get an Object Conversion Failure error. Don't panic if this happens. LightWave will have already moved the entire object and image files for you, but will not have moved the scene file. Simply copy the scene file to the new content directory by hand, and things should be okay. (It's possible some images may not be linked, but these can easily be corrected manually by finding the correct images as requested, then saving all objects after the scene has loaded.)

7. Once done, double-click the shortcut and get the node running! If successful, you should see a console window as shown in Figure 26-12.

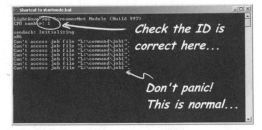

Figure 26-12: The node's alive!

If all looks well, move on to the next node and repeat, each time making sure that you increase the node ID by one so that each node has its own unique ID. Start each node, and build that farm!

With all nodes up and running, we'll want to see just how well it works by feeding it a scene and putting it through its paces. Scenes *must* be properly set up using content directories to work successfully on a render farm. This is where good habits and the new content directory features of LightWave v9 will play a big part in the successful use of a rendering farm.

8. Copy the images, objects, and scenes for one of your projects into the **L:\Content** folder. Open up LightWave on your server (or local machine with the L:\ drive mapped appropriately) and set the content directory to **L:\Content**. Load the scene file. Once the scene is loaded, we need to make sure the render path is set appropriately for the nodes to write to. Open the **Render | Render Globals** window, activate the **Save RGB** option, and set the filename to be saved to **L:\Render\test_**. Set the file type to be **LW_PNG24 (.png)** and save the scene to make sure it has these save options set for the nodes to use.

9. To get the ball rolling, we need a render farm controller. Lucky for us, LightWave itself has such a tool built right in! Click on **Render | Utilities | Network Render** to open the render control panel as displayed in Figure

26-13. Click on the **Command Directory** button, and set the directory to **L:\command**. Make sure that Maximum CPU Number is set to the highest node ID, and then click **Screamer Init** to initialize the render farm.

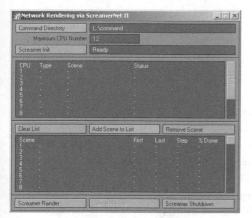

Figure 26-13: LightWave's render farm management tool.

One by one, each node should appear on the list in the window. Once initialized, the farm is ready and waiting for action!

10. Click the **Add Scene to List** button and add your scene file. Click **Screamer Render** and let the magic begin! Check the **L:\Render** folder as the render unfolds to ensure that the images are being created. Once all looks sweet, give yourself a pat on the back and congratulate yourself as a qualified render farmer!

Become a Better Farmer

The render farm controller that ships with LightWave is definitely not the most efficient of tools, and it's somewhat limited in its use. It also requires you to allocate your LightWave installation as a dedicated controller, losing you precious access to LightWave for doing work while it's busy. Luckily, there's a collection of alternate render controllers available to try and buy.

LightNet (Windows)

http://www.joejustice.org/lightwave/lightnet/

This is probably the best freebie you can get for your Windows-based render farm. It's open source, and loaded with features for managing your render farm. Resubmission and verification of renders, the ability to use multiple content directories, and node monitoring are just a few of the pros of this free software.

Note

One thing that can be difficult with a render farm is troubleshooting problems with scenes and renders. Sometimes it would be great if we could see just what render nodes had been up to, as often they'll display any errors that they hit but keep on attempting to process files. Lucky for us, LWSN actually has an option to pipe its output to disk, which can be extremely useful as logs later on for both troubleshooting and even analyzing performance if we feel the urge to process them. To create a log file for a node, simply add an -l logfilename parameter to the command line. Figure 26-14 shows how I updated the startnode.bat file to add logging to each node.

-l lets us create a log file

Figure 26-14: Log those nodes.

Mule (Windows)

http://www.epicsoft.net/products/mule

A feature-packed network rendering toolkit for LightWave. Not cheap, mind you, but well worth checking out.

TequilaScream (Windows)

http://www.digitaltoons.tv/shop/

A popular ScreamerNet controller that a lot of users seem to be working with, and worth a look. It has a 14-day trial, and there's a freeware node controller available as well.

ScreamerNet Controller (OS X)

http://www.catalystproductions.cc/screamernet/

While not free, this ScreamerNet controller for Mac OS X has had plenty of good reviews from the Mac community as being easy to use. There's a free Lite version to control a single node.

Renderfarm Commander (OS X)

http://www.brucerayne.com/renderfarm.html

Cheaper than ScreamerNet Controller, this is an alternative Mac OS X ScreamerNet controller worth looking at. Also has a free edition (with a two-node limit).

Planting the Crop

ScreamerNet was designed for network rendering, but it has a second functionality: It can be used to render on a single computer! You may be wondering why this would be useful. The first reason is low overhead. Because LWSN is the rendering engine only, it doesn't use up precious resources loading a big application and can actually render slightly faster than the Layout application itself.

The second reason is simple. Consider how many scenes you can load into Layout, and ask yourself how easy it would be to set up a handful of scenes to render out, say, overnight. That's correct — one is the answer here. And rendering a handful of scenes would require manual intervention on your part to load and start rendering each scene as needed.

This is where ScreamerNet can be used to our advantage in a mode called Standalone. This lets us batch-feed scenes into it and takes care of loading and rendering for us. While we could go into a tutorial on setting this up ourselves, creating such setups is time consuming and not overly user-friendly. I thoroughly recommend downloading some of the free batch rendering tools available for LightWave online.

LWSNController

http://www.dstorm.co.jp/english/plugin/other.htm

LWSNController comes in both Windows and Macintosh flavors, and is a nice simple click-and-add tool for setting up batch renders on a single computer. It also includes cool little features such as an email notification when rendering is done. I use this controller a lot for my own work, and it's well worth downloading.

LWSN Batch Render

http://jeremy.lwidof.net/lscript/

Jeremy Hardin has two sets of scripts for rendering files. One is for both Mac and PC in the form of a simple BG Render tool that starts up a render using LWSN in the background, and another is for Windows only for batch rendering with LWSN.

Conclusion

We've looked at what network rendering is and why it's good for both deadlines and just getting those render jobs completed in a timely fashion. We also managed to build a render farm, and have plenty of links to other useful software we can use. Network rendering is definitely cool and a lot less complex than you may have initially thought. It's a necessity in any studio, and with what we've covered in this chapter, you're probably already building up that rendering monster in preparation for your next big project.

Chapter 27

Plug-ins and Utilities

Plug-ins are utilities that run within a host application (such as Layout or Modeler) and extend its native capabilities, often in remarkable ways. LightWave ships with several hundred plug-ins (many of which we think of as native tools). There are also thousands of third-party plug-ins available for it. Some are commercial, but the vast majority of plug-ins for LightWave are free. Tools that would cost hundreds of dollars for applications like Maya, 3ds Max, or XSI can be downloaded at no cost thanks to the generosity of those in the LightWave community.

In this chapter we'll talk about how to add plug-ins and where to find them once

they're available within LightWave. We'll also talk about LScript, a programming language that allows users to make their own plug-ins. And finally, we'll take a look at some of the most useful third-party plug-ins and utilities, many of which are included on the DVD that came with this book.

We'd like to thank all the plug-in authors in the LightWave community whose work has made ours that much easier. But we'd especially like to thank the authors who gave us permission to include their valuable tools on the book's companion DVD. We are in your debt.

Adding Plug-ins

By default, Modeler and Layout scan the LightWave install directory for plug-ins when they start up. If you place plug-ins in the install directory, they will automatically be added when you run the program.

You can disable the auto-scan feature by opening the General tab of the Preferences window (in Layout) or the General Options window (in Modeler) (<o> for both) and unchecking the Autoscan Plugins option.

In most cases it's fine to leave the Autoscan option turned on, but if you have a lot of plug-ins installed, this

LAYOUT'S OPTIONS PANEL   MODELER'S OPTIONS PANEL

Figure 27-1: Layout and Modeler are configured to auto-scan the LightWave install directory for plug-ins.

can slow down the startup of each application. I prefer to turn auto-scanning off and add plug-ins manually.

Plug-ins can manually be added to both Modeler and Layout from the Utilities tab by clicking on either the Add Plugins or Edit Plugins button. Clicking the Add Plugins button will open a standard file browser window where you can locate the plug-ins you wish to add. Clicking on the Edit Plugins button will open a window where you can add and remove plug-ins from the program.

You can place plug-ins anywhere on your hard drive. Just make sure it's a fixed drive that the program will always have access to when it's run. I prefer to place my plug-ins in a folder on the root of my hard drive. This ensures that when it's time to upgrade, I won't lose or overwrite any existing plug-ins in the LightWave install directory.

If you need to add a lot of plug-ins, you can do so with ease via the Scan Directory option found in the Edit Plug-ins window. The Edit Plug-ins window also allows you to view installed plug-ins either by Category (where they fit into the program) or by File (the name of the plug-in). You can uninstall a plug-in by selecting it in the list and clicking on the Delete button. Deleted plug-ins will not be removed from the hard drive; they are simply removed from the program.

> **Note**
>
> When you use the Scan Directory option, all subdirectories will be scanned as well. If you have a lot of plug-ins in these directories, the scanning can take some time. Be patient. It's not uncommon for scanning to take several minutes to complete.

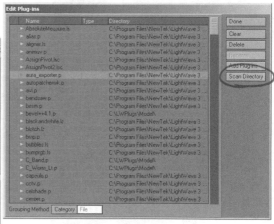

Figure 27-3: The Edit Plug-ins window lets you add an entire directory full of plug-ins via the Scan Directory option. You can also uninstall unwanted plug-ins by selecting them from the list and clicking on the Delete button.

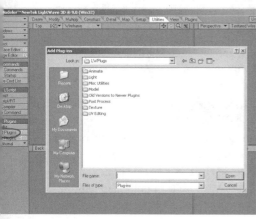

Figure 27-2: Clicking on the Add Plugins button lows you to manually add plug-ins. You can add ore than one plug-in at a time.

Accessing Plug-ins

Once plug-ins have been added to the program, they will be immediately available for use and can be accessed by clicking the Additional menu in the Plugins area. If you want to add buttons on the interface for your plug-ins, you will need to use the techniques described in Chapter 2.

In Modeler, plug-ins will be placed in the **Utilities | Plugins | Additional** menu regardless of whether you make a button for them. It's a good idea to look in this menu even if you haven't added any third-party plug-ins. LightWave ships with nearly 300 tools, and many of the ones that don't find their way onto the interface can be found here.

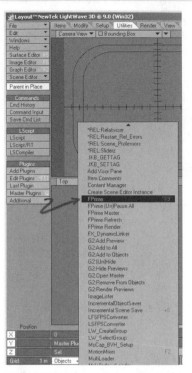

Figure 27-5: Layout stores many of its plug-ins in the Utilities | Plugins | Additional menu, although they can be found elsewhere throughout the program as well.

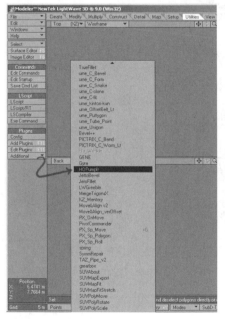

Figure 27-4: Modeler stores its plug-ins in the Utilities | Plugins | Additional menu.

Layout also has a Utilities | Plugins | Additional menu, and many of Layout's plug-ins can be found here as well.

The confusing thing about Layout is that not all plug-ins will appear in the Additional menu. Depending on the type of plug-in you add, it may appear in a number of different places. Here is a basic rundown of the common places that Layout adds plug-ins.

Master Plugins

The **Utilities | Master Plugins** button opens a window where you can view, add, and remove Master plug-ins. Master plug-ins are tools that affect the core operation of Layout. For example, the WindowConfigure plug-in that comes with LightWave allows you to set a specific window size and position for Layout's various panels.

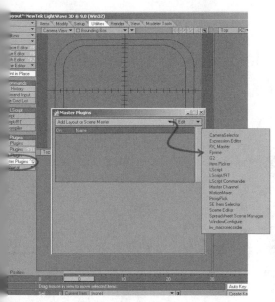

Tools that affect the core operation of yout can be found in the Utilities | Master Plugins ndow.

Custom Object

When you open the Object Properties window, the first tab is the Geometry tab. Here you'll find a pop-up menu called Add Custom Object. Plug-ins that affect how an object is displayed will appear in this menu.

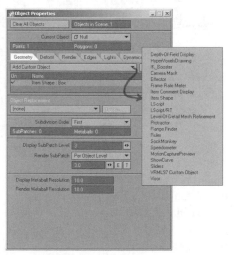

Figure 27-7: Tools that affect how an object is displayed can be found in the Add Custom Object menu.

For example, the Item Shape plug-in that comes with LightWave allows you to provide different shapes to null objects.

Displacements

On the Deform tab of the Object Properties window, you'll find an Add Displacement menu. Plug-ins that affect an object's shape can be found here. For example, the Morph Mixer tool that comes with LightWave allows you to easily blend various morph targets together to create things like lip sync and facial animation.

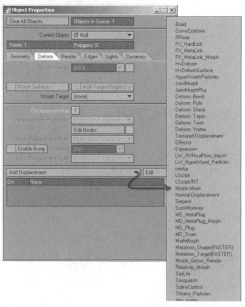

Figure 27-8: Tools that affect an object's shape can be found in the Add Displacement menu.

Motion

The IK and Modifiers tab of the Motion Options window (accessed by pressing the <m> key) is home to the Add Modifier pop-up menu. Here you'll find plug-ins that affect an object's movement. For example, the Jolt plug-in that comes with LightWave allows you to add a shaking motion. This is

925

perfect for camera shakes, such as when an asteroid flies by the camera.

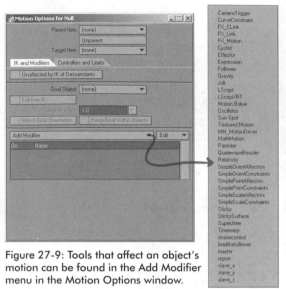

Backdrops

The Backdrop tab of the Effects panel contains an Add Environment pop-up menu. This menu contains plug-ins that create the sense of a world around the objects in your scene. For example, the SkyTracer plug-in that comes with LightWave allows you to add a sky, clouds, and a sun to your scene.

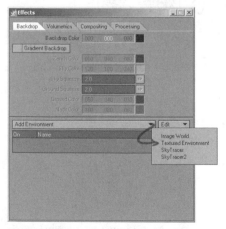

Figure 27-10: Tools that define the world around your 3D objects can be found in the Add Environment menu.

Volumetrics

The Volumetrics tab of the Effects panel contains the Add Volumetric pop-up menu. Here you'll find plug-ins that are typically used to define the appearance of particles. For example, the PixieDust plug-in that comes with LightWave is a great way to add stylized clouds, explosions, smoke, and other fanciful effects.

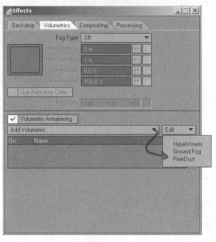

Figure 27-11: Tools that allow you to define the appearance of particles can be found in the Add Volumetric pop-up menu.

Image and Pixel Filters

The Processing tab of the Effects panel is home to two pop-up menus: Add Image Filter and Add Pixel Filter. The Add Pixel Filter menu gives you access to plug-ins that affect your image *while* it's being rendered. For example, the SasLite plug-in that comes with LightWave adds hair and fur to your objects during the rendering process, so it can be found here.

The Add Image Filter menu gives you access to tools that affect your image *after* it's been rendered. For example, the Corona plug-in (discussed in Chapter 7) that comes with LightWave allows you to add blooms to bright areas in your render, so it can be found here.

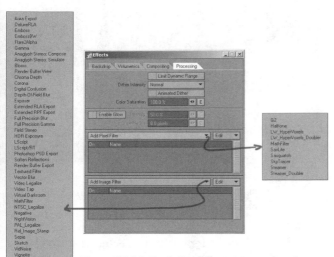

Figure 27-12: Tools that affect your rendered image can be found in the Add Pixel Filter and Add Image Filter pop-up menus.

LScript

LightWave plug-ins come in two varieties. The first are written in the C programming language and can be recognized by their .p extension. The second are written in the LScript language and have an extension of .ls or .lsc.

LScript is a programming language that allows users to write their own tools. It does not require any specialized programming software or language compilers. Since LScripts do not need to be compiled, they have the ability to run on both PC and Mac versions of LightWave. This makes LScript a popular format for many plug-in authors.

You can install and use LScripts as you would any other plug-in; however, creating your own LScripts does require you to have a little knowledge of computer programming. Even so, there are methods to create tools without the need for programming know-how. We'll look at these methods later in this section.

Note

Writing about LScript programming is a huge task and is beyond the scope of this chapter. It requires not only information on creating LScripts, but a complete review of Computer Programming 101 to make it accessible to all users. The following section is intended to make you aware of the tools at your disposal for creating your own plug-ins with LScript. It is not intended to be an exposition on the language itself.

Programming Tools for LScript

LightWave ships with some great coding tools to help programmers create LScripts efficiently. Inside the Programs folder of your LightWave install directory are two very cool tools that you may not be aware of: LSED and LSID.

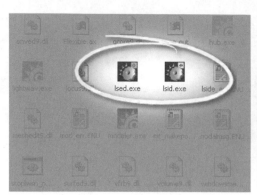

Figure 27-13: The LScript programming tools that ship with LightWave can be found in the Programs folder of the LightWave install directory.

Figure 27-14: Writing plug-ins is easy with the template provided in LSED.

LSED (LScript Editor) is a programming text editor. It's a specialized "word processor" that has been built to work with LScript code.

LSID (LScript Interface Designer) is a visual designer for creating interfaces and panels for LightWave tools.

I won't be going into a great amount detail about these programs here. If you're interested in learning more about the LScript language or the LSED and LSID tools, NewTek has a number of excellent resources available on their site. They can be downloaded from the Developer section of NewTek's website at http://www.new-tek.com/lightwave/developers.php.

LSED — Quick Starting Plug-in Code

The LSED tool is a feature-packed editor for writing LScript code. One of its great features worth mentioning here is that it allows you to start coding quickly by providing basic "templates" for all the common types of plug-ins you might develop for Modeler or Layout. Under the Tools menu you will find a list of templates to choose from.

When a template is selected, the code is automatically generated and ready for us to "fine-tune" to our liking. This feature is one of the reasons I find myself using LSED for creating LScripts.

LSID — Quick GUI Construction

The LSID tool is a great way to build your user interfaces visually. Traditionally, creating interfaces for your tools meant hand-scripting code and entering positions and sizes to lay them out. Not the most efficient of approaches! Using LSID, you can add, position, and size components on a panel directly. When LSED is running at the same time, you can export the panel as code directly into the editor to add it to your project!

Figure 27-15: Creating the look of your plug-ins is a snap, thanks to the LSID tool.

LScript Commander — Coding without Code

So, you don't know LScript or anything about the cryptic art of computer programming? Never fear, there's another way to create tools for LightWave that doesn't require you to be a techno-geek in the art of binary!

In Layout, most things we do are converted into commands that are called internally by the software. It's important to understand at this stage that these commands are not the same as the programming language of LScript. They are internal system commands for functions within Layout. Under the **Utilities | Commands** menu we have a handful of useful tools that allow us to watch what goes on as Layout does its thing.

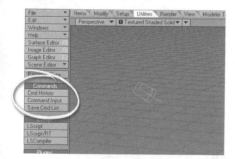

Figure 27-16: Layout's command center.

Cmd History displays a pop-up window with a list of commands that have been called in Layout as you've been working.

Command Input allows you to enter a command directly into Layout and execute it. For instance, entering the command CommandHistory and then clicking OK will open the pop-up window for Command History.

Save Cmd List saves a list of all known commands in Layout to a text file.

While you may never use these particular options while you work in Layout, there

is one tool in particular that you may find extremely useful. Under the **Utilities | Plugins | Additional** menu, you will find a great tool called the LS Commander (LScript Commander). This tool takes the command history and command input as well as the command list and puts them together into something quite powerful! Don't be fooled by the name: LScript Commander is a tool for working with Layout's internal commands (which, as we noted, are not the same as LScript). However, it can convert many of the Layout commands into their equivalent LScript syntax, which makes it an awesome tool for the non-programmers among us!

> **Note**
>
> The LScript Commander tool can also be added from the Master Plugins list (<Ctrl> + <q>).

Figure 27-17: LScript Commander is a utility that allows you to easily create your own custom Layout tools.

The top half of LScript Commander's interface is used to compile commands into a sequence, or session. This editable area is like the Command Input tool, except here you can create a more complex sequence of commands to run in Layout (instead of just one). Under the Session pop-up menu, you can also convert the commands into LScript so that you can use them later to program more powerful tools if you wish.

In the lower half of the LScript Commander interface are two tabs: Events and Command Sequence.

The Events tab contains a command history of what you have been doing in Layout since you activated LScript Commander.

The Command Sequence tab contains a complete list of available commands in Layout. It is like a library of every command within Layout.

To add any of the commands from the Events or Command Sequence lists to the session, simply right-click on it.

Creating a Plug-in with LScript Commander

Let's use LScript Commander to see how easy it is to create a new tool. We'll create a handy "Start new project" tool that not only creates a new empty scene, but saves the previously loaded scene and all of the objects prior to doing so.

> **Note**
>
> Unfortunately, the use of LScript Commander is limited to Layout only. It will not work with Modeler, nor are there tools like it for Modeler at the time of this writing. That's not to say there may not be in the future. LightWave v9 has had some pretty impressive changes to the way it works, and it's not unreasonable to think that we may see a Modeler version of LScript Commander in the future. Only time will tell.

1. Start a fresh new scene, or start a new instance of Layout. Add a null object (**<Ctrl>**+**<n>**) to make sure there is at least one object of some kind in

Layout. Without any objects, the options to save objects are disabled in Layout.

2. Save the scene. It doesn't matter what the filename is (call it **makesavetool.lws** for now). We need to save the scene first to make sure we can save again without the need to enter a filename.

3. Select the **Utilities | Plugins | Additional | LS Commander** tool. With the tool active, let's make this cool new project-saving tool!

4. In LScript Commander, click on the **Session** pop-up menu and select **Clear Session** to make sure we start with a clean slate.

5. Now we simply perform the actions we wish to record. Start with **File | Save | Save All Objects**. Click **Yes** when asked if we really want to save all objects. You should see the command SaveAllObjects appear under the Events list in LScript Commander.

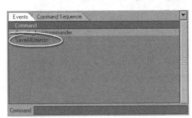

Figure 27-18: SaveAllObjects is our first command.

6. Select **File | Save | Save Scene Increment** to save the scene incrementally (rather than overwrite the original). This is a smart move in case the computer decides to crash during a save! Save Scene Increment is done through an LScript file; hence we see Generic_IncSceneSave added to our Events list. The word "Generic"

simply indicates what type of LScript was called. Generic LScripts are general "do whatever" nonspecific scripts in Layout.

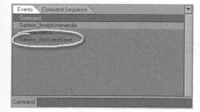

Figure 27-19: Saving the scene incrementally is our next command.

7. Finally, let's clear the scene to make it ready for our next project. Select **File | Clear Scene** and choose **Yes**. Two commands will be added to the Events list: PreClearScene and ClearScene.

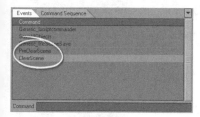

Figure 27-20: The scene is now cleared.

Now let's build our new tool from the sequence of events we just went through. To add any of the commands to our session from the Events list, we simply right-click on the command in the list.

8. Right-click on the following three commands in this order: **SaveAllObjects**, **Generic_IncSceneSave**, and **Clear-Scene**. This will copy them into the upper area of the LScript Commander interface to create the sequence of commands we wish to run.

Figure 27-21: The commands are listed in sequence and are ready to be added to the script pane by right-clicking them.

9. Select **Session | Convert to LScript** to see how these commands appear as LScript. This code is what we would have needed to enter manually if we were to write this without the assistance of LScript Commander.

Figure 27-22: Our commands are now listed as an LScript.

Note

If you know absolutely nothing about how to write LScript, you can use LScript Commander to assist your learning by seeing how certain sequences of operations in Layout would be handled as programming code. This is also useful should you know how to program LScript, but need a few clues to assist in solving a tricky programming situation in Layout. It's a great tool in many ways!

10. Click on the **Install** button in LScript Commander to save the sequence and set up a button for it in Layout automatically. Call the script something like **SuperSaveClear** and click **OK** to finish.

11. Close LScript Commander. If you are completely finished, it's not a bad idea to go to the Master Plugins list (**<Ctrl> + <q>**) and remove it completely.

When something has been installed from LScript Commander, Layout will generate a new tab called Macros (if one does not already exist). All scripts we create and install from LScript Commander will be added to this tab. This includes our new SuperSaveClear tool.

Finding Out More about LScript

As previously mentioned, LScript documentation is available in the Developer section of the NewTek website at http://www.newtek.com/lightwave/developers.php. LScript support is also available on their forum system, which allows you to ask questions freely.

Asking questions about LScript on most LightWave-related forums will often get answers as there are many people online who know and use this programming language.

Figure 27-23: Layout creates a Macros tab for tools created with LScript Commander and will automatically add buttons for the tools you create with it.

Third-Party Plug-ins and Utilities

Creating plug-ins may not be your cup of tea, but that's okay. There are hundreds of talented plug-in authors whose efforts can make your work that much easier. In this section we'll provide a list of some of our favorite tools and utilities. Many of these tools are free and are included on the DVD that came with this book. You can also find them on the websites listed here. We again wish to thank the plug-in authors for their outstanding contributions to the LightWave community. You have made all of our work so much more enjoyable.

LightWave Plug-ins — Freeware

Pictrix Tools by Masayuki Umezawa

http://www.pictrix.jp/lw/index_1.html
(✔ Included on the DVD)

If I had to list one plug-in developer whose tools consistently amaze me with their ingenuity and sheer usefulness, it would have to be those from Masayuki Umezawa. We saw how powerful his SP Move and SP Polygon tools were in Chapter 9. But Masayuki's Pictrix website contains dozens of additional tools, each as impressive as the next. Need to bend an object along a spline curve? Use his C_Bend tool. Need to move one object over the surface of another (such as placing rocks and trees over a terrain)? Try his OnMove tool. Need a turbo-charged rail extrude (for example, to create twisting ropes)? Check out his C_Worm utility. Need even more power than the free tools offer? Check out his low-priced commercial tools. They add unbelievable features to many of his free tools and will shave hours off your modeling work.

The PLG UV and IK Tools

http://homepage2.nifty.com/nif-hp/index2_english.htm
(✔ Included on the DVD)

We saw how powerful the PLG UV tools were in Chapter 11, but there are other tools available on the Nifty website as well. A handful offer advanced IK animation, including IK-spline deformation (rotating bones as if they lie along a spline) and a tool that does a job similar to IK Booster, giving each bone its own IK goal.

Denis Pontonnier RMan Procedural Textures

http://perso.orange.fr/dpont/plugins/Textures.htm
(✔ Included on the DVD)

Denis Pontonnier has created an amazing collection of free procedural textures based on Renderman shaders. If you thought LightWave's native procedurals were powerful, wait until you see what you can do with the RMan collection, which is available in both LW9 Node and standard procedural texture formats! Denis has gone so far as to include detailed samples and animated .gif files on his site showing what each texture can do. From creating fabric weaves to dusty sand dunes, Denis' RMan procedural

textures are a must-have addition to your LightWave texturing toolset.

Denis Pontonnier DPKit Nodes

http://perso.orange.fr/dpont/plugins/nodes/Additionnal_Nodes.html
(✔ Included on the DVD)

Denis Pontonnier has created an outstanding collection of nodes in what is called the DPKit. The DPKit offers node-based processing tools for other areas of LightWave v9 (image processing, HyperVoxels, etc.); modification tools for processing data; and a handful of shaders for creating rounded edges and adding relief maps (faking detail), quick skin tones, metallic surfaces, velvet, and more! As with his RMan Procedural textures, the DPKit is a must-have addition to your LightWave v9 toolset.

Kevman3D

http://www.kevman3d.com/lightwave.asp
(✔ Included on the DVD)

Kevin Phillips isn't just a talented LightWave user; he's also a talented programmer (and one hell of a co-author if you ask me)! On his Kevman website you'll find a collection of utilities ranging from scene cleaning tools to image filters, and handfuls of small Modeler tools to boot.

Highlights on his site include:

• Lean Clean Scene Machine — A batch processing scene error checking and fixer tool.

• FilmFX (Demo) — An image filter that adds film grain, scratches, and more to your renders.

• Letterboxer — Quickly apply a letterbox render region to match common film aspect ratios.

- DeMip all textures — Remove mipmap options and pixel blending en masse from surfaces.

- TGS Exporter — Use LightWave to animate Terragen v0.9 scenes.

- Layer tools — Quick slide and move tools for Modeler layers.

- Mask Morph Copy — Use weight maps to mass-copy morph targets in Modeler.

- Autosewer — A quick hack for a fast sewing tool for ClothFX.

Replace Beep by Jon Tindall/Binary Arts

http://www.binaryartsinc.com/LWave.htm
(✔ Included on the DVD)

Binary Arts, best known for its powerful Fiber Factory hair and fur plug-in, has released a fun and useful tool called Replace Beep. When you render a frame in LightWave, the computer will issue a small "beep" sound when it's finished. The Replace Beep tool allows you to replace the boring default beep with any audio file you choose. It's like getting a custom ringtone for LightWave.

CurveToPolychain by Terry Ford

http://www.aooe58.dsl.pipex.com/htm/frameplugins.shtml
(✔ Included on the DVD)

The CurveToPolychain tool is a fantastic utility for converting Modeler splines into two-point poly chains for use with Sasquatch and SasLite. Terry also has several other outstanding plug-ins on his site, including a nice set of UV tools that allow you to evenly space and distribute points in the UV Texture viewport.

Fi's Junk Box

http://f23.aaa.livedoor.jp/~fisjunk/plugin/plugin.php

Fi's Junk Box contains anything but junk. In fact, the plug-ins here (available for both PC and Mac versions of Modeler and Layout) are considered by many to be indispensable to their daily work. Much like the Pictrix site, Fi's Junk Box boasts dozens of unique tools. Standouts here include:

- Fi's Wrinkle — Allows you to add creases to subpatch objects.

- Fi's Weight Map Blur — Allows you to soften the falloff of weight maps. (See the Texturing with Weightmaps and Gradients bonus video on the companion DVD for an example of how powerful this plug-in can be.)

- Fi's Shaders — Adds several useful procedural textures such as scales and sci-fi ship panels.

- Fi's Crack-it Pack — Breaks an object into random chunks that can then be broken apart using LightWave's dynamics.

True Fillet 1.5

http://www.trueart.eu/?URIType=Directory&URI=Products/Plug-Ins/TrueFillet

LightWave's Rounder tool allows you to round the edges on a 3D object, but it cannot round points on a flat polygon. To do this, you need a point fillet tool. Enter True Fillet from True Art. This remarkably useful tool can shave hours off your modeling jobs by allowing you to soften the corners of polygons before they're extruded. Be sure to check out the other useful tools on True Art's website, including their powerful Wrinkle, True Bump, and Virtual Mirror tools.

The Cool Museum

http://colm.jp/plug/

This site offers a nice collection of additional camera types for LightWave v9, including a panorama camera and a fish-eye camera. The website is written in Japanese, so it pays to use a translation site like BabelFish to read the instructions!

Daniele Federico

http://www.danielefederico.it/works.php?pag=script

Daniele has created a great collection of plug-ins and scripts for LightWave, Maya, and XSI. Those available for LightWave include:

- DF_Sculpt_Tool — A modeling tool for sculpting geometry using spherical handles.
- Random Allocator — A tool that allows one object to be randomly cloned across the surface of another. A weight map can be used to control where these clones appear. Great for building forests on mountains!

Kevin MacPhail

http://www.kevinmacphail.com/index.html

Kevin has created a dynamics animation tool using the awesome Open Dynamics Engine (ODE). You can use this to create accurate and very slick dynamics effects for hard bodies!

Symmetrix Design Works

http://www.symmetrix.com.au/index.php?page=plugins.php

Here you'll find a nice little collection of tools for LightWave v9 by LightWave master James Willmott. Standouts here include:

- ObjectID — A node that lets you create various "instances" of an item so that you can texture various copies of it differently.

An example of how to use this node should be online shortly.

- Tiltshift Lens shader — A new camera type for LightWave v9 that is designed to create perspective renders where the vertical lines remain straight. A great tool for rendering architecture.
- EdgePack Modeler tools — A collection of great little tools to add power and ease to working with edges.

LightWave Plug-ins — Commercial

Worley Labs

http://www.worley.com/

Perhaps the most legendary plug-in developer for LightWave is Steve Worley. And for good reason. Worley's tools are without a doubt the most powerful and impressive on the market. And I'm not just talking about the LightWave market. Users of Maya, XSI, and 3ds Max often gape when they see what his plug-ins can do.

You're already familiar with Worley's SasLite from Chapter 20. When you're ready to take your hair simulation to the next level, consider purchasing the full version of Sasquatch. It's been used in countless feature films and independent animations around the world and is an industry-proven tool for adding hair and fur to your characters.

If you want to increase your productivity across the board, you should seriously consider purchasing a copy of FPrime. This real-time rendering engine allows you to make F9 test renders a thing of the past. And it can rip through tough rendering jobs that use time-consuming features such as area lights, radiosity, and LightWave v9.2's new node materials. If you're going to

935

purchase one plug-in for LightWave, this should be it.

LWCAD

http://www.wtools3d.com/

The Pictrix tools let you tackle most architectural modeling projects with confidence, but if you're going to make a living doing architectural visualization, you should seriously consider an investment in the LWCAD tools. This utterly fantastic suite of modeling tools provides CAD-style functionality and ease. They offer amazing spline modeling capabilities, extrusion tools, and libraries of great moldings and architectural motifs to choose from.

Third-party Utilities

Itty-Bitty Animation Timer

An *Essential LightWave* exclusive!
(Included on the DVD)

Tim Albee's Flash-based animation timer is a great utility for "acting out" a scene and then converting the time into a variety of formats, including frames and feet.

DOF PRO

http://www.dofpro.com/
(Included on the DVD)

Adding depth-of-field (DOF) effects can increase the realism of any scene, but it can also increase the rendering time in the process. If you've got time to spare, then it's not a problem. But if you need beautiful DOF that's fast and flexible, Depth of Field Generator PRO is the way to go.

DOF PRO is a Photoshop plug-in that allows you to add depth-of-field, bokeh, and film-grain effects to your renders. It accepts LightWave depth buffer output (as described in Chapter 7). It also allows batch processing, so it can handle animations. And since it's a post-production process, you can easily make changes without having to re-render your entire scene. The fact that it's a Photoshop plug-in means you can use it on any image, not just LightWave renders. And at only $59.99 (U.S.), DOF PRO is a steal. Check out the fully functional demo included on the DVD.

FileHamster

http://www.mogware.com/filehamster/
(Included on the DVD)

FileHamster is a version tracking application designed to meet the needs of digital content creators. It provides real-time backup and archiving of your files while you work. It enables you to monitor specific files on your hard drive and automatically create incremental backups whenever those files are modified. It also enables you to store notes about the changes that have been made, allowing you to quickly locate a specific revision or provide a detailed account of the work you've done on a project.

FileHamster is one of my favorite workflow utilities. You can forget about trying to figure out which version of your file is the latest and greatest. Just save one version and let FileHamster do the rest. It will monitor your files and create automatic backups for you whenever you modify them. You can quickly get back to an earlier version of any watched file and you can keep notes about the progress you've made while working.

A full version of FileHamster is provided on the *Essential LightWave v9* DVD free of charge courtesy of Mogware Software.

Appendix A

Resources

The Renaissance poet John Donne said, "No man is an island." How right he was! This chapter will provide you with resources to keep you informed, introduce you to other users, aid you in finding additional tutorials, and provide you with free or low-cost software to assist your development as a CG artist.

News and Information

Flay

http://www.flay.com

Christopher Stewart's venerable Flay.com should be your first stop when looking for the latest and greatest LightWave news, plug-ins, and more. The site is home to the largest database of plug-ins around. If you're looking for a tool to make a particular task a bit easier, Flay will help you find it.

CG Focus

http://www.cgfocus.com/

CG Focus is an excellent general news and information site, providing daily updates on all things 3D/CGI. While there are many CG news sites on the web, CG Focus has excellent support for LightWave info and helpful reviews of products.

Ultimate 3D Links

http://www.3dlinks.com/

Similar to CG Focus, the Ultimate 3D Links site is an amazing portal to all things 3D. Here you'll find links to news, tutorials, textures, and more.

Forums and Community

SpinQuad

http://www.spinquad.com

SpinQuad is one of the most popular LightWave forums on the web, providing industry news, artist interviews, a jaw-dropping gallery, and a robust forum with a huge LightWave user base. You can also get great deals on LightWave products and tutorials via their online store.

LightWave Group

http://www.lwg3d.com/v3/index.php

The LWG website is home to many talented LightWave artists and is known for its great tutorials. Drop by and take a peek at some of the amazing art being posted here.

NewTek Forums

http://www.newtek.com/forums/

A forum for all things NewTek, which means you'll find plenty of discussion about LightWave here. This is a great place to get info straight from the horse's mouth.

CGTalk

http://www.cgtalk.com

CGTalk is one of the most highly respected CG forums on the web. It is frequented by leading artists and hosts some of the liveliest "challenges" that push artists to come up with the best artwork they can in a given time frame. Discussions on nearly every application and discipline in computer art can be found here.

3D Fight Club

http://www.3dfightclub.com/

There's nothing like a challenge to bring out the best in a person, and 3D Fight Club does a great job of providing users with just that. Born out of a desire to extol the powers of LightWave over Maya, the site now includes users of every 3D application. Members participate in a variety of challenges, ranging from several minutes to several hours in length. The idea is to work quickly toward your goal and produce better work than your competitors within the time allowed. If you really want to hone your skills, I highly recommend a workout at 3D Fight Club.

Friends of NewTek

http://www.friendsofnewtek.com/

Looking for a user group where you can learn great tips, see demos of new software, and get to know other users in your area? You can find user groups via the Friends of NewTek site. No user group in your area? Start one and get the word out by signing up here.

Scifi-Meshes

http://www.scifi-meshes.com/

If spaceships, robots, and aliens are your thing, then check out the amazing work being done by the talented artists at Scifi-Meshes. You can download objects from popular sci-fi shows and post renders of your own work for critique by other artists as well.

Tweak

http://www.tweakcg.com/forum/

An excellent online modeling forum where modelers and artists can discuss and show off their CG sculptured creations. The work here is amazing, so come to be inspired. If you're up for it, post your best work and inspire others.

3D Buzz

http://www.3dbuzz.com/

3D Buzz is the home of a huge training community, offering forums, downloadable tutorials, and a whole lot more. Buzz became famous for producing large amounts of free video training tutorials. They cover a lot of CG products as well as topics ranging from game development to operating systems.

Spiraloid

http://cube.phlatt.net/forums/spiraloid/index.php

Spiraloid is a small discussion forum set up by artist extraordinaire Bay Raitt (perhaps most notably famous for being the creator of the Gollum facial system for *Lord of the Rings*). If digital sculpting of detailed characters is your passion, this site is well worth checking out for critique and inspiration!

Tutorials

LightWave Tutorials on the Web

http://members.shaw.ca/lightwavetutorials/Main_Menu.htm

When you need a tutorial on a specific topic, there's only one place to go. LightWave Tutorials on the Web is arguably the most comprehensive collection of LightWave tutorials around. Add this to your favorites list and check back often.

Kurv Studios

http://www.kurvstudios.com/

Kurv Studios has quickly become one of the leading suppliers of high-quality computer-based training material. Their LightWave series is hosted by industry-recognized artists and offers training on nearly every aspect of the software. What makes Kurv Studios really stand out from the competition, however, are the low prices. Videos typically range from $24.95 to $49.95 and contain more than 10 hours of training material. That's less than $5 per hour of training, making Kurv's videos some of the most cost-effective sources of training you'll find.

3D Tutorials

http://www.3dtutorials.sk/

The 3d.sk line of websites offers a wealth of resources for CG artists. Their tutorial site offers an expansive collection of tutorials for a variety of applications.

Simply LightWave

http://www.simplylightwave.com/

A site dedicated to providing downloadable video tutorials for LightWave artists. Some are free; however, many must be purchased. There are some great tutorials online here that are worth taking a look at.

IK Boost

http://www.ikboost.com/

Colin Larkin's outstanding tutorials show advanced uses for the IK Booster tool. If you thought IK Booster was just for characters, think again. The hidden gems of this powerful tool are exposed in Colin's free video tutorials.

3D Resources and Textures

HDR Light Probes

http://www.unparent.com/gallery_probeThumbs.htm

Keith Bruns' fantastic collection of HDR images can be found on this site along with sample renders showing their use. When you're in need of high-quality HDR images, this is the place to go.

Planet Pixel Emporium

http://planetpixelemporium.com/planets.html

A great collection of excellent textures for the planets within our solar system. For those science fiction projects, this site is a must.

Got 3D

http://free-textures.got3d.com/natural/free-character-references/index.html

Got 3D offers a totally awesome photo reference collection of real people taken from the side/front/back. This is a terrific resource for all character modelers.

Mayang's Free Textures

http://mayang.com/textures/index.htm

With over 3,400 free high-res textures in a variety of categories, Mayang's Free Textures is a great place to locate images for your texturing projects.

Open Footage

http://www.openfootage.net/

This site offers a great collection of high-res textures, panoramas, and time-lapse footage free for commercial and personal use.

Get Brushes

http://getbrushes.com/

You can never get enough brushes. Brushes allow you to easily create complex textures. The Get Brushes site provides links to free brushes in a variety of categories.

Monitor Calibration

http://www.3drender.com/light/calibration.htm

Jeremy Birn, author of the book *Digital Lighting and Rendering*, has a terrific calibration chart on his site that allows you to ensure your monitor's contrast and gamma settings aren't off. Jeremy was kind enough to give us permission to include a copy of this web page on the book's companion DVD. You can also get to it via the direct link listed here.

Archidom

http://www.archidom.net

A great resource for architectural materials for projects, from textures to models. Most models are in 3D Studio format; however, LightWave can import .3DS files easily. Well worth checking out.

Metanoia

http://www2.odn.ne.jp/metanoia-style/freetx/freetx.htm

A nice page of free textures, from cloth to Japanese street signs. Many are seamless for tiling over the surface of 3D objects.

NewTek's Free Textures Collections

http://www.newtek.com/freestuff/index.php

NewTek, creators of LightWave, have a fantastic collection of high-resolution image maps available for free download from their website. Requires registration, but worth the downloads.

Detonation Films

http://www.detonationfilms.com

Detonation Films creates clean video footage of explosions, smoke, fire, and pretty much anything that goes boom! Whether you need something to spice up your sci-fi space action or perhaps to bring that flying logo to life, these are your guys! Some of these videos can be freely downloaded from the website, though the files can also be purchased at insanely cheap prices (around $9 U.S.) on CD as well!

Textures.Forrest.cz

http://textures.forrest.cz/

A nice site loaded with texture maps that are nicely categorized for easy navigation. While not all textures are free, many are, and are worth a look through the library.

Digitalin.fr

http://www.digitalin.fr/index.php?page=goodies

Need to create that showroom appeal for the next CG sports car project? This page contains 58 free "artificial" HDR reflection probes, great for use when rendering metallic surfaces such as those of a car in a showroom environment.

Photo Resources

Flickr

http://www.flickr.com

Flickr is an amazing and huge online photo-blog system. While all images on this site are the property of their respective artist and should be respected, this site is an invaluable "research" tool for finding photographs and images of almost any subject.

Fotolog

http://www.fotolog.net

A long-running photo-blog service. A running count on the home page gives you the latest stats of the site. When I last visited, there were over 171 million photos on the system. Another great research site when looking for reference material.

Morguefile

http://www.morguefile.com

Morguefile offers royalty-free stock photographs for download, donated by online photographers around the world. If ever in need of a background plate or material for creating matte paintings, images for a texture, or even just for research purposes, this site is an invaluable resource.

Model Sheets/Blueprints

Disney Cartoon Characters

http://www.animationarchive.net/Model%20Sheets/

Want to create your favorite Disney character in Modeler but need reference? Look no further than Animationarchive.net, the Unofficial Disney Animation Archive since 1996! A bit of everything from early cartoons to Disney/Pixar films.

Anime-style Cartoon Characters

http://www.anime-model-sheets.com/

A gigantic resource of model sheets from many, many Japanese cartoon series. Nothing is categorized, so it can take a little time to find exactly what you want, but the amount of material here is well worth the time to look through for your next anime/manga-style modeling project!

Airwar

http://www.airwar.ru/other/drawe.html

A fantastic collection of often high-resolution plans and schematics of many aircraft, from early world war planes to modern jet fighters.

Richard Ferrieres' Aircaft 3-vues

http://richard.ferriere.free.fr/3vues/3vues.html

A very impressive (and long) web page containing a huge library of aircraft listed alphabetically. If you can't find a particular type of aircraft that you want to model elsewhere, it's highly likely you will find it in here!

Suurland

http://www.suurland.com/

This is perhaps one of the first blueprint sites on the web. Thomas Suurland is an artist from Denmark who has provided blueprints of aircraft, vehicles, ships, and even buildings for many years.

Sound Resources

DeusX

http://www.deusx.com

DeusX produces very inexpensive audio DVD-ROMs, loaded with several hundred effects and music loops. They also offer a great collection of freely downloadable samples on their website, which are perfect for those show reels or other animation projects.

Tools

Image Editing Tools

ArtWeaver

http://www.artweaver.de

A great little free paint tool, developed as a natural medium (pencil, etc.) painter, ArtWeaver works brilliantly with a graphics tablet and is very easy to use. It's great for painting textures that require a more "painterly" appearance!

IrfanView

http://www.irfanview.com/

When you're a CG artist, you typically deal with a wide assortment of graphics files, most of which cannot be previewed in Windows. The freely available IrfanView program allows you to view files in dozens of formats as well as edit, batch convert, and batch rename them. This is the Swiss Army knife of image viewing and editing.

The Gimp

http://www.gimp.org/

The Gimp is an open-source, free paint tool, and is probably the closest thing to Adobe Photoshop in terms of features. It comes with some very cool effects and plug-ins that you *won't* find in Photoshop for generating video screen effects and more. I've used this product many times in jobs where Photoshop wasn't available or when an effect was needed that Photoshop couldn't quickly produce.

Inkscape

http://www.inkscape.org/

If you need to develop vector art and can't afford something like Adobe Illustrator, then Inkscape is your free, open-source alternative. It's very easy to use. Check out the stunning pieces of art in the gallery to see what it can produce!

HDRI Editing Tools

AHDRIA

http://www2.cs.uh.edu/~somalley/hdri_images.html

Here you'll find a couple of nice HDRI editing and creation tools, free for personal use. Note that there are many, many links in this page to tutorials and other HDRI resources (including software, images, and more).

Texturing and Mesh Editing Tools

Tattoo

http://www.terabit-software.co.uk/

Tattoo is a 3D paint tool designed for painting a texture directly onto the surface of UV-mapped (including LWO) objects. It's free for non-commercial and personal use, and costs a paltry £ 25 (roughly $49 U.S.) for commercial use.

SharpConstruct

http://sharp3d.sourceforge.net/mediawiki/index.php/Main_Page

SharpConstruct is an open-source modeling tool with brush editing tools similar to Mudbox and ZBrush. It also provides native support for LightWave objects.

3D Object Conversion Tools

Biturn

http://mirex.mypage.sk/index.php?selected=1

Biturn is a nice little free converter that can read and write several 3D model and texture formats. It supports LightWave 6.5 upward and can also convert from various game formats.

Video Tools

JahShaka

http://www.jahshaka.org/

This is a great open-source (free) compositing tool. The interface is a little quirky at first, but if you're in need of something for compositing work on an extremely low budget (i.e., cheaper than After Effects, Digital Fusion, or Combustion), then check it out!

Virtual Dub

http://www.virtualdub.org/

Virtual Dub is the Swiss Army knife of video tools. Virtual Dub isn't a true video editor (although you can use it to trim and join files). Its focus is on capturing video from any source and recompressing existing video files. Being open source, it's free to download and use. I've used Virtual Dub many times to quickly compress my uncompressed renders or to add audio to a silent clip. It's extremely fast in processing video (much faster than many commercial video tools that have to "re-render" their footage), and includes a filter plug-in interface to process video footage as it

compresses it. Like IrfanView is great for images, Virtual Dub is essential for video!

Wax

http://www.debugmode.com/wax/

Wax is a freeware video editing and compositing package for Windows. Well worth the download, it can also work as a plug-in to some other non-linear editing tools such as Adobe Premiere and Sony Vegas.

Art Design Tools

Color Blender

http://www.colorblender.com/

This is a very nice web page that automatically assists in creating color palettes for your design work. Choose a color, and let this page offer up to six complementary colors to work with.

Panorama Creation Tools

Autostitch

http://www.cs.ubc.ca/~mbrown/autostitch/autostitch.html

A free demo for personal and non-commercial use, this tool automatically analyzes and stitches pictures into panoramic images for you! Amazingly clever technology, and well worth testing with your favorite folder of snapshots that you've yet to stitch together. The demo has a time expiration that requires you to pop back and grab the next update, but it's an amazing piece of software worth trying for yourself.

Game Development

Gamasutra

http://www.gamasutra.com

As the site says, the art and business of gaming. A site full of articles and information on game development and technology. This is a site that all game developers should be aware of.

NVidia's online documentation

http://developer.nvidia.com/page/documentation.html

Here you'll find a collection of great information on developing game graphics from NVidia, one of the leaders in video chip technology.

GameDev

http://www.gamedev.net/

GameDev is a game developer's portal, dedicated to the tools and techniques needed by game developers.

Filmmaking Tools

Springboard

http://6sys.com/springboard/

Springboard is an awesome little storyboard creation tool. Extremely cheap, it can even create an animatic from the storyboard for you, complete with camera moves and animation.

Celtx

http://www.celtx.com/

Probably the nicest, most complete script making tool that you can get for free! Script formatting and writing tools, character histories, time planner, online collaboration tools, and more! It's all in here. (Did I mention it was free?)

Sound and Music

Audacity

http://audacity.sourceforge.net/

One of the best open-source free sound editing tools around for tweaking your audio files. Edit, modify, repair, and add effects and more with Audacity.

Psycle

http://sourceforge.net/projects/psycle/

A very nice (and free) open-source music making package with advanced synthesis tools that works in the style of the old "tracker" music programs like Fastracker (from the "demo scene," a craze back in the 1990s where programmers would write programs that mixed music and graphics together in code). A web portal with a forum, skins, and music can be found at http://psycle.pastnotecut.org/portal.php.

If you're feeling in that audibly artistic mood and need to create the cutting-edge soundtrack for your animated short film, then this is a fairly well-featured package.

ModPlug Tracker

http://www.modplug.com/

ModPlug Tracker is another free open-source music creation tool, developed for creating tracked music like Psycle (but only using audio samples, unlike Psycle's advanced synthesis features).

Need More?

CyberGadget 3DXtra

http://www.3dxtra.cygad.ne

CyberGadget 3DXtra is a fantastic portal of links to resources all over the web ranging from models to plug-ins and magazines. If you can't find something, or just want to look for more sites to explore, then check this out.

Stonewashed

http://www.stonewashed.net/sfx.html

Stonewashed has an extensive portal of links to hundreds of free effects and music sites. If you need more audio resources, then check this site out.

Appendix B

Refraction Index

Material	Refraction Index	Material	Refraction Index
Acetone	1.36	Ice	1.309
Air	1.00029	Iodine Crystal	3.34
Alcohol	1.329	Lapis Lazuli	1.61
Amorphous Selenium	2.92	Light Flint Glass	1.575
Calspar1	1.66	Liquid Carbon Dioxide	1.20
Calspar2	1.486	Polystyrene	1.55
Carbon Disulfide	1.63	Quartz 1	1.644
Chromium Oxide	2.705	Quartz 2	1.553
Copper Oxide	2.705	Ruby	1.77
Crown Glass	1.52	Sapphire	1.77
Crystal	2.00	Sodium Chloride (Salt) 1	1.544
Diamond	2.417	Sodium Chloride (Salt) 2	1.644
Emerald	1.57	Sugar Solution (30%)	1.38
Ethyl Alcohol	1.36	Sugar Solution (80%)	1.49
Flourite	1.434	Topaz	1.61
Fused Quartz	1.46	Vacuum	1.00000
Glass	1.5	Water (20° C)	1.333
Heaviest Flint Glass	1.89	Zinc Crown Glass	1.517
Heavy Flint Glass	1.65		

Appendix C

LightWave's Default Hot Keys

Remember that all hot keys are CASE SENSITIVE. This list is also included as a PDF file on the companion DVD in the Keyboard Shortcuts Document folder.

Modeler

Description	Hot Key
Modeler: General	
New Object	N
Load Object	\<Ctrl\>+o
Save Object	s
Save Object As	\<Ctrl\>+s
Save Incremental	S
Quit	Q
Cut	\<Ctrl\>+x
Copy	\<Ctrl\>+c
Paste	\<Ctrl\>+v
Delete	\<Delete\>
Undo	\<Ctrl\>+z
Redo	z
Edit Keyboard Shortcuts	\<Alt\>+\<F9\>
Edit Menu Layout	\<Alt\>+\<F10\>
General Options	o
Display Options	d
Surface Editor	\<F5\>
Image Editor	\<F6\>
Layers Panel	\<F7\>
Vertex Maps Panel	\<F8\>
Presets Panel	\<F9\>
Hide Floating Windows On/Off	\<Alt\>+\<F1\>
Hide Toolbar On/Off	\<Alt\>+\<F2\>
Help	\<F1\>
Points Selection Mode	\<Ctrl\>+g
Polygons Selection Mode	\<Ctrl\>+h
Inclusive Volume Select Mode	\<Ctrl\>+j

Symmetry Mode	Y
Numeric panel	n
Statistics panel	w
Point/Polygon Info panel	i
Change Surface window	q
Toggle Fullscreen Viewport	Numeric keypad 0

Modeler: Create

Box	X
Ball	O
Manage Fonts	\<F10\>
Text	W
Points	+
Make Polygon	p
Sketch Curve	`
Make Open Curve	\<Ctrl\>+p

Modeler: Modify

Move	t
Drag	\<Ctrl\>+t
Snap Drag	G
DragNet	;
Magnet	:
Shear	[
Center	\<F2\>
Rest on Ground	\<F3\>
Rotate	y
Rotate to Ground	\<F4\>
Rotate selection 90° clockwise	r
Bend	~
Size	H
Stretch	h
Jitter	J
Smooth	M

Modeler: Multiply

Bevel	b
Edge Bevel	\<Ctrl\>+b
Extrude	E
Extender Plus	e
Lathe	L
Smooth Shift	F
Rail Extrude	\<Ctrl\>+r
Motion Path Extrude	P
Mirror	V
Array	\<Ctrl\>+y
Clone	c

Knife	K
Subdivide	D
Triple	T
Cut-Saw	U

Modeler: Construct

Remove Polygons (Leave Points)	k
Boolean	B
Solid Drill	C
Drill	R
Connect	l
SubPatch Activate/Deactivate	\<Tab\>

Modeler: Detail

Merge Points	m
Merge Polygons	Z
Unweld Points	\<Ctrl\>+u
Weld Points	\<Ctrl\>+w
Set Value	v
Flip	f
Spin Quads	\<Ctrl\>+k
Unify Polygons	I
Measure	\<Ctrl\>+e

Modeler: Map

| Clear Map from Selection | _ |
| Guess UV Viewport | \<Shift\>+\<F9\> |

Modeler: Utilities

| Add Plugins | \<F11\> |
| Edit Plugins | \<Alt\>+\<F11\> |

Modeler: View

Pan	\<Alt\>+click and drag
Magnify \<Ctrl\>+	\<Alt\>+click and drag left/right
Zoom	\<Ctrl\>+q
Fit All	a
Fit Selected	A
Center view around Cursor	g
Zoom In	.
Zoom In x 2	\>
Zoom out	,
Zoom Out x2	\<
Insert Layer	\<Insert\>
Delete Layer	\<Home\>
Object Collapser	\<End\>

Swap Layers	'
Next Layer Bank	\<Page Up\>
Previous Layer Bank	\<Page Down\>
Select Connected	]
Invert Connected	?
Expand Selection	}
Contract Selection	{
Invert Selection	"
Drop Selection	/
Hide Selected	-
Hide Unselected	=
Invert Hidden	|
Unhide All	\

Layout

Layout: General

Clear Scene	N
Load Scene	\<Ctrl\>+o
Load Object	Numeric +
Save Scene	s
Save Scene As	\<Ctrl\>+s
Save Scene Increment	S
Show/Hide Floating Windows	\<Tab\>
Show/Hide Toolbar	\<Alt\>+\<F2\>
Show/Hide SubPatch Cages	\<Alt\>+\<F3\>
Show/Hide Motion Paths	\<Alt\>+\<F4\>
Show/Hide Handles	\<Alt\>+\<F5\>
Show/Hide IK Chains	\<Alt\>+\<F6\>
Motion Mixer	\<F2\>
Presets	\<F8\>
Backdrop Options	\<Ctrl\>+\<F5\>
Volumetrics and Fog Options	\<Ctrl\>+\<F6\>
Compositing Options	\<Ctrl\>+\<F7\>
Image Processing	\<Ctrl\>+\<F8\>
Motion Options	m
Scene Editor	\<Ctrl\>+\<F1\>
Graph Editor	\<Ctrl\>+\<F2\>
Surface Editor	\<F5\>
Image Editor	\<F6\>
Display Options	d
General Options	o
Select Objects	O
Select Bones	B

Select Lights	L
Select Cameras	C
Selected Item Properties	p
Auto Key Create	<Shift>+<F1>
Create Key	<Return>
Delete Key	<Del>
Undo	<Ctrl>+z
Redo	z
Statistics	w
Help	<F1>
Set Content Directory	<Alt>+<F12>
Quit	Q

Layout: Items

Load Scene	<Ctrl>+o
Load Object	Numeric +
Add Null	<Ctrl>+n
Clone Selected Item	<Ctrl>+c
Mirror	V
Clear Selected Item from Scene	-

Layout: Modify

Move	t
Rotate	y
Size	H
Stretch	h
Path Tool	<Ctrl>+y
Jump to Numeric Input Field	n
Coordinate System: World	<Shift>+<F5>
Coordinate System: Parent	<Shift>+<F6>
Coordinate System: Local	<Shift>+<F7>
IK Boost Tool	<Ctrl>+b
IKB Calculate	<Ctrl>+x
Move TCB	<Ctrl>+g
Sliders	<Ctrl>+d
Edit Tool	<Ctrl>+e

Layout: Setup

Enter Bone Edit Mode	E
Exit Bone Edit Mode	D
Enable IK	<Shift>+<F8>
Add Child Bone	=
Joint Move	<Ctrl>+j
Tip Move	<Ctrl>+t
Bone Twist	<Ctrl>+k
Record Pivot Rotation	P

Record Bone Rest Rotation	r
UnParent Bone	\<Ctrl>+u
Mirror Hierarchy	\<Ctrl>+w
Import Rig	I
Export Rig	J
Motion Options	m
Record Minimum Joint Angles	{
Record Maximum Joint Angles	}
Selected Bone Active/Inactive	\<Ctrl>+r

Layout: Utilities

| Edit Plugins | \<Alt>+\<F11> |
| Master Plugins | \<Ctrl>+q |

Layout: Render

Render Frame	\<F9>
Render Scene	\<F10>
Render Selected Object	\<F11>
Render Motion Builder Preview	\<Shift>+\<F9>

Layout: View

Zoom In	.
Zoom In x 2	>
Zoom Out	,
Zoom Out x2	<
View Mode: Back	1
View Mode: Top	2
View Mode: Right	3
View Mode: Perspective	4
View Mode: Light	5
View Mode: Camera	6
View Mode: Schematic	7
Previous View Layout	\<F3>
Next View Layout	\<F4>
Increase Grid	]
Decrease Grid	[
Select All Objects	\<Ctrl>+a
Select Item By Name	'
Select Next Item	down
Select Previous Item	up
Select First Item	\<Shift> up
Select Last Item	\<Shift> down
Select Next Sibling	\<Ctrl> down
Select Previous Sibling	\<Ctrl> up
Show/Hide Safe Areas	\<Alt>+\<F7>
Show/Hide Field Chart	\<Alt>+\<F8>
Toggle Fullscreen Viewport	Numeric keypad 0

Index

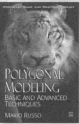

About the Companion DVD

The companion DVD contains images, objects, and scenes discussed throughout the book, as well as trial versions of LightWave v9.2, plug-ins and other utilities, and nearly 14 hours of video tutorials. The files are organized in the following folders:

- **Chapter Screen Shots** — All the figures from the book in color.
- **Keyboard Shortcuts Document** — A PDF version of Appendix C.
- **LightWave Book Content** — All the image, object, render, and scene files used in the projects throughout the book. This directory is further organized by chapter.
- **LightWave Trial Version** — Demo versions of LightWave v9.2 as well as pre-created materials from NewTek. The 30-day demos are available for Macintosh (for use with Mac OSX) and Windows (32-bit for Windows 2000/XP and 64-bit for Windows XP Pro x64). Additionally, the Content file contains a variety of royalty-free objects, scenes, and animations to give you a jump start on your LightWave learning experience. Unzip the Content file to your hard drive. Then in each project folder, locate the scene folder and double-click or load the .lws file into LightWave Layout.
- **LightWave Video Content** — Image, object, render, and scene files associated with the video tutorials.
- **Plug-ins and Utilities** — A variety of plug-ins and utilities that can help enhance your LightWave work. See Chapter 27 for more information about these tools.
- **Video Tutorials** — Nearly 14 hours of video tutorials that demonstrate how to use LightWave, including 18 videos that focus on updates made to LightWave v9.2.

 Warning:

By opening the DVD package, you accept the terms and conditions of the DVD/Source Code Usage License Agreement.
   Additionally, opening the DVD package makes this book nonreturnable.

DVD/Source Code Usage License Agreement

Please read the following DVD/Source Code usage license agreement before opening the DVD and using the contents therein:

1. By opening the accompanying software package, you are indicating that you have read and agree to be bound by all terms and conditions of this DVD/Source Code usage license agreement.

2. The compilation of code and utilities contained on the DVD and in the book are copyrighted and protected by both U.S. copyright law and international copyright treaties, and is owned by Wordware Publishing, Inc. Individual source code, example programs, help files, freeware, shareware, utilities, and evaluation packages, including their copyrights, are owned by the respective authors.

3. No part of the enclosed DVD or this book, including all source code, help files, shareware, freeware, utilities, example programs, or evaluation programs, may be made available on a public forum (such as a World Wide Web page, FTP site, bulletin board, or Internet news group) without the express written permission of Wordware Publishing, Inc. or the author of the respective source code, help files, shareware, freeware, utilities, example programs, or evaluation programs.

4. You may not decompile, reverse engineer, disassemble, create a derivative work, or otherwise use the enclosed programs, help files, freeware, shareware, utilities, or evaluation programs except as stated in this agreement.

5. The software, contained on the DVD and/or as source code in this book, is sold without warranty of any kind. Wordware Publishing, Inc. and the authors specifically disclaim all other warranties, express or implied, including but not limited to implied warranties of merchantability and fitness for a particular purpose with respect to defects in the disk, the program, source code, sample files, help files, freeware, shareware, utilities, and evaluation programs contained therein, and/or the techniques described in the book and implemented in the example programs. In no event shall Wordware Publishing, Inc., its dealers, its distributors, or the authors be liable or held responsible for any loss of profit or any other alleged or actual private or commercial damage, including but not limited to special, incidental, consequential, or other damages.

6. One (1) copy of the DVD or any source code therein may be created for backup purposes. The DVD and all accompanying source code, sample files, help files, freeware, shareware, utilities, and evaluation programs may be copied to your hard drive. With the exception of freeware and shareware programs, at no time can any part of the contents of this DVD reside on more than one computer at one time. The contents of the DVD can be copied to another computer, as long as the contents of the DVD contained on the original computer are deleted.

7. You may not include any part of the DVD contents, including all source code, example programs, shareware, freeware, help files, utilities, or evaluation programs in any compilation of source code, utilities, help files, example programs, freeware, shareware, or evaluation programs on any media, including but not limited to DVD, disk, or Internet distribution, without the express written permission of Wordware Publishing, Inc. or the owner of the individual source code, utilities, help files, example programs, freeware, shareware, or evaluation programs.

8. You may use the source code, techniques, and example programs in your own commercial or private applications unless otherwise noted by additional usage agreements as found on the DVD.

 Warning:

By opening the DVD package, you accept the terms and conditions of the DVD/Source Code Usage License Agreement.

Additionally, opening the DVD package makes this book nonreturnable.